POPULAR MEAT ROASTS

butchers may use different names. Learn to recognize
the shapes of various roasts. If you have difficulty
finding any of them, ask for them by the name given here.
Meat roasting timetables begin on page 44 of this book
and meat recipes will be found throughout Chapter IX.

Boneless Rolled Rump

Top Round

Bottom Round

Eye of Round

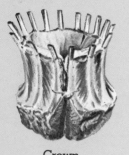

Crown

Leg

Leg, Sirloin Half, left
Shank Half, right

Boneless Leg

Blade Loin

Center Loin

Sirloin

Boneless Top Loin

VEAL

Rib

Loin

Leg

The
Redbook
Cookbook

THE REDBOOK COOKBOOK

Edited by

RUTH FAIRCHILD POMEROY

Women's Service Editor, *Redbook*

Grosset & Dunlap
A Filmways Co., Inc.
Publishers   New York

FOREWORD

To produce this Second Edition of the Redbook Cookbook has been an exciting project. We knew we were starting with a fine food handbook that readers—young women, older and more experienced women and men as well—have told us is their favorite basic cookbook.

Sey Chassler, our Editor-in-Chief, writing of the first Redbook Cookbook said, "As Editor of Redbook magazine, the largest circulation magazine in America specifically edited for young women, I have long felt that we had more reason than most magazines to produce a common-sense, plain-talking book of recipes and cooking information that would be of use to women for whom cooking is not simply a pastime or a hobby but one of the fundamental operations of their lives." So, under the guidance of Helen B. Mills (our Food Editor then), Elise Sticht and their staff of Home Economists, working in Redbook's Test Kitchens, the first Redbook Cookbook came into being—a basic, helpful, pleasurable book that many thousands of people welcomed in its first year of publication.

How then to improve on what seemed to us a book that already had classic proportions? In the short period since the first edition was published in 1971 until now, the life-style of the entire nation has changed, and everything from the way babies are delivered to the way we regard food and prepare it has been affected. Not only did we develop new food preferences, we also developed a greater concern for nutrition, a wider interest in interethnic recipes, a healthy concern for weight control. With the special expertise of Redbook's Food Editor Elizabeth Alston and her associates Freddi Greenberg and Amy Chatham Scotton and with the editorial vigilance of William A. Robbins, Redbook's Managing Editor, this second edition has been edited and expanded to fulfill the needs those new preferences produced.

We hope all who use this book will find it not only a good basic tool and a useful reference but a guide and an inspiration to the meaning and the pleasure of food. We hope you will find it good—and good for you.

Ruth Fairchild Pomeroy
Women's Service Editor, Redbook Magazine
(April, 1976)

CONTENTS

Foreword

I	To Begin	3
II	Food Facts for Easy Reference	25
III	Planning Menus	92
IV	Timing the Dinner	109
V	The Way It Looks	150
VI	Appetizers	162
VII	Soups	210
VIII	Beverages	242
IX	Meats	273
X	Poultry	356
XI	Fish	397
XII	Eggs	442
XIII	Cheese	467
XIV	Sauces	478
XV	Vegetables	495
XVI	Rice, Pasta, and Cereals	559
XVII	Salads and Salad Dressings	584
XVIII	Quick Breads	630
XIX	Yeast Bread	661
XX	Fruits	693
XXI	Desserts	719

XXII	Pies and Pastry	782
XXIII	Cakes	810
XXIV	Cookies	861
XXV	Candies and Confections	893
XXVI	Preserving Food	913
XXVII	Casseroles	937
XXVIII	Spices and Herbs	962
XXIX	About Wines with Food	980
XXX	About Food and Nutrition	992
	Index	1009

The
Redbook
Cookbook

CHAPTER I

TO BEGIN

There is no such thing as a "born cook." Cooking, like playing the piano, is an acquired skill that can become a creative art. But before you can improvise, you do have to have some basic techniques. Good cooking is really the sum of many simple operations; if each one of them is performed correctly, you can't fail to get good results. You must provide the desire to want to cook well, for it is a rewarding experience. In this book we will provide the words and the pictures that will show you how to "truss the bird," "clean the shrimp," or "whip until soft peaks form." These are a few of the simple procedures, simply stated in most recipes, but until you are familiar with these procedures and know how to go about them, they could just as well be written in Sanskrit. Be assured that all of these techniques—and many more—are fully described, or pictured, when you need them in this book. Now to begin.

How to Use a Recipe

For best results, recipes must be followed exactly.

Always read the recipe completely before you begin to cook—this means reading all the directions as well as the list of ingredients. Be sure that you are familiar with the cooking terms used; if you're not, check the procedure in Redbook's Guide to Cooking Terms on page 4, to see how to proceed.

Check the equipment you will need. When a specific size of pan is called for, the size given is the one that was used when the recipe was tested. Pan size and shape will affect the results of any dish; if you can't be exact, stay as close as possible to the size and shape described.

Assemble all the ingredients. Use the ones called for; they were chosen because they were best suited to the recipe. (One of the most common errors among young cooks is the use of a similar-sounding product instead of the exact one; for example, condensed milk instead of evaporated milk.) Don't alter amounts of key ingredients, such as flour, sugar, liquids, or shortening. Spices and seasoning may be varied, but until you are sure of yourself and your tastes, it is safer to follow the recipe exactly—at least the first time you prepare it. For best results in all recipes, butter, eggs, and milk should stand at room temperature a short time before you use them.

Assemble all the equipment. This will include measuring spoons and cups, mixing spoons and bowls, saucepans or baking pans, depending on the recipe being prepared.

Measure accurately. Tested recipes are based on the use of standard measuring cups and spoons. Be sure you know how to use these utensils properly (see How to Measure Ingredients Accurately on page 11).

Mix carefully. Follow directions exactly. Overmixing or undermixing, especially in baked goods, can give disastrous results.

Bake or cook as directed. Times and temperatures indicated in recipes should be carefully followed for complete success. All the recipes in this book give oven temperature in temperature degrees, and most recipes have top-of-range temperatures described both in words and in temperature degree. Top-of-range temperatures are noted for use with calibrated (temperature-controlled) burners.

Redbook's Guide to Cooking Terms

What does the recipe *really* mean when it says to *mince*? Isn't *chopping* the same thing? And what's the difference between *whip* and *beat*? If you've ever been frustrated by a recipe (and who hasn't?), you know how important cooking terminology is to the dish you bring to the table. At *Redbook* we never assume that everyone knows every nuance in the language of cooking, and we write our recipes so that you can understand them. But all recipe authors aren't always that explicit. What follows here is a guide to the most frequently used terms you'll come across in cooking, with complete definitions of each. When a term is new to you, refer to this guide.

À la king—served in a rich cream sauce (chicken à la king).

À la mode—usually describing cakes or pies served with ice cream (apple pie à la mode). Beef à la mode is a well-known dish in which the meat is larded before braising and simmering with vegetables. The vegetables are later served with the gravy.

Au gratin—foods creamed or moistened with milk or stock. The food is placed in a casserole or baking dish, covered with crumbs, butter, or cheese and baked or broiled until the top is brown (potatoes au gratin).

Au jus—meat served with its natural unthickened juices.

Bake—to cook by dry heat, usually in the oven (cakes). When applied to meats, the process is called roasting (roast beef).

Barbecue—to roast or broil on a rack or revolving spit over or under a source of cooking heat. The food is usually basted with a highly seasoned sauce (barbecued spareribs).

Baste—to moisten food, usually meat, while it is cooking. Melted fat or other liquid may be used. Basting adds flavor and prevents drying.

Batter—a mixture of flour and liquid, or a combination with other ingredients, of a consistency thin enough to pour (waffles).

Beat—to make a mixture smooth by rapid, regular motion that lifts it up and over. An electric mixer, rotary beater, wire whip, or mixing spoon may be used.

Blanch—to pour boiling water over food, or to place it in water, bring it to a boil, and drain. In some cases the food is then covered with cold water (removing skin from almonds).

Blend—to combine two or more ingredients thoroughly (sugar and shortening in cake batter).

Boil—to cook in liquid at boiling temperature. Boiling point is reached when bubbles rise continuously and break at the surface. Slow boiling will cook just as effectively as rapid boiling.

Bouquet garni—a bunch of herbs used to season soups, stews, braised dishes, and sauces. Parsley, thyme, and bay leaves are the foundation; other herbs may be added. They are wrapped together with a string or tied in cheesecloth, cooked with the food, and removed before serving.

Braise—to brown meat or vegetables in a small amount of hot fat and then cover and cook over very low heat (about 200° F.), sometimes adding a small amount of liquid (braised beef).

Bread—to coat the surface of food with fine dry bread, cracker, or cereal crumbs, or to coat with crumbs, then dip in diluted eggs or milk, and again coat with crumbs (breaded veal cutlets).

Broil—to cook under direct heat, as in a broiler, or over hot coals, as on a grill.

Brush—to spread butter (usually melted), margarine, eggs, etc., on top of food with a brush, paper towel, or cloth (egg glaze on cookies).

Candy—has two meanings. When applied to fruit and fruit peels, it means to cook in a heavy sugar syrup until transparent, then drain and dry (candied orange peel). The second meaning applies to vegetables that are cooked in a sugar syrup to give a coating or glaze (candied sweet potatoes).

Caramelize—to heat sugar slowly over low heat in a heavy utensil until sugar melts and develops a golden brown color and a caramel flavor (caramel syrup).

Chill—to allow to become thoroughly cold, usually in the refrigerator.

Chop—to cut into small pieces. If a French knife is used and you are right-handed, press two or three fingers from the left hand on the back of the blade near the point. With the handle in the right hand, cut up and down in a rocking motion, pivoting the point of the knife.

Clarify—as applied to liquid food or fat, it means to render clear or limpid, to suppress the solid parts or separate solids from liquid (clarified butter).

Coat—to cover the surface of food evenly with flour, sugar, crumbs, or nuts. Or to dip in slightly beaten egg or milk and then in seasoned crumbs or flour (croquettes).

Coat a spoon—indicates the thickness of a custard sauce. A metal spoon dipped in thickened sauce will be thoroughly coated with a thin film.

Coddle—to simmer gently in liquid over low heat (about 200° F.) for a short time (coddled eggs).

Cool—to let stand at room temperature until no longer warm to the touch.

Cream—to make soft, smooth, and creamy by beating with a spoon or electric beater; often applies to shortening and sugar as used in cakes.

Crimp—used in pastry-making; applies to formation of decorative edge on crust.

Crumb—to envelop a piece of food in bread crumbs or cracker crumbs after dipping it in egg or milk (see *Coat* and *Bread*).

Cube—to cut into small cubes (croutons).

Cut in—to distribute solid shortening through dry ingredients by using two knives, a pastry blender, or a fork (piecrust).

Dash—a scant ⅛ teaspoon of dry ingredients or liquid (a dash of nutmeg).

Deep-fat fry—to cook in a deep container in enough fat to cover food (croquettes or deep-fat-fried chicken).

Dice—to cut into ¼-inch cubes. Vegetables are cut into lengthwise or crosswise slices, then into slices ¼ inch wide and finally sliced crosswise into ¼-inch pieces (diced potatoes).

Diluted egg white or yolk—the separated egg white or yolk is slightly beaten and diluted with 2 tablespoons water.

Dissolve—to combine a dry substance with a liquid so that they merge and the dry substance liquefies (sugar syrup).

Dredge—to coat completely with a dry ingredient, such as with seasoned flour or sugar (stew meats).

Dress—to prepare for cooking, as to dress a chicken.

Dust—to sprinkle lightly with flour or sugar (confectioners' sugar on cookies).

Few drops—less than ⅛ of a teaspoon of a liquid ingredient.

Few grains—less than ⅛ of a teaspoon of a dry ingredient.

Flake—to break up into small pieces with a fork (canned tuna).

Flambé—to cover or combine food with alcoholic spirits (brandy or cognac) and burn with a flame (crêpe suzettes).

Fluting—an edging for pastry. Pastry dough is pressed around the rim of the pie plate into a standing rim and then formed into a fluted edge with the fingertips.

Fold in—to combine a delicate ingredient such as whipped cream or beaten egg whites with a solid mixture such as a batter, using a gentle under-and-over motion with a wire whip or rubber spatula.

Fricassee—meat or fowl cut into serving pieces, cooked in liquid, and thickened (chicken fricassee).

Frizzle—to fry in a pan with a little fat until edges curl (oysters).

Fry—to cook in hot fat (see *Sauté, Pan-fry,* and *Deep-fat fry*).

Garnish—to decorate.

Glaze—to coat with sugar syrup or melted jelly, either during or after cooking (glazed ham).

Grate—to rub on a grater to produce small particles (Parmesan cheese).

Grease—to rub a cooking utensil with a fat such as shortening or butter before filling with food.

Grill—another term for broiling.

Grind—to put through a food chopper (meat or vegetables).

Hull—to remove or strip off outer covering or stems of certain fruits and vegetables (to remove stem end from strawberries).

Julienne—to cut food into narrow, lengthwise, matchlike strips (julienne potatoes).

Larding—to cover meat, fish, or poultry with strips or slices of fat, or to insert fat under the skin or into the flesh with a skewer or larding needle (beef à la mode).

Level—applied to measurement of dry or solid ingredients in cooking. Ingredients should come to the top of the measuring utensil and then be leveled off with a straight-edged spatula or knife.

Lukewarm—in cooking, means the liquid or solid food is moderately warm to the touch (about 110° F.).

Marinate—to let food stand in a spicy, often acid, mixture (marinade) to improve flavor and texture (sauerbraten).

Mash—to make a soft or pulpy mass of food (mashed potatoes).

Mask—to cover a food completely with sauce, jelly, aspic, mayonnaise, or whipped cream (ham chaudfroid).

Melt—to reduce solids to liquids with the application of heat.

Mince—to cut or chop into very fine pieces.

Pan-broil—to cook uncovered in a hot skillet, pouring off fat as it accumulates (pan-broiled steak).

Pan-fry—to cook in a skillet with a small amount of fat (pan-fried fish fillets).

Parboil—to boil in liquid until partially cooked (green peppers for stuffing).

Parch—to brown by means of dry heat; applied to grains of corn.

Pare—to cut away the outer surface of vegetables and fruits with a knife or other utensil.

Pasta—this Italian term for paste and dough now generally includes all forms of macaroni, spaghetti, and noodles (ravioli).

Paste—once included the pasta products, but now usually means either a dough with a large amount of fat, used in making pastry for pie, or a smooth food product made by evaporation and grinding (almond paste).

Peel—to strip off the outer covering of certain vegetables and fruits; also, the rind or skin of certain fruits.

Pinch—the amount of a spice, herb, or condiment that can be held between thumb and forefinger.

Pipe—to ornament with a decorating tube (whipped cream on pumpkin pie).

Pit—to remove pits or seeds from fruit.

Poach—to cook in simmering liquid (poached fish or eggs).

Pot-roast—to cook by braising, usually over direct heat (pot roast of beef).

Precook—to simmer for a short time in water before cooking by some other method (see *Parboil*).

Preheat—to bring oven or broiler to desired temperature before using.

Purée—to press food through a fine sieve or food mill (applesauce).

Reduce—to lessen quantity of liquid by boiling it away over moderately high heat (about 325° F.) to the desired quantity.

Rehydrate—to soak, cook, or use other procedures with dehydrated foods to restore water lost through drying (dried minced onion).

Render—to heat fat, such as suet or salt pork, until melted, with only the crisp part (called cracklings) remaining.

Roast—to cook by dry heat, usually in the oven (meat or poultry).

Roll—has three meanings. First, to spread flat with a rolling pin, as rolling out pastry. Second, to roll up, as with a jelly roll. Third, a small piece of yeast dough baked in any of numerous forms.

Roux—a mixture of melted fat and flour used in making sauces and gravies.

Sauté—to cook in a small amount of hot fat in a skillet (sautéed onions).

Scald—to heat to just below the boiling point. Also, to pour boiling water over food or dip food quickly into boiling water (peeling tomatoes).

Scramble—to stir or mix gently while cooking (scrambled eggs).

Sear—to brown the surface of meat quickly by intense heat.

Season—to add a sprinkling of salt or pepper to taste.

Section—to remove neat segments of orange or grapefruit. After removing the peel in a continuous spiral, a cut (using a sawing motion) is made along the sides of each membrane so that the sections can be flipped out.

Shirr—to break into a dish with cream or crumbs, then bake (shirred eggs).

Shred—to cut or tear into long, narrow pieces (greens for salad) or to grate coarsely (cheese).

Sift—to put one or more dry ingredients through a fine sieve.

Simmer—to cook in liquid just below the boiling point.

Singe—to burn lightly or scorch the surface by passing over a flame. Usually done to remove hair and down from plucked poultry.

Skewer—to hold in place with metal or wooden pins (closing the cavity opening of a turkey).

Slit—to make a shallow incision in the surface, as in piecrust or meat.

Snip—to cut with a knife or scissors into small pieces (to snip chives).

Steam—to cook in a closed pot with only enough water to generate steam (rice).

Steam-bake—to cook in the oven in a pan or baking dish set in a pan of water (baked custard).

Steep—to cover with boiling water and let stand without additional heating (tea).

Stew—to cook foods in simmering liquid (meat-and-vegetable stew).

Tenderize—to make meat tender by pounding, marinating, or using a meat tenderizer.

Toast—to brown by direct heat in a toaster or the oven (bread toast or toasted coconut).

Toss—to tumble ingredients lightly with a fork and spoon (salad greens).

Truss—to fasten the leg and wing joints of fowl with skewers or twine before cooking.

Wedge—to cut fruit, meat, vegetables in the triangular shape of a wedge.

Whip—to beat rapidly with a rotary beater, electric mixer, or wire whip to incorporate air and increase volume (whipped cream or egg whites for meringue).

How to Measure Ingredients Accurately

A collection of basic measuring utensils is essential. For dry ingredients you need nested metal or plastic measuring cups from ¼-cup to 1-cup capacity; these should measure flush to the rim, enabling you to level off contents at the top. For liquid ingredients you need glass or plastic cup or quart measures that have fractional markings visible from the outside, a margin at the top, and a pouring spout. Other indispensables include a set of measuring spoons from ¼-teaspoon to 1-tablespoon capacity, a metal spatula or knife, and a rubber spatula. A flat surface on which to work (preferably one covered with clean waxed paper or foil to catch overflows) is also important.

Powdered ingredients: To measure the usual small quantities of baking powder, baking soda, salt, and other dry seasonings, first stir to break up small lumps, fill the measuring spoon to overflowing, then level it off with the straight edge of a spatula or knife.

White flour: Spoon either sifted or unsifted flour (depending on the recipe) into the dry measure until overflowing. Level off with the straight edge of a knife or metal spatula.

Whole-grain flours or meal: Stir lightly with a fork or spoon. Do not sift. Measure as you do white flour.

Liquids: Place the liquid measure on a level surface and fill it to the desired mark. Check the mark at eye level. Use measuring spoons to measure less than ¼ cup.

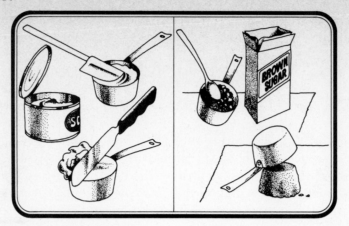

Solid shortening: If the shortening has been chilled, bring it to room temperature. With a rubber spatula, pack it firmly into a dry-measure cup. Level it off with the straight edge of a metal spatula or knife. Scrape out with a rubber spatula.

Sugar: Measure both granulated and confectioners' sugar as you do white flour. Spoon into the measure until overflowing, then level off.

Brown sugar: Break up any lumps by rolling or sifting. Pack into a dry-measure cup firmly with a spoon or rubber spatula. Level with the spatula or a knife, then turn out. (It should keep the shape of the cup.)

How to Choose the Right Pan Size

There is a reason why a specific pan size is called for in a recipe. A shallow baking dish will produce a different result from a deep casserole. In cake baking following suggested pan sizes is enormously important for good results.

If you don't know the size of your pan, look on the bottom. Many manufacturers imprint the pan size there. If the size is not there, you can use a ruler to measure height and diameter, or length and width. To determine the size of casseroles and molds, fill them with water, then measure the water. Be sure your casserole or mold will hold the quantity the recipe yields. Casserole measurements are usually given in cups, pints, or quarts.

How to Mix

Depending on what kind of mixing is called for, you'll need mixing spoons (either wooden or metal), mixing bowls in a variety of sizes, a wire whip (sometimes called a whisk), a rotary beater or an electric mixer, a pastry blender or two knives, and a level work surface.

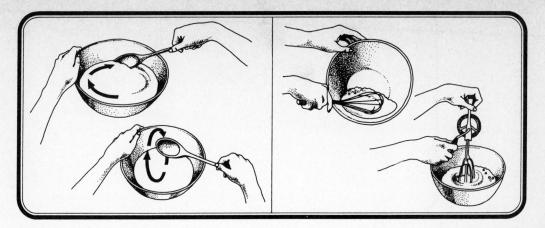

To stir: With a large mixing spoon, blend the ingredients together in a bowl, using a circular motion and widening the circles as you mix.

To cream *(not shown):* Work one or more ingredients (usually sugar and shortening) together in a bowl by pressing them against the bowl with the back of a spoon. Creaming can also be done with an electric mixer.

To beat: In a large bowl, mix the ingredients together with a vigorous, upward, circular motion with a mixing spoon or wire whip, lifting the mixture up and over to bring the under part to the surface. Tilt the bowl as you beat. Beating can also be done with an electric mixer.

To whip: In a bowl large enough to allow for the increased volume that results from whipping, beat the ingredients rapidly with a wire whip or rotary beater. This action aerates the mixture and increases its volume. (Ingredients that need whipping most frequently are heavy cream and egg whites.)

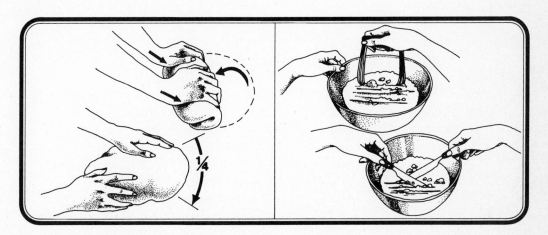

To knead: On a floured board or pastry cloth, shape the dough into a round, flat ball. Pick up the edge of the dough farthest away and fold it toward you. With the heels of both hands, press down gently but firmly at the same time pushing the dough away from you. Give the dough a quarter turn and repeat the folding, pressing, and pushing motions. Repeat—turning, folding, pressing, and pushing—until the dough is no longer sticky, looks and feels smooth, and has elasticity.

To cut in shortening: This term means to blend shortening and flour together until particles of shortening are flour coated and of a specific size. (For pastry the mixture should resemble coarse meal.) There are two standard methods: Make up-and-down chopping motions through the ingredients with a pastry blender; or use two crossed knives, one in each hand, and cut through the mixture in scissorlike strokes.

How to Change Recipe Quantities

To Cut a Recipe: In general it is better not to alter the size of a recipe; plan to use any leftovers for another meal. However, most recipes are made to serve either four or six, and many of them can be reduced to serve two by using only one half or one third the amount of each ingredient. Cooking times may need to be shortened and smaller utensils used.

When you divide a recipe, it sometimes helps to translate amounts into equivalent measures. One-third cup, for example, can be divided in half most accurately when you know that it equals 5 tablespoons plus 1 teaspoon, or 16 teaspoons; half will be 8 teaspoons or 2 tablespoons plus 2 teaspoons. Approach this division as the mathematical problem it is and do it carefully before you begin your recipe. Make a note of the halved figures in the page margin, or rewrite the recipe for future reference.

One problem in division puzzles many cooks: How do you halve an egg? Beat it with a fork until the white and yolk are mixed, then measure it with a standard tablespoon and use half for your recipe. Cover the remainder and store it in the refrigerator to supplement the breakfast scrambled eggs. One egg usually yields about 4 tablespoons. The following list includes the equivalents you'll need most often when dividing recipes.

Equivalent Weights and Measures

Dash	equals	2 to 3 drops or less than ⅛ teaspoon
Few drops	equals	less than ⅛ teaspoon
Few grains	equals	less than ⅛ teaspoon
1 tablespoon	equals	3 teaspoons or ½ fluid ounce
¼ cup	equals	4 tablespoons or 2 fluid ounces
⅓ cup	equals	5⅓ tablespoons or 2⅔ fluid ounces
½ cup	equals	8 tablespoons or 4 fluid ounces
¾ cup	equals	12 tablespoons or 6 fluid ounces
1 cup	equals	16 tablespoons or 8 fluid ounces
8 fluid ounces	equals	1 cup or ½ pint
16 fluid ounces	equals	2 cups or 1 pint
32 fluid ounces	equals	4 cups or 1 quart
1 gallon	equals	4 quarts

To Increase a Recipe: If a recipe yields six servings and you wish to serve eight persons, it is best to increase the recipe by half. Follow the procedure for cutting a recipe in half, then add the result to the original recipe.

Write down the amounts you plan to use. The most common mistake in altering recipes is to increase all but one ingredient.

How to Use Recipes and Metric Measures

The measuring units used in most of the world are based on the metric system and consequently recipes from foreign cookbooks use metric measurements. In the United States, packaged-food labels carry both the U.S. Standard measurements (ounces and/or pounds) and the metric measure (grams) to indicate the weight of the product. All nutrition labeling for protein, carbohydrates and fats in labeled food is given in grams.

The metric system, which is really more precise than the U.S. Standard, is based on the decimal system of numbers, which involves multiples of 10. Thus it is very easy to go from small units to large, or vice versa, simply by moving decimal points.

The basic metric units are grams (units of mass or weight), liters (units of volume) and meters (linear measures). Once the basic unit is determined, multiples are built on it with suitable prefixes:

Kilo- means 1000 times the basic unit, hence 1 kilogram equals 1000 grams and 1 kiloliter, 1000 liters.

Deci- means one tenth, so a decimeter is one tenth of a meter.

Centi- means one hundredth, so a centimeter is one hundredth of a meter.

Milli- means one thousandth, so a milligram is one thousandth of a gram.

Micro- means one millionth, so a microgram is one millionth of a gram.

In using recipes written with the metric system the major differences you will find will be in pan sizes, measured in centimenters rather than inches, and in liquid measures, given in liters, half liters, quarter liters and milliliters instead of quarts, pints, cups and portions of them. (Should the United States adopt the metric system, small measures such as tablespoons, teaspoons and fractions of them are not likely to change.) Dry ingredients such as flour and sugar usually are weighed in grams rather than measured in a cup. Meats, fruits and vegetables are purchased by the kilogram and are measured by gram weight in recipes. Oven temperatures are Celsius (°C.) rather than Fahrenheit (°F.).

It is relatively easy to convert recipes from U.S. Standard measurements to metric measurements or vice versa. Sets of measuring cups and spoons marked with both U.S. Standard and metric measurements are available. Kitchen scales for weight measurements also are available with dual markings.

To give you some feeling of the relationship between the two systems, it is helpful to keep in mind these two "benchmarks": a liter equals a little more than a quart (1 quart + 3 tablespoons); a kilogram equals a little more than two pounds (2.2 pounds). As a shopping aid, here are some approximate equivalents:

1 pound	= 454 grams
1 ounce	= 28 grams
1 cup	= 240 milliliters
1 tablespoon	= 15 milliliters
1 teaspoon	= 5 milliliters
1 inch	= 2½ centimeters

How to Equip Your Kitchen

Before you shop for housewares to equip your new kitchen, decide what you need. Although there are some items most cooks would agree are necessary, your entire list won't be exactly like anyone else's. And if you don't plan ahead, you may spend too much on attractive specialty pieces and end up without the basic tools you need.

The amount of money you can spend and the storage space in your kitchen will limit your list. If either is small, you must be especially careful to choose first those things you'll use most often. Even with a low budget it pays to buy good-quality cutlery, saucepans, frying pans, and measuring cups—things that you'll use day in and day out for years.

The type of food you expect to cook affects the make-up of your equipment list. If you don't intend to bake angel or chiffon cakes, you can get along without a tube cake pan; if you like homemade pizza, get a pizza pan. The extent to which you'll use prepared foods is another consideration. If you use instant mashed potatoes, you'll have little need for a potato masher. If you use frozen pie crusts or bakery pies, you won't need a pastry blender.

In some cases you'll need to decide what size utensils to buy. As for pots and pans, you'll probably do best to buy two 2-quart covered saucepans and a 10- or 12-inch covered frying pan. You'll find a small saucepan handy for melting butter, warming bits of leftovers, and for cooking other foods that would dry out in a large pan. Even when cooking for two, you'll need at least one large pot to cook foods such as spaghetti, corned beef, and corn on the cob. A 4- or 5-quart Dutch oven is excellent for pot roasts, stews, and a good many recipes suitable for buffet-style entertaining. A small frying pan is another useful item when you're cooking for one or two. Cookie sheets should be at least 2 inches smaller on all sides than your oven racks. A 13-x-9-x-2-inch cake pan is usable for many mixes and recipes and can double as an open roasting pan.

When you shop, you'll see displays of cookware in sets. There is economy in buying a set if the pieces are what you would select on an individual basis (and matching cookware does look nice when displayed). But remember that no one material is perfect for all cooking purposes; the pan that conducts heat well so that water boils quickly in it can't also be expected to hold heat so that food stays hot in it for serving. Many experienced cooks prefer to have an assortment of cookware from which they can choose the items best suited to each cooking job. You may want some utensils with nonstick linings, such as Teflon, and others without.

When possible, choose items that serve more than one purpose. Muffin pans can be used for many recipes, but corn-stick pans are limited; a ring mold is more versatile than a fish mold. Cook-and-serve ware that is both practical and good-looking is readily available and a good investment. Any uncovered dish can easily become a lidded one with a covering of heavy-duty foil.

Use our suggested list of equipment below as a starting point as you make your own list, planning an assortment that will let you work efficiently and accurately in following basic recipes. You can add the extras as your cooking skill improves.

STORAGE

Canister set with airtight covers
Refrigerator dishes, glass or plastic
Freezer containers, assorted sizes
Widemouthed, screw-top jars, also useful as refrigerator storage containers
Plastic bags, large and small

Reusable plastic containers, useful for refrigerator storage
Rolls of aluminum foil, plastic film and waxed paper

Useful but not essential

Breadbox
Spice rack
Root–vegetable bin

Dish-storage racks
Dispenser for paper towels, waxed paper, plastic wrap, foil

PREPARATION

Mixing bowls, graduated from 3 cups to 4 quarts
Metal cups for dry measure, 1-, ½-, ⅓-, and ¼-cup sizes
Glass cup for liquid measure, marked for fractions of cup
Measuring spoons, ⅛ teaspoon to 1 tablespoon

Metal spatulas, large and small
Beater, hand or electric
Can openers, regular and juice
Cutting board
Corkscrew
Juicer or reamer
Colander

TO BEGIN

Rubber or plastic spatulas, wide
and narrow
Cutting board
Cutlery
    paring knives
    5-inch utility knife
    carver
    slicer
Floating-blade parer

Strainers, large and small
String
Meat thermometer
Skewers
Grater
Molds
Vegetable brush
Toaster

Useful but not essential

Glass cups for liquid measure, 2-
cup and 4-cup
Kitchen shears
Cutlery
    grapefruit knife
    8-inch French chef's knife
Mixing fork
Flour sifter
Cheesecloth
Blender, electric
Cookie cutters, cookie press
Egg slicer
Kitchen scale with customary
    (U.S.) and metric (gram) markings

Wire whip or whisk
Pastry blender
Pastry cloth and rolling-pin cover
Rolling pin
Cutting wheel for pastry
Pastry brush
Garlic press
Candy thermometer
Deep-fat thermometer
Meat grinder
Food mill
Small funnel
Knife sharpener
Bottle opener

TOP OF RANGE

Saucepans, covered
    2-quart
    3-quart or second 2-quart
    1-quart or smaller
Dutch oven, 4- or 5-quart
Large kettle or pot, 6-quart or larger
Covered frying pan, 10- or 12-inch
Small frying pan
Coffeepot or electric coffee maker

Slotted spoon
Basting spoon
Turners
Two-tined fork
Ladle
Wooden or plastic spoons
Minute timer
Vegetable steamer

Useful but not essential

Electric frying pan
Griddle
Chicken fryer
Teakettle
Teapot

Carafe (for instant coffee)
Potato masher
Kitchen tongs
Kitchen clock with second hand
Double boiler

OVEN

Cake pans
    8- or 9-inch layers

Custard cups
Pie plate, 9-inch

13-x-9-x-2-inch
9-x-9-x-2-inch
tube cake pan
Loaf pan, 9-x-5-x-3-inch
Cookie sheets
Muffin pans

Casserole dish, 2-quart
Shallow baking dish, 1½-quart
Open roasting pan
Meat rack
Cake racks
Pot holders

Useful but not essential

Casserole dishes
1- or 1½-quart
3-quart
Soufflé dishes
Shallow baking dish, 2- or 2½-quart

Au gratin dish (shallow, broiler-
proof baking dish)
Covered roaster
Meat lifter

How to Choose a Stock of Staples

Staples are those basic food items that you keep on hand and use again and again as you prepare recipes and serve meals. Some are used alone; some, in recipes or as accompaniments to other foods. The ones we've listed here include the essentials—salt, sugar, shortening—and some optional ones that may not be to your taste—horseradish is a good example. We've also included some products, such as canned vegetables, that are good to have in the house for last-minute meals when you can't get out to shop. For efficiency's sake, keep your store of staples complete, replenishing as you run out of an item.

Baking powder
Baking soda
Biscuit mix
Bouillon cubes (beef and chicken)
Bread crumbs, dried
Cake frosting mixes
Cake mixes
Canned fish (tuna, salmon, sardines, crab meat, and shrimp)
Canned fruits (applesauce, cherries, cranberry sauce, fruit cocktail, grapefruit, peaches, pears, pineapple)
Canned juices (apple, cranberry, grapefruit, lemon, orange, pineapple, tomato)
Canned gravy (beef and chicken)
Canned meat (boned chicken, corned beef hash, luncheon meat)
Canned vegetables (asparagus; baked

beans; beets; corn; green beans; lima beans; mixed vegetables; peas; pimiento; potatoes, white and sweet; tomatoes)
Carbonated beverages
Catsup
Cereals, hot, and individual-serving boxes of dry cereals
Chocolate, unsweetened
Cocoa, unsweetened
Coconut, flaked or shredded
Coffee and instant coffee
Corn meal
Cornstarch
Crackers
Cream of tartar
Dehydrated soup mixes
Dehydrated vegetable flakes (parsley and onion)
Dried fruits (raisins and prunes)

Extracts (almond, lemon, pepper-
  mint, and vanilla)
Flour (all-purpose, instant-type, and
  cake)
Gelatin, unflavored and flavored
Herbs (see Spice-Shelf Shopping
  List, page 963)
Horseradish, prepared
Instant mashed potatoes
Jams and jellies
Macaroni
Meat tenderizer, instant
Milk (dried skim and evaporated)
Noodles
Nuts (almonds, peanuts, pecans, wal-
  nuts)
Olives
Peanut butter
Pickles and relish
Pudding mixes (cooked and instant)
Rice (regular and precooked)
Salad dressing (French and mayon-
  naise)

Salad oil
Salt
Sauce mixes, packaged dry
Seasoned salts
Shortening
Soy sauce
Spaghetti
Spices (see Spice-Shelf Shopping
  List, page 963)
Sugars (granulated, brown, confec-
  tioners')
Syrups (maple; honey; corn syrup,
  light and dark)
Tabasco sauce
Tapioca
Tea
Tomato sauce
Vinegar (cider and wine)
Vegetable oil
Worcestershire sauce

How to Buy and Use Food Wisely

When you first begin to shop, try all the stores convenient to you until you find the ones that carry the products you like at the lowest prices. Explore the small neighborhood stores, the large chains, the locally owned supermarkets. Many women divide their shopping among several stores when they discover that one consistently has fresh produce, another offers the best savings on canned goods, and so on. Because shopping is of such major importance in the whole business of food preparation, you will find shopping hints in every chapter of this book. However, these general rules may help you save money and time when you shop.

Planning the Weekly Shopping

1. *Watch newspaper ads, usually on Wednesdays, for supermarket weekend specials on foods you use frequently.* Make a shopping list based on several days' menus, listing the items in the order of the store's traffic pattern. This is a real step-saver.

2. Plan your weekly menus around the specials. Have menus made up before you shop, but be flexible. If the weekly meat special is beef, plan to use it. Be prepared to switch vegetables and fruits to take advantage of the best buys.

3. *Before you shop check your refrigerator and freezer for foods that should be used and plan menus that will use them. Remember that you can combine left-over vegetables in an omelet or soufflé or a cheese casserole that will substitute nicely for a more costly main dish.*

4. Shop in a supermarket for staples, canned goods, and frozen items. Chain stores can frequently offer better prices and a wider variety of brands and sizes than the independent grocer.

5. *Shop early in the day; the store will not be so crowded, the fresh produce will be fresher, and specials will be readily available.*

6. Make use of seasonal foods. Fresh fruits and vegetables in season are usually cheaper than those frozen or canned. Frozen orange juice concentrate is an exception: it is ordinarily lower in price than fresh orange juice.

7. *Buy fruits and vegetables only in quantities you can consume. Nothing is saved if you must throw away overripe, unused food.*

8. To help you keep track of the money you're spending before you reach the check-out counter, a small hand calculator to total your purchases as you fill your cart is a convenience. You will know immediately whether or not you can take advantage of extra food bargains you might otherwise pass by.

9. *Use coupons or discount slips you find in magazines or newspapers or receive in the mail.*

10. Shop alone if possible. You will be better able to concentrate, and other members of the family will not be adding unnecessary—and often expensive—items to the shopping cart.

What to Look for at the Store

11. *Watch for items on sale. Often they are used as "come-ons," but if they are things you use regularly, stock up.*

12. If an item is priced "2 for __," buy both to save a penny or two.

13. *Sometimes it is more economical to buy the smaller size if you are not going to use all the larger. Waste is no saving.*

14. When large quantities of meat are offered at a special price, take advantage of the saving. Buy a whole loin of pork, cut off enough chops for a meal, and roast the rest. Cut off part of a large pot roast and slice for a Stroganoff; make a pot roast with the remainder.

15. *Buy whole chickens and cut them up yourself. Use the meaty parts for oven frying; make a soup stock from the backs, wing tips, and necks.*

16. When buying meat, consider the cost per serving rather than the cost per pound. A boneless roast at a higher price per pound may yield more per serving than a bone-in roast that costs much less per pound.

17. *The cheapest ground meat is not always the best buy. Chuck, which is often fatty, will not yield as many servings as the more expensive and leaner ground round.*

18. Check into the smaller-sized fruits, especially apples. They may not look quite as handsome, but the price may be several cents a pound less than the other sizes.

19. *When buying potatoes, consider the types and relative costs. Baking-type potatoes will be more expensive than regular ones. If you use potatoes frequently for mashing, boiling, or making casseroles, you don't need the baking type. For a small family, however, the baking type may be the better buy to use for all purposes.*

20. When fresh fruits and vegetables are at their seasonal height, the frozen products will often be reduced in price. If you have an adequate freezer, this is the time to buy the frozen foods for later use.

21. *For some families, the large plastic bags of loose frozen vegetables and fruits are the best buy. Take out only what you need and keep the rest frozen.*

22. When shopping for eggs, compare the cost of the various sizes. Medium eggs priced seven cents per dozen less than large eggs are the best buy. Brown eggs usually cost less than white ones, and the color does not influence the quality. Purchase eggs from a refrigerated case. Refrigerate them promptly at home, large end up, to help maintain proper quality.

23. *If your family uses large quantities of fresh milk, select the half-gallon containers. Purchase at a supermarket, since home-delivered milk costs several cents more per quart.*

24. Shop for cereals carefully. If your family eats dry cereals often, buy big packages, as they are cheaper than individual boxes. For occasional cereal eaters, individual sizes may be the best buy. The sugar-coated variety costs more than the unsugared. Cereals to cook and serve hot are the best buys of all.

25. *If your freezer space allows, buy ice cream in large containers and ice-cream cones in bulk to provide inexpensive treats for the children.*

26. Buy uncut butter by the pound rather than the more expensive, quarter-pound sticks.

27. *Sometimes it is wise to buy canned goods by the case. If you use a lot of tomatoes for sauces and other dishes, ask the store manager for a case price.*

28. Don't ignore the second-day, specially priced baked goods at your supermarket. Rolls sprinkled with water and reheated in a paper bag at a low oven temperature will come out almost as good as fresh ones. Day-old bread is perfect for toasting, making stuffings, or making bread pudding. Sponge-cake layers with a warm lemon sauce could be the answer for dessert.

29. *Always check the price-per-unit weight of a giant economy-sized package or can to be sure it is really a saving. Sometimes the small size will be cheaper.*

30. Don't be an impulse buyer. If you are attracted to something unusual, ask yourself whether your family will eat it—and if they don't, can you afford to throw it away?

Ways to Save Money in Food Preparation

31. *The fanciest-graded product (usually the most expensive) is not always the best buy for every purpose. When a food is to be mixed with other ingredients, the quality is not as important as when it's to be served alone. For example, if only the drained fruit is to be used in a recipe, use halves and slices (whole fruits cost more) packed in a lighter syrup. Save the syrup to add to a gelatin salad or to blend with citrus juice.*

32. Homemade soups can be less expensive than the canned or dry soup mixes. Make soup stock from beef bones, which the butcher may even give free of charge. For chicken stock, use packaged wings; after cooking, carefully remove the meat from the bones. You'll be surprised at the amount of meat one pound of wings will produce. Add to the soup along with vegetables, or use in a dish calling for boned chicken.

33. *When making a stew, prepare enough for two meals. You save not only time but fuel costs as well.*

34. Instead of an expensive prepared dessert, serve fresh fruits when they are seasonally cheap.

35. *Save the water in which vegetables are cooked. Use to add to soup stock for additional food value and flavor.*

36. For casseroles, use a less expensive brand of canned vegetables, such as regular-pack tomatoes or mushroom stems and pieces, since appearance won't count so much.

37. *Save bits of jelly left in jars. They may be combined, melted down, and used to glaze a ham or pour over fruit tarts.*

38. Use nonfat dry milk or canned evaporated milk in prepared dishes.

39. *Mix together equal parts of reconstituted nonfat dry milk and fresh whole milk for drinking.*

40. Save celery leaves and scallion tops for use in stews and soups or to cut up in a salad.

41. *Leftovers that are too meager to be served by themselves (e.g., a few boiled potatoes, a small amount of rice or noodles) can often be combined with meat and other vegetables for a quick and—depending on your ingredients—surprisingly tasty meal.*

42. Use ends of French bread that have become hard to make bread crumbs. Crush them with a rolling pin or, easier still, whirl them in a blender.

43. *If a recipe calls for only the egg white, save the yolk to use later as a glaze or in making mayonnaise. (See How to Store Leftover Yolks, page 445.)*

44. Brown meat in the fat trimmed from the meat itself rather than in butter or other fat.

45. *Learn to stretch your meat; a meat loaf made with bread crumbs, egg,* *chopped celery, and onions will go much further than the same amount of chopped meat served by itself.*

46. Small, leftover pieces of cheese or cheese that has dried out can be grated and kept covered in the refrigerator. Use to add interest to casseroles, or melt to use in pasta, on potatoes, or on other vegetables.

47. *Cheaper cuts of beef may sometimes be broiled or pan-fried if you make use of a meat tenderizer.*

48. Be sure to use leftover foods promptly so that flavor and texture will not be impaired by long refrigeration.

49. *Freeze leftover rolls; reheat for another meal.*

50. Save bacon drippings in a covered jar in the refrigerator to use in cooking—for browning meats (when the flavor is compatible) or in a hot salad dressing.

High Altitude Cooking

Cooking at high altitudes presents the problem of adjusting the instructions in regular recipes to account for the lower boiling points and the rapid evaporation that take place when atmospheric pressure is decreased. If you live and cook in an area of the country that is 2000 or more feet above sea level you can expect that water will boil at a lower temperature than 212° F.; the higher the altitude, the lower the boiling temperature of liquids and the more rapid the evaporation. In general, you will find that for top-of-range cooking you will need to use more liquid than a sea-level recipe requires and increase the cooking time so ingredients will reach a desired degree of doneness.

Top-of-range cooking with little or no liquid will be most successful in heavy saucepans with tight-fitting covers and heavy skillets. Braised meats and vegetables must be tightly covered to avoid dryness; broiled meats need marinating or extra basting; deep-fat frying must be done at a lower temperature: 350° to 360° F.

Baked products—cakes and breads, particularly—need a readjustment of the recipe; cooked candies and canning procedures are also radically changed by altitude. If you live in an area over 2000 feet above sea level you should collect a specially devised set of recipes for these procedures. Your local utility (gas and electric) company or your state extension service will have recipes or be able to direct you to a good source in your area.

CHAPTER II

FOOD FACTS FOR EASY REFERENCE

There are a great many variables in shopping for and preparing food. Your steak may not be the same thickness and weight as ours; your market may be selling a different kind of apple than ours; you may have no baking chocolate on hand and wonder whether you can substitute cocoa. This chapter of charts along with those you'll find on the inside covers of this book are for handy reference when you wonder how to treat the particular food you have on hand.

This is a list of the charts you'll find in this book:

A GUIDE TO THE MOST POPULAR MEAT ROASTS (inside front and back covers).

TABLE OF EQUIVALENT AMOUNTS—How to judge recipe measurements in common foods.

TABLE OF SUBSTITUTIONS—Staples you can safely substitute in recipes.

CHEESE—The principal varieties, what they look like, what they taste like, and how to use them.

FRESH FRUITS—How much to buy and when to buy them.

Apples—Common varieties, what they look like and how to use them.

Pears—Common varieties, what they look like and how to use them.

Grapes—Common varieties, what they look like and how to use them.

Melons—Common varieties and how to recognize them.

Oranges—Common varieties, how to use them and when to buy them.

FRESH VEGETABLES—How much to buy and when to buy them.

MEATS—Roasting Timetable   Broiling Timetable
        Beef   Beef Steaks and Patties
        Fresh Pork   Smoked Pork
        Smoked Pork   Lamb
        Lamb
        Veal

FOOD FACTS FOR EASY REFERENCE

POULTRY—Roasting and Broiling Timetables

Chicken	Duck
Turkey	Goose

HOME FREEZING—How to prepare and freeze foods at home and how long to store them.

SAFE STORAGE CHART—How long to store common foods safely.

HOW MUCH TO BUY FOR TWO—A guide for brides learning to shop.

FOOD NUTRIENTS—What common foods contribute nutritionally.

CALORIE CHART—A listing of the calories in an average serving of common foods.

CARBOHYDRATE CHART—The carbohydrate values of common foods for persons choosing to use a low-carbohydrate diet.

Table of Equivalent Amounts

Recipes often vary in their language. One will call for a stick of butter, another will list the same measurement as ½ cup. Still another may ask for 8 tablespoons, depending often on how the butter is used in the recipe. It is sometimes easier both to shop for ingredients and to measure them when you know alternate equivalent amounts. If, for example, your recipe calls for 9 tablespoons of butter, you know this: you'll need one stick plus one tablespoon. This table translates some common measurements into other terms.

Apples, 1 medium . . . . *equals* . . . . 1 cup sliced

        1 pound . . . . *equals* . . . . 3 medium apples

Berries, 1 quart . . . . *equals* . . . . 3½ cups

Bread crumbs, 3 to 4 slices oven-dried

                 bread . . . . *equals* . . . . 1 cup fine dry crumbs

        1 slice fresh bread . . . . *equals* . . . . ¾ cup soft crumbs

Butter, ½ cup . . . . *equals* . . . . 1 stick or 8 tablespoons

        2 cups . . . . *equals* . . . . 4 sticks or 1 pound

Cheese, cottage, 8 ounces . . . . *equals* . . . . 1 cup

        cream, 3 ounces . . . . *equals* . . . . 6 tablespoons

        Cheddar, ¼ pound . . . . *equals* . . . . 1 cup shredded

Coconut, flaked, 3½-ounce can . . . . *equals* . . . . 1⅓ cups

Corn meal, 1 cup uncooked . . . . *equals* . . . . 4 cups cooked

Crackers, graham, 15 crackers . . . . *equals* . . . . 1 cup fine crumbs

Cream, heavy, 1 cup . . . . *equals* . . . . 2 cups whipped

Dates, pitted, 8-ounce package . . . . *equals* . . . . 1¼ cups, cut up

Eggs, 5 medium . . . . *equals* . . . . 1 cup

        8 medium egg whites . . . . *equals* . . . . 1 cup

        12 to 14 medium egg yolks . . . . *equals* . . . . 1 cup

Flour, 1 pound all-purpose .... *equals* .... 4 cups sifted
Gelatine, unflavored, 1 envelope .... *equals* .... 1 tablespoon
Lemon, 1 medium .... *equals* .... 2 to 3 tablespoons juice
Lemon peel, 1 medium lemon .... *equals* ...... 1 tablespoon grated peel
Lime, 1 medium .... *equals* ..... 1½ to 2 tablespoons juice
Macaroni, spaghetti, and noodles
  ½ pound .... *equals* .... 4 cups cooked
Milk, sweetened, condensed,
    15½-ounce can .... *equals* .... 1⅓ cups
  evaporated, 5⅓-fluid-ounce can .... *equals* .... ⅔ cup
  13-fluid-ounce can .... *equals* .... 1⅔ cups
Nuts, peanuts, 5 ounces .... *equals* .... 1 cup
  pecans, chopped, 4¼ ounces ...... *equals* .... 1 cup
  walnuts, chopped, 4½ ounces ..... *equals* .... 1 cup
  almonds, blanched, 5⅓ ounces .... *equals* .... 1 cup
Onion, 1 medium .... *equals* .... ½ cup chopped
Orange, 1 medium .... *equals* .... ⅓ to ½ cup juice
Orange peel, 1 medium orange .... *equals* 2 to 3 tablespoons grated peel
Potatoes, white, 1 pound raw,
    unpeeled .... *equals* .... 2 cups mashed
  sweet, 1 pound .... *equals* .... 3 medium
Raisins and currants, seedless, 16 ounces . *equals* .... 3 cups
Rice, regular white, 1 cup uncooked ..... *equals* .... 3 cups cooked
  parboiled (converted), 1 cup
    uncooked .... *equals* .... 4 cups cooked
  precooked, 1 cup uncooked .... *equals* .... 2 cups cooked
Shortening, hydrogenated, 1 pound .... *equals* .... 2½ cups
Sugar, granulated, 1 pound .... *equals* .... 2¼ to 2½ cups
  brown, 1 pound .... *equals* .... 2⅛ to 2¼ cups, firmly
      packed
  confectioners', 1 pound .... *equals* .... 4 cups unsifted or 4½ to 5
      cups sifted
Syrup, corn, light and dark, 1 pint ...... *equals* .... 2 cups
  honey, 16 ounces .... *equals* .... 1¼ cups
  maple syrup, 12 fluid ounces ..... *equals* .... 1½ cups
  molasses, light and dark,
    12 fluid ounces .... *equals* .... 1½ cups
Tomatoes, 1 pound .... *equals* .... 3 medium
Vegetable oil, 16 fluid ounces .... *equals* .... 2 cups

---

Table of Common Ingredient Substitutions

When you are cooking, it often is possible to make substitutions in your
list of ingredients. Substitutions help you save time and money because
you use what you already have on hand, instead of buying something

FOOD FACTS FOR EASY REFERENCE

new. And when you're caught short of a staple item, substitutions can save the day. These are some of the most useful ones.

AMOUNT	INGREDIENT	EQUIVALENT
1 tablespoon	Arrowroot	2 tablespoons flour or 1 tablespoon cornstarch or potato flour
1 teaspoon	Baking powder	¼ teaspoon baking soda plus ½ teaspoon cream of tartar
1 square (1 ounce)	Chocolate	3 tablespoons cocoa plus 1½ teaspoons shortening
1 tablespoon	Cornstarch	2 tablespoons flour
1 cup	Light cream	⅞ cup milk plus 3 tablespoons butter or margarine (for cooking only)
1 cup	Heavy cream	¾ cup milk plus ⅓ cup butter or margarine (for cooking only, not for whipping)
1 medium	Egg	2 egg yolks plus 1 tablespoon water, if used in baking recipes with flour; 2 egg yolks, if used in custards and puddings
1 tablespoon	Flour	½ tablespoon cornstarch or arrowroot or potato flour for thickening; 2 teaspoons quick-cooking tapioca in puddings or pies
1 cup (sifted)	Cake flour	1 cup all-purpose flour (sifted) less 2 tablespoons
1 tablespoon (chopped)	Fresh herbs	½ teaspoon dried herbs
1 cup	Milk (fresh, whole)	½ cup evaporated milk plus ½ cup water or 1 cup reconstituted nonfat dry milk plus 2 tablespoons butter or margarine or 1 cup sour milk or buttermilk plus ½ teaspoon baking soda

FOOD FACTS FOR EASY REFERENCE

AMOUNT	INGREDIENT	EQUIVALENT
1 cup	Sour milk (or buttermilk)	1 cup sweet milk plus 1 tablespoon lemon juice or white vinegar (let stand 5 minutes before using)
1 tablespoon	Potato Flour (or starch)	2 tablespoons flour or 1 tablespoon cornstarch or arrowroot

The Principal Varieties of Cheese

KIND	COLOR AND SHAPE	FLAVOR	USE
American Cheddar	White to yellow: wedges or bars	Mild to sharp	Sandwiches; in cooking
Asiago	Light yellow; cylinders	Piquant, sharp in aged cheese	General, grated when aged
Bel Paese	Creamy yellow interior, slightly gray surface; small wheels	Mild to moderately robust	Dessert; in sandwiches
Blue	White, marbled with blue-green veins; cylinders and wedges	Piquant, spicy	Canapés; table use; dessert; with fruits in salads; in dips
Brick	Creamy yellow; bricks or slices	Mild	Table use; in sandwiches
Brie	Whitish edible crust, creamy yellow interior; small wheels	Mild to pungent when very ripe	Canapés; dessert
Caciocavallo	Tan surface, light interior; beet or tenpin shapes; bound with cord	Sharp, similar to provolone	General, grated when aged
Camembert	Edible white crust, creamy yellow interior; small wheels or wedges	Mild to pungent	Cheese trays; dessert
Colby	Light yellow to orange; cylinders, wedges, or slices	Mild	Sandwiches; in cooking

FOOD FACTS FOR EASY REFERENCE

KIND	COLOR AND SHAPE	FLAVOR	USE
Cottage	White; large or small curd, packaged in cuplike containers. Also sold in bulk	Mild, slightly acid	In salads; in dips; in cooking
Cream	White; foil-wrapped, rectangular shapes	Mild	Sandwiches; in salads; on crackers
Edam	Creamy yellow; ball shapes, with red wax coat	Mild, nutlike	Cheese trays; on crackers; with fruit
Gjetost	Golden brown; cubes and rectangles	Sweetish, caramel	On crackers
Gorgonzola	Tan surface, light yellow interior marbled with blue-green veins; cylinders	Piquant, spicy like blue but less moist	Cheese trays; dessert
Gouda	Creamy yellow; flat round shapes, with or without red wax coat	Mild, nutlike similar to Edam	On crackers; with fruit for dessert
Gruyère	Light yellow; flat wheels	Nutlike, sweetish	Cheese trays; dessert
Liederkranz	Russet edible surface, creamy yellow interior; small foil-wrapped rectangles	Robust	Cheese trays; dessert
Limburger	Creamy white, edible white crust; foil-wrapped rectangles	Robust, highly aromatic	Sandwiches; on crackers
Monterey Jack	Creamy white; wheels	Mild	Sandwiches; in cooking
Mozzarella (pizza cheese)	Creamy white; rectangles or small spheres	Mild, delicate	Pizza; in cooking
Muenster	Yellow-tan exterior, creamy white interior; small wheels, blocks, or slices	Mild to mellow, between brick and Limburger	Sandwiches, cheese trays

KIND	COLOR AND SHAPE	FLAVOR	USE
Mysost (Primost)	Light brown; cubes and cylinders	Mild, sweetish, caramel	Cheese trays; in cooking
Neufchâtel	White; loaves or foil-wrapped rectangles	Mild, soft, smooth, and creamy	Sandwiches; in dips; in salads. Use as cream cheese
Parmesan (Reggiano)	Light yellow with brown or black coating; in wedges cut from cylinder, grated	Sharp, piquant	Usually grated as seasoning; sprinkled on salad or pasta
Port de Salut (Oka)	Russet surface, creamy yellow interior; small wheels	Mellow to robust	Dessert; on crackers; with fruit
Provolone	Light golden yellow to brown shiny exterior, yellowish white interior; pear, sausage, and salami shapes, bound with cord; slices or whole shapes	Mild to sharp and piquant, usually smoked	Sandwiches; in cooking
Ricotta	White; fresh in paper or plastic containers; when dry, grated	Bland, but semisweet, similar to cottage cheese when fresh	In cooking; as seasoning (like Parmesan) when dry and grated
Romano	Greenish black surface, yellowish white interior; wheels or grated	Sharp, piquant	As seasoning when grated; as such when fresh
Roquefort	White, marbled with blue-green veins; cylinders or wedges	Sharp, spicy, piquant	Cheese trays; dessert; on crackers; in salads; in cooking
Sapsago	Light green; small cone-shapes	Sweetish, flavored with clover leaves	Cheese trays; as seasoning when grated
Stilton	White, marbled with blue-green veins	Piquant, spicy, but milder than Roquefort	Cheese trays; dessert; in cooking; in salads

KIND		FLAVOR	USE
Swiss	Pale yellow; with large holes or eyes, usually rindless blocks and slices	Sweetish, nutlike	Cheese trays; sandwiches; salads; in cooking

Fresh Fruits

Recipes most often call for fruit ingredients in cup measures. This chart will guide you on retail amounts to buy to get the volume you need.

Fresh Fruit Conversion Chart

	WHEN YOU BUY			
KIND	*Weight*	*Volume or Pieces*	YOU'LL GET	WHEN TO BUY (PEAK SEASON)
Apples	1 lb.	3 medium		September through March
Pared, sliced, or diced	1 lb.	3 medium	about 3 cups	
Dried, cooked	1 lb.		about 8 cups	
Apricots	1 lb.	8 to 12	4 to 6 servings of 2 apricots each	June and July
Sliced or halved	1 lb.	8 to 12	2½ cups	
Dried, cooked	1 lb.	8 to 12	about 6 cups	
Avocado		1 medium	2 servings	November through April
Mashed		1¾ cups		
Bananas	1 lb.	3 or 4		All year
Sliced	1 lb.	3 or 4	about 2 cups (4 servings)	
Mashed	1 lb.	3 or 4	about 1⅓ cups	
Blueberries		1 pint	about 2 cups (4 servings)	June through August
Boysenberries		1 pint	about 2 cups (2 to 3 servings)	June through August
Cherries, red	1 lb.		about 2⅓ cups, pitted	June and July

FOOD FACTS FOR EASY REFERENCE

KIND	WHEN YOU BUY		YOU'LL GET	WHEN TO BUY (PEAK SEASON)
	Weight	*Volume or Pieces*		
Coconut		1 medium		All year
Shredded			3 to 4 cups	
Cranberries	1 lb.		4 cups	October through December
Sauce	1 lb.		16 ¼-cup servings	
Currants, dried	1 lb.		3¼ cups	All year
Dates, dried	1 lb.		2½ cups, whole or pitted and cut up	All year
Figs, fresh	1 lb.	12	4 servings of 3 figs each	June through November
Dried, whole	1 lb.	about 44	about 2 cups	
Cut fine	1 lb.		2⅔ cups	
Gooseberries	1 pint		about 2 cups	June through August
Grapefruit	1 lb.	1 medium	2 ½-grapefruit servings	All year, greatest supply
Sections	1 lb.	1 medium	10 or 12 sections	October through
Juice	1 lb.	1 medium	⅔ cup juice	July
Grapes				July through November
With seeds	1 lb.		2⅛ cups	
Seedless	1 lb.		2½ cups	
Lemons	1 lb.	4 lemons		All year
Juice	1 lb.	4 lemons	about ⅔ cup juice	
Limes	1 lb.	8 limes		June through December
Juice	1 lb.	8 limes	about 1 cup juice	
Oranges	6 lbs.	1 dozen		All year, greatest supply November through April
Sectioned	6 lbs.	1 dozen	4 cups	
Juice	6 lbs.	1 dozen	about 4 cups juice	
Peaches				June through September
Whole	1 lb.	4 medium		
Sliced	1 lb.	4 medium	2 cups	
Dried	1 lb.		3 cups	All year
Dried, cooked	1 lb.		6 cups	
Pears				August through November
Whole	1 lb.	4 medium		
Sliced	1 lb.	4 medium	2 cups	

FOOD FACTS FOR EASY REFERENCE

| | WHEN YOU BUY | | | |
KIND	Weight	Volume or Pieces	YOU'LL GET	WHEN TO BUY (PEAK SEASON)
Pineapple				March, April, and May
Whole	2 lbs.	1 medium		
Cubed	2 lbs.	1 medium	3 cups	
Plums	1 lb.	8 to 20		June through September
Halved and pitted	1 lb.	8 to 20	about 2 cups	
Prunes				
Dried	1 lb.		2¼ cups, pitted	All year
Dried, whole cooked	1 lb.		4 to 5 cups, 8 servings	
Quinces	1 lb.	3 medium		October to December
Chopped	1 lb.	3 medium	1½ cups	
Raisins, dried, seeded,				All year
Whole	1 lb.		3¼ cups	
Chopped	1 lb.		2½ cups	
Seedless, whole	1 lb.		2¾ cups	
Chopped	1 lb.		2 cups	
Raspberries	1 pint		about 2 cups (2 to 3 servings)	June through August
Rhubarb				February through June
Cut and cooked	1 lb.		2 cups	
Strawberries				April through June
Whole or sliced	1½ lbs.	1 quart	4 cups	

How to Select and Use the Most Popular Varieties of Apples

VARIETY	WHERE SOLD IN ABUNDANCE	WHEN MOST AVAILABLE	CHARACTERISTICS	USES
Baldwin	Northeastern and North Central states	November to May	Red skin. Tart, juicy, crisp. Firm when cooked.	All-purpose cooking apple. A favorite for pie and sauce.
Cortland	Northern and Central states as far west as the Mississippi	September to March	Brilliant red. Crisp, sweet. Does not turn brown easily upon exposure to air. Soft flesh when cooked, yet holds its shape.	General cooking when an apple that holds its shape is desired. Eating out of hand, fruit cocktails, salads.

FOOD FACTS FOR EASY REFERENCE

Variety	Where Sold in Abundance	When Most Available	Characteristics	Uses
Golden Delicious	Throughout the U.S.A.	October to April	Yellow, sweet, firm. Will not turn brown quickly when sliced.	Best for eating out of hand, though good for cooking when a firm shape is desired. Especially good in salads and fruit cocktails and as a dessert apple.
Red Delicious	Throughout the U.S.A.	September to May	Red, juicy, five knobs on blossom end, sweet, firm.	Most popular eating-out-of-hand apple. Crisp dessert apple in fruit cocktails and sliced with cheese. Salads.
Grimes Golden	North and South Midwestern states	September to January	Clear, deep yellow. Very firm, crisp, sweet. Moderately juicy. Firm when cooked.	General cooking when a firm-fleshed apple is desired. Eating out of hand.
Gravenstein	Northwestern states, Northeastern states	Formerly a mid-summer apple, now available much longer—possibly from July to October	Green with red stripes, also a red variety. Extremely juicy and crisp. Will not hold shape when cooked.	All-purpose. Applesauce, cooking when firm shape is not desired, eating out of hand.
Jonathan	Throughout the U.S.A.	September to February	Yellow, heavily overlaid with red. Juicy, crisp, moderately tart. Tender, yet holds shape well when cooked.	Baking, pies, puddings. Eating out of hand, salads.
McIntosh	All states east of the Mississippi	September to April	Red striped appearance. Hard, spicy, crisp, juicy. Will not hold shape when cooked.	All-purpose. Applesauce, pies, dumplings. Eating out of hand when a tart apple is desired, salads.
Northern Spy	Northeastern and Central states as far west as Minnesota	October to March	Yellow, heavily overlaid with red stripes. Crisp, tart, firm, juicy. Moderately soft when cooked.	General cooking, baking, sauce. Eating out of hand, salads.
Rhode Island Greening	Northeastern states, North Central states	September to February	Green and greenish yellow. Firm, crisp, tart, juicy; very soft when cooked.	General cooking where shape of slice is not important; pies when soft apples are desired; applesauce.

FOOD FACTS FOR EASY REFERENCE

VARIETY	WHERE SOLD IN ABUNDANCE	WHEN MOST AVAILABLE	CHARACTERISTICS	USES
Rome Beauty	Throughout the U.S.A.	November to May	Yellow mingled with red. Juicy, firm, tender, moderately tart. Holds shape beautifully when cooked.	Considered the prize as baking apple. Favorite for pie and sauce.
Stayman	East of the Mississippi except for northern New England. Favorite of the Chicago area	November to April	Red striped or mottled. Spicy, semifirm, moderately crisp, moderately tart. Tends to "mush" when cooked.	All-purpose. General cooking apple, sauce, pie, puddings. Eating out of hand, salads.
Winesap	Throughout the U.S.A.	December to July	Deep red, moderately crisp and tart, very juicy. Tender when cooked but not "mushy."	General cooking, cinnamon apple rings, pies, puddings. Eating out of hand, salads.
Yellow Newtown (Newtown Pippin)	Far West, Rocky Mountain area, Michigan, Middle Atlantic states	November to June	Bright yellow, juicy, crisp, medium tart. Holds shape well when cooked; one of the best keepers.	General cooking when an apple that holds its shape is desired. For pies, cinnamon apples, baking.
York	Southeastern and Middle Atlantic states	November to March	Light red, dotted with russet, firm, crisp, sweet. Holds shape well when cooked.	General cooking, apple rings, pies, baking, puddings.

How to Select and Use the Most Popular Varieties of Pears

VARIETY	WHEN MOST AVAILABLE	CHARACTERISTICS	USES
Anjou	October to May Available throughout the country	Medium to large in size. Globular shape with a short, thick neck. Yellowish green skin, sometimes sprinkled with russet. Yellowish white flesh is buttery and juicy. Spicy sweet flavor.	Eating out of hand, salads, desserts, general cooking.
Bartlett	August to January Available throughout the country	Medium to very large in size, shaped like an oblong bell. Clear yellow skin, fine, white flesh. Sweet and juicy.	Eating out of hand, desserts, and salads. Use fresh or cooked.

Variety	When Most Available	Characteristics	Uses
Bosc	October through March. Peak supply in October. Available throughout the country	Medium to large size, long tapering neck, and dark yellow skin overlaid with cinnamon—russet. Yellow-white flesh is buttery and very juicy.	Good dessert pear. May also be used in general cooking and salads.
Clapp Favorite	August through October. Available throughout the country	Medium to large size, shaped like an oblong bell with a clubbed stem end. Skin is greenish yellow, often blushed; flesh is fine, juicy, and sweet.	Eating out of hand, general cooking, and desserts.
Comice	August through January. Available throughout the country	Medium to large in size, heart-shaped with a fairly thick, granular skin that is greenish yellow, sometimes russeted. Flesh is fine-grained, very juicy with a sweet, aromatic flavor.	Eating out of hand, general cooking.
Easter	Late winter and early spring. Fruit is picked green in October and ripened under carefully controlled conditions. Available throughout the country	Medium in size, thick neck. The skin is thick and somewhat tough, deep green in color, occasionally russeted or blushed. Coarse, slightly gritty flesh.	Eating out of hand, general cooking.
Hardy	September and October, mostly in the Northeast	Medium to large size, oval in shape with a dull greenish yellow skin often dotted with russet. When ripe, this pear is too soft for commercial handling.	Used chiefly for home and commercial canning and spicing.
Kieffer	September, only in areas close to orchards where it is harvested	Medium-sized oval fruit with yellow skin. Coarse sandy flesh.	Canning, pickling, and preserves.
Seckel	August to December, in northeast sections of country	Small, heartshaped with a dull brownish red skin. Granular flesh but very juicy.	Best used cooked in desserts.
Winter Nelis	October to May. Available throughout the country	Small to medium size, round in shape. Fairly thick green or yellow skin. Fine, buttery flesh with a rich spicy flavor.	For desserts and general cooking.

How to Select and Use the Common Varieties of Grapes

Variety	When Most Available	Characteristics	Uses
Cardinal	June and July	A cross between Flame Tokay and Ribier. Sweet flavor, tight skin.	Dessert, salads, table use, juice, and jelly.
Catawba	September to November	Medium-sized oval with purple-red skin. Intense sweet flavor; slipskin.	Juice, jams, jelly, and table use.
Concord	August to early November	Round, blue, sweet; slipskin.	Juice, jelly.
Cornichon	September to November	Long, olive-shaped, blue; tight skin.	Dessert, salads, juices, jelly, table use.
Delaware	August to September	Small, light red, tender; slipskin. Very sweet, delicate flavor.	Juice, jam, jelly, table use.
Emperor	November and December	Firm, red; rather like Flame Tokay; tight skin. Neutral flavor.	Dessert, salads, table use.
Flame Tokay	September through November	Large, red, oval; tight skin. Neutral flavor.	Dessert, salads, table use.
Malaga	August through November	Round, very sweet, white, medium-sized. Red Malagas are larger and red in color; tight skin.	Dessert, salads, table use.
Niagara	September through November	White; slipskin. Sweet flavor.	Juice, jelly, table use.
Perlette	June and July	Small, white, oval, normally seedless grapes; tight skin. Mild flavor.	Dessert, salads, table use.
Ribier	August to October	Large, black, round; tight skin. Mild flavor.	Dessert, salads, table use.
Thompson seedless	July to October	Seedless, small, white, sweet, olive-shaped; tight skin.	Dessert, salads, table use, garnishes for meals.

How to Select and Use the Common Varieties of Melons

Variety	When Most Available	Characteristics	Uses
Cantaloupe	May to November	Salmon-colored, sweet flesh. Rind is grayish and netted.	Breakfast fruit, balls for salads and desserts. Halves with ice cream for dessert.
Casaba	August through November	Creamy, soft flesh with little aroma. Large melon with rough, ridged, yellowish rind, pointed at one end.	Wedges for first course or dessert.
Christmas or Santa Claus	December	Oval melon with mottled green and gold rind. Flesh is light green, mild, and sweet.	Wedges for first course or dessert, or peeled for fruit plates.
Cranshaw	July through October	Large green and gold melon, pointed at one end. Flesh is yellow orange, sweet, and spicy.	Wedges for first course or dessert.
Honeyball	June through November	Small, netted-rind melon. Soft fragrant flesh. Some varieties have pink flesh.	Breakfast fruit.
Honeydew	June through November	Large, smooth-skinned, creamy white melon. Pale green flesh is particularly sweet and aromatic.	Small wedges often served with prosciutto as first course.
Persian	July to October	Netted-rind melon, larger than cantaloupe. Flesh is deep salmon color, mild, and sweet.	As breakfast fruit or dessert.
Spanish	November and December	Large, green-skinned, ridged exterior. Pale green, delicate, sweet flesh.	Wedges, balls, peeled slices for fruit plate.
Watermelon	June through August	Large, oval melon with dark green exterior, sometimes with lighter stripes. Deep pink to red, juicy flesh. Midget watermelons are about the size of a honeydew.	Slices, wedges, balls.

How to Select and Use the Common Varieties of Oranges

Variety	When Most Available	Characteristics	Uses
Hamlin	October through December	Slightly rough peel, few seeds, very juicy.	Excellent juice oranges.
Navel	Western navels— December through May	Seedless; thick, bright, pebbly, orange skin.	Easy to peel, use for orange sections.
	Florida navels— October through January		
Parson Brown	October through December	Thin-skinned, pale orange color.	Good for sections or juice.
Pineapple	December through February	Bright, smooth, orange skin; seedless and juicy.	Excellent for juice or eating out of the half shell.
Temple	December through February	Actually part of the tangerine family with a zip-skin. Looks like a large orange with rounded top.	Eating out of hand or sectioning.
Valencia	Western Valencias— May through November	Seeded, lighter color orange skin and more juice than the navel orange.	For juice or cut up in fruit cup.
	Florida Valencias— October through January		

Fresh Vegetables

How Much to Buy and When to Buy Them

Kind	When You Buy	It Will Make	When to Buy (Peak Season)
Artichokes French, or globe	1 bud	1 cooked serving	All year—peaks in March, April, May
Jerusalem	1 lb.	4 cooked servings	Fall and winter months

FOOD FACTS FOR EASY REFERENCE

KIND	WHEN YOU BUY	IT WILL MAKE	WHEN TO BUY (PEAK SEASON)
Asparagus	2 lbs.	4 to 5 cooked servings	March through June
Beans			
Green or wax	1½ lbs.	4 cooked servings	All year—peaks in June through August
Lima	3 lbs.	4 cooked servings	Spring and summer months
Beets	2 bunches	4 cooked servings	All year—peaks in June and July
Broccoli	1½ lbs.	4 cooked servings	October through April
Brussels sprouts	1¼ lbs.	4 cooked servings	September through January
Cabbage			All year—peaks March through June
Green or red	1½ lbs.	4 cooked servings	
Shredded, raw	1 lb.	about 4 cups	
Carrots	1¼ lb.	4 cooked servings	All year
Shredded, raw	1 lb.	about 2½ cups	
Cauliflower	1 large head	4 servings	All year—peaks in September through November
Celery	1 medium bunch or stalk	4 cooked servings	All year
	1 long branch	about 1 cup, diced	
Celery Root or Celeriac	1½ lbs.	4 servings	October through April
Corn	1 dozen ears	6 to 12 servings	May through August
	2 ears	about 1 cup kernels	
Cucumbers	2 cucumbers	4 servings	All year—peaks in May, June, July
Eggplant	1½ lbs.	4 servings	All year—peaks in August and September
Diced, cooked	1½ lbs.	about 2½ cups	
Endive			October through May
Belgian or French	1 large head	1 cooked serving or 2 salad servings	

FOOD FACTS FOR EASY REFERENCE

KIND	WHEN YOU BUY	IT WILL MAKE	WHEN TO BUY (PEAK SEASON)
Greens Beet, turnip, collards, dandelion, kale, mustard, spinach, Swiss chard	2 lbs.	4 cooked servings	All year
Kohlrabi	1 medium bulb	1 cooked serving	June and July
Lettuce			All year
Butterhead type	1 head	2 servings for salad	
Iceberg or romaine	1 head	4 servings for salad	
Leeks	2 bunches	4 cooked servings	October through May
Mushrooms	1 lb.	4 cooked servings	November through April
Okra	1 lb.	4 cooked servings	June through November
Onions			
Green or scallions	2 bunches	4 servings	All year—peak May through August
White or yellow	1½ lbs.	4 servings	All year
Parsnips	1½ lbs.	4 servings	January through March
Peas	3 lbs.	4 servings	March through June
Pepper Green	1 lb. (3 to 6)	3 to 4 servings	All year
Chopped	1 lb.	4¾ cups	
Potatoes			
Sweet, or yams	1 lb.	3 medium potatoes	September through March
White	1 lb.	3 medium potatoes	All year—see pages 534–535 for availability of various types
Cooked and mashed	1 lb.	1¾ cups	

FOOD FACTS FOR EASY REFERENCE

Kind	When You Buy	It Will Make	When to Buy (Peak Season)

Pumpkin
  Cooked
  and
  mashed
	1 lb.	A little more than 1 cup	October

Radishes	2 bunches or bags	4 servings	All year—peak May, June, and July

Rutabaga,
  or yellow
  turnip
  Cooked
	1 lb.	2 cups, 2 to 3 servings	October through February

Salsify, or
  oyster
  plant
	1½ lbs.	4 servings	October and November

Shallots Minced	½ oz. (1 shallot)	1 tablespoon	All year in fine food markets

Spinach
  Raw
  Cooked
	
	1 lb.
	1 lb.
		
		4 cups leaves
		1½ cups
			All year

Squash
  Summer
  (includes
  zucchini)
  Winter
	
	2 lbs.
	
	3 lbs.
		
		4 servings
		
		4 servings
			
			Summer months
			
			Winter months

Tomatoes Cooked	2 lbs. 2 lbs.	4 servings 1½ cups	All year—peaks May through August
Turnips White	 2 lbs.	 4 to 5 servings	All year
Zucchini—See *Summer squash*			

Dried Vegetables

Kind	When You Buy	It Will Make	When to Buy (Peak Season)
Beans Cooked	 1 lb.	 5½ cups	All year
Peas Cooked	 1 lb.	 5 cups	All year
Lentils Cooked	 1 lb.	 5 cups	All year

Meat Roasting Timetables

Roasting times for meat will vary with the temperature of the meat at the time that it is put into the oven, with the desired degree of doneness you prefer, with the retail cut of meat and, of course, with the accuracy of your oven. Start by knowing the weight of your roast. An accurate meat thermometer is an invaluable aid to roasting meats.

Beef Roasting Chart

Cut	Weight	Oven Temperature	Internal Temperature (Thermometer Reading)	Approximate Cooking Time
*Rib roast, standing, bone in; ribs should measure no more than 7 inches from chine bone to rib ends see note at end of chart	4 lbs.	300° to 325° F.	140° F. (rare)	1¾ hrs. to 2 hrs. 10 min. (26 to 32 min./lb.)
			160° F. (medium)	2¼ hrs. to 2½ hrs. (34 to 38 min./lb.)
			170° F. (well done)	2 hrs. 40 min. to 2 hrs. 50 min. (40 to 42 min./lb.)
	6 lbs.	300° to 325° F.	140° F. (rare)	2 hrs. 18 min. to 2½ hrs. (23 to 25 min./lb.)
			160° F. (medium)	2 hrs. 40 min. to 3 hrs. (27 to 30 min./lb.)
			170° F. (well done)	3 hrs. 12 min. to 3½ hrs. (32 to 35 min./lb.)
	8 lbs.	300° to 325° F.	140° F. (rare)	3 hrs. 5 min. to 3 hrs. 20 min. (23 to 25 min./lb.

Cut	Weight	Oven Temperature	Internal Temperature (Thermometer Reading)	Approximate Cooking Time
			160° F. (medium)	3 hrs. 35 min. to 4 hrs. (27 to 30 min./lb.)
			170° F. (well done)	4 hrs. 16 min. to 4 hrs. 40 min. (32 to 35 min./lb.
Rib roast, rolled (boneless)	4 pounds (4½- to 5-inch diameter) **	300° to 325° F.	140° F. (rare)	2 hrs. 8 min. (32 min./lb.)
			160° F. (medium)	2½ hrs. (38 min./lb.)
			170° F. (well done)	3 hrs. 12 min. (48 min./lb.)
	6 pounds (5½- to 6-inch diameter) **	300° to 325° F.	140° F. (rare)	3¼ hrs. (32 min./lb.)
			160° F. (medium)	3¾ hrs. (38 min./lb.)
			170° F. (well done)	4¾ hrs. (48 min./lb)
Delmonico (rib eye)	4 to 6 lbs.	350° F.	140° F. (rare)	1¼ to 2 hrs. (18 to 20 min./lb.)
			160° F. (medium)	1 hr. 20 min. to 2¼ hrs. (20 to 22 min./lb.)
			170°F. (well done)	1½ to 2½ hrs. (22 to 24 min./lb.)
Tenderloin, whole	4 to 6 lbs.	425° F.	140° F. (rare)	45 minutes to 1 hour (total)
Tenderloin, half	2 to 3 lbs.	425° F.	140° F. (rare)	45 to 50 minutes (total)

CUT	WEIGHT	OVEN TEMPERATURE	INTERNAL TEMPERATURE (THERMOMETER READING)	APPROXIMATE COOKING TIME
Rolled rump (Choice or Prime grade)	4 to 6 lbs.	300° to 325° F.	170° F. (well done)	1¾ to 3 hrs. (25 to 30 min./lb.)
Sirloin tip (Choice or Prime grade)	3½ to 4 lbs.	300° to 325° F.	170° F. (well done)	2 to 2¾ hrs. (35 to 40 min./lb.)

*Times given are for ribs that measure 6 to 7 inches from chine bone to tip of rib. If ribs are cut longer, allow less time. The amount of the meat on the roast will be less. For these roasts count on 18 to 20 minutes per pound for rare; 22 to 25 minutes per pound for medium, and 27 to 30 minutes per pound for well done.

**Roasts of smaller diameter require less cooking time; roasts of larger diameter will require longer cooking time.

Fresh Pork Roasting Chart

CUT	WEIGHT	OVEN TEMPERATURE	INTERNAL TEMPERATURE (THERMOMETER READING)	APPROXIMATE COOKING TIME
Loin Center cut	3 to 5 lbs.	325° to 350° F.	170° F.	1½ to 2 hrs. 55 min. (30 to 35 min./lb.)
Half	5 to 7 lbs.	325° to 350° F.	170° F.	3 to 4¾ hrs. (35 to 40 min./lb.)
Blade loin or sirloin	3 to 4 lbs.	325° to 350° F.	170° F.	2 to 3 hrs. (40 to 45 min./lb.)
Rolled and boned	3 to 5 lbs.	325° to 350° F.	170° F.	1¾ to 3 hrs. 20 min. (35 to 40 min./lb.)
Picnic shoulder	5 to 8 lbs.	325° to 350° F.	170° F.	2½ to 4¾ hrs. (30 to 35 min./lb.)

CUT	WEIGHT	OVEN TEMPERATURE	INTERNAL TEMPERATURE (THERMOMETER READING)	APPROXIMATE COOKING TIME
Rolled	3 to 5 lbs.	325° to 350° F.	170° F.	1¾ to 3 hrs. 20 min. (35 to 40 min./lb.)
Cushion	3 to 5 lbs.	325° to 350° F.	170° F.	1¾ to 3 hrs. 20 min. (35 to 40 min./lb.)
Boston shoulder	4 to 6 lbs.	325° to 350° F.	170° F.	2 hrs. 40 min. to 4½ hrs. (40 to 45 min./lb.)
Leg (fresh ham)				
Whole (bone in)	12 to 16 lbs.	325° to 350° F.	170° F.	4 hrs. 24 min. to 7 hrs. (22 to 26 min./lb.)
Whole (boneless)	10 to 14 lbs.	325° to 350° F.	170° F.	4 to 6½ hrs. (24 to 28 min./lb.)
Half (bone in)	5 to 8 lbs.	325° to 350° F.	170° F.	2 hrs. 55 min. to 5 hrs. 20 min. (35 to 40 min./lb.)

Smoked Pork Roasting Chart

CUT	WEIGHT	OVEN TEMPERATURE	INTERNAL TEMPERATURE (THERMOMETER READING)	APPROXIMATE COOKING TIME
Ham (cook before eating)				
Whole	10 to 14 lbs.	300° to 325° F.	160° F.	3 to 4¾ hrs. (18 to 20 min./lb.)
Half	5 to 7 lbs.	300° to 325° F.	160° F.	1¾ to 3 hrs. (22 to 25 min./lb.)

Cut	Weight	Oven Temperature	Internal Temperature (Thermometer Reading)	Approximate Cooking Time
Shank or butt portion	3 to 4 lbs.	300° to 325° F.	160° F.	1¾ to 2¾ hrs. (35 to 40 min./lb.)
Ham (fully cooked)				
Whole (bone in)	12 to 15 lbs.	300° to 325° F.	130° F.	3 to 3¾ hrs. (15 min./lb.)
Half	5 to 7 lbs.	300° to 325° F.	130° F.	1½ to 2¾ hrs. (18 to 24 min./lb.)
Picnic shoulder (cook before eating)	5 to 8 lbs.	300° to 325° F.	170° F.	3 to 4¾ hrs. (35 min./lb.)
(fully cooked)	5 to 8 lbs.	300° to 325° F.	170° F.	2 hrs. 5 min. to 4 hrs. (25 to 30 min./lb.)
Shoulder roll	2 to 4 lbs.	300° to 325° F.	170° F.	1¼ to 2 hrs. 20 min. (35 min./lb.)
Canadian bacon	2 to 4 lbs.	300° to 325° F.	160° F.	1¼ to 2 hrs. 40 min. (35 to 40 min./lb.)

Lamb Roasting Chart

Cut	Weight	Oven Temperature	Internal Temperature (Thermometer Reading)	Approximate Cooking Time
Leg Whole	5 to 8 lbs.	300° to 325° F.	145° to 150° F. (very rare)	1 to 2 hrs. (12 to 15 min./lb.)

Cut	Weight	Oven Temperature	Internal Temperature (Thermometer Reading)	Approximate Cooking Time
			160° F. (medium)	1½ to 2¾ hrs. (18 to 20 min./lb.)
			175° F. (well done)	2½ to 4¾ hrs. (30 to 35 min./lb.)
Half	3 to 5 lbs.	300° to 325° F.	145° to 150° F. (rare)	¾ to 1¼ hrs. (15 min./lb.)
			160° F. (medium)	1 to 1½ hrs. (18 min./lb.)
			170° F. (well done)	1¼ to 2½ hrs. (25 to 30 min./lb.)
Shoulder Rolled	3 to 5 lbs.	300° to 325° F.	170° F.	1½ to 3¼ hrs. (30 to 40 min./lb.)
Cushion	3 to 5 lbs.	300° to 325° F.	170° F.	1¼ to 2½ hrs. (25 to 30 min./lb.)

Veal Roasting Chart

Cut	Weight	Oven Temperature	Internal Temperature (Thermometer Reading)	Approximate Cooking Time
Leg Whole	5 to 8 lbs.	300° to 325° F.	170° F.	2 to 4 hrs. (25 to 30 min./lb.)
Loin	4 to 6 lbs.	300° to 325° F.	170° F.	2 to 3½ hrs. (30 to 35 min./lb.)
Rib (rack)	3 to 5 lbs.	300° to 325° F.	170° F.	1¾ to 3¼ hrs. (35 to 40 min./lb.)
Shoulder, rolled or stuffed	4 to 6 lbs.	300° to 325° F.	170° F.	2¾ to 4½ hrs. (40 to 45 min./lb.)

Meat Broiling Timetables

Broiled Beef Steaks and Patties

This timetable is based on broiling at a moderate temperature; 1- and 1½-inch-thick steaks are placed 2 to 3 inches from the source of heat and steaks 2 inches and over are placed 3 to 5 inches from the heat source. This method produces a lightly browned, juicy steak that will have a 140° F. internal temperature for rare, 160° F. for medium, and 170° F. for well done. If you like a steak with a charred surface and rare interior, place the steak as close as possible to the source of high heat and reduce cooking time per side by approximately half.

CUT	WEIGHT	THICKNESS	APPROXIMATE COOKING TIME PER SIDE IN MINUTES		
			Rare	*Medium*	*Well Done*
Chuck steak (high quality or tenderized)	1½ to 2½ lbs.	1 inch	12	15	18
	2 to 4 lbs.	1½ inches	20	22	25
Club steak	1 to 1½ lbs.	1 inch	7	10	12 to 15
	1½ to 2 lbs.	1½ inches	12	15	18
	2 to 2½ lbs.	2 inches	17	22	25
Porterhouse steak and T-bone	1¼ to 2 lbs.	1 inch	10	12	15
	2 to 3 lbs.	1½ inches	15	17	20
	3 to 5 lbs.	2 inches	20	22	24
Rib steak and rib eye (Delmonico) and filet mignon	8 to 10 oz.	1 inch	7	10	12
	12 to 14 oz.	1½ inches	12	15	18
	1 to 1¼ lbs.	2 inches	17	22	25
Sirloin and wedge-bone steaks	1½ to 3 lbs.	1 inch	10	12	14
	2¼ to 4 lbs.	1½ inches	15	17	20
	3 to 5 lbs.	2 inches	20	22	24
Ground beef patties	4 oz.	1 inch	5 to 7	8 to 12	12 to 15

*Broiled Smoked Pork

CUT	WEIGHT	THICKNESS	APPROXIMATE COOKING TIME PER SIDE IN MINUTES
Ham slice (precooked)	¾ to 1 lb.	½ inch	5 to 6
	1½ to 2 lbs.	1 inch	8 to 10

Cut	Weight	Thickness	Approximate Cooking Time Per Side in Minutes
Canadian bacon		¼-inch slices	3 to 4
		½-inch slices	4 to 5
Bacon			2 to 3

*Broil 2 to 3 inches from source of heat.

Broiled Lamb

Cut	Weight	Thickness	Approximate Cooking Time Per Side in Minutes
Rib, shoulder, or loin chops	5 to 8 oz.	1 inch	6 (medium)
	8 to 10 oz.	1½ inches	9 (medium)
	10 to 16 oz.	2 inches	11 (medium)
English chops		2 inches	12 to 14 (medium)
Ground lamb patties	4 oz.	1 inch	8 to 9 (well done)

Poultry Roasting and Broiling Timetables

Roast Chicken

Cornish hens, plump broiler-fryers, capons, and roasting chickens may all be oven-roasted. Time is judged by weight of the bird and whether or not it is stuffed.

Weight	Temperature	Time Per Pound	*Approximate Total Time (Unstuffed)
1 to 1½ lbs.	400° F.	40 min.	1 hr.
2 lbs.	400° F.	35 min.	1 hr., 10 min.
2½ lbs.	375° F.	30 min.	1 hr., 15 min.
3 lbs.	375° F.	30 min.	1 hr., 30 min.
3½ lbs.	375° F.	30 min.	1 hr., 45 min.
4 lbs.	375° F.	30 min.	2 hrs.
4½ lbs.	375° F.	30 min.	2 hrs., 15 min.
5 lbs.	375° F.	30 min.	2 hrs., 30 min.

*Increase the roasting time by 15 minutes if chicken is stuffed.

Rotisseried Chicken

Ready-to-Cook Weight	Approximate Cooking Time
1½ to 2 lbs.	¾ to 1¼ hrs.
2 to 2½ lbs.	1¼ to 1½ hrs.
2½ to 3 lbs.	1½ to 1¾ hrs.

Broiled Chicken

Size of Bird	Distance from Heat Source		Broiling Time, Skin Side Down	Broiling Time, Skin Side Up
	Gas (set at 375° F.)	Electric (set at Broil)		
Broiler–fryer (1½ to 3 lbs.)	3 to 6 inches	6 to 9 inches	20 to 25 min.	15 to 20 min.

Roast Stuffed Whole Turkey (Uncovered)

Ready-to-Cook Weight	*Approximate Roasting Time in a 325° F. (slow) Oven	Internal Temperature
4 to 8 lbs.	2½ to 3½ hrs.	180° to 185° F.
8 to 12 lbs.	3½ to 4½ hrs.	180° to 185° F.
12 to 16 lbs.	4½ to 5½ hrs.	180° to 185° F.
16 to 20 lbs.	5½ to 6½ hrs.	180° to 185° F.
20 to 24 lbs.	6½ to 7 hrs.	180° to 185° F.

*Allow about ½ hour less for unstuffed turkey.

Roast Stuffed Whole Turkey (Foil-covered)

Ready-to-Cook Weight	Approximate Roasting Time in a 450° F. Oven		Internal Temperature
	Covered	Uncovered	
7 to 9 lbs.	1¾ to 2 hrs.	30 min.	180° to 185° F.
10 to 13 lbs.	2¼ to 2½ hrs.	30 min.	180° to 185° F.
14 to 17 lbs.	2½ to 2¾ hrs.	30 min.	180° to 185° F.
18 to 21 lbs.	2¾ to 3 hrs.	30 min.	180° to 185° F.
22 to 24 lbs.	3 to 3¼ hrs.	30 min.	180° to 185° F.

Roast Halves or Quarters of Turkey

Ready-to-Cook Weight	Approximate Roasting Time in a 325° F. (slow) Oven	Internal Temperature
5 to 8 lbs.	2½ to 3 hrs.	180° to 185° F.
8 to 10 lbs.	3 to 3½ hrs.	180° to 185° F.
10 to 12 lbs.	3½ to 4 hrs.	180° to 185° F.

Roast Boneless Turkey Roasts

Ready-to-Cook Weight	Approximate Roasting Time in a 325° F. (slow) Oven	Internal Temperature
3 to 5 lbs.	2½ to 3 hrs.	170° to 175° F.
5 to 7 lbs.	3 to 3½ hrs.	170° to 175° F.
7 to 9 lbs.	3½ to 4 hrs.	170° to 175° F.

Rotisseried Whole Turkey (Unstuffed)

Ready-to-Cook Weight	Approximate Cooking Time	Internal Temperature
4 to 6 lbs.	2 to 3 hrs.	180° to 185° F.
6 to 8 lbs.	3 to 3½ hrs.	180° to 185 F.
8 to 10 lbs.	3½ to 4 hrs.	180° to 185° F.
10 to 12 lbs.	4 to 5 hrs.	180° to 185° F.

Rotisseried Boneless Turkey Roasts

Ready-to-Cook Weight	Approximate Cooking Time	Internal Temperature
3 to 5 lbs.	2 to 2½ hrs.	170° to 175° F.
5 to 7 lbs.	2½ to 3 hrs.	170° to 175° F.
7 to 9 lbs.	3 to 3½ hrs.	170° to 175° F.

Whole Roast Duck

READY-TO-COOK WEIGHT	*APPROXIMATE ROASTING TIME IN A 325° F. (SLOW) OVEN
4 to 5 lbs. (stuffed or unstuffed)	2½ to 3 hrs.

*If crisp skin is desired, raise oven temperature to 425° F. for last half hour of cooking.

*Whole Roast Goose (Unstuffed)

READY-TO-COOK WEIGHT	APPROXIMATE ROASTING TIME IN A 325° F. (SLOW) OVEN
4 to 6 lbs.	2¾ to 3 hrs.
6 to 8 lbs.	3 to 3½ hrs.
8 to 10 lbs.	3½ to 3¾ hrs.
10 to 12 lbs.	3¾ to 4¼ hrs.
12 to 14 lbs.	4 to 4¾ hrs.

*Add ½ hour to cooking time for stuffed goose.

Freezing Foods at Home: How to Prepare Them and How Long to Keep Them

A Guide to the Freezing of Food

This chart is a general guide to freezing storage time and general preparation of common foods for freezing. If you have never prepared foods for freezer storage, check the introduction to freezing of foods on page 913.

Food	Storage Time	Preparation
COOKED FOODS		
Breads		
Quick (muffins, waffles, biscuits, fruit and nut breads)	1 to 2 months	Cool (if necessary); wrap in sheet wrapping or put into polyethylene bags. Seal and freeze.

FOOD	STORAGE TIME	PREPARATION
Yeast (loaves and rolls)	½ to 2 months (2 to 3 weeks, if purchased bread is frozen in original wrapper)	Cool; wrap in sheet wrapping or put into polyethylene bags. Seal and freeze.
Cakes (including butter, pound, fruit, sponge, angel food, and chiffon cakes)	Unfrosted, 4 to 6 months Frosted, 2 to 4 months Fruit, 12 months	Cool and remove from pan. Wrap unfrosted cakes in sheet wrapping or put into polyethylene bags. Seal and freeze. If desired, put into container to prevent crushing or freeze the cake unwrapped and package promptly once frozen. Cakes are better frozen unfrosted. If you do frost a cake, freeze before wrapping.
Cookies Baked	4 to 8 months	Cool. Pack in rigid containers with waxed paper between layers and in spaces. Seal and freeze.
Unbaked	4 to 6 months	Shape refrigerator-cookie dough into a roll or bar. Wrap in sheet wrapping. Seal and freeze.
Desserts In addition to pies, cakes, and ice cream described under their own headings, these desserts freeze well.		
Applesauce	9 to 12 months	Prepare as usual but do not add spices. Cool. Pack in containers, leaving headspace. Seal and freeze.
Baked apples	4 months	Prepare as usual (do not overcook). Pack in rigid containers, adding syrup from baking. Leave ½ inch headspace. Seal and freeze.
Custards		Not recommended for freezing.
Éclairs, cream puffs	1 to 2 months	Make éclairs or cream puffs; cool. Freeze unfilled or slit and fill with ice cream before freezing. Wrap with sheet wrapping. Seal and freeze.

FOOD FACTS FOR EASY REFERENCE

Food	Storage Time	Preparation
Gelatin		Not recommended for freezing.
Meringues Hard (baked)	½ month	Cool, then wrap in sheet wrapping, or follow recipe in which it will be used. Seal and freeze.
Soft		Not recommended for freezing.
Puddings, steamed or baked	4 months	Cool; remove from mold if desired. Package in covered can or wrap in sheet wrapping. Seal and freeze.
Sauces Dessert (such as chocolate, caramel, butterscotch, hard sauce)	4 months	Store in original container if moisture-vaporproof, or in rigid freezer container. Seal and freeze.
Fruit	9 to 12 months	Prepare as recipe directs. Cool. Pack in containers, leaving headspace. Seal and freeze.
Sherbets and fruit ices	½ to 1 month	If homemade, freeze in rigid freezer containers. If purchased, be sure lid is tightly sealed or transfer to freezer container.

Main dishes

Many main dishes can be frozen quite successfully. Appropriate dishes include the following:
  Chicken or Turkey
    à la king
  Chili
  Chop suey
  Chow mein
  Creamed dishes
  Croquettes and sticks
  Macaroni and cheese
  Meat, fish, and poultry:
    casserole dishes
  Newburgs and
    thermidors
  Oven-baked beans
  Pies
	2 to 3 months	Prepare a dish as usual, but omit ingredients that don't freeze well, such as hard-cooked eggs and boiled potatoes. Use less than usual of ingredients that develop a more intense flavor when frozen (onion, garlic, pepper, cloves, synthetic vanilla). Undercook the dish slightly since it will finish cooking when it is reheated for serving. Cool all cooked dishes quickly and thoroughly before preparing for freezing. Pack main dishes in the dish in which they will be served or in rigid freezer containers. Seal and freeze.

Food	Storage Time	Preparation
Ravioli		
Sauces		
Spaghetti		
Creole		
Barbecue		
Spaghetti, macaroni, noodle, or rice dishes		
Stews		
Stuffed green peppers		

Pies

  Pie dough and pie shells

Unbaked	2 months	Roll out dough; cut into circles. Stack circles flat in a freezer container or on a baking sheet or piece of cardboard. Separate each layer with two pieces of waxed paper. Cover the container, wrap in sheet wrapping or in plastic bags. Seal and freeze. Or shape pastry into pie plates and stack, separated by waxed paper or cellophane. Place an empty pie plate inside the top shell. Package in freezer bags or in sheet wrapping. Seal and freeze. Dough may also be frozen in bulk but this is less convenient because of the longer thawing time required.
Baked	2 months	Make pie shell and bake as usual. Cool, then wrap, seal, and freeze.
Chiffon pies	2 weeks	Make and set as usual. Freeze; then wrap with sheet wrapping or use freezer bag.
Cream and custard pies		Not recommended for freezing.
Fruit pies Unbaked (preferred)	3 to 4 months	Treat light-colored fruits with ascorbic acid solution (¼ teaspoon per pint of water) to prevent darkening. Prepare pie as usual, but do not cut vents in the top crust. Wrap in sheet wrapping or use freezer bags (for extra protection, cover the top before wrapping with paper or inverted aluminum foil

FOOD FACTS FOR EASY REFERENCE

Food	Storage Time	Preparation
		plate). Seal and freeze. These pies can be frozen before or after packaging.
Baked	3 to 4 months	Bake as usual. Cool. Package as for unbaked fruit pies.
Pecan and pumpkin	3 to 4 months	Pour filling into unbaked pie shell. Freeze; then wrap with sheet wrapping and seal. These pies can also be baked before freezing.
Pie meringue		Not recommended for freezing.

Sandwiches		
Meat, poultry, tuna or salmon, cheese spreads, egg yolk mixtures, nut pastes	1 month	Wrap each sandwich in sheet wrapping or use polyethylene bags. Seal and freeze.
Salad vegetables, hard-cooked egg whites, jelly		Not recommended for freezing.

Soups and Stews		
With base of meat or poultry stock	3 months	Many soups freeze well. To conserve space, freeze in concentrated form whenever possible, leaving liquids to be added at time of serving. Choose vegetables that freeze well (potatoes, for example, do not). Cool quickly after preparation. Package in rigid containers. Seal and freeze.
Navy bean soup		
Split pea soup		
Vegetable soup		
Fish chowder		

MEAT, POULTRY, AND FISH

Meat, *fresh*		
Beef, steaks and roasts	8 to 12 months	Wrap and seal with one of the suggested sheet wrappings. To avoid wasting freezer space, remove as many bones as possible. Pad any sharp points on bones with several layers of freezer wrapping material to prevent puncturing the outer wrapping.
Beef, ground	8 to 12 months	
Lamb	8 to 12 months	
Pork	4 to 8 months	
Pork sausage	1 to 3 months	
Beef or lamb liver	3 to 4 months	Separate individual steaks, patties, or slices of meat with two layers of
Pork liver	1 to 2 months	
Heart	1 to 4 months	

Food	Storage Time	Preparation
Veal	4 to 8 months	waxed paper so that they will be easy to separate for thawing and use. To facilitate later use, freeze ground meat in the form that it will be used—patties, meat loaf, etc.
Game	4 to 8 months	Handle as above with these suggestions: Remove all visible fat and as many bones as practical. Refrigerate at least 24 hours before freezing.
smoked Bacon, sliced Bacon, slab Ham, whole	 1 month 1 to 3 months, only 1 to 3 months, only	Though not recommended for freezing, it is permissible to freeze these meats for the short times listed here. Tight wrapping and sealing is important to prevent drying and to keep the smoked odor from spreading to other foods in freezer.
cooked Roasted Beef Pork	 4 to 6 months 1 to 3 months	Refrigerate to cool before freezing. Roasts or large pieces can be packaged in sheet wrapping. Slices or meats in sauces or gravy can be stored in freezer jars or containers. Seal and freeze.
Meat loaf, baked or unbaked	1 to 2 months	Package in sheet wrapping. Seal and freeze. If baked, refrigerate to cool quickly before freezing.
Poultry, *fresh* Chicken, ready-to-cook Giblets Turkey, ready-to-cook Duck Game birds Geese	 2 to 3 months 2 to 3 months 4 to 5 months 4 to 5 months 6 to 7 months 3 to 6 months	Package in suitable sheet wrapping or in polyethylene bags. Seal and freeze. Freshly killed birds, including game birds, should be dressed and refrigerated at least 24 hours before freezing. (Remove any excess fat from geese.)
cooked	4 to 6 months	Handle same as cooked meats.
Fish and Shellfish Lean fish Fatty fish	 4 to 6 months 3 to 4 months	Prepare fresh fish for freezing as you would for cooking—scale, remove en-

Food	Storage Time	Preparation
		trails, head, and fins; wash thoroughly and drain. Smaller fish can be frozen whole; larger fish can be frozen whole or cut into steaks or fillets. Whole fish can be immersed in water and frozen or ice-glazed for protection during freezer storage.
Clams, oysters, scallops	3 to 4 months	Pack washed scallops, shucked oysters, or clams in rigid freezer containers. Cover with a brine, using 1 tablespoon of salt to 1 cup of water; or substitute the liquid saved from shucking for part of the salt solution. Seal and freeze.
Crab and lobster	2 to 3 months	Cook as usual, cool, then remove meat from shells. Pack dry meat tightly in rigid freezer containers or in polyethylene bags. Remove as much air as possible. Seal and freeze.
Shrimp	1 to 2 months	Remove heads if necessary; wash and drain well. Freeze uncooked, either shelled or unshelled, in freezer containers. Shrimp can be cooked before freezing, but this often makes the meat slightly tough.
Commercially frozen fish	3 months	Needs no additional treatment.

DAIRY PRODUCTS AND EGGS

Food	Storage Time	Preparation
Butter	6 months	Overwrap with sheet wrapping. Seal and freeze. (Freeze only fresh creamery butter made from pasteurized sweet cream.)
Margarine	9 months	

Cheese

Food	Storage Time	Preparation
Cottage cheese Creamed		Not recommended for freezing.
Uncreamed	Commercial container, 1 to 2 weeks Freezer container, 3 to 4 months	Can be frozen, though not recommended for long storage. Do not exceed recommended storage time.

FOOD FACTS FOR EASY REFERENCE

FOOD	STORAGE TIME	PREPARATION
Cream cheese		Not recommended for freezing.
Hard or semi-hard cheeses	6 to 12 months	Wrap pieces no larger than ½ to 1 pound in sheet wrapping. Seal and freeze. May be crumbly when thawed.
Soft cheese	4 months	Wrap in moisture–vaporproof sheet wrap. Seal and freeze.
Cream		
Light		Not recommended for freezing.
Heavy	3 to 6 months	Put into rigid freezing containers, leaving ½-inch headspace. Seal and freeze. Will not whip well when thawed.
Whipped	3 to 6 months	Mound on freezer wrapping material on a baking sheet. Freeze. Remove frozen cream and place in plastic bag or carton. Seal and freeze. Do not thaw before serving.
Sour		Not recommended for freezing.
Eggs		
Whole	6 to 12 months	Remove from shell. Mix white and yolk (avoid incorporating air). Add 1 tablespoon sugar or 1 teaspoon salt for each cup of eggs. Pour into container, leaving ½-inch headspace. Seal and freeze.
Whites		Seal in airtight container, leaving headspace. Freeze.
Yolks		Handle same as whole eggs.
Cooked		Not recommended for freezing.
Ice cream	1 month	Freeze homemade in rigid containers; purchased, in original container or transfer to freezer container.
Milk	1 month	Freeze only pasteurized homogenized, using waxed container in which it was purchased. Freezing and thawing may affect quality.

VEGETABLES AND FRUITS

Vegetables — 8 to 12 months for all vegetables listed below, including commercially frozen ones. — (For information on how to blanch vegetables and package them, see page 934. Unless specified otherwise, vegetables should be dry-packed in the most convenient of the approved freezer containers leaving ½-inch headspace. Tray-frozen vegetables need no headspace when packaged.)

Asparagus — Break or cut off tough end of stalks. Wash thoroughly; sort according to thickness of stalk. Cut into pieces or leave as stalks. Blanch. Cool immediately. Pack into containers alternating large and small ends of stalks, leaving no headspace. Seal and freeze. (Blanch time: small, 2 min.; medium, 3 min.; large, 4 min.)

Beans
   Green or wax — Use young, tender, stringless beans that snap when broken. Wash and snip off ends. Leave whole, cut in two-inch lengths, or French cut. Blanch. Package by dry- or tray (loose)-pack methods into rigid container or plastic bags. Seal and freeze. (Blanch time: 3 min.)

   Lima — Shell, sort for size, discard immature, old, or split beans. Blanch. Chill; drain. Dry-pack in containers. Seal and freeze. (Blanch time: small, 1½ min.; large, 2½ min.)

Beets — Use young, tender beets, not more than three inches in diameter. Wash and sort according to size. Cut off all but ½ inch of stems. Cook in boiling water or steam until tender. Cool. Remove skins. Slice, dice, or leave smaller beets whole. Pack in containers. Seal and freeze.

FOOD	STORAGE TIME	PREPARATION
Broccoli	8 to 12 months for all vegetables listed below, including commercially frozen ones.	Use compact, dark green heads with tender stalks, free from woodiness. Wash; trim. Peel large stalks. Cut through entire stalk lengthwise so that the heads (flowerets) are no more than 1½ inches in diameter. Blanch. Cool; drain. Dry-pack in containers, leaving no headspace. Seal and freeze. (Blanch time: 3 min.)
Brussels sprouts		Cut sprouts from main stem; wash and trim away coarse outer leaves. Sort according to size. Blanch. Cool; drain; dry-pack, leaving no headspace. Seal and freeze. (Blanch time: small, 3 min.; medium, 4 min.; large, 5 min.)
Cabbage or Chinese cabbage		If frozen, can be used only in cooked dishes. Select fresh, compact heads; remove outer coarse leaves. Cut into medium or coarse shreds, thin wedges, or separate into leaves. Blanch. Cool; drain. Dry-pack in containers. Seal and freeze. (Blanch time: 1½ min.)
Carrots		Use young, tender carrots. Remove tops; scrape or pare. Leave whole, slice, or dice. Blanch. Cool, then package by dry- or tray-pack methods. Seal and freeze. (Blanch time: sliced, 3 min.; diced, 3 min.; whole, 5 min.)
Cauliflower		Trim; break into 1-inch flowerets. Wash and drain. Blanch. Chill; drain. Package, leaving no headspace. Seal and freeze. (Blanch time: 3 min.)
Celery		Frozen celery can be used only in cooked dishes. Use crisp, tender stalks. Wash and cut in 1-inch lengths. Blanch. Cool; drain. Package. Seal and freeze. (Blanch time: 3 min.)
Corn		Husk ears, remove silk. Wash and sort. Blanch; then chill thoroughly. For corn-on-the-cob, wrap each ear individually in sheet wrapping. For kernels, cut from cool cob; pack by

FOOD	STORAGE TIME	PREPARATION
		dry- or tray-pack methods. Seal and freeze. (Blanch time: small ears, 6 min.; medium, 8 min.; large, 10 min.)
Cucumbers	8 to 12 months for all vegetables listed below, including commercially frozen ones.	Not recommended for freezing.
Eggplant		Wash, pare, and cut into ⅓-inch slices or cubes. Blanch; then, to prevent darkening, dip into a solution of ½ teaspoon ascorbic acid in 1 quart of water. Chill in fresh water; drain. Package. Seal and freeze. Blanch time: 4 min.)
Greens (beet greens, chard, collards, dandelion greens, kale, mustard greens, spinach, turnip greens)		Use young, tender leaves. Wash thoroughly. Remove tough stems and imperfect leaves. Cut leaves of chard into pieces, as desired. Blanch. Cool, drain, pack into containers. Seal and freeze. (Blanch time: 2 min., except for collards, 3 min., and tender spinach, 1½ min.)
Kohlrabi		Use young, tender, mild-flavored kohlrabi, small to medium in size. Remove tops and roots. Wash, peel, cut into ½-inch pieces if desired. Blanch. Cool, drain, pack into containers. Seal and freeze. (Whole kohlrabi can be wrapped in sheet wrapping.) (Blanch time: whole, 2 min.; cubes, 1 min.)
Mushrooms		Sort according to size. Wash thoroughly in cold water. Trim stem ends. Slice or quarter mushrooms that are larger than 1 inch. To prevent darkening, dip for 5 minutes in a solution of 1 teaspoon lemon juice to 1 pint water. Blanch. Cool, drain, pack into containers. Seal and freeze. (Blanch time: whole, 5 min.; quarters, 3½ min.; slices, 3 min.)
Okra		Wash thoroughly. Cut off stems without cutting pods open. Sort for size. Blanch. Cool; drain; slice crosswise if desired. Pack into containers. Seal and freeze. (Blanch time: small pods, 3 min.; large pods, 4 min.)

Food	Storage Time	Preparation
Onions	8 to 12 months for all vegetables listed below, including commercially frozen ones.	Peel, wash, and chop. Package by dry- or tray-pack methods in rigid containers or freezer bags. Seal and freeze.
Parsnips		Remove tops, wash, and peel. Cut into ½-inch cubes or slices. Blanch. Cool, drain, and pack into containers. Seal and freeze. (Blanch time: 2 min.)
Peas		Shell peas. Discard immature or tough peas. Blanch. Cool and drain. Pack into containers. (Also suitable for tray-pack method.) Seal and freeze. (Blanch time: 1½ min.)
Peppers, Green		For use in uncooked foods, freeze raw: Wash, remove seeds, and chop. For easy use, freeze by tray-pack method. For use in cooked foods: Wash, remove stems, cut in half, and remove seeds. If desired, cut into strips or rings. Blanch. Cool; drain; pack into containers. Seal and freeze. (Blanch time: halves, 3 min.; slices or rings, 2 min.)
Red (hot)		Prepare as for green peppers, either raw or blanched.
Potatoes White		Only freeze raw, blanched potatoes. For freezing whole, use immature, small potatoes. Wash, scrub, but do not pare. For freezing in strips or cubes, use mature potatoes that have been stored at least one month. Blanch. Chill, drain, pack in containers. Seal and freeze. (Blanch time: sticks or cubes, 2 min.; whole, 4 min.)
Sweet		May be packed whole, sliced, or mashed. Wash and sort according to size. Cook until almost tender. Let stand at room temperature until cool. Peel, then cut into halves, slice, or mash. If desired, prevent darkening of whole or sliced sweet potatoes by dipping for five seconds in a solution of ½ teaspoon ascorbic acid, 1 tablespoon

Food	Storage Time	Preparation
		citric acid, or ½ cup lemon juice to 1 quart water. Keep mashed potatoes from darkening by mixing in two tablespoons orange or lemon juice per quart of mashed sweet potatoes. Pack in containers. Seal and freeze.
Pumpkin	8 to 12 months for all vegetables listed below, including commercially frozen ones.	Wash, cut in chunks, and remove seeds. Cook chunks until soft in boiling water, steam, pressure cooker, or in the oven. Remove pulp from rind and mash or press it through a sieve. Cool by placing pan containing pumpkin in cold water. Pack into containers. Seal and freeze.
Radishes		Not recommended for freezing.
Rutabaga		See turnips.
Squash Summer		Use small ones with a tender rind. Wash; cut into ½-inch slices. Blanch. Cool, drain, and pack into containers. Seal and freeze. (Blanch time: 3 min.)
Winter		Use firm, mature squash. Wash, cut into pieces, and remove seeds. Then prepare as for pumpkin. (See above.)
Tomatoes, stewed		(Raw tomatoes are not recommended for freezing.) Wash, remove stem ends, peel, and quarter. Cover and simmer until tender (about 10 to 20 minutes). Cool by placing pan containing tomatoes in cold water. Pack into containers, leaving 1-inch headspace. Seal and freeze.
Tomato juice		Wash, core, and cut into pieces. Simmer 5 to 10 minutes. Press through a sieve while hot. Add 1 teaspoon salt per quart of juice if desired. Pour into containers, leaving 1-inch headspace. Seal and freeze.
Turnips		Use small to medium young, tender turnips. Wash, peel, and cut into ½-inch cubes. Blanch. Cool and drain. Pack into containers. Seal and freeze. (Blanch time: 2 to 2½ min.)

Food	Storage Time	Preparation
Fruits	6 to 12 months for all fruits listed below, including commercially frozen ones. Fruits in a sugar pack keep better than those frozen unsweetened.	For information on preparation of sugar, syrup, dry, and tray packs, see page 914. Fruits to be packed in sugar or syrup should be packed in rigid freezer containers, leaving ½-inch headspace for pint containers, 1-inch for quarts. Fruits to be packed by the dry or tray method can go into either rigid containers (leaving ½-inch headspace) or plastic bags.
Apples		Peel, core, and slice. If fruit is to be served as is, cover with medium syrup (including ascorbic acid). If fruit is to be used in cooking, use either sugar pack or dry pack. Seal and freeze.
Apricots		Wash and remove pit. Freeze peeled or unpeeled. Cover with light to heavy syrup to which ascorbic acid has been added. Seal and freeze.
Avocados, mashed		Whole or sliced avocados cannot be frozen satisfactorily. Use soft-ripe fruit, free from blemishes. Peel, cut in half, remove pit, then mash. Pack unsweetened, adding ¼ teaspoon ascorbic acid per quart, or sweetened, adding 1 cup sugar per quart. Pack in containers. Seal and freeze.
Bananas		Not recommended for freezing.
Berries Blackberries Boysenberries Dewberries Loganberries Youngberries		Wash and sort, discarding immature or overripe berries. Use medium or heavy syrup pack, dry pack, or tray pack. Seal and freeze.
Blueberries Elderberries Huckleberries		Wash and sort. Use dry pack, tray pack, or medium syrup pack. Seal and freeze.
Cherries Sour		Sort, stem, wash, and pit. Use sugar pack, with ¾ cup of sugar to 1 quart fruit. Seal and freeze.
Sweet		Use light to medium syrup, plus ascorbic acid. Seal and freeze.

[67]

FOOD FACTS FOR EASY REFERENCE

FOOD	STORAGE TIME	PREPARATION
Coconut, fresh	6 to 12 months for all fruits listed below, including commercially frozen ones. Fruits in a sugar pack keep better than those frozen unsweetened.	Grate or grind finely. Pack tightly as dry coconut; add ½ cup sugar to 2 pounds grated coconut or cover with the coconut milk. Seal and freeze.
Cranberries		Wash and stem. Use dry pack, heavy syrup pack, or tray pack. Seal and freeze. Unopened packages of fresh berries can be frozen without further treatment.
Currants		Wash in cold water, drain, and stem. Pack unsweetened, cover with medium to heavy syrup, or add ¾ cup sugar per quart of fruit. Leave ½-inch headspace for any pack. Seal and freeze.
Dates		Wash, slit, remove pits. Pack into containers, leaving headspace. Seal and freeze.
Figs		Sort, discarding fruit that is immature or has become sour in the center. Wash; remove stems; peel if desired. Leave whole, cut in halves, or slice. Pack unsweetened, with or without water to cover, or cover with medium syrup. To prevent darkening, add ¾ teaspoon ascorbic acid to each quart of syrup or water. Seal and freeze.
Gooseberries		Sort, stem, wash, and remove soft fruit. For pie or preserves, package whole, using dry or tray pack. Or use sugar pack, adding ⅔ cup sugar to 4 or 5 cups crushed fruit. Seal and freeze.
Grapefruit and oranges		Peel, seed, and section, removing white membrane. Cover with heavy syrup, including ascorbic acid. Seal and freeze.
Grapes		Not generally recommended for freezing (they are very soft when thawed). If desired, they can be frozen in this way: Use firm-ripe grapes. Wash and stem. Cut table grapes and remove seeds; leave seedless grapes whole.

FOOD	STORAGE TIME	PREPARATION
		Pack unsweetened or cover with medium syrup. Seal and freeze.
Melons Cantaloupe Muskmelon Honeydew Persian Watermelon Cranshaw	6 to 12 months for all fruits listed below, including commercially frozen ones. Fruits in a sugar pack keep better than those frozen unsweetened.	Not particularly satisfactory for freezing since they become mushy when thawed. If frozen, serve barely thawed. Cut melon in half, remove seeds, and peel. Cut into balls, slices, cubes, or wedges. Pack in rigid container, covering with light syrup. Seal and freeze.
Nectarines		Use fully ripe, firm fruit. Sort, wash, and pit. Peel if desired. Cut into halves, quarters, or slices. Cut fruit directly into medium syrup (including ascorbic acid) in rigid freezer container. Press fruit down; add syrup to cover. Seal and freeze.
Oranges—See *Grapefruit*		
Peaches		Peel and pit. (Dipping fruits into boiling water for about ½ minute will make the skins easier to remove but will make the fruit less smooth.) Put ½ cup medium syrup and ascorbic acid into a rigid freezer container and slice or halve the fruit directly into the syrup. Press fruit down; add syrup to cover. Although syrup pack is best, sugar or water (no sweetening) pack can also be used. For sugar pack, dissolve ¼ teaspoon ascorbic acid crystals in ¼ cup cold water and sprinkle over 1 quart of fruit. Add ⅔ cup sugar for each quart of fruit. Mix well. For water pack, add 1 teaspoon of ascorbic acid for each quart of water. Slice fruit directly into water in freezer container. For all packs: To keep fruit submerged, put crumpled waxed paper on top. Seal and freeze.
Pears		Not recommended for freezing.
Persimmons		Best frozen as purée. Sort, wash, peel, and cut into sections. Press through sieve. To prevent darkening, add ⅛ teaspoon ascorbic acid per quart of

FOOD	STORAGE TIME	PREPARATION
		fruit and mix thoroughly. Pack unsweetened or add 1 cup sugar per quart of purée. Pack into containers. Seal and freeze.
Pineapple	6 to 12 months for all fruits listed below, including commercially frozen ones. Fruits in a sugar pack keep better than those frozen unsweetened.	Peel, core, and slice, cube, or crush. Fruit can be frozen either unsweetened or with a light syrup. In either case, pack tightly into a container. Seal and freeze.
Plums and prunes		Wash and sort; halve and pit. Cover with heavy syrup; use sugar pack, allowing ¾ cup sugar for each quart of fruit; or use tray pack. Seal and freeze.
Raspberries		Wash quickly in ice water, lifting berries out of water. They can be packed by any of the four methods: sugar, syrup, dry, or tray. For sugar pack, allow ¾ cup sugar per quart of fruit. For syrup pack, use medium syrup. Seal and freeze.
Rhubarb		Wash, trim, and cut into 1- or 2-inch pieces or lengths to fit container. For color and flavor retention, heat in boiling water for 1 minute, then promptly chill in cold water. Package unsweetened or cover with medium syrup. Seal and freeze.
Strawberries		Sort, wash, and hull. Slice or crush large berries. Cover with medium or heavy syrup (depending on tartness) or, for sugar pack, add ¾ cup sugar for each quart of berries. If necessary, pack unsweetened, adding water to cover and 1 teaspoon ascorbic acid per quart of water. Seal and freeze.

A Guide to the Safe Storage of Foods

To avoid waste and keep foods at their peak of freshness, proper food storage should be a primary concern. You can never improve the quality of foods by proper storage but you can preserve it. Detailed storage directions for specific foods are given in each chapter, but these are general methods you should memorize. Storage of foods involves more than putting perishable items into the refrigerator and nonperishable ones on the shelf. Here is some additional information that will help you keep all kinds of foods as fresh as they were when you brought them home from the market.

Here, listed in alphabetical order, are some of the major food categories, with suggestions about how to store specific foods and how long they may be kept safely.

Breads

Store unused bread in its original wrapper. It will keep in a ventilated breadbox for several days. To prevent formation of mold in hot, humid weather, store in the refrigerator for as long as a week. Bread may be stored in a freezer for 2 to 3 weeks.

Butter, Shortening, and Oils

Butter: Store, well wrapped, in refrigerator up to 2 weeks; in freezer, several months.
Hydrogenated shortening: May be stored at room temperature for several weeks.
Cooking and salad oils: May be stored at room temperature for a short period of time; in refrigerator, several months. Some oils may cloud and solidify in refrigerator but will become clear and liquid when warmed to room temperature.

Cakes

Cakes with whipped cream or custard cream fillings: Store covered in refrigerator both before and immediately after serving; use within 2 days. Plain or frosted cakes: Cover cut portion with waxed paper, store in tightly covered cakebox, or in refrigerator; use within a week.
Fruitcakes: Wrap tightly in waxed paper, plastic wrap, or aluminum foil; may be stored in refrigerator for several weeks.

Canned, Packaged and Jarred Dry Products

In general, these should be stored in a cool, dry place. Excess heat will destroy the flavor of spices and herbs; keep them tightly covered, away from the heat or sunlight.

FOOD FACTS FOR EASY REFERENCE

Cereals, Flour, Sugar, Spices

Store in tightly covered containers at room temperature.

Cheese

Hard cheeses, such as Cheddar, Swiss, and Parmesan: Wrap tightly and store in refrigerator; they will keep several weeks.
Soft cheeses such as cottage, cream, and Camembert: Store covered in coldest part of refrigerator. Use cottage cheese within 3 to 5 days, others within 2 weeks.
Cheese spreads: Store opened containers, covered, in refrigerator.

Eggs

In shell: Store in refrigerator in original carton or covered container. Use within 2 weeks.
Egg yolks: Store unbroken yolks in refrigerator in covered container with just enough cold water added to cover. Drain and use within 2 to 3 days.
Egg whites: Store in refrigerator in covered jar. Use within 10 days.

Frozen Foods

Frozen foods should always be kept in the freezer or freezer storage compartment of your refrigerator until you are ready to prepare them.

Fruits

Apples: Store mellow or ripe apples uncovered in refrigerator; use within a week. Hard or unripe apples may be stored at cool room temperature until ready to eat.
Apricots, avocados, grapes, nectarines, peaches, pears, plums: Store ripe fruit uncovered in refrigerator; use within 3 to 5 days. Allow unripe fruit to ripen at room temperature.
Berries: Sort and discard any damaged fruit. Store whole and uncovered in refrigerator; use within 1 to 2 days. Wash just before using.
Bananas: Store at room temperature; use within a few days.
Citrus fruits, melons, pineapple: Store at cool room temperature, 60° to 70° F. May be stored in refrigerator; use within a week.

Canned fruits and fruit juices: Store opened fruit or juice in refrigerator in covered glass jar. Use within a few days.

Frozen fruit juices: Store reconstituted juices in glass or plastic container. Use within 1 to 2 days.

Honey and Syrups

Store opened containers in refrigerator with covers on to protect from mold.

Jellies, Jams, Preserves

Store covered in refrigerator.

Mayonnaise, Salad Dressings

After opening jar, store covered in refrigerator.

Meat, Poultry, Fish

Uncooked: Wrap loosely; store in coldest part of refrigerator. Use ground meat, bulk sausage, liver, kidney, giblets, poultry, and fish within 1 to 2 days. Use roasts, chops, and steaks within 3 to 5 days.

Cooked: Cool quickly, wrap loosely, and refrigerate immediately. Whenever possible, separate meat from gravy or sauce and refrigerate each separately. Always remove stuffing from poultry and refrigerate it separately. Use fish within 1 day. Use gravies and sauces within 1 to 2 days, meat cooked in gravy or sauce within 3 days. Use roast meats within 4 to 5 days. Use poultry within 2 to 3 days; poultry stuffing, within 1 to 2 days.

Cold cuts: Wrap tightly and store in refrigerator; use within 3 to 5 days.

Cured and smoked meats: Wrap tightly; store in refrigerator. Use bacon, frankfurters, bologna, and smoked sausage within a week. Use half ham within 3 to 5 days; whole ham within a week; ham slices within 2 to 3 days.

Milk, Cream

Fresh milk and cream: Refrigerate immediately in original containers; use within a few days.

Evaporated and condensed milk: Store opened can, tightly covered, in refrigerator; use within a few days.

Dried milk: Store nonfat dry milk in closed container at room temperature; may be stored several months.

Sour cream and yogurt: Refrigerate, covered for one to two weeks; stir before using.

Nuts

Store shelled or unshelled nuts in tight container in refrigerator or freezer. May be kept several months.

Nut butters: Store opened jar, with cover on, in refrigerator.

Pies

Pies with cream or custard fillings: Store covered in refrigerator both before and after serving. Use within 2 days.

Fruit pies: Store covered in refrigerator; use within 4 to 5 days.

Relishes

Olives, pickles, etc.: Store opened jars, covered, in refrigerator.

Vegetables

Potatoes, onions, hard-rind squash, turnips, and eggplant: Store at cool room temperature with plenty of room for air to circulate.

Asparagus, broccoli, cabbage, cauliflower, Brussels sprouts, green beans, carrots, celery, beets, radishes, peppers, and cucumbers: Store in refrigerator in crisper or in plastic bags; use within a few days.

Green peas and lima beans: Leave in pods and store in refrigerator in crisper or plastic bags; use within 2 days.

Sweet corn: Store unhusked and uncovered in refrigerator; use within 1 to 2 days.

Tomatoes: Store ripe tomatoes uncovered in refrigerator. Keep unripe tomatoes at room temperature away from direct sunlight until ripened.

Lettuce and salad greens: Wash off surface dirt, shake dry, and store in refrigerator in crisper or plastic bags; use within a few days.

Spinach, kale, chard, and other leafy greens: Wash thoroughly, drain well, and store in refrigerator in crisper or plastic bags; use within 1 to 2 days.

Canned vegetables: Store opened vegetables in covered can or glass jar. Use within a few days.

How Much to Buy for Two

Shopping for two isn't as difficult as you might have heard. Many foods can be bought in small units; you can purchase just enough for two, though it is sometimes more practical to buy larger quantities and plan to use the food over a period of a few days. Other foods, such as roasts, must be bought in larger quantities; with these it helps to know the number of servings you're buying so that you can plan how to use them. Portions listed here are based on average-sized servings and can be used only as a general guide when you're shopping. If you know that you and your husband have big appetites and often like to have second portions, you may need to buy more.

FRUITS
Apples ....3 medium (1 lb.)
Apricots ....½ lb.
Avocados 1
Bananas ....2 large (1 lb.)
Berries ....1 pint
Cherries ....½ lb.
Grapefruit 1
Grapes ....½ to ¾ lb.
Melons . .1 small cantaloupe
         1 medium honeydew (4 servings)
Oranges 6
Peaches ....2 or 3 (½ to ¾ lb.)
Pears ....2 (½ to ¾ lb.)
Pineapple ....1 small
Plums ....½ lb.
Rhubarb ....¾ lb.

VEGETABLES
Asparagus ....¾ to 1 lb.
Beans, green or wax ....½ lb.
         lima . .1 lb. (makes 1 cup shelled)
Beets ....1 bunch (2 servings)
Broccoli ....1 bunch (4 servings)
Brussels sprouts ....1 pint or 1 lb.
Cabbage ....1 small head
Carrots ....1 bunch
Cauliflower ....1 small head

Celery ....1 small bunch
Corn ....4 ears
Cucumbers ....1 small
Eggplant ....1 small (½ to ¾ lb.)
Green peppers . .2 (for stuffed peppers)
Lettuce or greens ....1 small head
Mushrooms ....½ lb.
Onions ....½ lb.
Peas ....1 lb. (makes 1 cup shelled)
Potatoes, white or sweet .....¾ to 1 lb.
         (3 medium)
Spinach ....1 bag or 1 lb.
Squash, summer ....1 lb.
         zucchini ....1 lb.
         acorn ....1 (cut in half)
Tomatoes ....2 small to medium
         (½ to ¾ lb.)
Turnips ....½ to ¾ lb.

FISH AND SHELLFISH
Allow ⅓ to ½ lb. per serving of filleted (boned) fish; ½ lb. per serving of whole fish.
Clams (to serve as appetizer) . . .8 to 12
Crab meat, cooked ....½ lb.
Fillets ....¾ to 1 lb.
Lobsters ....2 small or 1 large
         (2 to 2½ lbs.)

tails ....2 large or 4 small
Mackerel ....1 small
Oysters (to serve as appetizer) ..8 to 12
Salmon steak ....¾ lb.
Scallops ....½ to ¾ lb.
Shrimp ....¾ to 1 lb. (in the shell)
Small fish (trout, perch, etc.) ..2 medium
Smelt ....1 lb.

MEAT
Allow ¼ lb. per serving of boneless meat; ½ lb. per serving of meat with bone; ¾ to 1 lb. per serving of bony meat (spareribs, breast of veal, etc.)
Beef
Club or short steak ....2 steaks of
    desired thickness
Flank steak ....1 (cut it in half and use
    for 2 meals)
Porterhouse or T-bone steak ..1, about
    1 inch thick
Rump, round, chuck, or blade
    for pot roast .....3 lbs. (4 to 6
    servings)
    for stew ....1½ lbs.
    for ground meat ....½ to ¾ lb.
Tongue, smoked ....1 (8 servings)
Tenderloin .....2, of desired thickness
Lamb
½ leg of lamb ....2½ to 3½ lbs.
    (4 servings)
Loin or rib chops ....2 to 4 chops
Loin roast ....4 to 6 chops in one piece
    (4 to 6 servings)
Shanks 2
Shoulder, for stew ....1½ lbs.
    for braising ..2 or 3 shoulder
    chops
Pork
Bacon ....½ lb. (8 to 10 slices)

Frankfurters 4
Loin, rib, or shoulder chops .....2 to 4
Loin roast .....2½ to 3 lbs. (6 servings)
Sausage ....½ lb.
Smoked ham slice ....1 slice, about
    ¾ inch thick
Smoked tenderloin ....1½ to 2 lbs.
    (4 servings)
Spareribs ....2 lbs.
Veal
Breast, shoulder, for stew ......1½ lbs.
Cutlet ....¾ to 1 lb.
Loin chops 2
Loin roast .....2 to 2½ lbs. (4 servings)
Variety
Kidneys, lamb 4
    veal 2
    beef 1
Liver ....½ lb.
Poultry
For chicken, allow ½ of a 1½-lb. broiler per serving; ¾ lb. per serving of frying chicken, roasting chicken, and stewing chicken.
Chicken, broiler .....1½ to 2 lbs., split
    fryer .....2 to 2½ lbs., cut in
    pieces (2 servings, plus)
    roasting ....3 to 4 lbs.
    (4 to 6 servings)
Duckling ....4 lbs. (4 servings)
Turkey .....4 to 8 lbs. (6 to 8 servings)

MISCELLANEOUS
Butter ....1 lb.
Canned fruits and vegetables .....8-oz.
    cans
Flour ....2 lbs.
Herbs and spices ....small jars
Shortening, hydrogenated ....1 lb.
Sugar, granulated ....2 lbs.

Calorie Count of Common Foods

This chart of calorie values will help you keep an accurate check on all the food you eat every day. To use it for either a weight-loss diet or a weight-maintenance diet, first ask your doctor what your daily calorie intake should be. Then refer to the listings in the chart and record calorie values of the food you eat; choose those foods that will keep you within your limit. Note that foods which are to be eaten cooked should be weighed after cooking in order to determine weight and calorie values.

FOOD	CALORIES
BEVERAGES	
Ale, 12 fluid ounces	144
Beer, 12 fluid ounces	150
Brandy, 1 fluid ounce	73
*Chocolate-flavored drink, 1 cup	190
Cider, sweet, 12 fluid ounces	188
Club soda, unsweetened	0
Cola-type carbonated beverages, 12 fluid ounces	145
Cocoa made with milk, 1 cup	245
Coffee, no cream or sugar, 1 cup	2–4
Fruit-flavored sodas and Tom Collins mix, 12 fluid ounces	170
Gin, rum, vodka, whisky	
80 proof, 1½ fluid ounces	100
90 proof, 1½ fluid ounces	110
100 proof, 1½ fluid ounces	125
Ginger ale, 12 fluid ounces	115
Lemonade, 1 cup	110
Limeade, 1 cup	100
Root beer, 12 fluid ounces	150
Tea, no cream or sugar, 1 cup	1
Tonic or quinine water, 12 fluid ounces	115
Wines, dessert, 3½ fluid ounces	140
Wines, table, 3½ fluid ounces	85
BREADS AND CRACKERS	
Bagel, 3-inch diameter	165
Biscuits, from mix, 2-inch diameter	90
Boston brown bread, 1 3-x-¾-inch slice	100

*All cup measures refer to standard measuring cups.

FOOD	CALORIES
Bread crumbs, dry, 1 cup	390
Butter cracker, 1 small round	18
Clover-leaf or pan roll (commercial), 1 average	85
Corn and molasses bread, 1 pound, 18 slices per loaf, 1 slice	71
Corn muffin, from mix, 2⅜-inch diameter	130
Cracked wheat bread, 1 average slice	65
Date-nut bread, 1 slice	100
Doughnut, 1 ounce	125
Frankfurter or hamburger roll	120
French or Vienna bread, 1 pound	1,315
Gluten bread, 1 slice	35
Graham cracker, 2½-inch square	28
Hard roll, 1 average	155
Italian bread, 1 pound	1,250
Muffin, 3-inch diameter	120
Protein bread, 1 slice	45
Pumpernickel bread, 1 average slice	79
Raisin bread, 1 average slice	65
Rye bread, 1 average slice	60
Rye wafers, 2	45
Soda cracker or saltine, 2-inch square	13
Sprouted rye bread, 1 pound, 18 slices per loaf, 1 slice	65
Sprouted wheat bread, 1 pound, 18 slices per loaf, 1 slice	65
Tortilla, 6-inch	63
White bread, firm crumb, 1 pound, 20 slices per loaf, 1 slice	65

FOOD FACTS FOR EASY REFERENCE

FOOD	CALORIES
White bread, soft crumb, 1 pound, 22 slices per loaf, 1 slice	.55
Whole-wheat bread, firm crumb, 1 pound, 18 slices per loaf, 1 slice	.60
Whole-wheat bread, soft crumb, 1 pound, 16 slices per loaf, 1 slice	.65

*CEREALS AND GRAIN PRODUCTS

FOOD	CALORIES
Bran flakes, 1 cup	105
Bran flakes with raisins, 1 cup	145
Buckwheat groats, uncooked, 1 cup	317
Bulgur, uncooked, 1 cup	559
Corn flakes, 1 cup	100
Corn flakes, sugar covered, 1 cup	155
Corn grits, cooked, 1 cup	125
Corn meal, cooked, 1 cup	120
Corn meal, uncooked, 1 cup	540
Corn, puffed, presweetened, 1 cup	115
Farina, cooked, 1 cup	105
Farina, uncooked, 1 cup	371
Granola, 1 cup	225
Macaroni, cooked, 1 cup	190
Macaroni, uncooked, 1 pound	1,674
Millet, uncooked, 1 cup	586
Noodles, cooked, 1 cup	200
Noodles, uncooked, 1 pound	1,760
Oatmeal or rolled oats, cooked, 1 cup	130
Oatmeal, uncooked, 1 cup	312
Oats, puffed, 1 cup	100
Pancakes, 1 cake, 4-inch diameter	.60
Rice, brown, cooked, 1 cup	203
Rice, brown, uncooked, 1 pound	1,633
Rice, instant, 1 cup	180
Rice, parboiled, cooked, 1 cup	185
Rice, puffed, 1 cup	.60
Rice, white, cooked, 1 cup	225
Rice, white, uncooked, 1 pound	1,647
Rye flour, 1 cup	286
Spaghetti, cooked, 1 cup	155

Note: Ready-to-eat cereals vary by brand in calorie values. Check the cereal package; each one has the calorie count for measured portions printed on the box.

FOOD	CALORIES
Spaghetti, uncooked, 1 pound	1,674
Waffle, 7-inch diameter	210
Wheat flakes, 1 cup	105
Wheat flour, cake, sifted, 1 cup	350
Wheat (white) flour, all-purpose, sifted, 1 cup	420
Wheat (white) flour, all-purpose, unsifted, 1 tablespoon	28
Wheat germ, toasted, ¼ cup	106
Wheat germ, toasted with honey, ¼ cup	107
Wheat, shredded, plain, 1 biscuit	.90
Whole-wheat flour, 1 cup	400
Wild rice, uncooked, 1 pound	1,601

CAKES, CANDY, ICE CREAM, PIES

Cakes

FOOD	CALORIES
Angel food, from mix, 1/12 of 10-inch diameter cake	135
Boston cream pie, homemade, 1/12 of 8-inch-diameter cake	210
Cupcakes, from mix, chocolate icing, 2½ inches	130
Devil's food, from mix, chocolate icing, 1/16 of 9-inch layer cake	235
Fruitcake, 1/30 of 8-inch loaf	.55
Gingerbread, from mix, 1/9 of 8-inch-square cake	175
Poundcake, homemade, ½-inch slice	140
Spongecake, homemade, 1/12 of 10-inch diameter cake	195
White, from mix, chocolate icing, 1/16 of 9-inch layer cake	250
Yellow, homemade, without icing, 1/16 of 9-inch layer cake	200

Candy

FOOD	CALORIES
Caramel candies, 1 ounce	115
Chocolate, sweet milk, 1 ounce	145
Chocolate, sweet milk, dietetic, 1 ounce	168
Chocolate-coated peanuts, 1 ounce	160
Fondant; mints, uncoated; candy corn, 1 ounce	105

Food	Calories
Fudge, plain or chocolate, 1 ounce	.115
Gumdrops, 1 ounce	.100
Hard candy, 1 ounce	.110
Hard candy, dietetic, 1 ounce	.108
Marshmallows, 1 ounce	.90
Mixed chocolates, dietetic, 1 ounce	.188

Frozen Desserts

Chocolate ice cream, ½ cup	.137
Iced milk, chocolate, ½ cup	.98
Iced milk, vanilla, ½ cup	.95
Sherbet, orange, ½ cup	.130
Strawberry ice cream, ½ cup	.133
Vanilla ice cream, ½ cup	.133

Pies (all portions are ⅛ of 9-inch pie)

Apple (2-crust)	.306
Butterscotch (1-crust)	.306
Cherry (2-crust)	.306
Custard (1-crust)	.249
Lemon meringue (1-crust)	.267
Mince (2-crust)	.319
Pecan (1-crust)	.429
Pineapple chiffon (1-crust)	.232
Pumpkin (1-crust)	.241
Turnover, frozen, apple	.290

Puddings

Chocolate, ½ cup	.193
Custard, baked, 1 cup	.305
Gelatin dessert, sweetened, 1 cup	.140
Vanilla, ½ cup	.143

FATS, OILS AND SALAD DRESSINGS

Food	Calories
Blue-cheese dressing, 1 tablespoon	.75
Butter, regular, 1 tablespoon	.100
Butter, whipped, 1 tablespoon	.65
French dressing, low-fat, artificial sweeteners, 1 tablespoon	.trace
French dressing, regular, 1 tablespoon	.65
Home-cooked salad dressing, boiled, 1 tablespoon	.25
Lard, 1 tablespoon	.115
Margarine, imitation, 1 tablespoon	.50
Margarine, regular, 1 tablespoon	.100

Food	Calories
Margarine, soft in tub, 1 tablespoon	.100
Margarine, whipped, 1 tablespoon	.68
Mayonnaise, 1 tablespoon	.100
Mayonnaise, low-calorie, 1 tablespoon	.20–33
Salad dressing, mayonnaise type, 1 tablespoon	.65
Thousand Island, 1 tablespoon	.80
Vegetable shortening, 1 tablespoon	.110
Vegetable oils: corn, cottonseed, olive, peanut, safflower, soybean, 1 tablespoon	.125

FISH AND SHELLFISH

Cooked or Canned

Bluefish, baked or broiled, 3-ounce (average) serving	.135
Clams, canned, solids and liquid, 3 ounces	.45
Clams, breaded and fried, 3½ ounces	.179
Crab, cooked, meat only, 1 pound	.422
Crabmeat, canned, 3 ounces	.85
Fish sticks, 5	.200
Haddock, fried, 3-ounce (average) serving	.140
Mackerel, broiled, 3-ounce (average) serving	.200
Ocean perch, breaded, fried, 3 ounces	.195
Salmon, canned, drained, 3 ounces	.120
Sardines, drained, 3 ounces	.175
Shad, baked, 3 ounces	.170
Shrimp, breaded, fried, 3 ounces	.192
Shrimp, canned, drained, ½ cup	.100
Swordfish, broiled, 3-ounce (average) serving	.150
Tuna, canned, drained, 3 ounces	.170
Tuna, water-packed, undrained, 3 ounces	.108

FOOD FACTS FOR EASY REFERENCE

Food	Calories
Uncooked	
Bass, flesh only, 1 pound	476
Bass, whole, 1 pound	205
Bluefish, flesh only, 1 pound	531
Bluefish, whole, 1 pound	271
Clams, hard, meat only, 1 pound	363
Clams, soft, meat only, 1 pound	372
Clams, meat only, 3 ounces	65
Cod, flesh only, 1 pound	354
Cod, whole, 1 pound	110
Flatfish (flounder, sole), flesh only, 1 pound	358
Flatfish (flounder, sole), whole, 1 pound	118
Haddock, flesh only, 1 pound	358
Halibut, flesh only, 1 pound	454
Lobster, meat only, 1 pound	413
Lobster, whole, 1 pound	107
Mackerel, Atlantic, flesh only, 1 pound	866
Mackerel, Pacific, flesh only, 1 pound	721
Mackerel, whole, 1 pound	468
Ocean perch, fillets, 1 pound	399
Oysters, meat only, ½ cup	80
Oysters, meat only, 1 pound	299
Perch, white, flesh only, 1 pound	193
Perch, yellow, flesh only, 1 pound	161
Salmon, steak, with bone, 1 pound	886
Scallops, bay and sea, 1 pound	367
Shad, flesh only, 1 pound	771
Shrimp, flesh only, 1 pound	413
Shrimp, in shell, 1 pound	285
Trout, brook, whole, 1 pound	224
FRUITS AND FRUIT JUICES	
Apple, raw, 1 medium	70
Apple juice, fresh or canned, 1 cup	120
Applesauce, sweetened, 1 cup	230
Applesauce, unsweetened or artificially sweetened, 1 cup	100
Apricot nectar, 1 cup	140
Apricots, canned in heavy syrup, halves and syrup, ½ cup	110
Apricots, dried, cooked, unsweetened, 1 cup	240
Apricots, dried, uncooked, 10 small halves	98
Apricots, raw, 3	55
Avocado, mashed, ¼ cup	76
Avocado, raw, ½ medium	132
Banana, 1 medium	100
Blackberries, raw, 1 cup	85
Blueberries, raw, 1 cup	85
Cantaloupe, raw, ½ medium	60
Cherries, red sour, water-packed, 1 cup	105
Cherries, sweet, raw, 1 cup	80
Cherries, sweet, raw, 1 pound	286
Cranberries, raw, 1 pound	200
Cranberry juice cocktail, 1 cup	165
Cranberry sauce, sweetened, 2 tablespoons	51
Dates, dried, pitted, cut up, ¼ cup	123
Figs, fresh, 3 small	80
Figs, fresh, 1 pound	363
Figs, dried, 3 small	123
Fruit cocktail, canned in heavy syrup, 1 cup	195
Grapefruit, canned in heavy syrup, 1 cup	180
Grapefruit, pink or red, raw, ½ medium	50
Grapefruit, water-packed, 1 cup	60
Grapefruit, white, raw, ½ medium	45
Grapefruit juice, canned, sweetened, 1 cup	130
Grapefruit juice, canned, unsweetened, or frozen, diluted, 1 cup	100
Grapefruit juice, fresh, 1 cup	95
Grape juice, bottled, 1 cup	165
Grape juice, frozen, diluted, 1 cup	135
Grapes, raw, 1 cup	65–95

Food	Calories
Grapes, raw, slip skin, 1 pound	197
Grapes, raw, adherent skin, 1 pound	270
Lemon juice, 1 tablespoon	4
Lime juice, fresh and canned, 1 tablespoon	4
Orange-flavored instant breakfast drink, 1 cup	118
Orange juice, canned, unsweetened or frozen, diluted, 1 cup	120
Orange juice, fresh, 1 cup	110
Orange and grapefruit juice, frozen, diluted, 1 cup	110
Oranges, raw, 1 large	65
Peaches, canned in heavy syrup, 1 cup	200
Peaches, frozen, sweetened, 1 cup	200
Peaches, raw, 1 medium	35
Peaches, raw, sliced, 1 cup	65
Peaches, water-packed, 1 cup	75
Pears, canned in heavy syrup, 1 cup	195
Pears, raw, 1 medium	100
Pears, water-packed, 1 cup	80
Pineapple, canned, crushed, 1 cup	195
Pineapple, canned, sliced, 1 large slice or 2 small	90
Pineapple, raw, diced, 1 cup	75
Pineapple juice, canned, 1 cup	135
Plums, canned in syrup, 1 cup	205
Plums, raw, 1 medium	25
Prune juice, canned, 1 cup	200
Prunes, dried, cooked, unsweetened, 1 cup	295
Prunes, dried, uncooked, 4 medium	70
Raisins, dried, ¼ cup	120
Raspberries, frozen, sweetened, ½ cup	110
Raspberries, red, raw, 1 cup	70
Rhubarb, cooked with sugar, ½ cup	193

Food	Calories
Strawberries, frozen, whole, sweetened, ½ cup	124
Strawberries, raw, unsweetened, 1 cup	55
Tangerines, raw, 1 medium	40
Watermelon, 4-x-8-inch wedge	115

MEATS
Beef, cooked

Food	Calories
Corned, canned, 3-ounce (average) serving	185
Corned beef hash, 3 ounces	155
Dried beef, 2 ounces	115
Enchiladas, frozen, each	150–280
Hamburger patty, lean ground round, 3 ounces	185
Hamburger patty, regular ground beef, 3 ounces	245
Potpie, frozen, 8 ounces	443
Pot roast, lean and fat, 3-ounce (average) serving	245
Pot roast, lean only, 2½-ounce serving	140
Roast beef, with a relatively large amount of fat, such as rib, 3-ounce slice	375
Roast beef, with a relatively small amount of fat, such as heel of round, 3-ounce slice	165
Steak, broiled, round, lean and fat, 3-ounce (average) serving	220
Steak, broiled, sirloin, lean and fat, 3-ounce (average) serving	330
Tongue, boiled, 3-ounce (average) serving	210

Beef, uncooked

Food	Calories
Beef, chuck, good grade, lean and fat, 1 pound	1,153
Beef, chuck, lean only, 1 pound	739
Club steak, good grade, lean and fat, 1 pound	1,210
Club steak, lean, 1 pound	717
Corned, medium fat, 1 pound	1,329

FOOD FACTS FOR EASY REFERENCE

Food	Calories
Flank, lean, 1 pound	631
Hamburger, lean, 1 pound	812
Hamburger, regular, 1 pound	1,216
Porterhouse, good grade, lean and fat, 1 pound	1,521
Porterhouse, lean, 1 pound	640
Rib, lean, 1 pound	753
Rib, with bone, good grade, lean and fat, 1 pound	1,535
Round, lean, 1 pound	612
Round, with bone, good grade, lean and fat, 1 pound	863
Rump, lean, 1 pound	640
Rump, with bone, good grade, lean and fat, 1 pound	1,037
Sirloin, good grade, lean and fat, 1 pound	1,175
Sirloin, lean, 1 pound	585
Tongue, cured, 1 pound	1,211
Tongue, whole, medium fat, 1 pound	714
T-bone, good grade, lean and fat, 1 pound	1,466
T-bone, lean, 1 pound	644
Kidneys	
Beef, raw, 1 pound	590
Calf, raw, 1 pound	513
Lamb, raw, 1 pound	476
Lamb, cooked	
Chop, lean and fat, 1 thick chop	400
Roast leg, lean and fat, 3-ounce (average) serving	235
Shoulder, roast or braised, fat and lean, 3-ounce (average) serving	285
Lamb, uncooked	
Leg, with bone, choice, 1 pound	845
Leg, without bone, choice, 1 pound	1,007
Loin, with bone, choice, 1 pound	1,146
Rib, with bone, choice, 1 pound	1,229
Shoulder, with bone, choice, 1 pound	1,082
Shoulder, without bone, choice, 1 pound	1,275

Food	Calories
Shoulder, without bone, lean, 1 pound	671
Liver	
Beef, fried, 2-ounce (average) serving	130
Beef and calf, uncooked, 1 pound	635
Calf, fried, 2-ounce (average) serving	148
Pork, cooked	
Bacon, broiled or fried, 2 slices	90
Chops, lean and fat, 1 3½-ounce chop	260
Fresh roast, lean and fat, 1 3-ounce (average) slice	310
Ham, boiled and sliced, 2 ounces	135
Ham, smoked, baked, 3-ounce (average) serving	245
Luncheon meat, canned, 2-ounce serving	165
Pork, simmered, lean and fat, 3 ounces	320
Pork, uncooked	
Bacon, sliced, 1 pound	3,016
Ham, lean only, 1 pound	694
Ham, with bone and skin, 1 pound	1,188
Pork, Boston butt, with bone, lean and fat, 1 pound	1,220
Pork, lean and fat, 1 pound	1,397
Pork, lean, 1 pound	789
Pork, loin, with bone, 1 pound	1,065
Pork, picnic, with bone, 1 pound	1,083
Pork, spareribs, with bone, medium fat, 1 pound	976
Pork, cured	
Ham, Boston butt, no bone or skin, 1 pound	1,320
Ham, Boston butt, with bone, medium fat, 1 pound	1,227
Ham, lean, 1 pound	762
Ham, picnic with bone, medium fat, 1 pound	1,060

Food	Calories
Ham, with bone, medium fat, 1 pound	1,100
Pork, salt, with skin, 1 pound	3,410
Sausages	
Bologna, 3-inch diameter, 2 slices	80
Braunschweiger, 2-inch diameter, 2 slices	65
Deviled ham, canned, 1 tablespoon	45
Frankfurter, cooked, 8 per pound, 1 frankfurter	170
Frankfurters, 1 pound	1,402
Pork links, cooked, 16 per pound, 2 links	125
Salami, cooked, 1 ounce	90
Salami, dry, 1 ounce	130
Vienna sausage, canned, 1	40
Veal, cooked	
Cutlet, broiled, 3-ounce (average) serving	185
Roast, 3-ounce (average) slice	230
Veal, uncooked	
Chuck, no bone, 1 pound	785
Loin, with bone, medium fat, 1 pound	681
Round and rump, with bone, medium fat, 1 pound	573
Round and rump, without bone, 1 pound	744
Sweetbreads, calf, 1 pound	426

MILK, EGGS AND CHEESE

Food	Calories
Buttermilk, 1 per cent fat, 1 cup	95
Buttermilk, from skim milk, 1 cup	90
Camembert (3 in 4-ounce package), 1 wedge	115
Cheddar cheese, 1 ounce	115
Cheddar cheese, shredded, 1 cup	458
Cottage cheese, creamed, 1 ounce	33
Cottage cheese, creamed, 1 cup	260
Cottage cheese, uncreamed, 1 ounce	21
Cottage cheese, uncreamed, 1 cup	170
Cream, dairy half-and-half, 1 tablespoon	20

Food	Calories
Cream, heavy or whipping, 1 tablespoon	55
Cream, light or coffee, 1 tablespoon	30
Creamer, imitation, powdered, 1 teaspoon	10
Cream cheese, 1 ounce	107
Eggs, 1 egg white	15
Eggs, 1 egg yolk	60
Eggs, fried or scrambled with fat, 1 medium	110
Eggs, raw, soft-cooked or poached, 1 medium	78
Milk, skim, 1 cup	90
Milk, skim, 1 per cent fat, 1 cup	114
Milk, sweetened condensed, 1 tablespoon	61
Milk, undiluted evaporated, 1 tablespoon	22
Milk, whole, 1 cup	160
Parmesan cheese, grated, 1 tablespoon	25
Process American cheese, 1 ounce	105
Process cheese food, 1 tablespoon	45
Process cheese spread, 1 ounce	80
Process Swiss cheese, 1 ounce	100
Roquefort or blue cheese, 1 ounce	105
Sour cream, 1 tablespoon	30
Sour dressing (imitation sour cream), 1 tablespoon	20
Swiss cheese, 1 ounce	105
Whipped topping, frozen, 1 tablespoon	10
Whipped topping, pressurized can, 1 tablespoon	10
Yogurt, from whole milk, 1 cup	150
Yogurt, from partially skimmed milk, 1 cup	125
Yogurt, fruit-flavored, 1 cup	225–260

NUTS, SEEDS

Food	Calories
Almonds, shelled, ¼ cup	213
Brazil nuts, broken, ¼ cup	229

FOOD FACTS FOR EASY REFERENCE

Food	Calories
Cashew nuts, ¼ cup	196
Coconut, fresh, shredded, ¼ cup	87
Coconut, dried, shredded, ¼ cup	166
Coconut, dried, shredded, sweetened, ¼ cup	125
Filberts, 10 to 12	97
Peanuts, ¼ cup	210
Peanut butter, 1 tablespoon	95
Pecans, halved, ¼ cup	185
Pignolias (pine nuts) ¼ cup	168
Pumpkin seeds, shelled, ¼ cup	184
Sesame seeds, hulled, ¼ cup	218
Sunflower seeds, shelled, ¼ cup	187
Walnuts, English, ¼ cup	198

*VEGETABLES AND VEGETABLE JUICES

Food	Calories
Artichokes, globe, cooked, 1 large	44
Artichokes, Jerusalem, raw, pared, 1 pound	300
Asparagus, canned, 1 cup	45
Asparagus, cooked, 4 medium spears	10
Asparagus, raw spears, 1 pound	66
Baked beans, with pork, 1 cup	310
Bean sprouts, mung, cooked, 1 cup	35
Beets, canned, 1 cup	85
Beets, cooked, diced or sliced, 1 cup	55
Beets, frozen, sliced in orange-flavored glaze, 1 cup	106
Beets, raw, with tops, 1 pound	78
Broccoli, chopped, yield from 10-ounce frozen package	65
Broccoli, cooked, 1 cup	40
Broccoli, raw spears, 1 pound	113
Broccoli, spears, frozen in hollandaise sauce, 1 cup	200
Brussels sprouts, cooked, 1 cup	55
Brussels sprouts, raw, 1 pound	188
Cabbage, green, cooked, 1 cup	30
Cabbage, green and savoy, raw, finely shredded, 1 cup	20

Note: Except where noted, vegetable calorie counts do not include added butter or dressing of any kind.

Food	Calories
Cabbage, green, raw, 1 pound	98
Cabbage, red, raw, coarsely shredded, 1 cup	20
Cabbage, red, raw, 1 pound	127
Carrots, cooked, 1 cup	45
Carrots, raw, 1 medium	20
Carrots, raw, grated, 1 cup	45
Carrots, raw, without tops, 1 pound	156
Cauliflower, cooked, 1 cup	25
Cauliflower, raw, trimmed, 1 pound	122
Celery, raw, diced, 1 cup	15
Celery, raw, 8-inch stalk	5
Chard, Swiss, raw, 1 pound	104
Chinese cabbage, cooked, 1 cup	16
Chinese cabbage, raw, 1 cup	10
Chinese cabbage, raw, 1 pound	62
Collards, raw, leaves, 1 pound	139
Corn, canned, 1 cup	170
Corn, canned, cream-style, 1 cup	204
Corn, 1 ear 5-inches long, cooked	70
Cucumber, raw, 6 slices	5
Cucumber, raw, pared, 1 medium	30
Dandelion greens, cooked, 1 cup	60
Dandelion greens, raw, trimmed, 1 pound	204
Eggplant, cooked, drained, diced, ½ cup	19
Eggplant, raw, 1 pound	92
Endive, raw, 2 ounces	10
Endive, raw, 1 pound	80
Escarole, raw, 1 pound	47
Garlic clove	2
Green beans, raw, 1 pound	128
Green beans and wax beans, canned, 1 cup	45
Green beans and wax beans, cooked, 1 cup	30
Green beans, frozen, with toasted almonds, 1 cup	44
Kale, cooked, 1 cup	30
Kale, raw, leaves and stems, 1 pound	128
Kohlrabi, raw, without leaves, 1 pound	96

Food	Calories
Leeks, raw, 1 pound	123
Lettuce, Boston, raw, 1 head	30
Lettuce, iceberg, raw, 2 large leaves	10
Lima beans, cooked, 1 cup	190
Mushrooms, canned, 1 cup	40
Mushrooms, raw, whole, 1 pound	123
Mustard greens, cooked, 1 cup	35
Mustard greens, raw, 1 pound	98
Okra, cooked, 8 pods	25
Okra, raw, 1 pound	140
Onion, dehydrated flakes, 1 tablespoon	17
Onions, cooked, 1 cup	60
Onions, frozen in cream-style sauce, 1 cup	254
Onion rings, French fried, frozen, 2 ounces	168
Onions, green, raw, 6	20
Onions, raw, 1 medium	40
Parsley, raw, chopped, 1 tablespoon	trace
Parsnips, cooked, 1 cup	100
Parsnips, raw, 1 pound	293
Peas, green, canned, 1 cup	165
Peas, green, cooked, 1 cup	115
Peas, green, frozen with sauteed mushrooms, 1 cup	134
Peas, green, raw, in pod, 1 pound	145
Peppers, green, raw, 1 pound	82
Peppers, red, raw, 1 pound	112
Peppers, sweet green, raw or cooked, 1 medium	15
Pimiento, canned, 1 medium	11
Potatoes, 1 pound	279
Potatoes, baked, 1 medium	90
Potatoes, French fried, frozen, 10 pieces	125
Potatoes, mashed with milk, ½ cup	63
Potatoes, mashed with milk and butter, ½ cup	93
Potatoes, peeled, boiled, 1 medium	80
Pumpkin, canned, 1 cup	75
Radishes, raw, 4 small	5

Food	Calories
Sauerkraut, canned, drained, 1 cup	45
Spinach, cooked, 1 cup	40
Spinach, raw, packaged, 1 pound	118
Spinach, raw, untrimmed, 1 pound	85
Squash, summer, cooked, 1 cup	30
Squash, summer varieties, raw, 1 pound	84
Squash, winter, cooked, 1 cup	130
Squash, winter varieties, raw, 1 pound	161
Sweet potatoes, baked or boiled, unpeeled, 1 medium	155
Sweet potatoes, candied, 1 medium	295
Sweet potatoes, canned, 1 cup	235
Sweet potatoes, raw, 1 pound	375
Tomato juice, canned, 1 cup	45
Tomatoes, canned or cooked, 1 cup	50
Tomatoes, raw, 1 medium	40
Tomatoes, raw, 1 pound	100
Turnip greens, cooked, 1 cup	30
Turnip greens, raw, untrimmed, 1 pound	107
Turnips, cooked, 1 cup	35
Turnips, raw, 1 pound	177
Vegetable juice, canned, 1 cup	43
Water chestnuts, 4	20
Water cress, 10 sprigs	2
Yams, raw, 1 pound	394

DRIED VEGETABLES

Food	Calories
Chick peas, cooked, 1 cup	272
Chick peas, uncooked, 1 pound	1,633
Great Northern beans, cooked, 1 cup	210
Kidney beans, cooked, 1 cup	268
Kidney beans, uncooked, 1 pound	1,556
Lentils, cooked, 1 cup	159
Lentils, uncooked, 1 pound	1,542
Lima beans, cooked, 1 cup	260
Lima beans, uncooked, 1 pound	1,565

Food	Calories
Navy (pea) beans, cooked, 1 cup ...225	
Navy beans, uncooked, 1 pound 1,542	
Soybeans, cooked, 1 cup 190	
Soybeans, uncooked, 1 pound 1,828	
Soy flour, defatted, 1 cup (5 ounces) 450	
Soy flour, full-fat, 1 cup (2½ ounces) 303	
Split peas, uncooked, 1 pound ...1,579	

POULTRY
Cooked
Food	Calories
Chicken, broiled, without bone, 3 ounces 115	
Chicken, ½ breast, fried 155	
Chicken, canned, boneless, 3 ounces 170	
Chicken, leg, fried 90	
Chicken potpie, frozen, 8 ounces ..460	
Duck, roasted, 3 slices (3 ounces) 310	
Turkey, roasted, without bone, 3 ounces 200	

Uncooked
Food	Calories
Capon, ready-to-cook, 1 pound 937	
Chicken, breasts, ready-to-cook, 1 pound 394	
Chicken, drumsticks, ready-to-cook, 1 pound 313	
Chicken, fryer, ready-to-cook, 1 pound 382	
Chicken, hen, ready-to-cook, 1 pound 987	
Chicken, liver, 1 pound 585	
Chicken, roaster, ready-to-cook, 1 pound 791	
Chicken, thighs, ready-to-cook, 1 pound 435	
Chicken, wings, ready-to-cook, 1 pound 325	
Duck, ready-to-cook, 1 pound 1,213	
Goose, ready-to-cook, 1 pound 803	
Turkey, ready-to-cook, 1 pound ...722	

SOUPS (canned, condensed, ready-to-serve) AND SAUCES
Food	Calories
*Bean soup with pork, 1 cup 170	
*Beef bouillon, broth and consommé, 1 cup 30	
*Beef noodle soup, 1 cup 70	
Borsch, 1 cup 72	
*Chicken noodle soup, 1 cup 65	
*Clam chowder, 1 cup 80	
Cream of chicken soup, prepared with milk, 1 cup 180	
*Cream of chicken soup, 1 cup 95	
Cream of mushroom soup, prepared with milk, 1 cup 215	
*Cream of mushroom soup, 1 cup ..135	
*Minestrone, 1 cup 105	
*Split pea soup, 1 cup 145	
Tomato soup, prepared with milk, 1 cup 175	
*Tomato soup, 1 cup 90	
*Turkey noodle soup, 1 cup 82	
*Vegetable beef soup, 1 cup 80	
*Vegetarian vegetable soup, 1 cup ...80	
Won ton soup, frozen, 2 won tons ..76	
Barbecue sauce, ¼ cup 58	
Beef gravy, canned, ¼ cup 45	
Cheese sauce, ¼ cup 130	
Chicken gravy, canned, ¼ cup 50	
Hollandaise sauce, 1 tablespoon 45	
Mushroom gravy, canned, ¼ cup ...29	
Tartar sauce, 1 tablespoon 75	
Tomato sauce, ¼ cup 79	
White sauce, medium, ¼ cup 101	

*Prepared with water

SPREADS AND SUGARS
Food	Calories
Chocolate, light syrup, 1 fluid ounce 90	
Honey, strained, 1 tablespoon 65	
Jams, marmalades, preserves, 1 tablespoon 55	
Jellies, 1 tablespoon 50	
Molasses, 1 tablespoon 50	
Syrup, table blends, 1 tablespoon ...60	

FOOD	CALORIES	FOOD	CALORIES
Brown sugar, 1 tablespoon	51	Miso paste, 4 ounces	194
Confectioners' sugar, 1 tablespoon	29	Mustard, prepared, 1 teaspoon	4
Granulated sugar, 1 tablespoon	48	Olives, green, 4 medium	15
		Olives, ripe, 3 small	15

MISCELLANEOUS

FOOD	CALORIES	FOOD	CALORIES
Arrowroot, 1 tablespoon	29	Pickle relish, 1 tablespoon	20
Bouillon cube	5	Pickles, dill, 1 medium	10
Carob flour, 1 ounce	51	Pickles, sweet, 1	20
Catsup, tomato, 1 tablespoon	15	Pizza, ⅛ of 14-inch pie	185
Chili sauce, 1 tablespoon	17	Popcorn, popped, with oil and salt, 1 cup	40
Chocolate, semisweet, small pieces, 1 cup	860	Potato chips, 10 medium	115
Chocolate, unsweetened, 1 square	145	Potato flour, 1 tablespoon	25
Cocoa, unsweetened, 1 tablespoon	21	Pretzels, small sticks, 10	10
Corn chips, 1 ounce	164	Pretzels, thin twist, 1	25
Cornstarch, 1 tablespoon	29	Rice flour, 1 tablespoon	29
Gelatine, 1 envelope plain	25	Vinegar, 1 tablespoon	trace
		Worcestershire, 1 teaspoon	4

Carbohydrate Gram Count of Common Foods

Many people choose to cut down on carbohydrate intake when dieting. Restrictions on this diet usually limit carbohydrate grams to 60 per day for a weight-reduction diet. Consult your doctor before electing to use any reducing diet.

FOOD	CARBOHYDRATE GRAMS	FOOD	CARBOHYDRATE GRAMS
BEVERAGES, CARBONATED		Cocoa, 1 cup	27
Cola type, 12 fl. oz.	37	Malted milk, 1 cup	28
Ginger ale, 12 fl. oz.	29		
		BREADS	
BEVERAGES, ALCOHOLIC		Bagel, egg, 1	28
Beer, 12 fl. oz	14	Baking powder biscuits, 2½ inches in diameter, 1	13
Gin	0	Bread: raisin, rye, white, whole wheat, 1 slice (toasted or not)	13
Red wine, 1 wine glass	4	Bread crumbs, dry, grated, ¼ cup	17
Rum	0	Corn muffin, 2¾ inches diameter, made with degermed, enriched corn meal, 1 muffin	19
Whisky	0		
		Crisp rye cracker, 1 cracker	5
BEVERAGES, MILK			
Chocolate-flavored milk drink, 1 cup	27		

FOOD FACTS FOR EASY REFERENCE

FOOD	CARBOHYDRATE GRAMS
English muffin	15
French or Italian bread, 1-lb. loaf	251
Gluten bread, 1 slice	6
Graham cracker, 1 cracker	5
Oyster crackers, 10 crackers	7
Pancakes, 4 inches in diameter,	
buckwheat mix	6
home recipe	9
Piecrust, 9-inch shell (1 crust)	79
Protein bread, 1 slice	9
Pumpernickel, dark, 1-lb. loaf	241
Rolls, 1 hard, medium-sized	30
1 plain, small	15
1 sweet, small	21
Saltines, 1 cracker	2
Soda cracker	4
Waffle, 7 inches in diameter	28
White muffins, 2¾ inches in	
diameter, made with	
white flour, 1	17

CAKES

FOOD	CARBOHYDRATE GRAMS
Angel food, 1/12 of 10-inch cake	32
Chocolate cake, iced, 1/16 of 9-inch	
layer cake	40
Cookie, 2 inches in diameter	7
Cupcake, 2¾ inches in diameter,	
without icing	14
Doughnut, plain	16
Gingerbread, 1/9 of 8-inch square	32
Poundcake, 2¾-x-3-x-⅝-inch slice	14
Sponge, 1/12 of 10-inch cake	36

CEREALS AND PASTAS

FOOD	CARBOHYDRATE GRAMS
Bran flakes, 1 cup	28
Corn flakes, 1 cup	21
presweetened, 1 cup	36
Corn meal, white or yellow, de-	
germed, enriched, 1 cup, cooked	26
Macaroni, cooked, ½ cup	20
Macaroni and cheese, baked,	
½ cup	20
Noodles, cooked, ½ cup	19
Oatmeal, cooked, ½ cup	12

FOOD	CARBOHYDRATE GRAMS
Puffed rice, 1 cup	13
Puffed wheat, 1 cup	12
Shredded wheat, 1 biscuit	20
Spaghetti, cooked, ½ cup	16
Spaghetti with meat sauce, ½ cup	19
with tomato sauce and cheese,	
½ cup	19
Wheat flakes, 1 cup	24
Wheat germ, 1 tablespoon	2
White rice, cooked, ½ cup	25

CHEESE

FOOD	CARBOHYDRATE GRAMS
Blue, 1 oz.	1
Cheddar, 1 cup, grated	2
Cheese foods, Cheddar, 1 oz.	2
Cottage, creamed, 1 cup	7
Cottage, uncreamed, 1 cup	5
Cream, 1 oz.	1
Parmesan, 1 oz.	1
Swiss, 1 oz.	1

EGGS

FOOD	CARBOHYDRATE GRAMS
1 egg, boiled or fried	trace
scrambled, with milk and fat	1

FATS

FOOD	CARBOHYDRATE GRAMS
Butter, 1 tablespoon	trace
Margarine, 1 tablespoon	trace
Oils: corn, cottonseed, olive, peanut,	
and soybean	0
Salad dressing, 1 tablespoon	
Blue cheese	1
Commercial, plain (mayonnaise	
type)	2
French	3
Mayonnaise	trace
Thousand Island	3
Salad oil	0
Vegetable fats (solid)	0

FISH AND SHELLFISH

FOOD	CARBOHYDRATE GRAMS
Clams, 3 oz.	2
Crabmeat, 3 oz.	1

Food	Carbohydrate Grams
Fish, broiled or fried without breading	0
Lobster, boiled or broiled	0
Oysters, 4 oysters	2
Salmon, shrimp, or tuna, canned	0
Sardines, 3 oz.	0
Scallops, 2 or 3 raw	4

FRUIT JUICES

Food	Carbohydrate Grams
Apple or cider, ½ cup	15
Apricot nectar, ½ cup	18
Cranberry, ½ cup	21
Grapefruit, fresh, frozen, or unsweetened, canned, ½ cup	12
Grape, ½ cup	21
Lemonade or limeade, frozen, ½ cup	14
Orange, fresh, frozen, or unsweetened, canned, ½ cup	15
Peach nectar, ½ cup	16
Pear nectar, ½ cup	17
Pineapple, ½ cup	17
Prune, ½ cup	25
Tangerine, unsweetened, canned, ½ cup	15
Tomato juice, ½ cup	5

FRUITS, CANNED

Food	Carbohydrate Grams
Applesauce, unsweetened, ½ cup	13
sweetened, ½ cup	31
Apricots, syrup-packed, 3 whole	14
Cherries (red, sour), ½ cup	13
Cranberry sauce, 1 tablespoon	5
Fruit cocktail, ½ cup	25
Grapefruit, ½ cup, syrup-packed	23
water-packed	9
Peaches, syrup-packed, ½ cup	26
water-packed, 2 halves	10
Pears, syrup-packed, 2 halves	25
water-packed, 2 halves	10
Pineapple, syrup-packed, 1 slice	24
crushed, ½ cup	25
Plums, syrup-packed, ½ cup	27

FRUITS, DRIED

Food	Carbohydrate Grams
Apricots, uncooked, 5 halves	13
cooked, unsweetened, ¼ cup	16
Dates, ¼ cup	35
Figs, 1	15
Peaches, dried, cooked, unsweetened, ½ cup	29
Prunes, uncooked, 4 whole	18
cooked, unsweetened, ¼ cup	20
Raisins, ¼ cup	32

FRUITS, FRESH

Food	Carbohydrate Grams
Apples, 1 medium (3 per pound)	18
Apricots, 3 (12 per pound)	14
Avocado, ½ medium	7
Banana, 1 small	26
Blueberries, ½ cup	11
Cantaloupe, ½ melon	14
Cherries, ½ cup	8
Grapefruit, ½ small	12
Grapes, 1 cup	15 to 25
Lemons, 1 tablespoon juice	1
Nectarines, 1 medium	8
Oranges, 1 small	16
Peaches, 1 medium	10
frozen, 12-oz. package	77
Pears, 1 medium	25
Pineapple, diced, ½ cup	10
Plums, 1 medium	7
Raspberries, ½ cup	9
frozen, 10-oz. package	70
Rhubarb, cooked, sweetened, ½ cup	49
Strawberries, ½ cup	7
frozen, 10-oz. package	79
Tangerines, 1 medium	10
Watermelon, 1 slice, 4 x 8 inches	27

MEAT AND POULTRY

Food	Carbohydrate Grams
Bacon, 2 slices	1
Beef heart, 3 oz.	1
Bologna, thin slices, 4 inches in diameter, 4	trace
Chicken livers, 1 medium	1

FOOD FACTS FOR EASY REFERENCE

Food	Carbohydrate Grams
Chili con carne, 1 cup, with beans . . .30	
without beans 15	
Frankfurters, 1 1	
Hash, canned, 3 oz. 9	
Liver, 2 oz. 3	
Luncheon meat, 2 oz. 1	
Meat: beef, lamb, pork, and veal (broiled, braised, fried, roasted, or simmered) 0	
Poultry (broiled, braised, fried, roasted, or simmered) 0	
Sausage, 1 link 0	
Smoked ham, 3 oz. 0	
Tongue, 3 oz. . . . . .trace	

MILK AND MILK PRODUCTS

Food	Carbohydrate Grams
Buttermilk, 1 cup 12	
Condensed milk, sweetened, undiluted, 1 cup 166	
Evaporated milk, undiluted, 1 cup . .24	
Half-and-half (milk and cream), 1 cup 11	
Heavy cream, 1 cup 7	
Ice cream, 1 cup 28	
Ice milk, 1 cup 29	
Light cream, 1 cup 10	
Nonfat dry milk solids, 1 cup 54	
Sherbet, 1 cup 59	
Skim milk, 1 cup 12	
Sour cream, 1 cup 10	
Whole milk, 1 cup 12	
Yogurt, 1 cup 13	

NUTS

Food	Carbohydrate Grams
Almonds, ½ cup 14	
Brazil nuts, ½ cup 8	
Cashews, ½ cup 21	
Filberts, 10 to 12 3	
Peanuts, ½ cup 14	
Peanut butter, 1 tablespoon 3	
Pecans, ½ cup 8	
Pistachios, 30 3	
Walnuts, ½ cup 10	

PIES

Food	Carbohydrate Grams
Apple, 4-inch wedge 51	
Cherry, 4-inch wedge 52	
Custard, 4-inch wedge 30	
Lemon meringue, 4-inch wedge 45	
Pumpkin, 4-inch wedge 32	

SOUPS *(canned, condensed, ready-to-serve, diluted with water)*

Food	Carbohydrate Grams
Bean with pork, 1 cup 22	
Beef, 1 cup 11	
Bouillon, consommé, 1 cup 3	
Cream of chicken, 1 cup 8	
Clam chowder, 1 cup 12	
Cream of mushroom, 1 cup 10	
Noodle, rice, barley, 1 cup 13	
Pea, 1 cup 21	
Tomato, 1 cup 16	
Vegetable, 1 cup 13	

SUGARS AND SWEETS

Food	Carbohydrate Grams
Caramels, 1 oz. 22	
Chocolate syrup, 1 tablespoon 12	
Hard candy, 1 oz. 28	
Honey, 1 tablespoon 17	
Jams, jellies, marmalades, preserves, 1 tablespoon 14	
Marshmallow, 1 oz. 23	
Maple syrup, 1 tablespoon 15	
Milk chocolate, 1 oz. 16	
Molasses, 1 tablespoon, dark 11	
light 13	
Sugar, brown, 1 tablespoon 13	
confectioners', ½ cup 60	
granulated, 1 tablespoon 11	
Table syrup, 1 tablespoon 15	

VEGETABLES, CANNED

Food	Carbohydrate Grams
Asparagus, ½ cup 4	
Baked beans, with tomato or molasses, ½ cup, with pork 27	
without pork 30	
Corn, ½ cup .20	
Green beans, ½ cup 5	

FOOD	CARBOHYDRATE GRAMS
Peas, ½ cup	16
Pumpkin, ½ cup	9
Red beans, ½ cup	21
Sauerkraut, drained, ½ cup	5
Tomatoes, ½ cup	5

VEGETABLES, DRIED

Black-eyed peas, cooked, ½ cup	17
Lima beans, cooked, ½ cup	24
Split peas, cooked, ½ cup	26

VEGETABLES, FRESH

Artichokes, 1 artichoke	6
Asparagus, 4 spears	2
Bean sprouts, ½ cup	4
Beets, ½ cup	6
Broccoli, ½ cup	4
Brussels sprouts, ½ cup	5
Cabbage, cooked, ½ cup	3
Carrots, 1 large	5
Cauliflower, ½ cup	3
Celery, 2 stalks	4
Cole slaw, ½ cup	5
Collards, ½ cup	5
Corn, 1 ear	16
Cucumbers, ½ large	4
Dandelion greens, ½ cup	6
Eggplant, ½ cup	4
Green beans, ½ cup	3
Green pepper, 1 medium	4
Kale, ½ cup	2
Lentils, ½ cup	18
Lettuce, 2 large leaves	2
Lima beans, ½ cup	17
Mushrooms, cooked, canned, ½ cup	3
Okra, 8 pods	5
Onions, cooked, ½ cup	7
green (scallions), 6 small	5
Parsley, chopped, 1 tablespoon	trace
Parsnips, ½ cup	12
Peas, ½ cup	10
Potatoes, 1 medium, boiled or baked	21

FOOD	CARBOHYDRATE GRAMS
½ cup mashed, milk and butter added	12
Radishes, 4 radishes	1
Sauerkraut, ½ cup	5
Spinach, ½ cup	3
Squash, summer (yellow or green), ½ cup	4
Squash, winter, ½ cup	16
Sweet potatoes, 1 small, boiled or baked	36
candied	60
Tomatoes, 1 medium (3 per pound)	9
Turnips, cooked, diced, ½ cup	4

MISCELLANEOUS

Barley, pearled, uncooked, ½ cup	79
Bouillon cube	trace
Chili sauce, 1 tablespoon	4
Chocolate, bitter, 1 oz.	8
sweetened, 1 oz.	12
Coconut, shredded, ½ cup, dried, sweetened	6
fresh	7
Flour, 1 tablespoon	6
French fries, 10 pieces	20
Gelatine, dry, unflavored	0
dessert (ready to eat), 1 cup, plain	34
Olives, green, extra large, 12	trace
ripe, extra large, 12	trace
Pickles, dill, 4 inches long	1
sweet, 2¾ inches long	6
Pizza, 5½-inch wedge of 14-inch diameter pie	27
Popcorn, ½ cup	3
Potato chips, 10 chips	10
Pretzels, 5 sticks	1
Starch, arrowroot or corn, 1 tablespoon	7
Tapioca, quick-cooking, granulated, 1 tablespoon	8
Tomato catsup, 1 tablespoon	4
Vinegar, 1 tablespoon	1
White sauce, medium, 1 cup	22

CHAPTER III

PLANNING MENUS

Menu planning can be a pleasure or a chore—it's all a matter of your approach to it. There are definite guides to follow for planning well-balanced meals. You'll find that putting together nutritious and appetizing meals becomes almost automatic with just a little practice.

The first rule of menu planning is to plan menus ahead as much as a week at a time—or more, if you want to shop less frequently than once a week. There are many advantages to this kind of preplanning besides making shopping much easier for yourself. You will avoid monotony and duplication of foods, and you won't get stuck with a small supply of foods that simply do not add up to a pleasant meal.

When you plan ahead, do it with the aid of store ads. They feature the specials and keep you up to date on the seasonal, low-priced fruits and vegetables in the market. Planning meals around the items that are well priced will help save you food-budget money.

While you are planning, keep these additional rules in mind to make the best combinations of food:

1. Do not repeat the same food or flavor in the same meal—don't, for instance, serve baked apples for dessert if you are using apples in the salad.

2. Food texture, color, and flavor should be varied. Try to combine a crisp texture with a soft one. Visualize how the food will look when it is served: Will the colors be pleasing together? And plan a tart flavor as a contrast to a sweet one.

3. Be sure to serve hot foods really hot and cold ones ice-cold; heat or refrigerate the serving plates.

4. Arrange the food carefully on plates and in serving dishes. Add a simple garnish to make it look prettier.

5. When planning a menu, choose the main dish first, for you will be building your meal around it. Next come the vegetables. If the main dish is a casserole with a sauce, or includes rice or macaroni, you will not want potatoes; choose two nonstarchy vegetables instead. One of them should be green or yellow, for good eye appeal. If the meat is plain, choose a potato or a macaroni and one nonstarchy vegetable. Again, keep in mind the desirability of color and texture contrast.

6. A salad is always a nice addition to a meal. Tossed green salad with a simple dressing will go well with almost any main dish, but for variety, try raw vegetable sticks or a jelled fruit or vegetable salad.

7. The addition of a bread to the menu is a matter of family preference. Sometimes the crispness of French bread or the glamour of hot muffins or rolls will add just the texture or flavor that is needed.

8. Plan desserts that are really a part of the meal. If the main dish is a salad or a hearty soup, you may use a heavy dessert—a pie, cobbler, or cake. When the main dish is heavy, a light dessert, such as fruit, ice cream, or fruit gelatin, is in order.

9. A first course is not necessary, but it will add a pleasant note, especially if the meal is to be a leisurely one. If the rest of the meal is hearty, a glass of chilled fruit juice is a good choice. With a cold-salad meal, serve a hot soup.

10. Consider the preparation time. Plan simple and quickly prepared meals for the days when you know time will be limited. Save the more complicated dishes for the days when you will be free to enjoy preparing them.

11. Consider the budget. Meals that stretch the food budget can be just as exciting as you care to make them. Many of the most inexpensive meats, when used with imagination, can be the basis of memorable meals. Budget-priced chicken adapts to almost any seasoning. When you shop, watch fluctuating prices; foods in season—and therefore in good supply—cost considerably less.

12. Keep in mind the equipment you have. The size, shape, and versatility of your cooking utensils and appliances should be considered. If you have a single oven and plan a meal that includes two or more baked dishes, be sure that the oven temperature for each of them is the same.

13. It goes without saying that a carefully planned and well-cooked meal should be served attractively and enjoyed with congenial company in pleasant surroundings.

14. Have fun with menu planning. Try to introduce something brand-new at least once a week. Collect new recipes—and use them. You'll increase your repertoire and gain confidence in your cooking ability.

Nutrition and Menu Planning

Good menu planning and good nutrition go hand in hand. It's easy to plan nutritious meals if you familiarize yourself with the four basic food groups listed below. Each day's menu should include a certain number of servings from each food group.

1. *Breads and cereals.* This group also includes pastas and rice. Recommended daily servings: four or more per person.
2. *Meats, poultry, fish, eggs, and cheese.* This group also includes dry beans, peas, and nuts. Recommended daily servings: two or more per person.
3. *Fruits and vegetables.* For vitamin A, include a dark green, leafy vegetable or a deep yellow vegetable; for vitamin C, a citrus fruit or tomatoes. Recommended daily servings: four or more per person.
4. *Dairy foods.* These include milk, milk products, and cheese. Recommended daily servings: two or more glasses of milk, or the equivalent, per adult. Children should have three or more glasses and teenagers four or more. Products made from milk, such as ice cream and cheese, can substitute for milk by the glass.

Fats, oils, and sugar are the "extra" foods. Besides providing energy they add to our enjoyment of food. However, we do need some fats and oils and they are present in many of the basic foods: meats, eggs, some fish, whole milk as well as butter or margarine. Fats are essential in the absorption of certain vitamins (see Food Nutrients and What They Do for You on page 992).

Classic Menu Mates

There is no rule that says applesauce *must* be served with roast pork or that fish must be served with chips (French fried potatoes); it is simply that many food combinations are so pleasing to so many people that they have become go-togethers. The fourteen sample dinner menus that follow include several of these time-tested combinations. To each menu we've added footnotes with suggestions for individuality—a simple addition of an herb to a vegetable, a little wine in the sauce for the meat, or a special topping for the dessert. If you have time and want to make the meal special, do try them.

BEEF STEW DINNER

*Beef Stew
Buttered Broccoli or Buttered Carrots
Dumplings or French Bread
Tossed Green Salad with
French Dressing
Baked Apple

Note: Stuff apples with raisins and chopped walnuts before baking.
*Recipe on page 298.

BEEF LIVER DINNER

*Broiled Beef or Calf's Liver
Spinach and Mushrooms with Bacon Bits
or French Fried Onions
Hashed Brown Potatoes or Hard Rolls
Pickled Watermelon Rind
Chocolate Ice Cream and Cookies

Note: Marinate liver in bottled French dressing; brush frequently with dressing while broiling.
*Recipe on page 346.

ROAST CHICKEN DINNER

*Roast Stuffed Chicken or Turkey
Gravy
Creamed Onions or Mashed Turnips
Candied Sweet Potatoes or Biscuits
Carrot and Celery Sticks
Mincemeat Pie

Note: Serve pie warm topped with brandied hard sauce.
*Recipe on page 359.

FRIED CHICKEN DINNER

Fried Chicken
Buttered Cauliflower or
*Swiss Spinach
Corn Fritters or Corn Sticks
Cheese-Stuffed Celery Hearts
Frozen Raspberries and Poundcake

Note: Serve chilled cranberry-apple juice as an appetizer.
*Recipe on page 523.

LEG OF LAMB DINNER

Roast Leg of Lamb
*Succotash
Buttered Peas
Baked Sweet Potatoes or Corn Sticks
Pear Halves Filled with Mint Jelly
Angel Food Cake à la Mode

Note: Serve marinated artichoke hearts on watercress as an appetizer.
*Recipe on page 518.

BROILED LAMB CHOP DINNER

Broiled Lamb Chops
Mashed Yellow Turnips or Buttered
Asparagus
French Fried Potatoes or Hard Rolls
Tossed Green Salad
*Southern Pecan Pie

Note: Serve chops with marjoram-herbed butter sauce.
*Recipe on page 795.

PORK CHOP DINNER

Baked Pork Chops
Buttered Kale or *Corn on the Cob*
**Rice with Fruit*
or Hard Rolls
Cole Slaw
Custard Pie

Note: Add shredded carrot and green pepper to cole slaw.
*Recipe on page 565.

ROAST PORK DINNER

**Roast Pork with Herb Dressing*
**Milk Gravy*
Harvard Beets or *Buttered Spinach*
Parsley Potatoes or *Corn Bread*
Pickled Watermelon Rind
Butterscotch Pudding with Cream

Note: Add a pinch of freshly ground nutmeg to spinach.
*Recipe on page 311.

BAKED HAM DINNER

Baked Virginia Ham
**Cabbage Amandine* or *Buttered*
Green Beans
Candied Sweet Potatoes or *Corn Muffins*
Jellied Fruit Salad
Chocolate Cream Pie

Note: Glaze ham with a mixture of orange marmalade and mustard.
*Recipe on page 511.

FRIED FISH DINNER

Fried Fish Steaks or *Fish Fillets*
Tartar Sauce
**Succotash* or *Baked Tomato Halves*
Scalloped Potatoes or
Garlic French Bread
Watercress Salad
Pineapple Upside-down Cake

Note: Serve upside-down cake with a scoop of coffee ice cream.
*Recipe on page 518.

ROAST VEAL DINNER

Roast Veal
**Eggplant-and-Tomato Scallop*
Buttered Carrots
Baked Potatoes or *Soft Rolls*
Jellied Vegetable Salad
Blueberry Pie

Note: Serve fruit cup topped with lemon sherbet as an appetizer.
*Recipe on page 520.

STEAK DINNER

Broiled Steak
**Corn Pudding* or *Sautéed Fresh*
Mushrooms
Baked Potatoes with Chive
Sour Cream or *Soft Rolls*
Lettuce Wedge with Blue Cheese
Dressing
Baked Custard

Note: Substitute cream for half of the milk in the custard; top each serving with coffee liqueur.
*Recipe on page 517.

ROAST BEEF DINNER

Roast Beef
Buttered Asparagus or *Corn on the Cob*
Oven-Browned Potatoes or *Popovers*
*Spinach Salad with Hot Bacon
Dressing
Ice Cream and Cookies

Note: Add some toasted sesame seeds to butter sauce for asparagus.
*Recipe on page 596.

POT ROAST DINNER

Pot Roast
Buttered Spinach or *Red Cabbage*
Mashed Potatoes or *Potato Pancakes*
Spiced Crab Apples
*Peanut Brittle Mousse

Note: Add a little Burgundy to pot roast drippings before making gravy.
*Recipe on page 747.

When Company's Coming

It really isn't necessary to have an elaborate or an expensive meal for company, although most of us feel more hospitable if a company dinner seems to show that we've made a special effort.

There is one rule for company planning that you should never break: Don't try a new recipe for the first time. That is living dangerously and can result in disaster.

Think about your time element. It's best not to plan meals that need a lot of last-minute preparation at a time when you'd like to be with guests.

Think about the serving dishes you have. Plan a meal that will fit them. Also, consider how and where you're going to serve the meal. If guests will be eating on laps or trays, it's better to serve fork food. Having to cut food on a tottering surface makes guests uncomfortable.

When you do plan a large party, it makes it merrier—and the menu easier—if you select a party theme to build the entire party around. The following three easy-to-serve and easy-to-eat themed party menus provide food that is a bit unusual, and has a reason for being so. (For holiday menu-planning see the menus and work schedule starting on page 131.)

HAWAIIAN LUAU

*Sautéed Shrimp and Scallops
Celery, Scallions, Radishes
*Curried Chicken
*Pork Kabobs

Party decorations: Cover buffet table with a fishnet cloth. Decorate table with fish shapes cut from construction paper and with fresh fruits and flowers. Give each guest a paper lei and decorate room with artificial flowers. Play South Sea records.

PLANNING MENUS

Fried Rice
Chutney, Peanuts, Raisins
Hawaiian Salad
Pineapple Cheesecake
Coffee, Tea

The day before the party: 1. Prepare and marinate shrimp and scallops; refrigerate. 2. Cook chicken and remove meat from bones ready for Curried Chicken; refrigerate chicken and broth. 3. Cook pork; cool and refrigerate ready for Pork Kabobs. 4. Cook rice for Fried Rice; refrigerate. 5. Prepare Hawaiian Salad Dressing and refrigerate. 6. Prepare and refrigerate Pineapple Cheesecake and Pineapple Sauce.

*Recipe follows.

Sautéed Shrimp and Scallops

1½ pounds fresh shrimp
1½ pounds fresh scallops
3 tablespoons lemon juice
6 tablespoons olive oil
½ teaspoon dried oregano leaves
3 cloves garlic, finely minced
2 teaspoons salt
1½ teaspoons paprika

Shell and devein shrimp. Cut very large scallops in half. Put shrimp and scallops together in a large bowl. Combine lemon juice, olive oil, oregano, garlic, and salt; pour over fish and marinate at least 2 hours, or overnight, in refrigerator, stirring occasionally. Pour into a large skillet and sprinkle with paprika; cook over moderately low heat (about 225° F.) 10 to 15 minutes, or until fish is tender. Spoon into scallop shells or individual casseroles. Serves 12.

Curried Chicken

2 3- to 3½-pound broiler-fryer chickens, cut up
6 cups water
2 carrots, peeled
1 medium-sized onion, peeled
1 stalk celery
Sprig parsley
2 teaspoons salt
⅛ teaspoon pepper
1 cup milk
1 3½-ounce can flaked coconut
6 tablespoons butter or margarine
6 green onions or scallions, thinly sliced
6 tablespoons flour
2 tablespoons curry powder

Place chicken, water, carrots, onion, celery, parsley, 2 teaspoons salt, and pepper in a 5-quart Dutch oven. Cover and bring to a boil; simmer over low heat (about 200° F.) 45 minutes, or until fork-tender. Remove chicken and strain broth; boil broth over moderately high heat (about 375° F.) to reduce it to 1 quart. Cool chicken and remove skin and bones; cut meat into bite-sized pieces. Place milk and coconut in the container of an electric blender and blend at high speed 40 seconds. Melt butter in saucepan over moderate heat (about 250° F.); add green onions and cook until tender. Blend in flour, curry, ginger, and the 1 teaspoon salt. Gradually add coconut milk, cream, and the 1 quart chicken broth. Cook, stirring constantly, until thickened. Add chicken and water chestnuts. Heat just before serving. Serve with Fried Rice. Serves 12.

½ *teaspoon ground ginger*
1 *teaspoon salt*
1 *cup light cream*
2 *5-ounce cans sliced water*
  chestnuts

❧ *Pork Kabobs*

1 *11-ounce can*
  mandarin orange
  sections
1 *teaspoon lemon juice*
¼ *cup vegetable oil*
1½ *teaspoons ground*
  ginger
2 *teaspoons soy sauce*
2 *chicken bouillon cubes*
2 *cups boiling water*
3 *pounds boneless*
  lean pork, cut into
  1-inch cubes
2 *green peppers, cut into*
  pieces about 1 inch
  square

Drain orange sections and reserve syrup. Blend together the syrup, lemon juice, vegetable oil, ginger, and soy sauce for basting sauce. Dissolve bouillon cubes in boiling water; add pork, cover and simmer over moderately low heat (about 225° F.) 1 hour, or until fork-tender. Drain. Arrange pork pieces, green pepper, and orange sections alternately on 12 skewers. Place on broiler rack; baste with the orange sauce. Place in preheated broiler 3 to 4 inches from heat and broil 5 to 8 minutes on each side, basting occasionally. Serves 12.

❧ *Fried Rice*

¼ *cup vegetable oil*
½ *cup finely chopped onion*
4 *cups cooked rice (1⅓*
  cups uncooked rice)
½ *teaspoon salt*
3 *tablespoons soy sauce*
¼ *cup toasted, slivered*
  almonds

Heat oil in large skillet over moderate heat (about 250° F.); add onion and cook about 5 minutes, until tender. Add remaining ingredients. Cook, stirring constantly, until hot. Serves 12.

❧ *Hawaiian Salad*

4 *quarts salad greens, torn*
  into bite-sized pieces
  (lettuce, romaine, and
  chicory)
1 *firm, ripe avocado*

Wash and dry greens thoroughly; wrap in towel and chill well. A half hour before serving, peel avocado, slice, and then cut slices in half. Place in bowl and barely cover with Hawaiian Salad Dressing; let stand 10 minutes. Toss greens and tomatoes together in a large salad bowl.

(Ingredients continued on page 100)

Hawaiian Salad Dressing
(recipe follows)
3 *tomatoes, quartered*

Drain avocado and add dressing to salad, with enough additional dressing to coat greens lightly. Arrange sliced avocado over top of salad. Serves 12.

Hawaiian Salad Dressing

½ *cup pineapple juice*
½ *cup wine vinegar*
2 *tablespoons lemon juice*
1 *cup vegetable oil*
1 *teaspoon salt*
¼ *cup sugar*
1 *teaspoon paprika*
½ *teaspoon dry mustard*
½ *teaspoon garlic powder*

Place all ingredients in jar with a tight lid and shake until blended. Chill. Shake well before using. Makes 2 cups dressing.

❧ Pineapple Cheesecake

1 *cup sugar*
3 *tablespoons unflavored gelatine*
¼ *teaspoon salt*
4 *eggs, separated*
1 *cup milk*
2 *teaspoons grated lemon peel*
4 *teaspoons lemon juice*
4 *cups cottage cheese*
1 *cup heavy cream, whipped*
1 *cup flaked coconut*
Pineapple Sauce *(recipe follows)*

Mix sugar, gelatine, and salt in top of double boiler. Beat egg yolks and milk together slightly; stir into gelatine mixture. Cook over simmering water, stirring constantly, until gelatine is dissolved and mixture thickens, about 10 to 15 minutes. Cool slightly and stir in lemon peel and juice. Beat cottage cheese until almost smooth with an electric mixer set at high speed, or put cheese through a fine sieve. Mix gelatine mixture and cheese together and chill in refrigerator until mixture mounds up when lifted with a spoon. Beat egg whites until stiff but not dry. Fold beaten egg whites and whipped cream into cheese mixture. Pour into a 13-x-9-x-2-inch pan. Toast coconut in a preheated 325° F. oven for 15 minutes, or until lightly browned, stirring occasionally. Cool and sprinkle over top of cheesecake. Chill 3 to 4 hours, or until set. Serve with Pineapple Sauce. Serves 12.

Pineapple Sauce

2 *20-ounce cans pineapple tidbits*
2 *tablespoons cornstarch*
Pinch of salt
½ *teaspoon ground ginger*
2 *teaspoons lemon juice*

Drain pineapple and reserve juice. Stir together cornstarch, salt, and ginger in saucepan. Gradually stir in pineapple juice and lemon juice; cook over moderate heat (about 250° F.), stirring constantly, until smooth and thickened. Fold in drained pineapple and cherries. Chill before serving. Makes 5½ cups sauce.

½ cup slivered maraschino
cherries

CONTINENTAL BUFFET

Dry Sherry   Sweet Vermouth
Miniature Quiches Lorraine
Apricot-Glazed Ham
Frosted Grapes
Meat Loaf
Mushroom Wine Sauce
Vegetable Medley Casserole
Tomato Aspic Salad
Hot Buttered Rolls
Chilled Rosé Wine
Fruit Ambrosia
Pineapple Chiffon Cake
Port   Cream Sherry
Demitasse

*Recipe follows.

Party decorations: Cover buffet table with a damask or lace cloth. Use candles and flowers on buffet and around the room. Use your best china, wineglasses, and silver serving dishes.

The day before the party: 1. Prepare and refrigerate Miniature Quiches Lorraine. 2. Prepare and chill Apricot-Glazed Ham and Frosted Grapes. 3. Prepare and refrigerate Meat Loaf ready to bake. 4. Prepare and refrigerate Vegetable Medley Casserole ready to bake. 5. Prepare and chill Tomato Aspic Salad. 6. Prepare Pineapple Chiffon Cake.

Miniature Quiches Lorraine

1 package pie-crust mix
4 slices raw bacon
1 small onion, thinly sliced
¼ cup shredded Swiss cheese
1 egg, slightly beaten
½ cup light cream or milk, heated
2 tablespoons grated Parmesan cheese
¼ teaspoon ground nutmeg
½ teaspoon salt
¼ teaspoon white pepper

Heat oven to 450° F. Prepare pastry according to package directions. Roll pastry out ⅛ inch thick on a lightly floured board. Cut into rounds with a 3-inch cookie cutter (there will be approximately 24 rounds). Fit rounds into the bottoms and sides of 2½-inch muffin cups. Prick lightly with the tines of a fork. Bake 5 minutes, or until lightly browned. In a skillet over moderately high heat (about 325° F.) cook bacon until crisp; drain and crumble into small pieces. Cook onion in the bacon fat over moderate heat (about 250° F.) until soft. Into each baked pastry cup, equally divide bacon, onion, and Swiss cheese. In a small bowl combine egg, cream, Parmesan cheese, nutmeg, salt, and pepper and blend well; pour over onion–cheese mixture in the pastry cups. Bake 15 minutes; reduce oven temperature to 350° F. and bake 5 to 7 minutes longer, or until silver knife inserted in mixture comes out clean. Serve hot. May be reheated in a 350° F. oven about 5 minutes. Makes 24 individual quiches.

᣾ Apricot-Glazed Ham

1 8-pound ready-to-serve
   canned ham
⅓ cup sugar
⅛ teaspoon ground cloves
1 tablespoon cornstarch
1 cup apricot nectar
1½ tablespoons lemon juice

Heat ham as directed on can; cool. Mix sugar, cloves, and cornstarch in a saucepan. Stir in apricot nectar and lemon juice; cook and stir over moderate heat (about 250° F.) until clear and thick. Chill thoroughly. Spread glaze evenly over ham. Chill several hours or overnight. Garnish with Frosted Grapes. Serves 24.

Frosted Grapes

1 egg white
About 1 pound purple or
   green grapes divided
   into several small
   bunches
About ½ cup granulated
   sugar

Beat egg white till frothy. Dip bunches of grapes in egg white and sprinkle generously with sugar. Spread on waxed paper to dry.

᣾ Meat Loaf

2 eggs
6 tablespoons milk
2½ cups soft bread crumbs
1½ pounds ground beef chuck
1½ pounds ground lean pork
½ cup finely chopped onion
½ cup chopped green pepper
½ cup chili sauce
1 tablespoon salt
½ teaspoon pepper
Watercress
Mushroom Wine Sauce (recipe
   follows)

Beat eggs and milk together slightly; add bread crumbs and stir to blend. Add beef, pork, onion, green pepper, chili sauce, salt, and pepper; mix lightly. Divide meat mixture in half and pack each into a 9-x-5-x-3-inch loaf pan. Cover and refrigerate until ready to bake. Bake 1¼ hours in a preheated 350° F. oven. Cool a few minutes before removing from pan. Slice and arrange on platter. Garnish with watercress. Serve with Mushroom Wine Sauce. Serves 12.

Mushroom Wine Sauce

6 tablespoons butter or
   margarine
1 pound mushrooms, sliced

Heat butter in skillet over moderate heat (about 250° F.); add mushrooms and cook until lightly browned. Sprinkle flour over mushrooms and stir to blend. Stir in

2 tablespoons flour
2 10¾-ounce cans beef
gravy
1 cup dry red wine

gravy and wine; cook and stir until thickened. Makes 4½ cups sauce.

❧ Vegetable Medley Casserole

3 tablespoons butter or
margarine
1 pound mushrooms, sliced
2 cans condensed cream of
mushroom soup
1 cup light cream
2 teaspoons ground
dillseed
2 cups cooked green
beans, fresh or frozen
2 cups cooked lima beans,
fresh or frozen
1 cup canned whole kernel
corn
1 cup coarsely grated raw
carrot
½ cup grated Parmesan
cheese

Melt butter in skillet over moderate heat (about 250° F.); add mushrooms and cook until lightly browned. Blend soup, light cream, and dill together; fold in mushrooms, green beans, lima beans, corn, and carrot. Pour into greased, deep 2½-quart casserole. Sprinkle Parmesan cheese over top of vegetables; cover and refrigerate until ready to bake. Bake in preheated 350° F. oven 35 to 40 minutes, or until bubbling hot. Serves 12.

❧ Tomato Aspic Salad

2 28-ounce cans whole
tomatoes
½ cup chopped onion
2 stalks celery
¼ cup lemon juice
2 bay leaves
½ teaspoon dried oregano
leaves
3 tablespoons sugar
2 teaspoons salt
4 envelopes unflavored
gelatine
Salad greens
Carrot curls
Sliced cucumbers
Tomato wedges

Combine tomatoes, onion, celery, lemon juice, bay leaves, oregano, sugar, and salt in a large saucepan; cover and simmer over moderately low heat (about 225° F.) 30 minutes. Remove celery and bay leaf. Put tomato mixture through a food mill or a fine sieve. Measure juice and add water, if needed, to make 2 quarts. Sprinkle gelatine over 1 cup of the tomato juice to soften, then stir over moderately low heat (about 225° F.) until gelatine is dissolved. Stir into remaining juice. Pour into 2-quart gelatine mold and chill until set. Unmold on salad greens. Garnish with carrot curls, sliced cucumbers, and tomato wedges. Serves 12.

PLANNING MENUS

⌁ *Fruit Ambrosia*

2 *12-ounce packages frozen mixed fruits, thawed*
1 *17-ounce can pitted Bing cherries*
1 *16-ounce can grapefruit sections*
2 *11-ounce cans mandarin orange sections*
3 *tablespoons cornstarch*
2 *teaspoons lemon juice*
½ *cup kirsch*
2 *bananas, sliced*

Drain frozen fruits; reserve juice. Drain Bing cherries, grapefruit sections, and mandarin oranges; add enough of the drained canned juices to the juice from the frozen fruits to measure 3 cups liquid. Blend cornstarch and lemon juice in a small bowl until smooth. Combine fruit juices and cornstarch mixture in a saucepan. Cook over moderate heat (about 250° F.), stirring constantly, until thickened and clear. Remove from heat and cool. Stir in kirsch; fold in fruits and bananas. Chill. Serves 12.

⌁ *Pineapple Chiffon Cake*

2¼ *cups sifted cake flour*
1½ *cups sugar*
3 *teaspoons baking powder*
1 *teaspoon salt*
5 *egg yolks*
½ *cup vegetable oil*
¾ *cup pineapple juice*
1 *cup egg whites (7 to 8)*
½ *teaspoon cream of tartar*
About 2 tablespoons confectioners' sugar

Heat oven to 350° F. Sift flour, sugar, baking powder, and salt together into a bowl. Make a well in center of flour mixture; add egg yolks, oil, and pineapple juice. Beat until smooth and creamy. Beat egg whites and cream of tartar together until stiff peaks form. Gradually fold in egg yolk mixture; blend thoroughly. Pour into an ungreased 10-inch tube cake pan. Bake 45 to 55 minutes or until top springs back when touched lightly with finger. Invert pan over funnel or neck of a bottle until completely cooled. Cut around sides and tube with thin spatula. Turn out and dust with sifted confectioners' sugar. Serves 12.

MEXICAN FIESTA

Guacamole   Corn Chips
Paella
Mexican Turnovers
Bean Salad
Cucumber Salad
Tostadas
Cinnamon–Chocolate Mousse
Coffee   Tea

Party decorations: Cover buffet table with a brightly striped cloth. Decorate buffet with Mexican flags and with flowers in a sombrero. Decorate room with travel posters, tambourines, fans, and paper lanterns. Play Mexican or Spanish records.
The day before the party: 1. Cook chicken and remove meat from bones ready for Paella; refrigerate meat and broth. 2. Prepare and refrigerate Bean Salad. 3. Prepare Tostadas. 4. Prepare and refrigerate Cinnamon–Chocolate Mousse.

*Recipe follows

[104]

✒ Guacamole

2 ripe avocados
2 medium-sized tomatoes
1 bunch green onions or
   scallions, finely chopped
½ teaspoon Tabasco
2 tablespoons lemon juice
2 teaspoons salt

Peel avocados; remove pits and save one. Mash pulp with a fork into fairly small pieces. Place tomatoes in boiling water for 1 minute, rinse in cold water, peel off skin, and finely chop. Combine all ingredients. Spoon into a serving bowl and place an avocado pit in center of guacamole. This will keep mixture from darkening. Cover and chill in refrigerator until serving time. Remove pit and stir before serving. Makes 3 cups, or enough to serve 12.

✒ Paella

1 3- to 3½-pound
   broiler-fryer chicken,
   cut up
4 cups hot water
1 medium-sized carrot,
   peeled
1 medium-sized onion,
   peeled
1 stalk celery
3 sprigs parsley
2 teaspoons salt
½ pound link pork
   sausage, cut into
   ½-inch slices
½ cup finely chopped
   onion
4 chicken bouillon cubes
Boiling water
2 cloves garlic, crushed
1 8-ounce can tomato
   sauce
2 teaspoons paprika
1½ pounds fresh shrimp,
   shelled and deveined, or
   ¾ pound frozen shelled
   and deveined shrimp
1 10-ounce can whole
   littleneck clams,
   drained and liquid
   reserved

Place chicken, the 4 cups water, carrot, onion, celery, parsley sprigs, and the 2 teaspoons salt in a 5-quart Dutch oven. Cover and bring to boil; simmer over moderately low heat (about 225° F.) about 1 hour, or until chicken is fork-tender. Remove chicken and strain broth. Cool chicken and remove meat from bones; cut meat into bite-sized pieces. Cook sausage over moderately high heat (about 275° F.) in the Dutch oven until lightly browned. Add onion and cook about 5 minutes, until tender. Measure broth from chicken and reserved clam liquid; add chicken bouillon cubes and enough boiling water to make 2 quarts liquid. Stir to dissolve bouillon. Add garlic, tomato sauce, paprika, and chicken pieces; cook over moderately low heat (about 225° F.) 15 minutes. Add remaining ingredients except clams; cover and cook 30 minutes, stirring occasionally, until most of the liquid is absorbed. Stir in clams. Cover and cook 5 minutes longer. Serves 12.

(Ingredients continued on page 106)

1 cup fresh or frozen
  peas
1 9-ounce package
  artichoke hearts,
  thawed
1 4-ounce can pimientos,
  diced
¼ cup minced parsley
3 cups uncooked rice
Pinch of powdered saffron
1½ teaspoons salt
¼ teaspoon pepper

✎ Mexican Turnovers

2 cups sifted all-purpose
  flour
1 teaspoon salt
2 teaspoons baking powder
½ cup shortening
⅓ cup cold water
Crab Meat Filling (recipe
  follows)

Heat oven to 400° F. Sift flour, salt, and baking powder together into a bowl. Cut in shortening with 2 knives or pastry blender until mixture resembles coarse corn meal. Sprinkle water, 1 tablespoon at a time, over flour mixture, tossing with fork until mixture clings together. Roll out dough ⅛ inch thick on lightly floured board. Cut out pastry rounds with a 3¼-inch cookie cutter or a 6-ounce custard cup. Spoon a heaping teaspoonful of the Crab Meat Filling onto half of each pastry round. Wet edge of pastry with water and fold in half; press edge together with fork to seal in filling. Prick tops with fork; arrange on cookie sheet and bake 15 to 20 minutes. Makes 2 dozen.

Crab Meat Filling

1½ teaspoons butter or
  margarine
2 tablespoons chopped
  onion
¾ cup crab meat, flaked
1 small tomato, peeled
  and chopped
¼ cup chopped stuffed
  olives
2 teaspoons chopped
  fresh parsley
½ teaspoon lemon juice
¼ teaspoon salt

Heat butter in skillet over moderate heat (about 250° F.); add onion and cook until tender. Combine cooked onion and remaining ingredients. Makes filling for 24 turnovers.

❧ Bean Salad

3 tablespoons finely
  chopped onion
3 cups finely chopped
  celery
3 15½-ounce cans kidney
  beans, drained
2 tablespoons chopped
  fresh parsley
⅓ cup lemon juice
3 tablespoons wine
  vinegar
¾ cup olive oil
1½ teaspoons crushed
  dried red pepper
¼ teaspoon dried thyme
  leaves
¾ teaspoon dried
  oregano leaves
¾ teaspoon salt

Combine onion, celery, beans, and parsley in a large bowl. Blend lemon juice, wine vinegar, olive oil, red pepper, thyme, oregano, and salt; fold into beans. Marinate in refrigerator several hours or overnight. Serves 12.

❧ Cucumber Salad

2 large cucumbers, thinly
  sliced
4 4-ounce cans pimientos,
  drained and sliced
⅔ cup vegetable oil
¼ cup wine vinegar
½ teaspoon salt
2 cups commercial sour
  cream

Fold together cucumber and pimientoes. Blend oil, wine vinegar, and salt; pour over cucumber mixture and chill 1 hour. Drain and serve with sour cream. Serves 12.

❧ Tostadas

4 cups sifted all-purpose
  flour
2 teaspoons salt
½ cup shortening
1 cup lukewarm water
Shortening or vegetable oil

Sift flour and salt together into bowl. Cut in the ½ cup shortening with 2 knives or pastry blender until mixture resembles coarse corn meal. Gradually add water, tossing with fork until mixture clings together. Turn out on lightly floured board and knead 75 times, or until mixture is well blended and smooth. Divide dough into 24 equal portions and form each into a ball. Cover with a dish towel and let stand 15 minutes. Roll each ball into a 5-inch circle. Heat shortening or oil to a depth of 4 inches in a deep-fat fryer. When temperature registers 380° F. on a deep-fat thermometer, fry tostadas, a few at a time, about 3 minutes on each side, until lightly browned. Drain well on paper toweling. If made a day ahead, reheat in a preheated, 350° F. oven for 5 minutes. Makes 24 tostadas.

❧ Cinnamon–Chocolate Mousse

1 cup sugar
1 teaspoon ground cinnamon
1 teaspoon salt
2 envelopes unflavored gelatine
2 13-fluid-ounce cans evaporated milk
1 12-ounce package semisweet chocolate pieces
4 eggs, separated
2 teaspoons vanilla extract
¼ cup sugar
Sweetened whipped cream (optional)

Mix the 1 cup sugar, cinnamon, salt, and gelatine in the top of a double boiler. Gradually add 1⅓ cups of the evaporated milk and the chocolate pieces. Place over simmering water and cook until gelatine is dissolved and chocolate is melted and smooth. Beat egg yolks slightly; gradually stir in chocolate mixture. Pour back into double boiler and cook and stir 1 minute. Stir in vanilla. Chill until mixture is the consistency of unbeaten egg white. While the gelatine is chilling, pour the remaining 2 cups evaporated milk into a refrigerator freezer tray or loaf pan. Freeze until ice crystals form around edges. Pour into chilled bowl and whip with rotary beater until mixture forms soft peaks. Beat egg whites until soft peaks form; gradually add the ¼ cup sugar and beat until stiff peaks form. Fold whipped milk and egg whites into chocolate mixture. Pour into a 3-quart gelatine mold and chill 3 to 4 hours, or until set. Unmold and garnish with sweetened whipped cream if desired. Serves 12.

CHAPTER IV

TIMING THE DINNER

The most common problem for new cooks is planning preparation of a meal so that everything will be done and ready to serve at the same time. The secret—until practice makes the planning second nature—is to clock your menus and make a written schedule.

To make a work-planned menu, set a serving time for your dinner. Now list each menu item in a column. Check all the recipes and estimate the preparation time necessary—that is, the time it will take to prepare the recipe to the point of cooking (or chilling). To the right of each menu item enter the preparation time plus cooking (or chilling) time. If you are working without recipes and don't know the cooking time for the fresh vegetables or meat you are preparing, check the time in the chapters on vegetables and meats. When you've entered a time for each item, you are ready to make a clocked work plan. The recipe that takes the longest to prepare and cook will be the key to when to start working. If, for example, the casserole you plan to make will take fifteen minutes to prepare and one hour to cook, you would start to make it at 4:45 to serve at 6 o'clock. Proceed through the menu, listing items in order of the amount of preparation and cooking time they require. Enter a starting time for each.

In the beginning, preparation of food may take longer than you anticipate. You can beat the clock by doing as much preparation as you can manage earlier in the day—such jobs as chopping nuts, washing salad greens, making salad dressing.

Timing the Dinner for Two

These three time-planned menus (to serve two people) are examples of the way to time-plan family meals.

*Baked Chicken with
Herb Gravy
Green Beans with Almonds
Baked Potato
Green Salad
Cranberry Sauce
Frozen Chocolate Éclair
Coffee   Milk*

In the morning or the night before: Check all ingredients needed. Wash and dry salad ingredients. Wash chicken; cover and refrigerate. Wash and cut beans; cover tightly and place in refrigerator. Wash and scrub potatoes. Place cranberry sauce in refrigerator to chill.

1½ hours before serving: Set table; get out serving dishes.

1¼ hours before serving: Heat oven to 325° F. Brown chicken in skillet; place in casserole with seasonings and bouillon. Place potatoes in oven to bake.

1 hour before serving: Place chicken in oven with potatoes to bake.

50 minutes before serving: Place cranberry sauce on serving dish and chill until serving time.

25 minutes before serving: Uncover chicken in oven. Put salad dressing and greens in bowl; do not toss, refrigerate. Remove frozen éclairs from freezer; place on serving plates and refrigerate.

20 minutes before serving: Start cooking green beans.

15 minutes before serving: Make coffee. Place butter, water, and cranberry sauce on table.

10 minutes before serving: Make the gravy for the chicken.

5 minutes before serving: Drain beans; add 1 tablespoon butter or margarine and 2 tablespoons toasted almonds. Remove potatoes from oven. Serve dinner. Toss salad at the table.

*Recipe follows

✒ Baked Chicken with Herb Gravy

1½ **tablespoons butter or
margarine**
2 **chicken legs or 1
chicken breast, split, or
half a frying chicken,**

Heat oven to 325° F. Melt butter in skillet over moderately high heat (about 325° F.) and brown chicken lightly on all sides. Place chicken in a casserole. Sprinkle with salt, pepper, and rosemary. Dissolve bouillon cube in boiling water and pour over chicken. Cover and bake 35

cut into 2 quarters
Salt and pepper
¼ teaspoon dried
   rosemary leaves
 1 chicken bouillon cube
¾ cup boiling water
⅓ cup commercial sour
   cream

minutes. Uncover and bake 15 to 20 minutes, or until fork-tender. Pour juices from casserole into a saucepan and cook over moderately high heat (about 375° F.) until reduced to ⅓ cup. Remove from heat. Gradually stir in sour cream; serve over hot chicken. Serves 2.

---

*Pork Chop Casserole
Steamed Rice
Buttered Spinach
*Apple–Celery Salad
*Apricot Delight
Shortcake
Coffee   Milk

In the morning or the night before: Check all ingredients needed. Wash salad greens and spinach; drain and place in plastic bags. Refrigerate.

1 ½ hours before serving: Set table; get out serving dishes.

1 ¼ hours before serving: Whip cream; fold in apricot jam and almonds for dessert. Refrigerate.

1 hour before serving: Prepare Pork Chop Casserole (takes 10 minutes).

50 minutes before serving: Start baking Pork Chop Casserole.

45 minutes before serving: Prepare Apple–Celery Salad and chill.

25 minutes before serving: Boil water for rice; add rice and cook.

20 minutes before serving: Cook the spinach.

10 minutes before serving: Prepare coffee. Finish preparing salad and arrange on greens.

5 minutes before serving: Drain spinach. Serve dinner. Toast poundcake and top with the cream mixture just before serving.

*Recipe follows

Pork Chop Casserole

2 loin pork chops, 1 inch
   thick
Salt and pepper
1 medium-sized onion,
   thinly sliced
1 8-ounce can tomatoes

Heat oven to 350° F. Place chops in a heavy skillet over moderately high heat (about 325° F.) and brown slowly on both sides. Place in a 1-quart casserole. Sprinkle with salt and pepper. Add onion and tomatoes. Cover. Bake 45 to 50 minutes, until chops are tender. Serves 2.

Apple–Celery Salad

½ cup diced apple
½ cup chopped celery
3 tablespoons French dressing
2 tablespoons mayonnaise or salad dressing
Salad greens

Combine apple, celery, and French dressing. Chill 30 to 35 minutes in refrigerator, stirring occasionally. Fold in mayonnaise. Serve on salad greens. Serves 2.

Apricot Delight Shortcake

⅓ cup chilled heavy cream
2½ tablespoons apricot jam
2 tablespoons slivered almonds
2 slices raisin poundcake

Whip heavy cream until it holds its shape. Fold in apricot jam and slivered almonds; chill. Toast poundcake and top with cream mixture. Serves 2.

Tomato Juice Crackers
*Lobster Newburg
Buttered Noodles
Canned Peas
*Cherry Cobbler
Coffee Milk

In the morning or the night before: Check all ingredients needed. Chill tomato juice.
1 hour before serving: Set table; get out serving dishes.
45 minutes before serving: Cook lobster tails if you are using them rather than canned or frozen lobster.
35 minutes before serving: Prepare Cherry Cobbler and put in oven to bake.
25 minutes before serving: Prepare Lobster Newburg.
20 minutes before serving: Start heating water for noodles.
15 minutes before serving: Start cooking noodles. Open peas and heat over low heat.
10 minutes before serving: Make coffee. Open tomato juice and put in glasses.
5 minutes before serving: Drain noodles and add 1 tablespoon butter or margarine. Season peas. Remove cobbler from oven. Serve dinner.

*Recipe follows

Lobster Newburg

1 tablespoon butter or margarine
1 cup cooked lobster

Melt butter in saucepan over moderate heat (about 250° F.); add lobster meat and cook 3 minutes. Add sherry and heat 1 minute. Beat egg yolk and cream together;

meat (frozen lobster tails
may be used)
1 tablespoon dry sherry
1 egg yolk
6 tablespoons heavy cream
¼ teaspoon salt
Few grains cayenne pepper
Few grains ground nutmeg

gradually stir into lobster mixture. Cook over low heat (about 200° F.), stirring constantly, until sauce just starts to thicken, about 4 to 5 minutes. If sauce boils, it will separate. Stir in salt, cayenne, and nutmeg. Serves 2.

✒ Cherry Cobbler

¾ cup prepared biscuit
mix
¼ cup sugar
1 egg
2 tablespoons milk
¼ teaspoon almond extract
1 21-ounce can cherry pie
filling

Heat oven to 375° F. Combine biscuit mix and sugar in a bowl. Beat together egg, milk, and extract in another bowl and stir into biscuit mixture. Spoon filling into a 1-quart baking dish. Spoon biscuit mixture over cherries. Bake 30 to 35 minutes. Serves 4.

Timing the Dinner for Company

These five dinner menus (three of them serve six people and two serve four people) are time-planned to make everything come out at one time and to leave very little last-minute work in the kitchen. Making at least a rough time schedule is something experienced hostesses do to be sure everything goes smoothly.

*Honeydew-and-Pear Cup
*Tongue with Raisin Sauce
    and Vegetables
  *Lemon Drop Freeze
    Coffee   Milk

In the morning or about 6 hours before serving time: allow about 1 hour's preparation time: Check all ingredients needed. Prepare and freeze Lemon Drop Freeze. Prepare Honeydew-and-Pear Cup and refrigerate. Prepare all the vegetables, except potatoes, for Tongue with Raisin Sauce; cover and refrigerate.
4½ hours before serving: Soak tongue in cold water 1 hour.
3½ hours before serving: Drain tongue and start it cooking as directed in recipe.
1 hour before serving: Prepare potatoes and add with seasonings and other vegetables, except cabbage, to tongue.

*Recipe follows

40 minutes before serving (or earlier if you prefer): Set table; get out serving dishes.

30 minutes before serving: Add cabbage to tongue and vegetables. Dish out honeydew and pears and garnish with mint; keep in refrigerator.

15 minutes before serving: Prepare coffee. Remove tongue and vegetables from saucepan. Slice tongue and arrange on serving platter. Keep hot in a warm oven. Prepare raisin sauce. Serve dinner.

◆§ Honeydew-and-Pear Cup

2 *firm ripe pears*
2 *cups honeydew melon balls (see page 707)*
⅓ *cup sugar*
⅓ *cup lemon juice*
1 *tablespoon finely chopped mint leaves*
6 *mint sprigs*

Peel pears, core, slice, and then cut slices into halves. Toss together with melon balls, sugar, lemon juice, and chopped mint leaves. Cover and store in refrigerator 3 to 4 hours, or longer. Serve garnished with mint sprigs. Serves 6.

◆§ Tongue with Raisin Sauce and Vegetables

1 *4-pound smoked beef tongue*
½ *teaspoon whole thyme leaves*
1 *bay leaf*
6 *peppercorns*
6 *small carrots*
6 *medium-sized onions*
3 *small white turnips, cut into halves*
6 *medium-sized potatoes, cut into halves*
1 *medium-sized cabbage, cut into 6 wedges*
2 *tablespoons butter or margarine*
2 *tablespoons flour*
½ *cup dry white wine*
1 *tablespoon sugar*
⅓ *cup raisins*

Cover tongue with cold water and soak 1 hour. Drain and place in large saucepan with enough cold water to cover. Place over moderately high heat (about 275° F.) and bring to boil; cover and simmer over low heat (about 200° F.) 2¼ hours. Add thyme, bay leaf, peppercorns, carrots, onions, turnips, and potatoes; cover and cook 30 minutes. Arrange cabbage over tongue and vegetables and cook, covered, 15 minutes longer. Remove vegetables with slotted spoon and arrange on large, warm platter. Keep warm in very low oven. Reserve 1½ cups of broth for raisin sauce. Remove roots from tongue: peel off all outer skin. Slice and arrange on platter with vegetables. Melt butter in saucepan over moderate heat (about 250° F.); stir in flour. Stir in the 1½ cups reserved tongue broth and the wine. Add sugar, raisins, lemon peel, and juice; cook until thickened. Serve with tongue. Serves 6.

¼ teaspoon grated lemon
    peel
1 tablespoon lemon juice

❧ Lemon Drop Freeze

1 cup evaporated milk
1 egg
1 tablespoon grated lemon
    peel
2 tablespoons lemon juice
½ cup sugar
⅛ teaspoon salt
3 tablespoons butter or
    margarine
⅓ cup firmly packed brown
    sugar
Few grains ground cinnamon
⅔ cup crushed shredded
    corn bite-sized biscuits
⅓ cup chopped walnuts
½ cup flaked coconut

Line bottom and sides of a 9-x-5-x-3-inch loaf pan with waxed paper. Pour evaporated milk into ice-cube tray or loaf pan and place in freezer until ice crystals form 1 inch around edge of pan. Beat egg well in top of double boiler; add grated lemon peel and juice, sugar and salt; beat until blended. Cook 12 to 15 minutes over simmering water until thickened, stirring occasionally. Place pan in a bowl of ice water and cool to room temperature. Pour chilled milk into chilled bowl and beat with rotary beater or electric mixer until mixture forms soft peaks. Fold whipped milk into lemon custard. Cut butter into brown sugar and cinnamon with pastry blender or 2 knives. Fold in cereal crumbs, nuts, and coconut. Pat half of the crumb mixture into the bottom of loaf pan. Pour in lemon filling. Sprinkle top with the remaining crumbs and press lightly into pudding. Cover with aluminum foil. Freeze until firm, 5 hours or longer. Serves 8.

Apple Juice
*Sweet-and-Pungent Shrimp
Rice
*Vegetable Medley Salad
*Chocolate Turnover
Custards
Coffee   Milk

In the morning or about 2½ hours before serving time: Allow about 30 minutes' preparation time. Check all ingredients needed. Chill apple juice. Cook and clean shrimp for Sweet-and-Pungent Shrimp; refrigerate.
2 hours before serving: Prepare peas, cucumber, and green onions for Vegetable Medley Salad; marinate in French dressing.
1½ hours before serving: Set table; get out serving dishes.
1¼ hours before serving: Prepare and bake Chocolate Turnover Custards.
1 hour before serving: Peel and slice avocado; marinate in lemon juice. Grate carrot; refrigerate.
40 minutes before serving: Prepare Sweet-and-Pungent Shrimp. Cook 1½ cups raw rice or 2 cups packaged precooked rice according to package directions.

*Recipe follows

10 minutes before serving: Prepare coffee. Unmold custards, arrange salad, and pour apple juice. Serve dinner.

Sweet-and-Pungent Shrimp

2 pounds fresh shrimp in shell or 1 pound frozen cleaned shrimp
1 8¼-ounce can sliced pineapple
½ cup firmly packed brown sugar
¼ cup vinegar
2 tablespoons soy sauce
1 cup water
1 medium-sized green pepper, cut into strips
1 tomato, cut into wedges
3 tablespoons cornstarch
¼ cup water
About 3 cups cooked rice

Cook fresh shrimp in boiling salted water over moderate heat (about 250° F.) 5 minutes. Cook frozen shrimp following package directions. Drain and cool in cold water. If in shell, clean and devein. Drain pineapple and reserve juice. Mix pineapple juice, brown sugar, vinegar, soy sauce, and the 1 cup water in saucepan. Bring to a boil over moderately high heat (about 275° F.). Add green pepper, pineapple, and tomato; cook over moderately low heat (about 225° F.) 20 to 25 minutes, or until green pepper is almost tender. Blend cornstarch and the ¼ cup water together; stir into sauce. Cook, stirring constantly, until thickened. Add shrimp and heat to serving temperature. Serve over rice. Serves 6.

Vegetable Medley Salad

1 10-ounce package frozen peas, cooked
1 medium-sized cucumber, sliced
½ cup sliced green onions or scallions
½ cup bottled French dressing
1 avocado
¼ cup lemon juice
½ teaspoon salt
Salad greens
1 cup coarsely grated carrot

Combine peas, cucumber, green onions, and French dressing. Cover and chill about 2 hours. Peel and slice avocado and marinate with lemon juice and salt, about 30 minutes or longer. To serve, line salad bowl with salad greens. Spoon pea mixture into bowl and arrange avocado slices in ring around edge of salad. Spoon carrots into center. Serves 6.

Chocolate Turnover Custards

18 mint chocolate wafers
4 eggs

Heat oven to 350° F. Butter six 6-ounce custard cups; place 3 chocolate wafers in bottom of each. Beat eggs

⅓ cup sugar
½ teaspoon salt
2 cups milk
1 teaspoon vanilla extract
¼ teaspoon grated lemon
   peel

slightly; stir in sugar, salt, milk, and vanilla. Strain mixture; stir in lemon peel. Pour into custard cups. Place custard cups in shallow baking pan; fill pan two-thirds full with hot water. Bake 40 to 45 minutes, or until set. Remove from hot water; cool 20 minutes. Loosen custards from edge of cups with a small spatula and carefully invert on serving dishes. Serves 6.

Tomato Juice
*South American Lamb Stew
*Poppy Seed Rice Pudding
*Piquant Apple Salad
*Peanut Ripple Ice Cream
   Coffee   Milk

In the morning or about 5 hours before serving time: Allow about 1½ hours' preparation time. Check all ingredients needed. Remove ice cream from freezer to soften for about 15 to 20 minutes. Prepare vegetables and gelatine mixture for Piquant Apple Salad. Chill gelatine and finish salad. Prepare and freeze Peanut Ripple Ice Cream. Prepare Poppy Seed Rice Pudding, cover and refrigerate. Brown meat for South American Lamb Stew and add marinade; cover and let stand until later. Wash, dry, and chill salad greens. Chill tomato juice.

2 hours before serving: Heat oven to 350° F. Finish stew and place in oven to bake. Remove rice pudding from refrigerator to warm at room temperature.

55 minutes before serving: Set table and get out serving dishes.

40 minutes before serving: Unmold salad on greens and refrigerate.

30 minutes before serving: Put rice pudding in oven to bake with stew.

10 minutes before serving: Pour tomato juice and make coffee.

5 minutes before serving: Remove stew from oven. Spoon meat and vegetables into serving dish; keep warm while making gravy. Remove rice pudding from oven. Serve dinner.

*Recipe follows

South American Lamb Stew

2 tablespoons vegetable
   oil
3 pounds cubed, boneless
   lamb
1 beef bouillon cube
1½ cups boiling water
⅛ teaspoon chili powder

Heat oil in a large skillet over moderately high heat (about 300° F.) and brown meat well on all sides. Dissolve bouillon cube in boiling water; add chili powder, saffron, ginger, turmeric, onion, garlic, and salt. Pour marinade over meat; refrigerate for 2 hours or longer to marinate, stirring occasionally. Put meat, marinade, and tomatoes in ovenproof casserole. Place in preheated

Pinch of saffron
¾ teaspoon ground
ginger
¾ teaspoon ground
turmeric
¾ cup chopped onion
2 cloves garlic, finely
minced
1½ teaspoons salt
1 16-ounce can tomatoes
2 tablespoons flour
1 tablespoon cold water
Chopped fresh parsley
(optional)

350° F. oven. Bake 1½ to 2 hours, or until tender. Remove meat to serving dish. Blend flour and cold water together. Gradually add to gravy, stirring vigorously. Cook over moderate heat (about 250° F.), stirring constantly, until thickened. Serve over meat. Sprinkle with chopped parsley if desired. Serves 6.

✑ Poppy Seed Rice Pudding

2 cups water
1 cup uncooked rice
1½ teaspoons salt
1 cup milk
1 egg, slightly beaten
⅛ teaspoon pepper
2 teaspoons prepared
mustard
½ teaspoon Worcestershire
sauce
1 cup coarsely shredded
Cheddar cheese
1 tablespoon poppy seeds
2 tablespoons butter or
margarine

Put water, rice, and salt in 2-quart saucepan. Bring to boil; cover and simmer over moderately low heat (about 225° F.) 14 minutes. Remove from heat and let stand 10 minutes, covered. Combine milk, egg, pepper, mustard, Worcestershire, and ½ cup of the shredded cheese; stir into rice. Spoon into a shallow 1½-quart baking dish. Sprinkle with poppy seeds and the remaining ½ cup cheese; dot with butter. Cover and refrigerate until ready to bake. Place in oven heated to 350° F. Bake 30 minutes, or until set. Serves 6.

✑ Piquant Apple Salad

1 envelope unflavored
gelatine
2 cups apple juice
¼ teaspoon salt
½ cup mayonnaise or salad
dressing
1 teaspoon grated onion
½ cup diced cucumber
½ cup diced celery
½ cup coarsely grated carrot

Sprinkle gelatine over ½ cup of the apple juice in a saucepan to soften. Place over moderate heat (about 250° F.), stirring constantly until gelatine is dissolved. Remove from heat and stir in remaining apple juice and salt. Add mayonnaise; beat until blended with rotary beater. Chill over a bowl of ice water, stirring constantly, until slightly thickened. Fold in onion, cucumber, celery, carrot, and cabbage. Pour into 1-quart mold and chill at least 4 hours, until set. Unmold on salad greens. Serves 6.

½ *cup chopped cabbage*
Salad greens

✑ *Peanut Ripple Ice Cream*

1 quart vanilla ice cream
½ *cup peanut butter*
½ *cup honey*

Remove ice cream from freezer and keep at room temperature for about 15 to 20 minutes, or until slightly soft. Spoon into loaf pan. Blend peanut butter and honey together and swirl through ice cream. Freeze several hours, or until firm. Serves 6.

Tuna–Cashew Casserole
Baked Potatoes
Buttered Green Beans
Celery Hearts
and Stuffed Olives
Banana–Rum Cream Cake
Coffee   Milk

In the morning or about 3 hours before serving time: Allow about 1½ hours' preparation time. Check all ingredients needed. Drizzle rum over sponge layers for Banana–Rum Cream Cake and prepare the banana filling. Chill filling in ice water. Prepare and refrigerate Tuna–Cashew Casserole. Wash 1 pound green beans; remove ends and cut into 1½-inch pieces. Refrigerate beans until ready to cook. Wash 4 large baking potatoes and rub skins with butter; refrigerate. Wash and cut celery hearts. Chill. Spread banana filling on cake as directed in recipe; chill.

1½ hours before serving: Heat oven to 350° F. Place potatoes in oven to bake about 1½ hours. Remove tuna casserole from refrigerator to warm at room temperature.

55 minutes before serving (or earlier if you prefer): Set table and get out serving dishes.

45 minutes before serving: Sprinkle reserved noodles over tuna casserole and place in oven to bake. Arrange celery and olives in serving dish; keep in refrigerator.

30 minutes before serving: Cook beans in boiling salted water over moderately low heat (about 225° F.) for 20 to 25 minutes, or until tender. Whip cream and spread over top of cake; refrigerate.

10 minutes before serving: Prepare coffee.

5 minutes before serving: Remove potatoes and casserole from oven. Cut a cross in each potato and press sides of potato to spread it open; top with butter. Drain and season beans. Serve dinner.

*Recipe follows

TIMING THE DINNER

❧ Tuna–Cashew Casserole

1 3-ounce can chow mein
  noodles
1 can condensed cream of
  mushroom soup
¼ cup water
1 6½-ounce can tuna,
  drained
¾ cup chopped salted
  cashew nuts
⅓ cup diced celery
¼ cup minced onion
¼ cup chopped ripe olives
½ teaspoon salt
Few grains pepper

Heat oven to 350° F. Reserve ¾ cup of the noodles. Combine rest of noodles and the remaining ingredients. Pour into greased deep 1½-quart casserole. Sprinkle with reserved noodles just before baking. Bake 40 minutes. Serves 4.

❧ Banana–Rum Cream Cake

¼ cup light rum
2 8-inch packaged sponge
  cake layers
⅓ cup sugar
2½ tablespoons cornstarch
¼ teaspoon salt
1½ cups milk
2 eggs
¼ teaspoon ground
  nutmeg
½ teaspoon vanilla
  extract
1¼ cups mashed banana
½ cup heavy cream,
  whipped

Drizzle rum over cake layers and let stand while preparing filling. Combine sugar, cornstarch, and salt in saucepan. Gradually add milk and cook over moderately low heat (about 225° F.), stirring constantly until thickened. Beat eggs slightly; stir in a little of the hot pudding mixture. Pour back into saucepan and cook 2 minutes. Remove from heat; add nutmeg, vanilla, and banana. Set pan in a bowl of ice water to cool. Place a cake layer in a 9-inch layer cake pan and top with half of the banana filling. Top with second layer and remaining filling. Chill 2 hours or longer. Top with cream before serving. Serves 6.

Half Grapefruit
Crunchy Baked Chicken
Hawaiian Sweet Potatoes
Brussels Sprouts
with Sour Cream Sauce
Strawberry–Banana Dessert
Coffee Milk

In the morning or about 2 hours before serving time: Allow about 30 minutes' preparation time. Check all ingredients needed. Prepare and refrigerate Strawberry–Banana Dessert and Hawaiian Sweet Potatoes. Put grapefruit in refrigerator to chill.
1½ hours before serving: Set table; get out serving dishes.
1¼ hours before serving: Heat oven to 400° F. Prepare

*Recipe follows

[120]

Crunchy Baked Chicken and place in oven to bake.

1 hour before serving: Remove sweet potatoes from refrigerator to warm at room temperature. Prepare grapefruit; pour 1 teaspoon crème de menthe over each serving. Garnish with a sprig of mint and chill until serving time. Wash and soak Brussels sprouts.

30 minutes before serving: Turn chicken and place sweet potatoes in oven to bake.

25 minutes before serving: Cook Brussels sprouts.

10 minutes before serving: Prepare coffee.

5 minutes before serving: Remove chicken and sweet potatoes from oven. Prepare sauce for Brussels sprouts. Drain sprouts; arrange in serving dish and top with sauce. Serve dinner.

Crunchy Baked Chicken

½ cup butter or margarine
1 3-pound broiler–fryer chicken, cut up
1 egg, slightly beaten
2 tablespoons milk
1 cup dehydrated potato flakes
½ cup grated Parmesan cheese
½ teaspoon salt
⅛ teaspoon pepper

Heat oven to 400° F. Melt butter and place in flat baking dish. Wash and dry chicken. Combine egg and milk. Mix potato flakes and Parmesan cheese. Dip chicken pieces in the milk mixture, then roll in potato flakes to coat thoroughly. Place chicken skin side down in baking dish. Save any leftover potato-flakes mixture. Sprinkle chicken with salt and pepper. Bake uncovered 30 minutes. Turn pieces and sprinkle again with salt and pepper and any leftover potato-flakes mixture. Bake 30 minutes longer, or until fork-tender. Serves 4.

Hawaiian Sweet Potatoes

1 16-ounce can vacuum-packed sweet potatoes
1 8¼-ounce can sliced pineapple, drained
¼ cup firmly packed brown sugar
¼ teaspoon salt
¼ cup coarsely chopped salted peanuts
2 tablespoons butter or margarine

Heat oven to 400° F. Arrange sweet potatoes in a deep 1-quart casserole. Cut pineapple slices into halves and arrange between sweet potatoes. Sprinkle with brown sugar, salt, and peanuts; dot with butter. Bake 25 minutes. Serves 4.

✑ *Brussels Sprouts with Sour Cream Sauce*

1 pound Brussels sprouts
½ cup commercial sour
   cream
¼ cup mayonnaise or salad
   dressing
1 teaspoon lemon juice
¼ teaspoon salt
Few grains pepper
½ teaspoon paprika

Wash Brussels sprouts, trim and soak in salted water 20 minutes. Drain and place in 1 inch of boiling, salted water. Bring to boil and simmer uncovered over moderately low heat (about 225° F.) 5 minutes. Cover and cook 10 to 15 minutes longer. Drain. Mix sour cream, mayonnaise, lemon juice, salt, pepper, and paprika in a saucepan; cook over low heat (about 200° F.), stirring constantly, until warm but not boiling. Serve over Brussels sprouts. Serves 4.

✑ *Strawberry–Banana Dessert*

1 3-ounce package
   strawberry-flavored
   gelatin
1 cup boiling water
1 10-ounce package frozen
   sliced strawberries,
   unthawed
1 ripe banana, sliced
Light cream

Dissolve gelatin in boiling water. Add frozen strawberries immediately and stir until melted and mixture is slightly thickened. Fold in bananas. Spoon into serving dishes. Chill. Serve with cream. Serves 4.

Last-Minute Meals

There are days of the week when you can anticipate that there'll be no time for much food preparation ahead and you'll need to plan menus that can be put together swiftly. These seven menus that follow (three of these are planned for two people and four of them serve four people) can all be ready to serve in less than an hour. Follow the numbered work schedule for the quickest procedure.

LESS-THAN-AN-HOUR DINNER FOR 2

*Fillet of Sole with
   White Wine Sauce
*Buttered Spinach with
   Nutmeg
*New Potatoes in Parsley–
   Butter Sauce

Work Schedule: (Put frozen fish in refrigerator in the morning to thaw.) 1. Boil water for potatoes; add potatoes. 2. Chop mushrooms and shallots and start cooking fish. 3. Prepare spinach. 4. While spinach is cooking, prepare fruit salad and dressing; refrigerate. 5. Prepare white wine sauce after fish is cooked; cover fish

*Recipe follows

*Fresh Fruit Salad
Ice cream with
Chocolate Sauce
Coffee Tea*

to keep it warm. 6. Melt butter and add parsley; drain potatoes and mix with butter sauce. 7. Add butter seasoning, and nutmeg to spinach. 8. Make coffee. 9. Spoon chocolate sauce over ice cream just before serving.

Fillet of Sole with White Wine Sauce

2 tablespoons butter or
  margarine
1 tablespoon chopped
  shallots or onion
⅓ cup sliced fresh
  mushrooms
Salt
1 12-ounce package
  frozen fillets of sole,
  thawed
½ cup dry white wine
1½ tablespoons butter or
  margarine
1½ tablespoons flour
2 tablespoons light
  cream

Melt the 2 tablespoons butter in a 10-inch skillet over moderately low heat (about 225° F.). Arrange shallots and mushrooms evenly on bottom of pan. Salt fish lightly; place on top of vegetables. Pour wine over fish. Bring the liquid in the pan to a boil over moderate heat (about 250° F.). Reduce heat to moderately low (about 225° F.) and cook the fish 10 to 12 minutes, until fish flakes easily when tested with a fork. Pour liquid into a measuring cup; add water, if necessary, to make ⅓ cup. In a small saucepan, melt the 1½ tablespoons butter over moderately low heat (about 225° F.). Gradually add the flour, stirring constantly. Continue to cook until mixture bubbles. Gradually stir in the ⅓ cup fish liquid, stirring vigorously until thoroughly blended. Stir in cream and heat until mixture is smooth and heated through. Serve over fish. Serves 2.

Buttered Spinach with Nutmeg

1 1-pound package fresh
  spinach leaves
⅓ cup water
Butter or margarine
Salt
Freshly ground nutmeg

Combine spinach leaves and ⅓ cup water in a large saucepan. Partially cover so that some steam can escape; cook over moderately low heat (about 225° F.) about 10 minutes. Drain thoroughly and season with butter and salt; sprinkle with nutmeg. Serves 2.

New Potatoes in Parsley–Butter Sauce

¾ pound unpeeled new
  potatoes, scrubbed
  (about 5 small ones)
4 cups water
3 tablespoons butter or
  margarine

Boil potatoes in the 4 cups water over moderate heat (about 250° F.) until potatoes are fork-tender, about 30 to 35 minutes. Melt butter over moderately low heat (about 225° F.) in a saucepan. Stir in parsley. Heat 1 to 2 minutes more; pour over potatoes. Toss gently. Serves 2.

(Ingredients continued on page 124)

1½ teaspoons dried
    parsley flakes

———————————

❧ Fresh Fruit Salad

Fresh nectarine wedges
Banana slices
Lettuce leaves
Crumbled walnuts
2 maraschino cherries
2 tablespoons mayonnaise
    or salad dressing
2 teaspoons milk

Place fruit on lettuce leaves on 2 salad plates. Top each with walnuts and a cherry. Combine mayonnaise and milk. Spoon dressing over each salad. Serves 2.

LESS-THAN-AN-HOUR DINNER FOR 2

*Minute Steaks Diane
*Spinach Egg Noodles
*French Fried Onion Rings
Tomato Slices
Hard Rolls
Chocolate Éclairs
Coffee   Tea

Work Schedule: 1. Boil water for noodles. 2. Place frozen French Fried Onion Rings in the oven. 3. Add noodles to boiling water. 4. Prepare steaks. 5. Slice tomatoes. 6. Set out rolls and butter. 7. Make coffee. 8. Place éclairs on dessert dishes just before serving time.

*Recipe follows

———————————

❧ Minute Steaks Diane

1 tablespoon butter or
    margarine
1 tablespoon chopped
    green onions or scallions
2 8-ounce minute steaks
Instant meat tenderizer
1 tablespoon freeze-dried
    chives
1 tablespoon Worcester-
    shire sauce
1 tablespoon bottled steak
    sauce

Melt butter in a skillet over moderate heat (about 250° F.). Add onions and cook 1 minute. Sprinkle steaks with meat tenderizer according to directions on jar. Place steaks in skillet and brown quickly on both sides over moderately high heat (about 325° F.). Remove steaks to a platter. Add chives, Worcestershire, and steak sauce to skillet; cook 1 to 2 minutes over moderate heat (about 250° F.), stirring constantly. Add steaks and any meat juices from platter. Cook about 1 minute, or until steaks are cooked to desired degree of doneness. Remove steaks to warm serving plates and pour sauce over them. Serves 2.

❧ *Spinach Egg Noodles*

Prepare *spinach egg noodles* according to directions on the box, using ½ cup dry noodles. Dot with *butter* and season to taste. Serves 2.

❧ *French Fried Onion Rings*

Prepare *1 4-ounce package frozen French fried onion rings* according to package directions. Serves 2.

LESS-THAN-AN-HOUR DINNER FOR 2

*Chicken Livers with
Bacon and Peppers
Buttered Broccoli Spears
*Chicken-Seasoned Rice
Lettuce Wedges with
Russian Dressing
*Cantaloupe with
Lime Sherbet
Iced Coffee
Iced Tea

*Recipe follows

Work Schedule: 1. Prepare chicken livers and peppers. 2. About 10 minutes before liver mixture is finished, prepare frozen broccoli and rice. 3. Cut lettuce wedges; arrange stuffed olive slices and dressing on top. 4. Make coffee. 5. Cantaloupe and sherbet may be prepared just before serving.

❧ *Chicken Livers with Bacon and Peppers*

1 8-ounce package frozen
  chicken livers
8 slices raw bacon
⅓ cup chopped onion
4 slices red pepper
4 slices green pepper
Few grains of cayenne
  pepper
1½ teaspoons salt
¼ teaspoon ground
  marjoram

Thaw chicken livers in water according to package directions. Cook bacon in a 10-inch skillet over moderately high heat (about 325° F.) until crisp. Remove bacon and drain. Reserve 3 tablespoons of the bacon fat. Cook livers and onion in the fat over moderately high heat (about 275° F.) 5 to 6 minutes, until livers are browned on both sides and onion is cooked. Remove livers and onion to a warm platter. Place red and green pepper slices in skillet; add cayenne, salt, and marjoram. Combine thoroughly. Cook over moderately high heat (about 300° F.), stirring frequently, about 8 minutes, until peppers are fork-tender. Add livers, bacon, and onion to peppers. Heat 2 to 3 minutes over moderately low heat (about 225° F.). Serves 2.

Chicken-Seasoned Rice

1 chicken bouillon cube
⅔ cup boiling water
⅔ cup packaged precooked rice
Dash of poultry seasoning

Dissolve bouillon cube in boiling water. Bring water back to a boil; stir in precooked rice. Cover; remove from heat. Let stand 5 minutes. Add poultry seasoning. Fluff with a fork to combine rice and seasoning thoroughly. Serves 2.

Cantaloupe with Lime Sherbet

Serve 2 *fresh cantaloupe wedges* with *a scoop of lime sherbet* on top.

LESS-THAN-AN-HOUR DINNER FOR 4

*Italian Veal Cutlets with
Tomato–Mushroom Sauce
Buttered Zucchini
*Fettucini
Italian Bread
*Relish Bowl
Spumoni
Coffee Tea

Work Schedule: 1. Heat water to boiling for noodles. 2. Coat veal with bread-crumb mixture and place in skillet. 3. Add noodles to the boiling water. 4. While veal is cooking, slice zucchini and place in 1 cup hot water. Cover and boil in saucepan. 5. Check veal. 6. Prepare relish bowl and heat tomato sauce. 7. Just before serving time add butter and seasoning to drained zucchini; drain noodles and combine thoroughly with remaining ingredients. 8. Make coffee. 9. Spumoni may be placed on dessert dishes just before serving.

*Recipe follows

Italian Veal Cutlets

½ cup fine dry bread crumbs
¼ cup grated Parmesan cheese
4 teaspoons paprika
1¼ pounds veal cutlet
3 tablespoons butter or margarine
Tomato–Mushroom Sauce (recipe follows)

Combine bread crumbs, grated cheese, and paprika in a pie plate; mix thoroughly. Coat veal cutlets lightly with the bread mixture. Melt butter in a 10-inch skillet over moderately low heat (about 225° F.). Add cutlets and brown 4 to 5 minutes on each side, until meat is fork-tender. Serve immediately with the Tomato–Mushroom Sauce. Serves 4.

Tomato–Mushroom Sauce

2 8-ounce cans tomato

Combine all ingredients in a saucepan. Heat over mod-

sauce with mushrooms
½ teaspoon dried
oregano leaves
1 teaspoon sugar

erately low heat (about 225° F.), stirring occasionally, until heated through. Serve with veal. Serves 4.

 *Fettucini*

2 cups medium egg
noodles
2 tablespoons melted
butter or margarine
½ cup grated Romano
cheese
½ cup heavy cream,
slightly whipped
Few grains pepper
Parsley sprigs

Cook noodles according to package directions. Drain thoroughly. Mix butter, cheese, and cream together; pour over noodles and mix gently. Serve immediately with a few grains of ground pepper and a sprig of parsley. Serves 4.

Relish Bowl

Watercress
Carrot sticks
Celery slices
Radish rosettes

Arrange all ingredients in a bowl. Chill.

LESS-THAN-AN-HOUR DINNER FOR 4

*Corned Beef–Macaroni
Casserole
Buttered Peas and Carrots
*Pineapple Slaw with
Mustard Dressing
Hot Buttered Rolls
Minted Pear Halves
Chocolate Chip Cookies
Coffee   Tea

Work Schedule: 1. Prepare macaroni casserole. 2. While casserole is baking, prepare pineapple slaw salad; chill. 3. Cook peas and carrots according to package directions; add drained 4-ounce can of mushrooms. 4. Heat rolls for a few minutes in the oven with the casserole. 5. Make Coffee. 6. Prepare pear halves—two per serving—by placing a spoonful of mint jelly in each just before serving.

*Recipe follows

✍ Corned Beef–Macaroni Casserole

1 7¼-ounce package
   macaroni and cheese
   dinner
1 can condensed cream of
   celery soup
½ cup milk
1 tablespoon prepared
   mustard
¼ cup drained chopped
   pimiento
Few grains pepper
1 teaspoon dried dillweed
1 teaspoon instant minced
   onion
1 12-ounce can corned
   beef, cubed
½ cup herb-seasoned stuffing
   croutons
2 teaspoons melted butter or
   margarine

Heat oven to 350° F. Prepare macaroni and cheese dinner in a large saucepan according to package directions. Add soup and milk to macaroni mixture; combine thoroughly. Stir in mustard, pimiento, pepper, dill, onion, and corned beef; mix well. Pour mixture into a buttered deep 1½-quart casserole. Combine herb croutons and butter in a bowl; toss well with a fork. Sprinkle herb crouton mixture on top of macaroni mixture. Bake 25 minutes, or until mixture is bubbling and top is lightly browned. Serves 4.

✍ Pineapple Slaw with Mustard Dressing

3 cups shredded cabbage
1½ teaspoons vinegar
½ teaspoon prepared
   mustard
2 tablespoons
   mayonnaise
Few grains salt
Few grains pepper
1 8¼-ounce can
   pineapple tidbits,
   drained
1 teaspoon pineapple
   syrup
Paprika

Combine cabbage, vinegar, mustard, and mayonnaise in a bowl. Add salt and pepper; mix well. Add pineapple and syrup; toss well. Garnish with paprika just before serving. Serves 4.

LESS-THAN-AN-HOUR DINNER FOR 4

*Crabmeat Divan
*Citrus Salad with

Work Schedule: 1. Set oven. 2. Cook asparagus. 3. While asparagus is cooking, combine crab mixture. 4. Butter

Creamy Dressing
Hot Rolls
Cream Puffs with Bottled
Caramel Ice Cream Topping
Coffee   Tea

casserole dishes; place drained asparagus on bottom of each. 5. Place crab, egg, cheese, and bread crumb layers on top. Bake casseroles. 6. Prepare salads and dressing; chill. 7. Heat rolls. 8. Make coffee. 9. Cream puffs may be topped with caramel topping just before serving time.

*Recipe follows

🔊 Crabmeat Divan

1 10-ounce package frozen whole asparagus spears, cooked and drained
2 7½-ounce cans Alaska king crab, drained and flaked
⅔ cup commercial sour cream
⅓ cup bottled French-style dressing
2 teaspoons finely chopped, fresh parsley
2 hard-cooked eggs, sliced
2 slices American cheese, each cut in half
2 tablespoons seasoned fine dry bread crumbs
Butter or margarine

Heat oven to 350° F. Arrange asparagus spears on the bottom of each of 4 buttered individual casserole dishes. Combine crab meat, sour cream, dressing, and parsley in a bowl; mix thoroughly. Using half of the crab mixture, spoon it over the asparagus in each casserole; top with some of the egg slices. Pour remaining crab mixture over the egg slices. Place half a cheese slice on top of each casserole; sprinkle each with bread crumbs and dot with butter. Bake 15 to 20 minutes, until mixture bubbles. Serves 4.

🔊 Citrus Salad with Creamy Dressing

1 16-ounce can grapefruit and orange sections, chilled
Salad greens
1 tablespoon mayonnaise or salad dressing
4 maraschino cherries

Drain grapefruit and orange sections, reserving syrup. Arrange fruit on salad greens on 4 serving plates. Combine 2 tablespoons of fruit syrup with mayonnaise; blend well. Spoon over salads. Top each with a cherry. Serves 4.

LESS-THAN-AN-HOUR DINNER FOR 4

Broiled Ham with Mustard Pickles

Work Schedule: 1. Preheat broiler and start ham broiling. 2. Prepare potato puffs according to package direc-

Creamy Onion Spinach
Frozen Potato Puffs
Cucumber Salad with
Tangy Sour Cream Dressing
Cherry–Almond Angel
Cake
Coffee   Tea

*Recipe follows

tions. 3. Cook spinach according to package directions. 4. When first side of ham is done, turn it over and broil other side. 5. Prepare cucumber salad and dressing. 6. Finish preparing spinach. 7. Make coffee. 8. The angel cake dessert may be prepared just before serving.

⋐ Broiled Ham with Mustard Pickles

1½ *pounds center-cut,*
   ready-to-eat ham, 1¼ to
   1½ inches thick
Mustard pickles

Preheat broiler. Slash edges of ham every 2 inches. Place ham on rack in broiler pan; set in broiler 3 inches from heat. Broil 10 minutes on each side. Cut ham into individual pieces. Serve immediately with mustard pickles or other condiments, if desired. Serves 4.

⋐ Creamy Onion Spinach

1 *10-ounce package frozen*
  chopped spinach
1 *teaspoon instant minced*
  onion
2 *teaspoons water*
1 *3-ounce package cream*
  cheese, at room
  temperature

Prepare spinach according to package directions. While spinach is cooking, soak onion in water 5 minutes. Drain any excess water from cooked spinach. Add rehydrated onion and cream cheese; stir constantly until cream cheese is entirely melted. Reheat if necessary. Serves 4.

⋐ Cucumber Salad with Tangy Sour Cream Dressing

1 *medium-sized cucumber,*
  sliced
Lettuce leaves
¼ *cup commercial sour*
  cream
½ *teaspoon dried dillweed*
½ *teaspoon prepared*
  horseradish
4 *stuffed green olives*

Arrange cucumber slices on lettuce leaves on 4 individual plates. Combine sour cream, dillweed, and horseradish in a bowl; blend thoroughly. Top each salad with some of the dressing and an olive. Serves 4.

❧ Cherry–Almond Angel Cake

1 21-ounce can cherry pie
filling
¼ teaspoon almond extract
4 slices angel food cake
(cut from small
packaged cake)
Roasted slivered almonds

Combine pie filling and almond extract in a saucepan. Heat over moderate heat (about 250° F.) just until thoroughly warmed, stirring constantly, 3 to 4 minutes. Serve warmed cherry filling on angel cake slices, topped with a few slivered almonds. Serve immediately. Serves 4.

Holiday Dinners

Cooking and serving your first big, traditional, family holiday dinner is an undertaking that's exciting—and rather awesome—to contemplate, even for those with some cooking experience. A holiday dinner presents complications: cooking in larger quantities than usual; having many different dishes to serve at the same time; and, most important, at the right moment producing a beautiful roast—juicy, crackling, golden brown, and done to a turn.

You need reassurance that the food will be perfect and the service will go smoothly. And so it will, if you begin planning by thinking your entire menu through from start to finish, from the shopping to the serving. Mentally prepare and serve each dish, and ask yourself all the crucial questions ahead of time. Decide what kinds of cooking utensils you'll need—what sizes and how many. Do you have enough serving dishes? Is your biggest platter large enough to hold the meat comfortably?

Plan to buy, borrow, or improvise everything you need in advance, so there will be no last-minute crises. Even though you may want a full traditional dinner with many vegetables and extras, if your cooking facilities, work space, and dining area are limited, it's best to limit your menu to suit them. Simplify whenever you can. Substitute an uncomplicated appetizer in the living room for a first course at the table; pass a relish tray and cranberry sauce instead of having a salad.

Let modern foods simplify preparations too. No one is apt to criticize (or even know the difference) if you use canned onions for a creamed onion dish, packaged bread stuffing as the basis for a giblet stuffing, or dehydrated potatoes for the mashed potatoes.

Holiday dinners traditionally offer a larger menu choice than usual company dinners. You need not serve everything on our menus. Tailor your dinner to your tastes and your family.

TIMING THE DINNER

There are many jobs that can be done well in advance of Christmas or Thanksgiving to lighten the work just before dinner. Although the over-all plans that follow are especially suited to Christmas, they can be used for any other traditional, big dinner.

At Least a Week Before the Dinner: Choose the menu you wish to use. Read over the recipes and be sure you understand them. Do you have the necessary equipment to prepare them? If not, perhaps you can borrow a mold or a roasting pan. Perhaps you will want to substitute a vegetable or make a family-favorite dessert rather than the ones we have suggested. Once the menu has been selected, make a market order from the recipe ingredients. Shopping will be easier if you break down the market order into categories—meat, dairy products, vegetables, fruits, canned foods, frozen foods, and staples. Check the pantry shelves for staples, those items you normally will have in good supply, before you shop. If you wish to serve wine with dinner, put that on the shopping list too.

Decide how and where dinner will be served. If possible, try to seat your guests at a table, even if it means putting two card tables together. If space is limited, the vegetables may be served from a small table or serving cart. The main dish may be carved in the kitchen or on a side table if there is not room on the dining table.

Plan the table setting. Be sure you have enough linens, china, silver, glassware, and serving dishes. Check the linens to see that they are clean and pressed. Check the silver and serving pieces and polish them if necessary. Plan a simple table decoration. Gay Christmas balls and a few sprays of pine in a low bowl make a pleasing arrangement. Candles are always a welcome addition. (Add candles to the shopping list if you are going to use them.) Work out a seating plan for the table. Place cards are fun; they eliminate confusion and they're decorative too.

Organize the kitchen. For a large dinner of this kind, you will need all the work space you can find. Put away any equipment that you will not need. Clear as much space as possible in the refrigerator and in the freezer section of the refrigerator.

ROAST TURKEY OR CHICKEN DINNER

Jellied Gazpacho
Sesame Wafers
Roast Turkey with
Sage Stuffing
or
Pineapple–Glazed Roast
Chickens with
Sausage-Rice Stuffing

Several Days Before Christmas:
1. Shop for staple items.
2. Order turkey or chickens from butcher.
Two Days Before:
1. Shop for rest of groceries.
2. If turkey is frozen, take it home and thaw as directed on wrapper. (The chickens probably will be fresh, not frozen.)

*Fluffy Stuffed Sweet
Potatoes
*Creamed Onions
*Broccoli Beurre Noir
*Citrus Salad
Rolls   Butter
*Pumpkin Pie
Coffee   Tea

3. Make clarified butter for Broccoli Beurre Noir.

The Day Before:
1. Prepare Jellied Gazpacho; cover and refrigerate.
*2. Make Sage Stuffing; cool, cover, and refrigerate.
3. Prepare Fluffy Stuffed Sweet Potatoes. Do not add marshmallows. Cover and refrigerate.
4. Prepare Creamed Onions; cool, cover, and refrigerate.
5. Prepare Pumpkin Pie. Cover and refrigerate.
6. Section grapefruit and slice oranges for the salad; cover and refrigerate.
7. Wash watercress; stand it in a bowl of ice water. Cover and refrigerate.

Early Christmas Morning:
*1. Wash and dry turkey; stuff with the Sage Stuffing. Start turkey roasting so it will be done about 30 minutes before serving time (see recipe).
2. Set table; arrange table decorations.
3. Get out china, glasses, and serving dishes.

About 1½ Hours Before Dinner:
1. Remove Fluffy Stuffed Sweet Potatoes and Creamed Onions from refrigerator. Top sweet potatoes with marshmallows.
2. Spoon Jellied Gazpacho into serving dishes; garnish and refrigerate.
3. Wash broccoli and separate into stalks.

About One Hour Before Dinner:
1. Arrange watercress on individual salad plates. Top with orange slices and grapefruit sections. Cover with plastic wrap and refrigerate.
2. Wrap rolls in foil to heat later.
3. Whip heavy cream for pie; spoon over filling and decorate top. Refrigerate until serving time.
4. Put dinner plates on range or another heated place to warm.

About 30 minutes Before Dinner:
*1. Remove turkey from oven and place on a large platter. Keep warm.
*2. *Increase* oven temperature to 350° F.
3. Place sweet potatoes and onion casserole in oven.
4. Heat water for broccoli.

About 20 Minutes Before Dinner:
1. Cook broccoli and drain well.
2. Top onion casserole with pimiento strips.
3. Place rolls in oven to heat.
4. Prepare Beurre Noir from clarified butter and toss with the broccoli in a warm serving dish.

*Recipe follows

5. Make coffee.
6. Fill water glasses on table.
Just Before Serving:
1. Pour dressing over salad and place on the table.
2. Set sherbet glasses filled with gazpacho on small plates with wafers on each and place on table.
3. Turn off oven and leave vegetables, including broccoli, and rolls in oven to keep warm while the gazpacho is being eaten.
4. Place butter on table.

Note: If you are serving the roast chickens instead of the roast turkey, eliminate the steps marked with an asterisk and substitute the following:

The Day Before:
1. Prepare Sausage-Rice Stuffing. Cool, cover, and store in the refrigerator.
Early Christmas Morning:
1. Wash and dry chickens; stuff with Sausage-Rice Stuffing. Start chickens roasting so they will be done about 30 minutes before serving time (see recipe). Keep stuffed chickens refrigerated until ready to start roasting them.
2. Prepare Pineapple Glaze.
About 30 Minutes Before Dinner:
1. After chickens are removed from oven, *reduce* oven temperature to 350° F. before putting in the sweet potatoes, onions, and extra stuffing.

Jellied Gazpacho

6 tablespoons cold water
2 packages unflavored gelatine
3 cups cocktail vegetable juice (about one 24-ounce can)
1½ teaspoons Worcestershire sauce
3 drops Tabasco
¼ teaspoon garlic powder
1½ tablespoons lemon juice
¼ teaspoon salt
3 tablespoons finely chopped onion

Place the water in a small saucepan. Sprinkle gelatine over water to soften. Place over boiling water and stir until dissolved. Combine vegetable juice, Worcestershire, Tabasco, garlic powder, lemon juice, and salt in a large metal bowl. Add gelatine and blend well. Place bowl in a larger bowl of ice water and stir until the consistency of unbeaten egg white. Stir in onion, green pepper, and cucumber. Chill in refrigerator until set. Spoon into sherbet glasses. Garnish each with a sprig of parsley and a lemon wedge. Serves 8.

1 large green pepper,
    coarsely chopped
1 large cucumber, peeled
    and coarsely chopped
    (about 1½ cups)
Parsley sprigs
Thin lemon wedges

❧ Roast Turkey with Sage Stuffing

1 12-pound frozen ready-to-
    cook turkey, thawed as
    directed on wrapper
Sage Stuffing (recipe follows)
Melted shortening or oil

Heat oven to 325° F. Rinse thawed turkey with cold water; drain and pat dry. Stuff neck cavity loosely with some of the stuffing. Fasten the neck skin to the back of the turkey with a skewer. Fold wing tips onto back. Stuff body cavity loosely with stuffing. Push drumsticks under band of skin at tail, if present, or tie them to tail with cord. Put remaining stuffing in a small casserole to be baked along with turkey the last hour of baking time. Place turkey on a rack in a shallow roasting pan, breast side up. Brush skin with melted shortening or oil. Do not add water to pan. Place in oven and roast, uncovered, 4½ to 5½ hours. Baste occasionally with pan drippings. Baste extra stuffing in casserole also after it goes into oven. When turkey is about two-thirds done, cut cord or band of skin at tail to release legs. Turkey is done when the thickest part of the drumstick feels very soft when pressed between protected fingers and the thigh joint moves freely. A meat thermometer placed in the thickest part of the thigh muscle should register 185° F. Remove turkey to a heated platter and keep warm. Serves 8 to 10, with leftovers.

Sage Stuffing

1 cup butter or
    margarine
¾ cup finely chopped
    onion
1 cup chopped celery
2 teaspoons salt
1½ teaspoons poultry
    seasoning
¼ cup chopped fresh
    parsley

Melt butter in saucepan over moderately low heat (about 225° F.). Add onion and celery; cook until onion is soft, stirring occasionally. Remove from heat; add salt, poultry seasoning, and parsley. Gradually pour butter mixture over bread cubes in a large bowl, stirring constantly to mix well. This will make a dry stuffing. For moist stuffing, add enough hot water or broth to moisten crumbs slightly. Cover and refrigerate until ready to use. Makes about 12 cups.

(Ingredients continued on page 136)

12 cups bread cubes
(use 2-to-3-day-old bread.
Cut off crusts and pull or
cut into ½-inch
pieces)

⌇ Pineapple-Glazed Roast Chickens

2 5-pound roasting
  chickens
Sausage–Rice Stuffing
  (recipe follows)
Pineapple Glaze (recipe
  follows)
Melted shortening or oil
4 pineapple rings
4 maraschino cherries

Heat oven to 375° F. Clean insides of chickens well. Stuff neck cavities loosely with some of the stuffing. Fasten neck skins to backs of chickens with skewers. Fold wing tips onto backs. Stuff body cavities loosely with more of the stuffing. Push drumsticks under band of skin at tail, if present, or tie them to tail with cord. Put remaining stuffing in a small casserole to be baked along with chickens the last half hour of baking time. Place chickens on a rack in a large shallow roasting pan, breast sides up. Brush skin with melted shortening or oil. Do not add water to pan. Place in oven and roast 2½ hours, or until done. Baste occasionally with pan drippings. Baste extra stuffing in casserole also after it goes into the oven. A half hour before chickens are done, cut cord or band of skin at tail to release legs. Brush with Pineapple Glaze. Continue to roast, brushing occasionally with more glaze. Fifteen minutes before chickens are done, arrange pineapple rings and maraschino cherries on breasts of chickens; brush with glaze. Chickens are done when the leg joints move freely. Remove chickens to a heated platter and cover with aluminum foil. Reduce temperature to 350° F. to heat vegetables. Serves 8, with leftovers.

Sausage–Rice Stuffing

2 8-ounce packages
  chicken-flavored rice
  and vermicelli mix
1 cup sliced pitted ripe
  olives
1 8-ounce package
  brown-and-serve frozen
  sausage links, thawed
  and thinly sliced
⅓ cup chopped fresh
  parsley

Prepare rice mix according to package directions. In a large bowl combine the cooked rice mixture, ripe olives, sausage, and parsley. Blend well. Cool. Cover and refrigerate until ready to use.

Pineapple Glaze

½ of a 6-ounce can frozen
   pineapple juice
   concentrate, thawed
2 tablespoons firmly
   packed dark brown
   sugar
2 tablespoons wine
   vinegar
¼ cup honey

In a small bowl combine pineapple juice concentrate, brown sugar, wine vinegar, and honey, and blend well. Brush on chickens ½ hour before they are done, basting frequently.

Fluffy Stuffed Sweet Potatoes

8 medium-sized sweet
   potatoes
⅓ cup butter or
   margarine, melted
1½ tablespoons firmly
   packed dark brown
   sugar
1 teaspoon salt
Few grains pepper
1 cup jarred
   marshmallow creme
8 marshmallows

Scrub potatoes with a brush. Place in a large flat baking pan and bake 40 to 45 minutes, or until fork-tender. Make a slit in the top of each potato. Scoop out pulp carefully. Reserve shells. Combine pulp, butter, brown sugar, salt, pepper, and marshmallow creme in the bowl of an electric mixer. Beat at medium speed until light and fluffy. Spoon mixture into potato shells. Place in two 1½-quart shallow baking dishes. Cover and refrigerate. About 1½ hours before serving time, remove potatoes from refrigerator. Slice marshmallows in half and place 2 halves on top of each potato. Bake at 350° F. for 20 to 30 minutes, or until heated through and marshmallows are melted. Serves 8.

Creamed Onions

24 small white onions,
   peeled
¼ cup butter or
   margarine
¼ cup flour
½ teaspoon salt
Few grains pepper
1 cup canned chicken
   broth
1 cup light cream
3 tablespoons grated
   Parmesan cheese
   (optional)

Place onions in a large saucepan; add boiling salted water to cover. Cover and simmer over moderate heat (about 250° F.) about 30 minutes, or until fork-tender. Drain well. Melt butter in a medium-sized saucepan over moderately low heat (about 225° F.); blend in flour, salt, and pepper, stirring constantly. Gradually stir in chicken broth and cream and cook, stirring constantly, until thickened and smooth. Stir in Parmesan cheese and parsley and blend well. Remove from heat. Add onions and pour mixture into a 1½-quart casserole. Cool. Store, covered, in refrigerator until ready to use. Heat oven to 350° F. Bake, covered, for 10 to 15 minutes, stirring once or twice. Arrange pimiento strips on top of cas-

¼ *cup chopped fresh*
parsley
Pimiento strips

serole and bake 10 minutes longer, or until heated through and sauce bubbles. Serves 8.

✺ *Broccoli Beurre Noir*

4 *pounds fresh broccoli*
Beurre Noir (recipe follows)

Cut off large leaves of broccoli and part of the lower stalks. Separate larger stalks into uniform-sized pieces. Place in boiling salted water to cover in a large saucepan. Cook, uncovered, 5 minutes; then simmer, covered, 5 to 10 minutes, or until fork-tender. Toss with Beurre Noir. Serves 8.

Beurre Noir

1 *cup butter*
2 *teaspoons lemon juice*

Melt butter over low heat (about 225° F.) in a small saucepan. Remove from heat and let stand a few minutes, allowing the milk solids to settle to the bottom. Skim the butter fat from the top, place in a container and refrigerate. When ready to use, place clarified butter in a small saucepan over moderately low heat (about 225° F.) and heat until melted and butter turns very dark brown, stirring constantly. Heat lemon juice in a small saucepan. Gradually stir lemon juice into butter. Pour over broccoli. Makes about 1 cup.

✺ *Citrus Salad*

2 *large grapefruit*
4 *navel oranges*
1 *large bunch watercress,*
washed and dried
8 *green maraschino*
cherries
Creamy French dressing

Peel and section grapefruit and place in a large bowl. Peel oranges and slice into thin rounds; add to grapefruit in bowl. Cover and refrigerate. Near serving time, arrange watercress on plates. Place orange slices and grapefruit sections on top. Place a maraschino cherry in the center of each plate. Refrigerate. At serving time pour creamy French dressing over each. Serves 8.

✺ *Pumpkin Pie*

1 *9-inch unbaked pastry*
shell (recipe on page 786)

Heat oven to 450° F. Prepare pastry shell. Place cream and milk in a small saucepan over moderately low heat

¾ cup heavy cream
¾ cup milk
3 eggs, well beaten
¾ cup firmly packed light
  brown sugar
¾ teaspoon ground
  cinnamon
½ teaspoon ground
  nutmeg
¼ teaspoon ground cloves
⅛ teaspoon ground
  ginger
1 tablespoon molasses
½ teaspoon salt
1¼ cups canned pumpkin
½ cup heavy cream

(about 225° F.) and heat until small bubbles appear around edge. Remove from heat. Mix eggs, light brown sugar, cinnamon, nutmeg, cloves, ginger, molasses, salt, and pumpkin in a large mixing bowl. Stir in cream and milk. Pour into the prepared shell and bake 10 to 15 minutes, or until edge of crust is lightly browned. Reduce temperature to 350° F. and continue baking for 25 to 30 minutes, or until a knife inserted 1 inch from the center comes out clean. Let cool on wire rack. Whip cream and use to decorate before serving.

ROAST FRESH HAM DINNER

Cream of Tomato Soup
  Crackers
*Roast Fresh Ham with
  Frosted Grapes
*Pan-Roasted Potatoes
*Whipped Turnip
  Casserole
*Savory Spinach
*Cranberry-Waldorf Salad
  with Fruit Dressing
  Rolls   Butter
*Steamed Holiday Pudding
  with Lemon Sauce
  Coffee   Tea

*Recipe follows

Several Days Before Christmas:
1. Shop for staple items.
2. Order the fresh ham from the butcher.
Two Days Before:
1. Shop for rest of groceries.
2. Prepare Steamed Holiday Pudding. Cool, cover, and refrigerate.
The Day Before:
1. Pare potatoes; place in a bowl covered with water and refrigerate.
2. Prepare Whipped Turnip Casserole and Savory Spinach to the point of baking. Refrigerate.
3. Prepare Cranberry-Waldorf Salad and refrigerate. Wash and dry salad greens and store in a plastic bag in refrigerator.
4. Prepare Fruit Dressing; cover and refrigerate in serving bowl.
5. Make Lemon Sauce. Cool, cover, and refrigerate.
Early Christmas Morning:
1. Start fresh ham roasting (see recipe) so it will be done about 30 minutes before serving time. It will carve more easily if it stands out of the oven at least 15 minutes.
2. Set table; arrange table decorations.
3. Get out china and serving dishes.
About 1 ½ Hours Before Dinner:
1. Remove turnip and spinach casseroles from refrigerator.

TIMING THE DINNER

2. Parboil potatoes for Pan-Roasted Potatoes as directed in the recipe. Drain and place in a shallow 2-quart cassserole.

3. Prepare Frosted Grapes.

About One Hour Before Dinner:

1. Unmold Cranberry-Waldorf Salad; garnish with greens and refrigerate.

2. Put potatoes in oven to roast with ham.

3. Start glazing ham.

4. Put dinner plates on range or another heated place to warm them.

About 50 Minutes Before Dinner:

1. Place turnip casserole in oven.

2. Wrap rolls in foil so they will be ready to heat later.

About 30 Minutes Before Dinner:

1. Remove ham and place on large platter. Keep warm.

2. Place spinach casserole in oven.

3. Prepare 2 cans tomato soup and keep warm over very low heat.

About 10 Minutes Before Dinner:

1. Place rolls in oven to heat.

2. Make coffee.

3. Fill water glasses on the table.

Just Before Serving Dinner:

1. Put soup and crackers on the table.

2. Put salad and dressing on the table.

3. Turn off oven and leave vegetables and rolls in the oven to keep warm.

4. Place butter on table.

While Dinner Is Being Served:

1. Heat Steamed Holiday Pudding as directed in recipe.

2. Heat Lemon Sauce over very low heat.

✃ Roast Fresh Ham with Frosted Grapes

1 12-to-14-pound fresh
   ham, bone-in
Salt and pepper
¾ teaspoon ground thyme
1 10-ounce jar apricot
   jam
Frosted Grapes (recipe
   follows)

Heat oven to 325° F. Sprinkle the fat side of ham with salt, pepper, and thyme and rub into the ham. Place on a rack in a shallow roasting pan and roast 22 to 24 minutes per pound, or until a meat thermometer inserted in meaty portion registers 170° F. A 12-pound ham will take about 4½ hours. After about 1½ hours of roasting, remove the rind from the end of ham, if present, and with a sharp knife score the fat into a diamond pattern.

[140]

About 30 minutes before the end of the roasting time, raise the oven temperature to 375° F. Place the apricot jam in a small saucepan. Place over moderately low heat (about 225° F.) and heat, stirring occasionally, until melted. To glaze, brush ham frequently with the melted apricot jam during the last 30 minutes of roasting. Let ham stand about 30 minutes before carving. Garnish ham platter with Frosted Grapes. Serves 8 to 10, with leftovers.

Frosted Grapes

2 bunches green grapes (about 2 pounds)
1 egg white, slightly beaten
Granulated sugar

Wash grapes and dry well. Separate grapes into small clusters. Brush grapes with egg white and roll in sugar to coat. Place on wire rack to dry for about an hour.

Pan-Roasted Potatoes

3½ pounds whole small potatoes or medium-sized potatoes, quartered
½ cup Roast Fresh Ham drippings
Salt

Wash, pare, and quarter potatoes. Cook in boiling salted water for about 10 minutes (do not fully cook); drain well. Place potatoes in a shallow 2-quart casserole. About 1 hour before serving time, spoon or pour off ½ cup of the Roast Fresh Ham drippings. Spoon drippings over potatoes and turn them to coat evenly. Roast in a 375° F. oven, uncovered, about 1 hour, or until potatoes are very brown, turning occasionally. Sprinkle lightly with salt before serving. Serves 8 to 10.

Whipped Turnip Casserole

3 pounds fresh yellow turnips
¼ cup butter or margarine
1½ tablespoons sugar
1½ teaspoons salt
Few grains pepper
3 eggs
1 cup soft bread crumbs
1½ teaspoons lemon juice

Wash turnips; pare and cut into about ½-inch slices. Cook, covered, in a large pot in a small amount of boiling salted water over moderate heat (about 250° F.) until tender, about 20 to 25 minutes. Drain thoroughly. Mash turnips while still very hot. Add butter, sugar, salt, and pepper. Beat with an electric mixer until blended. Add eggs, one at a time, and continue beating until soft and fluffy. Stir in bread crumbs and lemon juice. Pour into a deep 1½-quart casserole. If preparing ahead, cool and chill, covered, until the next day. To bake, place, uncovered, in a 375° F. oven for 50 minutes, or until top is lightly browned. Serves 8.

⧳ Savory Spinach

4 10-ounce packages
   frozen chopped spinach
1 4-ounce can sliced
   mushrooms
1½ cups commercial sour
   cream
1 package dry blue cheese
   salad dressing mix

Cook spinach according to package directions; drain very thoroughly. Drain mushrooms and reserve 2 tablespoons of the mushroom liquid. Combine the sour cream, salad dressing mix, reserved mushroom liquid, and cooked spinach. Pour into a deep 1½-quart casserole. Arrange mushrooms around the edges of casserole. If preparing ahead, cool and chill, covered, until the next day. To heat, cover with aluminum foil and place in a 375° F. oven for 25 to 30 minutes, or until bubbling. Serves 8.

⧳ Cranberry-Waldorf Salad with Fruit Dressing

2 cups cranberry juice
   cocktail
2 3-ounce packages
   lemon-flavored gelatin
1¾ cups cranberry juice
   cocktail
½ teaspoon salt
2 cups diced unpeeled
   red apples
1 cup diced celery
½ cup coarsely chopped
   walnuts
½ cup seedless raisins
Chicory (optional)
Fruit Dressing (recipe
   follows)

Pour the 2 cups cranberry juice cocktail into a saucepan; place over moderately low heat (about 225° F.) and heat to boiling. Remove from heat. Add gelatin and stir until dissolved. Stir in the 1¾ cups cranberry juice cocktail and salt. Chill until the consistency of unbeaten egg white. Fold in apples, celery, walnuts, and raisins. Pour into a 2-quart mold or individual molds. Chill until firm. Unmold and garnish with chicory, if desired. Serve with Fruit Dressing. Serves 8 to 10.

Fruit Dressing

1 cup mayonnaise
¼ cup orange juice
1 teaspoon grated orange
   peel

Combine mayonnaise, orange juice, and orange peel. Chill until serving time. Makes about 1 cup.

⧳ Steamed Holiday Pudding with Lemon Sauce

1 package spice cake mix
   (making 2 layers)
⅓ cup shortening

Grease 2 deep ½-quart ovenproof casseroles. Blend dry cake mix, shortening, eggs, and rum in the large bowl of an electric mixer. Beat 2 minutes on medium speed. Stir

4 eggs
1 tablespoon rum
1 cup finely cut-up pitted
  dates
1 cup finely cut-up figs
½ cup chopped pecans or
  walnuts
Lemon Sauce (recipe
  follows)

in dates, figs, and pecans. Divide batter between the 2 casseroles. Cover each tightly with aluminum foil. Place a rack in each of 2 Dutch ovens or other large pots. Pour water to a depth of 1 inch into each of the pots. Set puddings on the racks. Place over moderate heat (about 250° F.) and steam, covered, about 2½ to 3 hours, or until a cake tester inserted in the center of a pudding comes out clean. If necessary, add more water to the pot during steaming. Puddings may be made a few days in advance and stored, covered, in the casseroles in the refrigerator. To reheat puddings, place the covered casseroles on racks in large pots each containing 1 inch of water. Place over moderate heat (about 250° F.) and steam about 30 minutes. Unmold onto a serving plate. Serve warm with Lemon Sauce. If desired, garnish plate with holly. Each pudding serves 6.

Lemon Sauce

2 cups sugar
¼ cup cornstarch
¼ teaspoon salt
4 cups water
½ cup butter or margarine
½ cup lemon juice

Combine sugar, cornstarch, and salt in a saucepan. Add the water slowly, stirring constantly. Place over moderately low heat (about 225° F.) and cook, stirring constantly, until thickened and clear. Remove from heat and add butter and lemon juice. Stir until butter is melted. Serve warm. Makes about 5 cups sauce.

ROAST GOOSE OR ROAST DUCKLING DINNER

*Cranberry Frost
*Roast Goose with Sausage-
  Fruit Stuffing and
*Squash-Filled Orange Cups
  or
*Roast Duckling with
  Brown Rice Dressing
*Brussels Sprouts in
  Celery Sauce
*Glazed Carrots Lyonnaise
*Belgian Endive with
  Mustard Dressing
  Rolls   Butter
*Bûche de Noël
  Coffee   Tea

*Recipe follows

About Ten Days Before Christmas:
1. Prepare Bûche de Noël and freeze according to directions in recipe.
2. Shop for staple items.
3. Order goose or duckling from butcher.
Two Days Before:
1. If goose or duckling is frozen, pick it up and thaw as directed. (If birds will be fresh, pick up the day before and refrigerate until Christmas morning.)
2. Shop for rest of groceries.
*3. Cut up prunes and apricots for stuffing for goose.
The Day Before:
1. Place cranberry juice cocktail in refrigerator.
*2. Prepare stuffing for goose.
3. Prepare Glazed Carrots Lyonnaise. Cool and store, covered, in the refrigerator.
4. Wash and dry endive; store in a plastic bag in re-

frigerator. Clean and slice radishes. Make radish fans; store in a bowl of ice in refrigerator.

5. Prepare salad dressing and chill.

6. Prepare celery sauce for Brussels sprouts; cover and refrigerate.

7. Remove Bûche de Noël from freezer and thaw in refrigerator as directed in recipe.

*8. Prepare Squash-Filled Orange Cups; cover and refrigerate.

Early Christmas Morning:

*1. Stuff goose and start roasting so it will be done about 20 minutes before serving time.

2. Set table; arrange table decorations.

3. Get out serving dishes.

About 1½ Hours Before Dinner:

1. Arrange Belgian endive on salad plates with sliced radishes; refrigerate.

2. Scoop sherbet into sherbet glasses and place in freezer until serving time.

3. Remove Glazed Carrots and Squash-Filled Orange Cups from refrigerator.

About One Hour Before Dinner:

1. Cook Brussels sprouts. Heat celery sauce and add drained sprouts. Keep warm in top of double boiler over simmering water.

2. Put dinner plates on range or other warm place.

About 40 Minutes Before Dinner:

1. Place carrots and orange cups in oven to heat thoroughly.

About 20 Minutes Before Dinner:

*1. Remove goose from oven and place on a platter; keep warm.

2. Place rolls in oven to heat.

Just Before Serving:

1. Make coffee.

*2. Arrange orange cups on platter with goose.

3. Pour cranberry juice cocktail over sherbet and place on table.

4. Turn off oven and leave vegetables and rolls in oven to keep warm.

Note: If you are serving the Roast Duckling, eliminate the steps marked with an asterisk and substitute the following:

The Day Before:

1. Prepare Brown Rice Dressing. Cool, cover, and store in the refrigerator. Chop parsley for dressing and refrigerate.

2. Cut duckling into quarters if butcher has not done it for you.

About 2½ Hours Before Dinner:

1. Start roasting duckling so it will be done 10 minutes before serving time.

2. Prepare glaze for duckling.

About 40 Minutes Before Dinner:

1. Place rice dressing in oven to heat.

Just Before Serving:

1. Spoon rice dressing onto large platter and arrange duckling quarters on rice. Garnish platter with apple rings and kumquats. Cover and keep warm.

⤳ Cranberry Frost

1 quart lime sherbet
1½ cups bottled cranberry juice cocktail

About 1½ hours before serving time, place a scoop of sherbet in each of 6 sherbet glasses and place in freezer. Just before serving, pour about ¼ cup cranberry juice cocktail over sherbet in each glass. Serve immediately. Serves 6.

⤳ Roast Goose with Sausage-Fruit Stuffing

1 12-pound fresh or frozen goose, thawed
1 pound bulk sausage
¾ cup finely chopped onion
1 teaspoon dried rosemary leaves
½ teaspoon dried thyme leaves
1 bay leaf, crushed
1 clove garlic, minced
1½ cups coarsely cut-up dried prunes
1½ cups coarsely cut-up dried apricots
3 cups finely chopped green apples
½ cup canned chicken broth
2 tablespoons finely chopped fresh parsley

Rinse goose in cold water; drain and pat dry with paper towels. Remove most of the loose fat from the body cavity. Place sausage in a skillet over moderately high heat (about 325° F.) and cook, breaking sausage up with the back of a spoon. Cook until sausage has lost its pink color. Remove sausage and all but about 2 tablespoons of the fat. Reduce heat to moderately low (about 225° F.); add onion and cook until tender. Combine cooked sausage, onion, rosemary, thyme, bay leaf, garlic, prunes, apricots, apples, chicken broth, and parsley. Stuff neck cavity loosely with some of the stuffing. Fasten neck skin to the back with a skewer. Fold wing tips onto back. Stuff body cavity loosely with stuffing. Push drumsticks under band of skin at tail, if present, or tie them to tail. Place the goose on a rack in a shallow roasting pan, breast side up. Prick skin of goose at intervals with a fork; do not prick meat. Place, uncovered, in a preheated 450° F. oven and roast 10 minutes. Reduce heat to 325° F. and continue roasting, uncovered, for 4 to 4½ hours or until leg moves easily in its joint. Con-

Squash-Filled Orange Cups
(recipe follows)

tinue pricking skin every 30 minutes. Pour off fat as it accumulates. Any excess stuffing may be placed in a small casserole and baked, covered, during the last 1 hour of roasting time. Garnish platter with Squash-Filled Orange Cups. Serves 6 to 8.

⇜ Squash-Filled Orange Cups

4 medium-sized oranges, halved
3 12-ounce packages frozen mashed squash
¼ cup butter or margarine
1½ teaspoons salt
⅛ teaspoon pepper
¼ cup firmly packed light brown sugar
¼ teaspoon ground allspice
Mint leaves or watercress (optional)

Remove pulp from oranges and reserve for another use. Place squash, butter, salt, and pepper in a saucepan. Cover and cook over low heat (about 200° F.), stirring frequently, until squash is thoroughly heated, about 10 minutes. Stir in brown sugar and allspice. Spoon about ½ cup of squash into each orange shell. If preparing the day before serving, place in a shallow casserole; cool, cover, and chill until the next day. To reheat, cover casserole with aluminum foil and place in a 325° F. oven for about 40 minutes, or until thoroughly heated. If desired, garnish each cup with a mint leaf or watercress sprig. Arrange orange cups around goose on a large platter. Serves 8.

⇜ Roast Duckling with Brown Rice Dressing

2 5-pound ducklings, quartered
Salt and pepper
1 14-ounce jar spiced apple rings, undrained
¼ cup jarred kumquat syrup
½ cup light corn syrup
¾ cup jarred kumquats
Parsley sprigs
Brown Rice Dressing (recipe follows)
3 tablespoons brandy (optional)

Heat oven to 350° F. Wash duckling quarters and pat dry; sprinkle with salt and pepper. Place quarters, skin side up, on a rack in a shallow roasting pan. Prick the skin of duckling at intervals with a fork. Roast, uncovered, about 2 hours, or until skin is browned and duckling is tender. While duckling is roasting, combine ¼ cup of the syrup from spiced apple rings, the ¼ cup of the syrup from the kumquats, and corn syrup in a saucepan. Place over moderately low heat (about 225° F.) and bring to a boil. Simmer 5 to 10 minutes, stirring occasionally. Brush duckling occasionally with glaze during the last 30 minutes of roasting. Serve duckling on bed of Brown Rice Dressing. Garnish platter with parsley sprigs and kumquats, arranged on apple rings. If desired, flame with brandy just before serving. To flame brandy, heat 3 tablespoons of brandy in a small saucepan. Ignite it with a match and pour flaming brandy over duckling. Serves 6.

Brown Rice Dressing

1½ cups uncooked brown
  rice
3 cups canned chicken
  broth
1½ teaspoons salt
¼ cup butter or
  margarine
1 cup sliced blanched
  almonds
1 5-ounce can water
  chestnuts, drained and
  coarsely chopped
1½ teaspoons dried thyme
¾ teaspoon dried
  rosemary leaves
¼ teaspoon ground
  pepper
¼ cup finely chopped
  fresh parsley

Combine rice, broth, and salt in a saucepan. Place over moderately low heat (about 225° F.) and heat until boiling. Stir once. Cover and cook 45 minutes or until rice is tender and liquid is absorbed. Heat butter in a skillet over moderate heat (about 250° F.). Add almonds and cook, stirring occasionally, until almonds are browned. Combine cooked rice, almonds, water chestnuts, thyme, rosemary, and pepper. Place in a 2-quart shallow casserole. If preparing the day before serving, cool, cover, and chill until the next day. To reheat, cover casserole with aluminum foil and place in a 350° F. oven for about 40 minutes, or until thoroughly heated. Stir in parsley just before serving. Serves 6.

Brussels Sprouts in Celery Sauce

1½ cups diced celery
1 can condensed cream
  of celery soup
½ cup commercial sour
  cream
3 10-ounce packages
  frozen Brussels sprouts

The day before serving, cook celery in a small amount of boiling salted water until tender, about 5 minutes. Drain, reserving ⅓ cup of the cooking water. Combine soup and the reserved cooking water in a small saucepan. Place over moderately low heat (about 225° F.) until heated. Remove from heat and stir in sour cream and celery. Cool and chill covered until the next day. About an hour before dinner, cook Brussels sprouts according to package directions, using unsalted water. Drain well and add the celery sauce. Place over moderately low heat (about 225° F.) until gently bubbling. Place in the top of a double boiler and keep warm over hot water until serving time. Serves 6 to 8.

Glazed Carrots Lyonnaise

6 cups julienne carrots or
  carrot rounds
¼ cup butter or margarine

Cook carrots in a large saucepan in lightly salted, boiling water until tender, about 10 minutes for julienne strips or 20 minutes for the rounds. Melt butter in a skillet

3 medium-sized onions,
    thinly sliced
2 tablespoons sugar
2 teaspoons cornstarch
½ teaspoon salt
¼ teaspoon ground ginger
½ cup orange juice

over moderately low heat (about 225° F.). Add onions and cook, stirring occasionally, until tender. Combine sugar, cornstarch, salt, and ginger in a small saucepan; gradually add orange juice. Place over moderately low heat (about 225° F.) and cook, stirring constantly, until mixture is thickened and smooth. Combine drained carrots, cooked onions, and orange sauce, tossing to coat evenly. Cool and chill covered in a shallow casserole until the next day. To reheat, cover casserole with aluminum foil and place in a 325° F. or 350° F. oven for about 40 minutes or until thoroughly heated. Serves 6 to 8.

Belgian Endive with Mustard Dressing

½ cup vegetable oil
1 tablespoon prepared
    mustard
½ teaspoon salt
½ teaspoon paprika
3 tablespoons wine vinegar
6 small heads Belgian
    endive
1 cup thinly sliced radishes
6 whole radishes

Place the oil, mustard, salt, and paprika in a small bowl. Combine with a wire whip or rotary beater. Let stand at least 1 hour. Add the vinegar and beat vigorously with a wire whip or rotary beater. Pour into jar and chill until serving time. Wash endive and drain well. Cut each head in half lengthwise. Loosen each leaf at stem end; fan leaves out on individual salad plates. Divide sliced radishes among salad plates. Chill until serving time. Make several crosswise cuts almost to the bottom in each of the 6 radishes to form fans. Chill in ice water. At serving time, shake prepared salad dressing and pour a small amount over each salad. Garnish each salad with a radish fan. Serves 6.

Bûche de Noël

6 eggs, separated
1 cup granulated sugar
3 tablespoons unsweetened
    cocoa
1 tablespoon flour
Mocha Butter (recipe
    follows)
French Chocolate Icing
    (recipe follows)

Heat oven to 400° F. Grease a 15½-x-10½-x-1-inch jelly roll pan; line with waxed paper. Grease and flour paper. Beat egg whites in the large bowl of an electric mixer until stiff but not dry. Beat egg yolks in the small bowl of the electric mixer until thick; gradually add the sugar and continue beating until well blended. Combine cocoa and flour; fold into beaten egg yolks. Fold egg yolk mixture gently into beaten egg whites. Pour into prepared pan. Bake 12 minutes, or until a cake tester inserted in the center of the cake comes out clean. Immediately turn cake out onto a damp tea towel and peel off the waxed paper. Immediately roll up cake and towel, starting at a short end. Cool cake. Unroll cake and spread Mocha Butter to within ½ inch of edges. Reroll cake, starting at a short end. Place cake on a serving plate or if freezing, place on a large piece of heavy aluminum foil. Frost top and sides of cake roll with French Chocolate Icing; with a fork make lines in icing to resemble bark; outline circle on end of log. Chill one day before serving or if freezing, place unwrapped on a piece of heavy aluminum foil in freezer. When frozen, wrap in aluminum foil, and return to freezer. Remove Bûche de Noël from freezer the day before serving. Unwrap and place while still frozen on a serving plate; thaw overnight in the refrigerator. Let stand at room temperature about an hour before serving. Decorate with holly leaves, if desired. Cut in ¾-inch slices to serve. Serves 10 to 12.

Mocha Butter

½ cup softened butter or
  margarine
1 cup confectioners' sugar
2 egg yolks
4 teaspoons instant coffee
  powder or granules
1 tablespoon hot water

Work butter until creamy; gradually blend in confectioners' sugar until mixture is very smooth. Add egg yolks and blend thoroughly. Dissolve the coffee powder in the hot water. Add to butter mixture and beat until mixture is of a good spreading consistency.

French Chocolate Icing

2 1-ounce squares
  unsweetened chocolate
2 cups sifted confectioners'
  sugar
3½ tablespoons hot water
3 egg yolks
¼ cup softened butter or
  margarine
½ teaspoon vanilla extract

Place chocolate in the top of a double boiler over simmering water and stir until melted. Remove from heat and cool slightly. Alternately add the sugar and the water, beating well after each addition. Add egg yolks and beat until blended. Add butter and vanilla and beat with a rotary beater until smooth and creamy. If icing is too soft, place pan of icing over bowl of ice water and stir icing until it is the proper consistency for spreading.

CHAPTER V

THE WAY IT LOOKS

Perhaps because food is served three times a day—at least—the presentation of food as a creative expression is often overlooked. The same women who seek needlework, painting, and flower arranging as outlets for their creative urges sometimes give little thought to the imaginative presentation of food.

No matter how well cooked food may be, the first impression family or guests have of the meal put before them is the way it looks.

Food hastily dished into the same bowls or onto the same platters, meal after meal, can distract from the impression of goodness and abundance most mothers wish to provide their families. But surprises, a pretty table, and nicely arranged food can make an everyday meal a joy to sit down to—an atmosphere that makes mealtime something to get excited about.

It's true that mealtimes are often so hurried that the catsup bottle and the milk cartons do get put directly on the dinner table. Yet it doesn't take any extra time to place food on the right dish, to select place mats and napkins compatible to your china, and it takes very little time to pour milk into a pretty pitcher. It does require a little extra time to create a center-piece or to make roses out of radishes. But don't needlepoint and knitting and flower arranging and an art class take time?

Setting an interesting table and using imagination, even imagery, in serving meals for your family and guests gives more pleasure to more people and offers more challenge to the creator than many other forms of art. And it offers it oftener—three times each day.

Shapes, Patterns, Colors for a Pretty Table

Think of the elements of a table setting much as you would decorate a room. Think of the shapes, patterns, and colors of the china, tablecloth, place mats, and napkins you use. Unless you have a very skilled eye, avoid pattern (of plates) on pattern (of cloth). Pattern combinations are either very good or very bad. There's no in-between.

Start with a major color, treat it as your background color, and spark it with accents of color. Adding excitement to your table settings does not necessitate a shopping spree. You can do wonders with a can of spray paint; you can cut napkin rings from a paper-towel tube and make them any color you need. Spray old salt and pepper shakers to match and give faded napkins a new life by dipping them in a matching or contrasting liquid dye.

Look around your house for objects that can add color and design to your table. A figurine that's been gathering dust on a knickknack shelf might be surrounded with tiny colorful strawflowers for a change-of-pace centerpiece.

Old pitchers or mugs holding greens or candles can be grouped to form a charming table decoration.

Plain berry baskets sprayed with a shiny lacquer can be lined up in the center of the table and filled with nuts and dried flowers.

Serving Dishes

The first consideration in the attractive service of food is the choice of the dish—its size and shape and the treatment of the food to be put on it.

The dish should be neither so small that it looks as though the food will dribble off nor so large that the food looks lost. Round platters (called chop plates in china service) often are more suitable for many meats—ham slices, Swiss steak—than the traditional oblong platter.

Variety for a Party Table

You can let your imagination meet your needs—nothing is sacred about serving only cakes on cake stands. A creative hostess might use:

A giant clam shell to hold potato salad at an informal buffet.

Champagne and parfait glasses for adding serving appeal to ice cream, fruit cups, gelatine desserts, and canned fruit slices or halves.

Brown pottery custard cups to serve dips or canned pâtés, or for individual use in serving baked beans or onion soup.

Baskets of all shapes and sizes can be lined with foil or plastic wrap to hold French fried potatoes or onion rings, fried chicken, fish sticks, raw vegetables.

Little footed compote and nut dishes—all those odd little things that came as shower gifts or wedding presents—are useful for serving catsup, mustard, grated cheese, little crackers or croutons for soup. And what an air of "I care" they add to a table! One word of caution: high-salt foods, for example olives in brine, or sulfur foods, such as egg yolk, will darken silver. In general, never store food in silver containers.

Cake stands can give added importance to a molded salad, individual portions of fruit salad, an assortment of cookies, or fresh fruit.

Soup dishes—the old-fashioned shallow variety—are often much better proportioned for serving vegetables for two than a large vegetable bowl or dish.

Odd linen napkins not only add an air of nicety when used to wrap hot asparagus spears or ears of corn, but also serve to keep the food at the best temperature for eating.

Wooden chopping boards in an informal setting can be used to serve hot corn or loaves of French or pumpernickel bread. They also look bountiful laden with assorted cheeses for hors d'oeuvre or dessert.

A fondue dish need not be used rarely. It can be filled with foliage to make a pretty centerpiece. It can be used to serve hot sauces with meats or cold fudge to spoon over ice cream.

Trays are useful for serving napkin-wrapped rolls, bread slices, assorted bowls of relishes. Put the breakfast butter, jams, and salt and pepper shakers on one center tray; it saves table-setting steps.

The way we shape, cut, and arrange food too often becomes a matter of habit. When you feel a meal is falling into a monotonous pattern, try some of these changes of pace:

Tomatoes cut in wedges have a more attractive appearance than those sliced crosswise.

Cucumbers sliced extremely thin, Oriental-fashion, can be frozen and served lightly defrosted as an accompaniment to meats.

Green beans tied in bundles for cooking and served whole look prettier.

Zucchini sliced lengthwise to look like little boats is more attractive than the commoner round slices.

Liver and onions can look careless when served together. Try putting the onions in an individual soufflé dish or cream soup dish at one end of the platter.

Bread—plain white bread—looks more attractive when cut into triangles and arranged overlapping on a long narrow plate or board.

Hamburgers, usually rather lonely looking on a platter, can look abundant on a plank surrounded with a ring of vegetables circled with mashed potatoes. You can brush the tops of the potatoes with melted butter and run the plank under a hot broiler for a few minutes for a brown glaze.

Frankfurters look nicer when you cut little bias slits across them before cooking. Or they can be quite fancy when slit, stuffed with cheese or a slender pickle, and wrapped in bacon before broiling.

Mashed potatoes, heated for a few minutes in a buttered ring mold in the oven, can be turned out to hold a center portion of a second vegetable such as green peas or carrots.

A rolled pot roast might best be sliced in the kitchen and arranged in a circle on a round platter. Center a bowl of gravy in the ring of meat.

Food and Color

Few people would choose a menu of poached fish, mashed potatoes, and boiled onions even though it might taste good, for it's an extreme example of lack of color planning in food. No amount of the old standby parsley would do much for such a plate. Choosing food combinations that include a variety of color is the beginning of pretty food.

Garnishes add a bright last touch to whatever dish they adorn. They are as important to food as the right earring or scarf is to the total look of fashion.

In general, garnishes should be edible: radish roses circling a dish of coleslaw, spiced crab apples arranged around a baked ham, pickle fans at either end of a chicken-salad platter, a sunburst of pimiento strips atop a fish salad.

You can begin to experiment with garnishes by using parts of food that often get thrown away, such as scallion tops, which make lovely stems and leaves. Topped with a few carrot circles, it's quite easy to fashion a "bouquet" on the flat surface of a canned ham.

When peeling the breakfast oranges, start at the tip and cut the peel in a continuous spiral. Then, holding the tip flat on a counter, curl one end of the peel tightly to form the center of a flower. Wind the rest of the peel round and round it. (See Tomato Rose illustration on page 155.) You'll have a rose that can be stored in a plastic seal-top refrigerator dish to be used when the occasion demands.

Garnishes for Soups: For chilled soups, drop *1 rounded tablespoonful* of *commercial sour cream* or *whipped cream* into soup and sprinkle with *paprika* or *chopped chives.* On cucumber soup, float thin crosswise slices of *cucumber* or *ripe olive*, a sprig of *parsley* or *watercress*. On clear soup, float very thin crosswise slices of *lemon* cut into fancy shapes, such as those shown.

For any type of soup, make Carrot Curls. Scrape and wash a *small carrot;* slice lengthwise into very thin strips with a vegetable parer or sharp knife. Curl carrot strips and fasten with toothpicks; place in ice water until curls are crisp and hold their shape, about 1 hour. Remove toothpicks and float carrot curls in soup.

For hot soups, sprinkle *1 tablespoon grated American cheese* or *Parmesan cheese* on individual servings of soup. Or make Buttered Croutons. Remove crusts from slices of *bread*. Spread both sides with *soft butter;* cut into ½-inch cubes. Spread in a single layer on a cookie sheet; toast in 375° F. oven for 15 minutes. Seasoned Croutons may be made by removing crusts from *4 slices day-old bread*. Cut bread into ½-inch cubes and toss in ⅓ *cup French dressing* until coated on all sides. Toast as directed for Buttered Croutons. You may also float a few shreds of *turkey, chicken, ham,* or *smoked meat* over cream soup; sprinkle *sieved* or *finely chopped hard-cooked egg* over tomato or pea soup; or sprinkle canned *French fried onion rings* over cream soup.

Garnishes for Main Dishes: Stuff *pitted ripe olives* with short *carrot sticks* and arrange with *parsley* on a fish platter.

Drain *1 8-ounce can whole onions*. Dry onions on paper towels and dip the tip of each in *paprika*. Place onions on thick slices of *cucumber*. Arrange in groups on meat platter.

Open both ends of *1 16-ounce can jellied cranberry sauce* and gently slide sauce onto waxed paper. Slice crosswise into ½-inch slices; cut into fancy shapes with small cookie cutters. Serve with poultry.

Cut *canned pineapple rings* in half and arrange halves around base of a hot baked ham on a heat-resistant serving plate. Remove cores from *canned spiced crab apples;* fill each crab apple with *3 blanched almonds*. Place a filled crab apple in the center of each pineapple half. Place garnished ham in 400° F. oven for 15 minutes.

Crush *1 tablespoon dried rosemary leaves* and add to *1 cup dried prunes*. Cook prunes according to package directions. This is especially nice with lamb.

Use large, firm red tomatoes to make roses. Beginning at smooth end, peel tomato carefully so that peel does not break. Firmly wind one end of peel (see illustration below). Fasten end of peel in place with a piece of toothpick, if necessary. Group roses on platter around poultry, roast beef, or pork.

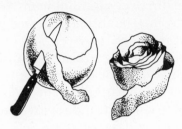

Use *canned preserved kumquats* that have no breaks in peel to make flowers. To make petals, make 5 evenly spaced cuts in stem end with point of sharp knife. Extend cuts two-thirds of the way down the sides, cutting just through peel. Carefully loosen peel with point of sharp knife and fold back. Cut a thin slice off blossom end of kumquat so that it will stand upright. Arrange in groups around poultry.

Make Flower Designs for Cold Ham, Poultry, or Fish by cutting thin crosswise slices of *carrot, turnip, white radish,* or *beet* into flower or petal shapes with hors d'oeuvre cutters, or by cutting around a pattern with the point of a sharp knife. Dip beets in *lemon juice* to prevent darkening. For flower centers use *whole cloves* or small shapes cut from vegetable slices, or both. Thinly peel a *cucumber* or *green pepper* and cut peel into stem and leaf shapes. Practice arranging flowers on waxed paper. When you have a design you like, transfer it to the cold meat or fish. Flowers may be set in glaze if desired.

To glaze a ham (same instructions apply for a 3- to 5-pound boneless turkey or a 4- to 5-pound poached salmon), chill a *3- to 5-pound ready-to-eat ham. Dissolve 1 4-serving package lemon gelatin* in *1 cup boiling water;* add *½ cup cold water.* Chill gelatin about 10 minutes, until it reaches the consistency of thick syrup, stirring occasionally. Place chilled ham on a cake rack over a tray; spoon gelatin over top and sides of ham in a thin, even layer. Do not refrigerate leftover gelatin. Chill ham until glaze sets, about 15 minutes. Spoon another thin layer of gelatin over ham; chill ham 15 minutes. Dip flower and leaf pieces (directions above) in gelatin and arrange on top and sides of ham. If flower slips, push back into place with toothpick. Chill ham 15 minutes. If necessary for a smooth surface, spoon another thin layer of gelatin over all. Chill ham until serving time. The gelatin that collects in tray may be strained, heated, and cooled to consistency of thick syrup and used for last layer.

Make a Lemon Basket by cutting a *lemon* lengthwise almost to center. Make crosswise cut down to first cut and remove ¼ of lemon. Repeat on opposite end. With point of sharp knife, cut around inside of rind on handle, being careful not to cut rind, and remove pulp. Scoop pulp out of basket. Fill with *chutney* and add a *sprig of parsley*.

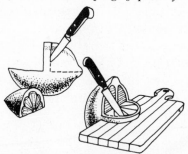

Garnishes for Sandwich and Cold-Meat Platters: Make a *Cucumber Flower* by cutting a 2-inch-long piece from one end of *cucumber*. Carefully scoop out pulp with a spoon, leaving peel ½ inch thick. To make petals, cut peel lengthwise into 5 equal sections, cutting to within 1 inch of end. Round off corners to form petals. Place in ice water for 1 hour to open petals. For center, use a 1-inch slice of *carrot*, cut with a small cocktail-size cutter.

Make Calla Lilies by cutting very thin slices from a *turnip.* Cut slices into 2- or 3-inch circles with a biscuit or cookie cutter. Roll each circle in the shape of a calla lily and fasten with a piece of toothpick. If turnip is too crisp to roll, leave at room temperature 15 to 20 minutes, until pliable. Place in cool water until ready to arrange on sandwich platter. Use long *carrot sticks* for stamens and *parsley* for foliage.

Cut *fresh cherries* in half and remove pits. Save stems. Place *1 teaspoon blue cheese spread* between the 2 halves and press halves together. Insert a stem in top. Arrange in groups at corners of plate.

Cut off top and base of *1 bunch celery* and carefully separate stalks to make celery rosettes. Wash stalks and pat dry. Add *1 tablespoon milk* to *8 ounces cream cheese* and beat until cheese is soft. Fill the center of each celery stalk with cheese. Regroup stalks, using smallest stalks in center, and press firmly into place. Wrap tightly and chill 2 to 3 hours. Shortly before serving, cut into crosswise slices.

To make pinwheels, use thin slices of round *bologna*. Cut each slice into quarters, cutting to within ½ inch of center. Fold every other corner to the center; fasten with a piece of colored toothpick and stick half a *stuffed olive* on top. Place each pinwheel on a *lettuce leaf*. Arrange 2 or 3 pinwheels at each end of platter.

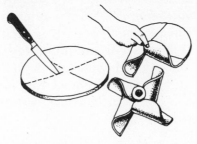

To make a Fancy Radish Rose, cut off the tip of a *medium-sized round radish*. Leave about 1 inch of the stem. Beginning at stem end, with sharp knife make horizontal slits ¼ inch deep and ½ to ¾ inch long, with smaller slits at tip end. Slant slits toward stem end so petals will point upward, as shown in illustration. For petals, slice *1 medium-sized* and *1 small radish* as thinly as possible. Insert slices in slits, using large slices at stem end and small slices at tip. Chill in ice water 1 hour. Arrange several roses in center of plate.

You can also make Cream Cheese Roses by dipping *firm, small tomatoes* in boiling water to loosen skin. Peel, then chill 30 minutes. With a fork beat *4 ounces cream cheese* until fluffy. Use a level, pointed teaspoonful of cream cheese for each petal. Hold tomato with rounded end at top. Press

teaspoon against side of tomato (step 1), then slide cheese onto tomato with a downward stroke of the spoon (step 2). Make 2 or 3 rows of petals, depending on size of tomato. Chill 1 hour. Place in center of platter on sprigs of parsley.

To make a Cherry-Tomato Mum use *1 small* and *3 medium-sized cherry tomatoes*. To make petals, cut each medium-sized tomato from blossom end almost to stem end, being careful not to cut through stem end of tomato; cut each half into 4 equal sections so that tomato will open to form 8 petals. Gently remove seeds and inner flesh of tomato. Cut small tomato in half as above; cut each half into 3 equal sections to form 6 petals. Remove seeds and inner flesh. Stack tomatoes with small tomato on top and fasten with a piece of toothpick. Cover with a damp paper towel until ready to use.

Jonquils can be made by cutting ⅛-inch-thick slices from a *turnip*. Make a pattern from stiff paper for the petal piece (see illustration); trace pattern onto turnip slice with point of a sharp knife. Cut out petal piece and cut a ½-inch-round hole in center. To form center of flower, cut a turnip slice into a circle 3 inches in diameter, then cut circle into 3 pie-shaped pieces. Roll each piece into a tube shape and slip small end through hole in petal piece. Trim small end so flower will stand upright. Use *3 short carrot sticks* for stamens. Place in cool water until ready to use.

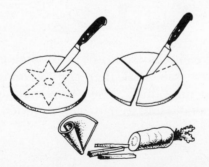

To make Frosted Grapes, snip *1 pound Tokay grapes* into small clusters; rinse and dry thoroughly. Beat *1 egg white* until foamy. Dip grapes in egg white, then in *granulated sugar*. Shake off excess sugar. Place clusters on a cake rack to dry.

Garnishes for Vegetables: Sprinkle green vegetables with Herbed Croutons (recipe on page 660) at serving time.

Sprinkle *grated orange rind* or *chopped mint* over *carrots* just before serving.

Crisp *bacon slices* or thin strips of *luncheon meat* may be arranged on top of *peas, green beans,* or *asparagus* at serving time.

Top individual servings of *asparagus* with a *green pepper* or *pimiento strip* before serving.

Sprinkle boiled *new potatoes* with *coarsely chopped parsley* or *fresh dill* just before serving.

Table Settings

There are "rules" for table setting, but what they amount to is making eating easy and pleasant for the diners. All the implements used should be convenient to reach, select, and use.

Beginning of meal | Ready for dessert and beverage | Placement of serving pieces

Without help in the kitchen and dining room it really isn't possible to serve a formal dinner. Don't attempt one. There are several acceptable alternatives; the fact that they are less formal doesn't mean that they are necessarily casual. That's up to you.

A sit-down dinner can be served with ease to six people or less. For sufficient room at the table, you'll need at least twenty-four inches for each place setting. In the traditional table setting (see sketch), forks are at the left, spoons and knives at the right; the only exception is the fish fork, placed at the right. Sharp edges of knives are turned toward the plate. The silver is set out in order of use; pieces used first are placed farthest from the plate. If salad is a separate course, include a salad fork, as shown here; if it is part of the main course, one dinner fork is sufficient. If you use steak knives, set the table with the regular knife too. Place the dessert silver (spoon or fork, or both) near the head of the plate and parallel to the table edge; or plan to bring the silver to the table when dessert is served, on a tray or with individual dessert portions. Spoons for after-dinner coffee or tea are brought to the table at the end of the meal in place on each cup and saucer. (See sketch.)

Silver and plates should be lined up evenly on the table about one inch from the edge. The butter plate, with the spreader across the outer edge (never with the blade resting in the center of the plate), is placed in front of the forks; the water glass, in front of the knives and spoons. If there's a wineglass, it should stand to the right of the water glass. Place napkins to the left of the forks, folded in oblongs, with the open corner at the lower right, next to the plate.

Serving pieces should be at the right of the person who will be serving. Two pieces used together look best parallel to each other. (See sketch.) Put out salt and pepper servers, trivets if necessary.

A serving cart or table is helpful beside the hostess's chair. For serving, it can hold the salad or dessert, tea or coffee, with all necessary dishes, silver, and serving pieces. When clearing the table, salt and pepper servers, relish trays, and other serving dishes can be placed on the top shelf; place the dishes on the lower shelves—never stack them. The cart can also hold a pitcher of ice water.

Just before your guests come to the table, fill the water glasses three-quarters full, put out pats of butter on the butter dishes, a bread or roll tray, and relishes. If you're serving the first course at the table, you can set this out too, unless it's a hot soup—this should be served when everyone is seated.

Sit-down dinners are easier to serve if the first course and/or dessert is served in the living room from a side table or tray. It is traditional to have after-dinner coffee in the living room too.

Your method for serving the main course depends a good deal on your menu. If it's a one-dish dinner (a stew, a casserole), you may want to serve it yourself. For other meals you may want to share the work with your husband. If he is carving (see sketch for alternate placements of the carving set), he may serve the vegetables too while you serve the salad. Plan whatever seems most comfortable—but have a plan and use it.

Buffet dinners are the solution when the guest list is long and space and help are limited. They can be served in a number of ways, with the food set out in one place and seating in another. All three buffet courses can be served from the sideboard or dining table or a living-room table—any large surface. In this arrangement your guests make three trips to the buffet.

Seating may be at the dining table, if it is large enough and you haven't already used it to hold the food. Or you may set up card tables in the living room. In either case, the tables are set as they would be for a sit-down dinner, with everything in place for service except the dinner plates.

Individual tray tables may also be used; these are not set. Or you can set a tray for each guest. As they serve themselves, guests place their filled plate on a tray and carry it into the living room.

Serving methods can be varied in a number of ways. You may want to serve your guests the first course and dessert—either from a serving cart in the living room or seated at the dining table—and have them help themselves to the main course set on the sideboard. Or you may want to serve your guests all three courses from the sideboard and then eat at the dining table.

Arrangement of the buffet spread should be planned for ease of service. From the starting point a possible order may be plates, food and relishes, salad, buttered rolls, silver, and napkins (if they aren't already at place settings), cups and saucers, beverage. Pieces of flatware should be placed in a row, never piled one on top of the other; serving pieces belong near the food to be served.

Table decoration is a matter of personal taste, but there are several points that are pertinent for your guests' enjoyment and comfort.

At sit-down dinners, centerpiece flowers should be low enough so that your guests can converse across the table with ease. Place cards can serve several purposes, especially if you are entertaining business friends. They "introduce" people who don't know each other and ensure that your guests will be seated in a way that provokes interesting conversation. Candles are a lovely addition to any table. Be sure the flames are higher than eye level. Light them just before you announce that dinner is served.

CHAPTER VI

APPETIZERS

Appetizers should be just what the name implies—tasty little morsels that whet the appetite but don't kill it. Serving a variety of three, two cold and one hot, is ample before a meal. It's best not to duplicate flavors; for example, if the hot appetizer is cheese puffs, the cold one should not also be cheese. When you have a dinner to prepare and serve, rely on the dips, dunks, and spreads that guests can help themselves to; they're easy and popular. It's thoughtful to plan one appetizer for weight-conscious people; serve some crisp cold vegetables, along with chips, for dunking or set out bowls of radishes or cherry tomatoes for people who can't resist nibbling but dread the weight gain.

Since at a large cocktail party appetizers may turn out to be the only meal people eat, it's a good idea to plan heavier hors d'oeuvre and canapés in quantity. You might center the appetizer table with a thinly sliced ham surrounded by small rye bread slices or a chafing dish of hot meatballs. Many of the hot canapés can be made up ahead of time and baked or broiled just before serving. You'll also find some in this chapter that can be frozen and reheated at the time of the party.

It's always important to take care with the appearance of any food, but it's perhaps most important that appetizers look appetizing. Select plates or trays or boards or bowls that fit the food you're serving and take time to garnish them and arrange them nicely. They'll taste infinitely better.

Dips and Spreads

There are excellent prepared spreads and dips available on the market. Arrange them in their own containers on a tray or spoon them into pretty bowls and surround them with chips of assorted flavors and raw vegetables. Or prepare a specially flavored dip of your own choosing from the following recipes.

❧ Avocado Dip

4 ripe avocados
3 to 4 cloves garlic
½ teaspoon dried red pepper flakes
½ cup lemon juice
1 cup olive oil
½ teaspoon salt

Peel and pit avocados (save one pit). Chop the pulp coarsely. Place half the avocados and about half of each ingredient in the top of an electric blender. Blend 30 seconds on high speed. Remove purée and repeat, using remaining ingredients. Mix both batches together and place the reserved pit in center of mixture. Cover and chill in the refrigerator for several hours. Serve with corn chips. Makes about 2 cups.

❧ Cubed Roast Beef with Horseradish–Whipped Cream Dip

1 cup chilled heavy cream
¼ cup prepared horseradish
Cold roast beef, cut into bite-sized cubes

Whip cream until stiff; fold in horseradish. Chill about ½ hour before serving. At serving time, place dip in a bowl in center of a large platter and surround with cubes of cold roast beef on toothpicks. Makes about 2 cups dip, or serves 8 to 10.

❧ Hot Curried Crabmeat Dip

2 3-ounce packages cream cheese, softened
1 6-ounce package frozen crabmeat, thawed and drained or 1 6½-ounce

(Ingredients continued on page 164)

Heat oven to 350° F. Combine all ingredients. Put in a small casserole or soufflé dish 4 to 5 inches in diameter. (This much can be done ahead.) Bake 15 to 20 minutes, until bubbly and lightly browned. Serve hot with raw vegetables or whole-wheat wafers for dipping. Makes 1½ cups.

can crabmeat, drained
3 tablespoons lemon juice
¼ to ½ teaspoon curry powder

⤜ऽ Chick-Pea Dip

1 cup dried chick peas
2 teaspoons salt
¾ cup canned ground sesame
    seeds (tahini)
¼ cup olive oil
⅓ cup lemon juice
1 teaspoon dried mint leaves
1 to 3 cloves garlic, peeled
    and crushed

In a large bowl cover dried chick peas with water and soak overnight. Drain peas. In a medium-sized saucepan combine soaked chick peas, 1½ quarts fresh water and 1 teaspoon of the salt. Place over moderately high heat (about 275° F.); cover and bring to a boil. Cook until peas are very tender, about 1 hour. Drain peas and reserve the liquid. Grind chick peas or press them through a food mill. In a bowl mix together ground peas, the remaining 1 teaspoon salt, sesame seeds, olive oil, lemon juice, mint leaves, 1 to 3 cloves (according to taste) crushed garlic; add enough (about 1 cup) of the reserved chick-pea liquid to make a creamy consistency. Blend well. Cover and chill at least 1 hour before serving. Makes 3 cups.

⤜ऽ Sherry Cheese Dip

1 cup ricotta cheese
¼ cup crumbled blue cheese
¼ pound (1 cup) shredded
    Port du Salut cheese
2 tablespoons snipped chives
¼ teaspoon dried tarragon
    leaves
5 tablespoons dry sherry
½ cup commercial sour cream
Raw vegetables or potato
    chips

Beat ricotta cheese with an electric mixer until smooth. Add blue cheese and beat until blended. Mix in Port du Salut, chives, tarragon, and sherry. Fold in sour cream. Chill. Serve as a dip with raw vegetables and potato chips. Makes about 2½ cups.

⤜ऽ Hot Jalapeno Bean Dip

2 10½-ounce cans jalapeño
    bean dip
2 tablespoons Worcestershire
    sauce
About ⅛ teaspoon Tabasco

Place bean dip in a heavy, medium-sized saucepan or fondue pot; stir in Worcestershire, Tabasco and cumin. Heat over moderate heat, stirring occasionally. When hot and bubbly, stir in cheese. Serve hot with raw vegetables and *tostadas* or corn chips. Makes 2⅓ cups dip.

¼ teaspoon ground cumin
  seed (optional)
⅔ cup shredded Monterey
  Jack or Muenster cheese

✑ Curried Vegetable Dip

1 8-ounce package cream
  cheese, at room
  temperature
1 cup commercial sour cream
½ teaspoon finely crumbled
  dried tarragon
1 teaspoon ground dillseed
1 teaspoon curry powder
1 teaspoon soy sauce
3 teaspoons lemon juice
Raw vegetables

Beat together cream cheese and sour cream. Stir in tarragon, dillseed, curry powder, soy sauce, and lemon juice. Chill until ready to serve. Serve as a dip for crisp raw vegetables. Makes about 2 cups.

✑ Fruits with Spiced Sour Cream Dip

1 cup commercial sour cream
2 tablespoons firmly packed
  light brown sugar
¼ teaspoon ground cinnamon
4 navel oranges
3 bananas
Bottled lemon juice
1 13¼-ounce can pineapple
  chunks, drained and
  chilled
1 10-ounce container pitted
  dates

Combine sour cream, brown sugar, and cinnamon; chill 1 to 2 hours. Peel oranges with a sharp knife, removing all the white membrane. Cut crosswise into ¼-inch slices; cut each slice in half. Peel bananas and cut into 1-inch diagonal slices; dip in lemon juice to prevent browning. Put sour cream mixture in a small dish in the center of a large platter. Arrange orange slices, banana pieces, pineapple chunks, and dates in groups around the dip. Other fruits in season, such as strawberries, peach slices, or melon wedges, may be used. Serves 8.

✑ Fresh Raw Vegetables with Low Calorie Dip

½ cup chili sauce
1 cup Low-Calorie Sour
  Cream (recipe below)
1½ teaspoons Worcestershire
  sauce

In a small bowl combine the chili sauce, low-calorie sour cream, Worcestershire sauce and horseradish. Blend well. Chill until ready to serve. Center the bowl on a serving platter and surround it with any of the raw vegetables listed. Recipe makes 1½ cups dip.

(Ingredients continued on page 166)

1½ teaspoons prepared
    horseradish
Cherry tomatoes, thin slices
    zucchini, cauliflowerettes,
    carrot strips, celery
    sticks, raw mushrooms,
    radishes, pepper strips

✑ Low-Calorie Sour Cream

1 *8-ounce container pot*
    cheese
¾ *cup buttermilk*
Few grains salt

Combine pot cheese, buttermilk and salt in the container of an electric blender. Blend mixture at high speed until smooth and creamy. Once during blending, stop blender and scrape down sides of the container with a rubber spatula. Refrigerate in a covered container. Mixture will keep for several days. Makes about 1½ cups.

Appetizer Spreads

Spreads are most suitable for parties small enough that each person can comfortably reach the tray and spread his own. You can spread several crackers to start serving and let guests take over as the party progresses.

✑ Beef Tartare

1 *pound lean ground round*
¼ *cup very finely chopped*
    onion
1 *tablespoon dried parsley*
    flakes
2 *egg yolks*
1 *teaspoon Worcestershire*
    sauce
¼ *teaspoon salt*
Few grains pepper
½ *teaspoon prepared*

Combine beef, onion, parsley flakes, the 2 egg yolks, Worcestershire, salt, pepper, and mustard in a medium-sized bowl. Toss lightly with a fork until combined. Stir in capers. Press mixture lightly into an oiled 2½-cup mixing bowl. Refrigerate, covered, until well chilled, at least 3 hours. Unmold in the center of a large serving platter. Make a slight indentation on the top with the back of a spoon. Slip the remaining egg yolk into the indentation. Arrange chopped parsley in a ring around the egg yolk. Butter the party rye lightly and arrange slices around the beef on the platter. Serve im-

mustard
1 tablespoon capers, well-
    drained
1 egg yolk
1 tablespoon very finely
    chopped fresh parsley
⅓ cup softened butter or
    margarine
1 8-ounce loaf sliced party
    rye bread

mediately with a knife for spreading. Makes about 3 dozen canapés.

❧ Ginger–Chicken Spread

2 3-ounce packages cream
    cheese, at room
    temperature
2 4¾-ounce cans chicken
    spread
4 teaspoons finely chopped
    candied ginger
¼ cup slivered almonds
Crackers

Combine all ingredients. Chill at least 1 hour. Serve as a spread with crackers. Makes about 2 cups.

❧ Liver Pâté Spread

2 tablespoons butter or
    margarine
¼ cup finely chopped onion
4 slices crisp-cooked bacon,
    crumbled
1 4½-ounce can liver spread
1 tablespoon brandy
¼ teaspoon dry mustard
¼ cup chopped fresh parsley
Caraway crackers

Melt butter in a small skillet over moderate heat (about 250° F.). Add onion and brown lightly. Place in a small bowl. Add crumbled bacon, liver spread, brandy, and mustard. Blend well. Oil a small 1-cup bowl well and pack mixture into it. Chill several hours, or overnight. Unmold onto a large plate. Cover with chopped parsley. Surround with caraway crackers. Makes one 3-inch mound. Serves 4 to 6.

❧ Party Pâté

1 envelope unflavored
    gelatine
¾ cup water
1 can condensed beef
    consommé, undiluted

Sprinkle gelatine over water and place over moderately low heat (about 225° F.), stirring occasionally until dissolved. Remove from heat; stir in consommé, lemon juice, and salt. Pour gelatine into a 1-quart mold to a depth of ½ inch and chill until set. Mash

1 teaspoon lemon juice
¼ teaspoon salt
2 8-ounce packages
   Braunschweiger liver
   sausage
1 tablespoon anchovy past
3 tablespoons cognac
Crackers

Braunschweiger and blend in anchovy paste and cognac. Shape into a ball and flatten ball on one side. Place in mold over gelatine, rounded side down, leaving about ½ inch space between pâté and edge of mold. Pour remaining gelatine around edge; cover and chill several hours, until firm. Unmold on serving plate and serve in small wedges with crackers. Serves 12.

Shrimp Paste

2½ cups water
2 teaspoons salt
2 teaspoons lemon juice
1 pound raw shrimp,
   shelled and deveined
⅓ cup crumbled blue cheese
1 cup mayonnaise
1 tablespoon prepared
   horseradish
Juice of ½ lemon
1 teaspoon Worcestershire
   sauce
2 drops Tabasco
Crisp crackers

Combine the water, salt, and the 2 teaspoons lemon juice in a large saucepan. Bring liquid to a boil. Add shrimp and return to boiling point. Reduce to moderately low heat (about 225° F.); cover and cook 3 to 5 minutes, or until shrimp are tender. Drain shrimp; cool. Grind shrimp and blue cheese together, using the fine blade of the grinder. Add mayonnaise, horseradish, lemon juice, Worcestershire sauce, and Tabasco to shrimp mixture. Combine thoroughly. Chill until ready to use. Serve with crisp crackers as a spread or dip. Makes 2⅓ cups.

Cheese Logs and Balls

Cheese logs and balls, centered on a wooden tray and surrounded by assorted crackers, are particularly attractive to serve for a large party.

Holiday Cheese Ball

6 ounces blue cheese, at room
   temperature
2 5-ounce jars process
   Cheddar cheese spread, at
   room temperature
4 3-ounce packages cream
   cheese, at room
   temperature

Place cheeses, onion, and Worcestershire sauce in the large bowl of an electric mixer. Mix until thoroughly blended. Stir in ½ cup of the pecans and ¼ cup of the parsley. Line a 1½-quart mixing bowl with foil or plastic wrap. Pack the cheese mixture in the bowl, smoothing the top flat; the flat part will be the bottom when the cheese ball is turned out. Cover tightly with foil or plastic wrap. Refrigerate about 4 hours or overnight, until

2 tablespoons grated onion
1 teaspoon Worcestershire
   sauce
1 cup ground pecans
½ cup finely chopped fresh
   parsley
Crackers

thoroughly chilled and hardened. About 1 hour before serving, roll the cheese ball in a mixture of the reserved ½ cup ground pecans and the ¼ cup chopped parsley. Pat the pecan–parsley mixture on with the hands to cover the cheese ball evenly. Place cheese ball on a platter and surround with a variety of crackers. If desired, cheese mixture may be shaped into three balls, wrapped, and chilled. Roll one ball in the chopped pecan–parsley mixture, another in chopped well-drained pimiento, and the third in finely chopped ripe olives. The mixture may also be shaped into rolls about 1½ inches in diameter before chilling. Serves 10 to 12.

◆§ Cheese Log

2 cups (½ pound) Cheddar
   cheese, coarsely shredded
1 hard-cooked egg, finely
   chopped
½ cup finely crushed soda
   crackers
¼ cup commercial sour cream
¼ cup finely chopped stuffed
   olives
2 tablespoons minced green
   pepper
2 tablespoons drained sweet
   pickle relish
1 tablespoon grated onion
2 teaspoons Worcestershire
   sauce
⅛ teaspoon Tabasco
¼ cup finely chopped fresh
   parsley
Melba rounds

Combine all ingredients except parsley in a bowl; shape into a roll about 2 inches in diameter. Roll in parsley. Wrap in plastic wrap and chill about 2 hours in refrigerator. Serve with Melba rounds. Serves 12.

◆§ Stuffed Gouda Cheese

1 Gouda cheese (about 10
   ounces), at room
   temperature
¼ cup dry sherry
½ teaspoon prepared
   mustard

(Ingredients continued on page 170)

Cut a wedge-shaped circle about 3 inches wide from top of cheese. Carefully scoop out cheese with a melon ball scoop, leaving a shell about ¼ inch thick. Chop cheese coarsely and measure. Measurements for wine and seasonings are for 1 cup tightly packed cheese. Increase amounts proportionately if there is more than 1 cup.

APPETIZERS

½ teaspoon Worcestershire
   sauce
⅛ teaspoon salt
⅛ teaspoon onion salt
⅛ teaspoon garlic salt
Few grains cayenne pepper

Place all ingredients in a bowl and blend. Spoon back into shell, replace top, and chill. Bring to room temperature before serving. Serves 4 to 6.

✑ Deviled Cream Cheese Balls

1 8-ounce package cream
   cheese, at room
   temperature
1 2¼-ounce can deviled ham
1 8½-ounce can pineapple
   tidbits, drained
Chopped fresh parsley or
   snipped chives

Blend cream cheese and deviled ham. Chill. Place pineapple tidbits on paper towels to drain well; cut each piece in half crosswise. Roll a spoonful of the cheese mixture around each pineapple piece to form a 1-inch ball. Chill. Roll balls in the chopped parsley or chives and chill until ready to serve. Serve on toothpicks. Makes about 30 cream cheese balls.

✑ California Cheese Rolls

1 cup (¼ pound) shredded
   American cheese, at room
   temperature
¼ pound blue cheese, at room
   temperature
1 3-ounce package cream
   cheese, at room
   temperature
2 tablespoons port wine
¼ cup finely chopped
   walnuts
½ teaspoon grated onion
2 tablespoons finely chopped
   fresh parsley
Few grains cayenne pepper
Crisp crackers

Blend cheeses thoroughly with an electric mixer. Add wine, nuts, onion, parsley, and cayenne. Chill until firm enough to shape into rolls. Form 2 rolls, about 1¼ inches in diameter. Wrap each in waxed paper and chill overnight or longer. To serve, unwrap rolls; slice with a sharp knife and arrange slices on crackers. Serves 8 to 10.

✑ Molded Roquefort Crème

¼ cup water
1 envelope unflavored
   gelatine
¼ pound Roquefort or blue

Pour the water into the top of a double boiler; sprinkle with gelatine and blend together. Place over simmering water and heat until gelatine is dissolved. In a bowl mash Roquefort cheese and cream cheese and beat together

cheese, at room
temperature
1 3-ounce package cream
cheese, at room
temperature
2 tablespoons white vinegar
2 tablespoons dried parsley
flakes
2 teaspoons onion salt
2 tablespoons chopped
pimiento
1 cup well-drained, grated,
unpeeled cucumber
1 cup heavy cream, whipped

until blended. Add vinegar, parsley, and onion salt; mix until blended. Stir in dissolved gelatine. Fold in pimiento and cucumber, then the whipped cream. Pour into a 3-to-4-cup mold and chill until set. The Roquefort Crème may be unmolded and used in a variety of ways. For an hors d'oeuvre, unmold on a plate and surround with crackers. Or unmold on salad greens garnished with tomato and cucumber slices and serve as a salad on a buffet table with cold meats. It may be cut into small wedges, arranged on a bed of lettuce, garnished with cucumber and tomato, and served with Melba rounds as a first course. Serves 8 to 10 as an hors d'oeuvre.

Finger-and-Toothpick Hors d'Oeuvre

These are favorites at all parties—easy to pick up and eat in one bite.

❧ Bacon Curls

2 tablespoons lemon juice
1 tablespoon Worcestershire
sauce
1 tablespoon seasoned salt
2 5-ounce cans water
chestnuts, drained
8 slices raw bacon, cut in half
crosswise

Mix lemon juice, Worcestershire, and seasoned salt; add water chestnuts and marinate for 10 minutes. Drain; wrap a half slice bacon around each chestnut and secure with a toothpick. Arrange on a rack in a broiler pan. Place in a preheated broiler about 3 to 4 inches from heat and broil about 2 minutes on each side, or until bacon is crisp. Serves 4 to 5.

❧ Hot Bacon–Onion Snacks

¼ cup grated onion
½ cup mayonnaise or salad
dressing
6 slices crisp-cooked bacon,
crumbled
¼ teaspoon Tabasco
½ teaspoon paprika
⅛ teaspoon salt
Few grains pepper
48 shredded whole wheat
wafers

Combine onion, mayonnaise, bacon, Tabasco, paprika, salt, and pepper. Drop a rounded ½ teaspoon of the mixture on each wafer. Place on broiler pan. Broil in preheated broiler 2 inches from heat 4 to 5 minutes. Makes 48 snacks.

APPETIZERS

ᏹᏣ *Crisp Cheese Appetizers*

1 cup plus 2 tablespoons
  sifted all-purpose flour
¼ teaspoon baking powder
½ teaspoon salt
6 tablespoons butter or
  margarine
1 cup shredded Cheddar
  cheese, lightly packed
3½ tablespoons water

Place flour, baking powder, and salt in a large mixing bowl. Cut in butter with a pastry blender or two knives until mixture looks like coarse meal. Stir in shredded cheese. Sprinkle water over mixture while tossing lightly with a fork. Pack together. Form into two bars about 3 inches by 6 inches. Wrap in waxed paper and chill at least 2 hours, or overnight. Heat oven to 425° F. Cut ¼-inch slices from the bars with a serrated potato slicer. Place on a lightly greased cookie sheet and bake 10 to 15 minutes, until golden brown. Makes 40 appetizers.

ᏹᏣ *Cheese-Stuffed Bologna Wedges*

2 3-ounce packages cream
  cheese, at room
  temperature
6 slices bologna
6 slices cooked salami

Spread some of the cream cheese on three slices of the bologna. Cover each with a slice of salami; spread salami slices with more of the cheese. Add a slice of bologna to each stack and spread bologna slices with the remaining cheese. Top each stack with remaining salami slices. Wrap stacks individually in waxed paper or plastic wrap. Chill several hours or overnight. Cut each stack into 8 wedges and serve wedges with toothpicks. Makes 24 wedges.

ᏹᏣ *Cheese-Stuffed Deviled Eggs*

8 hard-cooked eggs
¼ cup mayonnaise or
  salad dressing
1 tablespoon mashed blue
  cheese
¼ teaspoon Worcestershire
  sauce
¼ teaspoon salt

Cut eggs into halves lengthwise and remove yolks. Press egg yolks through a fine sieve; blend in the remaining ingredients. Spoon mixture into egg whites. Chill until serving time. Makes 16 halves.

❧ Crunchy Stuffed Celery

1 3-ounce package cream
cheese, at room
temperature
¼ cup chunk-style peanut
butter
3 tablespoons milk
⅛ teaspoon salt
3 or 4 cleaned celery stalks,
cut into 3-inch lengths
2 tablespoons chopped
peanuts (optional)
Paprika

Combine cream cheese, peanut butter, milk, and salt. Fill celery pieces with cream cheese mixture. Sprinkle with nuts, if desired. Garnish with paprika. Serves 4 to 6.

❧ Stuffed Cucumbers

2 large cucumbers
1 cup cottage cheese
2 tablespoons buttermilk
1 2-ounce can anchovy fillets,
finely chopped
2 tablespoons finely snipped
chives
2 tablespoons finely chopped
onion
2 tablespoons chopped fresh
parsley
1 tablespoon salt

Cut cucumbers in halves crosswise. With an apple corer, remove some of the inside of the cucumber pieces, leaving a shell about ¼ inch thick. Combine finely chopped cucumber pulp with the remaining ingredients. Blend thoroughly. Fill cucumber shells with cheese mixture. Chill several hours. Cut into ½-inch-thick slices. Makes about 32 slices.

❧ Cheese-Stuffed Mushrooms

1 pound small fresh
mushrooms
2 cups water
1 tablespoon lemon juice
1 8-ounce package cream
cheese, at room
temperature
4 teaspoons dry sherry

Wash mushrooms. Place water and lemon juice in a large saucepan. Bring to a boil and add whole mushrooms. Return to a boil and simmer over low heat (about 200° F.) 2 minutes. Remove, drain, and cool. Break stems from mushroom caps and reserve ½ cup finely chopped stems for filling. Blend cream cheese and sherry. Add the chopped mushroom stems, walnuts, curry powder, and Worcestershire. Place a small sprig of

½ cup finely chopped walnuts
1 teaspoon curry powder
1 teaspoon Worcestershire
   sauce
Parsley sprigs
Paprika

parsley in each mushroom cavity and fill with the cheese mixture; pile high. Sprinkle with paprika. Chill 2 hours before serving. Makes about 24 small mushroom appetizers.

❧ Stuffed Vegetable Relishes

1 6-ounce can broiled
   mushroom crowns, drained
1 8-ounce package cream
   cheese, at room
   temperature
1 tablespoon milk
2 tablespoons finely chopped
   radishes
2 tablespoons finely chopped
   green onions or scallions
2 tablespoons finely chopped
   fresh parsley
¼ teaspoon salt
1 small celery heart, cleaned
   and cut into 3½-x-½-inch
   sticks
1 pint cherry tomatoes
1 4¾-ounce can pasteurized
   process American cheese
   spread, packed in a pressurized can

Remove stems from mushroom caps with a grapefruit knife to form cups. Chop stems finely. Combine chopped mushroom stems, cream cheese, milk, radishes, green onion, parsley, and salt. Use mixture to stuff mushroom crowns and celery sticks. Holding a tomato, stem end down, cut out a circle from the bottom with a small sharp knife; scoop out pulp. Stuff tomatoes with cheese from pressurized can. Arrange stuffed celery, mushrooms, and tomatoes on a large serving platter. Serves 8.

❧ Sesame Chicken Bites

⅓ cup sesame seeds
2 chicken breasts, skinned
   and boned
½ cup dry white wine
½ cup soy sauce
½ cup vegetable oil
1 clove garlic, minced
1 tablespoon very finely cut
   crystallized ginger

Heat oven to 350° F. Place sesame seeds in a shallow pan. Heat in oven about 20 minutes, or until lightly browned, stirring 2 or 3 times. Cut chicken into 1-inch pieces. Combine wine, soy sauce, oil, garlic, and ginger in a medium-sized bowl. Add chicken pieces and stir to coat with the mixture. Let stand 20 to 30 minutes. Skewer chicken pieces on short wooden or metal skewers, allowing about 3 pieces per skewer. Place on grill over hot coals and cook about 15 minutes, or until chicken is cooked, turning a few times. Roll chicken in toasted sesame seeds immediately after removing from grill. Makes about 24 appetizers.

✌ Ham-and-Curry Turnovers

½ cup dried currants
3 2½-ounce cans deviled
    ham
⅓ cup chopped chutney
1½ tablespoons mayonnaise
    or salad dressing
1½ teaspoons curry powder
1 package pie-crust mix

Heat oven to 425° F. Mix currants, deviled ham, chutney, and mayonnaise. Add curry powder to pie-crust mix and prepare according to package directions. Roll pastry to a thickness of ⅛ inch on a lightly floured board. Cut out circles with a 3½-inch cookie cutter. Place a teaspoonful of filling on edge of each pastry circle. Fold other half of pastry over filling to form half circles. With fork tines, press edges together and prick tops. Place on an ungreased cookie sheet. Bake 20 to 25 minutes, or until lightly browned. Serve warm. Makes about 2 dozen.

✌ Asparagus–Ham Pinwheels

1 3-ounce package cream
    cheese, at room
    temperature
6 very thin slices boiled ham,
    6 by 4 inches
6 medium-sized stalks
    asparagus, cooked and
    chilled
Crackers (optional)

Cut cream cheese into 6 pieces and spread one piece on each slice of ham. Trim off the ends of the asparagus stalks so the stalks measure 4 inches and place one stalk on each ham slice. Roll ham tightly around asparagus. Chill well. With a very sharp knife, cut each roll into ½-inch pieces. Place on toothpicks or, if desired, serve on crackers. Makes about 42 appetizers.

✌ Ham Roulades

2 3-ounce packages cream
    cheese, at room
    temperature
1½ teaspoons prepared
    horseradish
2 teaspoons heavy cream
Few grains of salt
6 thin slices boiled ham

Combine cheese, horseradish, cream, and salt and beat until smooth; spread over slices of ham. Roll up ham jelly-roll fashion, starting at narrow end. Wrap each roll in waxed paper or plastic wrap and chill several hours or overnight. Cut into ½-inch slices. Serve on toothpicks. Makes 42 appetizers.

✌ Party Mix

½ cup melted butter or
    margarine
4 teaspoons Worcestershire
    sauce

Heat oven to 250° F. Combine butter, Worcestershire, seasoned salt, and celery salt. In a large, flat baking pan combine crackers, cereals, pretzels, and nuts. Gradually pour butter mixture over cereal mixture while stirring

1 teaspoon seasoned salt
1 teaspoon celery or onion
   salt
2 cups oyster crackers
3 cups bite-sized shredded
   rice biscuits
2 cups ready-to-eat oat
   cereal
2 cups thin pretzel sticks
8 ounces mixed salted nuts or
   peanuts

to coat pieces. Place pan on rack in center of oven. Bake 1 hour, stirring every 15 minutes. Cool and store in tightly covered container. Makes about 10 cups.

Hot Buttered Nuts

2 pounds unblanched walnut
   meats, pecan halves or
   whole blanched almonds
4 tablespoons butter or
   margarine
2 tablespoons salt

Heat oven to 350° F. Spread half the nuts on each of two large, shallow baking pans and dot with butter. Bake 10 minutes, stir nuts to distribute butter evenly, sprinkle with salt and stir again. Bake 5 to 10 minutes longer, until nuts are lightly toasted. Let walnuts and pecans cool before serving; almonds are good warm or cool. Store in airtight jars or tins. Makes about 8 cups.

Chili Peanuts

6½ cups roasted salted
   peanuts (about 2 pounds)
1 tablespoon chili powder

Heat oven to 350° F. Spread peanuts on a large, shallow baking pan and place in oven for 5 minutes. Remove from oven and sprinkle with chili powder. Stir to mix well and return to oven for 5 more minutes. Serve warm or cool. Makes 6½ cups.

Cheese-Dipped Pretzels

1 8-ounce package process
   American cheese slices
½ cup light cream
½ teaspoon Tabasco
1 15¾-ounce package
   miniature pretzels
1 tablespoon poppy seeds

Cut cheese into cubes. Put cheese, cream, and Tabasco in top of double boiler over simmering water. Cook, stirring constantly, until cheese is melted. Dip half of each pretzel in cheese and immediately sprinkle the cheese lightly with poppy seeds. Place on waxed paper until firm. Serves 16 to 18.

✑ Poppy-Seed Morsels

1 container refrigerated
  crescent dinner rolls
1 2¼-ounce can deviled ham
¼ cup shredded Cheddar
  cheese
1 tablespoon poppy seeds

Heat oven to 375° F. Open container, remove dough, and unroll. Separate the dough into the four rectangles. Pinch together the diagonal cuts in each rectangle. Spread two of the rectangles with deviled ham and sprinkle with the cheese. Top each with the two remaining rectangles and pat together lightly. Sprinkle with poppy seeds. Cut out rounds with a 1¼-inch cookie cutter. Place on a lightly greased cookie sheet. Bake about 10 minutes, until browned. Serve hot. Makes about 30 appetizers.

✑ Sesame Crisps

¼ cup butter or margarine
1 cup sifted all-purpose flour
1 teaspoon seasoned salt
2 tablespoons water
2 to 3 tablespoons sesame
  seeds

Heat oven to 425° F. Cut butter into flour and salt with a pastry blender or two knives until mixture looks like corn meal; sprinkle water over the mixture while stirring gently. Pack together and chill 10 minutes. Roll out very thin on a lightly floured board. Sprinkle pastry liberally with sesame seeds. Press seeds into dough with the hands. Cut out with a 1½-inch round cookie cutter. Bake on an ungreased cookie sheet 10 minutes, or until browned. Makes 45 sesame crisps.

✑ Italian Pickled Shrimp

2 quarts water
2 teaspoons salt
1 tablespoon mixed pickling
  spice
2 pounds fresh or frozen
  shrimp, shelled and
  deveined
¾ cup wine vinegar
6 tablespoons olive oil
2¼ cups water
⅓ cup finely chopped onion
¾ teaspoon salt

Place water in a large saucepan with the 2 teaspoons salt; add pickling spice. Bring to a boil. Add shrimp and cook 3 to 5 minutes after water returns to boil. Drain and cool shrimp. Combine vinegar, olive oil, the 2¼ cups water, onion, and the ¾ teaspoon salt in a saucepan; bring mixture to a boil. Reduce heat to moderately low (about 225° F.) and heat 5 minutes. Place shrimp in glass jars and add marinade to cover them. Refrigerate at least 24 hours before serving. Shrimp will keep about one week in the refrigerator. Serve on lettuce as a first course or on toothpicks as an hors d'oeuvre. Serves 6 to 8.

✑ Tiny Teriyaki

1 pound beef bottom round,
  cut 1 inch thick

Slice beef across the grain about ⅛ inch thick. Cut into 2-inch-long pieces. Sprinkle strips with meat tenderizer.

Instant meat tenderizer
1/4 *cup soy sauce*
1/4 *cup water*
1/4 *cup red wine*
1/4 *cup honey*
1/2 *teaspoon ground ginger*
2 *cloves garlic, minced*

Do not add salt. Combine soy sauce, water, red wine, honey, ginger, and garlic in a deep bowl. Add steak pieces and refrigerate 1 to 2 hours. Drain steak and thread on small bamboo skewers. Grill on hibachi about 1½ minutes. Makes about 30.

Canapés and Sandwiches

Canapés, cold or hot, are characteristically made up of a savory topping or filling placed on a piece of bread, toast, or cracker. These, which can be made ahead of time, are most useful when you want to set out pretty trays for a party.

Cold Canapés and Sandwiches

Crab-Meat Diamonds

1 *6½-ounce can crab meat*
1 *tablespoon lemon juice*
1/4 *cup mayonnaise*
1/2 *teaspoon salt*
Few grains pepper
Few drops Tabasco
16 *slices white or whole wheat bread*
Softened butter or margarine
1/3 *cup finely chopped fresh parsley*

Clean and flake crab meat. Toss together crab meat, lemon juice, mayonnaise, salt, pepper, and Tabasco. Chill. Cut out diamonds from bread with a cookie cutter or sharp knife. Spread with butter and then crab-meat filling. Sprinkle parsley around edge of each sandwich. Cover and chill until serving time. Makes 16 sandwiches.

Chicken Liver and Mushroom Canapés

6 *tablespoons butter or margarine*
1/2 *pound chicken livers*
1 *4-ounce can mushroom stems and pieces, drained*
1 *medium-sized onion,*

Heat the 6 tablespoons butter in skillet over moderately low heat (about 225° F.); add chicken livers, mushrooms, and onion and cook 40 minutes, or until very tender, stirring frequently. Mash liver mixture with a fork; add eggs, Worcestershire, salt, and pepper. Stir in sour cream. Chill. Trim crusts from bread and spread with

finely chopped
3 hard-cooked eggs, finely
   chopped
½ teaspoon Worcestershire
   sauce
1 teaspoon salt
⅛ teaspoon pepper
¼ cup commercial sour
   cream
7 slices white bread
Softened butter or margarine
Sliced scallions or green
   onions
Sliced, stuffed green olives

butter. Spread with chicken liver mixture and cut bread slices into quarters. Garnish with sliced scallions or olives. Makes 28 canapés.

ᕽ Bacon-and-Egg Circle Sandwiches

4 hard-cooked eggs, finely
   chopped
4 slices crisp-cooked bacon,
   crumbled
¼ teaspoon salt
⅛ teaspoon pepper
2 teaspoons minced onion
1 tablespoon chopped fresh
   parsley or 1 teaspoon
   dried parsley flakes
⅓ cup mayonnaise
1½ teaspoons curry powder
18 to 24 slices white or whole
   wheat bread
Mayonnaise
Chopped pimiento
Sliced ripe olives

In a medium-sized bowl, blend together eggs, bacon, salt, pepper, onion, and parsley. In a custard cup, blend the ⅓ cup mayonnaise and curry powder. Stir curry-mayonnaise into egg mixture. Using a 2-inch cookie cutter, cut two rounds from each slice of the bread. Spread half the rounds with mayonnaise. Cut out the center of the remaining bread rounds with a 1-inch cutter. Place cut-out rings on top of the rounds spread with mayonnaise. Fill centers with egg mixture. Arrange sandwiches on a cookie sheet or in a shallow pan. Cover with plastic wrap or foil and keep chilled until needed. Will keep in refrigerator about 24 hours. At serving time, garnish some circles with pimiento and others with sliced olive. Makes about 1½ cups filling, or enough for about 24 sandwiches. (If desired, bottom rounds may be of white bread and top rings of whole wheat.)

ᕽ Deviled Egg Canapés

Softened butter or margarine
20 Melba rounds
4 hard-cooked eggs
¼ cup chopped, stuffed
   green olives
¼ cup mayonnaise or salad

Spread butter lightly on Melba rounds. Cut each egg into 5 slices and remove yolks. Place a ring of egg white on each round. (Cut a circle out of the end egg-white slices without yolks to make a ring.) Press egg yolks through a fine sieve. Blend egg yolks, olives, mayonnaise, and mustard together. Mound yolk mixture in

dressing
½ *teaspoon prepared
mustard*
Parsley sprigs

center of egg-white rings. Garnish with sprig of parsley.
Makes 20 canapés.

ᴥᔲ Glazed Party Canapés

1½ *teaspoons unflavored
gelatine*
1 *12½-ounce can
consommé
madrilene*
Soft butter or margarine
32 *slices party rye bread*
Shrimp Filling (recipe follows)
*Radish and Egg Filling
(recipe follows)*

Dissolve gelatine in ½ cup of the consommé over moderately low heat (about 225° F.). Remove from heat. Add remaining consommé and set the pan in a bowl of ice cubes until consommé is the consistency of unbeaten egg white. Butter bread slices and top half the slices with Shrimp Filling and half with the Radish and Egg Filling. Place sandwiches on a cake rack over a large tray. Spoon a layer of gelatine over fillings. If gelatine becomes too stiff, place over moderately low heat (about 225° F.) to melt. If necessary, chill again and then continue spooning gelatine over sandwiches. Chill before serving. Makes 32 canapés.

Shrimp Filling

½ *cup commercial sour
cream*
1 *tablespoon chopped
fresh dill*
16 *large shrimp, cooked,
shelled, deveined, and
split*
16 *slices of cucumber, cut
in half*
Dill sprigs

Mix sour cream and chopped dill; spread over 16 of the buttered slices of bread. Arrange 2 pieces of shrimp and cucumber alternately on each slice; cover with gelatine, following directions above. At serving time, garnish with dill sprigs. Makes enough for 16 canapés.

Radish and Egg Filling

⅓ *cup commercial sour
cream*
1 *tablespoon chili sauce*
3 *hard-cooked eggs, sliced*
32 *radish slices*

Mix sour cream and chili sauce; spread over 16 of the buttered slices of bread. Arrange eggs and radish slices alternately on bread and cover with gelatine, following directions above. Makes enough for 16 canapés.

ᴥᔲ Curried Pastry Bites

1 *cup sifted all-purpose
flour*

Place flour, salt, and curry powder in a medium-sized bowl. Cut in shortening with a pastry blender or two

½ teaspoon salt
1½ teaspoons curry powder
⅓ cup shortening
2 tablespoons water
1 6-ounce can boneless chicken, chopped fine
¼ cup slivered toasted almonds
¼ cup well-drained crushed pineapple
3 tablespoons mayonnaise
1 teaspoon lemon juice

knives. Sprinkle water over flour mixture while stirring gently. Pack together, wrap in waxed paper, and chill 10 minutes. Heat oven to 425° F. Roll pastry on lightly floured board or cloth to a thickness of ⅛ inch. Cut rounds with a 1½-inch cutter and place on an ungreased cookie sheet. Bake 5 to 10 minutes, until lightly browned. Cool. Combine chicken, almonds, pineapple, mayonnaise, and lemon juice. Place a small amount of mixture on each pastry round. Serve at room temperature. Makes about 60 appetizers.

✑ Liver Pâté Ribbon Sandwiches

½ pound liverwurst
1 tablespoon butter or margarine
1 3¾-ounce package slivered blanched almonds (½ cup)
2 teaspoons grated onion
12 slices white bread
6 slices pumpernickel bread

Mash liverwurst in a bowl. Heat butter in a small skillet over moderately low heat (about 225° F.). Add nuts and cook, stirring, until nuts are golden brown. Combine liverwurst, nuts, and onion. Blend well. Spread 6 slices of the white bread and 6 slices pumpernickel bread with the pâté. Place pumpernickel slices on top of white. Top each pumpernickel slice with an unspread slice of white bread. Wrap each triple-decker sandwich in plastic wrap and chill at least 2 hours. Cut crusts from sandwiches. Cut each into ½-inch strips. Cut each strip in half crosswise, making 48 ribbon sandwiches about 2 inches by ½ inch.

✑ Salmon Pinwheels

1 16-ounce can salmon
2 tablespoons French dressing
1 loaf unsliced white bread
4 tablespoons soft butter or margarine

Drain salmon thoroughly; mash to a smooth paste with a fork. Add French dressing and blend thoroughly. Remove crusts from loaf of bread. Cut loaf into 6 horizontal slices. Spread slices lightly with butter. Spread each slice with some of the salmon mixture. Starting with a wide side, roll each slice tightly. Wrap in waxed paper and chill several hours or until needed. Cut into ¼-inch crosswise slices. Makes about 5 dozen pinwheels.

✑ Dried Beef and Watercress Canapés

1 5-ounce jar dried beef
Boiling water

Taste beef, and if it seems very salty, place it in a small bowl and cover with boiling water; let stand for up to 5

¼ cup mayonnaise

2 teaspoons Dijon-style mustard

2 teaspoons lemon juice

8 slices white bread, crusts removed

About 40 sprigs watercress

minutes, until as much salt has been removed as you wish; then drain the beef. Combine the mayonnaise, mustard and lemon juice; spread about 2 teaspoons on each slice of bread and then sandwich with beef and watercress. Cut each sandwich into quarters. Makes 16 canapés.

ᣠ French Radish Tartine

6 tablespoons lightly-salted butter

16 ½-inch thick slices French bread

12 or 14 medium-sized radishes, thinly sliced

Butter the bread and arrange radish slices evenly on each slice. Makes 16 good-sized canapés.

ᣠ Sardine–Cream Cheese Canapés

1 3-ounce package cream cheese, at room temperature

1 4⅜-ounce can skinless and boneless sardines, well drained

Soft butter or margarine

4 thin slices white or rye bread

Pimiento-stuffed olives

In a bowl blend together cream cheese and sardines. Butter bread slices lightly. Spread each with an equal amount of the cream cheese mixture. Cut each slice into 4 triangles. Garnish with slivers of olives in a decorative design. Makes 16 canapés, or serves 4.

ᣠ Curried Egg and Bean Sprout Sandwiches

6 hard-cooked eggs, peeled

⅓ cup mayonnaise

½ teaspoon curry powder

¼ teaspoon salt

½ teaspoon dry mustard (optional)

12 slices cracked-wheat bread, crusts removed

1 cup canned bean sprouts, drained and rinsed or 1

In a medium-sized mixing bowl mash eggs with mayonnaise, curry powder, salt and, if desired, the dry mustard. Spread the egg mixture on 6 slices of the bread (about ⅓ cup per slice); top with bean sprouts, grated carrots and remaining bread. Cut sandwiches into quarters. Makes 24 canapés.

cup fresh bean sprouts
½ cup coarsely grated
    carrots

◄§ Rolled Shrimp-and-Cucumber Sandwiches

¾ cup chopped cooked
    shrimp
1 8-ounce package cream
    cheese, at room
    temperature
1½ teaspoons snipped fresh
    dillweed or ½ teaspoon
    dried dillweed
½ cup finely diced, peeled
    cucumber
2 teaspoons snipped chives
¼ teaspoon salt
1 teaspoon lemon juice
About 18 slices whole wheat
    bread

Put chopped shrimp on paper towels and press out any excess moisture. Combine shrimp, cream cheese, dill, cucumber, chives, salt, and lemon juice. Trim crusts from bread. For each roll-up use two slices. Overlap them ¾ inch. Press together and roll lightly with a rolling pin to make bread more pliable and to seal more securely at the seam. Spread with shrimp mixture and roll up securely, jelly-roll fashion. Arrange roll-ups close together, seam side down, in a shallow pan. Cover with plastic wrap or foil and chill at least 2 hours. To serve, cut crosswise into ½-inch slices. Makes about 4 dozen.

◄§ Rolled Watercress Sandwiches

1 3-ounce package cream
    cheese, at room
    temperature
1 teaspoon lemon juice
⅓ cup commercial sour
    cream
⅛ teaspoon salt
1 teaspoon snipped chives
1 cup finely chopped
    watercress, lightly packed
18 slices fresh white bread
2 tablespoons soft butter or
    margarine
Sprigs of watercress

In a bowl blend together cream cheese, lemon juice, sour cream, salt, and chives. Stir in watercress. Makes about 1 cup mixture. Trim crusts from bread and roll slices lightly with a rolling pin to make them more pliable. Spread bread with soft butter, then with watercress mixture. Roll up jelly-roll fashion and arrange close together, seam side down, in a shallow pan. Cover with plastic wrap or foil and chill at least 1 hour. To serve, slice each roll-up crosswise into two lengths (each about 1½ inches long). Stand them upright and insert sprigs of watercress in the top. Makes 36.

Hot Canapés and Sandwiches

⤐ Bacon and Cheese Whirls

8 slices white bread
Softened butter or margarine
1 cup (¼ pound) shredded
   Cheddar cheese
8 slices raw bacon, cut in
   half
16 stuffed green olives

Heat oven to 400° F. Trim crusts from bread and roll with rolling pin to slightly flatten slices. Spread slices with butter and cut each in half crosswise. Spread each piece with some of the cheese and roll up jelly-roll fashion. Wrap a half slice of bacon around each sandwich and hold in place with a toothpick. Stand sandwiches on a cake rack over broiler pan. Bake 12 to 14 minutes. Garnish each with an olive placed on a toothpick. Makes 16 canapés.

⤐ Cheese Puffs

¼ cup mayonnaise
½ cup (2 ounces) grated
   process Cheddar cheese
¼ teaspoon Worcestershire
   sauce
Pinch of dry mustard
1 egg white
Round buttery crackers

Heat oven to 350° F. Combine mayonnaise, cheese, Worcestershire sauce, and mustard. Beat egg white with rotary beater until stiff but not dry. Fold mayonnaise mixture into beaten egg white. Spoon lightly onto crackers and bake 10 to 15 minutes, until puffy and golden brown. Serve warm. Makes about 1½ dozen.

⤐ Olive–Cheese Puffs

2 8-ounce packages cream
   cheese, at room
   temperature
1 egg yolk
2 teaspoons grated onion
1 teaspoon baking powder
3 tablespoons chopped stuffed
   green olives
About 40 round buttery
   crackers
About 40 stuffed green olive
   slices

Combine cream cheese, egg yolk, and onion in a bowl. Mix well with an electric mixer until thoroughly blended and smooth. Stir in the baking powder and olives; blend well. Cover and put in the refrigerator until ready to use. Mound about 1 teaspoon of the mixture evenly on each cracker. Bake in a preheated 350° F. oven about 9 minutes, or until cheese is puffed and lightly browned on top. Top each baked puff with an olive slice. Serve the puffs piping hot. Crackers may be spread 1 day in advance, covered, and kept in the refrigerator until ready to put into the oven. Or unbaked puffs may be covered well and frozen several days, then baked in the oven 12 to 13 minutes. Makes about 40 puffs.

❧ Creamy Clam Canapés

2 7½-ounce cans minced
  clams, very well drained
1 8-ounce package cream
  cheese
½ teaspoon grated onion
About 24 2-inch white bread
  rounds

Heat oven to 375° F. or preheat broiler. Mix together clams, cream cheese, and grated onion. Top each bread round with 1 tablespoon of the clam mixture. Place on cookie sheets and bake 22 to 25 minutes until lightly browned or place in a preheated broiler 4 inches from source of heat and broil 3 to 4 minutes until lightly browned. Makes about 24 canapés.

❧ Crab-Meat Puffs

24 2-inch bread rounds
Mayonnaise
24 thin small slices of tomato
Salt and pepper
1 6½-ounce can crab meat,
  drained and flaked
Lemon juice

Broil bread rounds on one side; cool. Spread untoasted side with mayonnaise. Fit a piece of tomato on bread. Sprinkle with salt and pepper. Top with 2 teaspoons crab meat, ½ teaspoon mayonnaise, and a few drops lemon juice. Broil until mayonnaise puffs and starts to brown. Makes 2 dozen.

❧ Ham Tartlets

10 slices white bread
Soft butter or margarine
1 4½-ounce can deviled ham
⅓ cup commercial sour
  cream
⅓ cup shredded Cheddar
  cheese

Heat oven to 400° F. Trim crusts from bread, butter lightly, and cut each slice into 4 squares. Press squares, buttered side down, into 1¾-inch muffin cups. Into each cup spoon a small amount of deviled ham and sour cream; sprinkle with cheese. Bake until bubbly. Serve hot. Makes 40 canapés.

❧ Mushroom Squares

1 4-ounce can mushroom
  stems and pieces, drained
  and chopped
2 slices crisp-cooked bacon,
  crumbled
2 tablespoons shredded Swiss
  cheese
2 tablespoons mayonnaise or
  salad dressing
1 tablespoon dried parsley

Mix mushrooms, bacon, cheese, mayonnaise, parsley, rosemary, and salt. Heat oven to 400° F. Trim crusts from bread, butter lightly, and cut each into 4 squares. Place squares, buttered side down, on a cookie sheet. Spoon small amount of mushroom filling onto each square. Bake 5 minutes. Serve hot. Makes 2 dozen canapés.

(Ingredients continued on page 186)

  flakes
⅛ *teaspoon crumbled, dried*
    rosemary leaves
Few grains salt
 6 *slices white bread*
Soft butter or margarine

✒ Shrimp Toast

1 *pound frozen shelled and*
   deveined shrimp, cooked
   and chilled
24 *slices party rye bread*
1 *cup mayonnaise or salad*
   dressing
½ *cup coarsely shredded*
   process American cheese
Dash of curry powder

Place 1 or 2 shrimp, depending on size, on each slice of bread. Mix mayonnaise, cheese, and curry powder. Spread some of the mixture over each canapé. Place on a cookie sheet in a preheated broiler, 3 to 4 inches from heat. Broil about 1 to 2 minutes, or until topping starts to brown. Serve at once. Makes 2 dozen canapés.

✒ Tuna Puffs

3 *dozen 1½-x-1¾-inch bread*
   rounds, white or whole
   wheat
1 *6½-ounce can tuna,*
   drained
2 *tablespoons finely chopped*
   onions
2 *tablespoons chopped green*
   pepper
1 *tablespoon chopped*
   pimiento
¼ *cup mayonnaise*
¼ *cup commercial sour*
   cream
1 *teaspoon Worcestershire*
   sauce
2 *teaspoons lemon juice*
Few grains pepper
¼ *cup grated American*
   cheese food
2 *egg whites, stiffly*
   beaten

Place bread rounds on a cookie sheet and broil in preheated broiler until lightly browned on one side. Combine tuna, onion, green pepper, pimiento, mayonnaise, sour cream, Worcestershire, lemon juice, pepper, and grated cheese. Blend. Fold in stiffly beaten egg whites. Top untoasted side of bread rounds with a mound of the mixture. Broil about 4 inches from heat until puffed and browned. Serve immediately. Makes 3 dozen canapés.

ᕦᕤ *Pizza Whole-Wheat Canapés*

1 8-ounce can tomato sauce
1 teaspoon dried basil leaves
9 cherry tomatoes, halved
¼ teaspoon salt
1 small clove garlic, peeled
and crushed
8 slices whole wheat or
cracked wheat bread,
lightly toasted, then cut
into quarters
4 ounces mozzarella cheese,
sliced thin and quartered
2 ounces Parmesan cheese,
freshly grated (½ cup)

Heat oven to 400° F. In a medium-sized mixing bowl combine tomato sauce, basil, tomatoes, salt and garlic mashing the tomatoes slightly while mixing. Arrange toast quarters on a baking sheet, spread a rounded teaspoon of the tomato mixture on each toast square, top with the mozzarella and sprinkle with Parmesan. Bake 7 to 10 minutes, until cheese melts. Makes 32 little pizza canapés.

Pastry Appetizers

Rich pastry crust flavored or filled makes an elegant hors d'oeuvre.

ᕦᕤ *Assorted Cheese Pastry Hors d'Oeuvre*

1 cup butter or margarine
2 cups sifted all-purpose
flour
½ teaspoon salt
½ teaspoon ground dillseed
1 cup cream-style cottage
cheese

Cut butter into flour, salt, and ground dillseed with pastry blender or two knives until mixture is the consistency of corn meal. Add cheese; mix with a fork until blended. Cover and chill one hour. Roll ¼ of the pastry at a time between sheets of waxed paper to a thickness of ⅛ inch. Cut and fill as directed in recipes following. Heat oven to 500° F. Bake pastries on cookie sheets 10 to 12 minutes, or until browned.

Franks in Blankets

Roll out ¼ of the pastry following directions above. Cut into strips 1¼ inches wide and 3 inches long. Wrap each around a *cocktail frankfurter;* seal ends of pastry. Reroll leftover pastry until all is used. Makes about 18 pastries.

Cornucopias

Roll out ¼ of the pastry following directions above. Cut into rounds 2½ inches in diameter. Place a *small strip of bologna or smoked ham* in center of each round. Fold over edges to center to form cornucopia. Moisten edges with water to seal. Makes about 16 pastries.

Liver Pâté Pastries

Roll out ¼ of the pastry following directions above. Cut into rounds 2½ inches in diameter. Spoon *½ teaspoon canned liver pêté* into center of each. Bring edges of circle up around filling and press firmly together. Reroll leftover pastry until all is used. Makes about 16 pastries.

Cheese Sticks

Roll ¼ of the pastry with palms of the hands into a rope ½ inch in diameter. Cut rope into 2-inch-long pieces and roll each in grated Parmesan cheese. Makes about 16 pastries.

✍ Rich Pastry

2 cups sifted all-purpose
  flour
1 teaspoon salt
⅔ cup soft shortening
4 tablespoons cold water

Sift flour and salt into a bowl. Cut in half of shortening with a pastry blender until mixture looks like coarse corn meal. Cut in rest of shortening until it looks like large peas. Sprinkle water, 1 tablespoon at a time, over flour mixture; toss with a fork until mixture clings together. Turn out on a floured board and shape into a ball. Roll out with a floured rolling pin as directed in recipes for Cheese Straws and Anchovy Tartlets.

Cheese Straws

Rich Pastry (see preceding
  recipe)
⅓ cup grated Parmesan
  cheese
⅛ teaspoon salt
⅛ teaspoon cayenne pepper

Heat oven to 400° F. Roll pastry out on a well-floured board into a rectangle about 12 by 17 inches. Mix cheese, salt, and cayenne together; sprinkle half the cheese mixture over half of the pastry to within about ½ inch of edge of dough. Fold plain half over onto cheese; press edges together. Roll again into a 12-x-17-inch rectangle and sprinkle half the pastry with remaining cheese; fold in half again and seal. Roll again into a 12-x-17-inch rectangle and cut into ½-inch strips and then into 4-to-5-inch sticks. Leave plain or twist and place on ungreased cookie sheet. Bake 8 minutes. Makes 7 dozen straws.

Anchovy Tartlets

1 8-ounce package cream cheese, at room temperature
*¼ cup anchovy paste
1 tablespoon chopped fresh dillweed
2 tablespoons finely snipped chives
Rich Pastry (see preceding recipe)

Cream the cheese, anchovy paste, dill, and chives together until smooth. Chill. Heat oven to 425° F. Trace about 4½ dozen 2-inch circles on heavy-duty aluminum foil, using a 2-inch biscuit cutter for a pattern. Cut out. Roll out pastry to ⅛ inch thickness and cut into 2-inch rounds with a biscuit cutter. Place a pastry round on a round of foil and pinch foil and pastry together to form a tart, or, if available, use small tart pans. Prick bottoms of tarts with tines of fork. Place on cookie sheet. Bake 8 minutes. Cool. Spoon cheese mixture into cake-decorating bag with a star tip and stuff tartlets. Makes 4½ dozen tartlets.

*Note: If more anchovy flavor is desired, increase amount of anchovy paste to taste.

Swiss Cheese Pie

1 9-inch unbaked pie shell (recipe on page 786)
2 cups (½ pound) Swiss cheese, grated
1 tablespoon flour
1 teaspoon butter or margarine
1 tablespoon finely chopped onion
3 eggs, well beaten
1 cup light cream or milk
½ teaspoon salt
Few grains cayenne pepper

Heat oven to 425° F. Lightly prick the bottom and sides of the pie shell. Bake pie shell about 10 minutes, or until crust is lightly browned. Remove shell from oven and reduce oven temperature to 325° F. Combine cheese and flour and mix well. Sprinkle cheese mixture evenly on bottom of baked pie shell. Melt butter in a small skillet over moderately low heat (about 225° F.). Cook onions in butter over moderately high heat (about 275° F.) until onions are translucent. Combine onions, beaten eggs, cream, salt, and cayenne pepper; pour over grated cheese mixture in pie shell. Bake 30 to 35 minutes, or until a knife inserted in center comes out clean. Serves 12 as an appetizer or 6 as a light supper entrée.

Crab-Meat Quiche

1 9-inch baked pie shell (recipe on page 786)

Heat oven to 300° F. Combine eggs, sour cream, Worcestershire, and salt. Stir in cheese, crab meat, and fried

3 eggs, slightly beaten
1 cup commercial sour cream
½ teaspoon Worcestershire
  sauce
¾ teaspoon salt
1 cup coarsely shredded
  Swiss cheese
1 6½-ounce can crab meat,
  drained and finely flaked
1 3½-ounce can French fried
  onions

onions. Pour into baked pie shell. Bake 55 to 60 minutes, or until custard is set and a silver knife inserted in center comes out clean. Serve hot. Serves 8 to 10 as an appetizer.

Chafing Dish Hors d'Oeuvre

These hot hors d'oeuvre are nice to serve from a chafing dish or candle-warmed dish.

Hors d'Oeuvre Mushrooms and Meatballs

1 egg
⅔ cup milk
3 slices white bread
3 tablespoons grated onion
3 tablespoons chopped fresh
  parsley
1 teaspoon salt
⅛ teaspoon pepper
¾ pound ground beef
¼ pound ground pork
¼ cup shortening
1 can condensed onion soup
2 3-ounce cans broiled
  mushroom crowns
¼ cup flour
½ cup light cream
½ cup dry white wine

Beat egg in a large bowl. Add milk and bread. Let bread soften; then beat with rotary beater to blend. Stir in onion, parsley, salt, and pepper. Add meat and blend. Form into small 1-inch balls. Turn heat control on electric skillet to 230° F. Add shortening and meatballs. Brown slowly, stirring occasionally. Remove when browned and drain on paper towels. Turn off skillet. Remove excess fat from pan. Strain onion soup; press pulp through sieve. Drain mushrooms, reserving liquid. Combine onion soup and mushroom liquid. Add enough water to make 2 cups liquid. Stir flour and some of the cold liquid together until smooth. Blend flour mixture and remaining liquid in the electric skillet. Stir in cream and wine. Turn dial to about 230° F. and cook, stirring constantly, until thickened. Add meatballs and mushrooms. Reduce heat to 150° F. Serve from skillet with toothpicks. Makes about 4½ dozen.

Swedish Meatballs for a Crowd

¼ cup butter or margarine
¾ cup finely chopped onion

Melt the ¼ cup butter in a skillet over moderately low heat (about 225° F.); add onion and cook over low heat

3 *eggs*
1⅓ *cups milk*
1½ *pounds ground beef round*
1½ *pounds ground pork*
1½ *teaspoons ground allspice*
½ *teaspoon ground nutmeg*
1 *tablespoon salt*
2 *cups finely crumbled soft bread crumbs*
½ *cup melted butter or margarine*
1 *beef bouillon cube*
1 *cup boiling water*
4 *tablespoons flour*
2 *cups light cream*
1½ *teaspoons salt*
Few grains pepper

until tender. Beat eggs and milk together. Lightly mix ground beef and pork, cooked onion, egg–milk mixture, allspice, nutmeg, the 1 tablespoon salt, and the bread crumbs. Chill in refrigerator for 1 hour before shaping into ¾-inch balls. Heat oven to 350° F. Meatballs are best baked in a single layer in a shallow baking pan. Use 2 baking pans and pour ¼ cup of the melted butter into each. Arrange meatballs in pans and bake 30 minutes. Turn meatballs and increase oven temperature to 400° F. Bake 20 to 25 minutes longer, turning meatballs occasionally. Remove meatballs from pans. Dissolve bouillon cube in the 1 cup boiling water. Add some of the bouillon mixture to each of the baking pans and stir to loosen meat particles. Then combine all the drippings in a saucepan. Blend the flour into ¼ cup of the drippings; stir into remaining drippings; add cream. Cook over moderately low heat (about 225° F.), stirring constantly, until thickened. Season with the 1½ teaspoons salt and the pepper. Meatballs and sauce may be prepared a day ahead of time and stored in the refrigerator. Heat before serving in a chafing dish or electric skillet. Makes about 9 dozen meatballs, or serves 24.

➳ *Sweet-and-Sour Cocktail Frankfurters*

3 *pounds small cocktail frankfurters*
2 *20-ounce cans pineapple chunks*
2 *tablespoons butter or margarine*
½ *cup finely chopped onion*
2 *cups chili sauce*
¼ *cup vinegar*
2 *tablespoons Worcestershire sauce*
½ *cup lemon juice*
¼ *cup firmly packed dark brown sugar*
½ *teaspoon paprika*
2 *teaspoons dry mustard*
1 *teaspoon salt*
½ *teaspoon pepper*

Place frankfurters in a saucepan; cover with water, bring to a boil, and drain. Drain pineapple chunks and reserve 1 cup of the juice. Heat butter in a large skillet over moderately low heat (about 225° F.); add onion and cook until tender. Add the reserved pineapple juice, the chili sauce, vinegar, Worcestershire, lemon juice, brown sugar, paprika, mustard, salt, and pepper to onions in skillet; mix together. Add frankfurters and pineapple; cover and place over moderately low heat (about 225° F.) and cook 20 minutes. At serving time, place in an electric skillet with heat control set at warm (about 150° F.) or place in a heated chafing dish. Serve with toothpicks. Serves 24.

Dinner First Courses

When you entertain, you can save an extra clearing of dishes from the table if you serve the first course of the dinner in the living room. Have the necessary serving dishes and silver on a side table and take the first course in on a tray.

✎§ Antipasto

1 9-ounce package frozen artichoke hearts
1 cup bottled Italian dressing
1 small head cauliflower
3 cups water
1 tablespoon lemon juice
½ teaspoon salt
6 large lettuce leaves
3 hard-cooked eggs, sliced
6 slices salami, cut into thin strips
2 ounces provolone cheese, cut into small strips
1 4-ounce jar pimientos, sliced
1 2-ounce can anchovies, rolled or flat
3 tablespoons mayonnaise
2 teaspoons milk
1 teaspoon prepared mustard

Cook artichoke hearts according to package directions. Drain thoroughly; cool. Pour ½ cup of the Italian dressing over hearts and chill at least two hours. Break cauliflower into bite-sized pieces. Bring water to a boil in a medium-sized saucepan. Add lemon juice, salt, and cauliflower, and return to boiling. Reduce heat to moderate (about 225° F.) and simmer gently 7 minutes. Drain and cool. Pour remaining ½ cup Italian dressing over cauliflower and chill 2 hours. Place lettuce leaves on 6 plates. Arrange artichoke hearts, cauliflower, sliced eggs, salami strips, cheese strips, pimiento slices, and anchovies on each lettuce leaf. Combine mayonnaise, milk, and mustard. Pour over egg slices. Serves 6.

✎§ Lemon-Marinated Artichokes

4 small artichokes, cooked and cooled (see directions on page 499)
¾ cup olive oil
⅓ cup lemon juice
1 hard-cooked egg, finely chopped
1 tabespoon capers
1 tablespoon chopped fresh parsley

Stand artichokes in a deep pan. Combine remaining ingredients; pour over artichokes. Chill several hours, basting occasionally. Drain and serve as an appetizer with marinade on the side as a dip. Serve 4.

¼ teaspoon dried oregano
   leaves
⅛ teaspoon garlic powder
2 teaspoons sugar
¾ teaspoon salt
Few grains pepper

❧ Eggs en Gelée

1 envelope unflavored
   gelatine
¼ cup cold water
1 chicken bouillon cube
¾ cup boiling water
6 hard-cooked eggs, shelled
6 lettuce leaves
⅓ cup mayonnaise or salad
   dressing
1 tablespoon lemon juice
1 tablespoon finely chopped
   green pepper

Soften gelatine in cold water. Dissolve bouillon cube in the boiling water. Add to gelatine and stir until dissolved. Chill until mixture begins to set. Place a small amount of gelatine mixture in the bottom of 6 oiled muffin cups. Place an egg in each cup. Cover with remaining gelatine. Chill until set. Unmold onto lettuce leaves. Combine mayonnaise, lemon juice, and green pepper. Pour over each mold. Serves 6.

❧ Ginger–Pear Appetizer

½ cup orange juice
1 tablespoon lemon juice
4 teaspoons sugar
¼ teaspoon ground ginger
2 ripe pears
½ cup sliced and seeded
   grapes

Mix orange juice, lemon juice, sugar, and ginger. Peel, core, and slice pears. Toss sliced pears and grapes in juice mixture and chill in refrigerator. Serve in sherbet glasses. Serves 4.

❧ Sherried Strawberries

1 package dry-packed whole
   frozen strawberries
½ cup sweet sherry
4 teaspoons confectioners'
   sugar

Thaw strawberries. Spoon strawberries into 4 fruit dishes. Pour 2 tablespoons sherry over each serving. Sprinkle each with about a teaspoon of sugar. Chill. Serves 4.

❧ Tuna Pâté

½ cup chicken broth, canned
   or homemade

Pour chicken broth into a small saucepan; stir in gelatine and let soak 2 to 3 minutes. Stir over low heat (about

2 envelopes unflavored
   gelatine
1 8-ounce carton plain
   yogurt (1 cup)
1 9¼-ounce can solid-packed
   tuna, drained
1 tablespoon lemon juice
2 tablespoons finely chopped
   fresh dillweed
1 tablespoon minced green
   onions or scallions

200° F.) 3 to 4 minutes, until gelatine is dissolved. Remove from heat and set aside to cool slightly. Place remaining ingredients in an electric blender; cover and blend at high speed. When smooth, pour mixture into a small bowl and stir in dissolved gelatine; when well mixed, pour into a 7½-x-3½-x-2¼-inch loaf pan and chill several hours, until firm. With a knife loosen tuna pâté from sides of pan and turn out onto a serving plate or board. Cut into thin slices. Serves 4.

✒ Pâté Au Porto

1 pound fresh chicken livers
Flour
6 ounces sweet butter (1½
   sticks)
3 tablespoons finely chopped
   shallots or green onions
   (white part only)
6 tablespoons port wine
⅛ teaspoon freshly grated
   nutmeg
1 teaspoon salt
¼ teaspoon freshly ground
   white pepper
Watercress or fresh parsley
Sour pickles
French bread

Remove any fat and connective tissue from livers before lightly coating them with flour. Melt butter in a large skillet over moderate heat. When butter foams, add the floured livers and chopped shallots. Cook the livers 10 to 12 minutes, stirring very frequently, until lightly browned; if necessary reduce heat to prevent too much browning. Add port, nutmeg and salt to livers and cook over low heat 3 to 4 minutes longer. Remove skillet from heat and stir in pepper. Mash the livers thoroughly with a fork. Grease a 7½-x-3½-x-2¼-inch loaf pan and line it with wax paper. Pack the chicken liver mixture firmly into the prepared loaf pan. Cover pan and chill 24 hours in refrigerator. To serve, turn out pâté onto a small platter, remove the paper and decorate with watercress or parsley. Slice pâté and serve as a first course or appetizer with *cornichons* (tiny sour pickles) and French bread or thin toast. Makes 8 to 10 servings.

✒ Country Meat Loaf

1 pound little pork sausage
   links, cut in 1-inch pieces
1 tablespoon vegetable oil
1 teaspoon minced, peeled
   garlic
1 cup finely chopped, peeled
   onion
2 pounds ground beef round
   or sirloin
3 eggs, lightly beaten

Heat oven to 350° F. In a large skillet fry sausage pieces over moderately high heat (about 325° F.) until lightly browned. Transfer sausage to a large mixing bowl and pour off fat from skillet. In same skillet heat oil over moderate heat (about 250° F.), add garlic and onion and cook, stirring occasionally, until soft. Add cooked onion to sausage; add remaining ingredients and mix together well. Pat mixture into a lightly oiled 9-x-5-x-2¾-inch loaf pan and bake 1 hour and 20 minutes. Cool in pan and refrigerate until serving time. Run a knife around the

2 teaspoons salt
½ teaspoon pepper
½ teaspoon dried thyme
leaves

loaf to loosen from the pan, invert pan onto a serving plate and rap bottom sharply until loaf drops out. Cut in thin slices to serve. Serves 12.

Note: Wrapped well, loaf will keep several days in the refrigerator.

✎§ Oysters on the Half Shell with Sauce

24 oysters on the half shell
1 12-ounce bottle chili sauce
2 tablespoons lemon juice
2 teaspoons prepared
horseradish
1 tablespoon finely chopped
celery
3 tablespoons finely chopped
onion
½ teaspoon salt
1 teaspoon Worcestershire
sauce
2 drops Tabasco
1 tablespoon bottled capers

Chill oysters thoroughly in the refrigerator. In a small bowl combine remaining ingredients and blend well. Chill until serving time. Place oysters on a bed of crushed ice and serve with the sauce. Serves 4.

✎§ Baked Clams Casino

2 cups fine soft bread crumbs
2 teaspoons paprika
2 tablespoons olive oil
1 clove garlic, very finely
chopped
3 dozen littleneck clams, on
the half shell
9 slices raw bacon
1 lemon, cut into wedges

Heat oven to 350° F. Toss together bread crumbs, paprika, olive oil, and garlic. Place clams in a flat baking dish. Mound some of the bread crumb mixture on each clam. Cut bacon slices into quarters and place a piece on each clam. Bake 25 minutes, or until bacon is crisp. If desired, the clams may be served on a bed of heated rock salt. Serve with lemon wedges. Serves 4 to 6.

✎§ Crab Cocktail

½ cup bottled cocktail sauce
1 tablespoon capers
⅓ cup commercial sour cream
¼ teaspoon prepared
horseradish

(Ingredients continued on page 196)

Combine cocktail sauce, capers, sour cream, and horseradish. Chill 1 to 2 hours, or until serving time. Arrange small lettuce cups in each of 6 cocktail glasses. Place a tablespoon diced celery in each. Arrange crab chunks in glasses, allowing about ¼ cup for each serving. Spoon some of the sauce in a ribbon over crab meat. Serves 6.

[195]

APPETIZERS

Small lettuce cups
6 tablespoons finely diced
   celery
2 6½-ounce cans chunk crab
   meat, drained

↣ Marinated Shrimp

1 cup white vinegar
1 cup olive oil
1 tablespoon creole mustard
   or hot prepared mustard
½ cup finely chopped
   scallions or green onions
1 clove garlic, crushed
½ cup chili sauce
⅛ teaspoon salt
2 tablespoons paprika
2 pounds fresh or frozen
   shrimp, cooked, shelled,
   deveined, and chilled
Bibb lettuce
Crisp toast points

Mix vinegar, olive oil, mustard, scallions, garlic, chili sauce, salt, and paprika together; pour over shrimp in a large bowl and marinate at least 8 hours or overnight. Turn shrimp several times during marinating. Drain and serve on bed of lettuce with toast points. Serves 10 to 12.

Appetizers for a Large Party

While you plan a menu for a party, check the appetizer recipes you wish to use for the quantity that each will make. You should allow a minimum of four to six assorted pieces per person. After you've decided on the menu, make a shopping list and plan to prepare as many of the foods as you can several days before the party, to freeze or refrigerate.

The recipes in this section are coded so that you can plan accordingly. Recipes marked "f" may be prepared at least a week in advance and frozen. (On the day of the party, thaw completely and reheat as directed in the recipe.) Those marked "sd" may be made several days ahead (three or four) and refrigerated. Those coded "db" are best made the day before and refrigerated. Those marked "d" should be make the day of the party. Plan for a minimum of preparation on the day of the party.

After you've chosen the menu, decide in advance just how many and what kind of platters and other serving dishes you'll need to borrow, buy, or improvise. If you're serving hot food, you will need a hot tray, an electric skillet, a chafing dish, or a candle warmer on the buffet table.

Otherwise you will have to make frequent trips from oven to table. Don't wait until you're ready to serve the food to discover your needs. It's better to overprovide than not to have enough serving equipment.

For parties of twenty or more, you will need not only serving trays for passing food among the guests but also someone to help you perform this additional courtesy.

Big occasion or small, simple or elaborate, a successful party always includes the same ingredients: a pleasant, relaxed atmosphere, congenial guests, and tempting "different" refreshments.

The cocktail appetizers that follow are planned for two kinds of menus—one simple, one elaborate—for groups of ten, twenty, and forty people.

Since most of these recipes can be prepared in advance, they will need only simple, last-minute attention before serving.

Simple Appetizer Menu for Ten:
Ham-and-Peanut Spread
Miniature Reuben Sandwiches
Wine–Cheese Spread
Fresh Raw Vegetables with
    Barbecue Dip

Elaborate Appetizer Menu for Ten:
Stuffed Mushroom Caps
Rumaki
Artichokes with Hollandaise Sauce
Crab-Meat Spread
Fresh Raw Vegetables with Barbecue
    Dip

Simple Appetizer Menu for Twenty:
Butterfly Franks or
    Beef Shish Kabobs
Cocktail Chicken Wings
Tuna Spread
Deviled Eggs
Fresh Raw Vegetables with Green
    Onion–Curry Dip

*Elaborate Appetizer Menu for
    Twenty:*
Hot Seafood Tartlets
Cocktail Chicken Wings
Glazed Corned Beef with Sweet-and-
    Sour Mustard Sauce
Eggplant Spread
Pinwheel Sandwiches
Fresh Raw Vegetables with Green
    Onion–Curry Dip

Simple Appetizer Menu for Forty:
Barbecued Spareribs
Miniature Reuben Sandwiches
Cheese Log
Shrimp-and-Cheese Spread
Fresh Raw Vegetables with Cheese
    Dip

Elaborate Appetizer Menu for Forty:
Profiteroles with Creamed Chicken
Hot Crab Fondue
Coconut Shrimp
Orange-Glazed Baked Ham
Chicken-Liver Pâté
Caviar Roll
Fresh Raw Vegetables with Cheese
    Dip

APPETIZERS

✐ *Ham-and-Peanut Spread (sd)*

1 4½-ounce can deviled ham
½ cup peanut butter
2 tablespoons mayonnaise
1 teaspoon prepared
   mustard
Assorted crackers and Melba
   rounds

In a small bowl mix all ingredients until well blended. Refrigerate until ready to serve. Serve with assorted crackers and Melba rounds. Makes 1 cup, enough for about 32 crackers.

✐ *Miniature Reuben Sandwiches (f)*

1 loaf party rye or
   pumpernickel bread
1 4½-ounce can corned beef
   spread or ¼ pound thinly
   sliced corned beef
1 4-ounce can sauerkraut,
   drained
3 slices Swiss cheese, cut into
   1-x-2-inch rectangles
Butter or margarine

Spread half the bread slices with the corned beef spread or sliced corned beef; top each with some of the sauerkraut and a rectangle of cheese. Cover with the remaining bread slices. In a large skillet over moderate heat (about 250° F.), melt about 2 tablespoons butter. Add sandwiches a few at a time and grill about 2 minutes on each side, until lightly browned and cheese is melted. Add additional butter as needed. Serve hot. May be reheated in a 350° F. oven about 5 minutes. Makes about 15.

✐ *Fresh Raw Vegetables with Dip (d)*

1 large celery stalk, cleaned
2 carrots, cleaned
2 bunches radishes
½ pound fresh mushrooms,
   washed
2 medium-sized green
   peppers
1 small head cauliflower,
   cleaned
1 pint cherry tomatoes
Cheese Dip, Barbecue Dip, or
   Green Onion-Curry Dip
   (recipes follow)

Cut celery and carrots into thin strips. Clean radishes and slice mushrooms. (If mushrooms are small, they may be left whole.) Clean and cut green peppers into thin strips. Separate cauliflower into flowerets. Wash tomatoes. Put desired dip in a bowl and place in the center of a large serving platter. Arrange vegtables in groups around the dip. Makes enough vegetables to serve 10 to 12.

Cheese Dip (sd)

1 4-ounce package blue
   cheese

In a small bowl soften blue cheese and cream cheese at room temperature. Add celery and garlic salts and mix

1 8-ounce package cream
  cheese
⅛ teaspoon celery salt
⅛ teaspoon garlic salt
½ cup heavy cream, whipped

well. Fold in whipped cream. Chill until ready to use. Serve with assorted raw vegetables. Makes 1½ cups dip, enough for 15 to 20.

Barbecue Dip (sd)

½ cup chili sauce
⅔ cup commercial sour cream
1 teaspoon prepared
  horseradish
2 teaspoons Worcestershire
  sauce
1 teaspoon lemon juice
Tabasco to taste

In a small bowl combine all ingredients and blend well. Chill until ready to serve. Serve with cocktail franks, chunks of ham, or vegetables for dipping. Makes 1⅓ cups, enough for 10.

Green Onion-Curry Dip (sd)

2 packages dried green onion
  dip mix
2 cups commercial sour cream
2 teaspoons curry powder
1 teaspoon onion salt
Milk (optional)

In a small bowl combine green onion mix with sour cream. Add curry and onion salt and blend well. Refrigerate at least 1 hour, or until ready to serve. If a thinner dip is desired, add a little milk. Serve with assorted raw vegetables. Makes 2 cups, enough for 20.

Wine-Cheese Spread (sd)

2 4-ounce packages blue
  cheese, at room
  temperature
2 8-ounce packages cream
  cheese, at room
  temperature
¼ teaspoon celery salt
½ teaspoon garlic salt
2½ tablespoons dry white
  wine
Assorted crackers

In a medium-sized bowl, beat blue cheese with an electric mixer at medium speed until smooth. Slowly beat in cream cheese and celery and garlic salts. Gradually blend in wine, beating well until smooth and creamy, about 3 minutes. Refrigerate tightly covered. This spread can be made days in advance. When ready to serve, spoon into a serving bowl and surround with assorted crackers. Makes 2 cups, enough for about 64 crackers.

✑ Stuffed Mushroom Caps (db)

12 large fresh whole
  mushrooms

Gently remove stems from mushrooms. Chop stems fine; put aside. Place mushroom caps on a cookie sheet.

2 tablespoons vegetable oil
1 small onion, finely chopped
¼ pound ground beef chuck
2 slices prosciutto ham, coarsely chopped
⅓ cup dry sherry
¼ cup seasoned dry bread crumbs
1 teaspoon garlic powder
1 teaspoon salt
½ teaspoon pepper
¼ cup grated Parmesan cheese

Heat oil in a large skillet over moderate heat (about 250° F.); cook onion and beef until lightly browned, stirring frequently. Add the chopped stems, ham, and sherry to onion–beef mixture and cook 5 minutes. Add bread crumbs, garlic powder, salt, and pepper and mix well. Stuff mixture into mushroom caps with a spoon. Sprinkle with cheese. Broil mushrooms in a preheated broiler 3 inches from source of heat for 2 to 5 minutes. Serve hot. May be reheated in a 350° F. oven about 5 minutes. Makes 12.

Rumaki (f)

½ pound chicken livers, 6 whole livers
1 cup chicken broth
2 tablespoons soy sauce
2 tablespoons dry sherry
9 slices raw bacon (½ pound), each cut crosswise into thirds
1 4-ounce can water chestnuts, drained and sliced

In a saucepan over moderately low heat (about 225° F.) simmer chicken livers in broth about 15 to 20 minutes, until firm. Drain well. In a small bowl combine soy sauce and sherry and add chicken livers. Marinate for 1 hour. Cut each liver into three pieces. Wrap a piece of bacon around each piece of chicken liver with 1 slice of water chestnut and secure with a toothpick. Place on rack in broiler pan and broil in preheated broiler 4 inches from source of heat for 15 minutes, or until bacon is crisp, turning once. Serve hot. May be reheated in a 350° F. oven about 5 minutes. Makes 18.

Artichokes with Hollandaise Sauce (d)

3 large artichokes
4 cups boiling water
¼ cup salt
1 teaspoon ground coriander
Hollandaise Sauce (recipe on page 488)

With a sharp knife, cut a 1-inch slice straight across from the top of each artichoke. Cut off stem flush with the base so that artichoke will stand upright. Pull off the tough leaves around the base. With scissors snip off the thorny tip of each leaf on the artichoke. Wash thoroughly. Place in a large saucepan; add boiling water, salt, and coriander. Cover and cook over moderate heat (about 250° F.) about 45 minutes, or until a leaf will easily pull away. Drain thoroughly and cool. When ready to serve, arrange artichokes on a large platter or tray. Spoon Hollandaise into a small bowl and place in center of tray. To eat: Guests pull off individual leaves and dip them in the Hollandaise. Serves 10 to 12.

✑ Crab-Meat Spread (d)

1 6½-ounce can crab meat,
  flaked
2 tablespoons finely chopped
  fresh parsley
1 tablespoon finely chopped
  onion
4 tablespoons mayonnaise
½ teaspoon lemon juice
1 tablespoon chili sauce
½ tablespoon prepared
  horseradish
Assorted crackers

In a small bowl combine all ingredients and mix until well blended. Refrigerate until ready to serve. Serve with assorted crackers. Makes 1 cup, enough for about 32 crackers.

✑ Butterfly Franks (f)

1 pound frankfurters
¾ cup bottled barbecue sauce
3 tablespoons prepared
  mustard
5 to 10 dashes Tabasco (to
  taste)

Cut a thin slice from both ends of the frankfurters and cut each frankfurter into 4 equal sections. Cut a cross about ¼ inch deep at each end of each section. In a large skillet over moderately high heat (about 375° F.), fry frankfurters until ends curl out and edges are brown, about 5 to 7 minutes. Reduce heat to low (about 200° F.). In a small bowl combine barbecue sauce, mustard, and Tabasco and add to frankfurters. Stir until frankfurters are well coated and sauce begins to thicken. Serve hot on toothpicks. May be reheated in a saucepan over moderate heat (about 250° F.) about 10 minutes. Makes 40 pieces.

✑ Beef Shish Kabobs (db)

¼ cup dry sherry
¼ cup soy sauce
½ teaspoon garlic powder
1 pound boneless beef chuck,
  cut into ½-inch cubes
1 tablespoon vegetable oil
2 large green peppers
30 4-inch wooden skewers
1 8-ounce can pineapple
  chunks, or 30 pieces
1 16-ounce jar stemless

In a bowl combine sherry, soy sauce, and garlic powder. Add beef cubes and marinate in the refrigerator for at least one hour. Drain cubes thoroughly. Heat oil in a skillet over moderately high heat (about 350° F.); cook beef cubes about 3 minutes, or until brown on all sides. Set aside. Cut peppers into pieces about 1 inch square. On each skewer arrange a pepper square, pineapple chunk, beef cube, cherry, onion, and mushroom. When ready to serve, place shish kabobs on a cookie sheet and bake 15 minutes in a 400° F. oven. Serve hot. Makes 30.

(Ingredients continued on page 202)

> *maraschino cherries, or*
> *30 pieces*
30 *cocktail onions*
 2 *8-ounce cans whole button*
> *mushrooms, drained*

✑ *Cocktail Chicken Wings (f)*

24 *chicken wings*
 2 *cloves garlic*
½ *teaspoon ground ginger*
½ *cup dry sherry*
¼ *cup soy sauce*
Vegetable oil for frying

Disjoint chicken wings into 3 sections. Discard the tip ends (or cook them for a soup stock). In a large bowl combine remaining ingredients, except oil, and add chicken pieces. Marinate chicken in refrigerator for at least 1 hour. Heat about ¾ inch oil in a deep saucepan over moderately high heat (about 375° F.). (An electric skillet may be used; set temperature control at 375° F.) Fry chicken pieces about 10 minutes, or until golden brown, turning once to brown all sides. Serve hot. May be reheated in a 350° F. oven about 10 minutes. Makes 48.

✑ *Tuna Spread (db)*

 1 *6½-ounce can tuna,*
> *drained*
 1 *3-ounce package cream*
> *cheese, at room*
> *temperature*
½ *teaspoon drained capers,*
> *chopped*
 1 *teaspoon prepared*
> *horseradish*
¼ *teaspoon Worcestershire*
> *sauce*
 2 *tablespoons finely*
> *chopped onion*
 1 *clove garlic, very finely*
> *chopped*
¼ *teaspoon celery salt*
1½ *tablespoons mayonnaise*
⅛ *teaspoon pepper*
Melba rounds or crackers

In a medium-sized bowl finely flake tuna. Add cream cheese and mix well. Combine rest of ingredients with the tuna mixture and blend until smooth and creamy. Refrigerate until ready to serve. Serve with assorted Melba rounds or crackers. Makes 1½ cups, enough for about 48 crackers.

ᵊ᷾ Deviled Eggs (db)

6 hard-cooked eggs, chilled
3 tablespoons mayonnaise
½ teaspoon dry mustard
¼ teaspoon pepper
⅛ teaspoon salt
⅛ teaspoon garlic salt
Parsley sprigs
Paprika (optional)
Anchovies (optional)

Cut eggs in half lengthwise. Remove yolks, being careful not to break whites; press yolks through a fine sieve. In a small bowl combine yolk and remaining ingredients. Mix well. Fill whites with the yolk mixture, using a spoon or pastry bag. Garnish with sprig of parsley, or dash of paprika or anchovy if desired. Makes 1 dozen halves.

ᵊ᷾ Hot Seafood Tartlets (f)

1 package pie-crust mix
¼ cup butter or margarine
⅓ cup sifted all-purpose flour
½ cup milk
½ cup chicken broth
2 tablespoons dry white wine
¼ cup finely chopped celery
2 tablespoons finely chopped
    fresh parsley
¼ teaspoon grated lemon peel
1 teaspoon lemon juice
½ cup flaked crab meat
½ cup fresh or frozen shrimp,
    cooked, peeled, deveined,
    and chopped
½ teaspoon salt
½ teaspoon pepper
½ teaspoon paprika

Heat oven to 450° F. Prepare pastry according to package directions. Roll pastry out on a lightly floured board to a thickness of ⅛ inch; cut 24 rounds with a floured 3-inch cookie cutter. Fit pastry rounds over the backs of 2½-inch muffin cups. Prick lightly with the tines of a fork. Bake 5 to 10 minutes, or until lightly browned. Remove from oven and cool a few minutes; gently remove pastry cups to a cookie sheet. Reduce oven temperature to 350° F. In a saucepan over moderate heat (about 250° F.) melt butter, add flour, and stir until foamy; gradually add milk and broth, stirring constantly. Cook until thickened and smooth. Add remaining ingredients except for paprika. Fill shells with the seafood mixture and sprinkle with paprika. Return to the oven and bake for 10 to 15 minutes, or until lightly browned. Serve hot. May be reheated in a 350° F. oven about 5 minutes. Makes 2 dozen.

ᵊ᷾ Glazed Corned Beef (db)

*4 pounds corned beef brisket
4 cups boiling water
1 large onion, sliced
2 whole garlic cloves
2 dried bay leaves
Whole cloves
1 tablespoon prepared
    mustard

Place beef in a large pot or Dutch oven. Cover with boiling water and add onion, garlic, and bay leaves. Bring water to a boil over moderately high heat (about 325° F.); then reduce heat to very low (about 175° F.). Cover tightly and cook approximately 3½ hours (50 minutes per pound, or until meat is fork-tender). Heat oven to 350° F. Remove meat and place in a shallow baking pan, fat side up. Score fat and stud with cloves.

2 tablespoons light brown
  sugar
Party rye
Sweet-and-Sour Mustard
  Sauce (recipe follows)

Brush fat with mustard; then sprinkle with sugar. Bake 15 to 20 minutes, or until well glazed. Cut into thin slices and serve with party rye bread and Sweet-and-Sour Mustard Sauce. Serves 20.

*Note: The corned beef may be cooked 2 days in advance. Remove beef from cooking liquid and refrigerate. When ready to use, let beef stand at room temperature at least 1 hour. Score fat, stud with cloves, spread with mustard, and sprinkle with sugar. Bake in 350° F. oven 30 minutes.

Sweet-and-Sour Mustard Sauce (sd)

3 tablespoons sugar
4½ tablespoons all-purpose
  flour
1 tablespoon dry mustard
1 cup heavy cream
1 egg yolk
3 tablespoons white vinegar

In the top of a small double boiler combine sugar, flour, and mustard. In a small bowl combine cream and egg yolk and beat slightly with a fork. Gradually add cream mixture to dry ingredients in top of double boiler; place over hot water. Cook over low heat (about 200° F.) for about 10 to 12 minutes, stirring constantly with a wire whip or wooden spoon. Remove from heat when sauce is thickened. Slowly add vinegar, beating constantly until well blended. Serve warm with corned beef. Makes 1 cup.

✎ Eggplant Spread (sd)

1 1-pound eggplant
¼ cup olive oil
½ cup thinly sliced onion
½ cup canned tomato sauce
½ cup finely diced celery
2 capers, chopped (optional)
3 stuffed green olives
2 teaspoons finely chopped
  almonds
2 tablespoons wine vinegar
1 teaspoon salt
1 teaspoon pepper
½ teaspoon garlic salt
Assorted Melba rounds and
  crackers

Peel eggplant and dice into small cubes. Heat oil in a skillet over moderate heat (about 250° F.), add eggplant and cook 10 minutes, or until eggplant is soft, stirring frequently. Remove eggplant and mash with a potato masher or fork. Add onion to skillet and cook for about 10 minutes, or until brown. Add a little more oil if necessary. Add tomato sauce and celery and cook for about 5 minutes, or until celery is tender. Add capers, olives, almonds, eggplant, vinegar, salt, pepper, and garlic salt. Reduce heat to low (about 200° F.) and simmer for 20 minutes. Remove from skillet and cool. Chill until ready to serve. Accompany with assorted Melba rounds and crackers. Makes 1½ cups, enough for about 48 crackers.

Pinwheel Sandwiches (f)

Egg Filling (recipe follows)
Deviled Ham Filling (recipe follows)
1 loaf unsliced white sandwich bread
¼ cup soft butter or margarine

Prepare Egg Filling and Deviled Ham Filling. Cut loaf of bread into 6 lengthwise slices. Trim off crusts. Lay slices between two slightly dampened tea towels and roll lightly with a rolling pin to make bread more pliable. Spread slices lightly with butter. Spread three slices with the Egg Filling and the other three with Deviled Ham Filling. Starting with the wide side, roll each slice tightly. Wrap each in plastic wrap and chill at least 2 hours, or until needed. To serve, cut rolls crosswise into ¼-inch slices. Makes about 6 dozen.

Egg Filling

2 hard-cooked eggs, finely chopped
2 tablespoons mayonnaise
1 tablespoon dry mustard
½ teaspoon garlic salt
1 tablespoon freeze-dried chives
¼ teaspoon white pepper

Combine all ingredients in a small bowl and blend well.

Deviled Ham Filling

1 4½-ounce can deviled ham
1 tablespoon drained sweet pickle relish
1 tablespoon prepared mustard

Combine all ingredients in a small bowl and blend well.

Barbecued Spareribs (f)

5 pounds fresh pork spareribs (2 strips)
1 cup bottled barbecue sauce
2 tablespoons wine vinegar
3 cloves garlic
¼ cup soy sauce
¼ teaspoon dry mustard
2 tablespoons red wine

With a sharp knife score the meat between the ribs, but do not cut all the way through. Place ribs in a shallow roasting pan large enough to let them lie flat. In a small bowl combine remaining ingredients and pour over meat. Let stand at least 1 hour, turning occasionally. For best results, let stand in refrigerator overnight. Heat oven to 350° F. Drain marinade from ribs into a small bowl and set aside. Roast meat in oven for 1 hour and 45

2 *tablespoons sugar*
¼ *teaspoon ground ginger*

minutes, basting occasionally with the marinade. When ready to serve, place under preheated broiler 3 inches from source of heat for about 5 minutes, until meat is crisp. Remove meat to a cutting board. Cut through between each rib, and with a meat cleaver or heavy knife cut each rib into 2 or 3 pieces. Serve hot. May be reheated in a 350° F. oven about 10 minutes. Makes approximately 50 pieces.

✑ Cheese Log (sd)

6 *ounces blue cheese, at room temperature*
2 *5-ounce jars pasteurized process bacon–cheese spread, at room temperature*
4 *3-ounce packages cream cheese, at room temperature*
2 *tablespoons instant minced onion*
1 *teaspoon Worcestershire sauce*
1 *cup finely chopped fresh parsley*
Assorted crackers

Combine cheeses, onion, and Worcestershire in the large bowl of an electric mixer. Mix at medium speed until well blended and smooth. Line a 1-quart loaf pan with aluminum foil. Pack the cheese mixture into the pan. Cover tightly and refrigerate at least 4 hours, or overnight, until well chilled and hardened. One hour before serving time, remove cheese from pan and roll cheese mixture with hands into a long, cylindrical roll about 2 inches in diameter. Peel off aluminum foil and pat parsley on all sides to cover evenly. Place cheese log on a large platter; chill until serving time. Serve with assorted crackers. Makes about 4 cups, enough for about 120 crackers.

✑ Shrimp-and-Cheese Spread (db)

2 *4½-ounce cans medium-sized shrimp, drained*
1 *cup ice water*
2 *tablespoons lemon juice*
1 *cup cream-style cottage cheese*
5 *tablespoons chili sauce*
1 *teaspoon finely chopped onion*
1 *teaspoon lemon juice*
½ *teaspoon Worcestershire sauce*
¼ *cup milk*
2 *tablespoons commercial sour cream*

In a small bowl soak shrimp in ice water and lemon juice for at least 30 minutes. Drain and finely chop shrimp. Mix with remaining ingredients until smooth and well blended. Chill until ready to serve. Spread on assorted crackers. Makes 2 cups, enough for about 64 crackers.

1 tablespoon chopped fresh
   parsley
¼ teaspoon salt
⅛ teaspoon white pepper
Assorted crackers

 Profiteroles with Creamed Chicken (f)

1 cup boiling water
½ cup butter or margarine
1 cup sifted all-purpose
   flour
¼ teaspoon salt
4 eggs
Creamed Chicken (recipe
   follows)

Heat oven to 450° F. In a medium-sized saucepan combine water and butter. Place over moderate heat (about 250° F.) and stir until butter is melted and mixture comes to a boil. Reduce heat to low (about 200° F.). Add flour and salt all at once. Stir vigorously over the heat until mixture forms a ball and leaves sides of pan. This will take about 1 minute. Remove from heat. Cool slightly. Add eggs one at a time, beating well after each addition. Continue beating until smooth and satiny. Drop level tablespoons of the batter onto greased cookie sheets about 1½ inches apart. Bake 20 minutes; then reduce temperature to 375° F. Bake 15 minutes longer, until sides of puffs feel rigid. Cool on wire racks. Cut a slice off top of each puff. Fill with Creamed Chicken. Replace tops and place puffs on cookie sheets. When ready to serve, heat in 250° F. oven about 5 minutes. Makes about 4 dozen.

Creamed Chicken

¼ cup milk
1 cup chicken broth
3 tablespoons butter or
   margarine
3 tablespoons all-purpose
   flour
1½ cups finely diced cooked
   chicken
¼ cup dry sherry
¼ teaspoon salt
⅛ teaspoon white pepper

Combine milk and chicken broth in a small saucepan over moderately low heat (about 225° F.) and heat until bubbles appear around the edge. In another saucepan over moderately low heat (about 225° F.) melt butter. Blend in flour with a wire whip or wooden spoon and cook until foamy. Remove from heat and add hot broth mixture, stirring constantly with a wire whip. Return to heat and cook and stir until sauce is thickened and smooth. Add chicken, sherry, salt, and pepper. Fill puffs with mixture. Makes 1⅔ cups.

Hot Crab Fondue (d)

1 5-ounce jar process sharp
   American cheese spread

In the top of a double boiler over boiling water, combine cheese spread and cream cheese. Stir constantly until

APPETIZERS

1 8-ounce package cream
  cheese
1 7½-ounce can Alaska king
  crab, drained and flaked
¼ cup light cream
½ teaspoon Worcestershire
  sauce
¼ teaspoon garlic salt
½ teaspoon cayenne pepper
French bread, Melba rounds,
  or toast points

blended and smooth. Add remaining ingredients except for breads and heat until well blended, stirring occasionally. Serve hot in a fondue pot or chafing dish with chunks of French bread, Melba rounds, or toast points. If fondue thickens on standing, stir in a little additional cream. Makes 2½ cups, enough for about 40.

Coconut Shrimp (f)

1 pound medium-sized
  fresh or frozen shrimp
  (about 20), peeled and
  deveined
1 egg
¾ cup milk
¼ cup firmly packed light
  brown sugar
1¼ cups all-purpose flour
Vegetable oil for frying
2 4-ounce packages
  shredded coconut

Cut each shrimp in half lengthwise. In a small bowl combine egg, milk, and brown sugar and beat until well blended. Gradually add flour and beat with a rotary beater until smooth. Pour oil into a deep saucepan to a depth of about 1 inch. Heat to a temperature of 375° F. on a deep-fat thermometer. (An electric skillet may be used; set temperature control at 375° F.) Place one package of the coconut in a shallow pan (add more as needed). Dip each shrimp half in egg mixture; then coat thoroughly with coconut. Fry in the hot oil about 5 minutes, or until golden brown. Serve hot. May be reheated in a 350° F. oven about 5 minutes. Makes about 40 pieces.

Orange-Glazed Baked Ham (d)

1 3-pound canned ham
Whole cloves
1¼ cups firmly packed light
  brown sugar
1 teaspoon dry mustard
¼ cup white vinegar
½ cup orange juice
1 tablespoon grated orange
  peel
1 large orange, cut into
  ¼-inch slices
Parsley sprigs
Party rye

Heat oven to 350° F. Place ham on a rack in a shallow baking pan and score the fat on the top. Stud fat with cloves. In a bowl combine sugar, mustard, vinegar, orange juice, and peel. Baste ham with some of the glaze and arrange some of the orange slices on top of ham. Bake about 45 minutes, allowing 15 minutes per pound. Baste with the glaze several times while cooking. Remove from pan and place on a large platter or tray. Cut about half of the ham into thin slices. Leave rest uncut, to be sliced as needed. Garnish platter with parsley and remaining orange slices and serve with party rye. Serves about 30.

ᷤ Chicken Liver Pâté (sd)

2 pounds chicken livers
1 cup chicken broth
8 slices raw bacon, coarsely
  chopped
2 cups finely chopped onions
5 hard-cooked eggs, cut into
  quarters
3 tablespoons butter or
  margarine
1 tablespoon salt
1 teaspoon pepper
2 teaspoons curry powder
2 tablespoons dry sherry
Assorted crackers

Combine chicken livers and broth in a saucepan and simmer over moderately low heat (about 225° F.) for 15 minutes. Drain thoroughly. In a skillet combine chicken livers and bacon and cook over moderate heat (about 250° F.) for about 5 to 7 minutes, or until bacon is crisp and golden brown. Remove livers and bacon with a slotted spoon; in the remaining fat cook onions for 10 minutes, or until soft and lightly browned. Combine liver, bacon, eggs, butter, salt, pepper, curry, and sherry in the large bowl of an electric mixer and mix at low speed about 5 minutes, or until fairly smooth. Or mixture may be put through a food chopper, using the fine blade. Refrigerate until ready to serve. If desired, the pâté may be firmly packed into a buttered 1-quart mold and chilled until firm. When ready to serve, loosen edges with a pointed knife; dip quickly into warm water and invert onto a tray. Surround with crackers. Makes about 4 cups pâté, enough for about 120 crackers.

ᷤ Caviar Roll (f)

¼ cup butter or margarine
⅔ cup sifted all-purpose flour
2 cups milk
4 eggs, separated
1 teaspoon salt
1 3-ounce package cream
  cheese, at room
  temperature
⅓ cup commercial sour cream
1 4-ounce jar red caviar

Heat oven to 325° F. Grease a 15½-x-10½-x-1-inch jelly-roll pan, line with waxed paper, grease paper, and sprinkle lightly with flour. In a saucepan over moderately low heat (about 225° F.) melt butter and stir in flour; add milk slowly, stirring constantly, and cook until mixture is thickened and smooth. Remove from heat. In a small bowl beat egg yolks well; add a small amount of the hot sauce (about ¼ cup) to the yolks. Then add egg mixture to hot sauce and blend well. In another bowl beat egg whites and salt until soft peaks form. Gently fold whites into hot mixture. Pour batter into prepared pan and bake 45 minutes, or until top is golden brown. Cool in pan 5 minutes; then turn out onto a clean tea towel. Peel off waxed paper; trim off edges. Starting at a narrow end, roll up cake with the towel and cool 30 to 45 minutes on a cake rack. In a bowl mix cream cheese, sour cream, and caviar. Gently unroll cake and remove towel. Spread caviar mixture on cake and roll it up again. Wrap in plastic wrap and refrigerate at least 1 hour. When ready to serve, cut roll into ¼-inch-thick slices and arrange on a serving plate. Makes about 2 dozen slices.

CHAPTER VII

SOUPS

Soups, most often thought of as a quick luncheon standby, can be—in consommé or bouillon form—a superb, almost calorie-free drink between meals or—in hearty chowder form—a satisfying supper meal. Except for a formal meal, where soup as a first course should be served at the table in either a soup plate or a cream soup dish with a serving plate under it, soup may be served hot in mugs or coffee cups or, chilled, in glasses and served in the living room before a meal.

While there is an infinite variety of soups available in canned, dry-mix, and frozen forms and clear broths can be quickly at hand with bouillon cubes, concentrated granules, or from a can, "dressing up" soups with a creative touch is one of the easiest ways for a new cook to start experimenting with cooking. Some suggestions for combining soup flavors are on pages 231–234 in this chapter. Garnishes are often added to soups not for appearance alone, but because the flavor combination is really part of the recipe. For example, a garnish of snipped chives is an integral part of cold vichyssoise, a slice of lemon and a sprinkling of sieved hard-cooked egg belong with hot black bean soup, a crisp slice of toasted French bread and a dash of grated Parmesan cheese should float on hot onion soup. You can experiment with dollops of unsweetened whipped cream or sour cream, snipped parsley or celery or watercress leaves, croutons, crumbled bacon, onion or green pepper rings as garnishes; experiment also with dried herbs (one at a time) to add an exotic flavor to ready-made soups. Dill is particularly compatible with potato soup; tarragon, with cream of chicken, and basil, with tomato soup. Try lacing any cream soup with a little dry sherry.

Stocks

When you start completely from scratch to make homemade soups, the first step is to make a broth, or stock. This is not difficult; it does require a large pot or kettle and long cooking, but very little of your attention once you put it on to cook. Stocks can be made ahead and refrigerated for a week or frozen for six months. They can be used to make soups, sauces, or gravies or combined with leftover meats, fish, or poultry and vegetables to make a thick soup or stew. Veal and chicken stocks can be used interchangeably but it's best to match the stock base to the meat or fish you're using in the soup.

All stocks should be clarified by straining through fine cheesecloth; chill so that fat, which rises to the top, can be easily lifted off. Frozen stock cubes are a great convenience to have on hand to add to sauces and gravies. Pour cooled stock into freezer trays; freeze. Store frozen cubes in plastic bags in the freezer.

 Beef Stock

4 *pounds beef shank slices (with meat on bones)*
2 *3-inch marrow bones*
3 *quarts water*
2 *medium-sized carrots, scrubbed and cut into thirds*
2 *medium-sized onions, quartered*
2 *stalks celery with leaves*
1 *bay leaf*
2 *whole cloves garlic*
4 *whole cloves*
6 *peppercorns*
½ *teaspoon dried thyme leaves*
2 *sprigs parsley*
2 *teaspoons salt*

Place meat and marrow bones in a large kettle with the water. Add remaining ingredients and bring to a boil over moderately high heat (about 275° F.). Simmer, covered, over low heat (about 200° F.) 4 hours. Strain stock. Cool. Chill overnight. Skim off fat from top before using. If stock gelatinizes on standing, warm slightly until it melts before measuring amount needed in recipe. Makes 3 quarts.

Chicken Stock

1 *5-pound stewing chicken, cut up*

Combine all ingredients in a large kettle. Bring to a boil over moderately high heat (about 275° F.). Simmer, cov-

1 stalk celery with leaves
3 medium-sized carrots, scrubbed and cut into thirds
1 medium-sized onion, quartered
1 bay leaf
1 sprig parsley
2 teaspoons salt
3 peppercorns
2 whole cloves
⅛ teaspoon dried marjoram leaves
2 quarts water

ered, over low heat (about 200° F.) 3 hours. Strain broth. Cool. Chill in refrigerator overnight. Skim off fat from top before using. If stock gelatinizes on standing, warm slightly until it melts before measuring amounts needed. Remove chicken from bones and use in salads and sandwiches. Makes 2 quarts.

Veal Stock

Substitute 1 pound veal neck or shoulder, cut into pieces, and 3 pounds veal knuckle bones for the chicken in recipe above.

_____

Fish Stock

1 cup sliced onions
¾ cup sliced leeks
2½ cups finely chopped fresh tomatoes
4 cloves garlic, crushed
⅓ cup olive oil
2½ quarts water
6 sprigs parsley
1 bay leaf
½ teaspoon dried thyme leaves
¼ teaspoon dried basil leaves
2 pinches dried saffron (optional)
⅛ teaspoon ground pepper
1 tablespoon salt
1 teaspoon grated orange peel
4 pounds fish heads, bones, and trimmings

Combine all ingredients in a large kettle. Bring to a boil. Skim off residue and simmer, covered, over low heat (about 200° F.) 35 to 40 minutes. Strain broth and reserve. Discard bones and vegetables. Makes about 2½ quarts.

Hearty Soups

Hearty soups, served with a hot bread, will make a complete supper or luncheon. They're especially good in chilly weather. They do take time to prepare but they may be made ahead and reheated at serving time. Most of these, like a good stew, will taste even better when the flavors have had a chance to meld.

❧ Minestrone

1 pound dried Great Northern white beans
¼ cup olive oil
¼ cup butter or margarine
1 large carrot, diced
2 cups diced celery
1½ cups sliced leeks
1 16-ounce can tomatoes
*3 quarts Beef Stock (recipe on page 211)
¼ pound sliced prosciutto ham, cut into bite-sized pieces
1½ tablespoons salt
1 clove garlic, crushed
3 sprigs parsley
1 tablespoon dried basil leaves
½ teaspoon dried oregano leaves
2 cups diced raw potatoes
2 9-ounce packages frozen Italian green beans
4 small zucchini, cut into ¼-inch slices
2 cups shredded white cabbage
½ cup raw elbow macaroni
Grated Parmesan cheese

Wash white beans; place in a large bowl. Cover with cold water and soak overnight. Drain. Place white beans in a large Dutch oven or kettle with water to cover. Cook, covered, over moderate heat (about 250° F.) about 1 hour, or until beans are soft. Drain. Combine olive oil and butter in bottom of Dutch oven and heat over moderate heat (about 250° F.). Add carrot, celery, and leeks and cook about 5 minutes, stirring occasionally. Stir in tomatoes, mashing them slightly with a fork. Simmer over moderately low heat (about 225° F.) 10 minutes. Add Beef Stock, prosciutto, and white beans. Simmer, covered, over moderate heat (about 250° F.) 30 minutes. Add salt, garlic, parsley, basil, and oregano. Stir in potatoes and Italian green beans. Simmer, uncovered, 10 minutes. Add zucchini, cabbage, and macaroni. Simmer 8 minutes longer. Serve in large bowls; sprinkle each serving with Parmesan cheese. Makes about 4½ quarts, or 12 1½-cup servings.

*Note: An equivalent amount of canned beef bouillon, or broth made from beef bouillon cubes, or instant beef broth plus water may be substituted for the Beef Stock.

Chinese Spinach Soup

½ pound fresh spinach
1 tablespoon cornstarch
*6 cups cold Chicken Stock
(recipe on page 211)
1 tablespoon vegetable oil
1 scallion or green onion,
thinly sliced
1 6-ounce can bamboo
shoots, drained (sliced, if
large)
¼ pound fresh mushrooms,
thinly sliced
¼ teaspoon ground ginger
1 7½-ounce can crab
meat, drained and flaked
1 tablespoon dry sherry
1 cup very fine egg noodles
1 teaspoon salt

Remove tough stems from spinach; chop leaves coarsely. In a small bowl blend cornstarch into ½ cup of the cold Chicken Stock. In a large Dutch oven heat oil over moderate heat (about 250° F.). Add scallion, bamboo shoots, mushrooms, and ginger and stir 1 minute. Add crab meat and cook 1 minute longer, stirring occasionally. Add sherry and blend well. Pour in the remaining 5½ cups stock and bring to a boil. Stir in noodles and salt and rapidly bring back to a boil. Reduce heat to moderately low (about 225° F.) and cook 5 minutes. Add cornstarch mixture and stir constantly until soup thickens slightly. Stir in spinach and heat until it wilts. Serve immediately. Makes 1½ quarts, or 6 1-cup servings.

*Note: An equivalent amount of canned chicken broth, or broth made from chicken bouillon cubes, or instant chicken broth plus water may be substituted for Chicken Stock.

Bouillabaisse

1¼ quarts Fish Stock (recipe
on page 212)
1 8-ounce package frozen
lobster tails
1 dozen small clams in
shells, scrubbed
¼ cup bottled clam juice
2 medium-sized tomatoes,
peeled and cut into
eighths
1½ pounds flounder or
halibut (or a combination
of both), cut into serving-
sized pieces
½ pound scallops, washed
½ pound fresh shrimp,
shelled and deveined,
with tails left on
1 7½-ounce can crab meat
drained and flaked

Bring Fish Stock to a boil. Cut membrane along both edges of each lobster tail and remove membranes. Cut each tail into 3 or 4 pieces, leaving meat in shells. Add lobster pieces to stock; cover and simmer over moderately low heat (about 225° F.) 10 minutes. Add clams in their shells, clam juice, and tomatoes and simmer, covered, 8 to 10 minutes longer. Stir in fish pieces, scallops, shrimp, and crab; cook 5 minutes, or until fish flakes easily and clam shells open. Do not overcook the fish. Serve immediately, with crusty rolls, if desired. Makes about 3 quarts, or 8 1½-cup servings.

✒️ Lentil-and-Split-Pea Soup

1½ cups dried lentils
½ cup dried green split peas
*2 quarts Beef Stock (recipe on page 211)
2 slices bacon, diced
¼ cup coarsely chopped carrot
½ cup coarsely chopped celery
3 tablespoons chopped fresh parsley
1 clove garlic, crushed
1 bay leaf
¼ teaspoon dried thyme leaves
2 teaspoons salt
⅛ teaspoon pepper
3 small potatoes, peeled and diced
1 tablespoon butter or margarine, melted
1 tablespoon flour
1 1-pound package bratwurst or bockwurst

Wash lentils and peas. Place in a large bowl, cover with cold water, and let stand overnight. Drain. In a large Dutch oven combine Beef Stock and drained lentils and peas; bring to a boil. Stir in bacon, carrot, celery, parsley, garlic, bay leaf, thyme, salt, and pepper. Simmer, covered, over low heat (about 200° F.) 2 hours, or until lentils are soft. Add potatoes and cook 20 minutes longer, or until potatoes are tender. In a small bowl combine butter and flour and blend well. Stir into soup and simmer 5 minutes. Meanwhile, cook the bratwurst according to package directions. Drain and slice. Place a few slices in each bowl. Pour soup over bratwurst. Makes 2½ quarts, or 7 1½-cup servings.

*Note: An equivalent amount of canned beef bouillon, or broth made from beef bouillon cubes, or instant beef broth plus water may be substituted for the Beef Stock.

✒️ New Orleans Seafood Gumbo

7 slices bacon, diced
1 small onion, finely chopped
2 garlic cloves, crushed
6 cups Fish Stock (recipe on page 212)
2 10-ounce packages frozen cut okra
1 pound tomatoes, peeled and quartered (3 medium-sized tomatoes)
2 lemon slices
1 bay leaf

Cook bacon in a large Dutch oven over moderately high heat (about 275° F.) until crisp. Drain bacon pieces on paper towels and reserve. Remove all but 2 tablespoons of the bacon fat from Dutch oven. Add onion and garlic and cook over moderately low heat (about 225° F.) until tender but not browned. Add Fish Stock to Dutch oven and bring to a boil over moderate heat (about 250° F.). Stir in the 2 packages okra and return to a boil. Add tomatoes, lemon slices, bay leaf, salt, and pepper. Simmer, covered, over low heat (about 200° F.) 20 minutes. Stir in crab meat, shrimp, rice, and bacon and simmer, covered, 5 minutes, or until shrimp turn pink and soup

1 tablespoon salt
¼ teaspoon pepper
1 7½-ounce can crab meat,
    drained and coarsely
    flaked
½ pound fresh or frozen
    cleaned and deveined
    shrimp
1 cup cooked rice

is thoroughly heated. Serve immediately. Makes about 3 quarts, or 8 1½-cup servings.

✑ Tomato–Fish Chowder

4 stalks celery, diced
2 medium-sized green
    peppers, diced coarsely
2 cups shredded cabbage
1 tablespoon instant minced
    onion
2 envelopes instant chicken
    broth mix
½ teaspoon dried thyme
    leaves
1 cup water
1 18-fluid-ounce can tomato
    juice
1 1-pound package frozen
    haddock fillets, partially
    thawed and cut into 1½-to
    2-inch chunks.

Combine all ingredients in a saucepan. Simmer, covered, over moderately low heat (about 225° F.) 10 minutes. Uncover and simmer 5 minutes longer. (If a thinner chowder is preferred, do not uncover last 5 minutes.) Serves 4.

✑ New England Fish Chowder

2 12-ounce packages frozen
    fillet of flounder, thawed
⅛ pound salt pork, diced
2 medium-sized onions,
    thinly sliced
2 medium-sized potatoes,
    peeled and diced
2 tablespoons butter or
    margarine
¼ cup flour
2 cups milk
1 teaspoon salt

Cut fish fillets into 6 to 8 pieces. Place in a heavy saucepan or Dutch oven. Add enough water to just cover bottom of pan. Cover tightly and simmer over moderately low heat (about 225° F.) about 15 minutes, or until fish flakes easily when tested with a fork. Remove fish. Strain and reserve fish stock. Add diced salt pork to Dutch oven and cook over moderate heat (about 250° F.) until lightly browned. Add sliced onion and cook until tender, about 10 minutes. Add reserved fish stock to Dutch oven. Add diced potatoes and enough water to barely cover the potatoes. Cover and cook about 20 minutes, until tender but not mushy. Melt butter in a

⅛ teaspoon pepper
¼ teaspoon sugar
Dash of dried thyme
Few grains cayenne pepper
Pinch of dried rosemary
½ cup light cream

saucepan over low heat. Gradually stir in flour and cook until bubbly. Slowly stir in milk. Cook over moderate heat, stirring constantly, until sauce is thickened and smooth. Add salt, pepper, sugar, thyme, cayenne pepper, and rosemary. Blend in the cream. Gradually stir white sauce into vegetable mixture in Dutch oven. Simmer very gently 15 minutes. Add cooked fish. Heat. Chowder may be stored in refrigerator 24 hours or longer to blend flavors. Reheat before serving. If necessary, add more salt and pepper. Drop in about 2 tablespoons butter and sprinkle with paprika before serving, if desired. Makes about 2 quarts, or 5 1½-cup servings.

ꬱ Manhattan Clam Chowder

2 10½-ounce cans minced clams
1 3-x-2-inch slice salt pork, finely diced (about 6 ounces)
1 large onion, coarsely chopped
1 medium-sized leek, sliced
2 medium-sized potatoes, peeled and cubed
4 large tomatoes, peeled and chopped
1 stalk celery, chopped
1 medium-sized green pepper, chopped
1 bay leaf
½ teaspoon dried thyme leaves
5 cups water
2 teaspoons salt
Few grains pepper
½ teaspoon caraway seeds (optional)

Drain clams and reserve both clams and liquid. Place salt pork in a large Dutch oven. Cook over moderately low heat (about 225° F.) about 2 minutes. Add onion and leek and cook until tender. Add potatoes, tomatoes, celery, green pepper, bay leaf, thyme, water, and liquid from clams. Add salt and pepper and blend well. Bring to a boil over moderate heat (about 250° F.). Simmer, covered, over moderately low heat (about 225° F.) 30 to 35 minutes, or until vegetables are tender. Add minced clams and caraway seeds. Cook 5 minutes. Makes 2 quarts, or 5 1½-cup servings.

ꬱ New England Clam Chowder

¼ cup finely chopped salt pork
¾ cup coarsely chopped onion

Cook salt pork in a heavy saucepan over moderate heat (about 250° F.) until crisp and brown. Drain crisp pieces on paper towels. Cook onion in the fat until tender. Add

[217]

2 cups diced potatoes
1 teaspoon salt
⅛ teaspoon pepper
2 7½-ounce cans minced
 clams or 1 pint shucked
 fresh clams, diced
2 cups milk
1 cup light cream or
 undiluted evaporated milk
1 tablespoon flour
2 tablespoons milk

diced potatoes, salt and pepper, and liquid drained from the clams. Add water, if necessary, just to cover potatoes; cook over moderately low heat (about 225° F.) until potatoes are tender. Add clams. Stir in the 2 cups milk and cream and set aside to ripen for a couple of hours. Reheat slowly over very low heat (about 175° F.). Stir flour and the 2 tablespoons milk together to form a smooth paste. Stir into chowder and cook slowly over moderately low heat (about 225° F.), stirring constantly, until slightly thickened. If possible allow chowder to stand in refrigerator for 24 hours, or longer, before serving. Reheat over very low heat (about 175° F.). Garnish each serving with crisp salt pork pieces. Serve with crackers. Makes 6 1½-cup servings.

Seafood Bisque

6 tablespoons butter or
 margarine
½ pound fresh or frozen
 shrimp, cleaned and
 deveined
½ pound scallops
 (optional)
1 pound fillet of sole
3 tablespoons flour
1 cup heavy cream
2½ cups milk
1 teaspoon salt
Few grains pepper
½ teaspoon Worcestershire
 sauce
1 tablespoon grated
 Parmesan cheese
¼ teaspoon paprika
1 7½-ounce can crab
 meat, drained and
 flaked
1 5-ounce can lobster,
 drained and flaked
2 tablespoons dry sherry
Chopped fresh parsley

Place butter in a large kettle or Dutch oven, and melt over moderate heat (about 225° F.). Cut shrimp, scallops, and sole into small pieces and add to butter. Cook 8 minutes, stirring occasionally. Remove from heat. Remove seafood with a slotted spoon and reserve. Stir the flour into the butter left in the kettle and blend well. Blend in ½ cup of the cream to form a thick paste. Gradually add the remaining cream and the milk and blend well. Add salt, pepper, Worcestershire, cheese, and paprika. Cook over moderate heat (about 250° F.) until mixture is smooth and thickened, stirring continuously. Add reserved seafood, crab meat, and lobster. Heat thoroughly. Just before serving, stir in sherry. Garnish each serving with a sprinkling of chopped parsley. Makes about 2 quarts, or 5 1½-cup servings.

◄§ Ukrainian Vegetable Borscht

2 pounds beef soup meat
1 marrow bone
2½ quarts water
1 half-pound ham slice
1 bay leaf
10 peppercorns
1 clove garlic, minced
3 sprigs parsley
1 medium-sized carrot, sliced
1 stalk celery, sliced
1 medium-sized leek, sliced
8 medium-sized beets
3 tablespoons water
2 large onions, quartered
1 cup shredded white cabbage
3 large potatoes, peeled and cut into eighths
⅓ cup tomato purée
2 tablespoons white vinegar
2 teaspoons sugar
1½ tablespoons salt
¾ cup canned white kidney beans
5 frankfurters, sliced
Commercial sour cream
Parsley sprigs

In a large kettle combine soup meat, bone, and the 2½ quarts water; bring to a boil. Simmer, covered, over low heat (about 200° F.) 1 hour. Add ham slice, bay leaf, peppercorns, garlic, parsley, carrot, celery, and leek. Cover and simmer 1½ hours longer. Meanwhile, place 7 beets in a large saucepan with water to cover. Bring to a boil. Simmer, covered, over moderately low heat (about 225° F.) 35 minutes, or until fork-tender. Peel and dice beets. Scrub remaining beet well; grate and mix in a small bowl with 3 tablespoons water; reserve. Remove meats and bone from broth. Cool meats and slice thinly. Add cooked beets, onion, cabbage, potatoes, tomato purée, vinegar, sugar, and salt to broth. Simmer, covered, over moderately low heat (about 225° F.) 40 minutes. Add beans and frankfurters and blend well. Simmer 15 minutes longer. Skim off fat from top of soup. Add the reserved grated beet and water mixture; blend well. Stir in meat slices and cook until heated through. Serve with a spoonful of sour cream on top of each serving. Garnish with a sprig of parsley. Makes about 6 quarts, or 16 1½-cup servings.

◄§ Potage St. Germain

4 10-ounce packages frozen peas
¼ cup coarsely chopped fresh parsley
1 small onion, quartered
2 large lettuce leaves, coarsely torn
3 cups canned chicken broth
½ teaspoon sugar

Cook peas according to package directions; drain. Reserve ¼ cup of the peas for garnish. Place about ⅓ of the peas in the container of an electric blender. Add to the container about ⅓ of the chopped parsley, onion, and lettuce and 1 cup of the chicken broth. Cover and blend at high speed about 45 seconds, or until peas are puréed. Pour mixture into a large saucepan. Repeat twice as above. Stir in the sugar, salt, and chervil. Cook over moderately low heat (about 225° F.) until heated thoroughly. Add cream and butter and blend well. Stir

1½ teaspoons salt
⅛ teaspoon dried chervil
  leaves
1 cup heavy cream
3 tablespoons butter or
  margarine
Parsley sprigs

until well heated. Garnish each serving with a sprig of parsley and a few of the reserved peas. Makes about 8½ cups, or 5 1½-cup servings.

✔ ✎ Lamb-Barley Soup

2 to 2½ pounds lamb neck,
  cut into pieces
2 stalks celery, halved
1 medium-sized onion,
  halved
1 bay leaf
2 teaspoons salt
10 peppercorns
5 whole cloves
2 quarts water
½ cup medium-sized barley
1 cup shredded carrots
¼ cup sliced leek

In a large saucepan combine lamb, celery, onion, bay leaf, salt, peppercorns, cloves, and water. Place over moderate heat (about 250° F.) and bring to a boil. Reduce heat to low (about 200° F.); cover and simmer 1¼ hours, or until lamb is fork-tender. Cool and chill several hours or overnight. Remove and discard the solidified fat. Remove meat pieces and cut meat from the bone. Strain stock. (Stock should measure about 1½ quarts; if it doesn't, add water to make 1½ quarts.) In a large saucepan combine stock and meat. Place over moderate heat (about 250° F.) and bring to a boil. Add barley and bring back to a boil, stirring constantly. Reduce heat to low (about 200° F.); cover and simmer 30 minutes, stirring occasionally. Add carrots and leek; season to taste and simmer 5 minutes. Serves 4 to 6.

✎ Quick-Supper Soup

1 pound ground lean lamb
¼ cup dry bread crumbs
1 egg, slightly beaten
¼ teaspoon dried rosemary
  leaves
¼ teaspoon celery salt
¼ teaspoon salt
⅛ teaspoon pepper
2 tablespoons butter or
  margarine
1 can condensed onion soup
1 can condensed vegetable
  soup
2 cups water

Combine lamb, bread crumbs, egg, rosemary, celery salt, salt, and pepper; chill. Shape into 1½-inch balls. Melt butter in saucepan over moderate heat (about 250° F.) and brown meat balls lightly. Remove balls and drain off drippings. Mix onion soup, vegetable soup, and water in saucepan; add lamb balls and cook over moderately low heat (about 225° F.) 30 minutes. Makes 7 cups, or serves 4 to 6.

◄§ Chicken-and-Dumpling Soup

2 1½- to 2-pound broiler–
   fryer chickens, cut up
2 quarts water
½ teaspoon dried rosemary
   leaves
1 tablespoon salt
⅛ teaspoon pepper
¼ cup chopped onion
1 cup sliced carrot
1 cup fresh, frozen, or
   canned corn
½ cup fresh or frozen lima
   beans
Parsley Dumplings (recipe
   follows)

Put chicken, water, rosemary, salt, and pepper in Dutch oven. Cover and bring to boil; simmer over low heat (about 200° F.) 40 to 45 minutes, or until fork-tender. Remove from heat; cool and chill in refrigerator several hours, or overnight, to allow fat to harden. Remove and discard fat. Cut chicken breasts in half and separate thighs from legs. Add chicken, onion, carrot, corn, and lima beans to stock. Cover and bring to boil; simmer over low heat (about 200° F.) 15 minutes. Drop spoonfuls of the Parsley Dumpling batter over top of soup. Cook uncovered over moderate heat (about 250° F.) 10 minutes. Cover tightly; reduce heat to moderately low (about 225° F.) and cook 10 minutes longer. Serve each portion with one or two dumplings. Makes about 3 quarts, or 8 1½-cup servings.

Parsley Dumplings

2 cups sifted all-purpose
   flour
4 teaspoons baking powder
1 teaspoon salt
¼ teaspoon pepper
1 egg
Milk
3 tablespoons melted butter
   or margarine
¼ cup chopped fresh parsley

Sift flour, baking powder, salt, and pepper together into a bowl. Break egg into measuring cup and add enough milk to make 1 cup liquid; beat together slightly. Stir milk mixture and melted butter into flour; mix well. Fold in parsley. Drop by spoonfuls over soup. Makes about 12 dumplings.

◄§ Quick Corn Chowder

4 tablespoons butter or
   margarine
⅔ cup coarsely chopped onion
½ cup coarsely chopped green
   pepper
2 cups Chicken Stock (recipe
   on page 211) or 2 chicken
   bouillon cubes dissolved in
   2 cups boiling water

Melt butter in a large saucepan over moderately low heat (about 225° F.). Add onion and green pepper and cook about 5 minutes, until golden. Combine Chicken Stock with chicken soup and add to onion mixture. Heat, stirring constantly, until smooth. Add corn, chicken, rice, milk, parsley, and paprika; heat thoroughly, stirring frequently. Season to taste with salt and pepper. Makes about 3 quarts, or 8 1½-cup servings.

(Ingredients continued on page 222)

2 cans condensed cream of
chicken soup
2 16-ounce cans cream-style
corn
1 cup diced, canned or fresh
cooked chicken
2 cups cooked rice
5 cups milk
4 tablespoons chopped fresh
parsley
¼ teaspoon paprika
Salt and pepper

⋑ Pepper Pot Soup

½ pound honeycomb tripe,
cut into ½-inch cubes
1 pound veal neck, sliced
1 quart water
Pinch of dried thyme leaves
¼ teaspoon dried oregano
leaves
¼ teaspoon dried basil
leaves
1¾ teaspoons salt
⅛ teaspoon pepper
1 cup canned tomatoes
¼ cup chopped onion
½ cup diced carrot
½ cup diced celery
½ cup chopped green pepper
½ cup diced potato
1½ tablespoons chopped fresh
parsley

Place tripe, veal, water, thyme, oregano, basil, salt, and pepper in a Dutch oven. Cover and bring to a boil; reduce heat to moderately low (about 225° F.) and cook 2½ to 3 hours, or until tripe is fork-tender. Remove from heat; cool; then chill in refrigerator several hours or overnight to allow fat to harden. Discard fat. Add tomatoes, onion, carrot, celery, green pepper, and potato; bring to a boil. Reduce heat to moderately low (about 225° F.) and cook ½ hour. Remove veal bones from soup and cut meat from bones into small pieces. Add meat and parsley to soup. Makes about 1½ quarts, or 4 1-cup servings.

⋑ Texas Beef Soup

2 pounds beef brisket
1 beef bone
2 quarts water
2½ teaspoons salt
Few grains pepper
1 cup chopped onion
1 cup chopped green pepper

Place meat, bone, water, salt, and pepper in Dutch oven. Cover and bring to boil; skim off the foam that will form on surface of the soup. Simmer over low heat (about 200° F.) 2 hours, or until meat is fork-tender. Cool and chill in refrigerator several hours, or overnight, to allow fat to harden. Remove and discard fat. Add onion, green pepper, carrot, celery, potato, tomatoes, chili

1 cup sliced carrot
1 cup diced celery
1 cup diced potatoes
1 16-ounce can tomatoes
1 to 1½ teaspoons chili
  powder
⅛ teaspoon ground cumin
  (optional)
½ pound zucchini, sliced
1 cup uncooked elbow
  macaroni

powder, and cumin; simmer over low heat (about 200° F.) 1 hour. Remove from heat. Remove bone and meat from stock. Trim fat from meat and cut meat into bite-sized pieces. Place meat, zucchini, and macaroni in stock; bring to boil and simmer over low heat (about 200° F.) ½ hour. Makes about 4 quarts, or 10 1½-cup servings.

✑ Oxtail Soup

2 tablespoons shortening
2 oxtails, cut into pieces
2 quarts water
1 cup sliced onion
1 bay leaf
1 tablespoon salt
⅛ teaspoon pepper
¼ cup chopped fresh parsley
1½ cups diced carrot
1 cup diced celery
⅓ cup pearl barley
1 small can tomato paste
1 teaspoon dried thyme
  leaves
½ cup dry red wine

Melt shortening in Dutch oven over moderate heat (about 250° F.); add oxtail pieces and cook until lightly browned. Add water, onion, bay leaf, salt, and pepper. Cover and bring to boil; simmer over low heat (about 200° F.) 1 hour. Add parsley, carrot, celery, barley, tomato paste, and thyme; continue to simmer ½ hour, or until meat is fork-tender. Stir in wine just before serving. Makes about 3 quarts, or 8 1½-cup servings.

✑ Czechoslovakian Soup Pot

2½ pounds medium-sized
  potatoes, peeled and
  quartered (about 7 or 8)
1 quart water
1 tablespoon salt
1 pound fresh green beans,
  broken in half, or two
  9-ounce packages frozen
  cut green beans
2 teaspoons salt
⅛ teaspoon pepper
2 tablespoons lemon juice

Place potatoes in a large Dutch oven with the 1 quart water and the 1 tablespoon salt. Bring to a boil; cook, covered, over moderately low heat (about 225° F.) 10 minutes. Add green beans and cook, covered, 15 minutes longer, or until vegetables are fork-tender. Drain. Return vegetables to Dutch oven. Sprinkle the 2 teaspoons salt, the pepper, and the lemon juice over the vegetables and toss lightly. Cover to keep warm. In a large saucepan melt the ½ cup butter over moderately low heat (about 225° F.). Stir in the ½ cup flour and cook until mixture is frothy, stirring constantly. Gradually stir in milk and cook, stirring constantly, until thickened and

½ cup butter or margarine
½ cup flour
1 quart milk
⅛ teaspoon paprika
1 cup commercial sour
    cream
1 tablespoon flour
1 tablespoon butter or
    margarine
Snipped chives

smooth. Stir in paprika. Add sauce to vegetables and blend well. In a small bowl combine sour cream and the 1 tablespoon flour and blend well. Stir sour cream slowly into hot soup and blend well. Place over low heat (about 200° F.) and heat until soup is heated through, stirring occasionally. Do not allow to boil. Stir in the 1 tablespoon butter before serving. Serve with a sprinkling of chives on top. Makes about 2½ quarts, or about 7 1½-cup servings.

❧ Soupe Au Pistou (French Vegetable Soup)

6 cups water
1 16-ounce can whole peeled
    Italian tomatoes, drained
    and liquid reserved
2 teaspoons salt
1 16-ounce can navy beans,
    rinsed and drained
1 pound green beans,
    trimmed and cut into
    1-inch pieces (about 3½
    cups)
1 cup macaroni
1 pound zucchini, washed
    and cut into ½-inch slices
    (about 3⅓ cups)
½ pound yellow squash,
    washed and cut into
    ½-inch slices (about 1⅔
    cups)
Pistou (recipe below)
Grated Parmesan cheese
(preferably freshly grated)

About 20 minutes before serving, in a large soup pot or Dutch oven bring water, tomato liquid and salt to a boil over moderately high heat. Add canned beans and tomatoes and cook 5 minutes. Add green beans and macaroni and cook 5 minutes. Add squash and cook 5 minutes. Mix a little of the soup with the *Pistou*, add to the soup pot and stir over low heat a few seconds. Taste soup and add more salt if desired. Makes 12 cups or 8 1½-cup servings. Ladle from the pot into large soup bowls and serve the grated cheese separately.

Pistou

¼ cup olive oil
3 cloves garlic, peeled
¼ cup fresh dillweed, packed
    tight to measure
1 tablespoon dried basil
    leaves

Place oil and garlic in an electric blender; cover and blend at medium speed about 10 seconds, until garlic is crushed. Add dillweed and basil; cover and blend at medium speed until smooth. Add cheese and blend at medium speed to a green-flecked paste, stopping machine often and pushing down contents with a rubber

½ cup (2 ounces) grated
Parmesan cheese
(preferably freshly grated)

scraper. *Pistou* can be made up to a day ahead and stored, tightly covered, in the refrigerator. Makes a generous ½ cup.

✌ Short Rib–Vegetable Soup with Liver Balls

2 pounds beef short ribs
6 cups water
4 leeks, sliced, or ½ cup
    sliced onion
4 stalks celery, sliced
1 bay leaf
1 tablespoon salt
½ teaspoon pepper
3 medium-sized carrots,
    sliced
1 sprig parsley
1 16-ounce can tomatoes
Liver Balls (recipe follows)

Place short ribs in Dutch oven; add water, leeks, celery, bay leaf, salt, and pepper. Cover; bring to boil and simmer over moderately low heat (about 225° F.) 1½ hours. Add carrots, parsley, and tomatoes; cook 1 hour, or until meat is tender. Remove from heat; cool and chill in refrigerator several hours, or overnight, to allow fat to harden. Prepare Liver Balls while soup is chilling. Remove and discard fat from soup. Remove bones and fat from meat and cut meat into bite-sized pieces. Add meat to soup and heat to boiling. Add Liver Balls; cover and simmer over moderately low heat (about 225° F.) 10 minutes. Makes about 9 cups.

Liver Balls

½ pound Braunschweiger,
    mashed
½ cup fine dry bread crumbs
1 egg
3 tablespoons chopped fresh
    parsley
½ teaspoon salt
⅛ teaspoon garlic powder
¼ teaspoon ground marjoram

Mix all ingredients together and chill 1 to 2 hours in refrigerator. Shape into 1¼-inch balls. Makes about 25 liver balls.

Hot Soups for a First Course

Formal, sit-down dinners, especially on cool evenings, can start off beautifully with a cup or small bowl of flavorful hot soup. Choose a flavor that will enhance, and not repeat, other foods on the menu. When soup is served as a first course, count on a serving of about ¾ cup per person.

❧ Broccoli Soup

3 slices bacon
¼ cup finely chopped onion
2 tablespoons bacon drippings
1 chicken bouillon cube
1 cup boiling water
1 cup thinly sliced carrot
½ cup coarsely chopped celery
3 tablespoons flour
1 quart milk
1½ cups cooked, coarsely chopped broccoli
2 teaspoons salt
⅛ teaspoon pepper
Paprika (optional)

Fry bacon in small skillet over moderately high heat (about 325° F.) until crisp. Remove bacon and crumble coarsely. Cook onion in the bacon drippings over moderate heat (about 250° F.) until lightly browned. Dissolve bouillon cube in the boiling water in a large saucepan; add onion, carrot, and celery. Cover and cook 10 minutes over moderate heat (about 250° F.). Stir flour into a little of the milk. Add flour, the remaining milk, broccoli, salt, and pepper to vegetables. Cook over moderate heat (about 250° F.) stirring constantly, until mixture thickens and begins to bubble, about 10 minutes. Stir in crumbled bacon and spoon into soup bowls. Garnish with paprika, if desired. Makes about 7 cups, or serves 6 to 8.

❧ Japanese Shrimp Soup

½ teaspoon ground ginger
Water
24 medium-sized frozen peeled and deveined raw shrimp
1 13¾-fluid-ounce can chicken broth, chilled and fat skimmed off
2 tablespoons lemon juice
1 teaspoon soy sauce
1 8-fluid-ounce bottle clam juice, not shaken
½ cucumber, peeled
⅓ cup shredded, peeled carrot
2 large mushrooms, sliced ¼-inch thick
4 to 6 springs watercress

In a 2-quart saucepan bring ginger and 3 cups of water to a boil over moderately high heat; add shrimp, turn off heat and let stand 2 minutes. Drain shrimp and rinse with cold water. Rinse pan and in it put 1½ cups of water, the chicken broth, lemon juice and soy sauce; carefully add the clam juice, leaving any sediment in the bottle. Bring mixture to a boil over moderate heat, stirring occasionally. Halve cucumber lengthwise, scrape out and discard seeds; slice cucumber into ¼-inch-thick pieces. When broth boils, add cucumber, carrot, mushrooms and shrimp; cook 1 minute and then remove pan from heat. Place a sprig of watercress in each soup bowl before ladling in the soup. Makes 5 cups; serves 4.

❧ Cream of Carrot Soup

2½ cups milk
1 tablespoon flour
1 teaspoon salt

Place milk, flour, salt, pepper, cooked carrots, and the peanut butter in the container of an electric blender. Blend on low speed about 2 minutes, until carrots are

⅛ teaspoon pepper
1½ cups diced cooked carrots
4 tablespoons peanut butter

thoroughly puréed. Pour soup into saucepan. Bring to a boil over moderate heat (about 250° F.). Cook, stirring constantly, about 1 minute. Makes about 3 cups, or serves 4.

ᴈᔆ Lentil-Spinach Soup

1 cup dried lentils
7½ cups water
2 tablespoons vegetable oil
1 cup minced, peeled onion
1 10-ounce package frozen chopped spinach, thawed
2 tablespoons tomato paste
1½ teaspoons salt
Few grains of cayenne pepper

In a large saucepot bring lentils and water to a boil over moderately high heat. Reduce heat to low, cover pot and simmer 30 minutes, or until lentils are very tender. About 10 minutes before lentils are done, heat oil in a medium-sized skillet over moderately high heat; add onion and cook about 4 minutes, stirring often, until onion is soft and golden. Add the spinach, breaking it up with a spoon. Reduce heat to low, cover pan and let onion and spinach stew for 5 minutes. Stir spinach mixture, tomato paste, salt and cayenne into the lentils and simmer uncovered 15 minutes to blend flavors. Makes 7½ cups soup, or serves 4 to 5.

ᴈᔆ Borscht

3 pounds beef foreshank, cut into 1½- to 2-inch slices
1½ quarts water
½ cup chopped onion
1 cup diced celery
1 clove garlic, minced
1 bay leaf
¼ teaspoon dried thyme leaves
3½ teaspoons salt
⅛ teaspoon pepper
1 cup diced carrot
2 bunches beets, scrubbed and coarsely grated
1 cup chopped cabbage
Commercial sour cream

Place meat in Dutch oven; add water, onion, celery, garlic, bay leaf, thyme, salt, and pepper. Cover and bring to boil; reduce heat and simmer over low heat (about 200° F.) 2 hours. Remove from heat, cool and chill several hours, or overnight, to allow fat to harden. Remove and discard fat. Add carrot, beets, and cabbage; bring to boil, and simmer over moderately low heat (about 225° F.) 20 minutes. Serve garnished with sour cream. Makes about 3 quarts, or serves 12 to 14.

ᴈᔆ Black Bean Soup

1 pound dried black turtle beans

Place beans in Dutch oven; cover with cold water; bring to a boil; reduce heat to moderate (about 250° F.) and

6 cups cold water
½ pound salt pork, sliced
2 medium sized onions,
    coarsely chopped
1 clove garlic, minced
1 bay leaf
½ teaspoon dried thyme
    leaves
2½ teaspoons salt
¼ teaspoon pepper
¼ cup dry sherry (optional)
Sliced hard-cooked egg

boil 2 minutes. Remove from heat and let stand 1 hour, covered. Cook salt pork in skillet over moderate heat (about 250° F.) until lightly browned. Add salt pork pieces, onion, garlic, bay leaf, thyme, salt, and pepper to the beans; cover and simmer over moderately low heat (about 225° F.) 2 hours or until beans are tender. Press soup through a sieve or food mill. Thin with water to desired consistency. If desired, add ¼ cup sherry. Heat before serving. Serve garnished with sliced hard-cooked egg. Makes about 2 quarts, or serves 8 to 10.

Oyster Stew

¼ cup butter or margarine
1 pint shucked oysters,
    drained and liquid
    reserved, or 2 8-ounce
    cans oysters
Milk
1¼ teaspoons salt
¼ teaspoon celery salt
Few drops Tabasco
Paprika

Melt butter in a saucepan over moderately low heat (about 225° F.). Add drained oysters and cook until edges curl, about 3 minutes. Pour oyster liquid into a 1-quart measuring cup and add enough milk to measure 3 cups. Add to oysters with salt, celery salt and Tabasco. Heat to serving temperature. Serve with a dash of paprika. Serves 3 to 4.

Split Pea Soup

1 tablespoon butter or
    margarine
⅓ cup sliced onion
1 cup slivered leftover
    baked ham
1 leftover ham bone
1½ quarts water
1 cup green or yellow split
    peas, well rinsed
1 large bay leaf
Dash of ground allspice
½ teaspoon salt
⅛ teaspoon pepper

In a heavy Dutch oven or large saucepan over moderately high heat (about 275° F.) melt butter. Add onion and ham and cook until onion is lightly browned. Add ham bone and remaining ingredients. Bring to a boil. Reduce heat to moderate (about 250° F.). Cover tightly and boil gently until peas have cooked apart, about 1½ to 2 hours, stirring occasionally. Remove bone and bay leaf before serving. Add more salt to taste if necessary. Soup may separate on standing; stir well before serving. Serves 6 to 8.

◄§ Tomato Bisque

1 16-ounce can tomatoes
⅓ cup finely chopped onion
1 teaspoon sugar
½ teaspoon salt
Few grains pepper
2 tablespoons butter or
   margarine
2 tablespoons flour
2 cups milk
Croutons (optional)
Commercial sour cream
   (optional)

Place tomatoes, onion, sugar, salt, and pepper in a saucepan; cook over moderately low heat (about 225° F.) 20 minutes, stirring occasionally. Press mixture through a food mill to purée. Melt butter in a saucepan over moderate heat (about 250° F.); blend in flour. Gradually add milk and cook until thickened, stirring constantly. Stir in tomato mixture and heat. If desired, serve garnished with croutons or sour cream. Makes about 3 cups, or serves 4.

◄§ Potato Soup

½ cup butter or margarine
½ cup minced onion
1 tablespoon salt
4 cups cubed raw potatoes
   (about 4 medium-sized
   potatoes)
1½ cups water
2 cups hot milk
1 egg yolk, slightly beaten
½ cup cold milk
Few grains cayenne pepper
⅛ teaspoon pepper
2 tablespoons chopped fresh
   parsley

Melt butter in a heavy saucepan over moderately low heat (about 225° F.). Add onion and cook until soft but not browned. Add salt, potatoes, and water. Cover; cook over moderately low heat (about 225° F.), stirring occasionally, until potatoes are tender, about 30 minutes. Stir in hot milk. Combine egg yolk and cold milk; gradually add to hot soup, stirring constantly. Add cayenne pepper and pepper. Garnish with parsley before serving. Serves 6 to 8.

◄§ Onion Soup with Gruyère French Bread

1 cup butter or margarine
10 cups thinly sliced onion
6 cans condensed beef broth
6¼ cups water
2 teaspoons Worcestershire
   sauce
2 teaspoons sugar
1 teaspoon salt
⅛ teaspoon pepper

Melt butter in a large skillet over moderately low heat (about 225° F.); add onion and cook until tender and golden brown. Remove onion from skillet and place in a large saucepan or Dutch oven. Add beef broth, water, Worcestershire, sugar, salt, and pepper; mix together. Cover and place over moderate heat (about 250° F.) and cook 45 minutes. Add wine and heat 10 minutes. Place bread slices on a cookie sheet and sprinkle with cheese. Place bread in preheated broiler about 3 inches from

2 cups dry white wine
16 slices French bread
10 ounces process Gruyère
cheese, shredded

heat for 2 to 3 minutes, or just until lightly browned. Spoon soup into bowls and top each with a slice of bread. Serves 12 to 16.

🦢 Fresh Vegetable Soup

3 pounds beef bones
3 quarts cold water
3 tablespoons butter or
margarine
¼ cup chopped onion
¼ cup diced carrot
¼ cup diced celery
¼ cup finely shredded
cabbage
¼ cup chopped green pepper
1 16-ounce can tomatoes
5 teaspoons salt
⅛ teaspoon pepper
¼ cup cooked peas
Chopped fresh parsley

Place bones in large saucepan or Dutch oven. Add cold water; cover and simmer over low heat (about 200° F.) 3 to 4 hours. Strain and skim off fat. Cook uncovered over moderate heat (about 250° F.) until stock is reduced to 1½ quarts. Melt butter in skillet. Add onion, carrots, celery, cabbage, and green pepper and cook over moderate heat (about 250° F.) 5 minutes. Add cooked vegetables, tomatoes, salt, and pepper to beef stock; cover and simmer over low heat (about 200° F.) 1 to 1½ hours. Add peas just before serving. Garnish with chopped parsley. Serves 8 to 10.

🦢 Tomato Consommé

1 16-ounce can peeled whole
tomatoes, drained
4 cups chicken broth
Juice of 1 lemon
1 teaspoon tomato paste
½ teaspoon dried thyme
leaves
½ teaspoon dried basil
leaves
1 bay leaf
2 tablespoons Madeira wine

Combine the tomatoes, chicken broth, lemon juice, tomato paste and herbs in a saucepan. Place over moderately low heat (about 225° F.) and cook covered for 20 minutes after mixture begins to simmer. Strain the soup and return it to the saucepan. Stir in Madeira and serve. Makes 3½ cups, or serves 4.

🦢 Egg Drop Soup

*1½ quarts chicken or beef
broth
1 egg
1 teaspoon flour

Heat broth to boiling. Beat egg and flour together and gradually pour in a thin steady stream into the boiling broth. Cook for 2 minutes. Serves 6.

*Note: You may use canned broth or 6 bouillon cubes and 6 cups hot water.

Quick Hot Soups

Using canned, frozen, or dry-mix soups or flavored bouillon cubes, you can make delightfully quick dinner soups that taste much more complicated than they really are.

❧ Consommé Julienne

4 chicken bouillon cubes
4 cups boiling water
2 small carrots, scraped
1 leek
1 stalk celery
2 slices turnip
1 tablespoon butter or margarine
3 outside cabbage leaves, shredded
½ medium-sized onion, thinly sliced
⅛ teaspoon salt
Few grains pepper
⅛ teaspoon sugar
Chopped fresh parsley

Dissolve bouillon cubes in boiling water. Set aside. Cut carrots, leek, celery, and turnip into very thin strips about 2 inches long. Melt butter in a small saucepan over moderate heat (about 250° F.). Add carrots, leek, celery, turnip, cabbage, onion, salt, pepper, and sugar; cook covered for 5 minutes, until vegetables are tender. Combine with chicken bouillon; simmer over moderately low heat (about 225° F.) 5 minutes. Serve with a garnish of chopped parsley. Serves 6.

❧ Crab Bisque

1 chicken bouillon cube
¾ cup boiling water
1 can condensed green pea soup
1 can condensed tomato soup
1 cup light cream
1 7½-ounce can Alaska king crab, drained
¼ cup dry sherry

Dissolve the chicken bouillon cube in the ¾ cup boiling water. Combine bouillon and soup in a medium-sized saucepan and blend well. Cook over moderately low heat (about 225° F.) just until soup reaches the boiling point, stirring frequently. Add cream, crab meat, and sherry and heat thoroughly. Makes about 6 cups, or serves 8.

❧ Chicken–Chestnut Soup

1 can condensed cream of chicken soup
1 12½-ounce can chicken consommé

Combine cream of chicken soup, chicken consommé, and water chestnuts in saucepan; heat over low heat (about 200° F.) stirring frequently. Just before serving, stir in sherry. Makes 4 1-cup servings.

(Ingredients continued on page 232)

1 5-ounce can water
chestnuts, drained and
finely chopped
2 tablespoons dry sherry

✑ Hot Tomato–Clam Soup

3 cans condensed tomato soup
1 soup can water
2 8-ounce bottles clam juice

Combine soup, water, and clam juice in a large saucepan. Cook over moderately low heat (about 225° F.) until thoroughly heated, about 6 to 8 minutes, stirring frequently. Serve in warm cups. Serves 8.

✑ Lady Curzon Soup

2 10½-ounce cans clear
turtle soup
1 to 2 teaspoons curry
powder
2 tablespoons cognac
½ cup heavy cream, slightly
heated

In a saucepan over low heat (about 200° F.) heat turtle soup with the curry powder to serving temperature. Remove from heat and stir in cognac. Pour into serving cups and top each serving with 1 tablespoon warm cream. Serves 5 to 6.

✑ Hot Turtle–Pea Soup

2 20-ounce cans green
turtle soup with sherry
1 can condensed green pea
soup
1¼ cups water
Thin lemon peel strips

Combine soups and water in a saucepan; blend thoroughly. Cook over moderately low heat (about 225° F.) 10 to 12 minutes. stirring frequently, until thoroughly heated. Serve immediately. Garnish with lemon peel. Serves 8.

✑ Buttered Black Bean Soup

1 can condensed black bean
soup
1 soup can water
½ teaspoon Worcestershire
sauce
2 tablespoons butter or
margarine
Lemon slices

Combine soup, water, Worcestershire, and butter in saucepan. Heat over moderately low heat (about 225° F.), stirring frequently, until soup bubbles. Put a thin lemon slice in each soup cup. Pour hot soup over lemon to serve. Serves 3.

ᕙᔑ Tomato Bouillon Medley

1 can condensed tomato
   soup
1 can condensed pea soup
1 can condensed beef
   bouillon
2½ cups water
¼ cup dry sherry
Commercial sour cream

Combine tomato soup, pea soup, bouillon, and water in a saucepan. Heat slowly over moderately low heat (about 225° F.), stirring frequently, until mixture boils. Add sherry. Serve in mugs with a garnish of sour cream. Makes 8 6-ounce servings.

ᕙᔑ Tomato-Asparagus Bisque

1 can condensed bisque of
   tomato soup
1 can condensed cream of
   asparagus soup
1 soup can water
½ soup can milk

Combine and blend soups in a medium-sized saucepan. Add the 1 soup can water and the ½ soup can milk a little at a time, stirring to blend. Cook over moderate heat (about 250° F.), stirring occasionally, until soup is heated thoroughly. Serves 6.

ᕙᔑ Vegetable–Pea Soup

3 tablespoons butter or
   margarine
½ cup coarsely grated carrot
½ cup coarsely grated
   cabbage
⅓ cup finely chopped onion
2 cans condensed frozen
   green-pea-with-ham soup
2 soup cans water

Heat butter in a saucepan over moderately low heat (about 225° F.); add carrot, cabbage, and onion and cook until tender, stirring frequently. Add soup and water and blend together. Heat to boiling and serve immediately. Serves 4.

ᕙᔑ Vegetable–Leek Soup

2 tablespoons butter or
   margarine
2 leeks, washed and thinly
   sliced
2 cans condensed vegetable
   and beef stockpot soup
2 soup cans water
4 pitted prunes, diced
½ teaspoon salt
Few grains pepper

Heat butter in a saucepan over moderately low heat (about 225° F.); add leeks and cook until tender but not browned. Add remaining ingredients; heat and serve. Serves 4.

SOUPS

~§ Petite Marmite

1 2½-ounce package
  prepared onion soup mix
1 cup diced cooked chicken
3 cups boiling water
1 can condensed chicken
  gumbo soup
Packaged cheese-flavored
  croutons

Place onion soup and chicken in 2 cups of the boiling water. Cook over moderately high heat (about 300° F.) for 10 minutes. Add remaining 1 cup of water and the chicken gumbo soup; simmer over moderately low heat (about 225° F.) for 5 minutes. Serve topped with cheese croutons. Serves 6.

~§ Chicken–Almond Soup

¼ cup butter or margarine
¾ cup ground blanched
  almonds
Few grains salt
Few grains pepper
¼ cup finely chopped celery
  hearts
1 tablespoon cornstarch
1 12½-ounce can clear
  chicken broth
1 cup light cream
Snipped chives

Melt butter in a saucepan over moderately low heat (about 225° F.). Add ground almonds and cook over moderately high heat (about 275° F.) about 5 minutes, stirring occasionally, until ground almonds are lightly browned. Add salt, pepper, and celery; stir well. In a bowl combine cornstarch with a little of the chicken broth. Stir until smooth. Add remainder of broth; mix well. Slowly add broth mixture to almond mixture, stirring constantly. Cook over moderately low heat (about 225° F.) about 10 minutes, stirring occasionally. Remove from heat. Add cream slowly to soup mixture, stirring constantly. Place over low heat (about 200° F.) just until soup is thoroughly heated; do not boil. Soup may be served hot or chilled with chives. Serves 4.

~§ Mexican Foam Soup

2 tablespoons butter or
  margarine
½ cup finely chopped onion
¼ cup finely chopped green
  pepper
2 cans condensed tomato
  soup
2 soup cans milk
Few grains cayenne pepper
¼ teaspoon salt
2 eggs, separated

Melt butter in a saucepan over moderately low heat (about 225° F.). Add onion and green pepper and cook until vegetables are tender, 5 to 8 minutes, stirring frequently. Add soup; stir in milk gradually. Add cayenne pepper and salt; blend thoroughly. Heat over moderately low heat (about 225° F.) 4 to 5 minutes, stirring occasionally. Do not let mixture boil. Beat egg yolks slightly; stir in about ½ cup of the hot soup. Gradually stir egg yolk mixture back into soup in saucepan. Beat egg whites with rotary beater until soft peaks form; add about ½ cup of the soup mixture and beat slightly. Pour egg white mixture on top of soup. Heat 2 to 3 minutes more. Serves 6.

Cold Soups

Chilled soups are not presented as frequently as hot soups, so there's a pleasant-change feeling about them. They are a refreshing way to start a summer dinner and a superb contrast of tastes with a hot sandwich at luncheons. Some of the following are quick to make, others take a little longer. All must be ice-cold and served in chilled cups to taste best.

Iced Asparagus Soup

1 can condensed cream of asparagus soup
1 can condensed cream of chicken soup
2 teaspoons freeze-dried shallot powder or 1 teaspoon onion powder
1½ cups milk
1 cup light cream
1 tablespoon lemon juice
2 tablespoons dry sherry
½ cup commercial sour cream

Blend soups together; stir in shallot powder, milk, cream, lemon juice, and sherry; mix well. Chill overnight or longer, until ice-cold. Serve garnished with sour cream. Serves 7.

Jellied Borscht

2 1-pound cans julienne beets
1 envelope unflavored gelatine
2 cans condensed beef consommé
1 teaspoon instant minced onion
2 tablespoons lemon juice
2 teaspoons prepared horseradish
1½ cups commercial sour cream

Drain beets, reserving juice. Soften gelatine in 1 cup of the beet juice in a saucepan. Place over low heat (about 200° F.), stirring constantly, until gelatine is dissolved. Add consommé, onion, and lemon juice; chill until the consistency of unbeaten egg whites. Mix the horseradish and 1 cup of the sour cream; stir in the remaining beet juice. Gradually stir the sour cream mixture into the consommé mixture. Fold in the drained beets and chill at least 3 to 4 hours, or longer, until the soup is slightly jellied. Serve garnished with the remaining ½ cup sour cream. Serves 8.

SOUPS

⋙ Consommé à la Ritz

1 12½-ounce can jellied
   consommé madrilène
1 12½-ounce can jellied
   chicken consommé
½ cup commercial sour cream
Curry powder
2 tablespoons red caviar

Chill madrilène and chicken consommé several hours. Spoon madrilène and chicken consommé side by side into bouillon cups. Garnish each serving with a generous spoonful of sour cream, a sprinkling of curry powder, and a small spoonful of caviar. Serves 4 to 6.

⋙ East Indian Curry Soup

1⅓ cups flaked coconut
1⅓ cups milk
1 tablespoon cornstarch
½ teaspoon curry powder
⅛ teaspoon salt
1 12½-ounce can clear
   chicken broth
Toasted coconut
Commercial sour cream
   (optional)
Ground ginger (optional)

Place flaked coconut and milk in the container of an electric blender. Cover and blend 40 seconds at high speed. Strain and press coconut to remove milk. Discard coconut. Mix cornstarch, curry, and salt in saucepan. Stir in coconut milk and chicken broth. Cook over moderate heat (about 250° F.), stirring constantly, until thickened. Chill several hours until ice-cold. Serve garnished with toasted coconut. If preferred, garnish with sour cream and a sprinkling of ground ginger. Serves 3.

⋙ Cream of Cucumber Soup

2 tablespoons butter or
   margarine
¼ cup chopped onion
2 cups diced, unpeeled
   cucumbers
½ cup watercress leaves
1 can condensed cream of
   potato soup
1 soup can water
2 sprigs parsley
½ teaspoon salt
⅛ teaspoon pepper
¼ teaspoon dry mustard
Unsweetened whipped cream
Radish slices (optional)

Melt butter in a saucepan over moderately low heat (about 225° F.). Add onion and cook until tender, 3 or 4 minutes, stirring frequently. Add cucumber, watercress, soup, water, and parsley; combine thoroughly. Stir in salt, pepper, and dry mustard. Bring to a boil over moderate heat (about 250° F.). Cook over moderately low heat (about 225° F.) 10 to 12 minutes, stirring occasionally. Place mixture in an electric blender. Cover and blend 40 seconds at low speed. Sieve blended mixture into a bowl. Chill until ice-cold. Serve garnished with whipped cream, and if desired, a radish slice. Serves 4.

ᴄᵇ Gazpacho

2 cloves garlic
⅛ teaspoon ground cumin
1 teaspoon salt
¼ cup olive oil
8 large ripe tomatoes, peeled
1 tablespoon cider vinegar
2 tablespoons olive oil
1 cup ¼-inch soft bread
   cubes
½ cup finely chopped, peeled
   cucumber
1 medium-sized green
   pepper, finely chopped
4 green onions or scallions,
   finely chopped

Mash garlic in a garlic press. Combine garlic, cumin, and salt in a small bowl and blend together. Stir in the ¼ cup olive oil. Remove stems from tomatoes, cut in quarters, and remove seeds. Place about 4 pieces of tomato at a time in the container of an electric blender and blend at high speed. Continue adding tomato until all is blended. It may be necessary to remove some of puréed mixture to a bowl. If blender is not available, press tomatoes through a food mill. Place puréed tomatoes in a bowl and mix in garlic–olive oil mixture and vinegar. Chill until ice-cold. While soup is chilling, heat the 2 table-spoons olive oil in a skillet over moderately high heat (about 300° F.); cook bread cubes until lightly browned, stirring occasionally. Serve Gazpacho in individual soup bowls. Place bread cubes, chopped cucumber, chopped green pepper, and scallions in individual bowls to be spooned as desired on soup. Makes 4¼ cups, or serves 5.

ᴄᵇ Iced Tomato Soup

2 chicken bouillon cubes
2 cups boiling water
6 large ripe tomatoes,
   coarsely chopped
1 medium-sized onion,
   chopped
¼ cup water
½ teaspoon salt
Few grains pepper
2 tablespoons tomato paste
2 tablespoons flour
1 cup heavy cream
1 large tomato, sliced thin
(optional)

Dissolve chicken bouillon cubes in boiling water. Combine tomatoes, onion, water, salt, and pepper in a sauce-pan; cook over moderate heat (about 250° F.) 5 minutes. Combine tomato paste with flour and add to tomatoes with chicken bouillon; simmer gently over low heat (about 200° F.) 3 minutes. Rub mixture through a fine sieve. Chill several hours. Before serving, add cream. Season to taste with more salt if necessary. Garnish each serving with a thin tomato slice, if desired. Serves 6.

ᴄᵇ Iced Raspberry Soup

2 chicken bouillon cubes
1¼ cups boiling water
2 10-ounce packages frozen
   raspberries, thawed,

(Ingredients continued on page 238)

Dissolve bouillon cubes in boiling water. Rub raspberries through a food mill or sieve. Add bouillon, pineapple juice, and sugar; stir until sugar is dissolved. Chill. Top each serving with a spoonful of sour cream and chopped almonds. Serves 5.

with juice
½ cup pineapple juice
2 tablespoons sugar
½ cup commercial sour
  cream
2 tablespoons chopped
  toasted almonds

ᕯ Vichyssoise

1½ quarts Chicken Stock
   (recipe on page 211) or
   canned chicken broth
1½ pounds potatoes, peeled
   and thinly sliced (about 3
   to 3½ cups)
2 bunches leeks, white
  portion thinly sliced,
  (about 3 cups)
1 teaspoon salt
1 cup heavy cream
¼ teaspoon salt
Few grains white pepper
2 to 3 tablespoons snipped
  chives

Place Chicken Stock, potatoes, leeks, and the 1 teaspoon salt in a saucepan. Cook over moderately low heat (about 225° F.) for 40 to 50 minutes or until vegetables are tender. Press soup mixture through a food mill to purée, or blend in the container of an electric blender until smooth. Stir in cream. Season with the ¼ teaspoon salt and the white pepper; add additional salt if necessary. Chill until ice-cold. Serve garnished with chives. Makes about 9 cups, or serves 10 to 12.

ᕯ Emerald Vichyssoise

3 tablespoons butter or
  margarine
1½ cups chopped scallions or
   green onions
1 10-ounce package frozen
  chopped spinach, thawed
2 10¼-ounce cans frozen
  cream of potato soup,
  thawed
1 cup nondairy powdered
  creamer
2½ cups boiling chicken broth
2 tablespoons lemon juice
½ teaspoon salt
¼ teaspoon pepper
Snipped chives for garnish

In a heavy saucepan melt butter over low heat (about 225° F.) until frothy. Add scallions and sauté about 3 minutes, until soft. Add spinach, potato soup, powdered creamer, and boiling chicken broth; blend well. Cover and cook 15 minutes. Put through food mill, or purée in electric blender, a little at a time, until mixture is smooth. Add lemon juice, salt, and pepper. Chill several hours. When ready to serve, sprinkle top with snipped chives. Serves 8.

Iced Watercress Soup

2 chicken bouillon cubes
2 cups boiling water
2 cups coarsely chopped
   watercress (about 1
   bunch, leaves and stems)
¼ cup chopped celery
2 tablespoons grated
   Parmesan cheese
1 teaspoon salt
Few grains pepper
2 tablespoons flour
1 cup light cream
Sliced stuffed olives

Dissolve bouillon cubes in boiling water in a saucepan. Add watercress, celery, Parmesan cheese, salt, and pepper; cover and cook over moderately low heat (about 225° F.) 10 minutes. Cool slightly and place in the container of an electric blender. Cover and blend 30 seconds at high speed. Blend flour and cream together in a saucepan. Gradually add blended vegetable–bouillon mixture. Cook over moderate heat (about 250° F.), stirring constantly, until thickened. Chill until ice-cold. Serve topped with sliced olives. Serves 4.

Jellied Garden Consommé

2 teaspoons instant minced
   onion
2 teaspoons water
½ cup finely chopped green
   pepper
3 tablespoons chopped fresh
   parsley
2 13-ounce cans consommé
   madrilène
Commercial sour cream

Sprinkle onion over water for 1 minute to soften. Combine onion, green pepper, parsley, and consommé. Chill in refrigerator for 2 to 3 hours until partially set. Stir gently to distribute vegetables evenly; continue chilling until set. Serve garnished with a spoonful of sour cream. Serves 4 to 5.

Senegalese Cream Soup

1 10½-ounce can cream of
   chicken soup
1 teaspoon curry powder
½ cup milk
1 cup cracked ice
½ cup heavy cream
Snipped chives (optional)
Cucumber slices (optional)

Put soup, curry powder, and milk in the container of an electric blender. Cover and blend at high speed for 15 seconds. Remove cover and add cracked ice and cream. Cover and blend a few seconds only until cream is blended in. Let stand a few minutes so that bubbles can settle out. Serve cold, garnished with chives or cucumber. Serves 4.

[239]

⤳ Green Goddess Soup

1½ cups diced peeled
   avocado
 3 tablespoons lime juice
 ½ teaspoon salt
Few grains pepper
Few grains ground nutmeg
 2 12½-ounce cans clear
   chicken broth
 ¼ cup heavy cream,
   whipped
Ground nutmeg

Place avocado, lime juice, salt, pepper, and nutmeg in the container of an electric blender. Add 1 can of the chicken broth. Cover and blend 30 seconds at high speed. Stir in remaining 1 can broth and chill until ice-cold. Serve garnished with a spoonful of whipped cream and a sprinkling of nutmeg. Serves 5 to 6.

⤳ Frosted Pea Soup

 1 can condensed green pea
   soup
 1 soup can light cream
 1 teaspoon Worcestershire
   sauce
 ½ teaspoon lemon juice
 ¾ teaspoon ground dillseed
 ¼ cup heavy cream, whipped
Paprika

Beat soup with a rotary beater until smooth. Gradually add the 1 soup can of light cream; beat until blended. Stir in Worcestershire, lemon juice, and dill. Chill several hours. Serve garnished with whipped cream and a dash of paprika. Serves 3 to 4.

⤳ Icy Cucumber Soup

 2 13¾-fluid-ounce cans
   chicken broth
2½ cups finely chopped
   cucumber, peeled and
   seeded
 2 tablespoons chopped
   green onions or scallions
 2 teaspoons snipped fresh
   dill
 1 teaspoon salt
Few grains pepper
 ¼ cup flour
 1 cup heavy cream
 1 cup milk
 2 teaspoons lemon juice

Pour 1½ cans of the broth into a saucepan, reserving remaining ½ can. Add chopped cucumber, green onions, dill, salt and pepper; simmer covered over low heat (about 200° F.) about 20 minutes, until cucumber is tender. Blend flour and the remaining broth together; stir into cucumber mixture. Cook over moderately low heat (about 225° F.), stirring constantly until thickened. Remove from heat. Rub mixture through a food mill or sieve. Stir in cream, milk and lemon juice. Cool. Stir in grated cucumber and chill soup until ice-cold. Serve garnished with a thin cucumber slice. Makes 8 to 10 servings.

½ cup coarsely grated
    cucumber
Thin cucumber slices

✍ Cold Borscht

2 bunches beets (2 to 2½
    pounds)
2 quarts water
1 tablespoon salt
½ teaspoon pepper
3 tablespoons sugar
¾ cup lemon juice
Commercial sour cream

Wash, scrape and coarsely grate beets. Place beets, water, salt, pepper, sugar and lemon juice in a large saucepan. Heat over moderate heat (about 250° F.) until mixture comes to a boil. Cover and reduce heat to low (about 200° F.) and simmer until beets are tender. Cover soup and chill several hours or overnight. Serve either in tall glasses or bowls and top with dollops of sour cream. This soup may be stored in a covered container in the refrigerator for about a week. Makes 16 to 20 servings.

CHAPTER VIII

BEVERAGES

"Stop by for coffee, a cup of tea, a drink . . ." is probably our most often verbalized invitation to neighborly visiting. Sharing a beverage break with someone is a signal for relaxation, conversation, and at least five minutes to put work or worries aside.

Beverage breaks may be as varied as the time of day, the season of the year, and the social occasion. In this chapter you will find variety: hot and cold versions of coffee, tea, and chocolate drinks; elaborate punches and perfect ice-cream sodas; beverages for the cocktail hour, with and without alcohol, and an array of flavorful fruit coolers.

Coffee

When people speak of a good cup of coffee, the emphasis is on the *good*. Some people prefer coffee strong; some like it weak. Either way, a "good" cup of coffee should be clear, have a fresh aroma and a full-bodied taste, and be served hot. This is how to get that result:

1. Start with fresh coffee. Buy coffee in the size of can or package that will be used within a week after opening. After opening, store coffee in a tightly lidded can or a glass jar with a screw-on top in the refrigerator.

2. Always use a thoroughly clean coffee maker. Rinse it with hot water before using. Wash coffee maker thoroughly after each use.

3. Use freshly drawn cold water. For best results use the full capacity of the coffee maker.

4. Measure the coffee and water accurately. The usual measurement is one level standard coffee measure or two level tablespoons of coffee to each three-fourths *measuring* cup of water.

5. Once you find the exact timing to obtain the desired strength with your coffee maker, stick to it for uniform results.

6. Serve the coffee as soon as possible after brewing.

What Kind of Coffee to Buy: The blend or brand of coffee you buy will have to be of your own choosing. There are more than a hundred different types of coffee beans grown. Most brands are a blend of several different beans; the roasting process may differ for each blend. Some have a stronger flavor; some are more aromatic. Find the blend that suits your taste.

The grind you select will depend upon your coffee maker, although the drip grind is a medium, all-purpose grind that works well in any type of coffee maker. If the manufacturer of your coffee maker suggests a particular grind, use that one.

Instant coffee comes in two forms: powdered and freeze-dried granules. The latter form produces a more aromatic cup of coffee.

Decaffeinated coffees have had almost all the caffein removed from them. They come in two forms: a regular grind to be prepared in a coffee maker and an instant powdered or granule form.

Cereal beverages are excellent coffee substitutes if you do not drink coffee. They come in two forms: one is like a ground coffee and the other is an instant type of beverage made with hot water.

The Ways to Make Coffee: No matter what kind of coffee maker you choose, follow the six rules listed above for making coffee. It is always best to follow the manufacturer's directions when you use any equipment. However, if you've inherited a coffee maker without directions, or if you're about to decide which kind you want, the following descriptions detail the various types.

Percolated coffee may be made in either an automatic (electric) percolator or a nonautomatic one that is used on the top of the range. Coffee is measured into a basket that sits, over water, at the top of the pot. As the water is heated, it sprays up and over the grounds to make a flavorful, aromatic brew. Automatic percolators will shut off when coffee is done to the desired strength. Always use the nonautomatic percolators over low heat and do not percolate more than six to eight minutes. In either case, remove the basket of grounds as soon as brewing is completed. Automatic percolators are available in two-cup to thirty-cup, or larger, sizes for party service. Nonautomatic percolators are generally available in two-cup to eight-cup sizes.

Vacuum-type coffee is brewed in a coffee maker that looks like two bowls set one on top of the other. In the top bowl, there will be a filter of cloth or stainless steel or a movable glass rod. Measure water into the lower bowl; coffee into the upper bowl. When heat is applied to the lower bowl, the water will rise to the upper bowl. Turn off the heat, stir the coffee once with the grounds, and allow it to stand. When the coffee has re-turned, slowly, to the lower bowl, it is ready to serve. Remove the top bowl for serving. These coffee makers are available in sizes up to twelve cups. Some models are automatic (electric).

Drip-type and/or filtered makers, favored by many coffee lovers, have an upper cone or basket to hold the coffee grounds and hot (boiling point) water and a lower, serving container into which the brewed coffee drips. In cone types and in some with baskets you insert a filter, usually paper, into the upper section to hold the grounds. Paper filters are disposable; you use a fresh one each time. Other types have a permanent, washable fine mesh filter. Depending on the quality of the coffee you use, and the quality of the pot's design, filtered coffee is an excellent brew. It is clear, with no stray grounds floating in it. Since the water passes through the grounds just once and the brew does not boil, the coffee is never bitter. Drip and filter coffee makers come in both electric and nonelectric versions. Capacities range from 1 to 20 cups.

Old-fashioned "boiled," or steeped, coffee can be made in a coffeepot that has no basket. Measure coffee into the pot. Add water, cold or hot. Place over heat and bring *just* to a boil. Turn heat to very low and stir well. Add a bit of cold water to settle the grounds. Let coffee sit over very low heat for five minutes; then strain through cheesecloth, if desired, to serve.

Instant coffee requires only a pan of boiling water. To make one or two cups, measure the coffee directly into the cups and pour boiling water over. To make four or more cups, measure coffee into a clean pot, pour boiling water over, and let stand over low heat for three to five minutes. Do not boil.

Espresso coffee has become very popular as an after-dinner coffee. It is made with Italian-roast coffee in a drip pot, which is called a *macchinetta*. It differs from an American drip in that the water is brought to boiling in the bottom of the pot; the whole assembly is then turned over to let the water drip through. Use four level measuring tablespoons of coffee to three-quarters cup of water. Espresso can be made in an American drip pot also. Espresso is served in demitasse cups with a twist of lemon and sugar if desired, never cream.

Coffeehouses have made popular many variations of hot coffee drinks. These are a few worth trying.

 *Demitasse*

8 *level tablespoons coffee* 2 *cups of water*	Brew this extra-strength coffee by any method you pre-fer. Serve in demitasse cups. Pass cream and sugar. Makes four 4-ounce servings. This coffee is usually served after dinner in the living room.

🫘 Café au Lait

2 cups scalded milk
2 cups strong hot coffee

Pour the milk and coffee together, letting the two liquids meet as they stream into the cup. Serves 4 to 5.

🫘 Viennese Coffee

½ cup heavy cream
3¾ cups hot coffee
Grated orange peel

Whip cream until it holds its shape. Pour coffee into demitasse cups. Place a generous spoonful of cream on top of each serving of coffee. Garnish cream with a sprinkle of freshly grated orange peel. Serves 6.

🫘 Café Brûlot

1 3-inch stick cinnamon, broken up
Grated peel of 1 orange
Grated peel of ½ lemon
¼ teaspoon ground allspice
Pinch of ground nutmeg
8 small sugar cubes
8 tablespoons cognac
3 cups freshly brewed espresso coffee (see page 244)

In the blazer pan of a chafing dish, combine cinnamon, orange and lemon peels, allspice, and nutmeg. Add sugar cubes and 6 tablespoons of the cognac. Place pan over heating unit until mixture is warm. Slightly warm the remaining 2 tablespoons cognac in a small pan over low heat (about 200° F.). Ignite cognac with a match and pour the flaming liquid over the sugar in the pan to melt it. Add coffee and stir well. Serve hot in demitasse cups. Serves 6.

🫘 Mexican Coffee

½ teaspoon quick chocolate-flavored mix
About ½ cup freshly-brewed espresso coffee (see page 244)
1 tablespoon whipped cream

Put the chocolate-flavored mix in the bottom of a demitasse cup. Fill cup with hot espresso coffee and top with whipped cream. Serves 1.

🫘 Caffe Cappuccino*

⅓ cup hot milk
⅓ cup hot espresso coffee (see

Pour equal quantities of hot milk and hot espresso into cappuccino cups. Sprinkle with ground cinnamon and

page 244)
Ground cinnamon
Ground nutmeg
Sugar

ground nutmeg. Serve with sugar to individual taste. Serves 1.

Note: Cappuccino cups are larger than demitasse cups but smaller than coffee mugs. You can serve this recipe in demitasse cups, using less coffee and milk, or in mugs, using more coffee and milk.

✑ *Caffe Cioccolaccino*

½ *cup hot milk*
½ *cup hot espresso coffee (see page 244)*
Ground cinnamon
Ground nutmeg
1 *tablespoon whipped cream*
Shaved semisweet chocolate
Sugar

Pour the hot milk and espresso into a tall mug. Sprinkle with cinnamon and nutmeg. Top with the whipped cream and sprinkle shaved chocolate over the cream. Serve with sugar added for individual taste. Serves 1.

✑ *Caffe Borgia*

½ *cup hot espresso coffee (see page 244)*
½ *cup hot chocolate (recipe on page 252)*
2 *tablespoons sweetened whipped cream*
Grated orange peel

Combine coffee and chocolate in a tall mug. Top with sweetened whipped cream. Sprinkle orange peel over cream. Serves 1.

✑ *Irish Coffee*

2 *teaspoons sugar*
½ *cup hot coffee*
2 *tablespoons Irish whiskey*
2 *tablespoons whipped cream*

Put the sugar into a warmed table-wine glass. Add the hot coffee and stir until sugar is dissolved. Add the whiskey, stir, and top with whipped cream. Serves 1.

✑ *Café Chantilly*

1 *cup hot black coffee*
½ *ounce cognac*
1 *teaspoon sweetened whipped cream*

Pour coffee into a warm mug. Add cognac and float whipped cream on the top. Serves 1.

❧ Iced Coffee (three ways)

1. Make double-strength coffee by using 4 level measuring tablespoons of coffee to each ¾ measuring cup of water. Pour freshly brewed coffee over ice cubes in a tall glass.
2. Use regular-strength coffee which has cooled to room temperature to make coffee ice cubes. Use these anytime with regular-strength hot coffee to make iced coffee.
3. Make regular-strength coffee. Pour it into a glass jar. Refrigerate until cool (not more than 3 hours or it will lose flavor). Pour it over plain ice cubes in a tall glass.

❧ Coffee Mocha Frosted

2½ cups regular-strength
    coffee, chilled
6 tablespoons canned
    chocolate syrup
1 pint vanilla ice cream

Place all ingredients in bowl and blend with rotary beater. Serve in tall glasses. This recipe may be prepared in an electric blender, but make only half the recipe at one time. Makes 4 large glasses.

❧ Iced Spiced Coffee

3 cups water
2 tablespoons instant coffee
    powder or granules
2 tablespoons sugar
2 cinnamon sticks,
    each about 3¼ inches long
8 whole cloves
8 whole dried allspice
Cracked ice or ice cubes
Milk, cream or vanilla ice
    cream
Long cinnamon sticks
    (optional)

Bring water to a boil in a small pan. Remove pan from heat, add coffee powder, sugar, cinnamon sticks, cloves and allspice. Stir to dissolve sugar and then cover and let stand 30 to 45 minutes. Strain mixture. Serve at once or refrigerate until needed. To serve, pour coffee mixture over cracked ice or ice cubes in a tall glass. Serve with milk, cream or a scoop of vanilla ice cream. Use long cinnamon sticks as stirrers. Makes 3 cups; serves 3 or 4.

❧ Coffee Tropicale

Finely chopped ice
1½ cups cool espresso coffee
    (see page 244)
1 tablespoon granulated
    sugar

Fill the container of an electric blender half full of chopped ice. Add coffee and sugar and blend until thick and foamy. Serve in tall chilled glasses. Serves 4.

❧ Creamed Cinnamon Coffee

4 cups extra-strength hot
coffee
3 sticks cinnamon
Sugar
½ cup heavy cream
Cracked ice

Pour hot coffee over cinnamon sticks in a large jar or bowl. Let stand for 1 hour. Remove cinnamon sticks and sweeten coffee to taste. Add cream and chill. Pour over cracked ice in tall glasses and use cinnamon sticks as stirrers. Serves 4 to 5.

❧ Brazilian Coffee–Chocolate

2 1-ounce squares
unsweetened chocolate
3 tablespoons sugar
1 cup extra-strength hot
coffee
3 cups milk
1 quart coffee ice cream

Melt chocolate in the top of a double boiler over hot water. Add sugar. Blend well. Add hot coffee slowly, stirring constantly. Scald milk in a saucepan (heat it just until bubbles form around the edge of the milk). Add scalded milk to coffee mixture and cook over hot water for 10 minutes. Remove from heat and beat with a rotary beater until frothy. Chill thoroughly. Serve in tall chilled glasses with a large scoop of coffee ice cream. Serves 5 to 6.

Tea

Tea is not exclusively an afternoon drink for ladies. Many people prefer it as a breakfast and lunchtime beverage and as a soothing evening drink. When iced, tea is a light cooling summer drink and especially good with summer picnic meals.

There are three general tea classifications: Green tea, which brews light in color; oolong tea, partly green and partly brown, which also brews light in color; and black tea, which is a clear amber color when brewed. These classifications refer to the processing of the tea after it has been picked. Within these three classifications, there are literally thousands of varieties of tea. Most of the teas bought in a food store are a blend of some twenty or thirty varieties selected for flavor, color, body, and aroma. There are many specialty teas, such as minted tea, spiced tea, and orange-flavored tea. If you are a tea-drinker, experiment with these, which are nice for a change.

Tea is available in these forms:

Tea bags contain a premeasured teaspoonful of tea in a special filter paper. They are convenient and easy to dispose of.

Loose tea is the classic form of tea. One pound of loose tea will make about two hundred cups.

Instant tea is a soluble powder that may be blended with hot or cold water.

How to Make Tea

1. Start with the freshest tea you can buy. Once a foil-wrapped container of tea is opened, it should be put in a clean, dry, airtight container and kept in a cool, dry place.

2. Always use a teapot; it will keep the water temperature at the highest possible level. China, glass, or earthenware teapots are preferable to metal ones. Rinse the pot with boiling water before adding the tea.

3. Use freshly drawn cold water in kettle or saucepan. Bring to a full, rolling boil.

4. In teapot, use 1 teaspoonful of tea leaves or one tea bag for each cup of boiling water to be added.

5. Let the tea brew for at least three minutes, but no more than five minutes. The color of the tea is no indication of strength and flavor because some teas brew darker than others.

6. Serve the hot tea immediately with a choice of milk (never cream—it overrides the flavor of the tea), lemon slices, and sugar.

◆§ Hot Cinnamon Tea

4 cups boiling water
8 tea bags
½ cup sugar
2 lemons
2 oranges
⅛ teaspoon ground cinnamon
4 whole cloves
8 thin slices lemon
8 whole cloves

Pour boiling water over tea. Brew 4 minutes. Remove tea bags; add sugar. Squeeze juice from lemons and oranges and stir into tea. Add cinnamon and cloves and heat over low heat (about 200° F.). Garnish each serving with a slice of lemon speared with a clove. Serves 8.

◆§ Midnight Tea

3 cups boiling water
1 tablespoon tea or 3 tea bags

Pour boiling water over tea. Brew 4 minutes. Strain. Return strained tea to saucepan; add marmalade; place over moderate heat (about 250° F.). Bring to boil. Re-

½ cup orange marmalade
2 tablespoons lemon juice
Thin lemon slices

duce heat to moderately low (about 225° F.) and simmer 10 minutes. Add lemon juice. Serve in pottery mugs or teacups. Garnish each with a thin slice of lemon. Makes about 3½ cups, or serves 4 to 5.

❧ Festive Hot Tea Punch

1 orange
1 lemon
4 quarts cold water
3 2-inch sticks cinnamon
20 whole cloves
4 tea bags
3 cups orange juice
½ cup lemon juice
2 cups pineapple juice
1½ cups sugar

Cut peel off orange and lemon. Place peel, water, cinnamon, and cloves in saucepan. Heat to boiling and cool. Cover and place in refrigerator 6 to 8 hours or overnight. Strain and again bring to a boil. Remove from heat, add tea, and steep 5 minutes. Remove tea bags and add fruit juices and sugar. Bring to boil and stir until sugar is dissolved. Pour into heatproof punch bowl. Makes about 4½ quarts, or 28 5-ounce servings.

❧ Iced Tea*—The Boiling Water Method

8 teaspoons loose tea or 8 tea bags
1 quart (4 measuring cups) freshly boiled water

Put the tea in a glass or ceramic pitcher. Pour the boiling water over it. Let stand 5 minutes. Serve in tall glasses over ice cubes. Pass lemon, milk, and sugar. Serves 6.

*Note: If tea clouds when refrigerated, add a little boiling water to restore it to a clear amber color.

❧ Iced Tea by the Pitcher*

1 quart freshly drawn cold water
⅓ cup loose tea or 15 tea bags
1 quart freshly drawn cold water

Bring the 1 quart of freshly drawn cold water to boil in a saucepan. Remove from heat and add the tea or tea bags to the water while it's still bubbling. Stir, cover, and let stand 5 minutes. Put the second quart of cold water into a large pitcher (at least 2-quart size). When tea has brewed, strain it into the quart of cold water in the pitcher. Serve over ice cubes in tall glasses. Pass lemon and sugar and milk if desired. Serves 8.

*Note: Iced tea may also be made with instant tea. Follow label directions to prepare. There are also instant iced-tea mixes that come with such flavorings as lemon and mint and sugar or sugar substitute already in them. These are made with cold water and ice.

❧ Iced Tea—The Cold Water Method (for tea bags only)

1 quart (4 measuring cups)
    cold water
8 to 10 tea bags, tags removed

This method produces clear iced tea that never clouds. Start it at least 6 hours before you plan to serve. Fill a quart pitcher with the cold water. Add tea bags. Cover and let stand at room temperature or in the refrigerator at least 6 hours. Remove tea bags, squeezing them against the side of the container. To serve, pour into ice-filled glasses. Serves 4 or 5.

❧ Spiced Iced Tea

2 3-inch sticks cinnamon
8 whole cloves
2½ cups boiling water
4 tea bags
1 6-ounce can frozen
    lemonade concentrate,
    unthawed
Thin lemon slices, cut into
    quarters
Fresh mint sprigs
4 cups cold Iced Tea (recipe
    above)

Place cinnamon sticks and cloves in a medium-sized saucepan. Pour boiling water over spices; simmer over moderately low heat (about 225° F.) for 5 minutes. Remove pan from heat and add the 4 tea bags; let stand 5 minutes. Strain tea into a bowl; add lemonade concentrate to tea, stirring until concentrate is melted. Pour tea mixture into an ice-cube tray. Place a quarter lemon slice, and a mint sprig in each cube. Place tray in freezing compartment and freeze until solid. Place 3 to 4 of the tea-flavored cubes in each tall, chilled glass and fill glasses with cold Iced Tea. Serves 4 to 6.

Hot Chocolate and Cocoa

For children, chocolate-flavored drinks are welcome anytime; adults may find the spiced or richer chocolate drinks warming after winter sports. There are numerous instant cocoa mixes on the market to make hot or iced chocolate drinks. Use them as the package directs. When you use a recipe for cocoa or chocolate drinks, be sure to note whether it calls for cocoa mix; unsweetened cocoa; semisweet, sweet, or bitter chocolate.

❧ Hot Cocoa

⅓ cup unsweetened cocoa
3 to 4 tablespoons sugar
Few grains salt
½ cup water
3½ cups milk

In a saucepan mix cocoa, sugar, and salt; add water. Place over moderately low heat (about 225° F.) and bring to a boil, stirring constantly. Reduce heat to low (about 200° F.) and continue cooking 1 minute. Remove from heat and stir in milk. Increase temperature to moderately low (about 225° F.) and heat until cocoa just starts to boil. Beat with a rotary beater until blended and serve immediately. Makes 4 cups, or serves 4 to 6.

❧ Hot Chocolate

2 1-ounce squares
  unsweetened chocolate
3 to 4 tablespoons sugar
Few grains salt
1 cup water
3 cups milk

In a saucepan mix chocolate, sugar, salt, and water. Place over moderately low heat (about 225° F.) and heat until chocolate is melted, stirring constantly. Gradually stir in milk; heat until mixture just starts to boil. Beat with a rotary beater until blended and serve immediately. Makes 4 cups, or serves 4 to 6.

❧ French Chocolate

¼ cup packaged semisweet
  chocolate pieces
¼ cup light corn syrup
2 tablespoons water
¼ teaspoon vanilla extract
1 cup heavy cream
3 cups milk, scalded

Mix chocolate pieces, syrup, and water in a small saucepan; place over low heat (about 200° F.) and heat until chocolate is melted, stirring constantly. Cool and stir in vanilla. Chill until cold and thickened. Whip cream with a rotary beater until it is slightly thickened. Gradually add chilled chocolate syrup and beat until it holds it shape and forms soft peaks. To serve, spoon about 5 tablespoonfuls of the chocolate–cream mixture into cups and fill with hot scalded milk. Stir together before drinking. Serves 6 to 8.

❧ Cocoa Syrup for Hot or Iced Cocoa

½ cup unsweetened cocoa
1 cup sugar
⅛ teaspoon salt
1 cup boiling water
1 teaspoon vanilla extract
Milk

In a small saucepan combine cocoa, sugar, and salt. Gradually add boiling water, stirring until smooth. Cook over moderately low heat (about 225° F.) until syrup reaches boiling point, stirring constantly. Reduce heat to low (about 200° F.) and heat for 1 minute without stirring. Cool and add vanilla. Chill. Allow 2 tablespoons syrup for each serving. For hot cocoa, stir syrup into 1 cup scalded milk and serve topped with whipped cream or a marshmallow. For iced cocoa, stir syrup into 1 cup cold milk and serve over ice cubes in a tall glass. Makes 1½ cups syrup, or enough for 12 1-cup servings.

❧ Hot Mocha Froth

1 cup hot coffee
½ cup heavy cream
¼ cup semisweet chocolate
    pieces

Combine coffee and cream and heat over low heat (about 200° F.) until steaming hot. Pour into the container of an electric blender; add chocolate pieces. Cover tightly and blend on high speed for 20 seconds. Pour into warmed mugs. Serves 2.

❧ Mexican Hot Chocolate

2 cups milk
2 ounces sweet cooking
    chocolate, broken up
2 small cinnamon sticks
2 egg whites, stiffly beaten

Heat 1 cup of the milk; add chocolate and heat, stirring over low heat (about 200° F.) until chocolate is melted. Add remaining milk and cinnamon sticks. Bring to boiling point. Remove from heat. Remove cinnamon; beat liquid with a rotary beater or wire whip until smooth. Gradually add beaten egg whites. Continue to beat mixture until frothy. Serve in chocolate cups. Serves 3.

❧ Hot Rum–Cocoa

½ cup quick
    chocolate-flavored mix
½ cup dark rum
1 quart milk, heated
Sweetened whipped cream or
    whipped topping

Stir chocolate-flavored mix and rum into the heated milk. Place a dollop of whipped cream in each of 4 to 6 mugs and pour the hot mixture over it. Makes 5 cups; serves 4 to 6.

Cool Summer Drinks

Many of these drinks are nice to serve with a summer luncheon or supper. Or they make satisfying teatime beverages to serve with cookies or crackers, depending upon the sweetness of the drink. Many of the sweet drinks, especially the coffee-based ones, can serve as both dessert and after-dinner drinks.

BEVERAGES

❧ Brazilian Cooler

1½ cups milk
2½ tablespoons quick
   chocolate-flavored mix
2 12-fluid-ounce bottles or
   cans cola beverage,
   chilled
1 pint chocolate ice cream

Sprinkle chocolate-flavored mix over milk and stir until blended. Pour equal amounts (about 6 tablespoons) of flavored milk into 4 tall glasses. Fill glasses with cola beverage and top with a generous scoop of chocolate ice cream. Serves 4.

❧ Chocolate–Spice Shake

¾ cup milk
1½ tablespoons canned
   chocolate syrup
⅛ teaspoon ground nutmeg
⅛ teaspoon ground
   cinnamon
1 scoop vanilla ice cream

Place all ingredients in electric drink mixer. Turn on until blended, about 30 seconds. Alternatively, an electric blender may be used; blend for about 15 seconds. Serves 1.

❧ Banana Breakfast Shake

2 cups skim milk
½ cup low-fat plain yogurt
1 egg
1 tablespoon vanilla extract
2 teaspoons ground nutmeg
1 cup instant nonfat dry milk
1 medium-sized banana,
   peeled and cut in chunks
1 6-ounce can frozen orange
   juice concentrate,
   undiluted

Place all ingredients in container of an electric blender. Blend at high speed for 10 seconds, until ingredients are well mixed and slightly frothy. Pour into glasses and serve. Makes 4 cups. Serves 4.

❧ Razzberry Yogurt

⅓ cup water
2 8-ounce cartons plain
   yogurt
1 10-ounce package frozen
   sweetened raspberries,
   broken in pieces
3 tablespoons lemon juice

Place all ingredients in an electric blender. Cover and blend at high speed about 30 seconds; stop machine once or twice and push raspberries down. If desired, strain drink before serving to remove seeds. Drink keeps several days in refrigerator. Makes 3½ cups; serves 3 or 4.

✍ Apricot Flip

3¾ cups apricot nectar,
    chilled
2½ cups lemon sherbet
Lemon slices

Beat apricot nectar and lemon sherbet together with a rotary beater until blended. Serve in tall glasses garnished with lemon slice. This recipe may be prepared in an electric blender, but make only half the recipe at one time. Serves 4.

✍ Grape Ade Cooler

2 cups grape juice, chilled
2 cups apple juice, chilled
4 teaspoons lemon juice
1 pint lemon sherbet

Mix juices together and pour into tall glasses. Top with generous scoop of lemon sherbet. Serves 4.

✍ Lemonade

Ice cubes
1⅓ to 2 cups Lemonade Base
    (recipe below)
*3 cups cold water
 4 lemon slices

Place 3 or 4 ice cubes in each of 4 tall, chilled glasses. Add ⅓ to ½ cup of the Lemonade Base, depending on desired strength. Stir about ¾ cup of cold water into each glass. Garnish each with a lemon slice. Makes 4 servings.

*Note: Chilled ginger ale, lemon-lime soda or carbonated water may be substituted for the water in recipe above.

Lemonade Base

1½ cups fine granulated
    sugar
½ cup boiling water
1½ cups fresh or bottled
    lemon juice

Place all ingredients in a large jar with a tight-fitting cover. Cover jar and shake until sugar is dissolved. Store mixture in the refrigerator. Makes 2¾ cups syrup.

✍ Cranberry Frosted

1 quart cranberry juice
    cocktail, chilled
1 pint lemon or orange
    sherbet

Pour cranberry juice into glasses. Place a scoop of sherbet on top and serve immediately. Makes 8 6-ounce servings.

✑ Fruit Shrub

1 10-ounce package frozen
raspberries, thawed
1 cup pineapple–grapefruit
juice
4 lemon wedges

Place raspberries and pineapple–grapefruit juice in blender container. Blend for about 30 seconds on low speed, or until thoroughly blended. Strain mixture to remove seeds. Chill until serving time. Serve in cocktail glasses. Garnish with lemon. Makes 2 cups, or 4 ½-cup servings.

✑ Honey–Peanut-Butter Shake

2 cups milk
⅓ cup creamy peanut butter
¼ cup honey
1 cup vanilla ice cream

Combine all ingredients in the container of an electric blender and blend together 5 seconds. Pour into tall glasses. Makes 1 quart; serves 4.

✑ Strawberry Milk

1 10-ounce package frozen
strawberries, thawed
1 4½-ounce container frozen
whipped topping, thawed
2 cups milk

Press strawberries through a coarse sieve. Stir the puréed strawberries into the whipped topping. Gradually stir in milk. Pour into tall glasses. Makes 5 cups; serves 4.

✑ Pineapple Cress

2 cups unsweetened canned
pineapple juice
1 cup chopped watercress
Thin lemon slices (optional)

Place juice and watercress in an electric blender. Cover and blend at high speed 30 to 40 seconds, until cress liquefies and drink is dark green. Garnish with lemon slices if desired. Makes 3⅔ cups. Serves 3 or 4.

✑ Peach Thaw

1 10-ounce package frozen
sliced peaches, thawed
2 tablespoons lemon juice
⅔ cup sugar
¼ teaspoon ground nutmeg
¼ teaspoon ground ginger
1 1-pint-12-fluid-ounce
bottle ginger ale, chilled
4 slices navel orange

Combine peaches, lemon juice, sugar, nutmeg, and ginger. Mash together thoroughly or blend in an electric blender. Put equal amounts into 4 tall, chilled glasses (10 ounces). Add ginger ale. Put thin slice of orange into each glass. Serves 4.

✑ Rhubarb Lemonade

1 pound fresh or frozen
rhubarb
1 6-ounce can frozen
lemonade concentrate
2 cups water
3 or more tablespoons sugar
1 cup cold water

If using fresh rhubarb, cut off and discard green leaves and cut stalks into 2-inch pieces. In a large saucepan place the rhubarb, lemonade concentrate, the 2 cups water and the 3 tablespoons sugar. Bring to a boil over moderately high heat (about 350° F.), stirring to melt lemonade and dissolve sugar. Reduce heat to moderately low (about 225° F.), cover pan and cook 10 to 15 minutes, or until rhubarb is mushy and falling apart. (Take care not to let the sticky mixture boil over.) When done, strain rhubarb mixture into a widemouthed pitcher or jar, pressing pulp against the sides of the strainer with a spoon to extract all the juice. Taste mixture and add more sugar if desired; drink should be tart. Add the 1 cup cold water to the rhubarb mixture and chill well. Serve over ice. Makes about 3½ cups. Serves 4.

✑ Raspberry Fruit Refresher

1 10-ounce package frozen
raspberries, thawed
3 cups pineapple juice, chilled
4 large scoops lemon sherbet
2 cups carbonated water,
chilled

Press raspberries through a fine sieve or food mill to remove seeds. For each serving, place about ¼ cup of the raspberry juice in electric drink mixer or the container of an electric blender. Add ¾ cup of the pineapple juice and 1 scoop of the sherbet. Turn on mixer until blended, about 1 minute, or blend 30 seconds in electric blender. Pour into a tall glass. Slowly pour in about ½ cup carbonated water. Serves 6.

✑ Vegetable–Fruit Blend

1½ cups pineapple juice
2 medium-sized carrots,
peeled and coarsely cut up
⅓ banana
½ cup crushed ice

Place all ingredients in the container of an electric blender. Blend until thick and foamy. Pour into 8-ounce glasses. Serves 3.

✑ Strawberry–Buttermilk Frosted

1 quart buttermilk, chilled
1 pint strawberry ice cream
¼ cup confectioners' sugar

Beat ingredients together with rotary beater until blended. Serve in tall glasses garnished with whole strawberry if desired. This recipe may be prepared in an

Whole strawberries (optional)

electric blender, but make only half the recipe at one time. Serves 4.

❧ Beet Buttermilk

2 *cups buttermilk*
1 *8¼-ounce can sliced beets, undrained*
⅛ *teaspoon salt*
⅛ *teaspoon pepper*
4 *teaspoons lemon juice*
¼ *teaspoon sugar (optional)*

Place all ingredients in an electric blender; cover and blend at high speed until smooth. Makes 3⅓ cups; serves 2.

Ice-Cream Sodas

Sodas are year-round favorites. You can make them as the professionals do with this recipe. Important: Have the carbonated water or soda thoroughly chilled.

❧ Basic Ice-Cream Soda

4 *tablespoons flavored sauce or syrup*
1 *tablespoon light cream or milk*
Carbonated water, chilled
2 *scoops of ice cream*
Whipped cream, if desired

In a tall glass, mix together the syrup or sauce and cream or milk. Fill ¾ full with *chilled* carbonated water and stir. Add ice cream and fill glass with carbonated water. Top with a spoonful of whipped cream, if desired. Makes 1 soda.

Black and White Soda

Use canned chocolate syrup and vanilla ice cream.

Chocolate Soda

Use canned chocolate syrup and chocolate ice cream.

Strawberry Soda

Use Strawberry Syrup (recipe follows) and strawberry ice cream.

Strawberry Syrup

1 **10-ounce package frozen strawberries, thawed**
½ **cup light corn syrup**

Drain thawed strawberries and reserve juice. Combine juice and corn syrup in a saucepan. Bring to a boil over moderate heat (about 250° F.) and boil 5 minutes. Cool. Press the berries through a sieve or purée them in a blender. Stir the pulp into the cooled syrup. Chill. Makes 1⅓ cups syrup, enough for about 5 sodas.

Note: Frozen raspberries or peaches may be used in place of the strawberries. Peaches must be coarsely chopped before puréeing. Use either vanilla ice cream or a flavor to match the sauce when you make a fruit soda.

Punch

Punch is an easy way to serve drinks to a crowd. It can be self-service and it also eliminates the need to stock a variety of drinks.

The punch bowl: Any large glass or enamel bowl or a soup tureen will do nicely for serving punch. You can surround it with leaves or center it on a pretty tray. For cold punch, be sure the bowl is chilled well.

The ice: It's better to use a block of ice rather than ice cubes in punch because cubes melt quickly, diluting the flavor of the punch. If you can't buy a small chunk of ice, you can make your own blocks of ice in a loaf pan or in molds. When you make your own, you have a chance to put your artistic talent to work. Half-fill a mold with water. Freeze. Lay cubes of pineapple, fresh strawberries, mint sprigs, red or green maraschino cherries, cutouts of lemon, orange, or lime peel on the ice. Cover with water and finish freezing. To unmold, dip pan in warm water until ice slips out easily. Ring molds and heart-shaped molds can be decorated for appropriate holidays.

Parties large enough to warrant serving punch may include children and, most likely, nondrinkers. If you are serving an alcoholic punch, have one also that isn't alcoholic rather than serving individual soft drinks. Count on 2 to 3 ½-cup servings per person when you serve punch.

Children's Candy Stick Punch

1½ **pints softened vanilla ice cream**

Spoon ice cream into punch bowl. Stir in eggnog and carbonated water. Top with puffs of whipped cream

6 cups dairy eggnog drink
5¼ cups chilled carbonated water
1½ cups heavy cream, whipped
½ cup crushed peppermint stick candy

and sprinkle cream with crushed peppermint. Makes about 24 ½-cup servings.

◄§ Cranberry–Lemon Punch

2 cups ice water
⅓ cup sugar
⅓ cup lemon juice, chilled
1 pint cranberry juice, chilled
1 pint ginger ale, chilled
1 pint lemon sherbet

Combine water, sugar, lemon juice, and cranberry juice in a small punch bowl. Slowly pour in ginger ale. Top with small scoops of sherbet just before serving. Makes 13 ½-cup servings.

◄§ Fruit Syllabub

12 tablespoons sugar
3 cups apple juice
⅓ cup lemon juice
¼ cup grated lemon peel
¾ teaspoon ground nutmeg
4½ cups milk
1½ cups light cream
6 egg whites

Mix 6 tablespoons of the sugar with the apple juice, lemon juice, lemon peel, and nutmeg in a large bowl. Stir well to dissolve sugar. In a medium-sized bowl, combine milk and cream and blend well. Refrigerate apple juice mixture and milk–cream mixture separately until serving time. At serving time, beat egg whites with an electric mixer until soft peaks form. Gradually add the remaining 6 tablespoons sugar and beat until stiff peaks form. Set aside. Add milk–cream mixture to apple juice mixture and beat with electric mixer until frothy. Gently fold in egg whites. Pour into serving pitchers and sprinkle tops lightly with nutmeg. Makes about 3¾ quarts, or 30 ½-cup servings.

◄§ Kris Kringle Punch

6 cups chilled bottled cranberry juice
3 cups chilled bottled apple juice
¾ cup chilled lemon juice
1½ cups chilled orange juice
2 1-pint-12-fluid-ounce bottles ginger ale

Combine cranberry juice, apple juice, lemon juice, and orange juice in a punch bowl. Just before serving, pour in ginger ale; stir well. Garnish with Ice Ring or use Fruit Ice Cubes in individual cups. Makes 4½ quarts, or about 36 ½-cup servings.

Ice Ring or Fruit Ice Cubes
  (recipes follow)

Ice Ring

Half-fill a ring mold with *cold water* and freeze until solid. Arrange one or more of the following fruits in a design over surface of ice: *red and green maraschino cherries, mandarin orange segments, pineapple chunks, lemon or lime slices.* Just cover with *water* and freeze. To unmold, dip in warm water until loosened and slip into punch bowl.

Fruit Ice Cubes

Place a piece of one of the above fruits listed in the Ice Ring recipe in each section of an ice-cube tray. Fill with cold water and freeze.

✑ Minted Chocolate Cola Punch

4 6-fluid-ounce bottles or 2 12-fluid-ounce bottles chilled cola beverage
1 1-pint-12-fluid-ounce bottle chilled carbonated water
1 cup canned chocolate syrup
Few drops peppermint flavoring
Vanilla ice cream or whipped cream (optional)

Combine cola beverage and carbonated water in punch bowl. Stir in chocolate syrup and peppermint flavoring to taste. Add a few ice cubes. If desired, garnish with spoonfuls of vanilla ice cream or whipped cream. Makes 7½ cups, or about 15 ½-cup servings.

✑ Mock Pink Champagne

3 6-ounce cans frozen orange juice concentrate, thawed
3 6-ounce cans frozen grapefruit juice concentrate, thawed
2 18-ounce cans pineapple juice, chilled
1 cup grenadine syrup
3 28-fluid-ounce bottles ginger ale, chilled
Fresh strawberries (optional)

Place orange and grapefruit juice concentrates, pineapple juice, and grenadine syrup in a punch bowl or other large container. Just before serving, add ginger ale and stir to mix thoroughly. If desired, float a few fresh strawberries on top of punch. Makes about 4 quarts punch or 32 ½-cup servings.

✑ *Orange Eggnog Punch*

1 quart dairy eggnog, chilled
1 6-ounce can frozen orange
    juice concentrate, thawed
¼ cup maple-blended syrup
¼ cup honey
Orange slices (optional)

In a large mixing bowl, combine eggnog, orange juice concentrate, syrup, and honey. With an electric mixer, beat until well blended and very thick. Chill for at least 1 hour. Serve in a punch bowl garnished with orange slices, if desired. Makes 1½ quarts, or 12 ½-cup servings.

Alcoholic Punches

Among the punch recipes that follow you will find that the first several are made with wines. These are lighter and far less lethal than the more alcoholic punches. They are particularly nice for daytime parties and they serve well with both sweet and spicy side foods.

✑ *California Punch*

1½ cups water
2 cups sugar
2 sticks cinnamon
2 teaspoons whole cloves
⅛ teaspoon salt
2 fifths Burgundy wine,
    chilled
6 cups cranberry-apple
    juice
1 12-fluid-ounce bottle
    carbonated water
Ice cubes
Lemon slices
Orange slices
Maraschino cherries

Place water, sugar, cinnamon, cloves, and salt in a saucepan over moderately low heat (about 225° F.); cook 10 minutes. Strain and discard spices; cool and chill syrup mixture in refrigerator. Combine syrup mixture, wine, cranberry-apple juice, and carbonated water in a punch bowl. Add ice cubes. Garnish with lemon slices, orange slices, and maraschino cherries. Makes about 4½ quarts, or 36 ½-cup servings.

✑ *Champagne Punch*

1 6-ounce can frozen
    lemonade concentrate,
    thawed
8 cups chilled pineapple juice
2 fifths Riesling wine, chilled

Pour lemonade and pineapple juice into punch bowl. Add wine and champagne just before serving. Unmold Cranberry Hearts and float on punch. Makes 18½ cups, or about 37 ½-cup servings.

1 fifth champagne, chilled
Cranberry Hearts (recipe
follows)

Cranberry Hearts

1 quart cranberry juice
2 cups water

Mix cranberry juice and water; pour into individual heart-shaped gelatin molds. Place in freezer for several hours, until frozen. Unmold by dipping in cold water to loosen. Makes about 12 hearts.

✑ La Fonda Sangría

4 lemons
4 navel oranges
6 tablespoons water
1 cup plus 2 tablespoons sugar
3 cups cracked ice
2 cups semidry red or white table wine, chilled
2 cups carbonated water, chilled

Slice lemons into round slices. Cut oranges into thin slices; then cut slices in half. Put half the fruit in the bottom of each of two 2-quart pitchers. In a small saucepan combine water and sugar and cook over moderate heat (about 250° F.) until mixture comes to a boil and sugar is dissolved, stirring constantly. Cool. Pour half the sugar syrup, 1½ cups cracked ice, and 1 cup wine into each pitcher. Add 1 cup carbonated water to each. Stir with a wooden spoon to blend mixture. Serve in 14- to 16-ounce glasses with a slice of lemon and orange in each glass. Serves 8.

✑ Wine Syllabub

2 cups sugar
1 fifth chilled sauterne wine
⅓ cup grated lemon peel
⅔ cup lemon juice
1½ quarts milk
1 quart light cream
8 egg whites
1 cup sugar
Ground nutmeg

Mix the 2 cups sugar, sauterne, and lemon peel and juice in bowl. Let stand until sugar is dissolved. Pour milk and cream into a punch bowl. Gradually add wine mixture, beating constantly with rotary beater until blended and frothy. Beat egg whites until soft peaks form. Gradually add the 1 cup sugar and beat until stiff peaks form. Spoon beaten egg whites in puffs over top of punch. Sprinkle with nutmeg. Makes about 3¾ quarts, or 30 ½-cup servings.

✑ Snowy Eggnog

5 egg yolks
5 tablespoons sugar
7 cups dairy half-and-half
¾ cup cognac

Beat egg yolks with the 5 tablespoons sugar until thick and lemon-colored. Stir in half-and-half and cognac; blend well. Chill several hours. Just before serving, pour mixture into chilled punch bowl. Beat egg whites until

5 *egg whites*
5 *tablespoons sugar*
Grated nutmeg

soft peaks form. Gradually add the remaining 5 tablespoons sugar and beat until stiff peaks form. Fold ⅔ of the meringue into chilled eggnog. Spoon out remaining meringue into large mounds on top. Sprinkle mounds generously with freshly grated nutmeg. Makes about 25 ½-cup servings.

❧ Holiday Wine Punch

1 *6-ounce can frozen pink*
  lemonade concentrate,
  thawed and prepared
  according to label
  directions
1 *fifth rosé wine, chilled*
1 *quart bottle port wine,*
  chilled
1 *pint raspberry sherbet,*
  slightly softened

Pour prepared lemonade into a 1- or 1½-quart ring mold and freeze several hours, or overnight. When ready to serve, unmold ice ring and place in a punch bowl. Pour wines over ring and allow it to melt slightly. Spoon in dollops of sherbet and serve. Makes about 2½ quarts, about 20 ½-cup servings.

❧ Caribbean Punch Bowl

4 *cups orange juice*
1½ *cups bottled lemon juice*
1½ *cups light rum*
1 *cup grenadine*
1 *cup apricot brandy*
¾ *cup banana liqueur or*
  Cointreau
¼ *cup rye whiskey (optional)*
1 *lemon, sliced (optional)*
1 *orange, sliced (optional)*

Combine all ingredients except sliced lemon and orange in a punch bowl and chill until serving time. When ready to serve, add ice. Lemon and orange slices may be floated on it as a garnishing touch, if desired. Makes about 10 cups, or 20 ½-cup servings.

❧ Holiday Eggnog

6 *eggs, separated*
½ *cup sugar (or to taste)*
1½ *cups bourbon whiskey*
½ *cup rum*
½ *cup brandy or Cointreau*
2 *teaspoons vanilla extract*
1 *pint milk*
3 *cups heavy cream*

In the large bowl of an electric mixer, beat egg yolks well. Gradually add the ½ cup sugar and beat until light and fluffy. While still beating, gradually add bourbon, rum, and brandy. Stir in vanilla. Chill in refrigerator at least 1 hour before adding milk and cream. Add about ⅓ of the milk and cream every half hour, stirring well after each addition. When ready to serve, beat egg whites until stiff peaks form. Fold half the egg white

3 *tablespoons sugar*
Ground nutmeg

mixture into cream mixture in bowl. Pour mixture into punch bowl. Beat the 3 tablespoons sugar into the remaining egg whites and swirl on top of eggnog or drop in spoonfuls on top of individual servings. Sprinkle with nutmeg. Makes 20 to 25 ½-cup servings.

❧ Tom and Jerry

1 *envelope unflavored*
  gelatine
½ *cup cold water*
8 *eggs, separated*
½ *cup confectioners' sugar*
Few grains salt
1½ *cups confectioners' sugar*
Brandy
Rum
Hot water
Ground nutmeg

Sprinkle gelatine over water to soften. Place over low heat (about 200° F.) and stir until gelatine is dissolved. Cool until slightly thickened. Beat egg yolks until they begin to thicken. Gradually add the ½ cup sugar; continue beating until thick. Stir in gelatine. Beat egg whites and salt until soft peaks form. Gradually add the 1½ cups sugar, beating until stiff peaks form. Fold egg yolk mixture into beaten egg whites. To serve: Pour 1 jigger brandy and 1 teaspoon rum into each cup or mug. Add 2 heaping tablespoons of the egg mixture. Pour ⅓ to ½ cup very hot water into each cup; sprinkle with ground nutmeg. Egg mixture may be stored in a covered jar in the refrigerator, where it will keep for several days. Makes 2 quarts egg mixture, or enough for about 36 servings.

❧ Texas, or Bourbon, Punch

12 *medium-sized lemons*
1 *cup sugar*
1 *quart water*
1 *fifth bourbon whiskey*

Cut lemons in half and squeeze the juice into a large saucepan. Add sugar, water, and the squeezed half-lemons to the juice; bring to a boil over moderate heat (about 250° F.). Remove from heat and cool slightly. Add bourbon and let stand several hours or overnight. Remove lemon peels, squeezing out any liquid. Strain punch and store, covered, in refrigerator (will keep refrigerated for a month). Stir well before serving. Serve over ice. Makes about 2 quarts or 16 ½-cup servings.

❧ Wassail Bowl

1 *cup water*
½ *teaspoon ground nutmeg*
1 *teaspoon ground ginger*
1 *2-inch stick cinnamon*
3 *whole cloves*

Combine water, nutmeg, ginger, cinnamon, the 3 whole cloves, allspice, and cardamom in a saucepan over moderately low heat (about 225° F.). Bring to a boil and simmer 10 minutes. Strain. Add sherry, ale, and sugar. Stir over low heat (about 200° F.) a few minutes to dis-

6 whole allspice
2 whole cardamom seeds
1 fifth sweet sherry wine
2 10-fluid-ounce cans ale
2 cups sugar
6 eggs, separated
½ cup cognac
3 dozen whole cloves
12 canned, spiced, whole crab
apples

solve sugar. Beat egg yolks well. Beat egg whites until stiff but not dry; fold them into yolks. Gradually stir in half of the sherry mixture; pour into heatproof punch bowl. Place remaining sherry mixture over moderate heat (about 250° F.) until it comes to a boil. Gradually stir into punch bowl. Stir in cognac. Place 3 whole cloves in each crab apple. Add to punch. Makes about 3½ quarts, or 28 ½-cup servings.

The Cocktail Hour

Cocktail time is a boon to those who are entertaining and to guests. It gives your friends a chance to unwind and to feel at home in your house and with one another—and it gives you time to take care of last-minute details of food preparation and table setting. For cocktails, one person takes over and needs to see that everyone has a drink. Lacking a partner, you can prevail upon a good friend to help or let guests mix their own drinks.

Bar needs vary according to the drinks, but in addition to the necessary ingredients, here are some supplies that you should have on hand: ice bucket and tongs, two or three bottle and can openers (one always gets misplaced), a corkscrew, a measuring glass, a martini pitcher, a long spoon or stirrer, a cocktail shaker (or a blender), a bar strainer, a paring knife (for lemon peels), a lemon-and-lime squeezer, an ice crusher, and a pitcher of water.

Before-dinner drinks don't have to include a variety of exotic drinks and elaborate cocktails. If you stock up on the makings of several of the most popular drinks, plus tomato juice, beer, and a few soft drinks, no one should criticize the hospitality of the house. Martinis, Manhattans, and whiskey sours are three popular before-dinner drinks, but the choices you offer should depend on local customs and individual tastes.

It's better to overbuy liquor than to be short because you can always use the excess for entertaining at another time. To help you estimate amounts: a fifth of liquor contains 25 ounces; a quart, 32 ounces. Experienced party givers usually count on each person's having three drinks, even though some people may not drink at all.

Following are recipes for the most popular cocktails.

ᏌᏫ Manhattan Cocktail (Dry)

1 dash Angostura bitters
¾ ounce dry vermouth
1½ ounces rye whiskey
Strip of lemon peel

Stir all ingredients except lemon peel with cracked ice and strain into a 3-ounce chilled cocktail glass. Twist the lemon peel over glass and drop into glass. Serves 1.

ᏌᏫ Manhattan Cocktail (Sweet)

1 dash orange bitters
¾ ounce sweet vermouth
1½ ounces rye whiskey
1 maraschino cherry

Stir all the ingredients except cherry with cracked ice and strain into a chilled 3-ounce cocktail glass. Garnish with cherry. Serves 1.

ᏌᏫ Manhattan Cocktail (Perfect)

Use same recipe as for Sweet Manhattan, but for the sweet vermouth, substitute *½ ounce sweet vermouth* and *½ ounce dry vermouth.*

ᏌᏫ Martini (Traditional 3 to 1)

1½ ounces gin
½ ounce dry vermouth
Olive or twist of lemon peel

Fill a Martini pitcher with cracked, not crushed, ice. Add gin and then vermouth. Stir briskly until very cold. Strain into an ice-cold 3-ounce glass. Add olive or a twist of lemon peel. May also be served on the rocks by pouring over ice cubes into an Old-Fashioned glass. Serves 1.

Dry Martini (5 to 1)

Use 1⅔ *ounces gin* and ⅓ *ounce dry vermouth.*

Extra-Dry Martini (7 to 1)

Use 1¾ *ounces gin* and ¼ *ounce dry vermouth.*

ᏌᏫ Screwdriver

4 ice cubes
1 tablespoon lime juice
¾ cup orange juice
1½ ounces (3 tablespoons) Vodka

Place all ingredients in a chilled 12-ounce glass. Stir with a long handled spoon to blend. Serves 1.

BEVERAGES

✌ Bloody Mary

1½ ounces vodka
3 ounces tomato juice
Juice of ½ lemon
Pinch each of salt, pepper,
    and celery salt
½ teaspoon Worcestershire
    sauce
Dash of Tabasco

Shake ingredients well with cracked ice and strain into a 6-ounce Old-Fashioned glass. Serves 1.

✌ Bar Syrup

(Bar syrup is easily prepared; it makes a smoother drink than one made with granulated sugar.)

4 cups sugar
1 cup water

Combine sugar and water in a saucepan. Bring to a boil over moderate heat (about 250° F.), stirring only until sugar is dissolved. Reduce heat to moderately low (about 225° F.); cook until clear. Cool and store in a tightly covered jar.

✌ Whiskey Sour

Juice of ½ lemon
½ teaspoon confectioners'
    sugar or bar syrup (recipe
    above)
2 ounces rye whiskey
½ slice orange
1 maraschino cherry

Shake lemon juice, sugar, and whiskey with crushed ice. Strain into a 6-ounce Whiskey Sour glass. Garnish with orange slice and cherry. May also be served on the rocks by pouring over ice cubes into an Old-Fashioned glass. Serves 1.

Scotch Sour

Substitute 2 ounces Scotch for rye whiskey.

✌ Tom Collins

Juice of ½ lemon
1 teaspoon confectioners'
    sugar or bar syrup (recipe
    above)
2 ounces gin

Shake lemon juice, sugar, and gin with cracked ice. Strain into a 12-ounce glass. Add several cubes of ice and fill with carbonated water. Garnish with orange and lemon slices and the cherry. Serve with a straw. Serves 1.

Carbonated water
½ slice orange
½ slice lemon
1 maraschino cherry

Rum Collins

Substitute *2 ounces rum* for gin.

John Collins

Substitute *2 ounces rye whiskey* for gin.

Vodka Collins

Substitute *2 ounces vodka* for gin.

✑ Shandygaff

Chilled beer
Chilled ginger ale

Fill a large, well-chilled highball or pilsner glass or beer mug halfway with beer. Top with ginger ale. Serves 1.

✑ Old-Fashioned Cocktail

½ *lump sugar*
2 *dashes Angostura bitters*
1 *teaspoon water*
2 *cubes ice*
2 *ounces rye, bourbon, or Scotch whiskey*
1 *slice orange*
1 *slice lemon*
1 *maraschino cherry*

Place sugar in bottom of an Old-Fashioned glass. Add bitters and water; muddle well. Add ice and pour in whiskey. Garnish with orange, lemon, and cherry. Serves 1.

✑ Mint Julep

1 *long sprig fresh mint*
Confectioners' sugar
2 *teaspoons bar syrup (recipe on page 268)*
6 *medium-sized mint leaves*
Dash of Angostura bitters (optional)

Chill a 14- to 16-ounce glass or silver mug in the refrigerator. Wash the mint sprig and dry partially. Dip in confectioners' sugar. Reserve for garnish. Place bar syrup, the 6 mint leaves, and the bitters in a glass; bruise the leaves with a muddler. Stir in the 2 ounces bourbon. Place ice in the chilled mug. Strain the bruised mint leaves and bourbon mixture and pour over the crushed

2 ounces bourbon whiskey
Crushed ice
1 ounce bourbon whiskey

ice. With a bar spoon, churn ice up and down; add more ice to within ¾ inch from top of glass. Add the 1 ounce bourbon and repeat churning process until glass is completely frosted. Garnish with the sugared mint sprig. If more than one julep is being made, do not prechill glasses, but chill the individual juleps in the refrigerator after last churning until frosted, allowing about 30 minutes. To keep glass or mug frosted while serving the julep, use a towel when handling it. Serves 1.

Daiquiri

Juice of 1 lime
  1 teaspoon confectioners'
  sugar or bar syrup (recipe
  on page 268)
1½ ounces light rum

Shake ingredients well with cracked ice and strain into a chilled 3-ounce cocktail glass. Serves 1.

Frozen Daiquiri

Juice of 1 lime
  1 teaspoon confectioners'
  sugar or bar syrup (recipe
  on page 268)
2 ounces light rum

Agitate ingredients in an electric mixer or blender filled with shaved ice (2 minutes in mixer or 30 seconds in blender). Strain through a coarse-meshed strainer into a 6-ounce champagne glass. Serve with a straw. Serves 1.

Gimlet Cocktail

Juice of 1 lime
  1 teaspoon confectioners'
  sugar or bar syrup (recipe
  on page 268)
1½ ounces gin

Shake ingredients well with cracked ice and strain into a champagne glass containing an ice cube. Serve with a short straw. Serves 1.

Champagne Cocktail

1 lump sugar
2 dashes Angostura bitters
Champagne
Strip of lemon peel

Place the lump of sugar in a 6-ounce champagne glass and saturate it with the bitters. Fill with champagne. Add twisted lemon peel. Serves 1.

ᕙ Sidecar Cocktail

¾ ounce triple sec or
   Cointreau
1¾ ounces brandy
Juice of ½ lemon

Shake ingredients with cracked ice and strain into a chilled 3-ounce cocktail glass. Serves 1.

ᕙ Rob Roy Cocktail (Sweet)*

¾ ounce sweet vermouth
1½ ounces Scotch whiskey
1 dash orange bitters
1 maraschino cherry

Stir vermouth, Scotch, and bitters with cracked ice and strain into a 3-ounce chilled cocktail glass. Garnish with cherry. Serves 1.

Note: For a Dry Rob Roy, substitute dry vermouth for the sweet vermouth.

ᕙ Gin Fizz

Juice of ½ lemon
1 teaspoon confectioners'
   sugar or bar syrup (recipe
   on page 268)
2 ounces gin
Carbonated water

Shake lemon juice, sugar, and gin with cracked ice and strain into a 7-ounce glass. Fill with carbonated water and stir. Serves 1.

ᕙ Bacardi Cocktail

1½ ounces light rum
Juice of ½ lime
  ½ teaspoon grenadine

Shake ingredients well with cracked ice and strain into a chilled 3-ounce cocktail glass. Serves 1.

ᕙ Grasshopper Cocktail

¾ ounce green crème de
   menthe
¾ ounce white crème de
   cacao
¾ ounce light cream

Shake ingredients with cracked ice and strain into a 3-ounce chilled cocktail glass. Serves 1.

BEVERAGES

✒ Stinger Cocktail

1 ounce white crème de
   menthe
2 ounces brandy

Shake ingredients with cracked ice and strain into a chilled 3-ounce cocktail glass. Serves 1.

✒ Alexander Cocktail

1 ounce crème de cacao
1 ounce brandy
1 ounce heavy sweet cream

Shake ingredients well with cracked ice and strain into a chilled 4-ounce cocktail glass. Serves 1.

CHAPTER IX

MEATS

Meat is, for most Americans, the heart of a dinner meal. People plan their menus around the meat they have selected to serve—the vegetables, the salad, the starch, and dessert usually follow. Since meat does consume the greatest part of a food budget, knowing how to buy meat and how to prepare it is enormously important.

Grading and Labeling

Because so much of the fresh meat sold today is precut and prepackaged, it is not often possible to rely on the United States Department of Agriculture's inspection and grading labels. All meat that is shipped between states must be inspected for wholesomeness; the round purple stamp that reads "U.S. Inspected and Passed" must appear on the carcass. The shield-shaped grade label may appear on larger cuts of meat you purchase since the stamp is applied repeatedly along the entire length of the carcass. Most of the meat you purchase in a supermarket will be graded Choice or Good. The short supply of Prime grade meats is directed mostly to the fine restaurant trade. The fourth and fifth meat grades are Standard and Commercial, or Utility. Both of these grades have a thin fat covering and very little marbling. They are best cooked in liquids, as in braised dishes or stews. All graded meats must have first been pronounced wholesome.

The Appearance of Fresh Meat

It takes an expert to look at a piece of meat and tell just how tender, juicy, and flavorful it will be. These are guides: The lean portion should be fine-grained, firm-looking, and bright in color without dark streaks. The fat should be clear and white. The amount of marbling—the flecks of fat through the lean—affects juiciness and flavor; well-marbled meat will be more tender.

Market Labels

One needs only to go into supermarkets in various parts of this country to realize that butchers are creative: Beauty steaks, butterfly steaks, his-and-her steaks, are just a few of the colorful local names assigned to given cuts of meat. If you are moving from one part of the country to another, you may have to do some research to be able to follow the local labeling; however, in some states it is required that the "primal" cut name must also appear on the label. There are seven primal cuts of meat, whether applied to beef, pork, veal, or lamb. If you know these cuts you can

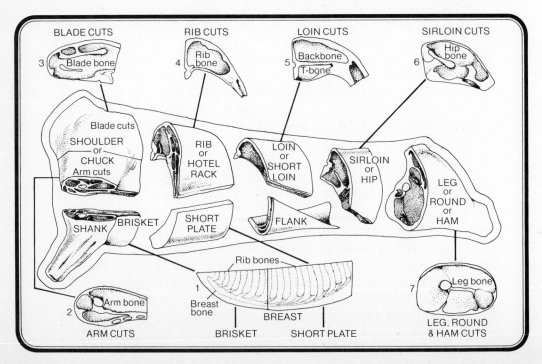

converse more knowledgeably with the butcher or market manager. Also, the primal cut will usually suggest how the meat is best cooked. If you ask, the butcher or the market manager will tell you where a given piece of meat comes from. Don't be afraid to try meats that are not in great demand. They are often the best way to lick the budget problem.

The Seven Basic Retail Cuts of Meat

In all meat animals, the most tender meat is taken from that portion of the animal where the muscles have been least used, the rib, loin, and sirloin cuts. These are the most in demand and frequently the most expensive.

Breast cuts are interlaced layers of fat and lean, many of which contain the lower portions of the rib bones. These are the cuts that will take long cooking with the addition of moisture or a basting marinade.

The common breast cuts in the market are as follows:

In beef:

Brisket, fresh or corned
Beef short ribs
Flank steak
Plate beef, rolled or in pieces

In pork:

Bacon, slab or sliced
Salt pork
Spareribs

In veal:

Veal breast, bone-in or boneless
  rolled
Veal brisket pieces
Veal riblets

In lamb:

Lamb breast, bone-in or boneless
  rolled
Lamb riblets

Arm cuts, unless they are boneless, have a characteristic round arm bone. They are best cooked in moist heat or tenderized with meat tenderizer or a marinade before barbecuing or broiling.

The common arm cuts in the market are as follows:

In beef:

Arm steak, short or full cut
Boneless shoulder steak
Boston cut
Chuck short ribs

In pork:

Arm steak
Arm roast
Fresh picnic, bone-in or rolled
Smoked picnic ham
Hocks, fresh or smoked

[275]

MEATS

In veal:

Veal arm steak
Arm roast
Foreshank

In lamb:

Arm or shoulder chops
Foreshank

Blade cuts, with bone in, can be identified by the long blade bone. They, like the arm cuts, are best cooked in moist heat unless tenderized with a marinade or meat tenderizer.

The common blade cuts in the market are as follows:

In beef:

Blade pot roast or steak
Petite steak, also called chicken steak
Inside chuck roll
Chuck short ribs

In pork:

Blade steak
Boston butt, may be rolled
Smoked shoulder butt
Jowl bacon

In veal:

Blade steak
Blade roast
Rolled shoulder
Neck

In lamb:

Blade chop
Square shoulder
Rolled shoulder
Cushion shoulder
Saratoga chops, boneless blade chops

Rib cuts are the beginning of the most tender cuts of meat. They may be broiled, pan-fried, or roasted without liquid.

The most common rib cuts in the market are as follows:

In beef:

Delmonico (rib eye) roast or steak
Rib steak, boneless or bone-in
Standing or rolled rib roast

In pork:

Butterfly chop
Rib chop
Canadian-style bacon, whole or sliced

In veal:

Rib chops, may be Frenched
Rib roast
Crown roast

In lamb:

Rib chops, may be Frenched
Rib roast
Crown roast

Loin cuts are succulent cuts in great demand. They are best broiled or roasted.

The common loin cuts in the market are as follows:

In beef:

Club steak
T-bone steak
Porterhouse steak
Tenderloin, whole or steak

In pork:

Tenderloin, boneless
Loin chop, may be smoked
Loin roast

In veal:

Loin chop
Loin roast, may be rolled
Kidney chop (kidney centered in a
    boned chop)

In lamb:

Loin chop
Loin roast, may be rolled
English chop (kidney centered in a
    boned chop)

Sirloin (or hip) cuts yield tender meat that may be broiled, pan-fried, or roasted without liquid.

The common sirloin cuts in the market are as follows:

In beef:

Sirloin steak, either wedge bone,
    pin bone, flat bone, or boneless
Tenderloin steak

In pork:

Sirloin chop

In veal:

Sirloin steak
Sirloin roast
Double sirloin roast, boneless

In lamb:

Sirloin chop
Sirloin roast
Rolled double sirloin roast

Leg (round and ham) cuts, from the solid, meaty portion of the animal, are less tender than rib, loin, and sirloin cuts but have excellent flavor. The top cuts (round) of this portion, nearest to the loin are, of course, the tenderest. Top round is more tender than bottom round. Roasts and steaks of beef need marinade, tenderizing, or moisture. Fresh or smoked hams and leg of lamb are usually roasted. Veal roasts are best with some additional fat for moisture.

The common leg cuts in the market are as follows:

In beef:

Top round steak
Bottom round steak

In pork:

Fresh ham steak
Smoked ham steak

MEATS

Beef tip steak
Eye round roast
Standing rump roast
Rolled rump roast
Tip steak
Sirloin tip roast
Cube steak
Ground round steak

Fresh ham, bone-in and boneless
Smoked ham roll
Smoked ham, bone-in and boneless

In veal:

Round steak
Leg roast
Rolled leg
Boneless cutlets, may be rolled
Heel of round

In lamb:

Leg steak or chop
Leg of lamb, whole or half
Rolled leg
Butterflied leg, to barbecue

Cubed meats for stew and ground meats may come from any portion of the animal unless you specify "ground round" or "cubed round" or "cubed chuck" or "lamb shoulder cut in cubes." Ground meat must, by law, contain no more than 30 percent fat and must have no other substance added unless it is so labeled. Regular ground beef has 20 to 25 percent fat; ground chuck, 10 to 20 percent; and ground round, 10 percent fat.

In addition to the primal cuts, there are a number of variety meats.

Liver of beef, pork, lamb, or veal is an exceptional source of essential food nutrients. Beef and pork liver are best cooked in moist heat; calf's (veal) liver and lamb liver may be broiled or pan-fried.

Heart of beef, pork, lamb, or veal is an excellent food. This is essentially a muscle and needs long, slow cooking in moisture.

Sweetbreads are a great delicacy. They are usually precooked in water seasoned with salt and lemon juice or vinegar (to keep them white and firm). They may then be sauced or rolled in crumbs and pan-fried.

Kidneys of beef, pork, lamb, or veal are a source of good nutrition and good eating. Beef kidneys must be cooked in moist heat. All others may be broiled or pan-fried.

Tripe may be purchased fresh, pickled, or canned. Fresh tripe has usually been partially cooked before marketing; however, further cooking in liquid is preliminary to all methods of preparation.

Tongue is sold fresh, pickled, corned, or smoked. Tongue should be cooked slowly in liquid—usually water with added seasonings or flavorings.

Brains are much like sweetbreads in tenderness and texture and are prepared in much the same way.

How to Store Meat

It is imperative that all meats be stored properly. When you get meat home, remove the store wrappings; do not wash. Wrap the meat in clear plastic wrap, waxed paper, or foil, leaving ends open so air can circulate, and store in the refrigerator. Ground meats and variety meats are more perishable than other meats and should be used within one or two days or frozen for later use (see page 58).

Cured and smoked meats, including sausages and bacon, and the ready-to-serve meats, such as cold cuts, may be left in their original wrappings and refrigerated.

Canned meats and canned meat products may or may not need to be refrigerated. See directions on the can.

Frozen meats should be stored in your freezer or the freezer compartment of your refrigerator. Thaw them according to package directions. Some are cooked or reheated from the frozen state, without first thawing.

When a particular fresh meat is a good buy, get extra and freeze it. See page 58 for how to wrap meat for freezing.

How to Cook Meat

There are two general ways to cook meat: with liquid or without. The dry-heat method is used for the tender cuts of meat. The liquid method is used for less-tender cuts.

Dry-heat methods include the following:

Roasting: This is reserved for large tender cuts and legs of fresh or smoked pork (hams), lamb, and veal. Meat is roasted in the oven in a shallow open pan without water added. Salt, pepper, and desired herbs should be added before roasting. The once-popular searing method of roasting meats, which called for a high temperature for the first ten minutes of cooking and a reduced temperature to finish cooking, is no longer considered as desirable as a constant roasting temperature for most roasts. (Time and temperature charts for roasting meats begin on page 44).

Broiling: This is reserved for tender steaks and chops. Place meat on broiler rack and put it in a preheated broiler. Position the meat away from the heat source as directed in the Meat Broiling Timetables, which begin on page 50. Broil on one side; season meat if desired; then turn and broil on the other side until desired degree of doneness is reached.

Pan-broiling: Steaks and chops may be cooked in a heavy, preheated skillet without fat or water over medium heat. Put meat in hot skillet, turn occasionally to brown on both sides. Pour off fat as it collects. Season meat after cooking.

Pan-frying: Place a small amount of fat in a heavy skillet over medium heat. When fat is melted, add steaks or chops and cook to brown on both sides. Season after cooking.

The moist-heat methods include the following:

Braising: This is an excellent method for the less-tender steaks, short ribs, or riblets. Brown meat slowly on all sides in a small amount of fat in a heavy skillet over medium heat. After browning, pour off collected fat, if any, and season the meat. Add a small amount of liquid (water, tomato juice, bouillon, wine) and seasonings. Cover and cook over low heat until meat is tender. You may want to thicken the liquid or serve it as is over rice or noodles.

Pot-roasting: Larger, less-tender cuts of meat make excellent pot roasts. In a large Dutch oven or heavy kettle, brown the meat on all sides slowly over medium heat. Use a small amount of fat if meat is not covered with a layer of fat. Add a small amount of liquid, cover and continue to cook over low heat or in a medium (325° F.) oven until meat is tender. Thicken juices if gravy is desired.

Simmering: Usually the meats for "boiled" dinners are not browned before cooking in liquid. Tongue and beef brisket, corned or fresh, are the meats most commonly cooked in liquid to cover. They are simmered in a covered kettle over low heat until tender (approximately 3½ to 4½ hours for a 4- to 6-pound piece of meat).

Stewing: Meat for stews should be cut into uniform one- to two-inch pieces. For white stews the meat is not browned before cooking. For brown stews, cubes (sometimes dusted with flour) should be browned, a few at a time, in a small amount of fat. If you fry too many cubes at one time, they stew in their own juice rather than browning evenly. Put browned cubes and water (or other liquid) in a kettle; cover and cook until meat begins to feel tender. Add vegetables near the end of the cooking time so they won't get mushy.

Cooking frozen meats: You have a choice between defrosting frozen meat before cooking or cooking it from the frozen state. The exception is, of course, commercially frozen products that have been precooked. Some cooks prefer doing roasts from the frozen state because this method produces a juicy interior and a brown, crispy crust.

If emergency requires, you can cook roasts from the frozen state. Allow half again as long for roasting time. Frozen hamburgers, steaks, and chops to broil must be placed farther from the heat source so they will not burn on the outside before they've reached the desired doneness on the inside. Meats to be pan-broiled, coated, or braised will be much better if allowed to thaw until the outside is defrosted.

Tenderized beef is now available in many markets. It is beef from animals that have had the food enzyme papain, from the papaya fruit, introduced into their circulatory systems before slaughtering. This process makes it possible to treat blade, arm, and leg cuts like the loin, rib, and sirloin cuts. This beef is marketed under a national brand name and is called tendered beef.

Meat tenderizers are powdered products that contain papain and will tenderize less expensive cuts of meat like shoulder and rump steaks so they may be broiled like the more expensive cuts.

Marinades, either commercially packaged or homemade, will also tenderize the less-expensive steaks and chops so that they may be broiled.

Roast Beef

Be sure you have read the first four sections of this chapter before you select your recipe. There are several cuts of beef for roasting. The tenderest, juiciest, and most expensive are the rib roasts.

A *standing rib roast* can have from two to seven ribs. Ribs can be from six inches to seven or more inches long. If you ask, the butcher will trim off three to four inches from the longer ribs which you can use later for braising (these are called short ribs). Trimmed roasts are called oven-ready or Newport roasts. A two-rib roast is the smallest you can buy. It will weigh about four pounds.

A *rolled rib roast* is a standing rib roast that has been boned and rolled.

Rib eye roast (Delmonico) is the boneless eye of the rib roast.

Beef tenderloin or *fillet* is a succulent, long, slender piece of meat, which may be roasted whole. It is often cut into tender filet mignon boneless steaks.

You may also roast rump roasts and sirloin tips of quality meats. Use the Meat Roasting Timetables on page 44 for time and temperatures.

✌ *Standing Rib Roast**

1 4-pound standing rib of beef, rib bones trimmed to 6 inches or less
Salt, pepper, and flour
Gravy (recipe follows)

Heat oven to 325° F. Wipe meat with paper towels and rub with salt, pepper, and flour. Place roast, fat side up, on a rack in a shallow roasting pan. Insert a meat thermometer so that it goes halfway through the eye muscle (the thick rounded portion) of the meat. Roast until the desired doneness; allow 26 to 32 minutes per pound for

*Note: A boned, rolled rib roast may be roasted in the same way. (See Meat Roasting Timetables on page 45 for roasting time.)

[281]

rare, or 140° F. on the meat thermometer; 34 to 38 minutes per pound for medium well done, or 160° F.; 40 to 42 minutes per pound for well done, or 170° F. Baste occasionally with meat drippings. Serve beef with pan juices or prepare gravy from drippings and serve with roast or make Yorkshire Pudding (recipe on page 635) with pan drippings. Serves 4 to 6.

Gravy

Skim fat from drippings in roasting pan and reserve the fat. Add *1 cup water* to pan juices; bring to a boil over moderate heat (about 250° F.) and stir to loosen brown particles. Measure the drippings from the pan; for each cup of drippings measure *2 tablespoons of the fat, 2 tablespoons flour,* and *½ cup milk or water.* Heat the fat in a heavy saucepan over moderate heat (about 250° F.). Add the flour and cook until bubbly. Gradually add the milk and pan drippings; cook, stirring constantly, until smooth and thickened. Season to taste with salt and pepper.

The Searing Method for Roasting Beef

There are fine cooks who believe the only way to prepare a choice cut of beef is to roast it at a very high temperature for a brief time then leave it in a warm, *unopened* oven to finish cooking. In our testing we've found this method does indeed produce a crunchy, brown exterior and a juicy rare interior and is a particularly good method for meat that is to be used cold. Beef to be prepared this way must be a good tender cut of high quality and must be started *at room temperature.* To do a Standing Rib Roast by this method prepare the meat for the oven as described in the recipe on page 281. Preheat your oven to 500° F. Cook meat for 15 minutes per rib. Turn the oven off, *do not open* the oven door and let the meat cook in the warm oven for two hours.

⌘ Beef Wellington

1 3- to 3½-pound fillet of
  beef, fat removed
Salt and pepper
6 slices raw bacon
3 tablespoons butter or
  margarine
1 cup finely chopped
  mushrooms
1 4¾-ounce can liver pâté
2 cups sifted all-purpose
  flour
1 teaspoon salt

Heat oven to 450° F. Sprinkle beef lightly with salt and pepper and place it on a rack in a shallow roasting pan. Lay bacon strips over top of beef. Roast for a total of 15 minutes for rare, or 20 to 25 minutes for medium well done. Remove from oven and remove beef from rack. Remove bacon strips from meat and arrange on the rack in the roasting pan. Return to oven for about 10 minutes, or until bacon is crisp. Crumble bacon and reserve. Cool beef to room temperature. Melt butter in a skillet over moderately low heat (about 225° F.). Add mushrooms and cook, stirring occasionally, until mushrooms are tender. Cool mushrooms. Combine with

¾ *cup shortening*
6 *tablespoons water*
1 *egg, slightly beaten*

crumbled bacon and liver pâté. Reserve mixture. Sift together flour and salt. Cut in shortening with 2 knives or a pastry blender until mixture is the size of small peas. Sprinkle water, a tablespoon at a time, over mixture, tossing and stirring lightly with a fork. Add water to driest particles, pushing lumps to the side, until dough is just moist enough to hold together. Form into a ball. Place dough on a lightly floured board and roll out into a 12-x-18-inch rectangle about ⅛ inch thick. Place the cooled fillet on the pastry, about 2 inches from one long side. Spread reserved pâté mixture over top, sides, and ends of beef. Fold larger portion of pastry over beef, covering it completely. Cut off excess pastry from sides and ends, leaving just enough to allow for sealing. Brush beaten egg on edges; pinch edges together to seal. Place the pastry-wrapped fillet on a cookie sheet. Brush pastry with the beaten egg. Reroll excess pastry and cut out leaf shapes; arrange on top of pastry in a decorative design; brush with beaten egg. Place in a preheated 425° F. oven. Bake about 30 minutes, or until pastry is golden brown. Cut into thick slices. Serves 6 to 8.

Pot Roasts

Pot roasts are usually made with boneless roasts taken from the leg or shoulder cuts of beef, although bone-in blade roasts are popular for pot-roasting in many parts of the country. This method of long cooking produces a wonderfully flavorful roast. Leftovers are good cold or reheated in the gravy.

Basic Pot Roast

2 *tablespoons flour*
2 *teaspoons salt*
¼ *teaspoon pepper*
1 *3- to 4-pound boneless beef*
  pot roast
3 *tablespoons vegetable oil*
½ *cup water or beef bouillon*
Additional flour and water for
  gravy

Combine the 2 tablespoons of flour, salt, and pepper. Rub outside of meat with this mixture. Heat oil in a heavy saucepan or Dutch oven over moderately high heat (about 300° F.). Add meat and cook until lightly brown. Turn meat to brown on all sides. Add water or bouillon. Cover tightly; cook over low heat (about 200° F.) about 3 hours until meat is fork-tender. Add a little more water if necessary. Remove meat. Measure liquid left in pan. For each cup of liquid, combine 1 tablespoon flour and 4 tablespoons water. Add flour mixture gradually to hot liquid. Cook and stir over low heat (about 200° F.) until thickened. Serve with meat. Serves 6 to 8.

⋙ Carne Mechada

1 4-pound beef eye round roast
1 7½-ounce jar roasted sweet red peppers, drained and cut into strips
1 3-ounce jar pimiento-stuffed olives, drained
¼ pound raw bacon, diced
¼ pound boiled ham, diced
2 medium-sized onions, chopped
2 small cloves garlic, crushed
1 tablespoon drained capers
½ cup vinegar
⅓ cup olive oil
1 teaspoon salt
Freshly ground pepper to taste
1 tablespoon olive oil
1 can condensed beef bouillon, undiluted
1 8-ounce can tomato sauce
½ cup cold water
⅓ cup flour

Using a knife with a long, narrow, sharp blade, cut 3 lengthwise triangles (about 1 inch wide at base) in the roast, removing the meat from the slits and forming 3 long "tunnels." (The meat that is removed may be ground for a hamburger patty.) Mix together peppers, olives, bacon, ham, onions, garlic, capers, vinegar, the ⅓ cup olive oil, salt, and pepper. With the fingers stuff this mixture into each tunnel; reserve any that may be left over. Heat the 1 tablespoon oil in a Dutch oven over moderately high heat (about 300° F.) and brown the roast on all sides. Remove from heat and cut roast into eight ¾- to 1-inch slices. Return slices to Dutch oven, adding any of the leftover stuffing, the beef bouillon, and tomato sauce. Cook, tightly covered, over low heat (about 200° F.) about 1¾ hours, or until fork-tender. Place meat slices on a serving platter and keep hot. Remove any excess fat from pan juices. The remaining juices should measure 1 quart; if necessary add water. Bring to a boil. Blend together water and flour; gradually stir mixture into the gravy, stirring constantly. Boil 1 minute, again stirring constantly. Serve meat slices with the gravy. Serves 8.

⋙ Oven Pot Roast

1 3- to 4-pound boneless beef pot roast
1 1⅜-ounce envelope dry onion soup mix
1 4-ounce can sliced mushrooms
Flour

Heat oven to 350° F. Arrange a long sheet of heavy-duty aluminum foil in a shallow baking dish. Place meat in center of foil and sprinkle onion soup mix over top and sides of meat. Add mushrooms. Bring long ends of foil over meat and seal with a double fold. Fold edges of foil together to seal. Bake 2½ to 3 hours, or until meat is fork-tender. When roast is tender, remove meat to a warm platter. Pour meat juices into a 1-quart measuring cup and skim off fat. To thicken gravy, allow 2 tablespoons flour blended with 2 tablespoons of the skimmed fat for each 1 cup meat juices. Gradually add to meat juices. Stir over moderate heat (about 250° F.) until thickened. Serves 6 to 8.

✑ Boeuf en Daube

4 slices raw bacon, halved
1 medium-sized onion, chopped
2 carrots, peeled and chopped
3½ cups peeled, diced yellow turnip, about 1¼ pounds (optional)
1 bay leaf
⅛ teaspoon ground marjoram or thyme
1 3- to 4-pound boneless beef pot roast
1½ teaspoons salt
¼ teaspoon pepper
1 cup dry red wine
⅓ cup cold water
2 tablespoons flour
¼ teaspoon salt

Place bacon in bottom of a Dutch oven or heavy saucepan; top with onion, carrot, turnip, bay leaf, and marjoram. Place meat over vegetables; add the 1½ teaspoons salt, the pepper, and the wine. Cover and simmer gently over low heat (about 200° F.) 3 to 4 hours, or until meat is fork-tender, stirring occasionally. Remove meat and discard bay leaf. Place water and flour in a small jar with a tight cover and shake to blend; gradually add to vegetable mixture in saucepan. Cook over moderate heat (about 250° F.), stirring occasionally until thickened. Season with the ¼ teaspoon salt. Slice meat and serve with vegetable gravy. Serves 6 to 8.

✑ Beef à la Mode

2 cups of dry red wine
1 can condensed beef consommé
2 medium-sized onions, thinly sliced
2 cloves garlic, minced
2 bay leaves
½ teaspoon dried oregano leaves
¼ teaspoon celery seeds
1 teaspoon salt
¼ teaspoon pepper
1 4-pound beef eye round roast
2 tablespoons shortening

Mix wine, consommé, onion, garlic, bay leaves, oregano, celery seed, salt, and pepper. Place meat in bowl or enamel pot just large enough to hold it. Pour marinade over meat; cover and store in refrigerator overnight. Turn meat occasionally. Remove meat and reserve marinade. Melt shortening in large ovenproof pot or Dutch oven over moderately high heat (about 300° F.). Brown meat on all sides. Add marinade; cover and heat until liquid comes to a boil. Heat oven to 350° F. Place meat in oven and bake 2½ hours, or until meat is fork-tender. Remove meat to warm platter. Strain gravy. Skim off fat and pour 3 tablespoons fat back into pot (discard remaining fat). Blend in flour and sugar. Measure gravy and add enough water to make 2½ cups liquid. Gradually stir into flour mixture. Cook over

3 *tablespoons flour*
½ *teaspoon sugar*

moderate heat (about 250° F.), stirring constantly, until thickened. Serve over meat. Serves 8 to 10.

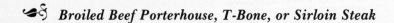 Sauerbraten

3 to 4 pounds bottom beef round
1 teaspoon salt
½ teaspoon freshly ground pepper
2 medium-sized onions, thinly sliced
1 carrot, peeled and sliced
1 stalk celery, chopped
4 whole cloves
4 whole black peppercorns
2 cups red wine vinegar
2 bay leaves
2 tablespoons olive oil
6 tablespoons butter or margarine
5 tablespoons flour
1 tablespoon sugar
10 gingersnaps, crushed
    Dumplings
    (recipe on page 644)

Sprinkle meat with the salt and pepper. Place in a porcelain, glass, enamel, or stainless-steel bowl. Combine onion, carrot, celery, cloves, peppercorns, vinegar, and bay leaves; pour over meat. Add enough water to bowl to cover meat. Cover and store in the refrigerator for 2 to 4 days to marinate. Heat olive oil and 1 tablespoon of the butter in a Dutch oven over moderate heat (about 250° F.). Increase temperature to moderately high (about 325° F.); add meat and brown on all sides. Add 3 cups of the marinade and the vegetables from it. Place over moderate heat (about 250° F.) and bring to a boil; reduce heat to moderately low (about 225° F.) and cook for 3 hours. Melt the remaining 5 tablespoons butter in a small saucepan over moderately low heat (about 225° F.); blend in the flour and sugar. Cook for 8 to 10 minutes, or until mixture just starts to brown, stirring frequently. Blend into hot marinade mixture in pot. Cover and continue cooking for 1 hour longer, or until meat is very tender. Remove meat to a warm platter. Stir crushed gingersnaps into the gravy and cook over moderate heat (about 250° F.), stirring constantly, until thickened. Serve gravy with the meat and Dumplings. Serves 6 to 8.

Steaks

Steaks of tender quality may be broiled or pan-fried (see page 279). Less tender steaks, with the use of tenderizers, may also be broiled or pan-fried. For steak-broiling time, see the chart on page 50.

Broiled Beef Porterhouse, T-Bone, or Sirloin Steak

1 *steak, cut 1 to 2 inches thick*
Salt and pepper

Preheat broiler. Slash fat edges of steak at 2-inch intervals to prevent curling. Put steak on a broiler pan placed

2 to 3 inches from source of heat for a 1-inch-thick steak and from 3 to 5 inches from heat for a 2-inch-thick steak. Broil until lightly browned; sprinkle with salt and pepper and turn and broil other side. Season second side with salt and pepper before serving. Broil a 1-inch steak 18 to 20 minutes for rare; turn after 10 minutes of broiling. For medium, allow 20 to 25 minutes, turning after 12 minutes of broiling. Broil a 2-inch steak for 30 to 40 minutes for rare; turn after 18 minutes. For medium, allow 35 to 45 minutes; turn after 20 minutes of broiling. This produces a lightly browned, juicy steak. If you prefer a charred exterior and a rare interior, place the meat as close as possible to the source of high heat and reduce the cooking time by approximately half.

Beef Tournedos with Béarnaise Sauce

Béarnaise Sauce (recipe follows)
2 slices white bread
1 tablespoon butter or margarine
2 slices beef fillet, cut 1 inch thick
1 tablespoon melted butter or margarine
Salt and pepper

Prepare Béarnaise Sauce and keep warm in the top of a double boiler. Cut two 3-inch bread rounds from slices of bread. Heat the 1 tablespoon butter in a small skillet over moderately high heat (about 300° F.); add bread rounds and fry until lightly browned on both sides. Wipe meat with a damp towel and place on broiler rack. Brush meat with ½ of the melted butter and sprinkle with salt and pepper. Place in a preheated broiler 4 inches from source of heat and broil 4 to 5 minutes. Turn and brush with the remaining butter and sprinkle with salt and pepper. Broil about 4 minutes longer, to the desired degree of doneness. Arrange on bread rounds and serve with Béarnaise Sauce. Serves 2.

Béarnaise Sauce

2 tablespoons tarragon vinegar
2 tablespoons dry white wine
1 teaspoon dried tarragon leaves
1½ teaspoons finely chopped shallots
2 egg yolks
¼ cup butter

Place vinegar, wine, ½ teaspoon of the dried tarragon and shallots in a saucepan; place over moderately low heat (about 225° F.) and heat until just simmering. Continue to heat until liquid is reduced to half, about 2 tablespoons. Strain mixture and return liquid to saucepan. Add egg yolks one at a time to vinegar mixture, beating with a wire whip until blended. Heat over moderately low heat (about 225° F.), whipping constantly until mixture thickens. Add the remaining ½ teaspoon dried tarragon. Add butter, 1 tablespoon at a time; whip until blended. Makes ½ cup.

MEATS

❧ Entrecôte with Watercress Garnish

4 8-ounce entrecôtes (beef rib
    steaks), cut 1 inch thick
Salt and pepper
¼ cup butter or margarine
½ tablespoon chopped fresh
    parsley
1 teaspoon lemon juice
Watercress

Cut a few bits of fat from meat and place in a heavy skillet over moderately high heat (about 375° F.) until fat melts. Add steaks; cook about 1½ minutes on each side for rare or about 2 minutes on each side for medium well done. Remove skillet from heat. Remove steaks to a heated platter. Season with salt and pepper. Add butter, parsley, and lemon juice to skillet; heat over moderately low heat (about 225° F.) until butter is melted. Pour mixture over steaks; garnish with watercress. Serves 4.

❧ Sliced Steak, Wine Sauce, and Glazed Onions

2 tablespoons butter or
    margarine
⅔ cup chopped mushrooms
½ cup chopped scallions or
    green onions
1 cup dry red wine
1 10¾-ounce can beef
    gravy
2½ to 3 pounds bottom beef
    round, cut 1½ inches
    thick
2 16-ounce cans whole
    boiled onions, drained
1 tablespoon sugar
2 tablespoons lemon juice

Heat the butter in a heavy skillet over moderate heat (about 250° F.). Add mushrooms and scallions and brown lightly. Stir in wine. Cook about 5 minutes, until liquid is reduced to about one half. Stir in beef gravy; cook and stir until blended. Keep sauce hot over very low heat (about 175° F.). Put steak on broiler rack and place in a preheated broiler about 3 inches from heat. Broil about 8 minutes on one side. Turn steak. Arrange onions around steak on broiler; sprinkle them with sugar. Continue to broil steak and onions about 5 minutes for medium rare. Remove steak to cutting board and slice diagonally into thin slices. Stir lemon juice into sauce and bring it to a boil. Serve steak topped with sauce and garnished with onions. Serves 5 to 6.

❧ Steak au Poivre

1 3- to 3½-pound beef chuck
    steak, cut 1 to 1¼ inches
    thick
Meat tenderizer
2 tablespoons cracked black
    pepper
¼ cup butter or margarine
¼ cup cognac or brandy

Slash fat edge of meat at 1-inch intervals. Prepare meat with tenderizer following label directions. Press 1 tablespoon of cracked pepper into each side of meat with heel of hand. Heat butter in skillet over moderate heat (about 250° F.). Add steak and cook over moderately high heat (about 325° F.) until browned on each side. Reduce heat to moderate (about 250° F.) and cook 10 to 12 minutes for rare, or longer, as desired. Remove meat to serving platter and cut in thin diagonal slices across the grain. Add cognac to drippings in skillet; heat and stir to loosen brown particles. Serve over meat. Serves 6 to 8.

Skillet London Broil

½ cup olive oil
¼ cup lemon juice
¼ cup vinegar
1 bay leaf, crushed
1 clove garlic, crushed
1 medium-sized onion, thinly sliced
½ teaspoon dried oregano leaves
1 teaspoon salt
½ teaspoon pepper
1 2½-pound beef round steak, cut 1 to 1½ inches thick

Mix oil, lemon juice, vinegar, bay leaf, garlic, onion, oregano, salt, and pepper. Place meat in a large baking pan; pour oil mixture over meat. Cover and let stand at room temperature for 4 hours, turning occasionally. Remove meat from marinade and drain well. Heat a large skillet over moderately high heat (about 375° F.). Sprinkle pan with salt and brown meat 5 to 6 minutes on each side. Reduce heat to moderately low (about 225° F.); cook about 10 minutes, or until cooked to the desired degree of doneness. To serve, cut across the grain into thin diagonal slices. Serves 6 to 8.

Note: Marinated meat may be broiled. See Meat Broiling Timetables on page 50.

Mock Filet Mignon with Broiled Parmesan Toast

1½ pounds beef round steak, cut 1½ inches thick
Meat tenderizer
2 tablespoons grated onion
½ teaspoon celery salt
⅛ teaspoon pepper
4 thin slices raw bacon
2 tablespoons butter or margarine
4 1-inch-thick slices French bread
Garlic powder or salt (optional)
2 tablespoons grated Parmesan cheese
2 tablespoons melted butter or margarine
1 teaspoon lemon juice
1 teaspoon bottled steak sauce

Trim excess fat from steak and cut steak into 4 serving portions. Prepare meat with tenderizer following label directions. Combine onion, celery salt, and pepper. Rub into all sides of the steak. Wrap a piece of bacon around the outside of each portion and fasten tightly with toothpicks. Spread butter thickly on both sides of the French bread. If desired, sprinkle with garlic powder. Sprinkle both sides with Parmesan cheese and press cheese into butter. Plug in electric rotisserie–broiler. When heated, place steaks on grill. Broil 8 to 10 minutes on each side for rare steaks, or longer as desired. Place bread on grill during last 10 minutes of cooking time. Broil until golden brown, about 5 minutes on each side. Combine the melted butter, lemon juice, and meat sauce. Remove steaks to a heated platter, pour the butter sauce over them, and serve with hot Parmesan toast. Serves 4.

Swiss Steak

2 tablespoons flour
¾ teaspoon salt

Heat oven to 350° F. Mix flour, the ¾ teaspoon salt, and the pepper; pound flour into meat with a mallet or edge

Few grains pepper
1½ pounds beef rump, round,
    or chuck steak, cut 1 inch
    thick
3 tablespoons vegetable oil
1 16-ounce can stewed
    tomatoes
1 medium-sized onion,
    thinly sliced
½ cup thinly sliced peeled
    carrot
½ cup sliced celery
¼ cup chopped green pepper
½ teaspoon salt
Few grains pepper

of heavy saucer. Cut meat into serving-sized pieces. Heat oil in an ovenproof Dutch oven over moderately high heat (about 300° F.); add meat and cook over moderate heat until browned on both sides. (If Dutch oven is not available, brown meat in a skillet and transfer it to a casserole.) Mix tomatoes, onion, carrot, celery, green pepper, the ½ teaspoon salt, and the pepper; pour over meat. Cover and bake 1 to 1½ hours, or until meat is fork-tender. Serves 4 to 6.

Chuck Steak de Luxe

1 5-pound blade-bone chuck
    steak, cut 1½ inches thick
Meat tenderizer
¼ cup chili sauce
2 tablespoons minced onion
1 tablespoon dark brown
    sugar
½ teaspoon Worcestershire
    sauce
1 tablespoon vegetable oil

Prepare meat with tenderizer according to label directions. Place steak on broiler pan. Mix together remaining ingredients; spoon half over steak. Place in preheated broiler and broil 4 inches from source of heat 20 minutes. Turn and spoon remaining chili mixture over steak. Broil 10 minutes longer or until desired doneness is reached. Serves 6.

Barbecued Flank Steak

1 2-pound lean beef flank
    steak
Salt
½ cup bottled Italian salad
    dressing
1 clove garlic, pressed
½ teaspoon prepared
    mustard
¼ teaspoon dried oregano
    leaves
⅛ teaspoon Tabasco

Score the meat by making shallow diagonal cuts at 1-inch intervals across the meat with the tip of a sharp knife. Score it in the opposite direction to make a diamond pattern on the face of the meat. Sprinkle the steak lightly with salt. Combine all remaining ingredients. Place steak on broiler rack and broil in preheated broiler about 4 inches from source of heat 5 to 8 minutes on each side for medium rare, or until cooked to desired degree of doneness, brushing frequently with some of the sauce. Cut the steak across the grain into thin diagonal slices. Serves 4 to 6.

⊰ Beef Roulades

6 slices raw bacon, diced
¾ cup finely chopped onion
6 slices white bread, toasted
  and cubed
3 tablespoons chopped fresh
  parsley
½ teaspoon dried basil
  leaves
½ teaspoon salt
¼ cup melted butter or
  margarine
1¾ pounds beef round steak,
  cut into ½-inch-thick
  slices (about 3 slices)
Salt and pepper
1½ cups diluted canned beef
  bouillon
1 15-ounce can tomato
  sauce
2 tablespoons butter or
  margarine
¾ pound mushrooms, thinly
  sliced

Place skillet over moderately high heat (about 275° F.); add bacon and onion and cook until onion is tender and bacon is crisp, stirring frequently. Toss bread, parsley, basil, and the ½ teaspoon salt together in a bowl; stir in cooked bacon mixture and the ¼ cup melted butter. Reserve to use as stuffing for meat. Cut each slice of meat into about 3 portions. (Portions may vary slightly in size.) Place meat on a wooden board and pound with a meat mallet until very thin (about 1/16-inch thick), or place between sheets of waxed paper and pound with a rolling pin. Season meat lightly on both sides with salt and pepper. Spoon 1 to 2 tablespoons of the stuffing mixture on each slice of meat. Roll up and tie together with string or secure with a toothpick. Place meat rolls in a large skillet; add bouillon. Cover and cook over moderately low heat (about 225° F.) for 1 hour, turning meat occasionally. Stir in tomato sauce and continue cooking 45 to 60 minutes, or until meat is fork-tender, stirring occasionally. Heat the 2 tablespoons butter in a second skillet over moderately low heat (about 225° F.). Add mushrooms and cook until tender. Stir into meat mixture. If a thicker sauce is desired, remove meat to a warm platter. Pour ¼ cup water into a jar with a tight cover and add 1 tablespoon flour; cover and shake until blended. Gradually add to tomato sauce mixture and cook over moderately low heat (about 225° F.), stirring constantly, until thickened. Serve sauce over meat. Serves 6.

⊰ Tenderloin Tips Deutsch

6 tablespoons butter or
  margarine
1½ pounds beef tenderloin
  tips, cut into 2- to 3-inch
  strips
2 medium-sized onions,
  chopped
2 green peppers, chopped
1 10¾-ounce can beef gravy
1 cup red burgundy wine
1 tablespoon cornstarch
Noodles (optional)

Heat 2 tablespoons of the butter in a skillet over moderately low heat (about 225° F.); add some of the meat and brown quickly over moderately high heat (about 325° F.). Remove meat as soon as it is browned. Add the remaining 4 tablespoons butter, as needed, to brown remaining meat. When all the meat is browned, add onion and green pepper to the skillet and cook until tender. Reduce heat to moderate (about 250° F.); add gravy. Combine wine and cornstarch and gradually stir into gravy. Cook and stir about 2 minutes, until thickened. Add browned meat and heat thoroughly. Serve with noodles, if desired. Serves 4.

❧ *Sirloin Pepper Steak*

¼ *cup vegetable oil*
½ *cup sliced onion*
2 *medium-sized green peppers, cut into ¾-inch-wide strips*
1½ *pounds sirloin tip, cut into 4-x-¾-x-¼-inch strips*
1¼ *cups water*
1 *tablespoon soy sauce*
½ *teaspoon salt*
½ *teaspoon garlic salt*
1 *teaspoon ground ginger*
1 *tablespoon cornstarch*
2 *tablespoons cold water*
¼ *cup dry sherry*
Hot cooked rice

Heat oil in a large skillet over moderate heat (about 250° F.). Quickly cook onion and green pepper until crisp-tender. Remove with a slotted spoon. In the same skillet place a single layer of meat strips and brown them quickly, adding a little more oil if necessary. (Meat strips should be slightly pink inside when cut.) Remove meat and pour off any excess fat from the skillet. Stir water into the skillet, loosening any brown particles. Stir in soy sauce, salt, garlic salt, and ginger. Blend cornstarch into the 2 tablespoons cold water. Stir into the liquid in the skillet. Return to heat and boil ½ minute, stirring constantly. Stir in sherry, meat, pepper, and onion. Reduce heat to low (about 200° F.). Cover and heat to serving temperature. Serve over hot cooked rice. Serves 4 to 6.

❧ *Sukiyaki*

¾ *pound boneless beef sirloin steak*
Meat tenderizer
3 *tablespoons vegetable oil*
1 *medium-sized onion, thinly sliced*
½ *cup thinly sliced celery*
4 *scallions or green onions, sliced lengthwise*
4 *large fresh mushrooms, sliced*
¼ *pound fresh spinach, cleaned and coarsely torn*
1 *tablespoon sugar*
3 *tablespoons soy sauce*
1 *cup canned beef bouillon*
1½ *cups hot cooked rice*

Prepare meat with tenderizer following label directions. Cut meat across the grain into very thin slices. Heat the oil in an electric skillet to 325° F. A large skillet may be used; in this case, heat over moderately high heat (about 325° F.). Add meat slices and brown quickly on all sides. Remove from skillet. Add onion, celery, and scallions to skillet and cook 2 minutes, or until crisp-tender. Add mushrooms and cook 1 minute. Return meat to the skillet. Add spinach. Sprinkle the sugar over top, then add the soy sauce. Pour beef bouillon over spinach and stir gently to blend. Heat just until spinach wilts and mixture is piping hot. Serve immediately over hot rice. Serves 2.*

Note: This recipe may be doubled or tripled, but because meat and vegetables should cook quickly, it is best not to cook more than 2 portions at a time.

❧ *Steak Kabobs*

2 *pounds beef round steak, cut 1½ inches thick*

Cut meat into 1½-inch cubes. Sprinkle cubes with meat tenderizer as directed on label. Alternate meat cubes,

Meat tenderizer
12 cherry tomatoes
1 4-ounce can mushroom
caps, drained
1 green pepper, cut into
1½-inch strips
1 16-ounce can boiled
onions, drained
Wine Sauce (recipe follows)

tomatoes, mushrooms, green pepper, and onions on skewers. Brush with Wine Sauce. Place on hibachi grill and broil 8 to 10 minutes, turning frequently to brown evenly. Heat remaining Wine Sauce to serve with kabobs if desired. Serves 6.

Wine Sauce

½ cup dry white wine
½ cup catsup
1 tablespoon prepared
mustard
1 tablespoon Worcestershire
sauce
1 clove garlic, minced
½ teaspoon dried rosemary
leaves
2 tablespoons vinegar
2 tablespoons brown sugar

Combine all ingredients in a jar and shake to blend thoroughly. Makes 1½ cups.

Barbecued Beef Ribs

2 tablespoons olive oil
1 large onion, sliced
½ cup molasses
1 cup catsup
½ cup water
¼ cup Worcestershire sauce
¼ cup prepared mustard
1 tablespoon salt
3 pounds beef short ribs

Heat oil in a 10-inch skillet over moderately low heat (about 225° F.). Add onion and cook until tender. Add molasses, catsup, water, Worcestershire, mustard, and salt. Cook 10 minutes until ingredients are blended. Heat oven to 350° F. Place short ribs in a shallow 3-quart baking dish. Brush ribs on all sides with the barbecue sauce. Bake 1½ to 2 hours, or until fork-tender, basting with sauce every half hour. Turn ribs occasionally. Place the remaining sauce in a small saucepan and heat over low heat (about 200° F.), stirring occasionally. Serve the hot sauce with the ribs. Serves 4.

Beef Fondue

Beef fondue is the meat version of the popular fondue service. It's a cook-your-own meal. You will need fondue forks and a fondue pan to hold hot oil or hot consommé (Oriental version). Use tender cubes of beef cut from beef tenderloin or sirloin tip.

MEATS

⌒ Beef Fondue

Vegetable oil
* A choice of sauces (recipes follow)
2 pounds beef tenderloin or sirloin, cut into ¾-inch cubes

Heat 1½ inches of oil in a fondue pot over high heat (about 400° F.) until temperature reaches 400° F. on a deep-fat-frying thermometer. Then bring pot to the table and place over its heat source. Put sauces in individual dishes at each place setting (or use sectioned fondue dishes). Each person places a cube of meat on a fondue fork and cooks the meat to the desired degree of doneness by holding it in the hot oil. (Cook about 20 seconds for rare.) To keep oil hot enough, only two persons at a time should brown meat (this precaution is usually not necessary with electric fondues). Reheat oil on range, if needed. The cooked meat is then dipped in sauce before being eaten. Serves 4 to 6.

*Note: Three sauces are usually served with beef fondue; at least one of them should be hot. Any of the following sauces is superb.

Quick Béarnaise Sauce

2 teaspoons dried tarragon leaves
2 tablespoons tarragon vinegar
2 cups mayonnaise or salad dressing
6 peeled green onions or scallions
¼ teaspoon dry mustard
Dash of Tabasco

Mix tarragon leaves and vinegar and let stand 30 minutes. Combine all ingredients in an electric blender; cover and blend at high speed for 30 seconds. Chill. Serve cold. Makes about 2 cups.

Curry Sauce

2 10¾-ounce cans beef gravy
2 tablespoons curry powder
1 clove garlic, mashed
½ teaspoon Worcestershire sauce
1 tablespoon lemon juice

Mix all ingredients together. Place over moderately low heat (about 225° F.) and stir until heated. Serve warm. Makes about 2½ cups.

Tomato Sauce

1½ tablespoons olive oil
½ cup finely chopped onion
⅓ cup finely chopped celery

Heat olive oil over moderate heat (about 250° F.); add onion, celery, and green pepper and cook until tender, stirring occasionally. Add tomatoes, basil, sugar, salt, and

¼ green pepper, chopped
1 16-ounce can whole
   tomatoes
½ teaspoon dried basil
   leaves
½ teaspoon sugar
½ teaspoon salt
Few grains pepper

pepper; cook over low heat (about 200° F.) for 45 minutes. Press through a fine strainer or a food mill. Serve sauce warm or cold. Makes about 1⅓ cups.

Cumberland Sauce

2 strips orange peel, cut 1½
   inches wide and 4 inches
   long
½ cup currant jelly
3 tablespoons dry sherry
¼ cup orange juice
2½ tablespoons lemon juice
1 teaspoon dry mustard
1 teaspoon cornstarch

Put all ingredients in the blender container. Cover and blend on high speed for 30 seconds, or until orange peel is finely chopped. Pour into a medium-sized saucepan and cook over moderately low heat (about 225° F.), stirring constantly, until thickened. Serve hot. Makes about 1 cup.

Horseradish–Chive Sauce

1 cup commercial sour
   cream
3 tablespoons well-drained
   prepared horseradish
¼ teaspoon salt
Dash paprika
1½ tablespoons freeze-dried
   chives

Combine all ingredients in a small bowl and stir to blend well. Cover and chill 1 hour. Makes about 1 cup.

✒ Fondue Oriental

2 pounds lean beef, veal, or
   pork, or lamb kidneys (or
   a combination of these
   meats)
Béarnaise Sauce (recipe on
   page 489)
Mushroom–Catsup Sauce
   (recipe follows)
Curried Mayonnaise (recipe
   follows)

Have the butcher cut the desired meats into very thin, bite-sized slices. (If desired, meat may be sliced at home by freezing slightly before slicing. Cut kidneys in half and remove the hard cores before making thin slices.) Divide the meat, sauces, and chopped onion equally among 6 sectioned fondue plates or other plates. Pour the consommé into a deep saucepan or other flame-proof pot. Bring the consommé to a boil in the kitchen; place pot of hot consommé on a heating element at the table. Each guest spears 1 or 2 pieces of meat on a fondue fork and puts

¾ *cup finely chopped onion*
5 *cans condensed beef consommé*

it into the boiling consommé until cooked to desired degree of doneness (pork must be well cooked). The cooked meat is then dipped in the sauces and chopped onion, as desired, and eaten with a dinner fork. In the meantime, spear another 1 or 2 pieces of meat and place in the boiling consommé. The fondue fork need not be held; stand it against the edge of the pot. Reheat consommé on range, if needed. If desired, serve with rice. After the meat is eaten, the consommé may be diluted with water to the desired strength (taste before serving) and served as a soup. Serves 6.

Mushroom–Catsup Sauce

2 *tablespoons chopped fresh parsley*
1 *4-ounce can mushroom stems and pieces, drained and finely chopped*
1 *cup catsup*

Combine ingredients and chill until serving time. Makes about 1½ cups.

Curried Mayonnaise

1 *cup mayonnaise*
1 *tablespoon curry powder*

Combine and chill until serving time. Makes 1 cup.

Boiled Beef Dinners

Boiled dinners are hearty and the majority of them are easy on your time and your budget. They're a meal in one pot and take little preparation and no close watching. They're especially welcome on wintery days.

Boiled Brisket of Beef with Horseradish Sauce

3 *pounds fresh boneless beef brisket*
2 *carrots, peeled and cut up*
2 *medium-sized onions, halved*
2 *stalks celery, cut up*
2 *teaspoons salt*
¼ *teaspoon pepper*

Place brisket in a large pot or Dutch oven. Add carrots, onions, celery, salt, pepper, and cloves. Add enough water to just cover beef. Simmer, covered, over low heat (about 200° F.) 3 to 4 hours, or until fork-tender. Transfer meat to a hot serving platter. If desired, surround meat with steamed cabbage, small cooked whole carrots, and cooked new potatoes. Serve with Horseradish Sauce. Serves 6 to 8.

10 whole cloves
Horseradish Sauce (recipe
  follows)
Assorted vegetables (optional)

Horseradish Sauce

¼ cup butter or margarine
2 tablespoons all-purpose
  flour
1 cup hot beef broth from
  Boiled Brisket of Beef
  (recipe on page 296)
1 4-ounce jar prepared
  horseradish
¼ cup commercial sour cream
¼ teaspoon sugar
Few grains of salt

Melt butter in a saucepan over moderately low heat; stir in flour and cook 2 to 3 minutes, until bubbly but not brown. With a wire whisk gradually mix hot beef broth into butter mixture. When sauce is smooth, stir in horseradish and then sour cream, sugar and salt. Stir sauce over moderately low heat until hot but not boiling. Serve with Boiled Brisket of Beef. Makes 1¾ cups sauce.

New England Boiled Dinner

2 pounds corned beef brisket
2 pounds fresh beef brisket
Boiling water
1 pound salt pork
12 small onions, peeled
12 small whole carrots, peeled
6 medium-sized potatoes,
  peeled
1 medium-sized cabbage, cut
  into 6 wedges
12 small beets

Put corned beef and fresh brisket in a large saucepan. Add boiling water to just cover meat. Cover and cook over low heat (about 200° F.) 2 hours. Add salt pork and cook 1½ to 2 hours longer, until meat is fork-tender. Cool slightly and skim off excess fat. Add onions, carrots, and potatoes. Cook uncovered 20 to 30 minutes or until vegetables are almost tender. Arrange cabbage over top of meat; cover and cook 15 to 20 minutes. While vegetables are cooking with the meat, trim off all but 1 inch of the stem and root ends of the beets and cook separately in boiling salted water over moderately low heat (about 225° F.), about 40 minutes, until fork-tender. Drain and slip off skins. Place meat in center of large platter and arrange vegetables around meat. Serves 6 to 8.

Corned Beef Hash

1 tablespoon butter or
  margarine
¼ cup chopped, peeled onion
2 cups chopped leftover
  corned beef

Melt the 1 tablespoon butter in a skillet over moderate heat (about 250° F.); add onion and cook just until limp. Flake corned beef into a medium-sized bowl, add potatoes, cooked onions, pepper and milk and mix well. Taste mixture and add salt if needed. (This much can be done

2 cups cooked potatoes cut
into ½-inch cubes
¼ teaspoon pepper
1 tablespoon milk
¼ teaspoon salt (optional)
2 tablespoons butter or
margarine

ahead.) Melt the 2 tablespoons butter in a skillet (same one used for onions). Scoop corned beef mixture ⅓ cup at a time and form into 3-inch patties; add to hot oil and cook slowly until brown on both sides and heated through. Makes 9 patties, ⅓ cup each.

⊷ Beef Stew

1½ pounds boneless beef
chuck, cut into 1½-inch
cubes
1½ tablespoons flour
2 tablespoons vegetable oil
1 cup water
1 16-ounce can tomatoes
4 whole cloves
1 bay leaf
1½ teaspoons salt
⅛ teaspoon pepper
½ cup diced celery
2 small onions, quartered
2 medium-sized carrots,
peeled and quartered
2 medium-sized potatoes,
peeled and cut into
eighths
1 medium-sized green
pepper, cut into 8 squares

Roll beef cubes in flour to thoroughly coat them. Heat oil in a Dutch oven over moderately high heat (about 300° F.); add beef; cook until browned on all sides. Add water and tomatoes; stir in cloves, bay leaf, salt, and pepper. Simmer, covered, over low heat (about 200° F.) 1½ hours. Add celery, onions, carrots, and potatoes. Continue to simmer, covered, ½ hour longer, or until meat and vegetables are almost tender. Add green pepper during last 10 minutes of cooking. Serves 4 to 6.

⊷ "Old-Fashioned" Beef Stew

½ cup flour
1½ teaspoons ground cloves
½ teaspoon ground allspice
½ teaspoon ground
cinnamon
½ teaspoon salt
Few grains pepper
3½ to 4 pounds beef chuck or
rump, cut for stew
6 tablespoons butter or
margarine

Mix flour, cloves, allspice, cinnamon, the ½ teaspoon salt, and the pepper. Pour into a small paper bag; add a few pieces of meat at a time and shake to coat pieces. Melt butter in a Dutch oven or heavy saucepan over moderately high heat (about 300° F.); add meat pieces a few at a time and cook until all are lightly browned. Remove meat as it is browned. When all the meat is browned, return it to the Dutch oven. Add consommé and the 1½ teaspoons salt; cover and simmer over low heat (about 200° F.) 1½ hours. Mix the sugar, bitters, and bourbon together; pour over meat. Cover and simmer 15 minutes. Add carrots and

1 can condensed beef
   consommé
1½ teaspoons salt
1 double old-fashioned (1
   tablespoon sugar, 4
   dashes Angostura bitters,
   and 4 ounces bourbon)
8 carrots, peeled and cut
   into 2-inch pieces
1½ pounds new potatoes,
   scrubbed and unpeeled
1 8-ounce can boiled
   onions, drained

potatoes; simmer, covered, 1 hour. Add onions and cook 15 minutes more, until vegetables are tender. Skim off fat. Serves 8 to 12.

✑ Carbonade Beef Stew

⅓ cup flour
1½ teaspoons salt
Few grains pepper
1¾ pounds boneless beef for
   stew, cut into 1½-inch
   cubes
¼ cup vegetable oil
3 cups thinly sliced onions
1 cup beer
1 clove garlic, crushed
1 tablespoon chopped fresh
   parsley
⅛ teaspoon dried thyme
   leaves
1 bay leaf
1½ teaspoons salt
⅛ teaspoon pepper

Place flour, the 1½ teaspoons salt, and the few grains of pepper in a plastic or paper bag. Shake meat, a few pieces at a time, in bag until coated with flour mixture. Heat oil in Dutch oven or a heavy saucepan over moderately high heat (about 300° F.); add beef cubes and cook until lightly browned. Remove meat; add onions and cook until tender over moderate heat (about 250° F.). Return meat to pot; add beer, garlic, parsley, thyme, bay leaf, the 1½ teaspoons salt, and the ⅛ teaspoon pepper. Cover and simmer over low heat (about 200° F.) 2½ to 3 hours, or until fork-tender. Serves 4.

✑ Beef in Wine

Salt
1½ pounds beef sirloin or top
   round, cut into 1-inch
   cubes
¼ teaspoon sugar
2 large onions, thinly sliced
1 large tomato, peeled and
   quartered

Heat a Dutch oven over moderately high heat (about 375° F.); sprinkle pot with a layer of salt and brown meat cubes on all sides. Sprinkle with sugar. Reduce heat slightly to moderately high heat (about 325° F.), add onion, tomato, Worcestershire, Tabasco, the ½ teaspoon salt, and pepper. Stir in the 1½ cups wine. Cover and bring to a boil; reduce heat to moderately low (about 225° F.) and cook 1½ hours, or until meat is almost

2 teaspoons Worcestershire
    sauce
Dash of Tabasco
½ *teaspoon salt*
Few grains pepper
1½ *cups dry red wine*
  2 *cups dry red wine*
½ *pound mushrooms, sliced*

tender. Remove from heat. Cool and chill in refrigerator overnight. The next day place meat over moderate heat (about 250° F.) and cook, uncovered, for 1 hour, or until most of the liquid boils away. Add the remaining 2 cups wine and the mushrooms; cook 20 minutes. Serves 4.

Hungarian Beef Goulash

6 *to 8 tablespoons vegetable*
    oil
4 *pounds boneless beef*
    round or chuck, cut into
    1½-inch cubes
2 *tablespoons flour*
1 *can undiluted condensed*
    beef bouillon
3 *cups chopped Spanish red*
    onions (3 medium-sized
    onions)
6 *cloves garlic, crushed or*
    finely chopped
3 *cups finely chopped, peeled*
    tomatoes (3 or 4
    medium-sized tomatoes)
2 *to 3 tablespoons*
    Hungarian paprika
1 *teaspoon salt*
⅛ *teaspoon pepper*
16 *to 18 small new potatoes,*
    peeled and cooked, or ¾
    pound broad egg noodles,
    cooked according to
    package directions

Heat 2 tablespoons of the oil in a large skillet over moderately high heat (about 300° F.) and brown meat cubes on all sides; add additional oil as needed. As meat cubes are browned, transfer them to a Dutch oven or heavy saucepan. Sprinkle meat with flour and toss to coat meat. Add beef bouillon to skillet and heat until meat particles are loosened. Heat the remaining ¼ cup oil in skillet over moderate heat (about 250° F.); cook onions and garlic until tender. Add cooked onion mixture, tomatoes, paprika, salt, and pepper to meat and stir together. Bring to boil; cover and simmer over low heat (about 200° F.) 2¼ hours, or until meat is fork-tender. Skim off fat. If desired, thin gravy with a little hot water. Serve with potatoes or noodles. Serves 8 to 10.

Beef Burgundy

3 *pounds boneless beef*
    chuck
2 *tablespoons flour*
2 *tablespoons butter or*
    margarine

Cut meat into 1-inch cubes. Roll in the 2 tablespoons flour. Heat butter and oil in a heavy skillet over moderately high heat (about 300° F.). Add meat, 6 or 8 cubes at a time, and cook until lightly browned on all sides. Transfer browned cubes to a 2½-quart casserole. Con-

2 tablespoons olive oil
¼ cup cognac, warmed
5 slices raw bacon, diced
1 small clove garlic, minced
½ cup chopped onions
½ cup diced, peeled carrots
⅓ cup chopped celery
2 cups Burgundy wine
1 bay leaf
½ teaspoon thyme leaves
½ teaspoon salt
Few grains pepper
3 tablespoons flour

tinue browning cubes a few at a time. When all cubes are browned return them to skillet. Pour cognac over meat and ignite with a match. When cognac stops flaming, put meat into casserole. Cook bacon in skillet over moderately high heat (about 325° F.) until it just starts to brown. Add garlic, onions, carrots, and celery; cook until onions are tender over moderate heat (about 250° F.). Add Burgundy, bay leaf, thyme, salt, and pepper; mix well. Pour over beef. If necessary, add water so that meat is just barely covered with wine mixture. Heat oven to 350° F. Cover casserole and bake 2 hours. Drain wine mixture from casserole into a 1-quart measuring cup. Skim off fat and pour 3 tablespoons fat into a saucepan; blend in the 3 tablespoons flour. Cook over moderately low heat (about 225° F.) 3 minutes, stirring constantly. Gradually add wine mixture and cook over low heat, stirring constantly, until thickened. Pour gravy over meat and bake 1¼ hours more, or until meat is very tender. Serves 6 to 8.

✑ German-Style Short Ribs

3 pounds beef short ribs, cut
   into serving-sized pieces
Meat tenderizer
⅓ cup flour
½ teaspoon salt
Few grains pepper
4 tablespoons vegetable oil
1 medium-sized onion,
   thinly sliced
1 can undiluted condensed
   beef consommé
½ cup water
3 tablespoons vinegar
1 teaspoon prepared
   horseradish
1 bay leaf
⅛ teaspoon ground allspice
⅛ teaspoon ground cloves

Prepare meat with meat tenderizer following directions on label. Mix flour, salt, and pepper; coat meat with mixture. Heat 2 tablespoons of the oil in skillet over moderately high heat (about 325° F.); brown meat well on all sides. Place meat in a deep 2½-quart casserole. Heat oven to 350° F. Add the remaining 2 tablespoons oil to skillet over moderate heat (about 250° F.) and cook onion until tender. Stir in consommé, vinegar, horseradish, bay leaf, allspice, and cloves; pour over meat. Cover and bake 1¾ to 2 hours, or until meat is fork-tender. Serves 4.

✑ Oxtail Ragout

4 pounds oxtails, cut into
   pieces

Heat oven to 325° F. Wash and dry oxtails. Combine flour, salt, and pepper in a paper bag; add meat pieces, a

¼ *cup flour*
¼ *teaspoon salt*
Few grains pepper
 4 *tablespoons butter or*
   margarine
 2 *medium-sized onions,*
   sliced
 6 *carrots, peeled and cut into*
   1-inch pieces
¼ *cup diced celery*
 1 *cup dry red wine*
 1 *teaspoon salt*
 1 *16-ounce can tomatoes*
 6 *peppercorns*
 1 *teaspoon paprika*
 2 *whole cloves*
 1 *bay leaf*
 1 *4-ounce can sliced*
   mushrooms

few at a time, and shake to coat meat evenly. Melt butter in a heavy skillet over moderately high heat (about 275° F.); add oxtails and onions and cook until meat is browned on all sides. Remove to a deep 2-quart casserole. Combine all remaining ingredients except mushrooms; add to oxtails. Cover tightly and bake 3 hours. Skim off fat; add mushrooms and continue to bake, covered, 30 minutes more. Serves 4.

Ground Beef or Hamburger

Hamburger is that marvelous, versatile meat that frequently makes many of the meals during the early years of newly-formed households. The only way to avoid resulting monotony is to have an array of recipes that make hamburger acceptable by varying its presentation. The following recipes will prove the point.

If you can have your beef ground to order, select it for the use you plan. Regular ground beef, which is most fatty (legally), is usually lowest in price; it is fine for making meat loaf or meatballs where the cooking time will cook out the fat. Because fat weighs, it is, perhaps, not cheaper in the long run than ground chuck or ground round. For hamburgers, meat should be ground only once to make juicy hamburgers. Store ground meat carefully: It is more fragile than the larger cuts and will spoil more quickly (see A Guide to the Safe Storage of Foods, page 73).

❧ Juicy Hamburgers

 1 *pound ground beef chuck,*
   round, or sirloin
Salt and pepper

Shape meat loosely into 4 1-inch thick patties. Pan-fry or broil as directed in the following recipes. Sprinkle with salt and pepper after broiling. Makes 4 patties.

Pan-Fried Hamburgers

Heat *2 tablespoons butter or margarine* in a skillet over moderately high heat (about 325° F.). Cook patties for about 4 to 8 minutes depending on desired degree of doneness. Turn once during cooking. If a nonstick skillet is used, no butter is required, but lightly salt the skillet.

Broiled Hamburgers

Preheat broiler. Place hamburgers on a broiler rack and place 3 inches from source of heat. Broil 12 to 20 minutes depending on desired degree of doneness. Turn once during broiling.

✌ Cheese-Stuffed Hamburgers

2½ **tablespoons butter or margarine**
⅓ **cup finely chopped onions**
⅓ **cup crumbled blue cheese**
2½ **tablespoons commercial sour cream**
2 **pounds ground beef round**
Salt and pepper

Melt butter in skillet over moderate heat (about 250° F.), add onions and cook until tender. Combine onion mixture, cheese, and sour cream. Divide meat into 8 portions and flatten into patties about 4 inches in diameter. Mound cheese mixture in center of 4 of them. Top with a second meat patty; pinch edges to seal and shape into a thick meat patty. Place on broiler rack. Broil in a preheated broiler 3 inches from heat for 7 minutes; sprinkle with salt and pepper. Turn and broil 5 minutes, or until cooked to the desired degree of doneness. Sprinkle with salt and pepper before serving. Makes 4 generous servings.

✌ Hamburgers with Garlic Butter

2 **tablespoons softened butter or margarine**
¼ **teaspoon minced, peeled garlic**
2 **teaspoons lemon juice**
Few grains of pepper
¾ **teaspoon salt**
1 **tablespoon chopped fresh parsley (optional)**
¾ **pound ground beef round**
2 **slices Italian bread, toasted**

In a small bowl mix butter with garlic, lemon juice, pepper, ¼ teaspoon of the salt and the parsley, if desired. Shape beef into 2 1-inch-thick burgers. Sprinkle remaining ½ teaspoon of salt in the bottom of a small, heavy skillet and place over high heat. When pan is very hot (when a drop of water skips across the bottom, it's ready), add burgers, reduce heat to moderately high and cook about 3½ minutes. Turn burgers and cook about 3½ minutes longer for medium rare. Spread half the garlic butter on the toasted bread, place a cooked burger on each slice and top with remaining garlic butter. Serves 2.

MEATS

✍ Salisbury Steaks

1 tablespoon butter or
  margarine
¼ cup chopped onion
1 can condensed cream of
  mushroom soup,
  undiluted
1 egg
½ cup Italian-style seasoned
  fine bread crumbs
¼ teaspoon salt
1½ pounds ground beef round
⅓ cup water

Heat oven to 350° F. In a large skillet over moderate heat (about 250° F.) melt butter and cook onion until lightly browned; cool slightly. In a large bowl beat together ⅓ cup of the undiluted cream of mushroom soup and the egg. Stir in bread crumbs and salt. Let crumbs soften about 5 minutes. Add cooked onion and the beef; mix well. Shape into six ½-inch-thick patties. Arrange in a lightly greased, shallow, rectangular 3-quart baking dish. Bake 30 minutes. Drain off excess fat. Blend together remaining undiluted soup with the water and pour over the patties. Return to oven and bake 10 minutes longer. Serves 6.

✍ Swedish Meatballs

2 tablespoons butter or
  margarine
½ cup finely chopped onion
1 cup water
3 slices thinly sliced white
  bread
1½ pounds ground beef round
  (ground twice)
1 teaspoon ground nutmeg
¾ teaspoon salt
⅛ teaspoon pepper
Flour
2 tablespoons butter or
  margarine
3 beef bouillon cubes
2½ cups boiling water
1 cup light cream
3 tablespoons flour
Chopped fresh parsley

Heat the 2 tablespoons butter in a skillet over moderately low heat (about 225° F.); add onion and cook until tender, stirring occasionally. Remove from heat. Pour the 1 cup water over bread slices and let stand 5 minutes. Squeeze bread dry and crumble into a bowl. Add ground beef, cooked onion, nutmeg, salt, and pepper; mix well. Shape level tablespoons of the meat mixture into balls and roll each in flour. Heat the remaining 2 tablespoons butter in the skillet over moderately low heat (about 225° F.). Increase temperature to moderately high (about 325° F.); add some of the meatballs and brown on all sides. Continue removing meatballs as they are browned and adding additional ones until all are browned. Reduce temperature to moderately low (about 225° F.) and return all the balls to the skillet. Dissolve bouillon cubes in the boiling water and add to meatballs; cook 30 minutes, stirring occasionally. Remove from heat. Remove meatballs from skillet and pour meat juices into a bowl or measuring cup; skim off fat. Just 1 cup of meat juices is needed; if necessary, boil the juices to reduce to 1 cup. Pour into skillet. Place cream and the 3 tablespoons flour in a jar with a tight lid and shake until blended. Gradually add to juices in skillet, mixing until blended. Cook over moderately low heat (about 225° F.), stirring constantly, until thickened. Add meatballs and heat about 10 minutes. Serve garnished with chopped parsley. Serves 6.

◈ Hamburger Stroganoff

¼ cup butter or margarine
½ cup finely chopped onion
1 clove garlic, minced
1 pound ground beef
chuck
2 tablespoons flour
1 pound fresh mushrooms,
sliced, or one 8-ounce
can sliced mushrooms,
drained
2 teaspoons salt
¼ teaspoon pepper
1 can condensed cream of
chicken soup
1 cup commercial sour
cream
2 cups cooked noodles or
rice
3 tablespoons finely
chopped fresh parsley

Heat butter in a large skillet over moderate heat (about 250° F.); add onion and garlic and cook until tender, stirring occasionally. Increase heat to moderately high (about 275° F.). Add ground beef and cook until lightly brown, or until meat loses its pink color, stirring frequently with a fork to break up meat. Stir in flour, mushrooms, salt, and pepper. Cover and cook 10 minutes over moderately low heat (about 225° F.) if using fresh mushrooms, or 5 minutes if using canned mushrooms; stir frequently. Uncover and blend in soup; continue cooking 10 minutes, stirring occasionally. Stir in sour cream and heat until mixture is piping hot. (Do not allow mixture to boil after sour cream is added.) Serve over cooked noodles or rice. Garnish with chopped parsley. Serves 4.

◈ Easy Beef Goulash

1 to 2 tablespoons vegetable
oil
1 pound ground beef chuck
3 cups uncooked medium egg
noodles
2 cups water
1 8-ounce can tomato sauce
1 envelope dry onion soup mix

Heat oil in a medium-sized skillet over moderately high heat (about 300° F.); add ground beef and cook until lightly browned, stirring occasionally with a fork to break up meat. Drain off any excess fat. Sprinkle uncooked noodles over meat. Combine water, tomato sauce, and onion soup mix. Pour over noodles in skillet. Do not stir. Cover and bring to a boil. Reduce heat to moderately low (about 225° F.) and simmer about 30 minutes, or until noodles are tender. Stir and serve. Serves 4.

◈ Southwest Chili

1 tablespoon vegetable oil
1 pound ground beef round
¼ cup sliced onion
1 clove garlic, pressed

Heat oil in a saucepan over moderate heat (about 250° F.). Cook beef, onion, and garlic until onion is soft and beef is browned, stirring frequently. Stir in chili powder, salt, cumin, and tomatoes. Break up any large tomato

2 teaspoons chili powder or
  ¼ teaspoon chili powder
  and 1 canned green chili
  pepper pod, seeded and
  sliced
½ teaspoon salt
Dash of ground cumin
  (optional)
1 16-ounce can tomatoes
1 16-ounce can pinto or red
  kidney beans, well
  drained

pieces with a wooden spoon. Stir in beans. Bring to a boil; reduce heat to moderately low (about 225° F.) and simmer, uncovered, for 10 minutes. Makes 1 quart or serves 4.

⊰ Beef Pilaf

¼ cup butter or margarine
½ cup sliced onion
1½ pounds ground beef round
1 teaspoon salt
⅛ teaspoon pepper
⅛ to ¼ teaspoon dried
  rosemary leaves
3 cups cooked rice (loosely
  packed)
1 4-ounce can mushroom
  stems and pieces,
  undrained
1 16-ounce can stewed
  tomatoes

Melt butter in a very large skillet over moderately low heat (about 225° F.); add onion and cook until lightly browned. Remove onion with a slotted spoon and add beef to skillet. Cook beef, stirring frequently, until it is no longer pink and juices have cooked down. Add onion to meat; sprinkle with salt, pepper, and rosemary. Stir in remaining ingredients, and heat to serving temperature. Serves 6.

⊰ Goulash Paprikash

2 pounds ground beef chuck
1½ teaspoons salt
2½ tablespoons flour
1 tablespoon paprika
¼ teaspoon pepper
2 tablespoons vegetable oil
½ cup sliced onion
1 16-ounce can stewed
  tomatoes
2 tablespoons cold water
Noodles (optional)

Sprinkle beef with 1 teaspoon of the salt. Shape into six 1-inch-thick oval patties. Combine 1 tablespoon of the flour with paprika, the remaining ½ teaspoon salt, and the pepper. Mix well. Coat patties lightly with this mixture. In a large saucepot or Dutch oven over moderately high heat (about 300° F.), heat oil and brown onion. Remove onion with a slotted spoon. In the same pot, brown patties on both sides, adding a little more oil if necessary. For ease of handling, brown 3 patties at a time. Remove from heat. Drain off any excess fat. Reduce heat to moderate (about 250° F.) and stir in stewed tomatoes. Bring to a boil. Blend remaining 1½ tablespoons flour with cold water and stir into simmering mixture, loosening any browned bits in the bottom of the pot. Add onions and patties; cover and simmer ½ hour. If desired, serve with buttered poppy-seed noodles. Serves 6.

Polynesian Beef

1 pound ground beef chuck
1 tablespoon curry powder
½ teaspoon salt
2 tablespoons vegetable oil
1 cup thinly sliced onion
1 green pepper, thinly sliced
½ cup seedless raisins
½ cup chopped salted peanuts
2 bay leaves
⅔ cup water
⅔ cup uncooked rice, cooked according to package directions

Mix ground beef, curry, and salt. Heat oil in skillet over moderately low heat (about 225° F.); add onion and green pepper and cook until tender. Add ground beef mixture and cook and stir over moderate heat (about 250° F.) until lightly browned. Add raisins, nuts, bay leaves, and water. Cover and simmer over low heat (about 200° F.) 20 minutes, stirring occasionally. Serve meat over hot cooked rice. Serves 4.

Hamburger Hash

1 pound ground beef chuck
3 cups chopped cold cooked potatoes (about 1 pound raw)
2 tablespoons finely chopped onion
1 teaspoon salt
⅛ teaspoon rubbed dried sage
Few grains pepper
¼ cup milk
2 tablespoons flour
¼ cup butter or margarine

In a large bowl mix together beef, potatoes, onion, salt, sage, pepper, and milk; blend well. Shape into eight ½-inch-thick patties and coat each lightly with flour. Chill 1 hour. Melt butter in a large skillet over moderate heat on a range. (Do not use controlled-heat burner.) Add patties and brown about 5 to 8 minutes on each side. Use a pancake turner to turn patties and to press together, if necessary. Serves 4.

Meat Loaves

There are so many recipes for meat loaf that it's possible to think any meats, liquids, seasonings and additions will do. That's not necessarily so. To be tender, juicy and slice well you do need a delicate balance of meats, crumbs, and liquids. But that ratio established, as it is in Our Best Meat Loaf below, you can improvise with a variety of ingredients as suggested. You can roll the meat around hard-boiled eggs before baking to make an attractive gold and white center to each slice. You can wrap it in a crescent-roll crust to make a mock Beef Wellington. You can frost it after baking with mashed potatoes brushed with a beaten egg and browned to a golden color. You can glaze it with a fruit sauce or top it with overlapping slices of cheese. You can make it your own. Be inventive.

✑ Our Best Meat Loaf*

2 cups fine soft bread crumbs made from enriched or whole grain bread
⅔ cup finely chopped peeled onion
2 teaspoons salt
¼ teaspoon pepper
⅓ cup milk
2 eggs
1 pound ground beef chuck
½ pound ground lean pork
½ pound ground veal

Heat oven to 350° F. Place bread crumbs, onion, salt, pepper and milk in a large bowl; combine thoroughly, using a rubber spatula. Add the eggs and combine thoroughly. Break about ¼ of the ground meats into small pieces and scatter the pieces over the bread crumb mixture. With a large cooking fork or the hands, gently mix in the meat until mixture is thoroughly combined. Repeat with the remaining portions of the meats. After all the meat is added, gently work the mixture with the hands to blend thoroughly. Place meat mixture in a 9-x-5-x-3-inch loaf pan. With the hands, pack the mixture firmly into the pan to form a loaf with a slightly rounded top. If preferred, meat loaf may be baked in an ungreased, shallow baking dish; shape the meat mixture with the hands into a loaf about 9 x 5 inches in a baking dish that is at least 1 inch larger in all dimensions than the loaf. Bake uncovered 1 hour and 20 minutes to 1 hour and 30 minutes. Pour off excess fat and meat juices. For easy slicing let meat loaf stand 10 minutes before serving. Serves 8.

*Note: For a smaller loaf to serve 4 use ½ of all ingredients. Bake in a 7½-x-3½-x-2¼-inch loaf pan or shape into an 8-x-4-inch loaf in a shallow baking dish. Reduce the baking time by about 15 minutes.

Meat Variations

All beef: Follow recipe for Best Meat Loaf, substituting 2 pounds ground beef chuck for the meats called for in the recipe. Bake uncovered 1 hour and 20 minutes.

Beef and Pork: Follow recipe for Best Meat Loaf, substituting 1 pound ground beef chuck and 1 pound ground lean pork for the meats called for in the recipe. Bake uncovered 1 hour and 20 minutes to 1 hour and 30 minutes.

Beef and Veal: Follow recipe for Best Meat Loaf, substituting 1½ pounds ground beef chuck and ½ pound ground veal for the meats called for in the recipe. Bake uncovered 1 hour and 20 minutes.

Ham and Pork: Follow recipe for Best Meat Loaf, omitting the salt and substituting 1 pound ground cooked ham and 1 pound ground lean pork for the meats called for in the recipe. Bake loaf uncovered in a shallow baking dish 1 hour and 30 minutes.

Lamb and Pork: Follow recipe for Best Meat Loaf, substituting 1½ pounds ground lean pork for the meats called for in the recipe. Bake uncovered 1 hour and 20 minutes to 1 hour and 30 minutes.

Beef and Sausage: Follow recipe for Best Meat Loaf, substituting 1½ pounds ground beef chuck and ½ pound bulk sausage for the meats called for in the recipe. Bake uncovered 1 hour and 20 minutes to 1 hour and 30 minutes.

Liquid Variations

Catsup: Follow recipe for Best Meat Loaf, substituting ¼ cup catsup for ¼ cup of the milk.

Tomato Soup: Follow recipe for Best Meat Loaf, reducing salt to 1 teaspoon and substituting ½ cup undiluted tomato soup from a 10¾-ounce can for the milk. Pour remainder of soup over the loaf and spread evenly over top before baking as directed.

Tomato Juice: Follow recipe for Best Meat Loaf, substituting ½ cup tomato juice for the milk.

Water: Follow recipe for Best Meat Loaf, substituting ½ cup water for the milk.

Chili Sauce: Follow recipe for Best Meat Loaf, omitting pepper and substituting ¼ cup chili sauce for ¼ cup of the milk.

Seasoning Variations

Dry Mustard: Follow recipe for Best Meat Loaf, omitting pepper and adding 2 teaspoons dry mustard to the bread crumb mixture.

Horseradish: Follow recipe for Best Meat Loaf, adding 2 tablespoons prepared horseradish to the bread crumb mixture.

Horseradish Mustard: Follow recipe for Basic Meat Loaf, omitting pepper and adding ¼ cup prepared horseradish mustard to the bread crumb mixture.

Lemon Juice: Follow recipe for Best Meat Loaf, adding 1 tablespoon lemon juice to the bread crumb mixture.

Garlic: Follow recipe for Best Meat Loaf, adding ½ teaspoon finely minced peeled garlic to the bread crumb mixture.

Any of the following may be added to the bread crumb mixture:

Green pepper: Add ⅔ cup finely chopped green pepper.
Cheese: Add 1 cup shredded Cheddar cheese.
Peanuts: Add ½ cup coarsely chopped salted peanuts.
Celery: Add ½ cup finely chopped celery.
Mushrooms: Add 1 8-ounce can mushroom stems and pieces, drained.
Vegetables: Add 1 10-ounce package frozen mixed vegetables, thawed, or 1 8½-ounce can mixed vegetables, drained.

~§ *Meat Loaf with Textured Protein*

Unseasoned textured vegetable protein (use amount recommended on package for mixing with 1 pound of ground meat)
Tomato juice or bouillon, instead of water, for rehydrating (use amount recommended on package)
 1 *cup firmly packed soft bread crumbs*
 ½ *cup finely chopped, peeled onion*
 1½ *teaspoons salt*
 ⅛ *teaspoon pepper*
 ⅓ *cup tomato juice or bouillon*
 1 *egg*
 1 *pound ground beef chuck*

Heat oven to 350° F. Place textured vegetable protein and desired liquid in a large mixing bowl. When textured protein is rehydrated, add the bread crumbs, onion, salt, pepper and tomato juice and mix well; add egg and meat and mix thoroughly. (Hands are best tools.) Place meat in a shallow baking pan (about 6-x-10 inches) and shape into a loaf about 9-x-5 inches. Bake uncovered 1 hour and 15 minutes. For easier slicing, remove loaf from oven and let stand about 10 minutes before cutting. Serves 6 to 8.

Roast Pork

Today's pork has been adjusted to modern tastes. Through breeding and research, pork today has a much smaller ratio of fat to lean. Pork for roasting has been affected most by research. Old recipes call for roast pork to be cooked to an internal temperature of 185° F., whereas newer recipes require only 170° F. However, all fresh pork should be well done.

There are several cuts of pork suitable for roasting.

Loin roasts are available as the whole loin; the loin end, which is more difficult to carve; the rib end; and the center cut, which is exactly like pork chops strung together. Have the butcher free the backbone from the ribs for easier carving.

Shoulder roasts are available with or without bone. The boneless roasts are easy to carve but the bone-in shoulder roasts are difficult and you can't count on neat, appealing slices.

Leg roasts are also called fresh ham. Fresh hams are frequently forgotten amid the great variety of precooked and canned smoked hams. This is succulent meat that needs long cooking but it is a delightful change of pace. See the Fresh Pork Roasting Chart, page 47, for cooking time and temperatures.

Crown roasts are made from the center rib sections of two or more loins. These are shaped into a circle with the rib ends up. These may be Frenched—meat removed from rib ends—and decorated, after cooking, with paper frills.

To make plain pork roasts, see the time and temperature chart for roasting pork beginning on page 46.

✒ *Roast Pork with Herb Dressing*

1 *4-pound pork loin roast*
2 *tablespoons butter or margarine*
¾ *cup finely chopped onion*
½ *cup chopped celery*
1 *cup soft bread crumbs*
¼ *teaspoon ground marjoram*
⅛ *teaspoon dried thyme leaves*
¼ *teaspoon salt*
Salt and pepper
½ *cup thinly sliced onion*
Milk Gravy (recipe follows)

Cut deep slits in fat side of roast about 1¼ inches apart, but do not cut through bone. Melt butter in skillet over moderate heat (about 250° F.); add onion and celery and cook until tender. Toss together bread crumbs, onion and celery, marjoram, thyme, and the ¼ teaspoon salt. Fill slits in roast with dressing and tie with string to hold stuffing in place. Sprinkle with salt and pepper. Heat oven to 325° F. Place roast on a rack in a shallow baking pan. Roast 2¼ hours. Place onion slices over meat and roast about ½ hour longer, allowing a total of 35 to 40 minutes per pound, or until a meat thermometer inserted in the meat registers 170° F. Prepare gravy if desired. Serves 4 to 5.

Milk Gravy

¼ *cup meat drippings from roast*
3 *tablespoons flour*
1 *teaspoon salt*
Few grains pepper
2 *cups milk*
1 *tablespoon chopped fresh parsley*

Pour meat drippings into saucepan; blend in flour, salt, and pepper. Gradually add milk and cook over moderately low heat (about 225° F.), stirring constantly, until thickened. Add parsley. Makes 2¼ cups.

✑ Crown Roast of Pork with Corn Bread Stuffing

1 8- to 9-pound crown roast
   of pork (about 14 to 16
   chops)
Salt and pepper
1 cup water
1 cup butter or margarine
2 8-ounce packages corn
   bread stuffing
½ cup chopped celery and
   celery leaves
¼ cup chopped fresh parsley
½ cup coarsely chopped
   pecans
2 eggs, beaten
Crab apples (optional)
Parsley sprigs (optional)

Have the butcher shape the crown roast from a loin of pork. Heat oven to 325° F. Place roast in a large, shallow, open roasting pan without a rack, rib ends up. Season with salt and pepper. Bone ends may be wrapped in aluminum foil to prevent excessive browning, if desired. Insert a meat thermometer between 2 ribs in center of meat; thermometer should not touch bone. Roast, uncovered, allowing 35 to 40 minutes per pound, or until the meat thermometer registers 170° F. (This will take 4¾ to 6 hours.) About 1½ hours before the roast is done, heat the water to boiling in a large saucepan. Remove from heat. Melt butter in the hot water. Add stuffing, celery and celery leaves, parsley, and pecans. Toss lightly to combine. Add the beaten eggs and toss lightly again to combine thoroughly. Remove roast from oven and mound some of the stuffing in center of roast, just up to where meat ends and bone begins. Cover stuffing loosely with foil. Return roast to oven. Place remaining stuffing in a buttered casserole and bake, covered, the last hour with roast. Carefully lift crown roast to a heated serving platter. Garnish with crab apples slipped over the rib ends and arrange parsley sprigs around base of roast, if desired. Serves 14 to 16, 1 chop per person.

✑ Half-Crown Roast with Spinach Dressing

1 3- to 3½-pound center-cut
   pork loin roast (about 8
   ribs)
6 tablespoons butter or
   margarine
3 tablespoons chopped
   onion
3 tablespoons chopped
   celery
3 cups soft bread crumbs
1½ cups crumbled corn bread
¾ cup chopped raw spinach
1½ teaspoons crumbled dried
   sage leaves
⅛ teaspoon crumbled dried
   rosemary leaves
¾ teaspoon salt

Have butcher cut ribs partially through, as for a crown roast, so that meat can be formed into a semicircle with bone on top. Place skewers at the ends and tie with cord to hold it in shape. Heat oven to 325° F. Melt butter in skillet over moderate heat (about 250° F.); add onion and celery and cook until tender. Toss together bread crumbs, crumbled corn bread, spinach, onion and celery mixture, sage, rosemary, and salt. Mound dressing in center of a shallow 2-quart baking dish. Place roast over dressing. Roast uncovered, 30 to 35 minutes per pound, or until a meat thermometer inserted in center of meat registers 170° F., about 1½ to 2 hours. Serves 8, one rib per person.

❧ Fruited Pork Roast

1 12-ounce package mixed
   dried fruits
1 3-inch stick cinnamon
½ lemon, sliced
2 cups apple juice
2 tablespoons orange juice
2 tablespoons honey
1 4- to 5-pound fresh pork
   shoulder, boned and rolled

Cook dried fruits as directed on package, adding cinnamon and lemon to water. Add apple juice, orange juice, and honey to cooked fruits. Heat oven to 325° F. Place pork on a rack in a shallow roasting pan. Insert meat thermometer into center of thickest part of meat. Pour fruit mixture over pork. Bake uncovered 35 to 40 minutes per pound, or until meat thermometer registers 170° F., about 2½ to 3½ hours. Baste pork frequently with pan drippings. Serves 8 to 10.

❧ Roast Shoulder of Pork

1 5-pound pork shoulder,
   boned, rolled, and tied
½ cup Madeira wine
1 teaspoon salt
⅛ teaspoon ground nutmeg
Few grains pepper
3 cups cold water
¼ teaspoon prepared
   horseradish
¼ cup flour
⅓ cup cold water

Heat oven to 325° F. Place pork on a rack in a shallow roasting pan and insert a meat thermometer in the thickest part of the roast. Roast 35 to 40 minutes per pound until the meat thermometer registers 170° F., about 3 to 3½ hours. Meanwhile mix together wine, ¼ teaspoon of the salt, the nutmeg, and pepper. Brush this mixture on the roast frequently during the last ½ hour of roasting time. When the roast is cooked, remove it to a serving platter and keep it warm. Drain off fat from the roasting pan and add the 3 cups of water to the pan. Stir to loosen all the brown bits from the bottom of the pan. Pour into a saucepan and add any remaining wine basting sauce. Add the remaining ¾ teaspoon salt and the horseradish. Blend the flour into the ⅓ cup water. Gradually stir into the sauce mixture. Place over moderately low heat (about 225° F.) and bring to a boil. Boil 1 minute, stirring constantly. Serve with roast. Serves 8 to 10.

❧ Pork Loin Roast with Spiced Apple-Plum Sauce

1 3- to 5-pound center-cut
   pork loin roast
Salt and pepper
1 17-ounce can whole purple
   plums
1 15-ounce jar sweetened
   applesauce
¼ teaspoon ground
   pumpkin-pie spices or ⅛

Heat oven to 325° F. Sprinkle pork lightly with salt and pepper and place on a rack in a shallow roasting pan. Insert meat thermometer into the meatiest part of the roast. Roast 30 to 35 minutes per pound or until thermometer registers 170° F. Remove roast to a warm platter and let stand in warm place 10 to 15 minutes before carving. Meanwhile, drain plums and reserve ¼ cup of the syrup. Remove pits from plums and place plums in the container of an electric blender with the reserved

*teaspoon ground nutmeg
and ⅛ teaspoon ground
allspice*
⅛ *teaspoon ground cinnamon*
Salt to taste

syrup. Blend at medium speed for 60 seconds or until smooth. In a saucepan combine plum purée with applesauce, pumpkin-pie spices, cinnamon and salt to taste. Place mixture over moderate heat (about 250° F.) and heat to serving temperature. Serve sauce over carved portions of pork. Serves 6 to 8.

Pork Chops and Steaks

Pork chops and steaks are best braised because they tend to get dry when broiled. Choose any of the chops or steaks listed under Pork in the section of this chapter dealing with the seven basic cuts of meat (page 275). Rib and loin are the most popular and the most expensive types of chops.

✑ Braised Pork Chops or Pork Steaks

4 *shoulder pork chops or
pork steaks*
2 *tablespoons flour*
½ *teaspoon salt*
3 *to 4 tablespoons water*
Salt and pepper

Trim excess fat from chops. Cook fat in a skillet over moderate heat (about 250° F.) until lightly browned and a thin layer of melted fat forms in skillet. Remove pieces of fat. Mix flour and the ½ teaspoon salt; dip chops in mixture to coat them. Cook in the skillet over moderately high heat (about 300° F.) until lightly browned on all sides. Reduce heat to low (about 200° F.). Drain fat drippings from pan. Add water. Sprinkle with salt and pepper. Cover and cook 45 to 60 minutes or until fork-tender. Serves 4.

✑ Orange-Glazed Pork Chops

4 *shoulder, loin, or rib chops,
cut ½ inch thick*
Salt and pepper
⅓ *cup frozen orange juice
concentrate*
¼ *teaspoon ground cinnamon*
1 *teaspoon grated orange
peel*
⅛ *teaspoon dried thyme
leaves*

Trim a bit of fat off chops. Heat it in a heavy skillet over moderately high heat (about 325° F.). Add chops and brown on both sides. Pour off excess fat. Season chops with salt and pepper. Reduce heat to moderately low (about 225° F.). Add remaining ingredients. Cover and cook 45 minutes, until chops are fork-tender. Serves 4.

✑ Pork Chops with Mustard Sauce

4 center-cut loin pork chops,
  cut 1 inch thick
2 tablespoons flour
½ teaspoon salt
Few grains pepper
¼ cup dry white wine
2 tablespoons butter or
  margarine
2 tablespoons flour
2 teaspoons prepared
  mustard
½ teaspoon salt
1 cup light cream

Trim off excess fat from chops. Cook fat in skillet over moderate heat (about 250° F.) until lightly browned and a thin layer of melted fat forms in skillet. Remove pieces of fat. Mix the 2 tablespoons flour, the ½ teaspoon salt, and the pepper; dip chops in mixture to coat them. Cook chops in the melted fat over moderately high heat (about 325° F.) until lightly browned on both sides. Add wine; cover and simmer over moderately low heat (about 225° F.), turning occasionally, for 45 minutes. Remove chops to a warm serving platter. Reserve drippings. Melt butter in a small saucepan over moderate heat (about 250° F.); blend in the 2 tablespoons flour, the mustard, and the ½ teaspoon salt. Gradually add cream and cook, stirring constantly, until thickened. Stir in drippings from skillet; heat. Serve sauce over chops. Serves 4.

✑ Stuffed Pork Chops

1½ cups soft bread crumbs
½ cup tart apple, peeled and
  shredded
½ cup diced orange sections
2 tablespoons dark seedless
  raisins
1 tablespoon butter or
  margarine
2 tablespoons chopped
  onion
2 tablespoons chopped
  green pepper
⅓ cup finely diced celery
⅛ teaspoon salt
⅛ teaspoon rubbed dried
  sage
Dash of ground nutmeg
Few grains pepper
6 double-bone rib pork
  chops with a pocket cut
  for stuffing
Salt
1 tablespoon vegetable oil
½ cup orange juice

Heat oven to 350° F. In a large bowl mix together crumbs, apple, orange, and raisins. Melt butter in a saucepan over moderate heat (about 250° F.). Add onion, green pepper, and celery. Cook until onion is lightly browned. Pour over crumb mixture and add the salt, sage, nutmeg, and pepper. Stir with a tossing motion to mix well. Sprinkle pork chops lightly on both sides and in pockets with additional salt. Stuff each pocket with about ⅓ cup of the stuffing mixture. Secure openings with toothpicks. Heat oil in a large skillet over moderately high heat (about 350° F.) and brown chops on all sides, adding a little more oil if necessary. Arrange chops in a shallow rectangular 3-quart baking dish. Add orange juice. Cover (use aluminum foil if appropriate-sized cover is not available) and bake 1 hour. Uncover and bake 15 minutes longer, or until chops are fork-tender. Place chops in a serving dish. Skim fat from pan; serve liquid over chops. Serves 6.

❧ Pork Chops and Sweet Potatoes

6 *loin chops, cut 1 inch thick*
Salt and pepper
1½ *pounds sweet potatoes, peeled and cut into ½-inch slices*
2 *cooking apples, peeled, cored, and sliced*
1 *teaspoon salt*
⅛ *teaspoon pepper*
¼ *cup water*
½ *teaspoon Worcestershire sauce*
½ *cup chopped onion*
4 *slices raw bacon, cut in half*

Heat oven to 350° F. Trim off excess fat from chops. Cook fat in skillet over moderate heat (about 250° F.) until lightly browned and a thin layer of melted fat forms in skillet; remove pieces of fat. Add chops and cook over moderately high heat (about 325° F.) until browned on both sides; sprinkle with salt and pepper. Arrange chops in bottom of a shallow 3-quart baking dish. Arrange a layer of sweet potatoes and apple slices over chops. Sprinkle with the 1 teaspoon salt and the pepper. Mix water and Worcestershire and pour over apples. Sprinkle with onion and top with the bacon slices. Cover and bake 1¼ hours. Uncover and bake 15 minutes. Serves 6.

❧ Sweet–Sour Pork Chops

2 *tablespoons shortening*
6 *pork rib chops or pork blade steaks, about ¾ inch thick*
2 *tablespoons flour*
1 *cup water*
1 *tablespoon vinegar*
1 *teaspoon salt*
1 *teaspoon rubbed dried sage*
3 *medium-sized baking apples, cored (not peeled), and cut into ½-inch crosswise slices*
¼ *cup firmly packed light brown sugar*
½ *cup seedless raisins*

Heat shortening in a large skillet over moderately high heat (about 325° F.). Add pork chops in a single layer and brown on both sides. Remove chops from the skillet and reduce heat to moderate (about 250° F.). Blend flour into drippings in skillet. Gradually stir in the water and vinegar. Cook, stirring constantly, until thickened. Return pork chops to skillet; sprinkle with salt and sage. Arrange apple slices on top of pork chops. Sprinkle with brown sugar and raisins. Cover tightly and simmer 45 minutes, or until pork is tender. Serves 6.

Pork Tenderloin

Pork tenderloin is the long, tapering, tender piece of pork that lies inside the loin next to the backbone. Tenderloins are small (from three-fourths of a pound to a pound and a half each) and are sold whole, cut into thick slices, or flattened into fillets. Tenderloin in all forms is available smoked or cured, as well as fresh.

⋙ Braised Tenderloin and Snow Peas

3 tablespoons shortening or vegetable oil
½ cup finely chopped onion
1 ¾-pound whole pork tenderloin
½ cup semidry white wine
2 8-ounce packages frozen Chinese pea pods, partly thawed
¼ cup water

Melt shortening in skillet over moderate heat (about 250° F.); add onion and cook until tender. Remove onion and reserve. Cut tenderloin into 1-inch diagonal slices and flatten slightly with a mallet or heavy can. Cook meat in skillet over moderately high heat (about 275° F.) until lightly browned on both sides. Add reserved onion and wine; cover and simmer 30 minutes over low heat (about 200° F.). Remove meat. Add peas and water to skillet; mix well. Place meat over vegetables. Cover and simmer 3 to 4 minutes, until peas are just tender. Spoon vegetables onto serving platter and arrange meat pieces over them. Serves 3 to 4.

⋙ Chinese Pork Tenderloin

1 chicken bouillon cube
½ cup boiling water
1 teaspoon soy sauce
2 tablespoons honey
1 tablespoon dry sherry
⅛ teaspoon ground ginger
Few grains ground cinnamon
1 ¾-pound whole pork tenderloin, cut into ½-inch slices
3 tablespoons flour
1 tablespoon butter or margarine
1 green pepper, cleaned and cut into ¼-inch strips
1 16-ounce can bean sprouts
2 cups cooked rice

Dissolve bouillon cube in boiling water; add soy sauce, honey, sherry, ginger, and cinnamon. Pour over sliced tenderloin; cover and marinate in refrigerator 2 hours. Drain meat and reserve marinade. Dip meat in flour to coat pieces. Melt butter in skillet over moderately high heat (about 275° F.); add meat and cook until lightly browned. Add reserved marinade and green pepper; cover and simmer over low heat (about 200° F.) 20 minutes. Drain bean sprouts and add ¼ cup of the bean liquid to meat mixture. Stir in bean sprouts and heat. Serve over rice. Serves 4.

Spareribs

Spareribs are sold by the sheet, or side. There are two sheets to one animal. Fresh ribs are meaty and pink in color. Have the butcher cut them into individual ribs or, if you prepare them by the sheet, have him crack through the ribs at the large end so they will be easier to cut into serving portions.

✑ Glazed Spareribs

8 pounds spareribs, cut into serving-sized pieces
4 teaspoons salt
4 8-ounce cans tomato sauce
16 whole cloves
4 stalks celery, finely chopped
2 cloves garlic, finely minced
8 dashes Tabasco
4 tablespoons Worcestershire sauce
½ cup vinegar
4 tablespoons sugar
2 teaspoons chili powder
½ teaspoon dry mustard
4 tablespoons raspberry jam

Place spareribs in a large saucepan. Add salt and barely enough water to cover ribs. Cover and simmer over low heat (about 200° F.) 45 minutes, until almost tender. Remove and drain thoroughly. Combine remaining ingredients. Brush ribs with the tomato mixture; cover and refrigerate until ready to use. Place ribs on grill over hot coals and cook about 15 minutes on each side, until browned and well glazed. Brush meat occasionally with some of the tomato mixture. Serves 8 to 10.

✑ Barbecued Spareribs

5 pounds spareribs, cut into serving-sized pieces
½ cup bottled barbecue sauce
3 tablespoons light corn syrup
1 8¼-ounce can pineapple slices, drained
1 8-ounce can apricot halves, drained

Divide spareribs between 2 large saucepans or Dutch ovens. Add water to cover and place over moderate heat (about 250° F.). Simmer, covered, 1½ hours, or until meat is fork-tender. Drain spareribs and place on a rack in a broiling pan. Combine barbecue sauce and corn syrup; brush meat with some of the sauce. Place in pre-heated broiler about 5 inches from the heat. Broil about 10 minutes, or until browned. Remove from oven and turn all spareribs to unbrowned side; brush again with the sauce. Arrange pineapple slices around meat, place an apricot half on each pineapple slice, and brush lightly with the sauce. Place under broiler for another 10 minutes. Serves 5 to 6.

✑ Chinese Spareribs

1 sheet spareribs, cut into 4 portions (about 3 pounds)
1 bay leaf

Combine spareribs, bay leaf, 1 teaspoon of the salt, peppercorns, and enough water to just cover in a Dutch oven. Place over moderately low heat (about 225° F.) and

1¼ teaspoons salt
¼ teaspoon peppercorns
½ cup canned chicken broth, diluted
¼ cup honey
2 tablespoons soy sauce
½ teaspoon ground ginger

bring to a boil. Cover and simmer 45 minutes, or until fork-tender. Drain and place in a large shallow baking pan. Combine remaining ingredients and pour over spareribs. Let stand to marinate 45 minutes, turning occasionally and spooning the marinade over the ribs. Remove ribs from marinade. Grill or broil 4 inches from source of heat 10 minutes, brushing frequently with remaining marinade. Turn ribs and continue to brush and broil 8 minutes longer, or until crisp and browned. Serves 4.

Ground and Cubed Pork

Usually cubed pork is readily available in markets but ground pork may not be. By law, pork must be ground in a separate grinder or the meat grinder must be washed after it has been used for pork to prevent passing any trichinosis bacteria into meats that may be cooked rare. If you plan to use ground pork order it a few days ahead so the butcher has time to prepare the quantity you need.

Ground Pork Patties

1 cup soft rye bread crumbs
¼ cup dry white wine
1 pound lean ground pork
½ teaspoon salt
¼ teaspoon pepper
1 tablespoon butter or margarine
½ cup firmly packed light brown sugar
½ teaspoon dry mustard
2 tablespoons lemon juice
¼ cup water

Moisten bread crumbs with the wine. Add pork, salt, and pepper; mix well. Shape into 1½-inch balls. Melt butter in a skillet over moderately low heat (about 225° F.). Increase temperature to moderately high (about 300° F.) and brown balls on all sides. Heat oven to 350° F. While meatballs are browning, mix brown sugar, dry mustard, lemon juice, and water in a small saucepan. Place over moderate heat (about 250° F.) and heat until brown sugar is dissolved. Arrange browned meatballs in a shallow 1-quart baking dish; pour the brown sugar mixture over them and bake uncovered for 30 minutes. Serves 3 to 4.

Chop Suey

3 tablespoons vegetable oil
1½ pounds lean pork, cut into ¾-inch cubes
2½ cups water

Turn heat control on a 3-quart electric saucepan to 360° F. A large saucepan over moderately high heat (about 350° F.) may be used. Place oil and pork in saucepan and brown lightly. Add the 2½ cups water, chicken bouillon

3 *chicken bouillon cubes*
1 *cup thinly sliced onions*
2 *cups diced celery*
½ *teaspoon salt*
⅛ *teaspoon pepper*
1 *teaspoon ground ginger*
⅓ *cup thinly sliced green*
   pepper
1 *16-ounce can bean*
   sprouts, drained
2 *tablespoons soy sauce*
1 *4-ounce can button*
   mushrooms, undrained
1 *5-ounce can water*
   chestnuts, drained
¼ *cup toasted slivered*
   almonds
5 *tablespoons cornstarch*
⅓ *cup water*
2 *3-ounce cans chow mein*
   noodles

cubes, onions, celery, salt, pepper, and ginger. When mixture boils reduce heat to 225° F.; cover and simmer 40 minutes. Add green pepper, bean sprouts, soy sauce, mushrooms with liquid, water chestnuts, and almonds. Stir cornstarch and the ⅓ cup water together; add to chop suey. Simmer 5 minutes after mixture boils. Serve over chow mein noodles. Serves 6.

৺§ Pork Hocks and Sauerkraut

4 *large pork hocks, fresh or*
   smoked
1 *teaspoon salt*
¼ *teaspoon pepper*
1 *bay leaf*
1 *27-ounce can sauerkraut,*
   drained
1 *large green apple, peeled,*
   cored, and quartered

Wash hocks and place in a large saucepan. Cover hocks with cold water; add salt, pepper, and bay leaf. Cover tightly. Place over moderately low heat (about 225° F.) and cook slowly 1½ to 2 hours, until fork-tender. Add sauerkraut and apple. Continue to cook 30 minutes more. Serves 4.

৺§ Sweet-and-Sour Pork

1½ *to 2 pounds boneless lean*
   pork shoulder
2 *tablespoons shortening*
1 *20-ounce can pineapple*
   chunks
¾ *cup water*
¼ *cup vinegar*
1 *tablespoon soy sauce*

Cut meat into strips about 3 to 4 inches long and 1 inch wide. Melt shortening in skillet over moderately high heat (about 275° F.) and cook meat until lightly browned. Drain pineapple and mix juice with the ¾ cup water, the vinegar, soy sauce, brown sugar, and salt. Pour over meat; cover and simmer over low heat (about 200° F.) 1 hour, or until tender. Combine cornstarch and the 2 tablespoons water; add to meat and cook,

¼ *cup firmly packed dark brown sugar*
½ *teaspoon salt*
2 *tablespoons cornstarch*
2 *tablespoons water*
⅓ *cup thinly sliced onions*
¾ *cup thinly sliced green pepper strips*
2 *to 3 cups cooked rice*

stirring constantly, until thickened. Add pineapple chunks, onions, and green pepper. Cover and cook 10 to 15 minutes, until vegetables are tender. Serve on rice. Serves 4 to 6.

Pork Sausage

Fresh pork sausage comes in links, patties, sausage meat rolls and in packaged, fully cooked links or patties that need only to be browned. The fresh uncooked products vary greatly in amount and kinds of seasonings. You'll have to see which suits your taste. All fresh sausage must be cooked until it is well done and loses its pink color.

To pan-fry sausage links: Arrange links in a large skillet that has a tight-fitting cover. Add ¼ cup water, cover pan, and put it over *low* heat for five minutes. Remove lid and let the water evaporate. Brown links slowly on all sides. Turn with a spoon or tongs to prevent piercing sausages. Brown slowly; this will take five to ten minutes.

To bake sausage links: This is an easy way to prepare a pound or more of sausage at one time. Spread links in one layer in a shallow baking pan. Bake in a preheated 400° F. oven for twenty to thirty minutes. Turn over with a spoon or tongs to brown evenly.

To pan-fry sausage patties: Shape or cut packaged meat into patties one-half inch thick, or use preshaped patties. Cook slowly in a heavy skillet over low heat for fifteen minutes. Turn occasionally and pour off fat as it accumulates.

⤳ Sausage and Red Cabbage

1 *tablespoon butter or margarine*
1½ *teaspoons flour*
1 *cup dry red wine*
1 *small head red cabbage, shredded*
2 *teaspoons salt*

Melt butter in a medium-sized skillet over moderately low heat (about 225° F.). Blend in flour. Gradually add wine; cook and stir until smooth. Add cabbage, salt, pepper, sugar, lemon juice, and vinegar. Cover tightly; simmer over low heat (about 200° F.) 30 minutes. Add sausage links; cover tightly and continue to cook 15 minutes. Serves 4.

(Ingredients continued on page 322)

¼ *teaspoon pepper*
¼ *cup firmly packed brown*
   sugar
3 *tablespoons lemon juice*
2 *tablespoons vinegar*
1 *pound pork sausage links*

❧ Pork-Sausage Pie

1 *pound pork sausage links*
½ *cup finely chopped onion*
¼ *cup coarsely chopped green*
   pepper
2 *16-ounce cans whole,*
   peeled tomatoes, drained
1 *12-ounce can whole-kernel*
   corn, drained
1 *10-ounce package frozen*
   lima beans
½ *cup chili sauce*
1 *teaspoon salt*
1 *12-ounce package corn*
   muffin mix

Place sausage links in a cold, medium-sized skillet over moderately high heat (about 275° F.). Cook until browned on all sides. Remove sausage and drain off all but 2 tablespoons of the fat from the skillet. Add onion and green pepper to skillet. Cook until onions are soft. Cut sausages into 1-inch pieces. Add sausage, tomatoes, corn, lima beans, chili sauce, and salt to onion mixture. Cover and simmer over low heat (about 200° F.) 30 minutes. Pour mixture into a greased, deep 3-quart casserole. Heat oven to 400° F. Prepare corn muffin mix as directed on package. Spoon batter over sausage mixture. Bake 20 to 25 minutes, until topping is golden brown. Serves 6 to 8.

Hams

Most meat packers wrap and label their hams with information as to type and cooking methods. Be sure to check the wrapper on the ham you buy. If it is not labeled, ask the butcher to tell you what it is. The following are the most common types of hams available.

Cook-before-eating hams have been heated to an internal temperature of at least 137° F. They require thorough cooking before eating. These hams should be heated to an internal temperature of 160° F.

Fully cooked hams have been processed to an internal temperature of 150° F. and may be eaten without further cooking. To serve hot they may be heated to an internal temperature of 140° F.

Country-style hams have been heavily cured, sometimes smoked. They require soaking and parboiling; after this they may be glazed and baked as other hams.

Canned hams are completely cooked. They may be eaten cold or may be removed from the can, glazed, and baked.

The following are the most common styles of hams available.

Bone-in hams are available whole, cut in half as butt and shank ends, or as ham slices. Shank bone, skin, and excess fat are sometimes removed. They are available as cook-before-eating, ready-to-eat, and fully cooked hams.

Boneless, skinless hams have been boned and shaped into rolls. They are available either whole or in pieces. They may be purchased as cook-before-eating and ready-to-eat hams.

Smoked picnic butt, or cottage roll, is the shoulder or foreleg; it is similar to ham in appearance and flavor but is smaller. Picnic butt is available either with bone-in or boneless.

When cooking smoked ham, follow the cooking directions on the wrapper. If not available, use a meat thermometer. Insert thermometer into the thickest part of the meat, away from the bone, and roast in a 325° F. oven (moderately low) until thermometer registers 160° F. for cook-before-eating ham, 140° F. for the fully cooked or canned ham. Check the estimated time and temperature for roasting ham in the chart beginning on page 47.

Canned hams always contain some gelatine and other hams tend to shrink when cooked. When you buy ham, it's best to allow ½ pound boned ham per person and about 1 pound bone-in ham per person.

✎ Glazed Baked Ham

1　*16-pound fully cooked bone-in ham*
½　*cup strained orange marmalade*
1　*cup dark corn syrup*
2　*teaspoons dry mustard*
Whole cloves
Frosted Grapes (optional, recipe on page 141)

Heat oven to 325° F. Place ham, fat side up, on a rack in a shallow roasting pan. Roast about 15 to 18 minutes per pound or until a meat thermometer registers 140° F., about 4 to 4¾ hours. While ham is roasting, mix orange marmalade, corn syrup, and dry mustard together. Remove ham from oven and cut off rind. Increase oven temperature to 375° F. Score ham with a sharp knife, making diagonal cuts ⅛ inch deep and about ¾ inch apart in one direction and then in a crosswise direction. Stud ham with cloves and brush with some of the glaze. Bake 15 to 20 minutes, basting frequently with more glaze, until glaze is golden brown. Remove the ham to a warm serving platter and garnish with the frosted grapes, if desired. Serves 16 generously.

Other Glazes for Ham

Use *½ cup orange* or *apricot marmalade; 1 cup cranberry* or *currant jelly; 2 cups apple cider* and *1 cup firmly packed brown sugar; 1 cup honey; 1 cup firmly packed brown sugar* and *¾ cup drained crushed pineapple.*

◄§ Pecan-Topped Picnic Ham

1 4- to 6-pound smoked
   picnic butt
1 cup firmly packed dark
   brown sugar
3 tablespoons flour
¼ teaspoon ground cloves
¼ teaspoon ground cinnamon
2 tablespoons vinegar
½ cup pecan halves

Heat oven to 325° F. Place ham, fat side up, on a rack in a shallow baking pan. Cover loosely with aluminum foil. Bake 35 minutes per pound, about 2½ to 3½ hours. Remove from oven. Slit rind and peel it off. Score fat in diamonds 1 inch wide. Combine sugar, flour, cloves, cinnamon, and vinegar. Spread mixture evenly over ham. Continue baking about 30 minutes. Before serving place a pecan half in center of each diamond. Serves 8 to 12.

◄§ Ham in Crust

1 5-pound canned ham
1 container refrigerated
   crescent dinner rolls
1 egg yolk
2 teaspoons prepared
   mustard
1 tablespoon milk

Remove ham from can; place in a large roasting pan and let stand at room temperature for 1½ hours. Heat oven to 200° F. Place ham in oven for 15 minutes, or until gelatine on ham is melted. Drain gelatine from pan and blot ham with paper towels to remove moisture from surface. Increase oven temperature to 375° F. Open container of rolls; cut into 8 triangles as directed. Use 6 of the triangles on ham as follows: Place a triangle of dough on the ham, holding it so that the longest tip of the triangle is at the center top of ham and the remaining part hangs down the side of the ham. Arrange a second triangle in the same way, leaving about 1½ inches space between them; tips should overlap at center top and at the one bottom edge. Continue arranging the next 4 triangles, leaving 1½ inches space between each. Press all overlapping edges at top and sides firmly together with floured fingertips. Cut the 2 remaining triangles in half to make 4 smaller triangles. Roll each into a small crescent roll and arrange on top of ham. Place egg yolk, mustard, and milk in a bowl and beat together with a rotary beater until blended. Brush dough surfaces with egg mixture. Bake 20 minutes, or until golden brown. Reduce oven temperature to 325° F. Continue baking 60 to 70 minutes, or until a meat thermometer inserted in the center of the ham registers 125° F. Slice ham into thin slices. Serve warm. Serves 10 generously.

Ham Slices

Ham slices cut ½ to 1 inch thick from the center section of ready-to-eat or fully cooked ham may be broiled, pan-broiled, or baked. You may have thicker slices especially cut. Trim rind from slices and slash edges of fat to prevent curling.

To broil: Preheat broiler. Arrange ham slice, cut one inch thick, on broiler rack about three inches from heat. Broil about five minutes on each side.

To pan-broil: Rub a preheated heavy skillet with a little fat. Place ham slice, cut ½ inch thick, in skillet and cook over moderately high heat (about 275° F.) about three minutes on each side.

To bake: Place ham slice, cut at least 1 inch thick, in a baking pan. Bake uncovered in a moderately low oven (325° F.) about twenty-five minutes.

Ready-to-eat, thinly sliced or boiled ham may be bought in packages or from your butcher.

⇜ Broiled Ham Steak

½ *cup apricot jam*
1½ *tablespoons prepared mustard*
⅛ *teaspoon ground cinnamon*
1 *center-cut slice of ham, 1½ to 2 inches thick (about 2 pounds)*
1 *24¼-ounce can sliced pineapple, drained*

Mix apricot jam, mustard, and cinnamon. Slash fat around ham slice and place ham on broiler rack. Place in preheated broiler about 4 inches from heat. Broil 6 to 7 minutes; turn. Arrange pineapple slices around ham. Brush apricot glaze over ham slice and pineapple. Broil 5 to 6 minutes. Serves 4 to 5.

⇜ Baked Glazed Ham Steak

1 *center-cut slice of ham, 2 inches thick (about 2½ pounds)*
Whole cloves
1 *29-ounce can cling peach halves*
½ *cup firmly packed brown sugar*
1 *tablespoon lemon juice*

Heat oven to 350° F. Score fat edge of ham and stud fat with cloves. Place in a shallow baking pan. Drain peaches and reserve ½ cup of the syrup. Combine syrup, brown sugar, lemon juice, and mustard. Mix about 1 tablespoonful of the glaze with the almonds and set aside. Brush ham generously with some of the remaining glaze. Bake 40 minutes. Remove ham from oven and arrange peach halves, cut side up, around ham. Brush ham and peaches with glaze. Spoon

½ teaspoon dry mustard
½ cup toasted diced almonds

almonds into peaches. Return to oven and bake 20 minutes longer. Serves 5.

❧ Barbecued Ham Steaks

4 slices boned and rolled
  ham, cut ¾ inch thick
  (about 3 pounds)
½ cup dry white wine
½ cup olive oil
2 cloves garlic, crushed
½ teaspoon pepper
¼ teaspoon Worcestershire
  sauce

Cut ham slices in halves crosswise. Place in a flat pan. Combine remaining ingredients and pour over ham. Let stand at room temperature 2 hours, turning frequently. Remove ham steaks from marinade. Place on broiler rack in preheated oven about 4 inches from heat. Broil about 5 minutes on each side; brush frequently with marinade. Serves 6 to 8.

❧ Stuffed Ham Slices

1 cup peeled, cored, and
  chopped apples
¼ cup orange marmalade
¼ teaspoon salt
2 cups corn flakes
3 tablespoons melted butter
  or margarine
2 center-cut fully-cooked
  ham slices, cut ½ inch
  thick

Heat oven to 350° F. Mix together apples, marmalade, and salt. Toss together corn flakes and butter; stir in apple mixture. Place one of the ham slices in a shallow baking dish; spoon half the crumb mixture over ham. Top with the second ham slice and the remaining crumb mixture. Bake 45 minutes, or until crumbs are lightly browned. Serves 6.

❧ Honey-Broiled Ham Steak with Sweet Potatoes

1 center-cut slice of
  fully-cooked ham, 1 inch
  thick (about 1½ pounds)
1 16-ounce can sweet
  potatoes, drained
½ cup apricot nectar
¼ cup honey
½ teaspoon grated lemon peel
2 tablespoons lemon juice
⅛ teaspoon ground
  cinnamon

Slash edges of ham steak at 1-inch intervals to prevent curling. Place ham on rack of broiler pan and arrange sweet potatoes around it. Combine remaining ingredients and brush on ham and sweet potatoes. Broil 4 inches from source of heat a total of 15 to 20 minutes; turn ham once during broiling. Brush ham and potatoes frequently with the honey sauce. Serves 4.

Ground Ham

Ground ham may be purchased from the market; you may have to order it specially; or you may grind it at home. The recipes that follow are an especially good way to use leftovers from a baked ham.

◅§ Orange-Glazed Ham Loaf

1½ pounds finely ground
    cooked ham
1½ cups fresh bread crumbs
    (about 3 slices)
¾ cup buttermilk
1 egg, slightly beaten
1½ tablespoons prepared
    horseradish
¼ cup orange marmalade

Heat oven to 350° F. Place ground ham, bread crumbs, buttermilk, beaten egg, and horseradish in a bowl. Toss gently with a fork to combine. Shape ham mixture into a round loaf about 8 inches in diameter; place on an ovenproof platter or small shallow roasting pan. Bake 1¼ hours. Spread orange marmalade over top of loaf. Preheat broiler. Place ham loaf about 4 inches below the source of heat. Broil about 3 to 5 minutes, or until topping bubbles. Serves 6.

◅§ Glazed Ham Balls

1½ pounds lean ground pork
1 pound ground ham
2 cups soft bread crumbs
1 teaspoon salt
1 cup milk
1 20-ounce can pineapple
    chunks
1 cup firmly packed dark
    brown sugar
½ cup cider vinegar
1 teaspoon dry mustard
4 to 5 cups cooked rice

Heat oven to 350° F. Have butcher grind the pork and ham together. Mix meat, bread crumbs, salt, and milk; shape level tablespoonfuls of the mixture into balls. Arrange balls in a single layer in a large baking pan. Bake uncovered 30 minutes. While meat is baking, drain pineapple and reserve ½ cup juice. Place juice, brown sugar, vinegar, and mustard in a saucepan; heat to boiling over moderate heat (about 250° F.). Remove ham balls to a 3-quart casserole, discarding fat. Pour pineapple juice mixture over balls. Bake uncovered 30 minutes, stirring occasionally. Add pineapple chunks and bake 15 minutes longer. Serve with rice. Serves 8 to 10.

◅§ Ham Balls with Sour-Cream–Mustard Sauce

4 cups ground cooked ham
    (about 2 pounds)
1 cup fine dry bread crumbs
2 eggs, well beaten
2 teaspoons dry mustard

In a large bowl combine ham, bread crumbs, eggs, mustard, and pepper and blend well. With your hands shape mixture into 1½-inch balls. In a skillet over moderate heat (about 250° F.) melt the 4 tablespoons butter and add ham balls. Cook about 10 minutes, or

⅛ teaspoon pepper
4 tablespoons butter or
  margarine
2 tablespoons butter or
  margarine
3 tablespoons flour
1½ cups canned chicken
  broth
1 cup commercial sour
  cream
3 teaspoons dry mustard
2 tablespoons chopped fresh
  parsley
4 to 5 cups cooked rice

until balls are brown on all sides. Remove from heat. In a saucepan over moderately low heat (about 225° F.) melt the 2 tablespoons of butter, stir in flour, and cook until bubbly. Gradually pour in chicken broth, stirring constantly with a wire whip. Boil 1 minute. Add sour cream, mustard, and 1 tablespoon parsley; blend well. Pour sauce over ham balls and mix gently. Transfer balls to a chafing dish and sprinkle the remaining 1 tablespoon parsley over top. Serve over cooked rice. Makes about 3 dozen. Serves 8 to 10.

Bacon

Most bacon is prepackaged in slices and sold by the pound or half pound. Some is sold in cans or jars. These vary in flavor, thickness of slices, and proportion of lean to fat. Slab bacon comes in one piece—slice it yourself or have the butcher slice to the thickness you prefer. Sliced bacon may be cooked in a variety of ways.

To pan-fry: Place desired number of bacon slices in an unheated skillet over moderate heat (about 250° F.). As bacon heats, separate slices. Increase temperature to moderately high (about 325° F.). Cook, turning frequently, until golden and brown. Do not pour off fat during cooking. Drain slices on soft paper.

To broil: Arrange separated bacon slices on broiler rack. Broil four to five minutes, three inches from heat. Turn once.

To bake: Arrange separated bacon slices on wire rack set in pan. Bake in hot oven (400° F.) for ten minutes without turning.

Canadian bacon is a smoked, boneless strip of pork loin, much leaner than bacon. It is sold in one piece, in a roll, or sliced. Much of it is prepackaged, sliced. Some is also sold whole, canned.

✑ *Piquant Glazed Canadian Bacon*

1 3-pound fully cooked
  canned Canadian bacon
½ cup red currant jelly

Place bacon on a rack in a roasting pan. In a small bowl combine jelly, mustard, and horseradish; blend well. Brush bacon well with the glaze. Heat oven to 325° F.

½ teaspoon dry mustard
1 tablespoon prepared
   horseradish

Roast bacon 60 minutes, or until heated through, basting frequently with glaze. Cut into thin slices and serve warm. Serves 12.

Roast Lamb

Lamb is the meat of a young sheep. It is tender, flavorful, and usually quite lean; consequently, the shoulder and leg cuts as well as the rib, loin, and sirloin cuts (see page 276) lend themselves to the dry-heat methods of cooking.

These are the kinds of lamb roasts you might find in your market:

Leg of lamb: The whole leg of lamb includes the sirloin, leg, and shank. You can have it cut into two roasts, the sirloin roast and the short leg (round) roast; often called half legs, they weigh two to three pounds each. If you buy a whole leg you may want to have the shank removed and a few steaks or chops cut from the sirloin end to freeze for later use. Legs may also be boned and rolled to make a compact roast, or boned and butterflied for broiling or barbecuing.

Shoulder roast: The bone-in shoulder is difficult to carve. It's best to buy a boned, rolled shoulder or a cushion roast, which has a pocket for stuffing.

Crown roast: This is made by tying rib pieces, usually fourteen ribs, together in a circle with the rib bones up. The tips of the bones are often Frenched (meat removed). They may be garnished with fruit or paper frills after cooking.

≈§ Herbed Roast Leg of Lamb

1 3¼-pound partially
   boned leg of lamb
Garlic powder
1 teaspoon crumbled dried
   rosemary leaves
1 teaspoon salt
¼ teaspoon pepper
1 teaspoon crumbled dried
   rosemary leaves
⅓ cup olive oil
2 tablespoons lemon juice
½ teaspoon salt

Heat oven to 325° F. Make 4 slits ½ inch wide and 2 inches deep in top of roast. Fill each slit with a pinch of garlic powder. Mix the 1 teaspoon rosemary leaves, the 1 teaspoon salt, and the ¼ teaspoon pepper; rub over surface of meat. Combine the remaining 1 teaspoon rosemary, olive oil, lemon juice, the ½ teaspoon salt, and the ¼ teaspoon pepper in saucepan. Heat 5 minutes over low heat (about 200° F.). Place lamb, skin side up, on a rack in a shallow roasting pan. If a meat thermometer is available, insert it in the center of the thickest part. Pour a little of the olive oil mixture over roast. Roast, basting occasionally with olive oil mixture,

¼ *teaspoon pepper*
1½ *cups water*
3 *tablespoons flour*
1 *tablespoon chopped fresh parsley*

until thermometer reaches 175° F. for medium done and 180° F. for well done, or 35 minutes per pound for medium done and 40 minutes per pound for well done.* Remove meat to a warm platter. Pour the 1½ cups water into pan and place over moderately low heat (about 225° F.), stirring constantly, to loosen any brown particles. Pour drippings into a 2-cup measuring cup and skim off all the fat and reserve 3 tablespoons. Spoon the 3 tablespoons fat back into roasting pan; blend in flour. Cook and stir until bubbly. Gradually add meat drippings; there should be about 1½ cups. Cook and stir until thickened and smooth. Stir in chopped parsley. Serve with lamb. Serves 4, with leftovers.

Note: If you like lamb pink or rare, roast it 18 to 20 minutes per pound.

❧ Crown Roast of Lamb

½ *cup butter or margarine*
½ *cup finely chopped onion*
½ *pound mushrooms, sliced*
¼ *cup chopped fresh parsley*
¼ *teaspoon ground rosemary*
1½ *teaspoons salt*
½ *teaspoon pepper*
1½ *pounds ground lamb*
2 *cups crumbled corn bread (made from a mix)*
1 *4- to 5-pound shaped and tied crown roast of lamb*

Heat oven to 325° F. Melt butter in a large skillet over moderately low heat (about 225° F.). Add onion; cook until tender. Add mushrooms, parsley, rosemary, salt, and pepper. Cook until mushrooms are soft. Remove vegetables and add ground lamb. Cook over moderate heat (about 250° F.), stirring frequently. Pour off excess fat. Combine mushroom mixture, lamb, and corn bread crumbs. Toss together lightly. Place roast on a rack in a shallow roasting pan. Spoon stuffing into center. Roast about 2½ to 3¾ hours, allowing 40 to 45 minutes per pound, or until meat thermometer inserted between 2 ribs in thickest part of meat registers 175° F. to 180° F. Remove to heated platter. Serves 8 to 10.

❧ Grilled Butterfly Leg of Lamb

1 *6- to 7-pound leg of lamb*
2 *cups dry vermouth*
½ *cup vegetable oil*
2 *tablespoons tarragon vinegar*
⅓ *cup finely chopped onion*
1 *tablespoon finely chopped fresh parsley*
1 *teaspoon dried basil leaves*
1 *teaspoon garlic powder*
1 *bay leaf, crumbled*

Have butcher butterfly the leg of lamb (the bones are removed and the meat is split lengthwise part-way through, then spread flat like a thick steak). Combine vermouth, oil, vinegar, onion, parsley, basil, garlic powder, bay leaf, pepper, and Worcestershire sauce. Pour into a large shallow dish or roasting pan. Add meat to marinade. Cover and refrigerate about 2 days, turning meat occasionally. Remove meat from marinade and place on grill over medium-hot coals. Reserve marinade. Cook about 50 minutes, turning every 10 to 15 minutes. Brush occasionally with marinade. Cut

½ teaspoon pepper
½ teaspoon Worcestershire
  sauce
1 lemon, thinly sliced

crosswise into thin slices to serve. Garnish with lemon slices. Serves 10.

ᕅᔢ Marinated Roast Lamb

1 tablespoon olive oil
1½ teaspoons lemon juice
1 medium-sized onion,
  finely chopped
¼ cup chopped fresh parsley
1 teaspoon salt
½ teaspoon pepper
1 teaspoon dried marjoram
  leaves
1 teaspoon dried thyme
  leaves
1 clove garlic, finely
  chopped
1 4-pound square-cut lamb
  shoulder

Combine all ingredients except lamb. Cut shallow slits in lamb; rub oil mixture into meat. Wrap in aluminum foil; place in refrigerator for 12 to 24 hours. Heat oven to 325° F. Remove foil and place roast on rack in a shallow roasting pan. Roast about 2 to 2½ hours, allowing 30 to 35 minutes per pound, basting occasionally with pan juices, until meat thermometer inserted in center of roast registers 175° F. to 180° F. Serves 6.

Lamb Chops or Steaks

These succulent cuts of lamb are relatively expensive meat. The loin and shoulder chops are usually less expensive than the rib chops and usually have more meat on them.

ᕅᔢ Lamb Chops with Herb Butter

8 rib lamb chops, cut 1 inch
  thick
¼ cup butter or margarine
1 tablespoon lemon juice
⅛ teaspoon ground marjoram

Place chops on a broiler rack in a preheated broiler 3 inches from heat. Broil 6 minutes on each side, or until cooked to the desired degree of doneness. While chops are cooking, heat butter, lemon juice, and marjoram just until butter is melted. Serve butter sauce over chops. Serves 4, 2 rib chops per person.

[331]

❧ Baked Lamb-Leg Chops

4 lamb-leg chops, cut ½ inch
   thick (about 1½ pounds)
1 clove garlic, cut in half
Salt and pepper
3 tablespoons butter or
   margarine
2 medium-sized tomatoes,
   sliced
1 cup sliced fresh mushrooms
¼ cup dry sherry
¾ cup finely chopped onion
1 cup chopped green pepper
½ teaspoon dried basil leaves
2 teaspoons paprika
¾ teaspoon salt
Few grains pepper

Heat oven to 325° F. Rub chops with garlic clove and sprinkle with salt and pepper. Melt butter in skillet over moderate heat (about 250° F.); brown chops. Place in a single layer in a shallow 1½-quart casserole. Arrange tomato slices over chops. Mix mushrooms, sherry, onion, green pepper, basil, paprika, the ¾ teaspoon salt, and the pepper; spoon over tomato slices. Cover and bake 20 minutes; remove cover and bake 20 to 30 minutes longer, until fork-tender. Serves 4.

❧ Braised Shoulder Lamb Chops

¼ cup vegetable oil
½ cup sliced onion
6 shoulder lamb chops,
   ¾-inch thick
¾ cup hot water
1 envelope instant vegetable
   broth mix
¼ teaspoon dried marjoram
   leaves
Few grains pepper
1 can condensed golden
   mushroom soup, undiluted

Heat oil in a large skillet over moderate heat (about 250° F.); add onion and cook until lightly browned. Remove with a slotted spoon. Add chops and brown well on both sides over moderately high heat (about 300° F.). Remove chops and drain off any excess fat. Return skillet to heat and reduce to low (about 200° F.); stir in hot water, broth mix, marjoram, and pepper. Stir to loosen browned bits on the bottom of the skillet. Return chops and onion to the skillet with the mushroom soup. Cover and simmer 50 minutes, or until chops are fork-tender. Remove cover and simmer 10 minutes longer. Serves 6.

❧ English Grill

8 link sausages
4 lamb kidneys
4 loin lamb chops, 1 inch
   thick
⅓ cup melted butter or
   margarine
Salt and pepper

Cover sausage with boiling water and simmer over low heat (about 200° F.) 5 minutes. Drain. Cut lamb kidneys in halves lengthwise, wash well, and remove fat and white veins with scissors. Dry on paper towels. Arrange kidneys on broiler rack with lamb chops; brush kidneys with melted butter and sprinkle both with salt and pepper. Place in preheated broiler 3 inches from heat.

2 *medium-sized tomatoes, cut*
  into halves
8 *large mushroom caps*
Ground dillseed
2 *bananas*
2 *tablespoons dark brown*
  sugar
1 *tablespoon lemon juice*
2 *tablespoons chopped*
  fresh parsley

Broil 8 minutes; turn chops and kidneys and brush kidneys with butter. Arrange sausages, tomato halves, and mushrooms (rounded side up) on rack. Brush vegetables with butter; sprinkle with salt, pepper, and dill. Broil 3 minutes. Peel bananas and cut in half lengthwise and then in half crosswise. Arrange bananas on rack, brush with butter, and sprinkle with brown sugar and lemon juice. Turn mushrooms and brush with butter. Continue to broil 4 minutes, or until chops are cooked to the desired degree of doneness. Before serving, sprinkle mushroom caps with chopped parsley. Serves 4.

⊰ Spicy Lamb Steaks

2 *tablespoons vegetable oil*
1 *tablespoon vinegar*
2 *teaspoons Worcestershire*
  sauce
1 *clove garlic, crushed*
1 *teaspoon salt*
¼ *teaspoon pepper*
½ *teaspoon celery seed*
2 *lamb steaks, cut 1 inch*
  thick

Combine all ingredients except lamb in a large bowl. Add lamb steaks. Cover and refrigerate at least 3 hours; turn steaks occasionally. Preheat broiler. Arrange well-drained steaks on broiler rack. Broil 4 inches from heat 6 minutes on each side for medium, 7 minutes for well done. Serves 2 to 3.

⊰ Shish Kabob

1½ *cups vegetable oil or olive*
  oil
⅓ *cup wine vinegar*
⅓ *cup lemon juice*
1 *clove garlic, minced*
1 *cup chopped onion*
¼ *cup chopped fresh parsley*
2 *teaspoons salt*
1 *teaspoon pepper*
1½ *teaspoons dried oregano*
  leaves
½ *teaspoon ground thyme*
*5 *to 7 pounds leg of lamb,*
  boned and cut into
  1½-inch cubes
(Ingredients continued on page 334)

Combine oil, vinegar, lemon juice, garlic, onion, parsley, salt, pepper, oregano, and thyme in a large bowl. Add meat cubes and stir to coat thoroughly. Cover and let stand in the refrigerator overnight. Drain meat thoroughly. Arrange a mushroom cap, a square of green pepper, and a tomato alternately with 4 cubes of meat on each 6-inch skewer. Place skewers on broiler rack and place in a preheated broiler 3 to 4 inches from heat. Broil 8 to 10 minutes on one side; turn and broil on other side about 5 minutes. Serves 8 to 10.

Note: 4 pounds cubed beef round steak may be substituted for the lamb in recipe above.

16 *small mushroom caps*
 1 *large green pepper cut*
   into 1-inch pieces
16 *very small tomatoes or*
   cherry tomatoes

Lamb Shanks

The meat on the lamb shank is particularly sweet and often a good buy. One shank makes one generous serving. Shanks need some moisture added to prevent drying during cooking.

◄§ Braised Lamb Shanks

4 *lamb shanks (about ¾ to 1 pound each)*
2 *tablespoons flour*
¼ *cup vegetable oil*
½ *cup sliced onion*
½ *cup water*
1 *can condensed cream of celery soup, undiluted*
½ *cup dry sherry*
½ *teaspoon salt*
⅛ *teaspoon pepper*
Dash of ground allspice
2 *cups hot cooked rice*

Coat lamb with flour. In a wide saucepot or Dutch oven heat oil and cook onion over moderately low heat (about 225° F.) until lightly browned. Remove with a slotted spoon. Add lamb shanks and brown on all sides over moderately high heat (about 300° F.). Remove pot from heat and remove lamb shanks. Drain off any excess fat. Stir in water and loosen any browned bits from bottom of pot. Stir in celery soup, sherry, salt, pepper, and allspice. Add lamb shanks and cooked onion. Return to heat and bring to a boil. Reduce heat to low (about 200° F.); cover and simmer 1½ to 2 hours, or until lamb is fork-tender, stirring occasionally. Serve with rice. Serves 4.

◄§ Lamb Shanks de Luxe

4 *lamb shanks (about ¾ to 1 pound each)*
½ *lemon*
¼ *teaspoon garlic powder*
1 *cup all-purpose flour*
2 *teaspoons salt*
½ *teaspoon pepper*
½ *cup vegetable oil*
1 *can condensed beef consommé, undiluted*

Rub lamb shanks with lemon and sprinkle with garlic powder. Combine flour, salt, and pepper in a paper or plastic bag and shake shanks, one at a time, until well coated with flour. Reserve flour mixture. Heat oil in a large, heavy skillet over moderately high heat (about 300° F.); add shanks and cook until lightly browned on all sides. turning occasionally. Remove shanks and place in a single layer in a shallow 3-quart baking dish. Add 4 tablespoons of the reserved flour mixture to drippings in skillet; blend well with a wire whip; cook and stir over

1 cup water
½ cup dry vermouth
1 medium-sized onion,
   chopped
4 medium-sized carrots,
   peeled and sliced into
   2-inch pieces
4 stalks celery, cut into
   2-inch pieces
Mashed potatoes (optional)
Noodles (optional)

moderate heat (about 250° F.) until flour is lightly browned. Add consommé, water, and vermouth; cook until thickened, stirring constantly. Add onion to the sauce; pour over lamb shanks. Heat oven to 350° F. Bake shanks, uncovered, 1½ hours. Turn shanks, add carrots and celery; bake 1 hour longer, or until meat is fork-tender. If desired, serve the gravy over mashed potatoes or noodles. Serves 4.

Breast of Lamb

Breast of lamb, like lamb shank, is often a good buy because it is not in great demand. Many people do not know how good the sweet meat is. Breast of lamb is sold in a sheet or cut into riblets.

✑ Baked Breast of Lamb with Pears

2 pounds breast of lamb,
   bone-in
1 17-ounce can pear halves
1 teaspoon whole cloves
¼ cup honey
¼ cup lemon juice
1 teaspoon salt
Fresh parsley

Heat oven to 325° F. Place lamb breasts on rack in a shallow roasting pan. Roast 1 hour and 45 minutes. Drain off excess fat. Drain pears; reserve ¼ cup of the syrup. Stud pears with cloves and arrange around lamb. Combine pear syrup, honey, lemon juice, and salt; pour over lamb and pears. Roast 15 minutes longer. Remove to heated platter and garnish with parsley. Serves 4.

✑ Lamb Riblets with Orange Sauce

3 pounds lamb riblets, cut
   into 2-rib portions
Salt and pepper
2 oranges, sliced and halved
2 medium-sized onions, sliced
1 tablespoon cornstarch
2 tablespoons sugar
Dash of ground allspice
1 cup orange juice
2 tablespoons lemon juice

Heat oven to 400° F. Arrange lamb riblets on a rack in a shallow baking pan; sprinkle with salt and pepper. Bake about 45 minutes, until lightly browned. Pour off fat and remove rack. Reduce oven temperature to 350° F. Arrange lamb riblets in bottom of pan and place orange and onion slices between and on top of lamb pieces, reserving a few orange slices for garnish. Bake about 1½ hours, or until lamb is fork-tender. Combine cornstarch, sugar, and allspice in a saucepan. Gradually stir in orange and lemon juices. Cook over moderate heat (about 250° F.) until thickened and clear, stirring constantly. Remove from heat. At serving time, arrange lamb riblets on a platter. Discard cooked onion and orange slices. Heat orange sauce and pour over lamb. Garnish with reserved orange slices. Serves 6.

☙ Barbecued Lamb Spareribs

6 lamb spareribs (about 4½ pounds)
Garlic salt
½ cup apricot nectar
¼ cup peach preserves, sieved
1 tablespoon lemon juice
¼ teaspoon salt
¼ teaspoon ground ginger
2 tablespoons vegetable oil

Sprinkle lamb with garlic salt to taste. Mix together remaining ingredients. Place spareribs on a rack in a broiler pan; brush with some of the fruit sauce. Broil or grill spareribs 6 to 7 inches from source of heat 15 to 20 minutes on each side, or until fork-tender, brushing frequently with the fruit sauce. Serves 6.

Ground and Cubed Lamb

Ground lamb is often marketed in ready-formed lamb patties or you may purchase it in bulk. Cubed lamb, unless you have it cut to order, may be labeled lamb-for-stew.

☙ Spring Lamb Stew

2 pounds boneless lamb shoulder, cubed
4 cups water
2½ teaspoons salt
¼ teaspoon pepper
1 small bay leaf
4 medium-sized carrots, peeled and cut in ½-inch slices
2 medium onions, sliced
4 medium-sized potatoes, peeled and halved
⅓ cup all-purpose flour
¼ cup cold water
1 cup fresh or frozen peas, cooked

Place lamb in a deep saucepan and add water, salt, pepper, and bay leaf. Bring to a boil over moderate heat (about 250° F.) and cook uncovered for 5 minutes. Skim foam from top as it forms. Add carrots and onions; cover and cook over moderately low heat (about 225° F.) 45 minutes, or until lamb is fork-tender. Add potatoes and continue to cook about 30 minutes longer until lamb and potatoes are fork-tender. Remove bay leaf. Combine flour and water and stir to a smooth paste. Add about ½ cup of the hot stew liquid to the flour-water mixture and blend thoroughly. Gradually add the flour mixture to the boiling stew, stirring constantly until smooth and thickened. Simmer, uncovered, 4 to 5 minutes. Just before serving add peas. Serves 6 to 8.

Barbecued Lamb Patties

1½ pounds ground lean lamb
½ cup chopped fresh parsley
½ cup chopped onion
¼ cup prepared mustard
¼ cup catsup
¼ cup chili sauce
2 tablespoons vinegar
½ teaspoon garlic salt
1 teaspoon sugar

Combine lamb, parsley and onion; mix well. Shape into 6 patties. Combine remaining ingredients; mix well. Brush half of mustard mixture over patties. Cook on grill 8 to 10 minutes. Turn and top with remaining mustard mixture. Cook 5 to 7 minutes longer. Serves 6.

Lamb and Kidney Kabobs

¼ cup olive oil
¼ cup dry sherry
½ teaspoon salt
¼ teaspoon dried oregano leaves
¼ teaspoon dried thyme leaves
6 lamb kidneys, cut into quarters
1 pound boneless lamb, cut into 1-inch cubes
12 slices raw bacon, cut into thirds

Combine oil, sherry, salt, oregano, and thyme in a small bowl. Marinate kidney pieces in oil mixture at least 1 hour. Preheat broiler. On long skewers alternate kidney pieces and lamb cubes, separating each piece with bacon. Place skewers 3 inches from heat; broil until lightly browned on all sides, about 12 to 15 minutes. Turn skewers frequently and baste with marinade. Serves 4.

Lamb Curry

1½ pounds lean lamb shoulder, cut into 1-inch cubes
1 teaspoon salt
Few grains pepper
⅛ teaspoon cumin seed
1 bay leaf
1½ cups water
¼ cup butter or margarine
1 small onion, sliced
¼ cup flour
2 teaspoons curry powder
¼ teaspoon ground turmeric
2 cups milk

Combine lamb, ½ teaspoon of the salt, pepper, cumin seed, bay leaf and water in a large saucepan. Place over moderate heat (about 250° F.) and bring to a boil. Reduce heat to low (about 200° F.); cover and simmer 1½ hours, or until lamb is fork-tender. Remove lamb and strain liquid; skim off fat. There should be ½ cup liquid left. If there is more, place over moderate heat and boil until reduced to ½ cup; set aside. In a saucepan over moderately low heat (about 225° F.) melt butter and cook onion until crisp-tender. Quickly stir in flour, the remaining ½ teaspoon salt, curry powder, and turmeric. Remove from heat and gradually stir in milk and the ½ cup stock. Return to heat; bring to a boil and boil 1 minute, stirring constantly. Add apple, raisins, and

½ cup peeled shredded tart
  apple
¼ cup golden raisins
1½ to 2 cups hot cooked rice
Fresh parsley

cooked lamb. Heat to serving temperature, stirring occasionally. Serve over cooked rice. Garnish with parsley. Serves 3 to 4.

✌ Lamb with Lemon Sauce

1 teaspoon salt
⅛ teaspoon pepper
¼ teaspoon garlic powder
3 pounds lean boneless lamb
  shoulder, cut into 1½-inch
  cubes
3 tablespoons vegetable oil
2 tablespoons butter or
  margarine
1 large onion, finely chopped
2 tablespoons flour
½ cup water
½ cup dry white wine
2 tablespoons chopped fresh
  dill
2 tablespoons chopped fresh
  parsley
½ teaspoon salt
3 stalks celery with leaves
3 small zucchini, sliced
4 egg yolks
6 tablespoons lemon juice

Combine the 1 teaspoon salt, the pepper, and the garlic powder in a small bowl. Add lamb cubes a few at a time and turn to coat pieces well. Heat oil in a Dutch oven over moderately high heat (about 275° F.). Add lamb cubes and brown meat on all sides. Remove meat with a slotted spoon as it browns. Add butter to Dutch oven and reduce heat to moderately low (about 225° F.). Add onion and cook until tender. Add flour and stir to blend well. Pour in water and wine and cook, stirring constantly, until thickened and smooth. Return meat to Dutch oven. Add dill, parsley, and the ½ teaspoon salt; cover and simmer 1 hour. Cut celery diagonally into 2-inch slices. Chop celery leaves. Add zucchini, celery, and leaves to Dutch oven. Cover and simmer 10 minutes. In a small bowl beat egg yolks until thick. Beat in lemon juice, 1 tablespoon at a time. Gradually pour 1 cup of the hot liquid from lamb mixture into the egg yolk mixture while beating vigorously. Slowly pour egg yolk mixture back into Dutch oven, stirring constantly, until mixture is smooth and thickened. Do not let mixture come to a boil. Serves 6 to 8.

Roast Veal

Veal is the meat of a very young calf. It is pale pink in color and tastes much more like chicken than like beef. Because veal has very little exterior fat and no marbling, it is better roasted, braised, or stewed rather than broiled. It is a delicate meat and, usually, an expensive one.

The loin or rib roast is a delicate roast, though not often available since it is usually cut into chops.

Leg roast has only one small bone and carves well. It may be purchased whole but is often cut into steaks and cutlets.

Rump roast is easier to carve if it has been boned and rolled.

Shoulder roast is also easier to carve if it has been boned and rolled.

ᔏ Roast Leg or Loin of Veal

1 5- to 8-pound leg of veal or
1 4- to 6-pound loin of
veal
Salt and pepper
Raw bacon, salt pork, or
vegetable oil

Heat oven to 325° F. Sprinkle salt and pepper over meat and place on a rack in a shallow roasting pan. Insert a meat thermometer into the thickest muscle of the roast. Arrange bacon slices or slices of salt pork over fat or brush with vegetable oil. Roast uncovered, allowing 30 to 35 minutes per pound, or until the internal temperature reaches 180° F. Leg of veal serves 7 to 10. Loin of veal serves 5 to 8.

Breast of Veal

Breast of veal may also be boned and used for roasting; it is particularly nice stuffed and rolled.

ᔏ Stuffed Rolled Breast of Veal

1 2½-pound boned breast of
veal (about 5 pounds
before boning)
2 tablespoons butter or
margarine
¼ cup finely chopped onion
¼ cup chopped mushrooms
1 10-ounce package frozen
chopped spinach, cooked
according to package
directions and drained
2 cups soft bread crumbs
1 egg, slightly beaten
⅛ teaspoon ground savory
½ teaspoon salt
Salt and pepper
1 medium-sized carrot,
peeled and quartered
1 medium-sized onion,
quartered
½ cup dry white wine
2 tablespoons flour
½ teaspoon salt

Have butcher bone breast for stuffing and reserve the bones. Melt butter in skillet over moderately low heat (about 225° F.); cook onion and mushrooms until tender. Mix together the cooked vegetables, thoroughly drained spinach, bread crumbs, egg, savory, and the ½ teaspoon salt. Spread dressing over veal and roll up, starting at the wide side. Tie with string at 1½-inch intervals. Place veal in a large shallow roasting pan. Sprinkle with salt and pepper. Arrange carrot, onion, and bones in pan around meat. Add wine and ½ cup water. Heat oven to 300° F. Roast meat uncovered, allowing 40 to 45 minutes per pound. Remove meat to warm platter. Discard bones. Reserve vegetables for gravy. Pour 1 cup water into roasting pan and stir over moderately low heat (about 225° F.) to loosen meat drippings. Pour into a 2-cup measuring cup and skim off fat; pour back into roasting pan. Pour ⅓ cup water into a jar or gravy maker; add flour and shake until blended. Gradually add to meat juices. Add the ½ teaspoon salt and cook over low heat (about 200° F.), stirring constantly, until thickened. Add reserved vegetables and heat. Serve with veal. Serves 6.

✑ *Barbecued Breast of Veal*

6 *pounds veal riblets*
2 *tablespoons salt*
Boiling water
1 *cup catsup*
1 *cup water*
¼ *cup vinegar*
¼ *cup firmly packed light
    brown sugar*
1½ *teaspoons Worcestershire
    sauce*
1 *teaspoon chili powder*
½ *teaspoon dry mustard*
½ *teaspoon salt*

Have butcher cut riblets into rib portions and then cut each rib in half crosswise to make 3- or 4-inch-long pieces. Place in a large pot or Dutch oven. Sprinkle with the 2 tablespoons salt; add boiling water to cover. Place over moderately low heat (about 225° F.) and cook 2 hours, or until tender. Drain. While riblets are cooking, mix catsup, the 1 cup water, vinegar, light brown sugar, Worcestershire, chili powder, mustard, and the ½ teaspoon salt in a saucepan. Place over moderately low heat (about 225° F.) and heat 10 minutes. Line a broiler pan with aluminum foil. Place veal riblets in a single layer on the broiler rack. Brush riblets with some of the glaze. Place pan in a preheated broiler about 4 inches from the heat. Broil 10 to 15 minutes, turning occasionally and brushing with more of the glaze, until riblets are lightly browned. Arrange riblets on a heated platter and pour any remaining glaze over them. Serves 8.

✑ *Veal Riblets and Noodles*

⅓ *cup flour*
1¼ *teaspoons paprika*
1½ *teaspoons salt*
⅛ *teaspoon pepper*
2 *to 2½ pounds veal riblets,
    cut into rib portions*
3 *tablespoons vegetable oil*
1 *can condensed cream of
    mushroom soup*
¾ *cup milk*
1 *clove garlic, finely
    chopped*
1 *cup thinly sliced onion*
½ *teaspoon salt*
2 *tablespoons chili sauce*
8 *ounces noodles, cooked*

Place flour, paprika, the 1½ teaspoons salt, and the pepper in a plastic or paper bag. Shake riblets, a few pieces at a time, in bag until coated with flour mixture. Heat oil in Dutch oven or a heavy saucepan over moderately high heat (about 300° F.); add riblets and cook until browned. Combine soup, milk, garlic, onion, and the ½ teaspoon salt; pour over riblets. Cover and cook over low heat (about 200° F.) 2 hours, or until fork-tender, stirring constantly. Skim off fat and stir in chili sauce. Serve over hot cooked noodles. Serves 4.

Veal Chops, Steaks, and Cutlets

Veal cutlets, when cut very thin and pounded flat, are often called veal for scaloppine. Do not broil these cutlets unless they have been well marinated. The meat is dry and broiling makes it drier.

✌ Veal Parmigiana

1 pound thin veal cutlets
(about 6 cutlets)
1 egg, slightly beaten
¾ cup seasoned fine dry bread
crumbs
¼ cup butter or margarine
1 14- to 16-ounce jar
meatless spaghetti sauce
1 8-ounce package
mozzarella cheese, sliced
Grated Parmesan cheese

Heat oven to 350° F. Dip veal cutlets first in egg and then coat well with bread crumbs. Heat butter in a skillet over moderately low heat (about 225° F.); add veal and increase temperature to moderately high (about 325° F.); cook veal until well browned on both sides. Pour a layer of spaghetti sauce into the bottom of a shallow, rectangular, 2-quart baking dish. Arrange veal in a single layer over sauce. Arrange the sliced mozzarella cheese over veal and pour the remaining sauce over the cheese. Sprinkle generously with Parmesan cheese and bake 30 minutes. Serves 3 to 4.

✌ Lemon-Braised Veal Steak

1 tablespoon butter or
margarine
1 veal bone-in round steak
(about 2 pounds)
1 clove garlic, pressed
¼ to ½ teaspoon salt
¼ teaspoon dried basil leaves
⅛ teaspoon pepper
½ teaspoon grated lemon peel
2 tablespoons lemon juice
1 envelope instant beef broth
mix
¾ cup water

Melt butter in a skillet over moderately high heat (about 275° F.) and brown veal steak on both sides. Add remaining ingredients and simmer, covered, over moderately low heat (about 225° F.) 45 minutes. Uncover and cook 5 minutes longer, or until fork-tender. Serves 4 to 6.

✌ Veal Scaloppine

Vegetable oil
1½ pounds veal for
scaloppine
1 cup water
1 cup dry white wine
1 clove garlic, crushed
¼ teaspoon crushed dried
rosemary leaves
½ teaspoon salt
Few grains pepper
½ pound mushrooms, thinly
sliced
2 tablespoons finely
chopped fresh parsley

Place a large skillet over moderately high heat (about 325° F.). Brush pan lightly with oil; add veal pieces and brown quickly on both sides. Remove from heat. Remove meat from skillet; add the water and stir over moderate heat (about 250° F.) to loosen browned particles. Add wine, garlic, rosemary, salt, and pepper; mix together. Return meat to skillet; sprinkle with mushrooms. Cover and cook over moderately low heat (about 225° F.) for 20 minutes, or until veal is tender. Skim off any fat from surface of sauce. Serve garnished with chopped parsley. Serves 6.

MEATS

～ Veal Birds with Wine Sauce

3 tablespoons butter or
   margarine
2 tablespoons finely chopped
   onion
¼ cup chopped green pepper
½ teaspoon ground poultry
   seasoning
½ teaspoon salt
Few grains pepper
 2 cups cubed day-old white
   bread
1½ pounds veal steak, cut
   ½ inch thick
Salt and pepper
 2 tablespoons vegetable oil
⅓ cup water
½ cup dry white wine

Melt butter in skillet over moderately low heat (about 225° F.); add onion and green pepper and cook until tender. Stir in poultry seasoning, the ½ teaspoon salt, and the pepper; mix with bread cubes. Cut meat into 8 portions and pound each with a mallet until doubled in size. Divide stuffing among the portions of meat; roll up meat and stuffing and secure with a toothpick or tie with string. Sprinkle with salt and pepper. Heat oven to 325° F. Heat oil in skillet over moderately high heat (about 325° F.); brown meat rolls on all sides. Place rolls in a shallow 1½-quart casserole. Add water to skillet and heat to loosen meat drippings; stir in wine. Pour wine mixture over meat; cover and bake 1 hour, basting occasionally. Serves 4 to 6.

～ Veal Piccata

Salt
1½ pounds veal cutlet,
   pounded very thin and cut
   into 12 pieces
Flour
 4 tablespoons butter or
   margarine
¼ cup lemon juice
¼ cup dry white wine
 2 tablespoons finely
   chopped fresh parsley
Lemon slices (optional)
Chopped parsley (optional)

Sprinkle salt lightly on both sides of the veal. Coat veal pieces with flour and shake off any excess. Melt 2 table-spoons of the butter in a large skillet over moderately high heat (about 350° F.). Add veal pieces and brown about 4 minutes on each side. Add the remaining 2 ta-blespoons butter as needed during browning. Reduce heat to moderately low (about 225° F.); add lemon juice, wine, and parsley. Cook for about 8 minutes. If desired, garnish each serving with a lemon slice and additional chopped parsley. Serves 4 to 6.

～ Stuffed Veal Rolls

6 slices boiled ham, cut
   about ⅛ inch thick
1 8-ounce package
   mozzarella cheese

Cut ham slices in half. Slice cheese into 3 equal slices and then cut each slice into four sticks. On each slice of veal place a slice of ham and a stick of cheese. Roll up meats and cheese and tie rolls at both ends with string or heavy

1½ *pounds sliced veal for scaloppine (12 slices)*
3 *tablespoons butter or margarine*
½ *cup rosé wine*
1 *12-ounce package fettucine noodles, cooked as directed on package*
Chopped fresh parsley (optional)

thread. Heat oven to 350° F. Heat butter in a large skillet over moderate heat (about 250° F.). Add veal rolls and increase heat to moderately high (about 300° F.); brown rolls well on all sides. Place rolls in a flat baking dish. Add wine to drippings left in skillet; heat and stir over moderately low heat (about 225° F.) until drippings are loosened from pan. Pour over veal. Bake, uncovered, 35 to 40 minutes, or until veal is fork-tender. Remove strings from rolls. Spoon noodles into bottom of a heated serving dish and arrange stuffed veal rolls on top. Pour meat juices over the rolls and garnish with chopped parsley, if desired. Serves 6.

✎§ Zesty Veal Chops

3 *to 5 tablespoons butter or olive oil*
4 *thick shoulder veal chops*
1 *10½-ounce can tomato purée*
1 *cup dry white wine*
1 *teaspoon salt*
¼ *teaspoon pepper*
½ *cup finely chopped fresh parsley*
2 *or 3 garlic cloves, crushed*
1 *tablespoon grated lemon peel*

Heat 3 tablespoons of the butter in skillet over moderate heat (about 250° F.); add meat and increase heat to moderately high (about 300° F.); cook until lightly browned (add more butter as needed). Mix tomato purée, wine, salt, and pepper; pour over meat. Cover and simmer over low heat (about 200° F.) 55 to 75 minutes, or until fork-tender. Combine parsley, garlic, and lemon peel; spoon over chops. Cover and simmer 10 minutes longer. Serves 4.

✎§ Veal Chop Broil

½ *cup catsup*
⅓ *cup vinegar*
¼ *cup firmly packed brown sugar*
2 *tablespoons soy sauce*
1 *clove garlic, very finely chopped*
1 *tablespoon prepared mustard*
1 *tablespoon vegetable oil*
4 *veal chops, cut ¾ inch thick*

Combine catsup, vinegar, brown sugar, soy sauce, garlic, mustard, and oil. Place veal chops in a flat pan; pour sauce over them. Let stand in refrigerator 2 hours or longer, turning occasionally. Place chops on hibachi grill or in a preheated broiler 3 to 6 inches from heat. Broil about 10 minutes on each side, until fork-tender and browned, basting occasionally with some of the marinade. Serves 4.

Cubed Veal

Veal for stewing is usually cut from the shoulder portion. Since all veal is quite lean it is not necessary to specify the cut desired. Any boneless veal cubes will work perfectly well in the recipes that follow.

⊸§ Veal Blanquette

2 pounds boneless veal
   shoulder, cut into 2-inch
   cubes
Boiling water
1 small clove garlic
3 sprigs parsley
1 bay leaf
Pinch of dried thyme leaves
1 teaspoon salt
2 peppercorns
4 medium-sized carrots,
   peeled
12 small white onions
3 tablespoons butter or
   margarine
2 tablespoons flour
¼ pound mushrooms, sliced
2 egg yolks
1 tablespoon water
2 to 3 cups cooked rice or
   noodles

In a large saucepan, cover meat with about 1 quart boiling water. Add garlic, parsley, bay leaf, thyme, salt, and peppercorns. Cover and simmer over low heat (about 200° F.) ½ hour. Add carrots and onions; simmer ½ hour longer. Remove meat and vegetables. Strain broth. Melt 2 tablespoons of the butter in a saucepan over moderately low heat (about 225° F.). Add flour and cook 5 minutes, stirring constantly. Gradually add strained broth, stirring constantly until thickened. Cook 15 to 20 minutes, stirring occasionally. While sauce is cooking, melt the remaining 1 tablespoon butter in a skillet over moderate heat (about 250° F.) and cook mushrooms until tender. Add meat and vegetables to sauce and heat. Just before serving, beat egg yolks and water together. Gradually add ¼ cup of the hot sauce to egg yolks; mix well. Gradually stir into remaining sauce and cook about 2 minutes over low heat (about 200° F.). Serve on rice or noodles. Serves 4 to 6.

⊸§ Veal and Peppers

4 medium-sized green peppers
1 tablespoon vegetable oil
1 medium-sized onion, sliced
1 tablespoon vegetable oil
1 pound veal shoulder, cut
   into 1-inch cubes
2 cups canned whole, peeled
   tomatoes
1 teaspoon salt
Few grains pepper
6 tablespoons dry white wine

Wash, stem, and seed green peppers; cut each into six sections. Heat the 1 tablespoon oil in skillet over moderately low heat (about 225° F.); add onion and green pepper and cook until tender, stirring frequently. Remove onion and green pepper. Add the remaining 1 tablespoon oil to the skillet and heat; add veal and cook over moderately high heat (about 300° F.) until lightly browned, stirring occasionally. Add tomatoes, salt, and pepper; cover and cook over low heat (about 200° F.) 30 minutes. Add green pepper, onion, and wine; cover and cook 30 minutes longer. Serves 4.

 **Veal Stew**

2 whole cloves
1 small onion
1½ cups undiluted chicken or beef broth
1 bay leaf
1 small lemon slice
1 teaspoon vinegar
½ teaspoon salt
1 pound lean boneless veal, cut into 1-inch cubes
1 tablespoon cornstarch
2 tablespoons water
2 tablespoons dry white wine

Stick cloves into onion and place in saucepan with broth, bay leaf, lemon, vinegar, and salt; heat to boiling. Add veal and simmer over low heat (about 200° F.) 1½ hours or until fork-tender. Remove meat; strain and skim off fat from broth. Measure broth and add water if necessary to make 1 cup of liquid. Mix cornstarch and the 2 tablespoons water together; gradually add to hot broth. Cook over moderately low heat (about 225° F.), stirring constantly, until thickened. Stir in wine. Add cooked veal and heat thoroughly but do not boil. Serves 3 to 4.

Veal Shanks

Veal shanks are often overlooked and shouldn't be. They are the basic ingredient in this classic Italian dish.

Osso Buco

3 whole shanks of veal, cut into 3-inch pieces
Flour
½ cup vegetable oil
½ cup dry white wine
½ cup water
1 recipe Tomato (Portugaise) Sauce (recipe on page 487)
½ teaspoon salt
1 8-ounce package broad egg noodles, cooked according to package directions

Roll shank pieces in flour. Heat oil in a large skillet over moderately high heat (about 300° F.) and cook shanks until browned on all sides. Add wine, water, Portugaise Sauce, and salt; cover and bring to a boil. Reduce heat to low (about 200° F.) and simmer 2 hours, or until fork-tender, stirring occasionally. Serve with hot noodles. Serves 6.

Variety Meats

The following section presents good ways to cook the nutritious variety meats described on page 278.

❧ Pan-Fried Calf's Liver

¼ cup flour
¼ teaspoon salt
Few grains pepper
1 pound calf's liver, cut ½ inch thick
3 tablespoons vegetable oil or bacon drippings

Mix flour, salt, and pepper together. Dredge slices of liver with flour mixture. Heat oil in a skillet over moderately high heat (about 300° F.). Add liver and cook about 3 minutes, or until lightly browned. Turn, add additional oil if necessary, and continue cooking about 2 to 3 minutes or until lightly browned. Serves 4.

❧ Broiled Beef or Calf's Liver

1 pound baby beef or calf's liver, cut ¾ inch thick
¼ cup melted butter or margarine
Salt and pepper

Dip slices of liver in melted butter, coating both sides. Sprinkle lightly with salt and pepper. Place on broiler pan in a preheated broiler about 3 inches from heat. Broil 2 to 3 minutes on each side, broiling just long enough for liver to change color and be lightly browned. Serves 4.

❧ Smothered Liver and Onions

1½ pounds beef liver, sliced
¼ cup flour
3 strips raw bacon, halved
½ cup sliced onion
¾ cup canned beef broth, diluted
⅛ teaspoon pepper
⅛ teaspoon dried tarragon leaves

Coat liver slices with flour; set aside. In a large skillet brown bacon over moderately high heat (about 325° F.). Drain on paper towels. In same skillet lightly brown the onion in the bacon drippings; remove onion with a slotted spoon. Then brown liver quickly in the same skillet, about 1 minute on each side, adding a little vegetable oil if necessary. Remove liver and drain off any excess fat. Reduce heat to moderately low (about 225° F.). In skillet combine broth, liver, pepper, and tarragon. Cover and simmer 20 minutes, or until liver is fork-tender. Uncover and top with bacon. Simmer uncovered 5 to 10 minutes, or until pan liquid is the consistency of gravy. Add salt if necessary. Serves 4 to 6.

❧ Baked Stuffed Heart

¾ cup uncooked rice
2 tablespoons butter or margarine
⅓ cup finely chopped onion
2 tablespoons chopped green pepper

Cook rice according to package directions. Melt the 2 tablespoons butter in a small skillet over moderately low heat (about 225° F.); add the ⅓ cup chopped onion and green pepper and cook until tender, stirring frequently. Remove from heat and stir in rice, prunes, marjoram, and salt. Wash heart and remove hard parts and mem-

1 cup pitted dried prunes,
    cooked and chopped
⅛ teaspoon ground marjoram
¼ teaspoon salt
1 3- to 4-pound beef heart
Meat tenderizer
¼ cup vegetable oil
Flour
1 small onion, chopped
1 cup hot water

branes. Sprinkle all surfaces of heart with tenderizer and pierce deeply with tines of a fork. Fill cavity of heart with some of the dressing; skewer and tie together. Spoon leftover dressing into an ovenproof bowl and cover with foil. Heat oven to 350° F. Heat the oil in an ovenproof Dutch oven over moderately high heat (about 350° F.). Dust heart with flour and brown lightly on all sides. Add the chopped onion and hot water. Cover and place in oven; bake 1 hour and 45 minutes, or until heart is fork-tender. Place bowl of dressing in oven with the heart for the last 45 minutes of baking time. Remove heart to a platter and cut into crosswise slices. Serves 8 to 10.

✑ Heart Andalouse

1 pound veal, lamb, or pork
    heart
1 cup water
1 teaspoon salt
1 can condensed tomato
    soup
1 teaspoon Worcestershire
    sauce
½ cup milk
2 tablespoons flour
1¼ cups (about 5 ounces)
    Cheddar cheese, coarsely
    shredded
2 cups hot cooked rice

Wash heart and remove hard parts and membranes. Cut into ¾-inch cubes. Place in a saucepan with water and salt. Cover and cook over moderately low heat (about 225° F.) for 1½ to 2 hours or until tender, stirring occasionally. Add a little more water if necessary. Remove from heat. Stir in tomato soup and Worcestershire. Place milk and flour in a jar with a tight lid and shake together until blended. Gradually add milk mixture to saucepan, and cook over moderately low heat (about 225° F.) until thickened, stirring constantly. Add cheese and stir until melted. Serve over hot rice. Serves 4.

✑ Sweetbreads in Wine

2 pairs veal sweetbreads
1 teaspoon salt
1 cup chicken broth
1 medium-sized onion, sliced
1 medium-sized carrot,
    peeled and sliced
3 sprigs parsley
1 bay leaf
Pinch dried thyme leaves
½ teaspoon salt
½ cup dry white wine

Drop sweetbreads into boiling water to cover; add the 1 teaspoon salt. Cover and cook over low heat (about 200° F.) for 25 minutes. While sweetbreads are cooking, place chicken broth, onion, carrot, parsley, bay leaf, thyme, and the ½ teaspoon salt in a small saucepan. Cook over low heat (about 200° F.) for 15 minutes, or until vegetables are almost tender. Heat oven to 350° F. Drain sweetbreads; hold them under cold running water and slip off the thin outside membrane with your fingers. With a paring knife cut out any dark veins and thick connective tissue. Place sweetbreads in a shallow 1½-

1 tablespoon water
1 tablespoon cornstarch

quart baking dish. Stir wine into the vegetable broth mixture and pour over sweetbreads. Cover and bake 20 minutes; uncover and bake 10 minutes longer. Place sweetbreads on a warm platter. Remove parsley and pour vegetable-broth mixture into a small saucepan. Blend the water and cornstarch together and stir into vegetable mixture. Cook over moderately low heat (about 225° F.) until mixture thickens, stirring constantly. Serve over sweetbreads. Serves 6 to 8.

❧ Chicken Terrapin

1 pair veal sweetbreads
1 tablespoon lemon juice
1 teaspoon salt
2 tablespoons butter or
  margarine
2 tablespoons flour
½ teaspoon salt
Few grains pepper
1 cup light cream
1 cup chicken broth, canned
  or fresh
2 egg yolks
½ cup dry sherry
3 cups diced cooked chicken
  or turkey

Cover sweetbreads with water; add lemon juice and the 1 teaspoon salt. Cover and cook over low heat (about 200° F.) for 25 minutes. Drain; hold them under cold running water and slip off the thin outside membrane with your fingers. With a paring knife cut out any dark veins and thick connective tissue. Cool sweetbreads and chop finely. Melt butter in saucepan over moderate heat (about 250° F.); blend in flour, the ½ teaspoon salt, and the pepper. Gradually add cream and chicken broth; cook, stirring constantly, until thickened. Beat egg yolks; gradually stir in ½ cup of the cream sauce. Pour back into sauce in saucepan, stirring constantly. Cook and stir over low heat (about 200° F.) until thickened. Add sherry, sweetbreads, and chicken; heat, stirring constantly. Serves 6 to 8.

❧ Broiled Lamb Kidneys

1 pound lamb kidneys
  (about 8)
⅓ cup bottled Italian dressing
Salt and pepper
2 medium-sized tomatoes, cut
  in half
8 large mushroom caps
¼ cup melted butter or
  margarine

Cut lamb kidneys in half lengthwise; wash well and remove fat and white veins with scissors. Dry on paper towels. Place in a bowl and pour dressing over them. Chill in refrigerator 1 hour. Drain and reserve dressing. Arrange kidneys on broiler pan. Brush with some of the dressing and sprinkle with salt and pepper. Place in a preheated broiler 3 inches from source of heat, and broil 8 minutes. Turn kidneys, brush with more dressing, and sprinkle with salt and pepper. Arrange tomatoes, cut side up, and mushrooms, rounded side up, on broiler pan; brush with melted butter and sprinkle with salt and pepper. Broil 4 minutes and turn mushrooms; brush again with butter and broil 3 minutes more, or until vegetables and kidneys are tender. Serves 4.

❧ Steak-and-Kidney Pie

2 pounds boneless beef chuck
2 tablespoons butter or margarine
1¼ cups chopped onions
1 can condensed beef broth, undiluted
1 teaspoon Worcestershire sauce
¼ teaspoon salt
Few grains pepper
Few grains cayenne pepper
¼ cup dry red wine
¾ pound lamb kidneys
¼ cup flour
1 pie-crust stick or enough pastry for a 9-inch pie shell (recipe on page 786)

Cut beef into 1-inch cubes. Melt butter in Dutch oven over moderate heat (about 250° F.), add onions, and cook over moderate heat until tender. Add beef cubes and cook until lightly browned. Add beef broth, Worcestershire sauce, salt, pepper, and cayenne. Pour wine into soup can and add enough water to fill can; pour over meat. Cover and cook over moderately low heat (about 225° F.) 2 hours. Cut kidneys in quarters and remove all fat and white tubes with scissors. Soak kidneys in salted water for ½ hour while meat is cooking. Drain kidneys and add to meat. Cook ½ hour. Drain meat and kidneys and place in a shallow 2-quart baking dish. Pour broth into a 1-quart measuring cup. Skim off fat and measure 4 tablespoons fat into a saucepan; blend in flour. Cook over moderately low heat (about 225° F.) 5 minutes, stirring constantly. Add meat broth gradually, stirring constantly until thickened. Cook 20 minutes, stirring occasionally. Pour gravy over meat. Heat oven to 450° F. Prepare pastry, following package directions. Roll out on a floured pastry cloth into an area 1 inch wider than the baking dish. Lay pastry over meat. Roll edge of pastry to make a standing rim and flute edge. Prick top of pastry with tines of fork or make several slits. Bake 20 to 25 minutes, until lightly browned. Serves 6.

❧ Savory Kidneys

1½ pounds veal kidneys (about 2)
1 egg, slightly beaten
2 tablespoons milk
¼ teaspoon dry mustard
1 teaspoon dried dillweed
1 teaspoon salt
2 tablespoons vinegar
½ cup fine dry bread crumbs
¼ cup vegetable oil

Wash kidneys well, remove membrane, and cut out white veins and hard fat parts with scissors. Slice into ½-inch slices; rinse well and dry on paper towels. Combine egg, milk, mustard, dill, and salt. Dip kidney slices first in vinegar and then in the egg mixture; coat evenly with bread crumbs. Heat oil in a skillet over moderately high heat (about 275° F.); brown slices well on all sides. Serves 4 to 6.

❧ Breaded Tripe

1½ pounds honeycomb tripe
1 tablespoon salt
1 bay leaf

Place tripe in a saucepan and cover with water. Add the 1 tablespoon salt, bay leaf, onion, and peppercorns. Cover and cook over moderately low heat (about 225°

1 *small onion, sliced*
3 *peppercorns*
1 *egg, slightly beaten*
1 *tablespoon milk*
½ *cup fine dry seasoned
   bread crumbs*
About 5 *tablespoons vegetable
   oil*
Salt and pepper

F.) for 2 to 2½ hours or until surface of tripe has a clear, jellylike appearance. Drain and cut into serving-sized pieces. Mix egg and milk. Dip pieces of tripe first in egg–milk mixture and then coat evenly with crumbs. Heat 2 tablespoons of the oil in a skillet over moderately high heat (about 300° F.). Cook tripe until lightly browned, adding more oil to pan as needed. Sprinkle with salt and pepper. Serves 6.

✌ Sliced Smoked Tongue with Raisin Sauce

*1 *4½-pound smoked tongue*
1 *medium-sized onion,
   halved*
1 *large bay leaf*
¼ *teaspoon peppercorns*
¼ *teaspoon whole allspice*
½ *cup firmly packed dark
   brown sugar*
1 *tablespoon cornstarch*
¼ *teaspoon ground
   cinnamon*
¼ *cup orange marmalade*
½ *cup seedless raisins*
2 *tablespoons lemon juice*

Place tongue in a large Dutch oven and add onion, bay leaf, peppercorns, and allspice. Cover tongue with water. Place over moderately low heat (about 225° F.) and bring to a boil; cover and simmer about 3 hours, or until tongue is fork-tender. Remove tongue from pan liquid and cool until it can be handled easily. Meanwhile strain 1½ cups of the tongue stock and set aside. In a saucepan mix together brown sugar, cornstarch, and cinnamon. Gradually stir in stock and blend smooth. Add orange marmalade and raisins. Place over moderately low heat (about 225° F.) and bring to a boil; boil ½ minute, or until sauce is translucent and thickened, stirring constantly. Stir in lemon juice and remove from heat. Cut off thick root end of tongue and reserve any meaty portions of it for another use. Peel skin from rest of tongue. Slice and serve with raisin sauce. Serves 4 to 6.

Note: Fully cooked tongue is also available. Heat as directed on the label. Substitute beef bouillon for the 1½ cups stock used to make the raisin sauce.

✌ Deviled Beef Tongue

1 *egg yolk, slightly beaten*
2 *teaspoons prepared
   mustard*
½ *teaspoon curry powder*
½ *teaspoon Tabasco*
2 *tablespoons olive oil or
   vegetable oil*
3 *tablespoons bottled lemon
   juice*
1 *16-ounce jar beef tongue*
½ *cup fine dry bread crumbs*
2 *tablespoons butter or
   margarine*

Combine egg yolk, mustard, curry powder, Tabasco, olive oil, and lemon juice in a pie plate. Cut tongue in crosswise slices about ¼ inch thick. Dip slices in egg yolk mixture and then in bread crumbs. Melt butter in medium-sized skillet over moderately high heat (about 275° F.); add tongue slices. Brown lightly on both sides. Remove to a warm platter. Serves 4.

✑ *Brains au Beurre Noir*

1½ **pounds calf's brains**
1 **quart water**
1 **tablespoon vinegar**
1 **teaspoon salt**
¼ **cup flour**
3 **tablespoons butter or margarine**
⅓ **cup clarified butter (recipe on page 490)**
3 **tablespoons capers**
3 **tablespoons chopped fresh parsley**

Wash brains and place in a saucepan with water, vinegar, and salt; cover and cook over moderately low heat (about 225° F.) for 15 minutes after water boils. Drain and cool quickly in cold water. Remove white membrane and cut brains into slices about ½ inch thick. Coat with flour. Heat the 3 tablespoons butter in a skillet over moderately high heat (about 275° F.); cook brains 2 to 3 minutes or until lightly browned. Remove to a hot serving dish. Pour the clarified butter into a clean skillet and cook over moderately high heat (about 325° F.) until butter is lightly browned. Add capers and parsley. Pour butter over brains. Serve immediately. Serves 4 to 5.

Frankfurters and Sausages

The seasoned sausages come in both ready-to-eat and uncooked forms; the ready-to-eat varieties may be used in combinations with other foods. In addition to the assortment of recipes incorporating them in this chapter, they are used in recipes throughout this book. (See the index for a complete listing.) These, like hamburger, are great budget foods boasting a variety of flavors.

Following is a list of the uncooked smoked sausages:

Smoked country style is fresh pork sausage that has been cured and smoked. It is usually sold in links.

Mettwurst is a spiced beef-and-pork sausage sold in casings and in links.

Polish Sausage (Kielbasa) is a garlic-flavored pork-and-beef sausage sold in large rings weighing one pound or more.

The list below describes the varieties of cooked sausages:

Frankfurters (wieners) are usually a blend of seasoned beef and pork or of beef, pork, and veal. There are also all-beef frankfurters. Check the package label or ask your butcher for a certain type. Frankfurters come either with casings or skinless. These also come canned or packaged in small sizes for appetizers.

Bologna is a highly seasoned beef, veal, and pork sausage that may be purchased either sliced or in a chunk.

Pickle-and-pimiento loaf and *olive loaf* are bologna with the name ingredients added.

Cervelat is a spiced sausage that resembles Lebanon bologna but is not quite so smoky.

Chorizo is a Spanish and Mexican pork sausage which comes in long links. It is highly seasoned with garlic, cayenne, and chili powder.

Lebanon bologna is a coarsely ground beef, heavily smoked and sharp in taste, which is either sliced or sold in the chunk. It was originally made in Lebanon, Pennsylvania.

Ham-bologna is a bologna that has large pieces of smoked ham in the roll. It may be purchased sliced or in the chunk.

Knackwurst is a large frankfurter flavored with garlic. These need further cooking before serving.

Bauernwurst is a mixture of pork and beef cooked and ready to serve.

Blutwurst, or blood sausage, contains diced cooked meats, beef, blood, and seasonings in a gelatine. It comes sliced and ready to use.

Bratwurst is a small German sausage made mainly of pork and sometimes a little veal, flavored with salt, pepper, nutmeg, caraway, marjoram, and sometimes mace. It must be cooked before eating.

Liverwurst, or liver sausage, is a ready-to-use pale pink, soft-textured mixture of ground liver, especially pork liver.

Liver cheese is made of ground liver and veal in a spiced gelatine. It is ready to use.

Mortadella, a spicy Italian smoked sausage, is a mixture of pork and beef and pork fat and highly seasoned with garlic.

Thuringer is made of ground pork with beef and veal sometimes added. This may be either fresh or cooked. Since it is similar to cervelat, be sure you know which you're buying.

Peperoni is a highly spiced dry sausage, which usually comes in small, round links. Available in two varieties—hot and sweet—it is often used in Italian hero sandwiches.

Salami is a dry sausage made of finely chopped pork, beef, and spices. Because there are many varieties of salami and variously seasoned ones, experiment to find the one that best suits your taste.

Souse (head cheese) is made of chunks of pork or beef or veal in flavored gelatine.

Spiced Luncheon Meat is usually a ground pork pressed into a gelatine mixture.

৺ৡ *Polish Sausage Ring*

1½ to 1¾ pounds Polish sausage or Kielbasa
Boiling water
6 large green peppers
2 large sweet red peppers

Place sausage in a large pot of boiling water; cover and cook over low heat (about 200 ° F.) for 20 minutes. Wash green and red peppers and remove stems and seeds; cut into strips ½ inch wide. Heat the 2 tablespoons of butter in skillet over moderately low heat (about 225° F.); add

2 tablespoons butter or
 margarine
1 clove garlic, finely minced
Salt and pepper to taste
3 cups hot mashed potatoes
 (prepared from packaged
 instant mashed potatoes)
2 or 3 tablespoons butter or
 margarine

garlic and green and red peppers and cook 5 minutes, stirring frequently. Reduce heat to low (about 200° F.); cover and cook 15 to 20 minutes, until peppers are just tender. Sprinkle with salt and pepper. Prepare potatoes, following directions on package. Spoon peppers onto a large platter. Arrange sausage over peppers; mound potatoes in center. Dot potatoes with the 2 or 3 tablespoons of butter. Serves 6.

✑§ Knackwurst-with-Sauerkraut Dinner

1½ pounds sweet potatoes
1 16-ounce can sauerkraut,
 drained
1 teaspoon caraway seeds
8 knackwurst
3 tablespoons melted butter
 or margarine
1 medium-sized cooking
 apple, peeled, cored, and
 thinly sliced

Wash sweet potatoes and cook in boiling salted water until tender, about 35 to 40 minutes. Cool. Peel sweet potatoes and cut into 1-inch crosswise slices. Mix sauerkraut and caraway seeds. Split knackwurst lengthwise, but not all the way through. Spoon 2 tablespoons of the sauerkraut mixture into each knackwurst and place toothpick or skewer in each to hold together. Place knackwurst on broiler rack, filled side down; brush with some of the melted butter. Make a small pan with a double thickness of aluminum foil, about 8 x 4 inches; spoon leftover sauerkraut into pan and top with apple slices. Brush apple slices with melted butter. Place aluminum foil pan on broiler rack. Place in preheated broiler (or as manufacturer directs) 3 inches from heat. Broil 5 minutes. Carefully turn knackwurst and brush again with butter. Arrange sweet potatoes on rack and brush with some of the butter. Broil 4 to 5 minutes, or until knackwurst is lightly browned and sweet potatoes are heated. Serves 4.

✑§ Baked Beans and Frankfurters

3 16-ounce jars New
 England-style baked
 beans
1 cup diced process
 American cheese
⅓ cup drained sweet pickle
 relish
¼ cup catsup
2 tablespoons prepared
 mustard

Heat oven to 375° F. In a large bowl mix together beans, diced cheese, pickle relish, catsup, and mustard. Blend well and turn into a shallow, rectangular 2-quart baking dish. Arrange frankfurters over the bean mixture. Bake 15 to 20 minutes, or until beans are bubbling and frankfurters are lightly browned. Sprinkle the shredded cheese over the frankfurters and bake 2 to 3 minutes longer, or until the cheese is melted. Serves 6.

(Ingredients continued on page 354)

1½ pounds frankfurters
½ cup coarsely shredded
   process American cheese

✑ Oven-Barbecued Frankfurters

1 can condensed tomato
  soup
1 1⅜-ounce envelope dry
  onion soup mix
1 2-ounce can mushrooms,
  drained
½ soup can water
16 frankfurters
4 slices process American
  cheese

Heat oven to 350° F. Combine tomato soup, dry onion soup mix, mushrooms, and water. Place 8 frankfurters in a single layer in a shallow 1½-quart baking dish. Spoon half the soup mixture over frankfurters. Place 2 of the cheese slices on frankfurters. Repeat layers. Bake 30 minutes, or until mixture bubbles at the edges. Serves 6 to 8.

✑ Franks on a Stick

1 cup packaged pancake mix
¾ cup milk
1 egg
1 teaspoon prepared
  mustard
Vegetable oil for frying
12 frankfurters (about 1½
  pounds)

In a bowl mix together pancake mix, milk, egg, and mustard just until blended smooth. Pour oil into a shallow saucepan or electric skillet to a depth of about 1½ inches. Heat oil to 375° F. Using tongs, dip frankfurters in the batter, making sure they are coated on all sides. Add frankfurters to hot oil a few at a time and brown on all sides, about 2 minutes. Drain on paper towels. Insert a small wooden skewer at one end of each. Serves 6.

✑ Frankfurter–Lentil Stew

1½ cups dried lentils, well
  rinsed
7 cups cold water
2 teaspoons salt
1 tablespoon vegetable oil
1 cup thinly sliced celery
⅓ cup coarsely chopped
  onion
1 16-ounce can whole
  tomatoes
½ teaspoon garlic salt
½ teaspoon dried marjoram
  leaves

In a large saucepot or Dutch oven over moderately high heat (about 300° F.) bring lentils, 6 cups of the water, and 1½ teaspoons of the salt to a full boil. Reduce heat to moderate (about 250° F.) and simmer, uncovered, 20 to 30 minutes, or until lentils are just tender. (Do not overcook.) Drain well. In a large saucepan over moderate heat (about 250° F.) heat oil and brown celery and onion lightly. Stir in tomatoes, the remaining 1 cup water, lentils, the remaining ½ teaspoon salt, garlic salt, marjoram, pepper, bay leaf, carrot, and parsley. Simmer, uncovered, 10 minutes. Add frankfurter slices and simmer 5 minutes longer. If a thinner stew is desired, add a little additional water. Serves 6.

¼ *teaspoon pepper*
1 *bay leaf*
1 *cup peeled and shredded carrot*
2 *tablespoons chopped fresh parsley*
½ *pound frankfurters, sliced*

🐦 *Lyonnaise Potatoes and Frankfurters*

1 *pound potatoes, peeled*
¼ *cup butter or margarine*
½ *pound frankfurters, thinly sliced*
½ *cup sliced onion*
1 *tablespoon finely chopped fresh parsley*
¼ *teaspoon salt*
Few grains pepper
Dash of nutmeg

Cook potatoes in boiling salted water until almost tender when tested with a fork. Do not overcook. Cool and cut into thin slices. In a 12-inch skillet over moderately high heat (about 350° F.) melt butter and add frankfurter slices and onion. Cook, stirring frequently, until frankfurters are lightly browned and onion is crisp-tender. Add potatoes and remaining ingredients and cook until potato slices are tender and lightly browned, turning frequently with a pancake turner. Add a little more butter, if necessary, to keep mixture from sticking to pan. Serves 4.

🐦 *Frankfurter–Potato Puff*

1 *tablespoon butter or margarine*
¼ *cup chopped onion*
1 *cup mashed potatoes, slightly cooled (prepared from packaged instant mashed potatoes)*
½ *cup coarsely shredded Cheddar cheese*
1 *tablespoon prepared mustard*
4 *eggs, separated and at room temperature*
4 *frankfurters (about ½ pound), thinly sliced*

Heat oven to 350° F. In a small saucepan over moderate heat (about 250° F.) melt butter and cook onion until lightly browned. In a large bowl mix together cooked onion, mashed potatoes, cheese, and mustard. Beat in egg yolks one at a time. Stir in frankfurter slices. Beat egg whites until stiff. Fold into frankfurter mixture. Turn into an ungreased, deep, 2-quart casserole. Bake 30 minutes, or until a silver knife inserted in the center comes out clean. Serve immediately. Serves 4 to 6.

CHAPTER X

POULTRY

At once elegant and economical, poultry has outgrown traditional Sunday and holiday menus and is used often for dinner parties and family meals. Poultry meat is an excellent protein food. Although lower in calories than most meats, it is equal to them in protein content.

There are five kinds of poultry generally available today: Chicken and turkey, which come in numerous forms, are almost always in butchers' cases. Duckling is usually available, but may have to be ordered ahead. Goose and guinea are stocked in some markets, but in most parts of the country they must be ordered. Squab (pigeons) are also available in some poultry stores. Most of the poultry you buy in a retail market today has been inspected for wholesomeness and will bear a wing tag or a stamp on the wrapping to that effect. Much of the poultry you buy will also be graded. The United States Department of Agriculture's grading label is in the form of a shield and is found on a tag or the outer wrapping. To be graded, poultry must have first been inspected for wholesomeness. "U.S. Grade A" is the grade given to a fowl that is fully fleshed and has pale, moist skin and clear, yellow fat. Look for the grade or for those characteristics when you buy poultry.

Storing Poultry

It is important to store poultry in the correct manner. If frozen, keep it frozen in its original wrappings until time to thaw it for cooking. In a true freezer (0° F. or less), frozen poultry may be held for several months. Be sure the original wrapping has not been punctured. If it has, rewrap the bird in moisture-vaporproof paper.

To defrost frozen poultry, follow the package directions for defrosting or use one of these methods: Puncture the wrapping and place the bird in a shallow pan in the food compartment of the refrigerator; allow one to three days for complete defrosting, depending upon the size of the bird. A Cornish hen will thaw in a day; a roasting chicken will take twenty-four hours, and a large turkey will take three days. Figure about twenty-four hours per five pounds of bird.

For faster defrosting, put the bird, *wrapping intact,* in a large pan under cold running water. This method will take a half hour for Cornish hens and up to six hours for a large turkey. Another quick method is to place the turkey, still in its *unopened* plastic wrap, in a paper bag; close the bag and thaw the turkey at room temperature. Allow sixteen hours of thawing time for large birds (twenty to twenty-five pounds) and about twelve hours for smaller ones (eight to twelve pounds). U.S. Department of Agriculture research shows that this method allows the turkey to thaw completely while keeping the outside surface temperature low enough for safety.

Once poultry is thawed, remove the wrappings, take the neck and giblets out of the body cavity, and prepare for cooking immediately.

If fresh, poultry should always be kept refrigerated. Buy only from a market that keeps poultry in a refrigerated (32° F.) case. When you get fresh poultry home, remove the market wrappings immediately and wrap the bird *loosely* in waxed paper or other wrap, leaving paper ends open because fresh, uncooked poultry should not be tightly wrapped for refrigerator storage. It increases chance of spoilage. Refrigerate immediately. Plan to use fresh poultry within twenty-four hours.

Cooked poultry should be refrigerated as soon as possible after the meal. Always remove remaining stuffing from a roasted bird and store it separately in a tightly covered container in the refrigerator. Gravy should also be stored separately in a covered jar in the refrigerator. If most of the bird has been carved, it is best to take the remaining meat off the bones to store it and to use the bones for broth and soup while they are fresh and moist and will yield more flavor. Wrap the meat tightly in plastic wrap or waxed paper to keep it fresh and flavorful. This storage method not only retains the flavor of the freshly cooked chicken but also takes up much less refrigerator space. Poultry cooked to use in salads or prepared dishes should be refrigerated within a half hour after cooking.

Chicken

In general, the younger the chicken the more tender it will be. The age of the chicken will govern the way in which you cook it.

Cornish Hens: These are the smallest chickens on the market. They are a special breed of small chicken usually marketed at six weeks of age. They may be bought fresh or frozen. If they are frozen they should be defrosted before cooking. These birds range in size from one to two pounds; they are usually roasted, stuffed or unstuffed, and served one to a person. They may also be done on a rotisserie; the larger sizes may be split and broiled to serve two.

Broiler–Fryer Chickens: These are young chickens (usually nine weeks old) that may be simply called frying chickens or broilers in your market. They will weigh from one and a half to four pounds. Cut up, they can be simmered, baked, broiled, barbecued, or, of course, fried. They can also be roasted whole, stuffed or not; they are really the all-purpose chicken but, because they are tender, do not need such long cooking as an older bird of comparable size.

Roasting Chickens: Older and larger than broiler–fryers, roasting chickens will run three and a half to five pounds. Roasting chickens are not "old" chickens. They have tender meat and are excellent for roasting, barbecuing, or frying.

Stewing Chickens or Fowl: These are mature hens that weigh from three to five pounds. They are less tender and more fatty than other kinds of chicken. They are flavorful and particularly good in such dishes as chicken pot pie and chicken fricassee.

Bro-hens: Mature hens that can run from five to eight pounds, bro-hens are the laying hens from which the young broiler–fryers are produced. They may take less time to cook than the stewing chickens. Use them too for long cooking in liquid.

Capons: These are young, desexed male chickens that are highly prized for roasting. They have a large quantity of light meat and superb flavor and tenderness. They usually weigh from four to seven pounds.

About Giblets: Don't throw them away. They are used primarily to make a broth that can be used for Roast Chicken Gravy (recipe on page 360) or to moisten stuffing.

To make the broth, wash the giblets—*heart, liver, gizzard*—and the *neck* thoroughly. Put them in a saucepan with a *stalk of celery, leaves and all;* add a *small, diced onion* and a few *peppercorns.* Add *water* to cover, and simmer covered over low heat about 15 minutes. Remove the liver, which should be done in this time, and continue cooking until the gizzard is easily pierced with a fork (thirty minutes to one hour depending upon age of the bird). Reserve the stock for gravy or stuffing or to use as part of the liquid in creamed chicken dishes. If covered and placed in the refrigerator it will keep for three days; frozen, it will keep for several months.

To use the giblets for gravy, remove the neck meat from the bones (discard the skin) and chop it and the giblets coarsely. Refrigerate covered if you will not be using them within an hour.

Giblets can be used in many ways: The neck meat and heart are sweet and can be added to soups or used for a sandwich spread; chicken livers can be mixed with mayonnaise and seasonings to make an appetizer or sandwich spread. Freeze the giblets, fresh or cooked, as you get them until you collect enough for a special use. They're filled with good food value—and you've paid for them.

To Roast a Chicken: Check the Roast Chicken timetable (page 51). Plan to have the chicken done twenty minutes before you serve dinner; this will allow you time to make a gravy if you wish, and the bird will carve more easily if it's been out of the oven this length of time.

Prepare a whole chicken for roasting exactly as you would prepare a turkey: See the pictured directions on page 379. Chicken may be roasted with or without stuffing. The following recipes are for a given size of bird. The roasting time can be adjusted for any size chicken by consulting the timetable.

ꝫ Savory Roast Chicken, Unstuffed

1 4-pound roasting chicken
1½ teaspoons seasoned salt
¼ cup celery leaves
1 medium-sized onion, quartered
¼ cup melted butter or margarine

Heat oven to 325° F. Wash chicken; drain and pat dry. Rub cavity of chicken lightly with some of the seasoned salt. Place celery leaves and onion pieces in cavity. Fasten the neck skin to the back with a skewer. Turn wing tips onto back. Tie drumsticks together and then to tail. Place chicken on a rack in a shallow roasting pan, breast up. Brush skin with melted butter. Sprinkle with the remaining seasoned salt. Roast, uncovered, about 2 hours, or 30 minutes per pound. Baste chicken several times with drippings from roasting pan. Serves 4 to 5.

ꝫ Roast Stuffed Chicken

1 5-pound roasting chicken
Salt and pepper
*Stuffing
⅓ cup melted butter or margarine

Heat oven to 375° F. Wash chicken; drain and pat dry. Rub inside of cavity with salt and pepper. Stuff chicken lightly with desired stuffing. Insert skewers at body openings; lace with string and tie legs together. Place chicken, breast side up, in shallow roasting pan. Dip cheesecloth in butter and place loosely over chicken. Roast 2¾ hours, or until drumstick–thigh joint will move easily and meat on drumstick is soft when pressed, basting occasionally with drippings in the pan. Serves 4 to 5.

Note: Any of the stuffing recipes starting on page 392 will be suitable. A recipe that yields 5 cups of stuffing will be enough for a 5-pound bird. A recipe that yields 12 cups may be cut in half. About 1 cup of stuffing will be left over, which may be baked separately in a small covered casserole for 30 minutes.

🥢 Roast Chicken Gravy

2 *tablespoons drippings*
from roasting pan
2 *tablespoons flour*
1 *cup hot broth from*
giblets or canned
chicken broth

Remove the chicken from the roasting pan and place it on a heated platter. Pour all the drippings from the pan into a measuring cup. Place the roasting pan on top of the range over low heat (about 200° F.) and return 2 tablespoons of the drippings to it. Stir in the flour to blend into a smooth paste. Remove the pan from the heat and slowly pour the hot liquid into the flour–fat mixture, stirring as you pour. Replace the pan over the low heat and scrape all the browned bits into the gravy. Cook for at least 1 minute after the gravy starts to bubble.

This makes a medium-thick gravy. For thin gravy, reduce the fat and flour to 1 tablespoon each. For thick gravy increase the fat and flour to 3 tablespoons each. Makes 1 cup of gravy.

Giblet Gravy

Stir coarsely chopped cooked neck and giblet meat (see page 358) into the gravy.

Cream Gravy

Substitute *1 cup of milk* for the broth or use *½ cup of broth* and *½ cup of light cream* for the liquid.

🥢 Basic Fried Chicken

1 *3- to 3½-pound broiler–*
fryer chicken, cut up
½ *cup flour*
2 *teaspoons salt*
⅛ *teaspoon pepper*
Vegetable oil or shortening

Wash and pat chicken dry. Place flour, salt, and pepper in a plastic or paper bag. Shake chicken in bag until coated with flour mixture. Pour vegetable oil or shortening into a large skillet to a depth of ½ to 1 inch and heat. Cook chicken over moderately high heat (about 350° F.) until lightly browned on all sides. Cover pan and cook 25 to 30 minutes over moderately low heat (about 225° F.), until fork-tender. Serves 4.

🥢 Kansas Fried Chicken

2 *2½- to 3-pound broiler–*
fryer chickens, cut up
⅔ *cup flour*
1 *teaspoon salt*

Wipe washed chicken pieces dry with paper towels. Combine flour and salt. Roll chicken pieces in flour mixture and pat on evenly with fingertips. Reserve any leftover flour for gravy. Melt butter and lard in a large,

2 *tablespoons butter or*
  margarine
4 *tablespoons lard or*
  shortening
2 *cups milk*

heavy skillet over moderately high heat (about 300° F.). When fat is hot, but not smoking, add chicken, the largest pieces first; allow room for turning. Keep skillet partly covered to avoid splatters. As chicken pieces brown, turn them. When pieces are fork-tender, drain on a rack set in a baking pan. Keep hot in a warm oven while making gravy. Pour off all but 3 tablespoons of the fat in the skillet. Add 3 tablespoons of the seasoned flour and cook over moderate heat (about 250° F.) until mixture bubbles. Slowly add milk; cook and stir constantly until thickened. Continue to cook about 5 minutes. Season with salt and pepper. Serves 4 to 6.

❧ Maryland Fried Chicken

1 *3- to 3½-pound broiler–*
  fryer chicken, cut up
1½ *cups water*
1 *medium-sized onion,*
  quartered
1 *carrot, cut up*
1 *parsley sprig*
½ *teaspoon salt*
¼ *cup flour*
½ *teaspoon salt*
Few grains pepper
2 *eggs, slightly beaten*
¼ *cup water*
1¼ *cups fine dry bread*
  crumbs
½ *cup butter or margarine*
¼ *cup flour*
½ *cup light cream*
¾ *cup milk*
½ *teaspoon salt*

Wash and pat chicken dry. Place chicken neck, backbone, and giblets in a small saucepan. Add the 1½ cups water, onion, carrot, parsley, and the ½ teaspoon salt. Cover and simmer over moderately low heat (about 225° F.) 1 to 1½ hours. Mix the ¼ cup flour, the ½ teaspoon salt, and pepper. Coat chicken pieces first in flour mixture and then in a mixture of egg and the ¼ cup water. Finally, coat with bread crumbs. Heat oven to 350° F. Melt butter in skillet over moderately high heat (about 300° F.) and cook chicken until lightly browned on all sides. Place chicken and pan drippings in shallow baking dish. Sprinkle with salt and pepper. Cover and bake 1 hour, or until fork-tender. Remove from oven. Strain the stock from the giblets into a measuring cup and skim off fat. Add enough water to make 1¼ cups. Spoon 4 tablespoons of the fat into a saucepan, using the fat from stock and the fat from the drippings in the baking dish. Blend in the remaining ¼ cup flour. Gradually add light cream and milk, stirring constantly. Gradually add chicken stock. Cook over moderate heat (about 250° F.) until thickened, stirring constantly. Season with the ½ teaspoon salt. Serve over chicken. Serves 4 to 6.

❧ Deep-Fat-Fried Chicken

1 *3- to 3½-pound broiler–*
  fryer chicken, cut up

In a deep-fat fryer, a heavy, deep saucepan, or an electric saucepan, heat 2 to 3 inches of oil or shortening to

POULTRY

Coating (select one of the
coating recipes that follow)
Vegetable oil or shortening for
frying

350° F. Wash and dry chicken pieces. Coat chicken with the desired coating. Fry a few pieces at a time until fork-tender. Fry drumsticks and thighs for about 20 minutes and the other pieces for about 15 minutes. Drain on paper towel. Keep fried chicken warm in 300° F. oven. Serves 4.

Herb-Flour Coating

Mix 1¼ cups all-purpose flour, 1 teaspoon dried thyme leaves, 2 teaspoons paprika, 2 teaspoons salt, and a few grains pepper; pour into a paper or plastic bag. Wash chicken and shake off any excess water, but do not dry thoroughly. Put chicken in the bag, a few pieces at a time, and shake until thoroughly coated. Fry as directed.

Batter Coating

Combine 1 cup sifted all-purpose flour and ½ teaspoon salt. Add 1 egg, slightly beaten, ¾ cup milk, and 1 tablespoon melted butter or margarine; stir until smooth. Dip well-dried chicken pieces in batter, letting excess batter drop off before putting into fat. Fry as directed.

✒ Oven-Fried Chicken

1 3- to 3½-pound broiler–
fryer chicken, cut
up for frying
Coating (select one of the
coating recipes that follow)

Heat oven to 400° F. Wash and pat chicken pieces dry. Coat chicken with the desired coating. Place in a single layer in a large, shallow baking pan. Bake 55 to 60 minutes, or according to coating recipe, until chicken is fork-tender. Serves 4.

Potato Coating

Place ¼ cup butter or margarine in a large baking pan and heat in oven to melt while preparing chicken. Mix 2 tablespoons instant minced onion with 2 tablespoons water and let stand 1 minute. Mix 1 cup instant potato buds or flakes, onion, ¼ cup grated Parmesan cheese, and ½ teaspoon chili powder. Dip chicken first in mixture of 1 egg, slightly beaten, and 2 tablespoons milk. Then coat with potato mixture, reserving any leftover mixture for later. Place chicken, skin side down, in buttered baking pan. Sprinkle with ½ teaspoon salt and a few grains pepper. Bake 30 minutes; turn chicken and sprinkle with any remaining potato mixture. Bake 25 to 30 minutes longer.

Corn Flake Crumb Coating

Dip chicken first in ⅔ cup undiluted evaporated milk and then in a mixture of 1¼ cups corn flake crumbs, 1¼ teaspoons salt, and a few grains pepper. Pour ⅓ cup *melted butter or margarine* in baking pan. Place chicken in pan, skin side up. Bake as directed.

Sour Cream Coating

Combine *1 cup commercial sour cream, 1 teaspoon lemon juice, 1 teaspoon Worcestershire sauce, 1 teaspoon celery salt, 1 teaspoon paprika, ¾ teaspoon salt,* and *¼ teaspoon pepper.* Dip chicken pieces in sour cream mixture, spreading it over chicken with a spatula to coat thoroughly. Finally, coat in *1 cup fine dry bread crumbs.* Pour *⅓ cup melted butter or margarine* into baking pan. Place chicken, skin side up, in pan. Bake as directed.

Biscuit-Pecan Coating

Combine *1 cup prepared buttermilk biscuit mix, 1½ teaspoons salt, 1 teaspoon paprika, ½ teaspoon poultry seasoning,* and *½ cup finely chopped pecans.* Dip chicken first in *½ cup undiluted evaporated milk* and then in dry mixture. Place chicken, skin side up, in pan. Pour *½ cup melted butter or margarine* over chicken. Bake as directed.

Sesame Seed Coating

Heat oven to 400° F. Place *3 tablespoons sesame seeds* in a flat pan and toast about 15 minutes, stirring 2 or 3 times. Combine sesame seeds, *1¼ cups packaged corn flake crumbs, 1 teaspoon salt,* and *⅛ teaspoon poultry seasoning.* Dip chicken pieces in *⅔ cup undiluted evaporated milk* and then roll in corn flake mixture. Place chicken, skin side up, in baking pan. Pour *4 tablespoons melted butter or margarine* over chicken. Bake as directed.

Herbed Baked Chicken

2 **2½- to 3-pound broiler–fryer chickens, quartered**
¼ **cup lemon juice**
1¼ **cups dry sherry**
3 **tablespoons olive oil**
1 **clove garlic, crushed**
1 **teaspoon dried tarragon leaves**
1½ **teaspoons salt**
Paprika

Wash and pat chicken dry. Arrange chicken in 2 shallow 2-quart baking dishes. Mix lemon juice, sherry, olive oil, garlic, tarragon, and salt; pour half the mixture over the chicken in each dish. Marinate in refrigerator about 3 hours, turning frequently. Heat oven to 375° F. Sprinkle chicken with paprika and bake about 1 hour until fork-tender. Serves 8.

Broiled Chicken

2 **2½-pound broiler–fryer chickens, split**

Wash and pat chicken dry. Place chicken halves, skin side down, on broiler pan; sprinkle with salt and pepper.

Salt and pepper
Glaze (select one of the
  recipes that follow)

Set temperature control on gas range to 375° F. and place pan 3 to 4 inches from broiler unit. Leave oven door slightly opened. Or set temperature control to BROIL on electric range and place pan 7 to 8 inches from heat. Leave oven door slightly opened. Brush chicken with one of the glazes and broil 20 to 25 minutes, until lightly browned, brushing with glaze occasionally. Turn and broil 10 to 15 minutes, or until tender, brushing occasionally with glaze. If some parts of the chicken are browning too quickly, place small pieces of foil over the dark areas. Serves 4.

Wine Glaze

Blend *½ cup vegetable oil, ½ cup dry white wine, 2 tablespoons minced shallots,* and *1 tablespoon dried crumbled rosemary leaves* together. Pour over chicken and marinate 1 hour in refrigerator before broiling. Broil as directed. Brush chicken with the marinade during broiling. Makes 1 cup.

Herb Glaze

Blend *¼ cup vegetable oil, ¼ cup lemon juice,* and *2 teaspoons ground marjoram* together. Chill in refrigerator for ½ hour before using. Brush chicken with the glaze and broil as directed. Makes about ½ cup.

Barbecue Sauce Glaze

Blend *¼ cup vegetable oil, 1 8-ounce can tomato sauce, 2 tablespoons wine vinegar, 1 teaspoon Worcestershire sauce, 3 tablespoons dark corn syrup,* and *2 teaspoons prepared mustard* together. Brush chicken with the glaze and broil as directed. Heat any extra sauce and serve with chicken. Makes about 1½ cups.

ᕘ Barbecued Chicken

2 3-pound broiler–fryer
  chickens, quartered
2 cups bottled barbecue sauce
4 tablespoons water
Juice of 1 lemon
4 tablespoons vegetable oil
2 16-ounce cans small onions,
  drained

Rinse chicken with cold water and pat dry. Combine barbecue sauce, water, lemon juice, and oil. Brush chicken pieces on all sides with some of the sauce mixture. Place on grill over hot coals and broil about 30 minutes on each side, until fork-tender, brushing frequently with more of the sauce. About 15 minutes before the chicken is done, brush onions with some of the sauce mixture. Wrap onions tightly in squares of heavy aluminum foil; place on grill with chicken and heat thoroughly. Serve onions with chicken. Serves 8.

✑ Pineapple Chicken on a Spit

2 2½- to 3-pound broiler–
  fryer chickens
1 lemon, cut in half
1 clove garlic, cut in half
2 teaspoons salt
½ teaspoon pepper
2 cups drained, crushed
  pineapple
4 tablespoons cornstarch
2 tablespoons soy sauce
1 teaspoon ground ginger
4 tablespoons melted butter
  or margarine

Wash and pat chickens thoroughly dry. Rub them inside and out with the cut lemon and garlic. Sprinkle with salt and pepper. Combine pineapple, cornstarch, soy sauce, and ginger. Spoon half of the mixture into cavity of each chicken. Close openings with skewers and lace with string. Tie wings and legs close to the body. Place chickens on spit, being sure to balance them properly. Set spit in place over hot coals. Brush chickens with some of the melted butter. Cook about 1½ hours, until fork-tender; brush occasionally with remaining butter. Serves 8.

✑ Hibachi Chicken

2 2½-pound broiler–fryer
  chickens, quartered
¼ cup vegetable oil
Salt and pepper
Paprika
Orange Marmalade Sauce
  (recipe follows)

Wash and pat chicken dry. Brush chicken quarters with vegetable oil. Sprinkle with salt, pepper, and paprika. Place chicken quarters, skin side up, on hibachi grill set 3 to 6 inches from heat. Cook until tender, turning occasionally and brushing with a little oil. Allow 45 minutes to 1 hour total cooking time, depending on weight of chicken and distance from heat. When chicken is done, leg should twist easily out of thigh joint and pieces should be fork-tender. Serve with Orange Marmalade Sauce. Serves 4 to 6.

Orange Marmalade Sauce

1 cup orange marmalade
¼ cup light corn syrup
¼ cup vinegar
1 tablespoon Worcestershire
  sauce
1 tablespoon curry powder
1 teaspoon salt
½ teaspoon ground ginger
Few grains cayenne pepper

Combine all ingredients in a small saucepan. Cook over moderate heat (about 250° F.), stirring occasionally, until marmalade is melted and mixture is heated through. Makes about 1½ cups sauce.

✑ Orange Baked Chicken

1 2- to 2½-pound broiler–
  fryer chicken, cut up
½ cup flour
1 teaspoon salt
⅛ teaspoon pepper
⅓ cup vegetable oil
½ teaspoon celery seed
½ cup thinly sliced onion
1 cup orange juice
1 unpeeled orange, cut into 8
  wedges

Heat oven to 350° F. Wash and pat chicken pieces dry. Combine flour, salt, and pepper in a small paper bag. Put in chicken pieces a few at a time and shake to coat evenly. Heat oil in a large heavy skillet over moderately high heat (about 300° F.); add chicken and sprinkle pieces with celery seed. Brown chicken well on both sides. Remove pieces to a deep 2-quart casserole. Pour off all but 1 tablespoon of the fat in the skillet; add onion to skillet and cook until tender but not browned. Add orange juice and bring to a boil, stirring to loosen brown particles from skillet. Pour orange juice mixture over chicken; arrange orange wedges around edge of casserole. Cover and bake 1 hour, or until chicken is fork-tender. Serves 4.

✑ Coq au Vin

2 2- to 2½-pound broiler–
  fryer chickens, cut up
4 tablespoons flour
2 teaspoons salt
½ teaspoon pepper
6 tablespoons butter or
  margarine
4 tablespoons brandy
1 clove garlic, mashed
1 bay leaf
1 stalk celery, cut into 1-inch
  slices
1 fifth dry red table wine
⅛ pound salt pork, finely
  diced
12 small white onions, peeled
12 mushroom caps

Heat oven to 350° F. Wash and dry chicken. Combine flour, salt, and pepper. Roll chicken in flour mixture to coat evenly. Melt butter in a heavy skillet over moderate heat (about 250° F.). Add chicken. Brown evenly on all sides over moderately high heat (about 325° F.). Add brandy; cook 2 minutes. Remove chicken and liquid to a deep 2-quart casserole. Place garlic, bay leaf, and celery in a small square of cheesecloth; bring corners together and tie securely. Add to chicken. Pour wine over all; cover tightly. Place in oven. Heat salt pork in a skillet over moderately low heat (about 225° F.) until some of the fat melts. Add whole onions and mushroom caps. Cook and stir until onions and mushrooms are lightly browned. When chicken has baked 40 minutes, add to it the salt pork, onions, mushrooms, and liquid from skillet. Cover casserole tightly; return to oven. Bake 30 minutes more, or until chicken is fork-tender. Serves 4.

✑ Chicken Véronique

2 2½-pound broiler–fryer
  chickens, quartered
Salt and pepper
½ cup butter or margarine
½ cup finely chopped onion

Wash and pat chicken dry. Sprinkle chicken with salt and pepper. Melt ¼ cup of the butter in a large skillet over moderately high heat (about 300° F.); add chicken and cook until lightly browned on all sides. Remove chicken. Add the remaining ¼ cup butter; cook onion,

¼ *pound mushrooms, sliced*
1 *clove garlic, finely chopped*
1 *12-ounce can chicken broth*
1 *tablespoon lemon juice*
1 *teaspoon sugar*
2 *tablespoons chopped*
  crystallized ginger
1 *cup white seedless grapes,*
  cut into halves
6 *tablespoons water*
¼ *cup flour*
¾ *teaspoon salt*

mushrooms, and garlic about 5 minutes over moderate heat (about 250° F.) until tender. Stir in broth, lemon juice, sugar, and ginger. Add chicken; cover and cook over moderately low heat (about 225° F.) 40 minutes, stirring occasionally. Add grapes and cook 5 minutes. Remove from heat. Remove chicken to serving dish. Blend water and flour together in a jar or gravymaker; stir into broth mixture. Cook and stir over moderately low heat (about 225° F.) until thickened. Season with the ¾ teaspoon salt. Serve sauce over chicken. Serves 4 to 6.

❧ Chicken Cacciatore

½ *cup flour*
2 *teaspoons salt*
½ *teaspoon pepper*
1 *3½- to 4-pound broiler–*
  fryer chicken, cut up
⅓ *cup olive oil*
¼ *cup finely chopped onion*
1 *clove garlic, minced*
1 *20-ounce can tomatoes*
1 *small can tomato paste*
½ *cup water*
1 *teaspoon dried basil leaves*
1 *bay leaf*
¼ *cup dry sherry*
1 *teaspoon sugar*

Mix flour, salt, and pepper together and pour into a paper or plastic bag. Wash and pat chicken pieces dry. Put chicken into bag, a few pieces at a time, and shake to coat evenly. Heat olive oil in skillet over moderately high heat (about 350° F.); lightly brown chicken pieces on all sides. Remove chicken; add onion and garlic and cook over moderately low heat (about 225° F.) about 5 minutes, until tender. Return chicken to skillet; add tomatoes, tomato paste, water, basil, and bay leaf. Cover and simmer over moderately low heat (about 225° F.) for 1 hour, stirring occasionally. Stir in sherry and sugar. Cook 15 minutes longer, or until fork-tender. Serves 4 to 6.

❧ Sautéed Chicken with Forty Cloves of Garlic

1 *2½- to 3½-pound broiler–*
  fryer chicken, cut up
1 *small lemon, cut in half*
Salt
Pepper
4 *tablespoons olive oil*
4 *tablespoons sweet butter*
1 *to 2 heads of garlic*

Rinse chicken and pat dry with paper towels. Rub cut lemon over pieces of chicken and sprinkle chicken lightly with salt and pepper. Heat olive oil and butter in a large sauté pan or skillet over moderately high heat; add chicken and cook about 15 minutes, until lightly browned on all sides. Reduce heat to moderately low, lightly sprinkle chicken again with salt and pepper, cover and cook 15 minutes. While chicken is cooking, prepare the garlic cloves. Place a whole head of garlic in one hand and with both thumbs press away dry outer skin. Be careful not to damage the shiny inner skin enclosing each clove with your fingernails. Carefully remove all outer skin and do not use any clove of which the tight inner skin is cracked or gouged. Prepare 40 cloves of garlic. Add garlic cloves to chicken, making sure all cloves are immersed in the pan juices. Cover skillet and simmer chicken 30 minutes longer, or until tender. Arrange drained chicken pieces on a heated platter and surround with garlic cloves. To eat garlic, simply press each clove with a knife or a fork to squeeze out the aromatic purée. Serves 4.

✑ Polynesian Chicken

6 pieces broiler–fryer
  chicken (legs, breasts,
  thighs)
2 to 3 tablespoons bottled
  French dressing
Salt and pepper
1 20-ounce can pineapple
  chunks
½ cup canned chicken broth
2 tablespoons soy sauce
3 tablespoons lemon juice
1 tablespoon cornstarch
1 7-ounce package frozen
  pea pods, thawed
1 5-ounce can water
  chestnuts, drained and
  sliced
⅓ cup sliced scallions or
  green onions
About 2 cups hot cooked rice

Heat oven to 450° F. Wash and pat chicken dry. Brush chicken pieces with French dressing; sprinkle with salt and pepper. Arrange skin side down in a shallow 2-quart baking dish. Bake, uncovered, 10 minutes. Drain syrup from pineapple into a small bowl; reserve pineapple. Add chicken broth and soy sauce to pineapple syrup and combine. Gradually stir lemon juice into cornstarch; add to pineapple syrup mixture. Pour over chicken. Return to 450° F. oven and bake about 30 minutes, or until chicken is lightly browned and tender. Cook pea pods according to package directions. Just before serving, combine reserved pineapple, cooked pea pods, drained water chestnuts, and scallions with chicken. Arrange the chicken pieces and the sauce on a large warm platter. Serve with hot rice. Serves 4.

✑ Chicken Marengo

1 1½- to 2-pound
  broiler–fryer chicken, cut
  into pieces
1 teaspoon salt
¼ teaspoon pepper
2 tablespoons flour
¼ cup butter or margarine
2 cloves garlic, chopped

Wash and pat chicken dry. Sprinkle chicken with salt and pepper, then with flour. Heat butter in a heavy skillet over moderately high heat (about 300° F.) and brown chicken, turning frequently. Add chopped garlic, sherry, tomato sauce, and juice drained from mushrooms. Cook, covered, over moderately low heat (about 225° F.) 30 minutes, or until chicken is fork-tender. Add mushrooms and continue to cook until mushrooms are

½ cup dry sherry or dry white
   wine
1 8-ounce can tomato sauce
1 6-ounce can broiled
   mushroom crowns
1 tablespoon chopped fresh
   parsley

hot. Serve sprinkled with freshly chopped parsley. Serves 4.

✑ Mexican Chicken

1 5- to 6-pound fowl, cut up
5 cups water
1½ teaspoons salt
¼ cup butter or margarine
½ cup finely chopped onion
1 clove garlic, minced
1 tablespoon flour
1 teaspoon ground cumin
½ teaspoon chili powder
1 tablespoon sugar
⅓ cup cream-style peanut
   butter
1 1-ounce square
   unsweetened chocolate,
   melted
2 tablespoons toasted
   sesame seeds

Wash chicken; cover with water. Add salt and cook over moderately low heat (about 225° F.) 3 hours, or until fork-tender. Drain and measure stock; there should be about 2½ cups. If necessary, boil to reduce to that amount. Skim off fat. Melt butter in saucepan over moderate heat (about 250° F.); add onion and garlic and cook until tender. Blend in flour, stir in cumin, chili powder, sugar, peanut butter, and chocolate. Gradually add the 2½ cups stock and cook until thickened, stirring constantly. Add sesame seeds and serve over chicken. Serves 6.

✑ Chicken Raphael Weill

1 2½- to 3-pound broiler–
   fryer chicken, cut up
Salt and white pepper
¼ cup butter or margarine
1 9-ounce package frozen
   artichoke hearts
2 teaspoons chopped
   shallots or onion
¼ pound mushrooms, sliced
1 teaspoon snipped chives
¾ cup heavy cream
2 tablespoons dry sherry
2 tablespoons water
1 tablespoon flour

Wash and pat chicken dry. Season chicken with salt and pepper. Heat butter in skillet over moderately high heat (about 300° F.); add chicken and cook until lightly browned. Drain all but 1 tablespoon butter from skillet; add artichoke hearts, shallots, mushrooms, chives, cream, and sherry. Cover skillet and cook over moderately low heat (about 225° F.) 25 minutes, or until chicken is fork-tender. Remove chicken and vegetables to a platter and keep warm. Place water and flour in a small jar and shake to blend; gradually add to the cream mixture in skillet. Cook and stir over moderately low heat (about 225° F.) until thickened and smooth. Continue to cook sauce about 5 minutes, stirring occasionally. Serve over chicken. Serves 4 to 6.

POULTRY

❧ Lemon-Fricasseed Chicken

2 2½-pound broiler–fryer
chickens, cut up
Salt and pepper
¼ cup olive oil
¼ cup butter or margarine
2 thin slices of garlic
(optional)
4 tablespoons flour
2 chicken bouillon cubes
1½ cups boiling water
1 cup dry white wine
⅓ cup lemon juice
¼ cup chopped fresh parsley

Wash and pat chicken pieces dry. Sprinkle with salt and pepper. Put olive oil, butter, and garlic slices in a large, heavy skillet and heat. Add chicken and lightly brown on all sides over moderately high heat (about 300° F.). Cover and cook about 25 minutes, or until fork-tender. Remove chicken pieces. Pour or spoon off excess fat from the skillet. Reduce heat to moderate (about 250° F.). Blend flour into drippings in skillet. Dissolve chicken bouillon cubes in boiling water and add gradually to skillet. Add wine and lemon juice, stirring to blend. Cook, stirring constantly, until thickened and smooth. Add chicken pieces to gravy and simmer a few minutes to heat thoroughly. Arrange chicken on serving platter. Sprinkle with chopped parsley. Serve with extra gravy. Serves 4 to 6.

❧ Chicken Stew with Matzo Balls

1 3½- to 4-pound broiler–
fryer chicken, cut up
3 tablespoons vegetable oil
1 can condensed cream of
mushroom soup
⅓ cup milk
⅛ teaspoon pepper
1 16-ounce can mixed
vegetables or mixed peas
and carrots with liquid
1 4-ounce can sliced
mushrooms with liquid
1 tablespoon dried parsley
flakes
1 tablespoon instant minced
onion
Matzo Balls (recipe follows)

Wash and pat chicken dry. Heat oil in skillet over moderately high heat (about 325° F.). Add chicken and cook until browned on all sides. Mix soup, milk, pepper, liquid from vegetables and mushrooms, parsley, and onion and pour over chicken. Cover and place over moderately low heat (about 225° F.); simmer 35 minutes, stirring occasionally. Prepare Matzo Balls according to following directions. Add vegetables and mushrooms to stew. Drop the Matzo Balls over chicken; cover tightly and simmer 15 minutes or until chicken is fork-tender. Serves 6.

Matzo Balls

1 cup hot chicken broth
1 cup matzo meal
2 tablespoons vegetable oil
1 egg, slightly beaten
½ teaspoon salt
Few grains ground nutmeg

Pour hot broth over meal; mix well. Add oil, egg, and seasonings; mix until blended. Chill. Form rounded tablespoons of batter into balls. Add balls to chicken stew. Makes 12 balls.

Brunswick Stew

1 4- to 5-pound fowl or
  stewing chicken, cut up
6 cups water
1 cup chopped onion
½ cup chopped green pepper
1 tablespoon salt
1 16-ounce can tomatoes
1 small can tomato paste
1 10-ounce package frozen
  lima beans
1 12-ounce can whole-kernel
  corn
2 tablespoons chopped fresh
  parsley
⅛ teaspoon dried thyme
  leaves
1 bay leaf
¼ teaspoon pepper

Wash chicken; place in Dutch oven. Add water, onion, green pepper, and salt. Cover and simmer over moderately low heat (about 225° F.) 2 hours. Add tomatoes, tomato paste, lima beans, corn, parsley, thyme, bay leaf, and pepper; cover and simmer about 1 hour longer, or until chicken is fork-tender. Remove bay leaf. Skim off fat. Serves 6.

Chicken Pot Pie

Simmered Chicken and Stock
  (recipe follows)
1 8-ounce can small whole
  white onions, well drained
1 16-ounce can small whole
  white potatoes, drained
1 10-ounce package frozen
  peas, cooked until almost
  tender and drained
1 cup sliced carrots, cooked
  until almost tender and
  drained
2 cups chicken stock
2 cups milk
⅓ cup flour
1 tablespoon chopped
  pimiento
2 teaspoons salt
⅛ teaspoon pepper
Pastry Topping or Biscuit
  Crust (recipes follow)

Combine cooked chicken pieces, onions, potatoes, peas, and carrots in a 13-x-9-x-2-inch baking dish; set aside. Bring to a boil over moderate heat (about 250° F.) the chicken stock and 1½ cups of the milk. Blend together the remaining ½ cup milk and the flour; quickly stir into boiling mixture. Boil 1 minute, stirring constantly. Remove from heat; stir in pimiento and add salt and pepper, if necessary. Pour sauce over chicken and vegetables; cool. Roll out pastry or biscuit crust into a 15-x-10-inch rectangle. Cover casserole with pastry, press pastry down over edges of dish, and trim if necessary to fit casserole. Cut an X in the center of the pastry. Make each stroke of the X about 4 inches long. Fold the loose center points back over the pastry to make a square opening in the center of the pie. Heat oven to 400° F. Bake 30 to 35 minutes, until mixture is thoroughly heated and crust is golden brown. Serves 4 to 6.

Simmered Chicken and Stock

1 3- to 3½-pound broiler–
   fryer chicken, whole
2 stalks celery with leaves,
   halved crosswise
1 whole medium-sized onion
3 sprigs parsley
½ teaspoon dried rosemary
   leaves
1 bay leaf
1 teaspoon salt
¼ teaspoon peppercorns

Wash chicken. In a large saucepan or Dutch oven combine chicken, celery, onion, parsley, rosemary, bay leaf, salt, and peppercorns. Add water to cover chicken halfway—about 1½ quarts. Bring to boil over moderate heat (about 250° F.); then reduce the heat to low (about 200° F.). Cover; simmer 30 to 40 minutes, or until chicken is fork-tender. Remove chicken and strain stock; set aside and cool. Bone chicken and cut into large pieces. Measure stock—there should be 2 cups. If necessary place over moderately high heat (about 275° F.) to reduce.

Pastry Topping

1½ cups sifted all-purpose
    flour
¾   teaspoon salt
½   cup shortening
3   to 4 tablespoons cold
    water

Sift together flour and salt. Cut in shortening with 2 knives or a pastry blender until mixture resembles coarse corn meal. Sprinkle water over mixture a tablespoon at a time. Toss with a fork and push moistened portion to one side. Repeat with dry portion until dough just holds in a ball. Follow directions for rolling pastry given in Chicken Pot Pie.

Biscuit Crust

3   cups sifted all-purpose
    flour
4½ teaspoons baking powder
1½ teaspoons salt
6   tablespoons butter or
    margarine
¾   to 1 cup milk

Sift together flour, baking powder, and salt into a bowl. Cut in butter with 2 knives or a pastry blender until mixture resembles coarse corn meal. Stir in milk until mixture forms a soft dough and leaves sides of bowl. Follow directions for rolling crust given in Chicken Pot Pie.

Chicken Parts

Whatever part of the chicken you want is available today either in fresh form or packaged frozen. Chicken breasts, the most favored pieces, usually cost more per pound than the dark-fleshed thigh and drumsticks. Wings, necks, and backs that can be used in simmered dishes or casseroles are much cheaper; they yield less meat per pound but, because of their bony structure, make a great soup.

Boned chicken breasts are popular for many dishes but the boning adds to the cost. With a little practice and a small sharp knife you can bone a chicken breast at home.

How to Bone a Chicken Breast

Place a whole raw chicken breast skin side down on a cutting board. Cut through the membrane to expose the breastbone (keel). Bend the breast back to free the breastbone from the meat, making it easy to remove both bone and gristle with your fingers.

Using the tip of a sharp knife, cut the meat away from the rib cage of one side while lifting the bones with the fingers. Repeat this procedure on the opposite side.

With the knife, scrape the meat away from the wishbone and lift it out. To remove the skin from the chicken breast, simply pull it off with your fingers.

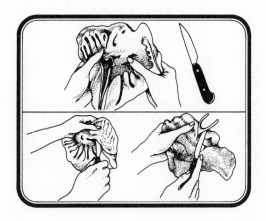

⊷ Chicken Breasts Baked in Mushroom Cream Sauce

4 large whole chicken breasts, boned and halved (if desired, remove skin)
Salt
Garlic salt
Paprika
1 can condensed cream of mushroom soup

Heat oven to 350° F. Wash and pat chicken dry. Sprinkle both sides of chicken with salt, garlic salt, and paprika. Arrange chicken, skin side up, in a shallow, rectangular 2-quart baking dish. Mix soup and cream together; pour over chicken. Sprinkle with parsley. Bake, uncovered, 1 hour, or until chicken is tender. Serve with hot cooked rice. Serves 6.

(Ingredients continued on page 374)

1 cup heavy cream
2 tablespoons chopped fresh
parsley
About 3 cups cooked rice

ᴥᶘ Chicken Breasts in Wine

¼ cup flour
½ teaspoon salt
Few grains pepper
 4 whole chicken breasts, split
½ cup butter or margarine
1 cup semidry white wine
¼ cup finely chopped onion
¼ cup flour
1 teaspoon salt
Few grains pepper
1 cup milk
1 cup light cream
4 slices boneless ham, cut ¼
inch thick
1 small avocado, peeled and
sliced

Mix together the ¼ cup flour, the ½ teaspoon salt, and the pepper. Wash and pat chicken dry. Remove skin from chicken breasts and coat chicken lightly in flour mixture. Melt half the butter in a skillet over moderately high heat (about 300° F.); add chicken and cook until lightly browned on both sides. Sprinkle lightly with salt and pepper. Add wine, cover, and cook over moderately low heat (about 225° F.) 20 minutes, turning occasionally. While chicken is cooking, melt the remaining ¼ cup butter in saucepan over moderate heat (about 250° F.); add onion and cook until tender. Blend in the remaining ¼ cup flour, the 1 teaspoon salt, and the pepper. Gradually add milk and cream; cook, stirring constantly, until thickened. Cut ham slices in half and arrange over bottom of a 3-quart shallow baking dish. Arrange chicken breasts over ham. Gradually stir wine mixture from skillet in which chicken was cooked into cream sauce; heat until blended. Pour over chicken breasts. Heat oven to 325° F. Bake about 15 minutes until chicken is fork-tender. Arrange avocado slices over chicken and return to oven for 5 minutes, until avocado is just heated. Serves 8.

ᴥᶘ Moo Goo Gai Pien

2 tablespoons cornstarch
½ teaspoon salt
2 whole boned and skinned
chicken breasts, split
3 tablespoons vegetable oil
2 scallions or green onions,
diagonally sliced
¼ pound fresh mushrooms,
sliced
⅛ teaspoon garlic powder
¼ teaspoon ground ginger

In a medium-sized bowl combine 1 tablespoon of the cornstarch and the salt. Wash chicken and pat dry. Cut chicken breasts into 1-inch cubes. (An electric knife works well for cutting both the chicken and the vegetables.) Place chicken in bowl with cornstarch and toss lightly to coat pieces well. Heat oil in an electric skillet to 375° F. Add chicken pieces and cook, stirring constantly, until chicken is done and lightly browned, about 2 to 3 minutes. Remove chicken; add scallions, mushrooms, garlic powder, and ginger and cook, stirring occasionally, about 1 minute. In a small bowl combine soy sauce,

1 tablespoon soy sauce
1 tablespoon dry sherry
1 can condensed chicken
    broth
1 7-ounce package frozen
    pea pods, thawed
About 2 cups hot cooked rice

sherry, and the remaining 1 tablespoon cornstarch and blend well. Stir chicken broth into skillet. Add cornstarch mixture gradually, stirring constantly, and cook until mixture thickens. Stir in pea pods. Simmer 30 seconds. Stir in chicken. Cook a few minutes, until thoroughly heated. Serve over rice. Serves 4.

❧ Chicken Scaloppine

1½ to 2 pounds chicken
    cutlets (sliced, boned, raw
    chicken breasts)
Salt
Pepper
Lemon
2 eggs, beaten
About 2½ cups seasoned fine
    dry bread crumbs
6 tablespoons butter or
    margarine
Lemon wedges

Wash chicken and pat dry. Place chicken pieces between two sheets of waxed paper. Flatten pieces slightly with the side of a meat mallet or meat cleaver. Sprinkle pieces lightly with salt and pepper. Squeeze a little lemon juice over each piece. Dip chicken pieces in egg, then in bread crumbs to coat well on both sides. Melt butter in a large skillet over moderately high heat (about 275° F.). Fry chicken pieces until golden brown, about 3 to 4 minutes on each side. Do not overcook or chicken will become tough. Serve with lemon wedges. Serves 4.

❧ Chicken Breasts in Tarragon Cream

4 to 6 whole chicken
    breasts, skinned, boned
    and cut in half
Salt
Freshly ground pepper
3 cups chicken broth
1 teaspoon dried tarragon
    leaves
5 tablespoons butter or
    margarine
5 tablespoons flour
1½ cups heavy cream
Juice of 1½ lemons
3 cups cooked rice
2 tablespoons finely
    chopped fresh parsley

Sprinkle both sides of each chicken breast lightly with salt and pepper. Arrange breasts in a large Dutch oven or saucepot. Mix the chicken broth with half the tarragon and pour over the chicken breasts. Cut circle of wax paper to fit the size of the pot, butter it and place over the chicken. Bring the liquid to a simmer over moderately high heat (about 275° F.). Turn heat to moderately low (about 225° F.) and simmer about 10 minutes, until the chicken breasts are tender. Remove breasts from the pot and keep warm. Boil the broth in the pot over high heat (about 400° F.) until just 2 cups remain; strain broth into measuring cup. Rinse and dry the pot and then melt the 5 tablespoons of butter in it over moderately low heat (about 225° F.). Add the flour and cook for 1 minute, stirring constantly. Gradually add the 2 cups of reduced chicken broth and the cream, stirring constantly with a wire whisk or wooden spoon. When the sauce is thickened and smooth, stir in the lemon juice and the remaining tarragon; return chicken breasts to pot. Simmer a minute or two while spooning sauce over the breasts. Make a bed of rice on a shallow serving platter; arrange breasts on rice. Spoon a little sauce over chicken breasts and sprinkle with parsley. Serve remaining sauce separately. Serves 4 to 6.

✌ Chicken Legs with Skillet Macaroni

8 chicken legs
Vegetable oil
½ cup sliced onion
Salt to taste
3 cups water
2 cups uncooked elbow
 macaroni (about ½
 pound)
1 can condensed cream of
 celery soup, undiluted
2 tablespoons chopped
 pimiento

Wash and pat chicken legs dry. Heat 1 tablespoon vegetable oil in a large skillet over moderately low heat (about 225° F.). Add onion and cook until lightly browned. Remove onion with slotted spoon and set aside. Add oil to skillet to a depth of about ¼ inch. Increase heat to moderately high (about 350° F.). While oil is heating to temperature, sprinkle chicken legs with salt to taste. Fry chicken legs 10 to 15 minutes on each side, or until well browned and fork-tender. Remove and drain on paper towels. Drain oil from skillet; reduce heat to moderate (about 250° F.). Stir in 1 cup of the water, loosening browned bits in the bottom of the pan. Add remaining 2 cups water and bring to a boil. Gradually stir in macaroni so water does not stop boiling. Cover and cook about 15 minutes, or until macaroni is tender, stirring occasionally. Stir in soup, pimiento, and cooked onion. Top with chicken legs. Cover and heat to serving temperature. Serves 4.

✌ Chicken Wings Oriental

2 pounds chicken wings
3 tablespoons vegetable oil
½ teaspoon salt
¼ teaspoon pepper
2 chicken bouillon cubes
2 cups boiling water
¾ cup sliced green onion or
 scallions
1 8-ounce can tomato sauce
2 tablespoons soy sauce
1 teaspoon sugar
2 tablespoons cornstarch
2 tablespoons water

Wash and pat chicken wings dry. Heat oil in a 10-inch skillet over moderately high heat (about 275° F.). Add wings and cook until browned on all sides, turning occasionally. Sprinkle with salt and pepper. Dissolve chicken bouillon cubes in the boiling water. Pour liquid over wings in skillet. Reduce heat to moderately low (about 225° F.); cover and simmer 45 minutes, or until chicken is tender. Add onion and tomato sauce. Stir to blend well, and simmer 5 minutes. In a small bowl combine soy sauce, sugar, cornstarch, and water and blend well. Gradually pour into skillet, stirring constantly until mixture is thickened and smooth. Serve with cooked rice; garnish with parsley. Serves 4.

About 2 cups cooked rice
Chopped fresh parsley

⁊ Savory Chicken Livers

2 tablespoons butter or
   margarine
1 pound chicken livers
2 chicken bouillon cubes
1½ cups boiling water
½ pound mushrooms, sliced
½ teaspoon salt
Pinch of dried rosemary leaves
Few grains pepper
2 tablespoons cornstarch
2 tablespoons water

Heat butter in a skillet over moderate heat (about 250° F.). Add chicken livers and cook until lightly browned, turning frequently. Dissolve bouillon cubes in the boiling water. Add bouillon, mushrooms, salt, rosemary, and pepper to livers. Cover and cook over moderately low heat (about 225° F.) for 10 minutes, or until chicken livers are cooked through. Mix cornstarch and the 2 tablespoons water together and stir into liquid in pan; cook 5 minutes, stirring constantly. Serves 4.

⁊ Roast Cornish Hens with Rice Stuffing

¾ cup butter or margarine
⅔ cup finely chopped onion
⅔ cup chopped celery
3¾ cups cooked brown rice
   (about 1¼ cups raw)
1 4-ounce can sliced
   mushrooms, drained
1 cup seedless raisins
¾ teaspoon salt
6 frozen Cornish hens,
   about 1¼ pounds each,
   thawed
Salt and pepper
6 slices raw bacon, cut into
   halves

Melt butter in skillet over moderately low heat (about 225° F.); add onion and celery and cook until tender. Mix cooked rice, mushrooms, cooked vegetables, raisins, and salt. Cool. Wash and dry hens. Sprinkle inside and outside with salt and pepper. Stuff hens loosely with the stuffing and secure closing with toothpicks. Tie legs together. Place in shallow roasting pan and lay bacon slices over hens. Spoon any leftover dressing into a small covered casserole and heat with hens. Heat oven to 350° F. Roast 30 minutes and remove bacon slices. Baste with drippings in pan. Bake 20 minutes longer, or until fork-tender and brown. Remove toothpicks and untie legs before serving. Serves 6.

⁊ Cornish Hens on a Spit

2½ tablespoons butter or
   margarine
⅓ cup chopped pecans
½ cup seedless raisins

Place the 2½ tablespoons butter in a skillet. Cook over moderately low heat (about 225° F.) until melted. Add pecans, raisins, celery, and rosemary and cook until celery is fork-tender. Add stuffing mix and water and stir

¼ *cup finely chopped celery*
¼ *teaspoon dried rosemary leaves*
1 *cup packaged herb-seasoned stuffing mix*
⅓ *cup water*
3 *Cornish hens, about 1 pound each*
3 *tablespoons melted butter or margarine*

to blend well. Remove from heat. Heat broiler–rotisserie until the heating element is red. Divide the stuffing mixture evenly among the 3 hens and stuff them. Secure openings with skewers. Tie legs together securely and tie wings to the body. Thread the hens close together on the spit. Secure tightly with prongs at each end of the spit. Make sure the hens are properly balanced to avoid strain on the motor when the spit is turning. Brush the hens with the 3 tablespoons melted butter. Place spit on rotisserie about 3 inches from source of heat. Turn on rotisserie motor. Roast 1¼ to 1½ hours. The drumstick will move easily when hens are done. Remove skewers and string before serving. Serves 3.

Turkey

Before you buy turkey, read the poultry labeling and storage information at the beginning of this chapter. It will tell you what to look for when you buy and how to handle fresh and frozen birds when you bring them home from the market. How much to buy? Small turkeys weigh from four to nine pounds, large birds weigh up to twenty-four pounds. Large turkeys are usually more economical than small ones; that is, they have more meat in relation to the total weight of the bird. The general rule is to allow about one pound per person if you're buying a bird under nine pounds, and three-quarters of a pound per person for heavier birds. Turkey leftovers are nice to have around and you can plan for them, but before you buy the biggest turkey in the case, be sure you have a roasting pan that will hold the large size and that the pan will fit your oven rack with enough air space left so that the heat will circulate freely.

If your turkey is frozen (90 percent are today), buy it two to four days before you plan to serve it and defrost it by one of the methods described on page 357. Once it is thawed, cover the turkey loosely with plastic wrap or aluminum foil and refrigerate until you are ready to roast it. Preferably, a turkey should be refrigerated immediately and cooked within three hours after thawing. However, a thawed, ready-to-cook turkey can be kept for two to three days in a refrigerator, if necessary.

If your turkey is fresh, store and use it as directed for fresh poultry on page 357.

When You Roast a Turkey

Timing is an important calculation when you're roasting a large turkey; stuffing and trussing the turkey will take anywhere from thirty minutes to an hour, depending upon the kind of stuffing you choose to make. First check the roasting time for your size turkey on the Poultry Roasting and Broiling Timetable (page 52). Add one hour and thirty minutes to the longest time given. This allows an hour for preparation of the bird and twenty to thirty minutes *after* roasting for the turkey to absorb its juices and be at its best for carving. Cooking times for turkeys will vary for any number of reasons—the accuracy of your oven thermostat, the starting temperature of the bird, the number of oven-door openings during cooking, and the age of the turkey.

Stuffing the Turkey

When you're ready to stuff the turkey, rinse it inside and out with cold water and pat it dry with paper towels. Stuff the turkey just before it is to be cooked, never the day before. Moistened stuffing does not keep well; handle it carefully. If you wish, prepare the dry ingredients a day ahead, then add the liquid just before stuffing the bird. Allow ½ to ¾ cup of stuffing for each serving. Stuffing expands while cooking, so you should never pack it tightly. A turkey will hold about 1 cup of stuffing per pound of bird weight. (Instead of overstuffing the bird, bake extra stuffing in a separate covered dish the last hour the turkey roasts, basting it with drippings from the roasting pan.)

First fill the neck cavity lightly. Fasten the neck skin to the back of the turkey with a skewer (Figure 2), hold it in place with the wing tips or sew the skin to the back. Then stuff the body cavity. To close up the bird, use poultry pins and lace them with string (Figure 3, page 380), or sew with a needle and thread. Many turkeys today are processed with a band of skin that fits tightly over the ends of the legs. To stuff these birds, pull the legs loose from the skin band, then tuck them back under it after stuffing. This eliminates lacing or sewing.

TRUSSING THE TURKEY

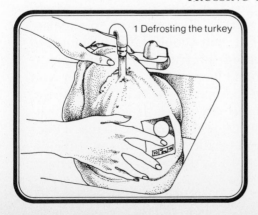
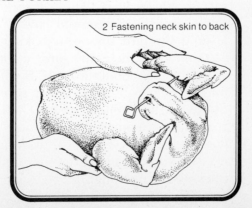

1 Defrosting the turkey

2 Fastening neck skin to back

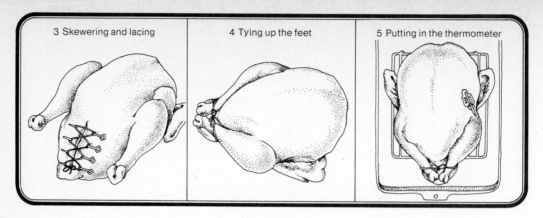

3 Skewering and lacing   4 Tying up the feet   5 Putting in the thermometer

Trussing

Trussing, which means binding the legs and wings to the body, makes the turkey more compact, easier to handle, easier to cook, and more attractive. To truss, fold the wings back, twisting the wing tips so that they snap into position on the turkey's back (Figure 2, page 379). With the wings in this position, the meaty breast of a modern bird has a chance to cook through, and the wings help balance the bird throughout the roasting and the carving. Tie a string securely around the tail as an anchor, then tie the ends of the legs to the same string (Figure 4, above). Or you may insert the tips of the legs through the natural band of skin formed about the tail.

Preparing the Turkey for the Oven

Brush the entire turkey with shortening, oil, or melted butter, using a twist of cheesecloth or paper towel if you haven't a brush.

Place the bird breast side up on a rack in a shallow roasting pan. The rack should be at least one-half inch high to keep the turkey out of its own juices, and the pan should have low sides to allow the heat to circulate around the bird for even cooking. The pan should be big enough to accommodate the entire bird, without legs protruding from the pan to spatter grease about the oven. If you don't have a large open roaster, you may be able to use the broiler pan from your range or an inexpensive, disposable, aluminum foil pan, and improvise a rack. If you use a meat-roasting thermometer, insert it into the inside thigh muscle so that it does not touch bone (Figure 5, above): For small turkeys this is difficult; instead, you can insert the thermometer into the center of the stuffing, through the opening.

Place the turkey in the oven, which has been preheated to 325° F. This low temperature is recommended for better flavor and appearance, less shrinkage, and less loss of juices.

Always roast the turkey in one continuous cooking period. Baste or brush it occasionally with pan drippings or butter, giving special attention to dry areas. When the turkey has been in the oven two-thirds of the estimated cooking time, cut the string or band of skin at the tail to release the legs and permit the heat to reach the thick, meaty part. When the turkey begins to turn golden brown, cover it with a loose tent of aluminum foil, or lay a fat-moistened cloth over legs and breast to prevent excessive browning.

The turkey is done when the meat thermometer registers 180° F. to 185° F. in the thigh or 165° F. in the stuffing. A less accurate test for doneness is to press the thickest part of the drumstick with your fingers (protect them with paper towels). When the thigh meat feels very soft and you can move the drumstick readily up and down, the turkey is done. (For complete directions for carving, turn to page 383).

Following is a complete recipe for Roast Turkey that has a choice of stuffings and is served with Giblet Gravy. You may substitute any of the stuffings from the recipes starting on this page; be sure cup-measurement of stuffing matches the weight of your bird.

❧ *Roast Turkey with Chestnut and Oyster Stuffings*

1 12- to 15-pound ready-to-cook frozen turkey, thawed as directed on page 378
Oyster Stuffing (recipe follows)
Chestnut Stuffing (recipe follows)
¼ cup melted shortening or vegetable oil

Heat oven to 325° F. Rinse thawed turkey with cold water; drain and pat dry. Fill wishbone area of the turkey loosely with the Oyster Stuffing. Fill the body cavity with the Chestnut Stuffing. Fasten neck skin to back with a skewer. Fold wing tips onto back. Push drumsticks under band of skin at tail, if present, or tie them to tail. Put any remaining stuffing in a small casserole to be baked along with turkey during the last hour of baking time. Place turkey on a rack in a shallow roasting pan, breast side up. Brush skin with melted shortening or oil. Do not add water to pan. Place in oven and roast, uncovered, 4½ to 5½ hours. Baste occasionally with pan drippings. When turkey is about two-thirds done, cut cord or band of skin at tail to release legs. Turkey is done when the thickest part of the drumstick feels very soft when pressed between protected fingers. A meat thermometer placed in the thickest part of the thigh muscle should register approximately 185° F. Remove turkey to heated platter and make gravy. (Pan drippings from turkey should be reserved for gravy.) Serves 8 to 10.

POULTRY

Chestnut Stuffing

½ pound chestnuts
1¾ cups water
1 cup butter or margarine
2 7-ounce packages herb-seasoned cubed stuffing
⅓ cup finely chopped fresh parsley

Wash chestnuts. Make a slit on the flat side of each with a sharp knife. Heat oven to 450° F. Bake chestnuts 20 minutes. Cool and remove shells and inner skin. Cover chestnuts with boiling water and cook over moderately low heat (about 225° F.) 10 to 15 minutes, until tender. Drain and chop coarsely. Heat the 1¾ cups water in a large saucepan; melt butter in hot water. Add stuffing, parsley, and chopped chestnuts; toss lightly until well blended. Makes about 6 cups stuffing.

Oyster Stuffing

*1 8-ounce can oysters
Water
½ cup butter or margarine
2 tablespoons lemon juice
1 7-ounce package herb-seasoned cubed stuffing

Drain can of oysters, reserving liquid. Pour liquid into measuring cup; add enough water to make 1 cup. Heat liquid in a large saucepan; melt butter in hot liquid. Stir in lemon juice. Add stuffing and toss lightly until stuffing is moistened. Chop oysters coarsely. Add oysters to stuffing and toss to blend well. Makes 3 cups stuffing.

*Note: 1 cup fresh or thawed frozen oysters with oyster liquid may be substituted.

Giblet Gravy

½ cup fat from turkey drippings
½ cup unsifted all-purpose flour
5 cups liquid (including reserved giblet broth)
Salt and pepper to taste
Cooked Giblets, chopped (recipe follows)

After turkey is removed from roasting pan, pour drippings from pan into a bowl, leaving most of the brown particles in the pan. Let the fat rise to the top of the drippings. Skim off ½ cup fat and pour into a large skillet. Skim off remaining fat and discard. Add rest of drippings to reserved giblet broth; pour into the roasting pan. Place over moderate heat (about 250° F.) and stir, scraping to remove brown particles from the bottom. Measure liquid from roasting pan and add enough water to make 5 cups. Heat the ½ cup turkey fat in the skillet over moderate heat (about 250° F.); gradually blend in flour. Cook until mixture bubbles. Remove skillet from heat and add the 5 cups liquid gradually, stirring constantly. Cook over moderate heat (about 250° F.), stirring constantly, until thickened and smooth. Add salt and pepper. Add chopped giblets to gravy and cook over moderately low heat (about 225° F.) about 5 minutes. Makes 5 cups.

Cooked Giblets

Giblets from turkey
- **1 teaspoon salt**
- **2 whole peppercorns**
- **2 whole cloves**
- **½ bay leaf**
- **2 thin slices onion**
- **1 stalk celery, cut up (about ⅓ cup)**
- **1 carrot, cut up (about ⅓ cup)**

Remove heart, liver, and gizzard from turkey. Rinse in cold water. Place giblets in saucepan and add boiling water to cover. Add remaining ingredients. Cover and cook over moderately low heat (about 225° F.) about 15 minutes. Remove liver and set aside. Continue to cook heart and gizzard over low heat (about 200° F.) until tender, about 2 to 3 hours. Chop giblets coarsely. Strain broth and reserve.

Carving a Turkey or Roasting Chicken

Carving a turkey or large roasting chicken expertly—and with complete assurance—is a skill worth acquiring. Following is a foolproof guide to the techniques and tools of carving the turkey or chicken to perfection.

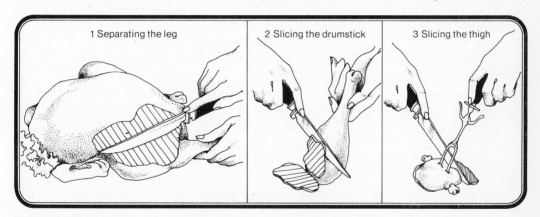

1 Separating the leg

2 Slicing the drumstick

3 Slicing the thigh

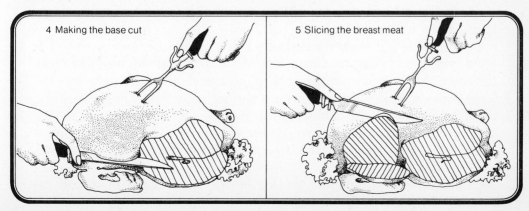

4 Making the base cut

5 Slicing the breast meat

Successful carving really begins in the kitchen, with a bird that is at the perfect degree of doneness and that has been allowed to stand 15 to 20 minutes, to absorb its own juices. Poultry roasts, like meat roasts, will carve more easily if they sit at room temperature a brief time before carving. Usually the time it takes to make gravy and get the other food on the table will be sufficient time for the turkey to be ready for carving. Before bringing in the bird, remove skewers and sewing string. Place the turkey or chicken on a warm platter that has room to spare. Keep garnishes at a minimum—they will only make carving more difficult.

Carving must be done on a steady table, and the area around the turkey platter must be kept clear. Don't offset the steady surface of the table by putting a wobbly trivet under the platter. If the tabletop needs protection, use a large hot pad; if necessary, improvise with cork or straw place mats, or use a large magazine wrapped in a clean towel.

There are other accessories that make carving go smoothly: a small, warm platter or serving plate next to the turkey platter; a warm vegetable dish for stuffing; a long-handled spoon, also for the stuffing; foil or paper ruffles, either bought or homemade, to put on the drumsticks (these are not as chichi as they may sound; they keep your hands from getting greasy in the very first step). You may also place a small, unobtrusive, dampened fingertip towel or napkin on a small plate, for the carver's hands. When you do the carving yourself, you will appreciate these thoughtful extra touches.

What expert carving really depends on is the knife. Use the very best carving knife you can find, freshly sharpened. You also need a long-handled carving fork with a guard on the handle. Many carvers find they can carve better and faster with an electric slicing knife, and at a large gathering with all waiting to be served, speed is welcome.

Carving Steps

If you're right-handed, place the bird so that its legs are at your right hand. Then follow these steps:

1. *Remove the leg:* Hold the drumstick firmly with the fingers of the left hand and gently pull the entire leg—drumstick and thigh—away from the body. At the same time, cut through the skin between the leg and body with the knife (Figure 1). Press the leg away from the body, using the flat side of the knife. Then cut through the joint that connects the leg to the back bone and cut through the skin on the back. Cut the meat completely away from the body by following the body contour carefully with the knife.

2. *Slice the drumstick:* Place the leg on the warm small plate and cut through the joint, dividing the leg into drumstick and thigh. Slice each

piece individually, starting with the drumstick. Hold it at a convenient angle, slicing toward the plate (Figure 2). If the tendons were not removed when the bird was processed, you will not be able to get perfect slices.

3. *Slice the thigh:* Hold the thigh firmly on the plate with the fork. Cut even slices parallel to the bone (Figure 3). Arrange all the dark meat slices neatly on the second serving plate or platter.

4. *Prepare the breast for slicing:* Before you begin to slice, make a base cut: Place the knife as close to the wing as possible and make a deep, horizontal cut into the breast meat, cutting to the bone (Figure 4). All the downward slices will stop at this cut. It's easier to leave the wing on at this point; if you wish to serve it, cut through the joint.

5. *Carve the breast meat:* Start halfway up the side, carving downward and ending at the base cut. Start each new slice at a slightly higher point on the breast. Keep all the slices thin and even (Figure 5). Continue carving until enough meat is sliced for first servings. Carve additional meat as needed.

To remove the stuffing, enlarge the opening of the body cavity at the tail, or cut into the side of the turkey where the leg has been removed, and spoon out stuffing. Serve the remaining stuffing from the wishbone area.

Leftover Turkey: This is both inevitable and desirable. Always remove the remaining stuffing from the body and neck cavities before you store cooked turkey (see page 357). If you plan to freeze the leftovers, see the freezing chart, page 59. Store leftover gravy, tightly covered, in the refrigerator. You will find recipes for leftover turkey in other chapters in this book. Check the index for recipes.

Broiled Turkey: Four- to six-pound turkeys may be quartered and broiled like chicken (page 363). Place turkey about nine inches from source of heat; regulate if necessary so turkey doesn't become too brown. Allow twenty to thirty minutes on each side.

Fried Turkey: Turkeys that weigh between four and six pounds may also be cut into serving pieces and fried like Basic Fried Chicken (page 360), except that they will have to cook longer.

Turkey Rolls: Frozen boneless turkey rolls are available nationally. They come in white meat only and a mixture of light and dark meat.

Turkey Parts: In many parts of the country turkey parts are available both fresh and frozen. Turkey breasts, legs and thighs can be bought separately. Turkey steaks (inch-thick slices of breast), turkey scallopine (thin slices of breast), turkey sausage, turkey chops, (ground turkey formed into chop shape) and ground turkey to use like hamburgers are offered at many meat counters. Following are some interesting ways to use turkey parts.

🦆 Turkey Breast with Pecan Dressing

½ pound butter or
  margarine
½ cup frozen or fresh
  chopped onion
1 16-ounce package
  herb-seasoned stuffing
1½ cups hot water
½ cup dry white wine
¼ cup dried parsley flakes
1 cup chopped pecans
1 10- to 11-pound frozen
  turkey breast, thawed
Salt and pepper
2 tablespoons softened
  butter or margarine
2 10½-ounce cans chicken
  giblet gravy

Heat oven to 325° F. Melt the ½ pound butter in a skillet over moderately low heat (about 225° F.). Add onion and cook until tender, stirring occasionally. Remove from heat. Mix together stuffing, hot water, wine, cooked onion, parsley, and pecans. Place a rack in a shallow roasting pan and cover it with aluminum foil to within 1 inch of edges. Place dressing on foil and mound it to fit cavity of turkey breast. Wash and dry turkey breast and sprinkle inside with salt and pepper. Place turkey over dressing. Spread the 2 tablespoons butter over skin of breast. Cover loosely with foil. (Do not tuck foil around turkey.) Roast 4¾ to 5 hours, or until fork-tender. Remove rack with turkey from pan. Add giblet gravy to drippings in pan. Place over moderately low heat (about 225° F.) and cook until gravy is heated, stirring constantly. Place turkey on platter; serve with dressing and gravy. Serves 8 to 10.

🦆 Turkey Kiev

1 stick (4 ounces) sweet
  butter, chilled
1½ pounds turkey breast,
  sliced into 8 to 12 ¼-inch
  slices
1 teaspoon salt
¼ teaspoon pepper
¼ cup finely chopped chives
  or green onions
Flour for dredging
2 eggs, slightly beaten
1 cup soft fresh bread
  crumbs
Vegetable oil for deep frying

Cut the stick of butter in half and then cut each half lengthwise into quarters.* Place a piece of butter in the middle of each turkey slice, sprinkle with salt, pepper and chives. Roll up each slice, pressing meat together firmly and enclosing butter completely. (The meat will adhere to itself.) Dredge each turkey roll in flour, dip in beaten egg and then roll in bread crumbs to coat completely. Set rolls on a plate and refrigerate 1 hour or longer. Heat 2 inches of oil in a deep skillet or deep-fat fryer until a frying thermometer registers 350° F. Cook half the turkey rolls at a time in the oil about 10 minutes, until browned all over and cooked through. Drain rolls on paper towels and serve. Serves 6.

*Note: The size of turkey slices may vary. If they are small, adjust the number of pieces of butter by cutting it in thirds.

Chicken Kiev

Use 4 boneless chicken breasts instead of turkey slices. Cut each breast in half and flatten slightly by pounding between pieces of waxed paper.

◈ Cold Poached Turkey with Curry Cream Dressing

2 turkey thighs (about 3
   pounds total)
2 teaspoons salt
Water
Lettuce leaves or watercress
Curry Cream Dressing (recipe
   follows)

Pull skin off thighs and discard. Put thighs side by side in a small saucepan; they should fit closely so that you won't need a lot of water. Add salt and just enough water to cover thighs; bring to a simmer over moderate heat (about 250° F.). Cover pan tightly and cook over low heat (about 200° F.) 55 minutes. Let turkey cool in broth and then chill for several hours if possible. Remove meat from bones. Slice turkey into very thin strips and arrange on a platter. Garnish with lettuce leaves or watercress and serve with Curry Cream Dressing. Yields about 4 cups cooked turkey; serves 4 to 6.

Curry Cream Dressing

¼ cup finely chopped, peeled
   onion
1½ tablespoons vegetable oil
2 tablespoons curry powder
½ cup water or turkey broth
1 bay leaf
¾ teaspoon salt
2 slices lemon, peel included
¼ cup apricot preserves
1½ cups mayonnaise
2 tablespoons lemon juice

In a small, heavy saucepan cook onion in oil over moderate heat (about 250° F.) about 30 seconds without browning. Add curry powder and stir over low heat (about 200° F.) 2 minutes. Add water, bay leaf, ½ teaspoon of the salt, the lemon slices and the preserves; cook over low heat about 10 minutes, stirring occasionally. Cool. Place mayonnaise in a bowl. Strain and stir in the cooled curry mixture half at a time; mix in the lemon juice and the remaining ¼ teaspoon salt. Taste dressing, add more salt or lemon juice if desired. Chill dressing. Makes about 1½ cups.

◈ Turkey Scallopini with Mushrooms, Ham and Cheese

¼ cup sweet butter
1 tablespoon vegetable oil
1 1¼- to 1½- pound turkey
   breast, cut into ¼-inch-
   thick slices, thawed if
   frozen
¾ cup all-purpose flour, for
   dredging
¼ teaspoon freshly ground
   pepper
⅓ cup chicken broth
⅓ cup dry white wine
1 cup freshly grated
   Parmesan cheese (about 1

Heat oven to 400° F. Heat the ¼ cup of butter and the oil in a medium-sized skillet over moderately high heat (about 275° F.) until foam subsides. Coat turkey slices with flour and shake off the excess. Turn heat up to moderately high (about 350° F.); cook the turkey slices in the butter a few at a time for 1 to 1½ minutes on each side, until lightly browned. As the pieces are done, remove them to a shallow ovenproof dish large enough to hold all the slices in a single layer; sprinkle with pepper. Add broth and wine to butter left in skillet to loosen all the browned particles. Boil broth mixture 1 minute over moderately high heat (about 300° F.); remove skillet from heat. Sprinkle half of the cheese over the turkey slices and then cover each slice with a slice of ham

cup plus 2 tablespoons)
¼ pound thinly sliced
prosciutto or Virginia
ham
1½ cups fresh mushrooms,
thinly sliced (about 6
ounces)
1 tablespoon sweet butter

trimmed to cover turkey neatly. Spoon mushrooms over ham and then cover with remaining cheese. Spoon the broth mixture carefully over the cheese and top with the 1 tablespoon butter cut into tiny pieces. Place the baking dish in the upper part of the oven and bake 6 to 8 minutes, or until cheese melts. Serve turkey from baking dish, spooning a little of the pan sauce on each serving. Serves 5 or 6.

 *Stir-Fried Turkey with Almonds and Zucchini*

1 pound turkey meat (light,
dark or both), boned,
skinned and cut into
¾-x-2-inch strips
½ egg white (beat the egg
white slightly and divide
in half)
1 tablespoon cornstarch
½ teaspoon salt
½ teaspoon sugar
6 tablespoons vegetable oil
2 cups ¼-inch-thick slices
unpeeled zucchini, cut on
the diagonal
1 cup whole blanched
almonds
4 thin slices peeled fresh
ginger or ½ teaspoon
ground ginger*
4 cloves garlic, peeled and
flattened but left whole
1½ tablespoons dry sherry
wine
1½ tablespoons soy sauce
¼ cup chopped fresh sweet
red pepper or drained
canned pimiento

Put the turkey strips in a small bowl and mix in the egg white, cornstarch, salt and sugar. Cover and refrigerate at least 30 minutes. Measure and prepare remaining ingredients before starting the cooking. To cook, heat 3 tablespoons of the oil in a large, heavy skillet, *wok* or electric *wok* over moderately high heat (about 375° F.); add the turkey and stir-fry about 2 minutes, until pieces turn white. With a slotted spoon, transfer turkey to a bowl. Add another tablespoon of oil to the skillet and heat; add zucchini and stir-fry over moderately high heat about 1 minute, until the pieces color slightly but remain crisp. Transfer zucchini to a second bowl. Heat another tablespoon of oil in the skillet, add the almonds and stir-fry about one minute, until they are golden brown; add almonds to zucchini. Heat remaining tablespoon of oil in skillet, add ginger and garlic, stir-fry about 30 seconds and then scoop them out and discard them. Add turkey, sherry and soy sauce to the garlic-flavored oil in the skillet and stir over moderately high heat (about 375° F.) about 15 seconds. Add zucchini and almonds and heat, stirring well to combine. Sprinkle with chopped red pepper and turn out onto a serving dish. Serves 4.

Note: If using ground ginger, mix and add it with the sherry and soy sauce.

Dilled MacTurkey

1 pound ground turkey
¼ cup packaged dry bread

Place turkey, the ¼ cup bread crumbs, dillweed, onion, sour cream, unbeaten egg, salt and pepper in a mixing

crumbs
2 teaspoons dried dillweed
¼ cup finely chopped, peeled
   onion
¼ cup commercial sour
   cream
1 egg
1 teaspoon salt
⅛ teaspoon pepper
1 egg, slightly beaten
Packaged dry bread crumbs
3 tablespoons vegetable oil

bowl. Mix well and then shape mixture into four oval patties, each about one inch thick. Place beaten egg in a pie plate and bread crumbs in a second plate. Dip turkey patties in beaten egg and then in bread crumbs to coat evenly. Heat oil in a skillet over moderately high heat (about 300° F.), add patties and cook about 7 minutes on each side, until cooked through and evenly browned; do not overcook. Remove patties from pan, drain on paper towels and serve immediately. Serves 4.

➳ Turkey Legs Milanese

6 small turkey legs (about 3
   pounds)
2 tablespoons butter
¾ cup finely chopped, peeled
   onion
¼ cup finely chopped, peeled
   carrot
¼ cup finely chopped celery
½ teaspoon finely chopped,
   peeled garlic
1 teaspoon salt
¼ teaspoon pepper
¼ cup olive oil
½ cup dry white wine
⅓ cup chicken broth
¼ teaspoon dried basil
   leaves
¼ teaspoon dried thyme
   leaves
1½ cups canned whole
   tomatoes, drained and
   coarsely chopped
½ cup finely chopped fresh
   parsley
1 bay leaf
1 tablespoon grated lemon
   peel
4 tablespoons finely
   chopped fresh parsley

Heat oven to 350° F. Rinse turkey legs and pat dry with paper towels. Melt the butter in a heavy, 3-quart Dutch oven or casserole over moderate heat (about 250° F.); add the onion, carrot, celery and garlic and cook, stirring occasionally, until lightly browned, about 10 minutes. Remove pot from heat. Meanwhile sprinkle legs with salt and pepper. Heat 3 tablespoons of the oil in a 12-inch skillet over moderately high heat (about 325° F.). Brown the legs in the oil 3 at a time, adding a little more oil if needed. Arrange browned legs side by side on top of vegetables in Dutch oven. Pour off and discard most of the fat from the skillet. Add wine to skillet and bring to a boil over moderately high heat (about 275° F.), stirring to scrape in the brown bits that cling to the skillet; boil until about ¼ cup of liquid remains. Add broth, basil, thyme, tomatoes, the ½ cup parsley and the bay leaf. Bring mixture to a boil and then pour it over the turkey legs. Place Dutch oven over moderately high heat (about 275° F.) and bring to a boil. Cover Dutch oven and bake for 1 to 1½ hours, basting every 30 minutes with pan liquid. Mix lemon peel and the 4 tablespoons parsley and sprinkle over legs. Serves 6.

Duckling

Duckling is delicious when it is properly cooked. To get it ready for cooking, thaw it (if frozen) or store it according to the directions for handling poultry (page 357). Duckling may be roasted whole, stuffed or unstuffed, or it can be quartered before cooking. Whichever way you choose, allow one quarter of a duckling per serving when you use the usual 4- to 5-pound weight.

Duckling will shed a large amount of fat in the cooking. This fat lies just beneath the skin. In order to get a crisp finished skin, prick the skin gently (don't pierce the meat) with the tines of a fork or score the skin lightly with a sharp knife at one-inch intervals.

Carving a duckling is not recommended. Remove the stuffing to a serving dish and cut the duckling into quarters with heavy poultry shears to serve.

✑ *Orange-Glazed Roast Duckling*

1 **4- to 5-pound ready-to-cook duckling**
4 **cups soft bread crumbs**
½ **cup chicken broth or bouillon**
½ **cup chopped green pepper**
1 **medium-sized onion, chopped**
½ **teaspoon rubbed dried sage**
½ **teaspoon dried thyme leaves**
¾ **teaspoon salt**
⅛ **teaspoon pepper**
2 **cups firmly packed light brown sugar**
1 **tablespoon cornstarch**
2 **tablespoons sliced orange peel**
1 **cup orange juice**

Heat oven to 325° F. Wash and dry duckling. Mix bread crumbs, chicken broth, green pepper, onion, sage, thyme, salt, and pepper. Spoon stuffing lightly into body cavity of duckling. Close opening with skewers and lace with string. Place duckling in a shallow roasting pan and prick skin with tines of a fork. Roast, allowing 30 minutes per pound. While duckling is roasting, prepare sauce. Mix together brown sugar, cornstarch, orange peel, and juice; place over moderate heat (about 250° F.) and cook 5 to 10 minutes until sauce is slightly thickened. About 30 minutes before end of roasting time, remove duckling from oven and drain off fat. Pour orange mixture over duckling and continue to roast, basting frequently with sauce from bottom of pan, until duckling is tender and glazed. Serves 3 to 4.

✑ *Roast Duckling with Green Grape Stuffing*

1 **4- to 5-pound ready to cook duckling**
Giblets from duckling

Wash and dry duckling. Refrigerate while making stuffing. Place giblets in a saucepan and add 2 cups boiling salted water. Cook over moderately low heat (about

½ *pound fresh mushrooms,*
sliced
½ *cup chopped onion*
¼ *cup butter or margarine*
5 *cups day-old bread cubes*
½ *cup chopped Brazil nuts*
½ *teaspoon salt*
½ *cup chopped fresh parsley*
⅛ *teaspoon dried marjoram*
leaves
1 *cup seedless green grapes*

225° F.) about 15 minutes. Remove liver and set aside. Continue to cook heart and gizzard until tender, about 2 to 3 hours. Add more water if needed as giblets cook. Cook mushrooms and onions in butter in a small skillet over moderately low heat (about 225° F.) until tender but not brown. Add ¼ cup of the giblet broth and cook a few minutes more, until liquid is absorbed. Chop giblets and combine lightly with remaining ingredients. (For moist stuffing add ½ cup of giblet broth.) Fill cavities of duckling with stuffing. Skewer neck skin over back. Close opening with skewers and lace with string. Prick skin with tines of fork. Heat oven to 325° F. Place duckling on rack in shallow pan, breast up. Roast 2 to 2½ hours. Serves 4.

Goose

Geese are available both frozen and fresh, but they are not usually carried on a day-to-day basis by most markets. You can usually order them, however, from any butcher. Like duckling, goose has a smaller ratio of meat to bone than chicken or turkey. Allow 1½ pounds of ready-to-cook weight per person. Because of the amount of fat in a goose, you will need to prick the skin before roasting; do not add fat or baste.

Store cooked and uncooked goose as directed in Storing Poultry on page 356.

Here is a favorite way to prepare Roast Goose.

✑ Roast Goose with Chestnut Stuffing

1 *12-pound fresh or frozen*
ready-to-cook goose
Goose fat
¾ *cup finely chopped onion*
1 *pound bulk sausage*
1 *goose liver, ground or*
finely chopped
1 *goose heart, ground or*
finely chopped
1 *teaspoon dried rosemary*
leaves
½ *teaspoon dried thyme*
leaves
1 *bay leaf, crushed*

If goose is frozen, thaw as directed on wrapper. Rinse goose in cold water; drain and pat dry with paper towels. Remove most of the loose fat from the body cavity. Heat a piece of the goose fat in a large skillet over moderate heat (about 250° F.) until fat melts. Measure and reserve 2 tablespoons melted fat; discard the rest. Add the onion to the melted fat and cook until tender. Add the sausage and break up with the back of a wooden spoon. Cook sausage until it has lost its pink color. Pour off most of the excess fat. Add goose liver and heart, rosemary, thyme, bay leaf, and garlic. Return to moderate heat (about 250° F.) and cook about 5 minutes, stirring occasionally. Add the chestnuts, apples, chicken stock, bread crumbs, parsley, and, if desired, the brandy. Combine

1 clove garlic, minced
3 cups cooked chestnuts
   (recipe follows)
3 cups finely chopped green
   apples
½ cup canned chicken stock
½ cup soft bread crumbs
2 tablespoons finely chopped
   fresh parsley
1 tablespoon applejack
   brandy (optional)

thoroughly. Fill wishbone area and body cavity of goose loosely with the prepared stuffing. Fasten neck skin to the back with a skewer. Fold wing tips onto back. Push drumsticks under band of skin at tail, if present, or tie them to tail. Place the goose on a rack in a shallow roasting pan, breast side up. Prick skin of goose at intervals with a fork; do not prick meat. Place, uncovered, in a preheated 450° F. oven and roast 10 minutes. Reduce heat to 325° F. and continue roasting, uncovered, for 4 to 4½ hours, or until leg moves easily in its joint. Continue pricking skin every 30 minutes. Pour off fat as it accumulates. Serves 6 to 8.

Boiled Chestnuts

1 quart chestnuts

With a sharp knife cut a cross on the flat side of the shells of the chestnuts. Place in a saucepan; add enough water to cover and place over moderate heat (about 250° F.). Bring to a boil and simmer about 5 minutes. Peel the chestnuts. If chestnuts are not fork-tender, add water to cover and simmer about 5 minutes longer. Older chestnuts will require more cooking. Makes about 3 cups chestnuts.

Note: If a fruit stuffing is preferred, prepare goose as directed. Stuff with Fruit Stuffing (recipe on page 394) and roast as directed above.

Stuffing

Many people feel that roast poultry is not complete without a flavorful stuffing. The variety of stuffings given here can be used interchangeably in chicken, turkey, duck, or goose. Note, however, that these stuffings yield different quantities, depending upon whether they were planned for a medium turkey or a roasting chicken. You may have to adapt them to your individual needs. The rules: Allow 1 cup stuffing mixture for each pound of ready-for-oven poultry. Any extra stuffing mixture may be placed in a covered casserole and baked in the oven with the bird for the last hour of cooking.

Bread that is one or two days old will make better stuffing than fresh bread. If you can get day-old bread, sliced or unsliced, at your market, it may be marked down in price and be just what you want. Many markets also have bags of unseasoned bread cubes to be used for stuffing.

Bread and seasonings may be mixed ahead of time and kept at room temperature. Do not add moisture to the stuffing before you are ready to use it and never stuff the bird until you are ready to roast it.

ঌ *Classic Herb Stuffing*

½ *cup butter or margarine*
1 *cup chopped onion*
1 *cup chopped celery, with leaves*
1½ *teaspoons salt*
½ *teaspoon pepper*
1 *teaspoon poultry seasoning*
3 *quarts (12 cups) cubed or torn day-old white bread*
2 *tablespoons chopped fresh parsley*
½ *cup fresh water*

Melt butter in skillet over moderately low heat (about 225° F.). Add onion and celery; cook until onion is soft, stirring occasionally. Remove from heat; add salt, pepper, and poultry seasoning. Gradually pour butter mixture over bread and parsley in a bowl; toss together. Moisten with water. Makes about 12 cups, enough for a 12-pound turkey.

Sausage Stuffing

Break up *1 pound sausage meat* in a skillet; cook over moderate heat (about 250° F.) 5 to 8 minutes, until lightly browned. Remove sausage from skillet. Add only 3 tablespoons of the butter called for in the Classic Herb Stuffing recipe. Brown onions and celery as directed and add to the bread mixture with the sausage. Reduce the salt to 1 teaspoon and the water to ¼ cup. Makes about 12 cups.

Oyster Stuffing

Gently simmer *1 quart oysters* over low heat (about 200° F.) until the edges curl. Drain and reserve ½ cup of the liquid. Chop the oysters coarsely and add to the bread mixture with the cooked onions and celery. Use the ½ cup oyster liquid in place of the water in Classic Herb Stuffing recipe. Makes about 12 cups.

Chestnut Stuffing

Wash ¾ *pound chestnuts;* make a slit on the flat side of each with a sharp knife. Heat oven to 450° F. Bake chestnuts 20 minutes. Cool and remove shells and inner skin. Cover chestnuts with boiling water and cook over moderately low heat (about 225° F.) 10 to 15 minutes, until tender. Drain and chop coarsely. Prepare Classic Herb Stuffing as directed, except reduce bread cubes to 9 cups. Add chestnuts with the onion and celery mixture. Makes about 12 cups.

Giblet Stuffing

Add chopped, cooked giblets (recipe on page 383) to Classic Herb Stuffing.
Makes about 12 cups.

✺ Fruit Stuffing

⅔ cup butter or margarine
¾ cup chopped onion
1¼ cups diced celery, with
    leaves
2¼ teaspoons salt
½ teaspoon pepper
1¼ teaspoons poultry
    seasoning
3 quarts (12 cups) cubed or
    torn day-old white and
    whole wheat bread
1½ cups seedless raisins
1¼ cups diced dried apricots
3 tablespoons chopped fresh
    parsley
⅓ cup stock or water

Melt butter in skillet over moderately low heat (about 225° F.). Add onion and celery; cook until onion is soft, stirring occasionally. Remove from heat; add salt, pepper, and poultry seasoning. Toss together bread, raisins, apricots, and parsley in a large bowl. Gradually add butter mixture and stock; toss together. Makes about 12 cups, enough for a 12-pound turkey.

✺ Corn Bread Stuffing

⅔ cup butter or margarine
1¼ cups chopped onion
1¼ cups chopped celery, with
    leaves
1¾ teaspoons salt
½ teaspoon pepper
½ teaspoon rubbed dried
    sage
½ teaspoon powdered thyme
4½ cups crumbled corn bread
7 cups cubed or torn
    day-old white bread
⅓ cup chopped fresh parsley
½ cup stock or water

Melt butter in skillet over moderately low heat (about 225° F.). Add onion and celery; cook until onion is soft, stirring occasionally. Remove from heat; add salt, pepper, sage, and thyme. Toss together corn bread, white bread, and parsley in a large bowl. Gradually add butter mixture and stock; toss together. Makes about 12 cups, enough for a 12-pound turkey.

❧ Cranberry–Nut Stuffing

½ cup butter or margarine
¾ cup finely chopped celery
¾ cup finely chopped onion
2 cups chopped fresh or
frozen cranberries
1 cup coarsely chopped
pecans
2 8-ounce packages corn
bread stuffing
1 cup water

Melt butter in a large skillet over moderately low heat (about 225° F.). Add celery and onion and cook until tender, about 10 minutes. Add cranberries and pecans and blend well. Remove from heat. Combine butter mixture, corn bread stuffing, and water in a large bowl; toss well with a fork to blend. Makes about 12 cups stuffing, enough for a 12-pound turkey.

❧ Sage and Onion Stuffing

4 medium-sized onions,
peeled
8 cups coarse, stale bread
crumbs
2 teaspoons rubbed dried
sage
1 teaspoon salt
¼ teaspoon pepper
¼ cup melted butter or
margarine
1 egg, slightly beaten

Pour boiling water over onions and let stand 5 minutes. Drain and rinse with cold water. Cover with more boiling water and cook over moderately low heat (about 225° F.) until tender, about 20 minutes. Drain onions; place between sheets of paper toweling and squeeze out all the moisture. Chop onions finely. Toss together onion, bread crumbs, sage, salt, and pepper. Blend in butter and egg. Makes about 8 cups stuffing, enough for an 8- to 10-pound turkey.

❧ Pecan–Bread Stuffing

½ cup butter or margarine
¼ cup chopped onion
¼ cup chopped celery
5 cups cubed day-old bread
¾ cup chopped pecans
½ teaspoon salt
¼ cup dry white wine

Melt butter in a skillet over moderately low heat (about 225° F.). Add onion and celery and cook until tender, stirring occasionally. Remove from heat. Place cubed bread in a large bowl; stir in vegetable mixture, pecans, salt, and wine. Makes about 5 cups stuffing, enough for a 5-pound chicken.

❧ Vegetable Stuffing

¾ cup butter or margarine
⅔ cup chopped onion

Melt butter in a skillet over moderately low heat (about 225° F.). Add onion and green pepper, and cook until

⅔ cup chopped green pepper
¾ teaspoon salt
¼ teaspoon pepper
½ teaspoon crumbled dried rosemary leaves
1 teaspoon rubbed dried sage
¼ teaspoon poultry seasoning
4⅓ cups coarsely grated carrot
⅓ cup chopped celery

tender, stirring occasionally. Remove from heat; add salt, pepper, rosemary, sage, and poultry seasoning. Place carrot and celery in a large bowl; gradually pour in butter mixture and toss together. Makes about 5 cups stuffing, enough for a 5-pound chicken.

CHAPTER XI

FISH

Once upon a time fish was a once-a-week menu item in this country, if it was served at all. Today, primarily because of the research that is probing the relationship between our health and what we eat, fish is becoming a most desirable food. Calorie-counters have learned that seafood is a superb choice for weight control and people who must restrict their fat intake can rely on many varieties of fish as a "safe" main course.

Many people think they don't like fish because they have been exposed only to fried fish (the least desirable way to treat it) or to overcooked fish (a process which renders it tasteless). Fish can be utterly delicious but it is, and must be handled as, a delicate food. Swimming comes easily to a fish so even the large varieties do not develop tough muscles.

Freshness is synonymous with quality in fish, and people living near coastal cities where salt-water catches come in daily or near enough to inland lakes and streams to get fresh trout, bass, perch, or pickerel are indeed fortunate. However, newly developed methods for the quick-freezing of fish are so good that the quality of frozen steaks and fillets of many varieties is excellent.

How to Buy Fish

Fish may be purchased in a variety of forms.

Whole or Round: These fish are marketed just as they come from the water. They must be scaled and eviscerated. With larger fish the head, tail, and fins are usually removed and the fish are either split or cut into serving-size portions, except when fish are to be used for baking. Small fish, such as smelt, are often cooked with only the entrails removed. Fish in the whole or round form will always be sold fresh.

Drawn: This means that the entrails have been removed. Before cooking, these fish should be scaled, if necessary, and the head, tail, and fins removed. They may be split, cut into serving-sized pieces, or left whole for baking. Drawn fish are usually sold fresh.

Dressed: These fish are scaled and eviscerated, usually with head, tail, and fins removed. Smaller sizes are ready for cooking as purchased, although they may be cut into steaks or serving-sized portions. Dressed fish may be purchased fresh or frozen.

Steaks: These are cross-section slices of large fish. They are ready to cook as purchased, but may be divided into serving-sized portions before or after cooking. A cross section of the backbone is usually the only bone in a fish steak. Fish steaks may be purchased fresh or frozen.

Fillets: These are the sides of the fish, cut lengthwise away from the backbone. They are practically boneless and require no preparation for cooking. Some fillets are skinned. A fillet cut from one side of a fish is known as a single fillet, the most common type. Fish fillets may be purchased fresh or frozen.

Butterfly Fillets: These are the two sides of the fish corresponding to two single fillets held together by uncut flesh and skin. Butterfly fillets are usually sold fresh.

Sticks and Other Precut Products: These are fish fillets or steaks frozen into blocks and then cut into portions of uniform size. These products are usually sold frozen.

When you buy whole or drawn fish, look for flesh that springs back when pressed; bright, clean eyes; tight, shining scales; and reddish-pink gills.

When you buy fillets and steaks, look for flesh that appears freshly cut and has no browning around edges. All fresh fish will have a fresh, mild odor. If wrapped, the wrapping should be of moisture-vaporproof material. There should be little or no air space between fish and wrapping.

When deciding upon quantity, count on one-third pound per person when serving steaks, fillets, or sticks; one-half pound per person for dressed fish; and one pound per person for whole fish.

How to Store Fish

Fish will spoil easily if not handled carefully. It should be wrapped in moistureproof paper or placed in a tightly covered container, stored immediately in the refrigerator, and cooked as soon as possible.

Frozen fish varieties are usually packed during seasons of abundance and can be purchased at reasonable prices. Frozen fish may be used interchangeably with fresh fish. Check to be sure frozen fish is solidly frozen when purchased. Deterioration in quality is prevented when fish is properly held in the frozen state, but frozen fish that has thawed and been refrozen is poor in quality. There should be no ice crystals or discoloration and little or no odor.

If frozen fish is to be kept several days, place the unopened package in your freezing unit. It will keep as long as it is solidly frozen. Once it has thawed, it should be used immediately. Never refreeze fish. If frozen fish is to be used shortly after purchase, it should be placed in the refrigerator in the unopened package.

Frozen fish is best thawed on the refrigerator shelf. Thawing may be hastened by leaving fish at room temperature until it can be easily handled. For quick thawing, the unopened package may be immersed in cold water. The last two methods tend to make the fish flesh less firm.

How to Cook Fish

There are hundreds of recipes and several basic methods for cooking fish but they all have one thing in common: Do not overcook. You can judge doneness partly by appearance; when cooked, fish loses its translucent appearance and becomes opaque. Also, when fish is cooked it flakes easily with a fork. Remove it from the heat at once.

Fish are classified as lean or fat. In general, the white-fleshed fish such as halibut, sole, and cod are lean; fish with colored flesh such as salmon and mackerel are fat. More butter or oil may be used to baste or prepare lean fish than fat fish. It is best to serve fish immediately after cooking. Otherwise it becomes dry and less flavorful.

These are the basic ways to cook fish:

Baked: Place steaks, fillets, or whole fish in a greased baking dish. Brush with seasoned butter and bake until fork-tender in a preheated oven at approximately 350° F. or at the temperature suggested in the recipe. Stuff whole fish with an herb and bread or shrimp stuffing, or marinate fish before baking. Bake breaded frozen fish sticks and portions according to package directions.

Broiled: Arrange steaks, fillets, or whole fish on a preheated, well-greased broiler rack. Brush with melted butter or basting sauce. For steaks and fillets, place rack about two inches from heat; for whole or split fish, place rack three to six inches from heat. Fillets and split fish do not need to be turned. Turn steaks and whole fish once, basting again.

Pan-Fried: Frying is usually reserved for small whole fish, such as trout. Fish fillets, steaks, and drawn fish may be pan fried although broiling is preferable. Bread the fish, if desired, by dipping into milk, then into corn

FISH

flake, cracker, or bread crumbs; corn meal; or seasoned flour. Use melted shortening—a combination of butter and vegetable oil is best—to cover the bottom of the pan. Fry fish until light brown, turn, and brown other side. Use a moderate temperature to fry fish.

Oven-Fried: This is the method most often used to cook frozen or breaded fillets, sticks, or portions. Place the breaded fish in a shallow, lightly greased pan or on a baking sheet and bake according to package directions.

Deep-Fried: Use a deep, heavy, 3- to 4-quart saucepan. Fill the saucepan about half full with shortening or vegetable oil and heat slowly. Heat the fat to about 375° F.; check the temperature with a thermometer if possible. Frying at too low a temperature causes foods to soak up shortening; at a too-high temperature, shortening will smoke and cause disagreeable odors and flavors. Place the fish in the bottom of a fryer basket or on a large slotted spoon and lower into the hot fat. Fry the fish just until it is golden brown; drain and serve immediately. Allow shortening to return to 375° F. before adding second batch.

Poached or Boiled: Tie the fish in a length of cheesecloth, place it on a flat, greased tray of a fish poacher or on a strip of greased, heavy-duty foil, lower it into a pan that is large enough to allow the fish to be removed easily, and cover the fish with a seasoned liquid. Simmer gently until the fish flakes easily. Remove it from the hot liquid immediately. The liquid in which the fish is poached might be a fish stock (court bouillon) or wine. These liquids are often boiled down (reduced) and used as a base for a sauce to serve with the fish.

Steamed: Steaming is much like poaching, except that the fish is cooked over the liquid instead of in it. Place the fish in a deep pan on a greased perforated rack or tray that will hold it above the level of the liquid. Bring liquid to a boil and cover the pan tightly. Cook just until fish flakes easily. Season and salt fish *after* steaming. The liquid used in steaming can be the base for sauce to serve with fish.

Planked: Whole fish, steaks, or fillets may be used in planking. Oil the plank or board carefully and heat it in a moderately hot oven (350° F.). Arrange the fish on the warmed plank, brush with butter, and bake in a moderate oven until it is nearly done. Arrange cooked vegetables around fish or pipe mashed potatoes around the edge, and return to oven for final baking. Serve on the plank.

✒ Pan-Fried Whole Fish

1 egg
2 tablespoons milk
1 teaspoon salt

Beat egg slightly and stir in milk, salt, pepper, and paprika; set aside. Mix together flour and corn meal. Wash and dry fish. Dip each fish into egg mixture and then

Few grains pepper
½ teaspoon paprika
⅓ cup flour
¼ cup yellow corn meal
*6 small whole dressed fish, about ½ pound each
Vegetable oil for frying

into flour mixture, making sure fish is well coated. In a large skillet add oil to a depth of ¼ inch and heat over moderately high heat (about 350° F.). Add fish and cook 5 to 8 minutes on each side, or until golden brown and fish flakes easily when tested with a fork. Drain on paper towels. Fish may be cooked over hot coals or on an outdoor camp stove. Serves 4 to 6.

*Note: For smaller fish, such as smelts, fry about 3 minutes on each side.

Sautéed Fish Fillets

½ cup flour
⅛ teaspoon paprika
½ teaspoon salt
1½ pounds fish fillets
¼ cup milk
3 tablespoons butter or margarine
Tartar Sauce (recipe follows)

Stir together flour, paprika, and salt. Dip fish fillets in milk and then thoroughly coat with flour mixture. Melt butter in skillet over moderately high heat (about 275° F.). Add fish fillets and cook about 5 minutes, until lightly browned on both sides. Serve with Tartar Sauce. Serves 4.

Tartar Sauce

½ cup mayonnaise or salad dressing
¼ cup commercial sour cream
2 tablespoons chopped fresh parsley
2 tablespoons chopped dill pickle
½ teaspoon instant minced onion
½ teaspoon dried tarragon leaves

Fold together all ingredients. Makes ¾ cup sauce.

Batter-Fried Fish

2 pounds boneless fish, cut into serving-size pieces not more than 1½ inches thick
Garlic salt (optional)
1 egg
⅓ cup milk
⅛ teaspoon Tabasco

Rinse fish and pat dry with paper towels. Sprinkle lightly with garlic salt and set aside. In a bowl beat egg slightly, then stir in milk and Tabasco. Mix together flour, salt, and mustard. Stir into egg mixture and beat until smooth. In a heavy deep saucepan or electric skillet heat oil to 375° F. (For best results, have the oil at least 1½ inches deep.) Coat fish with the batter and fry 3 to 5

½ cup all-purpose flour
¼ teaspoon salt
⅛ teaspoon dry mustard
Vegetable oil

minutes on each side, or until well browned and fish flakes easily when tested with a fork. This same batter may be used with shrimp or scallops. Serves 4 to 6.

✑ Trout Meunière

¼ cup flour
½ teaspoon salt
*4 brook trout, about ¾ pound each
Salt and pepper
½ cup butter or margarine
1 tablespoon chopped fresh parsley
¼ teaspoon dried tarragon leaves
1 teaspoon grated lemon peel
2 tablespoons lemon juice

Mix flour and the ½ teaspoon salt. Sprinkle insides of trout with salt and pepper. Thoroughly coat trout in flour mixture. Melt half of the butter in skillet over moderate heat (about 250° F.). Add fish and brown well, about 5 minutes on each side. Remove to warm platter. Add the remaining butter, parsley, tarragon, lemon peel, and lemon juice; heat until butter foams. Serve over trout. Serves 4.

*Note: Other small whole fish of comparable size may be used.

✑ Fillet of Sole Amandine

1½ pounds fillet of sole
Salt and pepper
4 tablespoons butter or margarine
2 tablespoons butter or margarine
3 tablespoons sliced blanched almonds
Lemon wedges
Parsley

If necessary, cut fish into serving-sized portions and sprinkle with salt and pepper. Heat the 4 tablespoons butter in a large skillet over moderate heat (about 250° F.). Add fish and cook until delicately browned on both sides, about 8 minutes. (Add additional butter if necessary.) Remove fish to a warm platter. Add the remaining 2 tablespoons butter and increase temperature to moderately high (about 300° F.); add almonds and cook until lightly browned. Pour over fish and garnish with lemon wedges and parsley. Serves 4.

✑ Broiled Trout

*6 pan-dressed brook trout, about ¾ pound each
2 tablespoons lemon juice
2 teaspoons salt

Clean and wash fish. Brush insides of fish with lemon juice and sprinkle with salt and pepper. Wrap 2 slices of bacon around each fish and secure with toothpicks. Place on well-greased barbecue grill and cook over hot

Few grains pepper
12 slices bacon

coals 10 to 15 minutes on each side, or until lightly browned and fish flakes easily. Trout may be placed in preheated broiler 3 to 4 inches from heat and broiled 8 to 10 minutes on each side. Serves 6.

Note: Other small whole fish of comparable size may be used.

Broiled Fish Steaks

1½ pounds fish steaks
2 tablespoons melted butter
  or margarine
Salt and pepper

Place fish on greased broiler rack. Brush with butter. Sprinkle lightly with a little salt and pepper. Place in preheated broiler, 2½ to 3 inches from heat; broil 5 minutes. Turn; brush with butter and sprinkle lightly with a little salt and pepper. Broil 6 to 8 minutes, or until fish is easily flaked with a fork. Serve with one of the sauces that follow. Serves 4.

Wine-Butter Sauce

Melt ¼ *cup butter* or *margarine* in a saucepan over low heat (about 200° F.). Stir in ½ *cup white wine, 1 tablespoon lemon juice, 1 tablespoon chopped parsley,* and ¼ *teaspoon salt.* Heat before serving. Makes ¾ cup sauce.

Anchovy-Butter Sauce

Melt ¼ *cup butter* or *margarine* in a saucepan over low heat (about 200° F.). Blend in *1 teaspoon anchovy paste,* ½ *teaspoon lemon juice,* ⅛ *teaspoon onion salt,* and *few grains cayenne pepper.* Heat before serving. Makes ¼ cup sauce.

Broiled Marinated Swordfish

¼ cup vegetable oil
¼ cup bottled teriyaki sauce
¼ cup dry sherry
2 tablespoons lime juice
1 small clove garlic, pressed
2 ¾-inch pieces dried ginger
  root
4 1-inch-thick slices
  swordfish, about 2 pounds
Lemon wedges

Combine oil, teriyaki sauce, sherry, lime juice, garlic, and ginger; mix to blend. Place fish slices in a single layer in a shallow baking dish. Pour marinade over fish. Marinate in the refrigerator 1 hour or longer, turning occasionally. Place fish on a rack in a broiler pan. Broil in a preheated broiler 5 inches from the source of heat for 5 minutes, brushing frequently with the marinade. Turn and broil 5 to 8 minutes longer, or until fish flakes easily when tested with a fork. Serve with lemon wedges. Serves 4.

Note: Other fish steaks of comparable size may be used.

FISH

❧ Delicious Poached Fish

2 1-pound blocks frozen cod
or other fish fillets, slightly
thawed
Water
¾ cup cider vinegar
1 carrot, peeled and cut in 4
pieces
1 onion, peeled and stuck
with 3 cloves
1 sprig parsley
1 2-inch bay leaf
8 to 10 whole peppercorns
1 teaspoon dried thyme
leaves
¼ lemon
¼ cup lemon juice

Place blocks of fish side by side in a large pot or skillet. Add enough water to barely cover fish and then remove fish to a plate. Add the vinegar, carrot, onion, parsley, bay leaf, peppercorns and thyme to water in pot. Cover and bring to a boil over moderately high heat; reduce heat to moderately low and simmer 20 minutes to make a well-flavored broth. While broth simmers rub the blocks of fish with the lemon quarter, squeezing to release the juice. Cut each block of fish into 3 pieces and wrap each group of 3 in 2 thicknesses of cheesecloth; twist cloth to close at each end of the fish and tie with long pieces of string. Place fish in hot broth, cover and simmer over moderately low heat for 12 to 15 minutes (5 to 7 minutes if fish is completely thawed); do not let water boil—just an occasional bubble should break the surface. Lift fish out of pan, untie one end of cheesecloth and check for doneness—flesh should be white and opaque in the middle, not translucent.

❧ Poached Fish with Mustard Caper Sauce

¾ cup mayonnaise
⅓ cup Dijon-style or brown
mustard
1 teaspoon capers, drained
and chopped
2 teaspoons dried dillweed
¼ cup lemon juice
¼ teaspoon sugar
Delicious Poached Fish
(recipe above)
Fresh spinach leaves, washed
and drained

In a small bowl combine all ingredients except fish and spinach leaves. Chill well. Arrange fish on spinach leaves and serve sauce separately. Makes 1⅓ cups sauce. Serves 6 to 8 as a main dish salad.

❧ Caribbean Fish Soufflé

1 pound fish, poached
according to directions for
Delicious Poached Fish
(use ½ recipe) or 2 cups
cooked, flaked fish

Heat oven to 350° F. Generously butter a 5-cup soufflé or baking dish 6 to 7 inches in diameter. In a medium-sized mixing bowl mix the fish, bread crumbs and onion with a fork. In a small bowl beat the egg yolks lightly with a fork or wire whisk; then beat in the melted butter,

⅔ cup white bread crumbs, made from stale bread
½ cup finely chopped, peeled onion
3 eggs, yolks and whites separated
3 tablespoons melted butter or margarine
2 tablespoons lime or lemon juice
¼ teaspoon cayenne pepper
¼ teaspoon salt
Lime or lemon wedges
Lemon-Curry Sauce (recipe follows)

lime juice, cayenne and salt. Stir yolk mixture into fish mixture. In another bowl beat the egg whites with an electric mixer or rotary beater until stiff peaks form when the beater is lifted. Using a rubber spatula, fold egg whites into the fish mixture. Pour mixture into the prepared baking dish and level the top. Bake 30 to 35 minutes, until pudding is firm and lightly browned on top. Serve with lime or lemon wedges and Lemon-Curry Sauce. Serves 4.

Lemon-Curry Sauce

⅓ cup butter, cut into 4 pieces
3 tablespoons lemon juice
¼ to ½ teaspoon curry powder
2 tablespoons chopped fresh parsley

Heat butter in a small saucepan over very low heat. When butter starts to melt, remove pan from heat and mash and stir butter until smooth. Stir in lemon juice and curry powder. Just before serving stir in parsley. Makes ½ cup sauce, or enough for 4 servings.

✑ Baked Stuffed Fish

1 2½-pound dressed fish (striped bass, carp, or red snapper)
2 tablespoons butter or margarine
¼ cup chopped celery
2 tablespoons chopped onion
1 tablespoon chopped green pepper
1 small clove garlic, pressed
2 cups soft bread cubes
½ teaspoon salt
¼ teaspoon dried thyme leaves
⅛ teaspoon rubbed dried sage
Few grains pepper
¼ cup diced tomato
2 slices bacon, halved

Heat oven to 350° F. Rinse the fish and pat dry with paper towels. Using a sharp knife, cut two ⅛-inch-deep gashes diagonally across the fish on both sides. Set aside. In a saucepan over moderately low heat (about 225° F.) melt butter and add celery, onion, green pepper, and garlic. Cook until onion is lightly browned. In a large bowl combine cooked vegetable–butter mixture with the soft bread cubes, salt, thyme, sage, pepper, and tomato. Mix together with a tossing motion. Place fish in a lightly buttered shallow baking dish and stuff loosely with bread mixture. Place bacon across top of fish. Bake 45 minutes, or until fish flakes easily when tested with a fork. Serves 2 to 3.

FISH

✒ Vegetable-Stuffed Baked Whole Fish

*1 4- to 6-pound whole
    dressed red snapper
6 tablespoons melted butter
    or margarine
Salt and pepper
¼ cup coarsely grated carrot
¼ cup chopped green pepper
¼ cup chopped celery
⅛ teaspoon garlic powder
¼ cup chopped onion
1 vegetable bouillon cube
1 cup boiling water

Heat oven to 350° F. Brush fish inside and out with 2 tablespoons of the butter; sprinkle well with salt and pepper. Arrange in a large, flat baking dish. Cut deep crosswise gashes in fish 1½ inches apart. Stir together 2 tablespoons of the remaining butter, carrot, green pepper, celery, and garlic powder. Spoon vegetable mixture into gashes. Cook onion in the remaining 2 tablespoons butter over moderate heat (about 250° F.) until tender. Dissolve bouillon cube in boiling water; stir into cooked onions. Pour into bottom of baking dish with fish. Bake 55 to 60 minutes, or until fish is fork-tender. Serve pan juices over fish. Serves 5 to 6.

*Note: Other whole fish of comparable size may be used.

✒ Sweet-and-Sour Baked Flounder

1 pound fresh or frozen
    flounder fillets
Salt and pepper
1 tablespoon vegetable oil
¼ cup finely chopped onion
1 clove garlic, finely chopped
½ cup water
¼ cup cider vinegar
2 tablespoons dark corn
    syrup
½ teaspoon ground ginger
½ teaspoon salt
6 ¼-inch-thick green pepper
    rings

Heat oven to 400° F. Place fish fillets in a single layer in a lightly oiled 1- or 1½-quart shallow baking dish. Sprinkle with salt and pepper. Heat the 1 tablespoon oil in a skillet over moderate heat (about 250° F.); add onion and garlic and cook until tender. Add water, vinegar, corn syrup, ginger, and salt; bring to a boil. Remove from heat and pour over fish; top with green pepper rings. Bake 20 minutes, or until fish flakes easily. Serves 3.

✒ Fillet of Flounder Florentine

3 pounds fresh spinach
1½ teaspoons salt
2¼ pounds fillet of flounder
Salt and pepper
Egg Stuffing (recipe follows)
Wine Sauce (recipe follows)

Heat oven to 375° F. Wash spinach in several changes of water; without drying leaves, place them in a large kettle. Sprinkle with the 1½ teaspoons salt. Cover and cook over moderately low heat (about 225° F.) 12 to 15 minutes, or until tender. Drain very thoroughly and chop coarsely. Place in the bottom of a shallow 3-quart baking dish. Sprinkle fillets with salt and pepper. Place a spoon-ful of the Egg Stuffing at one end of each fillet and roll up jelly-roll fashion. Arrange fillets in rows on spinach. Cover with the Wine Sauce. Bake 25 to 30 minutes. Serves 6 to 8.

Egg Stuffing

¼ cup butter or margarine
½ cup finely chopped onion
1 cup soft bread crumbs
3 hard-cooked eggs, coarsely chopped
1 teaspoon dried parsley flakes
¼ teaspoon dried marjoram leaves
½ teaspoon salt

Heat butter in a skillet over moderately low heat (about 225° F.). Add onion and cook until tender, stirring frequently. Add remaining ingredients and mix. Use for stuffing fillets. Makes about 1½ cups.

Wine Sauce

¼ cup butter or margarine
¼ cup flour
1 teaspoon salt
Few grains pepper
1¾ cups milk, scalded
¼ cup dry white wine
¼ cup grated Parmesan cheese

Place butter in a saucepan directly over moderately low heat (about 225° F.). Remove from heat and blend in flour, salt, and pepper. Return to heat and cook for 3 minutes, stirring constantly. Remove from heat and gradually add scalded milk, stirring constantly until all liquid has been added and sauce is smooth. Cook over low heat (about 200° F.) for 20 minutes, stirring very frequently. Remove from heat and gradually stir in wine and Parmesan cheese. Makes about 1¾ cups sauce.

Batter-Baked Fillets

⅔ cup pancake mix
¾ teaspoon salt
1 egg, slightly beaten
1½ teaspoons vegetable oil or melted shortening
¾ cup milk
5 or 6 drops Tabasco
2 tablespoons melted butter or margarine
2 cups crushed bite-sized shredded corn cereal
1½ pounds fish fillets

Heat oven to 400° F. Combine pancake mix and salt in a bowl. Mix together egg, oil, milk, and Tabasco. Add to dry ingredients and beat until smooth. Combine butter and cereal in a flat pan. Dip fillets in batter and roll in cereal mixture to coat thoroughly. Bake on ungreased cookie sheet 15 minutes. Turn with a broad spatula. Bake 10 minutes longer, or until crumbs are lightly browned. Serves 4.

✑ Cold Poached Bass with Watercress Sauce

1 **4-pound striped bass or any fresh, firm-fleshed fish, cleaned, scaled, head removed and tail left intact**
2 **onions, peeled and quartered**
2 **teaspoons salt**
¼ **teaspoon pepper**
1 **2-inch bay leaf**
¼ **teaspoon dried thyme leaves**
5 **sprigs fresh parsley**
2 **cups dry white wine**
2 **cups water**
1 **tablespoon lemon juice**
Watercress Sauce (recipe follows)

Choose a pan that will hold the whole fish and put the fish and 1 quart of cold water in it. If the quart of water does not almost completely cover fish, you will need to make double the quantity of broth. Pour water off fish (it was for measuring purposes only). To make broth: In a large saucepan place onions, salt, pepper, bay leaf, thyme, parsley, wine and water; bring to a boil over moderately high heat (about 325° F.). Reduce heat to low (about 200° F.) and simmer broth 15 minutes. Meanwhile, sprinkle inside cavity of fish with lemon juice and wrap fish in cheesecloth—candy-wrapper style, twisting ends and tying with white string. When broth is done, strain it into the pan in which fish will be cooked. Bring to a boil, add fish and simmer over moderate heat (about 250° F.) 8 minutes per pound of whole fish. When done, remove cooked fish from pan using two wide spatulas, taking care not to tear the skin. Lay fish on a plate, cover and chill several hours. To serve, carefully lift off skin with a knife and fork; then lift top layer of fish away from backbone and onto serving plates. Turn fish over and repeat with other side. Serve with Watercress Sauce. Serves 4.

Note: Any whole fresh fish of comparable size may be used.

Watercress Sauce

1 **bunch watercress, stems and leaves, coarsely chopped (about 2 cups)**
2 **tablespoons finely chopped fresh dillweed**
3 **tablespoons finely chopped green onions or scallions**
1 **tablespoon lemon juice**
1 **cup mayonnaise**
½ **teaspoon salt**
⅛ **teaspoon pepper**

Combine half of each ingredient in an electric blender and blend at high speed to a smooth, green-flecked cream. Remove mixture to a small bowl and repeat with remaining ingredients. Combine both batches of sauce; stir and chill several hours. Serve with poached fish, cold seafood or chicken. Makes about 2 cups sauce.

✑ Red Snapper à la Franey

2 **1½- to 2-pound red snapper, bluefish, or sea bass**

Heat oven to 425° F. Have fish cleaned and scaled, but leave head and tail intact. Dry fish well with paper towels. Sprinkle rosemary in cavity of fish; salt and pepper

2 teaspoons dried rosemary
  leaves
Salt
Freshly ground pepper
½ cup butter or margarine
¼ cup drained capers
¼ cup finely chopped whole
  lemon
Lemon slices (optional)

inside and outside of fish. Melt butter in a skillet with ovenproof handle over moderate heat (about 250° F.). Add fish to skillet and cook about 5 minutes, or until fish is lightly browned on one side; tilt pan frequently and spoon the hot butter over the fish. Turn fish in skillet. Bake uncovered in the oven for 20 to 25 minutes, until easily flaked with a fork. If skillet does not have oven-proof handle, transfer browned fish to a flat casserole, pour hot butter from skillet over fish, and bake as directed. Before serving, sprinkle with capers and chopped lemon. Garnish with lemon slices, if desired. Serves 4.

✑ Stuffed Salmon Turbans with Béarnaise Sauce

6 salmon steaks, cut 1 to 1½
  inches thick, about 6
  ounces each
3 fillets of sole (about 1½
  pounds)
2 tablespoons vegetable oil
Butter or margarine
Few grains salt
Few grains pepper
Béarnaise Sauce—Classic or
  Less-Rich (see recipes
  page 489)
Parsley

Heat oven to 375° F. Remove bones and skin from salmon steaks. Form each steak into a firm round. Cut fillet of sole into 6 1- to 1½-inch strips. Wrap a fillet strip around each of the 6 steaks and secure with toothpicks in about 3 places. Spread the vegetable oil on the bottom of a 12¾-x-9-x-2-inch baking dish; place the salmon steaks in the pan. Dot each steak with butter and sprinkle with salt and pepper. Place in oven and bake 25 minutes. Baste steaks occasionally with some of the juices in the pan. Prepare Béarnaise Sauce. Remove steaks from oven. Preheat broiler. Place steaks about 3 inches from heat and broil until lightly browned, about 10 to 12 minutes. Place steaks on a large heated platter; remove toothpicks. Top each with some of the Béarnaise Sauce and garnish with parsley. Serves 6.

✑ Baked Fillet of Sole Stuffed with Lobster

3 slices white bread, crusts
  removed
1 tablespoon cracker crumbs
2 tablespoons dry sherry
1 tablespoon shredded
  Cheddar cheese
⅛ teaspoon salt
8 ounces cubed cooked
  lobster meat
2 pounds fillet of sole

Heat oven to 350° F. Coarsely crumble bread and combine with cracker crumbs, sherry, cheese, salt, and lobster meat. Spoon some of the stuffing mixture along one end of each fillet and roll up tightly; fasten with toothpicks. Arrange rolled fillets in flat baking pan; pour butter and milk over them. Sprinkle with salt. Bake 25 minutes. Serve with Lobster-Newburg Sauce. Serves 8.

(Ingredients continued on page 410)

2 tablespoons melted butter
  or margarine
½ cup milk
Salt
Lobster-Newburg Sauce
  (recipe follows)

Lobster-Newburg Sauce

4 tablespoons butter or
  margarine
2 tablespoons flour
1 cup milk, heated
1 cup heavy cream, heated
1 teaspoon salt
⅛ teaspoon paprika
8 ounces cubed cooked
  lobster meat
2 tablespoons dry sherry

Melt 2 tablespoons of the butter in a saucepan over moderate heat (about 250° F.). Blend in flour. Gradually add the combined milk and cream; cook and stir constantly until smooth and thickened. Add salt and paprika. Melt the remaining 2 tablespoons butter in a small skillet over moderately low heat (about 225° F.). Add the lobster and sherry and cook about 5 minutes, until liquid is absorbed. Stir lobster into the cream sauce. Heat gently just before serving. Makes about 3 cups.

⊷ Mustard-Broiled Mackerel Fillets

1 pound frozen mackerel
  fillets, thawed enough to
  separate
2 tablespoons butter
2 tablespoons lemon juice
2 tablespoons Dijon-style
  mustard
¼ teaspoon fennel seeds,
  crushed with the back of a
  spoon
⅛ teaspoon pepper
Lemon slices

Heat broiler. Place mackerel fillets skin side down in an oiled baking dish. Melt butter in a small saucepan; stir in lemon juice, mustard, fennel and pepper. Spread over fillets with a spoon. Broil fillets 2 to 3 inches from the heat for 5 to 8 minutes, until fillets are opaque. Do not turn fillets. Garnish with lemon slices. Serves 4.

⊷ Poached Fish Steaks

1 cup water
1 tablespoon lemon juice
4 peppercorns
½ small onion, thinly sliced
1 bay leaf
1 teaspoon vinegar
1 teaspoon salt

Place all ingredients except fish and Mustard Sauce in saucepan; bring to a boil over low heat (about 200° F.) and simmer 5 minutes. Strain stock into a large skillet; add fish and simmer 10 to 15 minutes, or until fish is easily flaked. Remove fish and keep warm in oven. Strain broth and use in Mustard Sauce. Serve fish with Mustard Sauce. Serves 3.

1 pound cod, halibut, or
  haddock steaks, fresh or
  frozen, thawed
  Mustard Sauce (recipe
  follows)

Mustard Sauce

1 tablespoon vegetable oil
1 tablespoon finely chopped
  onion
1 tablespoon flour
Fish stock
Milk
1 tablespoon prepared
  mustard

Heat oil in saucepan over moderate heat (about 250° F.); add onion and cook until tender. Blend in flour and cook 1 minute. Measure fish stock and add enough milk to make 1 cup liquid. Gradually stir stock into flour mixture. Cook, stirring constantly, until thickened. Blend in mustard. Makes 1 cup sauce.

🦆 Fish and Chips

Shortening or vegetable oil for
  frying
2 pounds potatoes, peeled
  and cut into ¼-inch strips
2 12-ounce packages frozen
  cod fillets, partially thawed
1 cup sifted all-purpose flour
½ teaspoon salt
⅛ teaspoon pepper
1 teaspoon paprika
2 egg whites, at room
  temperature
2 egg yolks
⅔ cup beer
2 tablespoons melted butter
  or margarine
Salt
Malt vinegar (optional)

Fill deep-fat fryer or large, heavy saucepan half full with shortening or vegetable oil. Heat oil slowly to 350° F. Heat oven to 250° F. Add one third of the potatoes to the hot oil and cook 7 or 8 minutes, until tender and lightly browned. Remove potatoes and drain on paper towels. Repeat with remaining portions. While the potatoes are frying, separate and cut fish into serving portions; rinse and pat each piece dry with paper towels. Set aside. Prepare fish-coating batter. Sift flour, the ½ teaspoon salt, pepper and paprika together. In a small bowl beat egg whites until stiff but not dry. In another bowl beat egg yolks thoroughly. Stir in beer, sifted dry ingredients and melted butter. Gently fold in beaten egg whites. Set batter aside. Increase temperature of oil to 400° F. Return portions of potatoes to oil to brown, 1 to 2 minutes. When all the potatoes are browned, place them on a paper-towel-lined cookie sheet and place in oven to keep warm. Reduce oil temperature to 375° F. Dip pieces of the fish in the batter and fry 2 to 3 minutes on each side, until well browned. Drain on paper towels. Serve fish and potatoes with salt and malt vinegar if desired. Serves 6.

🦆 Salmon or Swordfish Steaks Béarnaise

¾ cup milk
2 12-ounce packages frozen

Pour milk into a large skillet. Place steaks in skillet. Bring milk almost to the boiling point. Reduce heat to

salmon or swordfish
steaks, thawed
Classic Béarnaise Sauce (see
  recipe page 489)
3 tablespoons chopped fresh
  parsley

low (about 200° F.). Cover and simmer 10 to 15 minutes, until fish flakes easily when tested with a fork. Turn once during cooking. Remove steaks to a heated serving platter. Top each steak with hot Béarnaise Sauce. Garnish with chopped parsley and serve immediately. Serves 4.

⤜ Fillets with Marguéry Sauce

1½ cups water
1 medium-sized onion,
  sliced
1 carrot, cut into 1½-inch
  pieces
1 stalk celery, cut into
  3-inch pieces
1 bay leaf
2 peppercorns
2 whole cloves
¾ teaspoon salt
1 cup dry white wine
1½ pounds fish fillets
5 tablespoons butter or
  margarine
1 4-ounce can sliced
  mushrooms, drained
1 cup cooked, cleaned
  shrimp
¼ cup flour
1 egg yolk
½ cup heavy cream,
  whipped

In large saucepan combine water, onion, carrot, celery, bay leaf, peppercorns, cloves, and salt; cook over moderately low heat (about 225° F.) for 15 minutes. Add wine. Put a double thickness of foil 10 by 8 inches on a large square of cheesecloth. Lay fillets on foil and fold cheesecloth over fish. Place in stock mixture and simmer over low heat (about 200° F.) 10 minutes. Remove from heat. Carefully remove fillets from cheesecloth and foil and place on heatproof platter or baking dish. Strain fish stock and reserve 1½ cups of the stock for sauce. Melt butter in saucepan over moderate heat (about 250° F.). Add mushrooms and shrimp and cook 5 minutes. Spoon out mushrooms and shrimp and place around fish on platter. Blend flour into butter in saucepan. Gradually add stock and cook, stirring constantly, until thickened. Beat egg yolk slightly and stir in ½ cup of the sauce. Pour back into saucepan and cook until thickened. Fold sauce into cream; pour over fish. Preheat broiler. Broil 3 inches from heat 2 to 3 minutes until sauce is lightly browned. Serves 6.

⤜ Fillet of Sole Bonne Femme

4 tablespoons butter or
  margarine
2 shallots, chopped
¾ cup thinly sliced fresh
  mushrooms
1½ pounds fillets of sole
Salt
¾ cup dry white wine
1 tablespoon flour

Melt 2 tablespoons of the butter in a large, shallow skillet over low heat (about 200° F.). Remove from heat. Arrange shallots and half the mushrooms on the bottom of the skillet. Sprinkle the sole fillets with salt and place them on the mushrooms. Arrange the remaining mushrooms on top of the fish. Pour wine over fish. Cut a small hole in center of a piece of waxed paper which is the size of the skillet. Butter waxed paper and place, buttered side down, on top of fish. Bring the liquid in the pan to a

2 **egg yolks, slightly beaten**
⅓ **cup light cream**
1 **tablespoon snipped chives**
1 **tablespoon chopped fresh parsley**

boil. Simmer over low heat (about 200° F.) 10 to 12 minutes, until fish flakes easily when tested with a fork. Using a large, broad spatula, remove the fish and mushrooms to a heatproof serving platter. Place in a warm oven. Reserve cooking liquid. Melt the remaining 2 tablespoons butter in a saucepan over moderate heat (about 250° F.). Add flour gradually and cook until mixture is golden. Stir fish liquid gradually into the butter–flour mixture. Cook, stirring constantly with a wire whip or wooden spoon, until sauce is thickened and smooth. There should be about 1 cup of sauce. Blend egg yolks with cream and add to the sauce. Heat to just below boiling point. Remove sauce from heat and pour over fish fillets. Sprinkle with chives and parsley. Serves 4 to 5.

Fillet of Sole Véronique

Follow directions for preceding recipe, but omit mushrooms, chives, and parsley. Add *1 8-ounce can seedless grapes, drained,* or *¾ cup fresh seedless grapes* to the sauce with the egg yolks and cream.

✒ Quick Bouillabaisse

¼ **cup olive oil**
¼ **cup chopped onion**
4 **leeks, chopped**
1 **clove garlic, minced**
½ **teaspoon dried thyme leaves**
½ **bay leaf**
1 **7½-ounce jar whole clams**
2 **cups crushed whole canned tomatoes**
½ **cup bottled clam juice**
1 **cup dry white wine**
1 **teaspoon grated orange peel**
2 **tablespoons chopped fresh parsley**
Pinch of curry powder
½ **teaspoon salt**
Few grains pepper
1 **12-ounce package frozen perch fillets, thawed**

Heat oil in a large, heavy saucepan or a Dutch oven over moderate heat (about 250° F.). Add the onion, leeks, garlic, thyme, and bay leaf. Cook 5 minutes. Drain clams and add the liquor to ingredients in Dutch oven. Add tomatoes, the ½ cup clam juice, wine, orange peel, parsley, curry powder, salt, and pepper. Simmer over low heat (about 200° F.) 15 minutes. Cut each perch fillet into 3 or 4 pieces. Cut membrane along both edges of each lobster tail and remove membranes. Cut each tail into 3 or 4 pieces, leaving meat in shell. Add clams, perch, lobster, and frozen shrimp to other ingredients in Dutch oven. Simmer 15 minutes longer. Serve in heated soup bowls. Serves 4 as a main course.

(Ingredients continued on page 414)

FISH

1 8-ounce package frozen
  lobster tails, thawed
1 pound frozen shelled and
  deveined shrimp

❧ Fish Gumbo

¼ cup butter or margarine
½ cup chopped onion
1 medium-sized green
  pepper, chopped
½ cup chopped celery
1 28-ounce can tomatoes
1 15½-ounce can okra
1 cup water
¼ teaspoon dried thyme
  leaves
1 teaspoon salt
1 pound fish fillets, cut into
  bite-sized pieces
2 cups cooked rice

Melt butter in large saucepan over moderately low heat (about 225° F.). Add onion, green pepper, and celery; cook until tender. Add tomatoes, okra, water, thyme, and salt. Simmer 15 minutes, stirring occasionally. Add fish and cook 10 minutes, or until fish is easily flaked. Spoon ½ cup hot rice into each soup bowl before filling with the fish mixture. Serves 4.

❧ Cioppino

¼ cup vegetable oil
2 cloves garlic, minced
½ cup chopped onion
½ cup chopped green pepper
½ pound mushrooms, sliced
1 28-ounce can tomatoes
1 small can tomato paste
1 7½-ounce bottle clam
  juice
2 tablespoons lemon juice
1 bay leaf
½ teaspoon dried oregano
  leaves
1 teaspoon sugar
1 teaspoon salt
⅛ teaspoon pepper
1 pound halibut, cut into
  bite-sized pieces
1 pound fillet of sole, cut into
  bite-sized pieces

Heat oil in Dutch oven over moderate heat (about 250° F.); add garlic, onion, and green pepper; cook 5 minutes. Add mushrooms, tomatoes, tomato paste, clam juice, lemon juice, bay leaf, oregano, sugar, salt, and pepper. Bring to a boil and simmer over moderately low heat (about 225° F.) 20 minutes, stirring occasionally. Add fish and lobster and simmer 20 minutes longer, stirring occasionally. Stir in wine and heat. Serve with toasted French bread. Makes about 9 cups, or 5 to 6 servings.

1 ½-pound lobster tail, meat
   removed from shell and
   cut up
½ cup dry white wine

◄§ Mixed Seafood Casserole

2 quarts water
2 tablespoons salt
1 pound medium-sized
   shrimp, shelled and
   deveined
1 pound scallops
1 pound fillet of sole
⅓ cup butter or margarine
⅓ cup flour
2 13-fluid-ounce cans
   evaporated milk
2 tablespoons dry sherry
1 tablespoon
   Worcestershire sauce
1 tablespoon capers
2 tablespoons grated
   Parmesan cheese
1½ teaspoons salt
1 teaspoon paprika
1 7½-ounce can crab meat,
   flaked
¼ cup grated Parmesan
   cheese
½ cup fine dry bread crumbs
⅛ teaspoon paprika

Heat water and the 2 tablespoons salt to boiling in a large saucepan; add shrimp and scallops and cook 2 minutes. Add fillet of sole and cook 3 minutes longer. Drain. Coarsely chop scallops and flake sole with a fork. Melt butter in large saucepan over moderately low heat (225° F.); blend in flour. Gradually add the evaporated milk. Cook, stirring constantly, until thickened. Add the sherry, Worcestershire, capers, the 2 tablespoons Parmesan cheese, the 1½ teaspoons salt, and the 1 teaspoon paprika. Fold in shrimp, scallops, sole, and crab meat. Heat until mixture is thoroughly heated, stirring constantly. Pour into a 2½-quart shallow casserole. Mix together the ¼ cup Parmesan cheese, bread crumbs, and the ⅛ teaspoon paprika; sprinkle over casserole. Place in a preheated broiler 4 inches from heat for 3 to 4 minutes until top is brown. Serves 8 to 10.

Shellfish

Lobster, shrimp, and crabs (the crustaceans) and oysters, clams, scallops, and mussels (the mollusks) are the darlings of the fish family. Many people who claim not to like fish will list shrimp cocktail as their favorite appetizer. All the shellfish are high in nutrients and low in calories—an unbeatable combination. They are extremely delicate and, in their fresh form particularly, must be kept ice-cold until cooked and should be purchased only from a dependable market. Frozen shellfish should not be thawed until you are ready to use it. Once thawed, it should not be refrozen.

Shrimp

Shrimp are in season year-round. Most of the shrimp sold across the country are the large varieties from the Gulf waters. These include the greenish gray varieties; the brown, or Brazilian shrimp, and the pink or coral colored. Pacific coast and some Maine varieties are mostly small, varying in color. All shrimp turn pink when cooked. Except for size, which may be a consideration for your recipe, the different varieties of shrimp are completely interchangeable; their taste and texture are the same.

How to Buy Shrimp

Fresh shrimp are sold by the pound, uncooked in the shell, cooked in the shell, or cooked and shelled, and sometimes deveined. They are also sold according to size. Jumbo, or large, shrimp usually cost the most but take the least time to shell and devein. In the large size you will get about fifteen shrimps per pound, unshelled. You'll get the same number in one half pound of shelled shrimp. Medium shrimp will run from twenty to twenty-five per unshelled pound; very small shrimp, up to as many as forty or fifty per pound. In general, count on getting about six main-course servings from two pounds of unshelled shrimp or one to one and a half pounds of cooked and shelled shrimp. Shrimp should have a mild odor, and when cooked and shelled, a firm texture.

Shrimp are also sold frozen or canned. Frozen shrimp are available in various stages of preparation, including uncooked in the shell; shelled and uncooked; cooked, shelled, and deveined; breaded and uncooked, and breaded and cooked. Shrimp in packages are subject to U.S. government grading. Look for Grade A packages.

Preparation of Shrimp

If you buy fresh or frozen shrimp in the shell, they can be shelled and cleaned either before or after cooking. The method remains the same: With pointed scissors snip the shell from head to tail along the back. Slip off the shell and rinse off any grit. Remove the black sand vein down the back. Rinse again and dry. If you use canned shrimp, you can freshen the taste by soaking them for an hour in a cup of ice water to which 2 tablespoons of lemon juice have been added.

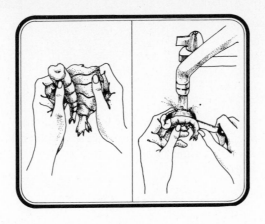

✑ Boiled Shrimp

1 quart water
1 stalk celery
1 small onion, sliced
4 peppercorns
1 bay leaf
1 teaspoon salt
1½ pounds raw shrimp
3 thin lemon slices

Combine water, celery, onion, peppercorns, bay leaf, and salt in saucepan. Bring to boil over moderately low heat (about 225° F.) and allow to simmer while preparing shrimp. Shell and devein shrimp.* Add shrimp and lemon slices to water. Cover, bring to boil, and simmer 5 minutes. Drain; reserve stock, if desired, to use in soups and sauces. Serves 6. Use shrimp in recipes calling for cooked shrimp, or chill and serve with your choice of cocktail sauce as an appetizer.

*Note: If preferred, shrimp may be cooked in the shell and then shelled and deveined.

✑ Butterfly Shrimp

1 to 1½ pounds raw jumbo shrimp
Pepper
Garlic salt
6 tablespoons (approximately) cornstarch
1 tablespoon dry sherry
1 tablespoon soy sauce

Shell and devein shrimp and pat dry with paper towel. Split shrimp lengthwise almost through, being careful to leave the two halves attached. Sprinkle both sides of shrimp lightly with pepper and garlic salt. Dust shrimp lightly with cornstarch. In a bowl combine sherry and soy sauce. Add shrimp and stir to coat them. In another bowl combine eggs, flour, and baking powder and stir until just smooth. Heat 3 inches of oil in an electric skillet to 375° F. Dip shrimp in the egg batter and fry in

4 *eggs, slightly beaten*
½ *cup all-purpose flour*
½ *teaspoon baking powder*
Vegetable oil for frying
Lemon wedges
Mustard Dip (recipe follows)
Cheese Dip (recipe follows)
Chili Dip (recipe follows)

heated oil about 3 or 4 minutes on each side, or until golden brown. Serve with lemon wedges or one or more of the dips as desired. Serves 4.

Mustard Dip

1 *cup mayonnaise*
2 *tablespoons prepared mustard*
¼ *teaspoon Worcestershire sauce*

In a small bowl combine mayonnaise, mustard, and Worcestershire sauce and blend well. Chill until serving time. Makes about 1 cup.

Cheese Dip

2 *3-ounce packages cream cheese*
¼ *cup milk*
2 *teaspoons frozen snipped chives*

Combine cheese, milk, and chives in a small bowl and blend well. Chill until serving time. Makes about ⅔ cup.

Chili Dip

1 *cup bottled chili sauce*
1 *teaspoon prepared horseradish*

In a small bowl combine chili sauce and horseradish and blend well. Chill until serving time. Makes about 1 cup.

Sherried Shrimp

2 *pounds raw shrimp*
Seasoned salt
¼ *cup butter or margarine, melted*
1 *tablespoon lemon juice*
2 *tablespoons dry sherry*
2 *tablespoons finely chopped fresh parsley*

Remove shells from shrimp, leaving the tails intact. Clean shrimp and wash well. Dry with paper towels. Arrange shrimp in rows in a shallow 1½-quart casserole with tails sticking up out of the dish. Sprinkle lightly with seasoned salt. In a small bowl combine butter, lemon juice, and sherry and blend well. Pour over shrimp in casserole. Preheat broiler. Broil 4 inches from source of heat for 8 minutes, or until shrimp are pink in color and tails are curled and slightly browned at tips. Sprinkle with parsley. Serves 6.

⋙ *Tempura*

10 *raw jumbo shrimp,*
      shelled and deveined
      (about ¾ pound)
  1 *egg*
  6 *tablespoons all-purpose*
      flour
  ½ *cup water*
1½ *tablespoons cornstarch*
  ¼ *teaspoon baking powder*
  ¼ *teaspoon salt*
Vegetable oil
  2 *large mushrooms, washed*
      and thinly sliced
  1 *small sweet potato, peeled*
      and cut into ⅛-inch-thick
      slices
  2 *stalks celery, cut into thin*
      strips
Tempura Sauce (recipe
      follows)

Cut shrimp down the center, almost through, and flatten out. In a small bowl combine egg, flour, water, cornstarch, baking powder, and salt and stir until mixture is almost smooth. (Batter should be just thick enough to coat the food with a thin film.) Pour oil into an electric skillet to a depth of 1½ inches. Heat oil to 375° F. Dip vegetables and shrimp in batter and place in hot oil. Fry until lightly browned, about 2 to 3 minutes on each side, or until cooked through. Drain on paper towels. Serve immediately. Dip vegetables and shrimp in Tempura Sauce. Serves 2.

Tempura Sauce

1 *tablespoon soy sauce*
1 *tablespoon dry sherry*
2 *tablespoons water*
Dash of sugar

Combine all ingredients in a small bowl and stir to blend well. Makes ¼ cup.

⋙ *Shrimp Chow Mein*

  1 *tablespoon vegetable oil*
  2 *pounds raw shrimp,*
      shelled and deveined
  1 *large stalk celery,*
      diagonally sliced
  ½ *cup sliced onion*
  ½ *cup slivered green pepper*
1½ *cups water*
  2 *envelopes instant chicken*
      broth mix
  2 *tablespoons soy sauce*
  ¼ *teaspoon ground ginger*

Over moderate heat (about 250° F.), heat oil in a skillet and cook shrimp just until it turns pink, stirring frequently. (All the oil may be absorbed; do not add additional oil.) Remove shrimp. In the same skillet combine celery, onion, green pepper, 1¼ cups of the water, broth mix, soy sauce, and ginger. Bring to a boil, stirring to loosen any of the browned bits. Blend together cornstarch and remaining ¼ cup water; quickly stir into boiling mixture. Boil ½ minute, stirring constantly. Add bean sprouts, lettuce, bamboo shoots, water chestnuts, and shrimp. Cover tightly and cook over moderately low heat (about 225° F.) 3 to 5 minutes,

1½ tablespoons cornstarch
1 16-ounce can bean
  sprouts, well drained
2 cups shredded romaine
  lettuce or Chinese
  cabbage
¼ cup sliced bamboo shoots
3 water chestnuts, sliced
2 cans chow mein noodles
3 cups cooked rice

or until lettuce is wilted and mixture is heated to serving temperature. Serve with additional soy sauce, noodles, and rice. Serves 6.

✧ Shrimp Newburg on Toast

¼ cup butter or margarine
3 tablespoons flour
2 cups light cream
¾ teaspoon salt
Dash of ground allspice
Dash of paprika
Dash of Tabasco
2 egg yolks, slightly beaten
½ cup dry sherry
2 pounds raw shrimp,
  cooked, shelled, and
  deveined
Toast

Melt butter in a saucepan over moderate heat (about 250° F.); quickly stir in flour. Gradually add cream, stirring constantly. (A wire whip is helpful.) Bring to a boil and boil 1 minute, stirring constantly. Add salt, allspice, paprika, and Tabasco. Gradually add a little of this hot mixture to the beaten egg yolks, stirring vigorously. Return to sauce in saucepan and place over low heat (about 200° F.). Stir in sherry and shrimp. Heat to serving temperature, about 5 minutes, stirring occasionally. Serve over toast. Serves 4 to 6.

✧ Shrimp Creole

2 tablespoons olive oil
1½ pounds raw shrimp,
  shelled and deveined
½ cup thinly sliced onion
1 8-ounce can tomato sauce
  with tomato bits
1 cup slivered green pepper
  (about 1 medium)
½ cup sliced celery
¾ teaspoon salt
¾ teaspoon garlic powder
Dash of chili powder
About 2 cups cooked rice or
  noodles

Heat the oil in a large skillet over moderate heat (about 250° F.). Add shrimp and cook just until shrimp turns pink, stirring frequently. Remove with a slotted spoon. To the same skillet, add onion and cook until lightly browned. Stir in tomato sauce, pepper, celery, salt, garlic powder, and chili powder. Simmer gently, uncovered, over moderately low heat (about 225° F.) 10 minutes. Add shrimp and heat thoroughly. Serve over cooked rice or noodles. Serves 3 to 4.

❧ Italian-Style Broiled Shrimp (Scampi)

1 pound fresh jumbo shrimp
⅓ cup olive oil
2 tablespoons lemon juice
1 tablespoon finely chopped
   parsley
1 clove garlic, peeled and
   pressed
½ teaspoon seasoned salt
⅛ teaspoon paprika

Under cold running water remove the shells from the shrimp up to the last tail section. Cut lengthwise down the back of each shrimp, cutting it almost completely through, and remove the sand veins. Place shrimp flattened out on a broiler pan, cut sides up. Mix together remaining ingredients and brush mixture over shrimp. Broil in preheated broiler, 4 inches from source of heat, 8 to 10 minutes. Serves 2 to 3.

❧ Shrimp Curry

3 pounds shrimp, frozen,
   shelled, and deveined
3 tablespoons butter or
   margarine
1½ cups finely chopped onion
2 tablespoons curry
   powder
3 cans frozen cream of
   shrimp soup, thawed
⅓ cup milk
3 cups commercial sour
   cream
About 5 cups cooked rice
Chopped cashew nuts
Chopped hard-cooked egg
Flaked coconut
Chutney

Place shrimp in enough boiling salted water to cover and cook over low heat (about 200° F.) 3 to 5 minutes after water returns to boil. Melt butter in a large skillet or Dutch oven over moderately low heat (about 225° F.). Add onion and curry and cook, stirring frequently, until onion is tender. Remove from heat and blend in soup and milk; add cooked shrimp. Return to heat and cook until hot, stirring constantly. Just before serving, fold in sour cream and cook over moderately low heat (about 225° F.), stirring constantly, until thoroughly heated. Do not allow mixture to boil. Serve over hot rice. Serve the condiments on the side to be sprinkled over each serving as desired. Serves 8 to 10.

❧ Sweet and Sour Shrimp

1½ pounds frozen shrimp,
   shelled and deveined
2 13¼-ounce cans
   pineapple tidbits
⅓ cup firmly packed light
   brown sugar
3 tablespoons cornstarch
¼ teaspoon ground ginger
(Ingredients continued on page 422)

Cook shrimp according to package directions and drain. Drain pineapple and add enough water to the syrup to make 1½ cups liquid. Mix brown sugar, cornstarch, ginger, and salt in a saucepan. Gradually add pineapple syrup, vinegar, and soy sauce. Cook over moderately high heat (about 275° F.), stirring constantly, until thickened. Add green pepper, pineapple, and shrimp; heat 5 minutes. Serves 4 to 6.

¼ *teaspoon salt*
⅓ *cup vinegar*
1½ *teaspoons soy sauce*
 2 *small green peppers,*
     cored and cut into strips

Lobster

Lobster—that is, the Northern lobster caught in the cold Atlantic waters from Labrador to North Carolina—is in season all year but is most plentiful in the summer months. The spiny, or rock, lobster is found in the warmer waters around the world; in this country, in Florida and California. In some areas of those states it is always in season.

How to Buy Lobster

Northern lobster is sold live or cooked in the shell. The cooked meat is sold fresh, frozen, or canned. Rock lobster tails, either from this country or imported from South Africa, Australia, the Caribbean, and the Mediterranean, are available frozen raw in the shell. The meat is also sold canned.

Live Northern lobsters should have a dark bluish green hard shell. They must be alive when you buy them and will be quite active unless they have been in very cold storage. The tail should curl quickly under the body when the lobster is picked up. Cooked lobsters have a bright red shell. They should have a fresh seashore odor. The tail should spring back under the body when straightened out—this will prove the lobster was alive just before it was cooked.

A one-pound live lobster or a five- to eight-ounce lobster tail will be enough for one dinner serving. One-half pound of cooked lobster meat will serve as an appetizer for six. Two one-pound live lobsters will yield one-half pound cooked meat. One and a half pounds of frozen lobster tails yield three quarters of a pound of cooked meat. It is easiest to buy the cooked meat (fresh, canned, or frozen) if you will be using it in a recipe.

 **Boiled Lobster**

4 *1- to 1½-pound live lobsters*
6 *quarts boiling water*

Plunge lobsters headfirst into a large pot of boiling salted water. Cover and return to boiling point; reduce

6 tablespoons salt
Melted butter

heat and simmer over low heat (about 200° F.) 20 minutes. Drain. Place lobsters on their backs and cut in half lengthwise with a sharp knife. Remove the head and the stomach (which is just back of the head) and the dark vein that runs from the stomach to the tip of the tail. Do not discard the green liver (tomalley) and any coral roe. Crack claws with a lobster cracker and provide small forks for removing meat. Serve with small custard cups of melted butter for dipping. Serves 4.

⮜ Broiled Lobster

4 1- to 1½-pound live
  lobsters, split for broiling
2 tablespoons melted butter
  or margarine
½ teaspoon salt
Pepper
Paprika
½ cup melted butter or
  margarine
2 tablespoons lemon juice

Have lobsters split for broiling and claws cracked at the fish market. Lay lobsters open on broiler pan as flat as possible. Brush with the 2 tablespoons butter and sprinkle with salt, pepper, and paprika. Place in preheated broiler 4 inches from heat and broil 12 to 15 minutes. Mix the ½ cup melted butter and lemon juice and serve with lobsters. Serves 4.

⮜ Baked Lobster

4 1½- to 2-pound live
  lobsters, split
2 cups finely crushed round
  buttery crackers
½ cup melted butter or
  margarine
Few grains pepper
2½ tablespoons
  Worcestershire sauce
Melted butter

Have lobsters split and claws cracked at fish market. Remove green liver (tomalley) to use in stuffing. Place lobsters in a large flat baking pan. Toss together cracker crumbs, the ½ cup melted butter, pepper, Worcestershire, and green liver. Spoon stuffing lightly into body cavities. Heat oven to 375° F. Bake lobsters 35 to 40 minutes. Serve with melted butter. Serves 4.

⮜ Broiled Lobster Tails

6 5- to 8-ounce frozen lobster
  tails, thawed
⅓ cup melted butter or
  margarine

Preheat broiler. Split lobster tails lengthwise. Lay as flat as possible on broiler pan, cut side up. Brush with the ⅓ cup melted butter and sprinkle with salt, pepper, and paprika. Place in broiler 4 inches from heat and broil 10

½ teaspoon salt
Few grains pepper
Dash of paprika
¾ cup melted butter or
  margarine
3 tablespoons lemon juice

to 15 minutes. Mix the ¾ cup butter and lemon juice and serve with lobster tails. Serves 6.

✑ Lobster Tails in Butter Sauce

2 8- or 9-ounce packages
  frozen lobster tails
¼ cup butter or margarine
1 small clove garlic, minced
¼ teaspoon dried oregano
  leaves
½ teaspoon salt
Few grains pepper
⅓ cup chopped fresh parsley
1 tablespoon grated
  Parmesan cheese

Cook lobster tails according to directions on package. Cut membrane along both edges of shell and remove membrane. Lift meat out of shell and reserve shell. Dice lobster meat coarsely. Melt butter in skillet over moderate heat (about 225° F.); mix in garlic, oregano, salt, and pepper. Add lobster meat and cook until heated. Fold in parsley and spoon into lobster shells. Sprinkle with cheese. Place in preheated broiler 3 inches from heat; broil 3 to 4 minutes, until lightly browned. Serves 3.

✑ Stuffed Lobster Tails

6 large frozen lobster tails
2 tablespoons butter or
  margarine
2 tablespoons flour
½ cup milk
½ cup dry white wine
¼ teaspoon salt
1 cup packaged seasoned
  bread stuffing
3 tablespoons water
½ cup flaked crab meat
2 tablespoons finely chopped
  onion
1 tablespoon chopped fresh
  parsley
⅛ teaspoon garlic salt
Few grains pepper
¼ cup grated Parmesan
  cheese

Cook lobster tails in boiling salted water 6 to 8 minutes, or until tender; drain and cool. Melt butter in saucepan over moderately low heat (about 225° F.); remove from heat and blend in flour. Gradually add milk; return to heat and cook, stirring constantly, until thickened. Gradually stir wine into sauce; mix in salt. Heat oven to 350° F. Cut membrane along both edges of lobster tail and remove membrane. Lift meat out of shells and reserve shells. Cut lobster into bite-sized pieces. Mix bread stuffing and water together to moisten; stir into lobster with crab meat, onion, parsley, garlic salt, and pepper. Mix in white sauce. Spoon lobster mixture into shells; sprinkle with Parmesan cheese. Bake 20 minutes. Serves 6.

❧ Rock Lobster Casserole

3 8-ounce packages frozen
lobster tails
1 10-ounce package frozen
lima beans
1 4-ounce can sliced
mushrooms
Milk
4 tablespoons butter or
margarine
4 tablespoons flour
½ teaspoon salt
½ teaspoon paprika
1 egg yolk
1 tablespoon dry sherry
(optional)

Heat oven to 400° F. Drop frozen lobster tails into boiling salted water to cover. When water comes to a boil again, cook tails 3 minutes. Drain and drench with cold water. Using scissors, cut lengthwise through center of membrane covering flesh. Insert fingers under meat at open end and pull out meat in one piece. Arrange in a shallow 2-quart casserole. Cook lima beans as directed on package. Drain mushrooms; measure broth and add enough milk to make 2 cups liquid. Melt butter in a saucepan over moderately low heat (about 225° F.); blend in flour, salt, and paprika. Gradually add combined milk and mushroom broth. Cook over moderately low heat, stirring constantly, until smooth and thickened. Remove from heat. Beat egg yolk slightly; add sherry. Stir the egg mixture slowly into sauce. Add mushrooms and lima beans. Pour sauce around lobster tails. Cover casserole tightly with aluminum foil and bake 15 to 20 minutes until thoroughly heated. Serves 6.

Crab

Crabs are either hard-shelled or soft-shelled. The soft-shelled crab, or "shedder," which is eaten shell and all, is not a separate species, but a molting crab that has shed its shell and is in the process of forming another. Soft-shelled crabs are available in the warm months, from May to October. Fresh hard-shelled crabs are available year-round but are most plentiful in the summer. About three-fourths of the crabs consumed in this country are blue crabs, which have bright blue claws before they are cooked and are found all along the Atlantic coast. Most soft-shelled crabs are blue crabs. The Dungeness crab is taken from Pacific coast waters and is named for a town in the state of Washington. Rock crab is caught off the New England and California shores. Alaska king crab, from the north Pacific, is named for its size; king crabs sometimes weigh up to twenty pounds. Only the leg meat is eaten. The meat from different types of crabs can be used interchangeably in most recipes.

How to Buy Crab

Cooked crab meat, picked from the shell, is available fresh, frozen, or canned. It is packed in several grades: lump meat, with solid pieces from the body of the crab; flake meat, or small pieces from the rest of the body; lump meat and flake meat combined; and claw meat. Your recipe will determine which you will want to buy. Lump meat is the most attractive—especially for use in salads—and it is the most expensive. Live hard-shelled crabs are sold only in the areas where they are caught, and therefore are not available across the country. Soft-shelled crabs are more frequently found inland (in their season) because they can be safely shipped long distances. If you are planning to serve hard-shelled crabs in the shell, the number you will need will depend on the weight of the crabs. With soft-shelled crabs, plan on two per person. One pound (a scant 3 cups) of crab meat will make six main-course portions or eight to ten appetizer portions.

How to Prepare Crabs

Hard-shelled crabs should be alive and active before they are cooked. Hold the crab with tongs and rinse it under cold water. Then drop it headfirst into boiling water. Cook a minimum of fifteen minutes, or, for large crabs, about eight minutes per pound. To remove meat from hard-shelled crabs: Twist off claws and legs, crack shell with a hammer, and pick out the meat. Break off the "apron" on the underside, pull upper and lower shells apart, and break body in half down center. Snip off membrane covering, cutting around edges, and remove meat. Soft-shelled crabs are usually cleaned by your fish dealer and are sold ready to cook. Always remove the stiff tendons from canned crab meat before using.

Fried Soft-Shelled Blue Crabs

12 *soft-shelled blue crabs, cleaned*
 2 *eggs, beaten*
¼ *cup milk*
 2 *teaspoons salt*
¾ *cup all-purpose flour*
¾ *cup fine dry bread crumbs*
Shortening or oil for frying
Tartar Sauce (recipe on page 401)

Have crabs cleaned at the fish market. Rinse in cold water; drain and dry between paper towels. Combine eggs, milk, and salt. Mix flour and crumbs. Dip crabs in egg mixture and then roll in flour–crumb mixture.

To pan-fry: Heat shortening or oil to a depth of ⅛ inch in a large skillet over moderate heat (about 250° F.). Add crabs and cook until browned on both sides, about 8 to 10 minutes. Drain on paper towels. Serves 6.

To deep-fat fry: Heat shortening or oil to a depth of 4 inches in a deep-fat fryer. When temperature registers

375° F. on deep-fat thermometer, fry crabs 3 to 4 minutes, or until golden brown. Drain on paper towels. Serve with Tartar Sauce. Serves 6.

ᛓ Chesapeake Crab Imperial

*1 pound fresh or frozen
fancy lump crab meat
¼ cup butter or margarine
2 tablespoons finely chopped
onion
1 tablespoon finely chopped
green pepper
2 tablespoons flour
½ teaspoon salt
½ teaspoon celery salt
Few grains white pepper
1 cup milk or dairy
half-and-half
2 tablespoons dry sherry
Dash of Tabasco
1 egg
1 tablespoon chopped fresh
parsley
1 pimiento, chopped
⅛ teaspoon grated orange
peel
1 cup soft bread crumbs
2 tablespoons melted butter
or margarine
Paprika

Heat oven to 350° F. Remove any shell and cartilage from crab meat, being careful to keep meat in large pieces. Melt butter in saucepan over moderate heat (about 250° F.); add onion and green pepper and cook until tender. Blend in flour, salt, celery salt, and white pepper. Gradually add milk and cook until thickened, stirring constantly. Remove from heat and stir in sherry and Tabasco. Beat egg slightly in a medium-sized bowl. Gradually add cream sauce to beaten egg; fold in crab meat, parsley, pimiento, and orange peel. Spoon crab meat mixture into 6 well-buttered scallop shells or 5-ounce custard cups. Toss bread crumbs and melted butter together and sprinkle over crab meat. Sprinkle with paprika. Bake 20 to 25 minutes, or until crumbs are lightly browned. Serves 6.

*Note: 3 6½-ounce cans white crab meat, well drained, may be substituted for fresh or frozen crab meat. Reduce salt to ¼ teaspoon.

ᛓ Crab Soufflé

4 slices white bread, cubed
2 cups flaked fresh, frozen, or
canned crab meat
½ cup mayonnaise or salad
dressing
1 medium-sized onion,
chopped
1 cup chopped celery

Arrange the cubed bread evenly in the bottom of a 2-quart baking dish. Fold together crab meat, mayonnaise, onion, celery, and green pepper; spoon over bread cubes. Trim crusts from the remaining slices of bread and arrange over crab meat mixture to cover top (if bread slices are small, 6 slices may be needed). Beat eggs and milk together and pour over bread. Cover and chill in refrigerator 8 hours, or longer, until baking

1 medium-sized green
   pepper, chopped
4 to 6 slices white bread
4 eggs
3 cups milk
1 can condensed cream of
   mushroom soup
¾ cup coarsely shredded
   Cheddar cheese
Paprika

time. Heat oven to 325° F. Bake soufflé, uncovered, 15 minutes. Spread soup evenly over bread slices; top with shredded cheese and a sprinkling of paprika. Bake 1 hour longer. Serves 8.

Oysters

Oysters are available year-round, but the best season is from the first of September to the first of May. Oysters are found in shallow bay waters, in sounds, and at river mouths where the fresh water of tributary streams reduces the saltiness of the ocean water. Every state that borders on the sea, with the exceptions of Maine and New Hampshire, has an abundance of oysters. Varieties found on the Pacific coast include the small Olympia oyster and the large Pacific, or Japanese, oyster; but the Eastern oyster, from the Atlantic, represents almost 90 percent of the oyster catch in this country.

How to Buy Oysters

Oysters are sold raw by the dozen, in the shell or on the half shell; or shucked, by the pint or quart. They are also sold canned or frozen. If you plan to cook them, it is easiest to buy them already shucked. If you buy them in the shell, they should be alive, the shell tightly closed. The oyster should be plump, shiny, and fresh-smelling. For six main-dish portions you'll need three dozen oysters in the shell or one quart of shucked oysters.

How to Prepare Oysters

To shuck oysters, rinse them well in iced water. Place the oyster on the table flat side up and hold it with one hand. With the other, force an oyster or clam knife between the shells at the thin end. The shell can be broken with a hammer to make it easier to insert the knife. Cut the large muscle where it is attached to the flat upper shell and remove the shell. Cut the muscle where it is attached to the lower, deeper half of the shell, to serve the oyster in the shell or to remove it for use in your recipe. Be sure to remove any shell particles.

Scalloped Oysters

1 3½-ounce box unsalted soda crackers
1 pint oysters, fresh or frozen, or 3 7-ounce cans of oysters
1¾ cups oyster liquid plus light cream or milk
1 teaspoon salt
¼ teaspoon pepper
4 tablespoons butter or margarine

Heat oven to 375° F. Crumble crackers coarsely. Drain oysters and measure oyster liquid. Add enough light cream or milk to make 1¾ cups. In the bottom of a deep, well-buttered 1½-quart casserole, put about ¼ of the cracker crumbs. Arrange about ⅓ of the oysters over the crumbs. Sprinkle with some of the salt and pepper and dot with 1 tablespoon of the butter. Repeat layers, ending with crackers and butter. Pour the 1¾ cups oyster liquid over all. Bake about 1 hour, until top is crusty. Serves 4.

Oysters Rockefeller

Rock salt
24 oysters on the half shell
1 10-ounce package frozen chopped spinach
½ cup butter or margarine
¼ cup chopped green onions or scallions
1 teaspoon anchovy paste (optional)
¼ cup finely chopped celery
1 clove garlic, very finely chopped
½ teaspoon celery salt
¼ teaspoon salt
2 tablespoons lime juice
Dash of Tabasco
⅓ cup fine soft bread crumbs

Heat oven to 450° F. Spread rock salt in an even layer in the bottom of 2 jelly-roll pans or other large, shallow baking dishes. (The rock salt will help to keep the shells level.) Arrange oysters on the half shell in the pans. Cook spinach according to package directions and drain very well. Melt butter in a large skillet over moderately low heat (about 225° F.). Remove from heat. Add green onions, anchovy paste, celery, garlic, celery salt, salt, lime juice, and Tabasco and blend well. Add well-drained spinach and bread crumbs and stir to blend. Spoon some of the spinach mixture over each oyster. Bake 5 to 7 minutes, or until oysters curl at edges. Serve immediately. Serves 4.

[429]

Clams

Clams are most abundant from October to April. There are two basic types: hard-shelled, which have a rounded shell, and soft-shelled, which have a more oval shape. Clams are found all along the Atlantic coast and along the coast of the Gulf of Mexico to Texas. Every region on our coastlines has its particular varieties. On the Pacific coast, where clams are found from California north to Alaska, the sharp-shelled razor clam has made the town of Long Beach, Washington, famous.

How to Buy Clams

Clams are sold fresh in the shell or shucked; also frozen or canned, whole or minced. You can buy clams in the shell by the pound, shucked clams by the quart. Small hard-shelled clams, such as littlenecks and cherrystones, are most often served raw on the half shell. Large hard-shelled clams, such as quahogs or chowders, are used in chowder and other recipes. Soft-shelled clams are used for steaming (the smallest ones are called steamers). Razor clams, which most of the country knows only in the canned form, are used for clam bisque and chowder. If you plan to use clams in a recipe and not in the shell, it is easiest to buy them already shucked, either fresh, canned, or frozen. For six main-dish portions you will need about a quart of shucked clams, three dozen shell clams, or two 7-ounce cans. When buying shell clams, they should be alive, the shells unbroken and tightly closed; if the clam inside is alive, an open shell will close quickly when touched. Shucked clams should be plump, with clear liquor and a good fresh odor. They should always be free from any shell particles.

How to Prepare Clams

If you are going to steam clams, scrub them well and let them stand in salt water (⅓ cup of salt to a gallon of cold water) for twenty minutes. Cook until shells are open. Discard any clams that do not open in cooking. To open hard-shelled clams, use one of the patented gadgets that works well; or, using a clam knife, follow this method: Hold the clam in your hand with the hinge edge against your palm, large end up. Insert the knife between the shell halves and cut around the clam, twisting the knife slightly to pry open the shell. If you are serving clams on the half shell, remove and discard one shell half and leave the clam in the other. Loosen it from the shell, but be careful to preserve the liquor.

❧ Steamed Clams

6 pounds soft-shelled clams
Water
Melted butter or margarine

Scrub clams thoroughly. Heat ½ inch water in large Dutch oven to boiling. Add clams. Cover and cook over moderate heat (about 250° F.) 15 minutes, or until shells open. (Discard any clams with unopened shells.) Strain broth through several thicknesses of cheesecloth to remove any sand. Serve with broth and melted butter. Serves 6.

❧ Fried Clams

1 quart shucked clams
3 eggs
3 tablespoons milk
1½ teaspoons salt
Few grains pepper
1½ cups fine dry bread
    crumbs
Vegetable oil or shortening for
    frying

Drain clams; (reserve liquor for soups, or chill and use as an appetizer). Dry clams well between paper towels. Beat together eggs, milk, salt, and pepper. Dip clams in egg mixture and then in bread crumbs. Recoat with egg and bread crumbs. Prick clams several times with a fork. Allow to stand 30 minutes before frying. Heat shortening or oil to a depth of 4 inches in a deep-fat fryer. When temperature registers 350° F. on a deep-fat thermometer, place 4 or 5 clams at a time in frying basket and gradually lower into fat. Fry about 5 minutes until golden brown. Drain will on paper towels. Serves 6.

Fried Oysters

Substitute *1 quart of frying-size oysters, drained,* for the clams in preceding recipe.

❧ Roasted Clams

6 pounds soft-shelled clams
Melted butter or margarine

Heat oven to 450° F. Scrub clams and drain well. Place in a flat baking pan. Bake 15 minutes, or until shells open. Serve hot in shell with melted butter. Serves 6.

❧ Baked Stuffed Clams

2 dozen cherrystone clams,
    shucked, with 24 half
    shells reserved

Heat oven to 400° F. Drain raw clams well and finely chop them; place in mixing bowl. Chop the mushrooms finely and add to the clams. Stir in onions, salt, Tabasco,

1 3-ounce can chopped
  broiled mushrooms,
  drained
2 tablespoons chopped
  green onions or scallions
¼ teaspoon salt
⅛ teaspoon Tabasco
⅛ teaspoon celery seed
1½ tablespoons melted butter
  or margarine
⅓ cup Italian-style seasoned
  dry bread crumbs
Lemon wedges

and celery seed; mix well. Rinse clam shells in cold water and pat dry. Spoon clam mixture into shells. Toss together the butter and bread crumbs. Sprinkle each stuffed shell with the buttered crumbs. Place in a shallow baking pan and bake 10 to 15 minutes, or until crumbs are browned. Serve hot with lemon wedges. Makes 24; serves 4.

Scallops

Scallops are available year-round, but they are at their best from November to April. Americans generally use only the scallop's large muscle, which opens and closes the shell. Whereas we regard this as the only edible part, Europeans eat the entire scallop. (Scallop shells are often sold separately for use as small baking dishes.) There are two types of scallops: bay scallops, found in inshore waters from New England to the Gulf of Mexico; and sea scallops, which are brought in from the deep waters off the Northern and Middle Atlantic states. Sea scallops are large, sometimes as big as two inches in diameter. Bay scallops are small, about one-half inch in diameter; they are especially tender and sweet—and higher in price than the more widely available sea scallop.

How to Buy Scallops

Sea scallops are sold both fresh and frozen; bay scallops are sold only fresh. Both varieties should have a sweet odor and be practically free from liquid. One pound of scallops will serve three to four. Scallops are ready for use just as you buy them. Rinse them in cold water and dry thoroughly.

Broiled Scallops or Shrimp

¼ cup olive oil
1 tablespoon lemon juice
¼ cup dry white wine

Blend together olive oil, lemon juice, wine, basil, garlic powder, salt, and pepper. Pour mixture over scallops or shrimp and place in refrigerator for at least 2 hours to

1 *teaspoon dried basil leaves*
¼ *teaspoon garlic powder*
1 *teaspoon salt*
⅛ *teaspoon pepper*
1 *pound fresh scallops or fresh or frozen shrimp, shelled and deveined*
1 *tablespoon chopped fresh parsley*

marinate. Drain and reserve marinade. Preheat broiler. Place scallops or shrimp on broiler rack and brush with some of the marinade. Broil 3 inches from heat for 5 minutes; turn and brush with remaining marinade. Broil 5 minutes longer. Serve garnished with parsley. Serves 3 to 4.

Batter-Fried Scallops or Shrimp

1 *pound scallops or shrimp*
2 *eggs, slightly beaten*
⅓ *cup ice-cold water*
⅔ *cup sifted all-purpose flour*
¾ *teaspoon salt*
Vegetable oil or shortening for frying

Shell and devein shrimp or wash scallops; dry thoroughly between paper towels. Mix eggs and water in a small bowl; add flour and salt and mix together lightly. Heat oil to a depth of 4 inches in a deep-fat fryer. When temperature registers 375° F. on a deep-fat thermometer, place shrimp or scallops one at a time on a skewer and coat with batter. Let excess batter run off. Lower gently into hot fat and fry until golden brown, about 4 minutes. Drain on paper towels. Serves 3 to 4.

Scallops Coquille

⅔ *cup dry white wine*
⅓ *cup water*
2 *parsley sprigs*
1 *small onion, cut in half*
1 *pound scallops*
3 *tablespoons butter or margarine*
¼ *pound mushrooms, chopped*
2 *tablespoons flour*
Few grains pepper
1 *can condensed cream of mushroom soup*
⅓ *cup heavy cream*
2 *tablespoons lemon juice*
2 *tablespoons melted butter or margarine*
¼ *cup grated Parmesan cheese*
½ *cup fine dry bread crumbs*

Combine wine, water, parsley, and onion in small saucepan; heat to boiling over moderately low heat (about 225° F.), add scallops, and simmer 5 minutes. Drain and reserve ½ cup of the wine broth. Chop scallops coarsely. Melt butter in the saucepan over moderate heat (about 250° F.); add mushrooms and cook until lightly browned. Blend in flour and pepper. Gradually add soup, cream, and lemon juice; cook, stirring constantly, until thickened. Gradually stir in the reserved wine broth. Fold in scallops. Spoon into individual scallop shells or serving dishes. Mix melted butter, grated Parmesan cheese, and bread crumbs. Sprinkle over scallop mixture. Place in preheated broiler 2 to 3 inches from heat and broil for 4 to 5 minutes, or until lightly browned. Serves 4.

❧ *Scallop Kabobs*

½ *pound small mushrooms*
1 *large green pepper, cut*
   into 1-inch squares
1 *pound scallops*
4 *slices raw bacon, cut into*
   1-inch pieces
3 *tablespoons melted butter*
   or margarine
¼ *teaspoon dried tarragon*
   leaves
½ *teaspoon salt*
Few grains pepper

Cook mushrooms and green pepper in boiling salted water to cover over moderately low heat (about 225° F.) for 4 minutes, or until almost tender. Drain well. If scallops are large, cut in half. Arrange scallops, mushrooms, green pepper, and bacon alternately on 6- or 7-inch skewers and place on broiler rack. Mix butter, tarragon, salt, and pepper; brush over scallops. Place in preheated broiler 3 inches from heat; broil 3 to 5 minutes, or until lightly browned. Turn, brush with butter mixture, and broil 3 to 5 minutes longer. Serves 4 to 6.

Mussels

Mussels are not nationally distributed. They are harvested commercially from fall until spring only on the northeastern and western shores of this country so distribution is limited although fresh mussels are flown into specialty stores and restaurants throughout the country. These sweet mollusks in their midnight blue shells are always eaten cooked whether they are served hot or cold.

How to Buy Mussels

Mussels are usually marketed live although they may be purchased canned in some specialty shops. Always buy mussels that feel heavy; discard any that are open or do not close when tapped; they are not edible. If you find mussels growing in fresh or salt water, check with the local health authorities or the state fish and wild life agency to see if they are safe to collect and eat.

How to Prepare Mussels

Exceptional care should be taken when cleaning mussels. With a sturdy knife cut or yank off "beards," the strawlike threads at the hinged edge where the mussel was attached to the rocks. Scrape off any barnacles that may be on the shells. Scrub thoroughly with a very stiff brush in cold running water. Rinse several times in clean water.

✑ Cold Marinated Mussels

2 *dozen large mussels*
Water
½ *cup vegetable oil*
¼ *cup fresh lime juice*
2 *tablespoons chopped fresh parsley*
½ *teaspoon salt*
¼ *teaspoon pepper*
⅔ *cup coarsely chopped, peeled red onion*
½ *cup coarsely chopped, seeded green pepper*
½ *cup coarsely chopped, seeded red pepper*
8 *drops (or more) Tabasco sauce*
Lime wedges

With a short-bladed, sturdy knife clean mussels by scraping off barnacles and yanking out beards. Then scrub shells with a stiff brush under cold water and rinse well. Pour about ½ inch of water into a wide saucepot or skillet. Place the mussels in the water, cover and bring to a boil over moderately high heat (about 275° F.); when water boils, immediately turn heat down to moderately low (about 225° F.) and simmer 5 to 7 minutes, until all the mussels have opened. Place remaining ingredients except lime wedges in a medium-sized bowl and stir to mix. Remove mussels from shells, add to oil-lime mixture and stir gently to coat mussels with the dressing. Cover and refrigerate 6 to 8 hours, stirring occasionally. To serve, arrange 24 mussel half-shells in a serving dish or on individual plates and spoon a mussel plus some dressing into each half-shell. Serve with lime wedges. Serves 4 as an appetizer.

✑ Mussels with Garlic Butter

2 *dozen large fresh mussels*
½ *cup butter or margarine, softened*
1 *teaspoon finely minced peeled garlic*
1 *tablespoon very finely chopped peeled onion*
2 *tablespoons chopped fresh parsley*
¼ *cup fine dry bread crumbs*
Few grains pepper

Scrub mussels thoroughly with a stiff brush. Yank off any "beard" and rinse well. Put mussels in a large saucepot; add enough boiling water to just cover bottom of pot. Cover and place over moderate heat (about 250° F.). Cook about 5 minutes, until shells open. Cool until mussels are comfortable to handle. Remove top shell of each mussel and leave the meat on the bottom-half shell. In a small bowl beat together the butter and garlic. Add remaining ingredients and beat until fluffy. Spread some of the butter mixture over each mussel. Arrange mussels on a broiler pan. Place in preheated broiler 4 inches from the source of heat and broil 2 to 3 minutes, or until topping is lightly browned. Serve hot. Serves 4 as an appetizer.

Canned Fish

Canned fish is a true convenience food. It includes many varieties of fish and shellfish and can be used in numerous dishes: appetizers, salads, fish loaves, casseroles, and soups. Canned fish, because of little or no waste, is economical to use, and it is desirable to keep on an emergency shelf. These are a few of the excellent dishes you can make with canned (or packaged) fish; check the index for a great variety of uses.

ᴥᵹ Clam-and-Corn Soufflé

1¼ cups crumbled soda
   crackers
1 cup milk
2 eggs, beaten
1 7-ounce can minced
   clams, undrained
1 cup thawed frozen corn
   niblets (½ package)
3 tablespoons melted butter
   or margarine
2 tablespoons minced onion
¼ teaspoon salt
½ teaspoon Worcestershire
   sauce
½ cup coarsely shredded
   Cheddar cheese

Place crackers in a bowl. Combine milk and eggs; pour over crackers and soak about 30 minutes. Add all the remaining ingredients except the cheese; fold together gently. Pour into a 1½-quart greased casserole. Cover and refrigerate. About 1¼ hours before serving time, heat oven to 300° F. Uncover casserole and bake 50 minutes; sprinkle top with cheese and bake 10 minutes longer, or until cheese is melted. Serves 4.

ᴥᵹ Deviled Crab

1 cup milk
¼ cup butter or margarine
2 tablespoons flour
1 tablespoon snipped fresh
   parsley
2 teaspoons lemon juice
1 teaspoon prepared
   mustard
½ teaspoon prepared
   horseradish
Dash of Tabasco
½ teaspoon salt
2 6½-ounce cans crab meat,
   drained and flaked
½ cup soft bread crumbs
2 tablespoons melted butter
   or margarine
Lemon wedges

Heat milk over very low heat (about 175° F.) until bubbles appear around edge of pan. Melt the ¼ cup butter in a saucepan over moderately low heat (about 225° F.). Remove from heat and blend in flour, parsley, lemon juice, mustard, horseradish, Tabasco, and salt. Gradually add hot milk, stirring constantly, until all liquid has been added and sauce is smooth. Cook over low heat (about 200° F.) for 20 minutes, stirring very frequently. Remove from heat. Stir in crab meat. Spoon mixture into individual scallop shells or flameproof ramekins. Combine bread crumbs and the 2 tablespoons melted butter. Sprinkle over crab mixture. Heat oven to 400° F. Bake about 10 minutes, until mixture bubbles at edges and crumbs are browned. Serve with lemon wedges. Serves 6.

ᴈ Baked Lobster and Shrimp

¼ cup finely chopped green pepper
¼ cup finely chopped onion
1 cup finely chopped celery
1 5-ounce can lobster, drained and cut into chunks
1 4½-ounce can shrimp, drained
¼ teaspoon salt
⅛ teaspoon pepper
1 teaspoon Worcestershire sauce
1 cup mayonnaise
1 cup soft bread crumbs
2 tablespoons melted butter or margarine

Heat oven to 350° F. Combine green pepper, onion, celery, lobster, shrimp, salt, pepper, Worcestershire sauce, and mayonnaise. Place in a deep 1-quart casserole. Toss bread crumbs together with melted butter and sprinkle over top. Bake 30 minutes, or until top is lightly browned. Serve warm. Serves 4.

ᴈ Crab Coquille

1 cup dry white wine
⅔ cup water
3 parsley sprigs
1 small onion
3 7½-ounce cans Alaska king crab meat
2 tablespoons butter
½ pound fresh mushrooms, chopped
2 tablespoons flour
1 can condensed cream of chicken soup
¾ cup heavy cream
3 tablespoons lemon juice
3 tablespoons melted butter or margarine
3 tablespoons grated Parmesan cheese
6 tablespoons fine dry bread crumbs

Combine wine, water, parsley sprigs, and onion in a small saucepan and heat over moderate heat (about 250° F.) until boiling. Add crab meat and simmer 5 minutes over moderately low heat (about 225° F.). Drain, reserving ¾ cup of the wine broth. Cut larger pieces of crab meat into bite-sized pieces. Melt the 2 tablespoons butter in a saucepan over moderately low heat (about 225° F.); add mushrooms and cook until lightly browned. Blend in flour. Gradually add soup, cream, and lemon juice; cook, stirring constantly, until thickened. Gradually stir in the wine broth. Fold in crab meat. Spoon into individual scallop shells or heatproof serving dishes. Mix the 3 tablespoons melted butter, the grated cheese, and the bread crumbs. Sprinkle over crab mixture. Place in preheated broiler 2 to 3 inches from heat for 3 to 4 minutes, or until lightly browned. Serves 8.

FISH

✑ Shrimp Foo Yung

2 cups ice-cold water
2 tablespoons lemon juice
2 4½-ounce cans shrimp
1 tablespoon vegetable oil
¼ cup chopped green onions
   or scallions
⅔ cup thinly sliced celery
1 16-ounce can bean sprouts,
   drained
½ teaspoon salt
¼ teaspoon pepper
6 eggs, well beaten
2 tablespoons vegetable oil
Foo Yung Sauce (recipe
   follows)

Combine ice-cold water and lemon juice in a bowl; let shrimp stand in mixture 20 minutes. Heat the 1 table-spoon oil in a medium-sized skillet over moderate heat (about 250° F.). Add green onion and celery; cook until celery is translucent. Remove from skillet and combine with bean sprouts. Drain shrimp and chop coarsely; add to bean-sprout mixture. Stir salt and pepper into beaten eggs; combine with shrimp mixture. Heat the 2 table-spoons oil in the skillet over moderate heat (about 250° F.). Drop Foo Yung mixture by ⅓-cup amounts into hot greased skillet. As mixture cooks push edges in slightly, using a spatula. Fry until golden brown on both sides. Makes 9 cakes. Serve with Foo Yung Sauce. Serves 4.

Foo Yung Sauce

2 envelopes instant chicken
   broth or 2 chicken
   bouillon cubes
1½ cups hot water
1½ teaspoons sugar
2 tablespoons soy sauce
6 tablespoons cold water
1½ tablespoons cornstarch

Combine chicken broth with bullion cubes, hot water, sugar, and soy sauce in a saucepan. Stir cold water slowly into cornstarch. Add to mixture in saucepan. Cook and stir over moderately low heat (about 225° F.), until thickened and smooth. Makes about 1¾ cups sauce.

✑ Tuna-Chip Bake

3 cups slightly crushed
   potato chips
1 10-ounce package frozen
   asparagus spears
1 6½-ounce can tuna,
   drained and flaked
½ cup sliced blanched
   almonds
1 cup process American
   cheese, shredded
2 tablespoons lemon juice
1 teaspoon seasoned salt
1 13-fluid-ounce can
   undiluted evaporated milk

Heat oven to 350° F. Place 2 cups of the potato chips in the bottom of an 8-inch-square pan. Layer half the asparagus, tuna, almonds, and cheese over chips. Repeat asparagus, tuna, almond, and cheese layers. Sprinkle with lemon juice and seasoned salt. Top with the remaining 1 cup potato chips. Pour evaporated milk over all. Bake 20 to 25 minutes. Serve at once. Serves 4.

❧ Tuna à la King

⅓ cup butter or margarine
¼ pound mushrooms, sliced
½ cup slivered green pepper
1 small onion, thinly sliced
⅓ cup all-purpose flour
2½ cups milk
½ cup light cream
1 teaspoon Worcestershire
sauce
¾ teaspoon salt
⅛ teaspoon dry mustard
Dash of ground nutmeg
Dash of Tabasco
2 pimientos, cut into strips
3 6½-ounce cans tuna, well
drained and broken into
large pieces
Toast or patty shells

Melt butter in a saucepan over moderate heat (about 250° F.). Cook mushrooms, green pepper, and onion until crisp-tender, about 3 minutes. Quickly stir in flour and blend until smooth. Gradually stir in milk, blending well. Stir in cream. Bring mixture to a boil. Stir in Worcestershire, salt, mustard, nutmeg, and Tabasco; boil 1 minute, stirring constantly. Remove from heat and stir in pimiento and tuna. Serve over toast or in patty shells. Serves 6.

❧ Skillet Potato–Tuna Pie

3 medium-sized potatoes
(about 1¼ pounds), peeled
and thinly sliced
1 teaspoon salt
⅛ teaspoon pepper
¼ teaspoon garlic powder
3 tablespoons butter or
margarine
¼ cup chopped onion
¼ cup chopped green pepper
2 tablespoons chopped
pimiento
2 tablespoons sliced, pitted
ripe olives
1 6½-ounce can light tuna,
well drained and flaked
¾ cup coarsely shredded
Cheddar cheese
3 eggs, well beaten

In a medium-sized bowl combine potato slices, salt, pepper, and garlic powder and blend well. Melt 2 tablespoons of the butter in an 8-inch skillet over moderately low heat (about 225° F.). Add onion, green pepper, and pimiento and cook until tender. Remove vegetables with a slotted spoon. Melt the remaining 1 tablespoon butter in the same skillet over moderately low heat (about 225° F.). Remove skillet from heat. Arrange ⅓ of the potatoes in the bottom of the skillet. Spoon ½ the onion mixture over top of potatoes. Sprinkle 1 tablespoon of the olives over onion mixture. Arrange ½ the tuna over top. Sprinkle with ⅓ of the cheese. Repeat layers, ending with a layer of potatoes. Sprinkle remaining cheese over top. Cover and cook over moderately low heat (about 225° F.) 25 minutes, or until potatoes are fork-tender. Pour eggs over top of potatoes. Cover and cook 8 to 10 minutes longer, or until eggs are set. Serves 2 or 3.

✑ Sauced Salmon Loaf

1 16-ounce can salmon
⅔ cup undiluted evaporated milk
2 cups soft bread crumbs
1 egg, slightly beaten
½ teaspoon salt
¼ teaspoon poultry seasoning
⅓ cup finely chopped celery
¼ cup finely chopped green pepper
1 tablespoon lemon juice
1 tablespoon instant dried minced onion
1 1⅛-ounce package Hollandaise-sauce mix
Parsley (optional)

Heat oven to 375° F. Turn the salmon with the liquid into a bowl; remove skin and bones and flake salmon. Combine milk and bread crumbs; add to salmon and mix gently with a fork. Add egg, salt, poultry seasoning, celery, green pepper, lemon juice, and onion. Combine gently. Turn mixture into a well-greased 1-quart ring mold. Bake 30 minutes, or until firm. Prepare Hollandaise sauce as directed on package of mix. Let salmon loaf stand about 5 minutes after removing from oven. Loosen around edges with a spatula and remove to a serving platter. Spoon warm Hollandaise sauce over ring. Garnish with parsley, if desired. Serves 4 to 6.

✑ Fish Croquettes

1 16-ounce can salmon, drained
3 tablespoons butter or margarine
3 tablespoons flour
1 cup milk, heated
¾ teaspoon salt
1 teaspoon lemon juice
1 teaspoon Worcestershire sauce
2 egg yolks, slightly beaten
1 6½-ounce can tuna, drained and flaked
1½ cups soft bread crumbs
Flour
2 whole eggs, slightly beaten
4 teaspoons milk
1 cup fine dry bread crumbs
Vegetable oil for frying
1 cup milk
1 1½-ounce package sour-cream-sauce mix

Remove skin and bones from salmon and flake it. Place between paper towels to remove excess moisture. Melt butter in saucepan over moderately low heat (225° F.); blend in flour. Gradually add milk and cook, stirring constantly, until it is thickened. Stir in salt, lemon juice, and Worcestershire sauce. Remove from heat. Blend a small portion of sauce into the 2 slightly beaten egg yolks and return to sauce in saucepan. Add salmon, tuna, and soft bread crumbs. Spread mixture on a flat tray; cover and chill at least 2 hours. Divide chilled mixture into 8 to 10 portions. Shape each with hands into a cone shape. Roll lightly in flour. Shake off excess. Blend together the slightly beaten whole eggs and the 4 teaspoons milk. Dip croquettes into egg batter, letting excess drip off. Coat croquettes thoroughly with the bread crumbs. Let stand about 10 minutes. If cracks appear, coat lightly with bread crumbs again. Chill several hours, or until firm. Place oil to a depth of 3 inches in a deep-fat fryer. Heat over high heat (380° F.) or until a temperature of 380° F. is reached on a deep-fat thermometer. Place 2 or 3 croquettes in basket and lower in hot fat. Fry 2 to 4 minutes, until golden brown. Drain on paper towels. Stir the remaining 1 cup milk into sour-cream-sauce mixture. Place over very low heat (about 175° F.) for a few minutes, until warm. Serve over croquettes. Serves 4 to 5.

⊰ Fried Kippered Herring

8 slices bacon
2 7-ounce cans kippered herring, drained
½ cup corn meal

Place bacon in a skillet and cook over moderately high heat (about 325° F.) until crisp. While bacon is frying, cut larger pieces of herring in half lengthwise; dip pieces in corn meal. Remove bacon from skillet and drain on paper towels. Leave bacon fat in skillet. Place fish in hot bacon fat over moderately high heat (about 325° F.) and fry for a few minutes on both sides until browned. Serve with bacon as a breakfast dish. Serves 4 to 6.

⊰ Creamed Finnan Haddie

1 pound smoked finnan haddie
4 tablespoons butter or margarine
1 teaspoon grated onion
3 tablespoons flour
2 cups milk, heated
⅛ teaspoon pepper
Toast points (optional)

Place fish in a heavy saucepan; cover with cold water. Place over low heat (about 200° F.) and simmer 15 to 20 minutes, until fish flakes easily with a fork. Remove fish and discard water. Remove any bones, if necessary, from fish and break into large pieces. Melt butter in the saucepan over moderate heat (about 250° F.); add onion and cook until onion is soft. Stir in flour. Remove from heat and gradually add milk, stirring constantly until well blended. Return to moderate heat and cook, stirring constantly, until smooth and thickened. Add fish and pepper to sauce; heat thoroughly. Serve on toast points, if desired. Serves 3 to 4.

CHAPTER XII

EGGS

To most Americans, nature's small wonder, the egg, is a breakfast mainstay. To great chefs, it is a food staple that defies the improbable—it makes oil and water mix, it makes fine crumbs cling to a piece of meat, and it raises angel cakes and soufflés to great heights.

To an aspiring cook an egg should be thought of always as exactly what it is: fragile and temperamental about temperature. To preserve quality, eggs must be stored cold, broad end up; a day at room temperature will age eggs more quickly than a week's storage in the refrigerator. They should be one of the first foods to be put away when you unpack the market basket. To separate easily and beat up well, they must be brought to room temperature. Even out of the shell an egg must still be treated tenderly; it should never be exposed to high temperatures (except in omelets, which require moderately high heat) or it will become tough and rubbery.

How to Buy Eggs

Buying eggs in a retail market may at first seem utterly confusing. All eggs you buy in the market should be cartoned and refrigerated; don't buy them if they're not. Most eggs marketed today have been graded for quality and size under federal-state supervision and will be labeled in accordance with the United States Department of Agriculture's standards. Information on the carton should tell you two things: *grade,* which stands for quality, and *size,* which stands for quantity. They are not necessarily related.

The two top grades of eggs are AA (also called fancy fresh) and A (the most commonly available grade). These eggs have a large amount of firm white and a round, high-standing yolk centered in the white—characteristics of a fresh egg. This quality of freshness is not so dependent upon the age of the egg as it is on the conditions under which the eggs have been kept. These are the most desirable eggs for poaching, frying, baking, and cooking in the shell.

The two lesser grades of eggs are B and C. They have a thinner white that spreads out when the egg is out of the shell; the yolk is fairly flat and may not be centered. These lower grades are lower priced and just fine for omelets, scrambled eggs, sauces, custards, and the like. They have exactly the same nutritive value as the higher grades.

The sale of cracked or checked (slight shell punctures) eggs is prohibited by many states but you may find them on sale at considerably lower cost. You may also find checked eggs in the carton when you get home; this can happen in the handling of the eggs from the time they're unpacked at the store until you get them home. Eggs that have had the inner membrane broken so that some of the white is leaking out are a potential source of bacterial contamination. The only safe way they can be used is to hard-cook them or use them as an ingredient in a food that is to be thoroughly cooked. A single egg, broken into a custard cup—or several broken into a baking dish—with a little water added, may be covered and baked for twenty minutes in a 350° F. oven. They can then be used like hard-cooked eggs for egg salad or creamed dishes. Checked eggs that are nonleakers may be used the same as any other clean, fresh egg.

Egg sizing is calculated by weight in three-ounce gradations. A dozen Large eggs must weigh at least twenty-four ounces. A dozen Extra Large will weigh twenty-seven ounces, and Jumbos will weigh thirty ounces. Medium eggs weigh three ounces less than Large per dozen, or twenty-one ounces, and Smalls weigh eighteen ounces. If you're mathematically inclined and scrupulous about your budget, you can translate cost per dozen to cost per pound to figure which size is the best buy.

Eggshell color doesn't make a particle of difference. If you live in an area where brown-shelled eggs are thought to be better and are consequently more expensive, buy white, and vice versa. Egg whites may sometimes have a straw or greenish color; this is due to the presence of a desirable nutrient, riboflavin (a B vitamin). Cloudiness in egg whites indicates that carbon dioxide, naturally present in fresh eggs, has not yet escaped through the shell. The paleness or deepness of the yellow yolk is almost wholly dependent upon the feed the hen eats; it doesn't affect the flavor or food value.

If you have a choice, use a utensil other than aluminum for egg mixing, cooking, and molding. The sulfur content of the egg will discolor aluminum utensils and tarnish silver. Stainless steel, heat-resistant glass, or enameled utensils are fine.

There are several inexpensive gadgets on the market that make egg cooking and handling easier. The most useful are a small pincer with a needle point on one side that punctures a hole in the broad end of the egg so it will not crack while it is being cooked in the shell, a plastic egg separator that has a well in the center to hold the yolk while the white runs off into a bowl, and slicers that will neatly cut a hard-cooked egg into thin, even slices or into wedges (sixths) for garnishing. Many cooks prefer a small or medium wire whip for mixing eggs to scramble or to make into omelets, and a large balloon whip for beating egg whites. Sophisticated cooks have a pan used only for omelets and a copper bowl for beating egg whites.

How to Separate Eggs

Separating eggs is a technique that must be learned; practice it before you launch into a recipe that calls for the separate use of whites and yolks. Allow the eggs to reach room temperature; about fifteen minutes out of the refrigerator will do.

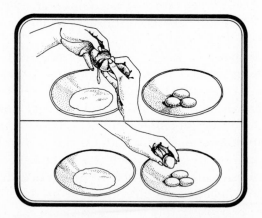

To separate an egg: Rap the egg in the center firmly and sharply with a knife edge or on the rim of a bowl. Put the tips of your thumbs in the crack and pull the halves apart, letting the yolk rest in one half of the shell; allow the white to run into a clean, dry bowl. (Egg whites that have one bit of fat or grease in them will not whip up.) Rock the yolk back and forth from one shell half to the other until all the white has been separated from the yolk. Ideally, the yolk should remain unbroken. If the yolk does break and a bit of it gets into the whites, take a piece of the clean eggshell and scoop it out immediately. You can also use a small piece of clean paper towel; the yolk will stick to the toweling. If you can't get the yolk out, save that egg for another use. When separating several eggs, break each, one at a time, over a custard cup or sauce dish. Pour the white into one bowl and put the yolk into another bowl.

How to Store Leftover Yolks and Whites

Both leftover yolks and whites need to be refrigerated in covered jars. If yolks are to be stored, cover them with cold water; drain and use in two or three days. Whites will keep, cold and covered, for about ten days. You can also freeze egg whites successfully; after thawing, use them exactly as you would fresh egg whites. They can be frozen in quantity in any moistureproof container or, for handier use, they can be frozen individually in plastic ice-cube containers. One egg white fits neatly into a single ice-cube compartment. When frozen, transfer them to a polyethylene bag. This way you thaw only as many as you plan to use for a recipe. Egg yolks will not freeze successfully without salt or sugar added. If you want to freeze yolks to use in desserts, stir (do not beat) 2 tablespoons of sugar or light corn syrup into 1 cup of yolks. For main-dish cooking, stir 1 tablespoon of salt into 1 cup of yolks. Whole eggs may be frozen using the same proportions of sugar or syrup or salt.

How to Use Eggs in Cooking

When using eggs as ingredients there are four often-encountered processes with which most inexperienced cooks have difficulty. With whites, the difficulties arise in whipping or beating them into a snowy foam of a desired stiffness and then in folding them into another mixture in a way so as not to lose the volume. The correct way to do this is describe in the portion of this chapter that deals with soufflés (pages 452 to 459). Problems may arise with yolks when using them as a thickener in hot sauces and as a binder (emulsifier) in such sauces as Hollandaise and mayonnaise. These two operations are discussed in detail in the chapter dealing with sauces (pages 478 to 494).

Eggs are delicate objects and should always be cooked gently over low or moderate heat. Eggs cooked over high heat become rubbery, lose their flavor, and are difficult to digest. Following are the preferred ways to cook breakfast eggs and the basic ways to prepare eggs for further use in recipes.

To fry (traditional way): In a skillet over moderate heat (about 250° F.), heat butter, margarine, or bacon fat until it is just hot enough to sizzle a drop of water. Quantity of fat will depend on size of skillet; estimate 1 tablespoon of fat for two eggs. Break and slip eggs, from a sauce dish if you prefer, into the hot skillet. Cook slowly three or four minutes to desired doneness. For sunny-side up eggs, baste with hot fat or cover skillet tightly during cooking. If you prefer fried eggs over, flip the eggs with a broad spatula, being careful not to break the yolk, and let them cook briefly on the other side. Either way, lift them gently out of the pan onto a warm (not hot) serving plate.

To steam-fry: Use just enough fat to grease the skillet. Put the eggs into the pan as described above. As soon as edges turn white, add ½ teaspoon of water per egg and cover the pan tightly. Cook three to five minutes.

To fry without fat: You can use a Teflon-lined skillet to "fry" an egg without fat. Technically, this is not frying, but it does help calorie- and cholesterol-watchers. Use the methods for frying or steam-frying described.

To fry in electric skillets: Follow manufacturer's directions; the most commonly recommended temperature is 275° F.

To soft-cook: There are two basic methods for cooking eggs in the shell: the cold-water method and the boiling-water method. It's easier and quicker to use the cold-water method because eggs can go directly from the refrigerator into the cooking pot without the risk of cracking shells.

To cook by the cold-water method, put the egg or eggs in a saucepan deep enough to hold them without crowding and add enough cold water to cover them by at least one inch. Bring to boil, uncovered. Turn off heat; set pan off burner, cover, and let stand two to four minutes, depending on how firm or soft you like your eggs. Cool eggs at once in cold water to prevent further cooking.

For the boiling-water method, eggs must be at room temperature—leave them out of the refrigerator forty-five minutes or place them in a pan of warm (not hot) water. Otherwise the shells may crack in cooking. For reassurance you can pierce the broad end of the egg, if you have the necessary utensil. This allows the air to ooze out of that end of the egg rather than expanding and cracking the egg in cooking. Fill a pan with enough water to cover the eggs by at least one inch and bring the water to a boil over moderately high heat (about 275° F.). Lower eggs gently into the boiling water; turn off heat. Set pan off burner, cover, and let stand six to eight minutes. Cool briefly in cold water and serve.

To hard-cook: The two basic methods for soft-cooking apply to hard-cooking. For the cold-water method, follow the same procedure, except allow the eggs to stand fifteen minutes after you remove them from the heat. After fifteen minutes, plunge them immediately into cold water. This makes the shells easier to remove and prevents the yolks from discoloring on the surface.

To use the boiling-water method, follow the directions for soft-cooked eggs, but when you have placed the eggs in the boiling water, reduce heat to low (about 200° F.) to keep water *below* simmering (no bubbles will be rising in the water at all) and hold at that heat for twenty minutes. Cool promptly in cold water.

To use an egg-cooker: There are several electric, time-controlled cookers on the market today for preparing soft- and hard-cooked eggs. Follow manufacturer's directions for their use.

To peel a hard-cooked egg: As soon as the eggs are cooked, pour off the hot water and cool quickly and thoroughly under cold running water. Crack the shell by rolling the egg on a flat surface, or hold the egg in your palm and tap the shell all over with the back of a spoon to crack and loosen the shell. Hold the egg under cold running water while you peel it, starting at the larger end and pulling away both the shell and the membrane with your fingers. (The water speeds this operation and helps remove those unwanted bits of shell.) Very fresh eggs can be hard to shell. It is safer to use eggs that have been refrigerated one or two days or left at room temperature a few hours before cooking.

To store shelled eggs: Shelled hard-cooked eggs may be stored covered in the refrigerator for no more than two days.

To poach: For best results, use only Grade AA or A fresh eggs. Poached eggs are usually cooked in hot water, although they can be done in hot milk or broth. Fill a shallow pan or skillet three-fourths full of water—it should be at least two inches deep. Bring water to a boil over moderately high heat (275° F.), then reduce the heat to simmering (about 200° F.). Break each egg separately into a saucer or sauce dish; bring the rim of the dish to touch the surface of the water and tilt to slip the egg quickly and gently into the water. Cook three to five minutes, depending upon the firmness desired. Remove eggs with a slotted spoon or pancake turner and drain on paper towels for later use, or serve directly on toast or warm plates.

Electric egg poachers are available. They do not really "poach" an egg; they steam it. However, the end product is very good. Use this appliance according to manufacturer's directions. Poaching rings, which may be placed in the simmering pan of water, will give poached eggs a perfectly rounded, if somewhat mechanical, appearance.

To bake eggs: Eggs baked in the oven in buttered, shallow dishes are sometimes called shirred eggs, although this method does not produce what the French call shirred eggs.

Baked, or shirred, eggs: Preheat oven to 325° F. (If the oven is too hot, the eggs will become tough.) Generously butter round or oval shallow baking dishes. Break two eggs into each dish. Bake twelve to fifteen minutes. Serve from the baking dish.

Baked eggs in ramekins: Preheat oven to 350° F. Fill a baking pan half full of hot water. Set individual, buttered ramekins or custard cups into the hot water (this water bath is called a bain-marie). Break one or two eggs into each ramekin. Dot with butter and pour a tablespoon of cream over the eggs in each ramekin. Bake five to ten minutes, depending upon firmness desired. Serve in ramekins.

To scramble: There are as many methods to make scrambled eggs as there are opinionated cooks. These are the rules on which everyone seems to agree: Allow two eggs per serving and cook over moderately low heat (about 225° F.) in butter or margarine. Choose the proper pan size for the number of eggs you wish to cook. An eight-inch skillet is right for four eggs. If the pan is too large, the eggs will solidify too quickly; if it's too small, the eggs will not be moist.

To add liquid or not is the question. Either way, start by breaking the required number of eggs into a bowl and blending the eggs well with a fork or wire whip. Add salt (about ¼ teaspoon for 2 eggs), a few grains of pepper (white if you don't want to see it), and any other herbs or seasonings you desire. Now, if you wish, add 1 tablespoon of milk, cream, or water per egg, and blend it in. Heat 1 teaspoon of butter per egg in a skillet over low heat. Pour all the egg mixture into the skillet. As the mixture begins to thicken, lift cooked portion from bottom and sides, allowing the thin, uncooked portion to flow to the bottom of the pan. Avoid constant stirring. Cook about five to eight minutes until eggs are firm but moist throughout. Scrambled eggs may also be made in the top of a double boiler placed over simmering water. Melt butter in the top of a double boiler, pour in egg mixture, and cook, using a spoon to lift cooked portion from sides and bottom. Cook until eggs are firm but moist.

Creamy Scrambled Eggs

6 eggs
6 tablespoons milk
1 teaspoon salt
¼ teaspoon pepper
2 tablespoons butter or margarine
2 eggs, well beaten

Heat water in bottom of double boiler and keep warm. Combine the 6 eggs, milk, salt, and pepper, using a fork, whip, or rotary beater. Melt the butter in a skillet over moderately low heat (about 225° F.). Pour in egg mixture. Lift the eggs with a spoon from the bottom and sides as the mixture thickens. This allows the uncooked portion to flow to the bottom. Avoid constant stirring. Remove from heat when eggs are thickened throughout but still very moist. Place eggs in the top part of double boiler and blend in the 2 well-beaten eggs. Cover and hold over low heat until serving time. Serves 4.

Baked Scrambled Eggs

In a bowl combine *6 eggs, ⅓ cup milk, 1 teaspoon salt,* and *⅛ teaspoon pepper;* beat with a rotary beater until frothy. Stir in *¼ pound process American cheese, cubed.* Pour into a greased deep 1-quart casserole and bake in a 350° F. oven about 30 minutes, until golden brown and puffy. Serve immediately. Serves 3 to 4.

Omelets

To make an omelet: Omelets perfectly made are a kind of culinary triumph; they can establish your reputation as a great cook. They are extremely quick to make—a marvelous impromptu luncheon dish and, in the sweet versions, a great last-minute dessert. Omelets are easy to make once you've got the feel of the technique. You must first read the directions carefully, visualizing what you're about to do, because there will be no time to check directions once you begin. By all means, practice on your family or yourself before you attempt omelets for company.

French omelets: The secrets of making a good plain omelet are speed, cooking at the proper temperature, and using the right pan. Most good cooks insist that you must have a pan used only for omelets, one that has sides that round into the bottom in an 8- to 10-inch size. (This size is perfect for a 4-egg omelet that serves two. It's not a good idea to make a larger omelet; they take so little time that it's better to make several.) The reason for keeping a pan for making only omelets is that the surface of the pan must be completely smooth and seasoned. It should be wiped, not washed, after each use. If you must use a pan that is used for other cooking, scrub it with a soapy steel-wool pad until it is shining smooth. Put an inch of salad oil in the pan and set it over moderate heat for twenty minutes. Pour off the oil, which you can use in other cooking, and wipe the skillet dry. It's now ready for omelet-making.

◞ *Plain (French) Omelet*

Put *4 eggs, ¼ teaspoon salt,* and *a few grains white pepper* in a bowl and beat with a fork until eggs are well blended but not frothy. Place the seasoned skillet over moderately high heat (about 350° F.) and stir *1½ tablespoons butter or margarine* quickly around in the pan to completely coat bottom and sides. The butter will foam quickly; as soon as the foam subsides, pour the egg mixture into the skillet. Now, with the flat side of the fork, stir the eggs briskly in a circular motion while you shake the pan back and forth over the heat. Stir just until the liquid begins to set. Let it cook less than a minute. (This is the point at which you decide whether you want to make it soft or very creamy in the center—a matter of taste.) Shake the pan; the omelet should move freely. Tilt the handle of the pan up; with the fork begin to roll the edge nearest the handle toward the center—you're going to roll it approximately into thirds. Complete the rolling by tilting the omelet out onto a warm serving plate. Serves 2.

Plain omelets may be seasoned in a variety of ways. A favorite is the Herb Omelet: You can experiment with adding snipped chives, oregano, basil, tarragon, dillweed, parsley, or marjoram. As a rule of thumb, don't use more than three herbs at once; use a teaspoon of chives or parsley to a 4-egg omelet and not more than a ¼ teaspoon of the stronger herbs. Stir the herbs into the egg mixture before cooking.

Plain omelets may be filled in an infinite variety of ways; be sure to have the filling ready before you make the omelet.

Spinach Omelet

Combine *1 cup chopped, cooked, hot spinach, 6 tablespoons commercial sour cream,* and ¼ *teaspoon ground nutmeg.* Prepare and cook Plain Omelet as directed. Just before folding omelet, spread spinach mixture over half the top. Serves 2.

Chicken Liver Omelet

Melt *3 tablespoons butter or margarine* in skillet; add ¼ *cup finely chopped onion* and ¼ *pound fresh mushrooms, sliced;* cook over moderate heat (about 250° F.) about 5 minutes, until tender. *Add 1 8-ounce package frozen chicken livers, thawed and cut in halves,* ¼ *teaspoon salt,* and *a few grains pepper;* cook about 5 minutes, until lightly browned. Prepare and cook Plain Omelet as directed. Just before folding omelet spoon some of the chicken-liver mixture over half the top. Serve remaining livers over omelet. Serves 2 to 3.

Mushroom Omelet

Cook ½ *pound mushrooms, coarsely chopped,* in *2 tablespoons butter or margarine* over moderate heat (about 250° F.) about 5 minutes, or until tender. Sprinkle with *2 tablespoons brandy,* ¼ *cup light cream,* and ¼ *teaspoon salt.* Heat. Prepare and cook Plain Omelet as directed. Just before folding omelet, spread mushroom mixture over half the top. Serves 2.

Spanish Omelet

Melt 1½ *tablespoons butter or margarine* in skillet over moderately low heat (about 225° F.) Add ¼ *cup finely chopped onion* and ¼ *cup finely chopped green pepper;* cook until vegetables are tender. Add *1 8-ounce can tomatoes,* ½ *bay leaf,* ½ *teaspoon sugar,* ½ *teaspoon chili powder, dash of ground clove,* and *a few grains pepper.* Cook 30 minutes or until most of the liquid has evaporated. Prepare and cook Plain Omelet as directed. Just before folding omelet, spread some of the sauce mixture over half the top. Serve with remaining sauce. Serves 2.

Fluffy Omelets

These are somewhat more akin to a soufflé than to a French omelet. The only secrets to making them are to get as much volume as possible from the beaten egg whites and to get the yolks thoroughly folded through the beaten whites. Because this omelet is cooked both on the top of the range and in the oven, be sure to use a skillet that has an ovenproof handle. If skillet is not ovenproof, cover handle with several thicknesses of aluminum foil.

✥ Fluffy Omelet

4 eggs, separated and at
   room temperature
¼ cup water
¼ teaspoon salt
Few grains pepper
1½ tablespoons butter or
   margarine

Heat oven to 325° F. Beat egg whites until stiff but not dry. (See page 452.) Beat egg yolks until thick and lemon-colored. Add water, salt, and pepper to yolks; beat until blended. Fold in beaten egg whites. Melt butter in a heavy 8-inch skillet with an ovenproof handle over moderate heat (about 250° F.) until it starts to foam. Add egg mixture and cook 3 minutes, or until omelet puffs up and is firm and lightly browned on the bottom. Place omelet in oven and bake 12 to 15 minutes, until top is dry and lightly browned. Cut halfway down across center and fold in half. Remove to serving plate. Serves 2.

✥ Flaming Dessert Omelet

3 eggs, separated and at room
   temperature
3 tablespoons sugar
3 tablespoons peach preserves
1 tablespoon butter or
   margarine
Sugar
3 tablespoons brandy

Beat egg whites with rotary beater or electric mixer until soft peaks form. Gradually add 2 tablespoons of the sugar and beat until stiff peaks form. Beat egg yolks until thick; add the remaining 1 tablespoon sugar and beat until thick and lemon-colored. Fold beaten yolks into whites. Spread peach preserves over a warm platter and set in a warm place. Preheat broiler. Place a 10-inch omelet pan over moderately low heat (do not use a thermostatically controlled burner). Butter pan well on bottom and sides. Turn in egg mixture and spread over bottom; with a rubber spatula pull mixture up to cover sides of pan. Cook until bottom and sides are lightly browned, about 2 minutes. Place in broiler about 4 inches from heat for about 1 minute, until top is just set. Hold omelet pan at one side of the platter; with a spatula roll omelet over from top and side and roll it out onto the platter. Sprinkle lightly with sugar. Heat brandy in a small saucepan over low heat (about 200° F.); ignite and pour over omelet. Serve immediately. Serves 4.

Soufflés

Of all the ooh- and ah-producing admiration beautiful foods can provoke, a towering, delicate soufflé probably tops the list. However, making one frightens even many experienced cooks. It shouldn't because once you've mastered the technique of getting great volume out of beaten egg whites and learned how to fold them into the heavier sauce without losing that volume, you will come to rely on a soufflé as being a marvelous luncheon or supper dish and a most attractive way to use an infinite variety of leftover meats, fish, and vegetables.

Soufflés are most dependent upon well-beaten egg whites. The first rule to remember about beating whites is that they will not whip up if there is any presence of fat. The utensils you use must be perfectly clean and dry and there must not be a speck of yolk in the whites. To get maximum volume from egg whites, allow them to come to room temperature before beating. Beat the whites in a clean, deep bowl with a wire whip, a rotary beater, or an electric mixer. Serious cooks insist that you need a balloon whip and a copper bowl in which to whip egg whites. You do get measurably greater volume using a balloon whip than you get using a rotary hand beater or an electric mixer. There is a chemical reaction between the copper bowl and the egg whites that tends to make the foam sturdier and with less tendency to flake. Lacking the copper bowl, you can use any clean, fatfree glass, enameled, or stainless steel bowl (aluminum will darken) and add a small amount of cream of tartar (¼ teaspoon for 4 eggs) to the egg whites. The acid will also help to make a less fragile foam.

Folding egg whites into a heavier mixture must be done very gently so that as much of the air in the particles of egg white is retained as possible.

When directions say "beat until soft peaks are formed," you should whip until rounded, glossy peaks remain in the bowl when the beater is lifted out. (The tip of the peak will be soft enough to fold over.) "Stiff peaks" will form as the whites are beaten longer. The peaks will remain pointed as the beater is lifted, but they still will be moist and glossy. (Stiffly beaten whites will not flow from the bowl when it is tipped.)

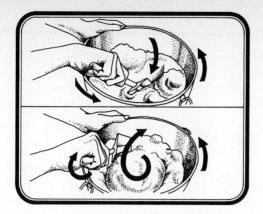

To fold stiffly beaten egg whites into a batter or other ingredients, pile all the whites on top of the batter at once. (Some recipes will call for stirring a few spoonfuls of beaten whites into the batter to lighten it before folding remaining whites into the batter.) With a rubber spatula or large spoon, carefully cut down through the center of the mixture across the bottom of the bowl and up the side, gently lifting some of the batter mixture up and over the egg whites. Continue this down-across-up-over motion until all the whites are blended in. Turn the bowl as you work. Stiffly beaten heavy cream is folded into a mixture in the same way.

The soufflé baking dish is classically a straight-sided round dish. However, any straight-sided ovenproof dish of the proper volume will do. The important consideration is to prepare the dish so that the rising soufflé will have something to cling to as it bakes. For main-dish soufflés, the mold should be well buttered and the sides and bottom coated with finely grated Parmesan or Swiss cheese or fine dry bread crumbs. For dessert soufflés, butter dish and coat with superfine granulated sugar.

At the point that a soufflé is ready to go into the oven, it may be covered and let stand up to an hour. But once a soufflé has been baked, it must be served promptly for it will begin to lose volume.

❧ Cheese Soufflé

5 egg whites
1 teaspoon butter or margarine
2 tablespoons grated Parmesan cheese
3 tablespoons butter or margarine
3 tablespoons flour
1 cup hot milk
½ teaspoon salt
¼ teaspoon dry mustard
Few grains cayenne pepper
¼ teaspoon Worcestershire sauce
4 egg yolks

Place egg whites in a large bowl and let stand at room temperature 1 hour. Heat oven to 400° F. Butter a 1½-quart soufflé dish or deep casserole with the 1 teaspoon butter; sprinkle bottom and sides evenly with Parmesan cheese. Melt the 3 tablespoons butter in a saucepan over moderately low heat (about 225° F.). Add the flour all at once and stir with a wire whip until well blended. Cook over moderate heat (about 250° F.), stirring constantly about 2 minutes, until mixture begins to foam and bubble. Remove from heat and add the milk, beating vigorously with a wire whip until mixture is thickened and smooth. Beat in the ½ teaspoon salt, the dry mustard, cayenne, and Worcestershire. Return to heat and cook 1 minute, stirring constantly, until sauce is very thick. Remove from heat and add egg yolks one at a

Pinch of salt
1 cup (¼ pound) Cheddar
    cheese, coarsely shredded

time, beating well after each addition. Pour egg yolk mixture into a large bowl. Beat egg whites and the pinch of salt with an electric mixer, whip, or rotary beater until stiff—but not dry—peaks form. Add 1 large tablespoonful of the beaten egg whites to the egg yolk mixture and stir until well blended. Add all but 1 tablespoon of the shredded cheese. Spoon remaining egg whites on top. Fold in with a rubber spatula to blend well. Pour into prepared soufflé dish; smooth surface with a small spatula. Sprinkle reserved cheese over top of mixture. Run a metal spatula through the mixture in a circle 1 inch from edge of dish. Place in center of oven and immediately reduce temperature to 375° F. Bake 35 to 40 minutes, or until soufflé is puffed about 2 inches above rim of dish and a knife inserted in the side comes out clean. Serve immediately. Serves 4.

Swiss–Parmesan Cheese Soufflé

Substitute ¾ *cup (3 ounces) shredded Swiss cheese and* ¾ *cup (3 ounces) grated Parmesan cheese* for the Cheddar cheese. Reduce *salt to* ¼ *teaspoon.* Reserve 1 tablespoon Swiss cheese to sprinkle over top of soufflé.

Camembert Cheese Soufflé

Substitute *4 1⅓-ounce wedges Camembert cheese* for the Cheddar cheese. Dice finely before adding it to the sauce.

✑ Soufflé Florentine

5 egg whites
1 teaspoon butter or
    margarine
1 tablespoon grated
    Parmesan cheese
1 10-ounce package frozen
    chopped spinach
3 tablespoons butter or
    margarine
4 tablespoons flour
1 cup milk, scalded
Dash of ground nutmeg
¾ teaspoon salt
Few grains pepper
  4 egg yolks

Place egg whites in a large bowl and let stand at room temperature 1 hour. Heat oven to 400° F. Butter a 1½-quart soufflé dish or deep casserole with the 1 teaspoon butter; sprinkle bottom and sides evenly with Parmesan cheese. Cook spinach according to package directions and drain well. Melt the 3 tablespoons butter in a saucepan over moderately low heat (about 225° F.). Add the flour all at once and stir with a wire whip until blended. Cook over moderate heat (about 250° F.), stirring constantly about 2 minutes, until mixture begins to foam and bubble. Remove from heat and add the milk, beating vigorously with a wire whip until mixture is thickened and smooth. Beat in nutmeg, the ¾ teaspoon salt, and pepper. Return to heat and cook 1 minute, stirring constantly, until sauce is very thick.

Pinch of salt
1 cup (¼ pound) Cheddar
    cheese, coarsely shredded

Remove from heat and add egg yolks one at a time, beating well after each addition. Pour egg yolk mixture into a large bowl. Beat egg whites and the pinch of salt with an electric mixer, whip, or rotary beater until stiff—but not dry—peaks form. Add 1 large tablespoonful of the beaten egg whites to the egg yolk mixture and stir until well blended. Add all but 1 tablespoon of the shredded cheese. Stir in the spinach. Spoon remaining egg whites on top. Fold in with a rubber spatula to blend well. Pour into prepared soufflé dish; smooth surface with a small spatula. Sprinkle reserved cheese over top of mixture. Run a metal spatula through the mixture in a circle 1 inch from edge of dish. Place in center of oven and immediately reduce temperature to 375° F. Bake 35 to 40 minutes, or until soufflé is puffed about 2 inches above rim of dish and a knife inserted in the side comes out clean. Serve immediately. Serves 4.

ᏍᏃ Shrimp–Cheese Soufflé

5 egg whites
1 cup ice-cold water
1 tablespoon lemon juice
1 4½-ounce can shrimp,
    drained
1 teaspoon butter or
    margarine
1 tablespoon grated
    Parmesan cheese
3 tablespoons butter or
    margarine
3 tablespoons flour
1 cup hot milk
½ teaspoon salt
Few grains cayenne pepper
4 egg yolks
Pinch of salt
1 cup (¼ pound) Cheddar
    cheese, coarsely shredded

Place egg whites in a large bowl and let stand at room temperature 1 hour. Combine water and lemon juice in a bowl, add shrimp, and let stand in mixture 20 minutes. Drain shrimp well and chop them finely. Heat oven to 400° F. Butter a 1½-quart soufflé dish or deep casserole with the 1 teaspoon butter; sprinkle bottom and sides evenly with Parmesan cheese. Melt the 3 tablespoons butter in a saucepan over moderately low heat (about 225° F.). When butter begins to bubble, add flour all at once and stir vigorously with a wire whip to blend well. Cook over moderate heat (about 250° F.) about 2 minutes, until mixture begins to foam and bubble. Remove from heat and pour in hot milk all at once, beating vigorously with whip until mixture is thickened and smooth. Beat in the ½ teaspoon salt and the cayenne. Return to heat and cook about 1 minute, stirring constantly, until sauce is very thick. Remove from heat and add egg yolks one at a time, beating well after each addition. Pour egg mixture into a large bowl. Beat egg whites and the pinch of salt with an electric mixer, whip, or rotary beater until stiff—but not dry—peaks form. Add 1 large tablespoonful of beaten egg white to the egg yolk mixture and stir until mixture is well blended. Stir in all but 1 tablespoon of the shredded Cheddar cheese;

add the shrimp. Spoon remaining egg whites on top. Fold in the egg whites with a rubber spatula to blend well. Pour into prepared soufflé dish. Smooth surface of soufflé with a spatula. Run a metal spatula through the mixture in a circle 1 inch from side of dish. Sprinkle reserved cheese over top of mixture. Place in center of oven. Bake 35 to 40 minutes, or until soufflé is puffed about 2 inches above rim of dish and a knife inserted in the side comes out clean. Serve immediately. Serves 4.

✿ Lobster Soufflé

5 egg whites
1 8-ounce package frozen lobster tails
1 teaspoon butter or margarine
1 tablespoon grated Parmesan cheese
3 tablespoons butter or margarine
3 tablespoons flour
1 cup hot milk
Dash of ground nutmeg
½ teaspoon salt
⅛ teaspoon pepper
Few drops Worcestershire sauce
1 small onion, peeled
1 bay leaf
4 egg yolks
¼ cup finely chopped fresh parsley
Pinch of salt

Place egg whites in a large bowl and let stand at room temperature 1 hour. Cook lobster tails according to directions on package. Cool and remove meat from shells. Flake lobster meat with a fork and drain well between paper towels. Heat oven to 400° F. Butter a 1½-quart soufflé dish or deep casserole with the 1 teaspoon butter; sprinkle bottom and sides evenly with Parmesan cheese. Melt the 3 tablespoons butter in a saucepan over moderately low heat (about 225° F.). When butter begins to bubble, add flour all at once and stir vigorously with a whip to blend well. Cook over moderate heat (about 250° F.) about 2 minutes, until mixture begins to foam and bubble. Remove from heat and pour in milk all at once; beat vigorously with a whip until mixture is thickened and smooth. Beat in nutmeg, the ½ teaspoon salt, the pepper, and Worcestershire; add whole onion and bay leaf. Return to heat and cook about 1 minute, stirring constantly, until sauce is very thick. Remove from heat; remove and discard onion and bay leaf. Add egg yolks one at a time, beating well after each addition. Stir in lobster and chopped parsley. Pour egg mixture into a large bowl. Beat egg whites and the pinch of salt with an electric mixer, whip, or rotary beater until stiff—but not dry—peaks form. Add 1 large tablespoon of beaten egg white to the egg yolk mixture and stir until mixture is well blended. Spoon remaining egg whites on top. Fold in with a rubber spatula to blend well. Pour into prepared soufflé dish. Smooth surface of soufflé with a spatula. Run a metal spatula through the mixture in a circle 1 inch from side of dish. Place in center of oven and immediately reduce temperature to 375° F. Bake 35 to 40 minutes, or until soufflé is puffed about 2 inches above rim of dish and a knife inserted in the side comes out clean. Serve immediately. Serves 4.

❧ Chicken Soufflé

5 egg whites
1 teaspoon butter or
    margarine
2 tablespoons grated
    Parmesan cheese
¼ cup butter or margarine
2 tablespoons finely chopped
    onion
¼ cup flour
1 cup hot milk
⅓ cup grated Parmesan
    cheese
½ teaspoon salt
⅛ teaspoon pepper
4 egg yolks
¾ cup ground cooked chicken
    or turkey
Creamy Mushroom Sauce
    (recipe follows)

Place egg whites in a large bowl and let stand at room temperature 1 hour. Heat oven to 400° F. Butter a 1½-quart soufflé dish well with the 1 teaspoon butter. Sprinkle the 2 tablespoons Parmesan cheese in buttered dish to coat sides and bottom evenly. Shake out excess cheese. Melt the ¼ cup butter in a 1½-quart saucepan over moderately low heat (about 225° F.). Add onion and cook until tender. Add flour all at once and stir vigorously with a wire whip to blend well. Cook over moderate heat (about 250° F.), stirring constantly about 2 minutes or until mixture begins to foam and bubble. Remove from heat and pour in hot milk all at once, beating vigorously with whip until mixture is thickened and smooth. Return to heat and cook 1 minute, stirring constantly, until sauce begins to boil. Remove from heat and stir in the ⅓ cup grated Parmesan cheese, the salt, and the pepper. Immediately stir in egg yolks one at a time, beating well after each addition. Stir in ground chicken to blend well. Pour egg yolk mixture into a large bowl. Beat egg whites with an electric mixer, whip, or rotary beater until stiff—but not dry—peaks form. Add 1 large tablespoonful of the beaten egg whites to the egg yolk mixture and stir until mixture is well blended. Spoon remaining egg whites on top. Gently fold in egg whites with a rubber spatula to blend well. Pour mixture into soufflé dish. Smooth surface with a spatula. Run a metal spatula through the mixture in a circle 1 inch from side of dish. Place in center of oven and immediately reduce temperature to 375° F. Bake 35 to 40 minutes, or until soufflé is puffed about 2 inches above rim of dish and a knife inserted in the side comes out clean. Serve immediately with Creamy Mushroom Sauce. Serves 4.

Creamy Mushroom Sauce

¼ cup butter or margarine
1 cup sliced fresh
    mushrooms
2 tablespoons flour
¼ teaspoon salt
Few grains pepper
1¾ cup hot milk
1 envelope instant chicken
    broth mix

Melt butter in a saucepan over moderately low heat (about 225° F.). Add mushrooms and cook until tender, stirring frequently. Remove from heat; blend in flour, salt, and pepper. Return to heat and cook 3 minutes, stirring constantly. Remove from heat and add hot milk, stirring constantly until all liquid is added and sauce is smooth. Add broth mix and cook over low heat (about 200° F.) for 20 minutes, stirring very frequently. Serve over Chicken Soufflé. Makes 1⅔ cups sauce.

✍ Asparagus Soufflé

5 egg whites
1 teaspoon butter or
　margarine
2 tablespoons fine dry bread
　crumbs
¼ cup butter or margarine
¼ cup flour
1⅓ cups hot milk
1 teaspoon salt
⅛ teaspoon pepper
1 teaspoon grated onion
¼ cup shredded sharp
　Cheddar cheese
2 tablespoons chopped
　pimiento
4 egg yolks
1¼ cups finely chopped raw
　asparagus (about 1
　pound) or chopped raw
　broccoli (about ½ pound)

Place egg whites in a large bowl and let stand at room temperature 1 hour. Heat oven to 400° F. Butter a 1½-quart soufflé dish well with the 1 teaspoon butter. Sprinkle crumbs in buttered dish to coat sides and bottom evenly. Shake out excess crumbs. Melt the ¼ cup butter in a 1½-quart saucepan over moderately low heat (about 225° F.). When butter begins to bubble, add flour all at once and stir vigorously with a wire whip to blend well. Cook over moderate heat (about 250° F.), stirring constantly about 2 minutes, until mixture begins to foam and bubble. Remove from heat and pour in hot milk all at once, beating vigorously with whip until mixture is thickened and smooth. Return to heat and cook 1 minute, stirring constantly, until sauce begins to boil. Remove from heat and stir in salt, pepper, onion, cheese, and pimiento; stir until cheese is melted. Immediately add egg yolks one at a time, beating well after each addition. Stir in asparagus to blend well. Pour egg yolk mixture into a large bowl. Beat egg whites with an electric mixer, whip, or rotary beater until stiff—but not dry—peaks form. Add 1 large tablespoonful of the beaten egg whites to the egg yolk mixture and stir until mixture is well blended. Spoon remaining egg whites on top. Gently fold in egg whites with a rubber spatula to blend well. Pour mixture into prepared soufflé dish. Smooth surface with a spatula. Run a metal spatula through the mixture in a circle 1 inch from side of dish. Place in center of oven and immediately reduce temperature to 375° F. Bake 35 to 40 minutes, or until soufflé is puffed about 2 inches above rim of dish and a knife inserted in the side comes out clean. Serve immediately. Serves 4.

✍ Fresh Mushroom Soufflé

5 egg whites
1 teaspoon butter or
　margarine
2 tablespoons fine dry bread
　crumbs
¼ cup butter or margarine

Place egg whites in a large bowl and let stand at room temperature 1 hour. Heat oven to 400° F. Butter a 1½-quart soufflé dish with the 1 teaspoon butter. Sprinkle the bread crumbs in buttered dish to coat sides and bottom evenly. Shake out excess crumbs. Melt the ¼ cup butter in a 1½-quart saucepan over moderately low heat

¼ *cup chopped onion*
¼ *cup flour*
¾ *cup hot milk*
¼ *cup dry white wine*
 1 *teaspoon salt*
⅛ *teaspoon pepper*
¼ *cup chopped fresh parsley*
¼ *teaspoon dried thyme*
 leaves
 4 *egg yolks*
1½ *cups finely chopped fresh mushrooms (about ½ pound)*

(about 225° F.). Add onion and cook until tender. Add flour all at once and stir vigorously with a wire whip to blend well. Cook over moderate heat (about 250° F.), stirring constantly about 2 minutes, or until mixture begins to foam and bubble. Remove from heat and pour in hot milk all at once, beating vigorously with a wire whip until mixture thickens and is smooth. Return to heat and cook 1 minute, stirring constantly, until sauce begins to boil. Remove from heat and stir in wine and blend well. Stir in salt, pepper, parsley, and thyme. Immediately stir in egg yolks one at a time, beating well after each addition. Stir in mushrooms and blend well. Pour egg yolk mixture into a large bowl. Beat egg whites with an electric mixer, whip, or rotary beater until stiff—but not dry—peaks form. Add 1 large table-spoonful of the beaten egg whites to the egg yolk mixture and stir until mixture is well blended. Spoon remaining egg whites on top. Gently fold in egg whites with a rubber spatula to blend well. Pour mixture into prepared soufflé dish. Smooth surface with a spatula. Run a metal spatula through the mixture in a circle 1 inch from side of dish. Place in center of oven and immediately reduce temperature to 375° F. Bake 35 to 40 minutes, or until soufflé is puffed about 2 inches from rim of dish and a knife inserted in the side comes out clean. Serve immediately. Serves 4.

Eggs for Special Breakfasts and Luncheons

Poached Eggs Benedict

4 *English muffins*
Butter or margarine
8 *thin slices boiled ham*
8 *eggs, to be poached*
1 *cup Hollandaise Sauce (recipe on page 488)*

Split English muffins; arrange them, split side up, on a broiler tray. Put in a preheated broiler about 3 inches from heat and broil until muffins are lightly toasted. Remove muffins, and butter. Broil ham until lightly browned. Meanwhile, poach eggs in salted water or in buttered cups of an egg poacher. Arrange 2 muffin halves, buttered side up, on a luncheon plate. Put a slice of ham on each muffin half; put a poached egg on ham. Spoon Hollandaise Sauce over eggs. Serves 4.

❧ Cheese–Bacon Custards

8 slices raw bacon
2 cups (½ pound) Swiss
   cheese, coarsely shredded
1 cup (¼ pound) Parmesan
   cheese, grated
2 large eggs or 3 small eggs,
   well beaten
2 cups light cream
½ teaspoon salt
½ teaspoon ground nutmeg

Heat oven to 350° F. Cook bacon until crisp over moderately high heat (about 325° F.); drain and crumble into pieces. Sprinkle bacon over bottoms of 6 6-ounce custard cups. Combine Swiss and Parmesan cheese, eggs, cream, salt, and nutmeg. Pour an equal amount into each cup. Set cups in a shallow pan. Pour water around the custard cups in pan so that water level is halfway up sides of custard cups. Bake custards for 55 minutes, until a silver knife inserted in outer edge of custard comes out clean. If desired, custards may be covered and kept on warming tray in pan of hot water until serving time. Serves 6.

❧ Shirred Eggs with Bacon

10 slices raw bacon
Butter or margarine
2½ tablespoons fine dry bread
   crumbs
2 tablespoons grated
   Parmesan cheese
4 to 5 eggs
¼ cup heavy cream
Pinch of salt
Few grains white pepper
Dash of paprika

Heat oven to 400° F. Place bacon on a wire rack in rows with the fat edges overlapping the lean edges. Place rack in a flat baking pan or broiler pan; bake 10 minutes. While bacon is cooking, butter a 1-quart shallow baking dish generously. Mix bread crumbs and cheese together; press over bottom and sides of dish. Break eggs one at a time into a custard cup and carefully pour eggs onto crumb mixture, placing them evenly over bottom of dish. Pour cream around egg yolks. Sprinkle with salt, pepper, and paprika. Reduce oven temperature to 350° F. Bake eggs and bacon for about 15 to 20 minutes, or until eggs are just set and bacon is crisp. Serves 4 to 5.

❧ Scotch Woodcock

4 eggs
¼ teaspoon salt
Few grains pepper
¼ cup milk
1½ tablespoons butter or
   margarine
4 thin slices white bread,
   toasted
Butter or margarine
8 anchovy fillets

Beat eggs, salt, pepper, and milk together with rotary beater. Melt butter in skillet over moderately low heat (about 225° F.). Pour in egg mixture. As eggs cook, lift cooked portion and sides with a wooden spoon to allow uncooked portion to flow to bottom of the pan. Cook until just set but not dry. Spread toast with butter and cut slices in halves. Allow one slice of bread for each serving. Spoon eggs over toast. Crisscross 2 anchovy fillets over each serving. Garnish each with 6 capers and chopped parsley. Serve immediately. Serves 4.

24 capers
Chopped fresh parsley

 **Eggs Foo Yung**

2 *tablespoons butter or*
margarine
1 *large onion, thinly sliced*
1 *cup thinly sliced celery*
6 *eggs*
1 *teaspoon salt*
1 *4-ounce can sliced*
mushrooms, drained
1 *cup drained canned bean*
sprouts
1 *tablespoon chopped fresh*
parsley
2 *4½-ounce cans shrimp,*
drained and coarsely
chopped
3 *tablespoons water*
4 *to 6 tablespoons shortening*
or vegetable oil
Soy sauce

Heat butter in a skillet over moderately low heat (about 225° F.). Add onion and cook until golden brown. Remove from heat and add celery; cool. Beat eggs and salt together until just blended. Add cooled onion mixture, mushrooms, bean sprouts, parsley, shrimp, and water. Heat about a tablespoonful of the shortening in a large skillet over moderately high heat (about 275° F.). Drop mixture by large tablespoonfuls into skillet. When lightly browned on one side, turn and brown other side. Drain on paper towel and keep hot. Add more shortening to skillet before cooking the rest of the egg mixture. Serve hot with soy sauce. Serves 6.

Eggs for Picnics and Salad Platters

Special Stuffed Eggs

6 *hard-cooked eggs*
2 *tablespoons chopped*
toasted almonds
1 *tablespoon finely chopped*
green pepper
1 *teaspoon grated onion*
1 *tablespoon finely chopped*
pimiento
⅛ *teaspoon Tabasco*
3 *tablespoons mayonnaise*
¼ *teaspoon salt*
⅛ *teaspoon pepper*

Cut eggs in halves lengthwise; remove yolks and press them through a fine sieve. Add remaining ingredients. Mix well. Fill egg-white halves with this mixture. Chill if desired. Makes 12 halves. Serves 6.

EGGS

✒ Egg Salad

6 hard-cooked eggs, coarsely
   chopped
¼ cup drained pickle relish
3 tablespoons mayonnaise or
   salad dressing
⅓ cup chopped celery
½ teaspoon salt

Combine all ingredients in a bowl. Cover and chill thoroughly. Serve on crisp lettuce. Serves 4.

✒ Stuffed Eggs à la Russe

4 hard-cooked eggs
1 tablespoon melted butter or
   margarine
1 tablespoon mayonnaise
¼ teaspoon prepared
   mustard
¼ teaspoon salt
⅛ teaspoon pepper
¼ cup mayonnaise
¼ cup chili sauce
2 tablespoons chopped,
   blanched almonds
Watercress

Cut eggs in halves lengthwise; take out yolks and press them through a fine sieve. Add butter, the 1 tablespoon mayonnaise, mustard, salt, and pepper. Blend thoroughly. Fill whites with yolk mixture. Chill. Combine the ¼ cup mayonnaise, chili sauce, and almonds. Arrange 2 egg halves on watercress; top with dressing. Serves 4.

✒ Bacon-and-Egg Salad

6 hard-cooked eggs, coarsely
   chopped
8 slices crisp-cooked bacon,
   crumbled
1 tablespoon chopped fresh
   parsley
¼ cup mayonnaise or salad
   dressing
3 tablespoons bottled
   Russian dressing
Few grains pepper
Crisp lettuce

Place chopped eggs, bacon, and parsley in a mixing bowl. Combine mayonnaise, Russian dressing, and pepper and add to egg mixture. Toss to combine all ingredients. Chill thoroughly. Serve on lettuce. Serves 4.

Note: This salad may be used as a sandwich filling. Makes filling for 4 sandwiches.

Eggs for Dinner Dishes

✑ Sliced Eggs with Tarragon Mushroom Sauce

10 hard-cooked eggs, sliced
2 tablespoons butter or
  margarine
2 tablespoons flour
½ teaspoon salt
⅛ teaspoon pepper
1½ cups milk
½ teaspoon dried tarragon
  leaves
1 tablespoon instant minced
  onion
½ cup dry white wine
1 4-ounce can sliced
  mushrooms, drained
Toast (optional)

Arrange sliced eggs on a serving plate. Melt butter in a medium-sized saucepan over moderately low heat (about 225° F.). Blend in flour, salt, and pepper, beating constantly with a wire whip or wooden spoon to prevent lumping. Gradually add milk, stirring constantly, until sauce thickens and comes to a boil. Blend in the tarragon and onion. Gradually add wine, stirring well. Stir in mushrooms and heat throughly. Serve hot sauce over sliced eggs on toast, if desired. Serves 5.

✑ Deviled Egg Casserole

½ teaspoon instant minced
  onion
1 teaspoon water
6 hard-cooked eggs
2 teaspoons dried parsley
  flakes
¼ cup mayonnaise or salad
  dressing
3 tablespoons butter or
  margarine
3 tablespoons flour
½ teaspoon salt
Few grains pepper
2 cups milk
2 cups (½ pound) Cheddar
  cheese, coarsely shredded
4 cups raw spinach egg
  noodles, cooked according
  to package directions
½ cup fine dry bread crumbs
2 tablespoons melted butter
  or margarine
¼ teaspoon paprika

Heat oven to 350° F. Soak onion in water 5 minutes. Cut eggs in half lengthwise. Remove yolks and mash; add parsley, onion, and mayonnaise, mixing well. Mound into egg whites. Melt the 3 tablespoons butter in a saucepan over moderately low heat (about 225° F.); blend in flour, salt, and pepper. Gradually add milk and cook, stirring constantly, until thickened. Add cheese and stir until melted. Mix half of the cheese sauce with the cooked noodles; pour into a greased deep 2-quart casserole. Arrange stuffed egg halves over noodles and pour remaining cheese sauce over eggs. Mix bread crumbs, the 2 tablespoons melted butter, and the paprika. Sprinkle over top. Bake 30 to 40 minutes until thoroughly heated. Serves 4.

Eggs with Cheese Sauce

¼ cup butter or margarine
¼ cup flour
1 teaspoon salt
¼ teaspoon pepper
2 cups milk
1 teaspoon prepared
    mustard
2 cups (½ pound) sharp
    American cheese,
    shredded
8 hard-cooked eggs
8 slices toast
Paprika (optional)

Melt butter in a small saucepan over moderately low heat (about 225° F.); blend in flour, salt, and pepper. Gradually add milk and cook, stirring constantly, until thickened and smooth. Add mustard and cheese. Stir until cheese is melted. Cut eggs in half lengthwise. Arrange two halves on each slice of toast. Top with cheese sauce. Sprinkle with paprika, if desired. Serves 4.

Green Island Casserole

1 can condensed green pea
    soup
¼ cup milk
6 hard-cooked eggs
2 tablespoons minced fresh
    parsley
1 tablespoon minced chives
3 tablespoons mayonnaise
½ teaspoon prepared
    mustard
¼ teaspoon Tabasco
¼ teaspoon salt

Heat oven to 350° F. Heat soup and milk in top of double boiler over gently boiling water. Halve eggs lengthwise; remove the yolks to a small bowl and mash with a fork. Work remaining ingredients into yolks to make a smooth paste. Refill whites with yolk mixture. Grease a shallow 1½-quart baking dish. Arrange eggs, filled side up, in dish. Carefully pour soup around them. Bake about 10 minutes, until hot and bubbly. Serves 4.

Ham-and-Egg Scallop

4 medium-sized onions,
    very thinly sliced
3 tablespoons butter or
    margarine
2 tablespoons flour
¼ teaspoon salt
⅛ teaspoon pepper
1½ cup milk
1 4½-ounce can deviled
    ham

Fry onions in butter in skillet over moderate heat (about 225° F.) until tender. Blend in flour, salt, and pepper. Gradually add milk and cook about 5 minutes; stir constantly until mixture is thick. Blend in ham and eggs. Pour into a greased shallow 1½-quart baking dish. Place in preheated broiler about 3 inches from heat and broil a few minutes until top is lightly browned. Serves 4.

6 hard-cooked eggs, cut into
eighths

✑ Chinese Slivered Eggs

Egg Pancakes
 4 eggs
 1 teaspoon soy sauce
 ¼ teaspoon salt
 ½ teaspoon sugar
 2 teaspoons vegetable oil
Vegetables
 1 tablespoon vegetable oil
 1 cup thinly sliced fresh
  mushrooms
 4 cups shredded iceberg
  lettuce
 1 teaspoon soy sauce
 ½ teaspoon sugar
 ¼ teaspoon salt
 ½ cup thinly sliced green
  onions or scallions
 ⅓ cup toasted slivered
  almonds

Egg Pancakes. In a small bowl beat eggs lightly with the soy sauce, salt and sugar. In a heavy, 10-inch skillet heat 1 teaspoon of the oil over moderately high heat; when a drop of water skips across the bottom of the pan, it's ready. Pour ¼ cup of the egg mixture into the skillet, or enough to thinly coat the bottom. Cook 20 to 30 seconds, until "pancake" is set. Working quickly, lift edge of pancake, then grasp with fingers and turn over. Cook 20 seconds longer, until underside is lightly browned; turn onto a plate to cool. Repeat with remaining egg mixture, using remaining 1 teaspoon of oil when necessary. Stack pancakes and with a very sharp knife slice into very thin slivers.

Vegetables. In the same skillet heat the 1 tablespoon of oil over moderately high heat. Add mushrooms, lettuce, soy sauce, sugar and salt and cook, stirring constantly, about 3 minutes, until lettuce wilts. Add egg slivers and green onions, and toss gently until heated through. Sprinkle with almonds and serve. Serves 4.

✑ Lobster-and-Egg Newburg

 4 tablespoons butter or
  margarine
 2 teaspoons grated onion
 2 tablespoons flour
 ½ teaspoon salt
 ⅛ teaspoon pepper
 1 cup milk
 ½ cup light cream
 2 tablespoons chopped fresh
  parsley
 2 tablespoons chopped
  pimiento
 ¼ cup dry sherry
 1 5-ounce can rock lobster
  meat, diced
 6 hard-cooked eggs, coarsely
  diced
 3 cups hot cooked rice

Melt butter in a saucepan over moderately low heat (about 225° F.). Add onion and cook 1 minute. Stir in flour, salt, and pepper. Gradually add milk and cream. Cook, stirring constantly, until thickened. Add parsley, pimiento, sherry, lobster, and eggs. Serve on hot rice. Serves 4 to 6.

❧ Egg-Salad Casserole

6 hard-cooked eggs,
  coarsely chopped
2 tablespoons chopped
  pimiento
½ cup finely chopped celery
1½ cups finely crushed pilot
  crackers
1 cup mayonnaise or salad
  dressing
¼ cup milk
½ teaspoon salt
¾ teaspoon garlic salt
¼ teaspoon pepper
2 tablespoons melted butter
  or margarine

Heat oven to 400° F. Mix eggs, pimiento, celery, 1 cup of the crushed crackers, mayonnaise, milk, salt, garlic salt, and pepper. Spread mixture in a greased, shallow 1-quart casserole or a 9-inch pie pan. Toss together the remaining ½ cup cracker crumbs and butter; sprinkle over egg mixture. Bake about 20 minutes, until lightly browned. Serves 6.

❧ Curried Eggs

2 tablespoons butter or
  margarine
¼ cup finely chopped onion
1 can condensed cream of
  celery soup, undiluted
⅓ cup light cream
½ teaspoon salt
Few grains pepper
1 teaspoon curry powder
6 hard-cooked eggs,
  quartered
Chutney
Banana Tidbits (recipe
  follows)

Melt butter in skillet over moderately low heat (about 225° F.); add onion and cook until tender but not browned. Add celery soup, cream, salt, pepper, and curry powder; stir to combine. Simmer mixture 10 minutes. Carefully fold in quartered eggs and heat gently for about 5 more minutes. Serve garnished with chutney and Banana Tidbits if desired. Serves 4.

Banana Tidbits

2 medium-sized bananas,
  fully ripe
½ cup undiluted evaporated
  milk
½ cup finely chopped peanuts
½ cup flaked coconut

Cut bananas crosswise into 1-inch pieces. Dip each piece in evaporated milk. Roll half of the banana pieces in the peanuts and half in the coconut. Serve as an accompaniment to Curried Eggs. Serves 4.

CHAPTER XIII

CHEESE

"The only way to learn about cheese is to eat it" is old but sound advice. This ancient food—history records it as a diet staple in 2000 B.C.—has traveled with people and civilizations, each one has added so many varieties to the basic "recipe" that a handbook of the United States Department of Agriculture gives a descriptive list of more than four hundred cheeses marketed in this country and a famous New York cheese store offers more than a thousand different cheeses in its mail order catalog. In this chapter you will find only a few descriptions of, and some recipes for using, the most commonly available natural cheeses and the processed cheeses popular in this country. However, there are recipes using cheese throughout this book; if you wish to become more adventuresome with cheese, turn to page 29 for a guide to a great variety of cheeses.

Because of its infinite variety of tastes, cheese is a delight to gourmets who never tire of "discovering" a new cheese or finding new ways to serve the known ones. But cheese has more everyday values: It is both a budget food, because there is little or no waste, and a nutritious food. A pound of whole-milk cheese, such as Cheddar, contains the same amount of protein as a gallon of milk, along with its vitamins and minerals. Any cheese that is not too hard to cut needs virtually no preparation. It can be left in one piece to be cut as served for appetizers, desserts, or snacks.

Natural cheeses are all made from fluid milk (or whey, in a few instances). Since texture dictates their use somewhat, they are classified according to texture.

Very Hard Cheeses

The very hard cheeses are used for grating. They can be blended with bread crumbs for breading meats or topping casseroles or used in cooking to add flavor to omelets, soufflés, or sauces. They are most commonly used as sprinkle-on flavorings for spaghetti; soups, such as onion and minestrone; green salads; or for making cheese croutons.

Parmesan: This is the best-known grating cheese. So hard that it has been called the Rock of Gibraltar of cheeses, it keeps almost indefinitely in its hardest form. It has been made in Italy for centuries, first in the vicinity of Parma. Its flavor is sharp, its texture granular. You can buy it already grated or by the piece to grate as you need it.

Romano: Another grating cheese from Italy, this cheese is similar to Parmesan but sharper and saltier. The well-aged cheese has a brittle texture.

Sapsago (sap-say-go): This hard green cheese has a sharp, pungent flavor, some of which is derived from the powdered clover leaves that give it its sage color. It has a pleasant aroma.

Hard Cheeses

Cheeses of this type are the most popular varieties in this country. They are most often used for cooking and sandwiches.

Cheddar: Also known as American Cheddar, American, or "store" cheese, Cheddar is a direct descendant of the English Cheddar, made in the village of that name since the sixteenth century. Since most cheese-making in America has been dominated by Cheddar-type cheeses, everyone is familiar with its several gradations in flavor and texture. There are the semihard Cheddars with a nutty, piquant flavor and the flaky hard Cheddars with a more pronounced flavor. The hardest ones can be used for grating; the softer ones, served on a cheese tray with crackers or pie or cobbler desserts. Cheddar is versatile in cooking too, alone or combined with other cheeses.

Swiss Cheese: This is the well-known hard cheese with the "eyes"—the round, shiny holes that develop in the cheese curd as it ripens. Switzerland Swiss is called Emmenthaler; its production in the valley of that name dates from approximately the mid-fifteenth century. Its sweet, nutlike flavor can range from mild to sharp. Use Swiss sliced thin for sandwiches on dark breads, as an appetizer, in salads, or on cold-meat platters. The Swiss use it to prepare many national dishes—one of them is Cheese Fondue.

Gruyère (grew-yair): Named after the Swiss village of Gruyères near the French border, this cheese has been made in Europe for over two hundred years. Although similar to Swiss in its nut-sweet flavor and dry, firm texture, it is a bit sharper. Serve it with crackers or fruit or use it in cooking.

Provolone (proh-vo-loh-nay): One of Italy's best-known cheeses, this cheese is easily recognized in its whole form by its rope-tied packaging. It is also sold by the wedge or sliced. The texture is smooth and firm; the flavor has a distinctive smoky tang. Serve it for a snack or dessert, with crackers or fruit. It adds a unique flavor to cooked dishes, too.

Caciocavallo (cah-choh-ca-val-lo): Although much like Provolone, this cheese is not smoked. When it is aged, it is often used for grating.

Edam and *Gouda:* These semihard cheeses from North and South Holland, respectively, are often confused because of their similar mild flavor and firm, smooth texture. There are some small differences, however. Edam is available in a loaf shape as well as in the familiar ball shape; its bright red covering is an identifying mark. Gouda, not always dressed in red, contains more fat than Edam and is therefore a slightly softer cheese. A popular size is the baby Gouda, an oval-shaped cheese weighing a pound or less. But here the main differences end; they can be used interchangeably. The Dutch eat them at every meal, including breakfast. Serve the cheese whole, preparing it by cutting a slice off the top; everyone then helps himself with a cheese scoop. Or you can slice the round into small pie-shaped wedges to serve with crackers.

Semisoft Cheeses

According to their individual characteristics, the semisoft cheeses are used as is on cheese trays or to add flavor to other cooked and uncooked dishes.

Brick: One of the few cheeses of American origin, this cheese is a rather pungent sweet-flavored cheese—about midway between Cheddar and Limburger. It has smaller holes than Swiss and is a good slicing cheese.

Blue Cheese: This cheese is the American version of a type of blue-veined cheese made in many countries. The classic imported blues are the English Stilton, the Italian Gorgonzola (also made in the United States), the French Roquefort, and, recently, the Danish Blue. Blue cheese, made with cow's or goat's milk, is named after the French *bleu*—the name for many Roquefort-type cheeses made throughout France. (The Roquefort name is limited by government regulation to describe blue cheese made with sheep's milk in the Roquefort area.) Blue cheese is generally cream-colored, distinguished by its blue-green mottling, a piquant flavor, and a smooth, rich texture. Use it sliced with fruit or crackers for dessert or as a flavoring, crumbled into tossed salad or salad dressing. It is also an excellent appetizer cheese and can be creamed for dips or canapés.

Bel Paese (bell-pa-azey): The name of this cheese, in Italian, means "beautiful country." It is a relatively modern cheese, first made in 1920. The texture is soft but firm; the flavor is similar to Muenster but more delicate. Similar cheeses made in Europe are often called butter cheese. Some authorities list it as a soft cheese. If you can't find Bel Paese under this name, ask for a Bel Paese type of cheese—there are several made. Slice it for cheese and crackers or cheese and fruit. It can also be used in cooking.

Port du Salut (port-du-saloo): Created by Trappist monks at the Abbey at Port du Salut in France, this cheese is now made in other Trappist monasteries in Europe, Canada, and this country. Commercial versions are also available. It is a semisoft cheese with a mild flavor, similar to that of Gouda, a smooth, creamy texture, and an aroma sometimes comparable to that of a mild Limburger. Serve it alone or with crackers, as an appetizer or snack cheese; with fruit for dessert, or shred it for use in a dip.

Muenster: A semisoft cheese of German origin, this variety has a mild but distinctive flavor and a firm but soft texture dotted with tiny holes. You can buy it by the wheel, in small ball shapes, by the wedge, or sliced. Use it for sandwiches or on a cheese-and-fruit tray. It is sometimes served with caraway seeds on the side, for extra seasoning.

Soft Cheeses

Soft cheeses are divided into two categories, ripened and unripened, that are totally different in taste. Ripened cheese has had bacteria, mold, or surface microorganisms added to it during processing. Unripened cheeses have no additions; hence their milder flavor and fresh taste. The varieties that follow are the most commonly used soft ripened cheeses in this country.

Brie (bree) and *Camembert* (kam-em-bear): These are the classic dessert cheeses of France. Brie has been made for centuries. Camembert was first made in 1791; a legend has it that Napoleon discovered the yet-unnamed cheese in its native hamlet of Camembert and named it. Both cheeses are soft ripened. They have a pungent, flavorful crust and a rich, creamy interior, which should be of almost liquid consistency when the cheese is served at room temperature. Brie has a sharp characteristic taste;

Camembert is similar but somewhat milder. Both cheeses are available in circular rounds or portion-sized wedges. Serve them for dessert with crackers or dark bread or thin slices of fruit—pineapple, pear, apple. Or use them as a salad cheese.

Limburger: The aroma of this cheese is somewhat more overpowering than its flavor. It is a soft open-textured cheese that is best eaten on unflavored bread or crackers.

Liederkranz: This is a trade name for a soft cheese, American in origin, that looks like Limburger but has a milder flavor and aroma.

The unripened soft cheeses are familiar to everyone. Cream cheese and cottage cheese, both the creamed and uncreamed varieties, are in this category. Some less familiar varieties that are becoming popular follow.

Ricotta: This Italian cottage cheese is somewhat finer grained than our variety. Made from whole milk, it is fresh (uncured) and moist, with a characteristic bland flavor. It mixes well with other cheeses and ingredients. Use it in baked dishes, in sandwiches, and in salads. Mix it with sweet ingredients for desserts.

Mozzarella (mutz-a-rel-la): Originally made in Italy from buffalo's milk, this cheese is a soft, mild-flavored cooking cheese that comes in small, irregularly shaped spheres. Used for topping pizza and in other baked dishes, it melts to a smooth, pleasantly elastic consistency.

Neufchâtel (new-sha-tell): Originated in Normandy, this soft cheese has a mild flavor and creamy texture. It is so similar to cream cheese that the two can be used interchangeably—for sandwiches, on crackers, or in recipes. Neufchâtel, however, has a lower fat content and a moister, less crumbly consistency. An imported Neufchâtel will probably be ripened; a domestic one will not be.

Process Cheeses

Process cheese is made by cooking together a variety of cheeses along with an emulsifying agent to produce a plastic cheese of uniform texture and flavor. Process cheese may be smoked or have smoked flavor added or may have fruits, vegetables, or meats added to it for flavor. Process cheese is a favorite melting and sandwich cheese. Process cheese food is made in the same way as process cheese except that dairy products, such as milk or whey, have been added in the blending. By law, more than half of the finished product must be natural cheese. It has about half as much fat as process cheese. Process cheese spreads are made like process cheese food except that they have more moisture and less fat.

Storing Cheese

The refrigerator is the place to keep cheese. To prevent it from transferring odor to other foods, or from picking up other strong odors, and from drying out, cheese should always be tightly wrapped in its original container or in foil or plastic wrap or placed in a covered container. Ends of cheese or grated cheese may be stored in a tightly covered jar.

Since all the ripened cheeses are more flavorful and easier to serve at room temperature, they should be put out an hour before you plan to use them. The soft, unripened cheeses, such as cottage and cream, are quite perishable; they should be kept refrigerated until served. Plan to use them within a week from the time you purchase them.

All process cheeses may be stored unopened at room temperature. Once opened, they must be refrigerated.

Cheeses may develop a mold, even under refrigeration. It is harmless; simply cut it off or scrape it off and use the cheese as planned. It is best not to freeze cheese.

Cooking Cheese

Cooking cheese, like eggs, requires gentle heat. High heat and overcooking toughen cheese and diminish its flavor. When you melt cheese, heat it in the top of a double boiler over simmering water. When you broil it, keep it four or five inches from direct heat until it just begins to melt. When you use it in a baked dish, keep oven temperature low to moderate, 300° to 350° F.

When you grate cheese to add to recipes, use a coarse grater for soft cheeses and a fine grater for hard cheeses, such as Parmesan.

Of all the dishes made with cheese, from appetizers to desserts, possibly the three most popular, after the ubiquitous cheese sandwich, are Fondue, Rarebit, and a cheese pie named Quiche Lorraine. These and variations of them introduce our list of luncheon or light supper dishes made with cheese.

Cheese Fondue

½ *pound Emmenthaler Swiss cheese*
½ *pound Gruyère cheese*
3 *tablespoons flour*

Cut cheeses into about ½-inch cubes. (An electric knife works well for this.) In a large bowl toss cheeses and flour until well coated. Rub a heavy earthenware pot with the garlic clove halves. Pour in the wine and place

1 garlic clove, cut in half
2 cups dry white wine
1 tablespoon lemon juice
Dash of ground nutmeg
2 tablespoons kirsch
2 loaves French bread, cut
into cubes with some crust
on each cube

pot on its stand over moderate heat. When tiny air bubbles rise to the surface, add the lemon juice. Add the cheese gradually, stirring constantly with a wooden spoon until cheese is melted and mixture is smooth. Add nutmeg and kirsch and stir well to blend. Keep bubbling over heat during serving. With their fondue forks, guests should spear the bread cubes through the soft portion to the crust and dip into the fondue. Serves 4.

✑ Yankee Cheese Fondue

1 clove garlic, cut in half
6 tablespoons butter or
margarine
6 tablespoons flour
4 teaspoons prepared
mustard
3 cups dairy half-and-half
3 cups (¾ pound) Cheddar
cheese, coarsely shredded
4½ cups (1⅛ pounds) Swiss
cheese, coarsely shredded
1 or 2 loaves French or
Italian bread, broken into
bite-sized pieces, each
with part of the crust

Rub inside of a large saucepan with the cut surface of garlic. Melt the butter in the saucepan over moderately low heat (about 225° F.); blend in flour and mustard. Gradually add half-and-half; cook and stir constantly until thickened. Add shredded Cheddar cheese and shredded Swiss cheese. Heat and stir until cheeses are melted. Pour into a chafing dish set over a heating unit. With a fondue fork, each guest should spear a piece of bread and dip it into the fondue. Serves 6.

✑ Welsh Rarebit

2 tablespoons butter or
margarine
2 teaspoons flour
½ teaspoon dry mustard
Few grains cayenne pepper
1 teaspoon Worcestershire
sauce
¼ teaspoon salt
½ cup beer or ale
3 cups (¾ pound) Cheddar
cheese, shredded
4 slices toast

Melt butter in top of double boiler over simmering water; blend in flour, mustard, cayenne pepper, Worcestershire, and salt. Gradually add beer and cook and stir until thickened. Add cheese and heat until cheese is melted. Just before serving beat with a rotary beater until smooth. Serve on toast. Makes about 1¾ cups and serves 3 to 4.

CHEESE

Golden Buck

Prepare Welsh Rarebit. Top each serving with a *poached egg*.

⋊ Rum Tum Tiddy

1 tablespoon butter or
 margarine
¼ cup finely chopped onion
¼ cup chopped green pepper
1 can condensed tomato soup
¾ cup milk
3 cups (¾ pound) Cheddar
 cheese, shredded
½ teaspoon Worcestershire
 sauce
1 egg, slightly beaten
¼ cup dry sherry
Toast or crackers

Melt butter in a saucepan over moderately low heat (about 225° F.); add onion and green pepper and cook until tender; remove from heat. Mix in tomato soup, milk, cheese, and Worcestershire. Cook, stirring constantly, until cheese is melted. Remove from heat. Blend ½ cup of the cheese sauce into beaten egg in a bowl. Pour egg mixture back into the remainder of the cheese sauce in the saucepan and heat over moderately low heat (about 225° F.). Stir in sherry and spoon over toast or crackers. Serves 4 to 6.

⋊ Quiche Lorraine

1 baked 9-inch pie shell
 (recipe on page 786)
½ pound sliced raw bacon
2 cups (½ pound) Swiss
 cheese, shredded
5 eggs, slightly beaten
1 cup milk
1 cup light cream
½ teaspoon ground nutmeg
½ teaspoon salt
⅛ teaspoon white pepper
Few grains cayenne pepper

Heat oven to 350° F. Cut bacon slices in half and cook in a skillet over moderately high heat (about 325° F.) until crisp. Drain well and crumble; sprinkle bacon and cheese in alternate layers in baked pie shell. Combine remaining ingredients in a medium-sized bowl and beat until well blended. Carefully pour over cheese and bacon. Bake in center of oven for 40 to 45 minutes, or until a silver knife inserted in center comes out clean. Cut into small or large wedges, as desired. Serves 12 as an appetizer or 6 as a light luncheon dish.

⋊ Quick Quiche Lorraine

1 baked 9-inch pie shell
 (recipe on page 786)
8 slices raw bacon
3 eggs, slightly beaten
1 cup commercial sour cream

Heat oven to 300° F. Cook bacon over moderately high heat (about 325° F.) until crisp. Drain and crumble coarsely. Combine eggs, sour cream, salt, Worcestershire, cheese, and onions. Add crumbled bacon. Pour into baked pie shell. Bake 30 minutes. If brown-

¾ *teaspoon salt*
½ *teaspoon Worcestershire sauce*
1 *cup (¼ pound) Swiss cheese, coarsely shredded*
1 *3½-ounce can French fried onions*

ed top is desired, place under preheated broiler 1 to 2 minutes. Cut into wedges. Serves 6.

ৰ্চ Cheese Soup

2 *tablespoons butter or margarine*
2 *tablespoons flour*
¼ *teaspoon salt*
Few grains pepper
⅛ *teaspoon garlic powder*
Dash of ground nutmeg
3 *cups milk, scalded*
1 *cup (¼ pound) Cheddar cheese, shredded*
2 *egg yolks*
½ *cup dry white wine*
2 *tablespoons Cheddar cheese, shredded*

Melt butter in a saucepan over moderately low heat (about 225° F.). Blend in flour, salt, pepper, garlic powder, and nutmeg. Cook 3 minutes, stirring constantly. Gradually add hot milk, stirring constantly, until all liquid has been added and sauce is smooth. Cook over low heat (about 200° F.) for 20 minutes, stirring very frequently. Add the 1 cup shredded cheese and heat until cheese is melted, stirring constantly. Beat egg yolks slightly; blend in 1 cup of the cheese sauce. Pour back into saucepan and mix until blended. Heat 1 minute, stirring constantly. Gradually add wine. Serve garnished with the 2 tablespoons shredded cheese. Serves 3 to 4.

ৰ্চ Vegetable–Cheese Chowder

3 *tablespoons butter or margarine*
½ *cup coarsely chopped onion*
½ *cup coarsely chopped celery*
1 *cup peeled, sliced carrots (about 3 small)*
1 *cup boiling water*
1 *10-ounce package frozen chopped broccoli, partially thawed*
4 *tablespoons flour*
1 *quart milk*
2 *teaspoons salt*
1½ *cups (6 ounces) sharp American cheese, shredded*

Melt butter in a large, heavy saucepan over moderately low heat (about 225° F.). Add onion and cook until lightly browned. Add celery, carrots, and boiling water. Cover and simmer over low heat (about 200° F.) 10 minutes. Break up broccoli and add; cook 5 minutes more, until just tender. Mix flour with a little of the milk and add to vegetables with rest of milk. Add salt. Cook and stir until slightly thickened. Add cheese and stir until melted. Serves 6.

CHEESE

⋙ *Cheese Strata*

12 slices white bread
½ pound sliced Cheddar
    cheese
4 eggs, well beaten
2½ cups milk
1 teaspoon salt
⅛ teaspoon pepper
¼ teaspoon prepared
    mustard
1 tablespoon instant minced
    onion
½ teaspoon Worcestershire
    sauce

Arrange bread slices over bottom of a greased shallow 2-quart baking dish, cutting slices to fit. Place cheese slices over bread and top with remaining slices of bread. Combine eggs, milk, and seasonings in a bowl. Pour over bread and cheese. Chill in the refrigerator for at least 1 hour. Heat oven to 350° F. Bake 1 hour, or until silver knife, inserted in center, comes out clean. Serves 6 to 8.

⋙ *Lobster-Cheese Custard*

6 slices white bread, crusts
    removed
3 slices packaged, sliced
    Swiss cheese, cut into
    halves
1 8-ounce package lobster
    tails, cooked according to
    package directions
2 eggs
2 cups milk, scalded
¼ teaspoon salt
Few grains pepper
Dash of ground nutmeg

Heat oven to 375° F. Place bread in a single layer in the bottom of a buttered shallow 1½-quart baking dish. Top each bread slice with a slice of Swiss cheese. Remove lobster meat from shells and dice; sprinkle over cheese. Beat eggs slightly; gradually stir in scalded milk, salt, pepper, and nutmeg. Pour milk mixture over bread, cheese, and lobster. Bake 40 to 45 minutes, or until set. Serve immediately. Serves 4.

⋙ *Corn-and-Cheese Pie*

1 9-inch pie shell, baked
    and cooled (recipe on
    page 786)
2 eggs, well beaten
1 teaspoon salt
Few grains pepper
1½ cups milk, heated
1 12-ounce can
    vacuum-packed corn with

Heat oven to 350° F. Combine eggs, salt, and pepper. Gradually stir in hot milk. Add corn and cheese. Pour into baked pie shell. Bake about 45 minutes, until a silver knife inserted in the center comes out clean. Cut into wedges to serve. Serves 4 to 6.

[476]

*green pepper and
pimiento*
2 *cups (½ pound) sharp
American cheese,
shredded*

◀ᷤ *Six-Cheese Spaghetti Casserole*

1 *1-pound package no. 8
spaghetti*
¼ *cup butter or margarine*
1 *tablespoon Worcestershire
sauce*
1 *teaspoon dry mustard*
⅛ *teaspoon cayenne pepper*
¼ *clove garlic, finely chopped*
2 *cups (½ pound) Cheddar
cheese, finely diced*
¾ *cup (3 ounces) Parmesan
cheese, finely diced*
¾ *cup (3 ounces) provolone
cheese, finely diced*
½ *cup (2 ounces) Swiss
cheese, finely diced*
½ *cup (2 ounces) Romano
cheese, finely diced*
½ *cup (2 ounces) hard smoky
cheese, finely diced*
Salt and pepper
Cayenne pepper (optional)
1 *quart milk*
Paprika (optional)

Cook spaghetti in boiling salted water according to package directions. Drain. Toss with 2 tablespoons of the butter. Grease a deep 3-quart casserole. Place Worcestershire sauce, mustard, the ⅛ teaspoon cayenne pepper, and the garlic in bottom of casserole. Spread over bottom and sides of casserole with the back of a spoon. Combine Cheddar, Parmesan, provolone, Swiss, Romano, and smoky cheeses. Place half the spaghetti in the casserole. Sprinkle with half the mixed cheeses. Dot with 1 tablespoon of the butter and sprinkle lightly with salt and pepper. If desired, sprinkle very lightly with cayenne. Repeat layers. Pour milk over mixture. With 2 forks, lift spaghetti to permit milk to seep through mixture. Cover and place in a 350° F. oven. Bake 20 minutes, or until milk begins to bubble. Remove from oven; with 2 forks or tongs, lift spaghetti from bottom of casserole, completely turning over the entire contents of the casserole. Return casserole to oven uncovered; bake 20 minutes. Remove from oven and repeat the turning-over process. Bake, uncovered, another 20 minutes. Repeat the turning-over process before serving. All the cheese should be melted and mixed thoroughly with the spaghetti. Add a little more milk, if necessary, during cooking to keep mixture moist. If desired, sprinkle with paprika. May be kept warm on an electric hot tray. Serves 8 generously.

CHAPTER XIV

SAUCES

A well-made sauce can make the difference between a humdrum dish and an exquisite one. It can transform such everyday, economical foods as poached fish and hard-cooked eggs and many leftovers into dishes to be proud of. And there are many favorite dishes that are not possible without the skill of making the sauce that enhances them. Eggs Benedict require a velvety Hollandaise Sauce, Lobster Newburg needs a rich, sherried white sauce, and Beef Stroganoff depends upon the flavor of a hearty brown sauce.

In this chapter you will find the six classic hot sauces. Most of them can be made two ways: a classic method and a shortcut method. Which you use will depend upon your time and your taste. From these six basic sauces there are a host of variations. At the end of the chapter there is a collection of barbecue basting sauces. In all the recipes in this chapter, look for serving suggestions at the end of the recipe. Mayonnaise and vinaigrette sauces, usually served with cold foods, are described in the salad chapter.

White (Béchamel) Sauce

This is probably the most commonly used sauce in this country; it is the sauce most often used to cream vegetables and fish, meat, or poultry. At its worst, it is a rather tasteless, gluey, and even lumpy sauce. The secret to making perfect white sauce is in combining the few ingredients (flour, butter, and milk) for the proper time at the proper temperature. It is important to cook the flour and butter together over low heat for at least three minutes *without browning*. (This result is called a white roux.) Take roux *off the heat* and gradually stir in the hot milk before returning the sauce to the heat for further cooking. By either the long or the short methods, these steps are important to achieve a smooth, fully cooked sauce. If you make white sauce ahead, keep it closely covered or float a little butter over the top to prevent a skin from forming. White sauces may be kept refrigerated, tightly covered, for three days or may be frozen for later use.

To Make Satin-Smooth White Sauce

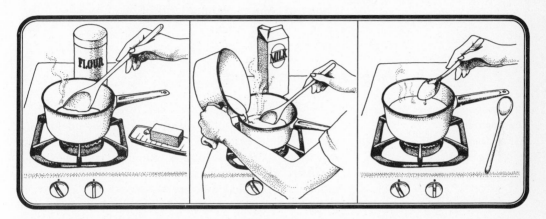

Don't hurry the cooking of the flour and butter before adding liquid. Cook the fat–flour mixture at least 3 minutes over low heat; stir constantly to make a smooth paste.

Add hot liquid to the cooked flour–fat mixture (called a roux). Stir in a little liquid at a time, stirring constantly. Do not use cold liquid; it can cause lumping.

Cook over lowest heat 20 minutes; stir just occasionally. The basic sauce will coat the back of a silver spoon when done.

In every white sauce, thick or thin, the amounts of butter and flour remain equal to each other.

To make a thinner sauce, reduce the proportions of flour and butter to milk. For example, for a very thin sauce you would use two tablespoons of butter and two tablespoons of flour to two cups of milk. This would make a thin soup consistency. Using three tablespoons each of butter and flour to two cups of milk would make a thick cream-soup consistency.

To make a thicker sauce increase the proportions of butter and flour. For example, a thick white sauce used to bind a croquette mixture would use eight tablespoons (one-half cup) each of butter and flour to two cups of milk.

The basic medium white sauce is an all-purpose sauce. It can be used as it is or seasoned to cream vegetables, eggs, meat, poultry, or fish. Often it is combined with egg yolks or cream or butter to make a richer sauce or with other flavors to make the popular variations that follow the basic recipes.

SAUCES

White (Béchamel) Sauce, Long Method

4 tablespoons butter or
margarine
4 tablespoons flour
1 teaspoon salt
2½ cups milk, scalded

Melt butter in a saucepan over moderately low heat (about 225° F.). Remove from heat and blend in flour and salt. Return to heat and cook for 3 minutes, without browning, stirring constantly. Remove from heat and gradually add hot milk, stirring constantly, until all liquid has been added and sauce is smooth. Cook over low heat (about 200° F.) for 20 minutes, stirring frequently. Makes about 2 cups of medium sauce.

White (Béchamel) Sauce, Short Method

4 tablespoons butter or
margarine
4 tablespoons flour
1 teaspoon salt
2 cups milk, scalded

Melt butter in a saucepan over moderately low heat (about 225° F.). Remove from heat and blend in flour and salt. Return to heat and cook 3 minutes, without browning, stirring constantly. Remove from heat and gradually add hot milk, stirring constantly, until all the milk has been added and sauce is smooth. Return to heat and cook for about 5 minutes, stirring constantly, until mixture is smooth and thickened. Makes 2 cups of medium white sauce.

Newburg Sauce

2 cups White Sauce (recipe
above)
½ cup heavy cream
3 egg yolks
Few grains cayenne pepper
3 tablespoons dry sherry

Heat White Sauce in top of double boiler over boiling water for 15 minutes, or until reduced to 1⅓ cups, stirring occasionally. Stir cream into sauce and heat 5 minutes, stirring occasionally. Strain sauce. Beat egg yolks slightly and gradually stir in sauce and cayenne. Pour back into top of double boiler and heat 2 minutes. Stir in sherry before serving. Serve with fish. Makes about 2¾ cups.

Chantilly Sauce

½ cup heavy cream, whipped
2 cups hot White Sauce
(recipe above)

Fold heavy cream into White Sauce and serve immediately. Serve with baked or boiled fish and croquettes. Makes about 3 cups sauce.

☙ Onion Sauce

1½ cups finely chopped onion
1½ cups boiling water
  2 tablespoons butter or
    margarine
  2 cups hot White Sauce
    (recipe on page 480)
  ½ cup heavy cream

Cover onion with boiling water and let stand 3 minutes. Drain. Melt butter in saucepan over moderately low heat (about 225° F.); add onion and cook about 5 minutes, or until soft. Stir into White Sauce and heat over simmering water for 15 minutes, stirring occasionally. Strain and gradually stir in cream. Heat. Serve with fish, poultry, or vegetables. Makes about 2 cups sauce.

☙ Cream Sauce

  2 cups hot White Sauce
    (recipe on page 480)
  ½ cup heavy cream

Heat sauce in top of double boiler over boiling water for about 15 minutes, or until reduced to 1½ cups, stirring occasionally. Strain sauce. Gradually add cream. Heat over low heat (about 200° F.), about 10 minutes, stirring constantly. Serve with vegetables or fish. Makes about 2 cups.

How to Thicken Sauces with Egg Yolks

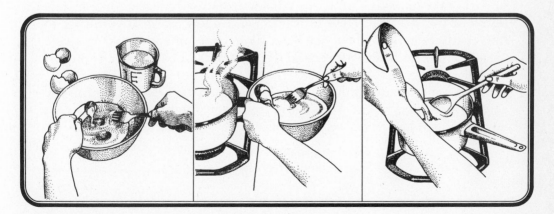

Separate the eggs carefully; put the yolks in a small bowl. Beat briskly with a fork; then add 1 teaspoon of cold water for each egg yolk. Beat to blend water and yolks.

Spoon hot sauce, allowing 1 tablespoon of sauce for each egg yolk, into the yolk-water mixture. Add hot sauce slowly to the yolks and blend with a fork as you add it.

Slowly stir yolk–sauce mixture into hot sauce and stir to blend well. Sauce should now cook another 5 minutes, but never be allowed to boil after eggs are added.

Frequently basic sauces are enriched or thickened further with egg yolks. Here the basic Béchamel Sauce is enriched to make the Mornay Sauce which follows. Because eggs cook quickly at low temperature, care must be taken when they are added to a hot sauce. The technique illustrated on page 481 works well.

Note: If the recipe calls for cream, milk, or other liquid to be added with eggs, omit the water called for on page 481.

✑ *Mornay Sauce*

2 **egg yolks**
2 **tablespoons heavy cream**
2 **cups hot White Sauce (recipe on page 480)**
2 **tablespoons grated Parmesan cheese**

Beat egg yolks and cream together; stir in ¼ cup of the White Sauce. Pour back into remaining sauce and heat over moderately low heat (about 225° F.) about 10 minutes. Strain and stir in Parmesan cheese before serving. Makes about 2¼ cups. Serve over poultry, fish, vegetables, and egg dishes.

Blond (Velouté) Sauce

Blond Sauce is a close sister to White Sauce; the main difference is that all or part of the liquid is a white stock made from veal, chicken, or fish. The flavor of the stock you choose will depend upon the dish you want to dress with the sauce. The white roux (flour and butter) should be made exactly as it is for White Sauce, and the stock should be hot when you add it to the roux.

Blond Sauce made completely with stock may be kept covered in the refrigerator for a week; it may also be frozen for future use. It keeps longer than White Sauce because there is no milk in the base.

✑ *Blond (Velouté) Sauce, Long Method*

4 **tablespoons butter or margarine**
5 **tablespoons flour**
2 **cups hot veal, chicken, or fish stock (recipes on pages 211–212)**

Melt butter in a saucepan over moderately low heat (about 225° F.). Remove from heat. Blend in flour; return to heat and cook for 4 minutes, or until golden, stirring constantly. Remove from heat and gradually add hot stock, stirring constantly, until all stock has been added and sauce is smooth. Cook over low heat (about 200° F.) for 20 minutes, stirring frequently. Strain through a fine-mesh sieve. Use in egg, chicken, veal, or fish dishes. Makes about 1⅔ cups.

✑ Blond (Velouté) Sauce, Short Method

¼ cup butter or margarine
4 tablespoons flour
*2 chicken bouillon cubes
*2½ cups boiling water
3 tablespoons chopped onion
1 whole clove
2 parsley sprigs
½ bay leaf

Melt butter in a heavy saucepan over moderately low heat (about 225° F.). Remove from heat. Blend in flour. Return to heat and cook for 4 minutes, or until golden, stirring constantly. Remove from heat. Dissolve chicken bouillon cubes in the boiling water; gradually add to flour mixture, stirring constantly, until smooth. Add remaining ingredients; cook over low heat (about 200° F.) for 20 minutes, stirring frequently. Strain through a fine-mesh sieve. Makes about 1½ cups.

*Note: 2½ cups boiling canned chicken broth may be substituted for the bouillon cubes and boiling water.

✑ Supreme Sauce

1 chicken bouillon cube
¼ pound mushrooms, sliced
¼ cup water
1½ cups hot Velouté Sauce (recipe on page 482)
½ cup light cream

Add bouillon cube, mushrooms, and water to Velouté Sauce. Place over boiling water and cook 20 minutes, or until reduced to 1½ cups, stirring occasionally. Strain and stir in light cream. Heat and serve. Serve with fish, poultry, and eggs. Makes about 2 cups sauce.

✑ Smitaine Sauce

1½ cups hot Velouté Sauce (recipe on page 482)
1 tablespoon butter or margarine
¼ cup finely chopped onion
⅓ cup dry white wine
½ cup commercial sour cream

Place Velouté Sauce in top of double boiler over boiling water for 15 minutes, or until reduced to 1⅓ cups, stirring occasionally. Melt butter in saucepan over moderately low heat (about 225° F.); add onion and cook until tender. Add wine and simmer about 5 minutes, or until reduced to ¼ cup. Stir into sauce and heat over boiling water 5 minutes. Stir in sour cream; reduce heat so that water is just simmering and cook about 5 minutes, until thoroughly heated. Serve with poultry or game. Makes about 2 cups.

Brown (Espagnole) Sauce

Brown or Espagnole Sauce is really a flavorful beef gravy which can be used to dress leftover meats in such dishes as hot, open-faced beef sandwiches or as a sauce in which you'd reheat and serve leftover cubed meat on noodles. It is also the base for many of the following flavorful sauces. This sauce is also made with a roux (butter and flour cooked together); the roux is cooked for six to eight minutes over very low heat until it takes on an even, golden brown color. It must not burn or turn dark or the finished sauce will be bitter.

Hot beef stock is then stirred into the brown roux before the sauce is cooked further. You may use either canned beef bouillon or bouillon cubes and boiling water. Do not use beef consommé. For a shorter shortcut, use canned beef gravy for the brown sauces in the recipes for variations which follow.

Brown Sauce may be kept covered and refrigerated for one week. It may also be frozen for future use.

✌ Brown (Espagnole) Sauce, Long Method

¼ cup butter or margarine
6 tablespoons flour
2 cups hot Beef Stock (recipe on page 211)

Melt butter in a saucepan over moderately low heat (about 225° F.). Blend in 4 tablespoons of the flour; return to heat and cook 6 to 8 minutes, or until medium golden brown or cinnamon-colored, stirring constantly. Remove from heat and stir in the remaining 2 tablespoons flour. Gradually add hot stock, stirring constantly, until all the stock has been added and sauce is smooth. Cook over low heat (about 200° F.) for 20 minutes, stirring frequently. Strain through a fine-mesh sieve. Makes about 1½ cups sauce.

✌ Brown (Espagnole) Sauce, Short Method

¼ cup butter or margarine
6 tablespoons flour
2 beef bouillon cubes
2½ cups boiling water
2 parsley sprigs
½ small bay leaf
Pinch of dried thyme leaves

Melt butter in a heavy saucepan over moderately low heat (about 225° F.). Add 4 tablespoons of the flour; cook about 6 to 8 minutes, stirring constantly, until medium brown or cinnamon-colored. Remove from heat and stir in the remaining 2 tablespoons flour. Dissolve bouillon cubes in the boiling water; gradually add to the flour mixture, stirring constantly, until thickened and smooth. Add remaining ingredients; cook over low heat (about 200° F.) for 20 minutes, stirring occasionally. Strain through a fine-mesh sieve. Makes about 1½ cups.

✑ Sauce Diable

3 tablespoons minced
   shallots or onions
⅛ teaspoon cracked pepper
⅓ cup dry white wine
1½ cups hot Brown Sauce
   (recipe on page 484)
1½ teaspoons Worcestershire
   sauce
1 teaspoon chopped fresh
   parsley

Place shallots, pepper, and wine in top of double boiler; cook over low heat (about 200° F.) for 5 minutes. Add Brown Sauce and Worcestershire; heat over simmering water for 15 minutes. Strain and stir in parsley. Serve with broiled meat and poultry. Makes about 1⅓ cups.

✑ Bordelaise Sauce

2 tablespoons minced
   shallots or onions
¾ cup dry red wine
1 teaspoon chopped fresh
   parsley
1½ cups hot Brown Sauce
   (recipe on page 484)

Place shallots, wine, and parsley in top of double boiler; place over low heat (about 200° F.) and cook about 8 minutes, or until reduced to 6 tablespoons. Add Brown Sauce and cook over simmering water for 15 minutes. Serve with sweetbreads, steaks, and grilled meats. Makes about 1½ cups.

✑ Piquant Sauce

1 tablespoon butter or
   margarine
2 tablespoons finely
   chopped onion
2 tablespoons chopped
   green pepper
1 tablespoon dry white wine
1 tablespoon lemon juice
1 tablespoon capers
Few grains cayenne pepper
1½ cups hot Brown Sauce
   (recipe on page 484)

Melt butter in saucepan over moderately low heat (about 225° F.); add onion and green pepper and cook until tender. Add wine, lemon juice, capers, cayenne, and Brown Sauce. Heat over low heat (about 200° F.). Serve with pork, leftover meats, and smoked meats. Makes about 2 cups.

✑ Brown Mushroom Sauce

¼ cup sliced mushroom caps
   (reserve stems and
   trimmings)

Place mushroom stems and trimmings in saucepan; add water, onion, celery, carrot, and sprig of parsley. Cover and simmer over low heat (about 200° F.) for 30 min-

3 cups water
½ medium-sized onion
½ stalk celery, sliced
½ carrot, peeled and sliced
1 parsley sprig
1 tablespoon butter or margarine
1½ cups hot Brown Sauce (recipe on page 484)
1 teaspoon minced fresh parsley

utes. Strain and measure broth. There should be ¾ cup; if necessary, boil to reduce to that amount. Melt butter in top of double boiler over moderately low heat (about 225° F.), add sliced mushrooms and cook until tender. Stir in Brown Sauce. Place over boiling water and heat 15 minutes, until reduced to 1¼ cups. Stir in mushroom stock and minced parsley; heat. Serve with meats, poultry, and smoked meats. Makes about 2 cups.

✥ Sauce Robert

1½ tablespoons butter or margarine
3 tablespoons finely chopped onion
⅓ cup dry white wine
½ teaspoon vinegar
1½ cups hot Brown Sauce (recipe on page 484)
3 tablespoons tomato paste
1½ teaspoons prepared mustard
1½ tablespoons finely chopped dill pickle
1½ teaspoons chopped fresh parsley

Melt butter in top of double boiler over moderately low heat (about 225° F.). Add onion and cook until tender. Add wine and vinegar; cook over low heat (about 200° F.) for 5 minutes. Add Brown Sauce and tomato paste; cook over simmering water 15 minutes. Strain. Stir in mustard, pickle, and parsley. Serve with pork and left-over meats. Makes about 2 cups.

Tomato (Portugaise) Sauce

This Tomato Sauce may either be used as it is on meatballs or cubed leftover meat or on spaghetti, noodles, or rice. It may be put through a fine-mesh sieve to produce a smooth sauce to use in such dishes as Veal or Eggplant Parmigiana. Or you can add a tablespoon or two of smooth Tomato Sauce to a White Sauce or Blond Sauce for flavor and color. Either strained or unstrained sauce will keep covered and refrigerated for a week. Or they may be frozen for later use.

~ *Tomato (Portugaise) Sauce*

¼ cup butter or margarine
½ cup finely chopped onion
1 clove garlic, crushed
2 tablespoons flour
1 16-ounce can tomatoes
1⅓ cups water
1 8-ounce can tomato sauce
¼ cup dry white wine (optional)
1 beef bouillon cube
1½ teaspoons sugar
½ teaspoon dried oregano leaves
½ teaspoon salt
Few grains pepper
¼ cup chopped fresh parsley

Melt butter in saucepan over moderately low heat (about 225° F.); add onion and garlic and cook until tender and soft. Blend in flour; cook for about 5 minutes, stirring constantly, until lightly browned. Add tomatoes, water, tomato sauce, wine, bouillon cube, sugar, oregano, salt, and pepper; cover and cook over low heat (about 200° F.) for 20 minutes, stirring occasionally. Stir in parsley. Use in meat and poultry dishes. Makes about 2½ cups.

Note: If smooth sauce is desired, press the hot sauce through a fine sieve. Be sure to press out all the juices from the vegetables.

Hollandaise Sauce

This is one of the most popular sauces, and probably the most feared by inexperienced cooks. It isn't hard to make; it is simply warm egg yolks flavored with lemon juice into which butter is gradually beaten. The proper result is a rich, creamy, yellow sauce with a light velvety texture.

There are many recipes for Hollandaise; they differ in the proportion of butter used to that of egg yolks and in the amount of water (if any) used in making the sauce. But these rules apply to any handmade Hollandaise Sauce. (1) The egg yolks must be warmed over hot (not boiling) water or over *very* low heat. (The water method is safer.) (2) The butter must be added slowly enough that the eggs have a chance to absorb it or hold it in suspension. Once sauce has started to thicken, the butter may be added a little faster. (3) The butter must not exceed the amount the yolks can absorb, roughly three-quarters of a stick of butter per large egg yolk. A small wire whip and a double boiler (you can improvise by putting a bowl over a small saucepan) are desirable equipment for making Hollandaise. Though Hollandaise is a cooked sauce, it is never really hot. It is served tepid, or warm, over hot vegetables or other hot foods.

Leftover Hollandaise may be kept refrigerated two to three days. It can be reheated by putting a tablespoon of sauce in a pan over hot water. Whip it well; then add sauce by the tablespoonful, beating well with each addition.

⮒ Classic Hollandaise Sauce

3 egg yolks
1 tablespoon cold water
*1 cup (2 sticks) sweet butter
4 teaspoons lemon juice
½ teaspoon salt
Few grains cayenne pepper

Place egg yolks and water in the top of a double boiler and beat well with a wire whip or fork. Put all but 2 tablespoons of the butter in a small saucepan over moderately low heat (about 225° F.) until just melted. Add 1 tablespoon of the cold butter to the egg and water mixture and place over hot, not boiling, water. Whip constantly until egg yolks thicken slightly. Remove from heat and whip in the second tablespoon of cold butter. Gradually pour the melted butter into the egg mixture, beating constantly. Place over hot, not boiling, water (water below should not touch bottom of pan) and cook until thickened, whipping constantly. Thickened Hollandaise should hold the imprint when a fork or whip is drawn across the surface. Remove from heat and stir in lemon juice, salt, and cayenne. Sauce may be placed in top of double boiler over hot, not boiling, water, covered, and kept until serving time. Serve with vegetables, baked or broiled fish, and shellfish. Makes about 1½ cups.

*Note: If you use salted butter, omit the salt in the recipe. However, this is a better sauce when made with sweet butter.

⮒ Less-Rich Hollandaise Sauce

4 egg yolks
½ cup butter or margarine
½ cup boiling water
2 tablespoons lemon juice
½ teaspoon salt
Few grains cayenne pepper

Place egg yolks in top of double boiler and beat slightly with wire whip or fork. Heat butter in saucepan over low heat (about 200° F.) until just melted. Gradually add butter to egg yolks, mixing with whip until blended. Gradually stir in water. Place over hot, not boiling, water (water below should not touch bottom of pan) and cook until thickened, stirring constantly. Remove from heat and stir in lemon juice, salt, and cayenne. Sauce may be placed in top of double boiler over hot water, covered, and kept until serving time. Serve with vegetables, baked or broiled fish, and shellfish. Makes about 1⅓ cups.

Blender Hollandaise Sauce

½ cup butter or margarine
3 egg yolks
2 tablespoons lemon juice
⅛ teaspoon salt
Few grains cayenne pepper

Place butter in a small saucepan or a 1-cup measuring cup over moderately low heat (about 225° F.) until bubbling hot. Put egg yolks, lemon juice, salt, and cayenne pepper in blender; cover, and switch on and off to blend. With motor at high speed, gradually add hot butter in a steady stream until all butter is added. Turn off at once. Serve immediately or place Hollandaise in saucepan over hot water to keep warm. Makes a generous ½ cup. (Allow about 2 tablespoons per serving.)

Classic Béarnaise Sauce

¼ cup wine vinegar
¼ cup dry white wine
1 tablespoon minced shallots or scallions
1 tablespoon minced fresh tarragon or ½ tablespoon crumbled dried tarragon
½ teaspoon salt
⅛ teaspoon pepper
⅔ cup sweet butter
3 egg yolks
2 tablespoons cold sweet butter

Combine vinegar, wine, shallots, tarragon, salt, and pepper in a small saucepan. Cook over moderate heat (about 250° F.) until the liquid is reduced to 2 tablespoons. Set aside to cool. Melt the ⅔ cup butter in a small saucepan over moderate heat (about 250° F.). Place the egg yolks in the top of a double boiler and beat with a fork or wire whip until well blended. Set over hot, not boiling, water and add 1 tablespoon of the cold butter and cook, beating constantly until egg yolks are slightly thickened. Remove from hot water and whip in the second tablespoon of cold butter. Gradually add the melted butter to the egg yolk mixture, beating constantly. Put back over hot water and cook, beating frequently until sauce is thickened. (Thickened Béarnaise will hold an imprint when a fork or whip is drawn across the surface.) Remove from heat and stir the cooled, seasoned wine and vinegar with the herbs into the sauce. Serve with baked, broiled, or poached fish, broiled steaks, or eggs. Makes about 1¼ cups.

Less-Rich Béarnaise Sauce

½ cup tarragon vinegar
⅓ cup dry white wine
1 tablespoon finely chopped onion
½ teaspoon crushed dried tarragon leaves
4 egg yolks
½ cup butter or margarine
Pinch salt

Place vinegar, wine, onion, and tarragon in a small saucepan over moderately low heat (about 225° F.); bring to boil and cook 6 to 8 minutes, or until reduced to ½ cup. Strain and reserve liquid. Place egg yolks in top of double boiler and beat slightly with wire whip or fork. Melt butter in saucepan over low heat (about 200° F.) until just melted. Gradually add butter to egg yolks, mixing until blended. Gradually stir in wine mixture. Place over hot, not boiling, water (water below should

Few grains cayenne pepper

not touch bottom of pan) and cook until thickened, stirring constantly. Remove from heat and season with salt and cayenne. Serve with baked, broiled, or poached fish, broiled beef, or eggs. Makes about 1¼ cups.

Butter Sauces

These butter sauces are simple ones, easy to make, yet they can particularly enhance the flavor of vegetables and fish.

⋖§ Clarified Butter

Place ½ *cup butter (1 stick)* in top of a double boiler over hot water. When butter is melted, pour off clear layer and discard milky sediment left. Makes about 5 tablespoons. Serve as a sauce for lobster and use in recipes calling for clarified butter.

⋖§ Herb Butter Sauce

½ **cup butter (1 stick), at room temperature**
1 **tablespoon flour**
2 **tablespoons milk**
⅛ **teaspoon salt**
Few grains pepper
Few grains cayenne pepper
1 **teaspoon minced fresh parsley**
1 **teaspoon snipped chives**
¼ **teaspoon ground dillseed**

Blend butter and flour together in top of double boiler. Stir in milk, salt, pepper, and cayenne; cook over boiling water until smooth. Add parsley, chives, and dill; mix well. Serve on vegetables or broiled fish. Makes about ½ cup sauce.

⋖§ Black Butter Sauce

¼ **cup butter (½ stick)**
1 **teaspoon lemon juice**
Chopped fresh parsley

Heat butter in a small saucepan over moderately low heat (about 225° F.) until dark brown. Stir in lemon juice. Use on vegetables, fish, or brains. First sprinkle

Capers

food with parsley and capers and then pour on Black Butter Sauce. Makes ¼ cup.

✍ *Maître d'Hôtel Butter*

¼ cup butter (½ stick), at
  room temperature
1 teaspoon chopped fresh
  parsley
¼ teaspoon salt
⅛ teaspoon pepper
2 teaspoons lemon juice

Beat butter with a fork until creamy. Add parsley, salt, and pepper and mix until blended. Blend in lemon juice. Chill. Serve cold on broiled steaks, fish, and chops. Makes ¼ cup.

Basting, or Barbecue, Sauces

A whole body of sauces, to prepare both indoors and out, has grown up around the American love of barbecued foods. The following assortment provides a variety of flavors.

✍ *Basting Sauce de Luxe*

¾ cup catsup
½ cup olive oil
½ cup red wine vinegar
1 tablespoon tarragon
  vinegar
½ cup water
1 tablespoon Worcestershire
  sauce
1 small onion, chopped
2 teaspoons brown sugar
¼ teaspoon celery salt
¼ teaspoon garlic salt
½ teaspoon salt
¼ teaspoon mustard seed

Combine catsup, olive oil, vinegars, water, and Worcestershire sauce in heavy saucepan. Place over moderately low heat (about 225° F.). Add onion. Blend remaining ingredients and add to the liquid. Stir vigorously until well blended. Simmer gently 25 minutes. Stir occasionally to prevent sticking. This sauce is suitable for basting almost any barbecued meat. It may be covered and stored in the refrigerator. Makes about 1½ cups.

(Ingredients continued on page 492)

SAUCES

¼ teaspoon celery seed
¼ teaspoon ground cloves
1 teaspoon chili powder
1 teaspoon dried oregano
leaves
1 small bay leaf, crushed

✌ Marmalade Basting Sauce

1 tablespoon butter or
margarine
1 tablespoon flour
¾ cup dry white wine
1 tablespoon vinegar
1 chicken bouillon cube
¼ cup water
¼ teaspoon black pepper
½ cup orange marmalade
1 tablespoon soy sauce

Heat butter in small saucepan over moderate heat (about 250° F.) until frothy. Add flour and stir until lightly browned. Add wine, vinegar, bouillon cube, water, and pepper. Blend thoroughly. Cover and simmer over moderately low heat (about 225° F.) 8 to 10 minutes. Add marmalade and soy sauce. Cover and simmer 5 minutes longer. Use to baste pork or poultry while barbecuing. Makes about 1 cup.

✌ Lemon Basting Sauce

½ cup butter or margarine
½ clove garlic, finely
chopped
2 teaspoons flour
1½ teaspoons sugar
1 teaspoon salt
⅛ teaspoon pepper
⅛ teaspoon poultry
seasoning
⅓ cup water
3 tablespoons lemon juice
⅛ teaspoon Tabasco

Melt butter in small saucepan over moderate heat (about 250° F.). Cook garlic in butter a few minutes. Stir in flour and remove from heat. Add the remaining ingredients. Cook until slightly thickened, stirring constantly. Cool and refrigerate until ready to use. Use to baste chicken or fish while barbecuing. Makes about 1 cup.

✌ Basting Sauce Diable

¼ cup chopped green onions
or scallions

Cook onions in butter over moderately low heat (about 225° F.) until tender. Remove from heat. Blend in water,

2 tablespoons butter or
margarine
½ cup water
1 beef bouillon cube
½ cup dry white wine
2 tablespoons Worcestershire
sauce
¼ teaspoon crushed dried
tarragon leaves
1 teaspoon dry mustard
½ teaspoon cracked black
pepper
2 tablespoons chopped fresh
parsley
1 tablespoon lemon juice

bouillon cube, wine, Worcestershire sauce, tarragon, mustard, and pepper. Simmer about 10 minutes, stirring occasionally. Add parsley. Add lemon juice just before using. Use to baste steak, short ribs, veal chops, or lamp chops while barbecuing. Makes about ½ cup.

ꙮ Pungent Barbecue Sauce

1 29-ounce can solid-pack
tomatoes
½ cup all-purpose flour
⅓ cup coarsely chopped,
peeled onion
1 clove garlic, peeled
¼ cup firmly packed dark
brown sugar
2 teaspoons salt
1 tablespoon dry mustard
1 tablespoon paprika
3 tablespoons vegetable oil
⅛ to ¼ teaspoon
cayenne pepper
1 cup lemon juice
¾ cup cider vinegar
½ cup water

Place tomatoes, flour, onion, garlic, sugar, salt, mustard, paprika, oil and cayenne in the container of an electric blender; cover and blend at high speed 10 seconds or until smooth. Pour into a large saucepan. Stir in lemon juice, cider vinegar and water; bring to a boil, stirring occasionally. Cook, uncovered, over moderately low heat (about 225° F.) 5 to 10 minutes, until sauce is thickened and smooth. Use as a sauce for barbecuing meats, poultry or fish. Sauce will keep for several weeks in a covered container in the refrigerator. To reheat, place in a small saucepan over low heat (about 200° F.) and stir until heated. Makes 6 cups.

ꙮ Jiffy Basting Sauce

2 8-ounce cans tomato sauce
1 package onion salad-

Combine all ingredients in a small saucepan. Simmer gently over moderately low heat (about 225° F.) for 3

SAUCES

dressing mix

1 *teaspoon prepared mustard*

¼ *cup vinegar*

2 *tablespoons vegetable oil*

⅓ *cup light molasses*

minutes, stirring occasionally. Use to baste spareribs, beef, or lamb while barbecuing. Makes about 2 cups.

CHAPTER XV

VEGETABLES

All too often vegetables are not the choice for "seconds" at a meal, and every mother knows by heart the admonition, "Eat your vegetables." Indifference to vegetables can usually be overcome by making them taste good rather than by urging that they be eaten because they're good for you. Vegetables are not only a nutritional necessity—primarily for Vitamins A and C and for valuable minerals—but should appeal to a weight-conscious America because most boiled vegetables contain less than fifty calories per half cup. Even the starchy ones, such as peas, corn, lima beans, and plain boiled potatoes, yield between fifty and one hundred calories per half cup. Raw vegetables for snacks are a boon to anyone watching his weight and make excellent between-meal snacks for children.

The primary way to ensure the flavor of vegetables is to be sure they are not overcooked. Vegetables lose color and flavor as well as nutrients when cooked too long or cooked too far ahead and allowed to stand before serving. The idea is to preserve the original flavor of the fresh vegetable as much as possible, then add herbs, seasonings, and sauces that enhance that flavor rather than mask it.

A second reason for vegetable doldrums is that people get tired of sameness. Branch out and try some different varieties rather than relying on a half-dozen staples.

Buying fresh vegetables: Shop for fresh vegetables in a market that keeps them in a cold case or in a market that has a rapid turnover. Fresh vegetables are generally lowest in price and highest in quality when they are in season, especially if they are grown in your locality. (See the Fresh

VEGETABLES

Vegetables chart on page 40.) You can usually spot specials on vegetables through your local newspaper or radio station. Beware of marked-down vegetables that are dirty or wilted. There is no economy in buying old vegetables that may have an excessive amount of waste. New methods of cleaning and quickly cooling fresh vegetables after picking and the well-iced shipping conditions that are being used today bring a far greater variety of high-quality fresh vegetables into local markets.

Buying frozen vegetables: If you think vegetables can't present variety in preparation, take a look at the number of preseasoned vegetables that are being marketed in the frozen-food cases. You should buy frozen vegetables only from a dealer who has a properly cold cabinet made for the purpose of holding foods at 0° F. or colder. Never take home a package of frozen food that feels soft or has been damaged. Plan to pick up frozen food last when you shop, and carry along an insulated bag if the trip home will be long. Transfer frozen vegetables into your freezer or freezer compartment as soon as you get home. Don't overlook the large bags of frozen vegetables. You can use what you need and return the rest to the freezer.

Buying canned vegetables: Canned vegetables can readily be selected by their labels; the label will tell you, for example, the form of the vegetable—whether it is whole, sliced, or diced. It will give you the net contents in weight and may also give you the grade, the size and maturity of the vegetable, seasonings, the number of servings and, frequently, recipe ideas. When vegetables are graded, choose the grade according to the way you intend to use the vegetable:

U.S. Grade A, or Fancy: Grade A vegetables are carefully selected for color, tenderness, and freedom from blemishes. They are the most tender, succulent, and flavorful vegetables produced.

U.S. Grade B, or Extra Standard: Grade B vegetables are of excellent quality but are slightly inferior to Grade A in color and tenderness. They are usually slightly more mature and therefore have a slightly different taste from the more succulent vegetables in Grade A.

U.S. Grade C, or Standard: Grade C vegetables are not so uniform in color and flavor as vegetables in the higher grades, and they are usually more mature. They are a thrifty buy when appearance is not too important—for instance, if you're using the vegetables as an ingredient in soup or a casserole.

Storing fresh vegetables: Even under the best storage conditions most fresh vegetables retain top quality only a few days. All fresh vegetables, except potatoes, onions, and yellow turnips, should be refrigerated as soon as possible in plastic bags or in the vegetable crisper of your refrigerator. If you wash vegetables before storing them, shake or wipe dry before refrigeration. Leave the naturally protected vegetables, such as peas in pods and corn in husks, as they are until you're ready to use them. This prevents loss of moisture. Potatoes, onions, and yellow turnips should be stored in a cool, dry place where there is ample air circulation.

Storing frozen vegetables: Keep all frozen vegetables solidly frozen until you cook them. The one exception to this rule is corn on the cob, which should be defrosted about 1½ hours at room temperature before cooking.

Storing canned vegetables: Store unopened canned vegetables on any shelf that is not too warm or moist. Canned vegetables to be used for salads should be chilled before opening. Canned foods that have been opened may be stored in the refrigerator in the can, covered.

Storing dehydrated vegetables: Store dried foods, such as peas, beans, and lentils, in a tightly covered container in a cool, dry place. Dehydrated potatoes are usually used soon enough that they may be stored in their original container. If you plan to keep them for any length of time after opening the package, they should be transferred to a tightly closed jar.

Storing leftover vegetables: Store, covered, in the refrigerator and plan to use in a day or two.

Cooking fresh vegetables: Vegetables are quick and easy to cook but they do require love, respect and careful attention during their few minutes of cooking time. Vegetables—fresh, canned and frozen—are a rich source of certain vitamins and minerals. Preserve them by following these 6 basic rules: (1) Peel and cut up vegetables close to cooking time. If you cut them up sooner, cover and refrigerate. (2) Wash vegetables quickly, preferably shortly before cooking. Do not soak cut vegetables in water. (3) Cook vegetables (except when stir-frying) in a covered pot, preferably not glass. Use as little water as necessary. (4) Certain nutrients are just under the skin of vegetables. Cook appropriate vegetables such as potatoes, in their skins and peel after cooking. (5) Do not add baking soda to vegetables to improve color; it destroys some of the nutrients. (6) Cook vegetables for the shortest time necessary. Learn to taste-test vegetables. Cook most vegetables until they are just tender but still crisp and slightly crunchy. Beets, sweet potatoes and white potatoes, turnips and rutabagas taste best when cooked until soft.

To steam: Steaming vegetables brings out their subtle flavors and keeps nutrient loss to a minimum. Buy a steamer basket, the kind with a rigid base, three short legs and flexible sides so the basket can be used in pots of different dimensions. If you don't have one, you can improvise by placing a colander in a pot that fits it. Cover the pot with a tight-fitting lid. To steam vegetables, wash or scrub them, peel if desired, slice or leave whole. Bring about 1 inch of water to a boil in a pot—just enough to almost touch the base of the steamer. Put the steamer basket in the pot. Add the vegetables. Cover the pot and let water boil over moderately high heat so vegetables cook in steam. Pieces of vegetable 1 inch thick will take about 10 minutes; whole potatoes or beets, 25 to 40 minutes, depending on size. (When cooking time is long, check water level; add more if needed.) Test small pieces of vegetable for doneness by tasting; pierce whole roots with a small knife.

To skillet steam: You'll need a heavy skillet with a tight-fitting lid. Wash vegetables. Peel if necessary. Leave whole or cut into uniform pieces. Bring about ½ inch of water to a boil in a skillet; add vegetables; stir for a few seconds so they heat evenly; then cover and cook over high heat until steam builds up under the lid. Lower heat to moderate and cook vegetables until tender. Carrot slices and leafy greens will take from 5 to 8 minutes; large cubes of beets or sweet potatoes, 10 to 20 minutes. Check once or twice during cooking to make sure water has not evaporated.

To stir-fry: This method is especially suited to tender vegetables like zucchini, but almost any vegetable can be stir-fried if sliced thin enough, if the pan is very hot and if the vegetables are not too crowded. Wash the vegetables and peel if necessary; cut into uniform pieces, ¼- to ½-inch thick. Heat 1 to 2 tablespoons of oil per pound of vegetables in a large heavy skillet or wok. If desired add a little minced garlic or ginger root to the hot oil, and about 10 seconds later stir in the vegetables. Continue cooking, stirring constantly, until vegetables are crisp-tender, about 4 to 6 minutes.

To broil: When broiling vegetables such as tomatoes, onions, and potato slices, season them and dot them with a little butter or brush them with vegetable oil. Broil four to five inches from source of heat until tender. This is also a good method for reheating leftover vegetables.

To boil: Use water sparingly. Except for some root vegetables, ½ to 1 cup of water is generally enough to cook six servings of tender, fresh vegetables. Spinach and other greens need only the water that clings to leaves; watery vegetables, such as zucchini and tomatoes, need less water. You will need a saucepan with a tight-fitting cover for all vegetables.

To pressure-cook: Follow the directions given by the manufacturer and watch the time carefully so vegetables will not be overcooked. A minute makes a big difference in a pressure cooker.

To pan or braise: Put vegetables in a skillet with a little fat and a small amount of water and salt. Cover tightly and cook until vegetable is just tender. You may add a dissolved bouillon cube for flavor; reduce salt is you do. Slice or julienne carrots, summer squash, or zucchini; shred cabbage for this method of cooking. Celery hearts, young green beans, asparagus, and Belgian endive may be cooked whole by this method.

To bake: When baking vegetables other than potatoes, arrange them in a casserole or baking pan, season as desired, and add just enough water to cover the bottom of the container.

To pan-fry: Heat 2 to 3 tablespoons of butter or margarine in a heavy skillet over medium heat. Fry cooked diced potatoes or sweet potatoes or carrots until golden. Tomatoes, eggplant, summer squash, and zucchini may be fried raw. Dip slices in seasoned flour and cook until tender and browned.

To French fry: Many fresh vegetables may be French fried. Potatoes, of course, are a favorite, but eggplant sticks, onion rings, parsnip sticks, for example, are all good French fried. French frying is a method of cooking food in enough hot (about 375° F. for vegetables) melted shortening to cover the food being fried. Most of the vegetables, except potatoes, will fry best if they are first dipped in a batter (use batter recipe for French Fried Onion Rings on page 528).

Cooking frozen vegetables: It's usually best to follow package directions for preparing frozen vegetables, although they may be baked in a tightly covered casserole with a tablespoon of butter or margarine added to them. At a 350° F. temperature, most frozen vegetables will need forty-five to sixty minutes to bake. This method is a good one to use if you have other food for the meal in a hot oven.

Cooking canned vegetables: If vegetables have thin liquid with them, pour it off into a saucepan and cook it down with a little butter and seasonings or herbs if you like. Let it boil until it's reduced to about half the original quantity; heat the vegetable in this concentrated broth.

Cooking dehydrated vegetables: Prepare dehydrated potatoes as directed on the package. Follow label directions for dried peas, beans, and lentils. Some of these products no longer need overnight soaking before cooking.

Artichokes

The most common type of artichoke is the globe, or French, artichoke. When shopping for artichokes, look for plump artichokes that have green, fresh-looking scales (or leaves). They should feel heavy for their size and the bud (which the artichoke is) should be tightly closed. Avoid artichokes that have large areas of brown and spreading scales. They are old and will be dry and tough. Size does not affect quality.

Before cooking, wash artichokes well. Cut off stems at base and remove small bottom leaves and any bruised leaves. Cut off about one inch from tops of artichokes and, if desired, trim off the sharp tips of the leaves. Stand artichokes upright in a deep saucepan of a size that will hold them snugly in place. Add ¼ teaspoon salt for each artichoke and pour in two to three inches of boiling water. Cover and boil gently over moderately low heat thirty to forty-five minutes, depending on size of artichoke, or until base can be pierced easily with a fork and a leaf can be pulled easily from the stem. If necessary, add more boiling water. Remove artichokes from pan and turn upside down on a tray to drain. If artichokes are to be stuffed, gently spread leaves apart and remove choke (thistle portion) from center of artichoke with a teaspoon.

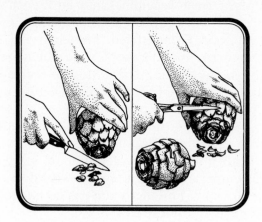

To eat artichokes, remove each leaf individually from outside of artichoke; pull it between your teeth to get only the tender pulp at the base, and discard the remainder. Leaves may be dipped in one of the sauces or dips given below. The choke, in the center, is a cluster of tiny, sharp, pointed leaves that should be discarded. Cut the remainder—the heart—into pieces and eat, dipping each piece into sauce if desired. Artichokes should be served on a separate plate since there is a great deal of waste that would clutter a dinner plate.

When artichokes are served hot, they are best dipped in a warm sauce that you can serve in individual demitasse cups or ramekins. Many people like Hollandaise Sauce (page 488) as an artichoke dip. This Savory Butter Sauce (recipe follows) is a particularly good dip.

Cold artichokes (or any leftovers) can be marinated or may be dipped in French dressing or mayonnaise to eat.

Jerusalem artichokes are not commonly available in all markets. They are shaped like fresh gingerroot. Look for firm tubers that are unblemished.

To cook Jerusalem artichokes, scrub well. Paring is not necessary, but if you prefer to pare them, use a floating blade parer and take off as little skin as possible. Slice or leave whole. Cook, covered, in a small amount of boiling, salted water about eight minutes for sliced artichokes and fifteen minutes for whole. The cooked flesh will look oyster gray. Serve dressed with lemon butter or a light Mornay Sauce (see page 482).

✌ Savory Butter Sauce

½ cup butter or margarine
2 tablespoons lemon juice
2 teaspoons dry mustard
¾ teaspoon salt
Few grains cayenne pepper

Melt butter in a small saucepan over moderately low heat (about 225° F.). Add lemon juice, mustard, salt, and cayenne pepper and blend well. Serve as a dip with hot artichokes. Makes ⅔ cup.

✌ Creamed Jerusalem Artichokes

2 pounds Jerusalem artichokes, washed, pared and diced
¾ teaspoon salt
3 cups water
1½ tablespoons butter or margarine
2 teaspoons finely chopped, peeled onion
1½ tablespoons flour
¼ to ½ teaspoon salt
⅛ teaspoon dry mustard
⅛ teaspoon dried parsley flakes
½ cup milk
½ cup light cream
¼ cup shredded sharp Cheddar cheese

In a heavy, medium-sized saucepan combine the diced Jerusalem artichokes, the ¾ teaspoon salt and the water. Place over moderate heat (about 250° F.). Cover and cook about 8 to 10 minutes until artichokes are fork-tender. Drain and set aside. Meanwhile in a saucepan melt butter over moderate heat (about 250° F.). Add onion and cook, stirring frequently, until lightly browned. Combine flour, salt, dry mustard and parsley flakes. Quickly stir the flour mixture into the onion and butter and blend smooth. Remove saucepan from heat and gradually stir in milk and cream, blending well after each addition. Return to heat and bring mixture to a boil; boil 1 minute, stirring constantly. Add cheese and cook, stirring occasionally, until cheese is melted. Add drained Jerusalem artichokes and heat to serving temperature. Serves 4 to 6.

✌ Swiss-Style Artichokes

2 9-ounce packages frozen artichoke hearts
1 chicken bouillon cube
½ cup hot water
2 tablespoons butter or margarine
2 tablespoons flour
½ cup milk
½ cup shredded Swiss cheese
1 tablespoon dry sherry
¼ teaspoon salt
Few grains pepper

Heat oven to 375° F. Cook artichokes according to directions on package; drain and arrange in a heatproof serving dish. Dissolve chicken bouillon cube in hot water. Melt butter in saucepan over moderate heat (about 250° F.) and blend in flour. Gradually add milk and chicken bouillon. Cook until thickened, stirring constantly. Remove from heat and add ¼ cup of the shredded cheese; stir until cheese is melted. Add sherry, salt, and pepper. Pour sauce over artichokes and sprinkle with the remaining shredded cheese. Bake 15 to 20 minutes, or until cheese is melted and lightly browned. Serves 6 to 8.

Asparagus

When shopping for asparagus, look for tightly closed tips, smooth stalks with green extending almost to the bottom of the stalk. Avoid open tips and stalks that have vertical ridges; these are signs of aging. Size does not influence tenderness.

To prepare asparagus for cooking, hold the stalk in both hands, bend with pressure on the base end. The stalk will snap just where the ends are tough. Discard the base. Remove the scales; this is where sand lodges. Scrub each stalk with a soft brush and pare thinly (paring is optional but it guarantees uniformly tender stalks). Stalks may be cooked whole or sliced diagonally in 1½-inch lengths.

To cook whole stalks, tie them together in serving-sized bundles. Stand them upright in a coffee pot or in the bottom of a double boiler. Add boiling water to cover lower third of stalks. Cover pot or invert top of double boiler over the lower part. Cook about ten minutes until bases of stalks are tender. Serve with lemon butter, Mornay Sauce (see page 482), Hollandaise Sauce (see page 488), or Cream Sauce (see page 481).

To braise or pan asparagus, cut it in diagonal slices. For each pound of asparagus put 2 tablespoons of butter and 2 tablespoons of water in a large skillet. Add cut asparagus, cover tightly, and cook five to seven minutes until just tender. Serve with salt and pepper and a wedge of lemon, or dress with a light Cream Sauce (page 481).

Cold asparagus makes a delicious salad. Marinate the cooked or canned spears in French Dressing (see page 626) in the refrigerator for at least two hours. Serve on lettuce leaves. Or lay chilled, fresh-cooked, or canned unmarinated stalks on shredded lettuce and spoon mayonnaise over them. Garnish with a strip of pimiento.

Asparagus Polonaise

3 pounds fresh asparagus
½ cup butter or margarine
¼ cup soft bread crumbs
2 hard-cooked eggs, finely chopped
1 tablespoon finely chopped fresh parsley

Wash asparagus; snap off tough ends. Cook in a small amount of boiling salted water 10 to 15 minutes, until just tender. Drain. Melt butter in a saucepan over moderately low heat (about 225° F.). Add crumbs; cook and stir until they are golden. Remove from heat. Stir in chopped eggs and parsley. Put asparagus on a warm platter; pour on sauce. Serves 6.

Asparagus Vinaigrette

2 pounds fresh asparagus
3 tablespoons vegetable oil

Wash asparagus; snap off tough ends. Cook in a small amount boiling salted water 10 to 15 minutes, until just

¼ *cup chopped fresh parsley*
2 *tablespoons snipped chives*
3 *tablespoons vinegar*
1 *teaspoon salt*
⅛ *teaspoon pepper*

tender. Drain. Place vegetable oil, parsley, chives, vinegar, salt, and pepper in a bowl; beat with a rotary beater until blended. Serve over asparagus. Serves 4.

Note: If desired, refrigerate asparagus in the vinaigrette sauce. Serve cold as a salad. Serves 6 to 8 as a salad.

Beans, Green, Wax or Pole

Look for clean slender pods that are free of blemishes. Green beans should have a fresh, bright green color. Wax beans should be a pale yellow. Pole beans resemble green beans but are slightly longer and coarser in appearance.

To cook green or wax beans, wash thoroughly and snip off both ends with a sharp knife. Beans may be cooked whole, snapped, cut in one-inch pieces, or slivered lengthwise for French-style beans. Cook cut beans uncovered in a half inch of boiling salted water for five to ten minutes. They should be just tender-crisp, never limp. Cook whole beans in the same way for five minutes; cover to finish cooking, about twenty minutes in all. Serve with slivered almonds or pimiento strips or mushrooms tossed with the beans.

Cold green or pole or wax beans are excellent salad vegetables. Use them like cold asparagus (page 502).

✒ Savory Green Beans

2 *pounds fresh whole green beans*
⅓ *cup butter or margarine*
½ *teaspoon salt*
Few grains pepper
1 *teaspoon dried summer savory leaves*

Wash beans and remove ends. Cook beans in a small amount of lightly salted boiling water over moderately low heat (about 225° F.) until fork-tender, about 20 to 25 minutes. (Cover for last 15 minutes of cooking.) Drain thoroughly. Melt butter in a saucepan over moderately low heat (about 225° F.). Add salt, pepper, and summer savory and stir. Pour butter mixture over drained beans and toss lightly to combine. Serves 8.

✒ Green Beans with Fried Onions and Thyme

3 *tablespoons vegetable oil*
1 *cup thinly sliced, peeled onion*

Heat oil in a medium-sized skillet over moderately high heat (about 300° F.); add onion and cook until lightly browned, stirring occasionally. Stir in remaining ingre-

1 *pound fresh whole green
   beans, trimmed and cut in
   1-inch pieces (about 4½
   cups)*
¼ *teaspoon dried thyme
   leaves*
½ *teaspoon salt*
⅛ *teaspoon pepper*
2 *tablespoons water*

dients, reduce heat to moderate (about 250° F.), cover skillet and cook 10 minutes; shake skillet occasionally to prevent vegetables from sticking. Uncover skillet, increase heat to moderately high (about 275° F.) and cook beans 3 to 5 minutes longer, until crisp-tender. Makes about 3 cups, or serves 4.

ᕍᶳ Green Bean Casserole

1 *can condensed cream of
   mushroom soup*
1 *teaspoon soy sauce*
2 *10-ounce packages frozen
   French-style green beans,
   cooked and drained*
1 *3½-ounce can French fried
   onions*
Few grains pepper

Heat oven to 350° F. In a deep 1½-quart casserole, mix the soup and soy sauce together until smooth. Add green beans, half the onions, and the pepper, mixing well. Bake uncovered 20 minutes. Sprinkle the remaining onions over beans and bake about 5 minutes longer, until onions are crisp. Serves 4 to 6.

ᕍᶳ Pole Beans Amandine

1 *pound green pole beans*
1 *teaspoon salt*
Water
¼ *cup butter or margarine*
2 *tablespoons coarsely
   chopped, peeled onion*
⅓ *cup thinly sliced celery*
2 *tablespoons slivered,
   blanched almonds*

Remove and discard ends from beans. Cut beans into 1-inch pieces. In a large saucepan combine beans, salt and enough water to barely cover beans. Place over moderate heat (about 250° F.). Cover and simmer about 15 minutes, until beans are fork-tender. Drain. Meanwhile in a small saucepan melt butter over moderate heat (about 250° F.). Add onion, celery and almonds. Cook, stirring frequently, until almonds are lightly browned. Toss drained beans with almond-butter mixture. Serves 4.

Lima Beans

Look for broad, thick green pods that are well-filled with large seeds. Avoid limp, pliable, yellowed pods; they are a sign of age.

To cook lima beans, it may be necessary to cut the thin outer edge of the shell with scissors. Snap open the pods and remove the beans. Rinse shelled beans quickly in cold water. Cook, covered, in one inch of boiling, salted water for twenty to twenty-five minutes. Drain and serve with butter. Lima beans are delicious sprinkled with a little garlic salt or onion salt.

✑ Spanish Lima Beans

1 tablespoon butter or margarine
1 tablespoon finely chopped onion
⅓ cup finely chopped green pepper
1 cup peeled, chopped tomatoes
1½ cups cooked fresh lima beans
Salt and pepper
Toasted bread cubes

Melt butter in a saucepan over moderate heat (about 250° F.). Add onion and green pepper; cook until lightly browned. Add tomatoes and cook over moderately low heat (about 225° F.) 15 minutes. Add lima beans; season with salt and pepper. Heat. Top with bread cubes. Serves 4.

✑ Lima Beans with Dill

3 10-ounce packages frozen lima beans
¼ cup butter or margarine
2 teaspoons ground dillseed
½ teaspoon salt

Cook lima beans according to package directions. While beans are cooking, melt butter over low heat (about 200° F.); add ground dillseed and salt. Pour seasoned butter over the well-drained lima beans and toss to mix. Serves 8.

✑ Continental Lima Beans

3 tablespoons butter or margarine
½ cup chopped onion
½ cup chopped green pepper
1 clove garlic, finely chopped
2 10-ounce packages frozen Fordhook lima beans, cooked and drained
1 10½-ounce can tomato purée

(Ingredients continued on page 506)

Heat oven to 350° F. Melt the 3 tablespoons butter in a saucepan over moderately low heat (about 225° F.). Add onion, green pepper, and garlic; cook until tender. Add lima beans, tomato purée, Worcestershire, salt, and pepper. Combine 2 tablespoons of the Parmesan cheese with the 1 tablespoon melted butter and the bread crumbs and set aside for topping. In a greased deep 1-quart casserole make layers of the bean mixture and the remaining 4 tablespoons Parmesan cheese. Sprinkle the seasoned bread crumbs over the top. Bake uncovered about 20 minutes, until mixture is hot and top is browned. Serves 6.

½ teaspoon Worcestershire
    sauce
½ teaspoon salt
Few grains pepper
 6 tablespoons grated
    Parmesan cheese
 1 tablespoon melted butter or
    margarine
⅓ cup soft bread crumbs

Beets

Look for young, small beets with smooth skin and fresh green tops. Larger beets are fine if they have smooth skins, a firm root, and green tops.

To cook beets, cut off tops two inches above crown. If beet greens (the leaves) are young and fresh, cook them as you would cook any fresh greens (see page 522). Leave the root end on the beets; scrub the beets with a soft brush. Cook whole in boiling, salted water to cover. Cover saucepan to speed up cooking. Small beets will take from thirty to fifty minutes to cook; larger ones may take up to two hours. Cook just until tender. Drain. Pour cold water over beets. As soon as you can handle them, slip off the skin and root with your fingers. Beets may be served whole, diced, or sliced, or as in the recipes that follow.

◆ᔈ Shredded Beets

1 bunch beets (about 1
   pound)
¼ cup butter or margarine
½ teaspoon salt
⅛ teaspoon pepper
2 tablespoons finely chopped
   fresh parsley
1 tablespoon lemon juice

Wash and peel beets; shred on a fine grater. Melt butter in a heavy skillet over moderate heat (about 250° F.). Add beets, salt, and pepper. Cover and cook about 15 minutes until beets are just tender, stirring occasionally. Before serving sprinkle with parsley and lemon juice. Serves 2 to 3.

◆ᔈ Harvard Beets

2 bunches beets (about 2
   pounds)

Prepare and cook beets as in directions above. Drain and reserve ¼ cup of the liquid. Slip off skins. Cut into thin,

⅓ cup sugar
2 teaspoons cornstarch
¼ cup beet liquid
¼ cup vinegar
1 tablespoon butter or
margarine

crosswise slices. Mix sugar and cornstarch in a saucepan; stir in reserved beet liquid and vinegar. Cook over moderately low heat (about 225° F.) until thickened, stirring constantly. Add beets and butter and heat thoroughly. Serves 4.

⮑ Baked Beets

2 bunches young beets (about
2 pounds), peeled and
thinly sliced
½ teaspoon grated orange
peel
1 cup orange juice
½ teaspoon prepared
horseradish
1 tablespoon sugar
1 teaspoon salt
2 tablespoons butter or
margarine

Heat oven to 425° F. Place beets in a deep 1-quart casserole. Mix orange peel, juice, horseradish, sugar, and salt; pour over beets. Dot with butter. Cover and bake 70 to 75 minutes, or until tender. Serves 4.

Broccoli

Look for broccoli that has a firm, compact cluster of flower buds with none opened enough to show the yellow flower. Bud clusters should be dark green or green with a purple cast.

To cook broccoli, cut off large leaves and tough base if any. Wash broccoli and cut large stalks into uniform pieces. Lay stalks in a large skillet in one inch of boiling, salted water. Cover, leaving lid ajar and cook until just fork-tender, ten to fifteen minutes. Drain and serve hot with Jiffy Hollandaise Sauce (recipe follows) or Black Butter Sauce (recipe on page 490).

⮑ Jiffy Hollandaise Sauce

1 cup mayonnaise or salad
dressing
¼ cup heavy cream, whipped
½ tablespoon snipped chives

Heat mayonnaise in a double boiler over simmering water, stirring constantly. Remove from heat; fold in whipped cream and chives. Stir until well blended. Serve hot over broccoli. Makes about 1½ cups sauce, enough for 4 to 6 servings.

Broccoli with Lemon Sauce

½ cup vegetable oil
½ cup lemon juice
½ teaspoon paprika
1 tablespoon instant minced
  onion
¾ teaspoon sugar
½ teaspoon salt
2 bunches fresh broccoli
  (about 2 pounds each)
2 hard-cooked eggs, finely
  chopped

Place vegetable oil, lemon juice, paprika, onion, sugar, and salt in a jar with a tight lid; cover and shake until blended. Let stand about 1 hour. Cook broccoli as directed on page 507. Drain broccoli and arrange on a large platter. Pour lemon sauce over broccoli and garnish with chopped egg. Serves 8.

Broccoli Timbales

1 10-ounce package frozen
  chopped broccoli
2 tablespoons butter or
  margarine
2 tablespoons flour
¾ cup milk
1 egg, slightly beaten
½ teaspoon salt
¼ teaspoon dried instant
  minced onion

Cook broccoli according to package directions. Drain thoroughly and chop finely. Press between paper towels to remove any excess moisture. Melt butter in saucepan over moderate heat (about 250° F.); blend in flour. Gradually add milk and cook, stirring constantly, until thickened. Cool slightly. Gradually pour sauce into beaten egg. Add salt and onion. Fold in drained chopped broccoli. Pour into four 6-ounce custard cups. Place in a shallow baking pan and add 1 inch hot water to pan. Heat oven to 350° F. Bake 40 minutes, or until firm. Turn out of cups to serve. Serves 4.

Brussels Sprouts

Look for Brussels sprouts that have a fresh, bright green color and firm tight little buds. Avoid those with loose outer leaves and a yellowing color.

Before cooking Brussels sprouts, wash thoroughly; take a small slice off the stem end and cut a little **x** in the end so sprouts will cook more quickly. Cook uncovered in one inch of boiling salted water eight to twelve minutes until tender. They will be mushy if overcooked. Drain and serve with butter or margarine; you may toss a few slivered almonds with them. They may also be served with Sour Cream Sauce (recipe follows).

✒ Sour Cream Sauce

2 tablespoons butter or
  margarine
2 tablespoons flour
½ cup water
½ cup commercial sour cream
½ teaspoon prepared
  horseradish
¼ teaspoon salt
Few grains pepper

Melt butter in small saucepan over moderate heat (about 250° F.); add flour and stir over low heat until smooth. Add water, sour cream, horseradish, salt, and pepper; mix until well blended. Cook sauce over low heat (about 200° F.), stirring frequently, 3 to 5 minutes. Serve over hot Brussels sprouts. Makes about ¾ cup sauce, enough for 4 servings.

✒ Brussels Sprouts with Cheese

2 10-ounce packages frozen
  Brussels sprouts or about
  2 pounds fresh
1 cup soft bread crumbs
3 tablespoons melted butter
  or margarine
2 tablespoons grated
  Parmesan cheese

Cook Brussels sprouts according to package directions or cooking directions for fresh Brussels sprouts above. Toss together bread crumbs, butter, and Parmesan cheese. Serve over sprouts. Serves 6.

Cabbage

There are three types of cabbage generally available: The familiar smooth-leafed green cabbage, crinkly leafed savoy cabbage, and red cabbage. They may be used interchangeably.

Look for firm, hard heads that are heavy for their size. Outer leaves should be a good green or red color, not wilted or yellowed. New cabbage which has not been in storage may have tough outer (called wrapper) leaves that are usually discarded. Old cabbage, sold from storage, will not have the wrapper leaves on it. Outer leaves from these heads are quite usable.

To cook cabbage, wash and discard any wilted leaves. Cut into wedges or wide shreds; remove core. Cook, covered, in one inch of boiling salt water five minutes for shredded cabbage, eight to twelve minutes for wedges. Red cabbage needs slightly longer cooking: follow timing in the red cabbage recipe that follows. Cabbage is one of the vegetables most often overcooked—it is best cooked just to the crisp-tender stage. Cooked cabbage is good with just salt and pepper and butter, though many people like a sprinkling of vinegar or lemon also.

Steamed Buttered Cabbage

1 medium-sized head
   cabbage
3 tablespoons butter or
   margarine
1 teaspoon salt
⅛ teaspoon pepper
1 teaspoon dried basil leaves

Cut cabbage into quarters. Soak in cold water until leaves are crisp; drain. Melt butter in a heavy skillet over moderately low heat (about 225° F.). Add cabbage and remaining ingredients; cover tightly. Cook until cabbage is just tender, about 10 minutes. Serves 4.

Braised Cabbage

1½ pounds green cabbage,
   shredded (8 cups)
2 tablespoons butter or
   margarine
1 teaspoon salt
⅛ teaspoon pepper

Trim, rinse and finely shred the cabbage. In a heavy, 12-inch skillet or medium-sized saucepot melt the butter over moderately high heat (about 350° F.). Add the cabbage, salt and pepper and stir 2 to 3 minutes, until cabbage is hot and well coated with butter. Lower heat to moderate (about 250° F.); cover pan and cook cabbage 6 to 8 minutes, until crisp-tender. Makes 4 cups, or 4 or 5 servings. Good with pork chops or pot roast, corn bread and fried apple rings.

Savoy Cabbage

¼ cup butter or margarine
1 medium-sized savoy
   cabbage, trimmed and cut
   into ½-inch-wide strips
1 cup pared, cored and sliced
   green apple
½ cup coarsely chopped,
   unsweetened canned
   chestnuts or cooked,
   peeled chestnuts
1 teaspoon salt
½ teaspoon monosodium
   glutamate

In a large skillet melt butter over moderately high heat (about 350° F.). Add cabbage and cook, uncovered, stirring frequently, for 5 minutes. Stir in remaining ingredients and cook, stirring occasionally, 5 to 10 minutes longer or until cabbage is crisp-tender. Serves 4 to 6.

✃ Cabbage Amandine

1 tablespoon butter or
   margarine
¼ cup chopped blanched
   almonds
1½ cups milk
5 cups coarsely shredded
   cabbage
1 teaspoon salt
2 tablespoons butter or
   margarine
2 tablespoons flour

Melt butter in a skillet over moderately low heat (about 225° F.); add almonds and cook until lightly browned. Set aside. Heat milk in a large saucepan over moderately low heat (about 225° F.). Add cabbage and salt; cover and simmer 2 minutes. Add the 2 tablespoons butter; sprinkle flour over cabbage. Mix and simmer 3 minutes, stirring frequently. Stir in almonds. Serves 6.

✃ Hot Cabbage Slaw

4 cups finely shredded
   cabbage
1 tablespoon butter or
   margarine
1 teaspoon instant minced
   onion
2 tablespoons vinegar
¼ teaspoon dry mustard
½ teaspoon salt

Cook cabbage in a small amount of boiling water over moderate heat (about 250° F.) 5 to 10 minutes. Drain. Mix butter, onion, vinegar, mustard, and salt; heat. Stir into cabbage and serve hot. Serves 4.

✃ Red Cabbage with Wine

4 tablespoons butter or
   margarine
2 tablespoons brown sugar
1 teaspoon salt
Few grains pepper
½ cup vinegar
1 medium-sized head red
   cabbage, finely shredded
¼ cup dry red wine

Heat butter in a heavy saucepan over moderate heat (about 250° F.). Add sugar, salt, pepper, and vinegar. Bring mixture to a boil and add cabbage. Cover and cook over moderately low heat (about 225° F.) about 15 minutes, until tender but still crisp. Stir occasionally. Just before serving stir in wine. Serves 4.

Carrots

Look for firm, bright, clean carrots. If there are leaves (most carrots now come topped), they should be bright green. When you can, buy young fresh (baby) carrots; they're superbly sweet.

Scrub carrots before cooking. Don't scrape or pare them if they are young and tender. If you do pare them, take off only a thin layer. Carrots may be cooked whole, sliced, chunked, diced, cut in strips (julienne), or shredded. Cook them covered in one inch of boiling salted water to which you may add ½ teaspoon of sugar per pound of carrots. (It gives them a sweet, fresh flavor.) Shredded carrots will cook in four to five minutes; cut pieces will take ten to fifteen minutes; and whole carrots, twenty minutes. You can purée carrots after cooking and mold them into a pretty ring to fill with peas at serving time; puréed carrots may also be served in individual mounds brushed with dill butter.

✺ Orange-Glazed Carrots

2 bunches small carrots, peeled
Juice of 1 orange (about 6 tablespoons)
¼ teaspoon salt
6 tablespoons water
¼ cup butter or margarine
2 tablespoons sugar
2 teaspoons Cointreau
¼ cup flaked coconut

Cook carrots in orange juice, salt, and water over moderately low heat (about 225° F.) until just tender, about 15 to 20 minutes; drain. Melt butter in skillet over moderate heat (about 250° F.); add sugar and Cointreau. Add carrots and cook until glazed, turning frequently. Garnish with coconut before serving. Serves 6.

✺ Baked Shredded Carrots

2 tablespoons butter or margarine
¼ cup finely chopped onion or green onions
1 bunch carrots, peeled and shredded
½ cup water
1 teaspoon lemon juice
½ teaspoon ground ginger
1 tablespoon sugar
¾ teaspoon salt
2 tablespoons butter or margarine

Heat oven to 400° F. Melt the 2 tablespoons butter in skillet over moderate heat (about 250° F.); add onion and cook until tender. Mix onion and carrot together; pour into a deep 1-quart casserole. Mix the water, lemon juice, ginger, sugar, and salt; pour over carrots. Dot with the 2 tablespoons butter. Cover and bake 50 to 55 minutes or until tender. Serves 4.

✒ Carrot and Spinach Timbales with Nutmeg Sauce

1½ cups peeled, raw carrots, coarsely grated
1 10-ounce package frozen chopped spinach, cooked and drained
¼ cup butter or margarine
¼ cup flour
1½ cups milk
2 eggs, slightly beaten
½ teaspoon instant minced onion
1 teaspoon salt
Nutmeg Sauce (recipe follows)

Heat oven to 350° F. Cook carrots 5 minutes in a small amount of boiling water over moderate heat (about 250° F.); drain. Chop drained, cooked spinach finely. Melt butter in saucepan over moderate heat (about 250° F.); blend in flour. Gradually add milk; cook and stir until thickened. Cool slightly. Gradually pour sauce into beaten eggs. Add onion and salt. Fold in spinach and carrots. Pour into greased, 6-ounce custard cups. Place in large baking pan and add 1 inch hot water to pan. Bake 40 minutes, or until set. Turn out on serving dish and serve with Nutmeg Sauce. Serves 6.

Nutmeg Sauce

1 tablespoon butter or margarine
1 tablespoon flour
1 cup milk
1 egg yolk
Few grains ground nutmeg
¼ teaspoon salt
Few grains pepper

Melt butter in saucepan over moderate heat (about 250° F.). Blend in flour. Gradually add milk; cook until thickened, stirring constantly. Cool slightly. Beat egg yolk slightly and stir in a little of the hot sauce; pour back into saucepan and add nutmeg, salt, and pepper. Heat over low heat (about 200° F.), stirring constantly. Serve hot over timbales. Makes about 1 cup sauce.

Cauliflower

When shopping for cauliflower, look for creamy white flowerets and a crisp, firm, heavy head with green outer leaves.

To cook cauliflower, wash, remove outer stalk leaves, and take out as much of the core as you can if you plan to cook the head whole. (It's prettiest served that way.) For quicker cooking, you can separate flowerets by snapping them apart. These crisp, raw flowerets make an excellent fresh vegetable for dip plates. Cook cauliflower, covered, in one inch of boiling salted water. Flowerets will take eight to ten minutes; whole head (cook it core side down) will take twenty to thirty minutes. Serve cauliflower sprinkled with a mixture of grated Parmesan cheese and fine bread crumbs, with Mornay Sauce (see page 482), or in the ways suggested below.

VEGETABLES

✺ Steamed Cauliflower with Salsa Verde

1 medium-sized cauliflower
Water
½ teaspoon salt
½ cup olive oil
2 tablespoons lemon juice
¼ cup chopped, pitted, unstuffed green olives
1 teaspoon minced, peeled garlic
½ cup finely chopped fresh parsley
½ teaspoon salt
¼ teaspoon pepper

Wash cauliflower, remove outer leaves and separate into flowerets by snapping them apart. Place cauliflowerets in a steamer basket over boiling water, sprinkle with the ½ teaspoon salt and steam, covered, 10 to 15 minutes. Meanwhile, place remaining ingredients in the container of an electric blender and blend at high speed until smooth. Makes ⅔ cup sauce. Serve with cauliflower. Good with baked fish and hot French bread. Serves 4.

✺ Garden Cauliflower

1 cup julienned carrots (2-inch strips)
1 medium-sized cauliflower
¼ cup light cream
1 can condensed cream of mushroom soup
½ cup soft bread crumbs
1 tablespoon melted butter or margarine

Cook carrots in a small amount of boiling salted water over moderately low heat (about 225° F.) 5 minutes; drain. Wash cauliflower and break into flowerets. Place in small amount of boiling salted water. Cover and cook over moderately low heat (about 225° F.) until tender, 8 to 10 minutes; drain. Mix light cream and mushroom soup together in a saucepan; place over moderate heat (about 250° F.) and stir until smooth. Stir in carrots. Arrange cauliflower in heatproof serving dish and pour vegetable sauce over it. Toss together bread crumbs and butter; sprinkle over top. Heat oven to 350° F. Bake 20 to 25 minutes, or until crumbs are lightly browned. Serves 6.

Celery

Look for celery that has crisp stalks with fresh green leaves. Pascal celery will have green stalks also. Avoid limp, wilted stalks. You will find celery hearts, which are frequently a good buy because there is no waste, are often sold trimmed and packaged.

To cook celery, separate branches and scrub with a soft brush. Trim off root and any blemishes. If outer stalks are particularly stringy, shave off the strings with a floating-blade vegetable parer. Use hearts and center stalks for salads or relish trays. Slice outer stalks diagonally into one-inch pieces or cut into julienne strips. Cook, covered, in one inch of boiling salted water fifteen to twenty minutes.

✑ Braised Celery

6 tablespoons butter or margarine
6 cups sliced celery and celery tops
2 medium-sized green peppers, cut into strips
1 teaspoon salt
¼ teaspoon pepper
¼ teaspoon dried oregano leaves
2 tablespoons finely chopped onion
½ cup water
¼ cup heavy cream

Melt butter in a large, heavy skillet over moderate heat (about 250° F.). Add celery, green peppers, salt, pepper, oregano, onion, and water. Cover and cook 8 to 10 minutes, until celery is almost done but still crisp. Remove cover and cook about 4 minutes, until liquid is absorbed. Stir in cream. Heat but do not boil. Serves 6.

✑ Celery au Gratin

4 cups 1-inch slices celery
2 tablespoons butter or margarine
2 tablespoons flour
1½ cups milk
1 cup shredded Cheddar cheese
½ teaspoon salt
⅛ teaspoon paprika
Few grains cayenne pepper

Cook celery in a small amount of boiling salted water over moderate heat (about 250° F.) until tender, about 10 minutes. Drain celery. Melt butter in a saucepan over moderately low heat (about 225° F.). Blend in flour; cook until bubbly. Gradually stir in milk; cook, stirring constantly, until sauce is thickened and smooth. Remove from heat. Add cheese, salt, paprika, and cayenne. Stir until cheese is melted. Arrange celery in a buttered, shallow 1½-quart baking dish. Pour cheese sauce over celery. Heat oven to 350° F. Bake 35 to 40 minutes, or until sauce bubbles. Serves 6.

Celery Root or Celeriac

Celery root is a delicious root vegetable that is often overlooked; buy only firm, clean roots.

To cook celery root, wash and scrub to remove all traces of black dirt. Celery root is easiest to cook whole, like beets, in a covered pan with enough boiling, salted water to cover; it takes forty to sixty minutes to cook. Peel the cooked root and slice, dice, or purée it. Serve hot with butter or margarine, lemon juice, and salt and pepper—or heat the diced vegetable in seasoned cream.

Celery root is also delicious raw. Peel the root and cut it into thin strips for a relish tray or to use with a vegetable dip. Shredded and tossed with mayonnaise, it makes a delicious first course to serve on a leaf of lettuce.

✌ Celeriac Salad

1 pound celeriac, washed and drained
½ teaspoon salt
Water
1 tablespoon vinegar
1 teaspoon finely minced, peeled onion
⅛ teaspoon dried dillweed
⅛ teaspoon dried tarragon leaves
1 cup thinly sliced, unpared cucumber
¼ cup finely diced, washed red radishes
2 tablespoons coarsely chopped, seeded sweet red pepper
2 tablespoons mayonnaise
2 tablespoons commercial sour cream
Crisp lettuce leaves

Cut celeriac into ½-inch-thick slices. Pare slices with a sharp knife. Cut each slice into ½-inch cubes. Place in a medium-sized saucepan and sprinkle with ¼ teaspoon of the salt. Add enough water to measure 1 inch in bottom of pan. Place over moderate heat (about 250° F.). Cover and simmer 5 to 8 minutes or until celeriac is fork-tender. Drain well. Meanwhile mix together vinegar, the remaining ¼ teaspoon salt, onion, dillweed and tarragon. While the celeriac is still warm, toss with the vinegar mixture. Cover and chill. When ready to serve, mix the celeriac with the cucumber slices, radishes, red pepper, mayonnaise and sour cream. Serve on crisp lettuce leaves. Serves 4.

Corn

Look for corn that has fresh green husks and plump kernels that spurt milk when pressed. Refrigerate fresh corn *in the husks.*

To cook corn-on-the-cob, remove husk and silk. Have ready a large pot of boiling, unsalted water (if you're cooking only two or three ears you can use a large skillet). Drop corn in the boiling water, cover, and cook three to six minutes, just until the milk in the kernels is set.

To cook corn-on-the-cob at a barbecue, do not husk the corn. Soak it in cold, salted water for an hour. Lay the wet corn in its husks about four or five inches from the coals; turn occasionally and let it cook until the husks are light brown on all sides.

To bake corn-on-the-cob, spread the husked ears with butter or margarine, sprinkle with salt and pepper, and wrap in a square of aluminum foil. Bake ten to fifteen minutes in a 350° F. oven. Turn and bake an additional ten to fifteen minutes.

When there's leftover corn, cut it off the cob and store it, covered, in the refrigerator. Use it for corn pudding, corn fritters, or combine it with lima beans to make succotash.

✒ *Corn Oysters*

2 egg yolks, slightly beaten
2 cups corn, cut from cob or drained, canned whole-kernel corn
½ teaspoon salt
¼ teaspoon pepper
¼ cup sifted all-purpose flour
¼ teaspoon baking powder
2 egg whites, stiffly beaten
Vegetable oil for frying

Combine egg yolk, corn, salt, and pepper. Stir in flour and baking powder. Fold in beaten egg whites. Heat about 2 tablespoons oil in a large skillet over moderately high heat (about 350° F.). Drop batter by tablespoonfuls into skillet and cook until golden brown on underside. Turn and brown other side. Remove and keep hot while cooking rest of batter. Add more oil as needed. Makes about 12.

✒ *Corn Pudding*

3 eggs
2 cups light cream
2 cups corn, cut from the cob
1 tablespoon melted butter or margarine
1 tablespoon sugar
1¼ teaspoons salt
¼ teaspoon pepper
½ teaspoon Worcestershire sauce

Heat oven to 350° F. Beat eggs and cream together. Stir in corn, butter, sugar, salt, pepper, and Worcestershire. Pour into buttered deep 1½-quart casserole. Place in a large baking pan and add 1 inch boiling water to pan. Bake 1 hour, or until set. Serves 6 to 8.

✑ Succotash

2 cups shelled lima beans
½ cup water
1 teaspoon salt
1 teaspoon sugar
¼ teaspoon pepper
3 tablespoons butter or
   margarine
2 cups fresh corn kernels cut
   off the cob (about 2 ears)
¼ cup light cream

Place lima beans, water, salt, sugar and pepper in a large saucepan; cover and cook over moderately low heat (about 225° F.) until beans are almost tender, about 20 to 25 minutes. Add butter and corn and cook uncovered about 5 minutes, until corn is tender and all the water is absorbed. Add the light cream and heat until the mixture is completely warmed through. Serves 6 to 8.

✑ Southern Corn Casserole

3 tablespoons butter or
   margarine
1 medium-sized onion,
   thinly sliced
1 medium-sized green
   pepper, thinly sliced
1 tablespoon cornstarch
1 16-ounce can stewed
   tomatoes
1½ teaspoons sugar
½ teaspoon salt
Few grains pepper
1 15½-ounce can whole
   okra
1 12-ounce can
   whole-kernel corn
2 tablespoons melted butter
   or margarine
½ cup fine dry bread crumbs
1 tablespoon dried parsley
   flakes

Heat oven to 375° F. Melt the 3 tablespoons butter in saucepan over moderately low heat (about 225° F.); add onion and green pepper and cook about 5 minutes, until almost tender. Blend in cornstarch. Gradually add tomatoes, mixing well. Cook, stirring constantly, until thickened. Remove from heat. Add sugar, salt and pepper. Combine okra, corn, and tomato mixture. Pour into a deep 2-quart casserole. Mix the 2 tablespoons melted butter, dry bread crumbs, and parsley. Sprinkle over vegetables. Bake 30 minutes. Serves 6.

Cucumbers

Look for firm cucumbers with dark green skin. Avoid fat cucumbers that feel pliable inside; they will be seedy and sometimes pithy or dry.

Although cucumbers are most often served raw, they may also be

cooked. Pare cucumbers—or score the peel with the ti[...]
off and discard ends that have no seeds, and slice or d[...]
also cut cucumbers in half lengthwise, remove the s[...]
cook the "boats" to fill with another vegetabl[...]
stuffing. Cook, covered, in one inch of boilin[...]
fifteen minutes. Tarragon or dill butter is par[...]
cucumbers.

❧ Fried Cucumber Rounds

2 large cucumbers
¼ cup flour
½ teaspoon salt
⅛ teaspoon pepper
¼ cup butter or margarine

Wash and peel cucumbers. Cut into eve[...]
crosswise slices. Combine flour, salt, and [...]
paper bag. Add a few cucumber slices at a [...]
shake bag to coat pieces. Heat butter in a large[...]
over moderate heat (about 250° F.). Add cucumber s[...]
and brown slowly on both sides. Serve hot. Serves 6.

Eggplant

Look for firm, heavy eggplants with shiny, tight, purple skins; avoid those with brown rust spots.

Eggplant is usually cooked in combination with other foods, although it may be fried alone: Wash the eggplant and peel if the skin is tough. Cut into slices about one inch thick. Dip in fine bread crumbs, then into an egg beaten with 2 tablespoons of water, and into crumbs once more. Fry slowly in a skillet with 2 tablespoons of vegetable oil. Turn when brown and cook until eggplant is golden and tender. Serve sprinkled with salt, pepper, and Parmesan cheese. Or use eggplant as described below.

❧ Eggplant Parmigiana

1 2-pound eggplant (1 large)
2 eggs, slightly beaten
3 tablespoons water
½ teaspoon salt
¼ cup flour
½ cup fine dry bread crumbs
1 cup olive oil
Basic Tomato Sauce (recipe on page 486)

Peel eggplant and cut into ⅓-inch slices. Mix eggs, water, and salt. Dip eggplant in flour, then in the egg mixture, and finally in the bread crumbs to coat evenly. Heat ¼ cup of the olive oil in a large skillet over moderate heat (about 250° F.); cook eggplant until lightly browned on both sides, adding the remaining olive oil as needed. Drain slices on paper towels. Heat oven to 350° F. Pour Tomato Sauce into bottom of a shallow 3-quart baking dish. Arrange a layer of eggplant

...d grated Parmesan
...ese (1 cup)
...ounce package
...ozzarella
cheese, diced
tablespoons butter or
margarine

slices over the bottom of dish. Sprinkle with some of the Parmesan cheese and then with part of the mozzarella cheese. Repeat layers with the remaining eggplant slices and the cheeses. (Reserve some of the mozzarella cheese for top.) Dot with butter. Bake 30 minutes, until cheese is lightly browned. Serves 8 to 10.

Herb-Broiled Eggplant

1 medium-sized eggplant
  (about 1½ pounds)
½ teaspoon minced, peeled
  garlic
¾ teaspoon salt
¼ teaspoon pepper
½ teaspoon dried basil or
  oregano leaves
4 tablespoons olive oil
¼ cup finely chopped fresh
  parsley

Wipe eggplant, trim ends and slice into ½-inch rounds; place on a cookie sheet. Place garlic and salt in a small bowl and mash to a smooth paste with the back of a spoon. Stir in pepper, basil, oil and 2 tablespoons of the parsley. Brush eggplant with half the herb mixture and broil 5 inches from the heat for about 8 minutes. Turn eggplant, brush with remaining herb mixture and broil 8 minutes longer, until brown and tender. Sprinkle with remaining parsley and serve hot. Serves 4.

Eggplant-and-Tomato Scallop

½ cup thinly sliced peeled
  carrot
1 1-pound eggplant
4 slices raw bacon, cut into
  pieces
½ cup chopped onion
1 can condensed tomato soup
1 4-ounce can sliced
  mushrooms, drained
1 teaspoon salt
Few grains pepper
¼ teaspoon ground marjoram
  leaves
4 ounces mozzarella cheese,
  thinly sliced

Cook carrot in boiling water over moderate heat (about 250° F.) until tender, about 10 minutes. Peel eggplant, cut into 1-inch cubes, and cook in boiling water over moderate heat (about 250° F.) 5 minutes. In a skillet fry bacon over moderately high heat (about 325° F.) until crisp; remove bacon pieces and all but 1 tablespoon of the bacon drippings. Add onion and cook over moderate heat (about 250° F.) until tender, about 5 minutes. Combine bacon, onion, tomato soup, mushrooms, salt, pepper, and marjoram in a bowl. Drain carrot and eggplant; add to tomato soup mixture. Spoon into a greased shallow 1½-quart casserole and arrange cheese slices over top. Heat oven to 375° F. Bake 15 to 20 minutes, until cheese melts and begins to brown. Serves 4 to 6.

Ratatouille

⅓ cup olive oil
2 cups sliced onion

Heat oil in a Dutch oven over moderately low heat (about 225° F.); add onion and garlic and cook until

1 large clove garlic, pressed
1½ quarts cubed, unpeeled
eggplant (about 1
medium-sized eggplant)
1 quart thickly sliced
unpeeled zucchini (about
4 medium-sized zucchini)
1½ cups 1-inch squares green
pepper (about 1 large
pepper)
¼ cup chopped fresh parsley
1 teaspoon salt
⅛ teaspoon pepper
1 teaspoon dried tarragon
leaves
3 large tomatoes, cut into
eighths

golden brown. Add eggplant, zucchini, green pepper, parsley, salt, pepper, and tarragon. Mix gently to coat with oil; if necessary, add a little more oil. Cover and cook 15 minutes. Stir in tomatoes; cover and cook 10 minutes longer, or until vegetables are fork-tender. If desired, Ratatouille may be served chilled as a meat accompaniment. Serves 8 to 10.

✦ Stuffed Eggplant Provençale

1 2-pound eggplant (1 large)
2 slices raw bacon, coarsely
chopped
½ cup finely chopped onion
½ cup coarsely chopped green
pepper
1 medium-sized tomato,
coarsely chopped
1 teaspoon dried basil leaves
½ teaspoon salt
Few grains pepper
2 tablespoons fine dry bread
crumbs
2 tablespoons melted butter
or margarine

Cut eggplant in half lengthwise. Cut around eggplant ½ inch from edges; carefully scoop out pulp leaving a shell about ½ inch thick. Parboil shells in boiling salted water 5 minutes; drain and reserve. Cut eggplant pulp into coarse cubes and reserve. Heat oven to 350° F. Cook bacon in a large skillet over moderate heat (about 250° F.) just until it starts to brown. Add cubed eggplant, onion, and green pepper; cook until eggplant is just tender, about 5 minutes, stirring frequently. Remove from heat and stir in tomato, basil, salt, and pepper. Spoon mixture into the 2 eggplant shells. Mix together bread crumbs and butter and sprinkle over filling. Bake 30 to 35 minutes, until thoroughly heated and slightly browned. Serves 4.

Endive, Belgian or French

When shopping for endive, look for pale white to slightly yellow heads that are firm and fresh-looking.

Before cooking endive, wash heads in water and discard any wilted leaves. Cut a small slice off the base of each head and cut the endive in half lengthwise. Belgian endive retains its flavor best if it is baked or braised as in the following recipes.

Belgian endive is also an excellent salad vegetable. There is a suggestion for its use in the salad chapter (page 594).

⌁ Braised Endive

4 large heads Belgian endive
1½ tablespoons melted butter
   or margarine
1 tablespoon lemon juice
¼ teaspoon salt
Few grains pepper
Roquefort Cream Sauce
   (recipe follows)

Remove any discolored part from the root end of endive. Split stalks lengthwise. Place cut-side up in a skillet. Sprinkle with melted butter, lemon juice, salt, and pepper. Place ½ inch water in the bottom of the skillet. Cover and simmer gently over moderately low heat (about 225° F.) for about 5 minutes. Drain well. Serve with Roquefort Cream Sauce. Serves 4.

Roquefort Cream Sauce

1 package white sauce mix
1 cup milk
⅓ cup crumbled Roquefort
   cheese

Prepare white sauce according to package directions, using the 1 cup milk. Stir Roquefort cheese into sauce. Makes 1 cup sauce.

⌁ Braised Endive with Walnuts

6 large heads Belgian endive
⅓ cup butter or margarine
½ teaspoon dried basil leaves
¼ teaspoon salt
Few grains white pepper
½ cup canned beef consommé
   or broth
2 tablespoons butter or
   margarine
3 tablespoons chopped
   walnuts

Remove any discolored outside leaves from endive; cut heads in half lengthwise. Melt the ⅓ cup butter in a 10-inch skillet over moderately low heat (about 225° F.). Arrange endive in butter and sprinkle with basil, salt, and pepper. Pour consommé into bottom of skillet. Cover and cook until fork-tender, about 8 to 10 minutes. Add a little more consommé if liquid in pan evaporates. In a second skillet melt the 2 tablespoons butter over moderately low heat (about 225° F.); add walnuts and cook until lightly browned, stirring occasionally. Serve over endive. Serves 6.

Greens

The greens that are frequently cooked are beet, turnip, collard, dandelion, kale, mustard, spinach, and Swiss chard. Salad greens are described in the chapter which deals with salads (pages 584 to 586).

Look for greens that have crisp leaves and bright green color.

Before cooking greens, cut off roots and trim out any heavy midribs on the leaves. Wash greens thoroughly in several waters. Greens will shed sand more easily if water is tepid. You should boil greens in a very small amount of salted water—not more than a quarter of an inch. Fresh spinach requires only the water that clings to its leaves to cook it. Cook, covered, five to fifteen minutes, depending upon the age of the greens. Drain thoroughly. Season with salt and pepper, butter and lemon, or bacon or ham drippings.

Greens may also be steamed. Take them from the rinse water and put them in a colander. Set the colander over a pan of boiling water and cover it. Depending upon the variety and age of the greens, this method will take five to twenty-five minutes.

Swiss Spinach

2 pounds fresh spinach
¼ teaspoon ground nutmeg
3 teaspoons salt
Few grains pepper
4 tablespoons butter or margarine

Wash spinach several times in warm water and discard roots and tough stems. Place in saucepan with only the water that clings to the leaves. Cover and cook over moderately low heat (about 225° F.) until spinach is wilted. Add nutmeg, salt, and pepper; cook 5 to 10 minutes, stirring occasionally. Drain and chop, if desired; stir in butter. Serves 4.

Creamed Spinach

2 10-ounce packages frozen chopped spinach
3 tablespoons butter or margarine
2 tablespoons finely chopped onion
2 tablespoons flour
1 cup milk or light cream
½ teaspoon salt
⅛ teaspoon ground nutmeg

Cook spinach according to package directions; drain thoroughly. Melt butter in saucepan over moderately low heat (about 225° F.); add onion and cook until tender, stirring occasionally. Remove from heat. Blend in flour; gradually add milk. Cook over moderately low heat (about 225° F.), stirring constantly, until thickened. Stir in salt and nutmeg; stir into drained spinach and heat gently. Serves 6.

Mustard Greens in Sour Cream

1 10-ounce package frozen mustard greens
¼ teaspoon salt

Cook mustard greens according to package directions. Drain well. Add salt, pepper, lemon juice, and sour cream. Stir gently to mix. Serves 3.

(Ingredients continued on page 524)

Few grains pepper
¾ teaspoon lemon juice
½ cup commercial sour cream

Kohlrabi

Kohlrabi bulbs are light green in color, about the size of a large beet, and the green tops are usually attached when purchased. The texture and flavor of the root bulb is rather like a white turnip. Kohlrabi greens may be cooked like other vegetable greens (page 522).

Look for small to medium-sized kohlrabi bulbs with fresh green leaves. Skin should be tender.

To cook kohlrabi, remove tops and pare off skin; wash. Cut into slices, cubes, or julienne strips. Slices and strips are nice for a raw vegetable relish plate; or cook them covered in one inch of boiling salted water. The julienne strips will cook in about fifteen minutes; larger slices take about twenty-five minutes. Serve with butter, salt, pepper, and a little thyme or tarragon.

Leeks

Leeks are a member of the onion family. They are larger than scallions and have broad, flat, dark green tops.

Look for white, clean bulbs with fresh crisp green tops.

Leeks are often used to flavor soups but may be poached or braised as a dinner vegetable. Cut a slice off the root end; peel off any tough outer layer from the bulb; wash thoroughly to remove any sand. Leave leeks whole or cut into two-inch portions and spread in a ten-inch skillet; add butter, ½ cup water, and a bouillon cube. Cover tightly and cook about fifteen minutes. Serve with butter or margarine and salt and pepper.

Mushrooms

Look for plump, unblemished, cream-colored or white mushrooms with short stems. Buy only the cultivated variety unless you're an expert botanist.

Mushrooms can be broiled, baked, or sautéed. They also add wonderful flavor to other vegetables. Mushrooms should be washed; they need not be peeled.

To broil: Remove the caps from the stems (reserve the stems to chop into other vegetables or soups). Place the caps hollow-side up on a broiler pan. Put a dot of butter in each cap; sprinkle with salt, pepper, and a little lemon juice. Broil about five inches away from heat source for five to eight minutes. Mushroom caps may be stuffed with seasoned bread crumbs. They are delicious filled with hot puréed peas that have been seasoned with nutmeg.

To bake: Arrange mushrooms in a shallow baking dish with just enough water to cover the bottom of the dish. Dot with butter and sprinkle with salt and pepper. Bake at 350° F. for about fifteen minutes.

To sautée or fry: Put one pound of sliced mushrooms in ¼ cup melted butter or margarine in a heavy skillet. Cook, covered, over moderate heat for about ten minutes. Uncover pan, sprinkle mushrooms with salt, pepper, and a little lemon juice. Cook and stir over high heat a few minutes to absorb the juices.

Creamed Mushrooms and Chestnuts

1 *pound fresh chestnuts*
5 *tablespoons butter or margarine*
1 *pound mushrooms, quartered*
2 *tablespoons flour*
½ *teaspoon salt*
⅛ *teaspoon pepper*
1½ *cups light cream*
1 *tablespoon chopped fresh parsley*

Prick chestnut shells with the tines of a fork; cover with cold water and bring to a boil over moderate heat (about 250° F.). Boil 15 minutes. Drain; cool and remove shells and skin; cut into quarters. Melt butter in skillet over moderate heat (about 250° F.); add mushrooms and cook until lightly browned. Add flour, salt, and pepper; stir until blended. Gradually add cream; cook, stirring constantly, until thickened. Fold in chestnuts and heat. Garnish with parsley. Serves 6.

Mushrooms and Herbs

1 *pound mushrooms*
½ *cup olive oil*
1 *tablespoon grated onion*
1 *tablespoon snipped chives*
1 *tablespoon chopped fresh parsley*
1 *clove garlic, finely chopped*

Wash and slice mushrooms; combine with remaining ingredients except butter. Cover and let stand 2 hours. Melt butter in a saucepan over moderately low heat (about 225° F.), add mushrooms and marinade, and simmer 10 minutes, stirring frequently. Serves 4.

(Ingredients continued on page 526)

¾ *teaspoon salt*
3 *tablespoons tarragon*
   vinegar
Dash of dried tarragon leaves
Dash of dried thyme leaves
Few grains pepper
4 *tablespoons butter or*
   margarine

Okra

When shopping for okra, look for crisp, bright green pods that are free from blemishes. Choose small to medium pods.

Before cooking okra, wash; do not trim off stem ends unless they are woody. Pods may be cooked whole or cut into half-inch rounds. Cook in a nine- or ten-inch skillet in one inch of boiling, salted water. Boil, uncovered, for five minutes; cover and cook another five minutes. Drain, season with salt, pepper, and butter or with French dressing.

Onions

Green onions are often called scallions. They should have crisp, green tops with medium-sized white roots two to three inches long.

To cook green onions, wash well; remove any loose layers of skin; cut off hairy roots and cut green stems to about three-inch lengths. Cook in a skillet in one inch of boiling, salted water until tender, eight to ten minutes. Serve as a buttered vegetable or on toast with White Sauce (see page 480).

White or yellow onions should be bright, clean, well shaped, and hard; they should have dry papery skins. Avoid onions with wet or soft necks.

Small white onions are often used as an ingredient in stews or they are parboiled and creamed as a vegetable dish. The larger white and yellow onions are more suitable for baking and slicing. Cut a thin slice off both the top and the bottom of the onion; then peel off the paper shell until you get down to the white outer layer. Small white onions are usually cooked whole. Larger ones may be sliced or used whole or separated into rings to French fry. Cook onions, uncovered, in enough boiling, salted water just to cover them. Small onions take fifteen to twenty minutes. Drain and serve with Mornay Sauce (page 482) or with butter and grated cheese.

Red onions vary in size. They may be as small as a large yellow onion or as large as a Spanish onion. They are mild in flavor and attractive in salads.

Spanish onions are large and mild in flavor. Judge them as you would the yellow and white onions. They make big sweet onion rings and are delicious in salads and sandwiches.

✑ Creamed Onions

24 small white onions, peeled (about 1¼ pounds)
¼ cup butter or margarine
¼ cup flour
½ teaspoon salt
Few grains pepper
1 cup canned chicken broth
1 cup light cream
3 tablespoons grated Parmesan cheese (optional)
¼ cup chopped fresh parsley
Pimiento strips

Place onions in a large saucepan; add boiling salted water to cover. Cover and simmer over moderate heat (about 250° F.) about 20 minutes, or until fork-tender. Drain well. Melt butter in a medium-sized saucepan over moderately low heat (about 225° F.); blend in flour, salt, and pepper, stirring constantly. Gradually stir in chicken broth and cream and cook, stirring constantly, until thickened and smooth. Stir in Parmesan cheese and parsley and blend well. Remove from heat. Add onions and pour mixture into a 1½-quart casserole. Heat oven to 350° F. Bake, covered, for 10 to 15 minutes, stirring once or twice. Arrange pimiento strips on top of casserole and bake 10 minutes longer, or until heated through and sauce bubbles. Serves 6.

✑ Stuffed Onions in Tomato Sauce

6 large yellow onions (about 3 pounds)
1 cup soft white or whole wheat bread crumbs, tightly packed
½ cup shredded Cheddar cheese
½ cup chopped walnuts
2 tablespoons chopped fresh parsley
1 egg, beaten
2 tablespoons melted butter or margarine
¼ teaspoon dried thyme leaves
½ teaspoon salt
1 can condensed bisque of tomato soup
½ cup milk
¼ cup heavy cream

Peel onions without cutting off root end. Cut a slice about 1 inch thick from top of each onion. Place onions and onion slices in a large amount of boiling salted water and cook over moderate heat (about 250° F.) until just tender, about 20 to 30 minutes. Drain and cool. Heat oven to 375° F. Scoop out centers of onions to form cups having a ½-inch wall; reserve onion centers for filling. Invert cups to drain. Chop reserved onion and onion slices; mix with bread crumbs, cheese, walnuts, parsley, egg, melted butter, thyme, and salt. Stuff the onions with mixture. Mix soup, milk, and cream; pour into bottom of a 1½-quart shallow baking dish. Place onions in sauce and bake 20 to 30 minutes, until tops are browned. Serves 6.

VEGETABLES

◄§ Glazed Onions

20 small white onions (1
    pound), peeled, or 1
    16-ounce can boiled
    onions, drained
 3 tablespoons butter or
    margarine
 6 tablespoons granulated
    sugar

Place peeled onions in a large saucepan; add boiling salted water to cover. Cover and cook over moderately low heat (about 225° F.) about 20 minutes, or until fork-tender. Drain well. Melt the butter in a large skillet over moderate heat (about 250° F.), add the onions and sprinkle them with the sugar. Cook, shaking the pan frequently to turn the onions, until they are golden on all sides. Use as a vegetable or a garnish for roasts. Serves 4 to 5.

◄§ Onions in Mustard Sauce

 3 16-ounce cans small
    whole boiled onions, well
    drained
¼ cup melted butter or
    margarine
 3 tablespoons sugar
 1 tablespoon dry mustard
⅛ teaspoon paprika
1½ teaspoons salt
⅓ cup chopped fresh parsley

Heat oven to 325° F. Place onions in a buttered shallow 1½-quart baking dish. Combine butter, sugar, mustard, paprika, and salt; pour over onions. Bake 30 to 40 minutes, until heated. Sprinkle with parsley before serving. Serves 8 to 10.

◄§ Scalloped Onions and Peppers

10 medium-sized onions,
    peeled (about 2½ pounds)
 1 cup small green pepper
    strips
 3 tablespoons butter or
    margarine
 3 tablespoons flour
½ teaspoon salt
1½ cups milk
¼ cup chopped salted
    peanuts

Cook onions in a large amount of boiling salted water over moderate heat (about 250° F.) about 10 minutes, or until almost tender. Add green pepper strips during the last 5 minutes. Drain and cool slightly. Cut onions into halves or quarters. Arrange onions and green pepper in a buttered, shallow 1½-quart baking dish. Melt butter in a saucepan over moderately low heat (about 225° F.). Blend in flour and salt; cook until bubbly. Gradually stir in milk. Cook, stirring constantly, until thickened and smooth. Pour sauce over vegetables in casserole. Sprinkle with chopped peanuts. Heat oven to 350° F. Bake 30 to 40 minutes, until bubbly. Serves 6.

◄§ French Fried Onion Rings

2 large sweet Spanish onions
1 cup sifted all-purpose flour

Cut off root ends of onions; peel and slice crosswise into ¼-inch slices. Separate slices into rings. Mix flour,

1 teaspoon baking powder
½ teaspoon salt
1 egg, slightly beaten
1 cup milk
1 tablespoon vegetable oil
Vegetable oil for frying

baking powder, and salt together in a bowl. Add the egg, milk, and the 1 tablespoon oil; mix until smooth. Pour oil into a skillet or deep-fat fryer to a depth of 1½ to 2 inches. Heat oil to 375° F. on a deep-fat-frying thermometer. Dip onion rings in batter and place, one at a time, in oil; add only enough rings to cover surface of oil. Cook rings until lightly browned on both sides. As rings brown, remove and drain on paper towels. Continue adding rings as there is room in skillet. Keep finished rings in a warm oven. Serves 4 to 6.

Parsnips

Look for small or medium parsnips that are smooth and firm. Avoid limp or shriveled ones and large ones, which will tend to have a woody core.

Before cooking parsnips, wash and cut off the tip end of the root; then take a slice off the top. Pare and cut in half. Take out the center core if it is tough and woody. Cook as halves, quarters, or slices. Cook, covered, in one inch of boiling, salted water until tender. Halves will take about twenty to thirty minutes. Quarters and slices take ten to twenty minutes; it depends on the size of the parsnip. Parsnips may be served in a cream sauce or mashed with butter and cream. After boiling, the halves may be browned in butter in a heavy skillet.

✒ Fried Parsnips

1 pound parsnips, pared
2 tablespoons butter or
   margarine
Salt and pepper

Cut parsnips in half lengthwise. Cut larger pieces again in half lengthwise and crosswise if necessary, to make pieces of uniform size. Place parsnips in boiling salted water in a large saucepan. Cover and cook over moderate heat (about 225° F.) about 20 minutes until fork-tender. Drain well on paper towels and cut pieces lengthwise into ¼-inch slices. Melt butter in a skillet over moderately high heat (about 275° F.). Add parsnips and fry until golden brown on both sides. Sprinkle with salt and pepper. Serves 4.

✒ Parsnips au Gratin

3 tablespoons butter or
   margarine
3 tablespoons flour

Melt the 3 tablespoons butter in a saucepan over moderately low heat (about 225° F.). Blend in flour and salt. Gradually add milk and cook, stirring constantly,

½ teaspoon salt
1½ cups milk
3 cups diced cooked parsnips
Few grains pepper
¼ pound shredded Cheddar cheese
1 cup soft bread crumbs
2 tablespoons melted butter or margarine

until thickened. Remove from heat and add diced cooked parsnips and pepper. Pour half of the parsnip mixture into a buttered shallow 1½-quart casserole. Sprinkle with half of the cheese. Repeat layers. Combine bread crumbs and the 2 tablespoons melted butter; sprinkle over top. Heat oven to 400° F. Bake 25 to 30 minutes, until crumbs are browned. Serves 6 to 8.

Peas

Look for peas that have well-filled, bright, fresh-looking green pods. Shell peas by pressing the pod between your thumb and forefinger to split it open. Take out peas and discard any with sprouts. Rinse shelled peas quickly in cold water. Drain. Cook peas covered in one inch of boiling, salted water eight to twelve minutes. It helps flavor greatly to add sugar to the cooking water; use ¼ teaspoon of sugar to one pound of unshelled peas. Serve drained peas dressed with butter or margarine, or with cream.

⊷ French Peas

12 large lettuce leaves, washed
4 pounds fresh peas, shelled
¼ cup thinly sliced scallions or green onions
1 teaspoon sugar
1 teaspoon salt
¼ teaspoon pepper
¼ teaspoon dried chervil
¼ teaspoon dried thyme leaves
¼ cup butter or margarine

Cover bottom and sides of a 10-inch skillet with some of the moist lettuce leaves. Top with peas and sprinkle with scallions, sugar, salt, pepper, chervil, and thyme and dot with butter. Cover peas with remaining lettuce leaves. Cover skillet tightly and cook over low heat (about 200° F.) for 10 to 15 minutes, or until peas are tender. Remove lettuce leaves. Toss well before serving. Serves 8.

⊷ Herbed Peas and Onions

3 10-ounce packages frozen peas

Place peas, water, butter, parsley, dillweed, and salt in a saucepan; cover and cook over moderately low heat

6 tablespoons water
3 tablespoons butter or
   margarine
1 tablespoon dried parsley
   flakes
1½ teaspoons dried dillweed
¾ teaspoon salt
1 16-ounce can small whole
   boiled onions, drained

(about 225° F.) until mixture starts to boil; separate peas with a fork. Reduce heat to low (about 200° F.) and simmer 5 to 7 minutes. Stir in onions and heat 4 to 5 minutes. Serves 9 to 10.

✍ Carrot Ring with French Peas

2 tablespoons butter or
   margarine
2 cups peeled and finely
   shredded carrots
1 teaspoon salt
⅛ teaspoon pepper
1 tablespoon finely grated
   onion
3 tablespoons butter or
   margarine
3 tablespoons flour
¼ teaspoon salt
Hot milk
3 eggs, separated
French Peas (recipe on page
   530)

Melt the 2 tablespoons butter in a heavy saucepan over moderately low heat (about 225° F.). Add carrots; cover tightly and cook until carrots are soft, about 8 to 10 minutes. Drain and measure liquid. Season carrots with the 1 teaspoon salt, pepper, and grated onion. Melt the 3 tablespoons butter in a saucepan over moderately low heat (about 225° F.). Stir in flour and the ¼ teaspoon salt. Add enough hot milk to carrot liquid to make 1 cup; gradually add to flour mixture, stirring constantly. Cook and stir until smooth and thickened. Slowly add the hot sauce to the well-beaten egg yolks. Add carrots. Cool mixture to room temperature. Heat oven to 350° F. Beat egg whites with rotary beater until stiff but not dry; fold into cooled carrot mixture. Pour into a very well-greased, 2-quart ring mold. Set mold in a large baking pan and fill pan to a depth of 1 inch with hot water. Bake 45 minutes. Carefully slip ring out onto a large chop plate. Fill center with French Peas. Serves 8 to 10.

Sweet Potatoes and Yams

Sweet potatoes and yams are interchangeable in recipes. Sweet potatoes have pale golden skins and yellow flesh that is dry and mealy when cooked. Yams have pale to reddish skins, orange flesh, and are moister when cooked.

Look for smooth-skinned potatoes that are free of blemishes and have a firm, bright appearance. Avoid withered-looking potatoes. Sweet potatoes and yams are far more perishable than white potatoes so plan to use them soon.

Sweet potatoes may be boiled, baked, fried, mashed, or oven roasted. Sweet potatoes cook more quickly than white potatoes.

To boil sweet potatoes, pare them thinly and cut into halves or quarters. Place them in boiling, salted water in a saucepan; allow about two cups of water for four potatoes. Cook, covered, thirty to forty minutes.

Whole baked sweet potatoes take about fifty to sixty minutes in a 400° F. oven. Scrub the potatoes well, prick the skin lightly in several places, and place the potatoes on an oven rack. When baked, they may be cut in half, dressed with butter, and served from the shell.

✌ Candied Sweet Potatoes

6 medium-sized sweet potatoes (about 2½ pounds)
¾ cup dark corn syrup
¼ cup butter or margarine
½ teaspoon grated lemon peel
⅛ teaspoon ground ginger
½ teaspoon salt

Wash potatoes and place in saucepan with boiling water to cover. Cover pan and cook over moderate heat (about 250° F.) about 30 minutes, or until just tender. Remove potatoes from water, cool, and peel. Cut potatoes into halves lengthwise. Heat oven to 375° F. Place potatoes in a shallow 2-quart baking dish. Heat corn syrup, butter, lemon peel, ginger, and salt in a small saucepan over moderate heat (about 250° F.) until butter is melted. Pour over potatoes. Bake uncovered 20 to 25 minutes, basting occasionally with sauce to glaze potatoes. Serves 6.

✌ Pecan-Stuffed Baked Sweet Potatoes

5 medium-sized sweet potatoes (about 2 pounds)
Vegetable oil
⅓ cup butter or margarine
3 to 4 tablespoons sweet sherry
2 tablespoons sugar
½ teaspoon salt
Few grains pepper
⅓ cup chopped pecans
5 teaspoons butter or margarine

Heat oven to 400° F. Wash potatoes, wipe dry, and rub skins with vegetable oil. Place in a shallow pan. Bake 50 to 60 minutes, or until tender. Remove from oven. Cut a thin slice from one side of each potato and carefully remove pulp, being careful not to break skins. Mash pulp; add the ⅓ cup butter, sherry, sugar, salt, and pepper. Beat until fluffy; fold in pecans. Spoon potato mixture back into skins. Top each potato with 1 teaspoon of butter. Bake 15 to 20 minutes. Serves 5.

✌ Southern-Style Fried Sweet Potatoes

3 medium-sized sweet potatoes (about 1¼

Wash potatoes and place in saucepan with boiling water to cover. Cover pan and cook over moderate heat (about

pounds)
Flour
3 to 4 tablespoons butter or margarine
Sugar

250° F.) about 30 minutes, or until just tender. Remove potatoes from water, cool and peel. Cut crosswise into ½-inch slices and coat both sides with flour. Melt butter in skillet over moderate heat (about 250° F.); add potatoes and cook until lightly browned on both sides. Sprinkle lightly with sugar. Serves 4.

৶ Orange Sweet Potatoes

2 18-ounce cans vacuum-packed sweet potatoes
1 6-ounce can frozen orange juice concentrate, thawed
½ cup milk
¼ cup melted butter or margarine
1 tablespoon grated orange peel
½ teaspoon ground nutmeg
½ teaspoon salt
4 eggs, separated
¼ cup sugar

Heat oven to 350° F. Mash the sweet potatoes in a large bowl; blend in concentrated orange juice, milk, butter, orange peel, nutmeg, and salt. Place egg whites in a large bowl and beat with a rotary beater or electric mixer until soft peaks form. Gradually add sugar and beat until stiff peaks form. Beat egg yolks until thick and lemon-colored; blend into sweet potato mixture. Fold in beaten egg whites. Pour into a buttered deep 2-quart casserole. Bake uncovered 1 to 1¼ hours, until browned. Serves 6 to 8.

৶ Glazed Sweet Potatoes

1 17-ounce can vacuum-packed sweet potatoes
¼ cup softened butter or margarine
½ cup firmly packed light brown sugar
½ cup heavy cream
½ cup chopped walnuts

Heat oven to 400° F. Place sweet potatoes in a 1½-quart casserole. Blend butter, sugar, and cream together; pour over sweet potatoes. Cover and bake 35 minutes. Remove cover, sprinkle with walnuts, and continue baking, uncovered, 5 to 10 minutes longer. Serves 4.

৶ Fluffy Stuffed Sweet Potatoes

8 medium-sized sweet potatoes
⅓ cup butter or margarine, melted
1½ tablespoons firmly packed dark brown sugar
1 teaspoon salt

Heat oven to 450° F. Scrub potatoes with a brush. Place in a large flat baking pan and bake 40 to 45 minutes, or until fork-tender. Make a slit in the top of each potato. Scoop out pulp carefully. Reserve shells. Combine pulp, butter, brown sugar, salt, pepper, and marshmallow creme in the large bowl of an electric mixer. Beat at medium speed until light and fluffy. Spoon mixture into

Few grains pepper
1 *cup jarred marshmallow*
  creme
8 *marshmallows*

potato shells. Place in two 1½-quart shallow baking dishes. Reduce oven to 350° F. Slice marshmallows in half and place 2 halves on top of each potato. Bake for 20 to 30 minutes, or until heated through and marshmallows are melted. Serves 8.

White Potatoes

Look for potatoes that are well shaped, firm, and free from blemishes and sunburn (a green discoloration under the skin). Avoid sprouted or shriveled potatoes. There are several varieties of potatoes on the market, and which you buy depends on how you plan to use them.

New potatoes are characterized by relatively thin or "feathering" skin. (It may be red or pale brown.) They are on the market in the late winter and early spring, though they may appear in some areas at other times of the year. They are best for boiling and creaming and are usually cooked with their skins on or with a narrow band of skin pared off around the middle. They must be well scrubbed with a stiff brush. Cook them, tightly covered, in two inches of salted boiling water for twenty-five or thirty minutes, just until tender. New potatoes are superb with only melted butter and one herb tossed with them. Try dill, parsley, or tarragon. Fresh herbs are best with the new potatoes; if you use a dried herb, let it stand in the butter while the potatoes cook. New potatoes are also good in a light Cream Sauce (see page 481), in a Mornay Sauce (see page 482), or combined with freshly cooked peas and dressed with hot dairy half-and-half.

Mature potatoes are the general-purpose potatoes of many varieties. They may be round or oval in shape, depending upon their breed. Mature potatoes are in the market year round. They may be *thinly* pared before cooking, or scrubbed and cooked with the skins on and skinned after cooking. These are the potatoes to boil, scallop, mash, fry, even bake, although most of these do not make the best baked potato. To boil, use about two cups of boiling, salted water for four medium potatoes. Cover tightly and cook thirty-five to forty minutes until tender.

The best-known baking potatoes are the long russet Idaho bakers. They are large, oval in shape, and have a fine scaly netting on the skin. The flesh is dry, mealy, and fluffy. (These make excellent French fries also.) To bake them, wash them well; dry the potatoes; and prick the skin with a fork in several places to prevent the potatoes from bursting. Preheat oven to 400° F.; place the potatoes on a center rack and bake for forty-five to sixty minutes, until tender. If you have other foods in the oven and want to bake potatoes at a lower temperature, you will have to allow a longer time. When potatoes are done, take them from the oven. With a sharp knife, cut an X in the top of each potato. Take the potato in your hand (you can use a clean tea towel to protect your hand) and squeeze from the bottom until the mealy interior starts to push its way through the X. Serve with salt, pepper, butter or sour cream, and a sprinkling of chives.

New Potatoes in Parsley–Butter Sauce

1½ pounds scrubbed, unpeeled new potatoes (about 10 small potatoes)
6 tablespoons butter or margarine
1 tablespoon chopped fresh parsley

Place scrubbed potatoes in a saucepan and cover with boiling salted water. Cook over moderately low heat (about 225° F.) until potatoes are fork-tender, about 25 to 30 minutes. Melt butter in a saucepan over moderately low heat (about 225° F.); stir in parsley. Heat and pour over potatoes. Serves 4.

Creamy Mashed Potatoes

5 cups hot diced cooked potatoes (about 6 medium-sized potatoes)
⅓ cup butter or margarine
1¼ cups hot milk or light cream
1½ teaspoons salt
⅛ teaspoon pepper

Partially mash potatoes with a potato masher. Add butter, hot milk, salt, and pepper. Beat with electric mixer until smooth and fluffy. Serves 4 to 6.

Scalloped Potatoes

4 cups thinly sliced raw potatoes (about 5 medium-sized potatoes)
1½ teaspoons salt
⅛ teaspoon pepper
⅛ teaspoon ground nutmeg
2 tablespoons flour
¾ cup sliced onion
2 tablespoons butter or margarine
1½ cups milk, heated

Heat oven to 350° F. Grease a shallow 1½-quart baking dish. Spread half the potatoes over bottom. Combine salt, pepper, nutmeg, and flour. Sprinkle potatoes with half of this mixture and all the onion. Dot with half the butter. Add remaining potatoes, the rest of the flour mixture, and the remaining 1 tablespoon butter. Pour hot milk over top. Cover and bake 65 minutes. Uncover and bake 15 minutes longer, until potatoes are fork-tender. Serves 4.

◄§ Stuffed Baked Potatoes

8 medium-sized baking
   potatoes
½ cup butter or margarine
1¼ teaspoons salt
⅛ teaspoon pepper
1 cup milk
¼ cup heavy cream
2 tablespoons snipped
   chives

Heat oven to 400° F. Scrub potatoes well with a vegetable brush. Puncture each with the tines of a fork. Place in oven and bake about 1 hour, or until potatoes feel soft when pressed between protected fingers. Cut a thin slice from one side of potatoes. Scoop out insides into a bowl and mash. Reserve potato shells for stuffing. Add butter, salt, and pepper. Combine milk and heavy cream in a small saucepan over moderately low heat (about 225° F.) and heat just to the boiling point; add to the potato mixture. Beat with an electric mixer until smooth and fluffy. Stir in chives. Spoon potato mixture into the reserved potato shells. If desired, decorate the top with some of the potato mixture piped through a pastry bag. Place, uncovered, in a 425° F. oven for about 25 minutes, or until thoroughly heated. Serves 8.

◄§ Cheese-Stuffed Baked Potato

4 small baking potatoes,
   about 3½ inches long
2 tablespoons butter or
   margarine
2 tablespoons heavy cream
½ teaspoon salt
6 tablespoons shredded
   American cheese

Heat oven to 400° F. Bake potatoes 40 to 45 minutes, or until fork-tender. Cut a thin slice off one side of potatoes and scoop out potato, being careful not to break shell. Place potato in a bowl and mash; add butter, cream, salt, and 2 tablespoons of the cheese. Beat until fluffy. Spoon potato mixture into shells. Sprinkle tops with the remaining 4 tablespoons cheese. Place in preheated broiler about 3 inches from heat and broil 3 to 4 minutes, or until cheese is lightly browned. Serves 4.

◄§ Hashed Brown Potatoes

1½ tablespoons flour
1½ teaspoons salt
⅛ teaspoon pepper
2 tablespoons milk
2 cups diced cooked
   potatoes (about 3
   medium-sized potatoes)
2 tablespoons finely
   chopped onion
2 tablespoons vegetable oil

Combine flour, salt, and pepper. Stir in milk and mix until smooth. Add potatoes and onion and stir until thoroughly mixed. Heat vegetable oil in a medium-sized skillet over moderate heat (about 250° F.). Add the potato mixture and spread evenly, making one large cake that does not touch sides of skillet. Cook until underside is brown. Cut into quarters and turn pieces to brown other side. Serves 4.

❧ Duchess Potatoes

5 cups hot diced cooked
   potatoes (about 6
   medium-sized potatoes)
1 egg yolk
4 tablespoons milk
¼ cup butter or margarine
1¼ teaspoons salt
⅛ teaspoon pepper

Heat oven to 400° F. Partially mash potatoes with a potato masher. Add egg yolk, milk, butter, salt, and pepper. Beat with an electric mixer until smooth. If mixture is too stiff to drop from a spoon, add a tablespoon more milk. Drop spoonfuls on a lightly greased cookie sheet. Bake 12 to 15 minutes, until golden brown. This mixture may be piped with a pastry tube around a broiled steak on a heatproof platter or plank and broiled until golden brown. Serves 4 to 6.

❧ Potatoes O'Brien

5 cups cubed cooked potatoes
   (about 6 medium-sized
   potatoes)
3 tablespoons finely chopped
   onion
3 tablespoons chopped
   pimiento
1 can condensed Cheddar
   cheese soup
⅓ cup milk
1 teaspoon salt
1 tablespoon fine dry bread
   crumbs

Heat oven to 350° F. Combine potatoes, onion, and pimiento and place in a lightly greased deep 1½-quart casserole. Combine cheese soup, milk, and salt. Pour over potatoes. Sprinkle top with bread crumbs. Bake uncovered 30 minutes, until heated. Serves 4 to 6.

❧ Potato Pancakes

2 cups grated raw potatoes
   (about 4 medium-sized
   potatoes)
2 eggs, well beaten
2 tablespoons flour
1 teaspoon baking powder
1 teaspoon salt
½ small onion, grated
   (optional)

Chill pared potatoes in ice water for 2 hours before grating (to prevent grated potatoes from turning color). Place grated potatoes in a clean tea towel and press out excess moisture until potatoes are quite dry. Combine potatoes, eggs, flour, baking powder, and salt. Stir in onion if desired. Heat a well-greased griddle over moderately high heat (about 350° F.). Drop batter by tablespoonfuls onto griddle. Cook about 5 minutes on each side, until golden brown. Serve with applesauce or as an accompaniment for sliced cold meat. Makes eight 3-inch pancakes.

VEGETABLES

✺ Crisp-Baked Potato Halves

4 medium-sized baking
   potatoes
4 tablespoons soft butter or
   margarine
Salt and pepper
Crumbled rosemary leaves
   (optional)

Heat oven to 400° F. Scrub potatoes thoroughly and cut into halves lengthwise. Score cut side of each half deeply with a fork; brush with soft butter and sprinkle with salt, pepper, and rosemary, if desired. Place potatoes on a cookie sheet, cut-side up, and bake 35 to 45 minutes, until fork-tender. Serves 4.

✺ Cheese-and-Potato Pie

¼ cup dry bread crumbs
1½ pounds unpeeled potatoes
   (4 medium-sized), well-
   scrubbed or 1½ pounds
   frozen peeled potatoes
Water
2 tablespoons butter or
   margarine
½ cup hot milk
1 egg
½ teaspoon salt
⅛ teaspoon pepper
½ pound mozzarella cheese,
   sliced thin
½ cup (2 ounces) freshly
   grated Parmesan cheese

Butter the inside of a 10-inch pie plate and sprinkle bread crumbs evenly over bottom and sides, tipping out any loose crumbs. Put potatoes in a large saucepan, cover with water and bring to a boil over moderately high heat; reduce heat to moderate and cook potatoes until tender, about 30 minutes. Heat oven to 375° F. Drain potatoes, peel them if unpeeled and put them back in the pot; add butter and milk and mash until smooth. Beat in egg, salt and pepper. Spread about half the potato mixture in an even layer in the pie plate and top with half the mozzarella cheese (if potatoes won't spread easily, press them down with the cheese). Top with remaining mashed potatoes and then the remaining mozzarella slices. Sprinkle top with Parmesan cheese and bake 35 to 40 minutes, until golden brown. Serves 4.

✺ Swiss Potato Cake

3 large (1 pound) baking or
   all-purpose potatoes,
   scrubbed
Boiling water
4 tablespoons butter or
   margarine
¾ teaspoon salt
⅛ teaspoon pepper

Place potatoes in a medium-sized saucepan and cover with boiling water. Cook covered over moderate heat (about 250° F.) 20 minutes. Drain potatoes, cool and chill in refrigerator. Peel potatoes and grate coarsely. In a heavy, medium-sized skillet melt 3 tablespoons of the butter over moderately high heat (about 350° F.); spread potatoes over bottom of pan and pat down gently with a spatula. Sprinkle potatoes with salt and pepper, reduce heat to moderate (about 250° F.) and cook uncovered 30 minutes, or until underside is browned; take care that potatoes do not burn. With a spatula carefully loosen potato cake from bottom and sides of pan; invert onto a plate, crusty side up. Melt remaining 1 tablespoon of butter in skillet and slip potato cake back into skillet, uncooked side down. Cook 15 minutes longer. Loosen potato cake with a spatula and slide onto a serving plate or cut in quarters and serve from skillet. Serves 4.

Peppers

The vegetable pepper is the sweet green or bell pepper that turns red when mature.

Look for firm peppers that have thick flesh and are shiny and bright green in color. Avoid withered or bruised peppers.

Peppers are frequently used raw or minced into other foods for color and flavor. When cooked they are usually stuffed and baked whole or cut into strips and pan-fried. To use them whole, wash the pepper and remove the stem and seeds. If peppers are to be cut up, it's easier to halve them to remove the seeds.

❧ Stuffed Green Peppers

4 or 5 large green peppers
3 tablespoons butter or margarine
1 small onion, finely chopped
½ cup raw rice
1 pound ground beef chuck
1½ teaspoons salt
¼ teaspoon pepper
1 egg
2 tablespoons butter or margarine
2 tablespoons flour
1 18-fluid-ounce can tomato juice

Cut a slice from the top of each pepper. Cut out membranes and seeds from the inside. Place peppers in a bowl and add boiling water to cover. Drain. Set aside. Melt the 3 tablespoons butter in a skillet over moderately low heat (about 225° F.). Add onion and rice. Cook about 5 minutes. Place meat in a bowl. Blend rice, onion, salt, pepper, and egg into the meat. Fill the green peppers with meat mixture. Melt the 2 tablespoons butter in a saucepan over moderately low heat (about 225° F.). Add flour and blend thoroughly. Slowly add tomato juice. Cook, stirring constantly, until mixture thickens, about 5 minutes. Remove from heat. Place stuffed peppers in a heavy saucepan or Dutch oven. Pour sauce over all. Cover and cook over low heat (about 200° F.) 1 hour. Stir occasionally to prevent sticking. Serves 4 to 5.

❧ Italian-Style Peppers

2 tablespoons vegetable oil
2 large green peppers, cut into strips

Heat oil in large skillet over moderate heat (about 250° F.). Add peppers and onion; cook until onion is tender, about 5 minutes. Push peppers and onion to one side of

1 medium-sized onion, thinly
   sliced
1 medium-sized zucchini, cut
   into ½-inch slices
½ medium-sized eggplant,
   peeled and cut into ½-inch
   slices
2 tomatoes, peeled and diced
1 teaspoon salt
¼ teaspoon pepper
¼ teaspoon dried basil leaves
1 clove garlic, minced
1 tablespoon chopped fresh
   parsley

skillet. Add zucchini and eggplant slices and cook until eggplant absorbs most of the oil. Add tomatoes, salt, pepper, basil, and garlic; stir gently to combine. Cover and cook over low heat (about 200° F.) about 10 minutes, or until vegetables are tender-crisp. Sprinkle with parsley. Serves 4 to 6.

Pumpkins

Technically a vegetable, most pumpkin is used as fruit in pies and custards.

Look for bright-colored, firm, unblemished pumpkins. Shape is unimportant.

To cook pumpkin, cut in half with a large, heavy knife. Remove the stem end; scoop out the seeds and all the stringy portion. If you like toasted pumpkin seeds, set them aside to use later. Cut the pumpkin pulp into small pieces and pare each piece thinly. Cook, covered, in one inch of boiling, salted water about thirty minutes, until tender. Drain pulp, mash, and drain well again. Pulp is now ready to use in recipes for pies and puddings (see index).

Roasted Pumpkin Seeds

2 cups washed, cleaned,
   and dried pumpkin seeds
1½ tablespoons melted
   butter or margarine
1¼ teaspoons salt

Heat oven to 250° F. Combine pumpkin seeds with butter and salt. Spread in the bottom of a shallow pan. Bake 30 to 40 minutes, stirring frequently, until seeds are browned and crisp. Makes about 2 cups.

Radishes

When shopping for radishes, look for smooth, firm crisp roots. Since most radishes are marketed in plastic bags and have had the green tops removed from the roots, you can rarely judge the freshness of radishes by the leaves. Avoid soft radishes; they will be pithy.

Radishes are usually eaten raw. Wash them and cut off the rootlets. A small portion of the stem end may be left on. Store in a plastic bag in the refrigerator. To cook, drop whole radishes into one inch of boiling, salted water; cover and cook six to eight minutes, until crisp-tender. Drain and serve with butter or margarine and salt and pepper. Sliced radishes with slivers of celery and green pepper are good panned or braised.

Salsify or Oyster Plant

When shopping for salsify, look for medium-sized roots that are firm and free of blemishes.

To cook salsify, scrub roots well; pare thinly or scrape them. Cut roots into thin slices or slivers. Cook, covered, ten to fifteen minutes in two inches of boiling salted water with a teaspoon of vinegar or lemon juice added to keep the salsify white. Drain and serve with butter or margarine and salt and pepper.

Sauerkraut

Sauerkraut is generally available in cans (several sizes) and in one-pound plastic bags in grocer's or butcher's cold cases.

To cook sauerkraut, pour canned sauerkraut with its juice into a saucepan; cover and steam twenty to thirty minutes. Drain and add caraway seeds, chopped apple, or onion; toss and serve. Cook packaged, fresh sauerkraut about forty minutes in just enough water to cover. Add any of the flavorings suggested above.

❧ Quick Choucroute

1 27-ounce can sauerkraut
1 8-ounce jar applesauce
1 cup dry white wine
1 teaspoon caraway seeds
    (optional)
1 pound knackwurst (about 4)
Mashed potatoes (optional)
Cooked noodles (optional)

In a large skillet combine sauerkraut, applesauce, wine, and caraway seeds; blend well. Top with the knackwurst. Cover and simmer over moderate heat (about 250° F.) 5 minutes. Remove cover and continue to cook until most of liquid is absorbed, about 15 minutes. Serve with mashed potatoes or noodles, if desired. Serves 4.

Shallots

Shallots, a mild member of the onion family, are usually marketed in dried form. They grow in clusters which are usually separated into cloves. Because shallots are not in great supply, they are rather expensive to use as a vegetable. Use them when you want a very mild onion flavor in omelets or soups.

Squash, Summer

Summer squash are immature squash; the entire squash, including the skin, is edible. There are several varieties: the yellow, which may be straight or crooknecked; the white patty pan, which is flat, scalloped, and disk-shaped; the green zucchini; the striped cocozelle; and the light green chayote.

Look for firm squash with glossy skin and a fresh appearance.

To cook summer squash, wash; do not pare. Cut a slice from the stem and blossom ends. Cut into cubes or slices (or lengthwise halves if recipe directs). Cook, covered, in one inch of boiling salted water ten to fifteen minutes, just until tender.

✑ Baked Stuffed Zucchini

4 zucchini or yellow summer squash, about 6 inches long
2 tablespoons instant minced onion
2 tablespoons water
¼ cup fine dry bread crumbs
2 tablespoons finely chopped green pepper
1 tablespoon chopped pimiento
½ teaspoon seasoned salt
Few grains pepper

Place whole washed zucchini in boiling water to barely cover; cover and cook over moderately low heat (about 225° F.) 7 minutes. Heat oven to 350° F. Drain zucchini and cool slightly. Cut into halves lengthwise. Scoop out pulp, leaving a ¼-inch shell, and reserve. Sprinkle onion over the water and let stand 1 minute. Coarsely chop the reserved zucchini pulp and mix with onion, bread crumbs, green pepper, pimiento, seasoned salt, and pepper. Spoon mixture into zucchini shells and sprinkle with additional crumbs, if desired. Bake 30 minutes. Serves 4.

✑ Sautéed Zucchini

1 medium-sized zucchini, cut into ¼-inch slices

Dip zucchini slices in egg, then in the bread crumbs to coat well on all sides. Melt butter in a large skillet over

1 egg, slightly beaten
Seasoned fine dry bread
crumbs (about 1 cup)
¼ cup butter or margarine

moderately low heat (about 225° F.). Add zucchini slices in a single layer and cook over moderately high heat (about 275° F.) until lightly brown on one side, about 2 minutes. Turn and brown lightly on the other side. Serves 2.

✎ Zucchini Parmigiana

2 pounds zucchini
3 tablespoons butter or
margarine
1½ teaspoons salt
2 teaspoons chopped fresh
parsley
½ cup grated Parmesan
cheese

Heat oven to 350° F. Wash zucchini thoroughly and thinly slice. Arrange a layer of zucchini in a greased shallow 1½-quart baking dish. Dot with some of the butter; sprinkle with some of the salt, parsley, and cheese. Repeat layers. Cover and bake 30 minutes; uncover and continue baking for 20 minutes or until crisp-tender. Serves 4 to 6.

✎ Sicilian Squash

2 pounds yellow summer
squash
2 tablespoons olive oil
1 clove garlic, minced
2 tablespoons wine vinegar
1 teaspoon sugar
1 teaspoon salt
2 teaspoons chopped mint
leaves

Wash squash and cut into thin, crosswise slices. Heat oil in large skillet over moderate heat (about 250° F.). Add squash and garlic; cook about 10 to 15 minutes, until just tender, stirring occasionally. Add remaining ingredients; cover and cook 5 minutes longer over moderately low heat (about 225° F.). Serves 4.

Squash, Winter

The winter squash are those varieties of squash that are marketed only when mature. The most common varieties are the green corrugated acorn; the pale yellow butternut; the green and gold banana; the green and blue Hubbard; and the buttercup, or turban.

Look for firm squash with thick rind. Squash should feel heavy for its size.

To boil squash, wash, cut in half lengthwise, and remove any seeds and stringy pulp. (Pare butternut squash.) Cut squash into three to four inch squares. Cook in a large, covered saucepan in two inches of boiling salted water about thirty minutes until tender. Drain thoroughly. Scrape pulp from rind and mash. Season to taste with butter, salt, and pepper. A two-pound squash yields about four cups mashed squash.

To bake squash (except acorn), rinse, cut in half lengthwise, and remove seeds. Cut into three to four inch squares and place in a large baking pan. Add two cups boiling salted water to pan. Cover and bake seventy to eighty minutes in a 400° F. oven, until skin is easily pierced with a fork and pulp is tender. Drain thoroughly. Scrape pulp from rind and mash. Season to taste with butter, salt and pepper.

To bake acorn squash, wash and cut in half lengthwise. Remove strings and seeds. Place, cut-side down, in a greased baking pan. Bake at 400° F. for thirty minutes. Remove from oven, turn squash halves cut-side up. Sprinkle with salt and put a pat of butter into the squash cavity. You may add brown sugar also. Bake another twenty to thirty minutes until tender. Serve in the shell. Acorn squash is best baked, not boiled, since it has a moist pulp. Butternut squash may also be baked in the same way.

 Nut-Topped Squash

2 12-ounce packages frozen winter squash
⅓ cup butter or margarine
¼ cup light cream or dairy half-and-half
2 tablespoons dark brown sugar
½ teaspoon salt
¼ teaspoon pepper
⅛ teaspoon ground cinnamon
⅛ teaspoon ground nutmeg
¼ cup firmly packed dark brown sugar
2 tablespoons light corn syrup
2 tablespoons melted butter or margarine
1 cup coarsely chopped walnuts

Cook squash according to package directions. Add the ⅓ cup butter, the cream, the 2 tablespoons brown sugar, the salt, pepper, cinnamon, and nutmeg; mix thoroughly. Place in buttered deep 1½-quart casserole. Combine the remaining ingredients. Spread over squash. Heat oven to 350° F. Bake casserole 25 to 30 minutes, until squash is hot and topping has melted. Serves 6 to 8.

Squash Creole

2 tablespoons butter or margarine
½ cup finely chopped onion

Heat oven to 375° F. Melt butter in skillet over moderate heat (about 250° F.); add onion, garlic, and green pepper and cook until tender. Blend in flour. Gradually add

1 *clove garlic, finely minced*
½ *cup chopped green pepper*
2 *tablespoons flour*
1 *16-ounce can stewed*
   tomatoes
1 *teaspoon sugar*
½ *teaspoon dried basil leaves*
1 *bay leaf*
½ *teaspoon salt*
Few grains pepper
2 *pounds acorn or butternut*
   squash

tomatoes, mixing well. Cook, stirring constantly, until thickened. Remove from heat. Add sugar, basil, bay leaf, salt, and pepper. Cut squash in half; cut into ¾-inch slices. Remove skin, seeds, and stringy portion from slices. Place squash in a 1½-quart casserole; pour in sauce. Cover and bake 55 to 60 minutes, or until tender. Serves 4 to 6.

🥬 Squash Custard

2 *cups mashed boiled or*
   baked Hubbard squash
¼ *cup grated American*
   cheese food
3 *eggs, beaten*
½ *teaspoon salt*
¼ *cup finely chopped onion*
2 *tablespoons vegetable oil or*
   shortening
1 *package white sauce mix*
   Milk
¼ *cup fine dry bread crumbs*

Heat oven to 350° F. Combine squash, cheese, eggs and salt; beat until thoroughly blended. Cook onion in the vegetable oil over moderately low heat (about 225° F.) until tender but not browned. Stir into squash mixture. Combine sauce mix and milk according to package directions and cook over moderate heat (about 250° F.), stirring constantly, until thickened. Stir into squash mixture and mix thoroughly. Pour into a greased, straight-sided 1½-quart casserole or soufflé dish and sprinkle with bread crumbs. Place the casserole in a deep 3-quart casserole and fill the large casserole with water to the level of the custard. Bake 70 to 75 minutes, until custard is firm. Replace water that evaporates from large casserole as needed. Serves 4 to 6.

Tomatoes

Hothouse tomatoes are available year-round. Vine-ripened tomatoes are available in the summer months. There are several varieties of round, red tomatoes, and a few yellow ones. The fresh red or yellow plum-shaped tomatoes are often in the market during summer months, and the little red cherry tomato or love apple is now marketed almost year-round.

Look for firm, heavy tomatoes that are not overripe. Sometimes tomatoes are purchased green for frying.

Tomatoes for salads need only be washed and cored for slicing or quartering. Many people prefer to skin them, however. To do it, dip the whole tomato into a pan of boiling water; leave about a half-minute. Spoon out of the water. Let cool a bit and skin will strip off easily. To cook, cut peeled tomatoes into quarters. Season with salt and pepper, simmer gently in their own juice for eight to ten minutes. Do not cover.

✒ Broiled Tomato Halves

4 whole ripe tomatoes
½ cup fine dry bread crumbs
¼ teaspoon salt
Few grains pepper
4 tablespoons melted butter
   or margarine
1 teaspoon finely chopped
   onion
1 teaspoon finely chopped
   green pepper

Preheat broiler. Wash tomatoes, remove stem end, and cut in half crosswise. Combine bread crumbs, salt, and pepper. Dip cut surfaces of tomatoes first in melted butter and then in crumb mixture. Sprinkle tops with onion and green pepper. Place in a shallow pan and broil about 5 inches from source of heat until tender and browned. Serves 4.

✒ Baked Tomato Halves

4 medium-sized tomatoes
¾ cup fine dry bread crumbs
⅓ cup Cheddar cheese,
   coarsely shredded
¼ cup melted butter or
   margarine

Heat oven to 375° F. Wash tomatoes and cut each in half crosswise. Toss together bread crumbs, cheese and butter; mound crumbs on top of tomato halves. Bake 25 to 30 minutes, or until the tomatoes are hot and the bread crumbs on top are lightly browned. Serves 4.

✒ Tomatoes Benedict

2 medium-sized tomatoes,
   cut in half
4 large mushroom caps
2 tablespoons melted butter
   or margarine
12 ¼-inch slices Canadian
   bacon
4 slices buttered toast, or 2
   English muffins split and
   toasted
1 recipe Hollandaise Sauce
   (recipe on page 488)
2 tablespoons chopped fresh
   parsley

Place tomatoes and mushroom caps (cup side up) on broiler rack. Spoon ½ teaspoon melted butter into each mushroom cap and brush tomatoes with melted butter. Place in preheated broiler about 3 inches from heat and broil for 4 minutes. Arrange Canadian bacon on the broiler rack with the tomatoes and mushrooms and continue to broil 3 to 4 minutes, or until tomatoes and mushrooms are tender. Place 3 slices of bacon on each slice of toast. Top each with a tomato half and a mushroom. Spoon Hollandaise Sauce over each and sprinkle with parsley. Serves 4.

✌ *Hearty Stuffed Tomatoes*

6 large, firm tomatoes
Salt and pepper
1 can condensed cream of
    mushroom soup
¾ cup shredded Cheddar
    cheese
1 4-ounce can sliced
    mushrooms, drained
1 tablespoon snipped chives
1 egg, slightly beaten
⅓ cup finely chopped celery
1 tablespoon chopped
    pimiento
1 tablespoon lemon juice
¼ teaspoon salt
¼ cup fine dry bread crumbs

Wash tomatoes; cut a slice from stem end of each and scoop out pulp, leaving a shell about ½ inch thick. Sprinkle inside with salt and pepper; invert and drain 10 minutes. In a saucepan mix soup, ½ cup of the shredded cheese, mushrooms, chives, egg, celery, pimiento, lemon juice, and the ¼ teaspoon salt. Stir, cooking over moderately low heat (about 225° F.), until mixture is smooth and blended. Stir in bread crumbs. Spoon mixture into tomatoes. Place tomatoes in shallow baking dish and sprinkle tops with the remaining ¼ cup cheese. Heat oven to 375° F. Bake 20 minutes, or until cheese is lightly browned. Serves 6.

✌ *Tomatoes à la Provençale*

8 medium-sized tomatoes
Salt and pepper
1 cup finely chopped fresh
    parsley
1½ cloves garlic, crushed
½ cup fine dry bread crumbs
½ cup olive oil

Heat oven to 375° F. Cut tomatoes in half and place, cut-sides up, in a large shallow baking pan. Sprinkle with salt and pepper. Mix parsley and garlic; spoon on top of tomato halves. Sprinkle bread crumbs over parsley. Pour olive oil over tomatoes. Bake 20 to 30 minutes. Serves 8.

White Turnips

White turnips are generally available year round.

Look for smooth, firm roots; the tops should be young, fresh, and green.

To cook turnips, remove tops and cook as greens (see page 522). Remove root and cut a slice from the rootlet end and a slice from the stem end of the turnip. Pare thinly. White turnips may be cooked whole but will cook more quickly sliced, diced, or cut into strips. Cook, covered, in two inches of boiling salted water. Whole turnips will take about thirty minutes. Sliced or diced turnips will take ten to twenty minutes. Cook just until tender. Serve with butter or margarine and salt and pepper.

Yellow Turnips, or Rutabagas

When shopping for yellow turnips, look for firm, heavy roots. Yellow turnips are usually marketed without tops. They may have a heavy wax coating on them to protect the moisture of the vegetable.

To cook yellow turnips, scrub well and pare thinly. Cut into slices, strips, or half-inch cubes. Cook in two inches of boiling salted water for thirty-five to forty minutes, until tender.

~§ Mashed Turnip

1½ *pounds yellow or white turnip*
2 *tablespoons butter or margarine*
½ *teaspoon salt*
⅛ *teaspoon pepper*

Wash turnip. Cut in half and place cut-side down on cutting board. Cut each half in about 3 slices. Peel slices and cut into cubes. Rinse thoroughly and place in a large kettle. Add 2 inches boiling salted water. Cover and cook over moderately low heat (about 225° F.) about 40 minutes, until fork-tender. Drain and mash with a potato masher. Add the butter, salt, and pepper and mix well. Place over low heat (about 200° F.) for a few minutes to evaporate excess moisture; serve hot. Makes about 2 cups mashed turnip, or serves 3 to 4.

Note: White turnips will need shorter cooking time.

~§ Turnip Soufflé

2 *cups cooked mashed yellow turnip (see preceding recipe)*
1 *cup soft bread crumbs*
1 *tablespoon sugar*
¼ *teaspoon ground mace*
⅛ *teaspoon ground ginger*
¼ *teaspoon salt*
½ *cup milk*
1 *egg*
1 *tablespoon butter or margarine*

Heat oven to 350° F. Combine mashed turnip, bread crumbs, sugar, mace, ginger, and salt. Combine milk and egg and stir into turnip mixture. Pour into a greased deep 1-quart casserole and dot with the 1 tablespoon butter. Bake 45 minutes, until top is lightly browned. Serves 3 to 4.

~§ Turnip Patties

3 *cups thinly sliced white or yellow turnip (about 1½ pounds)*

Simmer turnip and onion slices in boiling salted water over low heat (about 200° F.) until fork-tender, 20 to 40 minutes. Drain well and mash. Add soft bread crumbs,

¼ *cup sliced onion*
⅓ *cup soft bread crumbs*
¼ *cup finely chopped fresh parsley*
1 *egg, slightly beaten*
Few grains pepper
Fine dry bread crumbs
Vegetable oil or shortening for frying

parsley, egg, and pepper; mix well. Chill 2 to 3 hours. Shape into patties, using about ⅓ cup mixture for each. Coat patties well with dry bread crumbs. Heat a small amount of oil in a skillet over moderately high heat (about 300° F.). Add patties and brown on both sides. Serves 4.

✑ Turnip-and-Onion Casserole

2 *pounds yellow turnips*
4 *cups thinly sliced onion*
Salt and pepper
1 *chicken bouillon cube*
½ *cup boiling water*
2 *tablespoons butter or margarine*

Heat oven to 325° F. Pare turnips; cut in half and then into thin crosswise slices. Arrange alternate layers of turnip and onion in a greased 2½-quart casserole. Sprinkle layers lightly with salt and pepper. Dissolve bouillon cube in boiling water and pour over vegetables. Dot with butter. Cover casserole tightly and bake 2 to 2¼ hours, or until turnip is fork-tender. Serves 6.

Vegetable Platters

Mixed vegetables, seasoned and served together, can make a nice change of pace. These are a few examples.

✑ Steamed Vegetables with Cheese

2 *tablespoons vegetable oil*
1 *large onion, peeled and sliced thin*
1 *large green pepper, seeded and diced (1 cup)*
½ *pound fresh mushrooms, quartered (2½ cups)*
1 *pound (3 medium) zucchini, cut into 1-inch chunks (4 cups)*
½ *teaspoon salt*
½ *pound mozzarella, Fontina or Edam cheese, sliced thin*

In a large skillet heat oil over moderately high heat; stir in onion and cook about 5 minutes, until soft and yellow. Stir in green pepper, mushrooms, zucchini and salt; reduce heat to moderate, cover and steam 10 minutes, until vegetables are crisp-tender. Arrange cheese evenly on top of vegetables; remove skillet from heat, cover and leave 5 minutes, until cheese melts. Serves 4.

VEGETABLES

✒ Braised Mixed Vegetables

¼ cup butter or margarine
½ cup finely chopped onion
1 cup chopped green pepper
½ pound sliced mushrooms
8 stalks celery, thinly sliced
1 16-ounce can chop suey
  vegetables with bamboo
  shoots, undrained
1 beef bouillon cube
2 tablespoons soy sauce
2 10-ounce packages frozen
  chopped spinach, thawed

Melt butter in an electric skillet with temperature control set at 250° F., or in a large skillet over moderate heat (about 250° F.). Add onion, green pepper, and mushrooms; cook about 5 minutes. Add celery, chop suey vegetables, bouillon cube, and soy sauce. Cook 7 to 8 minutes, stirring occasionally. Add spinach; cover and heat 3 minutes, or until spinach is just wilted and hot. Serves 8.

✒ Vegetable Medley

¼ cup corn oil
1½ cups peeled, thinly sliced
  onion
¾ pound thinly sliced
  zucchini
¾ cup peeled, thinly sliced
  carrots
½ cup fresh peas (about ½
  pound unshelled)
½ pound fresh green beans,
  cut into 1-inch pieces
½ cup water
3 tablespoons dried
  currants
¾ teaspoon salt
2 teaspoons curry powder
1½ tablespoons soy sauce
2 cups hot cooked brown
  rice
¼ cup toasted sesame seeds

Heat 2 tablespoons of the oil in a *wok* over moderately high heat (about 300° F.). Add onion and zucchini. Stirring frequently, cook until onion is lightly browned, about 5 minutes. Remove vegetables with a slotted spoon; set aside. Add to the *wok* the remaining 2 tablespoons of oil, carrots, peas and beans; cook 5 minutes, stirring frequently. Reduce heat to moderate (about 250° F.). Add water, currants, salt, curry and soy sauce. Cover and, stirring occasionally, cook until beans are crisp-tender, about 15 minutes. Stir in onion and zucchini. Cover and cook 5 minutes. Serve over brown rice and sprinkle with sesame seeds. Serves 4.

✒ Foil-Baked Vegetables

3 medium-sized potatoes, cut
  into strips
2 medium-sized carrots, cut
  into ¼-inch rounds

Tear off four 18-inch squares heavy-duty aluminum foil. Place a quarter of the potatoes in the center of each square. Top each with a quarter of the carrot, green pepper, and onion slices. Sprinkle with celery salt and

½ *green pepper, cut into thin strips*
1 *medium-sized onion, sliced*
Celery salt
Few grains pepper
1 *cup packaged precooked rice*
1 *18-ounce can tomato juice*
¾ *cup chili sauce*
1 *teaspoon brown steak sauce*

pepper. Place ¼ cup of rice on each portion of vegetables. Combine tomato juice, chili sauce, and steak sauce. Pour about ⅔ cup of mixture over each portion of vegetables. Wrap each portion in the foil, sealing well. Leave room for rice to expand. Place in a 350° F. oven for 40 minutes, or on outdoor grill for 1 to 1½ hours, until vegetables are tender. Serves 4.

Vegetable Tempura

1 *cup unbleached white flour, unsifted*
1 *cup whole-wheat flour, unsifted*
1½ *teaspoons salt*
1½ *cups cold water*
1 *medium-sized carrot, peeled and diagonally sliced*
1 *medium-sized parsnip, peeled and thinly sliced*
1 *medium-sized peeled onion, cut into 8 wedges*
8 *small broccoli flowerettes (about ½ pound)*
8 *small cauliflowerettes (about ½ pound)*
8 *small mushrooms (about ¼ pound)*
About 2 quarts oil (half vegetable and half peanut oil)

In a medium-sized bowl mix together white flour, whole-wheat flour and salt until well blended. Add water and stir just enough to make a smooth batter. Chill batter 15 minutes. Meanwhile prepare vegetables. In a *wok* heat oil to 385° F. Dip individual pieces of vegetables a few at a time into the batter to coat evenly. Pieces should be coated with a thin layer of batter. If batter seems too thick, add a little more water. Fry in the hot oil until golden brown, about 5 minutes on each side. Drain pieces on paper towels and keep warm in a 200° F. oven until all the vegetables are done. Serves 4.

Dried Beans, Peas, and Lentils

Dried beans and their close cousins, dried peas and lentils, are bargain foods—nutritionally and budgetwise. A pound will make eight servings or more, depending upon what you add to them.

Split peas and lentils need no soaking before cooking. Whole peas and beans do need some soaking before use, usually overnight, to replace part of the water moisture lost in drying.

Overnight soaking of the dried vegetables isn't a chore, but the United States Agricultural Research Service recommends this shortcut if you need to save time: cover beans with boiling water; boil two minutes. Remove from heat and soak one hour before further cooking.

Boston Baked Beans

- *2 16-ounce packages dried pea beans*
- *1 teaspoon baking soda*
- *1 pound salt pork*
- *1 medium-sized onion, thinly sliced*
- *⅔ cup molasses*
- *½ cup sugar*
- *2 teaspoons dry mustard*
- *4 teaspoons salt*
- *½ teaspoon pepper*

Cover beans with cold water and let soak overnight. In the morning pour off water; cover with fresh water. Add soda and bring slowly to a boil over moderately low heat (about 225° F.); simmer 10 minutes. Drain and reserve bean liquid. Cut half the salt pork into 1-inch cubes; place in bottom of a 4-quart bean pot or casserole. Add onion. Pour in all the beans. Mix molasses, sugar, mustard, salt, pepper, and 2 cups of the reserved bean liquid. Pour over beans. Score remaining piece of salt pork at ½-inch intervals down to the rind; push it down into beans with fat side up until about ½ inch protrudes above beans. Add enough bean liquid to just cover beans. Heat oven to 300° F. Bake beans uncovered at least 6 hours. Add a little hot water as necessary to keep juice bubbling at top of pot during the entire baking time. Serves 10 to 12.

Burgundy Beans

- *1 pound dried red, pink, or pinto beans*
- *5 cups water*
- *2 tablespoons vegetable oil*
- *½ cup finely chopped onion*
- *1 clove garlic, minced*
- *2 teaspoons salt*
- *1 pound ground beef*
- *1 egg, slightly beaten*
- *½ cup dry seasoned bread crumbs*
- *2 tablespoons butter or margarine*

Wash beans. Heat water to boiling in a Dutch oven. Add beans, cover and boil 2 minutes. Remove from heat and let stand, covered, 1 hour. Add vegetable oil, onion, garlic and the 2 teaspoons salt. Cover and place over moderate heat (about 250° F.); bring to boil and simmer 1½ hours over moderately low heat (about 225° F.), or until almost tender. While beans are cooking, mix beef, egg, and bread crumbs; shape into 1½-inch balls. Melt butter in skillet over moderately high heat (about 275° F.) and brown meat balls lightly. Drain liquid from beans. Mix beans, tomatoes, wine, and the 2 teaspoons salt; pour into a 3-quart casserole. Arrange meat balls over top. Heat oven to 325° F. Bake beans 45 minutes.

1 16-ounce can stewed
    tomatoes
¾ cup Burgundy wine
2 teaspoons salt
½ 8-ounce package
    mozzarella cheese

Remove from oven. Slice mozzarella cheese thinly and place on top of meat balls. Bake about 15 minutes longer, or until cheese is melted and lightly browned. Serves 6 to 8.

❧ Italian Baked Beans

2 cups large white dried
    beans, washed
6 cups water
1 tablespoon salt
2 tablespoons butter or
    margarine
1 cup finely chopped onion
2 cloves garlic, minced
1½ cups finely chopped celery
½ cup vegetable oil
2 tablespoons chopped fresh
    parsley
½ teaspoon ground thyme
¼ teaspoon dried basil
    leaves
¼ teaspoon pepper
1 cup canned stewed
    tomatoes
½ cup grated Parmesan or
    Romano cheese

Cover beans with water. Bring to boiling point and boil 2 minutes. Remove from heat. Cover and let stand 1 hour. Add salt and butter. Place over moderately high heat (about 275° F.) and bring to boiling point; cover and reduce heat to moderately low (about 225° F.). Simmer 2 hours, or until tender. Drain beans and reserve liquid. Cook onion, garlic, and celery in oil in skillet over moderately low heat (about 225° F.) until tender; add parsley, thyme, basil, and pepper. Measure bean liquid and add water if needed to make ⅔ cup liquid. Add to vegetable mixture and heat to boiling point. Stir together beans, tomatoes, and the vegetable mixture. Pour into greased 2-quart deep casserole. Heat oven to 350° F. Bake 50 minutes. Remove from oven and sprinkle top with Parmesan cheese. Return to oven and bake 10 minutes longer. Serves 6 to 8.

❧ Split Pea Rarebit

½ cup green or yellow split
    peas, well rinsed
1¼ cups water
¼ teaspoon salt
1 tablespoon butter or
    margarine
2 tablespoons chopped
    onion
1 can condensed Cheddar
    cheese soup, undiluted

(Ingredients continued on page 554)

In a heavy saucepan over moderate heat (about 250° F.) combine peas, water, and salt. Bring to a boil. Cover tightly and boil gently until peas are tender but hold their shape, about 20 minutes, stirring occasionally. Drain and set aside. Return saucepan to heat and melt butter; add onion and cook until lightly browned. Stir in soup, beer, Worcestershire, and dry mustard. Blend smooth (a wire whip is helpful). Stir in cooked peas and heat to serving temperature. Serve on toast points or Melba toast. Serves 3 to 4.

½ *cup beer or ale*
½ *teaspoon Worcestershire*
   sauce
¼ *teaspoon dry mustard*
Toast or Melba toast

◅§ *Savory Supper Dish*

1⅓ *cups green or yellow*
   split peas, well rinsed
3 *cups water*
¾ *teaspoon salt*
6 *slices raw bacon (about*
   ¼ pound)
2 *tablespoons chopped*
   onion
2 *tablespoons chopped*
   green pepper
1 *small clove garlic, pressed*
1 *pound ground beef*
   round
1 *8-ounce can stewed*
   tomatoes
¼ *teaspoon chili powder*

In a heavy saucepan combine peas, water, and ½ teaspoon of the salt. Place over moderate heat (about 250° F.) and bring to a boil. Cover tightly and boil gently until peas are tender but hold their shape, about 20 to 25 minutes, stirring occasionally. Drain. Heat oven to 350° F. Meanwhile in a skillet over moderately high heat (about 325° F.) cook bacon until lightly browned but not crisp. Remove bacon and drain on paper towels. In the same skillet with the bacon drippings cook onion, green pepper, and garlic until onion is lightly browned. Remove with slotted spoon. Add ground beef to skillet and cook until no longer pink. Remove and drain off any excess fat. In a bowl mix together drained peas, onion mixture, beef, tomatoes, chili powder, and remaining ¼ teaspoon salt. Turn into a deep 1½-quart casserole and bake uncovered 25 minutes, or until bubbling hot, adding the bacon slices to the top the last 10 minutes. Serves 4 to 6.

◅§ *Lentil-Potato Soup*

½ *cup dried lentils*
3 *medium-sized potatoes*
   (about 1 pound), peeled
   and diced
2 *large onions, peeled and*
   diced (about 2½ cups)
1¼ *teaspoons salt*
⅛ *teaspoon pepper*
6 *cups water*
1 *hard-cooked egg, peeled*
   and sliced
¼ *cup chopped fresh parsley*

In a Dutch oven or large saucepot bring lentils, potatoes, onions, salt, pepper and water to a boil over high heat. Reduce heat to moderate and simmer 1 hour, until lentils are very tender. Place half the soup in an electric blender, cover and blend at medium speed until smooth. Repeat with remaining soup. Pour all the soup back into the pot and reheat, adding ½ cup water if soup is too thick. Taste soup, add more salt and pepper if desired. To serve, top each bowl of soup with egg slices and parsley. Makes 6 cups soup, or serves 4.

Lentils and Short Ribs

2 tablespoons vegetable oil
3 pounds beef short ribs, cut into serving pieces
4½ cups water
1 tablespoon salt
⅛ teaspoon pepper
1 bay leaf
1 medium-sized onion, thinly sliced
1 16-ounce package dried lentils
1 8-ounce package mixed dried fruits, cut up

Heat oven to 350° F. Heat oil in a large skillet over moderately high heat (about 300° F.); brown short ribs on all sides. Arrange short ribs in a deep 3-quart casserole. Add water, salt, pepper, bay leaf, and onion. Cover and bake 1 to 1½ hours, or until meat is tender. Remove from oven. Wash lentils thoroughly and add to short ribs with the mixed dried fruits. Cover and bake 1 hour, stirring occasionally during baking. Serves 6 to 8.

Baked Lentils

1⅓ cups lentils, well rinsed
2½ cups water
1 teaspoon salt
¼ to ⅓ cup honey
2 tablespoons butter or margarine

Heat oven to 375° F. In a heavy saucepan combine lentils, water, and salt. Place over moderate heat (about 250° F.) and bring to a boil. Cover tightly and boil gently until lentils are tender but still hold their shape, about 15 minutes. Remove from heat. Add honey and butter, stirring until butter is melted. Turn into a deep 1-quart casserole. Bake uncovered 20 minutes. Serves 4.

Brazilian Black Beans and Rice

1¼ cups dried black beans (½ pound)
4 cups water
1¼ teaspoons salt
1 large clove garlic, peeled and slightly flattened
1 small onion, peeled and stuck with 3 whole cloves
2 tablespoons olive or vegetable oil
1 cup diced, peeled onion
1 large green pepper, seeded and diced
2⅔ cups cooked rice (1 cup uncooked)
Salsa (recipe follows)

In a heavy, medium-sized, covered saucepan soak beans in water for 8 to 24 hours in a cool place. Add salt to pan and bring beans to a boil over moderately high heat; cover pan, reduce heat to moderately low and simmer 1 hour. Poke garlic and clove-studded onion under beans, cover pan and cook 30 minutes to 1 hour longer, checking beans every 15 minutes and adding more water if liquid falls below top layer of beans. About 15 minutes before beans are done, heat oil in a medium-sized skillet over moderately high heat; add diced onion and pepper and cook, stirring often, until onion begins to brown. Remove whole onion and garlic from cooked beans and discard; add beans and liquid to onion and pepper and cook a few minutes to blend flavors. Serve black beans over cooked rice and top with Salsa. Makes 3 cups beans, or serves 4.

VEGETABLES

Salsa

1 14½-ounce can sliced baby
   tomatoes, drained
¾ cup diced, peeled red or
   white sweet onion
1 teaspoon minced, peeled
   garlic
1 tablespoon wine vinegar
1 teaspoon olive or vegetable
   oil
½ teaspoon salt
3 dashes Tabasco sauce

In a small bowl break up tomatoes with a spoon. Mix in remaining ingredients, cover sauce and refrigerate up to 12 hours to let flavors blend. Serve with Brazilian Black Beans and Rice. Makes 1½ cups.

Note: Use liquid from canned tomatoes in a soup or sauce.

ঔ French Bean Pot

1¼ cups Great Northern
   beans (½ pound)
1 quart water
1 teaspoon salt
2 tablespoons olive oil
2 teaspoons minced, peeled
   garlic
2½ cups diced, peeled onion
1 1-pound can whole peeled
   tomatoes
1 small unpeeled eggplant
   (1 pound), cut into 1-inch
   cubes
1 teaspoon dried basil
   leaves
½ teaspoon salt
¼ cup chopped fresh parsley
   (optional)
Freshly grated Parmesan
   cheese (optional)

In a large, covered saucepot or Dutch oven soak beans in water for 8 to 24 hours in a cool place. Add the 1 teaspoon of salt to the soaked beans and bring to a boil over moderately high heat; reduce heat to moderate and simmer 1 hour, or until beans are tender but not mushy. Stir in oil, garlic, onion, tomatoes, eggplant, basil and the ½ teaspoon salt; increase heat to moderately high, and when mixture begins to bubble, reduce heat to moderate and simmer 30 minutes, stirring occasionally. Remove about ¼ cup of the beans from pot, mash with a fork and stir back into pot. Simmer 15 minutes longer, until mixture is thick and very little liquid remains. Sprinkle with parsley, and if desired, serve with grated cheese. Serves 4.

ঔ Falafel (Fried Chick-Pea Rounds)

1½ cups dried chick-peas
4 cups water

Rinse chick-peas and discard any bad ones. Soak chick-peas in the water in refrigerator from 8 to 24 hours;

1 medium-sized onion,
   peeled and chopped fine
¼ cup lemon juice
1½ teaspoons baking powder
2 teaspoons salt
¼ teaspoon pepper
2 cloves garlic, peeled and
   crushed
2 tablespoons finely
   chopped fresh parsley,
   preferably flat-leaf
1 teaspoon ground cumin
2 teaspoons ground
   coriander
Few grains of cayenne pepper
   (optional)
Vegetable oil for frying
Yogurt Sauce
   (recipe follows)

drain. Put chick-peas and onion through a meat grinder twice, using the fine blade. Put ground mixture into a medium-sized mixing bowl, add remaining ingredients except oil and Yogurt Sauce and mix well. (Mixture may be refrigerated 24 hours before cooking.) Shape level tablespoonfuls of the chick-pea mixture into cakes 1¾ inches in diameter. (This may be done several hours ahead.) Pour 2 inches of oil into a deep fryer or heavy, 1½-quart saucepan; heat over moderately high heat to 325° F. on a frying thermometer. Lower chick-pea cakes carefully into the hot oil, cooking about 6 at a time. Cook 4 to 5 minutes, or until well browned; lower heat if browning too quickly. Lift cakes out and drain on paper towels. Fry ahead, wrap loosely in foil and reheat for 20 minutes in a 300° F. oven. Serve with Yogurt Sauce. Makes about 32 cakes.

Yogurt Sauce

2 cups plain yogurt
1 teaspoon salt
2 tablespoons finely chopped
   fresh parsley, preferably
   flat-leaf

Mix yogurt and salt in a small bowl. Pour into serving bowl, sprinkle with parsley, cover and refrigerate until serving time. Makes about 2 cups sauce.

✑ Sweet and Pungent Chick-Peas

1¼ cups dried chick-peas or
   garbanzo beans (½
   pound)
5 cups water
2 tablespoons vegetable oil
2 cups chopped, peeled
   onion
1 teaspoon minced, peeled
   garlic

In a heavy, medium-sized covered saucepan soak chick-peas in the 5 cups water for 8 to 24 hours. Bring to a boil over moderately high heat; reduce heat to moderate and simmer gently 1 hour, or until chick-peas are tender. In a medium-sized skillet heat oil over moderately high heat; add onion and garlic, reduce heat to moderate and cook, stirring frequently, until golden brown. Stir in cayenne, cumin and salt and cook five minutes longer. Add the ½ cup water, the catsup and

⅛ *teaspoon cayenne pepper*
⅛ *teaspoon ground cumin*
 1 *teaspoon salt*
½ *cup water*
 2 *tablespoons catsup*

cooked chick-peas, plus any remaining liquid; mix well and then cover and simmer 10 minutes. Makes 3½ cups, or serves 4.

CHAPTER XVI

RICE, PASTA, AND CEREALS

These are members of the starch family that can provide unexpected variety in menus, a change from the old concept that all big meals had to start with meat and potatoes. Rice, pastas, and cereals combine well with small amounts of meat or poultry to make most acceptable main dishes and add their share of protein for the budget-minded cook.

Rice

Rice, most frequently served hot as the starch on a dinner menu, is far more versatile than most of us in this country have discovered. It's an excellent ingredient to use in making stuffings, salads, and desserts. Today the packaged rices we buy have been processed so that they do not need to be washed before cooking as old recipes direct; washing would only remove valuable minerals and vitamins. A bland food, rice lends itself to the addition of innumerable flavorings and seasonings—witness the great variety of packaged seasoned rices on the market today. In addition to being available in seasoned varieties, rice comes in several other forms, which vary greatly in cost.

Regular milled white rice has the inedible outer hull and inner coating of bran removed. It is the most popular and useful kind of rice available in long-, short-, and medium-grained varieties. The long-grained is light and fluffy when cooked; the grains tend to separate. It is useful in almost any rice dish—in soups, stuffings; mixed with vegetables, meats, or fruits; or served alone. Short- and medium-grained rice cooks tender and moist;

the grains have a tendency to cling together. They are especially useful for making puddings, croquettes, and rice rings—in any recipe requiring tender, easily molded rice. They are also less expensive than the long-grained variety. One cup of uncooked rice yields three cups cooked.

Parboiled (coverted) rice is long-grained rice that has been steam-treated before milling to retain much of the vitamin and mineral content of the whole grain. It takes longer to cook than regular milled rice and requires more water in the process. When cooked, the grains are fluffy and plump and separate. One cup uncooked will yield four cups cooked.

Precooked rice is a form of long-grained rice that has been cooked before packaging and has only to be steamed in boiling water to be ready to serve. It's the time-saver rice. One cup yields two cups cooked. Follow recipe directions on package.

Brown rice is rice closest to its natural state; only the hull and some of the bran have been removed. Because of this, it is rich in vitamins and minerals. The distinctly nutlike flavor and chewy texture limit its use to stuffings, main dishes, or side dishes; it is not particularly suitable in desserts. Since brown rice requires more liquid and a longer cooking time, it can be substituted for white rice only in recipes in which the rice is cooked before it is mixed with the other ingredients. One cup of un-cooked brown rice yields four cups cooked.

Wild rice is not really rice, but the seed of a grass that grows in the Great Lakes region. Dark brown, rich in flavor, it is excellent used as stuffing for game birds and animals and a favored side dish with all poultry. The annual wild-rice crop is so small that the price is always high. To prepare, follow recipe instructions on the package.

Storage of uncooked rice is no problem, since rice is relatively nonperishable, but keep it in a cool place in a tightly covered container. Brown rice has a shorter storage life than white; plan to use it within a few months.

Cooked rice will keep about a week when stored in a covered container in the refrigerator. It can be reheated in the top of a double boiler, used cold in salads, or folded into whipped cream with chopped fruits and nuts for dessert.

Prepared properly, rice will be firm yet tender, niether hard nor mushy. For best results always use a *heavy* saucepan with a tight-fitting lid. A heavy aluminum pot—a Dutch oven or a pressure cooker without the pressure gauge—is ideal, as is enameled ironware.

Don't stir rice once it has come to a boil. Stirring mashes the grains, making them gummy. And don't lift the pot lid to see how it's doing—steam will escape and the cooking temperature will be lowered, which will result in the rice's sticking.

To keep rice warm before serving, you can leave it in the pot, covered, for about five or ten minutes, but if you leave it longer, it will "pack." Or keep it in a just-warm oven. If it is too moist for the use you intend, steam out excess moisture by placing the uncovered pot over the lowest flame possible for a few minutes.

The bland flavor of rice can be varied by cooking it in liquids other than water. Try chicken or beef broth, which can be made from bouillon cubes; onion soup made from a mix; tomato juice; fruit juices. Follow the basic recipe proportions of liquid and rice.

For saffron rice, add one large pinch of saffron per one cup of white rice to the water just before covering. Too much saffron is overpowering, but used in moderation, it gives a savory taste and a rich golden color to the rice. It is good with chicken or seafood.

Rice with dill is an excellent accompaniment to lamb, beef, or pot roast. Add two teaspoons of dried dillweed, not dillseed, to one cup of rice just before covering.

Vegetables also enhance rice. Chop an onion finely and cook it gently in a small amount of oil in the same pot in which the rice will cook; add rice and water and a few grains of freshly ground black pepper; cook as usual. Or slice six to eight fresh mushrooms, cook them in butter until lightly browned, and fold them into a cup of cooked rice.

Many ingredients can be added to cooked rice for extra taste and texture: pine nuts or slivered almonds, unsweetened coconut, a generous portion of chopped fresh parsley. When mixing in additional ingredients, fold them in gently with a two-pronged fork; don't stir.

Basic Cooking Method for Rice

*1 cup long-grained rice
1¾ cups water or other liquid
1 tablespoon butter or margarine, olive oil or vegetable oil
1 teaspoon salt

Combine rice, water, butter, and salt in a heavy, 2-quart saucepan. Bring to a boil over moderately high heat (about 275° F.); reduce heat to low (about 200° F.) and cover saucepan with a tight-fitting lid. Simmer, without lifting lid, 25 to 30 minutes, or until rice is tender. For a moister rice, use ¼ cup additional water. Makes 3 cups, or serves 4.

*Note: If you use parboiled rice, allow ¼ cup more water per cup of rice. Yield will be 4 cups cooked rice for 1 cup raw rice.

Baked Rice

2 tablespoons butter or margarine

Heat oven to 350° F. Melt butter in skillet over moderately high heat (about 300° F.). Add rice and cook

1 cup long-grained rice
2 chicken bouillon cubes
2 cups boiling water
2 tablespoons chopped fresh
   parsley

until lightly browned, stirring frequently. Spoon into a deep 1½-quart casserole. Dissolve bouillon cubes in boiling water; pour over rice. Sprinkle with parsley. Cover and bake 30 minutes. Serves 4.

✍ Rice with Pine Nuts

1 cup brown rice
3 tablespoons butter or
   margarine
½ cup pine nuts
3 tablespoons sesame seeds
½ teaspoon salt
1 tablespoon soy sauce

Prepare rice according to package directions. Meanwhile melt 2 tablespoons of the butter in a saucepan over moderate heat (about 250° F.). Add pine nuts and, stirring frequently, toast them until golden brown; set aside. In a small, dry skillet combine sesame seeds and salt. Place over moderately high heat (about 275° F.) and, stirring frequently, toast until golden brown. Combine hot cooked rice, pine nuts, sesame seeds, soy sauce and the remaining 1 tablespoon butter. Place over moderately low heat; stir until butter is melted. Serves 4 to 6.

✍ Chinese Brown Rice

1 tablespoon peanut oil
1 cup brown rice
2½ cups water
1 teaspoon peanut oil
2 eggs, at room temperature
2 tablespoons peanut oil
1 cup peeled and thinly
   sliced onion
1 clove garlic, peeled and
   crushed
½ cup diagonally sliced
   scallions or green onions
½ cup drained canned bean
   sprouts
1 cup fresh peas (about 1
   pound unshelled)
½ pound fresh mushrooms,
   rinsed and sliced
1½ teaspoons dark sesame
   seed oil
1 tablespoon soy sauce
1 teaspoon salt

Heat the 1 tablespoon peanut oil in a large skillet over moderately high heat (about 325° F.). Add the rice. Stirring frequently, cook until it browns. Place the rice in a saucepan and add water. Place pan over moderately high heat (about 300° F.) and bring mixture to a boil. Reduce heat to low (about 200° F.). Cover tightly and cook 25 minutes, until water is all absorbed. Remove from heat and set aside. In an 8-inch skillet over moderately high heat (about 275° F.) heat the 1 teaspoon peanut oil. In a small bowl beat eggs slightly and pour them quickly into the skillet while tilting the pan to cover the bottom completely with the eggs; cook without stirring just long enough to brown the eggs lightly on the bottom. Turn eggs out onto two thicknesses of paper towel to dry. In a large skillet over moderately high heat (about 350° F.) heat the 2 tablespoons peanut oil. Add onion and garlic and, stirring frequently, cook until onion is crisp-tender. Add scallions, bean sprouts, peas and mushrooms and, stirring frequently, cook, uncovered, until vegetables are crisp-tender. Meanwhile cut the cooked egg into thin strips. Add rice, egg strips, sesame oil, soy sauce and salt to vegetable mixture. Heat, stirring frequently. Serves 6 to 8.

❧ Gourmet Spanish Rice

3 slices raw bacon
½ cup raw wild rice
½ cup raw brown rice
½ cup chopped onion
1 clove garlic, finely chopped
½ cup chopped green pepper
1 tablespoon butter or margarine
1 28-ounce can whole tomatoes
1 teaspoon salt
⅛ teaspoon pepper
1½ cups water
¼ cup sliced stuffed olives

Cook bacon in large skillet over moderately high heat (about 325° F.) until lightly browned. Remove bacon and crumble coarsely. Add all rice to bacon fat; cook over moderate heat (about 250° F.) 10 minutes, or until lightly browned, stirring frequently. Add onion, garlic, green pepper, and butter; cook until vegetables are tender. Add tomatoes, crumbled bacon, salt, pepper, and ½ cup of the water. Cover and simmer over low heat (about 200° F.) 25 minutes, stirring occasionally. Pour rice mixture into a greased 1½-quart casserole and stir in remaining 1 cup of water. Heat oven to 375° F. Bake casserole 30 minutes; fold in olives. Bake 15 minutes longer. Serves 6.

❧ Rice Casserole

6 tablespoons butter or margarine
1 medium-sized onion, finely chopped
1 clove garlic, mashed
1 medium-sized green pepper, finely chopped
1 cup long-grained rice
1 4-ounce can mushroom stems and pieces, undrained
2 tablespoons soy sauce
1 teaspoon dried oregano leaves
1 12½-ounce can chicken consommé
¾ cup water

Melt butter in skillet over moderate heat (about 250° F.); add onion, garlic, and green pepper, and cook until tender. Stir in rice and cook until lightly browned, stirring occasionally. Add mushrooms, soy sauce, and oregano; cover and simmer 20 minutes over low heat (about 200° F.), stirring occasionally. Heat oven to 350° F. Pour rice mixture into a deep buttered 1½-quart casserole; add consommé and water. Cover and bake 1¼ hours. Serves 6.

❧ Wild Rice Casserole

1 cup wild rice
1 beef or chicken bouillon cube
2 cups boiling water

Wash rice well and place in a 1½-quart casserole. Dissolve bouillon cube in the boiling water; pour over rice and let stand 2 to 3 hours. Heat oven to 350° F. Melt butter in a skillet over moderately low heat (about 225°

¼ cup butter or margarine
½ cup chopped onion
½ cup chopped celery
1 3-ounce can sliced broiled mushrooms
1½ teaspoons salt
Slivered almonds (optional)

F.); add onion and celery and cook until tender, stirring occasionally. Add cooked vegetables, mushrooms, and salt to rice and mix together. Cover and bake 30 minutes. Uncover and continue baking 20 minutes longer. Remove from oven and let stand 5 minutes before serving. Garnish with almonds, if desired. Serves 4.

✑ Risotto

2 tablespoons butter or margarine
6 tablespoons finely chopped onion
3 cups diluted canned chicken broth
¾ cup dry vermouth
1½ cups converted rice

Heat butter in a saucepan over moderately low heat (about 225° F.). Add onion and cook until tender, stirring frequently. Add broth and vermouth; cover and bring to a rolling boil. Add rice and reduce heat to low (about 200° F.); cook about 25 minutes, or until most of the liquid is absorbed. Remove from heat and fluff rice with a fork before serving. Serves 6 to 8.

✑ Rice Pilaf

2 tablespoons butter or margarine
1 cup long-grained rice
½ cup finely chopped onion
¾ teaspoon salt
⅛ teaspoon pepper
½ teaspoon dried oregano leaves
1¾ cups water
2 beef bouillon cubes
1 tablespoon butter or margarine
⅓ cup slivered, blanched almonds
2 teaspoons dried parsley flakes or 1 tablespoon finely chopped fresh parsley

Melt the 2 tablespoons butter in a 2-quart saucepan or Dutch oven with tight-fitting cover over moderate heat (about 250° F.). Add rice. Stir constantly until rice is golden brown. Stir in onion, salt, pepper, oregano, water, and bouillon cubes. Stir until cubes are dissolved. Cover and simmer over low heat (about 200° F.) 20 minutes, or until rice is tender and liquid is absorbed. Meanwhile melt remaining 1 tablespoon butter in a small saucepan over moderately low heat (about 225° F.). Stir in almonds and heat, stirring constantly, until almonds are lightly browned. Fold almonds and parsley into rice. Serves 6.

✑ Eastern Pilaf

½ cup butter or margarine
¼ cup unsalted pine nuts

Melt butter in a skillet over moderate heat (about 250° F.). Add nuts and cook until lightly browned, stirring

¼ cup shelled pistachio nuts
1 teaspoon ground mace
2 cups cold cooked rice

frequently. Add mace and rice and continue cooking, lifting rice with a large spoon until thoroughly heated and all the butter is absorbed. Serves 3 to 4.

❧ Nutted Rice

½ cup packaged wild rice
1 cup long-grained rice
2 cups water
3 tablespoons butter or
  margarine
1 teaspoon salt
½ cup chopped pecans

Cook wild rice according to package directions. Combine long-grained rice, water, butter, and salt in a heavy 2-quart saucepan. Bring to a boil; reduce heat to low (about 200° F.) and cover saucepan with a tight-fitting lid. Simmer, without lifting lid, 25 to 30 minutes, or until rice is tender. Combine white rice with cooked wild rice and pecans. Serves 6.

❧ Rice with Cashews and Peppers

1 cup long-grained rice
1¾ cups water
3 tablespoons butter or
  margarine
1½ cups sliced green pepper
¾ cup salted cashew nuts
Soy sauce (optional)

Combine rice, water, and 1 tablespoon of the butter in a heavy, 2-quart saucepan. Bring to a boil. Reduce heat to low (about 200° F.) and cover tightly. Simmer 25 to 30 minutes, or until rice is tender. While rice is cooking, melt the remaining 2 tablespoons butter in a skillet over moderately low heat (about 225° F.); add green pepper and cook, stirring occasionally, until tender. Add to cooked rice. Rinse nuts to remove salt and add to rice. Cover and heat 2 minutes. Serve with soy sauce, if desired. Serves 4 to 6.

❧ Rice with Fruit

1 cup long-grained or
  parboiled rice
2 tablespoons butter or
  margarine
⅛ teaspoon saffron
¾ teaspoon salt
1 12-ounce package mixed
  dried fruits
1 3-inch stick cinnamon
¼ teaspoon ground nutmeg
1 12-fluid-ounce can apricot
  nectar, plus enough water
  to make 2½ cups liquid

Combine all ingredients in a 2-quart saucepan with tight-fitting cover. Bring mixture to a boil; cover and simmer over low heat (about 200° F.) 25 to 30 minutes. Serve as an accompaniment for cold meat. Serves 6.

Rice–Carrot Casserole

2 eggs, well beaten
1¼ cups milk
1 tablespoon grated onion
½ teaspoon salt
⅛ teaspoon pepper
1 tablespoon melted butter
  or margarine
2 cups peeled, shredded
  carrots
2 cups Cheddar cheese,
  coarsely shredded
2 cups cooked long-grained
  rice

Heat oven to 350° F. In a bowl mix together eggs, milk, onion, salt, pepper, and butter. Stir in carrots, cheese and rice and mix thoroughly. Turn into a deep 1½-quart casserole. Cover and bake 20 minutes; uncover and bake 40 minutes longer. Let stand 10 minutes before serving. Serves 6.

Two-Cheese Rice Balls

3 cups water
2 chicken-flavored bouillon
  cubes
1 cup brown rice
½ cup chopped fresh parsley
1 cup (4 ounces) freshly
  grated Parmesan cheese
1 cup (4 ounces) finely diced
  mozzarella cheese
½ cup dry bread crumbs
Vegetable oil

In a medium-sized saucepot bring water and bouillon cubes to a boil over moderately high heat, stirring to dissolve bouillon cubes. Stir in rice, and when liquid is boiling again, reduce heat to low, cover pan and cook 45 minutes, until rice is very soft and sticky. Transfer rice to a large mixing bowl and refrigerate 1 hour or longer. Add parsley and cheeses and toss with a fork to mix. Using a ⅓-cup measuring cup, scoop up mixture and shape into balls. Roll each ball in bread crumbs, coating it evenly. Pour oil into a medium-sized saucepot to a depth of about 1 inch and heat over moderately high heat until oil registers 450° F. on a deep-frying thermometer. Fry 5 or 6 balls at a time in the oil for about 5 minutes, turning until they are browned all over. Remove balls to paper towels to drain. If desired, keep fried balls warm in a 250° F. oven while frying remaining balls. Makes 12 balls, or serves 4.

Hoppin' John

1 cup raw pea beans
4 cups water
2 teaspoons salt
4 to 6 slices raw bacon, diced
1 small onion, chopped (about
  ⅓ cup)
1 cup long-grained rice

Combine beans, the 4 cups water, and the salt in a large saucepan. Cover tightly and cook over moderately low heat (about 225° F.) until beans are tender, about 1½ hours. While beans are cooking, cook bacon in a skillet over moderately high heat (about 325° F.), stirring frequently, until crisp. Remove bacon bits from skillet with a slotted spoon; set aside. Cook onion in bacon drippings over moderate heat (about 250° F.) until golden brown. When beans are tender, drain them and reserve the liquid. Combine beans, rice, onion, and bacon drippings and bacon bits in the top of a double boiler; stir well. Measure reserved bean liquid and add enough water to make 2¼ cups liquid. Add the 2¼ cups liquid to bean mixture. Liquid should cover bean mixture completely; add a little additional water if necessary. Cover tightly and place over water boiling in bottom of double boiler. Cook over moderately low heat (about 225° F.) until rice is thoroughly cooked, about 1 hour and 15 minutes, carefully lifting bottom of rice to top about every 15 minutes. Add water to bottom of double boiler when necessary. Serve hot as a vegetable. Serves 6.

Pasta

Pasta is the family name for a group of cereal products more commonly broken down into spaghetti, macaroni, and noodles.

Spaghetti is formed in a solid rodlike shape and is always at least 8 inches long. It comes in several thicknesses; these are designated by number or name depending upon the brand.

Macaroni is tubular in shape. Although it does come in long, usually 8-inch, lengths, it is more commonly available in small arc-shapes called elbows. Manicotti, ziti, tufoli, and rigatoni are macaronis.

Noodles are shaped in flat strands in fine, medium, and broad widths. They also come in bow, ring, flake, and alphabet shapes. When these products are designated as egg noodles, they must, by law, contain 5½ percent egg solids. Green spinach noodles are also available.

Pasta comes in such a variety of shapes and forms and may be served with so many other food flavors that if your familiarity with them is limited to spaghetti and meatballs or macaroni and cheese, you should try some new ways with recipes in this chapter. Now frequently enriched with some of the B vitamins, these inexpensive foods, with the addition of meat, fish, or cheese, make a hearty meal that can stretch a limited budget.

Many pasta dishes are now available in canned and frozen form. Spaghetti, ravioli, lasagna, canneloni, manicotti, and macaroni flavored with cheese or tomato and meat are among the most popular. Homemade pastas are most satisfying dishes to produce and, although they are time-consuming, they are not tricky or difficult. They are simple doughs to make and doing the cut-outs can really be entertaining. In this chapter we give you instructions for making homemade noodles, cannelloni, and ravioli.

Storing pasta is not a problem. In the package, its shelf life is almost indefinite. After cooking, leftover pasta may be stored covered in the refrigerator for about a week. Leftovers may be fried with bits of vegetables or leftover meats or reheated in a sauce or used in salads.

Basic Method for Cooking Pasta

3 quarts boiling water
1 tablespoon salt
1 tablespoon vegetable oil
8 ounces pasta

In a large saucepan (at least 4 quarts) bring the 3 quarts of water to a rapid boil. Add the salt and oil. Gradually add the pasta (don't break up spaghetti—it will settle into the water as it becomes pliable). Be sure the water continues to boil rapidly. Stir occasionally with a wooden spoon to keep the pasta moving and prevent sticking. After 6 minutes of rapid boiling, taste for doneness. It generally takes from 8 to 10 minutes for pasta to reach the *al dente* ("to the tooth") stage when it will taste tender but still be firm. Overcooked pasta is mushy and far less flavorful than the *al dente*. Pasta that is to receive further cooking in a casserole should be boiled a shorter time. As a guide, allow 2 ounces of uncooked pasta per person. For a main course you may want to double that.

Immediately drain the pasta in a colander. Serve as quickly as possible, or mix with other ingredients in the recipe, for freshly cooked pasta is the very best kind there is. Do *not* rinse, unless the macaroni is to be used in a cold salad. Then, rinse with cold water and drain again.

Casserole Marie-Blanche

8 ounces medium-width egg noodles, cooked according to directions on package
1 cup cream-style cottage cheese
1 cup commercial sour cream
½ teaspoon salt
⅛ teaspoon white pepper
⅓ cup snipped chives
1 tablespoon butter or margarine

Heat oven to 350° F. Combine noodles, cheese, sour cream, salt, pepper, and chives. Pour into a buttered deep 2-quart casserole and dot top with the 1 tablespoon butter. Bake about 30 to 35 minutes, until noodles begin to brown. Serve immediately. Serves 6.

Garden Noodle Casserole

Add *1 tablespoon grated onion,* ¼ *teaspoon Tabasco sauce, 2 tablespoons chopped pimiento,* and *1 tablespoon chopped green pepper* to noodle mixture. Pour into casserole and sprinkle with ½ *cup coarsely shredded sharp Cheddar cheese.*

Noodles Romanoff

Add *1 teaspoon Worcestershire sauce* to noodle mixture before pouring into casserole. Sprinkle top with ¼ *cup grated Parmesan cheese.*

✺ Fettucine

1 *8-ounce package medium-width egg noodles*
¼ *cup melted butter or margarine*
1 *cup grated Romano cheese*
½ *cup heavy cream, slightly whipped*

Cook noodles according to package directions. Drain thoroughly. Mix butter, cheese, and cream together; pour over noodles and mix gently. Serve immediately. Serves 4.

✺ Fried Noodles

5 *tablespoons butter or margarine*
4 *ounces fine egg noodles, cooked according to directions on package*
¼ *teaspoon poppy seeds*
¼ *cup grated Romano cheese*

Melt 3 tablespoons of the butter in a 10-inch skillet over moderate heat (about 250° F.). Spread cooked noodles over butter. Sprinkle with poppy seeds. Cook until bottom of noodles is lightly browned. Loosen edge of noodles with spatula; place cookie sheet over skillet and invert to remove noodles. Melt the remaining 2 tablespoons butter in skillet. Carefully slide noodles into skillet and cook until bottom is lightly browned. Sprinkle with Romano cheese and cut into wedges to serve. Serves 3 to 4.

✺ Baked Noodle–Vegetable Casserole

3 *tablespoons butter or margarine*
½ *cup chopped onion*
½ *cup chopped green pepper*
4 *ounces spinach noodles, cooked according to directions on package*

Heat oven to 375° F. Melt the 3 tablespoons butter in skillet over moderate heat (about 250° F.); add onion and green pepper and cook until tender. Combine with noodles, tomato soup, corn, green beans, pimiento, olives, salt, and pepper. Pour into buttered, deep 2-quart casserole. Combine the 2 tablespoons melted butter, bread crumbs, and grated cheese. Sprinkle over

1 can condensed tomato soup
1 16-ounce can whole-kernel
  corn, drained
1 16-ounce can cut green
  beans, drained
¼ cup diced pimiento
½ cup chopped, pitted ripe
  olives
1 teaspoon salt
⅛ teaspoon pepper
2 tablespoons melted butter
  or margarine
⅓ cup fine dry bread crumbs
2 tablespoons grated
  American cheese food

top of casserole. Bake 40 to 45 minutes, or until lightly browned. Serves 6.

✑ Sukiyaki with Noodles and Sesame Seeds

1 10-ounce package fresh
  spinach
½ cup beef broth, made with
  ½ cup boiling water and 1
  beef bouillon cube
½ cup soy sauce
¼ cup dry sherry
4 teaspoons sugar
1 teaspoon vegetable oil
2 tablespoons sesame seeds
2 tablespoons vegetable oil
1 bunch green onions or
  scallions, cut into 2-inch
  lengths (about ¾ cup)
½ pound fresh mushrooms,
  sliced thin (3 cups)
1 pound Chinese celery
  cabbage, cut into
  1-inch-wide slices (5 cups)
1 tablespoon cornstarch
3 cups cooked vermicelli or
  thin spaghetti (½ pound
  uncooked)

Remove and discard tough stems from spinach, wash leaves in several changes of tepid water and drain. In a measuring cup combine the beef broth, soy sauce, sherry and sugar. In a large heavy skillet or *wok* heat the 1 teaspoon of oil over moderate heat; add sesame seeds and cook 5 minutes, stirring once, until lightly toasted. Remove seeds to a paper towel to drain. Add the 2 tablespoons of oil to skillet, increase heat to moderately high and add green onions; stir-fry 3 minutes. Add mushrooms to skillet and stir-fry 1 minute longer. Add cabbage and ½ cup of the soy-sherry mixture and stir over high heat 1 minute; then cover and cook 1 minute longer, until cabbage is crisp-tender. Mix cornstarch with remaining soy-sherry mixture and stir into vegetables in skillet. Reduce heat slightly, and when sauce begins to thicken, stir in spinach and noodles. Cover and cook about 3 minutes, stirring mixture once with 2 large spoons, until spinach wilts and noodles are hot. Sprinkle with sesame seeds and serve. Makes 4 servings.

✑ Baked Vermicelli

½ cup vegetable oil
8 ounces vermicelli

Heat oven to 300° F. Heat the oil in a large, heavy skillet over moderate heat (about 250° F.). Add uncooked ver-

1 tablespoon chopped onion
¾ cup canned tomatoes
1 4-ounce can mushroom
   stems and pieces, drained
2 cups chicken broth
½ teaspoon monosodium
   glutamate
Salt to taste
1 cup coarsely shredded
   Cheddar cheese

micelli and sauté until golden brown, stirring gently with a fork while cooking to prevent its becoming too dark. Remove vermicelli to a deep 2-quart casserole, pouring off all but 2 tablespoons of oil from the skillet. Add the chopped onion to this oil and cook until golden, then add the tomatoes, mushrooms, chicken broth and seasonings. Heat all to boiling and pour over vermicelli. Cover tightly and bake 45 minutes. Sprinkle cheese over the top and continue baking, uncovered, 15 minutes longer. Serves 6.

✒ Linguiné with Walnut Sauce

¼ cup olive oil
1 large clove garlic, peeled
¼ teaspoon pepper
1 teaspoon dried basil leaves
1 cup freshly grated
   Parmesan cheese (4
   ounces)
½ cup warm water
½ cup broken walnuts
6 cups hot, cooked linguiné
   (¾ pound uncooked)

Place oil, garlic, pepper and basil in an electric blender; cover and blend 3 seconds at high speed, until garlic is crushed. Add cheese and ¼ cup of the water and blend again until fairly smooth. Add nuts and remaining ¼ cup of water and blend until mixture is thick and smooth. Makes about 1 cup sauce. Serve sauce over hot, cooked *linguiné*. Serves 4.

✒ Manicotti

2 cups cream-style cottage
   cheese or ricotta cheese
1 8-ounce package
   mozzarella cheese, finely
   diced
⅓ cup grated Parmesan
   cheese
3 eggs, slightly beaten
½ teaspoon salt
⅛ teaspoon pepper
2 tablespoons melted butter
   or margarine
1 recipe Basic Tomato Sauce
   (recipe on page 574)
8 ounces manicotti, cooked
   according to directions on
   package
¼ cup grated Parmesan cheese

Heat oven to 350° F. Mix cottage cheese, mozzarella, the ⅓ cup Parmesan cheese, eggs, salt, pepper, and butter. Pour a thin layer of Tomato Sauce into bottom of a large, shallow baking dish. Spoon some of the cheese filling into each manicotti and place in a single layer over sauce. Pour remaining sauce over manicotti and sprinkle with the ¼ cup Parmesan. Bake 30 to 35 minutes. Serves 5 to 6.

RICE, PASTA, AND CEREALS

❧ Lasagna

1 16-ounce package lasagna
½ cup grated Parmesan
   cheese
2 cups ricotta or cottage
   cheese
1 8-ounce package
   mozzarella cheese, diced
Tomato Sauce (recipe follows)

Cook lasagna in boiling salted water and a few drops of oil over moderate heat (about 250° F.) for 12 minutes, or until tender. Rinse and drain. Arrange a single layer of lasagna in the bottom of a 3-quart shallow baking dish. Add a sprinkling of part of the Parmesan cheese, spoonfuls of ricotta, pieces of mozzarella cheese, and some of the Tomato Sauce. Repeat layers until all ingredients are used. Heat oven to 350° F. Bake 30 to 45 minutes, or until sauce is bubbly. Serves 6 to 8.

Tomato Sauce

¼ cup butter or margarine
2 cloves garlic, minced
1 medium-sized onion,
   chopped
1 28-ounce can Italian plum
   tomatoes
1 15-ounce can tomato sauce
1 12-ounce can tomato paste
1 teaspoon dried basil leaves
1 teaspoon dried oregano
   leaves
1 teaspoon dried thyme
   leaves
Pinch of rubbed dried sage
1 teaspoon salt
⅛ teaspoon pepper
¾ cup grated Parmesan
   cheese

Heat butter in a large saucepan over moderate heat (about 250° F.); add garlic and onion and cook until lightly browned. Add tomatoes, tomato sauce, tomato paste, basil, oregano, thyme, sage, salt, and pepper; cover and simmer over low heat (about 200° F.) 1 hour. Add Parmesan cheese and simmer 30 minutes. This recipe makes quite a thick sauce; if thinner sauce is desired, thin with a little water. Makes about 1½ quarts.

❧ Baked Macaroni

8 ounces elbow macaroni
½ cup butter or margarine
6 tablespoons all-purpose
   flour
1½ teaspoons salt
2½ cups milk
8 ounces sharp Cheddar
   cheese
6 thick slices tomato
   (optional)

Cook macaroni in boiling salted water as directed on package. Drain. Melt butter in a saucepan over moderate heat (about 250° F.); stir in flour and salt. Add milk gradually; cook, stirring constantly, until sauce is smooth and thickened. Measure out 1 cup of the sauce for use later. Pour rest of sauce over cooked macaroni and mix thoroughly. Cut half the cheese in ¼-inch cubes; fold into macaroni. Shred rest of cheese; add to the remaining 1 cup of sauce and heat until cheese melts. Pour macaroni mixture into a greased, shallow

2-quart baking dish. Arrange tomato slices on top. Pour sauce over. Heat oven to 400° F. Bake, covered, for about 25 minutes; then remove cover from casserole and bake, uncovered, for an additional 10 or 15 minutes, until hot and lightly browned. Serves 4 to 6.

❧ Skillet Macaroni

1 pound ground beef chuck
¼ cup finely chopped onion
1 small green pepper, finely chopped
2 8-ounce cans tomato sauce with cheese
1 cup water
1 8-ounce package elbow macaroni
1 cup commercial sour cream

Place ground meat, onion, and green pepper in a medium-sized skillet over moderately high heat (about 300° F.). Add a little oil, if necessary, to prevent sticking. Cook, stirring occasionally, until meat is browned and onion is tender. Reduce heat to moderate (about 250° F.); add tomato sauce, water, and macaroni. Cover and cook, stirring occasionally, until macaroni is tender, about 20 minutes. If necessary, add additional water during cooking to prevent sticking. Remove from heat and stir about 1 cup of the hot macaroni mixture into the sour cream. Return to mixture in skillet and stir to blend thoroughly. Season with salt, if necessary. Serves 4 to 6.

Spaghetti Sauces

Spaghetti sauce recipes are as numerous as the cooks that make them, and the variety of flavors can go on, seemingly, ad infinitum. The following recipes are for a few of the well-loved dressings to serve with freshly cooked spaghetti.

❧ Meatballs and Spaghetti with Tomato Sauce

4 slices day-old white bread
2 eggs, slightly beaten
1 pound ground beef
¼ cup grated Romano cheese
2 tablespoons instant minced onion
2 tablespoons dried parsley flakes

Cover bread slices with enough water to just barely cover; soak 2 minutes. Squeeze out moisture from bread. Mix together bread, eggs, beef, cheese, onion, parsley, oregano, and salt. Shape into 20 small balls. Melt butter in skillet over moderate heat (about 250° F.); brown meat balls on all sides. Remove from heat. Ten minutes before serving time, heat Tomato Sauce and meatballs over low heat until piping hot, stirring fre-

½ *teaspoon dried oregano leaves*

1 *teaspoon salt*

3 *tablespoons butter or margarine*

Basic Tomato Sauce (recipe follows)

1 *8-ounce package thin spaghetti*

quently. Cook one 8-ounce package thin spaghetti according to package directions. Drain. Serve sauce and meatballs over spaghetti. Serves 4.

Basic Tomato Sauce

2 *tablespoons olive oil*

1 *small clove garlic, minced*

¼ *cup finely chopped onion*

1 *8-ounce can tomato sauce*

1 *16-ounce can tomatoes*

1 *small can tomato paste*

½ *teaspoon dried basil leaves*

½ *teaspoon dried oregano leaves*

½ *teaspoon dried thyme leaves*

2 *teaspoons sugar*

½ *teaspoon salt*

Few grains pepper

Heat olive oil in large saucepan over moderate heat (about 250° F.); add garlic and onion and cook until lightly browned. Add the remaining ingredients and mix well. Cover and simmer over moderately low heat (about 225° F.) 1½ hours, stirring occasionally. Makes 4 cups sauce.

Meat Sauce

Use Basic Tomato Sauce recipe. *Cook 1 pound ground beef* with onion and garlic until lightly browned. Add remaining ingredients and follow directions above. Makes 5½ cups sauce to serve over 8 ounces cooked spaghetti; serves 4 to 6.

Summer Salad Sauce

½ *teaspoon minced, peeled garlic*

½ *teaspoon dry mustard*

¾ *teaspoon salt*

⅛ *teaspoon pepper*

¼ *teaspoon dried basil leaves*

4 *tablespoons finely chopped fresh parsley*

In a small mixing bowl place the garlic, dry mustard, salt, pepper, basil, 2 tablespoons of the chopped parsley, the vinegar and the oil; stir briskly to combine. Add tomatoes and onion and mix thoroughly with the dressing. If possible, refrigerate an hour or longer to allow flavors to blend. Just before serving, cook the pasta as directed in Basic Method for Cooking Pasta (page 568). Heap cooked, drained pasta in serving bowl or

1 tablespoon red wine
vinegar
3 tablespoons olive oil
2 cups coarsely chopped
fresh tomatoes (about 1
pound)
½ cup diced, peeled red onion

individual bowls, top with tomato-salad mixture and sprinkle with remaining parsley. Serve immediately. Makes enough sauce for 8 ounces cooked linguini or other pasta. Serves 4.

❧ Spicy Spaghetti Sauce

1½ pounds ground beef chuck
4 Italian sweet sausages,
sliced (about ½ pound)
1 stick peperoni, sliced
(about ½ pound)
4 28-ounce cans tomatoes,
mashed
1 large onion, chopped
2 cloves garlic, minced
3 bay leaves
1 teaspoon dried oregano
leaves
1 teaspoon salt
Grated Parmesan cheese

Cook beef, sausages, and peperoni in a large Dutch oven over moderate heat (about 250° F.), stirring constantly, until lightly browned and beef is crumbly. Add remaining ingredients and stir to blend well. Simmer, covered, over moderately low heat (about 225° F.) 3 hours, or until thick, stirring occasionally. Serve over cooked spaghetti and garnish with Parmesan cheese. Makes enough sauce for 16 ounces cooked spaghetti; serves 8 to 10.

❧ White Clam Sauce

½ cup olive or vegetable oil
3 cloves garlic, quartered
2 7-ounce cans minced
clams, undrained
¼ cup chopped fresh parsley

Heat oil in large skillet over moderate heat (about 250° F.). Add garlic and cook 5 minutes. Remove garlic. Add clams and broth; cover and simmer over low heat (about 200° F.) 5 minutes. Toss together with spaghetti and garnish with chopped parsley. Makes enough sauce for 8 ounces cooked spaghetti; serves 4 to 6.

❧ Spaghetti with Mediterranean Tuna Sauce

¼ cup olive oil
2 cloves garlic, peeled and
flattened but left whole
½ teaspoon dried oregano
leaves
1 7-ounce can white tuna,
drained

Heat oil in a medium-sized skillet over moderately high heat (about 325° F.). Add garlic to oil and cook until brown, about 30 seconds. Remove skillet from heat and discard garlic; add oregano and tuna to oil and break up with a spoon. Stir in olives, lemon juice and pepper; cover and cook over moderate heat (about 250° F.) just until mixture is hot. Turn drained, cooked pasta onto a

½ cup sliced pitted ripe olives
1 teaspoon lemon juice
⅛ teaspoon pepper

platter and pour the tuna mixture over it. Makes about 1½ cups tuna sauce, enough for 8 ounces cooked spaghetti. Serves 4.

❧ Garlic Butter Sauce

¾ cup butter or margarine
2 cloves garlic, quartered
½ teaspoon dried basil leaves
1 teaspoon salt
Grated Parmesan cheese

Melt butter in a saucepan over moderately low heat (about 225° F.). Add garlic, basil, and salt. Cook 10 minutes; press garlic cloves against edge of pan occasionally. Remove garlic before serving. Toss butter sauce with cooked spaghetti and serve with Parmesan cheese. Makes ¾ cup sauce, enough for 8 ounces cooked spaghetti; serves 4 to 6.

Homemade Pasta

To make homemade pasta you will need a fairly large work surface for rolling out the dough and a large saucepan for cooking the pasta. The method for mixing and rolling pasta dough is the same for all three recipes given in this section.

❧ Egg Noodles

2 cups sifted all-purpose flour
3 egg yolks
1 whole egg
2 teaspoons salt
¼ to ½ cup water

Mix and knead dough according to pictured directions on page 577. In making noodles, add 1½ tablespoons of the water with the eggs and the salt at the beginning of the mixing. Add just enough water, a tablespoon at a time, so dough can be formed into a ball. After kneading, cover dough with a damp towel and let rest 10 minutes. Divide dough into 4 equal portions. Place one portion on a well-floured board and roll out with a floured rolling pin into a paper-thin 8-x-12-inch rectangle. Starting at the 8-inch wide side of the rectangle fold the dough over 2½ inches. Pick up dough and fold over again 2½ inches. Fold over once more to make 4 layers. Cut into ¼-inch strips. Shake out strips and place on a towel to dry, about 2 hours. Roll out remaining portions of dough in same manner. When strips are dry cook in 3 quarts boiling salted water for 10 to 12 minutes or until tender. Drain thoroughly. Use as desired. Makes about 5½ cups of cooked noodles.

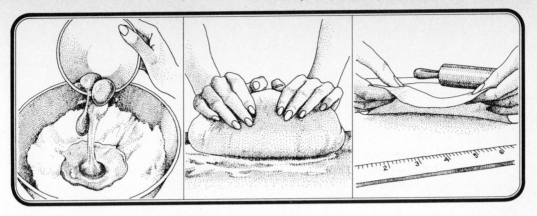

1. To make egg pasta dough: Place *flour* in a bowl. Make a well in the center of the flour. Break *eggs* into a small bowl; add *salt* and *water*. Add to flour all at once. Break up eggs with a fork and mix in the flour until mixture is too stiff to stir. With the fingers, work in rest of flour in the bowl. The dough should be just soft enough to be formed into a ball.

2. To knead dough: Remove dough to a well-floured pastry board. With floured hands, round up dough; fold it in half toward you. Press down lightly and push it away from you with the heels of the hands. Give the dough a quarter turn, fold, and press again. Continue to turn, fold, and press for 15 minutes, until dough is smooth and elastic. Sprinkle board and dough with enough flour to prevent sticking.

3. To roll dough: Divide dough into two or more portions according to recipe directions. Place one portion on a well-floured board. With a rolling pin roll dough into a rectangle. Then, rolling from the center out to the edges, continue to roll until dough is paper-thin. Turn dough frequently and stretch it gently with the fingers. Sprinkle the dough lightly with flour if it should stick to the rolling pin. Roll out other portion of dough.

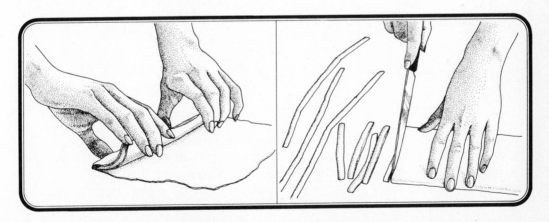

To shape noodles: Starting at the 8-inch wide side of the 8-x-12-inch rectangle of dough, turn 2½ inches of the dough back over itself. Fold this part over another 2½ inches. Continue folding the dough over once more to make 4 layers of dough.

To cut noodles: With a sharp knife cut noodle dough into ¼-inch strips through 4 layers at a time. It's easiest to use a ruler to measure the strips and as a guide to cutting straight strips. After strips are cut, shake off excess flour and lay them in a single layer on a clean tea towel to dry.

◀§ *Cannelloni*

2 *cups sifted all-purpose*
   flour
3 *large eggs*
¾ *teaspoon salt*
1½ *tablespoons lukewarm*
   water
Meat Filling (recipe follows)
Cream Sauce (recipe follows)
Grated Parmesan cheese

Mix and knead dough according to pictured directions on page 577. After kneading, cover dough with a damp towel and let rest 10 minutes. Divide dough into 2 portions. Place one portion on a well-floured board. With a floured rolling pin, roll dough into a paper-thin 12-x-16-inch rectangle. Stretch dough gently with the fingers as you roll. Sprinkle lightly with flour if dough should stick to rolling pin. Cut the dough into 3-x-4-inch rectangles. Lay each flat on a tea towel. Repeat with remaining portion of dough. Drop them, a few at a time, into a large quantity of boiling salted water and cook 5 minutes. Remove with a slotted spoon and put into a bowl of cold salted water. When ready to fill, drain on paper towels. Place about 2 tablespoons of the Meat Filling on longer edge and roll up. Spread a layer of Cream Sauce in individual casseroles. Lay 4 cannelloni in the sauce. Top with more sauce; sprinkle generously with Parmesan cheese. Bake in 375° F. oven 35 to 40 minutes. Makes about 2½ dozen. Serves 8.

To shape cannelloni: Cut the thinly rolled dough into 3-x-4-inch rectangles. Drop them, a few at a time, into a large quantity of boiling salted water and cook 5 minutes. Remove with a slotted spoon and put into a bowl of salted cold water. When ready to fill, drain on paper towels. Place 2 tablespoons Meat Filling (*recipe follows*) on longer edge and roll up.

Meat Filling

6 *tablespoons olive or*
   vegetable oil
⅓ *cup finely chopped onion*
1½ *cups peeled finely diced*
   carrot
2 *pounds ground beef chuck*
1 *cup dry white wine*
6 *egg yolks*
⅓ *cup grated Parmesan*
   cheese
2 *teaspoons salt*
¼ *teaspoon pepper*

Heat oil in a large skillet over moderate heat (about 250° F.). Add onion, carrot, and beef; cook and stir until lightly browned. Add wine; cover and cook 30 minutes, stirring occasionally. Cool to room temperature. In a large bowl beat egg yolks slightly; stir in Parmesan cheese, salt, and pepper; stir in cooled meat mixture. In the container of an electric blender blend 1 cup of the mixture at a time for about 20 seconds at high speed. Remove from container and repeat until all the mixture is blended. Makes about 4½ cups filling.

Cream Sauce

6 tablespoons butter or
    margarine
6 tablespoons all-purpose
    flour
2½ teaspoons salt
⅛ teaspoon pepper
1½ quarts (6 cups) milk
3 egg yolks

Melt butter in saucepan; blend in flour, salt, and pepper. Gradually add milk. Cook over moderate heat (about 250° F.), stirring constantly, until thickened. In a bowl beat egg yolks slightly; gradually stir in 1 cup of the milk mixture. Pour back into saucepan, stirring constantly. Cook and stir over moderately low heat (about 225° F.) until thickened. Makes about 6 cups sauce.

ᦇ Ravioli

2 cups sifted all-purpose
    flour
3 large eggs
¾ teaspoon salt
1½ tablespoons lukewarm
    water
Spinach Filling (recipe
    follows)
1 egg, slightly beaten
Basic Tomato Sauce (recipe on
    page 574
Grated Parmesan cheese

Mix and knead dough according to pictured directions on page 577. After kneading, cover dough with a damp towel and let rest 10 minutes. Divide dough into two portions. Place one portion on a well-floured board. With a floured rolling pin, roll dough into a paper-thin 12-x-16-inch rectangle. Stretch dough gently with the fingers as you roll. Sprinkle lightly with flour if dough should stick to rolling pin. Cut the dough into long ribbons 2 inches wide. Place a rounded teaspoon of the Spinach Filling at 2-inch intervals on one of the ribbons. Brush dough around filling with beaten egg. Lay a second strip of dough over the filling. With the fingers, gently press around each mound to seal. Cut between mounds with a knife or pastry wheel. Place ravioli flat on a tea towel. Repeat with remaining portion of dough. Drop them, a few at a time, into a large quantity of boiling salted water and cook about 15 minutes. Remove with a slotted spoon and drop into hot Basic Tomato Sauce. Heat thoroughly. Serve with Parmesan cheese. Makes about 4 dozen. Serves 6.

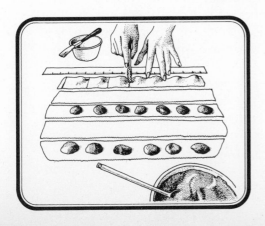

To shape ravioli: Cut the thinly rolled dough into long ribbons 2 inches wide. Place a rounded teaspoon of Spinach Filling (*recipe follows*) at 2-inch intervals on one of the ribbons. Brush dough around filling with beaten egg. Lay a second strip of dough over the filling. With the fingers, gently press around each mound to seal. Cut between mounds with knife or pastry wheel.

Spinach Filling

½ *pound ground beef chuck*
¼ *cup well-drained chopped*
  cooked spinach
¼ *cup grated Parmesan*
  cheese
2 *tablespoons finely chopped*
  fresh parsley
⅓ *cup fine dry bread crumbs*
⅓ *cup finely chopped salami*
2 *eggs, slightly beaten*
¼ *teaspoon salt*
Few grains pepper

Cook meat in a skillet over moderately high heat (about 300° F.), stirring with a fork to break up meat, until meat loses it color. Drain off excess fat and mix meat with remaining ingredients. Cool before using. Makes about 1¾ cups filling.

Other Cereals

In addition to rice and wheat (from which the pastas are made), there are several other cereals that may also be used as the starch element in a meal. Adding variety to everyday dinners, they are so good in themselves that you should add them to your menu plans.

Hominy grits are well known in the South where they are served as a breakfast accompaniment to ham and eggs and as a starch vegetable with a meal. They must be cooked in plenty of water (use 5 cups of salted water for 1 cup of grits). Stir the grits slowly into the boiling water so that it never stops bubbling. Cover and cook about a half hour, stirring frequently.

Corn meal comes in both yellow and white forms. Because they taste much the same, they can be used interchangeably in recipes though regional preferences may dictate otherwise. Corn meal mush, like hominy grits, may be served as a starch vegetable or a breakfast dish. It is also the ingredient used to make a delicious spoon bread, a superb accompaniment to a roast.

Farina is a wheat product that is often served as a hot breakfast cereal; it is also the basis for the excellent Italian side dish, gnocchi.

Buckwheat groats, sometimes called kasha, taste much like brown rice and are popular with people of Middle-European background.

Cracked wheat, which is also marketed under the names *wheat pilaf* and *bulgur*, is available in fine, medium and coarse grinds. The heart of the wheat, it is often cooked with other flavorings with bits of fruits and nuts stirred in. It is excellent as a hot dish and good in salads.

❧ Hominy Grits Soufflé

1 cup hominy grits
2 tablespoons butter or
  margarine
1 tablespoon sugar
4 cups milk
½ teaspoon salt
2 eggs, separated
1 tablespoon butter or
  margarine

Place grits, the 2 tablespoons butter, sugar, milk, and salt in the top of a double boiler. Cook over simmering water until thick, stirring occasionally, about 20 to 25 minutes. Let grits cool. Heat oven to 350° F. Beat egg yolks into cooled grits. Pour into a large bowl. Beat egg whites until stiff peaks form. Gently fold into grits. Pour into a buttered, 1½-quart, straight-sided baking dish. Dot top with the 1 tablespoon butter. Bake 40 to 45 minutes, or until lightly browned. Serves 6.

❧ Bulgur Salad

⅓ cup olive oil
2 cups bulgur
2 cloves garlic, peeled and
  crushed
1 quart water
½ teaspoon salt
3 ears fresh corn, cooked and
  with kernels cut off
½ cup sliced green onions
⅓ cup chopped peeled red
  onion
1 medium-sized unpeeled
  cucumber, thinly sliced
  (about 2 cups)
¾ cup coarsely chopped fresh
  parsley
⅓ cup lemon juice
¾ teaspoon salt
⅛ teaspoon pepper
⅛ teaspoon garlic powder
Crisp lettuce (optional)

Heat 2 tablespoons of the oil in a large, heavy skillet over moderately high heat (about 375° F.). Add the bulgur and crushed garlic. Stirring frequently, cook until bulgur begins to get golden and has a slight aroma resembling popcorn. Stir in water and the ½ teaspoon salt. Bring mixture to a boil. Reduce heat to moderate (about 250° F.); cover and, stirring occasionally, cook 20 minutes, or until bulgur is tender and the water is completely absorbed. Turn bulgur into a shallow pan and chill until completely cold. Meanwhile prepare remaining ingredients. When bulgur is chilled, toss all ingredients together. Serve on lettuce if desired. Makes 3 quarts, or six 2-cup servings as a main dish.

❧ Corn Meal Mush

3 cups water
1 cup yellow corn meal
1 teaspoon salt
1 cup cold water
Maple syrup, honey, molasses,
  or brown sugar

Heat the 3 cups water in a saucepan to boiling. Mix corn meal, salt, and the 1 cup cold water together; gradually pour into boiling water. Cook over moderately low heat (about 225° F.), stirring frequently until thickened. Cover and cook over low heat (about 200° F.) for about 10 minutes. Remove from heat and serve with maple syrup, honey, molasses, or brown sugar. Serves 4 to 6.

Fried Mush

Pour the cooked corn meal mush into a waxed-paper-lined 8½-x-4½-x-2½-inch loaf pan. Cool and chill until firm. Remove from pan onto a wooden board and slice into ½-inch slices. Melt *2 tablespoons butter or margarine* in a skillet over moderate heat (about 250° F.); fry slices of mush until lightly browned on both sides. Serve with the same toppings as suggested for Corn Meal Mush. Serves 4 to 6.

◄§ Southern Spoon Bread

3 cups milk
½ cup white corn meal
2 eggs, separated
2 tablespoons butter or margarine
½ teaspoon baking powder
1 teaspoon salt

Heat oven to 350° F. Heat 1½ cups of the milk to boiling point over moderately low heat (about 225° F.). Stir ½ cup of the cold milk into the corn meal. Stir corn meal mixture into scalded milk and cook over moderately low heat (about 225° F.), stirring occasionally, until the consistency of mush, about 5 minutes. Beat egg yolks slightly and add to corn meal with the remaining 1 cup cold milk, butter, baking powder, and salt; stir until butter is melted. Beat egg whites until stiff, but not dry, and fold into corn meal mixture. Pour into greased deep 1½-quart casserole. Bake about 1 hour and 10 minutes, until firm. Serves 8.

◄§ Gnocchi Romano

3 cups milk
1 cup farina
1 teaspoon salt
4 tablespoons butter or margarine
⅔ cup grated Parmesan cheese
Dash of nutmeg

Butter two 9-x-5-x-2¾ inch loaf pans lightly. Pour milk into a saucepan. Place over moderately low heat (about 225° F.) until milk is slightly warm. Sprinkle in farina and salt. Cook, stirring constantly, until thickened and smooth, about 5 minutes. Remove from heat. Stir in 2 tablespoons of the butter, 6 tablespoons of the cheese, and the nutmeg and blend well. Spread evenly in the bottoms of the two loaf pans. Chill until firm, about 3 hours. Cut contents of each pan into 6 slices. Arrange slices, slightly overlapping, on rack in a broiler pan. Melt the remaining 2 tablespoons butter and pour over slices. Sprinkle with the remaining cheese. Place in a preheated broiler about 3 inches from the source of heat; broil about 3 to 4 minutes, or until tops are golden brown and gnocchi is heated through. Serves 4.

✑ Kasha Varnishkis

1 tablespoon vegetable oil
½ cup buckwheat groats
½ teaspoon salt
1¼ cups water
3 ounces noodle bows
1 tablespoon vegetable oil
1 medium-sized onion,
   minced
½ pound mushrooms, sliced
½ teaspoon salt
Few grains pepper

Heat the 1 tablespoon oil in a large skillet over moderately low heat (about 225° F.); add groats and cook until brown, stirring occasionally. Sprinkle with the ½ teaspoon salt. Add the 1¼ cups water, or as much as groats will absorb. Cover and remove from heat. Heat oven to 350° F. Cook noodles in boiling salted water 10 to 12 minutes, or until just tender. Heat the 1 tablespoon oil in a second skillet; add onions and cook over moderate heat (about 250° F.) until tender. Add mushrooms and cook 5 minutes. Fold groats, noodles, vegetable mixture, the ½ teaspoon salt, and pepper together; pour into a deep 1-quart casserole. Bake 20 to 25 minutes. Serve hot. Serves 6 to 8.

✑ Rachel's Granola

⅔ cup sesame seeds
½ cup slivered blanched
   almonds
½ cup shelled sunflower seeds
¼ cup butter or margarine
¾ cup unroasted cashew nuts
1 cup unsweetened shredded
   coconut
⅓ cup light sesame seed oil
4 cups old-fashioned rolled
   oats
⅓ cup honey
¾ cup dried currants

Heat oven to 350° F. In a large skillet over moderately high heat (about 375° F.) dry-toast sesame seeds until lightly browned, stirring frequently. Turn seeds out into a bowl. In the same skillet dry-toast almonds until lightly browned, stirring frequently. Add sunflower seeds and continue to toast and stir until mixture is golden brown. Add mixture to sesame seeds. In the same skillet melt butter and add cashews; toast until lightly browned, stirring frequently. Add coconut and continue to toast and stir until mixture is golden brown. Add cashews and coconut to sesame mixture. In a *wok* or the same skillet heat oil over moderately high heat (about 375° F.). Add oats, and toast until lightly browned, stirring frequently. Add sesame seed mixture and honey to the oats and heat mixture 5 minutes, stirring frequently. Turn mixture into an ungreased 15½-x-10½-x-1-inch jelly-roll pan and spread it evenly. Bake 10 to 15 minutes or until mixture is a rich, golden-brown color. Remove pan from oven and stir in currants. Line a second jelly-roll pan with four thicknesses of paper towels and place pan on a wire cake rack. Turn mixture onto the paper towels and spread it evenly. Cover with four additional thicknesses of paper towels and allow mixture to cool completely. Break up granola into chunks. Makes about 3 quarts, or about 2¼ pounds.

CHAPTER XVII

SALADS AND SALAD DRESSINGS

There are very few good ingredients that haven't been used in a salad of one form or another. From the light tossed green salad that is an accompaniment to dinner to the chef's salads and fruit, vegetable, and meat salads that make a meal, these chilled dishes are great warm-weather favorites. Fortunately the salad greens that are the base for many salads and the edible garnish for most are in increasingly better year-round supply in this country in a wide variety and in garden-fresh condition.

When you shop for salad greens, it pays to go to a market where the vegetable storage area is cooled or refrigerated and delicate greens are handled with the care they deserve. Otherwise you will run the risk of getting "bruised" (brown outer leaves denote this) or "rusted" greens that will not be wholly usable.

A variety of greens will add interest, both in appearance and flavor, to your salads. These greens are commonly available now:

Crisp head lettuce (iceberg) is the compact, heavy head familiar to everyone. It has medium green outer leaves and an almost white center. Its flavor is rather sweet and mild and its texture should be very crisp.

Butterhead lettuce (Boston) has a smaller, softer head than crisp head and the leaves are thinner and smoother. It has pale green outer leaves and a pale yellow interior. Butterhead leaves are tender and not crisp.

Bibb lettuce has a small, open-type head. It has a delicate flavor and very tender rich green leaves on the outside that are whitish green near the core. A whole or half Bibb lettuce makes a superb single salad serving.

Cos lettuce (romaine) has a tall cylindrical head and stiff, coarse leaves. The leaves are usually medium dark green on the outside and greenish white near the center. Its flavor is sweet.

Leaf lettuce comes in many varieties and colors. Its loose leaves growing on a sturdy stalk do not form a head. When it is young, it is crisp, sweet, and tender.

Chicory (curly endive) has frondlike leaves growing from a center stalk. It's dark green on the outer leaves with a yellow heart. It adds a crunchiness and a biting flavor to a salad.

Escarole (broad-leaved endive) has broad spiny leaves growing from a center stalk. It's colored and flavored much like chicory.

Belgian endive (French) looks more like a cone than a head. It has tight, white leaves, a marvelous crisp texture, and a pleasantly sharp flavor.

Spinach may have crinkled or smooth leaves. Either type is suitable for salads, so long as the leaves are tender, crisp, and a bright green. They have a sweet, fresh taste and a chewy texture.

Watercress, usually sold bunched, grows in dark green lacy sprigs. It adds a flavor tang to green salads.

Cabbage, red or green, that is fresh and young can be used sparingly in green salads.

Chinese cabbage (celery cabbage), shaped much like romaine lettuce, has long thin leaves. The leaves are green-edged and nearly white in the center. This is somewhat milder in flavor than the familiar tight-head cabbage.

Other greens that may be used in salads are young turnip greens, young beet greens, tender celery leaves, young dandelion greens, mustard greens, kale, field salad, arugula, and nasturtium leaves.

What you do with salad greens when you get them home from a good market is an important step toward making "the perfect salad." If you are going to use the greens the same day, wash them thoroughly, dry them carefully, wrap them in a towel, and put them in the refrigerator to crisp. Greens washed in tepid (not hot, not cold) water will shed their sand more easily and will crisp more quickly than those washed in hot or cold water. If they are to be stored and used over a period of a few days, rinse them under the faucet, holding the stem end up to avoid letting water soak into the inner leaves (water can rust greens during storage). Or dunk loose lettuce heads in a pan of tepid water and let them drain stem-end up. Shake greens dry and store in the vegetable crisper of the refrigerator or wrap them in foil, plastic wrap, a kitchen towel, or plastic bag and store on a low shelf of the refrigerator.

Greens stored in this way must be washed again before using. At that time, separate iceberg lettuce by cutting out the core and fill the head with water by holding under the faucet. The force of the water will separate and wash the leaves. Separate Boston and Bibb lettuce leaves and wash carefully; the tender leaves bruise easily. When washing romaine, escarole, chicory, spinach, and dandelion greens, separate the leaves and break off and discard the thick midribs, if desired. All these leaf vegetables should again be wrapped and refrigerated so that they will be crisp and dry when you use them. Untie bunched watercress or parsley, rinse, and shake dry. Store stem-ends down in a tightly covered jar or a tightly closed plastic bag in the refrigerator. Belgian endive, which is very delicate, may be stored in a plastic bag and washed when used.

The Tossed Green Salad

If there is such a thing as "salad lore," it has grown out of the innumerable do's and don'ts of making a perfect tossed green salad. We stand on two do's: Always chill the serving plates and do tear, not cut, the greens. Also, don't add moisture-producing foods, such as tomatoes, before you coat the greens with dressing. Chopped chives, radish slices, well-drained artichoke hearts, slices of avocado, and the like may be tossed with the greens. This is our version of the classic green salad with two ways to achieve it. The first is simpler; the second will give a more vivid garlic tinge to the dressing. The ingredients are the same.

❧ Classic Green Salad

2 quarts torn salad greens
1 clove garlic, cut
6 tablespoons vegetable oil or olive oil
2 tablespoons tarragon, wine, or other vinegar, or lemon juice
½ teaspoon salt
¼ teaspoon freshly ground pepper
Pinch of dry mustard

For either version, dry washed greens thoroughly, wrap in a towel, and chill well. Put required number of salad plates and a wooden bowl large enough to hold the salad for tossing in the refrigerator to chill.

Version 1: Just before serving, rub the wooden salad bowl with the cut surface of the garlic. Discard the garlic. Combine the oil, vinegar or lemon juice, salt, pepper, and mustard in the bowl and stir with a fork to blend. Add the crisp, dry greens. Take the untossed salad to the table along with the chilled serving plates. At the table, toss the greens lightly just to coat each leaf with dressing. Serve at once. Makes 4 large salads or 6 small ones.

Version 2: Put the salt, pepper, and mustard, and several pieces of finely minced garlic (half a clove suits most tastes) into the salad bowl. Mash the garlic and seasonings with the back of a spoon until the garlic disappears.

Stir the vinegar or lemon juice into the seasonings; then stir in the oil. Add the crisp dry greens. Refrigerate until serving time. Do *not* toss until you are ready to serve the salad on chilled plates. Serves 4 to 6.

Chef's Salad

1 quart crisp, torn salad
  greens
1 hard-cooked egg, chopped
6 ounces Swiss cheese, cut
  into julienne strips
6 ounces boiled ham, cut into
  julienne strips
½ cup Chef's Dressing (recipe
  follows)
8 Garlic Bread Cubes (recipe
  follows)
1 tomato, peeled and
  quartered

Toss salad greens, egg, cheese, ham, and dressing together in salad bowl until greens are thoroughly coated. Sprinkle garlic bread cubes over salad and garnish with quarters of tomato. Serves 2.

Chef's Dressing

¼ clove garlic
1 tablespoon salt
1 tablespoon prepared
  mustard
1 egg
6 tablespoons cider vinegar
2 tablespoons tarragon
  vinegar
2 cups vegetable oil
½ cup water

Force garlic through garlic press or chop very fine; blend with salt in a bowl. Add mustard, egg, and 3 tablespoons of the cider vinegar; beat thoroughly with a rotary beater. Gradually add remaining vinegar and oil, beating after each addition until mixture is smooth and creamy. Add water. Store in covered glass jar in refrigerator. Remove from refrigerator 1 hour before serving. Shake well before measuring. Makes 3 cups dressing.

Garlic Bread Cubes

2 slices white bread
1 large clove garlic, cut in
  half

Heat oven to 300° F. Thoroughly rub both sides of bread with the cut garlic. Remove crusts from bread and cut into ¼-inch cubes. Cover with a damp towel and let stand 30 minutes. Spread cubes on a cookie sheet and bake 15 minutes in a 300° F. oven, or until lightly browned. Store cubes in a tightly covered jar for use as needed. Makes about ⅔ cup.

SALADS AND SALAD DRESSINGS

✑ Salad Mimosa

¼ cup olive oil
1 tablespoon wine vinegar
½ teaspoon salt
Few grains pepper
⅓ clove garlic, finely
   chopped
2 quarts crisp, torn salad
   greens
2 hard-cooked eggs, finely
   chopped

Combine oil, vinegar, salt, pepper, and garlic in a jar with tight lid. Shake vigorously. Arrange greens in salad bowl; add dressing and toss thoroughly. Sprinkle with chopped egg. Serves 4 to 6.

✑ Delicate Tossed Salad

1 small head Boston lettuce
1 small avocado
6 tablespoons olive oil
2 tablespoons wine vinegar
½ teaspoon salt
1 small celery heart, thinly
   sliced
1 medium-sized tomato, cut
   into wedges

Wash and dry lettuce; tear into bite-sized pieces. Peel avocado and thinly slice. Place oil, vinegar, and salt in bottom of salad bowl. Blend thoroughly. Place salad servers in dressing. Place lettuce and celery heart loosely on top of servers. Arrange avocado and tomato wedges on top. Toss together just before serving. Serves 4.

✑ Caesar Salad

6 slices white bread
½ cup butter, softened
2 eggs
⅓ cup olive oil
2 to 3 tablespoons lemon juice
½ cup grated Parmesan
   cheese
1 tablespoon prepared
   mustard
Few grains pepper
1½ cloves garlic, pressed
   through garlic press
3 anchovy fillets, minced
   (optional)
3 quarts crisp, dry, torn
   romaine leaves

Remove crusts from bread and spread butter lightly on both sides of bread. Place a large skillet over moderate heat (about 250° F.); add a little of the remaining butter. Brown bread slices on both sides, adding more of the butter as needed so that there is a thin layer of it in the skillet. Drain bread on paper towels and cut into cubes. Place eggs in a bowl and beat with a wire whip or rotary beater. Add olive oil, lemon juice, Parmesan cheese, mustard, pepper, garlic and anchovies, if desired; beat together until blended. Place the prepared romaine in a salad bowl and toss with the dressing and croutons. Serves 6.

❧ Hot Tossed Salad

1 head iceberg lettuce
1 12-ounce package fresh spinach
1 4-ounce can sliced mushrooms, undrained
2 tablespoons butter or margarine
½ cup water
1 teaspoon sugar
½ teaspoon salt
⅛ teaspoon ground nutmeg
1 tablespoon chopped pimiento
2 tablespoons lemon juice
1 tablespoon cornstarch

Core, rinse, and drain lettuce. Tear enough lettuce into bite-sized pieces to make about 2 quarts, lightly packed. Place in a large saucepan. Remove tough stems from spinach leaves. Wash leaves well; drain and toss lightly with lettuce in saucepan. Combine mushrooms, butter, water, sugar, salt, nutmeg, and pimiento in a small saucepan; place over moderately low heat (about 225° F.) and bring to a boil. Stir lemon juice into cornstarch, mixing until smooth. Add to mushroom mixture in saucepan. Cook, stirring constantly, until thickened. Hold sauce over low heat (about 200° F.). Cook lettuce and spinach over moderate heat (about 250° F.), tossing a few times, just until hot and leaves begin to soften (lettuce leaves should still be crunchy). Drain and place in heated bowl. Toss with warm mushroom dressing at table. Serve immediately. Serves 6 to 8.

❧ Special Spinach Salad

6 tablespoons olive oil
2 tablespoons lemon juice
1 clove garlic
½ teaspoon salt
Few grains pepper
8 slices raw bacon
1 pound raw spinach
3 hard-cooked eggs, coarsely chopped

Place olive oil, lemon juice, garlic, salt, and pepper in a jar or salad cruet. Shake vigorously to blend; store overnight in refrigerator. Remove garlic clove before using. Cook bacon over moderately high heat (about 325° F.) until golden brown and crisp. Place on paper towels to drain. Wash spinach well; drain and dry thoroughly with paper towels. Discard tough stems and tear leaves into bite-sized pieces. Crumble bacon and sprinkle over spinach with the chopped egg; toss with the dressing just before serving. Serves 6.

Fruit and Vegetable Salads

Many of the lighter fruit and vegetable salads are particularly good with dinners. They are a change-of-pace way of getting necessary fruits, vegetables, and leafy greens into family meals.

✒ Twenty-Four-Hour Fruit Salad

1 20-ounce can pineapple
chunks, drained
1 11-ounce can mandarin
oranges, drained
½ cup canned pitted sweet
dark cherries, well
drained
½ cup halved and seeded
green grapes
1¼ cups miniature
marshmallows or
quartered large
marshmallows
1 egg yolk, slightly beaten
2 tablespoons sugar
1 cup heavy cream
2 tablespoons lemon juice
⅛ teaspoon salt

Combine pineapple, oranges, cherries, grapes, and marshmallows. Chill thoroughly. Combine egg yolk, sugar, 2 tablespoons of the cream, lemon juice, and salt in the top of a double boiler. Place over boiling water and cook, stirring constantly, until thickened. Remove from heat and cool. Chill completely. Whip remainder of heavy cream until stiff. Fold into chilled dressing. Add to chilled fruit and combine. Cover and chill about 24 hours. Makes 4 cups. Serves 6.

✒ Five Cup Fruit Salad

1 11-ounce can mandarin
orange segments, drained
(1 cup)
1 cup fresh or canned seedless
white grapes, halved and
drained
1 cup miniature
marshmallows
1 cup flaked coconut
1 cup commercial sour cream

Place the first four ingredients in a bowl and mix well. Fold sour cream into fruit mixture and mix until all ingredients are well moistened. Cover and chill in refrigerator until serving time. Makes 3⅔ cups, or serves 4 to 6.

✒ Fruit Salad with Cardamom Cream Dressing

½ cup undiluted evaporated
milk
½ cup vegetable oil
¼ cup lemon juice
⅛ to ¼ teaspoon ground
cardamom seed
¼ teaspoon sugar
½ teaspoon salt

Place evaporated milk, vegetable oil, lemon juice, cardamom, sugar, and salt in the container of an electric blender. Blend a few seconds at high speed until smooth and thickened. Chill. Combine cantaloupe, bananas, peaches, grapes, and blueberries. Chill 1 hour. Arrange fruits on salad greens or in a small watermelon shell. Pour dressing over fruit. Serves 4.

1 cup diced cantaloupe
1 cup sliced bananas
1 cup fresh peach slices,
    sweetened to taste
½ cup halved seedless grapes
½ cup blueberries
Salad greens

❧ Orange-and-Artichoke Salad

8 small oranges
Salad greens
2 6-ounce jars marinated
    artichoke hearts
¼ cup grated Parmesan
    cheese

Peel oranges and slice thinly. Arrange salad greens on individual salad plates; top with sliced oranges. Place artichoke hearts over oranges. Spoon some of the marinade from the artichokes over each salad. Sprinkle with Parmesan cheese. Serves 8.

❧ Waldorf Salad

2 large eating apples
2 teaspoons lemon juice
1 cup diced celery
¼ teaspoon salt
½ cup mayonnaise
1 teaspoon confectioners'
    sugar
¼ cup commercial sour cream
Lettuce cups
⅓ cup coarsely broken
    walnuts

Core apples. Pare, if desired, or leave red-skinned apples unpeeled. Dice them and sprinkle with lemon juice. Combine apples with celery and salt. Blend together mayonnaise, sugar, and sour cream. Pour over apple mixture, tossing lightly with a fork until apple pieces are well coated. Arrange salad in lettuce cups. Sprinkle with walnuts. Serves 6 to 8.

❧ Cheese-Stuffed Fresh Pear Salad

4 large, firm ripe pears
1 tablespoon lemon juice
1 3-ounce package cream
    cheese, at room
    temperature
1 1¼-ounce wedge Roquefort
    cheese, crumbled (about
    ¼ cup)
Lettuce cups

(Ingredients continued on page 592)

Wash pears. Cut into halves lengthwise and remove cores. Peel if desired. Brush cut surfaces with lemon juice. Blend together the cream cheese and Roquefort cheese. Pack cheese mixture into core cavities in pear halves. Press two halves together and wrap each whole stuffed pear in transparent plastic wrap. Chill for several hours or overnight. Just before serving, cut pears in quarters or slices. Arrange in lettuce cups, and if desired, garnish with mint. Serve with French dressing. Serves 8.

Mint leaves (optional)
Basic French Dressing (recipe on page 626)

Frozen Fruit Salad

- 2 *3-ounce packages cream cheese, at room temperature*
- ⅓ *cup mayonnaise or salad dressing*
- 2 *tablespoons lemon juice*
- ¼ *cup sugar*
- 1 *teaspoon salt*
- 1½ *cups miniature marshmallows or quartered large marshmallows*
- 1 *13¼-ounce can pineapple chunks, well drained*
- ½ *cup coarsely chopped walnuts*
- 1 *medium-sized orange, peeled and cubed*
- ¼ *cup red maraschino cherries, halved*
- ¼ *cup green maraschino cherries, halved*
- 1 *cup heavy cream, whipped*
- *Salad greens*

Combine cream cheese, mayonnaise, lemon juice, sugar, and salt. Beat with a rotary beater until well blended. Stir in rest of ingredients except cream. Gently fold in cream. Spoon mixture into 2 8½-x-4½-x-2½-inch loaf pans and place in freezer 6 hours or overnight. To serve, let stand at room temperature several minutes; slice and serve on crisp greens. Serves 10 to 12.

Asparagus Salad

- 2 *10-ounce packages frozen asparagus spears*
- ¾ *cup bottled Italian dressing*
- 1 *5-ounce can water chestnuts, drained and sliced*
- 1 *medium-sized tomato, coarsely chopped*
- *Lettuce cups*

Cook asparagus according to package directions, but cook for only 5 minutes after water comes to boil, or just until asparagus is crisp-tender. Drain and cut each spear crosswise into 3 pieces. Place warm asparagus in a bowl with the salad dressing and chill 1 hour. Add water chestnuts and tomato to asparagus and chill 1 hour longer. Drain salad and serve in lettuce cups. Serves 6.

❧ Green Bean Salad

2 pounds green beans, cut in
  1-inch pieces and cooked
2 cups commercial sour
  cream
2 tablespoons ground
  dillseed
½ teaspoon salt
¼ teaspoon pepper
1 tablespoon lemon juice
2 cucumbers, thinly sliced

Chill beans. Combine cream, dill, salt, pepper, and lemon juice. Combine beans and cucumbers. Add sour cream mixture. Toss together. Chill several hours. Serves 6 to 8.

❧ Marinated Lima Bean Salad

2 10-ounce packages frozen
  lima beans
1 large red onion, cut into
  ⅛-inch slices
1 cup coarsely chopped fresh
  parsley
1 cup vegetable oil
1 cup cider vinegar
2 teaspoons sugar
1 teaspoon salt
½ teaspoon pepper
Lettuce
Parsley (optional)

Cook lima beans as directed on package. Drain thoroughly. Combine beans, onion, and parsley in a bowl. Combine oil, vinegar, sugar, salt, and pepper; beat with a rotary beater until well blended. Pour mixture over beans. Cover and chill 12 hours or longer. When ready to serve, drain well; remove a few onion rings for garnish. Arrange in a lettuce-lined bowl. Top with onion rings and more parsley, if desired. Serves 6 to 8.

❧ Four-Bean Salad

1 9-ounce package frozen cut
  green beans
1 9-ounce package frozen cut
  wax beans
¼ cup olive oil
¾ cup wine vinegar
Juice of ½ lemon
2 cloves garlic, crushed
1 teaspoon dried oregano
  leaves
2 teaspoons sugar

Cook green and wax beans according to package directions. Let cool. In a small bowl combine oil, vinegar, lemon juice, garlic, oregano, and sugar and mix well. In a large bowl, combine the four beans, onion, and celery and pour oil-and-vinegar mixture over them. Toss gently. Chill for several hours, or overnight. If desired, drain beans and serve in a lettuce-lined bowl. Serves 10 to 12.

(Ingredients continued on page 594)

SALADS AND SALAD DRESSINGS

1 15-ounce can Garbanzo
   beans, drained
1 15-ounce can red kidney
   beans, drained
1 small sweet onion, finely
   chopped
⅔ cup finely chopped celery
Lettuce (optional)

Belgian Endive Salad with Chiffonade Dressing

¾ teaspoon salt
½ teaspoon paprika
Few grains pepper
¼ cup white vinegar
¾ cup vegetable oil
2 canned pimientos, finely
   chopped
¼ cup peeled and shredded
   carrot
¼ cup finely chopped green
   pepper
1 teaspoon onion juice
8 small heads Belgian endive

If desired, salad dressing may be prepared a day in advance. Place salt, paprika, and pepper in a jar with a tight lid. Add vinegar and then oil. Cover tightly and shake vigorously to blend. Add pimientos, carrot, green pepper, and onion juice; stir to combine. Wash endive and drain well. Cut each head in half lengthwise. Loosen each leaf at stem end; fan leaves out on individual salad plates, allowing one head per person. Pour a small amount of prepared dressing over each. Serves 8.

Coleslaw

½ cup mayonnaise
2 tablespoons commercial
   sour cream
2 tablespoons finely chopped
   onion
2 teaspoons caraway seeds or
   ½ teaspoon celery seed
   (optional)
½ teaspoon salt
3 cups finely shredded
   cabbage
1 pimiento, chopped

Mix mayonnaise, sour cream, onion, caraway seeds, and salt. Combine cabbage and pimiento; add dressing and toss. Chill 1 hour. Serves 4.

Blender Coleslaw with Sour Cream Dressing

1 small head cabbage
½ green pepper

Quarter cabbage, remove core, and slice coarsely. Seed the green pepper and cut into strips. Slice onion and

[594]

½ medium onion, peeled
1 peeled carrot
Sour Cream Dressing (recipe
  follows)

carrot coarsely. Fill container of an electric blender with mixed vegetables and add water just to cover. Cover container and blend on high speed for 5 seconds, just until vegetables are coarsely chopped. Drain into colander and repeat until all vegetables are chopped. Empty well-drained vegetables onto paper towel to absorb excess moisture. Put dry vegetables into salad bowl. Serve with Sour Cream Dressing. Serves 6.

Sour Cream Dressing

1¼ cups mayonnaise
1 cup commercial sour
  cream
3 tablespoons lemon juice
1 teaspoon salt
¼ teaspoon pepper

Put all ingredients into blender container. Stir to combine and blend on high speed for 5 seconds. Pour dressing over vegetables in salad bowl; toss lightly.

Old-Fashioned Cauliflower Slaw

1 cup mayonnaise or salad
  dressing
1 cup commercial sour
  cream
1 package garlic-cheese
  salad dressing mix
4 teaspoons caraway seeds
  (optional)
1 large head cauliflower
1 cup thinly sliced radishes
¼ cup sliced green onions or
  scallions
½ cup snipped watercress

Stir together mayonnaise, sour cream, salad dressing mix, and caraway seeds; chill while preparing the remaining ingredients for salad. Cut cauliflower in half and discard core. Cut cauliflower into thin slices and combine with radishes, onions, and watercress. Add mayonnaise mixture and toss until vegetables are well coated with dressing. Chill 1 to 2 hours before serving. Serves 8 to 10.

Celery Victor

3 beef bouillon cubes
2½ cups hot water
2 small whole celery hearts
1 medium-sized onion,
  sliced
¾ cup bottled French
  dressing
Watercress or shredded
  lettuce

Dissolve bouillon cubes in hot water. Place celery hearts in a 10-inch skillet; arrange onion on top. Pour bouillon over vegetables. Cover and cook over low heat (about 200° F.) about 15 minutes. Cool vegetables in bouillon 15 to 20 minutes. Remove hearts and onion slices; cut each heart in half lengthwise. Place hearts in a 1-quart baking dish, cut-side up. Arrange the onion slices on top of and around hearts. Pour French dressing over vegetables. Cover and chill for 2 to 3 hours. Serve hearts on water-

Anchovy fillets
Pimiento strips
Tomato wedges
Ripe olives

cress or shredded lettuce. Arrange anchovy fillets, pimiento strips, and the onion slices from the marinade over the hearts. Garnish with tomato wedges and ripe olives. Pour the French dressing over each salad. Serves 4.

✌ Cucumber Salad

6 *large cucumbers*
1 *large sweet onion*
1 *cup white wine vinegar*
  with tarragon
2 *teaspoons dried dillweed*
  (optional)
½ *teaspoon ground pepper*
2 *tablespoons salt*
2 *tablespoons sugar*

Wash and scrub cucumbers well. Slice cucumbers into ⅛-inch-thick rounds. Slice onion thinly. In a small bowl combine vinegar, dillweed, pepper, salt, and sugar and blend well. Combine cucumbers and onions in a large bowl and pour vinegar mixture over them. Toss well to blend. Cover and chill 4 to 5 hours, stirring occasionally. Makes about 2 quarts.

✌ Cucumbers in Sour Cream

¾ *cup commercial sour*
  cream
2 *tablespoons finely chopped*
  onion
2 *tablespoons cider vinegar*
½ *teaspoon salt*
½ *teaspoon ground dillseed*
Few grains pepper
2 *medium-sized cucumbers,*
  peeled and thinly sliced
Paprika

Mix sour cream, onions, vinegar, salt, dill, and pepper; fold into cucumbers. Sprinkle with paprika. Chill. Serves 4.

✌ Spinach Salad with Hot Bacon Dressing

1 *pound fresh spinach,*
  washed, dried, and chilled
4 *slices raw bacon, diced*
2 *teaspoons brown sugar*
¼ *cup sliced green onions*
¼ *teaspoon salt*
1½ *tablespoons vinegar*
⅛ *teaspoon dry mustard*
Dash of paprika

With scissors, snip spinach coarsely into a salad bowl. Cook diced bacon in a skillet over moderately high heat (about 325° F.) until crisp. Reduce heat to moderate (about 250° F.), add sugar, green onions, salt, vinegar, mustard, and paprika. Bring to the boiling point and remove from heat. Just before serving, pour the hot dressing over the spinach and toss lightly until leaves are coated. Serves 4.

Potato, Macaroni, Rice, and Legume Salads

Potato salads and their close relations, macaroni and rice salads, may be the starch in many summer meals. They're particularly compatible with cold meats or poultry.

Potato Salad

4 cups cold diced cooked
    potatoes (about 5
    medium-sized potatoes)
¼ cup Basic French
    Dressing (recipe on page
    626)
½ cup diced celery
¼ cup coarsely chopped
    onion
1½ teaspoons salt
⅛ teaspoon pepper
½ cup mayonnaise or salad
    dressing
2 hard-cooked eggs, sliced
Stuffed olives
Paprika

Combine potatoes and French dressing; let stand 10 to 15 minutes to marinate. Add celery, onion, salt, and pepper. Toss until well blended. Add mayonnaise and toss lightly. Place in serving bowl; arrange egg slices and olives on top. Chill at least 2 hours. Sprinkle with paprika before serving. Serves 6.

Baked German Potato Salad

4 cups hot diced cooked
    potatoes (about 5
    medium-sized potatoes)
½ cup coarsely chopped
    celery
½ cup finely chopped onion
6 strips crisp-cooked bacon,
    crumbled
1 teaspoon salt
⅛ teaspoon pepper
⅓ cup cider vinegar
⅓ cup vegetable oil
1½ tablespoons sugar
1 tablespoon chopped fresh
    parsley

Heat oven to 350° F. Combine potatoes, celery, onion, bacon, salt, and pepper. Toss gently until well mixed. Place in a 2-quart casserole. Combine vinegar, vegetable oil, and sugar. Pour over potatoes. Toss lightly. Bake 25 minutes. Sprinkle with parsley before serving. Serves 4 to 6.

✑ Macaroni-and-Cheese Salad

8 ounces uncooked elbow
   macaroni
1 cup (¼ pound) sharp
   Cheddar cheese, finely
   diced
½ cup peeled finely diced
   carrot
¼ cup finely diced celery
2 tablespoons chopped
   pimiento
1 tablespoon grated onion
⅔ cup mayonnaise
Lettuce
1 green pepper, cut into thin
   rings

Cook macaroni in boiling salted water as directed on package. Drain and rinse thoroughly with cold water. Combine macaroni, cheese, carrot, celery, pimiento, and onion. Add mayonnaise and blend. Chill. Arrange on lettuce and garnish with pepper rings. Serves 6 to 8.

✑ Chilled Rice and Chick-Pea Salad

4 teaspoons vegetable oil
4 teaspoons wine vinegar
¾ teaspoon salt
½ teaspoon dried dillweed
2 cups cooked brown rice
2 cups cooked chick-peas
2 seeded green peppers,
   diced
2 medium-sized ripe
   tomatoes, cut into chunks
½ cup diced, peeled onion

In a medium-sized mixing bowl place oil, vinegar, salt and dill and stir to mix. Add remaining ingredients, toss gently, cover and refrigerate 1 hour or longer to let flavors blend. Toss again before serving. Serves 4.

✑ Minted Brown Rice Salad

2 13¾-ounce cans chicken
   broth
2 cups brown rice
¼ teaspoon salt
⅓ cup lemon juice
¼ cup olive oil
1½ teaspoons salt
1 cup thinly sliced green
   onions or scallions
1 cup finely chopped fresh
   parsley

In a heavy, medium-sized saucepan bring broth to a boil over moderately high heat; add rice and the ¼ teaspoon of salt. Reduce heat to low, cover pan and cook 40 to 45 minutes, until liquid is absorbed and rice is tender but still slightly firm. Remove pan from heat, add the lemon juice, olive oil and the 1½ teaspoons salt and toss gently to mix. Allow rice to sit 30 minutes and then mix in scallions, parsley and mint. Chill before serving in a large bowl with the romaine leaves stuck in for dippers. Makes about 6½ cups; serves 4 to 6.

½ cup chopped fresh mint or
  2 tablespoons dried mint
  leaves
Romaine leaves (optional)

☙ Tabouli and Chick-Pea Salad

½ cup bulgur wheat
½ cup boiling water
¼ cup lemon juice
¼ cup olive oil
½ teaspoon minced, peeled
  garlic
½ teaspoon dried oregano
  leaves
1½ teaspoons salt
¼ teaspoon pepper
1 cup canned chick-peas or
  garbanzo beans, drained
  and rinsed in cold water
1 cup sliced, peeled carrot
2 cups chopped red or green
  cabbage
2 tablespoons minced green
  onions or scallions
½ cup finely chopped fresh
  parsley
Lemon wedges (optional)

Place bulgur in a large mixing bowl and pour boiling water over it; let stand 10 minutes and then stir gently. In a small screw-top jar place lemon juice, oil, garlic, oregano, salt and pepper; cover and shake well to mix. Pour dressing over bulgur, add remaining ingredients, except lemon wedges, and toss gently to mix. Cover bowl and chill salad in refrigerator. Serve with lemon wedges. Makes 4 cups, or serves 3 to 4.

☙ Lentil Salad

3½ cups water
3 cups dried lentils
1½ teaspoons salt
1 medium-sized onion,
  peeled and stuck with
  four cloves
2 large bay leaves
1 teaspoon dried thyme
  leaves
1 cup finely chopped, peeled
  red or sweet yellow onion

(Ingredients continued on page 600)

In a large saucepan bring the water to a boil over high heat. Add lentils, the 1½ teaspoons salt, the onion stuck with cloves, the bay leaves and thyme. When water returns to a boil reduce heat to low, cover pan and simmer 25 to 30 minutes, until lentils are tender, stirring frequently during the last few minutes. Remove pan from heat and let stand 10 minutes with the lid on. Add remaining ingredients except green pepper and parsley. Toss to mix thoroughly. Let salad stand 45 minutes and then toss again. Serve warm or cover and chill in refrigerator up to 2 days. Add green pepper and parsley just before serving. Makes about 8 cups; serves 6 to 8.

1 large clove garlic, peeled
  and minced
¾ cup olive oil
½ cup wine vinegar
1 teaspoon pepper
1¼ teaspoons salt
¾ cup finely chopped, seeded
  green pepper
¾ cup chopped fresh parsley

Main-Dish Salads

Some of the hearty fruit salads, and all the vegetable, poultry, meat, and
fish salads, make good main dishes for a luncheon or a summer supper.
Serve them well chilled on cold plates with a hot, crusty bread on the side.

⇜ Fruit Salad Plate

Boston lettuce
8 ounces Cheddar cheese
2 peaches, peeled and sliced
3 bananas, quartered
Lemon juice
½ cup finely chopped walnuts
1 grapefruit, peeled and
  sectioned
1 orange, peeled and
  sectioned
1 3-ounce package cream
  cheese, at room
  temperature
2 tablespoons honey
¼ cup bottled French
  dressing
Strawberries
Packaged date-nut bread
Butter

Arrange lettuce leaves on individual salad plates. Cut
cheese into 1-inch cubes and place on colored toothpicks. Dip peach slices and bananas in lemon juice. Roll
bananas in walnuts. Arrange grapefruit and orange sections, peach slices, and bananas on the lettuce. Add
cheese cubes. Thoroughly blend cream cheese, honey,
and French dressing. Pour over fruit. Garnish with
strawberries. Slice date-nut bread and butter lightly.
Serve with salad. Serves 4.

⇜ Fresh Fruit Salad with Wine-Gelatin Cubes

1 3-ounce package
  raspberry-flavored gelatin

Put raspberry-flavored gelatin in a bowl. Add the boiling
water and stir until gelatin is dissolved. Stir in the port.

peeled onion
¼ *cup water*
1 *tablespoon curry powder*
1 *cup heavy cream*
1 *teaspoon lemon juice*
1 *tablespoon finely chopped
fresh parsley*

saucepan, ignite and pour flaming over the chicken. Sprinkle 1 teaspoon of the salt, the pepper and onion over the chicken. Add the water to the skillet and stir over low heat (about 200° F.) to loosen browned particles; add to the chicken. Cover pot tightly and cook over moderately low heat (about 225° F.) 1 hour, or until just tender. Sprinkle curry powder over chicken and baste with pan juices; remove pot from heat. When chicken is cool enough to handle, remove meat from bones; discard bones, skin and gristle and leave meat in large chunks. Arrange meat, smooth side down, in a 10-inch pie plate. To the juices left in the pan add cream, the remaining ½ teaspoon salt and the lemon juice; stir over moderately high heat (about 275° F.) until mixture comes to a boil. Strain liquid over chicken, covering the meat and filling the pie plate. Cover and chill several hours or overnight. Unmold onto a flat serving plate; sprinkle with parsley. Serves 4.

Chicken Tonnato

3 *medium-sized chicken
breasts, boned, skinned
and split (about 1½
pounds boneless)*
3 *cups water*
1 *small carrot, peeled and
quartered*
1 *stalk celery*
1 *small onion, peeled and
quartered*
1 *tablespoon lemon juice*
1 *tablespoon salt*
½ *cup mayonnaise*
½ *cup chicken broth, canned
or homemade*
½ *teaspoon salt*
¼ *teaspoon pepper*
1 *teaspoon lemon juice*
1 *teaspoon dried basil leaves*
1 *tablespoon drained capers*
1 *7-ounce can solid-packed
tuna, drained and flaked*
¼ *cup finely chopped fresh
parsley*
½ *cup sliced pitted ripe olives*

Cut each split breast in half crosswise and place between sheets of wax paper. With a mallet or rolling pin pound the chicken pieces to ¼-inch thickness. Place the water, carrot, celery, onion, 1 tablespoon lemon juice and 1 tablespoon salt in a large saucepan; bring to a boil over moderately high heat (about 350° F.). Reduce heat to moderate (about 250° F.), add chicken, cover pan and simmer gently 5 minutes, until chicken turns white and feels spongy. Remove pan from heat, lift out chicken pieces and pat with paper towels to remove excess moisture. Discard cooking liquid. Arrange chicken pieces on a serving plate. Place the mayonnaise, broth, the ½ teaspoon salt, the pepper, 1 teaspoon lemon juice, basil, capers, tuna and 2 tablespoons of the parsley in an electric blender. Cover and blend at high speed until smooth. Spoon sauce over chicken and chill several hours. Sprinkle with the remaining 2 tablespoons of parsley; garnish with olives. Serves 6.

✎§ Chicken Malibu

¾ cup mayonnaise or salad
    dressing
1 tablespoon lemon juice
½ teaspoon celery seed
½ teaspoon salt
2 cups diced cooked chicken
1 3-ounce jar marinated
    mushrooms, drained and
    cut into halves
½ cup chopped celery
1 tablespoon chopped fresh
    parsley
2 tablespoons chopped
    pimiento
2 tablespoons pine nuts or
    slivered almonds
6 small- to medium-sized
    artichokes
1 hard-cooked egg yolk
Salad greens
2 tomatoes, cut into wedges

Blend mayonnaise, lemon juice, celery seed, and salt together. Fold in chicken, mushrooms, celery, parsley, pimiento, and pine nuts. Chill for several hours. Cook artichokes as directed on page 499. Chill. Remove chokes from artichoke centers. Spoon in chicken salad. Sieve egg yolk and sprinkle over chicken salad. Serve on salad greens and garnish with wedges of tomato. Serves 6.

✎§ Ham and Melon Salad

¼ cup fresh lime juice
¼ cup honey
1 teaspoon poppy seeds
¾ pound baked or boiled
    ham, cut into julienne
    strips (about 3 cups)
1 medium-sized cucumber,
    peeled and sliced thin
    (about 2 cups)
1 medium-sized ripe
    cantaloupe, seeds and
    rind removed, cut into
    1-inch cubes (about 4
    cups)
¼ cup finely chopped green
    onions or scallions

In a small bowl place the lime juice, honey and poppy seeds; stir until well blended. Place remaining ingredients in a large bowl; add poppy-seed dressing and toss well. Makes 7 cups salad, or serves 4 to 6.

Macaroni–Ham Loaf

2 cups or 6 ounces
uncooked macaroni,
broken into 2-inch pieces
2 tablespoons butter or
margarine
2 tablespoons finely
chopped onion
2 tablespoons flour
½ teaspoon salt
1 cup milk
1 egg, slightly beaten
1½ pounds ground
ready-to-eat ham
2 teaspoons prepared
mustard
½ teaspoon pepper
¾ cup coarsely shredded
Cheddar cheese
⅓ cup chopped green pepper
¼ cup chopped pimiento

Lightly grease a 9-x-5-x-3-inch loaf pan and line with waxed paper. Cook macaroni according to package directions; drain. Melt butter in saucepan over moderate heat (about 250° F.); add onions and cook until tender. Blend in flour and salt. Gradually add milk and cook, stirring constantly, until thickened. Gradually stir hot sauce into beaten egg. Mix ham, mustard, pepper, and ⅓ cup of the cream sauce. Spread mixture evenly over bottom and sides of loaf pan. Add cheese to remaining sauce and place over low heat (about 200° F.), stirring constantly, until cheese is melted. Fold together cheese sauce, macaroni, green pepper, and pimiento. Pour into center of loaf. Pack firmly and smooth off the top. Cover and chill in refrigerator for at least 4 hours. Unmold on platter and slice with sharp knife. Serves 10.

Summer Salad

2 cups (1 pound) creamed
cottage cheese
¼ teaspoon dry mustard
2 teaspoons caraway seeds
½ teaspoon salt
¼ teaspoon pepper
1 tablespoon capers
1 medium-sized green
pepper, seeded and diced
1 cup diced celery
¼ cup minced green onions or
scallions
¼ cup sliced radishes
¼ cup chopped, canned or
jarred pimientos
Romaine lettuce leaves
2 or 4 hard-cooked eggs,
peeled and halved
2 ripe tomatoes, quartered

Place the cottage cheese in a medium-sized bowl; add and stir in the dry mustard, caraway seeds, salt, pepper and capers. Add green pepper, celery, green onions, radishes and pimientos and mix in. Mound cottage cheese mixture on a bed of lettuce leaves in the center of a serving plate; surround with egg halves and tomato quarters. Makes about 3 cups cottage cheese mixture, or serves 4.

✌ Hot Meat-and-Potato Salad

3 tablespoons dried mixed
   vegetable flakes
½ cup boiling water
1 tablespoon instant minced
   onion
2 tablespoons water
1 tablespoon shortening
1 12-ounce can luncheon
   meat, cut into ½-inch
   cubes
2 16-ounce cans tiny white
   potatoes, cubed
⅓ cup mayonnaise or salad
   dressing
½ teaspoon salt
⅛ teaspoon pepper
1 8-ounce package sliced
   process American cheese

Mix mixed vegetable flakes and boiling water; bring to boil and let stand 15 minutes. Mix onion and the 2 tablespoons water and let stand 5 minutes. Heat shortening in skillet over moderate heat (about 250° F.); add luncheon meat and cook until lightly browned. Add vegetable flakes, onion, potatoes, mayonnaise, salt, and pepper; heat over low heat (about 200° F.), stirring occasionally. Fold in cheese and heat 5 minutes, until cheese starts to melt. Serve hot. Serves 4 to 6.

✌ German-Style Franks and Potato Salad

2 tablespoons butter or
   margarine
¼ cup finely chopped onion
¼ cup chopped green pepper
½ cup water
¼ cup cider vinegar
4 cups diced cold cooked,
   peeled potatoes (about 2
   pounds)
½ teaspoon prepared
   horseradish
1 tablespoon sugar
¼ teaspoon salt
Few grains pepper
¼ cup chopped celery
6 frankfurters, sliced

Melt butter in large saucepan over moderate heat (about 250° F.); add onion and green pepper and cook until lightly browned. Add water and vinegar. Add diced potatoes and let stand at room temperature 1 hour to marinate; gently stir after 30 minutes. Add horseradish, sugar, salt, pepper, celery, and frankfurters; gently mix. Just before serving, pour into a large skillet and heat thoroughly over moderately low heat (about 225° F.) stirring occasionally. Serves 4 to 5.

✌ Avocado Stuffed with Crab

1 6-ounce package frozen
   Alaska king crab, thawed
2 tablespoons lemon juice
3 tablespoons mayonnaise or

Flake crab meat and dry well between paper towels. Sprinkle with the 2 tablespoons lemon juice. Blend mayonnaise, chili sauce, horseradish, Worcestershire, salt, and pepper. Fold in crab meat, celery, and egg. Cut

salad dressing
3 tablespoons chili sauce
¼ teaspoon prepared
    horseradish
¼ teaspoon Worcestershire
    sauce
¼ teaspoon salt
Few grains pepper
½ cup chopped celery
1 hard-cooked egg, chopped
2 avocados
Lemon juice
Chicory

avocados in half lengthwise; remove pits and brush the cut surfaces with lemon juice. Mound salad in avocado halves and serve on a bed of chicory. Serves 4.

🥄 Crab Louis

½ cup mayonnaise
3 tablespoons bottled French
    dressing
2 tablespoons chili sauce
1 tablespoon snipped chives
1 tablespoon chopped green
    olives
½ teaspoon prepared
    horseradish
½ teaspoon Worcestershire
    sauce
1 small head lettuce, washed
    and well drained
Salt
Pepper
2 6-ounce packages frozen
    crab meat, thawed and
    drained
3 hard-cooked eggs,
    quartered
Tomato wedges
Capers

Combine mayonnaise, French dressing, chili sauce, chives, olives, horseradish, and Worcestershire sauce. Chill. Divide lettuce into quarters and cut each crosswise into fine shreds. Cut shreds into 2-inch lengths. Pile about 1 quart of the shredded lettuce in a shallow, chilled salad bowl. Sprinkle lightly with salt and pepper. Press crab meat between paper towels to remove some of the excess moisture. Flake crab meat, using a fork; mound on top of lettuce. Spoon dressing over salad. Garnish with hard-cooked egg quarters, tomato wedges, and capers. Serves 4 to 5.

🥄 Stuffed Eggs with Rice Salad

6 hard-cooked eggs, peeled
    and halved
¼ cup mayonnaise
¼ teaspoon dry mustard
¼ teaspoon salt

Remove yolks and, using the back of a wooden spoon, press them through a strainer. Add mayonnaise, dry mustard, salt and pepper to sieved yolks; mix well. Fill egg-white halves with yolk mixture and sprinkle with parsley. Arrange Rice Salad in a shallow, round serving

⅛ teaspoon pepper
2 tablespoons finely chopped
fresh parsley
Rice Salad with Fresh Herbs
(recipe follows)
Watercress for garnish
(optional)
Tomato quarters for garnish
(optional)

dish; place stuffed eggs in a circle on top of rice. If desired, place a small bunch of watercress in the middle of the eggs and arrange the tomato quarters around the edge of the salad. Serves 4 to 6.

⨾ Rice Salad with Fresh Herbs

2 cups converted rice
4 cups chicken broth,
canned or homemade
¼ cup vegetable oil
¼ cup wine vinegar
1 teaspoon Dijon-style
mustard
1½ teaspoons salt
½ teaspoon pepper
2 tablespoons finely
chopped fresh dillweed
1 tablespoon finely chopped
fresh basil leaves or ¼
teaspoon dried basil
1 large tomato, cut in
eighths
¾ cup thinly sliced, peeled
carrot
1 large green pepper,
seeded and cut into
½-inch squares
6 Stuffed Eggs (see recipe
on page 607)

Cook the rice in the broth according to package directions, until tender but still slightly firm to the bite. In a screw-top jar place oil, vinegar, mustard, salt, pepper, dillweed and basil; cover and shake well. Place cooked rice in a large salad bowl, add dressing and toss gently. Cover and chill several hours. Just before serving add remaining ingredients, except the stuffed eggs; toss salad. Chill and garnish with stuffed eggs just before serving. Makes about 8 cups, or serves 6.

⨾ Salmon Salad and Eggs Platter

4 7¾-ounce cans salmon,
drained, boned, and
flaked
1 cup finely diced celery
2 teaspoons drained capers
2 teaspoons grated onion
2 teaspoons prepared
horseradish

In a mixing bowl combine salmon, celery, capers, onion, horseradish, Worcestershire, ginger, and mayonnaise. Mix to blend well. Arrange on each of 6 lettuce-lined plates a scoop of the salmon mixture, 2 egg halves, carrot sticks, a radish rose, and a gherkin. Serves 6.

¾ teaspoon Worcestershire
  sauce
¼ to ½ teaspoon ground
  ginger
⅓ to ½ cup mayonnaise or
  salad dressing
Lettuce leaves
  6 hard-cooked eggs, halved
  3 carrots, halved and cut
  into sticks
  6 radish roses
  6 sweet midget gherkins, cut
  into fans

⁓ Shrimp Salad

2½ cups cooked, shelled,
  deveined, and cut-up
  shrimp
  3 tablespoons bottled
  French dressing
¼ teaspoon salt
Few grains pepper
  1 cup diced celery
  2 tablespoons finely
  chopped stuffed olives
  1 tablespoon chopped green
  pepper
½ cup mayonnaise or salad
  dressing
Salad greens
  2 hard-cooked eggs
  (optional)

Mix together shrimp and French dressing. Chill 1 hour to marinate. Stir in salt, pepper, celery, olives, green pepper, and mayonnaise. Serve on salad greens. If desired, the 2 hard-cooked eggs, chopped, may be combined with shrimp before serving. Serves 4.

⁓ Shrimp-and-Macaroni Salad

1½ tablespoons lemon juice
  1 tablespoon vegetable oil
  1 cup elbow macaroni,
  cooked according to
  package directions
1½ cups cooked, shelled,
  deveined, and diced
  shrimp

Mix lemon juice and vegetable oil; combine with macaroni; chill several hours, stirring occasionally. Fold in shrimp, eggs, green pepper, onion, celery, tomato, and olives. Blend sour cream, salt, and mayonnaise together; fold into macaroni mixture. Arrange on crisp salad greens. Serves 4 to 6.

(Ingredients continued on page 610)

2 hard-cooked eggs
2 tablespoons chopped
green pepper
1 teaspoon chopped onion
½ cup chopped celery
½ cup diced fresh tomato
¼ cup chopped stuffed olives
2 tablespoons commercial
sour cream
½ teaspoon salt
¼ cup mayonnaise or salad
dressing
Salad greens

✎ Tuna–Avocado Luncheon Plate

2 6½-ounce cans tuna, well
drained and flaked
¼ cup finely diced celery
3 tablespoons finely chopped
onion
3 tablespoons finely chopped
green pepper
1 tablespoon drained capers
¼ teaspoon dried dillweed
½ cup diced orange sections
⅓ cup mayonnaise
3 large unpeeled avocados,
halved and pits removed
Lettuce cups
Radish Finger Sandwiches
(recipe follows)
Fresh parsley or watercress
Ripe olives

In a bowl mix together tuna, celery, onion, green pepper, capers, and dill. Just before serving, fold in diced orange and mayonnaise. Spoon equal amounts into 5 avocado halves. Arrange halves in lettuce cups on individual plates. Peel remaining avocado half. Cut into thin slices and garnish each avocado half with the slices. Arrange 3 Radish Finger Sandwiches on each salad plate and garnish plate with parsley or watercress and olives. Serves 5.

Radish Finger Sandwiches

10 thin slices white bread
Soft butter or margarine
10 to 12 large radishes, thinly
sliced
Salt and pepper

Spread bread slices with butter. Arrange radish slices on 5 of the buttered slices. Sprinkle radishes with salt and pepper to taste. Complete sandwiches with remaining buttered bread. Trim off crusts, if desired, and cut each sandwich into 3 fingers. Makes 15 sandwiches.

✒ Tuna Salad

1 6½-ounce cans tuna, well
  drained and flaked
¼ cup chopped celery
¼ cup sliced stuffed olives
1 tablespoon freeze-dried
  chopped chives
¼ cup mayonnaise
Salad greens
2 medium-sized tomatoes,
  sliced
2 hard-cooked eggs, sliced

Combine tuna, celery, olives, chives, and mayonnaise. Chill. Mound salad on lettuce leaves and garnish with tomato and egg slices. Serves 4.

✒ Hot Tuna Salad

2 6½-ounce cans tuna,
  drained and flaked
1 cup diced celery
1 cup halved and seeded
  green grapes
¼ cup sliced ripe pitted olives
½ cup toasted whole blanched
  almonds
⅔ cup mayonnaise
1 tablespoon lemon juice
1 teaspoon grated onion
¼ teaspoon celery salt
½ teaspoon salt
½ cup crushed bite-sized
  toasted corn cereal
2 tablespoons grated
  American cheese
1 tablespoon melted butter or
  margarine

Heat oven to 350° F. Combine tuna, celery, grapes, olives, and almonds in a mixing bowl. Blend mayonnaise, lemon juice, grated onion, celery salt, and salt. Add to tuna mixture and toss lightly. Turn into a shallow 8-inch-square ovenproof dish. Combine crushed cereal, grated cheese, and butter. Sprinkle over top of salad. Bake 10 minutes. Serve warm. Serves 4 to 6.

✒ Herring Salad

1 cup herring tidbits or 1
  cup fillet of herring
1 medium-sized apple,
  peeled and cored

Chop herring, apple, potato, and egg white. Place all ingredients in a bowl and fold together. Chill and serve with Mock Sour Cream. Serves 3 to 4.

(Ingredients continued on page 612)

1 *medium-sized potato,*
   peeled and boiled
White of 1 hard-cooked egg
¼ *cup diced dill pickle*
Few capers
1½ *teaspoons sugar*
Freshly ground pepper
Mock Sour Cream (recipe
   follows)

Mock Sour Cream

2 *tablespoons lemon juice*
3 *to 5 tablespoons skim milk*
1 *cup cottage cheese*
Pinch of salt

Place lemon juice and 3 tablespoons skim milk in the container of an electric blender. Gradually add cottage cheese and salt, blending at low speed. Blend a few minutes at high speed until smooth. Thin mixture if necessary with the remaining skim milk. Makes 1 cup mixture.

Molded Salads

Molded salads may be made in any size or shape you wish. They're often served because they look so pretty on a serving platter. If you have a good collection of molds, you can create a variety of beautiful salads; however, you can use anything that will hold liquids—a plain metal or glass mixing bowl or a baking dish will do.

There are just three tricks to making a molded or jellied salad. The first is to be certain all of the gelatine is dissolved in whatever hot liquid is designated. The second is to know just when to add other ingredients, such as chopped vegetables or whipped cream, to the partially cooled gelatine. If added too soon, the added ingredients will not stay in suspension; if they are added too late, the salad will be lumpy.

To speed the setting of gelatine mixtures, fill a deep pan with ice cubes. Put gelatine mixture in a bowl, preferably a metal one, and set bowl in the ice cubes. With a rubber spatula stir mixture constantly until it just holds its shape when dropped from the spatula or until it is the consistency of unbeaten egg white. This is the correct consistency for adding extra ingredients.

The third trick is to unmold the salad neatly onto a serving plate. To unmold gelatine molds, fill a sink or a large bowl with warm (not hot) water to the depth of the gelatine in the mold. Dip the mold in the water and hold it there for a few seconds. Loosen the edge of the gelatine with the tip of a paring knife. Place a serving plate over the top of the mold. Invert both mold and plate, holding them firmly. Shake the gelatine gently down onto the plate. If it does not slip out of the mold, dip the mold briefly in warm water again and repeat that procedure.

Molded salads should not be put out onto a serving plate more than an hour before you serve them. They must then again be refrigerated until serving time.

Cherry Coronet Salad

1 17-ounce can pitted Bing
   cherries
1 11-ounce can mandarin
   oranges
1 6-ounce package
   raspberry-flavored
   gelatin
½ cup port wine
½ cup coarsely chopped
   pecans
Salad greens
Mayonnaise or salad dressing

Drain cherries and oranges, reserving juices. Pour juices into a 1-quart measuring cup and add enough water to make 3¼ cups liquid. Heat juice mixture to boiling over moderate heat (about 250° F.); add gelatin and stir until dissolved. Cool slightly. Stir in wine. Chill until the consistency of unbeaten egg white. Fold in cherries, orange segments, and nuts. Pour into a 1½-quart gelatin mold. Chill several hours, or until set. Unmold on salad greens. Serve with mayonnaise. Serves 8 to 10.

Molded Cranberry Salad

3 cups fresh cranberries
¾ cup sugar
1 8½-ounce can crushed
   pineapple
1 6-ounce package
   raspberry-flavored
   gelatin
½ teaspoon grated lemon
   peel
3 tablespoons lemon juice
1½ cups unpeeled diced apple
Salad greens

Put cranberries through the coarse blade of a food chopper; stir in sugar; let stand while preparing the gelatin. Drain pineapple and add enough water to the juice to make 2 cups liquid. Heat juice mixture to boiling over moderate heat (about 250° F.); remove from heat. Add gelatin and stir until dissolved. Stir in 1 cup cold water, grated lemon peel, and lemon juice; chill until slightly thickened. Fold in drained pineapple, cranberries, and apple. Pour into a 1½-quart mold. Chill several hours, until set. Unmold on salad greens. Serves 8 to 10.

Molded Grapefruit Salad

1 16-ounce can grapefruit
   sections
Fruit juice or water

Drain grapefruit sections, reserving syrup. Measure syrup and add enough additional fruit juice to make 1½ cups liquid. Sprinkle gelatine over juice to soften. Place

1 *envelope unflavored*
  gelatine
2 *tablespoons sugar*
1 *teaspoon lemon juice*
⅛ *teaspoon salt*
½ *cup chopped celery*
½ *cup peeled and coarsely*
  grated carrot
Salad greens
Mayonnaise

over moderate heat (about 250° F.) and stir until dissolved. Add sugar, lemon juice, and salt; stir until dissolved. Chill until slightly thickened. Fold in grapefruit, celery, and carrot. Pour into individual ⅔-cup molds or large custard cups and chill until set. Unmold on salad greens and serve with mayonnaise. Serves 4.

⋑ Lime Cream Salad

1 *6-ounce package*
  lime-flavored gelatin
2 *teaspoons salt*
2 *cups boiling water*
2 *tablespoons cider vinegar*
2 *teaspoons grated onion*
⅛ *teaspoon pepper*
2 *cups commercial sour*
  cream
½ *cup mayonnaise*
2 *cups well-drained seeded,*
  shredded cucumber,
  peeled
Crisp lettuce
3 *tomatoes, thinly sliced*
Mayonnaise (optional)

Combine gelatin and salt in a large bowl. Add boiling water and stir until gelatin is dissolved. Add vinegar, onion, and pepper. Chill mixture until the consistency of unbeaten egg white. Add sour cream and mayonnaise and beat with a rotary beater to blend thoroughly. Fold in cucumber. Pour into a 2-quart mold. Chill about 3 hours, until firm. Unmold on crisp lettuce bed. Arrange tomato slices around edge of mold. Cut mold in wedges and serve with additional mayonnaise, if desired. Serves 8 to 10.

⋑ Spiced Peach Salad

2 *16-ounce cans sliced*
  peaches
12 *whole cloves*
2 *2-inch sticks cinnamon*
1 *6-ounce package*
  orange-flavored gelatin
¼ *cup white vinegar*
⅔ *cup mayonnaise or salad*
  dressing
Salad greens

Drain peaches and add enough water to syrup to make 2 cups liquid. Add cloves and cinnamon and simmer 10 minutes over low heat (about 200° F.). Strain into a medium-sized bowl. Dissolve gelatin in the hot syrup mixture. Stir in vinegar. Add mayonnaise; beat with rotary beater until well blended. Chill until slightly thickened. Fold in peaches. Pour into a 1-quart mold. Chill until firm. Unmold on a platter lined with salad greens. Serves 8.

🖎 Jellied Beet Salad

2 envelopes unflavored
  gelatine
⅓ cup cold water
1 16-ounce can diced beets
¼ cup sugar
1 teaspoon salt
2 small bay leaves, crushed
¼ cup cider vinegar
½ cup chopped sweet pickles
Mayonnaise (optional)
Milk (optional)

Soften gelatine in the ⅓ cup cold water. Drain beets and add enough water to beet liquid to make 2 cups; bring to a boil in a medium-sized saucepan over moderate heat (about 250° F.). Remove from heat and add gelatine, sugar, salt, bay leaves, and vinegar. Stir until gelatine is dissolved. Chill until slightly thickened. Mix in beets and pickles. Pour into a 1-quart mold. Chill about 3 hours, or until firm. Unmold on serving plate. If desired, serve with mayonnaise mixed with a little milk. Serves 6 to 8.

🖎 Molded Garden Salad

1 3-ounce package
  lemon-flavored gelatin
¾ cup boiling water
1 3-ounce package
  orange-flavored gelatin
1½ cups boiling water
2 tablespoons lemon juice
1 cup ginger ale
1¼ cups shredded chopped
  cabbage
¾ cup diced celery
1 8½-ounce can crushed
  pineapple
2 tablespoons lemon juice
1¼ cups coarsely shredded,
  peeled carrot
Salad greens

Dissolve lemon gelatin in the ¾ cup boiling water. In a second saucepan dissolve orange gelatin in the 1½ cups boiling water. Cool lemon gelatin to room temperature. Stir in the 2 tablespoons lemon juice and ginger ale. Place saucepan of lemon gelatin in a bowl of ice cubes and stir until slightly thickened. Fold in cabbage and celery. Pour into an 8-inch-square pan. Chill until almost set. Cool orange gelatin to room temperature. Drain crushed pineapple and add the pineapple juice and the 2 tablespoons lemon juice to the orange gelatin. Chill over ice cubes until slightly thickened. Fold in drained pineapple and shredded carrot. Pour over lemon layer and chill 3 to 4 hours, or until set. Unmold and cut into squares. Serve on salad greens. Serves 9.

🖎 Spinach–Cheese Mousse Ring

1 3-ounce package
  lemon-flavored gelatin
1 cup boiling water
½ cup cold water
1½ tablespoons white vinegar
½ cup mayonnaise or salad

Dissolve gelatin in boiling water. Add cold water, vinegar, mayonnaise, salt, and pepper. Blend well with rotary beater. Pour into freezer tray or loaf pan and chill in freezer 15 to 20 minutes, or until firm 1 inch around edge of pan. While gelatin is chilling, put cheese through a fine sieve or beat with an electric mixer until

dressing
½ *teaspoon salt*
Few grains pepper
 1 *cup cottage cheese*
 1 *cup cleaned, chopped raw*
 spinach
½ *cup finely chopped celery*
 2 *tablespoons finely*
 chopped onion
½ *cup heavy cream,*
 whipped
 4 *hard-cooked eggs, cut into*
 halves crosswise
Salad greens

almost smooth. Beat gelatin mixture until fluffy with a rotary beater or electric mixer. Gradually add cottage cheese, beating until blended. Fold in spinach, celery, and onion. Fold in whipped cream. Arrange egg halves in ring around bottom of a 5-cup or 8-inch ring gelatin mold. Carefully spoon in the gelatin mixture. Chill several hours, until firm. Unmold on a chilled platter lined with salad greens. Serves 4 to 6.

✑ Tomato Aspic

 1 *envelope unflavored*
 gelatine
1½ *cups tomato juice*
 2 *tablespoons lemon juice*
 1 *teaspoon sugar*
 1 *tablespoon instant minced*
 onion
½ *teaspoon dried basil*
 leaves
¼ *teaspoon salt*
Salad greens

Sprinkle gelatine over tomato juice in saucepan. Add lemon juice, sugar, onion, basil, and salt; place over moderate heat (about 250° F.) and heat until gelatine is dissolved. Pour into an 8-inch-square pan and chill until set. Cut into squares and serve on salad greens. Serves 6.

✑ Vegetable Aspic

 2 *envelopes unflavored*
 gelatine
¼ *cup cold water*
 1 *24-ounce can vegetable*
 juice cocktail
½ *teaspoon salt*
½ *teaspoon sugar*
 1 *tablespoon bottled clear*
 French dressing
Dash of Tabasco
Crisp lettuce leaves
Thin unpeeled cucumber slices
Basic French Dressing (recipe
 on page 626)

In a saucepan sprinkle gelatine over the cold water and ½ cup of the vegetable juice; allow gelatine to soften. Place over low heat (about 200° F.), stirring constantly, until gelatine is dissolved. Remove from heat and stir in salt and sugar to dissolve. Add remaining vegetable juice, French dressing, and Tabasco; stir to blend. Pour into 6 individual molds. Chill until firm. Unmold onto 6 lettuce-lined salad plates and garnish with cucumber slices. Serve with additional dressing, if desired. Serves 6.

Molded Main-Dish Salads

✒ Chicken–Almond Mousse

1 4- to 5-pound stewing
   chicken, cut up
4 cups hot water
1 tablespoon salt
1 onion, sliced
1½ tablespoons unflavored
   gelatine
3 cups chicken broth
1 teaspoon salt
½ teaspoon pepper
1 teaspoon finely chopped
   onion
3 egg yolks, well beaten
¼ cup sliced, stuffed olives
¼ cup chopped, blanched
   almonds
1 cup heavy cream,
   whipped
Melon balls (optional)
Strawberries (optional)

Cook chicken, hot water, salt, and onion over low heat (about 200° F.) until chicken is fork-tender, about 3½ hours. Cool chicken and broth separately. Remove chicken from bones and chop coarsely. Reserve 3 cups and save any leftovers for another use. Soften gelatine in ½ cup cold chicken broth. Heat remaining 2½ cups broth with salt, pepper, and onion in top of double boiler. Stir a little of the hot mixture into egg yolks and then combine with rest of hot mixture. Cook and stir over boiling water until thickened and smooth. Add softened gelatine. Cool until the consistency of unbeaten egg white. Fold in olives, nuts, chopped chicken, and cream. Pour into greased 1½-quart mold. Chill several hours until firm. Unmold on chilled plate. Garnish with melon balls and strawberries, if desired. Serves 6.

✒ Chicken-and-Ham Mousse

1 envelope unflavored
   gelatine
¼ cup cold water
1 chicken bouillon cube
1 cup hot water
⅛ teaspoon cayenne pepper
3 egg yolks
¼ cup mayonnaise or salad
   dressing
1 cup finely chopped, cooked
   chicken
1 cup finely chopped, cooked
   ham
2 tablespoons finely chopped
   scallions
2 tablespoons finely chopped
   pimiento

Sprinkle gelatine over the ¼ cup cold water to soften. Dissolve bouillon cube in hot water. Beat together cayenne and egg yolks in top of double boiler. Gradually stir in bouillon. Cook over simmering water until thickened, stirring constantly. Add gelatine and stir until gelatine is dissolved. Blend in mayonnaise. Chill until mixture is the consistency of unbeaten egg white. Fold in chicken, ham, scallions, pimiento and whipped cream. Pour into a 1-quart mold and chill several hours, until firm. Unmold on salad greens. Garnish with mayonnaise, if desired. Serves 4 to 6.

(Ingredients continued on page 618)

½ *cup heavy cream, whipped*
Salad greens
Mayonnaise (optional)

✍ *Polynesian Curry Salad*

Curried Rice Ring (recipe follows)
Chicken and Grape Salad (recipe on page 619)
Watercress
 6 *lettuce cups*
¾ *cup chopped green pepper*
½ *cup chopped candied ginger*
¾ *cup flaked coconut*
¾ *cup chutney*
 1 *11-ounce can mandarin oranges, drained*
 1 *cup salted peanuts*

Prepare Curried Rice Ring about 4 hours before serving time. Prepare Chicken and Grape Salad about 2 hours before serving time. Unmold rice ring on a round tray. Spoon Chicken and Grape Salad into center of ring. Garnish edges of Chicken and Grape Salad with a ring of watercress. Arrange the lettuce cups around ring; spoon one of the condiments (green pepper, ginger, coconut, chutney, oranges, and peanuts) into each cup. Serves 6.

Curried Rice Ring

 1 *cup uncooked long-grained rice*
2½ *cups chicken broth*
 ½ *teaspoon salt*
 ½ *cup chicken broth*
 1 *envelope unflavored gelatine*
 1 *tablespoon instant minced onion*
1¼ *cups chicken broth*
 ½ *cup mayonnaise or salad dressing*
 2 *teaspoons curry powder*
 ½ *teaspoon salt*
 ⅛ *teaspoon pepper*
 ½ *cup heavy cream, whipped*
 ½ *cup finely chopped celery*
 ¼ *cup chopped pimiento*
 2 *hard-cooked eggs, chopped*

Place rice, the 2½ cups chicken broth, and the ½ teaspoon salt in a 3-quart saucepan with a tight-fitting cover. Bring to a boil over moderately high heat (about 275° F.), stirring once or twice. Reduce heat to moderately low (about 225° F.) and cook 16 minutes without removing the cover, or until rice is tender. Cool. Pour the ½ cup chicken broth into a saucepan and sprinkle gelatine over broth. Add onion and heat over low heat (about 200° F.) until gelatine is dissolved. Add the remaining 1¼ cups chicken broth, the mayonnaise, curry powder, the ½ teaspoon salt, and the pepper; beat with a rotary beater until blended. Cool slightly and stir in rice. Place saucepan in a large bowl of ice cubes and chill until slightly thickened. Fold in the cream, celery, pimiento, and eggs. Pour into a 6½-cup ring mold and chill until set. Serves 6 in Polynesian Curry Salad.

Chicken and Grape Salad

½ cup mayonnaise or salad
  dressing
1 tablespoon instant minced
  onion
1 tablespoon lemon juice
½ teaspoon salt
⅛ teaspoon pepper
3 cups diced cooked chicken
1 cup thinly sliced celery
1 cup halved seedless grapes

Mix mayonnaise, onion, lemon juice, salt, and pepper in a bowl; fold in chicken, celery, and grapes. Chill. Serves 6 in Polynesian Curry Salad.

Holiday Ham Mold

1 6-ounce package
  lemon-flavored gelatin
2 cups boiling water
1½ cups commercial sour
  cream
½ cup pineapple juice
2 tablespoons lemon juice
1 cup chopped cooked ham
½ cup chopped green pepper
2 tablespoons minced onion
Pinch of dry mustard
¼ teaspoon salt
⅛ teaspoon pepper
Salad greens
6 canned pineapple slices
Pimiento strips

Dissolve gelatin in boiling water. Chill until the consistency of unbeaten egg white. Mix sour cream, pineapple juice, and lemon juice together; add to thickened gelatin and beat with rotary beater until blended. Mix in ham, green pepper, minced onion, mustard, salt, and pepper. Pour into a 1½-quart gelatin mold. Chill until firm. Unmold on salad greens. Garnish with half slices of pineapple and strips of pimiento. Serves 6.

Lamb Mousse

1 6-ounce package
  lemon-flavored gelatin
2 cups boiling water
1¼ cups cold water
¼ cup mayonnaise or salad
  dressing
*1 cup finely chopped, cooked
  lamb

(Ingredients continued on page 620)

Dissolve gelatin in boiling water. Add cold water and mayonnaise; beat with rotary beater until thoroughly blended. Chill until mixture is the consistency of unbeaten egg white. Fold in lamb, salt, green pepper, onion, pimiento, and apple. Fold in whipped cream. Pour mixture into a 2-quart mold or loaf pan and chill several hours, until firm. Unmold on greens. Serves 6 to 8.

*Note: 1 cup finely chopped, cooked veal, ham, or chicken may be substituted for the cooked lamb.

¼ teaspoon salt
½ cup chopped green pepper
3 tablespoons finely
   chopped onion
2 tablespoons chopped
   pimiento
1 medium-sized apple,
   cored, pared, and
   chopped
½ cup heavy cream,
   whipped
Salad greens

⌇ Turkey Salad in Cucumber Ring

1 cup unsweetened
   pineapple juice
1 3-ounce package
   lime-flavored gelatin
½ cup lemon juice
1 teaspoon salt
2 cups finely grated, peeled
   cucumber
1½ cups diced cooked turkey
   or chicken
1 cup chopped celery
2 tablespoons chopped
   green pepper
½ cup peeled, grated carrot
½ cup coarsely chopped
   cashew nuts
2 hard-cooked eggs,
   chopped
Salt and pepper
¾ cup mayonnaise
Lettuce

Heat pineapple juice in a saucepan over moderate heat (about 250° F.) until it comes to a boil. Remove from heat and add gelatin. Stir until gelatin is dissolved. Add lemon juice and salt. Chill until mixture is the consistency of unbeaten egg white. Fold in cucumber. Pour into a 1½-quart ring mold. Chill until firm. Combine turkey, celery, green pepper, carrot, nuts, and eggs. Season with salt and pepper. Add mayonnaise and toss to blend. Chill. Unmold cucumber ring on crisp lettuce. Fill center with salad mixture. Serves 6 to 8.

⌇ Lobster Mousse

2 envelopes unflavored
   gelatine
½ cup cold water
1 cup mayonnaise or salad
   dressing
2 tablespoons lemon juice

Sprinkle gelatine over cold water in a small saucepan. Place over low heat (about 200° F.) and stir until gelatine is dissolved. Blend mayonnaise, lemon juice, salt, and paprika in a large bowl. Stir in gelatine. Fold in lobster, celery, and cucumber. Fold in whipped cream. Pour into a 2-quart mold and chill until firm. Unmold onto a

1 teaspoon salt
¼ teaspoon paprika
2 5-ounce cans lobster,
  drained and flaked
1 cup chopped celery
1 cup coarsely grated
  cucumber
1 cup heavy cream, whipped
4 tablespoons finely chopped
  fresh parsley

chilled platter. If desired, save a few lobster claw pieces for garnish. Sprinkle chopped parsley around mold. Serves 8.

Cold Chicken with Walnut Sauce

2 3½-pound chickens, cut up
6 cups water
1 teaspoon salt
3 cups shelled walnuts
1 cup finely chopped, peeled
  onion
6 slices slightly stale bread,
  torn in pieces
2 teaspoons paprika
Few grains of pepper
2 teaspoons salt
Flat-leaf parsley
Canned pimiento

In a large pot place the chickens, water and the 1 teaspoon of salt; cover and bring to a boil over high heat. Reduce heat to moderate, leave lid half on and cook chicken 35 minutes, or until just tender. Remove chicken pieces from pot and let cool. Meanwhile, turn up heat under chicken broth and let it boil fast until just 3 cups remain; this will take about 30 minutes. Pour 1½ cups of the broth into an electric blender; add half the walnuts and onion. Cover and blend at high speed until smooth. Stop blender and add half the bread, pushing it down into the walnut purée. Cover and blend to a smooth purée, stopping blender 3 or 4 times to push mixture down. Transfer purée to a large bowl. Repeat blending procedure with remaining chicken broth, walnuts and onion; add the paprika, pepper and the 2 teaspoons salt with remaining bread. Combine both puréed mixtures in the bowl. Remove and discard chicken skin and bones. Cut or shred chicken into very small pieces, about ¾-inch long and ⅛-inch wide. Place shredded chicken in cooking pot with 3 cups of the walnut sauce; toss well to mix. Arrange chicken mixture smoothly on a platter in a crescent shape. Cover tightly and chill several hours or overnight. Coat surface of crescent with the remaining cup of walnut sauce and decorate with parsley leaves and pimiento just before serving. Serve with a spoon. Makes about 7 cups, or 14 to 16 servings as part of a buffet. Recipe may be halved to serve 8.

Deviled Egg Mold

2 envelopes unflavored
  gelatine

Sprinkle gelatine over water in a large saucepan; place over low heat (about 200° F.) and stir until gelatine dis-

1 cup cold water
2 teaspoons salt
3 tablespoons lemon juice
½ teaspoon Worcestershire
   sauce
¼ teaspoon pepper
½ teaspoon dry mustard
1½ cups mayonnaise
1 tablespoon grated, peeled
   onion
1 cup finely diced celery
½ cup finely diced, seeded
   green pepper
½ cup chopped canned or
   jarred pimiento
8 hard-cooked eggs, peeled
   and chopped
Salad greens or watercress
Cherry tomatoes

solves. Remove pan from heat and stir in salt, lemon juice, Worcestershire sauce, pepper and mustard; let cool. Stir mayonnaise into cooled gelatine mixture, and then add onion, celery, green pepper, pimiento and eggs. Spoon into a 6-cup mold; cover and chill in refrigerator 3 hours or more, until firm. To unmold, have ready a serving dish that has been rinsed with cold water and left wet. With a sharp knife loosen mold around edge. Dip bottom of mold into a pan of warm water, invert serving dish over mold and, holding them tightly, turn over both together. Hold mold and dish together firmly and shake gently until contents of mold fall onto plate. If it doesn't work, repeat the quick dip in water, but take care not to leave mold in water too long or gelatine mixture may begin to melt. Garnish unmolded mixture with salad greens and cherry tomatoes. Serves 6 to 8.

❧ Molded Tuna-and-Avocado Salad

2 envelopes unflavored
   gelatine
2½ cups cold water
1 envelope instant vegetable
   broth mix
½ teaspoon grated lemon
   peel
¼ cup lemon juice
3 6½-ounce cans tuna,
   drained and flaked
1 cup finely diced celery
¼ cup chopped
   pimiento-stuffed olives
1 tablespoon finely chopped
   onion
½ cup mayonnaise
1½ cups peeled and diced
   avocado (about 1
   medium-sized)
Tomato slices (optional)
Avocado slices (optional)

In a small saucepan sprinkle gelatine over 1 cup of the cold water. Place over very low heat (about 175° F.) and dissolve, stirring constantly. When dissolved blend in broth mix. Remove from heat. Combine gelatine mixture with remaining water, lemon peel, and juice. Chill until the consistency of unbeaten egg whites. Meanwhile, in a large bowl combine tuna, celery, olives, and onion. Mix in mayonnaise. Gently fold in avocado, being careful not to mash it. Fold in gelatine mixture. Turn into a 1½-quart mold. Chill until firm, several hours or overnight. Unmold onto a chilled platter. Garnish with tomato and avocado slices, if desired. Serves 6.

Salad Dressings

Although the number of excellent bottled dressings and mayonnaises and packaged mixes for salad dressings seems to grow daily, there are basically only three varieties of salad dressings. They are mayonnaise, French (vinaigrette), and cooked (or boiled) salad dressing. Sour cream dressings are usually a variation of one of the basic dressings.

Mayonnaise is an emulsion of oil and egg yolks (or whole eggs) with an acid (lemon or vinegar) and seasonings added. Homemade mayonnaise is not difficult to make once you get the feel of the point at which the egg yolks begin to absorb the oil and turn thick and creamy. Most important: Have all ingredients at room temperature before you start. You can use a small wire whip or an electric hand beater for blending.

Blender mayonnaise, a whole-egg mayonnaise, is a little lighter and thinner than basic mayonnaise.

Mayonnaise can be flavored with any fresh or powdered herbs. Fresh minced parsley, tarragon, basil, dill, or chives can be added in the proportion of 3 tablespoons of fresh herbs to 1 cup of mayonnaise. When using dried herbs, use 1 tablespoon dried herbs to one cup of mayonnaise.

French (Vinaigrette) dressing is made from an oil and an acid (usually vinegar or lemon juice) and seasonings. Since it will separate on standing, it must be shaken vigorously before adding to a salad.

Cooked salad dressing has a thickened white-sauce base that can be made with water or milk with acid, seasonings, and fat (usually butter) added. This is a particularly good dressing for meat, potato, and cabbage-slaw salads.

Cream-based dressings, which do not fall into the basic categories, are especially good with fruit salads.

❦ Basic Mayonnaise

3 egg yolks, at room
  temperature
½ teaspoon salt
½ teaspoon dry mustard
3 tablespoons vinegar or
  lemon juice
2 cups of salad oil or olive oil
Few grains cayenne pepper

Put egg yolks into a small bowl. Beat egg yolks until they are well blended and slightly thickened. Add salt and mustard and 1 tablespoon of vinegar or lemon juice; blend it in. Add the oil *very* slowly. If you are using an electric mixer, set it at medium speed. As you beat, add the oil by droplets, not more than a ½ teaspoon at a time. By the time you have beaten in ½ cup of the oil, you should have a very thick, creamy mixture. Now you can add the remainder of the oil by tablespoons and beat in the remaining vinegar or lemon juice. Add cayenne pepper last. Cover tightly and store in the refrigerator. Makes about 2¼ cups.

Note: If you plan to keep the mayonnaise any length of time before using it, you can beat *2 tablespoons of boiling water* into the finished mayonnaise before storing it. This prevents mayonnaise from separating.

❧ Blender Mayonnaise

1 egg
½ teaspoon dry mustard
½ teaspoon salt
2 tablespoons vinegar
1 cup vegetable oil

Place egg in container of electric blender. Add mustard, salt, and vinegar. Add ¼ cup of the oil. Cover and turn motor to low speed. Immediately uncover and, with motor still running, pour in remaining oil in a thin, steady stream (do not add drop by drop). Replace cover. Leave blender on about a minute after the last of the oil has been added. Mayonnaise may be stored in a tightly covered container in the refrigerator for up to 5 days. Makes about 1¼ cups.

❧ Thousand Island Dressing

1 cup Basic or Blender Mayonnaise (recipes on pages 623 and 624)
¼ cup chili sauce
2 tablespoons stuffed green olives, minced
1 tablespoon minced onion
1 hard-cooked egg, chopped
2 teaspoons chopped fresh parsley

Combine mayonnaise, chili sauce, olives, onion, chopped egg, and parsley. Use with green salads. Makes about 2 cups.

❧ Russian Dressing

⅓ cup chili sauce
⅔ cup Basic or Blender Mayonnaise (recipes on pages 623 and 624)
3½ tablespoons chopped dill pickle
⅛ teaspoon dry mustard
⅛ teaspoon onion powder

Combine all ingredients in a small bowl and blend well. Cover and chill at least 1 hour. Use with vegetable and green salads. Makes 1 cup.

⤳ Green Goddess Dressing

1 cup Basic or Blender
   Mayonnaise (recipes on
   pages 623 and 624)
¼ cup finely chopped fresh
   parsley
2 tablespoons finely snipped
   chives
3 anchovy fillets, minced
1 clove garlic, minced
1 tablespoon lemon juice
1 tablespoon tarragon
   vinegar
¼ teaspoon salt
Few grains ground black
   pepper
½ cup commercial sour cream

Combine mayonnaise, parsley, chives, anchovies, garlic, lemon juice, vinegar, salt, pepper, and sour cream. Use with seafood salads. Makes about 1½ cups.

⤳ Strawberry Cream Dressing

¼ cup Basic or Blender
   Mayonnaise (recipes on
   pages 623 and 624)
½ cup sliced fresh
   strawberries
2 tablespoons powdered
   sugar
1 tablespoon lemon juice
¼ cup heavy cream, whipped

Combine mayonnaise, strawberries, powdered sugar, and lemon juice thoroughly. Fold in whipped cream. Cover and refrigerate until serving time. Use with fruit salads. Makes about 1¼ cups.

⤳ Honey-Lime Dressing

½ cup Basic or Blender
   Mayonnaise (recipes on
   pages 623 and 624)
¼ cup honey
2 tablespoons lime juice
½ cup heavy cream, whipped

Combine mayonnaise, honey, and lime juice thoroughly. Fold in whipped cream. Cover and refrigerate until serving time. Use with fruit salads. Makes about 1¾ cups.

✍ Blue Cheese Mayonnaise

1 cup Basic or Blender
   Mayonnaise (recipes on
   pages 623 and 624)
¼ cup crumbled blue cheese
3 tablespoons milk
Few drops Tabasco

Combine mayonnaise, blue cheese, milk, and Tabasco. Use with green salads. Makes about 1½ cups.

✍ Pink Currant Dressing

½ cup currant jelly
½ cup Basic or Blender
   Mayonnaise (recipes on
   pages 623 and 624)
½ cup heavy cream, whipped

Beat currant jelly with rotary beater until soft and smooth. Blend in mayonnaise. Fold in whipped cream. Cover and refrigerate until serving time. Use with fruit salads. Makes about 2 cups.

✍ Basic French Dressing

¾ teaspoon salt
¼ teaspoon paprika
   (optional)
Few grains black pepper
¼ cup white, cider, or wine
   vinegar or lemon juice
¾ cup vegetable oil or olive
   oil

Measure salt, paprika, if desired, and black pepper into a jar or salad cruet. Add vinegar and then oil. Cover tightly. Shake vigorously or blend in the container of an electric blender at high speed for 20 seconds. Refrigerate overnight before using. Makes about 1 cup.

Sherry French Dressing

¼ cup dry sherry
1 cup Basic French Dressing
   (recipe above)

Add sherry to French dressing and shake vigorously to blend. Refrigerate to store. Use on fruit salads. Makes about 1¼ cups.

Blue Cheese French Dressing

¼ cup crumbled blue cheese
1 cup Basic French Dressing
   (recipe above)

Add blue cheese to French dressing and shake vigorously to blend. Refrigerate to store. Use with green salads. Makes about 1¼ cups.

Lime French Dressing

3 tablespoons lime juice
1 tablespoon lemon juice
1 cup Basic French Dressing
   (recipe above)

Substitute lime and lemon juices for the vinegar or lemon juice called for in Basic French Dressing. Refrigerate to store. Use on fruit salads. Makes about 1 cup.

Mint French Dressing

2 tablespoons finely chopped
mint leaves
1 cup Basic French Dressing
(recipe on page 626)

Add mint to French dressing and shake vigorously to blend. Refrigerate to store. Use with fruit salads. Makes about 1 cup.

Garlic French Dressing

2 cloves garlic, minced
1 cup Basic French Dressing
(recipe on page 626)

Add garlic to French dressing and shake vigorously to blend. Store in refrigerator for several days before using. Use with green salads. Makes about 1 cup.

Honey French Dressing

2 tablespoons honey
1 cup Basic French Dressing
(recipe on page 626)

Add honey to French dressing and shake vigorously to blend. Refrigerate to store. Use with fruit salads. Makes about 1 cup.

❧ Olive Oil French Dressing

⅔ cup olive oil
¼ cup lemon juice
¼ teaspoon dry mustard
½ teaspoon dried basil leaves
1 small clove garlic
½ teaspoon sugar
½ teaspoon salt
⅛ teaspoon pepper

Place all ingredients in a jar and shake together until well mixed. Makes a scant cup of dressing.

❧ Vinaigrette Dressing

7 tablespoons vegetable oil
7 tablespoons vinegar
½ cup finely chopped fresh
parsley
¼ cup finely snipped chives
2 teaspoons salt
¼ teaspoon pepper

Place oil, vinegar, parsley, chives, salt, and pepper in a small bowl; beat with a rotary beater until well blended. Serve over vegetable salads. Makes about 1 cup.

❧ Italian Dressing

1 teaspoon salt
⅛ teaspoon black pepper

Measure salt, black pepper, and cayenne into a jar. Add vinegar and then oil. Add onion, pimiento, parsley,

Few grains cayenne pepper
¼ cup wine vinegar
¾ cup olive oil
1 tablespoon finely chopped
   green onion
1 tablespoon finely chopped
   pimiento
1 tablespoon finely chopped
   fresh parsley
1 tablespoon finely chopped
   dill pickle
1 clove garlic

pickle, and garlic clove; shake vigorously to blend. Refrigerate several hours; remove garlic clove before serving. Use with green salads. Makes about 1¼ cups.

✑ Basic Cooked Salad Dressing

2 tablespoons sugar
2 tablespoons flour
1 teaspoon salt
1 teaspoon dry mustard
Few grains cayenne pepper
1 egg, slightly beaten
¾ cup milk
¼ cup cider vinegar
1½ teaspoons butter or
   margarine

Combine sugar, flour, salt, dry mustard, and cayenne in the top of a double boiler. Blend in egg and milk. Place over hot—not boiling—water and cook, stirring constantly, until thickened and smooth. Add vinegar and butter. Stir until butter melts. Cool and store in refrigerator. Makes about 1 cup. Use in potato salad or in variations given below.

Mustard Dressing

2 tablespoons prepared
   mustard
1 cup Basic Cooked Salad
   Dressing (recipe above)

Add mustard to cooked salad dressing and serve hot as a sauce for boiled beef or use cold as a dressing for coleslaw. Makes about 1 cup.

Sour Cream Dressing

½ cup commercial sour cream
1 cup Basic Cooked Salad
   Dressing (recipe above)

Add sour cream to cooked salad dressing. Beat with a rotary beater or wire whip to blend. Use as a dressing for coleslaw or potato salad. Makes about 1½ cups.

✑ Cucumber Dressing

⅔ cup chopped peeled
   cucumber
1½ tablespoons chopped
   onion

Place cucumber and onion in the container of an electric blender; blend on high speed until very finely chopped. Chill. Whip cream until stiff; fold in sour cream and salt. Fold in cucumber mixture. Serve immediately over

½ *cup chilled heavy cream*
½ *cup commercial sour cream*
½ *teaspoon salt*

sliced tomatoes or lettuce wedges or with cold or poached fish. Makes about 1¾ cups.

ᕫ Avocado Cream Dressing

1 *tablespoon lemon juice*
¼ *cup heavy cream*
⅛ *teaspoon salt*
⅛ *teaspoon ground ginger*
1½ *tablespoons confectioners' sugar*
½ *small ripe avocado, peeled and diced*
¼ *cup heavy cream, whipped*

Place lemon juice, the ¼ cup heavy cream, salt, ginger, confectioners' sugar, and avocado in container of electric blender. Cover and blend on high speed for about 20 seconds, until mixture is smooth and fluffy. Fold in whipped cream with a rubber spatula. Serve immediately. Use with fruit salads. Makes about 1 cup.

ᕫ Orange Cream Dressing

⅓ *cup orange juice*
1½ *teaspoons lemon juice*
¼ *cup sugar*
⅛ *teaspoon salt*
2 *egg yolks*
¾ *cup heavy cream, whipped*
1 *teaspoon grated orange peel*

Place orange juice, lemon juice, sugar, and salt in the top of a double boiler. Place over moderate heat (about 250° F.) and bring to a boil. Remove from heat and cool for about 5 minutes. Add the egg yolks one at a time, beating well after each addition. Place over hot—not boiling—water (water below should not touch bottom of pan) and cook until thickened and smooth, stirring constantly. Remove from heat and cool. Chill thoroughly. Fold in whipped cream and orange peel. Use with fruit salads. Makes about 1½ cups.

CHAPTER XVIII

QUICK BREADS

Nothing will add so much to a humdrum meal as a delicate hot bread. The breads in this chapter are called quick breads because they depend upon quick-acting leavening agents—baking soda, baking powder, or eggs—to make them rise. Tender hot biscuits and muffins, flavorful loaf breads, and sweet coffeecakes are all truly quick and easy to make. Doughnuts, dumplings for soups and stews, and light fruit or vegetable fritters are also in this category.

Although they are not technically breads, you will find waffles and pancakes—from the fat breakfast variety to the delicate crepes—in this chapter because the method for handling the batter is much the same as for other quick breads.

With the exception of the loaf breads, the term *quick* also applies to the way these breads should be served—immediately after baking while they are steaming hot.

The most important general rule for handling the quick bread batters: Don't overmix. The flour in pancakes and muffins should be stirred in just until it is dampened. The batter will look slightly lumpy. Biscuits should be handled only enough to pat them out for shaping. Use, if you like, the excellent mixes on the market. Follow the directions on the box but observe the rule for mixing.

Because of their texture, quick breads do not stay fresh for long. If you have leftovers, they should be wrapped tightly and kept at room temperature for a day. You can reheat them in a tight wrapping of aluminum foil in a 250° F. oven for 10 to 15 minutes.

Biscuits

There was a time when biscuits were the classic test of a bride's ability to cook. While a tender, fluffy biscuit may no longer be the only showcase for a new cook's talents, there are so many uses for biscuits—as a hot bread, as a casserole topping, as a pot-pie crust, or the base of a fruit shortcake—it's well worth knowing how to produce a tender, flaky, melt-in-your-mouth biscuit.

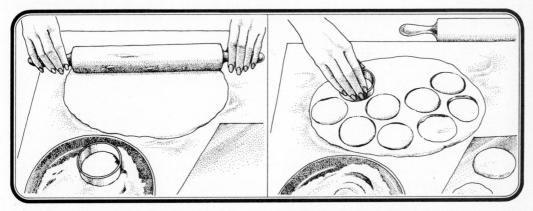

Any biscuit dough should be handled gently or the biscuits will be tough. On a lightly floured board roll out the dough ¼ inch thick for thin, crusty biscuits; roll out to ½-inch thickness for thicker softer ones.

Cut the biscuits with a well-floured biscuit cutter. Fit all the leftover bits of dough together. Pat it out and cut. Place biscuits close together for soft sides, or 1 inch apart for crusty sides, on ungreased baking pan.

✑ Basic Rolled Biscuits

2 cups sifted all-purpose flour
3 teaspoons baking powder
1 teaspoon salt
6 tablespoons soft shortening
⅔ cup milk

Heat oven to 450° F. Sift flour, baking powder, and salt into a bowl. Cut in shortening with a pastry blender or two knives until mixture resembles coarse corn meal. Make a well in center of mixture. Add milk all at once and mix lightly with a fork until a soft dough is formed. Knead dough lightly on floured board about 6 times. Handle dough lightly. Roll out to thickness of ½ inch. Flour a 2-inch biscuit cutter and cut biscuits close together. Pat together scraps of dough and cut out. Place biscuits on ungreased cookie sheet about 1 inch apart for crusty sides, or close together for soft sides. Bake 10 to 12 minutes, until golden brown. Makes about 12 2½-inch biscuits.

Watercress or Parsley Biscuits

Add ½ cup coarsely chopped watercress or fresh parsley with the milk to the above recipe. Dry watercress or parsley thoroughly before chopping.

QUICK BREADS

❧ Rolled Cheese Biscuits

2 cups prepared buttermilk
  biscuit mix
1 tablespoon instant minced
  onion
½ cup milk
1 cup (¼ pound) sharp
  Cheddar cheese, coarsely
  shredded

Heat oven to 425° F. Put biscuit mix in a bowl; add onion and milk. Stir with a fork until a soft dough forms. Beat 15 strokes. Turn out on a board lightly sprinkled with biscuit mix and knead dough lightly about 10 times. Roll out dough into a rectangle 9 x 12 inches. Sprinkle with cheese. Starting with the shorter side, roll up dough like a jelly roll. Cut into nine 1-inch slices. Arrange slices, cut-side down, on a greased cookie sheet. Bake 10 to 12 minutes, until golden brown. Makes 9 biscuits.

❧ Orange Tea Biscuits

1⅓ cups sifted all-purpose
  flour
1¼ teaspoons baking powder
½ teaspoon salt
3 teaspoons grated orange
  peel
½ cup soft shortening
½ cup milk
3 tablespoons sugar
1½ tablespoons melted butter
  or margarine

Heat oven to 450° F. Sift flour, baking powder, and salt together into a bowl. Stir in 1 teaspoon of the orange peel. Cut in shortening with pastry blender until mixture resembles coarse corn meal. Make a well in center and pour in milk. Mix until dough leaves sides of bowl. Knead lightly for about 5 strokes on floured board. Pat out to a thickness of ½ inch. Cut with a 2-inch biscuit cutter. Place biscuits on ungreased cookie sheet, 1 inch apart. Stir together the remaining 2 teaspoons orange peel, sugar, and butter. Crumble over tops of biscuits. Bake 15 minutes. Makes about 12 biscuits.

❧ Poppy Seed Spirals

¼ cup water
½ cup poppy seeds
2 tablespoons honey
½ teaspoon grated lemon peel
2 cups sifted all-purpose
  flour
3 teaspoons baking powder
½ teaspoon salt
2 tablespoons sugar
¼ cup soft shortening
¾ cup milk
¼ cup melted butter or
  margarine
2 tablespoons honey

Combine water, poppy seeds, and the 2 tablespoons honey in a small saucepan. Bring to a boil and cook over moderate heat (about 250° F.) 5 minutes, or until most of the water is evaporated. Add lemon peel and cool. Reserve for filling. Heat oven to 400° F. Sift flour, baking powder, salt, and sugar into a bowl. Cut in shortening with a pastry blender until mixture resembles coarse corn meal. Make a well in center of mixture. Add milk all at once and mix lightly with a fork until a soft dough forms. Knead about 6 times on a lightly floured board. Roll out into a 12-x-8-x-¼-inch rectangle. Brush surface with 2 tablespoons of the melted butter. Spread dough with the poppy seed filling. Starting at the 12-inch side, roll dough in jelly-roll fashion. Cut into 1-inch slices. Combine remaining 2 tablespoons melted butter and the

2 tablespoons honey and put 1 teaspoon of the mixture in each of twelve 2½-inch muffin cups. Place the biscuit slices, cut-side down, into muffin cups. Bake 20 minutes, until browned. Makes 12 biscuits.

Muffins

Perfect muffins should be rounded on the top, should be tender and evenly textured, and should not have tunnels in them. Following the illustrated directions below should give you this result. Unless your muffin tins are Teflon-lined, you will need to grease the cups or use paper baking cups to line each cup. If you are not using all of the spaces in a muffin tin, half-fill the empty cups with water so they won't burn.

To make perfect muffins, start by sifting the dry ingredients together into a medium-sized bowl. Make a little well in center of dry ingredients. Beat egg slightly with a fork in a small bowl; add milk and melted shortening or oil. Add to dry ingredients all at once. Stir with a spoon just enough to dampen flour particles. Batter will have small lumps in it which will disappear as muffins bake. Fill well-greased muffin cups two-thirds full. Fill any unused cups with water.

ᕦᕤ Basic Muffins

2 cups sifted all-purpose
  flour
3 teaspoons baking powder
3 tablespoons sugar
1 teaspoon salt
1 egg, slightly beaten

Heat oven to 400° F. Sift flour, baking powder, sugar, and salt together into a bowl. Make a well in center of dry ingredients. Combine egg, milk, and oil. Add all at once to dry ingredients. Stir only until flour is just moistened. Batter will be lumpy. Drop batter from tablespoon into greased cups of 2½-inch muffin pans. Fill

1 cup milk
¼ cup vegetable oil

muffin cups two-thirds full. Bake 15 to 20 minutes, until golden brown. Let muffins stand a few minutes before removing from pan. Serve warm with butter, jam, or marmalade. Makes 12 muffins.

Ginger Muffins

Add ½ cup finely cut candied ginger to dry ingredients before mixing with the liquid.

Cheese Muffins

Add ½ cup ¼-inch cubes sharp Cheddar cheese to dry ingredients before mixing with the liquid.

Banana Pecan Muffins

Prepare Basic Muffins but use only ⅓ cup milk. Add ½ cup chopped pecans and ¼ teaspoon ground nutmeg to sifted dry ingredients. Add 1 cup mashed banana with egg, milk, and oil.

Blueberry Muffins

Stir 1 cup washed and well drained fresh blueberries into sifted dry ingredients before adding liquid.

Orange Muffins

Peel 2 navel oranges and cut into sections. Drop batter into greased 2½-inch muffin cups. Place an orange section on top of each and sprinkle with 1 tablespoon sugar.

❧ Bacon Breakfast Muffins

6 slices raw bacon
1⅓ cups sifted all-purpose flour
3 teaspoons baking powder
3 tablespoons sugar
1 teaspoon salt
¾ cup crushed shredded wheat cereal
2 eggs, slightly beaten
⅔ cup milk
¼ cup vegetable oil

Cook bacon in skillet over moderately high heat (about 325° F.) until lightly browned. Drain and crumble. Heat oven to 400° F. Sift flour, baking powder, sugar, and salt together into a bowl. Stir in shredded wheat cereal and bacon. Combine eggs, milk, and oil. Add all at once to dry ingredients. Stir only until flour is just moistened. Batter will be lumpy. Drop batter from tablespoon into greased cups of 2½-inch muffin pans. Fill muffin cups two-thirds full. Bake 15 to 20 minutes, until golden brown. Let muffins stand a few minutes before removing from pan. Serve warm with butter, jam or marmalade. Makes 12 muffins.

❧ Date or Raisin Bran Muffins

1 cup bran cereal
¾ cup milk

Heat oven to 400° F. Combine cereal and milk; let stand until most of the milk is absorbed. Add egg and shorten-

1 egg
¼ cup soft shortening
1 cup sifted all-purpose flour
2½ teaspoons baking powder
½ teaspoon salt
¼ cup sugar
½ cup finely chopped pitted dates or whole seedless raisins
½ cup chopped walnuts

ing and beat well. Sift together flour, baking powder, salt, and sugar into a small bowl. Stir fruit and nuts into flour mixture. Add flour mixture to cereal mixture and stir only enough to moisten the dry ingredients. The mixture will be lumpy. Fill greased 2½-inch muffin pans two-thirds full. Bake about 30 minutes, or until browned. Serve hot. Makes about 12 muffins.

Popovers

Popovers are delicate, golden wonders that are high, crisp, and hollow. They are leavened by steam and should be timed to come from the oven just as dinner is served so butter will melt in them while they are piping hot.

✌ Popovers or Yorkshire Pudding

2 eggs
1 cup milk
1 cup sifted all-purpose flour
½ teaspoon salt

Heat oven to 425° F. Heavily grease 6 deep custard cups. Beat eggs slightly in a bowl. Add milk, flour, and salt and beat with a rotary beater until just smooth. Do not over-beat. Fill custard cups half full. Bake 40 to 45 minutes, or until golden brown. After removing popovers from oven, make a small slit in top of each to let steam escape. Serve hot. Makes 6.

To make Yorkshire Pudding to serve with Roast Beef, coat an 8- or 9-inch square baking pan with ¼ *cup of roast beef fat drippings*. Preheat pan for 5 minutes. Pour in batter and bake uncovered at 425° F. for 30 minutes. Serves 6.

Scones

Scones are really biscuits which may be sweetened or not but are always enriched with the addition of cream and eggs. They may be cut out in rounds, diamonds, or triangles. They are superb for breakfast.

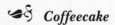 Scones

2 cups sifted all-purpose
   flour
4 teaspoons baking powder
1 tablespoon sugar
¾ teaspoon salt
¼ cup butter or margarine
2 eggs, well beaten
⅓ cup light cream
Sugar
2 tablespoons jelly or jam

Heat oven to 450° F. Sift flour, baking powder, the 1 tablespoon sugar, and salt into a bowl. Cut in butter with a pastry blender until the mixture looks like coarse meal. Make a well in center of dry ingredients. Reserve 2 tablespoons of the beaten egg. Combine remainder of egg with cream and add to flour mixture all at once. Stir only until dry ingredients are moistened. Turn dough out onto a lightly floured board. Divide dough in half. Roll each half into a 6-inch circle; cut each circle into 6 pie-shaped wedges and place on greased cookie sheets about 1 inch apart. Brush wedges with reserved egg and sprinkle with sugar. Bake 12 to 15 minutes, until lightly browned. Top each scone with jelly or jam. Serve warm. Makes 12.

Griddle Scones

2 cups sifted all-purpose
   flour
1 teaspoon sugar
1 teaspoon cream of tartar
1 teaspoon baking soda
¼ teaspoon salt
⅓ cup evaporated milk,
   undiluted
⅓ cup water
2 teaspoons white vinegar or
   lemon juice

Sift together flour, sugar, cream of tartar, baking soda, and salt. Combine evaporated milk, water, and vinegar in a small measuring cup. Let stand about 5 minutes. Empty sifted dry ingredients into a mixing bowl. Gradually add milk mixture, stirring with a fork until soft dough forms. Place dough on a piece of floured waxed paper or aluminum foil. Divide dough in half. Pat each half into a 6-inch circle; cut each circle into 6 pie-shaped wedges. Place wedges on a lightly floured griddle over moderate heat (about 250° F.). When browned on one side, turn and brown the other side. Makes 12 scones.

Coffeecakes

Coffeecakes are best served slightly warm. Despite their famil. name they're beautifully suited to afternoon tea service.

Coffeecake

1½ cups sifted all-purpose
   flour

Heat oven to 375° F. Sift together flour, baking powder, and salt. Grease and flour a 9-inch round cake pan.

2 teaspoons baking powder
½ teaspoon salt
⅓ cup soft shortening
¾ cup sugar
1 egg
½ cup milk
Jam or Crunch Topping
    (recipes follow)

Work shortening and sugar together until creamy; add egg and beat thoroughly. Add sifted dry ingredients to creamed mixture alternately with milk; beat well after each addition. Pour into prepared pan. Top with Jam or Crunch Topping. Bake 30 to 35 minutes. Serve warm. Serves 6 to 8.

Jam Topping

⅓ cup jam (raspberry,
    apricot, cherry, as desired)
2 tablespoons sugar
¼ teaspoon ground cinnamon
¼ teaspoon ground nutmeg
1 tablespoon softened butter
    or margarine

Beat jam with a fork. Drop by teaspoonfuls over batter. Run a knife through the batter several times around pan to marble slightly. Combine sugar, cinnamon, nutmeg, and butter. Crumble over batter.

Crunch Topping

4 tablespoons melted butter
    or margarine
½ cup firmly packed light
    brown sugar
2 tablespoons flour
2 teaspoons ground
    cinnamon
½ cup chopped nuts

Combine all ingredients thoroughly. Crumble over batter.

Old-Fashioned Coffeecake

2 cups sifted all-purpose
    flour
1½ teaspoons baking powder
½ teaspoon baking soda
1 teaspoon salt
1 cup butter or margarine
1¼ cups sugar
1 teaspoon vanilla extract
2 eggs
1 cup commercial sour
    cream
1 cup chopped walnuts
1 teaspoon ground
    cinnamon
2 tablespoons sugar

Heat oven to 350° F. Sift flour, baking powder, baking soda, and salt together. Grease a 10-inch tube pan. Blend butter and the 1¼ cups sugar in a large bowl; beat until mixture is light and fluffy. Add vanilla. Add eggs one at a time, beating well after addition. Blend in sour cream. Gradually add sifted dry ingredients to creamed mixture and beat until well blended. Spoon half of batter into prepared pan. Mix nuts, cinnamon, and the remaining 2 tablespoons sugar; sprinkle half of mixture over batter. Top with remaining batter and sprinkle with remaining nut mixture. With a knife, cut through batter several times to marble slightly. Bake 45 to 50 minutes. Cool on wire rack 10 minutes. Remove from pan and place on serving plate. Combine orange juice and the 2 tablespoons brown sugar in a saucepan; cook

⅓ cup orange juice

2 tablespoons dark brown
sugar

over low heat (about 225° F.) until sugar is dissolved.
Brush over top and sides of warm cake. Serve warm.
Serves 8 to 10.

🦢 Apricot Streusel Coffeecake

1 cup finely cut dried
apricots

1 6-ounce package (1 cup)
butterscotch pieces

½ cup water

¼ cup firmly packed dark
brown sugar

1 tablespoon flour

½ teaspoon ground
cinnamon

½ cup finely chopped pecans

1 tablespoon melted butter
or margarine

1½ cups sifted all-purpose
flour

2 teaspoons baking powder

½ teaspoon salt

¼ cup soft shortening

½ cup granulated sugar

1 egg, slightly beaten

½ cup milk

Combine apricots, butterscotch pieces, and water. Cook
over moderate heat (about 250° F.), stirring occasionally,
until thick, about 10 minutes. Cool. Combine brown
sugar, the 1 tablespoon flour, cinnamon, pecans, and
melted butter. Reserve for topping. Heat oven to 375° F.
Sift together the 1½ cups flour, the baking powder, and
salt. Work shortening in a bowl until creamy. Add ¼ cup
of the granulated sugar and beat until fluffy. Stir in the
remaining ¼ cup granulated sugar. Add egg and beat
thoroughly. Stir in milk and mix well. Add the sifted dry
ingredients to shortening mixture and mix well. Pour
about two-thirds of the batter into a greased and floured
9-inch-square cake pan. Spread cooled apricot filling
over surface of batter. Drop remaining batter in small
spoonfuls over filling. Sprinkle top with the streusel.
Bake 20 to 25 minutes. Cool slightly before cutting into
squares. Serves 8 to 10.

🦢 Date Nut Surprise Rolls

⅓ cup chopped pitted dates

⅓ cup chopped nuts

⅓ cup firmly packed light
brown sugar

1¼ teaspoons ground
cinnamon

3 tablespoons melted butter
or margarine

½ cup firmly packed light
brown sugar

½ cup melted butter or
margarine

15 whole walnut halves

8 candied cherries, halved

3 cups prepared buttermilk

Heat oven to 375° F. Combine dates, nuts, the ⅓ cup
brown sugar, cinnamon, and the 3 tablespoons melted
butter; set aside. Combine the ½ cup brown sugar and
the ½ cup melted butter and spread evenly over the
bottom of a shallow 1½-quart baking dish. Arrange walnuts and cherries cut-side up in rows over the sugar
mixture. Place biscuit mix in bowl; combine oil and milk
and add to biscuit mix all at once. Stir with a fork until
mixture forms a soft dough. Beat 15 strokes. Turn out
on a board lightly dusted with biscuit mix and knead
about 10 times. Roll out into a 12-x-15-inch rectangle.
Cut into fifteen 4-x-3-inch rectangles. Drop a heaping
teaspoonful of the date mixture in the center of each
rectangle. Bring the sides of the dough up over the
filling and roll gently with the hands to form a ball. Place

biscuit mix
¼ cup vegetable oil
¾ cup milk

balls in baking pan over nuts and cherries. Bake 35 minutes. Cool 2 minutes and invert pan on plate. Serve warm. Makes 15 rolls.

✎ Lemon Ball Coffeecake

3½ cups prepared buttermilk
   biscuit mix
¼ cup firmly packed light
   brown sugar
¼ cup granulated sugar
1 teaspoon ground
   cinnamon
½ teaspoon ground nutmeg
6 tablespoons melted butter
   or margarine
½ cup milk
1 egg, slightly beaten
¼ cup slivered toasted
   almonds
3 tablespoons light brown
   sugar
1 tablespoon grated lemon
   peel

Heat oven to 350° F. In a large bowl stir together biscuit mix, the ¼ cup light brown sugar, the sugar, cinnamon, and nutmeg. Combine 2 tablespoons of the melted butter with the milk and egg. Make a well in center of dry ingredients. Add liquid all at once. Using a fork, stir only until dry ingredients are moistened. Shape dough into balls the size of walnuts. Roll balls in the remaining 4 tablespoons melted butter. Arrange 2 rows of balls in a buttered 9-inch tube pan with removable bottom. Combine almonds, the 3 tablespoons brown sugar, and the lemon peel. Sprinkle half this mixture over balls in the pan. Beginning at the center of tube pan, arrange remaining balls over the first layer. Sprinkle remaining topping over balls. Bake 35 to 40 minutes, until lightly browned. Cool slightly. Cut around edges with a spatula and lift cake and bottom of pan to a flat tray. Separate balls with a fork. Serve warm. Makes about 8 servings.

✎ Sally Lunn

2 cups sifted all-purpose
   flour
2½ teaspoons baking powder
¾ teaspoon salt
⅓ cup soft shortening
⅓ cup sugar
1 egg
⅔ cup milk

Heat oven to 400° F. Sift flour, baking powder, and salt; sift again. Work shortening in a bowl until creamy. Add sugar and beat until fluffy. Add egg and beat well. Stir in milk, add flour mixture, and stir just enough to moisten dry ingredients. Pour into greased 8-inch-square pan. Bake 20 to 25 minutes. Cut into squares and serve hot. Serves 6 to 8.

Quick-Bread Loaves

Flavorful loaf quick breads are excellent for serving sliced with or without a spreading of sweet butter. They also lend themselves well to making special sandwiches. The fruit and nut breads are particularly compatible with mild cheese spreads.

QUICK BREADS

〜§ *Apple Nut Bread*

¼ *cup butter or margarine*
¾ *cup firmly packed light*
  brown sugar
2 *eggs*
2 *tablespoons milk*
1 *cup coarsely chopped*
  peeled tart apples
2 *cups sifted all-purpose*
  flour
2 *teaspoons baking powder*
1 *teaspoon baking soda*
½ *teaspoon ground cinnamon*
¼ *teaspoon ground nutmeg*
¼ *teaspoon ground ginger*
½ *teaspoon salt*
1 *cup coarsely chopped*
  walnuts

Work butter in a bowl until creamy. Add sugar and beat until well blended. Add eggs one at a time; beat well after each addition. Add milk and apples. Sift together flour, baking powder, baking soda, cinnamon, nutmeg, ginger, and salt. Add nuts to flour mixture. Add flour mixture to butter mixture and mix thoroughly. Pour into a greased 9-x-5-x-3-inch loaf pan. Let stand 20 minutes. Heat oven to 350° F. Bake bread 45 minutes. Let cool 10 minutes. Remove from pan and cool on wire rack. The flavor will be better if bread is allowed to stand overnight before cutting. Makes 1 loaf.

〜§ *Apricot Nut Bread*

2¼ *cups sifted all-purpose*
  flour
3 *teaspoons baking powder*
½ *teaspoon baking soda*
¾ *cup sugar*
½ *teaspoon salt*
2 *eggs*
⅓ *cup vegetable oil*
¾ *cup milk*
½ *cup chopped dried*
  apricots
1 *cup whole-bran cereal*
¾ *cup chopped walnuts*

Heat oven to 350° F. Grease a 9-x-5-x-3-inch loaf pan. Sift together flour, baking powder, baking soda, sugar, and salt. Place eggs in a bowl and beat slightly with a rotary beater; stir in oil, milk, and apricots. Add flour mixture and partially blend. Add cereal and nuts; stir until moistened. Pour into prepared pan. Bake 60 to 65 minutes. Let cool 10 minutes before removing from pan onto wire rack. Cool completely; wrap and store overnight before slicing. Makes 1 loaf.

〜§ *Banana Raisin Bread*

1½ *cups sifted all-purpose*
  flour
½ *cup sugar*
2 *teaspoons baking powder*
½ *teaspoon baking soda*

Heat oven to 350° F. Sift flour, sugar, baking powder, soda, and salt into a bowl. Stir in oats and raisins. Make a well in center of dry ingredients. Add eggs, oil, buttermilk, and bananas. Stir until just combined. Pour batter into a greased 9-x-5-x-3-inch loaf pan lined with waxed

1   *teaspoon salt*
1   *cup quick old-fashioned*
    rolled oats
½   *cup dark seedless raisins*
2   *eggs, well beaten*
⅓   *cup vegetable oil*
½   *cup buttermilk*
¾   *cup mashed bananas*

paper. Bake about 50 minutes, until a cake tester inserted in the center comes out clean. Remove from pan immediately and peel off waxed paper. Cool completely on a wire rack. Wrap bread and store 1 day before slicing. Makes 1 loaf.

⋰ Cheese Bread

¾   *cup (3 ounces) sharp*
    Cheddar cheese, coarsely
    shredded
3¾ *cups prepared buttermilk*
    biscuit mix
6   *strips bacon, cooked and*
    crumbled
1½ *cups milk*
1   *egg*

Heat oven to 350° F. Mix cheese, biscuit mix, and bacon together in a bowl. Beat milk and egg together; stir into dry ingredients. Pour into greased 9-x-5-x-3-inch loaf pan. Bake 1 hour. Remove from pan and cool on a wire rack about 10 minutes. Slice and serve warm. Makes 1 loaf.

⋰ Cranberry Orange Bread

2   *cups sifted all-purpose*
    flour
½   *teaspoon salt*
½   *teaspoon baking soda*
1½ *teaspoons baking powder*
1   *cup sugar*
Grated peel of 1 orange
½   *cup orange juice*
2   *tablespoons shortening*
¼   *cup boiling water*
1   *egg, beaten*
1   *cup chopped cranberries*
1   *cup chopped walnuts*

Heat oven to 350° F. Sift together flour, salt, baking soda, baking powder, and sugar. Combine orange peel, orange juice, shortening, and boiling water. Blend into dry ingredients. Add egg and beat well. Fold in cranberries and nuts. Pour into a greased 9-x-5-x-3-inch loaf pan. Bake 1 hour. Let cool 10 minutes before removing from pan onto wire rack. Cool completely; wrap and let stand overnight before cutting. Makes 1 loaf.

⋰ Graham Cracker Bread

1¾ *cups sifted all-purpose*
    flour
2   *teaspoons baking soda*
1½ *teaspoons salt*

Heat oven to 375° F. Grease and lightly flour two 9-x-5-x-3-inch loaf pans. Sift flour, baking soda, salt, and nutmeg together. Work shortening in a large bowl until creamy. Gradually add graham crackers and blend in

½ teaspoon ground nutmeg
½ cup soft shortening
2 cups fine graham cracker crumbs
¾ cup light molasses
2 eggs, slightly beaten
1¾ cups buttermilk
1 cup seedless raisins

well. Add molasses and eggs and beat well. Add sifted dry ingredients alternately with the buttermilk to the creamed mixture. Blend well after each addition. Stir in raisins. Turn batter into prepared pans and bake 35 to 45 minutes, until a cake tester inserted in center comes out clean. Let cool 10 minutes. Remove from pans to wire racks; cool completely. Makes 2 loaves.

Corn Breads

Devotees of corn bread still carry on the controversy of whether to sweeten or not to sweeten the batter. It is a matter of taste and regional preferences. In this section you'll find both variations and a number of interesting ways to flavor baked cornmeal products.

⇜ Corn Sticks

1 egg
1 cup milk
½ cup melted butter or margarine
½ cup sifted all-purpose flour
2 teaspoons baking powder
2 tablespoons sugar
½ teaspoon salt
1 cup yellow corn meal

Heat oven to 450° F. Beat together egg, milk, and butter. Sift flour, baking powder, sugar, and salt together into a bowl. Stir in corn meal. Make a well in center of dry ingredients; all milk mixture and stir until just blended. Spoon into greased corn-stick or muffin pans. Bake 15 to 20 minutes. Makes about 1 dozen 5-inch sticks or 1¼ dozen 2-inch muffins.

⇜ Cornmeal Muffins

1 cup sifted all-purpose flour
4 teaspoons baking powder
2 tablespoons sugar
1 teaspoon salt
1 cup yellow corn meal
2 eggs, slightly beaten
1 cup milk
¼ cup vegetable oil

Heat oven to 425° F. Sift flour, baking powder, sugar, and salt into a bowl. Stir corn meal into flour mixture. Make a well in the center of dry ingredients. Combine eggs, milk, and oil. Add all at once to dry ingredients. Stir until smooth. Fill greased cups of 2½-inch muffin pans two-thirds full. Bake 15 to 20 minutes, until golden brown. Let stand a few minutes before removing from pan. Makes 12 muffins.

Corn Bread

Bake muffin batter in well-greased 8-inch-square cake pan for 20 to 25 minutes. If you prefer corn bread unsweetened, eliminate the sugar in the preceding recipe.

❦ Cornmeal Crisps

½ cup sifted all-purpose flour
¼ teaspoon baking soda
⅛ teaspoon paprika
¼ teaspoon salt
1 cup yellow corn meal
2 tablespoons vegetable oil
½ cup milk
¼ cup melted butter or
    margarine
Salt

Heat oven to 350° F. Sift flour, baking soda, paprika, and salt into a bowl. Stir corn meal into flour mixture. Make a well in the center of dry ingredients. Mix vegetable oil and milk. Add all at once to dry ingredients, stirring until dry ingredients are moistened. Knead dough on a lightly floured board about 10 minutes. Shape dough into 1-inch balls; flatten each with palms of hands and roll with rolling pin on lightly floured board until paper-thin. Using a broad metal spatula, place circles on ungreased cookie sheets about 1 inch apart. Bake about 12 minutes. While still hot, brush with melted butter and sprinkle lightly with salt. Cool on wire racks. May be stored for several days in a tightly closed container. Makes about 18.

❦ Skillet Corn Bread

4 eggs
2 cups milk
2 cups yellow corn meal
2 teaspoons baking powder
1 teaspoon salt
2 tablespoons vegetable oil

Beat eggs slightly, add the remaining ingredients, and mix thoroughly. Grease a heavy 8-inch skillet. Place over moderately high heat (about 325° F.); when hot, pour in half the cornmeal mixture. Cook about 10 minutes, until bottom is browned and top is set. With a broad spatula turn cake and cook about 7 to 8 minutes to brown other side. Repeat with remaining cornmeal mixture. Serve hot. Makes 2 8-inch cakes or 8 to 10 servings.

Dumplings

The recipes that follow are for dumplings to be used in soups and stews. They are steamed or poached rather than baked. (For dessert dumplings, see Chapter XXI.) You can make excellent dumplings with a biscuit mix; simply follow package directions.

✌ Dumplings

1½ cups sifted all-purpose
    flour
2 teaspoons baking powder
½ teaspoon salt
1 egg, slightly beaten
½ cup milk
2 tablespoons vegetable oil

Sift flour, baking powder, and salt into a mixing bowl. Combine egg, milk, and oil; stir into dry ingredients, mixing just until flour is moistened. Spoon rounded tablespoonfuls of batter over top of simmering stew. Cook uncovered over low heat (about 200° F.) for 10 minutes; cover and continue cooking 10 minutes. Serve with stew. Makes 6 to 8 dumplings.

Parsley Dumplings

Add ⅓ *cup chopped fresh parsley* to egg, milk, and oil mixture in preceding recipe.

✌ Bread Dumplings for Soup

1 tablespoon instant minced
    onion
1 tablespoon water
2 cups ½-inch cubes rye
    bread, tightly packed
2 tablespoons flour
⅛ teaspoon baking powder
1 teaspoon chopped fresh
    parsley
Pinch ground nutmeg
¼ teaspoon salt
Few grains pepper
1 egg
2½ tablespoons milk
1 teaspoon melted butter
1½ quarts clear chicken broth

Mix onion and water together and let stand 5 minutes. Mix onion with bread cubes, flour, baking powder, parsley, nutmeg, salt, and pepper in a bowl. Beat together egg, milk, and butter in a bowl; stir into bread mixture. Let stand 10 minutes. Shape bread mixture into firm balls about 1 inch in diameter. Drop dumplings into boiling chicken broth and cook uncovered over moderate heat (about 250° F.) for 7 to 8 minutes. Serve with broth. Serves 6.

Fritters

Fritters are made from a basic batter that holds bits and pieces of food together so that they can be dropped by spoonfuls into hot fat for frying. They come in a variety of flavors, depending upon the food you choose to incorporate in the batter.

Fritters may be served as a breakfast dish, a dinner side dish or, when they contain meat, as a luncheon dish.

❧ Basic Fritters

1½ cups sifted all-purpose
    flour
 2 teaspoons baking powder
 ¾ teaspoon salt
 2 egg whites
 2 egg yolks
 ¾ cup milk
 1 tablespoon vegetable oil
Vegetable oil

Sift together flour, baking powder, and salt. Beat egg whites until stiff peaks form. Beat egg yolks, milk, and the 1 tablespoon vegetable oil together until blended. Add sifted dry ingredients and beat until smooth. Fold in egg whites and the desired filling for fritters. Pour oil to a depth of about 4 inches into a deep saucepan; heat over moderately high heat to a temperature of 375° F. on a deep-fat-frying thermometer. Spoon ¼ cupfuls of batter into hot fat and fry 10 minutes, allowing about 5 minutes on each side. Makes about 12 fritters.

Clam Fritters

Drain 2 7½- or 8-ounce cans minced clams and reserve ¼ cup cup of the liquor. Add ¼ teaspoon paprika to sifted dry ingredients. Substitute the reserved clam juice for ¼ cup of the milk. Fold in clams and prepare following the directions above. Makes about 14 fritters.

Oyster Fritters

Drain 1 pint oysters, fresh or frozen, and reserve ¼ cup of the liquor. Coarsely chop oysters. Add ¼ teaspoon paprika to the sifted dry ingredients. Substitute the reserved oyster liquor for ¼ cup of the milk. Fold in oysters and prepare following the directions above. Makes about 14 fritters.

Corn Fritters

Drain 1 12-ounce can vacuum-packed whole-kernel corn and fold into batter, or add 1¼ cups fresh corn cut from the cob. Prepare following directions above. Makes about 15 or 16 fritters.

❧ Apple-Ring Fritters

 1 cup sifted all-purpose flour
 1 teaspoon baking powder
 ½ teaspoon salt
 1 tablespoon sugar
 4 cooking apples that keep
   their shape when cooked
   (such as Cortland, Rome
   Beauty, or Yellow Newton)
 1 egg, separated
 ⅔ cup milk
 1 tablespoon vegetable oil

Sift together flour, baking powder, salt, and the 1 tablespoon sugar. Wash, peel, and core apples. Slice them into ½-inch rings. In a bowl beat egg yolk with a fork; add milk and the 1 tablespoon oil. Stir milk mixture into sifted dry ingredients; blend well. Beat egg white with rotary beater until stiff; fold into the batter. Heat oil to a depth of 1 inch in a large skillet over moderately high heat (about 325° F.) until it is hot enough to brown a large bread cube in 60 seconds. Dip apple slices in the batter, coating them well. Fry slices until golden brown, turning to brown both sides. Drain fritters on paper

Vegetable oil
⅛ teaspoon ground cinnamon
2 tablespoons sugar

towel. Combine cinnamon and the remaining 2 tablespoons sugar; sprinkle over fritters and serve hot. Makes about 20 fritters.

❧ Crunchy Tuna Fritters

Vegetable oil
1 6½-ounce can tuna, drained and flaked
1 2¼-ounce can potato sticks, crushed
1 tablespoon grated onion
½ cup sifted all-purpose flour
1 large egg
¼ teaspoon salt
⅛ teaspoon pepper
1 teaspoon baking powder

Heat about 3 inches of oil in a deep saucepan over moderately high heat (about 375° F.). Heat until deep-frying thermometer registers 375° F. In a medium-sized bowl combine tuna and crushed potato sticks. Add onion, flour, egg, salt, pepper, and baking powder; blend well. Drop mixture by tablespoonfuls into hot oil, a few at a time. Fry until golden brown on all sides, about 3 minutes. Drain on paper towels. Repeat with remaining mixture. Makes about 16 fritters.

Doughnuts

When making homemade doughnuts, it's most important to use a deep-fat-frying thermometer or a fryer with a thermostatic control, since the temperature influences the absorption of fat. To make crisp doughnuts that have no greasy coating, be sure the temperature of the fat is 370° F.

❧ Rich Doughnuts

2 eggs
1 cup sugar
2 tablespoons soft shortening or vegetable oil
¾ cup thick buttermilk
½ teaspoon lemon extract
3½ cups sifted all-purpose flour
2 teaspoons baking powder
1 teaspoon baking soda
½ teaspoon salt
1 teaspoon ground nutmeg
½ teaspoon ground cinnamon

Beat eggs well. Beat in sugar and shortening. Stir in buttermilk and lemon extract. Sift together flour, baking powder, baking soda, salt, nutmeg, and cinnamon. Add to egg mixture and beat until smooth. Dough will be soft. Cover bowl and chill at least 2 hours. Heat oil to a depth of 3 to 4 inches in a large, deep saucepan or deep-fat fryer over moderately high heat (about 375° F.) to a temperature of about 370° F. on a deep-fat-frying thermometer. Generously flour a board or pastry cloth. Remove about ¼ of the chilled dough; leave remaining dough in refrigerator until ready to roll. With floured fingers gently roll dough around on the board to shape it into a ball and lightly coat the surface with flour. Pat dough out to a thickness of about ⅓ inch. Cut with a well-floured 2½-inch doughnut cutter. With a wide,

Vegetable oil
Sugar or cinnamon (optional)

floured spatula carefully lift doughnut from board, remove center round, and slide doughnut ring into the hot oil. When it rises to the top, if necessary reshape it into a circle with a long-handled cooking fork. Cook about 1 minute until browned on one side. Flip it over and brown the other side. Remove to a pan lined with paper towels. Fry only 3 or 4 doughnuts at a time. Before working with each portion of chilled dough, scrape and reflour board or pastry cloth and clean doughnut cutter. While still warm, doughnuts may be rolled in sugar or cinnamon sugar, if desired. Makes about 24 doughnuts.

✒ Lemon Crullers

2½ cups sifted all-purpose
    flour
  2 teaspoons baking powder
  2 eggs
Grated peel of 2 lemons
  ½ cup sugar
  2 tablespoons water
Pinch of salt
  ¼ cup olive oil
  4 teaspoons lemon juice
Vegetable oil
Granulated sugar

Sift flour and baking powder. Beat eggs, lemon peel, sugar, water, and salt in a medium-sized bowl with a rotary beater until light and foamy. Add the olive oil and lemon juice and blend well. Stir sifted dry ingredients into egg mixture. In a heavy saucepan heat 3 inches of oil over moderately high heat (about 375° F.) to a temperature of 365° to 370° F. on a deep-fat-frying thermometer. Drop rounded balls of dough, one at a time, from a tablespoon into the oil. The crullers should puff and brown almost instantly. Turn them, cooking until a deep golden brown on all sides. Make only 2 or 3 crullers at a time. Remove each with a slotted spoon and drain on paper towels. Roll immediately in granulated sugar. If desired, crullers may be reheated in a pan covered with aluminum foil in a warm oven. Makes about 20 crullers.

Pancakes

Pancakes are easy to make because they contain few ingredients. The many excellent packaged pancake mixes available make the preparation even quicker. Whether you make your own or use a packaged mix according to the directions, there are a few general rules for making perfect pancakes.

Measure all ingredients carefully.

Add the liquid ingredients all at once and stir batter only until the dry ingredients are moistened. The small lumps in the batter will disappear during cooking.

Pancake preferences vary. If you prefer thin ones, add a little more liquid to the basic recipe. For thick ones, add a little flour or a little more packaged mix.

A heavy griddle is best for even browning. Some griddles need no greasing (follow manufacturer's directions). If griddle does need it, grease lightly with unsalted shortening. In general, if the batter contains 2 tablespoons or more of fat per cup of liquid, the griddle will not need greasing.

Heat griddle slowly over moderately high heat (about 350° F.). To test for correct temperature, sprinkle a few drops of cold water on the griddle; if it is hot enough, the water will dance on the surface before evaporating.

Pour batter from a small pitcher or dip with a ¼-cup measure onto a hot griddle. Allow space between cakes for easy turning.

Turn cakes with a large, flat turner when they are puffed and appear full of tiny bubbles. Turn and bake until underside is nicely browned. Turn only once.

Serve pancakes right from the griddle for best results. If it is necessary to keep them warm, place the pancakes between folds of a warm towel in a warm oven or put them separately on a rack in a very low oven with the door ajar. Never stack them—except on a plate for a hungry person.

Breakfast Pancakes

◆§ Basic Pancakes

1½ cups sifted all-purpose
    flour
2 teaspoons baking powder
1 teaspoon salt
2 tablespoons sugar
1 egg, well beaten
*1¼ cups milk
3 tablespoons vegetable oil

Sift together the flour, baking powder, salt, and sugar into a large bowl. Combine egg, milk, and oil. Add to flour mixture all at once and stir just until blended. Heat griddle over moderately high heat (about 350° F.) until a few drops cold water will dance in small beads before evaporating. Grease griddle lightly if necessary. Pour a scant ¼ cup batter onto griddle. Bake until center is full of unbroken bubbles. Turn with a broad spatula and brown other side. Makes about 12 5-inch pancakes.

*Note: Buttermilk or sour milk may be used. Substitute ½ teaspoon baking soda for ½ teaspoon of the baking powder.

Rich Pancakes

Add *1 additional egg* and ¼ *cup additional milk* to Basic Pancake recipe above.

✑ Apple-Filled Pancakes

⅓ cup butter or margarine
6 cups peeled, cored apples,
    sliced ¼ inch thick
1¼ teaspoons ground
    cinnamon
⅓ cup sugar
1 recipe Basic Pancakes
    (recipe on page 648)
Whipped Maple Butter (recipe
    follows)

Melt butter in a large skillet over moderate heat (about 250° F.). Add the apples and cook, stirring occasionally, until lightly browned. Stir together cinnamon and sugar and sprinkle over the browned apples. Cook about 3 minutes longer, until sugar is syrupy and apples are tender. Prepare and bake pancakes according to directions. Place some of the hot apple mixture in the center of each pancake and roll up loosely. Place seam side down on heated plates. Top with Whipped Maple Butter. Makes 12 filled pancakes.

Whipped Maple Butter

½ cup butter or margarine,
    at room temperature
2 tablespoons confectioners'
    sugar
2 tablespoons maple syrup
    or maple-flavored syrup

In a small bowl beat butter with an electric mixer until fluffy. Add confectioners' sugar and beat thoroughly. Slowly add maple syrup and beat until blended. Makes ¾ cup.

✑ Fruit Pancakes

1 recipe Basic Pancakes
    (recipe on page 648)
¾ cup quartered, sliced
    bananas or ½ cup
    blueberries
½ teaspoon ground nutmeg
Fruit Syrup (recipe follows)
Vanilla Butter Syrup (recipe
    follows)

Prepare pancake batter according to directions. Fold in bananas or blueberries and nutmeg. Bake according to directions. Serve banana pancakes with Fruit Syrup; serve blueberry pancakes with Vanilla Butter Syrup. Makes about 14 5-inch pancakes.

Fruit Syrup

½ cup currant jelly or
    raspberry jam

Combine jelly or jam and water in a medium-sized saucepan. Beat mixture with rotary beater and cook

¼ *cup water*
½ *cup light corn syrup*

over moderately low heat (about 225° F.) until smooth. Add corn syrup and heat thoroughly. Serve hot. Makes 1¼ cups syrup.

Vanilla Butter Syrup

1 *cup light corn syrup*
2 *tablespoons butter or*
   margarine
1 *teaspoon vanilla extract*

Combine corn syrup, butter, and vanilla. Bring to a boil over moderate heat (about 250° F.). Serve hot. Makes about 1 cup.

✑ Yeast Pancakes

2 *cups sifted all-purpose*
   flour
¾ *teaspoon baking soda*
1 *teaspoon baking powder*
3 *tablespoons sugar*
1 *teaspoon salt*
1 *package active dry yeast*
¼ *cup warm water*
3 *eggs, well beaten*
¼ *cup vegetable oil*
1½ *cups buttermilk*

Sift together the flour, baking soda, baking powder, sugar, and salt into a large bowl. Soften the yeast in warm water. Add eggs, oil, and buttermilk to yeast. Add to flour mixture all at once and stir just until blended. Batter will be thick. Heat griddle over moderately high heat (about 350° F.). Pour a scant ¼ cup batter onto griddle and spread into a 5-inch pancake. Bake until center is full of unbroken bubbles. Turn with a broad spatula. When underside is lightly browned, remove to heated plates. Makes about 16 5-inch pancakes.

Note: Batter for yeast pancakes will keep for 5 days if covered tightly and stored in the refrigerator.

✑ German Apple Pancake

4 *eggs, separated*
½ *cup sifted all-purpose flour*
½ *teaspoon baking powder*
½ *teaspoon salt*
¼ *cup sugar*
½ *cup milk*
½ *teaspoon grated lemon peel*
2 *tablespoons lemon juice*
1 *cup coarsely grated peeled*
   apple
2 *tablespoons butter or*
   margarine
Cinnamon sugar

Heat oven to 400° F. Beat egg yolks until light and fluffy. Sift flour, baking powder, salt, and sugar together. Add alternately with milk to egg yolks. Stir in lemon peel, lemon juice, and apple. Beat egg whites until stiff but not dry. Gently fold egg whites into the batter. Melt butter in an ovenproof 10-inch skillet. Pour in batter and bake 10 minutes. Reduce temperature to 350° F. and continue baking 15 minutes. Cut into wedges. Serve with a sprinkle of cinnamon sugar. Serves 4.

Luncheon or Supper Pancakes

◄§ Chicken Pancakes with Sour Cream Sauce

1 recipe Rich Pancakes
(recipe on page 649)
1 chicken bouillon cube
¾ cup boiling water
3 tablespoons butter or
margarine
¼ cup finely chopped onion
3 tablespoons flour
Few grains pepper
1 cup commercial sour cream
2 cups diced cooked chicken
1 4-ounce can sliced
mushrooms, drained
2 tablespoons Parmesan
cheese, grated
¼ teaspoon paprika

Prepare and bake pancakes as directed in recipe; while they are still hot, roll up loosely. Place on a wire cake rack until ready to use. Heat oven to 375° F. Dissolve bouillon cube in the boiling water. Put butter in a medium-sized saucepan. Add the onion and cook over moderate heat (about 250° F.) for 1 minute. Stir in the flour and cook 1 minute longer. Gradually stir in chicken bouillon. Add pepper. Cook, stirring constantly, until thickened. Remove from heat and stir in sour cream. Take out half the sauce and reserve for topping. To the remaining sauce, add the chicken and mushrooms. Unroll pancakes and spoon some of the chicken mixture into the center of each. Reroll and place, seam side down, in a shallow baking dish. Top with the remaining sauce. Stir together Parmesan cheese and paprika and sprinkle over sauce. Bake about 15 minutes, until pancakes are thoroughly heated and sauce is bubbly. Makes 12 filled pancakes to serve 4 or 6.

◄§ Chicken-Curry Pancakes

1 recipe Basic Pancakes
(recipe on page 648)
6 tablespoons butter or
margarine
6 tablespoons flour
1½ teaspoons instant minced
onion
1½ teaspoons salt
Few grains pepper
3 cups milk
1½ teaspoons curry powder
2 5-ounce cans boned
chicken
¼ cup seedless raisins
1⅓ cups diced peeled apple
2 teaspoons lemon juice
¼ cup grated Parmesan
cheese

Prepare pancakes as directed; while they are still hot, roll up loosely. Place on a wire rack until ready for use. Melt butter in saucepan over moderate heat (about 250° F.). Blend in flour, onion, salt, and pepper. Gradually add milk and cook over moderately low heat (about 225° F.) until thickened, stirring constantly. Measure 1 cup of the sauce and reserve for later. Add curry, chicken, raisins, apple, and lemon juice to remaining sauce. Heat. Unroll pancakes and spoon some of the mixture along the edges of each pancake. Roll loosely and place in a flat baking dish, seam side down. Pour the reserved sauce over pancakes and sprinkle with cheese. Place in preheated broiler, 3 to 4 inches from heat, until cheese is melted and lightly browned. Makes 12 filled pancakes to serve 4 or 6.

☙ Crab-Filled Luncheon Pancakes

1 recipe Rich Pancakes (recipe on page 649)
2 tablespoons butter or margarine
2 tablespoons grated onion
2 tablespoons lemon juice
2 6½-ounce cans crab meat
½ cup mayonnaise or salad dressing
½ teaspoon salt
Few grains pepper
3 slices process American cheese
½ cup commercial sour cream
2 tablespoons chopped fresh parsley

Prepare and bake pancakes as directed in recipe; while they are still hot, roll up loosely. Place on a wire cake rack until ready to use. Heat oven to 375° F. Cook butter and onion 1 minute in a small saucepan over moderate heat (about 250° F.); add lemon juice. Remove cartilage and coarsely flake crab meat. Add mayonnaise, salt, pepper, and butter mixture. Toss together lightly. Cut each cheese slice into four strips. Unroll pancakes; put a strip of cheese and some of the crab mixture on each and reroll. Place, seam side down, in a shallow baking dish. Bake uncovered about 15 minutes, until thoroughly heated. Remove to serving plates and garnish each serving with sour cream and parsley. Makes 12 filled pancakes to serve 4 or 6.

Crepes

Although crepes, or French pancakes, have an air of elegance attached to them in this country, they are an excellent way to use leftovers; the thin cakes are rolled around a filling, covered with a Mornay sauce, and browned under the broiler. As breakfast cakes they are particularly good filled with fruit or jelly and sprinkled with confectioners' sugar, or reheated in warm maple syrup or any of the flavored syrups in the pancake section. As a dessert, crepes may be used with a variety of fillings and sauces (see pages 774 to 776).

Crepe batter should be made at least one hour before baking. It may be made ahead and stored in the refrigerator in a tightly covered container overnight.

Crepes are cooked, one at a time, in a small iron skillet or in a crepe pan that is six to seven inches in diameter. Baking a crepe takes less than two minutes, but they can be kept warm in a slow oven or over simmering water on top of the range; or they can be reheated at serving time in the sauce designated in the recipe.

Perfect crepes should be tender and delicate and not more than one-sixteenth of an inch thick.

Basic Crepes

1 cup sifted all-purpose
   flour
Few grains salt
3 eggs
1½ cups milk
About ¼ cup vegetable oil for
   frying

To prepare batter with an electric mixer, combine flour and salt in the large bowl of an electric mixer and blend well. Add eggs one at a time and beat well after each addition. Beat until mixture is a smooth paste. Gradually add milk and beat until the batter is smooth. (The batter should be the consistency of heavy cream.) Strain the batter through a fine sieve to remove any lumps that may remain. Cover batter tightly with plastic wrap and chill in the refrigerator 1 to 2 hours.

To prepare batter with a wire whip, combine flour and salt in a medium-sized bowl and blend well. Place eggs in a small bowl and beat lightly with the wire whip. Add milk and stir to blend well. Gradually add milk–egg mixture to the dry ingredients, beating with the whip vigorously until the mixture is smooth. (The batter should be the consistency of heavy cream.) Strain batter through a fine sieve to remove any lumps that may remain. Cover batter tightly and chill in the refrigerator 1 to 2 hours.

To prepare crepes, lightly brush the bottom of a 6- to 7-inch crepe pan with oil. Place pan over moderately high heat (about 325° F.). The pan is hot enough when a few drops of water sprinkled on it will bounce about. Lift the pan off the heat. Using a ladle for easy measuring, pour about 2 tablespoons of the batter into the center of the pan. Immediately tip the pan in all directions, so as to cover the entire bottom surface evenly with a very thin layer of batter. The crepe should be as thin as possible. If there is too much batter in the pan, pour off the excess. If there is not enough to cover the bottom or if any holes are left, ladle a little more batter into the pan. Set the pan back over the heat. Cook about 1 minute, or until the top of the crepe is dry and the bottom is lightly browned. Check the crepe by lifting up one corner with a spatula. To turn the crepe, slide the spatula under the crepe and flip it over. Cook on the second side for about 20 seconds, or until lightly browned. Tip the crepe out of the pan onto a plate. The second side of a crepe is rarely as evenly browned as the first. It should be used as the inside of the crepe when filled. The batter is of the wrong consistency if it does not spread quickly and evenly in the pan and is thicker in spots. If this is the case, beat in a few teaspoonfuls of water to thin the batter. Repeat steps as above until all the batter is used. This amount of batter will make from 14 to 18 crepes, depending on how expert you become. If crepes are to be used within a 48-hour period, wrap unfilled crepes tightly in foil or plastic wrap, or place in a plastic bag, and refrigerate. If desired, crepes may be frozen; arrange them in layers of 6 to 8 with waxed paper between each crepe. Wrap each packet securely in freezer wrap and seal well. Crepes may be kept frozen for about 3 weeks. Thaw crepes completely before using.

❧ Cheese Fondue Crepes

12 to 14 cooked crepes (recipe on page 653)
½ cup Swiss cheese, shredded
1 3-ounce package cream cheese
1 8-ounce container cottage cheese
3 tablespoons butter or margarine
½ teaspoon salt
¼ teaspoon garlic powder
Few grains cayenne pepper
¼ cup dry white wine
1 egg
1 cup vegetable oil

Have the crepes ready. Combine Swiss cheese, cream cheese, cottage cheese, butter, salt, garlic powder, cayenne, and wine in the top of a double boiler. Cook over simmering water, stirring constantly, until cheeses are melted and mixture is smooth. Remove from heat. Spread about 2 tablespoons of the cheese mixture on each crepe. Roll up crepes into tight rolls. Beat egg in a small bowl to blend well. Heat oil in a 7-inch skillet to 375° F. Dip each crepe in the egg mixture to coat well on all sides. Place 2 crepes at a time in the skillet and cook in the oil until golden brown on one side, about 1 minute. Turn crepes over and cook 1 minute longer. Drain on paper towels. Repeat with remaining crepes. Serve hot. To reheat, place crepes on a broiler pan 6 inches from source of heat in a preheated broiler and broil 1 minute, or until heated through. Serves 6.

❧ Ham-and-Egg Crepes Benedict

12 cooked crepes (recipe on page 653)
Butter
2 tablespoons butter or margarine
1 tablespoon finely chopped onion
¼ clove garlic, crushed
¼ cup dry white wine
1 tablespoon cornstarch
½ cup heavy cream
½ cup Swiss cheese, shredded

Have crepes ready. Generously butter six 4½- to 5-inch individual ramekins. Melt the 2 tablespoons butter in a small skillet over moderately low heat (about 225° F.). Add onion and garlic and cook until tender. Add wine and simmer 1 minute. Combine cornstarch and cream in a small bowl and stir to blend well. Add cornstarch–cream mixture to skillet and cook, stirring constantly, until mixture thickens and is smooth. Add the ½ cup cheese and cook, stirring constantly, until melted. Remove from heat. Prepare each ramekin in the following way: Line ramekin with a crepe. Place a little of the sauce mixture over crepe. Then sprinkle evenly with about 2

1 cup finely chopped boiled
ham
6 cold poached eggs, well
drained
¼ cup Swiss cheese, shredded

tablespoons of the chopped ham. Place a cold drained poached egg over ham layer. Cover egg with another crepe. Sprinkle top with about 1½ teaspoons of the remaining ¼ cup cheese. Broil in a preheated broiler 6 inches from source of heat about 2 to 3 minutes, or until heated through and top is lightly browned. Serve immediately. Serves 6.

Chicken Livers in Madeira Sauce Crepes

12 to 14 cooked crepes (recipe
on page 653)
1½ pounds chicken livers
¼ cup vegetable oil
1 cup Madeira or port
½ teaspoon salt
¼ teaspoon pepper
½ clove garlic, crushed
2 chicken bouillon cubes
3 canned truffles, chopped,
liquid reserved (optional)
2 tablespoons butter or
margarine

Have crepes ready. Wash and drain livers thoroughly. Heat oil in a large skillet over moderately high heat (about 275° F.). Add livers and cook about 5 minutes, stirring occasionally, until browned on outside but slightly pink inside. Remove livers from skillet and chop coarsely. Add wine, salt, pepper, garlic, bouillon cubes, truffles, and their juice to the skillet. Bring mixture to a boil over moderately high heat (about 325° F.) and boil rapidly until reduced to ⅔ cup. Remove from heat. Add butter and chopped livers. Blend well. Place about 2 tablespoons of the mixture in the center of each crepe. Fold up sides of crepes to enclose filling in a packet. Place crepes seam side down in a buttered, shallow, 3-quart baking dish. Bake in a preheated 375° F. oven 10 to 15 minutes. Serves 6.

Creamed Spinach Crepes

12 to 14 cooked crepes (recipe
on page 653)
2 10-ounce packages frozen
chopped spinach
3 tablespoons butter or
margarine
3 tablespoons flour
1 cup milk, heated
½ teaspoon salt
¼ teaspoon pepper
¼ cup Swiss cheese, shredded

Have crepes ready. Cook spinach according to package directions. Drain very well. Place spinach in a blender and blend a few seconds on high speed to purée it, or force it through a food mill. Set aside. Melt butter in a medium-sized saucepan over moderately low heat (about 225° F.). Add flour and cook, stirring constantly, until mixture is frothy. Add milk, stirring vigorously, until mixture is thickened and smooth. Stir in salt, pepper, and spinach and blend well. Place about 2 tablespoons of the spinach mixture in the center of each crepe. Roll up crepes. Place seam side down in a buttered, shallow, 3-quart baking dish. Sprinkle top with cheese. Bake in a preheated 375° F. oven 10 to 15 minutes, or until heated through. Serve immediately. Serves 6.

❧ Salmon Velouté Crepes

12 to 14 cooked crepes (recipe on page 653)
1 16-ounce can salmon
3 tablespoons butter or margarine
3 tablespoons flour
⅔ cup milk, heated
2 egg yolks
½ teaspoon salt
¼ teaspoon pepper
½ teaspoon onion powder
¼ teaspoon dried oregano leaves
⅓ cup Swiss cheese, coarsely shredded

Have crepes ready. Drain salmon and reserve ⅓ cup of the liquid. Place salmon in a small bowl and remove bones. Flake salmon with a fork. Melt butter in a medium-sized saucepan over moderately low heat (about 225° F.). Add flour and cook, stirring constantly, until mixture is frothy. Add milk and reserved salmon liquid and stir constantly until mixture thickens and is smooth. Remove from heat. In a small bowl beat egg yolks slightly. Add a little of the hot sauce to the egg yolks and stir to blend well. Add egg yolk mixture to remaining sauce in saucepan and stir to blend well. Stir in salmon, salt, pepper, onion powder, and oregano and blend well. Place about 3 tablespoons of the sauce mixture in the center of each crepe. Roll up crepes. Place seam side down in a buttered, shallow, 3-quart baking dish. Sprinkle tops with cheese. Bake in a preheated 375° F. oven 10 to 15 minutes, or until heated through. Serve immediately. Serves 6.

French Toast

French toast should be golden-crisp on the outside and puffily soft on the inside. Dust hot toast with confectioners' sugar or serve it with maple syrup, jam, or any of the pancake syrups on pages 649 and 650.

❧ Basic French Toast

2 eggs, beaten
½ cup milk
¼ teaspoon salt
1 tablespoon sugar
¼ teaspoon ground cinnamon
Butter or margarine
8 to 10 slices bread
Confectioners' sugar, jam, or maple syrup

In a shallow dish combine eggs, milk, salt, sugar, and cinnamon. Melt 1 tablespoon of butter in a skillet over moderate heat (about 250° F.). Coat bread slices quickly on both sides in the egg mixture. Cook bread slices for 3 to 4 minutes on each side, or until golden brown. Add additional butter as needed. Serve hot with confectioners' sugar, jam, or maple syrup. Makes 8 to 10 slices.

[656]

❧ Crispy French Toast

4 eggs, slightly beaten
¾ cup light cream
½ teaspoon vanilla extract
6 slices day-old white bread
½ cup packaged corn flake
    crumbs
Strawberry Whipped Butter
    (recipe follows)

Combine eggs, light cream, and vanilla. Cut bread slices diagonally to make two triangles. Dip bread slices in egg mixture until thoroughly moistened; drain off excess liquid and place bread on tray. Sprinkle both sides lightly with corn flake crumbs. Heat oven to 450° F. Place on buttered baking sheet and bake 5 minutes on each side. Makes 12 toast triangles to serve 4.

Strawberry Whipped Butter

¼ cup softened butter or
    margarine
¼ cup strawberry jam

Whip butter and jam until fluffy. Serve with Crispy French Toast. Makes ½ cup.

Waffles

The perfect waffle is evenly browned and uniform in shape. It is crisp, light, and tender.

Waffle batters are thin and should be mixed just until smooth, but no more. Melted shortening should be cooled slightly before being added. The egg whites are often beaten separately and folded in. Excellent waffles may be made quickly from packaged pancake mix; follow the directions on the package.

Correct use of the waffle iron is most important. Follow the manufacturer's directions carefully for seasoning the grids, preheating, use of heat control, and care of iron after use. If the iron has no automatic heat control, test by sprinkling grids with a few drops of water. If the water immediately forms white balls and dances on the surface before evaporating, the temperature is correct for plain waffles. For special batters containing cheese, chocolate, or fruit, the temperature should be a little cooler and the drops of water should slowly bubble and boil away.

Pour the batter from a cup or pitcher into the center of the hot iron to about one inch from the outside edge. Close lid quickly and bake until all steaming stops, about four to six minutes. Lift off waffles with a fork and serve immediately, or cool on cake rack if they are to be used cold.

Store leftover batter in a covered container in the refrigerator.

Baked waffles may be cooled, tightly sealed in freezer wrap, and frozen. To reheat, unwrap and place frozen waffles directly on oven racks in a moderate oven (350° F.) until hot and crisp.

❧ Basic Waffles

1¾ cups sifted all-purpose
    flour
1 teaspoon baking soda
2 teaspoons baking powder
1 teaspoon salt
1 tablespoon sugar
3 eggs
½ cup vegetable oil
1½ cups buttermilk or 1½
    tablespoons vinegar and
    enough milk to make 1½
    cups

Heat waffle iron. In a small bowl sift together flour, soda, baking powder, salt, and sugar. Beat eggs well in a large bowl. Add oil, buttermilk, and the sifted dry ingredients. Beat until just blended. Pour batter onto the heated waffle iron. Close and bake until steaming stops, 4 to 6 minutes. Makes about 9 4½-inch waffles.

❧ Deluxe Waffles

1 cup sifted all-purpose
    flour
1½ teaspoons baking powder
½ teaspoon salt
1 tablespoon sugar
2 egg yolks
2 tablespoons melted butter
    or margarine
1 cup heavy cream
2 egg whites, stiffly beaten

Heat waffle iron. In a small bowl sift together flour, baking powder, salt, and sugar. Beat egg yolks in a medium-sized bowl. Add sifted dry ingredients, melted butter, and cream. Stir until blended. Fold in beaten egg whites. Pour onto heated waffle iron. Close and bake until steaming stops, 4 to 6 minutes. Makes about 7 4½-inch waffles.

❧ Sour Cream Waffles

2 eggs
⅔ cup commercial sour
    cream
⅔ cup milk
¼ cup melted butter or
    margarine
1½ cups sifted all-purpose
    flour
2¼ teaspoons baking powder
½ teaspoon baking soda

Heat waffle iron. Beat eggs with a rotary beater until thick and lemon-colored. Add sour cream, milk, and butter; beat until blended. Sift together flour, baking powder, baking soda, sugar, and salt. Gently fold into egg mixture. Fold in nuts. Pour onto heated waffle iron. Close and bake until steaming stops, 4 to 6 minutes. Makes 8 4½-inch waffles. Serve with maple syrup or with ice cream for a dessert, if desired. Makes 8 4½-inch waffles.

1 tablespoon sugar
¾ teaspoon salt
⅓ cup finely chopped
   walnuts
Maple syrup (optional)
Ice cream (optional)

⋘ Raisin Oatmeal Waffles

1 cup seedless raisins
1 recipe Basic Waffles
   (recipe on page 658)
½ cup quick cooking rolled
   oats
Maple-flavored syrup

Partially cover raisins with water in a small saucepan. Simmer gently 1 minute. Drain well. Prepare waffle batter according to recipe directions. Stir in oats and drained raisins. Bake as directed. Serve with maple-flavored syrup. Makes 10 4½-inch waffles.

⋘ Cornmeal Brunch Waffles

¾ cup sifted all-purpose
   flour
1 teaspoon baking soda
2 teaspoons baking powder
1½ teaspoons salt
1 tablespoon sugar
1½ cups yellow corn meal
3 eggs
½ cup vegetable oil
1½ cups buttermilk or sour
   milk
20 link sausages, cooked
2 16-ounce cans applesauce

Heat waffle iron. Sift together flour, soda, baking powder, salt, and sugar. Stir in corn meal. Beat eggs well in a large bowl. Add oil, sifted dry ingredients, and buttermilk. Beat until just blended. Pour batter onto the heated waffle iron. Bake until steaming stops. Makes 10 4½-inch waffles. Top each waffle with 2 sausages and a generous spoonful of applesauce. Serves 5 to 6.

Croutons

Croutons are flavored bread cubes that are especially good in green salads, soups, or served as appetizers with cold drinks.

Garlic Croutons

Rub bottom of a large skillet with a cut *clove of garlic.* Melt *¼ cup butter or margarine* in skillet over moderate heat (about 250° F.); add *2 cups ½-inch cubes of white or whole wheat bread.* Toss in butter to coat; heat and stir until lightly browned. Makes about 2 cups.

QUICK BREADS

Baked Croutons

Heat oven to 325° F. Remove crusts from *4 slices white or whole wheat bread.* Spread slices with *butter or margarine.* Cut bread into ½-inch cubes, place on cookie sheet and bake 25 minutes, or until lightly browned. Makes about 2 cups.

Cheese Croutons

Melt ¼ *cup butter or margarine* in a large skillet over moderate heat (about 250° F.); add *3 cups ½-inch cubes white or whole wheat bread.* Toss in butter to coat. Heat and stir until lightly browned. Mix ⅓ *cup grated Parmesan cheese,* ¾ *teaspoon salt,* and *1 teaspoon paprika* in a paper bag. Add hot croutons and shake in mixture to coat them thoroughly. Makes about 3 cups.

Herbed Croutons

Mix *1½ teaspoons instant minced onion* and *1½ teaspoons water* and let stand 5 minutes. Heat ⅓ *cup olive oil* and ¼ *cup butter or margarine* in a large skillet over moderate heat (about 250° F.); stir in minced onion, ½ *teaspoon salt, 1 teaspoon paprika* and ½ *teaspoon dried thyme leaves.* Add *4 cups ½-inch cubes of white or whole wheat bread;* toss in skillet to coat with herb mixture. Heat and stir until lightly browned. Makes about 4 cups.

Bacon Croutons

Heat ¼ *cup bacon drippings* in a large skillet over moderate heat (above 250° F.); add *2 cups ½-inch cubes of white or whole wheat bread.* Heat and stir until lightly browned. Makes about 2 cups.

CHAPTER XIX

YEAST BREAD

A few years ago a *Redbook* reader wrote asking for directions for making bread because, she told us, "I don't want my children to grow up without knowing what freshly baked homemade bread *smells* like." We know what she meant; the aroma of homemade bread and the flavor of that first warm crust lavished with butter is one of life's beautiful experiences. Bread-making is not tricky; the key to success is having the proper temperature. It must be controlled so that the yeast—the ingredient that makes bread rise—can do its job. There are several methods of mixing bread. The conventional, or old-fashioned, method calls for kneading the bread, which many people find a pleasant job—a good way to work off some nervous energy. The rapid-mix method is very close to the conventional method but the order of mixing the ingredients is easier and quicker. A shorter method is the batter method, which does not require kneading or a second rising. The cool-rise method allows you to make up the dough the day before and bake the bread the following day. You can choose the one that suits your needs best.

The Ingredients of Bread

Yeast is the key ingredient—and the touchy one. Yeast, which is a live but dormant plant in granular or cake form, is activated when it is combined with *warm* liquid. Yeast comes in two forms: active dry yeast (small granules that usually come in quarter-ounce packets) and cake yeast. Dry yeast will stay fresh and useful on a cool, dry cupboard shelf until the expiration date printed on each package. When dissolved in warm water, one package of dry yeast is equal to a three-fifths-ounce compressed yeast cake. Cake yeast must be kept refrigerated and used within two weeks. It should be crumbled before dissolving it in warm water.

Flour that has a fine gluten content is necessary for bread-making. Sifted all-purpose white flour will develop the gluten necessary to produce the elasticity that holds in the air bubbles the yeast produces. Even when other flours are used for flavor, a portion of the flour should be fine, all-purpose wheat flour.

Warm liquid is necessary to dissolve the yeast; in most cases, use water for this step. At 105° F. to 115° F., the liquid will feel neither hot nor cold when you place a drop of it on the inside of your wrist. If other liquids, usually milk, are scalded before adding to the yeast, be sure to let them cool to the required temperature before mixing them with the yeast.

It is best to use a thermometer for testing the temperature of the warm liquid because both the type of yeast and the methods of mixing influence the best temperature to use. Granular yeast that is dissolved directly in warm liquid (the conventional method) should be dissolved in liquid that is between 105° F. and 115° F. Cake yeast works best dissolved directly in warm liquid that is heated to 95° F. to 105° F. (Warm liquids used in the batter, rapid-mix, and cool-rise methods should be heated to a higher temperature because they will come in contact with the yeast after it has been mixed with the flour.)

Sugar, in addition to adding flavor to bread, is the necessary food on which the yeast feeds and grows as it produces the air bubbles that make the bread light.

Shortening and *eggs* add color and flavor to bread; eggs are not used in plain white breads.

Flavor additions, such as nuts and fruits, should be added as the recipe directs. Be sure to distribute them evenly throughout the loaf.

The Language of Bread-Baking

There are several descriptive phrases that are used in almost all bread recipes. This is what they mean.

Add only enough flour to make a soft dough. Many recipes for bread will give a range for the amount of flour to use because there are some differences between brands of flour. They have slightly different powers due to milling methods and the kinds of wheat used in making the flours.

Both the batter breads and the conventional white bread will usually call for enough flour to make a soft dough, which is the point at which the dough pulls away from the sides of the bowl to form a central mass. The batter bread is then ready for rising and the conventional bread is ready to knead.

Knead until the dough is smooth and elastic. To knead: Follow pictured instructions that follow for Kneading Dough. This process will take from eight to ten minutes. You may need to sprinkle more flour over the dough and on the work surface if it feels sticky. Too much flour will produce a heavy loaf and too little flour will make a soft, open-textured loaf that will not rise to great heights. This smooth-and-elastic stage is one you will be able to feel after a little practice.

KNEADING DOUGH

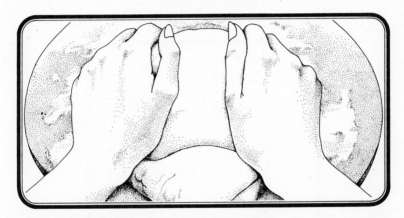

Kneading is necessary to develop texture in the finished bread. Round up dough on a floured board. Fold it in half toward you; then press down lightly and push it away from you with heels of hands. Give dough a quarter turn, fold, and press again. Continue to turn, fold, and press for about 10 minutes, until the dough feels springy and elastic and does not stick to board as it is kneaded.

Shape bread into a ball and place in a greased bowl. After the bread has been kneaded, wash and dry the bowl in which you mixed the dough. Grease it with vegetable oil or soft shortening. Place the ball of dough in it and turn it over once so that the whole ball is lightly covered with a shortening film, which will keep it from forming a dry skin.

Cover and let rise in a warm place free from drafts. Cover the bowl with a piece of waxed paper and put a clean tea towel over the paper. When a recipe calls for letting the dough rise in a warm place (85° F.), use one of the following methods to approximate that temperature.

1. Set bowl of dough on the upper rack of an unheated oven. Place a large pan of hot tap water on the rack beneath it. Replace water from time to time as it cools.

2. If you have a gas range with a pilot and oven light, turn the light on and place bowl of dough in oven to rise.

3. Fill a large pan two-thirds full with hot tap water; place a wire rack on top and the bowl of dough on the rack. Replace water as it cools.

4. Set the bowl of dough in a deep pan of warm water. (It is important that the water not be too hot.) Replace water as it cools.

5. Put the dough in a draft-free place near a hot range or radiator—never on top of it.

6. On hot summer days, room temperature may be more than 85° F. In this case, keep bread dough out of direct sunlight and place the bowl in a pan of cool water if necessary.

Let rise until double in bulk. To test whether dough has risen to double in bulk, press the tips of two fingers lightly and quickly into the top of the dough about half an inch deep. If the dents stay, the dough has doubled in bulk; if they don't, it needs more rising time.

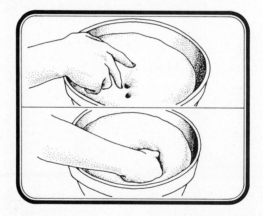

Test for "double in bulk": Press fingertips into risen dough about ½ inch deep. If indentations remain, dough has risen to double in bulk.

Punch down dough: When dough has doubled in bulk, press down firmly in the center with your fist. Then with your fingers fold edges toward the center to form a ball.

Punch down dough. To "punch down" dough, push your floured fist into the center of the dough. Pull the edges to the center with your fingers to form a ball; turn the dough over.

Shape into loaves one at a time. Divide the dough into equal portions according to the number of loaves you plan to make by cutting it through cleanly with a long sharp knife. Shape loaves this way: Roll the dough on a floured board into an oblong about nine by seven inches. Starting with the narrow ends, fold the oblong into thirds, overlapping them in the center. Press the dough down firmly, working with both hands to shape the loaf evenly. Pinch the dough together along the center fold and at the ends. Place the loaf, sealed side down, in a greased pan.

SHAPING LOAVES

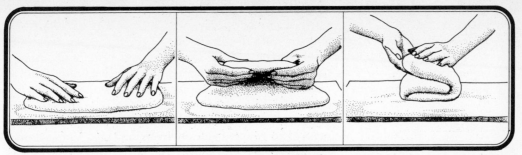

Another Loaf-Shaping Method is to flatten dough firmly and shape it into a rectangle.

Fold dough in half lengthwise. Press and shape into a rectangle about 15 by 5 inches.

Fold ends to middle in thirds. Press out bubbles. Keep loaf the length of bread pan.

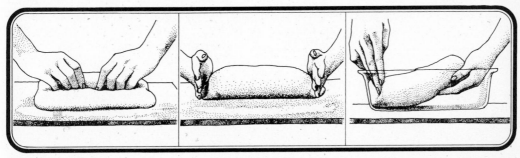

Starting with a narrow side, roll the dough tightly. Pinch edge of the last turn to seal.

Push ends of roll into loaf; then seal ends firmly with sides of hands. Tuck ends under.

Place the roll sealed side down in a greased pan. Grease the top, cover, and let rise.

Bake the bread on the center shelf of the oven with at least two inches between pans.

Test for doneness by tapping the bottom and sides of the loaf; there will be a hollow sound. If it is not done, put the loaf back in the pan and continue baking.

Cool the bread by turning the loaf out of the pan onto a wire rack. If you want a soft crust, brush the top while hot with soft shortening. If you want a crisp crust, don't brush it. Cool completely before storing.

Old-fashioned Homemade Bread

✍ White Bread, Conventional Method

6 cups sifted all-purpose flour

Sift and measure 6 cups flour. Heat milk in a small saucepan over moderately low heat (about 225° F.) until

1 cup milk
3 tablespoons sugar
2½ teaspoons salt
6 tablespoons butter or
margarine
1 cup warm water
1 package active dry yeast

bubbles appear around edge. Remove from heat; add sugar, salt, and butter. Cool until lukewarm. Pour the warm water into a large bowl; sprinkle with the yeast and stir until dissolved. Stir in the lukewarm milk mixture. Add 3 cups of the flour and beat until smooth. Gradually stir in just enough of the remaining flour to make a soft dough, scraping bowl occasionally. Turn out onto a floured board and knead 8 to 10 minutes, until dough is smooth and elastic, adding flour to board as needed to prevent dough from sticking. Shape dough into a ball and place in a greased bowl. Turn once to bring greased side up. Cover with a damp cloth and let rise in a warm place (85° F.) until double in bulk, about 1 hour. Punch down and turn out onto a lightly floured board. Cover and let rest for 15 minutes. Divide dough in half and shape into 2 loaves. Place in 2 greased 8½-x-4½-x-2½-inch loaf pans. Cover and let rise in a warm place until doubled in bulk, about 1 hour. Bake in a preheated 400° F. oven for 25 to 30 minutes, or until done. Remove from pan and cool on wire rack. Makes 2 loaves.

✤ Whole Wheat Bread, Conventional Method

4½ cups unsifted whole wheat
flour
2 cups sifted all-purpose
flour
¾ cup milk
3 tablespoons sugar
⅓ cup dark molasses
4 teaspoons salt
⅓ cup butter or margarine
1½ cups warm water
2 packages active dry yeast

Measure whole wheat flour and sifted all-purpose flour and mix together in a bowl. Heat milk in a small saucepan over moderately low heat (about 225° F.) until bubbles appear around edge. Remove from heat; add sugar, molasses, salt, and butter. Cool until lukewarm. Pour the warm water into a large bowl; sprinkle with yeast and stir until dissolved. Stir in the lukewarm milk mixture. Add 3 cups of the flour mixture and beat until smooth. Gradually stir in just enough of the remaining flour to make a soft dough, scraping bowl occasionally. Turn out onto a floured board (use some of the remaining flour mixture) and knead for 8 to 10 minutes, until dough is smooth and elastic, adding flour to board as needed to prevent dough from sticking. Shape dough into a ball and place in a greased bowl. Turn once to bring greased side up. Cover with a damp cloth and let rise in a warm place (85° F.) until double in bulk, about 1¼ hours. Punch down and turn out onto a lightly floured board. Divide dough in half and shape into 2 loaves. Place in 2 greased 8½-x-4½-x-2½-inch loaf pans. Cover and let rise in a warm place until doubled in bulk, about 1 hour. Bake in a preheated 400° F. oven for 25 to 30 minutes, or until done. Remove from pan and cool on wire rack. Makes 2 loaves.

❧ Rye Bread, Conventional Method

2½ cups unsifted rye flour
3 cups sifted all-purpose flour
1 cup milk
2 tablespoons dark molasses
2½ teaspoons salt
2 tablespoons butter or margarine
1 cup warm water
1 package active dry yeast
1 tablespoon caraway seeds
¼ cup yellow corn meal
Vegetable oil

Measure rye flour and sifted all-purpose flour and mix together in a bowl. Heat milk in a small saucepan over moderately low heat (about 225° F.) until bubbles appear around edge. Remove from heat; add molasses, salt, and butter. Cool until lukewarm. Pour the warm water into a large bowl; sprinkle with the yeast and stir until dissolved. Stir in the lukewarm milk mixture. Stir in 2½ cups of the flour mixture and the caraway seeds; beat until smooth. Gradually stir in just enough of the remaining flour to make a soft dough, scraping bowl occasionally. Turn out onto a floured board and knead for 8 to 10 minutes, until dough is smooth and elastic, adding flour to board as needed to prevent dough from sticking. Shape dough into a ball and place in a greased bowl. Turn once to bring greased side up. Cover with a damp cloth and let rise in a warm place (85° F.) until double in bulk, about 1¼ to 1½ hours. Punch down and turn out onto a lightly floured board. Divide dough in half and shape each half into a ball. Cover and let stand 10 minutes. Flatten each piece of dough slightly; roll lightly on a floured board with the hands to form a loaf about 8½ to 9 inches long with tapered ends. Grease 2 cookie sheets and sprinkle each with corn meal. Place shaped dough on cookie sheets and brush surfaces with oil. Let rise in a warm place until double in bulk, about 50 to 60 minutes. Bake in a preheated 400° F. oven for 25 minutes, or until done. Remove from sheets and cool on wire racks. Makes 2 loaves.

Rapid-Mix Breads

The rapid-mix method does not require dissolving the yeast or scalding the milk. Be sure liquids are heated to 125° F. to 135° F. and use active dry yeast, not cake yeast.

White Bread, Rapid-Mix Method

6 cups sifted all-purpose
  flour
3 tablespoons sugar
2½ teaspoons salt
1 package active dry yeast
1 cup milk
1 cup water
6 tablespoons butter or
  margarine

Sift and measure 6 cups flour. In the large bowl of an electric mixer, mix 2 cups of the flour, the sugar, salt, and yeast. Place milk, water, and butter in a small saucepan over moderately low heat (about 225° F.) and heat until liquids are warm (butter will be entirely melted and temperature should be about 125° F.). Gradually add liquid to dry ingredients and beat 2 minutes at medium speed of the electric mixer, scraping bowl occasionally with a rubber spatula. Add ½ cup of the flour, or enough flour to make a thick batter. Beat at high speed 2 minutes, scraping bowl occasionally. With a spoon gradually stir in just enough of the remaining flour to make a soft dough, scraping bowl occasionally. Turn out onto a floured board and knead for 8 to 10 minutes, until dough is smooth and elastic, adding flour to board as needed to prevent dough from sticking. Shape dough into a ball and place in a greased bowl. Turn once to bring greased side up. Cover with a damp cloth and let rise in a warm place (85° F.) until doubled in bulk, about 1 hour. Punch down and turn out onto a lightly floured board. Cover and let rise for 15 minutes. Divide dough in half and shape each half into a loaf. Place in 2 greased 8½-x-4½-x-2½-inch loaf pans. Cover and let rise in a warm place until doubled in bulk, about 1 hour. Bake in a preheated 400° F. oven for 25 to 30 minutes, or until done. Remove from pan and cool on wire racks. Makes 2 loaves.

Whole Wheat Bread, Rapid-Mix Method

4 cups unsifted whole wheat
  flour
2½ cups sifted all-purpose
  flour
3 tablespoons sugar
4 teaspoons salt
2 packages active dry yeast
¾ cup milk
1½ cups water
⅓ cup molasses
⅓ cup butter or margarine

Measure whole wheat flour and sifted all-purpose flour; mix together in a bowl. In the large bowl of an electric mixer, mix 2½ cups of the flour mixture, the sugar, salt, and yeast. Place milk, water, molasses, and butter in a small saucepan over moderately low heat (about 225° F.) and heat until liquids are warm (butter will be entirely melted and temperature should be about 125° F.). Gradually add liquid to dry ingredients and beat 2 minutes at medium speed of the electric mixer, scraping bowl occasionally with a rubber spatula. Add 1 cup of the flour mixture, or enough to make a thick batter. Beat at high speed 2 minutes, scraping bowl occasionally. Gradually stir in just enough of the remaining flour to make a soft dough, scraping bowl occasionally. Turn out onto a floured board (using some of the remaining flour mixture) and knead for 8 to 10 minutes, until dough is smooth and elastic, adding flour to board as needed to prevent dough from sticking. Shape dough into a ball and place in a greased bowl. Turn once to bring greased side up. Cover with a damp cloth and let rise in a warm place (85° F.) until doubled in bulk, about 1 hour. Punch down and turn out onto a lightly floured board. Divide dough in half and shape into 2 loaves. Place in 2 greased 8½-x-4½-x-2½-inch loaf pans. Cover and let rise in a warm place until doubled in bulk, about 1 hour. Bake in a preheated 400° F. oven for 25 to 30 minutes, or until done. Remove from pan and cool on wire rack. Makes 2 loaves.

❧ Rye Bread, Rapid-Mix Method

2½ cups unsifted rye flour
2½ cups sifted all-purpose flour
1 tablespoon sugar
1 tablespoon salt
1 tablespoon caraway seeds
1 package active dry yeast
1 cup milk
1 cup water
2 tablespoons honey
1 tablespoon butter or margarine
¼ cup corn meal
Vegetable oil

Measure rye flour and sifted all-purpose flour and mix together in a bowl. In the large bowl of an electric mixer, mix 1⅔ cups of the flour mixture, the sugar, salt, caraway, and yeast. Place milk, water, honey, and butter in a small saucepan over moderately low heat (about 225° F.) and heat until liquids are warm (butter will be entirely melted and temperature should be about 125° F.). Gradually add liquid to dry ingredients and beat 2 minutes on medium speed of the electric mixer, scraping bowl occasionally with a rubber spatula. Add 1¼ cups of the flour mixture, or enough to make a thick batter. Beat at high speed 2 minutes, scraping bowl occasionally. With a spoon gradually stir in just enough of the remaining flour mixture to make a soft dough, scraping bowl occasionally. Turn out onto a floured board (using some of the remaining flour mixture) and knead 8 to 10 minutes, until dough is smooth and elastic, adding flour to board as needed to prevent dough from sticking. Shape dough into a ball and place in a greased bowl. Turn once to bring greased side up. Cover with a damp cloth and let rise in a warm place (85° F.) until double in bulk, about 1¼ to 1½ hours. Punch down and turn out onto a lightly floured board. Divide dough in half and shape into 2 balls. Cover and let stand 10 minutes. Flatten each piece of dough slightly; roll lightly on floured board with the hands to form a loaf about 8½ to 9 inches long with tapered ends. Grease 2 cookie sheets and sprinkle each with corn meal. Place shaped dough on cookie sheets and brush surfaces with oil. Let rise in a warm place until double in bulk, about 50 to 60 minutes. Bake in a preheated 400° F. oven for 25 minutes, or until done. Remove from sheets and cool on wire racks. Makes 2 loaves.

◈§ Anadama Bread, Rapid-Mix Method

6½ cups sifted all-purpose flour
2 teaspoons salt
1 cup yellow corn meal
2 packages active dry yeast
1 cup water
1 cup milk
½ cup light molasses
3 tablespoons butter or margarine

Sift and measure 6½ cups flour. In the large bowl of an electric mixer, mix 2½ cups flour, salt, corn meal, and yeast. Place water, milk, molasses, and butter in a saucepan over moderately low heat (about 225° F.) and heat until liquids are warm (butter will be entirely melted and temperature should be about 125° F.). Gradually add liquid to dry ingredients and beat 2 minutes at medium speed of the electric mixer, scraping bowl occasionally with a rubber spatula. Add ½ cup flour or enough to make a thick batter. Beat at high speed 2 minutes, scraping bowl occasionally. With a spoon gradually stir in just enough flour to make a stiff dough, scraping bowl occasionally. Turn out onto a floured board and knead 8 to 10 minutes, until dough is smooth and elastic, adding flour to board as needed to prevent dough from sticking. Shape into a ball and place in a greased bowl. Turn once to bring greased side up. Cover with a damp cloth and let rise in a warm place (85° F.) until doubled in bulk, about 1 to 1½ hours. Punch down and turn out onto a lightly floured board. Cover and let rise 15 minutes. Divide dough in half and shape each half into a loaf. Place in 2 greased 9-x-5-x-3-inch pans. Cover and let rise in a warm place until double in bulk, about 30 to 45 minutes. Heat oven to 375° F.; bake 40 to 45 minutes, or until done. Remove loaves from pans; cool on racks. Makes 2 loaves.

◈§ French Bread, Rapid-Mix Method

3¾ cups sifted all-purpose flour
1½ teaspoons salt
1 package active dry yeast
1¼ cups warm water

Sift and measure 3¾ cups flour. In the large bowl of an electric mixer mix 1½ cups flour, salt, and yeast. Place water and butter in a saucepan over moderately low heat (about 225° F.) and heat until liquids are warm (butter will be entirely melted and temperature should be about

3 tablespoons butter or margarine

¼ cup corn meal

125° F.). Gradually add liquid to dry ingredients and beat 2 minutes at medium speed, scraping bowl occasionally with a rubber spatula. Add ½ cup flour or enough to make a thick batter. Beat at high speed 2 minutes, scraping bowl occasionally. With a spoon gradually stir in just enough flour to make a stiff dough, scraping bowl occasionally. Turn out onto a floured board and knead 8 to 10 minutes, until dough is smooth and elastic, adding flour to board as needed to prevent dough from sticking. Shape into a ball and place in a greased bowl. Turn once to bring greased side up. Cover with a damp cloth and let rise in a warm place (85° F.) until double in bulk, about 1 hour. Punch down and turn out onto a lightly floured board. Cover and let rise 15 minutes. Divide dough in half and roll each into a 15-x-10-inch oblong. Roll up tightly, starting with wider side. Seal edge by pinching together. With a hand on each end, roll gently back and forth to lengthen roll and taper ends. Place diagonally on a greased cookie sheet which has been sprinkled with corn meal. Make ¼-inch-deep slashes in top of loaves at 1-inch intervals. Brush top with cold water. Let rise uncovered in a warm place until double in bulk, about 1 hour. Heat oven to 375° F. Brush top of bread again with cold water and bake 40 to 45 minutes, or until golden brown. Makes 2 loaves.

Batter Breads

In batter-bread recipes, beating is very important. The dough should be beaten until it leaves the sides of the bowl. The term *stirring down* used in batter-bread recipes means to stir raised dough until it is reduced to almost its original volume.

⤸ White Batter Bread

4 to 4½ cups sifted all-purpose flour

3 tablespoons sugar

1 tablespoon salt

2 packages active dry yeast

Sift and measure 4½ cups flour. In the large bowl of an electric mixer, mix 1½ cups flour, the sugar, salt, and yeast. Place milk, water, and butter in a small saucepan over moderately low heat (about 225° F.) and heat until liquids are warm (butter will be entirely melted and

1 cup milk
1 cup water
2 tablespoons butter or
margarine

temperature should be about 125° F.). Gradually add liquid to dry ingredients and beat 2 minutes at medium speed of the electric mixer, scraping bowl occasionally with a rubber spatula. Add 1¼ cups flour, or enough to make a thick batter. Beat on high speed for 2 minutes, scraping bowl occasionally. Gradually stir in enough of remaining flour to make a stiff batter so that batter leaves sides of bowl. Cover with a damp cloth and let rise in a warm place (85° F.) until double in bulk, about 50 to 60 minutes. Heat oven to 375° F. Stir batter down with a spoon and beat vigorously ½ minute. Turn batter into a greased 9-x-5-x-3-inch loaf pan. Bake 40 to 50 minutes, or until done. Remove from pan and cool on wire rack. Makes 1 loaf.

✒️ Cheese Batter Bread

4¾ to 5½ cups sifted
   all-purpose flour
3 tablespoons sugar
1 tablespoon salt
2 packages active dry yeast
1 cup milk
1 cup water
2 tablespoons butter or
   margarine
1½ cups (6 ounces) sharp
   Cheddar cheese, coarsely
   shredded
1 egg, at room temperature

Sift and measure 5½ cups flour. In the large bowl of an electric mixer, mix 1¾ cups flour, the sugar, salt, and yeast. Place milk, water, and butter in a small saucepan over moderately low heat (about 225° F.) and heat until liquids are warm (butter will be entirely melted and temperature should be about 125° F.). Gradually add liquid to dry ingredients and beat 2 minutes on medium speed of the electric mixer, scraping bowl occasionally with a rubber spatula. Add cheese, egg, and ¾ cup flour, or enough to make a thick batter. Beat on high speed for 2 minutes, scraping bowl occasionally. Gradually stir in just enough of the remaining flour to make a stiff batter; batter will leave sides of bowl. Cover with a damp cloth and let rise in a warm place (85° F.) until double in bulk, about 50 to 60 minutes. Heat oven to 375° F. Stir batter down with a spoon and beat vigorously ½ minute. Turn batter into 2 deep, greased, 1-quart casseroles. Bake 50 to 50 minutes, or until done. Remove from casseroles and cool on wire racks. Makes 2 loaves.

✒️ Raisin Batter Bread

4½ to 4¾ cups sifted
   all-purpose flour
½ cup sugar
1 teaspoon salt
2 packages active dry yeast

Sift and measure 4¾ cups flour. In the large bowl of an electric mixer, mix 1½ cups flour, the sugar, salt, and yeast. Place milk, water, and butter in a small saucepan over moderately low heat (about 225° F.) and heat until liquids are warm (butter will be entirely melted and

1 cup milk
½ cup water
¼ cup butter or margarine
1 egg, at room temperature
1 cup seedless raisins

temperature should be about 125° F.). Gradually add liquid to dry ingredients and beat 2 minutes at medium speed of the electric mixer, scraping bowl occasionally with rubber spatula. Add egg and 1¼ cups flour, or enough to make a thick batter. Beat on high speed for 2 minutes, scraping bowl occasionally. Gradually stir in just enough of the remaining flour to make a stiff batter so that batter leaves sides of bowl. Cover with a damp cloth and let rise in a warm place (85° F.) until double in bulk, about 1 hour. Heat oven to 350° F. Stir batter down with a spoon and add raisins; beat vigorously ½ minute. Turn batter into 2 deep, greased, 1-quart casseroles. Bake 40 to 45 minutes, or until done. Remove from casseroles and cool on wire racks. Makes 2 loaves.

✍ Oatmeal Batter Bread

¾ cup boiling water
½ cup quick-cooking rolled oats
¼ cup light molasses
2¾ cups sifted all-purpose flour
2 teaspoons salt
1 package active dry yeast
½ cup water
3 tablespoons butter or margarine
1 egg, at room temperature

Combine the boiling water, oats, and molasses in a bowl and let stand until lukewarm. Sift and measure flour. In the large bowl of an electric mixer, mix 1½ cups of the flour, the salt, and yeast. Place the ½ cup of water and butter in a small saucepan over moderately low heat (about 225° F.) and heat until liquid is warm (butter will be melted entirely and temperature should be about 125° F.). Add the butter mixture and oats mixture to dry ingredients and beat 2 minutes on medium speed of electric mixer, scraping bowl occasionally. Add the egg and ¾ cup of the flour, or enough to make a thick batter. Beat on high speed 2 minutes, scraping bowl occasionally. Gradually stir in just enough of the remaining flour to make a stiff batter, so that batter leaves sides of bowl. Cover with a damp cloth and let rise in a warm place (85° F.) until double in bulk, about 50 to 60 minutes. Heat oven to 375° F. Stir batter down with a spoon and beat vigorously ½ minute. Turn batter into a greased 9-x-5-x-3-inch loaf pan. Bake 50 to 60 minutes, or until done. Remove from pan and cool on wire rack. Makes 1 loaf.

Cool-Rise Breads

The cool-rise method is most useful when you want to make up bread dough one day and bake it the next or when you want one loaf fresh one day and the other fresh a second day. Cool-rise dough should be refrigerated at a temperature between 38° F. and 41° F.

⊰ White Bread, Cool-Rise Method

6 or 7 cups sifted all-purpose
    flour
2 tablespoons sugar
1 tablespoon salt
2 packages active dry yeast
½ cup softened butter or
    margarine
2 cups very hot tap water
    (approximately 145° F.)
Vegetable oil

Sift and measure 7 cups flour. In the large bowl of an electric mixer, mix 2 cups of the flour, the sugar, salt, and yeast. Add butter. Pour in the hot water and beat 2 minutes at medium speed on the electric mixer, scraping bowl occasionally with a rubber spatula. Add 1¼ cups of the flour, or enough to make a thick batter. Beat at high speed for 2 minutes, scraping bowl occasionally. With a spoon gradually stir in just enough of the remaining flour to make a soft dough, scraping bowl occasionally. Turn out onto a floured board and knead for 8 to 10 minutes, until dough is smooth and elastic, adding flour to board as needed to prevent dough from sticking. Shape dough into a ball; cover first with plastic wrap, then with a towel; let stand for 20 minutes. Remove towel and plastic; punch dough down; divide in half and shape each half into a loaf. Place in 2 greased 8½-x-4½-x-2½-inch loaf pans. Brush tops with oil. Cover loosely with plastic wrap and refrigerate 2 to 24 hours. When ready to bake, remove from refrigerator. Uncover and let stand 10 minutes at room temperature; meanwhile heat oven to 400° F. Puncture any gas bubbles on top of dough with a greased toothpick or metal skewer. Bake 30 to 40 minutes, or until done. Remove from pan and cool on wire racks. Makes 2 loaves.

⊰ Whole Wheat Bread, Cool-Rise Method

2½ cups unsifted whole wheat
    flour
3 to 4 cups sifted
    all-purpose flour
2 tablespoons sugar
1 tablespoon salt
2 packages active dry yeast
1¾ cups milk
½ cup water
3 tablespoons butter or
    margarine
Vegetable oil

Measure whole wheat flour and sifted all-purpose flour into separate bowls. In the large bowl of an electric mixer, mix 1 cup of each of the flours, the sugar, salt, and yeast. Place milk, water, and butter in a small saucepan over moderately low heat (about 225° F.) and heat until liquids are warm (butter will be entirely melted and temperature should be about 125° F.). Gradually add liquid to dry ingredients and beat 2 minutes at medium speed on the electric mixer, scraping bowl occasionally with a rubber spatula. Add ¾ cup of the all-purpose flour, or enough to make a thick batter. Beat at high speed for 2 minutes, scraping bowl occasionally. Stir in the remaining whole wheat flour and enough of the all-purpose flour to make a soft dough, scraping bowl occasionally. Turn out onto a board and knead for 8 to 10 minutes, until dough is smooth and elastic, adding flour to board as needed to prevent dough from sticking. Shape dough into a ball; cover with plastic wrap, then with a towel; let rest 20 minutes. Remove towel and plastic; punch dough down; divide in half and shape into 2 loaves. Place in 2 greased 8½-x-4½-x-2½-inch loaf pans. Brush tops with oil. Cover loosely with plastic wrap and refrigerate 2 to 24 hours. Uncover and let stand 10 minutes at room temperature; meanwhile heat oven to 400° F. Puncture any gas bubbles on the top of dough with a greased toothpick or metal skewer. Bake 30 to 40 minutes, or until done. Remove from pan and cool on wire racks. Makes 2 loaves.

Whole Grain and Cereal Breads

❧ Currant Oatmeal Bread

2 cups water
1½ cups old-fashioned rolled oats
¼ cup soft butter or margarine
1 cup milk
½ cup honey
1 tablespoon salt
1 egg, slightly beaten
1 package active dry yeast
½ cup dried currants
About 5 cups sifted all-purpose flour
Melted butter or margarine
Cinnamon sugar

Bring water to a boil over moderately high heat (about 275° F.); stir in rolled oats and cook 5 minutes, stirring frequently. Remove oats from heat and stir in butter. Turn mixture into a large mixing bowl and stir in milk, honey and salt. Cool mixture to lukewarm. Beat in egg and yeast. Let stand 10 minutes; mixture should be bubbling. Stir in currants and flour, 1 cup at a time, beating vigorously until dough is sticky but stiff enough to knead. Turn out on a floured board or pastry cloth and knead 8 to 10 minutes, until dough has a smooth, satiny appearance. Add more of the flour to the board if dough becomes sticky. Place dough in a large, lightly greased bowl and cover with a damp, clean tea towel. Let rise in a warm place (85° F.) about 1 hour, until double in bulk. Punch down dough and turn it out onto a lightly floured board. Knead until smooth. Divide dough in half. Shape each half into a loaf and place each in a greased and floured 9-x-5-x-2¾-inch loaf pan. Cover and let rise in a warm place about ½ hour, until double in bulk. Heat oven to 350° F. Bake 40 to 45 minutes, or until the bread sounds hollow when tapped lightly on the bottom or side. Turn bread out onto a wire cake rack, and while still hot brush with melted butter and sprinkle generously with cinnamon sugar. When completely cooled, wrap and store for a day before cutting. Makes 2 loaves.

⋙ Cornell Bread

3 cups warm water
2 packages active dry yeast
2 tablespoons sugar or honey
7 cups all-purpose flour or more
3 tablespoons wheat germ
½ cup soy flour
¾ cup instant non-fat dry milk
4 teaspoons salt
2 tablespoons salad oil

Combine the water, yeast, and sugar or honey. Let stand for 5 minutes. Measure and sift the flour, wheat germ, soy flour, and skim-milk powder. Stir the yeast mixture and while stirring add the salt and 3 cups of the flour mixture. Beat 75 strokes by hand or 2 minutes with an electric mixer. Add the salad oil and 3 more cups flour mixture. Blend and then turn out onto a floured board, adding 1 cup or more additional flour as needed. Knead thoroughly, about 5 minutes or until dough is smooth and elastic. Place in a greased bowl, brush the top with soft butter or oil, cover, and let rise until doubled. Punch dough down, fold over the edges, and turn dough upside down. Let it rise another 20 minutes. Turn onto a board, shape into 2 loaves, place in 2 greased 9-x-5-x-3-inch bread pans, cover, and let rise until doubled. Bake in a 350° F. oven for 50 to 60 minutes. If loaves begin to brown too soon, in 15 or 20 minutes, reduce heat to 325° F.

Note: The soy flour, non-fat dry milk and wheat germ add protein to the popular bread developed by Cornell University.

⋙ Whole Wheat–Egg Bread

1 cup scalded milk
¼ cup vegetable oil
⅓ cup honey
1½ teaspoons salt
3 eggs, at room temperature
1 envelope active dry yeast
⅓ cup warm water (105° F. to 115° F.)
3½ cups unsifted whole wheat flour
½ cup unsifted soy flour

In a large mixing bowl combine milk, oil, honey and salt; cool slightly. Beat in 1 egg at a time. Mix together yeast and water. Stir yeast into egg mixture. Add 3 cups of the whole wheat flour, 1 cup at a time, beating vigorously after each addition. Add remaining ½ cup whole wheat flour and soy flour, beating vigorously. Turn batter into an oiled bowl and cover with a damp towel. Let dough rise in a warm place (85° F.) about 1¼ hours, until double in bulk. Heat oven to 350° F. Punch down dough and turn it into a greased 9-x-5-x-2¾-inch loaf pan. Let stand at room temperature 10 minutes. Bake 45 to 60 minutes, or until the bread sounds hollow when lightly tapped on the bottom or side. Turn bread out of the pan onto a wire cake rack and cool completely. Cut into slices with a serrated knife. Makes 1 loaf.

⌇ Cracked Wheat Bread

½ cup warm water
2 packages active dry yeast
1 tablespoon brown sugar or
  molasses
1 cup buttermilk
1 cup water
3 tablespoons butter or
  margarine
¼ cup honey
1 tablespoon salt
¼ teaspoon baking soda
4 cups whole wheat flour
1 cup cracked wheat
2 cups all-purpose flour

Combine the ½ cup water, the yeast and brown sugar in a large mixing bowl; let stand 10 minutes. In a medium-sized saucepan heat buttermilk, the 1 cup of water, the butter, honey and salt over low heat until lukewarm (about 110° F.); pour into yeast. Add baking soda, whole wheat flour and cracked wheat and mix thoroughly. Cover and let rise until double in bulk, about 1 hour. Stir dough until deflated and then work in 1 cup of the all-purpose flour. Turn out dough onto a well-floured surface (use some of remaining flour) and knead for 5 minutes, using only as much of remaining flour as needed to prevent dough from sticking. Place dough in a greased bowl; turn once to bring greased side up. Cover and let rise in a warm place until double in bulk, about 30 minutes. Grease 2 9-x-5-x-3-inch loaf pans or sprinkle 2 baking sheets with corn meal. Punch down dough, turn out onto a floured surface and cut in half. Shape each piece into a loaf and place in prepared pans or on baking sheets. Cover and let rise in a warm place until almost double in size, about 45 minutes. Put in an unheated oven and turn on oven to 375° F. Bake 55 to 60 minutes, or until done. Cool loaves on a wire rack. Makes 2 loaves.

⌇ Whole Wheat Bran Bread

1 cup all-purpose flour
1 cup whole wheat flour
1 cup wheat-bran cereal
1 tablespoon sugar
1 teaspoon salt
1 package active dry yeast
¾ cup milk
1 tablespoon molasses
3 tablespoons butter or
  margarine, softened
1 egg
Melted butter or margarine

In small mixing bowl, stir together all-purpose flour and whole wheat flour. In large bowl of electric mixer, combine ½ cup of the flour mixture, the bran cereal, sugar, salt and yeast. In small saucepan, combine milk, molasses and the 3 tablespoons margarine. Place over low heat until very warm (120° to 130° F.). Gradually add to cereal mixture and beat at medium speed on electric mixer for 2 minutes, scraping bowl occasionally. Add egg and ¼ cup of the flour mixture. Beat at high speed on electric mixer for 2 minutes. With spoon, stir in remaining flour mixture to make a stiff dough. Turn dough out onto lightly floured surface and knead 5 minutes or until smooth and elastic. Place in well-greased bowl, turning to grease top. Cover and let rise in warm place about 1 hour or until double in bulk. Punch down dough. Form into smooth round ball with hands, being careful not to create large folds in dough. Place on greased baking sheet. Cover and let rise in warm place about 1 hour or until doubled in bulk. Bake on center rack of oven at 375° F. about 30 minutes or until golden brown. Remove immediately from baking sheet. Place on wire rack. Brush with melted margarine. Cool. Makes 1 loaf.

Yeast Rolls, Plain and Sweet

❧ Cool-Rise Rolls

6½ cups sifted all-purpose flour
½ cup sugar
2 teaspoons salt
2 packages active dry yeast
¼ cup softened butter or margarine
2 cups very hot tap water (approximately 145° F.)
1 egg

Sift and measure 6½ cups flour. In the large bowl of an electric mixer, mix 2 cups of the flour, sugar, salt, and yeast. Add butter. Pour in the hot water and beat 2 minutes at medium speed on the electric mixer, scraping bowl occasionally with a rubber spatula. Add egg and 1½ cups flour, or enough to make a thick batter. Beat at high speed 2 minutes, scraping bowl occasionally. With a spoon gradually stir in just enough of the remaining flour to make a soft dough, scraping bowl occasionally. Turn out onto a floured board and knead for 8 to 10 minutes until dough is smooth and elastic, adding flour to board as needed to prevent dough from sticking. Shape dough into a ball; cover first with plastic wrap, then with a towel; let stand for 20 minutes. Remove towel and plastic; punch dough down and shape as described in How to Shape Rolls (pages 679 and 680). Cover rolls loosely with plastic wrap and refrigerate 2 to 24 hours. Heat oven to 400° F. Remove rolls from refrigerator and let stand at room temperature 10 minutes. Bake 10 to 15 minutes, or until golden brown. Remove from pan and cool on wire racks. Makes 16 Crescents, about 20 Cloverleafs or Lucky Clovers, about 36 Parker House Rolls, or 12 Fan-Tans.

❧ Yeast Rolls, Rapid-Mix Method

3 to 3½ cups sifted all-purpose flour
¼ cup sugar
½ teaspoon salt
1 package active dry yeast
5 tablespoons softened butter or margarine

Sift and measure 3½ cups flour. In the small bowl of an electric mixer, mix ¾ cup of the flour, the sugar, salt, and yeast. Add softened butter. Gradually add hot water to dry ingredients and beat 2 minutes at medium speed of the electric mixer, scraping bowl occasionally with a rubber spatula. Add egg and ½ cup of the flour, or enough flour to make a thick batter. Beat at high

⅔ *cup very hot water*
   (approximately 145° F.)
1 egg
Melted butter or margarine

speed 2 minutes, scraping bowl occasionally. With a spoon gradually stir in enough of the remaining flour to make a stiff dough, scraping bowl occasionally. Turn out onto a floured board and knead 8 to 10 minutes, until dough is smooth and elastic, adding flour to board as needed to prevent dough from sticking. Shape dough into a ball and place in a greased bowl. Turn once to bring greased side up. Cover with a damp cloth and let rise in a warm place (85° F.) until double in bulk, about 1 hour. Punch down and turn out onto a lightly floured board. Shape into rolls following directions given under How to Shape Rolls (pages 679 and 680). Brush tops of rolls with melted butter. Let rise covered in a warm place (85° F.) until double in bulk, about 45 to 60 minutes. Bake in a 400° F. oven for 10 to 15 minutes. Serve warm. Makes 16 Crescents, about 20 Cloverleafs or Lucky Clovers, about 36 Parker House Rolls, or about 12 Fan-Tans.

How to Shape Rolls

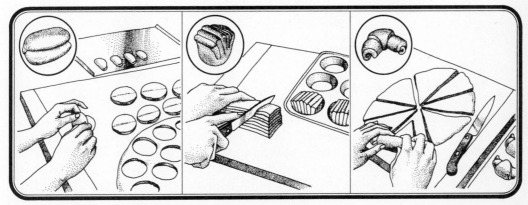

Parker House Rolls: Roll dough ¼ inch thick. Cut with a biscuit cutter 2½ inches in diameter. Make a slight indentation slightly off center of each circle with the back of a knife. Brush with melted butter. Fold larger half to overlap the other slightly. Place in the pan as recipe directs. (For soft-sided rolls, they should be close together in a pan. For crisp sides, they should be placed about 2 inches apart on a cookie sheet.)

Fan-Tans: Roll out enough dough to make a 9-x-10½-x-¼-inch rectangle. Brush it lightly with melted butter. Cut the dough into 7 strips 9 inches long and 1½ inches wide. Put one on top of another, and cut the stack crosswise into six 1½-inch pieces. Place each piece in a greased 2¾-inch muffin cup, cut-side up.

Crescents: Roll the dough into 2 rounds ¼ inch thick and 9 to 10 inches in diameter. Brush with melted butter. Cut each round into 8 wedge-shaped pieces. Roll up each piece, starting at wide side. Pinch the dough to seal the pointed side to the roll. Place on a greased cookie sheet about 2 inches apart, with point underneath. Curve each roll into a crescent shape.

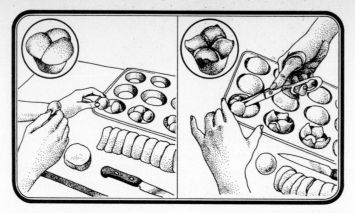

Cloverleaf Rolls: To make each roll, form 3 small balls of dough about 1 inch in diameter. Brush each thoroughly with melted butter. Place 3 in each greased muffin cup.

Lucky Clovers: Shape dough into balls slightly less in diameter than the bottom of the muffin cup. Place 1 ball of dough in each greased muffin cup. Hold scissors vertically and snip down almost to the bottom of the dough, cutting first into halves, then quarters. Brush tops lightly with melted butter.

☙ *Basic Sweet Dough*

7½ **cups sifted all-purpose flour**
½ **cup sugar**
2 **teaspoons salt**
2 **packages active dry yeast**
1 **cup milk**
1 **cup water**
½ **cup butter or margarine**
2 **eggs**

Sift and measure 7 ½ cups flour. In the large bowl of an electric mixer, mix 2 cups flour, sugar, salt, and yeast. Place milk, water, and butter in a small saucepan over moderately low heat (about 225° F.) and heat until liquids are warm (butter will be entirely melted and temperature should be about 125° F.). Gradually add liquid to dry ingredients and beat 2 minutes at medium speed of the electric mixer, scraping bowl occasionally with a rubber spatula. Add eggs and ¾ cup flour, or enough flour to make a thick batter. Beat at high speed 2 minutes, scraping bowl occasionally. With a spoon, gradually stir in just enough of the remaining flour to make a stiff dough, scraping bowl occasionally. Turn out onto a floured board and knead 8 to 10 minutes, until dough is smooth and elastic, adding flour to board as needed to prevent dough from sticking. Shape into a ball and place in a greased bowl. Turn once to bring greased side up. Cover with a damp cloth and let rise in a warm place (85° F.) until double in bulk, about 1 hour. Punch down, turn out onto a lightly floured board, and knead a few minutes. Use in recipes that follow.

ᴇᔑ Cinnamon Rolls

½ recipe Basic Sweet Dough (recipe above)
2 tablespoons softened butter or margarine
¾ cup firmly packed dark brown sugar
2 teaspoons ground cinnamon
White Icing (recipe follows)

Roll dough into a 13-x-9-inch oblong. Spread with softened butter. Combine sugar and cinnamon and sprinkle evenly over butter. Beginning with a wide side, roll up tightly in jelly-roll fashion. Pinch edge to seal. Cut roll into 1-inch slices. Place ¼ inch apart in a greased 13-x-9-x-2-inch pan. Cover with greased waxed paper and a towel and let rise in a warm place (85° F.) until double in bulk, about 30 to 45 minutes. Heat oven to 375° F. Bake rolls 25 minutes, until golden brown. Turn rolls out onto a rack. While still warm, spread tops with White Icing. Makes 15 rolls.

White Icing

1 cup sifted confectioners' sugar
4 teaspoons milk
¼ teaspoon vanilla extract

Combine sugar, milk, and vanilla. Beat until smooth. Makes 1 cup.

ᴇᔑ Honey Buns

½ recipe Basic Sweet Dough (recipe on page 680)
½ cup melted butter or margarine
¾ cup sugar
2 teaspoons ground cinnamon
1 tablespoon honey
½ cup pecan halves

Roll dough into a 15-x-15-inch square. Brush with 2 tablespoons of the melted butter. Sprinkle with ¼ cup of the sugar and the cinnamon. Beginning with a wide side, roll up tightly jelly-roll fashion. Pinch edge to seal. Combine remaining butter, remaining sugar, and honey. Spread evenly in the bottom of a 13-x-9-x-2-inch baking pan. Arrange nuts evenly over sugar mixture. Cut roll into 1-inch slices. Place roll slices, cut-side down, about 1 inch apart over nuts. Cover with greased waxed paper and a towel and let rise in a warm place (85° F.) until double in bulk, about 45 to 60 minutes. Heat oven to 375° F. Bake about 25 minutes. Remove from oven and immediately turn pan upside down on a flat tray. Let stand 1 minute. Remove pan. Makes 2 dozen buns.

Cinnamon Rolls: Roll ½ Basic Sweet Dough into oblong 13 x 9 inches. Spread with butter and sprinkle with sugar and cinnamon as directed on page 681. Starting with wide side, roll tightly. Pinch edge of last turn to seal.

Cut roll into 1-inch slices. Place cut-side up about ¼ inch apart in greased 13-x-9-x-2-inch pan or in two 8-inch round layer cake pans. Cover, let rise, and bake as directed. Turn buns out onto a rack, and while still warm, ice tops.

Swedish Coffee Ring: Roll and shape dough as directed in recipe that follows. On greased baking sheet bring ends of roll together; seal. Snip at 1-inch intervals two-thirds of the way through. Turn each slice on its side.

Swedish Coffee Ring

½ recipe Basic Sweet Dough (recipe on page 680)
2 tablespoons softened butter or margarine
½ cup firmly packed dark brown sugar
2 teaspoons ground cinnamon
½ cup seedless raisins
White Icing (recipe on page 681)

Roll dough into a 15-x-9-inch oblong. Spread with softened butter. Combine sugar and cinnamon and sprinkle over butter. Top with raisins. Beginning with a wide side, roll up tightly jelly-roll fashion. Pinch edge to seal. Place on greased cookie sheet. With scissors make cuts two-thirds of the way through ring at 1-inch intervals. Turn each slice on its side. Cover with greased waxed paper and a towel and let rise until double in bulk, about 45 to 60 minutes. Heat oven to 375° F. Bake 25 to 30 minutes. Frost with White Icing. Makes 1 ring.

Sweet Breads

These breads are superb with coffee or tea for a morning or afternoon break. Although many of these are traditionally used at Christmas and Easter times, nothing says that they won't taste as good any other time of the year.

✑ Hot Cross Buns

3 cups sifted all-purpose
   flour
¼ cup sugar
¾ teaspoon salt
½ teaspoon ground
   cinnamon
¼ teaspoon ground nutmeg
1 package active dry yeast
½ cup milk
¼ cup water
3 tablespoons butter or
   margarine
1 egg
½ cup dried currants
¼ cup diced citron
Egg Glaze (recipe follows)
1 cup confectioners' sugar
3½ teaspoons warm water
¼ teaspoon vanilla extract

Sift and measure 3 cups flour. In the large bowl of an electric mixer, mix ¾ cup flour, sugar, salt, cinnamon, nutmeg, and yeast. Place milk, water, and butter in a small saucepan over moderately low heat (about 225° F.) and heat until liquids are warm (butter will be entirely melted and temperature should be about 125° F.). Gradually add liquid to dry ingredients and beat 2 minutes at medium speed of the electric mixer, scraping bowl occasionally with a rubber spatula. Add egg and ⅓ cup of the flour, or enough flour to make a thick batter. Beat at high speed 2 minutes, scraping bowl occasionally. With a spoon, gradually stir in just enough of the remaining flour to make a soft dough, scraping bowl occasionally. Turn out onto a floured board and knead for 8 to 10 minutes, until dough is smooth and elastic, adding flour to board as needed to prevent dough from sticking. Shape into a ball and place in a greased bowl. Turn once to bring greased side up. Cover with a damp cloth and let rise in a warm place (85° F.) until double in bulk, about 1 to 1½ hours. Punch down and turn out onto a lightly floured board. Knead in currants and citron. Divide dough into 9 equal parts. Shape each into a smooth ball and place in a greased 8-inch square cake pan. Cover with a sheet of greased waxed paper and a tea towel and let rise in a warm place until double in bulk, about 30 to 40 minutes. Heat oven to 375° F. Brush with Egg Glaze. Bake 30 minutes, until golden brown. Cool slightly and remove from pan. Mix confectioners' sugar, warm water, and vanilla extract. Spoon icing over the buns in crossed pattern. Makes 9 buns.

Egg Glaze

Beat together *1 egg yolk* and *1 tablespoon warm water*.

✑ Cinnamon Bow Ties

1 14-ounce package hot-roll
   mix
2 tablespoons melted butter
   or margarine

Prepare hot-roll mix as directed on package. When it has doubled in bulk, punch down and turn out on a lightly floured board. Roll into an 18-x-7-inch oblong about ½ inch thick. Brush with butter. Combine raisins,

½ *cup seedless raisins*
⅓ *cup coarsely chopped pecans*
⅓ *cup firmly packed dark brown sugar*
1 *teaspoon ground cinnamon*

nuts, sugar, and cinnamon; sprinkle over dough. Starting with the wide side of oblong, roll up dough jelly-roll fashion. Cut into slices about 1 inch thick. Pick up each strip, holding one end in each hand, and twist tightly in opposite direction. Place about 1½ inches apart on greased cookie sheets. Cover with greased waxed paper and a towel and let rise in a warm place (85° F.) until doubled, about 30 minutes. Bake in a 375° F. oven about 18 minutes. Makes about 2 dozen bow ties.

⤳ Schnecken

½ *cup milk*
½ *cup sugar*
1 *teaspoon salt*
½ *cup warm water*
2 *packages active dry yeast*
4 *cups sifted all-purpose flour*
1 *whole egg*
1 *egg yolk*
10 *tablespoons melted butter*
1½ *cups sugar*
2 *teaspoons ground cinnamon*
⅔ *cup seeded raisins*
⅓ *cup chopped walnuts*

Scald milk; stir in the ½ cup sugar and the salt. Cool until lukewarm. Pour warm water into a large bowl; sprinkle with yeast and stir until dissolved. Add cooled milk mixture. Add ½ of the flour and beat until smooth. Pour into greased bowl; cover with damp cloth and let rise in a warm place (85° F.) until double in bulk, about 1 hour. Beat egg and egg yolk together slightly and stir into yeast dough. Add 4 tablespoons of the melted butter and enough of the remaining flour to handle easily. Turn out on lightly floured board or pastry cloth and knead, adding enough of the remaining flour to make a smooth dough. Knead until smooth and elastic, about 10 minutes. Shape dough into a ball and place in greased bowl. Turn once to bring greased side up. Cover with a damp cloth and let rise in warm place (85° F.) until double in bulk, about 1 hour. Punch down and turn out on floured board. Halve dough and roll ½ into a 14-x-9-inch rectangle. Brush with 2 tablespoons of the remaining melted butter. Mix the 1½ cups sugar and cinnamon; sprinkle ⅓ over the dough. Sprinkle with ½ of the raisins and nuts. Beginning with the wide side, roll up tightly in jelly-roll fashion. Pinch edges to seal. Cut roll into 1½-inch slices. Repeat with the remaining dough. Place slices, cut-side down, in a greased 13-x-9-x-2-inch pan. Brush with the remaining 2 tablespoons butter, and sprinkle with the remaining sugar-and-cinnamon mixture. Cover with greased waxed paper and a towel and let rise about 1 hour. Heat oven to 350° F. Bake rolls 35 to 40 minutes. Cool in pan a few minutes; then invert on flat tray. Makes about 1½ dozen rolls.

⋙ Brioches

¾ *cup lukewarm water*
1 *package active dry yeast*
½ *cup sugar*
½ *teaspoon salt*
3 *whole eggs*
1 *egg, separated*
½ *cup softened butter or*
   margarine
3½ *cups sifted all-purpose*
   flour
1 *tablespoon sugar*

Pour water into the large bowl of the electric mixer; add yeast and stir until dissolved. Add the ½ cup sugar, salt, whole eggs, egg yolk, butter, and 2 cups of the flour. Beat on low speed of the electric mixer for ½ minute until blended. Increase speed to medium and beat 10 minutes, scraping bowl occasionally with a rubber spatula. Stir in the remaining flour, mixing until smooth. Scrape dough from sides of bowl. Cover with a damp cloth and let rise in a warm place (about 85° F.) for 1 hour or until double in bulk. Stir down dough by beating 25 strokes with a wooden spoon. Cover bowl with plastic wrap and refrigerate 8 hours or overnight. Stir down dough. Divide in half and place one portion on a well-floured board. Keep remaining half of dough covered in refrigerator. Shape dough into a roll 8 inches long; cut into 16 slices about ½ inch thick. Shape 12 of the slices into balls with well-floured hands, and place in greased 2½-inch muffin cups. Flatten tops of balls and make a slight indentation in center of each. Cut each of the remaining 4 slices into 3 equal parts and shape each piece into a ball; place one in each indentation in the larger balls. Make 12 more brioches with the remaining dough. Cover with a damp cloth and let rise in a warm place about 40 minutes, or until double in bulk. Heat oven to 375° F. Beat the egg white and the 1 tablespoon sugar together until blended; brush over rolls. Bake 15 to 20 minutes, or until golden brown. Makes 2 dozen brioches.

⋙ French Croissants

1 *cup milk, scalded*
1 *tablespoon butter or*
   margarine
1 *tablespoon sugar*
¾ *teaspoon salt*
1 *package active dry yeast*
¼ *cup lukewarm water*
About 3 *cups sifted all-purpose*
   flour
1 *cup softened butter*
Cream

Combine hot milk, butter, sugar, and salt in a bowl. Cool to lukewarm. Sprinkle yeast into lukewarm water and stir until dissolved. Add to warm milk mixture. Stir in enough flour to make a dough that will handle easily. Turn dough out onto a lightly floured board or pastry cloth. Knead about 8 to 10 minutes until smooth and elastic. Place in greased bowl; turn once to bring greased side up. Cover with a damp cloth; let rise in a warm place (85° F.) until double in bulk, about 1 hour. Punch down with the fist and chill in refrigerator at least 1 hour. Turn out on lightly floured board and pat and roll into a 16-x-9-x-⅛-inch rectangle. Spread with 4 tablespoons of the softened butter. Starting with a narrow side of the rectangle, fold 1 side toward the center; then fold other side over it to make 3 layers. Give dough a quarter turn; roll out again, spread with 4 tablespoons of the butter, and fold into thirds. Repeat twice more. Wrap dough in waxed paper and a towel and refrigerate for 2 hours. Roll dough out on a lightly floured board into an 18-x-18-inch square. Cut into nine 6-inch squares. Cut each square in half diagonally, making 2 triangles. Starting with the wide side, roll each triangle loosely toward the point. Pinch the dough to seal the pointed side to the roll. Shape into crescents and place on a lightly greased cookie sheet. Chill 20 minutes. Heat oven to 375° F. Brush rolls with cream and bake 18 to 20 minutes, or until lightly browned. Makes about 18 croissants.

🌿 Fastnacht

4½ cups sifted all-purpose
    flour
⅓ cup sugar
½ teaspoon salt
1 package active dry yeast
¼ cup softened butter or
    margarine
1 cup very hot water
    (approximately 145° F.)
1 egg
Vegetable oil for frying
Cinnamon sugar or
    confectioners' sugar

Sift and measure 4½ cups flour. In the large bowl of an electric mixer, mix 1¼ cups flour, sugar, salt, and yeast. Add softened butter. Gradually add hot water to dry ingredients and beat 2 minutes at medium speed of the electric mixer, scraping bowl occasionally with a rubber spatula. Add egg and ½ cup of the flour, or enough flour to make a thick batter. Beat at high speed 2 minutes, scraping bowl occasionally. With a spoon gradually add enough flour to make a stiff dough, scraping bowl occasionally. Turn out onto a floured board and knead 8 to 10 minutes, until dough is smooth and elastic, adding flour to board as needed to prevent dough from sticking. Shape dough into a ball and place in a greased bowl. Turn once to bring greased side up. Cover with a damp cloth and let rise in a warm place (85° F.) until double in bulk, about 1 hour. Punch dough and turn onto a lightly floured board and knead a few minutes. Roll out into an 8-x-16-inch rectangle. Cut into 2-inch squares. Cut a slit about ¼ inch deep on the top of each square. Place on two ungreased cookie sheets leaving 2 to 3 inches between each square. Cover; let rise in a warm place (85° F.) until double in bulk, about 45 minutes. In a heavy saucepan heat 3 inches of oil over moderately high heat (about 375° F.) to a temperature of 375° F. on a deep-fat-frying thermometer. Fry fastnacht a few at a time 2 to 3 minutes on each side or until golden brown. Drain on paper towels. Sprinkle with cinnamon sugar or confectioners' sugar. Makes 32 fastnacht.

❧ Kuchen

¼ cup warm water
1 package active dry yeast
¾ cup milk, scalded
1 cup sifted all-purpose flour
½ cup butter or margarine
1 cup sugar
4 eggs
Grated peel of 1 lemon
1 cup seeded raisins
2¼ cups sifted all-purpose flour

Pour water into a large mixing bowl. Sprinkle yeast over water and stir until dissolved. Add milk and the 1 cup flour and mix thoroughly. Cover with a damp cloth and let rise in a warm place (85° F.) until mixture is bubbly, about 30 to 45 minutes. Work butter in a bowl until creamy; add sugar gradually and beat until light and fluffy. Add eggs, one at a time, beating well after each addition. Add the egg mixture to yeast mixture and blend well. Stir in lemon peel, raisins, and the remaining 2¼ cups flour. Generously butter a 3-quart fluted pan with center tube. Place dough in pan; cover with greased waxed paper and a towel and let rise in a warm place until double in bulk, about 1 hour. Heat oven to 350° F. Bake cake 40 to 45 minutes. Cool slightly; remove from pan and cool on a wire rack. Makes 1 cake.

❧ Moravian Sugar Cake (or Coffeecake)

½ pound potatoes, peeled
1 package active dry yeast
¼ cup warm water
¾ cup butter and lard or shortening, mixed
1 scant cup sugar (about 1 tablespoon less)
2 eggs
1 cup potato water, warm
2 teaspoons salt
5 to 7 cups sifted all-purpose flour
2 tablespoons butter, cut up
1 cup firmly packed dark brown sugar
1 teaspoon ground cinnamon
½ cup light cream

Cook potatoes in water to cover until tender; drain, reserving 1 cup of the water. Mash potatoes and measure out 1 cup to use in recipe. Add yeast to the ¼ cup warm water and stir until dissolved. Cream the ¾ cup butter mixture and sugar together well; beat in eggs one at a time. Mix in mashed potatoes, potato water, salt, and yeast. Gradually add flour, mixing in enough to make a soft, sticky dough. Cover bowl with a damp towel and let rise in a warm place (85° F.) until double in bulk, about 2 to 3 hours. Punch down and pat into 2 well-greased 13-x-9-x-2-inch pans. Cover with a damp towel and let rise again until double in bulk, about 1½ hours. Heat oven to 400° F. With a sharp knife punch small holes in top of dough and insert bits of butter. Sprinkle with brown sugar and cinnamon. Dribble cream over top. Bake 20 to 25 minutes, or until brown. Cake reheats very satisfactorily. Makes 2 coffeecakes.

YEAST BREAD

❧ Santa's Bread

1 cup sugar
½ cup soft shortening
2 teaspoons salt
1¾ cups milk, scalded
½ cup warm water
2 packages active dry yeast
2 eggs, slightly beaten
7¾ cups sifted all-purpose flour
2 cups mixed candied fruits and peels
1 cup dark seedless raisins
1½ teaspoons finely crushed cardamom seed
Melted shortening
Confectioners' Glaze (recipe follows)
Candied citron and cherries

Place sugar, shortening, salt, and milk in a large mixing bowl; stir until shortening is melted. Cool to lukewarm. Pour warm water into a small bowl; sprinkle in yeast and stir until dissolved. Add eggs and yeast to milk mixture and mix until blended. Add half the flour and beat with a spoon until smooth. Stir in fruits and peels, raisins, and cardamom. Add enough of the remaining flour to handle easily. Turn out on a lightly floured board or pastry cloth and knead, adding enough of the remaining flour to make a soft dough. Knead about 10 minutes, until smooth and elastic. Shape dough into a ball and place in a greased bowl; brush with melted shortening. Cover and let rise in a warm place (85° F.) until double in bulk, about 1½ to 2 hours. Punch down and divide dough into 3 equal portions. Shape each into a loaf and place each in a greased 8½-x-4½-x-2½-inch loaf pan. Cover and let rise in a warm place until almost double in bulk, about 1 hour. Heat oven to 450° F. Bake 10 minutes. Reduce heat to 350° F. and bake 35 to 40 minutes longer. Cool slightly and remove from pans. Place on wire racks. When thoroughly cooled, frost with Confectioners' Glaze and garnish with citron and cherries. Makes 3 loaves.

Confectioners' Glaze

Beat together 4½ cups confectioners' sugar, 6 tablespoons hot milk, and ½ teaspoon vanilla extract. Spread on cooled bread.

❧ Czechoslovakian or Bohemian Kolacky

1 cup milk
2 cups butter or margarine, or a mixture of both
1½ cups sugar
2 packages active dry yeast
½ cup warm water
7 cups sifted all-purpose flour
1 teaspoon salt
6 egg yolks
Poppy-Seed Filling or Nut Filling (recipes follow)
Confectioners' sugar

Heat milk in a saucepan over moderately low heat (about 225° F.) until small bubbles appear around edges; add butter and continue heating until butter is melted, stirring frequently. Remove from heat; mix in sugar and stir until dissolved. Cool until lukewarm. Add yeast to the warm water and stir until dissolved. Sift 2 cups of the flour and the salt into the large bowl of an electric mixer. Add yeast, milk mixture, and egg yolks and mix, using the low speed of the electric mixer, until blended. Gradually add the remaining 5 cups flour, continuing to mix at a low speed (if batter climbs up the beater, scrape it down with a rubber spatula). When all flour is added, beat for 5 minutes. Cover with a damp cloth and let rise in a warm place (85° F.) until almost double in bulk, about 4 hours. When dough has risen, do not punch down, but spoon out portions of dough onto a well-floured wooden board. Sprinkle dough with a little flour and pat out with well-floured fingertips to a thickness of about ⅜ inch. Cut into rounds about 3 inches in diameter. Lift from board with a wide spatula and place on a well-greased cookie sheet, leaving about 2 inches between each round. With the finger, make an indentation in center of each round and fill with a tablespoon of filling. Push in edges of dough to make a wall around filling. Cover with greased waxed paper and a tea towel and let rise in a warm place for about 1 hour, or until double in bulk. Heat oven to 375° F. and bake 20 to 30 minutes, or until golden brown. Dust with confectioners' sugar while still warm. Makes about 3½ dozen kolacky.

Poppy-Seed Filling

2 cups ground poppy seeds
1⅓ cups milk
1 teaspoon ground cinnamon
1 cup sugar
½ teaspoon ground cloves
½ teaspoon ground mace
⅔ cup seedless raisins
⅔ cup chopped walnuts or other nuts

Place all ingredients in a saucepan over moderately low heat (about 225° F.) until sugar is dissolved and ingredients are blended. Cool before using. Makes about 3½ cups.

Nut Filling

1 pound walnuts, ground
¾ to 1 cup warm water
¾ cup sugar

Place ingredients in a saucepan over moderately low heat (about 225° F.) until sugar is dissolved and ingredients are blended. Cool before using as a filling. Makes about 2¾ cups.

❧ Christmas Stollen

1½ packages active dry yeast
½ cup warm water
Pinch of salt
1 tablespoon sugar

In a large mixing bowl, mix yeast and warm water and stir until yeast is dissolved. Mix in the salt, the 1 tablespoon sugar, and the ½ cup flour; cover with a damp cloth and let rise in a warm place (85° F.) for 10 minutes.

½ cup sifted all-purpose
    flour
½ cup milk
¾ cup butter
½ cup sugar
2 egg yolks
1 whole egg
Grated peel of 1 lemon
2 cups sifted all-purpose
    flour
½ teaspoon salt
2 cups sifted all-purpose
    flour
3 ounces (½ cup) chopped
    mixed candied fruits and
    peels
1 ounce (¼ cup) slivered
    citron
3 ounces (½ cup) seedless
    raisins
1 ounce (2 tablespoons)
    dried currants
3 ounces (½ cup, heaping)
    slivered, blanched
    almonds
1 tablespoon flour
1 egg, slightly beaten
¼ cup soft sweet butter
Sugar

Meanwhile, heat milk over moderately low heat (about 225° F.) until small bubbles appear around edges. Remove from heat. Add the ¾ cup butter and the ½ cup sugar and stir until butter is melted. Cool to lukewarm. Beat egg yolks and whole egg together and mix into yeast mixture with lemon peel. Using an electric mixer, gradually add the 2 cups flour, the ½ teaspoon salt, and the warm milk alternately to yeast mixture, using a moderate speed. Beat for about 5 minutes. Gradually add the remaining 2 cups flour, lowering speed of mixer as batter gets thicker. It will be necessary to mix in some of the flour with a wooden spoon. After all the flour is added, continue beating until dough begins to leave sides of bowl. (This will not take long if dough has been beaten enough during the first addition of flour.) Cover with a damp cloth and let rise in a warm place for about 1 hour, or until double in bulk. Dredge fruits and nuts with the 1 tablespoon flour. Punch down dough and mix in fruit mixture. Cover with a damp cloth and let rise in a warm place for about 40 minutes, or until double in bulk. Turn out on a well-floured board and punch down. Divide dough in half and shape each portion into an oblong about 12-x-4 inches. Place each loaf on a large greased cookie sheet. Brush tops with slightly beaten egg. Cover with a damp towel and put in a warm place to rise for 30 to 40 minutes, or until double in bulk. Heat oven to 350° F. Bake loaves for 20 to 25 minutes, or until golden brown. Remove from oven; brush with softened sweet butter and sprinkle with sugar. Cool on wire cake racks. Makes 2 loaves.

✑ Italian Easter Bread

5 cups sifted all-purpose
    flour
½ cup sugar
2 tablespoons grated lemon
    peel
1 teaspoon salt
2 packages active dry yeast
½ cup milk
½ cup water
½ cup soft butter or
    margarine
2 eggs

Sift and measure 5 cups flour. In the large bowl of an electric mixer, mix 1½ cups flour, sugar, lemon peel, salt, and yeast. Place milk, water, and butter in a small saucepan over moderately low heat (about 225° F.) and heat until liquids are warm (butter will be entirely melted and temperature should be about 125° F.). Gradually add liquid to dry ingredients and beat 2 minutes at medium speed of the electric mixer, scraping bowl occasionally with a rubber spatula. Add eggs and ¾ cup of the flour, or enough flour to make a thick batter. Beat at high speed 2 minutes, scraping bowl occasionally. With a spoon, gradually stir in just enough

½ *cup white raisins (optional)*
12 *raw eggs in shell, colored with pure food Easter-egg coloring*
Egg Glaze (recipe on page 683)

of the remaining flour to make a soft dough, scraping bowl occasionally. Turn out onto a floured board and knead for 8 to 10 minutes, until dough is smooth and elastic, adding flour to board as needed to prevent dough from sticking. Shape dough into a ball and place in a greased bowl. Turn once to bring greased side up. Cover with a damp cloth and let rise in a warm place (85° F.) until double in bulk, about 1 to 1½ hours. Punch down and turn out onto a lightly floured board. Knead in raisins. Cover and let rise 15 minutes. Divide dough into 4 equal portions and roll each into an even 28-inch rope. On a greased cookie sheet, loosely twist 2 of the ropes together 6 times and bring ends together to form a circle. Seal ends firmly. Between the twists of the ropes, shape 6 nests and insert a colored egg in each nest. Make a second ring with the remaining ropes and eggs. Cover with a sheet of greased waxed paper and a tea towel and let rise in a warm place until double in bulk, about 30 to 45 minutes. Heat oven to 375° F. Brush ring with Egg Glaze, being careful not to brush the eggs. Bake 25 to 30 minutes, until golden brown. Serve the bread hot; cut between the eggs and serve each person an egg and the bread around it. Serves 12.

Colored Easter Eggs

The eggs in the Italian Easter Bread are used uncooked; they cook as the bread bakes. However, eggs to be used for other purposes should be hard-cooked before they are colored. Hot-water dyes work faster. Prepare the dye solution as directed on the package. Dip fresh, scrubbed white eggs until the desired shade is reached.

Russian Kulich

3¾ *cups sifted all-purpose flour*
¼ *cup sugar*
1 *teaspoon salt*
1 *package active dry yeast*
½ *cup milk*
½ *cup water*
¼ *cup butter or margarine*
1 *egg*
½ *teaspoon vanilla extract*
½ *cup seedless raisins*

Sift and measure 3¾ cups flour. In the large bowl of an electric mixer, mix 1 cup flour, sugar, salt, and yeast. Place milk, water, and butter in a small saucepan over moderately low heat (about 225° F.) and heat until liquids are warm (butter will be entirely melted and temperature should be about 125° F.). Gradually add liquid to dry ingredients and beat 2 minutes at medium speed of the electric mixer, scraping bowl occasionally with a rubber spatula. Add egg, vanilla, and ¾ cup flour, or enough to make a thick batter. Beat at high speed 2 minutes, scraping bowl occasionally. With a spoon,

¼ *cup chopped, blanched almonds*
Lemon Icing (recipe follows)

gradually stir in just enough of the remaining flour to make a stiff dough, scraping bowl occasionally. Turn out onto a floured board and knead 8 to 10 minutes, until dough is smooth and elastic, adding flour to board as needed to prevent dough from sticking. Shape into a ball and place in a greased bowl. Turn once to bring greased side up. Cover with a damp cloth and let rise in a warm place (85° F.) until double in bulk, about 1 to 1½ hours. Punch down and turn out onto a lightly floured board and knead in raisins and almonds. Divide into 2 equal portions. Shape each into a ball. Grease two 1-pound coffee cans and press half of the dough in each. Cover with greased waxed paper and a damp cloth and let rise 30 to 40 minutes, or until top of dough is slightly above rim of can. Heat oven to 375° F. Bake 25 to 30 minutes, or until golden brown. Cool slightly and remove from cans. While still warm, frost with Lemon Icing. Makes 2 loaves.

Lemon Icing

Mix *2 cups confectioners' sugar, 3 tablespoons warm water, 1 teaspoon lemon juice, 1 teaspoon grated lemon peel,* and *a few drops yellow food coloring* together until smooth. Spoon frosting onto top of loaf and let it run down sides.

CHAPTER XX

FRUITS

Artists, children, chefs, dieters, nutritionists, doctors—everybody loves fruits because they are beautiful to look at and delicious to eat. A bright bowl of fresh fruit on the coffee table, a pretty jar of dried fruits, or a chilled can of fruit in the refrigerator invites the kind of nibbling no mother can object to and it helps children form healthful food choices.

Although most fresh fruits have peak seasons (see pages 32 to 40), with improved storage and transportation conditions there is an increasing supply of fresh fruits in the market year-round. What is not available fresh will be conveniently available in canned, frozen, or dried form. If you have access to locally grown fruits, which will be relatively inexpensive in season, you can freeze or can them yourself (see pages 67 to 70).

Fresh fruits are perishable. When you shop, select only unblemished, mature fruits that look fresh and firm. Buy only the amount of ripe fruit you will use within three or four days. Many fresh fruits are picked when they are mature but not fully ripened. These fruits can be ripened at home, at room temperature. Once ripe, fresh fruits should be refrigerated to halt further ripening and prevent spoilage.

Frozen fruits should be picked up when you buy the frozen vegetables—last stop in the market. Buy them only from a frozen-food case that is not loaded above the safety line and that is kept at 0° F. or below. Never buy a package of frozen fruit that feels soggy; it is partially thawed. Get frozen fruits into your own freezer as soon as you get home. If the trip is a long one or if you plan other stops, take along an insulated bag to protect all frozen foods. Judge the quantity you will need by your recipe or by the number of servings you want; serving quantities are usually given in the label information.

Canned fruits come in a variety of sizes, shapes, and syrups. Look for descriptive information on the can label. It will tell you the form the fruit is in—sliced, whole, halves. It will describe the juice. *Light* or *heavy syrup* indicates the amount of sugar in the syrup; *water-pack* means no sugar has been added. It may tell you the number of servings and the size of the servings or the number of pieces. It may have a grade label—A, B, or C—which indicates the quality, size, color, and uniformity of the fruit in the can. A is the most select grade. Choose the grade according to the use you plan for the fruit. Store canned fruits on a cool, dry shelf, or refrigerate in the can if you plan to serve them as chilled fruit. Many canned fruits have been especially prepared and seasoned for use as relishes, garnishes, and ready-to-use pie fillings.

Dried fruits. Several popular fruits are available year-round in dried form (see pages 717 and 718).

Apples

Apples may be purchased fresh; canned in applesauce, slices, rings, or whole baked; or dried in slices. Fresh apples are sold prepackaged or loose by the pound, peck, half bushel, or bushel (approximately fifty pounds). Apples are prepackaged in plastic bags or in pulp-board trays with a plastic overwrap. Loose apples can be bought in quantities smaller than 1 pound; three medium-sized apples equal a pound.

To buy fresh, look for well-shaped apples that are free from blemishes or soft spots. Choose those that are well-colored for the particular variety. Choose the variety of apple that suits the purpose for which you plan to use it. On page 34, you will find a listing of commonly available apples and their best uses.

Store small quantities of apples in the crisping unit of the refrigerator. Apples packaged in plastic bags may be kept in the refrigerator in the bag. Larger quantities should be kept in a well-ventilated, cool area.

To core whole apples, insert an apple corer or a sharp-pointed knife halfway into stem end, aiming toward the blossom end. Make a complete turn. Remove half the core. Now push corer halfway into the opposite end; push halfway through. Make a complete turn and remove the rest of the core.

When a large quantity of sliced apples is being prepared, sprinkle slices with lemon juice or an ascorbic acid (vitamin C) mixture, as directed on the package. This will keep the slices from turning brown.

You will find many apple recipes throughout this book; see the index for a complete listing.

❧ *Rosy Baked Apples*

6 *medium-sized red baking apples*
¼ *cup coarsely broken walnuts*
¾ *cup sugar*
1 *cup water*
¼ *teaspoon ground nutmeg*
¼ *cup red cinnamon candies*
Heavy or light cream

Heat oven to 350° F. Wash and core apples. Starting at the stem end, pare apples ⅓ of the way down. Arrange apples in shallow baking pan with pared side up. Fill centers with nuts. Combine sugar, water, nutmeg, and cinnamon candies in a saucepan. Bring to a boil over moderate heat (about 250° F.) and cook 10 minutes. Pour mixture over apples. Bake uncovered about 45 minutes, until apples are soft. Spoon syrup from pan over apples frequently. Chill. Serve with plain cream. Serves 6.

❧ *Glazed Baked Apples*

6 *large red baking apples*
1¼ *cups sugar*
1 *cup water*
Few drops red food coloring
½ *teaspoon ground cinnamon*
½ *teaspoon ground nutmeg*
1 *tablespoon butter or margarine*
Heavy or light cream (optional)

Wash and core apples. Starting at the stem end, pare them about ⅓ of the way down. Put the peelings and cores into a medium-sized saucepan. Add 1 cup of the sugar, the water, and food coloring. Bring mixture to a boil over moderate heat (about 250° F.), stirring until sugar is dissolved. Cook, uncovered, for 10 minutes. Heat oven to 375° F. Arrange apples, stem end up, in a shallow baking dish. Combine the remaining ¼ cup sugar, cinnamon, and nutmeg. Spoon some of the sugar mixture into the center of each apple. Dot each with butter. Strain syrup. Baste apples with some of the syrup and pour the rest of it around them in the pan. Cover tightly and bake 30 to 45 minutes, or until apples are almost fork-tender. Remove cover and continue to bake, basting frequently with syrup in pan, until apples are very tender, about 20 minutes longer. Serve warm or chilled, with cream if desired. Serves 6.

❧ *Strained Applesauce*

6 *large cooking apples*
1 *cup water*

Wash apples and cut them into quarters. Combine apples, water, and lemon slices in a 4-quart saucepan.

2 slices lemon with peel
½ to 1 cup sugar
⅛ teaspoon ground nutmeg
¼ teaspoon ground cinnamon

Cover tightly and cook over moderately low heat (about 225° F.) 15 to 20 minutes, or until apples are tender. Add a little more water, if necessary, toward the end of the cooking period to prevent apples from sticking to the pan. Turn apples into a coarse strainer. Set strainer in a bowl. Using the back of a wooden spoon, rub apples through strainer until only the skins and lemon peel remain. Or use a food mill. Add sugar to taste, stirring until sugar is dissolved. Stir in nutmeg and cinnamon. Serve warm or chilled. Serves 6 to 8.

Breakfast Parfait

⅓ cup low-fat plain yogurt
⅓ cup uncreamed cottage cheese
⅓ cup unsweetened applesauce
¼ cup fresh orange segments
½ small, unpeeled apple, cored and chopped
½ medium banana, peeled and sliced
¼ cup wheat germ
2 tablespoons chopped nuts

Mix yogurt, cottage cheese and applesauce in a bowl. In 2 parfait glasses or other tall, slender glasses layer yogurt mixture with fruit, wheat germ and nuts. Top with some of the wheat germ and nuts. Serves 2.

Red Cinnamon Apple Rings

5 medium or large cooking apples
2 cups water
2 cups sugar
½ teaspoon red food coloring
2 to 3 sticks cinnamon, about 2½ inches long

Peel and core apples. Cut them into ¾-inch-thick rings. Combine water, sugar, food coloring, and cinnamon in a large skillet. Stir over moderately low heat (about 225° F.) until sugar is dissolved. Cook 10 minutes. Arrange apple rings in syrup. Cook, basting frequently with syrup in skillet, until apples are tender, about 6 to 10 minutes. Remove apples from syrup and use hot as garnish for meats or chilled as garnish for salads. Makes about 15 apple rings.

Apricots

Apricots may be purchased fresh, canned, peeled or unpeeled, whole or in halves, or dried in halves. To buy fresh, look for plump fruit that has a uniform, golden orange color. Ripe apricots will yield to gentle pressure on the skin. After purchasing, keep them in the refrigerator.

To prepare apricots, wash the fruit and eat it fresh, unpeeled, or plunge the fruit into boiling water for one or two minutes. Spoon it out and plunge it into cold water; the skin will then slip off easily. Cut it in half, remove the pit, and eat it raw or cook as the recipe directs.

Other apricot recipes appear throughout this book. See the index for a complete listing.

❧ *Apricot Parfait*

2 **16-ounce cans unpeeled apricot halves**
2 **egg whites**
¼ **teaspoon salt**
¼ **cup sugar**
Few grains ground nutmeg
2 **teaspoons lemon juice**
⅛ **teaspoon almond extract**
1 **pressurized can ready-whipped cream**
6 **pecan halves**

Drain apricots. Reserve 12 apricot halves and press remaining halves through a fine strainer (makes about 1 cup pulp). Beat egg whites and salt until soft peaks form. Gradually add sugar and beat until stiff peaks form. Add nutmeg, lemon juice, and almond extract to egg whites. Gradually add sieved apricots, beating with a rotary beater until blended. Spoon a layer of the apricot whip into each of 6 parfait glasses. Follow with an apricot half and a layer of ready-whipped cream in each. Repeat the 3 layers and top with a layer of apricot whip. Garnish with cream and a pecan. Serve immediately. Serves 6.

Avocados

Avocados are available most of the year; the California crop is on the market in the early months of the year and the Florida crop in the fall. Most of the varieties of this delicious fruit are pear-shaped but some are almost spherical. Some have a leathery, textured skin and others have a glossy, smooth skin. The skin color is usually some shade of green, but certain varieties turn purplish or brown as they ripen. These variations in appearance do not affect quality.

For immediate use, select avocados that yield to gentle pressure when you squeeze them between the palms of your hands. For later use, choose fruits that do not yield to the squeeze test. Avoid avocados that have dark sunken spots or cracked or broken surfaces. Irregular smooth brown markings are normal to some avocados.

To store avocados: if they are firm and unripened, keep them at room temperature until they yield to the squeeze test. Then refrigerate and use within a few days. Refrigerate ripe, soft avocados immediately.

To prepare an avocado, cut the avocado lengthwise or crosswise all the way around the shell, cutting down to the pit. Hold the avocado between your palms and twist it gently to separate the halves. To loosen the pit imbedded in one of the halves, rap it sharply with a knife, twist it slightly, lift it out, and discard. Peel off the thin green skin from each half. To slice, place halves, hollow side down, on a cutting board and cut into lengthwise or crosswise slices. If not to be served immediately, dip slices in lemon juice to prevent darkening. If you are using only a portion of an avocado, leave the pit in the remainder (it will prevent darkening) and wrap the unused portion in foil or plastic wrap and refrigerate.

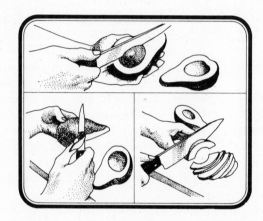

Avocados are usually served raw in salads or in halves to be eaten out of the shell with a squeezing of lemon juice or a bit of French dressing or mayonnaise. Or the halves can be stuffed with crab salad or chicken salad for a luncheon dish. When you use the halves in this fashion, do not peel the avocado. Ripe, mashed avocado is the basis for a marvelous dip called guacamole (see page 105), and you'll find slices of avocado cooked in several dishes—for instance, Chicken Breasts in Wine (see page 374).

Bananas

Look for firm, unblemished fruit that has a good clear color. You may find bananas in the market at several different stages of ripeness, which is indicated by the skin color. Bananas with green tips are partially ripe; these are ready for frying, baking, or broiling, but need to be ripened at room temperature for a few days before they are most flavorful for eating raw. When bananas are all yellow, they are ready to eat raw, to cook, or to use as a baking ingredient. Yellow bananas that are flecked with brown have developed their full flavor; many people prefer this degree of ripeness for eating and baking. These fully ripe bananas are best for infant feeding.

To store bananas, keep them at room temperature until they have reached the desired degree of ripeness. Then, in spite of all you've heard, refrigerate them to halt further ripening and prevent spoilage. Use refrigerated bananas within a few days.

To prepare bananas, peel and then slice to serve alone or combined with other fruits, or mash if recipe directs. Serve immediately or dip banana slices in an ascorbic acid (vitamin C) preparation or in acid fruit juices, such as lemon or pineapple juice, to prevent darkening.

Other banana recipes appear throughout this book. See index for complete listing.

❧ Baked Bananas

4 *firm green-tipped bananas*
2 *tablespoons melted butter or margarine*
Salt

Heat oven to 375° F. Peel bananas; place in a well-greased baking dish. Brush well with melted butter; sprinkle lightly with salt. Bake 18 to 20 minutes. Serve hot with ham, pork, or poultry. Serves 4.

Dessert Baked Bananas

After brushing bananas with the butter, sprinkle with *1 tablespoon lemon juice, 3 tablespoons light brown sugar,* and *¾ teaspoon ground cinnamon.* Bake as directed above and serve with *sweetened whipped cream* or *ice cream.*

❧ Bananas Flambé

3 *firm green-tipped bananas*
2 *tablespoons flour*
¼ *cup butter or margarine*
1 *tablespoon lemon juice*
3 *tablespoons confectioners' sugar*
¼ *cup light rum, warmed*

Peel bananas; cut in half lengthwise and then in half crosswise. Coat with flour. Heat 2 tablespoons of the butter in the blazer of a chafing dish. Place over high heat of alcohol burner and cook until butter is melted. Add bananas and cook until lightly browned; turn to brown both sides. Add the remaining 2 tablespoons butter as needed. Sprinkle with lemon juice and sugar. Pour rum over bananas and ignite. Serve immediately. Serves 4.

Berries

Except for strawberries, fresh berries are usually available only during peak seasons. All berries are available canned, and many of them are excellent frozen. In the frozen form, the berries may be packed in sugar syrup or frozen whole without sugar added. Consult the chart on page 32 to learn when various berries are in season.

Following is a list of what to look for when shopping for fresh berries: *Blueberries* that are plump and firm and have a dark blue color with a silvery bloom. *Blackberries, raspberries, boysenberries, and loganberries* that have a bright, clean appearance and a uniform good color. The individual small cells that make up these berries should be plump and tender. Avoid wet-looking or moldy berries. *Gooseberries* that are pale green in color, firm, and dry with no blemishes. *Strawberries* with a full, red color and firm flesh with the green cap stem attached. Berries should be dry and clean.

Do not wash berries until you are ready to use them. Pick over the berries, discarding any unripened or soft ones. Spread remainder in a shallow baking or storage dish and refrigerate, uncovered.

To prepare berries for serving or cooking, put them in a large sieve or colander and rinse them under a gentle stream of cold water. Hull or remove stems when necessary. Sprinkle fresh berries with sugar if they are tart. Serve with cream if desired.

Other berry recipes appear throughout this book. See index for a complete listing of them.

Orange-Flavored Strawberries

3 pints strawberries
1 large orange
2 tablespoons orange-flavored liqueur
2 tablespoons brandy
¼ cup sugar

Rinse the strawberries quickly; hull and dry them thoroughly on paper towels. Place strawberries in a serving bowl and finely grate the rind of the orange over them. Cover bowl with plastic wrap and chill until ready to serve. Squeeze the orange; combine the juice with the liqueur and brandy. At serving time sprinkle sugar and orange juice mixture over the strawberries. Toss gently but thoroughly and serve immediately. Serves 6.

Strawberries Romanoff

1 quart strawberries
¼ cup confectioners' sugar

Wash strawberries; hull and cut into halves. Sprinkle with sugar and the 1 tablespoon Cointreau; stir gently

1 tablespoon Cointreau
½ cup chilled heavy cream
2 cups softened vanilla ice
   cream
¼ cup Cointreau

and chill at least 30 minutes. At serving time, whip cream until stiff. Beat ice cream with a spoon until smooth and creamy; fold in whipped cream and the ¼ cup Cointreau. Drain strawberries and spoon into serving bowl; top with cream mixture and serve immediately. Serves 8 to 10.

Cherries

Although cherries come in many varieties, they may be generally classified as being either red sour cherries or sweet cherries. The red sours are for cooking in pies, puddings, and cakes; the sweet red, white, or black cherries are best for eating, although they are often used in recipes also. Both varieties are available either fresh or canned.

To buy, look for bright, glossy, plump cherries with fresh-looking stems.

To store cherries: wash them gently in cold water and dry them on a clean tea towel or paper towels. Do not remove stems if you plan to serve them on a fruit tray. Refrigerate.

To pit cherries, use the tip of a floating-blade vegetable parer. Force it into the stem end of the cherry and pry up the pit. A cherry pitter works very well too.

Other cherry recipes appear throughout this book. See the index for a complete listing.

Cherry Floating Island

2 eggs, separated
Pinch of salt
¼ cup sugar
3 cups milk
3 whole eggs
½ cup sugar
⅛ teaspoon salt
1½ teaspoons vanilla extract
2 cups pitted sweet cherries

Combine the 2 egg whites and pinch of salt in a bowl. Beat with rotary beater until soft peaks form. Gradually add the ¼ cup sugar, beating constantly until stiff peaks form. Pour milk into a large skillet; place over low heat (about 200° F.) and bring just to simmering point. Drop egg white mixture by tablespoonfuls into milk; there should be 6 meringues. Cook slowly, uncovered, until firm, about 5 minutes. Lift meringues from milk and drain on paper toweling. Reserve milk. Beat the 3 eggs and the 2 yolks slightly; add the ½ cup sugar and the ⅛ teaspoon salt. Stir in the 3 cups reserved milk; cook mixture in the top of a double boiler over hot—not boiling—water, stirring constantly, until mixture is thick enough to coat a metal spoon. Remove from heat, cool slightly, and add vanilla. Place cherries in bottom of a 2-quart serving dish; cover with custard and top with meringues. Chill. Serves 6.

Coconut

Fresh coconut is not always available, but when it is, it's worth taking the time to prepare, for it is richly flavorful. To buy, look for a coconut with no cracks in the outer shell. A ripe coconut should sound full of liquid when shaken and feel heavy for its size. Canned and packaged flaked and shredded coconut are available year-round.

To store coconut, keep opened canned or packaged coconut covered in the refrigerator. Fresh coconut, once cracked and cut or grated, should be refrigerated, covered.

To open a fresh coconut, puncture the three "eyes," or indentations, on one end of the shell with an ice pick or a heavy long nail and a hammer. Drain off the liquid and reserve it if you plan to use it. Put the whole, drained coconut in a shallow pan and bake it in a 350° F. oven for about 15 minutes to crack the shell. After baking, you can easily complete cracking the shell with a hammer. Pry the coconut meat away from the shell in large pieces using the blade of a firm knife. Use a vegetable paring knife to pare the brown skin off the chunks of coconut. Rinse the pared pieces under cold water if necessary. Dry on paper towels.

To grate fresh coconut, use the medium or medium-fine blade of a hand grater. Rub the dried pieces of fresh coconut over the grater. You will get long shreds if you use the full length of the grater. Use as recipe directs; it is especially good sprinkled over a White Cake (see page 817) that has been frosted with White Mountain Frosting (see page 859). The coconut liquid may be used as part of the milk in Rice Pudding (see page 739) or Baked Custard (see page 737).

Cranberries

Fresh cranberries are available from fall into spring; frozen cranberries, without sugar added, canned jellied, and whole cranberry sauce are always in the market. To buy, look for plump, firm berries with a lustrous red color. Refrigerate them unwashed or prepare them for freezing (see chart on page 68).

To prepare cranberries, pick out and discard immature or soft berries; wash remainder briefly in a bath of cold water. If berries are to be ground raw for use in relish or salad, it is not necessary to thaw the frozen ones.

Other cranberry recipes appear throughout this book. See the index for a complete listing of them.

❧ Cranberry Relish

4 cups fresh cranberries
2 oranges, quartered
½ cup canned, crushed pineapple
2 cups sugar

Put cranberries and oranges through fine blade of food chopper. Add remaining ingredients; mix thoroughly. Cover tightly and store in refrigerator. Serve as a relish with poultry or ham. May be kept refrigerated several weeks. Makes about 4 cups relish.

Currants

Fresh currants are in the market briefly in the summer. The red and white varieties are for eating out of hand or for combining with other fruits in salads or compotes. The black ones are used for jellies and jams. Dried currants are available year-round. To buy fresh currants, look for bright, plump berries that are firmly attached to their stems. Spread them in a shallow tray and refrigerate, uncovered. To prepare, wash them gently. Remove stems if you plan to use them in a recipe. Dry on paper towels before combining them with other fruits or adding them to a fruit tray.

Figs

Always available in canned and dried forms, figs are only available fresh from about June through December. They come in four popular colors: the Kadota are a pale yellow; the Calimyrna, greenish yellow; the Brown Turkey, reddish brown; and the Black Mission, dark purple. They are all good to eat out of hand or sliced. To purchase fresh figs, look for plump fruits that yield to a gentle pressure. Unlike other fresh fruits, underripe figs should be refrigerated until they are soft for eating. To prepare fresh figs for cooking, wash and pare off the outer skin. Figs need not be peeled for eating out of hand.

Grapefruit

Grapefruit is marketed either as whole fresh fruit or as sections packed in cans, in refrigerated jars, or frozen. It comes in white (pale yellow) and pink- or red-fleshed varieties, with or without seeds. The "seedless" variety may have a few small seeds in it. To buy fresh, look for firm, well-shaped fruits that feel heavy for their size—the weight comes from the juice. Thin-skinned fruits have more juice than thick-skinned fruits. Neither the skin color nor the size is a special indication of quality. Often the smaller fruits are sweeter and juicier than the larger fruits. Since grapefruit is picked "tree-ripe," these fruits are ripe when you buy them; they should be refrigerated immediately.

To prepare grapefruit, cut it in half. With a sharp knife or a grapefruit knife, which has a rounded blade, cut around each segment of fruit to release it from the membrane and the skin. To section a whole grapefruit, cut off the peel in a long spiral starting at the top or cut the peel off in sections (or see method for peeling and sectioning an orange on page 708). Peel deeply enough to get off the white membrane. Hold the fruit over a bowl and cut away the membrane from each side of a segment. Lift out the segment and drop it into the bowl. Remove seeds as you go.

Other grapefruit recipes appear throughout this book. See index for a complete listing.

✌ Honey-Baked Grapefruit

2 medium-sized grapefruits
⅓ cup honey
1 tablespoon butter or margarine

Heat oven to 400° F. Cut grapefruits in half crosswise and loosen each section from membrane and skin. Arrange halves in a shallow baking pan. Mix honey and butter together; spoon over grapefruit halves. Bake 5 to 8 minutes, or until lightly browned. Serves 4.

Grapes

Fresh grapes come in many varieties that vary in color from pale green to blue-black (see page 38). The pale green Thompson and sultana are seedless. Seedless grapes are used in canned fruit cocktail and canned alone in a variety of syrups. To buy fresh grapes, look for well-colored, plump grapes that are firmly attached to the stem. The white or green grapes will have a yellowish cast when they are fully ripe. Avoid soft or wrinkled skins and brittle stems.

To store grapes, refrigerate them unwashed. When ready to serve them, wash them and let them dry on paper towels. Leave them in clusters to add to a fruit bowl. If grapes are to be added to other fruits in a compote, seed them by slicing them in half with a sharp knife and, with the tip of the knife, flicking out the seeds.

There are grape recipes throughout this book. See the index for a complete listing. This is one of our favorite ways to serve fresh, seedless grapes.

❧ Continental Grapes

3 cups seedless green grapes
½ cup commercial sour cream
⅓ cup firmly packed brown sugar
Chocolate-Dipped Almonds (recipe follows)

Wash grapes; drain well and place in a large bowl. Fold in sour cream and blend until grapes are thoroughly coated. Chill for at least two hours. Spoon into dessert dishes. Sprinkle lightly with brown sugar and garnish with Chocolate-Dipped Almonds. Serves 6.

Chocolate-Dipped Almonds

1 1-ounce square semisweet chocolate
2 teaspoons butter or margarine
1½ dozen blanched whole almonds

Place chocolate and butter in the top of a double boiler and place over simmering water. Stir until melted, blending well. Dip almonds in mixture to cover just half of each almond. Place almonds on cookie sheet covered with waxed paper. Chill in refrigerator until chocolate is set.

Kumquats

Kumquats are the babies of the citrus family; they are shaped like large, unshelled pecans. They are never peeled; the entire fruit is edible. They are sold fresh for only the short season between Thanksgiving and New Year's, but preserved kumquats are available year-round in jars and cans. Either the fresh or preserved variety make a pretty, edible garnish for meats and poultry.

To buy fresh kumquats, look for plump, firm, golden fruit. The stems and leaves may still be attached. Keep them in the refrigerator. When ready to prepare, wash them. Leave stems and leaves attached if the kumquats are to be added to a fruit bowl. If they are to be used in a fruit compote, slice or quarter them.

Lemons

Fresh lemons are always available; lemon juice is marketed in bottles and plastic squeeze containers and canned frozen. Fresh lemons should have a rich yellow color and a smooth-textured skin that is relatively thin. Avoid dark yellow, dry-looking skins; these are a sign of age. Keep them refrigerated until ready to prepare. Then cut a thin slice off the blossom end. Cut in lengthwise quarters to serve along with fish, vegetables, or melon, or cut into thin round slices and remove seeds to serve with hot or iced tea.

See the index for many good lemon-flavored recipes.

Limes

Fresh limes are generally available from June through December. Lime juice may be purchased in cans or plastic squeeze containers or as a frozen concentrate. Limes (the dominant Persian variety) look like green lemons. The smaller, round, smooth-skinned variety are Key limes.

To buy, look for limes with glossy skin and good weight for their size. Avoid dull, dried skins. Keep them refrigerated until ready to use.

Limes are usually used for their juice, which you can extract with a reamer or any other fruit-juicing utensil. Vertical lime wedges or thin round slices may be used just as you use lemon wedges.

Mangoes

Fresh mangoes are available during the summer months. They are oval and vary in size from that of an apricot to six to eight inches long. They have a smooth, yellow to red skin and a soft, juicy, orange-yellow pulp. The mango flavor resembles a combination of apricot and pineapple. Buy plump, smooth-skinned fruits that yield to gentle pressure. Keep them in the refrigerator. To eat raw, peel back the skin in sections, squeeze a little lemon or lime juice onto the fruit, and spoon out of the shell. Mangoes may also be peeled and cut into chunks to add to fruit compotes. The unripened fruit is green and is used in making chutney.

Melons

There is a great variety of melons on the market, which range from the familiar golden-fleshed cantaloupe to the pale-green-fleshed honeydew to the miniature watermelon-shaped Christmas melon. For more descriptive details, see the chart on page 39.

Selection of melons for good quality and flavor is difficult. A ripe melon, ready to chill and use the day you buy it, should yield to gentle pressure on the blossom end and have a fragrant, fresh-melon aroma. Firmer melons can be kept at room temperature until they pass the pressure test; the increasing melon aroma is another indication that the melon is ready to chill and eat. Since melons tend to pass their aroma on to other foods, wrap ripe melons in plastic wrap first and then refrigerate.

To prepare melons, use a heavy knife to cut small melons in half and larger melons into lengthwise wedges. Remove seeds (except in watermelon). Serve with wedges of lemon or lime. To make melon balls, you may use a special melon-ball cutter that has two different scoop sizes, one on either end. Or you can use the half-teaspoon measure from a round-spoon measuring set. Press and turn the round scoop into the flesh of the melon and lift out little ball-shaped bites.

Other melon recipes appear throughout this book. See index for a complete listing.

✑ Melon Surprise

1 medium-sized cantaloupe or honeydew melon
3 cups melon balls (combination of cantaloupe, honeydew, casaba, or watermelon)
1 cup raspberries, strawberries, or blackberries
1 tablespoon kirsch
1 tablespoon grenadine syrup
Fresh mint sprigs

Wash well-chilled melon and cut off one end about ⅓ of the way down from the top. Scoop out seeds. With a melon-ball cutter or spoon, cut out bite-sized pieces of melon meat, leaving a shell about ½ inch thick. Mix together melon balls, berries, kirsch, and grenadine. Spoon fruit into shell. Replace top. Refrigerate 1 to 2 hours. At serving time, garnish with sprigs of mint. Serves 4.

✑ Fruit-Filled Watermelon

Half of a 13- to 15-pound watermelon (cut lengthwise)
1 quart strawberries
3 large oranges

Scoop out watermelon balls from the watermelon half with a melon-ball cutter and place balls in a large bowl. Remove excess liquid and seeds from watermelon and dry the inside of the shell well with paper towels. Wash and hull strawberries. Peel and section oranges. Cut

1 14¼-ounce can sliced
    pineapple, drained
1 pound seedless grapes
1 cup water
½ cup sugar
1 tablespoon lemon juice
Fresh mint sprigs

pineapple slices in half. Wash grapes and remove from stem. Combine fruits with watermelon balls in bowl. In a small bowl combine water, sugar, and lemon juice and blend well. Pour over fruit and stir gently to blend. Chill until serving time. Arrange fruit in watermelon shell at serving time and decorate with fresh mint sprigs. Serves 12 to 16.

Nectarines

This fresh summer fruit looks somewhat like a cross between a large plum and a smooth peach and tastes like a firm, juicy peach. Buy firm, but not hard, bright, smooth-skinned fruit. Most varieties have an orange-yellow ground color with red blushes. Ripe fruit yield to gentle pressure. Firm fruit may be held at room temperature to ripen; refrigerate ripe fruit.

Fresh nectarines do not need to be peeled. Wash and dry and eat them out of hand or slice and cube them to combine with other fruits.

Oranges

Fresh oranges are available year-round. They are sold loose, by the dozen, or marketed in bags. Those that peel easily are best for eating in sections or slices; others, which are thinner-skinned, are best for juice. For more descriptive detail, see How to Select and Use the Common Varieties of Oranges, page 40. To buy, look for oranges that feel heavy for their size. Skin color is not an indication of quality. Oranges are tree-ripe when picked so need no further ripening. To store, keep them

TO PEEL AND SECTION
AN ORANGE

To peel, place the orange on a cutting board and cut a slice from the top and bottom of the orange. With a sharp knife cut off the peel and white membrane from top to bottom, following the curve of the fruit. To section, hold the orange over a bowl and cut on either side of the membrane between segments. Lift out each segment and remove any seeds. Drop segments into the bowl. Squeeze juice from the membrane into the bowl.

in a cool place spread out in a single layer. Refrigerate them several hours before you plan to use them.

Other orange recipes appear throughout this book. See index for a complete listing.

⤙ Broiled Oranges

3 large oranges
2 tablespoons light brown sugar
1 tablespoon butter or margarine
30 miniature marshmallows

Slice the oranges in half and cut around sections with a sharp knife. Drop 1 teaspoon light brown sugar and ½ teaspoon butter on each half. Arrange in a shallow baking pan. Place in a preheated broiler about 4 inches from heat. Broil 5 minutes; remove and top each half with 5 miniature marshmallows. Return to broiler until marshmallows are melted and brown. Serve immediately. Serves 6.

Temple Oranges

This fruit sheds its skin easily and has loose segments that can be pulled apart with your fingers for eating. It is about the size of a large orange and looks like an orange except that is has a slightly raised rounded top. It should have fresh, bright skin and good weight for the size. Keep in the refrigerator. When ready to use, peel and eat, or add segments to fruit compotes. Remove any white strings that cling to the segments.

Mandarin Oranges

Mandarin oranges are marketed in canned form only. These tiny sweet seedless segments are excellent for adding to fruit compotes or for garnishing fowl.

⤙ Mandarin Orange Sundae Sauce

2 11-ounce cans mandarin orange sections
2 tablespoons cornstarch
Few drops yellow food coloring
Few grains salt
4 tablespoons Cointreau liqueur

Drain orange sections and reserve syrup. Stir a little of the drained syrup into cornstarch. Stir in rest of syrup. Cook over moderate heat (about 250° F.), stirring constantly, until mixture is smooth and thickened. Remove from heat; add yellow coloring and salt. Fold in orange sections and Cointreau. Serve over vanilla ice cream. Makes 2 cups sauce.

Papayas

Plentiful in the West and in some parts of the South, papayas are now being shipped into special markets. The sweet golden flesh is usually eaten with a spoon out of the shell. This small melon-shaped fruit varies in size from five to ten inches in length. Papaya juice is also available canned. It is a naturally sweet juice and is extremely high in vitamins A and C.

A ripe papaya will be soft and have a yellow skin. Refrigerate ripe fruits and use within a few days. Good firm green papayas will ripen at room temperature in a day or two.

To prepare papayas, cut in half and remove the black seeds. Eat out of the shell with a squeeze of lemon or lime juice, if desired. Green papayas may be peeled, seeded, and cooked as a vegetable.

Peaches

Peaches fall into two general classifications: the freestone (the flesh readily separates from the pit) and the clingstone (the flesh clings to the pit). Fresh peaches are available throughout the summer months. Canned peaches of both varieties are packed whole, halved, sliced, and diced. They are also available spiced in jars. Frozen peaches are usually packed in a sugar syrup.

To buy fresh peaches, look for plump, firm fruit that yields to gentle pressure. The skin color between the red blushes should be yellow or creamy white. Avoid hard peaches with a green color. They will not fully ripen at room temperature. If yellow peaches are firm and need to ripen a little more, keep them at room temperature until they are ready to eat.

TO PEEL AND SLICE A PEACH

To peel and slice a peach: If the skin does not peel off easily with a knife, spear the peach on a fork and dip it into boiling water for about 1 minute; then dip it into cold water. Insert the point of a knife under the skin and it will peel off easily. To slice, hold the peeled peach over a bowl and cut out lengthwise wedges. If the peach is a clingstone variety, pry wedges loose from the stone with the blade of a knife.

Refrigerate when ripe. If peaches are to be peeled and sliced and held for any length of time before using, sprinkle them with lemon juice or an ascorbic acid (vitamin C) mixture, as directed on the package.

Other peach recipes appear throughout this book. See the index for a complete listing.

~§ Pêches Flambées

1 cup water
⅓ cup sugar
Few grains salt
½ teaspoon vanilla extract
3 fresh medium-sized peaches, peeled and halved
1½ teaspoons cornstarch
2 tablespoons water
¼ cup kirsch

Place the 1 cup water in a large, 3-quart saucepan; bring water to a boil over moderately low heat (about 225° F.). Add sugar and continue cooking 1 to 2 minutes, until sugar is dissolved, stirring constantly. Mix in salt and vanilla. Place peaches in hot syrup, cut-side up. Poach over moderate heat (about 250° F.), stirring occasionally, until peaches are fork-tender, about 15 minutes. Baste fruit with syrup 2 or 3 times during cooking time. Strain peaches and place halves in a chafing dish or a deep 10-inch skillet; set aside. Return syrup to saucepan; heat over moderate heat (about 250° F.) 1 minute. Dissolve the cornstarch in the 2 tablespoons water; gradually mix into syrup in saucepan. Cook 2 to 3 minutes, or until mixture thickens, stirring constantly. Pour syrup over peaches; heat over moderately low heat (about 225° F.) or heating unit until small bubbles appear around edge. At the table, pour 1 teaspoon of kirsch into a warm tablespoon and ignite with a match; while still flaming, pour over peaches. Add the remaining kirsch and serve after flame goes out, allowing a peach half and a spoonful of syrup per serving. Serves 6.

~§ Poached Peaches

2½ cups water
½ cup sugar
½ cup orange marmalade
Few grains salt
8 small peaches (about 3 pounds)
⅓ cup Cointreau

Mix water, sugar, orange marmalade, and salt in saucepan. Place over moderately low heat (about 225° F.) and stir until sugar is dissolved. Remove from heat. Cover peaches with boiling water. Let stand 2 minutes. Drain and cover with cold water. Remove skins and cut peaches in half; remove pits. Place in syrup mixture in saucepan. Cook over moderate heat (about 250° F.) 10 minutes, basting peaches occasionally with syrup. Remove peaches and boil syrup until mixture is reduced to 1¼ cups. Stir in Cointreau and cool slightly. Pour into a serving bowl and chill thoroughly. Serves 8.

Pears

This delicate summer fruit comes in 3,000 known varieties. You will find the most popular ten, with a description of their appearance, in the chart on page 36. Besides being available fresh, pears also come canned whole, quartered, and sliced. They are also spiced in jars.

Pears you buy fresh may come individually wrapped in paper, cellophane-wrapped in cardboard trays, or loose. They will seldom be tree-ripened. Pears are picked when full-grown but still green and then ripened at the proper temperature and humidity for the particular pear variety. When buying, avoid fruit that has bruises or rough scaly areas. Fruit may need two to three days more ripening time at home.

To ripen properly, pears need temperatures between 60° F. and 70° F. and a high humidity. Place the pears in a paper bag, put a damp sponge in with them, and keep in a cool room. If you use a plastic bag, punch holes in it for adequate ventilation. Color is not a good test for ripeness; pears are ready for eating when they yield readily to slight pressure. After ripening, store them in the crisper compartment of the refrigerator, where the cold will keep them from ripening further. Avoid temperatures above 70° F.; at too high a temperature, the flesh around the core may soften and even decay before the outer flesh becomes soft.

Serve pears cool, but not ice-cold, since fruit when too cold loses some of its aroma and flavor. If pears are to be peeled and held for half an hour or longer, sprinkle them with lemon juice or an ascorbic acid (vitamin C) mixture, as directed on the package, to prevent discoloration. Ripe pears with attractive yellow or rosy skins may be diced unpeeled if you wish.

If skins are free from blemishes, pears may be baked or stewed unpeeled, though most people prefer them peeled. The exact time required to simmer or bake firm, ripe pears cannot be given. This depends on the variety of the pear and just how ripe it is. Bartlett pears take five minutes less cooking time, on the average, than other kinds. Most pears may be cooked and used interchangeably in recipes—even Bartletts, though they are primarily for out-of-hand eating. The grainier Kieffers and the Seckel pears are still found in abundance in local areas, but are usually limited in use to pickling and preserving. Other pear recipes appear throughout this book. See the index for a complete listing.

✑ *Pears in Wine*

¾ *cup dry red wine*
¾ *cup sugar*

Combine wine, sugar, and cinnamon in large saucepan. Bring to a boil and add pears. Cook covered, over mod-

½ *inch stick cinnamon or*
¼ *teaspoon ground*
   cinnamon
6 *pears, peeled*

erately low heat (about 225° F.), about 25 minutes, or until pears are fork-tender. Place pears and syrup in serving dish and chill thoroughly. Serves 6.

❧ Curried Fresh Pears

3 *medium-sized firm ripe*
   pears
3 *tablespoons soft butter or*
   margarine
3 *tablespoons firmly packed*
   brown sugar
1 *tablespoon curry powder*
½ *teaspoon grated lemon peel*
¼ *teaspoon salt*
¼ *cup water*

Heat oven to 350° F. Wash and peel pears. Cut them into halves lengthwise and remove cores. Grease a shallow baking pan. Arrange pears, cored side up, in the pan. Blend the butter, sugar, curry, lemon peel, and salt. Pack the mixture into the cavities in the pears where cores were removed. Pour water into the pan around the pears. Cover and bake 20 minutes. Uncover and continue to bake 10 to 15 minutes until pears are fork-tender and nicely glazed. Serve warm or chilled as an accompaniment for ham, pork, or poultry. Serves 6.

Persimmons

Persimmons are a smooth-skinned winter fruit of bright orange color. They are larger than plums and usually have no seeds. Their flavor is rich and sweet. Buy plump, firm fruit that yields to gentle pressure. Let them stand at room temperature until fully ripened (soft), then refrigerate.

This fruit need not be peeled to be served, but if you like, remove the skins by submerging them in boiling water for about a minute. Plunge them into cold water. Skins will slip off easily. Serve them whole or in halves or quarters.

Pineapple

Available fresh year-round, pineapple also comes canned in rings, slices, chunks, tidbits, spears, or crushed. Frozen pineapple chunks are also canned.

A pineapple should be heavy for its size. Its characteristic aroma will tell you when it is ripe. Or if the center leaves at the top pull out easily and color is a rich orange-brown, the pineapple is ready to use.

To store pineapple, wrap it with plastic wrap or aluminum foil to prevent its imparting its aroma to other foods. Store in the refrigerator. Refrigerate cut pineapple in a tightly covered container.

TO PEEL A PINEAPPLE AND REMOVE THE EYES

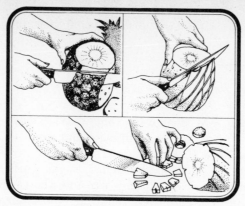

To peel a pineapple, cut off the crown and stem ends and stand the fruit on end. Holding it firmly, cut off the peel with a sharp knife from top to bottom, following the curve of the fruit. Pineapple "eyes" follow a natural curve down the fruit. Following this curve, make a long, slanted, V-shaped cut along both sides of a diagonally curved row of eyes, forming a long, V-shaped section. Lift out this entire section and repeat, thereby removing all the eyes. To slice, lay the peeled and "eyed" pineapple on its side, cut it into slices, and remove the core from each slice with a pointed knife. For cubes or small pieces, cut the slices to the size you wish. For spears, stand peeled whole pineapple, with eyes removed, upright. Cut lengthwise into eighths. Cut core from each wedge. Cut each wedge into lengthwise strips.

Other pineapple recipes appear throughout this book. See the index for a complete listing.

Stuffed Pineapple

1 pineapple
2 bananas, peeled and sliced
5 oranges, peeled and
   sectioned
1 cup grapes, halved and
   seeded
½ cup granulated sugar
2 tablespoons lemon juice
2 tablespoons dark rum
1 cup heavy cream
2 tablespoons confectioners'
   sugar
6 maraschino cherries

Cut pineapple in half lengthwise through fruit and leaves. Carve out pineapple meat and dice into 1-inch cubes. Mix together pineapple, banana, orange sections, grapes, granulated sugar, lemon juice, and rum. Mound fruit in the pineapple shells. Serve the remaining fruit in a bowl for seconds. Place cream and confectioners' sugar in a bowl and beat with a rotary beater until mixture holds its shape. Garnish fruit shells with cream and top with maraschino cherries. Serves 8.

Plums and Fresh Prunes

Both plums and fresh prunes (a variety of plum that can be dried) are available fresh in season and canned year-round. Plums come in three distinct colors. The small blue or purple plum is the prune plum; it is particularly sweet and has a freestone pit. It is in season in late summer and early fall. The large red plums and the green (greengage) plums are usually in the market in quantity in the summer months. Buy firm plums or prunes that yield to slight pressure and have good color for their variety. Keep them refrigerated until ready to wash and eat out of hand. Prepare them according to the plum recipes that appear throughout this book. See the index for a complete listing.

⌇ *Purple Plum Pie*

Pastry for 9-inch 2-crust pie
  (recipe on page 787)
4 cups halved, pitted purple
  plums
3 tablespoons flour
1 cup sugar
½ teaspoon ground cinnamon
½ teaspoon ground nutmeg
¼ teaspoon salt
2 tablespoons lemon juice
2 tablespoons melted butter
  or margarine
Vanilla ice cream (optional)

Heat oven to 425° F. Line a 9-inch pie plate with half the pastry. Cut plum halves once, crosswise. Arrange plums in pie plate. Combine flour, sugar, cinnamon, nutmeg, and salt; sprinkle over plums. Sprinkle with lemon juice. Cover with rest of pastry. Seal and flute edge. Brush crust with melted butter. Bake 35 to 40 minutes. If desired, serve slightly warm with vanilla ice cream. Serves 6 to 8.

Pomegranates

Pomegranates, which are about the size of an orange, have a tough skin that shades between an orangey red and a red brown. To buy, look for plump firm fruit that yields to slight pressure. Store pomegranates in the refrigerator. To prepare pomegranates, cut them in half—do not remove seeds. Eat out of the shell with a spoon. Seeds and their surrounding juice and pulp are all edible.

Quinces

This is one fruit that is not eaten raw; it is a hard yellow fruit that is available in the fall in some markets. To buy, look for plump, bright yellow fruit that will be hard though ripe. Store quinces in the refrigerator.

This fruit is most often used for jelly. It may also be poached or baked. Pare the fruit, cut into halves or quarters, and remove the core. Poach or bake until fruit is tender. Baking, at 325° F., will take about 2 hours; poaching 30 to 45 minutes. You will need to use ¾ to 1 cup sugar per pound of quinces and enough water to keep the fruit covered.

Rhubarb

Fresh rhubarb is available the first six months of the year. Frozen rhubarb in sugar syrup is available year-round. To buy, look for crisp long stalks that vary in color (depending upon the season) from light pink to dark reddish green. Keep, if necessary, in a cool dry place. It is best to prepare rhubarb while it is fresh. To prepare rhubarb, trim and discard the leaves. Wash well. Cook as recipe directs.

There are rhubarb recipes throughout this book; see the index for a complete listing.

 **Stewed Rhubarb**

1½ *pounds rhubarb*
¾ *cup sugar*
½ *cup water*
1 *teaspoon grated lemon peel*

Wash rhubarb; cut off root and leaf ends and cut into 1- or 2-inch pieces. In a saucepan combine all ingredients. Cook over moderately low heat (about 225° F.) for 10 minutes after mixture begins to boil, stirring occasionally. Serve warm or chilled. Serves 4 to 5.

Tangerines

Tangerines are the original citrus fruit with the "zipper" skin. Tangerines are fresh in the market in midwinter. Fruits should have a lustrous orange color; they will not feel firm because their characteristic skin is loose and puffy. Store tangerines in the refrigerator.

Prepare tangerines by peeling off the outer skin. Pull, don't cut, apart segments. Remove any loose white strings from the segments and eat them as they are or add them to fruit compotes.

Tangelos

Tangelos are a cross between a tangerine and a grapefruit, but taste more like an orange. Use them as you would use tangerines or temple oranges.

Dried Fruits

Prunes, apricots, peaches, pears, and apples are the commonly dried fruits. They come packaged and have been so processed that they are tender enough to eat just as they are. Mixed dried fruits are also available. Read the package label to find out what is in the package and whether the fruit is pitted or not. Keep unopened packages on a cool, dry shelf. Store opened packages, covered, in the refrigerator. To prepare, follow package directions. Most dried fruits today need no added sugar and no long soaking or long cooking.

❧ Baked Fruit Compote

2 *12-ounce packages mixed dried fruits*
1 *13¼-ounce can pineapple chunks, undrained*
1 *21-ounce can cherry pie filling*
2 *cups water*
¼ *cup dry sherry*
1 *tablespoon lemon juice*

Heat oven to 350° F. In a deep 2½-quart casserole, combine dried fruits and pineapple. Combine remaining ingredients in a bowl, blend well, and pour over fruit. Cover and bake 1½ hours. Serve warm. Serves 10.

Dates

Dates are usually in the market in boxes or trays with a clear overwrap or in rigid plastic containers. They come pitted or unpitted or cut in dice ready to add to salads, cakes, and cereals. Use kitchen scissors to chop dates. You can dip the blades in a little flour or cold water to keep the dates from sticking. To store, overwrap opened fruit and keep it refrigerated or frozen.

Figs

Two varieties of figs are often sold dried. When dried, they are packaged like dates. Most of the light Kadota figs are marketed fresh or canned. The dried varieties are Black Mission, which are black in color, and Calimyrna, which are a light brown color. To store figs, overwrap them and keep refrigerated.

Raisins and Currants

Raisins come in two varieties, seeded and seedless. The seedless come in two colors, dark and light or golden, depending upon the process used in drying the seedless grapes. These seedless raisins are dry and whole. They are packaged in 15-ounce sizes and in snack-size 1½-ounce cartons. The seeded raisins are made from grapes from which the seeds have been removed. They are usually sticky. Currants generally come in 11-ounce packages. Store on a cool, dry shelf. Once opened, it is best to shut air away from these dried fruits. Put them into jars with tight lids or tape clear plastic wrap over the boxes. They will also keep in the freezer.

✑ Sweet Raisin Kugel

½ *pound (6 cups) medium egg noodles (about 4 cups cooked)*
1 *cup pot cheese or dry curd cottage cheese*
½ *cup commercial sour cream*
2 *eggs*
3 *tablespoons melted butter or margarine*
½ *teaspoon salt*
½ *teaspoon vanilla extract*
2 *tablespoons sugar*
*1 *cup dark seedless raisins*
1 *tablespoon sugar*
⅛ *teaspoon ground cinnamon*

Cook noodles as directed on package. Meanwhile, heat oven to 350° F. Place the pot cheese, sour cream, eggs, butter, salt, vanilla and the 2 tablespoons sugar in the large bowl of an electric mixer. Beat cheese mixture at high speed one minute, or until smooth. Remove bowl from mixer; gently fold the drained, cooked noodles and the raisins into cheese mixture. Pour into a buttered, deep, 2-quart casserole. Mix the 1 tablespoon sugar with the cinnamon and sprinkle over the noodle mixture. Bake 40 minutes. Serve warm. Serves 6 to 8.

Note: 1 cup snipped, pitted prunes or dates may be used instead of raisins.

CHAPTER XXI

DESSERTS

In all the polls ever taken of what recipes people collect, one category always tops the list: Desserts. From the light fresh fruits, the cool gelatine desserts, the homey puddings, the fluffy mousses, the perennially favorite ice cream to such creations as rum-soaked Baba au Fraises, and flaming Crêpes Suzette—these are the concoctions that make everyone's mouth water.

Rich desserts are delightful on special occasions but are hardly for everyday. The desserts of fruits, eggs, amd milk are the ones that can help you balance meals for each day.

For busy days, explore the shelves and freezer case at your supermarket. You'll find a selection of quick-to-serve desserts such as canned and frozen puddings; frozen pies, cakes, and whipped toppings; and frozen fruits, ice-cream sherbets, and ice-cream cake rolls that are easy and delicious.

Fruit Desserts

Fruit desserts, cold or hot, are good for family meals and make a most acceptable light ending for a large company dinner.

DESSERTS

ᴥᶴ Ambrosia

6 large navel oranges
¼ cup confectioners' sugar
1 4¼-ounce can shredded
  coconut
⅓ cup orange juice

Peel oranges carefully, removing all membranes, and cut into thin slices. Place ⅓ of the sliced oranges in a serving dish and sprinkle with some of the sugar and coconut. Repeat layers twice, ending with coconut. Add orange juice and chill about 1 hour before serving. Serves 6.

ᴥᶴ Cloud Nine Cream

1 8¼-ounce can crushed
  pineapple
1 8-ounce package cream
  cheese, at room
  temperature
1 2-ounce package whipped
  topping mix
3 tablespoons sugar
½ cup chopped pecans
½ cup well-drained
  maraschino cherries

Drain pineapple well, reserving ¼ cup of the syrup. Place cream cheese in the small bowl of an electric mixer and beat until creamy. Gradually add the ¼ cup reserved syrup and beat until light and smooth. Prepare the whipped topping mix according to package directions. Fold in the cream cheese mixture, sugar, nuts, pineapple and cherries. Cover and chill 3 hours. Serves 6.

ᴥᶴ Coeur à la Crème

2 8-ounce packages cream
  cheese at room
  temperature
1 16-ounce container small-
  curd cream-style cottage
  cheese
¼ cup confectioners' sugar
1 cup heavy cream
1 pint strawberries, sliced
  and sweetened, or 1
  10-ounce package frozen
  strawberries, thawed

Beat cream cheese with rotary beater until fluffy. Gradually add cottage cheese and continue beating until almost smooth. Add sugar and heavy cream and beat until blended. Place a large colander in a cake pan. Line colander with several thicknesses of cheesecloth. Pour in cheese mixture; cover and let stand in refrigerator 8 hours or overnight, stirring mixture several times. Line 6 individual heart-shaped molds or a 3-cup heart-shaped mold with a double layer of cheesecloth, Spoon in cheese mixture and pack firmly. Chill 3 hours. Invert molds on dessert plates and peel off cheesecloth. Garnish with strawberries. Serves 6.

ᴥᶴ Exotic Fruited Cream

4 cups commercial sour
  cream

Cut a double thickness of cheesecloth about 30 x 15 inches. Place sour cream in the middle of cheesecloth.

¼ teaspoon ground
  cardamom seeds
1 cup firmly packed light
  brown sugar
*1 7-ounce package marrons
  glacés, coarsely chopped
1 10-ounce package frozen
  strawberries, partially
  thawed
2 tablespoons Grand
  Marnier
¼ cup slivered toasted
  almonds

Overlap 2 opposite sides of cheesecloth over sour cream. Bring the other 2 sides up and tie securely; place in a wire sieve over a bowl. Let stand overnight in the refrigerator. Discard liquid in the bottom of bowl. Remove curd from cheesecloth and combine with ground cardamom, brown sugar, and chopped marrons. Chill until serving time. Combine partially thawed strawberries and Grand Marnier. Spoon sour cream mixture into sherbet glasses; top each with some of the strawberry mixture and sprinkle with almonds. Serves 6 to 8.

*Note: If the packaged marrons glacés are not available, a 9½-ounce jar of vanilla-flavored marron pieces may be substituted. Drain off all the syrup, blot marrons dry with paper towel, and chop coarsely.

Fruits Mandarin

¼ cup orange marmalade
⅓ cup lime or lemon
  marmalade
1 tablespoon lemon juice
2 tablespoons orange juice
2 grapefruit, peeled and cut
  into sections
3 oranges, peeled and cut
  into sections
2 bananas
2 tablespoons slivered
  candied ginger

Place marmalades in saucepan over moderately low heat (about 225° F.); heat until marmalades are melted, stirring occasionally. Stir in lemon juice and orange juice; cool. Place grapefruit and orange sections in a bowl; stir in marmalade mixture. Chill. Just before serving, slice bananas; gently mix into fruit. Garnish with ginger. Serves 6.

Oranges in Cointreau

7 large navel oranges
1 lemon
2 tablespoons Cointreau
¾ cup sugar
½ cup water
2 tablespoons Cointreau
Ground nuts (optional)

Peel 6 of the oranges, removing all white membrane. Work over a bowl to save all juices. Squeeze and strain the juice from the remaining orange and the lemon; add to any juices from peeling the oranges. With a sharp knife cut between sections of oranges, working over the bowl to save juices. Don't cut quite to the bottom of each orange section. It is important that the oranges hold their shape and that the sections hold together. Set aside fruit juices. Place oranges in a large shallow dish;

sprinkle the 2 tablespoons Cointreau over tops of oranges. Combine sugar and water in a saucepan. Stirring constantly, cook over moderately low heat (about 225° F.) about 5 minutes, until sugar is dissolved. Stir in reserved fruit juices; cool about 10 minutes. Pour cooled syrup over and around oranges. Cover and refrigerate oranges several hours or overnight, basting oranges several times with syrup from the bottom of the dish. Oranges should be ice-cold when served. Just before serving, add the remaining 2 tablespoons of Cointreau to the syrup, stirring thoroughly. Serve each orange in a glass serving dish; spoon 3 to 4 tablespoons syrup mixture over each and sprinkle with ground nuts, if desired. Serves 6.

⊷§ Pears Hélène

Rum Sauce (recipe follows)
1 29-ounce can pear halves, drained
Fudge Sauce (recipe follows)

Spoon Rum Sauce into bottom of 8 dessert dishes. Arrange a pear half in each dish, cut-side down. Top with warm Fudge Sauce. Serves 8.

Rum Sauce

¾ cup milk
¼ cup rum
1 teaspoon vanilla extract
1 4-ounce package whipped topping mix

Place milk, rum, vanilla, and topping mix in a bowl and prepare according to directions on package. Makes 2¾ cups sauce.

Fudge Sauce

½ cup unsweetened cocoa
1 cup sugar
1 cup light corn syrup
½ cup undiluted evaporated milk
3 tablespoons butter or margarine
½ teaspoon salt
½ teaspoon vanilla extract

Mix cocoa, sugar, corn syrup, evaporated milk, butter, and salt in a saucepan. Place over moderately low heat (about 225° F.) and cook until mixture comes to a boil; boil 3 minutes. Remove from heat and add vanilla. Serve warm. To reheat, place sauce in top of double boiler over simmering water. Makes 2¼ cups sauce.

⊷§ Chocolate Pears Supreme

2 17-ounce cans pear halves
2 1-ounce squares semisweet

Drain pears; cover and chill. Break chocolate squares into quarters. Turn electric blender on Grate setting or

chocolate
¼ cup unsweetened cocoa
1 cup commercial sour cream
1 cup sugar
1 teaspoon vanilla extract
2 tablespoons crème de cacao

high speed. Drop a few chocolate pieces at a time through top of blender container, replacing cover each time. Blend 2 to 3 seconds. Turn off blender and scrape sides and bottom of container, turning out grated chocolate into a medium-sized bowl. Repeat process until all the chocolate is grated. Add cocoa, sour cream, and sugar to the grated chocolate in the bowl and blend well. Fill water pan of chafing dish with 1 inch of boiling water. Place blazer over water pan. Pour chocolate–sour cream mixture into blazer. Cook over highest heat of an alcohol burner, stirring occasionally, until chocolate is melted and mixture is thick and smooth, about 15 to 20 minutes. Stir in vanilla and crème de cacao. Blend well. Serve the sauce hot over the chilled pears. Serves 5 to 6.

❧ Peach Melba

1 10-ounce package frozen raspberries, thawed
½ cup currant jelly
¼ cup white rum (optional)
2 29-ounce cans cling peach halves, drained
1 quart vanilla ice cream
Blanched, slivered almonds

Press raspberries through a sieve to remove seeds. In a small saucepan combine raspberries and jelly and cook over moderately low heat (about 225° F.) for about 5 minutes, stirring constantly, until mixture is well blended. Remove from heat and cool. Add rum. Chill. To serve, place each peach half cut-side up in the center of a dessert dish. Place a scoop of vanilla ice cream on top; pour about 2 tablespoons of the raspberry sauce over each and sprinkle with almonds. Serves about 12.

❧ Raspberry Dream

1 cup commercial sour cream
1 10-ounce package frozen raspberries or quick-thaw pouch, thawed
1 cup sugar
1 teaspoon vanilla extract

Combine all ingredients in the small bowl of an electric mixer and beat at medium speed until smooth and creamy, about 3 minutes. Pour into an 8½-x-4½-x-2½-inch loaf pan; cover with aluminum foil and freeze until firm, 6 hours or overnight. Spoon into serving dishes. Serves 5 to 6.

❧ Low-Calorie Fruit Fluff

1 3-ounce package strawberry-flavored gelatin
½ cup boiling water
½ cup cold water

Place gelatin powder in an electric blender and add boiling water; cover and blend at medium speed until gelatin dissolves. Add cold water and blend a few seconds longer. Add nonfat dry milk to skim milk and stir to dissolve; add to gelatin mixture and blend a few sec-

⅓ cup instant nonfat dry milk
1 cup liquid skim milk
1 cup creamed cottage cheese

onds. Add cottage cheese to gelatin mixture and blend until fairly smooth. Pour mixture into a 1-quart bowl or 4 individual dishes and chill until firm, 3 hours or more. Serves 4.

Hot Fruit Desserts

✌ Apple Brown Betty

½ cup butter or margarine
4 cups ½-inch cubes white or whole wheat bread, tightly packed
6 cups peeled, cored, and sliced apples (about 6 medium-sized apples)
¾ cup firmly packed light brown sugar
¼ teaspoon ground cinnamon
½ teaspoon ground nutmeg
2 teaspoons grated lemon peel
2 tablespoons lemon juice
⅓ cup water
Sweetened whipped cream or Brandy Butter (recipe follows)

Heat oven to 375° F. Melt butter in skillet over moderate heat (about 250° F.); add bread cubes and toss together. Spoon one third of the bread into a greased deep 2½-quart casserole. Toss together sliced apples, brown sugar, cinnamon, nutmeg, and grated lemon peel. Cover layer of bread cubes with half the apple mixture. Repeat layers once again, reserving one third of the bread cubes for last layer. Mix lemon juice and water and pour over crumbs. Cover tightly and bake 30 minutes. Remove cover and bake 30 to 40 minutes. Serve warm with whipped cream or Brandy Butter. Serves 6 to 8.

Brandy Butter

½ cup butter or margarine
1½ cups confectioners' sugar
2 tablespoons brandy

Work butter in a bowl until creamy. Add sugar gradually and beat until smooth. Stir in brandy. Spoon into serving bowl; cover and refrigerate until serving time. Makes 1 cup.

✌ Apple Pandowdy

8 cups peeled, cored and sliced baking apples (about 8 medium-sized apples)

Heat oven to 400° F. Arrange a third of the apples in a deep 3-quart casserole. Combine the 1 cup sugar, cinnamon, nutmeg, and cloves; sprinkle about a third of the mixture over apples and dot with some of the butter.

1 cup sugar
2 teaspoons ground
    cinnamon
1 teaspoon ground nutmeg
½ teaspoon ground cloves
¼ cup butter or margarine
⅔ cup light molasses
2 cups sifted all-purpose
    flour
3 tablespoons sugar
3 teaspoons baking powder
¾ teaspoon salt
½ cup shortening
½ cup plus 1 tablespoon milk
1 egg
Light cream (optional)

Repeat layers twice. Pour molasses over the mixture. Bake 45 to 50 minutes, or until apples are almost tender. Stir apple mixture once or twice during baking. When apples are almost tender, sift together flour, the 3 tablespoons sugar, baking powder, and salt into a mixing bowl. Cut in shortening with a pastry blender or two knives until mixture resembles coarse corn meal. Combine milk and egg with a fork; add all at once to dry ingredients and stir with a fork until a soft dough forms. Drop dough by spoonfuls onto apples to form a ring around the edge of casserole. Return to oven and bake 15 to 20 minutes, or until biscuits are browned. Serve warm with plain cream, if desired. Serves 8.

Quick Apple Kuchen

1½ cups prepared buttermilk
    biscuit mix
2 tablespoons sugar
1 egg
1 tablespoon vegetable oil
½ cup milk
2 cups peeled, cored, and
    sliced tart cooking apples
    (about 2 medium-sized
    apples)
⅛ teaspoon ground nutmeg
¼ teaspoon ground
    cinnamon
2 tablespoons sugar
1 tablespoon melted butter
    or margarine
¼ cup crab apple jelly
Light cream (optional)

Heat oven to 400° F. Combine biscuit mix and the 2 tablespoons sugar in a bowl. Beat egg; add oil and milk and pour into biscuit mixture, stirring until just blended. Grease a 9-inch round layer cake pan. Spread batter evenly over bottom of pan. Arrange apple slices, rounded edges slightly overlapping over the surface of the dough. Combine spices and the remaining 2 tablespoons sugar. Sprinkle over apples. Drizzle apples with melted butter. Bake 35 minutes, or until apples are tender. Remove from oven. Beat jelly with a fork and spread it over apples. Return to oven for 3 to 4 minutes, or until jelly is melted. Serve warm with or without cream, as desired. Serves 8.

Rosy Apple Dumplings

1 cup sugar
1 cup water
⅛ teaspoon ground nutmeg
¼ cup red cinnamon candies

Combine sugar, water, nutmeg, and cinnamon candies in a saucepan. Cook over moderately low heat (225° F.) 5 minutes until candies are dissolved. Add butter. Cool slightly. Heat oven to 375° F. Mix together and sift flour,

2 tablespoons butter or
margarine
2 cups sifted all-purpose
flour
2 teaspoons baking powder
1 teaspoon salt
⅔ cup shortening
½ cup milk
6 small baking apples,
peeled and cored
¼ cup chopped walnuts
3 tablespoons cinnamon
sugar

baking powder, and salt into a bowl. Cut in shortening with a pastry blender or two knives until mixture looks like coarse corn meal. Add milk; stir with a fork only until flour is moistened. Roll out dough on a lightly floured board or pastry cloth into an 18-x-12-inch rectangle. Cut dough into 6-inch squares with a pastry wheel or knife. Place an apple in the center of each square; place chopped nuts in center of apple and sprinkle with cinnamon sugar. Bring the corners of the dough up over the apples, pressing edges of dough firmly to seal dumplings well on sides. Turn center corners back for petal effect. Place 1 inch apart in a greased shallow 3-quart baking dish. Pour the cinnamon syrup over all. Bake about 35 minutes, until apples are soft and pastry is golden brown. Serve warm. Serves 6.

How to Shape Fruit Dumplings

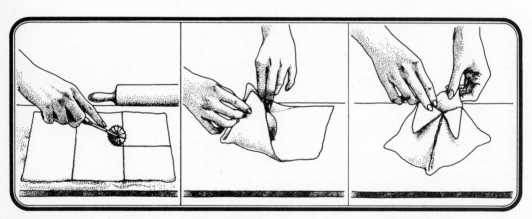

Roll out dough in a rectangle on a floured board. Cut into 6-inch squares with a fluted pastry wheel.

Moisten edges of square. Place whole fruit in center. Bring corners up to center and pinch sides together.

Gently turn back each of the center corners to form petals. Be sure sides stay pinched together firmly.

✑ Mrs. Chandler's Apple Roll

2 cups firmly packed light
brown sugar
2 cups water

Heat oven to 400° F. Place brown sugar and water in a 13-x-9-x-2-inch pan; heat in oven for 10 minutes, or until sugar is dissolved. Sift together flour, baking

2 cups sifted all-purpose flour

4 teaspoons baking powder

½ teaspoon salt

5 tablespoons butter or margarine

⅔ cup milk

3 tablespoons melted butter or margarine

3 cups coarsely chopped McIntosh apples (about 3 medium-sized apples)

½ teaspoon ground cinnamon

Light cream or vanilla ice cream

powder, and salt; cut in butter with a pastry blender or two knives until mixture resembles coarse corn meal. Stir in milk to make a soft dough. Turn out onto a well-floured board and knead lightly a few times. Roll out dough into a 12-x-8-inch rectangle. Brush with part of the melted butter, reserving some for tops of biscuit rolls. Spread apples over dough and sprinkle with cinnamon. Roll firmly as for a jelly roll, starting from 12-inch edge. Cut into 12 slices about ¾ inch thick and place in syrup in pan, leaving a space between each roll. Brush tops with melted butter. Bake 45 to 50 minutes, or until tops are lightly browned. Serve warm with light cream or vanilla ice cream. Serves 8 to 10.

 ## Fruit Flan

Pastry

1½ cups all-purpose flour

½ cup sugar

1 teaspoon baking powder

Few grains of salt

½ cup (1 stick) sweet butter

1 egg yolk

2 tablespoons milk

2 teaspoons finely grated lemon peel

Filling

2 pounds small freestone peaches or nectarines, peeled, halved and pitted (about 4 cups)

2 tablespoons lemon juice

2 tablespoons sugar

Glaze

½ cup apricot preserves

2 teaspoons water

Mix flour, sugar, baking powder and salt in a large mixing bowl. Add butter and cut in with a pastry blender or 2 knives until mixture resembles coarse corn meal. Add egg yolk, milk and lemon peel and stir with a fork until the mixture is moistened but still quite crumbly. Pat mixture into an 11-inch fluted quiche pan with a removable bottom; refrigerate while preparing fruit. Heat oven to 350° F. In a mixing bowl toss peaches with lemon juice and sugar. Arrange peaches cut side down on the dough in a circular pattern, so that the pieces of fruit touch but do not overlap. Pour any juice remaining in bowl over fruit and bake on shelf in center of oven 1 hour. Turn oven up to 400° F., place pan on shelf in lower third of oven and bake 20 minutes longer. Crust will be pale golden, not brown. Place pan on a wire cake rack to cool. Stir preserves and water in a small saucepan over moderately low heat 5 minutes, until syrupy; strain. Brush the apricot glaze over the peaches. Serve warm or cool. Serves 8.

Note: Instead of the quiche pan, a 13-x-9-x-2-inch aluminum baking pan can be used. Grease pan lightly and reduce baking time at 400° F. to 10 minutes. Unpeeled plums may be used instead of peaches; place them cut side up on pastry.

DESERTS

ᶟ Baked Cranberry Pears à la Mode

3 large ripe pears
6 tablespoons honey
1 16-ounce can whole berry
  cranberry sauce
Vanilla ice cream

Heat oven to 350° F. Peel pears, cut them into halves lengthwise, and remove cores. Arrange them, cut-side up, in a greased, shallow baking dish. Top each pear half with 1 tablespoon of the honey and spoon the cranberry sauce over and around them. Bake, covered, 20 minutes. Uncover and continue to bake until pears are fork-tender, 5 to 10 minutes, depending on size and degree of ripeness. Cool slightly. Serve topped with ice-cream. Serves 6.

ᶟ Hot Curried Fruit

1 17-ounce can apricot
  halves
1 17-ounce can pitted Bing
  cherries, drained
1 13¼-ounce can pineapple
  chunks, drained
1 8¼-ounce can sliced
  pineapple, drained
⅓ cup butter or margarine,
  melted
¾ cup firmly packed light
  brown sugar
1 to 2 teaspoons curry powder
1 cup commercial sour cream
Toasted coconut (directions on
  page 746)

Heat oven to 325° F. Drain apricots and reserve ¼ cup of the liquid. Place apricots, cherries, and pineapple chunks in a shallow 1½-quart baking dish. Pour in reserved apricot liquid. Cut pineapple slices in half and arrange in an overlapping ring on top of fruit. In a small bowl combine butter, brown sugar, and curry and spread over fruit in dish. Bake, uncovered, about 15 minutes, or until thoroughly heated. Serve warm, topped with sour cream and sprinkling of coconut. Serves 6.

ᶟ Fruit Betty

½ cup butter or margarine
8 slices white bread, cut into
  ½-inch cubes
1 16-ounce package frozen
  rhubarb, thawed
1 10-ounce package frozen
  halved or sliced
  strawberries, thawed
¼ cup sugar
1 tablespoon lemon juice
2 tablespoons sugar
Light cream (optional)

Heat oven to 375° F. Melt butter in a large skillet over moderately low heat (about 225° F.); add bread cubes and toss to coat with butter. Raise heat to moderately high (about 375° F.) and heat, stirring occasionally, until bread cubes are golden brown. Combine rhubarb, strawberries, the ¼ cup sugar, and lemon juice. Place half the fruit in a deep 1½-quart casserole; sprinkle with half the bread cubes. Repeat layers. Sprinkle with the 2 tablespoons sugar. Bake 40 minutes. Serve with light cream, if desired. Serves 6.

⋐§ Peach Crisp

1 cup unsifted all-purpose
   flour
½ cup sugar
¼ teaspoon ground nutmeg
¼ teaspoon salt
½ teaspoon ground
   cinnamon
½ cup firmly packed brown
   sugar
½ cup butter or margarine
1½ cups ½-inch bread cubes,
   cut from toasted white
   bread
4 cups sliced peeled fresh
   peaches (4 to 6 peaches)
¼ cup sugar
1 teaspoon grated lemon
   peel
Juice of ½ lemon
¼ teaspoon salt
Light cream or vanilla ice
   cream

Heat oven to 350° F. Sift flour, sugar, nutmeg, salt, and cinnamon into a bowl. Add brown sugar and mix well. With a pastry blender or two knives, cut butter into flour mixture until mixture looks like coarse crumbs. Generously butter bottom and sides of an 8-x-8-x-2-inch baking dish. Arrange bread cubes in dish. Combine peaches, the ¼ cup sugar, lemon peel, lemon juice, and salt; pour over bread cubes. Cover peaches with topping mixture; pat down well. Bake 45 minutes. Serve warm with plain cream or vanilla ice cream. Serves 6.

⋐§ Pears Streusel à la Mode

1 8¼-ounce can pear halves,
   well drained
6 gingersnaps, finely crushed
2 tablespoons sugar
2 tablespoons softened butter
   or margarine
Vanilla ice cream

Heat oven to 300° F. Place pears in a 2-cup casserole or baking dish. Combine gingersnap crumbs and sugar in a small bowl and blend well. Add butter and work with your fingers until mixture is crumbly. Sprinkle over the pears. Bake 20 minutes. Serve warm with a scoop of vanilla ice cream. Serves 2.

⋐§ Baked Rhubarb Pudding

¼ cup dark corn syrup
¼ cup softened butter or
   margarine
8 slices white bread
1 16-ounce package frozen
   rhubarb, cooked according
   to package directions

Heat oven to 400° F. Pour the ¼ cup corn syrup into bottom of a greased shallow 1½-quart baking dish. If necessary, tilt dish from side to side to cover the bottom completely. Spread butter on one side of each slice of bread. Arrange half the bread slices in bottom of dish, buttered side down. Cut slices where necessary so they entirely cover bottom of dish. Spoon rhubarb over bread

¼ *cup dark corn syrup*
Eggnog Sauce (recipe follows)

and top with remaining slices of bread, buttered side up, cutting if necessary. Pour the remaining ¼ cup corn syrup over bread. Bake 20 to 25 minutes, or until lightly browned. Serve warm with Eggnog Sauce. Serves 6.

Eggnog Sauce

1 *4-serving-size package vanilla pudding and pie filling*
2 *cups milk*
½ *cup heavy cream*
⅛ *teaspoon ground nutmeg*
½ *teaspoon rum extract*

Prepare pudding, following directions on package but substituting the amount of milk and cream given here. Add nutmeg and rum extract; mix well. Serve warm over pudding. Makes about 2½ cups sauce.

Fruit Shortcakes

Whether the base of a fruit shortcake should be biscuit or sponge cake will probably vary according to what your mother used to serve. We've given the universally popular rich biscuit first. If you prefer a homemade sponge layer, use the recipe for the cake base in Pineapple Sponge Shortcake (recipe on page 731).

Basic Shortcake Biscuits

2 *cups sifted all-purpose flour*
3 *teaspoons baking powder*
¾ *teaspoon salt*
3 *tablespoons sugar*
½ *cup shortening*
⅓ *cup undiluted evaporated milk or light cream*
1 *egg*

Heat oven to 425° F. Sift together flour, baking powder, salt, and sugar into a bowl. Cut in shortening with a pastry blender or two knives until mixture resembles coarse corn meal. Combine milk and egg and beat slightly; add to dry ingredients. Stir with a fork until all the flour is moistened. Turn out onto a lightly floured board and knead gently about 5 times. Roll dough to a thickness of ½ inch. Cut with a floured 3-inch cutter. Bake on an ungreased cookie sheet 12 to 15 minutes, until golden brown. For a large shortcake, pat dough into an 8-inch round cake pan. Bake 15 to 20 minutes until golden brown. Split shortcakes; fill and top with desired fruit. Makes 6 biscuits or 1 8-inch layer.

ᴄꜱ *Old-Fashioned Strawberry Shortcake*

1 quart fresh
   strawberries
½ cup sugar
1 recipe Basic Shortcake
   Biscuits (recipe on
   page 730)
1 cup heavy cream
2 tablespoons confectioners'
   sugar
2 tablespoons butter or
   margarine
Sweetened whipped cream

Wash strawberries and remove hulls. Slice; add the ½ cup sugar. Toss gently until berries are coated with sugar. Refrigerate 15 to 20 minutes. Make biscuits while strawberries are chilling in refrigerator. Combine cream and the 2 tablespoons confectioners' sugar; beat until stiff. To serve, split hot biscuits and spread with butter. Spoon berries between layers and over tops of biscuits. Top with sweetened whipped cream. Serves 6.

ᴄꜱ *Pineapple Sponge Shortcake*

For Cake Base:

1 cup sifted cake flour
1 teaspoon baking powder
¼ teaspoon salt
3 eggs, at room temperature
1 cup sugar
2 teaspoons lemon juice
6 tablespoons hot milk

For Filling:

1 29½-ounce can pineapple
   chunks
1 tablespoon cornstarch
2 tablespoons lemon juice
1 cup heavy cream
¼ cup maraschino cherry
   juice
¼ teaspoon almond extract
½ cup broken walnuts
Maraschino cherries

To Make Cake: Heat oven to 350° F. Line the bottoms of two ungreased 8-inch round cake pans with waxed paper. Sift together flour, baking powder, and salt. In a large bowl beat eggs at high speed until very thick, about 5 minutes. While continuing to beat, gradually add sugar and lemon juice; scrape sides and bottom of bowl often. Fold dry ingredients into egg mixture, a little at a time. Quickly add the hot milk and stir until thoroughly blended. Pour batter into prepared pans. Bake 20 to 25 minutes, until tops spring back when touched lightly with the finger. Cool cakes 15 to 20 minutes before removing from pans.

To Make Filling: Drain pineapple chunks, reserving 1 cup of syrup. Add cornstarch and lemon juice to syrup and cook over moderately low heat (about 225° F.), stirring frequently, until syrup thickens and begins to bubble. Remove from heat and add pineapple chunks. Let stand 10 to 15 minutes at room temperature. Combine cream, maraschino cherry juice, and almond extract; beat until cream holds its shape. To serve, spoon half of pineapple mixture and whipped cream over one layer of sponge cake and top with second layer. Spread remaining pineapple and whipped cream over top. Sprinkle with walnuts and garnish with maraschino cherries. Serves 8.

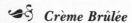 *Cranberry Clafouti*

1 *1-pound can whole cranberry sauce*
1 *8-ounce can juice-packed pineapple chunks, drained**
1 *tablespoon lemon juice*
⅓ *cup liquid skim milk*
2 *tablespoons plain yogurt*
2 *eggs*
¼ *cup all-purpose flour*
¼ *teaspoon salt*
1 *tablespoon finely grated lemon peel*
2 *teaspoons butter or vegetable oil*

In a medium-sized bowl place cranberry sauce, pineapple chunks and lemon juice and mix thoroughly. Place milk, yogurt, eggs, flour, salt and lemon peel in an electric blender; cover and blend at high speed 1 minute. Heat oven to 375° F. Melt butter in a heavy, 10-inch iron skillet or flameproof, ovenproof dish over moderate heat. When butter foams, add about one fourth of the yogurt batter; rotate pan so batter coats bottom evenly. Cook the "pancake" over moderately high heat until set, about 4 minutes; spread cranberry mixture over pancake and top with remaining batter. Place skillet in oven and bake 35 to 40 minutes. Cut in wedges and serve hot from skillet. Serves 6.

*Note: Save juice and use in a drink or fresh fruit compote.

Puddings

Crème Brûlée

2 *cups heavy cream*
4 *egg yolks*
4 *tablespoons sugar*
1½ *teaspoons vanilla extract*
¼ *cup firmly packed light brown sugar*

Heat oven to 350° F. Heat cream in a saucepan over low heat (about 200° F.) until bubbles appear around edge of the pan. Remove from heat. Beat egg yolks in a bowl until thick and lemon-colored. Beat in sugar and vanilla. Gradually add hot cream and stir to blend thoroughly. Pour mixture into a 1-quart soufflé dish. Set baking dish in a larger pan containing about 1 inch hot water. Bake 50 minutes, or until a knife inserted toward the side of the custard comes out clean. Cool and then chill about 1 hour. Sprinkle brown sugar evenly over top of chilled custard and place in a preheated broiler 3 inches from heat and broil 1 to 2 minutes, until sugar melts. Watch pudding carefully because the sugar burns easily. Serve immediately. Serves 6 generously.

⌐§ Chocolate Pot-de-Crème

8 ounces sweet cooking
  chocolate
5 tablespoons cold water
5 eggs, separated
2 tablespoons dark rum
Sweetened whipped cream
  (optional)

Break chocolate into small pieces. Place in a heavy saucepan; add water. Cook over moderately low heat (about 225° F.), stirring constantly, until chocolate is melted. Remove from heat. Beat egg yolks slightly. Add rum and stir to blend. Pour chocolate mixture into egg yolks. Mix gently until blended. Beat egg whites until stiff but not dry. Fold egg whites into chocolate mixture. Pour into a serving bowl or small individual serving dishes. Chill several hours. Serve topped with whipped cream, if desired. Serves 4 to 6.

⌐§ Floating Island

1½ cups milk
 3 eggs, separated
 6 tablespoons sugar
 1 teaspoon flour
¾ teaspoon vanilla extract
Caramelized Sugar (recipe
  follows)

Scald milk in the top of a double boiler over hot water. In a small bowl beat egg whites until soft peaks form. Gradually add 3 tablespoons of the sugar, beating constantly until stiff peaks form. Drop by heaping tablespoonfuls into the hot milk. Make only 2 or 3 puffs at a time. Cover and cook 4 minutes. Remove puffs with a perforated spoon and drain on a plate. Repeat with rest of egg-white mixture. In a small bowl beat egg yolks until thick and lemon-colored. Gradually add the remaining 3 tablespoons sugar and the flour; continue beating until well blended. Gradually add ¼ cup of the hot milk to egg yolk mixture; beating constantly until blended; pour this mixture back into hot milk. Cook over hot water, stirring constantly, until custard coats a metal spoon. Stir in the vanilla. Pour into serving dishes. Top each serving with an egg-white puff. Drizzle meringues with Caramelized Sugar. Chill, uncovered, until serving time. Serves 4 to 6.

Caramelized Sugar

Place ¼ *cup sugar* in a small skillet. Cook over low heat (do not use controlled-temperature burner), stirring constantly to prevent burning, until sugar melts and turns light golden brown. With a teaspoon, immediately drizzle Caramelized Sugar over meringues. Work quickly because sugar will harden in the skillet. If sugar in skillet does harden, place over very low heat just until it melts again, stirring constantly.

✑ Nesselrode Pudding

3 egg yolks
1½ cups light cream
¾ cup sugar
1 teaspoon unflavored gelatine
¼ teaspoon salt
½ cup canned crushed pineapple, undrained
1 cup heavy cream, whipped
½ cup seedless raisins
2 tablespoons well-drained, diced maraschino cherries
¼ cup chopped semisweet chocolate pieces

Set control of refrigerator at coldest setting. Beat egg yolks. In the top of a double boiler combine egg yolks, light cream, sugar, gelatine, salt, and pineapple. Cook, stirring constantly, over simmering water until custard is slightly thickened, about 7 minutes. Chill until mixture begins to thicken. Turn into an ice cube tray; cover and freeze until firm about 1 inch from sides of tray, about 2 hours. Break up mixture into a chilled bowl. Beat with an electric or rotary blender until smooth. Fold in whipped cream, raisins, maraschino cherries, and chocolate. Pour into a chilled 4- or 5-cup mold or 2 ice cube trays. Cover and freeze until firm, about 2½ to 3 hours. Serves 6 to 8.

✑ Brown-Rice Pudding

½ cup uncooked brown rice
2½ cups liquid skim milk
4 3-inch strips lemon peel
1 3-inch cinnamon stick
3 tablespoons brown sugar
¼ cup chopped pitted dates

Place rice, milk, lemon peel and cinnamon stick in a medium-sized, heavy saucepan and bring to a boil over moderately high heat, stirring once or twice. When mixture boils, reduce heat to low, cover pan and simmer gently 1 hour. Stir in sugar and dates and cook covered 15 minutes longer. Remove lemon peels and cinnamon stick before serving. Serve pudding hot or pour into a serving dish; cover and chill 3 hours or longer. Makes 2½ cups, or serves 4.

✑ Zabaglione

6 egg yolks
6 tablespoons sugar
⅔ cup Marsala wine

Combine all ingredients in the top of a double boiler. Place over simmering, not boiling, water. Beat with an electric hand mixer or rotary beater over hot water until very thick and foamy, about 5 minutes. Do not overcook or mixture will curdle. Serve warm in sherbet glasses or use as a sauce over fresh fruit. Serves 6 to 8.

Baked Puddings

✌ Custard Bread Pudding

3 cups milk
¼ cup melted butter or
  margarine
½ cup sugar
4 cups ½-inch soft bread
  cubes
3 eggs
¼ teaspoon salt
1 teaspoon vanilla extract
⅛ teaspoon ground nutmeg

Heat oven to 350° F. Grease a deep 1½-quart baking dish. Heat milk over low heat (about 200° F.) until little bubbles form at pan edge. Remove from heat. Add butter, sugar, and bread cubes. Let stand 5 minutes. Beat eggs well in a large bowl. Add salt, vanilla, and nutmeg. Slowly stir milk mixture into egg mixture. Pour into greased dish. Set dish in a baking pan and add 1 inch hot water to pan. Bake for 55 minutes until set. Serves 6.

✌ Queen of Bread Puddings

1½ cups ¼-inch cubes white
  bread, tightly packed
¼ cup firmly packed dark
  brown sugar
2 cups milk
2 tablespoons melted butter
  or margarine
¼ teaspoon salt
1 teaspoon vanilla extract
2 egg yolks
⅓ cup dried currants
1 cup seedless raisins
2 egg whites, at room
  temperature
¼ cup granulated sugar
¼ cup currant jelly

Heat oven to 375° F. Mix bread cubes, brown sugar, milk, butter, salt, and vanilla in a bowl. Beat egg yolks slightly and stir into bread mixture. Add currants and raisins. Pour into a greased 8-x-8-x-2-inch pan. Set in a larger pan and pour warm water into larger pan to a depth of 1 inch. Bake 50 minutes, or until set. Remove pudding from oven and increase oven temperature to 425° F. Beat egg whites until soft peaks form; gradually add sugar and beat until stiff peaks form. Spread currant jelly over pudding; cover with meringue. Bake 4 to 5 minutes, or until meringue is lightly browned. Serve slightly warm. Serves 4 to 6.

✌ Deluxe Chocolate Bread Pudding

1 cup soft white bread
  crumbs, tightly packed
⅔ cup sugar
½ teaspoon ground
  cinnamon
¼ teaspoon ground nutmeg

Heat oven to 325° F. Mix bread crumbs, sugar, cinnamon, nutmeg, and salt in a bowl; stir in milk, butter, and vanilla. Gradually add chocolate, stirring until blended. Beat eggs and coffee liqueur together; stir into chocolate mixture. Pour into greased deep 1-quart casserole. Bake 70 minutes, or until a knife

⅛ teaspoon salt
2½ cups milk, scalded
2 tablespoons melted butter
2 teaspoons vanilla extract
2 1-ounce squares
　unsweetened chocolate,
　melted
2 eggs
3 tablespoons coffee liqueur
Sweetened whipped cream

inserted near center comes out clean. Serve slightly warm or chilled with whipped cream. Serves 6.

ঞ Crème Caramel

¾ cup sugar
2 cups dairy half-and-half
4 eggs
⅛ teaspoon salt

Heat oven to 300° F. Heat ½ cup of the sugar in a small heavy skillet over low heat (do not use temperature-controlled burner), stirring constantly with a wooden spoon until the sugar melts, is free from lumps, and turns a light caramel color. Pour caramel into the bottom of a greased deep 1-quart casserole. In a medium-sized saucepan heat half-and-half over moderately low heat (about 225° F.) until tiny bubbles appear around the edges of the pan. In a medium-sized bowl beat eggs, the remaining ¼ cup sugar, and the salt with a rotary beater; gradually stir in scalded half-and-half and blend well. Pour mixture slowly through a fine strainer into the casserole. Place casserole in a larger pan. Pour hot water around casserole to within ¾ inch from top of casserole. Bake about 1¼ hours, or until a knife inserted in the custard ½ inch from edge of casserole comes out clean. Remove custard from hot water immediately and cool on wire rack. Chill several hours in refrigerator. Gently loosen custard from sides of dish with a spatula and invert onto a serving plate. Spoon some of the caramel sauce over each serving. Serves 6 to 8.

ঞ Cottage Pudding with Peach Sauce

1 29-ounce can sliced
　peaches
1¾ cups sifted all-purpose
　flour
2 teaspoons baking powder
½ teaspoon salt

Heat oven to 350° F. Grease and flour a 9-inch-square cake pan. Drain the peaches and reserve syrup. Coarsely chop enough sliced peaches to make 1 cup. Reserve remaining peaches for sauce. Sift together into a bowl the flour, baking powder, and salt. Add shortening, sugar, egg, milk, and vanilla and beat vigorously until

¼ *cup softened shortening*
¾ *cup sugar*
1 *egg*
⅔ *cup milk*
1 *teaspoon vanilla extract*
Peach Sauce (recipe follows)

well blended. Fold in the chopped peaches. Pour into prepared pan; bake 25 to 30 minutes. Cut into squares and serve warm with Peach Sauce. Serves 8.

Peach Sauce

¼ *cup sugar*
2 *tablespoons cornstarch*
Sliced peaches and syrup
 (from preceding recipe)
½ *cup orange marmalade*
1 *teaspoon lemon juice*
¼ *teaspoon almond extract*

Mix sugar and cornstarch in a saucepan. Pour reserved peach syrup into a 2-cup measuring cup; add enough water to make 1¾ cups liquid. Gradually add peach syrup mixture to saucepan; mix well. Cut peach slices in half and add to syrup. Cook over moderately low heat (about 225° F.), stirring constantly, until thickened and clear. Add orange marmalade, lemon juice, and almond extract; heat. Serve over pudding. Makes 3 cups sauce.

৵৽ Baked Custard

Butter
 4 *eggs*
¼ *cup sugar*
¼ *teaspoon salt*
2½ *cups milk, heated*
 1 *teaspoon vanilla extract*
Ground nutmeg

Heat oven to 300° F. Butter five 6-ounce custard cups. Beat eggs until foamy; add sugar and salt and stir until blended. Gradually stir in milk and vanilla. Pour into prepared cups. Sprinkle with nutmeg. Place cups in a large pan and add 1 inch hot water to large pan. Bake 45 to 50 minutes or until a knife inserted in center comes out clean. Remove at once from the hot water. Cool on wire cake racks and refrigerate before serving. Serves 5.

Note: This custard may be baked in a 1½-quart buttered baking dish. Increase baking time about 10 minutes or until a knife inserted one inch from the center comes out clean.

৵৽ Date Nut Torte

 2 *eggs*
½ *cup sugar*
 1 *teaspoon vanilla extract*
¾ *cup chopped walnuts*
¾ *cup chopped almonds*
1½ *cups cut-up pitted dates*
½ *cup packaged graham*
 cracker crumbs
 1 *teaspoon baking powder*

Heat oven to 325° F. Beat eggs and sugar until well combined; stir in vanilla, nuts, and dates. Combine cracker crumbs, baking powder, and salt and add to date–nut mixture. Blend well. Spread in the bottom of a greased 8-inch-square cake pan. Bake 50 minutes, or until firm. Let stand about 15 minutes before cutting. Serve warm with ice cream or Vanilla Custard Sauce. Serves 6 to 8.

¼ *teaspoon salt*
Vanilla ice cream or Vanilla
Custard Sauce (recipe
follows)

Vanilla Custard Sauce

1½ *cups milk*
2 *eggs, well beaten*
¼ *cup sugar*
¼ *teaspoon salt*
1 *teaspoon vanilla extract*

Scald milk in the top of a double boiler over low heat (about 200° F.). Combine eggs, sugar, and salt in a small bowl. Gradually stir in scalded milk. Return mixture to top of double boiler; cook over simmering, not boiling, water, (about 200° F.), stirring constantly. When custard will coat a metal spoon, remove from heat. Place pan in cold water to cool quickly. If custard should start to curdle, beat vigorously with a rotary beater until smooth. Blend in vanilla; cool. Makes about 2 cups.

Baked Indian Pudding

4 *cups milk*
½ *cup sugar*
½ *cup yellow corn meal*
3 *eggs, slightly beaten*
½ *teaspoon ground cinnamon*
1 *teaspoon ground ginger*
1 *teaspoon salt*
1 *cup molasses*
1 *teaspoon grated orange
peel*
Vanilla ice cream (optional)

Heat oven to 325° F. Heat milk and sugar in a saucepan over moderately low heat (about 225° F.) until tiny bubbles appear around edge of pan. Gradually stir in corn meal; cook and stir constantly until smooth and slightly thickened. Remove from heat. Stir in eggs, cinnamon, ginger, salt, molasses, and orange peel. Mix thoroughly. Pour into a greased deep 2-quart casserole. Bake 1½ hours. If desired, serve hot with vanilla ice cream. Serves 6.

Baked Lemon Pudding

1½ *cups sugar*
½ *cup sifted all-purpose
flour*
½ *teaspoon baking powder*
¼ *teaspoon salt*
3 *eggs, separated*
2 *teaspoons grated lemon
peel*
¼ *cup lemon juice*
2 *teaspoons melted butter
or margarine*
1½ *cups milk*

Heat oven to 350° F. Sift 1 cup of the sugar with flour, baking powder, and salt. Beat egg yolks until thick and lemon-colored; add lemon peel, lemon juice, butter, and milk. Beat thoroughly. Stir in flour mixture and beat until smooth. Beat egg whites until soft peaks form. Add the remaining ½ cup sugar, 1 tablespoon at a time, beating well after each addition until stiff peaks form. Fold beaten egg whites into flour mixture. Pour into a buttered deep 2-quart casserole. Set in a pan containing ½ inch hot water. Bake about 50 to 60 minutes, or until firm. Cool on wire cake rack; chill 1 hour. Makes 4 to 6 servings.

☙ *Piedmont Pudding*

1¼ cups water
3 tablespoons instant
   farina
1 pound ricotta cheese
1 whole egg
1 egg, separated
¼ cup sugar
¼ teaspoon ground
   cinnamon
¼ teaspoon ground nutmeg
½ teaspoon salt
3 tablespoons light rum
1 tablespoon seedless
   raisins
¼ cup diced mixed candied
   fruits and peels
½ cup packaged graham
   cracker crumbs
Confectioners' sugar

Bring water to a boil; gradually add instant farina and cook 10 minutes over low heat (about 200° F.), stirring constantly, until thickened. Remove from heat. Beat cheese with an electric mixer until smooth. Add whole egg, egg yolk, sugar, cinnamon, nutmeg, salt, and rum; beat 2 minutes. Fold in raisins, candied fruit, and instant farina. Heat oven to 300° F. Beat egg white until stiff but not dry; fold into cheese mixture. Butter a shallow 1½-quart baking dish; sprinkle graham cracker crumbs over bottom. Pour in cheese mixture and bake 1 hour. Turn off heat and cool in oven 1 hour with door closed. Sprinkle with confectioners' sugar before serving. Serves 6.

☙ *Rice Pudding*

3½ cups milk, scalded
¼ cup uncooked rice
⅓ cup sugar
½ teaspoon salt
1 teaspoon vanilla extract
¼ teaspoon ground nutmeg

Heat oven to 325° F. Combine all ingredients in a greased 1-quart casserole. Bake for 2 hours. When pudding has baked about 30 minutes, stir in brown crust that forms on top of pudding. Repeat at half-hour intervals. Bake pudding without stirring the last half hour. Serve warm. Serves 6.

Steamed Puddings

☙ *Chocolate Steamed Pudding*

1½ cups sifted all-purpose
   flour
1½ teaspoons baking powder
½ teaspoon salt
½ teaspoon ground

Sift together flour, baking powder, salt, and cinnamon. Work together shortening and sugar in a mixing bowl. Add vanilla. Beat in eggs. Melt chocolate in a small saucepan over low heat (about 200° F.); combine with mixture in mixing bowl. Add flour mixture alternately

cinnamon
3 tablespoons shortening, at
room temperature
¾ cup sugar
1½ teaspoons vanilla extract
2 eggs
2 1-ounce squares
unsweetened chocolate
¾ cup milk
Ice cream (optional)
Chocolate sauce (optional)

with milk to mixture in bowl, beating well after each addition. Butter a deep 1½-quart casserole; sprinkle with sugar to coat bottom and sides; shake out any excess sugar. Pour pudding batter into prepared casserole. Cover casserole with foil and tie securely around the edge with string. Place on a rack in a large, deep pot or Dutch oven. Pour water into pot to come halfway up the sides of casserole. Place over moderate heat (about 250° F.) until water comes to a boil. Cover pot and steam 1½ hours, or until a cake tester inserted in the center of pudding comes out clean. Place a serving plate over pudding and invert pudding onto it. Let cool about 15 minutes before cutting. Serve pudding warm with ice cream and chocolate sauce, if desired. Serves 6 to 8.

◄§ Christmas Plum Pudding

¾ cup sifted all-purpose
flour
1 teaspoon baking powder
½ teaspoon salt
½ teaspoon ground allspice
¼ teaspoon ground nutmeg
1 cup fine dry bread crumbs
1½ cups finely chopped beef
suet (about 6 ounces)
1¼ cups seeded raisins,
coarsely chopped
1 cup currants
1¼ cups seedless raisins
¾ cup blanched almonds,
chopped
⅓ cup diced, mixed candied
fruits and peels
1 tablespoon grated lemon
peel
4 eggs
¾ cup firmly packed light
brown sugar
2 tablespoons lemon juice
¼ cup brandy
¼ teaspoon almond extract

Sift together flour, baking powder, salt, allspice, and nutmeg in a large bowl. Stir in bread crumbs. Add suet, chopped raisins, currants, seedless raisins, almonds, mixed candied fruits, and lemon peel; toss together until fruits are thoroughly coated with flour mixture. Beat eggs well; add brown sugar, lemon juice, the ¼ cup brandy, almond extract, marmalade, and milk. Beat until mixture is blended. Gradually add to flour–fruit mixture; stir until all the flour is moistened. Spoon into a greased 2-quart mold or two small molds, filling each ¾ full. Cover well and place on rack in large pot with 1 inch of boiling water in the bottom. Cover and simmer 4½ to 5 hours. Add more boiling water if necessary. Store in cool place. Before serving, place covered mold in small amount of boiling water and steam 1 hour, until pudding is thoroughly heated. Remove pudding from mold and place on a heatproof serving dish. Just before serving, heat the 3 tablespoons brandy or rum and pour over pudding; set aflame. Serve with Custard Sauce or Brandy Butter. Serves 14 to 16.

1 tablespoon orange
    marmalade
1 cup milk
3 tablespoons brandy or
    rum
Custard Sauce (recipe follows)
    or Brandy Butter (recipe
    on page 724)

Custard Sauce

2 eggs
3 tablespoons superfine sugar
1 cup milk, scalded
1 tablespoon brandy

Beat eggs well. Add sugar and beat until blended. Gradually stir in milk. Pour into top of double boiler. Place over simmering water and cook, stirring constantly, until mixture coats a metal spoon. Remove from heat, stir in brandy. Serve immediately, or cover and store in refrigerator. Reheat over hot water. Makes 1¼ cups.

✑ English Christmas Pudding

4 cups seedless raisins
2 cups dried currants
4 cups finely chopped peeled
    apples
1 cup finely cut candied citron
4 cups sifted all-purpose flour
8 eggs, separated
2 cups sugar
2 teaspoons ground nutmeg
2 teaspoons salt
4 cups finely chopped beef
    suet (about 1 pound)
4 cups soft bread crumbs
3 cups milk, fruit juice, or
    cider
Vanilla Sauce (recipe follows)
Hard Sauce (recipe follows)

Combine raisins, currants, apples, and citron with 1 cup of the flour; coat fruits evenly with flour. Beat egg yolks until light in color; pour into a large pot or clean dishpan; gradually beat in sugar. Add 1 cup of the flour, the nutmeg, and the salt and stir to combine thoroughly. Add the combined fruits, suet, and crumbs alternately with the 3 cups liquid. Stir in remaining flour. Beat egg whites until stiff but not dry. Fold into batter. Fill greased plain (not fluted) molds of 1 quart or less capacity two-thirds full. Cover tightly and place on a rack in a large pot. Pour 1 inch of water into the pot. Place over moderate heat (about 250° F.) and steam about 4 hours, or until a cake tester inserted in center of pudding comes out clean. (Smaller molds will take less time.) Add more water to pot if necessary. Puddings may be made a few days in advance and stored in molds in the refrigerator. To reheat, place covered mold on a rack in a large pot. Pour 1 inch water into pot. Place over moderate heat (about 250° F.) and steam about 1 hour. Unmold onto a serving plate. Serve with Vanilla Sauce and Hard Sauce. Makes 6 pounds.

Vanilla Sauce

Combine ½ *cup sugar, a few grains salt,* and *1 tablespoon cornstarch.* Gradually add *1 cup water.* Place over moderate heat (about 250° F.); cook and stir until thickened and clear. Add *2 tablespoons butter, 1 teaspoon vanilla extract,* and *a few grains ground nutmeg.* Serve warm. Makes about 1 cup.

Hard Sauce

Work ⅓ *cup butter or margarine* in a bowl until creamy.   Gradually add *1 cup confectioners' sugar* and beat until blended. Add ½ *teaspoon vanilla extract* and *a dash of ground nutmeg,* if desired. Chill. Makes about ¾ cup.

Gelatine Desserts

Gelatine desserts are picture-pretty desserts to do in your most attractive molds. Some of them are relatively low in calories.

Hints for Perfect Gelatine Desserts

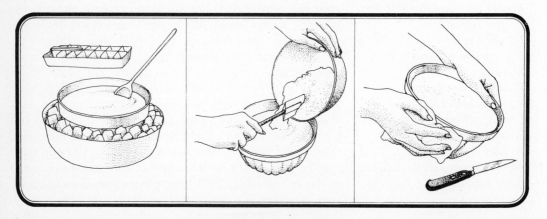

Set gelatine mixture in pan of ice cubes and water. Stir constantly until mixture begins to thicken.

Use a rubber spatula to fold any other ingredients called for into the slightly thickened gelatine.

To unmold gelatine, cut around top edge with a knife. Rub outside of mold with hot wet cloth to loosen.

How to Fold in Cream or Egg Whites

Whipped cream or whipped egg whites should be carefully folded into thickened gelatine so that the mixture will retain as much air as possible and the finished product will be light and spongy. Add the stiffly beaten cream or egg whites to the thickened gelatine mixture. With a rubber spatula make a cut down through the center of the mixture; bring spatula along the bottom of the bowl and up the side to the rim. Then fold spatula back to the center ready for the next cut. As you work, turn the bowl frequently. Continue to cut and fold only until the mixture is smooth. Don't overmix.

Coffee Jelly

1 envelope unflavored
   gelatine
¼ cup sugar
⅛ teaspoon salt
1¾ cups strong coffee
1 tablespoon brandy
   (optional)
½ recipe Vanilla Custard
   Sauce (recipe on page
   738)

Combine gelatine, sugar, and salt in a saucepan. Stir in coffee. Place over low heat (about 200° F.) and stir until gelatine is dissolved. Stir in brandy. Pour into a 9-x-5-x-3-inch loaf pan and cool about 30 minutes. Chill until firm. Cut into ½-inch cubes. Serve with Vanilla Custard Sauce. Serves 4.

Orange Cream in Orange Cups

8 large navel oranges
1⅓ cups sugar
2 tablespoons cognac
2 envelopes unflavored
   gelatine
½ cup cold water

Cut a thick slice from the navel end of each orange (slice should be approximately ¼ of the orange). Flute edges with a sharp knife, if desired. With a grapefruit knife and a teaspoon, scoop out orange pulp into a bowl. Put orange cups in a shallow dish. With a potato masher press out the juice from the pulp in the bowl. Strain the

[743]

1½ cups heavy cream
Grated unsweetened chocolate

juice into a 1-quart measuring cup. There should be 3 cups; if necessary, add additional orange juice. Stir sugar and cognac into juice. Sprinkle gelatine over the cold water in the top of a double boiler; place over simmering water and heat until gelatine is dissolved; pour into a medium-sized bowl. Slowly stir juice mixture into the dissolved gelatine. Stir in ¾ cup of the heavy cream and ladle into the orange cups. Chill until firm. Just before serving whip remaining cream and spoon onto each serving. Top with grated chocolate. Serves 8.

✑ Snow Pudding

1 envelope unflavored
  gelatine
½ cup sugar
1¼ cups hot water
¼ cup lemon juice
1 teaspoon grated lemon
  peel
¼ teaspoon salt
2 egg whites, at room
  temperature
2 tablespoons sugar
1 cup thinly sliced fresh or
  canned peaches
Fresh mint sprigs
Vanilla Custard Sauce (recipe
  on page 738)

Combine gelatine and the ½ cup sugar in a saucepan. Add hot water and place over low heat (about 200° F.); stir until gelatine is dissolved. Add lemon juice, lemon peel, and salt. Chill until the consistency of unbeaten egg white. Beat egg whites until soft peaks form. Gradually add the 2 tablespoons sugar and continue beating until peaks are stiff and glossy. Fold beaten egg whites into thickened gelatine mixture. Pour into a 3½-cup mold and chill until firm. Unmold pudding and garnish with peach slices and mint. Serve with Vanilla Custard Sauce. Serves 8.

✑ Strawberry Charlotte Russe

7 or 8 whole ladyfingers
1 6-ounce package
  strawberry-flavored
  gelatin
2 cups boiling water
1½ cups crushed strawberries
1 tablespoon lemon juice
½ cup sugar
⅛ teaspoon salt
2 cups heavy cream,
  whipped

Put a 3-inch strip of waxed paper around the inside of an 8-inch springform pan. (If a springform pan is not available, charlotte may be made in and served from a deep 2½-quart casserole.) Split ladyfingers; cut tips from one end of the halves so they will stand. Arrange, rounded end up, around edge of pan inside waxed paper. Put strawberry gelatin in a large bowl. Add boiling water and stir until dissolved. Combine strawberries, lemon juice, sugar, and salt; stir until sugar is dissolved. Combine with gelatin mixture. Chill until mixture is the consistency of unbeaten egg white. Fold in whipped cream. Carefully spoon into pan lined with ladyfingers; chill until firm—at least 5 hours or overnight. Remove the side of springform pan and the waxed paper; lift onto a large serving plate. Decorate top with additional whipped cream and whole strawberries, if desired. Serves 10 to 12.

Mousses

Light, fluffy mousses are ideal company desserts. Molded in a pretty shape, they may be decorated to make a beautiful presentation at a candlelit table.

How to Unfold Mousses

Gelatine and frozen mixtures must be carefully removed from the mold so that the smooth, firm texture of the surface will be retained.

To unmold gelatine mousse, fill a deep pan with lukewarm water; it should feel barely warm to the hand. Run a thin knife carefully around the top edge of the mold to break the air seal. Dip the mold carefully into the water until water comes up just to the rim. Hold it there for a few seconds; remove from the water and shake mold gently to loosen the mousse. Place a large, flat plate over the top of the mold; hold plate and mold firmly and invert them. Again shake gently and the mousse should slip out. If it doesn't, dip it in the warm water again.

To unmold frozen mousse, invert the mold on a large, flat plate. Cover the mold with a warm, damp towel for a few seconds, until the mold can be lifted off easily.

🦢 *Banana Mousse*

⅔ *cup evaporated milk*
⅓ *cup water*
3 *egg yolks*
¾ *teaspoon vanilla extract*
1 *cup evaporated milk*
½ *cup light corn syrup*

Combine the ⅔ cup evaporated milk and ⅓ cup water in a saucepan and heat to boiling point over moderate heat (about 250° F.). Beat egg yolks in top of double boiler and gradually add scalded evaporated milk and water. Cook over simmering water, stirring constantly until mixture thickens and coats a metal spoon. Add vanilla

¼ *cup sugar*
¼ *cup water*
3 *egg whites, at room
   temperature*
1½ *cups mashed banana*

and cool. Pour the 1 cup evaporated milk into freezer tray or loaf pan and freeze until ice crystals form around edges. Turn into chilled bowl and whip with an electric or rotary beater until stiff. Chill in refrigerator until ready to use. Combine corn syrup, sugar, and the ¼ cup water in saucepan. Bring to boil over moderate heat (about 250° F.) and boil 2 minutes. Beat egg whites until stiff. Gradually add sugar mixture, beating constantly until stiff peaks form. Fold bananas, beaten egg whites, and whipped evaporated milk into cooled custard. Pour into 10-cup mold or freezer trays or loaf pans. Freeze 3 to 4 hours, until firm. Unmold by placing warm cloth over mold until mold can be lifted off. Makes 2½ quarts or serves 12.

❧ Cherry–Brandy Mousse

1 *13-fluid-ounce can
  evaporated milk*
½ *cup confectioners' sugar*
⅔ *cup light corn syrup*
3 *tablespoons lemon juice*
2 *tablespoons brandy*
1 *16-ounce can sour red
  cherries, drained and
  chopped*

Pour evaporated milk into a freezer tray and freeze until ice crystals form around edges. Turn into a chilled bowl and whip with an electric or rotary beater until stiff. Add sugar, corn syrup, lemon juice, and brandy. Beat until blended. Fold in cherries. Pour into freezer trays and freeze until firm. Makes 2 quarts, or serves 10 to 12.

❧ Lemon Mousse

1 *egg white, at room
  temperature*
⅓ *cup water*
⅓ *cup nonfat dry milk solids*
1 *egg yolk*
⅓ *cup sugar*
Few grains salt
¼ *teaspoon grated lemon
  peel*
3 *tablespoons lemon juice*
⅟₄ cup toasted coconut

Place egg white, water, and dry milk in a bowl and beat with rotary beater or electric mixer until mixture stands in peaks. Place egg yolk, sugar, salt, lemon peel, and juice in a bowl and beat until blended. Gradually add lemon mixture to egg white mixture and beat until blended. Pour into ice-cube tray or loaf pan. Sprinkle with coconut and freeze 4 to 5 hours, until firm. Serves 6.

Note: If toasted coconut is not available, spread ¼ cup flaked coconut in a flat pan and place in a 325° F. oven 5 to 7 minutes, stirring occasionally until toasted.

Mocha Mousse Coronet Cake

16 to 18 ladyfingers, split
1 envelope unflavored
   gelatine
2 tablespoons cold water
1 6-ounce package
   semisweet chocolate
   pieces
1 8-ounce package cream
   cheese, at room
   temperature
½ cup firmly packed light
   brown sugar
1 teaspoon instant coffee
   powder
3 eggs, separated
½ cup firmly packed light
   brown sugar
1½ teaspoons vanilla
   extract
1½ cups heavy cream,
   whipped
Sweetened whipped cream
   (optional)
Chocolate curls (optional)

Arrange split ladyfingers around sides and over bottom of a 9-inch springform pan. Sprinkle gelatine over cold water to soften. Place over boiling water and stir until gelatine is dissolved. Melt chocolate over hot, not boiling, water. Cool 10 minutes. Beat cream cheese until fluffy. Gradually add the ½ cup brown sugar and the coffee; beat until blended. Add egg yolks, one at a time, beating well after each addition. Beat in melted chocolate and gelatine. Beat egg whites until soft peaks form. Gradually add the remaining ½ cup brown sugar and vanilla to egg whites and beat until stiff and satiny. Fold egg whites and cream into chocolate mixture. Pour into springform pan and chill at least 5 hours, or until set. Garnish with additional whipped cream and chocolate curls, if desired. Remove the side of springform pan. Serve cut into wedges. Serves 10.

Peanut Brittle Mousse

1 envelope unflavored
   gelatine
¼ cup sugar
⅛ teaspoon salt
2 eggs, separated
1¼ cups milk
½ teaspoon vanilla
   extract
¼ cup sugar
¾ cup crushed peanut
   brittle
1 cup heavy cream,
   whipped

Mix together gelatine, the ¼ cup of sugar, and the salt in a saucepan. Beat together egg yolks and milk; stir into gelatine mixture. Place over low heat (about 200° F.), stirring constantly, until gelatine is dissolved, about 6 minutes. Add vanilla and chill until mixture is the consistency of unbeaten egg white. Beat egg whites until soft peaks form. Gradually add the ¼ cup sugar, beating constantly until stiff peaks form. Fold egg whites, peanut brittle, and cream into gelatine mixture. Pour into a 1-quart mold; chill until set. Serves 4 to 6.

DESSERTS

Soufflé Froid au Chocolat

2 1-ounce squares
   unsweetened chocolate,
   melted
½ cup confectioners' sugar
1 cup hot milk
1 envelope unflavored
   gelatine, softened in 3
   tablespoons cold water
¾ cup granulated sugar
1 teaspoon vanilla extract
¼ teaspoon salt
2 cups heavy cream, whipped

Combine chocolate and confectioners' sugar in a saucepan. Gradually add hot milk, stirring constantly. Place over moderately low heat (about 225° F.) and stir until mixture reaches the boiling point. Do not boil. Remove from heat; stir in softened gelatine, sugar, vanilla, and salt. Mix until gelatine is entirely melted. Chill until slightly thickened. Beat with a rotary beater until light in color and smooth. Fold in whipped cream. Fold a sheet of aluminum foil in half lengthwise and tie around outside of a 1½-quart soufflé dish leaving 2 inches above edge. Pour gelatine mixture into the soufflé dish. Chill 2 to 3 hours. Serves 6 to 8.

Orange Grand Marnier Mousse

¼ cup orange juice
1 envelope unflavored
   gelatine
5 eggs
½ cup sugar
2 teaspoons grated orange
   peel
3 tablespoons Grand
   Marnier
1 cup heavy cream, whipped

Pour orange juice into a small saucepan and sprinkle gelatine over it to soften. Place eggs and sugar in the top of a 1½-quart double boiler over simmering water. Beat with an electric mixer about 10 minutes over the water, or until egg mixture is thick, very light in color, and almost fills the double boiler. Remove from heat and pour into a large bowl. Heat softened gelatine over low heat (about 200° F.) until gelatine is dissolved. Stir gelatine, orange peel, and Grand Marnier into egg mixture. Place bowl in a larger bowl filled with ice cubes and stir constantly until mixture is the consistency of unbeaten egg white. Fold whipped cream into gelatine mixture. Pour into a 5-cup serving dish. Chill several hours. Serves 6 to 8.

Fresh Strawberry Soufflé

2 pints fresh strawberries,
   hulled (2½ cups purée)
2 envelopes unflavored
   gelatine
¼ cup water
⅔ cup sugar
4 egg yolks, well beaten
⅛ teaspoon salt
1 tablespoon lemon juice

Cut a 3-inch band of brown paper long enough to go around top of a 1½-quart soufflé dish. Fasten to dish with cellophane tape, or tie with a string. Mash strawberries thoroughly in an electric blender. Soften gelatine in the water in the top of a double boiler. Add the ⅔ cup sugar, egg yolks, salt, and 1 cup of the mashed berries. Stir well. Cook over boiling water about 5 minutes, or until gelatine is dissolved. Remove from heat; cool slightly. Add lemon juice and remaining

4 *egg whites, at room*
  temperature
½ *cup sugar*
1 *cup heavy cream*
Whole strawberries (optional)
Whipped cream (optional)

mashed berries. Chill until the consistency of unbeaten egg white. Meanwhile, in a large bowl beat egg whites until soft peaks form; gradually add the ½ cup sugar, beating constantly, until egg whites form stiff peaks. Then whip heavy cream and fold into egg white mixture. Fold in chilled berry mixture. Pour into soufflé dish. (If soufflé dish is not available, mixture may be poured into a 1½- to 2-quart glass serving bowl.) Chill 3 to 4 hours, or until firm. To serve, remove paper collar. Garnish with strawberries and whipped cream, if desired. Serves 6 to 8.

Raspberry–Macaroon Mousse

⅓ *cup light corn syrup*
2½ *tablespoons sugar*
2½ *tablespoons cold water*
2 *eggs, separated*
¾ *teaspoon vanilla extract*
1 *10-ounce package frozen*
  raspberries, thawed and
  mashed
½ *cup finely crumbled soft*
  macaroons (about 4
  macaroons)
1 *cup heavy cream,*
  whipped

Combine corn syrup, sugar, and water in a saucepan. Bring to a boil over moderate heat (about 250° F.) and boil 2 minutes. Cool 10 minutes. Beat egg whites until just stiff. Gradually add syrup mixture to egg whites, beating constantly until stiff peaks form. Add vanilla. Beat egg yolks until thick and lemon-colored; fold into egg whites. Fold in remaining ingredients. Pour into 5-cup mold. Freeze until just firm, about 3 to 4 hours. Unmold by placing warm, wet cloth over mold until mold can be lifted off. Serves 5.

Strawberry Festival Mousse

1 *6-ounce package*
  strawberry-flavored
  gelatine
2 *cups boiling water*
1½ *cups crushed fresh*
  strawberries
1 *tablespoon lemon juice*
½ *cup sugar*
⅛ *teaspoon salt*
½ *cup sweet sherry*
2 *cups heavy cream,*
  whipped
Whole strawberries

Dissolve gelatine in boiling water. Stir together strawberries, lemon juice, sugar, and salt; stir until sugar is dissolved. Combine strawberry gelatine strawberry mixture, and sherry. Chill until mixture is the consistency of unbeaten egg white. Fold in whipped cream. Pour into a 2-quart mold and chill several hours, until set. Garnish with whole strawberries. Serves 10.

Meringues

Meringues are sweetened, stiffly beaten egg whites baked in a slow oven. They make a delicate crust that is delicious filled with fruit or ice cream. See pages 452 and 453 for instructions on how to beat egg whites.

How to Shape and Bake a Meringue Shell

Cover cookie sheet with brown wrapping paper. Draw a 9-inch circle; use plate or compass for a guide.

Shape meringue on circle. Make center about 1 inch thick, rim about 2 inches high.

Bake 1 hour in low oven (250° F.). Turn off heat, open oven door, and leave shell in oven until cool, about 1 hour.

 **Meringue Shell**

3 egg whites, at room temperature
⅛ teaspoon salt
¼ teaspoon cream of tartar
1 teaspoon vanilla extract
1 cup sugar

Heat oven to 250° F. Beat egg whites in a bowl until foamy. Add salt, cream of tartar, and vanilla. Continue to beat until soft peaks form. Add sugar, 2 tablespoons at a time, beating well after each addition. Continue to beat until stiff peaks form. Draw a circle 9 inches in diameter on a heavy piece of brown paper placed on a cookie sheet. Spoon meringue into circle. Push meringue from center to edge of circle so center is 1 inch thick and rim 2 inches high. Bake shell 1 hour. Turn off heat; open door and leave shell in oven 1 hour. Remove paper and place meringue on a flat plate. Fill as desired with fresh fruit, ice cream, or pudding.

❧ Meringue Nests

2 egg whites, at room
   temperature
½ teaspoon cream of tartar
¼ teaspoon salt
½ cup sugar
½ cup flaked coconut
Ice cream or fresh fruit

Heat oven to 225° F. Place egg whites in the small bowl of an electric mixer; add cream of tartar and salt. Beat at high speed until stiff peaks are formed but whites are not dry. Gradually beat in 1 tablespoon of the sugar at a time, beating well after each addition. Meringue mixture should appear glossy. Remove bowl from mixer and fold in coconut. Cover cookie sheets with ungreased brown paper. Spoon or pipe meringue into six 2½-inch-diameter "nests" on the cookie sheets, building up the sides of the nests as you work. Bake 70 minutes. Allow to cool thoroughly before removing from paper. Place on serving dishes and fill meringue centers with ice cream or fresh fruit. Serves 6.

Refrigerator Desserts

❧ Chocolate Refrigerator Cake

½ cup heavy cream
⅛ teaspoon vanilla extract
2 tablespoons mint-flavored
   apple jelly (optional)
20 thin chocolate wafers
½ cup heavy cream
2 tablespoons quick
   chocolate-flavored mix
Shaved chocolate (optional)

Whip the ½ cup cream and the vanilla extract until mixture holds its shape. Break up jelly into small pieces and fold into cream. Reserve ¼ cup of the cream filling and spread remaining cream mixture over 15 of the chocolate wafers. Arrange frosted wafers in stacks of 3. Top each with an unfrosted wafer. Chill in refrigerator 1 hour. Turn stacks of cookies on their sides in a row on a flat serving plate, joining them together with the reserved ¼ cup cream filling to make one long roll. Whip the remaining ½ cup cream and the chocolate mix until mixture holds its shape. Frost outside of chocolate roll. Chill in refrigerator 4 to 5 hours or overnight. If desired, garnish with shaved chocolate. Serves 6 to 8.

❧ Key Lime Dessert

1¼ cups packaged graham
   cracker crumbs
2 tablespoons sugar

Mix crumbs and the 2 tablespoons sugar. Cut butter into crumbs with pastry blender. Stir in water. Press over bottom and sides of buttered individual soufflé dishes.

DESSERTS

1/3 cup softened butter or
  margarine
1 tablespoon water
3 eggs, separated
1 14-ounce can sweetened
  condensed milk
1/2 cup lime juice
Green vegetable food coloring
6 tablespoons sugar
Sliced almonds

Chill. Beat egg yolks slightly; add condensed milk and beat until blended. Add lime juice and beat until smooth. Stir in a few drops green food coloring to give desired color. Pour into crumb-filled dishes and chill. Beat egg whites until soft peaks form. Gradually add the 6 tablespoons sugar and beat until stiff peaks form. Mound meringue over filling just before serving. Garnish with almonds. Serves 5.

❧ Toffee Refrigerator Dessert

1/2 cup butter, softened
1 cup confectioners' sugar
2 eggs, separated and at
  room temperature
1 1-ounce square
  unsweetened chocolate,
  melted
1/2 teaspoon vanilla extract
1/4 cup heavy cream, whipped
1 cup crushed vanilla wafers
1/4 cup toasted slivered
  almonds
Whipped cream (optional)

Work butter until creamy. Gradually beat in confectioners' sugar. Add egg yolks one at a time, beating well after each addition. Blend in melted chocolate and the vanilla extract. Beat egg whites until stiff but not dry; fold into butter mixture. Fold in whipped cream. Spread 1/2 cup crushed vanilla wafers in bottom of 1 1/2-quart shallow dish. Spoon chocolate mixture over crumbs. Mix remaining crumbs with almonds and sprinkle over the top. Refrigerate overnight. Cut into squares. Serve with additional whipped cream, if desired. Serves 6.

❧ Refrigerator Rum Pudding

2 dozen soft macaroons
1/4 cup light rum
2 cups heavy cream
2 teaspoons vanilla extract
1/8 teaspoon almond extract
Toasted almonds

Arrange macaroons on a cookie sheet. Sprinkle with rum. Cover and chill 30 minutes. Whip cream with a rotary beater until it holds its shape; stir in vanilla and almond extracts. Arrange about 8 of the chilled macaroons in the bottom of a 9-x-5-x-3-inch loaf pan—it may be necessary to cut macaroons to fit. Spread with 1/3 of the cream. Repeat layers of macaroons and cream, ending with cream. Cover and chill overnight. Spoon into serving dishes and garnish with toasted almonds. Serves 6.

Frozen Desserts

❧ *Biscuit Tortoni*

¾ cup crumbled soft
  macaroons (about 6
  macaroons)
¾ cup light cream
¼ cup confectioners' sugar
Few grains salt
 1 cup heavy cream, whipped
½ teaspoon vanilla extract
¼ teaspoon almond extract
¼ cup toasted blanched
  almonds, chopped

Set control of refrigerator at coldest setting. Combine macaroon crumbs, light cream, confectioners' sugar, and salt in a small bowl. Let stand 1 hour in refrigerator. Fold macaroon mixture into whipped cream. Fold in vanilla and almond extracts. Pour mixture into small paper cups set in refrigerator trays. Sprinkle with almonds; cover with foil or plastic wrap and freeze until firm, about 2 hours. Serves 8 to 10.

❧ *Crème de Menthe Parfaits*

24 large marshmallows
 ⅔ cup milk
3 to 4 tablespoons green crème
   de menthe
 2 tablespoons white crème de
   cacao
 1 cup heavy cream, whipped
½ cup heavy cream
Fresh mint (optional)

In a medium-sized saucepan combine the marshmallows and milk. Cook over moderately low heat (about 225° F.), stirring constantly, until marshmallows are melted. Cool. Fold in crème de menthe and crème de cacao. Gently fold in the 1 cup whipped cream. Pour into a 9-x-5-x-3-inch loaf pan. Cover and freeze until firm, about 3 hours. Remove from freezer and let stand 5 minutes, or until mixture can be spooned easily. Whip the remaining ½ cup cream until soft peaks form. Layer the crème de menthe mixture and the whipped cream alternately in parfait glasses. Top each with a dab of whipped cream. Parfaits may be served immediately or stored in the freezer until serving time. Garnish with mint, if desired. Serves 4.

❧ *Fruit-Studded Log*

2 3-ounce packages cream
  cheese, at room
  temperature
¾ cup sugar
2 tablespoons lemon juice

In a large bowl combine cream cheese, sugar, lemon juice, and sour cream; beat with a wooden spoon until well blended and light and fluffy. Add the red food coloring and stir to blend well. Stir in drained fruits, cherries, pecans, and marshmallows. Spoon mixture

2 cups commercial sour
 cream
2 drops red food coloring
1 29-ounce can fruits for
 salad, drained
⅓ cup coarsely chopped
 maraschino cherries
⅓ cup coarsely chopped
 pecans
2½ cups miniature
 marshmallows
Fresh mint (optional)

into two 1-pound coffee cans. Cover and freeze 8 hours or overnight. To serve, remove from freezer and let stand 5 minutes. Remove bottom of coffee can with a can opener and push log out onto a serving plate. If desired, decorate with fresh mint. Let stand 10 minutes before slicing. Serves 14 to 16.

✑ Lemon-Crunch Freeze

1 cup sifted all-purpose flour
¼ cup firmly packed dark
 brown sugar
½ cup coarsely chopped
 walnuts
½ cup melted butter or
 margarine
2 eggs, separated
1 14-ounce can sweetened
 condensed milk
½ cup fresh lemon juice
1 teaspoon grated lemon peel
¼ cup granulated sugar
Lemon twists (optional)

Heat oven to 350° F. In a medium-sized bowl combine flour, brown sugar, and walnuts. Pour in butter and stir until well blended and mixture is crumbly. Put mixture on a cookie sheet and with a fork break it up into small crumblike particles. Bake 20 minutes, stirring occasionally, until crumbs are crisp and golden brown. Cool crumbs. Spread ⅔ of the crumb mixture in the bottom of a 9-x-5-x-3-inch loaf pan. In a medium-sized bowl beat the 2 egg yolks until thick and lemon-colored. Add condensed milk, lemon juice, and lemon peel and stir until mixture thickens. In a small bowl beat the 2 egg whites until soft peaks form. Gradually add the ¼ cup granulated sugar and beat until stiff peaks form. Fold egg whites gently into lemon mixture until well blended. Pour over the crumbs in the loaf pan. Sprinkle remaining crumbs over top. Cover with aluminum foil and freeze until firm, about 4 to 6 hours. Spoon into sherbet glasses. If desired, garnish each with a twist of lemon. Serves 6 to 8.

✑ Mocha Bombe

¾ teaspoon unflavored
 gelatine
¼ cup cold water
⅔ cup milk
⅔ cup sugar
1 tablespoon unsweetened
 cocoa

Set control of refrigerator at coldest setting. Sprinkle gelatine over cold water. Combine milk, sugar, cocoa, and coffee in a small pan. Heat slowly over moderately low heat (about 225° F.), stirring occasionally, until mixture is smooth and blended and bubbles form around the edge of the pan. Stir in softened gelatine, stirring until gelatine is dissolved. Cool. Blend in vanilla.

1 teaspoon instant coffee
granules or powder
½ teaspoon vanilla extract
1 cup heavy cream, whipped

Chill until mixture is the consistency of unbeaten egg white. Whip chilled mixture with an electric or rotary beater until thick and fluffy. Fold in whipped cream. Pour into a 3- or 4-cup mold. Cover with foil or plastic wrap. Freeze about 3 hours, or until firm. Serves 5 to 6.

❧ Frozen Plum Pudding

¼ cup maraschino cherries
Brandy
2 cups milk
1 cup sugar
2 eggs, well beaten
⅛ teaspoon salt
1 cup seedless raisins
½ cup chopped candied
pineapple
½ cup chopped walnuts
1 tablespoon orange
marmalade
1 pint heavy cream, whipped

Place cherries in a small bowl with enough brandy to cover; soak overnight. In the top of a double boiler combine milk, sugar, and eggs. Cook over simmering water until mixture thickens and coats a metal spoon. Stir in salt. Pour into a large bowl and chill. Drain cherries. Fold cherries, raisins, candied pineapple, walnuts, and marmalade into custard. Gently fold in whipped cream and blend well. Pour into a 9-x-5-x-3-inch loaf pan. Cover with foil; freeze until firm. Makes about 1½ quarts or serves 9 to 10.

Ice Cream

Electric ice-cream freezers—including those designed to work in your refrigerator's freezer—have taken the work out of homemade ice cream but left the fun. You also can make ice cream in your refrigerator's freezer without this special equipment, using metal ice cube trays or a loaf pan. Pour the mixture into a metal pan or bowl and put it in the freezer. Use ice cube trays with removable grids and reserve them only for this purpose. Once used for ice cream, it may be difficult to release ice cubes from the trays.

❧ Vanilla Tub-Churn Ice Cream

1 14-ounce can sweetened
condensed milk
1 milk can water
3 eggs, well beaten

Combine condensed milk and water in top of a double boiler. Cook over simmering water until hot. Beat with rotary beater until smooth. Add a little of the hot milk to the beaten eggs; return egg mixture to rest of milk in

[755]

2 *cups heavy cream*
2½ *teaspoons vanilla extract*
Ice and rock salt for freezing

top of double boiler. Cook over simmering water, stirring constantly, until mixture thickens slightly. Remove from heat, cover, and cool to room temperature. Stir in cream and vanilla. Pour mixture into can of a 2-quart electric tub-churn freezer. Set covered can in tub. Pack tub half full with crushed ice; sprinkle with rock salt. Fill tub completely with ice; sprinkle with salt. Use a proportion of 6 parts ice to 1 part salt. (These are general directions for all ice-cream freezers; for best results, follow the instructions that come with each freezer.) Churn about 20 minutes, until motor begins to labor. Add more ice and salt as it melts down. When ice cream is finished, it will be the consistency of whipped cream. Remove motor head and dasher from can. Cover can with waxed paper; cover and insert cork in cover. Pack tub with more ice and salt. Let stand 2 hours or longer to harden ice cream. Makes about 2 quarts.

◄§ Vanilla Refrigerator-Tray Ice Cream

1 *envelope unflavored gelatine*
2 *cups light cream*
1 *cup sugar*
⅛ *teaspoon salt*
2 *cups heavy cream*
2 *teaspoons vanilla extract*

Sprinkle gelatine over ½ cup of the light cream in top of double boiler. Cook over simmering water until gelatine dissolves. Stir in sugar and salt. Remove from heat; stir in remaining light cream. Chill this mixture until it mounds when dropped from the tip of a spoon. Whip heavy cream; with a rotary beater beat chilled mixture smooth; fold it and vanilla into the whipped cream. Pour into 2 ice cube trays or a loaf pan. Cover with waxed paper or aluminum foil and freeze in ice-tray compartment of refrigerator, set at coldest. Makes about 1½ quarts.

Ice-Cream Flavor Variations

	IN A TUB CHURN	IN THE REFRIGERATOR TRAY
Chocolate	Reduce vanilla to 1 teaspoon. Add 4 1-ounce squares unsweetened chocolate to milk mixture before cooking.	Reduce vanilla to 1 teaspoon. Add 3½ 1-ounce squares unsweetened chocolate to cream before cooking.
Chocolate Rum Nut	Omit vanilla. Use chocolate as above. Add 2 teaspoons rum extract and ¾ cup chopped nuts to cooled custard.	Omit vanilla. Add chocolate as above. Fold 1½ teaspoons rum extract and ½ cup chopped nuts into chilled gelatine mixture.

Ice-Cream Flavor Variations

	IN A TUB CHURN	IN THE REFRIGERATOR TRAY
Chocolate Chip	Reduce vanilla to 1 teaspoon. Add 1 cup grated unsweetened chocolate to cooled custard.	Reduce vanilla to 1 teaspoon. Fold ¾ cup grated unsweetened chocolate into chilled gelatine mixture.
All Fresh Fruits	Reduce vanilla to 2 teaspoons. Add 2 cups sweetened crushed fruit to cooled custard.	Reduce vanilla to 1½ teaspoons. Add 1½ cups sweetened crushed fruit to chilled gelatine mixture.
Burnt Almond or Butter Pecan	Omit vanilla. Cook and stir ⅔ cup sugar and 2 tablespoons water in a heavy saucepan over low heat until sugar melts and turns a golden brown. Add browned sugar to milk before cooking. Add ⅔ cup chopped toasted almonds or pecans to cooled custard.	Omit vanilla. Cook ⅔ cup sugar and 2 tablespoons water in a heavy saucepan over low heat until sugar melts and is golden brown. Add browned sugar to hot cream. Fold ½ cup chopped toasted almonds or pecans to chilled gelatine mixture.
Toasted Coconut	Reduce vanilla to 1 teaspoon. Add ½ teaspoon almond extract. Toast 1 can flaked coconut. Fold into cooled custard.	Reduce vanilla to 1 teaspoon. Add ½ teaspoon almond extract. Toast ¾ cup flaked coconut. Fold into chilled gelatine mixture.
Peppermint Stick	Reduce vanilla to 1 teaspoon and add 1 cup crushed peppermint candy to cooled custard.	Reduce vanilla to 1 teaspoon. Fold ¾ cup finely crushed peppermint candy into chilled gelatine mixture.
Coffee Cognac	Omit vanilla. Add 1 tablespoon instant coffee to hot milk; stir 2 tablespoons cognac into cooled custard.	Omit vanilla. Add 1 tablespoon instant coffee to hot cream. Add 2 tablespoons cognac to whipped cream.

Sherbets and Ices

 **Emerald Milk Sherbet**

*1 envelope unflavored
   gelatine*
½ cup milk

Set control of refrigerator at coldest setting. Sprinkle gelatine on the ½ cup milk in a measuring cup. Set cup in a pan with about 1 inch hot water around it. Heat,

½ teaspoon salt
1⅓ cups sugar
¾ cup lime juice
2 tablespoons grated lime peel
1½ cups milk
1 cup heavy cream
Few drops green food coloring

stirring occasionally, until gelatine is dissolved. Combine salt, sugar, lime juice, and lime peel in a bowl; stir until sugar is dissolved. Blend together the 1½ cups milk, cream, and dissolved gelatine. Slowly pour lime mixture into cream mixture (mixture may curdle slightly). Blend in food coloring. Turn into ice cube tray; cover and freeze until firm 1 inch from sides of tray. Turn into chilled bowl; beat with an electric or rotary beater until smooth but not completely melted. Return mixture to tray; cover with foil or plastic wrap. Freeze until just firm enough to spoon out, about 2½ hours. Serves 4 to 5.

✒ Lemon Sherbet

2 egg whites, at room temperature
¼ cup sugar
1 cup light corn syrup
2 cups milk
½ teaspoon grated lemon peel
⅔ cup lemon juice

Beat egg whites in a bowl until soft peaks form. Add sugar, a tablespoon at a time, beating well after each addition. Continue to beat until stiff peaks form. Gradually add remaining ingredients, beating constantly. Pour into ice cube trays, cover with plastic wrap, and freeze until a layer 1 inch wide is frozen around sides of trays. Scrape mixture into a chilled bowl and beat with an electric or rotary beater until smooth but not melted. Pour back into trays, cover, and freeze until firm. Makes about 1 quart.

✒ Lemon Ice

4 cups water
3½ cups sugar
1 cup fresh or frozen lemon juice
1 tablespoon grated lemon peel

Combine water and sugar in a saucepan; bring to a boil over moderate heat (about 250° F.) and boil 5 minutes. Cool. Add lemon juice and peel. Pour into 2 ice cube trays. Cover trays and place in freezer. When mixture is frozen to a mush, remove to a cold bowl and quickly beat with an electric or rotary beater until smooth. Return to trays, cover, and freeze again; remove mixture to cold bowl and quickly beat again until smooth. Return to trays, cover, and freeze until firm, about 2 hours. Serves 6.

✒ Raspberry Ice

2 10-ounce packages frozen raspberries, thawed

Rub raspberries through a fine sieve. Stir in lemon and orange juices. Combine sugar and water in a saucepan

½ cup fresh, frozen, or
  bottled lemon juice
¼ cup fresh or frozen orange
  juice
1 cup sugar
2½ cups water

and cook over moderate heat (about 250° F.) 5 minutes. Cool mixture and add to raspberries. Pour into ice cube trays, cover, and freeze about 1 hour, until mixture is the consistency of thick mush. Remove mixture to a chilled bowl and whip with an electric or rotary beater until fluffy but not melted. Return to ice cube trays, cover, and freeze until firm. Serves 10 to 12.

✑ Orange Sherbet

1 cup undiluted evaporated
  milk
1 can (6 ounces) frozen
  concentrated orange juice,
  thawed
½ cup sugar
⅛ teaspoon salt

Chill evaporated milk in an ice cube tray or loaf pan until ice crystals form around edges. Turn into a chilled bowl and whip with rotary beater or at high speed of electric mixer until stiff. Combine orange juice concentrate, sugar, and salt; add to whipped milk 1 tablespoon at a time, whipping until very stiff. Pour mixture into loaf pan, cover with aluminum foil, and freeze until firm. Makes about 1 quart.

✑ Strawberry Sherbet Dolley Madison

3½ cups water
½ cup apricot brandy
1½ cups sugar
Few grains salt
1½ pints strawberries
2 tablespoons lemon juice
1 teaspoon grated orange
  peel

Mix water, apricot brandy, and sugar in a saucepan. Bring to a boil over moderate heat (about 250° F.) and boil 6 minutes; cool and add salt. Slice strawberries and press through a sieve or food mill. Strain through several thicknesses of cheesecloth to remove seeds. Stir strawberry juice, lemon juice, and grated orange peel into brandy mixture. Pour into a 9-x-5-x-3-inch loaf pan, cover, and place in freezer until firm about 1 inch around edge of pan. Remove from pan to a chilled bowl; beat with an electric or rotary beater until smooth. Return to pan; cover with plastic wrap and freeze until firm. Serves 8 to 10.

Ice-Cream Desserts

✑ Baked Alaska

1 packaged 8-inch sponge
  cake layer

Cut a cardboard round to measure slightly larger than the cake layer. Cover it with heavy-duty aluminum foil.

1 quart ice cream, any flavor
4 egg whites, at room
    temperature
½ cup sugar
Flaked coconut (optional)

Place the cake layer on the cardboard. Mound the ice cream on the cake. Cover and freeze until firm, several hours or overnight. When ready to serve, heat oven to 450° F. Beat egg whites until stiff but not dry, gradually adding the sugar. Place the frozen cake on a cookie sheet; do not remove it from the cardboard. Completely cover the cake and ice cream with the meringue. Sprinkle lightly with coconut, if desired. Bake 3 to 5 minutes. Serve immediately. Serves 6 to 8.

✑ Bombe Glacée

1 pint raspberry sherbet or
    ice, slightly softened
1 pint vanilla or pineapple
    ice cream, slightly
    softened

Set control of refrigerator at coldest setting. Spread about ⅔ of the sherbet over surface of a chilled 3- or 4-cup mold. Pack half the ice cream over the sherbet lining. Drop the remaining sherbet in tablespoonfuls over the ice cream in the mold. Firmly pack in the remaining ice cream. Cover and freeze about 1½ to 2 hours, or until firm. To unmold, place a warm, moist cloth over the outside surface of the mold. Invert it onto a chilled serving plate. Lift off mold. Serve at once. Serves 6.

✑ Jubilee Ice-Cream Bombe

2 quarts coffee ice cream
1 pint vanilla ice cream
1 cup chilled heavy cream
1 tablespoon confectioners'
    sugar
½ teaspoon vanilla extract
Pecans (optional)
Cherry Sauce (recipe follows)

Place a 1½-quart melon mold in freezer until well chilled. Let coffee ice cream stand in refrigerator for 15 minutes, or until slightly softened. Spoon coffee ice cream into mold to form an even layer over bottom and sides; pack firmly. Place in freezer for 1 hour, or until ice cream has hardened. Remove vanilla ice cream from freezer and place in refrigerator for 15 minutes to soften slightly. Spoon vanilla ice cream into mold over coffee layer, packing firmly. Cover and place in freezer for several hours or overnight, until hard. To unmold, place mold on serving plate. Dip a towel in hot water and wring it out; wrap around mold. Repeat until ice cream slips out of mold. Return to freezer for about a half hour. Whip cream, sugar, and vanilla together with rotary beater until stiff. Spoon into decorating bag and decorate mold, using the star tip. If desired, garnish with pecans. Mold may be kept in freezer for several hours after garnishing. Serve with flaming Cherry Sauce. Serves 10.

Cherry Sauce

1 22-ounce can cherry pie
   filling
½ cup orange juice
¼ cup kirsch

Heat cherry pie filling and orange juice together in a skillet or chafing dish over low heat (about 200° F.). Heat kirsch in a small pan over low heat (about 200° F.) and pour over cherries. Light with a match and serve flaming sauce over ice cream. Makes 2¾ cups sauce.

Rainbow Meringue Glacé

1 pint coffee ice cream
1 pint strawberry ice cream
1 pint chocolate-chip mint
   ice cream
About 2 cups toasted coconut
   (directions on page 746)
4 egg whites, at room
   temperature
¼ teaspoon cream of tartar
¾ teaspoon vanilla extract
¾ cup sugar
Bottled chocolate ice-cream
   topping

Line a jelly-roll pan with waxed paper. Scoop out a ball of ice cream from one of the pints and roll it quickly in toasted coconut to coat evenly. Place in the prepared pan. Repeat until you have scooped 5 balls out of each pint of ice cream, to make a total of 15. Freeze until firm, about 2 hours. Heat oven to 275° F. Place egg whites in the large bowl of an electric mixer and beat at high speed until foamy. Add cream of tartar and vanilla and beat until soft peaks form. Gradually add sugar, beating well after each addition. Continue beating until stiff peaks form and meringue is glossy. Cover a cookie sheet with brown paper. Spoon out about ⅓ of the meringue onto the center of the cookie sheet and shape into a 6-x-8-inch rectangle about ¼ inch thick. Spoon remaining meringue into a decorating bag with a star tip and make a border of rosettes around the edge of the rectangle. Bake 1 hour. Turn off oven. Loosen bottom of meringue carefully from brown paper with a spatula and replace on the paper. Return meringue to oven; close oven and let stand 2 hours. Cool completely. If desired, meringue shell may be wrapped in aluminum foil and placed in freezer until ready to use. At serving time, place meringue shell on a large serving platter. Arrange ice-cream balls in shell, piling them up. Pour chocolate ice-cream topping over ice-cream balls. Cut into wedges to serve. Serves 8.

Ice-Cream Sauces

With these sauces, some nuts and cream toppings, and a variety of ice creams, you can concoct sundaes of proportions to suit your own sweet tooth.

DESSERTS

✺ Chocolate Fudge Sauce

1 6-ounce package semisweet
  chocolate pieces
1 tablespoon butter or
  margarine
¼ cup hot water
¼ cup sugar
Few grains salt
¼ cup light corn syrup
1 teaspoon vanilla extract

Combine chocolate pieces, butter, and hot water in a small saucepan. Place over low heat (about 200° F.) and stir until chocolate is melted and mixture is smooth. Add sugar and salt, Cook and stir until sugar is dissolved. Remove from heat. Stir in corn syrup and vanilla and stir to blend well. Serve warm. Makes 1½ cups.

✺ Bittersweet Chocolate Sauce

2 teaspoons instant coffee
  granules or powder
½ cup boiling water
3 1-ounce squares
  unsweetened chocolate
¼ cup heavy cream
1 cup sugar
1 tablespoon butter or
  margarine
½ teaspoon vanilla extract

Dissolve the coffee powder in the boiling water. Combine the coffee, chocolate, and heavy cream in a medium-sized saucepan. Cook over moderately low heat (about 225° F.), stirring constantly, until chocolate is melted and mixture is smooth. Add sugar and butter and cook over moderate heat (about 250° F.), stirring constantly, until sugar is dissolved. Cook about 4 minutes longer, stirring constantly, until mixture is slightly thickened. Remove from heat. Add vanilla and stir to blend well. Pour into hot sterilized jar with tight-fitting lid. Cool. Serve sauce at room temperature or slightly warmed. Refrigerate unused sauce. Makes about 1½ cups.

✺ Chocolate Rum Sauce

3 1-ounce squares
  unsweetened chocolate,
  broken up
2 teaspoons instant coffee
  granules or powder
½ cup water
¼ cup milk
⅔ cup sugar
1 tablespoon butter or
  margarine
Few grains salt
½ teaspoon vanilla extract
3 to 4 tablespoons rum

Place chocolate squares in a saucepan. Add instant coffee powder, water, and milk to chocolate. Cook over low heat (about 200° F.), stirring constantly, until smooth, about 3 to 4 minutes. Add sugar, butter, and salt. Cook over moderate heat (about 250° F.), stirring constantly, until slightly thickened, 3 to 5 minutes. Remove from heat. Add vanilla and 3 to 4 tablespoons rum, as desired. Stir thoroughly. Serve warm or cold over ice cream. Sauce may be stored in a jar with a tight lid in refrigerator and reheated, if desired. Makes about 1¼ cups sauce.

✑ Rich Butterscotch Sauce

1 cup firmly packed dark
  brown sugar
½ cup granulated sugar
⅔ cup evaporated milk,
  undiluted
¼ cup butter or margarine
2 tablespoons light corn
  syrup
¼ teaspoon salt
1 teaspoon vanilla extract

Mix all ingredients in a saucepan except vanilla. Bring to a boil over moderately low heat (about 225° F.); cook slowly 3 minutes; stir constantly. Add vanilla. Use hot or pour into a covered container and store in refrigerator. Reheat over low heat (about 200° F.). Makes 1½ cups.

✑ Pineapple Syrup

1 13¼-ounce can crushed
  pineapple
1 teaspoon cornstarch
⅔ cup light corn syrup

Combine undrained pineapple and cornstarch in small saucepan. Cook over moderately low heat (about 225° F.), stirring constantly, until mixture boils and is clear and thickened. Remove from heat. Place corn syrup in a medium-sized saucepan. Heat over moderately low heat (about 225° F.) until syrup comes to a full boil. Cook, stirring constantly, for 2 minutes. Remove from heat, add pineapple, and blend. Makes 2 cups.

Pineapple Mint Syrup

Stir ⅔ cup mint jelly into hot, thickened Pineapple Syrup. Stir until jelly softens and melts.

✑ Strawberry Sauce

1 16-ounce package frozen
  whole strawberries
½ cup light corn syrup

Thaw berries; drain well. Combine syrup and juice drained from berries (½ cup) in saucepan. Bring to a full boil over moderate heat (250° F.) and boil 5 minutes. Cool and add drained berries. Makes 2 cups.

✑ Maple-Nut Syrup

1 cup maple syrup or
  maple-blended syrup
½ cup dark corn syrup
½ cup broken walnuts or
  blanched almonds

Combine syrups in a medium-sized saucepan. Bring to a full rolling boil over moderate heat (about 250° F.). Boil, stirring 1 minute. Skim if necessary. Remove from heat. Cool and add nuts. Store in covered jar. Makes 1⅔ cups.

Hot Dessert Soufflés

Hot dessert soufflés are made by the same techniques used for main-dish soufflés. Read the illustrated directions on page 452 before you attempt to make a hot dessert soufflé. Like all hot soufflés, these must be served as soon as they are baked.

✌ Chocolate Soufflé

4 egg whites
2 1-ounce squares
   unsweetened chocolate
⅓ cup sugar
2 tablespoons cold coffee
½ teaspoon vanilla extract
1 teaspoon butter or
   margarine
2 tablespoons sugar
¼ cup butter or margarine
¼ cup flour
1 cup hot milk
4 egg yolks

Place egg whites in a large bowl and let stand at room temperature 1 hour. Mix chocolate, the ⅓ cup sugar, and the coffee in the top of a double boiler; place over simmering water and heat until chocolate is melted. Stir in vanilla and cool. Heat oven to 350° F. Butter a 1½-quart soufflé dish with the 1 teaspoon butter. Sprinkle bottom and sides evenly with the 2 tablespoons sugar. Shake out any excess sugar. Melt the ¼ cup butter in a saucepan over moderately low heat (about 225° F.). Add the flour all at once and stir with a wire whip until well blended. Cook over moderate heat (about 250° F.), stirring constantly about 2 minutes, until mixture begins to foam and bubble. Remove from heat and add the hot milk, beating vigorously with whip until mixture is thickened and smooth. Return to heat and cook 1 minute, stirring constantly, until sauce begins to boil. Remove from heat. Add egg yolks one at a time, beating well after each addition. Pour egg yolk mixture into a large bowl. Stir in cooled chocolate mixture. Beat egg whites with an electric mixer, whip, or rotary beater until stiff—but not dry—peaks form. Add 1 large tablespoonful of the beaten whites to the egg yolk mixture and stir until well blended. Spoon remaining egg whites on top. Gently fold in beaten egg whites with a rubber spatula to blend well. Pour into prepared soufflé dish. Run a metal spatula through the mixture in a circle 1 inch from edge of dish. Place in center of oven and bake 45 to 50 minutes, or until puffed about 2 inches above rim of dish and a knife inserted in the side comes out clean. Serve immediately. Serves 6.

✌ Coconut Soufflé with Chocolate Sauce

4 egg whites
1 teaspoon butter or
   margarine

Place egg whites in a large bowl and let stand at room temperature 1 hour. Heat oven to 350° F. Butter a 1¼-quart soufflé dish with the 1 teaspoon butter; sprinkle

2 tablespoons sugar
¼ cup butter or margarine
¼ cup flour
1 cup hot milk
⅓ cup sugar
4 egg yolks
1 teaspoon vanilla extract
½ teaspoon almond extract
1 4-ounce can shredded
  coconut
*Chocolate Fudge Sauce (recipe
  on page 762)*

bottom and sides evenly with the 2 tablespoons sugar. Shake out any excess sugar. Melt the ¼ cup butter in a saucepan over moderately low heat (about 225° F.). Add the flour all at once and stir with a wire whip until well blended. Cook over moderate heat (about 250° F.), stirring constantly about 2 minutes, until mixture begins to foam and bubble. Remove from heat and add the hot milk all at once, beating vigorously with whip until mixture is thickened and smooth. Return to heat and cook 1 minute, stirring constantly, until sauce begins to boil. Remove from heat and stir in the ⅓ cup sugar. Add egg yolks one at a time, beating well after each addition. Add vanilla and almond extracts. Reserve 3 tablespoons of the coconut for topping the soufflé. Add the remainder to sauce mixture and combine thoroughly. Pour coconut mixture into a large bowl. Beat egg whites with an electric mixer, whip, or rotary beater until stiff—but not dry—peaks form. Add 1 large tablespoonful of the beaten egg whites to the egg yolk mixture and stir until mixture is well blended. Spoon remaining egg whites on top. Gently fold in egg whites with a rubber spatula to blend well. Pour into prepared soufflé dish. Run a metal spatula through the mixture in a circle 1 inch from edge of dish. Sprinkle top with the reserved 3 tablespoons coconut. Place in center of oven and bake 45 to 50 minutes, or until puffed about 2 inches above rim of dish and a knife inserted in the sides comes out clean. Serve immediately with the warm Chocolate Fudge Sauce. Serves 6.

◆§ Almond Soufflé

4 egg whites
1 4½-ounce can diced
  roasted almonds
1 teaspoon butter or
  margarine
2 tablespoons sugar
¼ cup butter or margarine
¼ cup flour
1 cup hot milk
⅓ cup sugar
1 teaspoon vanilla extract
½ teaspoon almond extract
4 egg yolks
*Whipped cream or vanilla ice
  cream (optional)*

Place egg whites in a large bowl and let stand at room temperature 1 hour. Heat oven to 350° F. Chop almonds finely and reserve 1 tablespoon for garnish. Butter a 1½-quart soufflé dish with the 1 teaspoon butter. Sprinkle with the 2 tablespoons sugar to coat sides and bottom evenly. Shake out excess sugar. Melt the ¼ cup butter in a 1½-quart saucepan over moderately low heat (about 225° F.). Add flour all at once and stir with a wire whip until well blended. Cook over moderate heat (about 250° F.), stirring constantly about 2 minutes, until mixture begins to foam and bubble. Remove from heat and pour in hot milk all at once, beating vigorously with a wire whip until mixture thickens and is smooth. Return to heat and cook 1 minute, stirring constantly, until sauce begins to boil. Remove from heat and stir in the ⅓ cup sugar and the vanilla and almond extracts. Immediately stir in egg yolks one at a time, beating well after each addition. Stir in almonds and blend well. Pour egg yolk mixture into a large bowl. Beat egg whites with an electric mixer, whip, or rotary beater until stiff—but not dry—peaks form. Add 1 large tablespoonful of the beaten egg whites to the egg yolk mixture and stir until mixture is well blended. Spoon remaining egg whites on top. Gently fold in egg whites with a rubber spatula to blend well. Pour mixture into prepared soufflé dish. Smooth surface with a spatula. Run a metal spatula through the mixture in a circle 1 inch from edge of dish. Sprinkle reserved 1 tablespoon almonds on top. Place in center of oven and bake 45 to 50 minutes, or until soufflé is puffed about 2 inches above rim of dish and a knife inserted in the side comes out clean. Serve immediately. Serve with whipped cream or vanilla ice cream, if desired. Serves 6.

✺ Orange Soufflé

4 egg whites
1 teaspoon butter or margarine
2 tablespoons sugar
¼ cup butter or margarine
¼ cup flour
½ cup hot milk
½ cup orange juice
⅓ cup sugar
½ teaspoon vanilla extract
1 teaspoon orange extract
1 teaspoon grated orange peel
4 egg yolks
Foamy Orange Sauce (recipe follows)

Place egg whites in a large bowl and let stand at room temperature 1 hour. Heat oven to 350° F. Butter a 1½-quart soufflé dish with the 1 teaspoon butter. Sprinkle bottom and sides evenly with the 2 tablespoons sugar. Shake out any excess sugar. Melt the ¼ cup butter in a saucepan over moderately low heat (about 225° F.). Add the flour all at once and stir with a wire whip until well blended. Cook over moderate heat (about 250° F.), stirring constantly about 2 minutes, until mixture begins to foam and bubble. Remove from heat and add the hot milk all at once, beating vigorously with whip until mixture is thickened and smooth. Stir in the orange juice until smooth. Return to heat and cook 1 minute, stirring constantly, until sauce begins to boil. Remove from heat and stir in the ⅓ cup sugar, the vanilla and orange extracts, and orange peel. Add egg yolks one at a time beating well after each addition. Pour egg yolk mixture into a large bowl. Beat egg whites with an electric mixer, whip, or rotary beater until stiff—but not dry—peaks form. Add 1 large tablespoonful of the beaten whites to the egg yolk mixture and stir until mixture is well blended. Spoon remaining egg whites on top. Gently fold in egg whites with a rubber spatula. Pour into prepared soufflé dish. Run a metal spatula through the mixture in a circle 1 inch from edge of dish. Place in center of oven and bake 45 to 50 minutes, or until puffed about 2 inches above rim of dish and a knife inserted in the side comes out clean. Serve with the foamy Orange Sauce. Serves 6.

Foamy Orange Sauce

Work ¼ *cup butter or margarine* in a bowl until creamy. Beat in 1 cup sifted confectioners' sugar gradually. Continue to beat until mixture is fluffy. Stir in *1 well-beaten egg yolk* and *4 tablespoons orange juice*. Fold in *1 stiffly beaten egg white.* Makes 1 cup.

✑ Vanilla Soufflé

4 *egg whites*
1 *teaspoon butter or*
   margarine
2 *tablespoons sugar*
¼ *cup butter or margarine*
¼ *cup flour*
1 *cup hot milk*
⅓ *cup sugar*
4 *egg yolks*
1½ *teaspoons vanilla extract*

Place egg whites in a large bowl and let stand at room temperature 1 hour. Heat oven to 350° F. Butter a 1½-quart soufflé dish with the 1 teaspoon butter; sprinkle bottom and sides evenly with the 2 tablespoons sugar. Shake out any excess sugar. Melt the ¼ cup butter in a saucepan over moderately low heat (about 225° F.). Add the flour all at once and stir with a wire whip until well blended. Cook over moderate heat (about 250° F.), stirring constantly about 2 minutes, until mixture begins to foam and bubble. Remove from heat and add the hot milk all at once, beating vigorously with whip until mixture is thickened and smooth. Return to heat and cook 1 minute, stirring constantly, until sauce begins to boil. Remove from heat and stir in the ⅓ cup sugar. Add egg yolks one at a time, beating well after each addition. Add vanilla. Pour egg mixture into a large bowl. Beat egg whites with an electric mixer, whip, or rotary beater until stiff—but not dry—peaks form. Add 1 large tablespoonful of the beaten egg whites to the egg yolk mixture and stir until mixture is well blended. Spoon remaining egg whites on top. Gently fold in egg whites with a rubber spatula to blend well. Pour into prepared soufflé dish. Run a metal spatula through the mixture in a circle 1 inch from edge of dish. Place in center of oven and bake 45 to 50 minutes, or until puffed about 2 inches above rim of dish and a knife inserted in the side comes out clean. Serve immediately. Serves 6.

Cream Puffs and Éclairs

These airy shells are called cream puffs when round shaped and éclairs when oblong. They are usually filled with a custard, whipped cream, or ice cream and may be glazed or frosted on top.

To Make Perfect Cream Puffs

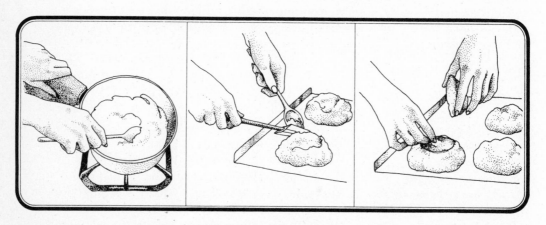

Stir flour and water mixture vigorously over moderate heat until it forms a ball and does not separate.

Shape spoonfuls of batter on an ungreased cookie sheet. Round up for puffs, make oblong for éclairs.

Cut tops off cooled puffs. Pull out a little of the soft center. Spoon in ice cream or a cream filling.

Sundae-Sauce Cream Puffs

1 cup water
½ cup butter or margarine (cut into small pieces)
¼ teaspoon salt
1 cup sifted all-purpose flour
4 eggs
1 recipe Custard Cream Filling (recipe follows)
1 double recipe Rich Butterscotch Sauce (recipe on page 763)

Heat oven to 400° F. Place water, butter, and salt in a heavy saucepan. Place over moderate heat (about 250° F.). Heat until butter melts and mixture comes to a rolling boil. Reduce heat to low (about 200° F.). Add flour all at once. Stir vigorously over heat about 1 minute, until mixture leaves sides of pan and clings to spoon. Remove from heat. Add unbeaten eggs, one at a time, beating well after each addition. Continue to beat vigorously until smooth and satiny. Drop mixture by large spoonfuls onto an ungreased baking sheet about 2 inches apart, making 10 mounds. Shape dough into rounds about 2 inches in diameter and pile slightly in the center. Bake until well browned and puffy, about 50 to 55 minutes. Remove cream puffs from oven and make a horizontal slit about a third of the way from top to allow steam to escape. Cool on wire racks. Cut off tops. If desired, remove some of the soft interior that remains in the center. Fill each cream puff with about ½ cup of Custard Cream Filling. Replace tops. Refrigerate. At serving time, heat butterscotch sauce as directed in recipe. Spoon some sauce over each cream puff before serving. Makes 10 puffs.

Custard Cream Filling

¾ teaspoon unflavored
    gelatine
2 cups milk
⅔ cup sugar
3 tablespoons cornstarch
⅛ teaspoon salt
2 egg yolks, beaten
2 tablespoons butter or
    margarine
1 teaspoon vanilla extract
1½ cups heavy cream,
    whipped

Soften gelatine in ¼ cup of the milk. Scald the remaining milk. Combine sugar, cornstarch, and salt. Add to the hot milk and stir to blend. Place over moderate heat (about 250° F.) and cook until mixture boils, stirring constantly. Blend about ½ cup of the hot mixture into egg yolks; return mixture to saucepan. Continue to cook over moderately low heat (about 225° F.) about 5 minutes, stirring constantly. Remove from heat and add gelatine mixture, butter, and vanilla; blend well. Cool thoroughly, stirring occasionally. Chill. Fold in whipped cream. Makes about 5 cups filling, enough to fill 10 large puffs.

✒ Brazilian Cream Puffs

1⅓ cups water
1 small package pie-crust
    mix or 2 pastry sticks
4 eggs
Coffee Crème (recipe follows)
⅓ cup instant cocoa mix
2½ teaspoons water

Heat oven to 400° F. Heat the 1⅓ cups water to a rolling boil over moderate heat (about 250° F.). Stir in pie-crust mix. Cook, stirring constantly, for 30 seconds after mixture leaves sides of pan. Remove from heat. Add eggs one at a time, beating well after each addition, until blended and smooth. Spoon ¼ cupfuls of batter 2 inches apart onto ungreased cookie sheets. Bake 30 to 35 minutes, or until golden brown. Remove from oven. Make a small slit in the side of each puff. Cool. Just before serving, cut off top of cream puff and fill with Coffee Crème. Blend instant cocoa and the 2½ teaspoons water together. Spoon over each puff. Makes 12.

Coffee Crème

1 4-serving-size package
    vanilla pudding and pie
    filling

Combine pudding mix and instant coffee. Gradually add milk. Cook over moderately low heat (about 225° F.), stirring constantly, until thickened. Cool and stir in

½ teaspoon instant coffee
   granules or powder
1½ cups milk
¼ cup coffee liqueur
½ cup heavy cream,
   whipped

coffee liqueur. Chill. Beat until smooth with rotary beat-er; fold in cream. Makes 2½ cups, or enough for 12 puffs.

☙ Cream Puff Swans

1 cup water
½ cup butter or margarine
1 cup sifted all-purpose flour
¼ teaspoon salt
1 teaspoon sugar
4 eggs
1 17½-ounce container
   frozen creamy vanilla
   pudding, thawed
½ cup confectioners' sugar

Heat oven to 450° F. In a medium-sized saucepan over moderately high heat (about 350° F.), combine water and butter and bring to a boil. Reduce heat to low (about 200° F.). Remove pan from heat and add flour, salt, and sugar all at once. Return to heat and stir vigorously until mixture forms a ball around the spoon, about 1 minute. Cool slightly. Add eggs, one at a time, beating well after each addition; continue to beat until mixture is smooth and glossy. Reserve ½ cup of mixture for the necks. Drop rest of mixture (approximately 2 tablespoons each) onto an ungreased cookie sheet, 1½ inches apart. Place the remaining ½ cup batter in a decorating bag with a small star tip. Onto another greased cookie sheet, press out batter into the form of a question mark, about 2½ inches long. Make as many necks as there are shells, adding, if possible, a few extras to allow for breakage. Place both cookie sheets in the oven for 20 minutes. Remove necks and cool. Reduce oven temperature to 350° F. and continue baking shells for another 15 min-utes, or until sides of shells are rigid. Cool on wire racks. Cut off the top ⅓ of each shell and reserve. Fill shells with spoonfuls of creamy vanilla pudding. Cut tops in half and press 2 halves into the filling of each shell on either side to make the wings. Insert necks into filling to complete the swans. Sprinkle confectioners' sugar over each swan. Makes about 12.

☙ Frozen Chocolate Éclairs

1 cup water
½ cup butter or margarine
¼ teaspoon salt
1 cup sifted all-purpose
   flour

Heat oven to 400° F. In a medium-sized saucepan combine water, butter, and salt. Cook over moderate heat (about 250° F.) until butter is melted and mixture comes to a rolling boil, stirring occasionally. Add flour all at once and cook over low heat (about 200° F.) about 1

4 large eggs
Chocolate Filling (recipe
  follows)
Whipped cream (optional
Chopped nuts (optional)

or 2 minutes, beating constantly with a wooden spoon, until mixture forms a ball in the center of pan. Remove from heat. Beat in eggs one at a time, beating well after each addition until mixture is smooth. After all the eggs are added, beat mixture until shiny and smooth. Press mixture through a large round decorating tube or shape with a spoon into ten 3-inch lengths about 2 inches apart on an ungreased cookie sheet. Bake 45 to 50 minutes, until puffed and golden brown. (Éclairs should sound hollow when tapped lightly with the fingertips.) Let cool completely on wire racks. Cut éclairs in half horizontally. Spoon Chocolate Filling into the bottom half of éclairs and replace tops. Freeze until firm. Wrap each éclair in aluminum foil and store in freezer until ready to use. At serving time decorate éclairs with whipped cream and chopped nuts, if desired. Let stand 10 minutes before serving. Serves 10.

Chocolate Filling

1 6-ounce package
  semisweet chocolate pieces
½ cup milk
¼ cup sugar
16 marshmallows
1 teaspoon vanilla extract
⅓ cup chopped walnuts
1 cup heavy cream, whipped

Place chocolate pieces, milk, sugar, and marshmallows in the top of a double boiler. Place over simmering water and cook, stirring constantly, until mixture is melted and smooth. Remove from heat. Stir in vanilla and nuts. Chill. Gently fold in whipped cream and fill éclairs. Makes about 3½ cups filling, or enough for 10 éclairs.

Chocolate Fondue

Chocolate fondue is the dessert version of popular fondue service—everyone chooses his own dunk and dips it in hot chocolate. This is a dessert to serve informally at a table that allows everyone to reach a pot of sauce.

Chocolate Fondue

5 3¾-ounce bars milk
  chocolate
1 cup heavy cream

Break the chocolate into small pieces in a small saucepan, fondue pot, or chafing dish. Add cream. Place over low heat (about 200° F.) and stir constantly until mixture

¼ *cup brandy*
Strawberries, washed and
hulled
Orange sections
Canned pineapple chunks,
well drained
Stemmed maraschino cherries,
well drained
Bananas, peeled and cut into
1½-inch pieces
Toasted pound-cake fingers

is melted and smooth. Stir in brandy. Arrange strawberries, orange sections, pineapple, cherries, bananas, and cake, or any desired selection, on a large platter, or arrange some of each on individual dessert plates. Allow about 10 to 12 pieces of fruit and cake per person. Supply guests with fondue forks with which to dip fruits and cake into the warm fondue. Serves 8.

Dessert Pancakes

❧ Coconut Pancakes with Cinnamon Whipped Cream

1 *3½-ounce can flaked*
coconut
½ *teaspoon almond extract*
1 *recipe Basic Pancakes*
(recipe on page 648)
3 *tablespoons sugar*
1 *teaspoon vanilla extract*
1 *teaspoon ground*
cinnamon
1½ *cups heavy cream,*
whipped
Cherry preserves

Add coconut and almond extract to Basic Pancakes. Spoon about 1½ tablespoons batter onto hot griddle heated over moderately high heat (about 325° F.) for each pancake. When done, place on cake rack until ready to use. Fold sugar, vanilla, and cinnamon into whipped cream. For each serving, stack 3 pancakes together with some of the whipped cream mixture between each layer and on top. Garnish with a spoonful of cherry preserves. Serve immediately, or refrigerate until serving time. Serves 6.

❧ Chocolate Pancakes with Peppermint Whipped Cream

6 *tablespoons unsweetened*
cocoa
¼ *cup sugar*
1 *recipe Basic Pancakes*
(recipe on page 648)
2 *tablespoons vegetable oil*
2 *tablespoons sugar*
1 *teaspoon vanilla extract*
¼ *cup finely crushed*
peppermint-stick candy

Add cocoa and the ¼ cup sugar to the dry ingredients in the Basic Pancakes recipe. Add the additional 2 tablespoons oil and mix as directed. Spoon about 1½ tablespoons batter onto hot griddle heated over moderately high heat (about 325° F.) for each pancake. Turn when puffy; do not overbake. Place on a cake rack until ready to use. Fold the 2 tablespoons sugar, vanilla, crushed candy, and red food coloring into whipped cream. For each serving, stack 3 pancakes together with some of the whipped cream mixture between each layer and on top.

1 drop red food coloring
1½ cups heavy cream,
 whipped

Serve immediately, or refrigerate until serving time.
Serves 6.

✑ Flaming Swedish Pancakes

3 eggs
¾ cup sifted all-purpose
 flour
1½ teaspoons sugar
⅛ teaspoon salt
⅔ cup water
⅔ cup milk
Melted butter
1 14¾-ounce jar
 lingonberries
Cinnamon sugar
½ cup warmed brandy

Beat eggs well and blend in flour, sugar, salt, water, and
milk. Cover and chill in refrigerator for 2 hours or
overnight. Place a 7-inch skillet over moderately high
heat (about 325° F.) and brush lightly with butter. Pour a
scant ¼ cup of the chilled batter into skillet and tip skillet until batter covers entire bottom surface. Cook until
lightly browned at edges; turn and cook until browned.
Remove from pan and roll up. Continue making crepes,
brushing pan occasionally with additional melted butter.
To serve, unroll crepes, spoon 2 tablespoons lingonberries on each crepe and reroll. Place in a shallow ovenproof dish. Sprinkle generously with cinnamon sugar.
Place in a preheated broiler about 4 to 5 inches from
heat until sugar is slightly caramelized. Remove from
broiler. Pour the ½ cup warmed brandy over the crepes
and ignite; spoon brandy over crepes until flame subsides. (Crepes may be made ahead of time. Stack unrolled between sheets of waxed paper. Keep in refrigerator
until ready to use. Spoon lingonberries on each crepe;
roll and heat as directed above.) Makes twelve 7-inch
crepes, or serves 6.

✑ Blintzes with Assorted Fillings

9 eggs
3 cups milk
1½ teaspoons salt
6 tablespoons vegetable oil
2¼ cups sifted all-purpose
 flour
Butter or margarine
Cheese Filling (recipe follows)
Blueberry Filling (recipe
 follows)
Apple Filling (recipe follows)

In a large bowl beat eggs, milk, salt, and vegetable oil
together well. Stir flour into egg–milk mixture until well
blended. Beat with a rotary beater until batter is smooth.
Melt about 1 teaspoon butter in a heavy 8-inch skillet
over moderately low heat (about 225° F.). Pour about ¼
cup batter into hot skillet heated over moderately high
heat (about 325° F.), tilting pan quickly to coat bottom.
Use just enough batter to make a very thin pancake.
Cook until batter sets and bottom is golden brown. Slide
onto a platter. Repeat with remaining batter. Place desired filling in center of each pancake. Fold the 4 sides
over to encase filling, making a square packet. Place
seam side down on platter and refrigerate. At serving
time, butter an electric skillet lightly and heat to 250° F.

Place several blintzes in skillet and cook 10 to 12 minutes, turning occasionally, until golden brown. Add more butter as needed. If desired, serve with sour cream, applesauce, fruit jam, or powdered sugar. Makes 2 dozen blintzes.

Cheese Filling

2 16-ounce containers small-curd cottage cheese
2 egg yolks
4 tablespoons sugar
½ teaspoon ground cinnamon
1 tablespoon lemon juice

Combine all ingredients in a bowl. Use ½ cup for each blintz. Makes enough filling for 8 blintzes.

Blueberry Filling

1 21-ounce can blueberry pie filling
⅛ teaspoon ground nutmeg
1½ teaspoons lemon juice

Combine all ingredients in a bowl. Use ¼ to ⅓ cup for each blintz. Makes enough filling for 8 blintzes.

Apple Filling

1 20-ounce can sliced apples
¼ teaspoon ground cinnamon

Combine both ingredients in a bowl. Use ¼ to ⅓ cup for each blintz. Makes enough filling for 8 blintzes.

Dessert Crepes

Dessert crepes are made exactly like main-dish crepes except that the fillings are sweet. See the techniques for making crepes on page 653.

Apple Crepes

12 to 14 cooked crepes (recipe on page 653)
1½ pounds cooking apples
¼ cup butter or margarine
½ teaspoon ground cinnamon
½ cup sugar
¼ cup seedless raisins
2 tablespoons brandy or apple brandy

Have crepes ready. Peel, core, and cut apples into thin slices. Melt butter in a large skillet over moderate heat (about 250° F.). Add apples and cook until fork-tender. Add cinnamon, sugar, raisins, and brandy and simmer about 4 minutes, or until most of the liquid has evaporated. Place about 2 tablespoons of the mixture in the center of each crepe. Roll up crepes. Place rolled crepes seam side down in a buttered, shallow, 3-quart baking dish. Bake in a preheated 375° F. oven 10 to 15 minutes, or until heated through. Serve immediately. Serves 6.

❧ Chestnut Custard Crepes

12 to 14 cooked crepes (recipe
on page 653)
1 tablespoon cornstarch
¼ cup sugar
2 egg yolks
⅔ cup milk, heated
2 tablespoons butter or
margarine
2 cups canned sweetened
chestnut purée

Have crepes ready. Combine cornstarch and sugar in a small bowl and stir to blend well. Beat egg yolks in the small bowl of an electric mixer until thick. Gradually add sugar–cornstarch mixture and beat until pale-colored and fluffy. While still beating, add the hot milk a few drops at a time and beat until mixture is light and fluffy. Pour mixture into the top of a double boiler and cook over simmering water, stirring constantly, for about 15 to 20 minutes, or until mixture is as thick as mayonnaise and will form soft ribbons when dropped from a spoon. Remove from heat. Add butter and chestnut purée and blend well. Spread each crepe with about 2 tablespoons of the mixture. Roll up crepes. Arrange crepes seam side down in a buttered, shallow, 3-quart baking dish. Bake in a preheated 350° F. oven 10 to 15 minutes, or until heated through. Serve immediately. Serves 6.

❧ Chocolate-Cream Crepes

12 to 14 cooked crepes (recipe
on page 653)
½ cup sugar
1 tablespoon cornstarch
2 egg yolks
¾ cup light cream, heated
2 1-ounce squares
unsweetened chocolate,
grated
2 tablespoons butter or
margarine
2 tablespoons confectioners'
sugar

Have crepes ready. Combine sugar and cornstarch in a small bowl and blend well. Beat egg yolks in the small bowl of an electric mixer until thick. Gradually add sugar–cornstarch mixture and beat until pale-colored and fluffy. While still beating, add the hot cream a few drops at a time and beat until mixture is light and fluffy. Pour mixture into the top of a double boiler and cook over simmering water, stirring constantly, for about 15 to 20 minutes, or until mixture is as thick as mayonnaise and will form soft ribbons when dropped from a spoon. Remove from heat. Add chocolate and butter and stir until melted and well blended. Place about 1 tablespoon of the chocolate mixture in the center of each crepe. Roll up crepes. Place crepes seam side down in a buttered, shallow, 3-quart baking dish. Bake in a preheated 350° F. oven 10 to 15 minutes, or until heated through. Sprinkle top with sugar. Serve immediately. Serves 6.

❧ Lemon-Cheese Crepes

12 to 14 cooked crepes (recipe
on page 653)

Have crepes ready. Combine whole egg, egg yolk, and sugar in the large bowl of an electric mixer and beat

1 *whole egg*
1 *egg yolk*
⅔ *cup sugar*
2 *8-ounce packages cream cheese, at room temperature*
2 *tablespoons grated lemon peel*
2 *tablespoons lemon juice*
½ *cup finely chopped mixed candied fruits and peels*
2 *tablespoons confectioners' sugar*

until pale-colored and thick. Add cream cheese, lemon peel, and lemon juice, and beat until smooth and creamy and well blended. Stir in candied fruit. Place about 2 tablespoons of this mixture in the center of each crepe. Roll up crepes. Place crepes seam side down in a buttered, shallow, 3-quart baking dish. Bake in a preheated 375° F. oven 10 to 15 minutes, or until heated through. Sprinkle with confectioners' sugar. Serve warm. Serves 6.

✒ *Crepes Suzette*

12 to 14 *cooked crepes (recipe on page 653)*
1 *cup butter*
½ *cup sugar*
¼ *cup fresh orange juice*
¼ *cup orange-flavored liqueur*
3 *tablespoons grated orange peel*
½ *cup coarsely cut orange sections*
¼ *cup brandy or cognac*
¼ *cup orange-flavored liqueur*

Have crepes ready. Beat butter in the large bowl of an electric mixer until creamy. Add sugar gradually and beat until pale-colored and fluffy. Gradually add orange juice and the ¼ cup orange liqueur; beat until thick and creamy. Stir in orange peel and orange sections and blend well. Refrigerate, covered, until ready to use. Shortly before serving, place the orange–butter mixture in the blazer of a chafing dish or crepes suzette pan. Cook over direct heat until butter mixture is melted and bubbly. Dip each crepe into the hot mixture and with 2 spoons fold each crepe in half, then in half again to form a wedge. Push each wedge to one side of the pan until all the crepes are folded, then arrange them in an overlapping layer in the pan. Place brandy and the ¼ cup liqueur in a small saucepan. Place over moderately low heat (about 225° F.) until slightly warm. Ignite and pour over crepes. Gently spoon flaming sauce over crepes until the flame dies out. Serve immediately. Serves 6.

Dessert Waffles

✒ *Sweet Dessert Waffles*

1 *cup sifted all-purpose flour*
¾ *teaspoon baking powder*
¼ *teaspoon salt*

Heat waffle baker according to manufacturer's directions. Sift together flour, baking powder, and salt. Beat eggs well in a medium-sized bowl. Add sugar and beat

3 eggs
1 cup sugar
¼ cup melted butter or
  margarine
¼ cup water
1 teaspoon vanilla extract
Sweetened sliced peaches
  (optional)
Sweetened strawberries
  (optional)
Confectioners' sugar
  (optional)

well. Stir in melted butter, water, vanilla, and sifted dry ingredients. Bake at a slightly cooler temperature than for regular waffles. When steaming stops, remove from the waffle baker and cool on cake racks. Serve with sweetened sliced peaches or strawberries or sprinkle hot waffles with confectioners' sugar. Makes ten 4½-inch waffles.

✌ Graham Waffles with Fudge Sauce

2 cups packaged graham
  cracker crumbs
½ teaspoon salt
3 teaspoons baking powder
1 teaspoon ground cinnamon
½ teaspoon ground nutmeg
3 eggs
½ cup sugar
1 cup milk
¼ cup vegetable oil
½ cup chopped walnuts
Vanilla ice cream
Chocolate Fudge Sauce (recipe
  on page 762)

Heat waffle baker according to manufacturer's directions. Mix together graham cracker crumbs, salt, baking powder, cinnamon, and nutmeg. Beat eggs in a large bowl. Add sugar and beat well. Stir in crumb mixture, milk, oil, and nuts. Bake as directed for regular waffles. (see page 657). Cool on a cake rack. Serve with a scoop of vanilla ice cream and fudge sauce. Makes eight 4½-inch waffles.

✌ Belgian Waffles

1 cup sifted all-purpose flour
¾ teaspoon baking powder
¼ teaspoon salt
3 eggs
1 cup sugar
¼ cup melted butter or
  margarine
¼ cup water
1 teaspoon vanilla extract
1 pint heavy cream
4 tablespoons confectioners'
  sugar

Heat regular or Belgian waffle baker according to manufacturer's directions. Sift together flour, baking powder, and salt. Beat eggs well in a medium-sized bowl; add sugar and beat well. Stir in melted butter, water, the 1 teaspoon vanilla, and sifted dry ingredients. Bake at a slightly cooler temperature than directed for regular waffles. When steaming stops, remove from waffle baker and cool on wire racks. Place waffles on serving plates. Whip the cream; stir in confectioners' sugar and the 2 teaspoons vanilla. Spoon whipped cream on top of waffles and top each with about ¼ to ⅓ cup sliced strawberries. Serve immediately. Makes ten 4½-inch waffles.

(Ingredients continued on page 778)

2 teaspoons vanilla extract
2 cups fresh strawberries,
    washed, drained, hulled,
    and sliced

Very Special Desserts

✃ Cannoli

2 cups sifted all-purpose
    flour
¼ teaspoon salt
¼ cup sugar
2 tablespoons butter or
    margarine
2 eggs, slightly beaten
1 tablespoon white vinegar
1 tablespoon water
1 egg yolk, slightly beaten
Vegetable oil
Cheese Filling (recipe follows)

Cut 6 circles out of heavy-duty aluminum foil, each 6 inches in diameter. Roll each circle into a cone shape. Set aside.* Sift flour, salt, and sugar together in a medium-sized bowl. With a pastry blender, cut in butter until mixture resembles coarse corn meal. In a small bowl, combine the 2 eggs, vinegar, and water and blend well. Add to flour mixture and mix with a fork until smooth. Turn out onto a floured board. Divide dough into 24 pieces. Roll each piece into a 5-inch round about ⅛ inch thick. Roll each circle around a foil cone to fit tightly. Seal edges with the slightly beaten egg yolk. Heat about 3 inches of oil in a heavy saucepan until it registers 375° F. on a deep-fat-frying thermometer. Fry 2 cones at a time (do not remove from foil), turning occasionally, until golden brown, about 3 to 4 minutes. Remove from fat with a slotted spoon and drain on paper towels. Cool slightly before removing from foil cones (foil cones may be reused). Fill with Cheese Filling just before serving. Makes 2 dozen cannoli.

*Note: In place of foil cones, you may use dowel sticks 1 inch in diameter and 5 inches long.

Cheese Filling

¾ pound (12 ounces) ricotta
    cheese
¼ cup finely chopped mixed
    candied fruits and peels
¼ cup coarsely chopped
    semisweet chocolate
⅛ teaspoon ground cinnamon
¼ cup coarsely chopped sliced
    blanched almonds
½ cup heavy cream
¼ cup confectioners' sugar

Rub cheese through a fine sieve. Fold in candied fruits, chocolate, cinnamon, and almonds. Place cream and sugar in the small bowl of an electric mixer and beat until cream holds its shape. Fold into cheese mixture. Makes about 2¼ cups filling, enough for 2 dozen cannoli.

⇜ Caramel Crème Frite

5 tablespoons cornstarch
3 tablespoons sugar
1½ cups milk
2 eggs
½ teaspoon vanilla extract
⅛ teaspoon lemon extract
½ cup sifted all-purpose
    flour
½ teaspoon baking powder
⅓ cup milk
1 egg
Vegetable oil
Caramel Syrup (recipe
    follows)

Combine cornstarch and sugar in a saucepan. Beat together the 1½ cups milk and the 2 eggs; gradually add to dry mixture in saucepan, stirring constantly. Place over moderately low heat (about 225° F.) and cook, stirring constantly with a wire whip, until thickened. Remove from heat and add vanilla and lemon extracts. Pour into a 9-x-5-x-3-inch loaf pan. Chill thoroughly. Cut chilled cream mixture into 10 equal portions. To make batter for coating, combine the flour and baking powder. Combine the ⅓ cup milk and the remaining egg; gradually stir into flour mixture, stirring constantly. Pour oil to a depth of 3 to 4 inches into a saucepan or deep-fat fryer. Heat to a temperature of 375° F. on a deep-fat frying thermometer. Dip each portion of chilled cream mixture into the batter; let any excess drip off. Fry in hot fat until golden brown, about 5 minutes. Drain on paper towels and keep warm while frying remainder of mixture. Serve with Caramel Syrup. Serves 6 to 8.

Caramel Syrup

1 cup sugar
⅓ cup water
⅓ cup plus 1 tablespoon
    water

Combine sugar and the ⅓ cup water in a saucepan. Place over moderate heat (about 250° F.), shaking pan occasionally until all of sugar is dissolved. Do not stir. Boil, watching carefully, until syrup turns a light caramel color. Remove immediately from heat and set in a large pan of cold water to stop further cooking. After syrup has cooled, add the ⅓ cup plus 1 tablespoon water. (Syrup may lump, but will dissolve upon heating.) Place again over moderate heat (about 250° F.) and cook, stirring constantly, until syrup is dissolved. Cool to room temperature before serving over Crème Frite.

⇜ Beignets Soufflés with Apricot Sauce

1 cup water
½ cup butter or margarine
¼ teaspoon salt
1 cup sifted all-purpose flour
4 eggs
½ teaspoon grated orange
    peel
Vegetable oil
Apricot Sauce (recipe follows)
Confectioners' sugar

Place water, butter, and salt in a heavy saucepan over moderate heat (about 250° F.). Cook, stirring occasionally, until butter melts and mixture comes to a rolling boil. Reduce heat to low (about 200° F.); add flour all at once and stir vigorously over heat about 1 minute, or until mixture leaves sides of pan and clings together. Remove from heat; add unbeaten eggs one at a time, beating well after each addition. Continue to beat vigorously until smooth and satiny. Stir in orange peel. Pour oil to a depth of 3 inches in a heavy saucepan or deep-fat fryer. Heat to 370° F. on a deep-fat-frying thermometer. Form level tablespoonfuls of the prepared batter into balls with the aid of a small metal spatula and drop into the hot fat. (Four or more may be fried at the same time, depending on the size of the fryer.) Fry about 5 to 8 minutes, or until puffed and golden brown. Beignets will turn automatically as they cook. (Keep warm while preparing remainder of beignets.) Pour about ½ cup of the Apricot Sauce into each dessert dish. Arrange 4 of the prepared beignets in each serving dish. Place a little confectioners' sugar in a small sieve and shake a small amount of sugar over each serving. (If desired, beignets may be made a few hours ahead. To reheat for serving, place on a cookie sheet in a 375° F. oven for about 10 minutes.) Serves 8.

Apricot Sauce

1 8-ounce package dried
   apricots
2 to 3 cups water
1 cup sugar
2 to 3 tablespoons kirsch or
   brandy (optional)

Place apricots in a saucepan and cover with water. Place over moderate heat (about 250° F.) and cook 30 to 40 minutes, or until apricots are very tender. Drain apricots, reserving apricot liquid. If necessary, add enough water to liquid to make 2 cups. Place about ⅓ of the apricots and ¼ cup of the apricot liquid in the container of an electric blender; blend on low speed until puréed. Repeat with remaining apricots. Return puréed apricots and remaining liquid to saucepan; add sugar and cook over moderate heat (about 250° F.), stirring occasionally, until sugar is dissolved. If desired, add kirsch or brandy. Serve warm with Beignets Soufflés. Makes about 3½ cups sauce, enough for 8 servings of beignets.

Baba au Fraises

2½ cups sifted all-purpose
   flour
¼ cup sugar
½ teaspoon salt
1 package active dry yeast
½ cup milk
¼ cup water
¼ cup butter or margarine
3 eggs, at room temperature
3 tablespoons dried
   currants

In the large bowl of an electric mixer mix ⅔ cup of the flour, the ¼ cup sugar, salt, and yeast. Place milk, water, and butter in a small saucepan over moderately low heat (about 225° F.) and heat until liquids are warm (butter will be entirely melted and temperature should be about 125° F.). Gradually add liquid to dry ingredients and beat 2 minutes at medium speed of the electric mixer, scraping bowl occasionally with a rubber spatula. Add eggs and ½ cup of the flour, or enough to make a thick batter. Beat at high speed 2 minutes, scraping bowl occasionally. With a spoon stir in just enough of the remain-

1 *cup sugar*
1 *cup water*
¼ *cup rum*
1 *quart strawberries,*
   washed and hulled
⅓ *cup sugar*

ing flour to make a thick batter. Cover with a damp cloth and let rise in a warm place (85° F.) until double in bulk, about 1 hour. Stir down batter amd mix in the currants. Pour into a well greased 2-quart ring mold. Cover and let rise 30 minutes, or until double in bulk. Heat oven to 350° F. and bake 35 to 40 minutes, or until golden brown. Cool on a wire cake rack for 5 minutes; invert cake onto a serving platter. While cake is baking, combine the 1 cup sugar and the 1 cup water in a saucepan. Place over moderate heat (about 250° F.) and cook 5 minutes after mixture comes to a boil, stirring occasionally. Remove from heat, cool, and stir in rum. Prick cake at ½-inch intervals with a toothpick or cake tester around top and sides. Spoon sauce over top and sides of warm cake until all of the sauce is used. To serve, reserve a few strawberries for garnish and slice remainder. Fold in remaining ⅓ cup sugar. Spoon sweetened strawberries in center and garnish with whole berries. Serves 8.

CHAPTER XXII

PIES AND PASTRY

"As easy as apple pie" was no doubt a meaningful expression to your great-grandmother who probably learned to make pastry before she was in her teens. But to young cooks today, the thought of making pastry and trying to turn out a perfect pie often produces uncertainty and dread. Actually, with the uniformly excellent packaged pastry mixes on the market today or with standard measuring equipment and good basic ingredients, cooks today can be more certain of turning out superb pies than could cooks of yesterday.

Pastry

There are many variations of pastry, as you will see as you proceed through this section. In its simplest form, it consists mainly of flour, shortening, and water. The trick is to combine them in the right quantities and to the right degree. Do use standard measuring cups and spoons and measure accurately. The pictured directions given here show how to mix both Flaky Solid-Shortening Pastry and Flaky Liquid-Shortening Pastry for one 9-inch pie shell. If you use packaged pie crust, follow package directions.

Mixing Pastry

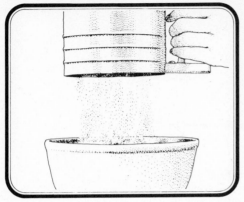

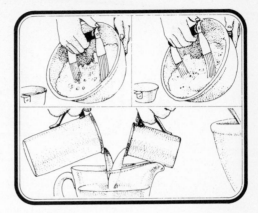

1. Sift flour before measuring. Spoon sifted flour into a 1-cup measure. Level off flour with the edge of a knife or spatula. Combine flour and salt in a sifter and sift again into a medium-sized bowl.

2a. If solid shortening is used: Add half the shortening to the flour mixture. Cut it in with a pastry blender or two knives until the mixture looks like coarse meal. Cut in rest of shortening until particles are the size of small peas.

2b. If liquid shortening is used: Measure out the correct amount of salad oil and the correct amount of milk. Pour oil and milk into a glass measuring cup but do not stir them together. The milk will stay at the bottom of the cup.

3a. Measure out water 1 tablespoon at a time and sprinkle it over the flour–shortening mixture. As the water is added, toss mixture lightly with a fork. Mix until all flour particles are moistened and mixture begins to leave side of bowl.

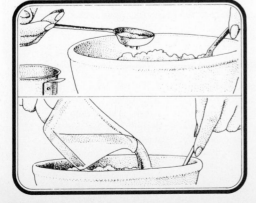

3b. Pour all the oil and milk in the center of the sifted flour-and-salt mixture. Stir vigorously with a fork until all the flour particles become moistened and the mixture forms a ball that will pull away from the side of the bowl.

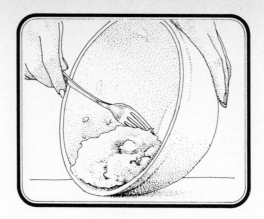

4. When all the flour is moistened, work dough together with the fork and turn it out onto a wooden board that has been lightly sprinkled with flour or a canvas pastry cloth well rubbed with flour.

Rolling Pastry

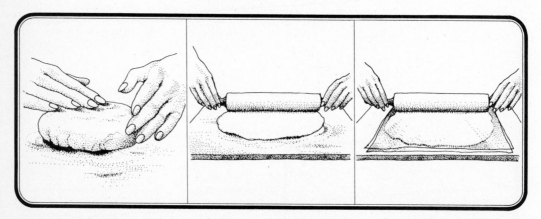

1. Shape the dough gently into a ball with the hands. For a two-crust pie, cut ball in half; set aside one half for the top crust. Reshape the other half; place on floured board and flatten slightly with the fingers, ready for rolling bottom crust.

2. Roll pastry made with solid shortening on a floured board or pastry cloth. Starting in center of flattened ball, roll with floured rolling pin from the center to outside edge. Roll dough in all directions to shape it into a smooth circle.

3. To roll liquid-shortening pastry: Cover board with waxed paper. Place flattened ball of dough on paper and cover with a second piece of waxed paper. Roll into a circle. Peel off top paper.

Fitting Pastry into a Plate

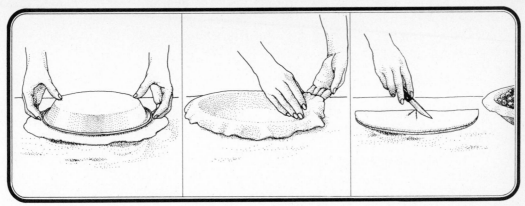

1. Roll out either type of pastry until it forms a circle that is about ⅛ inch thick and 1½ inches larger than the pie plate in which the pie is to be baked. To judge size easily, hold the inverted pie plate over the rolled-out circle of dough.

2. Fold the rolled-out circle of dough in half. Place fold in center of the pie plate, then unfold dough. Gently ease the dough into the plate with the fingers. Stretching the dough while putting it in the plate causes shrinkage. Pour in filling.

3. Roll out top crust the same size as bottom one. Fold in half; cut slits with a sharp knife to allow steam to escape as pie bakes. Moisten edge of bottom crust with water. Loosely fit crust over filling.

Sealing and Shaping Pastry Edge

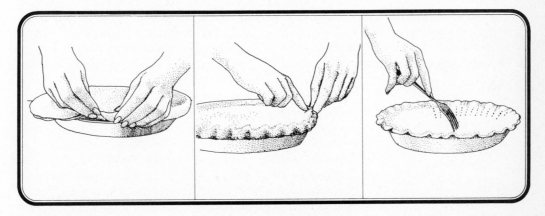

1. For two-crust pies: Press bottom and top crusts together along edge of plate. Trim with scissors to leave about 1 inch of pastry beyond plate. Roll pastry under with fingers until it is even with edge. Press to make a high stand-up rim.

2. To make fluted edge: Place the right index finger on inside of pastry rim and the left thumb and index finger on outside edge. Pinch fingers together. Repeat all around edge of pie. Sharpen the points by pinching each one firmly.

3. For unbaked or baked pastry shells: Fit pastry circle loosely into pie plate. Roll edge under to form high rim. Flute the edge. If shell is to be baked, prick bottom and sides with a fork.

To Make a Fluted Edge

Form a high-standing rim. Place left index finger inside pastry rim. Make flutes about every ½ inch by pushing pastry into the V shaped by the right thumb and index fingers on the outside of the rim. Pinch flutes to make clean, definite edges.

To Make a Rope Edge

Form a high-standing rim. Place thumb on pastry rim at an angle; press pastry against thumb with knuckle of index finger. Repeat around rim.

To Make a Leaf Edge

Form a high-standing rim. With scissors clip rim at an angle every ¼ inch. Press down the clipped rim sections alternately to left and right to form a leaf pattern.

To Make a Fork Edge

Form a high-standing rim. With floured 4-tined fork, press pastry firmly to plate rim at ½-inch intervals.

⊸ Flaky Solid-Shortening Pastry Shell

1 cup sifted all-purpose flour
½ teaspoon salt
⅓ cup soft shortening (not butter, margarine, or vegetable oil)
2 to 3 tablespoons cold water

Sift flour and salt into a bowl. Add half of the shortening and cut it in with a pastry blender or two knives until mixture looks like coarse meal. Cut in remaining shortening until it looks like large peas. Sprinkle water, 1 tablespoon at a time, over flour–shortening mixture; toss with a fork until mixture clings together. Roll out dough on a lightly floured board or pastry cloth. Form a flattened ball and, starting in the center, roll with floured rolling pin from center to outside edge. Roll out dough in all directions to shape into a smooth circle about 1½ inches larger than a 9-inch pie plate. Fold pastry in half; carefully lift from board and place fold across center of the pie plate; then unfold pastry. Gently ease dough into plate with fingertips. (Stretching dough while putting it in place causes shrinkage.) If necessary, trim pastry about 1 inch beyond edge of plate. Roll edge under to form a high-standing rim and use one of edges listed above. If recipe calls for a baked pastry shell, prick bottom and sides of pastry with a fork. Heat oven to 450° F. Bake 12 to 15 minutes. (For a perfectly shaped baked pastry shell, place a large round of waxed paper in pricked unbaked shell and pour in 2 cups of raw rice or beans. Bake in oven for 6 minutes. Take from oven, spoon out rice, and remove waxed paper. Prick shell again; return to oven and bake 6 to 7 minutes, or until lightly browned.) Makes one 9-inch pastry shell.

Nut Pastry

Mix *3 tablespoons finely chopped walnuts, pecans, or almonds* into flour before cutting in shortening.

Cheese Pastry

Mix *3 tablespoons grated Cheddar cheese* into flour before cutting in shortening.

Chocolate Pastry

Mix *3 tablespoons sugar* and *3 tablespoons unsweetened cocoa* with flour before cutting in shortening. Stir in *¼ teaspoon vanilla extract* with water in recipe on page 786.

Almond Pastry

Stir *3 tablespoons finely ground almonds* and *3 tablespoons confectioners' sugar* into flour mixture. Substitute *1 slightly beaten egg* and *1 teaspoon lemon juice* for water in recipe on page 786. If necessary, add *1 to 2 teaspoons water* if pastry is too dry to handle.

✒ Two-Crust Flaky Solid-Shortening Pastry

2 cups sifted all-purpose flour
1 teaspoon salt
⅔ cup soft shortening (not butter, margarine, or vegetable oil)
4 to 6 tablespoons cold water

Make pastry exactly as for Flaky Solid-Shortening Pastry Shell (on page 786) and divide pastry into 2 balls. Roll and fit into plate as shown in pictures on pages 784 and 785.

✒ Flaky Liquid-Shortening Pastry Shell

1⅓ cups sifted all-purpose flour
1 teaspoon salt
⅓ cup vegetable oil
3 tablespoons cold milk

Sift flour and salt together into a bowl. Pour oil and milk into a measuring cup, but do not stir. Add all at once to flour and stir until mixed. With the fingers, press into a smooth ball. Roll between two 12-inch squares of waxed paper. Dampen tabletop to keep paper from slipping. Roll dough in a circle to edges of paper. Peel off top paper. Invert pastry and paper over a 9-inch pie plate. Gently remove paper. Ease and fit pastry into plate. Trim and flute edge as desired. Bake as directed for solid-shortening pastry. Makes one 9-inch pastry shell.

Note: Double recipe above for a 2-crust pie; roll out and use as directed on pages 784 and 785.

ᕤ Lattice Top for Two-Crust Pies

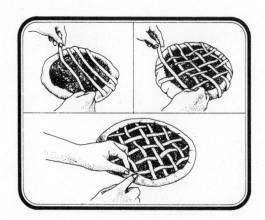

Lattice top: Roll the pastry dough into a round ⅛ inch thick. With a knife cut it into 10 strips ½ inch wide. (To make decorative edges, cut the strips with a pastry wheel.) Place 5 strips at equal intervals across the top of the filled, unbaked pie, using one of the longest strips for the center, the shorter ones at the sides. The ends will extend over the edge of the lower crust. Fold back the center strip and the 2 outside strips just past the middle of the pie. Lay 1 of the remaining long pastry strips across the center and unfold the first 3 strips over it. Fold back the 2 inside strips; lay another remaining strip across the pie and flip the folded strips over it. Repeat, folding back alternate sets of strips and placing the new ones, creating a woven top for the pie. For a quicker lattice effect, you can place the second 5 strips across the first without weaving. Trim strips to fit the edge of the lower crust. Turn the pastry edge from the lower crust over the ends of the strips. Pinch or flute to seal the edge.

Trellis Top

Make exactly like lattice top but twist pastry strips as you proceed.

Glazed Top

Brush top crust before baking with *milk,* or with *1 egg* beaten with *1 tablespoon ice water.*

For a sparkling effect, sprinkle with *granulated sugar,* or dust warm pie after baking with *sifted confectioners' sugar.*

ᵃ❦ Lard Pastry Shell

6 tablespoons lard
3 tablespoons boiling water
1 cup sifted all-purpose flour
¼ teaspoon baking powder
½ teaspoon salt

Mix lard and boiling water together with an electric mixer until mixture is creamy and cool. Sift flour, baking powder, and salt together into a bowl. Add lard mixture and stir with a fork until a ball is formed. Roll out dough and fit into pie plate. Trim and flute edge, as desired. Bake as directed for solid-shortening pastry. Makes one 9-inch shell.

Note: Double recipe above for a 2-crust pie; roll out and use as directed on pages 784 and 785.

ᵃ❦ Perfect Apple Pie

Pastry for 9-inch 2-crust pie
(recipes on page 787)
¾ cup sugar
1 tablespoon flour
½ teaspoon ground cinnamon
¼ teaspoon ground nutmeg
⅛ teaspoon salt
1 tablespoon grated lemon peel
5 cups peeled, cored, and thickly sliced apples for pie
1 tablespoon lemon juice
2 tablespoons butter or margarine

Heat oven to 425° F. Roll out half the pastry and line a 9-inch pie plate. Combine sugar, flour, cinnamon, nutmeg, salt, and lemon peel in a bowl. Add apples and toss to coat evenly. Arrange apples in pie plate. Sprinkle with lemon juice and dot with butter. Roll out rest of pastry and place over apples. Trim pastry rim and flute edge. Bake 40 to 45 minutes. Serves 6 to 8.

ᵃ❦ Blueberry Pie

Pastry for 9-inch 2-crust pie
(recipes on page 787)
4 cups fresh blueberries or 2 12-ounce packages frozen blueberries, thawed
¾ cup sugar
⅓ cup flour
½ teaspoon grated lemon peel
1 teaspoon lemon juice
¼ teaspoon ground nutmeg
½ teaspoon ground cinnamon
⅛ teaspoon salt
1 tablespoon butter or margarine

Heat oven to 425° F. Roll out half the pastry and line a 9-inch pie plate. Wash and drain fresh blueberries. Combine sugar, flour, lemon peel, lemon juice, nutmeg, cinnamon, and salt. Place half the berries in the lined pie plate. Sprinkle with half the sugar mixture. Add remaining berries and top with rest of sugar mixture. Dot top with butter. Roll out remaining pastry and place over berries. Trim and flute edge. Bake 35 to 40 minutes. Serves 6 to 8.

❧ Cherry Pie

Pastry for 9-inch 2-crust pie
(recipes on page 787)
2 16-ounce cans
water-packed, pitted, tart
red cherries
1 cup sugar
⅓ cup flour
⅛ teaspoon salt
½ teaspoon almond extract
Few drops red food coloring
2 tablespoons butter or
margarine

Heat oven to 425° F. Roll out half the pastry and line a 9-inch pie plate. Drain cherries and reserve ½ cup of the liquid. Mix together sugar, flour, and salt in a saucepan. Gradually add the ½ cup cherry liquid; mix until smooth. Cook over moderate heat (about 250° F.), stirring constantly, until smooth and thickened. Remove from heat and stir in almond extract and red food coloring. Pour sauce over cherries and mix gently. Pour into lined pie plate; dot top with butter. Roll out rest of pastry and place over cherries. Trim and flute edge. Bake 35 to 40 minutes, until crust is brown. Serves 6 to 8.

❧ Cranberry Pie

¾ cup seedless raisins
Hot water
1 pound fresh or frozen
cranberries
1¾ cups sugar
¼ cup all-purpose flour
¼ teaspoon salt
½ cup cold water
1 tablespoon grated orange
peel
Pastry for a 9-inch 2-crust pie
(recipes on page 787)
3 tablespoons butter or
margarine

Place raisins in a small bowl and pour hot water over to cover. Let stand 10 minutes and drain. Grind cranberries, using the coarsest blade of a food chopper or grinder. In a large bowl combine sugar, flour, and salt. Stir in ground cranberries, raisins, water, and orange peel. Blend well. Heat oven to 450° F. Prepare pastry. Roll out half the pastry on a lightly floured pastry cloth and line a 9-inch pie plate, leaving 1 inch of pastry beyond edge of plate. Add cranberry mixture and dot with butter. Roll out remaining pastry and place over filling. Trim pastry; fold top crust edges under bottom crust and flute edges. Cut slashes in top of pie to allow steam to escape. Bake 15 minutes; then lower heat to 375° F. and bake 35 to 40 minutes, or until golden brown. Serve at room temperature. Serves 6 to 8.

❧ Concord Grape Pie

4 cups Concord grapes
2½ tablespoons quick-cooking
tapioca
1¼ cups sugar
¼ teaspoon salt
⅛ teaspoon ground cloves
½ teaspoon grated lemon
peel

Heat oven to 425° F. Wash and stem Concord grapes. Slip off skins and reserve them. Put grape pulp in a saucepan. Cook over moderately low heat (about 225° F.) 3 to 4 minutes, or just long enough to soften. Rub hot pulp through a sieve to remove seeds. Combine sieved pulp, grape skins, tapioca, sugar, salt, cloves, lemon peel, lemon juice, and butter. Roll out half the pastry and line a 9-inch pie plate. Pour grape mixture into

1 tablespoon lemon juice
1 tablespoon butter or
  margarine
Pastry for 9-inch 2-crust pie
  (recipes on page 787)
Sugar

shell. Roll remaining pastry and cut into ½-inch-wide strips. Weave strips in lattice over top (see page 788). Sprinkle lightly with sugar. Trim and seal edge. Bake 45 minutes. Serves 6 to 8.

✜ Mincemeat Pie

⅓ cup dried currants
3 tablespoons dry sherry
1⅔ cups prepared mincemeat
  (1 18-ounce jar)
1½ cups peeled, cored, and
  chopped apples
⅓ cup chopped walnuts
1 package pastry mix or
  pastry for a 9-inch
  2-crust pie (recipes
  on page 787)

Heat oven to 425° F. Place currants and sherry in a small saucepan and simmer 5 minutes over low heat (about 200° F.). Combine mincemeat, currant mixture, apple, and walnuts. Prepare pastry. Roll out half the pastry on a lightly floured board and line a 9-inch pie plate, leaving 1 inch pastry beyond edge of plate. Pour in mincemeat mixture. Roll out remaining pastry and make a lattice top as directed on page 788. Bake 45 minutes. Serve warm. Serves 6 to 8.

✜ Strawberry–Rhubarb Pie

Pastry for a 9-inch 2-crust pie
  (recipes on page 787)
3 cups diced, unpeeled
  rhubarb
1 cup sliced strawberries
6 tablespoons flour
1¼ cups sugar
1 teaspoon grated orange
  peel
1 tablespoon butter or
  margarine

Heat oven to 425° F. Roll out half the pastry and line a 9-inch pie plate. Combine rhubarb and strawberries. Mix together flour, sugar, and orange peel. Sprinkle over fruits and toss lightly. Pour mixture into pastry-lined pie plate. Dot with butter. Roll out remaining pastry and place over fruit. Trim and flute edge. Bake 45 to 50 minutes. Serves 6 to 8.

One-Crust Pies

One-crust pies can have a variety of crusts and toppings. They may be chilled before serving; they may have whipped cream or meringue or any number of garnishes added as attractive toppings. Streusel or crumb toppings are favorites for one-crust fruit pies. Pies may have ice-cream fillings or have a thick meringue placed over ice cream and baked so that the meringue browns and the ice cream remains cold.

One-crust pies may begin with a simple pastry crust or they may start with any of the various crumb crusts that consist principally of cracker or cereal or cookie crumbs with nuts, coconut, or spices added. Although these are relatively simple to handle in the mixing, they are not so easy to shape as the pastry crust.

How to Shape a Crumb-Crust Shell

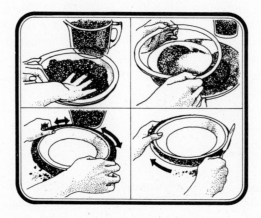

Crumb crust: Place crumb mixture evenly in the bottom of a 9-inch pie plate. Place an 8-inch pie plate on top of crumb mixture, and with a twisting motion press down gently to spread the mixture evenly to the sides. With a flexible metal spatula, press the crumbs into the space between the edges of the plates to form a rim. Remove the 8-inch plate. (If you don't have an 8-inch pie plate, use a spoon or your fingertips to press the crumb mixture evenly over the bottom and sides.) Bake in a preheated 375° F. oven 8 minutes for graham cracker crumbs. For other cookie crumbs, follow the recipe baking directions. Chill before filling.

◅§ Graham-Cracker-Crumb Shell

1⅓ cups fine graham-cracker crumbs
¼ cup sugar
6 tablespoons melted butter or margarine

Heat oven to 375° F. Mix crumbs and sugar in a bowl; add butter and stir until crumbs are moistened. Press crumbs evenly over bottom and sides of a buttered 9-inch pie plate. Bake 8 minutes. Chill before adding filling. Makes one 9-inch shell.

✌️ Corn-Flake-Crumb Shell

1 cup corn-flake cereal
   crumbs
¼ cup sugar
⅓ cup melted butter or
   margarine

Heat oven to 375° F. Mix crumbs and sugar in a bowl; gradually add butter and mix until crumbs are moistened. Press mixture evenly over bottom and sides of buttered 9-inch pie plate. Bake 8 minutes. Chill before adding filling. Makes one 9-inch shell.

✌️ Gingersnap-Crumb Shell

1½ cups fine gingersnap
    crumbs
 5 tablespoons melted butter
    or margarine

Heat oven to 375° F. Mix crumbs and butter together until crumbs are moistened. Press crumbs evenly over bottom and sides of a buttered 9-inch pie plate. Bake 8 minutes. Chill before adding filling. Makes one 9-inch shell.

✌️ Cookie Pie Shell

1 15-ounce roll refrigerated
   sugar or peanut butter
   cookie dough
Butter or margarine
Sugar

Heat oven to 375° F. Cut chilled cookie dough into ⅛-inch-thick slices, using about half the roll. Generously butter the bottom, sides, and edge of a 9-inch pie plate. Sprinkle well with sugar. Arrange cookie slices around sides of pie plate, overlapping them slightly to form a scalloped edge. Line bottom of pie plate with cookie slices. Bake 8 to 10 minutes, until golden brown. Chill completely before adding filling. Makes one 9-inch shell.

✌️ Meringue Shell

3 egg whites, at room
   temperature
¼ teaspoon cream of tartar
Few grains of salt
½ teaspoon vanilla extract
¾ cup sugar

Heat oven to 300° F. Place egg whites in a bowl and beat with rotary beater until foamy. Add cream of tartar, salt, and vanilla; beat until soft peaks form. Gradually add sugar, 2 tablespoons at a time, beating until stiff peaks form. Spread evenly over bottom and sides of a buttered 9-inch pie plate up to the rim. Bake 40 minutes, or until lightly browned. Cool away from drafts. Makes one 9-inch shell.

✌️ Toasted Coconut Shell

2 cups flaked coconut
¼ cup butter or margarine

Heat oven to 375° F. Place coconut and butter in a 9-inch pie plate. Bake 15 to 20 minutes, stirring very frequently, to brown coconut evenly. With the back of a spoon, press coconut mixture over bottom and sides of pie plate. Chill before adding filling. Makes one 9-inch shell.

✑ Chocolate-Crumb Shell

1⅓ cups chocolate wafer crumbs (made from packaged chocolate wafers)

3 tablespoons soft butter or margarine

Heat oven to 375° F. In a medium-sized bowl combine crumbs and butter and work mixture with fingers until well blended. Press mixture over bottom and sides of a 9-inch pie pan. Bake 8 minutes. Chill before adding filling. Makes one 9-inch shell.

✑ Nut Shell

1½ cups finely chopped walnuts or pecans

3 tablespoons sugar

3 tablespoons melted butter or margarine

Heat oven to 450° F. Mix nuts and sugar in a bowl. Gradually add butter and stir until nuts are moistened. Press mixture evenly over bottom and sides of a 9-inch pie plate. Bake 6 to 8 minutes. Chill before adding filling. Makes one 9-inch shell.

Favorite One-Crust Pies

One-crust, or open-faced, pies may be made in either a baked or unbaked pastry shell. Be sure to check the recipe before you begin, to allow time to make a baked pastry or crumb shell if needed.

✑ Honey–Apple Pie

1 9-inch unbaked pastry shell (recipes on pages 786 and 787)

½ cup sugar

3 tablespoons all-purpose flour

¼ cup honey

⅓ cup heavy cream

2 to 2½ pounds tart apples, peeled, cored, and cut into ¾-inch-thick slices

Prepare pastry shell. Heat oven to 425° F. Sprinkle bottom of pastry shell evenly with 1 tablespoon each of the sugar and flour. Combine remaining sugar and flour; stir in honey and cream. Pour mixture over apple slices in a bowl; mix gently until slices are well coated. Spoon into pie shell. Sprinkle with cinnamon and nutmeg; dot with butter. Bake 45 minutes, until apples are fork-tender. Serve warm or cold. Serves 6 to 8.

½ teaspoon ground cinnamon
¼ teaspoon ground nutmeg
1 tablespoon butter or
margarine

✐ Custard Pie

1 9-inch unbaked pastry
shell
(recipes on pages 786 and
787)
4 eggs, slightly beaten
½ cup sugar
¼ teaspoon salt
½ teaspoon vanilla extract
2½ cups milk, heated
Freshly grated nutmeg
Sweetened whipped cream
(optional)

Prepare pastry shell and chill one hour. Beat eggs, sugar, salt, and vanilla together; brush the chilled crust lightly with this mixture. Return crust to refrigerator while completing custard filling. Heat oven to 450° F. Gradually stir hot milk into remaining egg mixture. Pour filling into chilled pastry shell. Bake 20 minutes. Reduce oven temperature to 350° F.; bake 20 minutes, or until a knife inserted 1 inch from the center comes out clean. Remove from oven and grate a little fresh nutmeg over the top. Cool and then chill. Garnish with whipped cream, if desired. Serves 6 to 8.

✐ Southern Pecan Pie

1 9-inch unbaked pastry shell
(recipes on pages 786 and
787)
3 eggs
⅔ cup sugar
1 cup dark corn syrup
⅓ cup melted butter or
margarine
1 cup pecan halves

Prepare pastry shell. Heat oven to 350° F. In a medium-sized bowl combine eggs, sugar, corn syrup, and melted butter and blend well. Stir in pecans. Pour into pastry shell. Bake 50 to 55 minutes, or until knife inserted in center comes out clean. Serve slightly warm. Serves 8.

✐ Date–Pecan Pie

1 9-inch unbaked pastry shell
(recipes on pages 786 and
787)
3 eggs
⅔ cup sugar
½ teaspoon salt
⅓ cup melted butter or
margarine
1 cup dark corn syrup
1 tablespoon rum or 1

Heat oven to 450° F. Prepare pastry shell and bake about 5 to 7 minutes, just to set pastry. Shell should not brown. Remove from oven and cool. Reduce oven temperature to 375° F. Place eggs, sugar, salt, butter, corn syrup, and rum in a mixing bowl. Beat with a rotary beater until well blended. Stir in dates and pecan halves. Pour into pastry shell. Bake 40 to 50 minutes, or until pastry is browned and a knife inserted midway between edge and center of filling comes out clean. Cool. Garnish with sweetened whipped cream, if desired. Serves 8.

(Ingredients continued on page 796)

teaspoon rum extract
½ cup finely cut-up pitted
 dates
1 cup pecan halves
Sweetened whipped cream
 (optional)

✥ Sweet-Potato Pie

1 9-inch unbaked pastry
 shell (recipes on pages
 786 and 787)
2 cups mashed, cooked
 sweet potatoes (takes
 about 1½ pounds)
¾ cup sugar
1 teaspoon ground
 cinnamon
½ teaspoon ground nutmeg
½ teaspoon ground ginger
⅛ teaspoon ground cloves
¾ teaspoon grated lemon
 peel
½ teaspoon salt
3 eggs, slightly beaten
1¼ cups light cream, scalded
2 tablespoons melted butter
 or margarine
Sweetened whipped cream
 (optional)

Prepare pastry shell. Heat oven to 400° F. Place mashed sweet potatoes in mixing bowl; add sugar, cinnamon, nutmeg, ginger, cloves, lemon peel, and salt. Beat with rotary beater or electric mixer until blended. Add eggs, cream, and melted butter and beat until fluffy. Pour into prepared pastry shell. Bake 50 to 60 minutes, or until a knife inserted in center comes out clean. Cool. If desired, garnish with sweetened whipped cream. Serves 8.

✥ Raisin–Nut Pie

1 9-inch unbaked pastry
 shell (recipes on pages
 786 and 787)
1½ cups commercial sour
 cream
1 cup sugar
½ teaspoon ground cloves
2 eggs
1 egg yolk
1½ cups dark seedless raisins
½ cup chopped walnuts

Prepare pastry shell. Heat oven to 400° F. Combine sour cream, sugar, and cloves. Beat eggs and the egg yolk together with a rotary beater; gradually stir into sour-cream mixture. Stir in raisins, walnuts, almonds, vanilla, and sherry. Pour into shell. Bake 15 minutes. Reduce oven temperature to 350° F. and bake 35 to 40 minutes, or until a knife inserted midway between edge and center of filling comes out clean. Cool before serving. Serves 8.

¼ cup slivered blanched
    almonds
½ teaspoon vanilla extract
2 tablespoons sweet sherry

✑ Banana Cream Pie

1 9-inch pastry shell, baked
    and cooled (recipes on
    pages 786 and 787)
½ cup sugar
5 tablespoons flour
¼ teaspoon salt
2 cups milk, heated
2 egg yolks, slightly beaten
1 tablespoon butter or
    margarine
½ teaspoon vanilla extract
4 ripe bananas
Sweetened whipped cream
    (optional)

Prepare, bake, and cool pastry shell. Combine sugar, flour, and salt; gradually add hot milk, stirring constantly. Slowly add to beaten egg yolks and mix until smooth. Pour into the top of a double boiler. Cook over simmering water, stirring constantly, until mixture thickens, about 5 minutes. Cook 5 minutes more, stirring occasionally. Remove from simmering water; stir in butter and vanilla. Cool. Peel 3 bananas and slice into pastry shell. Cover immediately with filling so that bananas will not darken. Chill about 3 hours. Just before serving, peel and slice remaining banana over top. Garnish with whipped cream, if desired. Serves 8.

✑ Black-Bottom Pie

1 9-inch pastry shell, baked
    and cooled (recipes on
    pages 786 and 787)
1 1-ounce square
    unsweetened chocolate
1 4-serving-size package
    chocolate pudding and
    pie filling mix
1¾ cups milk
½ teaspoon vanilla extract
1 3½-ounce package
    vanilla-flavored whipped
    dessert mix
¾ cup light cream
¼ cup chilled light rum
1 cup frozen whipped
    topping, thawed
Additional whipped topping
    (optional)
Chocolate sprinkles (optional)

Prepare, bake, and cool pastry shell. Melt the chocolate in a small saucepan over low heat (about 200° F.). Prepare chocolate pudding according to package directions, using only the 1¾ cups milk. Stir melted chocolate and vanilla extract into pudding. Cool, stirring occasionally, until pudding no longer steams. Pour into the cooled pie shell and cool thoroughly. Combine whipped dessert mix and ½ cup of the light cream in the small bowl of the electric mixer. Whip at the highest speed of mixer about 1 minute, or until mixture is very thick. Blend in the remaining ¼ cup light cream and the rum; whip on the highest speed about 2 minutes. Fold in the whipped topping. Pour the mixture over the cooled chocolate layer. Chill 2 to 3 hours, or until firm. If desired, garnish with additional whipped topping and chocolate sprinkles. Serves 8.

✒ Chocolate Cream Pie

1 9-inch pastry shell, baked
  and cooled (recipes on
  pages 786 and 787)
3 1-ounce squares
  unsweetened chocolate
½ cup sugar
¼ cup water
6 tablespoons flour
¼ teaspoon salt
2 cups milk
1 egg, well beaten
1 teaspoon vanilla extract
1 tablespoon butter or
  margarine
Sweetened whipped cream
Shaved chocolate

Prepare, bake, and cool pastry shell. Combine chocolate, ¼ cup of the sugar, and water in the top of a double boiler. Cook over low heat (about 200° F.) until chocolate is melted, stirring occasionally. Remove from heat; add the remaining ¼ cup sugar, flour, salt, and milk. Cook over simmering water, stirring constantly, until thickened. Cover and continue to cook 10 minutes. Stir a little of the hot mixture into the beaten egg. Return egg to mixture in double boiler. Cook over simmering water, stirring constantly, 5 minutes. Remove from heat; add vanilla and butter. Cool slightly. Pour into baked pie shell. Chill. Garnish with whipped cream and chocolate. Serves 8.

✒ Chocolate-Almond Pie

1 9-inch Graham-Cracker-
  Crumb Shell, baked and
  chilled (recipe on page
  792)
6 ⁹/₁₆-ounce milk chocolate
  candy bars with almonds
15 large marshmallows
½ cup milk
1 cup heavy cream, whipped

Prepare and chill shell. In the top of a double boiler combine chocolate bars, marshmallows, and milk. Cook over simmering water, stirring constantly, until melted and smooth. Cool completely. Gently fold in whipped cream and pour into prepared crust. Chill 3 hours. Serves 8.

✒ Grasshopper Pie

1¼ cups finely crushed
   chocolate wafers
½ cup sugar
3 tablespoons melted butter
  or margarine
1½ teaspoons unflavored
   gelatine
6 tablespoons cold water
1 egg yolk, slightly beaten
⅓ cup crème de menthe

Heat oven to 450° F. Combine crushed wafers, ¼ cup of the sugar, and the melted butter. Press crumbs firmly onto the bottom and sides of a well-buttered 9-inch pie plate. Place in oven and bake 2 to 3 minutes. Cool. Sprinkle gelatine over the cold water in a small saucepan. Place over low heat (about 200° F.) and stir until dissolved. Combine the remaining ¼ cup sugar and the egg yolk in a mixing bowl. Add dissolved gelatine, crème de menthe, and crème de cacao. Chill until the consistency of unbeaten egg white. Prepare whipped topping

¼ *cup white crème de cocao*
1 *2-ounce package whipped topping mix*
Additional whipped topping (optional)
Shaved chocolate (optional)

mix according to package directions. Fold into the gelatine mixture. Pour into prepared chocolate wafer crust. Chill 3 to 4 hours, or until set. If desired, top with additional whipped topping and shaved chocolate before serving. Serves 8.

Lemon Angel Pie

3 *egg whites, at room temperature*
Few grains salt
¼ *teaspoon cream of tartar*
½ *teaspoon vanilla extract*
¾ *cup sugar*
4 *egg yolks*
½ *cup sugar*
1 *tablespoon grated lemon peel*
3 *tablespoons lemon juice*
1 *cup heavy cream, whipped*
¼ *cup raspberry or strawberry jam*

Heat oven to 275° F. Beat egg whites in a bowl until foamy. Add salt, cream of tartar, and vanilla. Continue to beat until soft peaks form. Add the ¾ cup sugar, 2 tablespoons at a time, beating well after each addition. Beat until stiff, glossy peaks form. All the sugar should be dissolved. Spread meringue over bottom and sides of a well-buttered 9-inch pie plate. Build up edges to form a high rim. Bake about 1 hour, or until light brown and crisp to the touch. Turn off oven. Leave shell in oven several hours to dry thoroughly. Beat egg yolks and the ½ cup sugar together in the top of a double boiler until thick. Stir in lemon peel and juice. Place over simmering water and cook until thickened, about 10 minutes. Cool, stirring occasionally. Chill. Fold half of the whipped cream into the lemon filling. Spread about a quarter of the remaining whipped cream in a thin layer over the bottom of the cooled meringue shell. Pour the lemon filling into the meringue shell. Spoon remainder of whipped cream into center of pie. Just before serving, spoon jam in a circle around whipped cream. Serves 8.

French Strawberry Pie

1 *9-inch pastry shell, baked and cooled (recipes on pages 786 and 787)*
1 *quart strawberries*
1 *3-ounce package cream cheese, at room temperature*
1¼ *cups granulated sugar*
3 *tablespoons cornstarch*
1 *tablespoon lemon juice*
Red food coloring

Prepare, bake, and cool pastry shell. Wash, drain, and hull strawberries. Beat cream cheese with a fork until smooth. Spread cheese over bottom of pastry shell. Stand half of the whole strawberries in the shell with tips up. Mash the rest of the strawberries and put through a sieve to remove seeds. Measure the juice and, if necessary, add water to make 1½ cups liquid. Mix granulated sugar and cornstarch in a saucepan; gradually stir in strawberry mixture and lemon juice. Cook over moderate heat (about 250° F.), stirring constantly, until thickened and clear, about 5 to 6 minutes. Stir in a few drops

½ *cup heavy cream*
1 *tablespoon confectioners'*
   sugar

red food coloring. Remove from heat. Cool about 10 minutes and pour over the strawberries in the shell. Chill about 3 hours, or until firm. Whip cream and confectioners' sugar together until mixture holds its shape, and spoon in a ring around edge of pie. Serves 6 to 8.

✑ Warm Apple Tart

1 *cup sugar*
½ *cup butter or margarine*
1 *teaspoon ground cinnamon*
8 *medium-sized tart apples*
Butter Pastry (recipe follows)
Whipped cream

Heat oven to 450° F. Place sugar in a 10-inch ovenproof skillet; place over low heat (do not use thermostatically controlled burner). Heat until sugar is melted and just lightly browned, stirring constantly. Remove from heat and add butter and cinnamon. Stir until butter is melted and well mixed with cinnamon and sugar. Pare, quarter and core apples. Arrange in skillet with rounded side down in sugar mixture. Make a second layer of apples, placing them rounded side up in the skillet. Prepare Butter Pastry and roll out on a floured board into a 10-inch circle and place over apples. Flute edge and prick top of pastry with the tines of a fork. Bake 25 to 30 minutes, or until crust is golden brown. Cool about 2 minutes before inverting into a shallow dish. Garnish with whipped cream. Serves 6.

Butter Pastry

¾ *cup plus 2 tablespoons*
   sifted all-purpose flour
1½ *teaspoons sugar*
⅛ *teaspoon salt*
¼ *cup butter or margarine*
2 *to 3 tablespoons cold*
   water

Sift together flour, sugar and salt into a bowl. Cut butter into flour with a pastry blender or two knives into pieces the size of small peas. Sprinkle water, 1 teaspoon at a time, over flour, mixing with a fork until all the flour is moistened. Shape into a ball and roll out, following above directions for Warm Apple Tart.

Meringue-Topped Pies

Meringue-topped pies are often a problem to make—soft meringue toppings can "weep," producing droplets of moisture that make the pie less attractive. This is the technique for ensuring a perfect meringue pie:

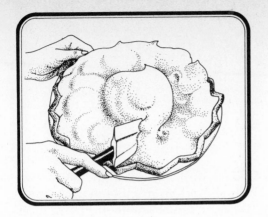

Spread the meringue over hot pie filling evenly, starting at the edges to seal the meringue to the crust. Don't leave any uncovered spaces between crust and meringue. Swirl the rest of the meringue evenly over the top. Bake in a preheated 350° F. oven 12 to 15 minutes. Cool at room temperature, away from drafts.

✑ Butterscotch Meringue Pie

1 9-inch pastry shell, baked and cooled (recipes on pages 786 and 787)
1½ cups firmly packed dark brown sugar
¼ cup butter or margarine
¼ cup heavy cream
1½ cups milk
6 tablespoons cornstarch
2 eggs, separated, at room temperature
½ teaspoon vanilla extract
4 tablespoons granulated sugar

Prepare baked pastry shell. Place brown sugar, butter, and cream in a heavy saucepan. Cook over moderate heat (about 225° F.) until thickened and golden brown, stirring constantly. Remove from heat. Place milk, cornstarch, and egg yolks in a bowl and beat together with a rotary beater. Gradually pour milk mixture into brown-sugar mixture. Cook over moderate heat (about 225° F.), stirring constantly, until thickened; add vanilla. Cool filling slightly. Pour into pie shell. Heat oven to 350° F. Beat egg whites until soft peaks form; gradually add granulated sugar and beat until stiff peaks form. Spread meringue over filling to edge of crust. Bake 12 to 15 minutes, or until lightly browned. Cool. Serves 8.

✑ Lemon Meringue Pie

1 9-inch pastry shell, baked and cooled (recipes on pages 786 and 787)
¼ cup cornstarch
2 tablespoons flour
1 cup sugar
¼ teaspoon salt
2 cups boiling water
3 eggs, separated, at room temperature

Prepare baked pastry shell. Mix cornstarch, flour, the 1 cup sugar, and salt in top of a double boiler; gradually stir in boiling water. Beat egg yolks slightly and gradually stir into cornstarch mixture. Place top of double boiler over boiling water and cook about 5 minutes, until filling is thickened, stirring constantly. Continue to cook 5 minutes more, stirring occasionally. Remove from boiling water. Mix in butter, lemon peel, and juice. Cover and cool slightly. Pour into pastry shell. Heat oven to 350° F. Beat egg whites until soft peaks form. Gradually

2 *tablespoons butter or*
margarine
1 *tablespoon grated lemon*
peel
6 *tablespoons lemon juice*
6 *tablespoons sugar*

add the 6 tablespoons sugar and beat until stiff peaks form. Spread meringue over lemon filling to edge of crust. Bake 12 to 15 minutes, or until lightly browned. Cool. Serves 8.

❧ Quick Lemon Meringue Pie

1 *9-inch pastry shell, baked*
and cooled (recipes on
pages 786 and 787)
4 *eggs, separated, at room*
temperature
½ *cup sugar*
2 *14-ounce cans sweetened*
condensed milk, undiluted
2 *teaspoons grated lemon*
peel
1 *cup lemon juice*

Prepare baked pastry shell. Heat oven to 350° F. Beat egg whites with an electric mixer until soft peaks form; gradually add the sugar and beat until stiff peaks form. Mix condensed milk, lemon peel, and lemon juice together until smooth and thickened. Beat egg yolks slightly and stir into condensed milk mixture. Pour into baked pastry shell. Spread the meringue over filling to edge of crust. Bake 12 to 15 minutes, or until meringue is lightly browned. Cool before serving. Serves 8.

Chiffon Pies

These airy pies derive their characteristic lightness from well-beaten egg whites folded into a gelatine mixture of the right consistency. If these are new to you, check the technique for beating egg whites on page 452 and test for folding ingredients into gelatine on page 612.

❧ Chocolate-Peppermint Chiffon Pie

1 *9-inch chocolate crumb*
shell baked and chilled
(recipe on page 794)
1 *envelope unflavored*
gelatine
¼ *cup cold water*
3 *egg whites*
1 *cup heavy cream*
1 *teaspoon vanilla extract*

Sprinkle gelatine over water in a small custard cup; set cup in a small pan of simmering water for a few minutes, until gelatine is dissolved and clear. Remove pan from heat. In a mixing bowl whip egg whites with an electric mixer or rotary beater until stiff peaks form when beater is lifted. Add remaining 2 tablespoons of sugar, 1 tablespoon at a time, beating well after each addition. In another bowl whip the cream (no need to wash beaters); when stiff, pour the warm gelatine into the cream while

¼ teaspoon peppermint
extract
½ cup finely crushed
red-and-white peppermint
candies
Few drops of red food coloring
Chocolate sprinkles or grated
chocolate, for decoration

beating or stirring the cream. Fold the beaten egg whites into the cream mixture. Fold in vanilla, peppermint extract, crushed candy and a few drops of red food coloring. Pour into prepared crumb crust. Chill 1 to 2 hours or longer. Just before serving, decorate with sprinkles or grated chocolate if desired. Serves 10 to 12.

Eggnog Pie

1 9-inch pastry shell, baked
and cooled (recipes on
pages 786 and 787)
1 envelope unflavored
gelatine
½ cup cold water
4 eggs, separated, at room
temperature
¼ cup sugar
2 cups light cream, heated
4 tablespoons brandy
Few grains salt
⅓ cup sugar

Prepare and bake pastry shell. Sprinkle gelatine over cold water to soften. Beat egg yolks in a small bowl; stir in the ¼ cup sugar. Slowly add the hot cream, stirring constantly. Pour into top of double boiler and cook over simmering water, stirring constantly, until slightly thickened. Remove from water and add softened gelatine; stir until dissolved. Stir in brandy. Chill until mixture is the consistency of unbeaten egg whites. Add salt to egg whites and beat until soft peaks form. Add the ⅓ cup sugar gradually, beating well after each addition until stiff peaks form. Fold in gelatine mixture. Pour into baked shell. Chill several hours, until firm. Serves 8.

Lime Chiffon Pie

1¼ cups crushed chocolate
wafers
¼ cup sugar
⅓ cup melted butter or
margarine
1 envelope unflavored
gelatine
½ cup sugar
Few grains salt
4 egg yolks
½ cup lime juice
¼ cup water
1½ teaspoons grated lemon or
lime peel

Combine cookie crumbs, sugar, and butter in a bowl. Mix until blended. Press mixture firmly into a greased 9-inch pie plate. Cover bottom and sides evenly. Chill about 1 hour. Combine gelatine, the ½ cup granulated sugar, and salt in a saucepan. Beat together egg yolks, lime juice, and water; stir into gelatine mixture. Place over moderately low heat (about 225° F.) and bring to a boil, stirring constantly. Remove from heat and stir in grated lemon peel and green food coloring. Place pan in large bowl of ice cubes. Stir frequently until filling is the consistency of unbeaten egg whites. Beat egg whites until soft peaks form. Gradually add the remaining ½ cup granulated sugar, beating until stiff peaks form. Fold beaten egg whites and the ¾ cup cream, whipped,

Few drops green food coloring
4 egg whites, at room
 temperature
½ cup sugar
¾ cup heavy cream,
 whipped
½ cup heavy cream
1½ teaspoons confectioners'
 sugar
¼ teaspoon vanilla extract
Chocolate curls

into gelatine mixture. Pour the mixture into cooled cookie shell. Chill several hours in refrigerator, until set. Whip the ½ cup cream with confectioners' sugar and vanilla until it holds its shape. Garnish edge of pie with spoonfuls of cream. Sprinkle with chocolate curls. Serves 8.

Note: To make Lemon Chiffon Pie, substitute lemon juice and lemon peel for the lime juice and peel and omit green food coloring.

✒ Pumpkin Chiffon Pie

1 Graham-Cracker-Crumb
 Shell, baked and cooled
 (recipe on page 792)
1½ teaspoons unflavored
 gelatine
½ cup milk
28 large marshmallows
1 cup canned pumpkin
1 teaspoon ground
 cinnamon
¼ teaspoon ground ginger
¼ teaspoon ground nutmeg
⅛ teaspoon ground cloves
¼ teaspoon salt
1 cup heavy cream,
 whipped
Additional whipped cream
 (optional)

Prepare Graham-Cracker-Crumb Shell. Sprinkle gelatine over milk in top of double boiler to soften. Place over simmering water and stir until gelatine is dissolved. Add marshmallows; cover and cook until marshmallows are melted, stirring occasionally. Mix pumpkin, cinnamon, ginger, nutmeg, cloves, and salt; gradually stir in marshmallow mixture. Chill in refrigerator until mixture is slightly thickened. Beat pumpkin mixture until smooth. Fold in cream. Pour into crumb crust and chill several hours until set. If desired, garnish with additional whipped cream. Serves 8.

✒ Raspberry Chiffon Pie

1 9-inch pastry shell, baked
 and cooled (recipes on
 pages 786 and 787)

Prepare and bake pastry shell. Combine gelatine, the ½ cup sugar, and the sat in a small saucepan. Drain raspberries. Measure juice and add water if necessary to

1 *envelope unflavored*
gelatine
½ *cup sugar*
¼ *teaspoon salt*
1 *10-ounce package frozen*
raspberries, thawed
2 *teaspoons lemon juice*
Few drops red food coloring
3 *egg whites, at room*
temperature
⅛ *teaspoon cream of tartar*
¼ *cup sugar*
½ *cup heavy cream, whipped*
Additional whipped cream
(optional)

make 1 cup liquid. Stir into gelatine mixture. Add lemon juice. Place over moderately low heat (about 225° F.) and bring to a boil, stirring constantly. Remove from heat; add red food coloring. Place pan in large bowl of ice cubes. Stir frequently until filling is the consistency of unbeaten egg white. Beat egg whites and cream of tartar until soft peaks form. Add the sugar 1 tablespoon at a time, beating well after each addition. Continue beating until stiff peaks form. Fold gelatine mixture gently into egg whites. Fold in whipped cream and drained raspberries. Pour mixture into baked pastry shell. Chill several hours until set. If desired, garnish with additional whipped cream. Serves 8.

Ice-Cream Pies

ᕥ Ribbon Alaska Pie

1 *Chocolate-Crumb Shell*
(recipe on page 794)
2 *pints strawberry or cherry*
ice cream
1 *cup bottled chocolate-*
fudge ice-cream topping
4 *egg whites, at room*
temperature
⅛ *teaspoon cream of tartar*
½ *cup sugar*
Granulated sugar

Prepare and cool Chocolate-Crumb Shell. Let 1 pint of the ice cream soften slightly; spoon evenly into the bottom of the cooled chocolate shell. Pour fudge topping over ice cream and spread evenly with a spatula. Freeze until firm, about 2 hours. Let remaining pint of ice cream soften and spoon over fudge layer in an even layer. Freeze until firm, about 2 hours. In the large bowl of an electric mixer beat egg whites until foamy. Add cream of tartar and beat at high speed until soft peaks form. Gradually add the ½ cup sugar, beating well after each addition. Continue to beat until stiff, glossy peaks form. Spread mixture over top of pie, being careful to seal the edges of the pie well with the meringue. Pie may be stored in freezer until serving time. Just before serving, heat oven to 525° F. Sprinkle the meringue lightly with sugar. Place pie on a wooden board and bake until meringue is lightly browned, about 1 minute. Serve immediately. If desired, pie may be served with additional fudge sauce over top. Serves 8.

✍ Chocolate Heavenly Pie

3 egg whites, at room
  temperature
¼ teaspoon cream of tartar
¼ teaspoon salt
¾ cup sugar
2 tablespoons
  unsweetened cocoa
1 pint chocolate ice cream
1 4-serving-size package
  instant chocolate-pudding
  mix
¼ cup milk
½ cup heavy cream, whipped
1 banana, sliced

Lightly butter a 9-inch pie plate. Heat oven to 275° F. Beat together egg whites, cream of tartar, and salt at high speed until soft peaks form. Sift together sugar and cocoa. Gradually add sugar mixture to egg whites, 2 tablespoons at a time, beating constantly, until meringue is very stiff and shiny. Spread meringue over bottom and sides of greased pie plate, bringing it well up onto the rim. Bake for 1 hour. Cool thoroughly on wire cake rack. When meringue shell is cool, remove ice cream from freezer and let it soften slightly at room temperature. Combine pudding mix, milk, and softened ice cream in a bowl. Beat 2 minutes, or until smooth and blended. Pour into meringue shell. Refrigerate at least 8 hours or overnight. Serve topped with whipped cream and sliced banana. Serves 8.

Tarts

✍ Flaming Apple Tart

1 9-inch unbaked Sweet Tart
  Shell (recipe on page 807)
1 teaspoon powdered
  ascorbic acid mixture
¾ cup sugar
¼ cup quick-cooking tapioca
¼ teaspoon salt
½ teaspoon ground
  cinnamon
5 cups peeled, cored, and
  sliced tart apples (about 5
  apples)
½ cup seedless raisins
3 tablespoons lemon juice
2 tablespoons butter or
  margarine
⅔ cup peach jam
3 tablespoons peach brandy

Heat oven to 425° F. Bake tart shell 10 to 15 minutes, or until edge of shell is lightly browned. Combine ascorbic acid mixture, sugar, tapioca, salt, and cinnamon. Add to apples and toss to coat apples with mixture. Stir in raisins and lemon juice. Arrange apple mixture in tart shell. Dot with the 2 tablespoons butter. Melt jam in a small saucepan over moderately low heat (about 225° F.); spoon over apples. Reduce oven temperature to 375° F. and bake 40 to 45 minutes. Remove tart from oven and cool about 20 minutes. Heat brandy in a small saucepan over moderate heat (about 250° F.) until bubbling. Ignite with a match and pour over apple tart while still flaming. Serves 6 to 8.

✑§ Continental Peach Pie

1 9-inch Sweet Tart Shell,
baked and cooled (recipe
follows)
2 3-ounce packages cream
cheese, at room
temperature
2 tablespoons confectioners'
sugar
1 29- or 30-ounce can
cling-peach halves, well
drained
2 10-ounce packages frozen
raspberries, thawed
2 tablespoons cornstarch
2 teaspoons grated lemon peel

Prepare baked tart shell. Work cheese and confectioners' sugar together until smooth. Spread over bottom of tart shell. Arrange peach halves over cheese, cut-side down. Drain raspberries; mix juice and cornstarch together in a saucepan. Cook over moderately low heat (about 200° F.) until thickened and clear. Remove from heat. Stir in lemon peel. Cool. Stir in raspberries. Pour over peaches and chill about 2 hours. Serves 6 to 8.

✑§ Sweet Tart Shell

1⅓ cups sifted all-purpose
flour
¼ cup sugar
½ teaspoon grated lemon
peel
2 egg yolks
½ cup softened butter or
margarine

Heat oven to 400° F. Mix flour, sugar, and lemon peel in a bowl. Make a well in the center; add egg yolks and butter; mix with a fork until well blended. With fingertips, press mixture over bottom and sides of a 9-inch round cake pan. Bake 10 minutes; reduce heat to 350° F. and bake 15 minutes. Makes one 9-inch tart shell.

Individual Tarts

✑§ Tart Shells

1 pie-crust stick or ½
package pie-crust mix or
enough pastry for a 9-inch
pastry shell (recipes on
pages 786 and 787)

Heat oven to 425° F. Prepare pastry according to package directions. Roll out on floured board and cut into four 4-inch circles. Shape over the backs of custard cups. Prick with fork and bake 8 to 10 minutes. Makes 4 tart shells.

How to Shape Tart Shells

Cut each pastry round 1 inch larger than the diameter of the inverted tart pan. Ease the pastry round into the pan, pressing gently to fit, and prick with a fork. Bake right side up. To make a slightly larger shell, place the pastry round on the *outside* of the inverted tart pan, pressing to fit the outer contour of the pan. Prick the entire surface with a fork. Place inverted pan on a cookie sheet. Bake tarts in a preheated 450° F. oven 10 to 12 minutes. Cool before filling.

If tart pans are unavailable, cut the pastry into rounds 4½ inches in diameter, using a paper pattern as a guide. Place the rounds over inverted 5-ounce custard cups or the backs of 2½-inch muffin cups. Pleat the pastry dough to fit the cups snugly. Prick with a fork on the bottoms and sides and place them, inverted, on cookie sheet. Bake in a preheated 450° F. oven 10 to 12 minutes. If a Teflon-lined muffin pan is used, bake at 400° F. Cool shells before filling.

To use foil as the tart pan, roll out pastry round about 4½ inches in diameter on a square of heavy-duty foil. Using a 4½-inch circular paper pattern, trim the edges of the pastry and foil evenly with kitchen shears. Prick the pastry with a fork at ½-inch intervals. Shape into tarts by turning up the edges all around and then pinch or flute to form a tart shape. Place on a cookie sheet right side up. Bake in a preheated 450° F. oven 10 to 12 minutes. Cool before filling.

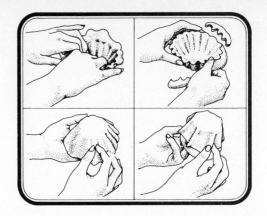

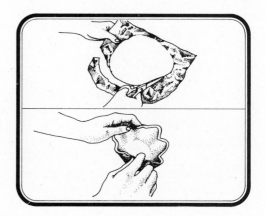

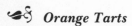 *Orange Tarts*

4 baked and cooled Tart Shells (recipe on page 807)
1 cup reconstituted frozen orange juice concentrate
1 tablespoon cornstarch
½ cup heavy cream
2 tablespoons confectioners' sugar
Grated peel of 1 orange
1 large orange, sectioned

Prepare and cool Tart Shells. Combine orange juice and cornstarch in a small saucepan. Cook over moderate heat (about 250° F.), stirring constantly, until thickened. Set aside until cool. Combine heavy cream and confectioners' sugar; beat until mixture holds its shape. Fold cream and 1 tablespoon grated orange rind into cooled orange juice mixture. Cut orange sections into quarters; add to orange juice mixture. Spoon into Tart Shells and garnish with grated peel. Chill 2 hours. Serves 4.

Strawberry-Vanilla Tarts

½ cup (4 ounces) cream
  cheese, at room
  temperature
½ cup sugar
2 teaspoons vanilla extract
1½ cups light cream
8 baked and cooled Tart
  Shells (recipe on page
  807)
3 cups sweetened, sliced
  fresh strawberries or
  thawed frozen sliced
  strawberries

Work together cheese, sugar, and vanilla in the small bowl of an electric mixer at low speed. Slowly add the cream, mixing on low speed of mixer until thoroughly blended. Cover bowl tightly with aluminum foil and freeze mixture until solidly frozen. This will take about 6 hours. Prepare and cool tart shells. Remove frozen mixture from freezer and break up into chunks with a spoon. Beat on low speed of electric mixer until fairly smooth. Whip at medium speed until mixture is very smooth, about 10 minutes. Divide mixture among tart shells, filling to within ¼ inch of top. Place tarts in aluminum cake pans; wrap pans in aluminum foil, sealing ends well. Freeze. Remove tarts from freezer about 5 to 10 minutes before serving time and place on individual serving plates. Spoon about ⅓ cup of sweetened strawberries over each tart. (Any other fresh or frozen fruit may be used.) Serves 8.

CHAPTER XXIII

CAKES

In the language of professional recipe testers, many cake recipes are not very "tolerant." What they mean is that any deviation from the original recipe or any mishandling of the ingredients will produce a less-than-perfect cake or perhaps a complete failure. This fact shouldn't discourage you from baking cakes; it should only discourage you from trying to be creative the first time you try a new cake recipe.

These twelve rules apply to cake-making whether you start from scratch or use a mix.

1. Read the recipe all the way through and assemble all the ingredients you need before you start to mix.
2. If you need chopped nuts or fruits or melted chocolate, get them ready before you start to put the cake together.
3. Have at hand all of the standard measuring cups and spoons that you will need. Use level measurements and be sure to measure liquid ingredients at eye level.
4. Get out the proper pans and prepare them according to recipe directions before you make the batter. Be sure aluminum pans are bright and shiny inside and out (unless they are Teflon-lined) to ensure even browning. If you use ovenproof glass pans you will have to reduce the oven temperature for baking by 25° F. If pans are to be lined with waxed paper, set the pan on a sheet of paper and trace around it. If you need liners for more than one pan, cut two or three at a time. If pans are to be

greased, brush a thin film of shortening over bottoms and sides. (If you don't have a pastry brush you can use a paper towel.) If pans are to be greased and floured, grease as described above, sprinkle flour into each pan, then shake to coat the pan evenly. Turn the pan upside down and knock it on the edge of the sink to remove any excess flour. Pans for angel, sponge, and chiffon cakes are never greased or floured. For chocolate cakes you may "flour" the pans with unsweetened cocoa (not a chocolate drink mix) so the chocolate layers won't have a pale film. It is best to use pans of the size and depth indicated in the recipe. If different pans are used, and you are not sure of the measurement, fill the pans only half full. Any leftover batter can be baked as cupcakes.

5. Use the exact ingredients the recipe calls for; don't, for example, substitute cream for milk to make a richer cake or two eggs for one to make it "better."

6. Start heating the oven ten minutes before you plan to have the batter ready. The oven must be at the proper temperature when the cake goes into the oven.

7. Don't overmix cakes once the dry ingredients have been added to the batter. You should mix just until the batter is smooth. Continued mixing at this point will reduce volume and cause tunnels or uneven texture in cakes.

8. Place pans in the oven so there is even heat circulation around them. Pans should not touch each other and should not touch the sides of the oven. If you're baking more than two layers you may need to use two oven racks. Place them in the middle third of the oven, allowing enough space for the cakes on the bottom rack to rise. Place the top pans on one back corner of the upper rack and one front corner. Place the pans on the bottom rack in opposite corners so top layers do not sit directly over bottom layers.

9. Bake cakes at the exact temperature and time called for in the recipe. If a range of time is given, test when cake has baked the shortest time suggested. Touch the top of the cake lightly with a finger. If an imprint remains, it needs more baking; if the top springs back, the cake is done. You can also use a cake tester or a toothpick. Stick it gently into the center of the cake. If it comes out with crumbs clinging to it, the cake needs to bake longer; if it comes out clean, the cake is done.

10. Layer or flat rectangular cakes should be cooled in the baking pans set on cake racks for at least ten minutes and no longer than twenty minutes. Loosen the edges of the cake with a spatula. Hold a cake rack over the top of the cake pan; then invert pan so rack will be under the top of the cake. Set the rack on the table, lift off the pan, and remove paper, if any, from the bottom of the cake. Peel paper off carefully to keep bottom crust intact. Take a second rack and place it lightly over the

bottom of the cake. Invert cake and racks again so that the bottom of the cake is resting on a cake rack. Let cakes cool completely in this position. Angel, chiffon, and sponge cakes need longer cooling in the pan in an upside-down position. Follow recipe directions for these.

11. To frost layer cakes, follow the pictured directions, How to Frost a Layer Cake, on pages 815 and 816. Cakes baked in tube pans are always frosted bottom side up.

12. To store cakes, cover them after they are cool whether they are frosted or not. A cake-keeper that has a domed lid is excellent. You can improvise one by placing a large bowl or saucepan or a clean box over the cake. Cakes with pudding or whipped cream fillings must be kept refrigerated. Fruit cakes need tight wrapping and aging as recipes direct.

Techniques for Butter Cakes

1. Sift flour onto a sheet of waxed paper before measuring it. Spoon it gently into a dry-measure cup; level off with edge of spatula. Usually the measured flour will be resifted with other dry ingredients.

2. To measure shortening, have it at room temperature. Pack firmly into a dry-measure cup; level with spatula.

3. Measure liquids in a marked glass measuring cup. Put cup on a level table; check measure at eye level.

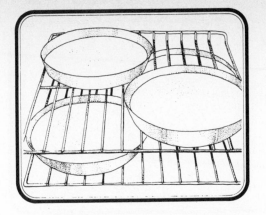

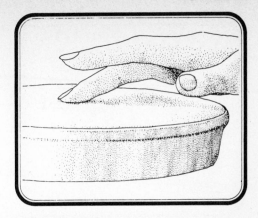

4. When placing pans in oven for baking, the general rule is to have center of cake as near to the center of oven as possible. Layers should be placed so they don't touch each other or oven sides and do not sit directly over each other if two shelves are used.

5. Cakes baked in shiny pans at accurate temperature should be done in required time. When done, top of cake will leave no impression when lightly pressed with finger. For glass pans, lower temperature 25° F.

Special Tips for Butter Cakes and Quick-Mix Cakes

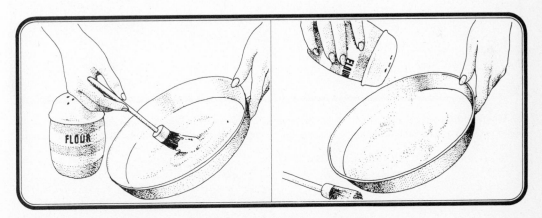

1. To prepare pans, grease the bottoms and sides with soft shortening or oil.

2. Coat greased surface lightly with flour; shake out excess.

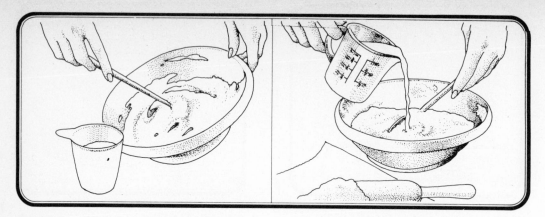

3. When recipes call for *creaming*—blending of shortening and sugar—mixture should be light and fluffy.

4. When a liquid and a flour mixture are added alternately, a little at a time, begin and end with the flour.

5. When adding beaten egg whites to batter, fold them in gently with a rubber spatula to make a light cake.

6. Quick-mix or one-bowl cakes do not call for creaming or beating eggs separately. Batters will be thinner.

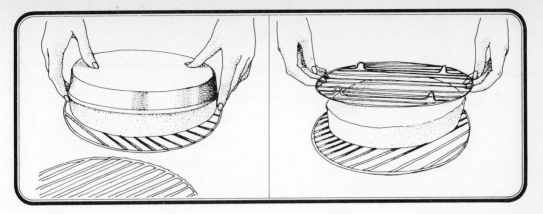

7. After cooling 10 minutes in the pan, loosen sides of cake, invert pan over cake rack to turn out the layer.

8. Turn cake top side up onto a second rack, not onto a plate, to cool.

How to Frost a Layer Cake

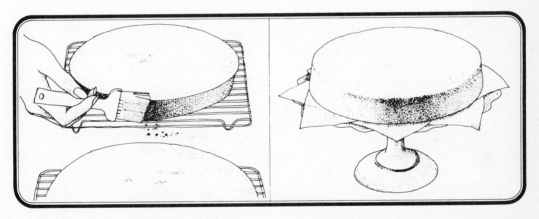

1. Always cool cake before frosting. Brush loose crumbs from sides of cake with a clean brush before placing the first layer, top side down, on a flat plate.

2. To keep the plate clean while frosting cake, place triangles of waxed paper under edges of cake. Slip paper out after the cake has been frosted.

3. Frost first layer. Allow to set slightly; add second layer, top side up. Frost sides with a "base coat" to seal in crumbs. Apply more frosting to sides.

4. Spread side frosting with upward strokes. Keep sides straight, leaving a ridge of frosting around top of cake. Swirl top with spatula or spoon.

How to Cut Cakes

A round cake usually is cut into wedge-shaped pieces. To cut 16 wedges from a 9-inch cake, mark the cake into 4 equal quarters by scoring the surface lightly with a knife. Mark each quarter into 4 equal wedges, dividing it first in half, then dividing each half. (To make 12 servings, mark each quarter into 3 equal wedges.) Insert the point of a thin, sharp knife into center of the cake, and with the point down and the handle up, slice by drawing the knife toward you. If the frosting sticks to the knife, dip it in hot water or wipe it with a damp paper towel before making a new cut.

For smaller, thinner pieces, cut the round cake into quarters. Cut each quarter into even slices, as shown. The longer slices closest to the center can be cut in half.

To split a single cake layer: Mark the halfway point of the cooled layer in several places with toothpicks. Using a long, thin, sharp knife and the toothpicks as a guide, cut the layer in two horizontally.

Another method: Cut the layer with a long piece of heavy-duty thread. With the toothpicks as a guide, cut the layer in half with a sawing motion of the thread.

To cut an oblong or square cake: Cut the cake lengthwise into thirds. Cut into rectangles of the de-

sired size. Or cut the cake diagonally and divide into diamonds and triangles.

Angel, sponge, and chiffon cakes cut best with a pronged cake separator, with two forks, or with a gentle sawing motion with a fine serrated knife. Jelly rolls cut best with a fine serrated knife or a piece of thin string.

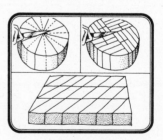

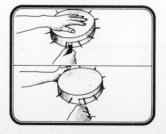

Butter Cakes

Butter cakes are superior cakes—not for busy days (the quicker one-bowl cakes starting on page 823 are better for a hurried time) but for occasions when you want to produce a very special cake. Take time to read, if you haven't already, the dozen rules for successful cake-making on page 810. Work carefully and accurately and you will produce a masterpiece.

White Cake

2⅔ cups sifted cake flour
3 teaspoons baking powder
1 teaspoon salt
¾ cup milk
½ cup water
1 teaspoon vanilla extract
¾ cup softened butter or margarine
1½ cups sugar
3 egg whites, stiffly beaten
White Mountain Frosting (recipe on page 859)

Heat oven to 350° F. Grease and flour two 8-inch round cake pans lightly. Sift together flour, baking powder, and salt onto a piece of waxed paper. Combine milk, water, and vanilla. Cream butter and sugar in a large bowl and beat until well blended, 4 minutes at medium speed with an electric mixer or 400 strokes by hand. Add ⅓ of dry ingredients and ½ of liquid ingredients to creamed mixture. Beat until well blended. Add ½ of remaining dry ingredients and the remaining liquid ingredients; beat well. Add remaining dry ingredients and beat 2 minutes at medium speed or 200 strokes by hand. Scrape sides of bowl often. Fold batter into beaten egg whites. Pour into prepared pans. Bake 35 to 40 minutes, or until top springs back when lightly touched with finger. Remove from oven and cool on a wire cake rack for 10 minutes. Remove from pans and cool completely. Fill layers and frost top and sides with White Mountain Frosting.

Devil's Food Cake

3 1-ounce squares unsweetened chocolate
2¼ cups sifted cake flour
2 teaspoons baking soda
1 teaspoon salt
½ cup softened butter or margarine
2 cups sugar
1 teaspoon vanilla extract
3 eggs
½ teaspoon red food coloring

Heat oven to 350° F. Melt chocolate over hot, not boiling, water or directly over very low heat (about 175° F.). Grease and flour two 9-inch round cake pans. Sift together flour, baking soda, and salt. In the large bowl of an electric mixer cream butter and sugar at medium speed until well blended. Add vanilla. Add eggs one at a time; beat well after each addition, scraping bowl occasionally with a rubber spatula. Reduce speed of mixer to low and add melted chocolate and red food coloring; beat until blended. Add sifted dry ingredients to butter mixture alternately with buttermilk. Add about a third of the flour mixture at a time; begin and end with it.

*½ cup buttermilk
1 cup boiling water

Beat well after each addition. Add boiling water and mix until just blended; batter will be thin. Pour equal amounts of batter into each prepared pan. Bake 30 to 35 minutes, or until top springs back when lightly touched with finger. Remove from oven and cool on wire cake racks 10 minutes. Remove from pans and cool completely. Fill and frost with desired frosting.

*Note: If buttermilk is not available, you can substitute sweet milk with lemon juice or vinegar added; see the chart on page 29.

✒ Dark Devil's Food Cake

2 cups sifted cake flour
1¾ cups sugar
¾ cup unsweetened cocoa
1¼ teaspoons baking soda
½ teaspoon baking powder
1 teaspoon salt
¾ cup soft shortening
¾ cup milk
1 teaspoon vanilla extract
½ cup milk
3 eggs
Four-Minute Fudge Frosting
  (recipe on page 858)

Heat oven to 350° F. Grease and flour two 9-inch round layer cake pans. Sift flour, sugar, cocoa, baking soda, baking powder, and salt into a large mixing bowl. Make a well in dry ingredients and add shortening, the ¾ cup milk, and vanilla. Beat until well blended. Add the ½ cup milk and eggs; beat thoroughly. Pour equal amounts of batter into each prepared pan. Bake 35 minutes, or until top springs back when lightly touched with finger. Remove from oven and cool on wire cake racks 10 minutes. Remove from pans and cool completely. When layers are cool, fill and frost with Four-Minute Fudge Frosting.

✒ Choco-Chip Lovelight Cake

2 eggs, at room temperature
1½ cups sugar
2¼ cups sifted cake flour
3 teaspoons baking powder
1 teaspoon salt
⅓ cup vegetable oil
1 cup milk
1½ teaspoons vanilla extract
2 1-ounce squares
  unsweetened chocolate,
  grated

Heat oven to 350° F. Grease two 9-inch round cake pans well and dust with flour. Separate eggs; put whites in a small, deep bowl; set yolks aside to use later. Beat whites until frothy. Gradually beat in ½ cup of the sugar, a tablespoon at a time. Continue to beat until meringue is stiff and glossy. In another bowl sift together the remaining 1 cup sugar, flour, baking powder, and salt. Pour in oil, ½ cup of milk, and the vanilla. Beat 1 minute at medium speed with an electric mixer or 150 strokes by hand. Scrape sides of bowl often. Add remaining milk and the 2 egg yolks. Beat 1 minute more. Fold in meringue, then grated chocolate. Pour into prepared cake pans and bake for 30 to 35 minutes, or until top springs back when lightly touched with finger. Cool on wire cake racks 10 minutes before removing from pans.

Cool completely before frosting. Fill layers and frost with your favorite white frosting.

⇜ Carrot Cake

2½ cups sifted all-purpose flour
1½ teaspoons baking soda
1½ teaspoons ground cinnamon
½ teaspoon ground mace
½ teaspoon salt
About 6 medium-sized carrots, peeled
*¼ cup buttermilk
1 cup softened butter or margarine
2 cups sugar
4 eggs
1 teaspoon vanilla extract
¾ cup chopped walnuts
Confectioners' sugar

Grease and flour a 10-inch tube pan. Heat oven to 350° F. Sift together flour, baking soda, cinnamon, mace, and salt. Cut carrots into 1-inch pieces. Put about ½ cup carrots into the container of an electric blender at one time. Cover container and turn motor to low speed for about 1 second. Turn off blender. If necessary, when blender is stopped push carrots toward blades with a rubber spatula. Repeat procedure several times until carrots are finely shredded. Empty shredded carrots into a small bowl. Repeat until there is enough shredded carrot to measure 1½ cups. Pour buttermilk into the shredded carrots and toss lightly to blend well. In the large bowl of an electric mixer beat butter until creamy. Add sugar gradually and beat until blended. Add eggs one at a time and beat after each addition until well blended. Stir in vanilla. At low speed, beat in flour mixture alternately with carrot mixture. Beat only until well blended. Stir in nuts. Turn into prepared pan. Bake 60 to 65 minutes, or until top springs back when lightly touched with finger. Cool in pan 10 minutes. Turn out on wire rack and cool completely. Sprinkle top with confectioners' sugar.

*Note: If buttermilk is not available, you can substitute sweet milk with lemon juice or vinegar added; see the chart on page 29.

⇜ Gold Cake

2¼ cups sifted cake flour
2½ teaspoons baking powder
1 teaspoon salt
½ cup softened butter or margarine
1½ cups sugar
1 teaspoon vanilla extract
2 eggs
1 cup milk
Hungarian Frosting (recipe on page 858)

Heat oven to 375° F. Grease and flour two 9-inch round cake pans. Sift together flour, baking powder, and salt. Mix butter and sugar in a large bowl; beat until mixture is well blended. Add vanilla. Add eggs one at a time; beat well after each addition. Add sifted dry ingredients to butter mixture alternately with milk. Add about a third of the flour mixture at a time; begin and end with it. Beat well after each addition. Pour equal amounts of batter into each prepared pan. Bake 25 to 30 minutes, or until top springs back when lightly touched with finger. Remove from oven and cool on a wire cake rack for 10 minutes. Remove from pans and cool completely. Fill layers and frost with Hungarian Frosting.

CAKES

✠ Chocolate Marmalade Cake

Cake
Butter and flour for
    preparing cake pan
1½ bars (6 ounces) sweet
    cooking chocolate, broken
    into small pieces
¾ cup butter
4 large eggs, yolks and
    whites separated
¾ cup sugar
5 tablespoons all-purpose
    flour
1 tablespoon finely grated
    orange peel
Few grains of salt

Glaze
½ cup orange marmalade
1 teaspoon water

Icing
1 bar (4 ounces) sweet
    cooking chocolate, broken
    into small pieces
3 tablespoons water
3 tablespoons butter
Blanched slivered almonds

Heat oven to 375° F. Lightly butter the inside of a 9-inch round cake pan. Lay a 9-inch circle of waxed paper in the bottom of the pan, butter the paper and dust cake pan with flour, removing any excess. Place the 6 ounces of chocolate and the ¾ cup of butter in the top of a double boiler over simmering water; stir often until chocolate melts. In a medium-sized mixing bowl beat the egg yolks and sugar with a wire whisk or rotary beater until thick and pale; add to melted chocolate and stir over low heat until well mixed. Remove from heat, stir in flour and orange peel. Using a clean, dry rotary beater or electric mixer, beat egg whites with salt until stiff peaks form when beaters are lifted. Stir about one fourth of the beaten whites into the chocolate mixture, add to the remaining beaten whites and gently fold in. Fill prepared pan with batter and bake 30 minutes, until cake is firm and pulls away slightly from the sides of the pan; center of cake will be quite moist. Place cake pan on wire cake rack to cool completely. When ready to ice, place the rack over a large pan (to catch drips) and invert cake onto rack. In a small saucepan heat marmalade and the 1 teaspoon of water over moderately low heat. When mixture is syrupy, remove from heat, cool slightly and then pour over cake; smooth over top and sides with a metal spatula and let excess run off. Let set while making icing. In the top of a double boiler over simmering water melt the 4 ounces of sweet chocolate with the 3 tablespoons of water, stirring often. Remove pan from heat and stir in the 3 tablespoons of butter. Pour warm icing over cake, spreading evenly with a spatula. Arrange almonds in daisy pattern on top of cake. Refrigerate 2 hours or longer before serving; allow icing to harden in refrigerator before wrapping cake loosely.

✠ Marble Cake

⅓ cup softened butter or
    margarine
1 cup sugar
1 teaspoon vanilla extract

Heat oven to 350° F. Grease an 8-inch-square cake pan; line with waxed paper and grease and flour paper. In a large bowl blend butter, sugar, and vanilla; beat until well blended. Add egg yolks one at a time, beating well

3 eggs, separated, at room
   temperature
2 cups sifted cake flour
2 teaspoons baking powder
¼ teaspoon salt
⅔ cup milk
1 1-ounce square
   unsweetened chocolate
2 tablespoons boiling water
¼ teaspoon baking soda
½ teaspoon ground cinnamon
⅛ teaspoon ground nutmeg
Butter Cream Frosting (recipe
   on page 856)
Chocolate curls

after each addition. Sift flour, baking powder, and salt together three times. Add to shortening mixture alternately with milk. Add about a third of the flour at a time; begin and end with it. Beat well after each addition. In another bowl beat egg whites until stiff. Gently fold them into the batter. Put half the batter into a second bowl. Melt chocolate over hot water or directly over very low heat (about 175° F.); mix in boiling water, baking soda, and spices and blend into half the batter. Drop tablespoons of plain and chocolate batter alternately into prepared pan. Bake 45 minutes, or until top springs back when lightly touched with finger. Cool on wire cake rack 10 minutes before removing from pan. Remove from pan and cool completely. Frost top and sides with Butter Cream Frosting. Garnish top with chocolate curls.

❧ Pound Cake

2 cups sifted all-purpose
   flour
½ teaspoon salt
1 cup softened butter or
   margarine
2 cups sugar
5 eggs, at room temperature
2 teaspoons vanilla extract

Heat oven to 325° F. Grease and flour a 9-x-5-x-3-inch loaf pan. Sift together flour and salt; set aside. In the large bowl of an electric mixer, beat the butter until creamy. Gradually add sugar, beating until light and fluffy. With mixer on Cream setting add eggs, one at a time, beating well after each addition. Add vanilla extract. Remove from mixer and with a spoon gently stir in flour mixture. Turn into prepared pan. Bake 60 to 75 minutes, or until top springs back when lightly touched with finger. Place on wire cake rack and cool 5 minutes. Loosen sides of cake from pan with a small metal spatula or a thin paring knife and turn out onto the cake rack and cool thoroughly.

❧ Spice Cake

2½ cups sifted cake flour
  1 teaspoon baking powder
  1 teaspoon baking soda
  1 teaspoon salt
  1 teaspoon ground
    cinnamon
  1 teaspoon ground nutmeg
  ½ teaspoon ground cloves

Heat oven to 350° F. Grease and flour two 8- or 9-inch round cake pans. Sift together flour, baking powder, baking soda, salt, cinnamon, nutmeg, cloves and ginger. In the large bowl of an electric mixer cream butter and sugar on medium speed until well blended. Add vanilla. Add eggs one at a time; beat well after each addition, scraping bowl occasionally. Add sifted dry ingredients to butter mixture alternately with buttermilk. Add about a

CAKES

¼ teaspoon ground ginger

½ cup softened butter or
margarine

1½ cups firmly packed light
brown sugar

1 teaspoon vanilla extract

3 eggs, at room temperature

*1 cup buttermilk

Maple-Nut Butter-Cream
Frosting (optional, recipe
on page 857)

third of the flour mixture at a time; begin and end with it. Beat well after each addition. Pour equal amounts of batter into each prepared pan. Bake 30 to 35 minutes, or until top springs back when lightly touched with finger. Remove from oven and cool on wire cake racks for 10 minutes. Remove from pans and cool completely before frosting. Frost, if desired, with Maple-Nut Butter-Cream Frosting.

*Note: If buttermilk is not available, you can substitute sweet milk with lemon juice or vinegar added; see the chart on page 29.

Boston Cream Pie

Cake:

1¾ cups sifted cake flour

2 teaspoons baking powder

½ teaspoon salt

⅓ cup softened butter or
margarine

1 cup sugar

2 eggs, well beaten

½ cup milk

Filling:

1 cup milk

½ cup sugar

¼ teaspoon salt

1½ teaspoons cornstarch

1 egg, slightly beaten

1 tablespoon butter or
margarine

1 teaspoon vanilla extract

Frosting:

1 1-ounce square
unsweetened chocolate

1½ teaspoons butter or
margarine

¼ cup milk

1 cup confectioners' sugar

¼ teaspoon vanilla extract

Heat oven to 375° F. To make cake: Grease and flour two 8-inch round cake pans. Sift together flour, baking powder, and salt. Mix butter and sugar in a large bowl until mixture is well blended. Gradually beat in eggs. Add sifted dry ingredients to butter mixture alternately with the ½ cup milk. Add about a third of the flour mixture at a time; begin and end with it. Beat well after each addition. Bake about 25 minutes, or until top springs back when lightly touched with finger. Cool on wire cake racks 10 minutes. Remove from pans and cool completely.

To make filling, scald the 1 cup milk in the top of a double boiler over moderately low heat (about 225° F.). Combine sugar, salt, and cornstarch; stir in egg. Add mixture gradually to hot milk. Place over boiling water and cook, stirring constantly, until mixture thickens and is clear, about 10 minutes. Add butter and vanilla. Cool thoroughly. Place a cake layer on a serving plate, crust side down. Spread with filling. Top with second layer.

To make frosting, combine chocolate, butter, and milk in a heavy saucepan. Cook over moderately low heat (about 225° F.), stirring constantly, until chocolate is melted. Cool to lukewarm. Gradually add confectioners' sugar and vanilla; beat until thick enough to spread. Spread over top of cake. Chill. Serves 6.

One-Bowl Cakes

ᔌ One-Bowl White Cake

2¼ cups sifted cake flour
1½ cups sugar
3½ teaspoons baking powder
1 teaspoon salt
½ cup soft shortening
1 teaspoon vanilla extract
1 cup milk
4 egg whites, at room
   temperature
White Mountain Frosting
   (recipe on page 859)

Heat oven to 350° F. Grease and flour two 8- or 9-inch round cake pans. Sift together flour, sugar, baking powder, and salt into a medium-sized mixing bowl. Add shortening, vanilla, and ¾ cup of the milk. Beat 2 minutes at medium speed with an electric mixer or 300 strokes by hand. Scrape sides of bowl often. Add the remaining ¼ cup milk and the egg whites and beat 2 minutes longer. Pour equal amounts of batter into each prepared pan. Bake 30 to 35 minutes, or until top springs back when lightly touched with finger. Remove from oven and cool on wire cake racks 10 minutes. Remove from pans and cool completely. Fill and frost with White Mountain Frosting.

Lady Baltimore Cake

In place of the 1 teaspoon vanilla extract called for above use ¾ teaspoon vanilla extract and ½ teaspoon almond extract. Frost with Lady Baltimore Frosting (recipe on page 860).

ᔌ One-Bowl Devil's Food Cake

1⅔ cups sifted cake flour
1½ cups sugar
½ teaspoon baking powder
1¼ teaspoons baking soda
1 teaspoon salt
½ cup unsweetened cocoa
½ cup softened butter or
   margarine
1 cup milk
1 teaspoon vanilla extract
3 eggs
White Mountain Frosting
   (optional, recipe on page
   859)

Heat oven to 350° F. Grease and flour two 8- or 9-inch round cake pans or one 13-x-9-x-2-inch pan. Sift together flour, sugar, baking powder, baking soda, salt, and cocoa into a medium-sized mixing bowl. Add butter, milk, and vanilla. Beat 2 minutes at medium speed with an electric mixer or 300 strokes by hand. Scrape sides of bowl often. Add eggs and beat 2 minutes longer. Pour batter into prepared pans. Bake 8-inch cakes 35 to 40 minutes, 9-inch cakes 30 to 35 minutes, and oblong cake 45 to 50 minutes; until top springs back when lightly touched with finger. Cool on wire cake racks 10 minutes before removing from pan. Remove from pan and cool completely before frosting.

[823]

CAKES

ᵛᶩ *Easy Banana Cake*

2¼ cups sifted cake flour
1¼ cups sugar
2½ teaspoons baking powder
½ teaspoon baking soda
½ teaspoon salt
½ cup softened butter or
    margarine
1 cup mashed banana
1½ teaspoons vanilla extract
2 eggs
*½ cup buttermilk
Sweetened whipped cream
    (optional)

Heat oven to 350° F. Grease and flour two 9-inch round cake pans. Sift together flour, sugar, baking powder, baking soda, and salt into a large mixing bowl. Add butter, banana, and vanilla. Beat 2 minutes at medium speed with an electric mixer or 300 strokes by hand. Scrape sides of bowl often. Add eggs and buttermilk and beat 2 minutes longer. Pour batter into prepared pans. Bake 30 to 35 minutes, or until top springs back when lightly touched with finger. Remove from oven and cool on wire cake racks 10 minutes. Remove from pans and cool completely. If desired, fill and top with sweetened whipped cream.

*Note: If buttermilk is not available, you can substitute sweet milk with lemon juice or vinegar added; see the chart on page 29.

ᵛᶩ *One-Bowl Golden Yellow Cake*

2½ cups sifted cake flour
1½ cups sugar
4 teaspoons baking powder
1 teaspoon salt
½ cup softened butter or
    margarine
1 teaspoon vanilla extract
⅔ cup milk
2 eggs, unbeaten
⅓ cup milk
Lemon Cream-Cheese Frosting
    (recipe on page 859)

Heat oven to 350° F. Grease and flour two 9-inch round cake pans or one 13-x-9-x-2-inch pan. Sift together flour, sugar, baking powder, and salt into a medium-sized mixing bowl. Add butter, vanilla, and the ⅔ cup milk. Beat 2 minutes at medium speed with an electric mixer or 300 strokes by hand. Scrape sides of bowl often. Add eggs and the ⅓ cup milk and beat 2 minutes longer. Pour batter into prepared pan. Bake round layers 30 to 35 minutes and oblong cake 35 to 40 minutes, or until top springs back when lightly touched with finger. Cool on wire cake racks 10 minutes before removing from pans. Remove from pans and cool completely. Frost with Lemon Cream-Cheese Frosting.

ᵛᶩ *Gingerbread*

2½ cups sifted all-purpose
    flour
1 teaspoon ground
    cinnamon
1 teaspoon ground ginger
½ teaspoon ground allspice
1 teaspoon salt
¾ teaspoon baking powder

Heat oven to 350° F. Grease a 9-inch-square cake pan, line with waxed paper, and grease and flour paper. Sift together flour, cinnamon, ginger, allspice, salt, baking powder, and baking soda. Mix shortening and sugar together in a large bowl; beat until mixture is well blended. Add molasses and eggs and beat until smooth. Add sifted dry ingredients to shortening mixture alternately with hot water. Add about a third of the flour

¾ teaspoon baking soda
⅔ cup soft shortening
⅔ cup firmly packed light
   brown sugar
⅔ cup dark molasses
2 eggs
⅔ cup hot water

mixture at a time; begin and end with it. Beat well after each addition. Pour into prepared pan. Bake 45 minutes, or until top springs back when lightly touched with finger. Remove from oven and cool on a wire cake rack for 10 minutes. Remove from pan and cool completely.

⤙ Quick Spice Cake

2¼ cups sifted cake flour
1½ cups sugar
3 teaspoons baking powder
1 teaspoon salt
1 teaspoon ground
   cinnamon
½ teaspoon ground cloves
¼ teaspoon ground nutmeg
½ cup softened butter or
   margarine
¾ cup milk
1 tablespoon molasses
1 teaspoon vanilla extract
2 eggs, unbeaten
¼ cup milk
Caramel Frosting (optional,
   recipe on page 858)

Heat oven to 375° F. Grease and flour two 8-inch-square cake pans. Sift together flour, sugar, baking powder, salt, cinnamon, cloves, and nutmeg into a medium-sized mixing bowl. Add butter, the ¾ cup milk, molasses, and vanilla. Beat 2 minutes at medium speed with an electric mixer or 300 strokes by hand. Scrape sides of bowl often. Add eggs and the ¼ cup milk and beat 2 minutes longer. Pour batter into prepared pans. Bake 25 to 30 minutes, or until top springs back when lightly touched with finger. Cool on wire cake racks 10 minutes. Cut around edges before removing from pans. Remove from pans and cool completely. Frost if desired with Caramel Frosting.

⤙ Tomato Soup Cake

2¼ cups sifted cake flour
1⅓ cups sugar
4 teaspoons baking powder
1 teaspoon baking soda
1½ teaspoons ground allspice
1 teaspoon ground
   cinnamon
½ teaspoon ground cloves
½ cup soft shortening
1 can condensed tomato
   soup
2 eggs
¼ cup water
Swirl Frosting (recipe on page
   859)

Heat oven to 350° F. Grease and flour two 8- or 9-inch round layer cake pans. Sift together flour, sugar, baking powder, baking soda, allspice, cinnamon, and cloves into the large bowl of an electric mixer. Add shortening and tomato soup; beat at medium speed 2 minutes or 300 strokes by hand, scraping sides of bowl often. Add eggs and water and beat 2 minutes longer, scraping bowl frequently. Pour into prepared pans. Bake 25 to 30 minutes, or until tops spring back when lightly touched with the finger. Let stand in pans 10 minutes. Remove from pans and cool on wire cake racks before frosting. Frost sides and top of cake with Swirl Frosting.

Foam Cakes

Foam cakes all depend upon well-beaten egg whites to give them volume. Check instructions on how to beat egg whites on page 452.

Special Tips for Foam Cakes (Angel, Sponge, and Chiffon)

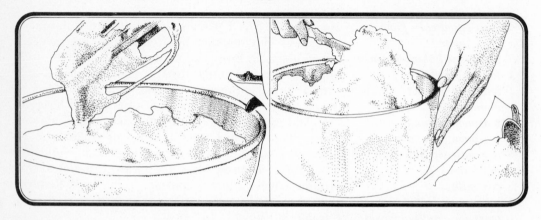

1. Properly beaten egg whites are essential to all foam cakes. Eggs at room temperature give greatest volume. The whites must be beaten until they hold stiff, straight peaks when lifted with beater.

2. When adding dry ingredients to beaten whites, use a gentle folding motion so you don't lose the air beaten into the eggs. With a rubber spatula cut down through middle of batter and up one side. Repeat motion, turning the bowl often.

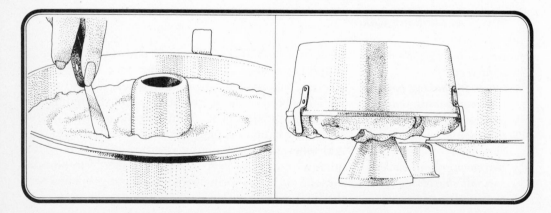

3. Carefully push foam-cake batter into an ungreased pan. Usually tube pans are used for foam cakes; they may be baked in loaves. In either case, gently cut through the batter in the pan to prevent large air bubbles from forming.

4. Invert foam cakes to cool. Center tube pans over a funnel or bottle; hang loaf pans on custard cups. Cool completely. Loosen cake sides from pan; rap pan rim sharply on table edge to release cake.

✒ Angel Food Cake

1 cup sifted cake flour
¾ cup sugar
1½ cups egg whites (about 12), at room temperature
1½ teaspoons cream of tartar
¼ teaspoon salt
1½ teaspoons vanilla extract
¾ cup sugar
Peppermint Glaze (recipe on page 860)

Heat oven to 375° F. Sift flour with ¾ cup sugar. In a large bowl beat egg whites with cream of tartar, salt, and vanilla until stiff enough to hold soft peaks. Add the remaining ¾ cup sugar, 2 tablespoons at a time, to egg whites, beating well after each addition. Continue beating until meringue holds stiff peaks. Sift about ¼ of the flour mixture over egg white mixture; fold in gently with a rubber spatula. Fold in remaining flour mixture by fourths. Carefully pour into an ungreased 10-inch tube pan. Gently cut through batter with a spatula to prevent large holes. Bake 30 to 35 minutes, or until top springs back when touched lightly with finger. Invert pan on funnel or bottle. Cool completely. Cut around sides and tube with a thin spatula. Rap rim of pan sharply on table edge to loosen cake. Spread with Peppermint Glaze, if desired.

✒ Feather Sponge Cake

6 eggs, separated, at room temperature
½ teaspoon cream of tartar
¼ teaspoon salt
1 cup sifted sugar
2 tablespoons cold water
1 tablespoon grated lemon peel
1 tablespoon lemon juice
½ teaspoon vanilla extract
1 cup sifted cake flour
White Mountain Frosting (recipe on page 859)

Heat oven to 325° F. Place egg whites, cream of tartar, and salt in a large bowl and beat with an electric mixer until stiff enough to hold its shape. Add ½ cup of the sugar, 2 tablespoons at a time, to egg whites, beating after each addition. Continue beating until meringue holds stiff peaks. Place egg yolks in a large mixing bowl; beat until thick and lemon-colored. Add the remaining ½ cup sugar, one tablespoon at a time, beating until creamy. Combine water, lemon peel, lemon juice, and vanilla; gradually mix into egg yolk. Gently fold flour into egg yolks with a rubber spatula; then carefully fold in meringue. Pour into an ungreased 10-inch tube pan. Gently cut through batter with spatula to break up large air bubbles. Bake 60 minutes, or until top springs back when touched lightly with finger. Invert pan on a funnel or bottle. Cool completely. Cut around sides and tube with a thin spatula. Rap rim of pan sharply on table edge to loosen cake. Invert on a cake plate and frost top and sides with White Mountain Frosting.

✒ Golden Chiffon Cake

2¼ cups sifted cake flour
1½ cups sugar

Heat oven to 350° F. Sift together flour, sugar, baking powder, and salt. Make a well in center of dry ingre-

3 teaspoons baking powder
1 teaspoon salt
½ cup vegetable oil
5 egg yolks
¾ cup cold water
2 teaspoons vanilla extract
1 tablespoon grated lemon peel
1 cup egg whites (about 7), at room temperature
½ teaspoon cream of tartar
Almond Butter-Cream Frosting (optional, recipe on page 856)

dients and add vegetable oil, egg yolks, water, vanilla, and lemon peel. Beat until smooth and creamy with rotary beater or electric mixer. Combine egg whites and cream of tartar; beat until very stiff peaks form. Fold egg yolk mixture into beaten egg whites and mix well. Pour into an ungreased 10-inch tube pan. Bake 50 to 55 minutes, or until top springs back when lightly touched with finger. Remove cake from oven, invert pan on funnel or bottle. When cake is completely cool, cut around sides and tube with a thin spatula. Carefully invert cake on flat tray. If desired, frost with Almond Butter-Cream Frosting.

❧ Daffodil Cake

½ teaspoon cream of tartar
¼ teaspoon salt
1 cup egg whites (about 7), at room temperature
1 cup sugar
4 egg yolks
1 teaspoon grated orange peel
1 teaspoon grated lemon peel
1 teaspoon orange juice
1 teaspoon lemon juice
1 cup sifted cake flour
¼ teaspoon almond extract
½ teaspoon vanilla extract
Cocoa Whipped Cream (recipe on page 860)

Heat oven to 325° F. Put cream of tartar, salt, and the cup of egg whites in a bowl; whip until soft peaks form. Add sugar, 2 tablespoons at a time, beating well after each addition until soft peaks form. Set aside while you beat the 4 egg yolks in another bowl until thick and lemon-colored. Stir orange and lemon peels and juices into beaten yolks. Now gently fold half the beaten egg whites into the yolks, using a rubber spatula; carefully add and fold in ½ cup of the flour. Add almond and vanilla extracts to the remaining egg whites and fold the remaining ½ cup of flour into them. Drop spoonfuls of the two mixtures alternately into an ungreased 9-inch tube pan. Cut through mixture with a knife to marble slightly. Bake 50 to 55 minutes, or until top springs back when lightly touched with a finger. Remove from oven and invert pan over a funnel or bottle. When cake is completely cool, cut around sides and tube with a thin spatula. Rap rim of pan sharply on table edge to loosen cake. Remove to a cake plate. Slice and serve with Cocoa Whipped Cream.

❧ Sugared Orange Chiffon Cake

2¼ cups sifted cake flour
1½ cups sugar
3 teaspoons baking powder
1 teaspoon salt

Heat oven to 350° F. Sift flour, the 1½ cups sugar, baking powder, and salt into a bowl; make a well in the center. Add oil, egg yolks, orange peel, and juice. Beat until mixture is smooth and creamy. In a large bowl,

½ cup vegetable oil
5 egg yolks
3 tablespoons grated
  orange peel
¾ cup orange juice
1 cup egg whites (about 7),
  at room temperature
½ teaspoon cream of tartar
½ teaspoon ground
  cinnamon
2 tablespoons sugar

whip egg whites and cream of tartar until very stiff peaks form. Pour egg yolk mixture gradually over whites, gently folding together with a rubber spatula. Combine cinnamon and the 2 tablespoons sugar in a cup. Pour ⅓ of the batter into an ungreased 10-inch tube pan; sprinkle with half the cinnamon–sugar mixture. Repeat. Top with remaining batter. Bake 45 to 55 minutes, or until delicately browned and top springs back when lightly touched with finger. Remove cake from oven and invert pan over a funnel or bottle. When cake is completely cool, cut around sides and tube with a thin spatula. Rap rim of pan sharply on edge of table to loosen cake from pan. Serve unfrosted with ice cream or fruit.

✑ Maple Pecan Chiffon Cake

2¼ cups sifted cake flour
 ¾ cup granulated sugar
 ¾ cup firmly packed brown
   sugar
 3 teaspoons baking powder
 1 teaspoon salt
 5 egg yolks, unbeaten
 ½ cup vegetable oil
 ¾ cup cold water
 2 teaspoons maple flavoring
 7 egg whites (about 1 cup),
   at room temperature
 ½ teaspoon cream of tartar
 1 cup very finely chopped
   pecans
Maple Swirl Frosting (recipe
   on page 859)
Coarsely chopped pecans

Heat oven to 350° F. Sift flour, sugars, baking powder, and salt together into a bowl. Make a well in center of flour mixture; add egg yolks, oil, water, and maple flavoring. Beat until smooth and creamy. Beat egg whites and cream of tartar together until stiff peaks form; gradually fold into egg yolk mixture; blend thoroughly. Fold in the 1 cup very finely chopped pecans and pour into an ungreased 10-inch tube pan. Bake 50 to 60 minutes, or until top springs back when touched lightly with finger. Invert pan over funnel or bottle until completely cooled. Cut around sides of tube with a thin spatula. Rap rim of pan sharply on table edge to loosen cake. Turn out on cake plate and frost with Maple Swirl Frosting. Sprinkle top of cake with coarsely chopped pecans.

Cheesecakes

Cheesecakes are really overgrown pies in a crumb crust. They are rich, often spectacular in appearance, and universally loved.

CAKES

❧ Velvet Cheesecake

18 zwieback, rolled into fine
    crumbs
3 tablespoons butter or
    margarine, melted
1 tablespoon sugar
2 8-ounce packages cream
    cheese, at room
    temperature
½ cup sugar
⅛ teaspoon ground
    cinnamon
½ teaspoon vanilla extract
1 teaspoon grated lemon
    peel
1 tablespoon lemon juice
2 eggs, separated, at room
    temperature
1 cup commercial sour
    cream
1 tablespoon sugar
1 teaspoon vanilla extract

Heat oven to 300° F. Blend crumbs, butter, and the 1 tablespoon sugar. Press into bottom of a well-buttered 9-inch springform pan. Bake 5 minutes. Cool. Blend cheese and the ½ cup sugar, cinnamon, the ½ teaspoon vanilla, lemon peel, and juice. Beat in yolks one at a time. Beat egg whites until stiff but not dry; fold into cheese mixture. Pour over crumbs in pan. Bake 45 minutes. Blend sour cream and the 1 tablespoon sugar and the 1 teaspoon vanilla. Remove cheesecake from oven; spread cream mixture over top; bake 10 minutes longer. Cool cheesecake thoroughly before removing rim of pan. Serves 8 to 10.

❧ Cheesecake Supreme

1¼ cups graham cracker
    crumbs
¼ cup sugar
¼ cup melted butter or
    margarine
5 8-ounce packages cream
    cheese, at room
    temperature
1¾ cups sugar
3 tablespoons flour
2 teaspoons grated lemon
    peel
1 tablespoon grated orange
    peel
5 whole eggs
2 egg yolks
¼ cup heavy cream
Fruit Glaze (recipe follows)

Heat oven to 500° F. Work graham cracker crumbs, sugar, and butter together until well blended. Butter a 9-inch springform pan and press crumb mixture over the bottom and about 2¼ inches up the sides of the pan. In the large bowl of an electric mixer combine cheese, sugar, flour, lemon peel, and orange peel on low speed. Add whole eggs and egg yolks one at a time, beating well after each addition. Add cream and beat at medium speed just until mixture is smooth. Pour cheese mixture into prepared pan. Bake for 10 minutes. Reduce oven temperature to 200° F. and continue baking for 1 hour. Remove from oven and cool on wire rack away from drafts. Refrigerate until cold. When cold, remove rim of pan and place cake on a serving plate. While cake is chilling, prepare Fruit Glaze. Arrange apricots in a ring in center of chilled cake. Surround with a circle of quartered pineapple slices. Halve strawberries and arrange in a ring around edge of cake. Spoon blueberries in

*4 or 5 canned apricot
halves, well drained
(reserve syrup)*
*1 8¼-ounce can sliced
pineapple, drained and
cut into quarters (reserve
syrup)*
1 pint strawberries, washed
*⅓ cup blueberries, fresh or
frozen*

center of cake and between fruits. Spoon glaze over fruits and refrigerate until serving time. Serves 10 to 12.

Fruit Glaze

Pour *apricot and pineapple syrup* into a measuring cup; ¾ *cup* is needed for the glaze. Place the ¾ *cup syrup* and *1 tablespoon lemon juice* in a small saucepan. Mix *1 tablespoon cornstarch* and *2 tablespoons water or syrup* until blended. Stir into juices in pan and cook over moderate heat (about 250° F.), stirring constantly, until thickened. If desired, add a few drops of yellow food coloring. Cool before using.

✑ Pineapple Cheesecake

*½ cup finely crushed sugar
honey graham crackers
(about 8 medium crackers)*
*¼ cup melted butter or
margarine*
¼ teaspoon ground cinnamon
*2 eggs, separated, at room
temperature*
6 tablespoons sugar
*2 cups cream-style cottage
cheese*
2 tablespoons milk
2 tablespoons flour
2 tablespoons lemon juice
¾ teaspoon grated lemon peel
*¼ teaspoon grated orange
peel*
¾ teaspoon vanilla extract
¼ teaspoon salt
**Pineapple Glaze (recipe
follows)**

Heat oven to 400° F. Combine crumbs, 2 tablespoons of the melted butter, and the cinnamon. Press into the bottom of a 9-inch springform pan. Bake 10 minutes. Remove from oven and cool. Reduce oven temperature to 300° F. Beat egg whites until soft peaks form. Gradually add 3 tablespoons of the sugar and continue beating until peaks are stiff and glossy. Set aside egg white mixture. Place cheese in the large bowl of an electric mixer and beat until smooth. Add the remaining 2 tablespoons melted butter and the egg yolks and mix well. Add the remaining 3 tablespoons sugar, the milk, flour, lemon juice, lemon and orange peel, vanilla, and salt; beat until well blended. Fold beaten egg whites into cheese mixture until thoroughly blended. Pour into springform pan. Bake 1 hour and 40 minutes, or until knife inserted about 2 inches from center comes out clean. Cool completely. Run a knife or spatula around edge of cheesecake to loosen. Remove rim from pan. Top with Pineapple Glaze. Chill. Serves 10.

Pineapple Glaze

1 tablespoon cornstarch
2 tablespoons sugar
1 8½-ounce can crushed
  pineapple

Combine the cornstarch and sugar in a small saucepan. Gradually stir in the undrained pineapple. Place over moderately low heat (about 225° F.) and cook, stirring constantly, until thickened. Remove from heat. Cool, stirring occasionally. Makes 1 cup.

Rolled Cakes

Rolled cakes are baked in a jelly-roll pan, which must be lined with waxed paper that is then greased and sometimes floured. Be free to work fast when these cakes come out of the oven; they must be rolled while they are warm and pliable.

How to roll a jelly roll: Spread a clean tea towel on a flat surface and generously dust the towel with confectioners' sugar. Run a spatula around the edge of the cake pan to loosen the cake. Invert the pan onto the towel, with the length of the pan corresponding to the length of the towel and leaving an even margin of towel all around. Lift off the pan (and waxed paper, if used). Trim away crisp edges of the cake with a sharp knife.

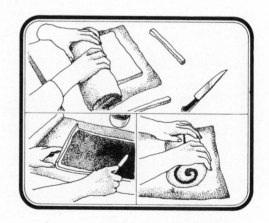

Starting at one end of the cake, turn the towel edge onto the cake and carefully roll up both cake and towel. Cool the roll on a rack, seam side down.

When it has cooled completely, remove it from the rack and place it on a flat surface. Unroll the cake very gently, leaving the towel underneath. Spread the filling over the cake to within ½ inch of all the edges. Carefully roll up the cake with its filling. Place the cake roll on a serving plate, seam side down.

Chocolate Cream Roll

6 eggs, separated, at room
  temperature
1 cup granulated sugar
3 tablespoons unsweetened
  cocoa
1 tablespoon flour
Confectioners' sugar

Heat oven to 400° F. Grease a 15½-x-10½-x-1-inch jelly-roll pan; line with waxed paper and grease and flour paper. Beat egg whites with an electric mixer until stiff but not dry. Beat egg yolks in another bowl with mixer until thick; gradually add the 1 cup granulated sugar; beat until thick and lemon-colored. Mix cocoa and flour together; fold into beaten egg yolks. Fold in

2 cups chilled heavy cream
¼ cup confectioners' sugar
1 teaspoon vanilla extract
Chocolate curls (optional)

egg whites. Pour into prepared pan. Bake 12 minutes, or until top springs back when lightly touched with finger. Loosen edges of cake and invert immediately on a tea towel sprinkled with confectioners' sugar. Peel off paper. Cut off crisp edges of cake. Immediately roll up cake and towel, starting at short end, and cool. Whip cream, confectioners' sugar, and vanilla with rotary beater until stiff. Reserve 1 cup of the whipped cream for garnish. Unroll cake and remove towel. Spread with remaining whipped cream to within ½ inch of edge. Roll up cake and place on serving plate. Spoon the 1 cup reserved cream into decorating bag and, using a star tip, decorate top of roll with rosettes of cream. Garnish with chocolate curls if desired. Serves 10 to 12.

ஜ Peppermint Cream Roll

5 eggs, separated, at room
temperature
½ teaspoon cream of tartar
1 cup sugar
¼ cup sifted all-purpose flour
3 tablespoons unsweetened
cocoa
¼ teaspoon salt
2 teaspoons vanilla extract
Confectioners' sugar
1 cup heavy cream, whipped
1 6-ounce package semisweet
chocolate pieces
1 cup coarsely crushed
peppermint candy
Confectioners' sugar

Heat oven to 325° F. Line bottom and sides of a 15½-x-10½-x-1-inch jelly-roll pan with waxed paper. Grease paper and sprinkle lightly with flour. Beat egg whites and cream of tartar in the large bowl of an electric mixer until stiff but not dry. Continue to beat and gradually add ½ cup of the sugar, 2 tablespoons at a time. Beat until mixture forms stiff, shiny peaks. Beat egg yolks until thick and lemon-colored. Sift the remaining ½ cup sugar with the flour, cocoa, and salt. Add beaten yolks and 1 teaspoon of the vanilla to flour mixture. Fold flour mixture into the beaten egg whites. Pour into prepared pan. Bake about 25 to 30 minutes, or until cake pulls away slightly from edges of pan. Loosen edges of cake and invert immediately onto a clean tea towel sprinkled with confectioners' sugar. Peel off waxed paper. Cut off crisp edges of cake and roll up immediately in the towel. Cool thoroughly, about 2 hours, at room temperature. Fold the remaining 1 teaspoon vanilla into the whipped cream. Place chocolate pieces in the top of a double boiler over hot, not boiling, water. Stir until melted. Remove from heat and cool about 10 minutes. Fold in ½ cup of the whipped cream. Gently unroll cake. Spread chocolate mixture over cake in a thin layer to edges. Cool. Reserve 2 tablespoons of the crushed peppermint. Combine remaining peppermint and remaining whipped cream. Reserve ½ cup of the peppermint–cream mixture. Spread remainder of mixture over cake to within ½ inch of edge. Roll up cake loosely. Spoon reserved peppermint filling over the top center of roll. Chill until serving time. Before serving, sprinkle with the reserved 2 tablespoons crushed mint candy and dust lightly with confectioners' sugar. Cut into 1-inch slices. Serves 8 to 10.

ᐱᔧ Pineapple Cake Roll

1 20-ounce can crushed pineapple
⅔ cup firmly packed brown sugar
4 eggs, separated, at room temperature
¼ cup granulated sugar
½ teaspoon vanilla extract
½ cup sugar
¾ cup sifted all-purpose flour
1 teaspoon baking powder
½ teaspoon salt
Confectioners' sugar, sifted
3 tablespoons sugar
1½ tablespoons cornstarch
⅔ cup orange juice

Heat oven to 375° F. Drain pineapple and reserve juice. Spread pineapple evenly on the bottom of an ungreased 15½-x-10½-x-1-inch jelly-roll pan. Sprinkle brown sugar over pineapple. Beat egg yolks until thick and lemon-colored. Gradually beat in the ¼ cup sugar. Add vanilla. Beat egg whites until soft peaks form; gradually add the ½ cup sugar and continue beating until stiff peaks form. Fold yolk mixture into beaten egg whites. Sift together flour, baking powder, and salt. Fold gently into egg mixture. Spread batter evenly over pineapple in pan. Bake about 20 minutes. Loosen sides with a small spatula and invert cake on a tea towel sprinkled with sifted confectioners' sugar. Cool 2 or 3 minutes. Roll up just the cake, starting at narrow end of cake. Wrap in the sugared towel and cool. Combine the 3 tablespoons sugar and cornstarch in a saucepan. Gradually stir in 1 cup of the reserved pineapple juice and the orange juice. Cook over moderate heat (about 250° F.), stirring constantly, until thickened and clear. Serve sauce warm or chilled over slices of cake roll. Serves 8 to 10.

ᐱᔧ Raspberry Jelly Roll

4 eggs
½ teaspoon salt
¾ cup sugar
¾ cup packaged pancake mix
¼ cup very finely chopped almonds
¼ teaspoon almond extract
Confectioners' sugar
1 10-ounce package frozen raspberries, thawed
1 3-ounce package raspberry-flavored gelatin

Heat oven to 400° F. Grease bottom and sides of 15½-x-10½-x-1-inch jelly-roll pan; line with waxed paper; grease paper and sprinkle with flour. Beat eggs and salt together in medium-sized bowl until thick and lemon-colored. Gradually add the ¾ cup sugar, beating well after each addition. Add pancake mix, almonds, and almond extract; stir until blended. Pour into prepared pan and bake 8 to 10 minutes. Loosen edges of cake and invert immediately on a tea towel sprinkled with confectioners' sugar. Peel off waxed paper. Cut off crisp edges of cake. Roll up immediately in towel. Cool and chill. Drain raspberries and add enough water to juice to

½ *cup cold water*
½ *cup heavy cream*
2 *tablespoons confectioners'
  sugar*

make 1 cup of liquid. Heat liquid to boiling; sprinkle with gelatin and stir until dissolved. Stir in the ½ cup cold water. Chill until slightly thickened. Whip cream and the confectioners' sugar together until it holds its shape. Fold cream and drained raspberries into gelatin; chill until mixture starts to thicken. Unroll cake and remove towel. Spread raspberry filling to within ½ inch of edge of cake. Roll up and sprinkle with additional confectioners' sugar. Serves 8 to 10.

Quick Bûche de Noël (Christmas Log)

4 *eggs*
½ *teaspoon salt*
¾ *cup sugar*
2 *tablespoons unsweetened
  cocoa*
¾ *cup pancake mix*
1 *teaspoon vanilla extract*
Confectioners' sugar
1 *2-ounce package whipped
  topping mix*
1 *teaspoon instant coffee
  powder*
1 *can ready-to-spread
  chocolate frosting*
4 *candied cherries, halved*
Silver dragées

Heat oven to 400° F. Grease bottom and sides of a 15½-x-10½-x-1-inch jelly-roll pan and line with waxed paper; grease paper and sprinkle with flour. Beat eggs and salt together in a medium-sized bowl with a rotary beater or electric mixer until thick and lemon-colored. Mix together sugar and cocoa; gradually add to beaten eggs, beating well after each addition. Stir in pancake mix and vanilla. Pour into prepared pan. Bake 8 to 10 minutes, or until cake just begins to break away from sides of pan. Loosen cake from edges of pan with a spatula. Invert cake immediately on a tea towel sprinkled with confectioners' sugar. Peel off waxed paper and roll up cake in the towel, starting at the 10½-inch end. Cool; then chill until cold. Prepare whipped topping mix, following directions on package, but add the coffee to the dry mixture before beating. Unroll cake and spread with the coffee filling; roll up and chill, covered, in the refrigerator several hours or overnight. At serving time place cake on serving plate and spread with chocolate frosting (there will be some frosting left over). Garnish top with halved cherries and silver dragées. Serves 8 to 10.

Upside-down Cakes

Upside-down cakes come from the pan all trimmed and ready to serve hot or cold.

◆§ Cherry Upside-down Cake

1 can cherry pie filling
⅓ cup slivered blanched
   almonds
1¼ cups sifted all-purpose
   flour
2 teaspoons baking powder
¼ teaspoon salt
¾ cup sugar
¼ cup soft shortening
½ cup milk
1 egg
1 teaspoon vanilla extract
Whipped cream (optional)

Heat oven to 350° F. Combine cherry pie filling and almonds in a 9-inch-square cake pan. Sift together flour, baking powder, and salt in the large bowl of an electric mixer; stir in sugar. Add shortening and milk and beat about 2 minutes on medium speed of mixer, scraping bowl frequently. Add egg and vanilla and beat an additional 2 minutes on medium speed. Spread cake batter over cherry filling. Bake 50 to 60 minutes, or until cake springs back when touched lightly in the center. Remove from oven and let stand about 5 minutes. Loosen cake from edge of pan. Place a large serving platter over cake pan and invert, turning cake out onto platter. Remove cake pan. Let cool about 10 minutes before serving. Serve warm with whipped cream, if desired. Makes nine 3-inch squares.

◆§ Chocolate Upside-down Cake

½ cup chopped walnuts
1 6-ounce package
   semisweet chocolate
   pieces
1 cup sifted confectioners'
   sugar
⅓ cup undiluted evaporated
   milk
¼ cup softened butter or
   margarine
¾ cup sugar
1 egg
1 cup plus 2 tablespoons
   sifted all-purpose flour
1½ teaspoons baking powder
½ teaspoon salt
½ cup milk
1 teaspoon vanilla extract

Heat oven to 350° F. Line an 8-inch-square baking pan with waxed paper. Sprinkle nuts in bottom of pan. Place chocolate pieces in top of double boiler. Place over hot, not boiling, water until chocolate melts. Add confectioners' sugar and evaporated milk and beat until smooth. Spread mixture evenly over nuts in bottom of pan. Work butter in a bowl until creamy. Add sugar and beat until well blended. Beat in egg. Sift together flour, baking powder, and salt. Add flour mixture alternately with milk to creamed mixture, beating well after each addition. Blend in vanilla. Pour batter over chocolate mixture in pan. Bake 45 to 50 minutes. Let stand in pan about 5 minutes. Loosen cake from edge of pan. Invert on a wire rack. Remove waxed paper. Cool. Cut into 2-inch squares. Makes 16 squares.

◆§ Pineapple Upside-down Cake

⅓ cup butter or margarine
½ cup firmly packed light
   brown sugar

Heat oven to 350° F. Melt the ⅓ cup butter in a 10-inch skillet with an ovenproof handle or a 9-x-9-x-2-inch pan over moderately low heat (about 225° F.). Remove from

1 15¼-ounce can sliced
   pineapple, drained
7 or 8 maraschino cherries
1½ cups sifted cake flour
2 teaspoons baking powder
½ teaspoon salt
1 cup sugar
⅓ cup softened butter or
   margarine
1 teaspoon vanilla extract
⅔ cup milk
1 egg
Sweetened whipped cream

heat. Sprinkle brown sugar evenly over butter. Arrange pineapple slices (about 7) over sugar and butter in skillet. Place a cherry in the center of each pineapple slice. Sift flour, baking powder, salt, and sugar into a medium-sized bowl. Add the ⅓ cup butter, vanilla, and milk. Beat 2 minutes at medium speed with an electric mixer or 300 strokes by hand, scraping sides of bowl often. Add the egg and beat 2 minutes longer. Pour over fruit in prepared pan. Bake 35 to 40 minutes or until top springs back when lightly touched with finger. Remove from oven and let cool 2 to 3 minutes on a wire rack. Loosen sides of cake with a spatula and invert onto a serving plate. Serve warm with whipped cream. Serves 8.

Tortes

Tortes are multilayered creations that may be as complicated as the St. Honoré cake that you'd prepare for a most special party or as easy as the two-layered Mocha Torte. They're superb combinations of cake and filling flavors.

⧈ Chocolate–Almond Torte

3 cups sifted all-purpose
   flour
¾ cup sugar
Few grains salt
1 cup butter or margarine
1 egg
1 6-ounce package
   semisweet chocolate
   pieces
2 cups commercial sour
   cream
2 cups finely chopped
   almonds
1½ cups confectioners' sugar
1 teaspoon vanilla extract
¼ cup apricot jam
12 whole almonds

Heat oven to 350° F. Sift flour, ¾ cup sugar, and salt into a mixing bowl. Cut in the butter with a pastry blender or two knives until mixture is mealy. Add the unbeaten egg and blend mixture with the hands until a dough forms. Divide dough into 7 equal parts. On lightly floured, inverted cookie sheet, roll a portion of dough into a 9-inch circle. Using a 9-inch cake pan as an aid, trim the layer evenly. Bake 10 to 12 minutes, until pastry is a golden brown. Let pastry layer remain on cookie sheet 3 or 4 minutes. Remove with a wide spatula and cool on wire rack. While layers are baking, cover unrolled portions of dough with a towel to prevent drying. Cool cookie sheet each time before rolling out another layer. Melt chocolate pieces in the top of a double boiler over hot, not boiling, water. Combine sour cream, almonds, confectioners' sugar, and vanilla. Blend in melted chocolate pieces. Assemble torte on a large serving plate by alternating pastry layers and about ⅔ cup of the chocolate–

almond mixture, beginning and ending with a pastry layer. Melt the apricot jam in a small saucepan over moderately low heat (about 225° F.). Add whole almonds and stir to coat thoroughly with glaze; remove nuts with a slotted spoon and place on waxed paper. Spread melted jam over top of torte. Arrange almonds in a circle about 2 inches from edge of torte. Serves 12.

❧ Chocolate Cream Torte

4 eggs, separated, at room
    temperature
Pinch of salt
½ cup sugar
4 1-ounce squares
    semisweet chocolate,
    melted
1½ tablespoons
    strong-brewed coffee
¾ teaspoon vanilla extract
Sugar
Chocolate–Almond Filling
    (recipe follows)
Almond Cream (recipe follows)
Chocolate curls

Heat oven to 375° F. Grease two 8-x-8-x-2-inch pans; line each with a single strip of waxed paper over the bottom and up 2 sides of the pan so that the paper extends over edges of pan. Grease and flour the paper. Beat egg whites and salt with a rotary beater or electric mixer until soft peaks form. Gradually add sugar, 1 tablespoon at a time, continuing to beat until stiff peaks form. Beat egg yolks well and stir in chocolate, coffee, and vanilla. Fold about ¼ of the beaten egg whites into the chocolate mixture, mixing until blended. Then fold chocolate mixture into the remaining beaten egg whites, blending well. Spread half the batter in each of the prepared pans. Bake 20 to 23 minutes, or until top of cake is firm and cake shrinks from sides of pan. Cool on wire rack for 2 to 3 minutes. Turn cakes out onto a tea towel sprinkled with sugar; peel off waxed paper and let cool 30 minutes, or until cake is thoroughly cool. Cut each cake in half to make 2 rectangular layers. *To Assemble:* Place a cake layer on a serving plate and spread with half the Chocolate–Almond Filling. Top with a second cake layer and spread with half the Almond Cream. Place a third layer over cream and spread with the remaining chocolate filling. Add the remaining layer and spread with the remaining cream. Garnish with chocolate curls and chill several hours. To serve, cut into slices. Serves 8.

Chocolate–Almond Filling

2 egg whites, at room
    temperature
¼ cup sugar
1 teaspoon vanilla extract
½ teaspoon almond extract
¼ cup finely ground almonds

Beat egg whites with a rotary beater or electric mixer until soft peaks form; gradually add sugar and beat until stiff peaks form. Stir in vanilla and almond extracts. Fold in almonds and chocolate.

2 1-ounce squares
    semisweet chocolate,
    melted

Almond Cream

½ cup heavy cream
1½ teaspoons sugar
¼ cup finely ground toasted
    almonds

Whip cream and sugar together until mixture holds its shape. Fold in almonds.

⪡ Mocha Torte

¾ cup sifted cake flour
1 teaspoon instant coffee
    powder
1 teaspoon baking powder
½ teaspoon salt
4 egg yolks
1 cup sifted confectioners'
    sugar
1 teaspoon vanilla extract
4 egg whites, at room
    temperature
Mocha Cream (recipe follows)
½ cup slivered Brazil nuts

Heat oven to 325° F. Grease two 9-inch round cake pans and line with waxed paper. Sift together flour, instant coffee powder, baking powder, and salt. Beat egg yolks with rotary beater or electric mixer until thick and lemon-colored. Gradually add confectioners' sugar, beating until blended. Add vanilla. Gently fold sifted dry ingredients into yolk mixture. Beat egg whites until stiff but not dry; fold into batter. Pour equal amounts of batter into prepared pans. Bake 25 minutes until top springs back when lightly touched with finger. Remove from oven and cool on wire cake rack for 10 minutes. Remove from pans and cool completely. Just before serving, spoon half of the Mocha Cream over bottom layer and sprinkle with half of the nuts. Top with second layer and frost with remaining Mocha Cream; sprinkle with nuts. Serves 8.

Mocha Cream

Whip *1 cup chilled heavy cream, 2 tablespoons confectioners' sugar, 1 teaspoon instant coffee powder,* and *1 teaspoon vanilla extract* together with rotary beater until mixture holds its shape.

⪡ Meringue Strawberry Torte

Almond Meringue Layers
    (recipe follows)
10 ladyfingers
¼ cup sweet sherry
1½ cups chilled heavy cream
¼ cup confectioners' sugar
½ teaspoon almond extract
1 pint strawberries,
    washed, hulled, and cut
    into halves

Prepare Almond Meringue Layers. Cool as directed. Split ladyfingers and sprinkle with sherry. Whip cream, confectioners' sugar, and almond extract with rotary beater until stiff. Reserve ½ cup of the whipped cream for garnish. Place a meringue layer on large serving plate and cover with about ⅓ of the whipped cream. Arrange half the ladyfingers over cream, spoke fashion. Reserve 6 halved strawberries for garnish and place half the remaining strawberries over ladyfingers and cream. Spread with another ⅓ of the cream and repeat ladyfinger and strawberry layers once again. Top with remaining ⅓ of the cream and the second meringue layer. Chill about 4 hours before serving. At serving time, mound reserved ½ cup whipped cream in center of top and garnish with the reserved strawberries. Serves 10.

Almond Meringue Layers

3 egg whites, at room
    temperature
Few grains salt
¾ cup sugar
½ cup finely ground almonds

Heat oven to 250° F. Beat egg whites and salt with a rotary beater until soft peaks form. Gradually add sugar and beat until stiff peaks form. Fold in almonds. Grease two cookie sheets. Using a 9-inch round cake pan for a pattern, trace a circle on two pieces of waxed paper. Place a piece of paper on each cookie sheet and spread half the meringue to within ½ inch of the edge of each circle. Bake 45 minutes, or until lightly browned. Turn off heat and leave in oven until cool. Carefully peel paper off meringue.

✍ St. Honoré Cake

1¼ cups sifted all-purpose
    flour
5 tablespoons granulated
    sugar
Few grains salt
1 egg
¼ cup soft butter or
    margarine
Cream Puff Dough (recipe
    follows)
Caramel Syrup (recipe
    follows)
1¼ cups chilled heavy cream
1 tablespoon confectioners'
    sugar
½ teaspoon almond extract
Chocolate Chiffon Filling
    (recipe follows)

Mix flour, granulated sugar, and salt in a bowl. Make a well in center and add egg and butter. Mix with a fork until blended; knead in bowl with fingertips until pastry is smooth. Wrap in waxed paper and chill in refrigerator for several hours. Place pastry between pieces of floured waxed paper and roll with a rolling pin into a circle 9 inches in diameter. Slip cookie sheet under waxed paper and dough; remove top sheet of paper. Place a second greased cookie sheet over pastry and invert on sheet. Remove remaining piece of waxed paper. Place a 9-inch round cake pan over pastry and, if necessary, trim pastry to make a perfect circle. Prepare Cream Puff Dough. Heat oven to 400° F. Drop teaspoonfuls of the Cream Puff Dough around edge of pastry circle to form a border about ¾ inch wide. Drop remaining dough in heaping teaspoonfuls about 1½ inches apart on a greased cookie sheet to form small, individual puffs. Bake small puffs about 20 to 25 minutes and the large cake 25 to 30 minutes, or until lightly browned. Remove large cake to a wire rack and cool. Cool small puffs and remove a slice from the top of each. Prepare Caramel Syrup. Dip bottoms of small puffs in the hot syrup and arrange around edge of large cake. Whip cream, confectioners' sugar, and almond extract with a rotary beater until stiff. Measure 1 cup of the whipped cream and reserve to use in Chocolate Chiffon Filling. Spoon remaining cream into the little puffs. If desired, cover with the tops. Refrigerate while making filling. Prepare Chocolate Chiffon Filling and pour into center of ring. Chill 3 to 4 hours, until set. Serves 10 to 12.

Cream Puff Dough

¾ cup water
6 tablespoons butter or margarine
⅛ teaspoon salt
¾ cup sifted all-purpose flour
3 eggs

Place water, butter, and salt in a heavy saucepan. Place over moderate heat (about 250° F.). Heat until butter melts and mixture comes to a rolling boil. Reduce heat to low (about 200° F.). Add flour all at once. Stir vigorously over heat about 1 minute until mixture leaves sides of pan and clings to spoon. Remove from heat. Add eggs one at a time and beat thoroughly after each addition until a thick dough is formed (about 3 minutes altogether). Do not be afraid that you will overbeat.

Caramel Syrup

½ cup granulated sugar
¼ cup water

Mix sugar and water in a small skillet. Place over moderate heat (do not use controlled-heat burner) and heat about 7 to 10 minutes, or until mixture starts to brown slightly. Remove from heat and use immediately. If syrup becomes hard before all the small puffs have been put into place, set pan over very low heat until syrup is melted.

Chocolate Chiffon Filling

1 envelope unflavored gelatine
2 tablespoons sugar
¼ teaspoon salt
2 eggs, separated, at room temperature
½ cup milk
¾ cup heavy cream
1 6-ounce package semisweet chocolate pieces
1 teaspoon vanilla extract
¼ cup sugar

Mix gelatine, the 2 tablespoons sugar, and the salt in top of double boiler. Beat egg yolks, milk, and cream together; stir into gelatine mixture. Add chocolate and cook 10 minutes over boiling water, stirring constantly until chocolate is melted and gelatine is dissolved. Remove from heat and stir in vanilla. Beat egg whites with rotary beater until soft peaks form. Gradually add the ¼ cup sugar and beat until stiff peaks form. Place top of double boiler with chocolate mixture in a large bowl filled with ice cubes. Stir frequently, until filling is cool and starts to thicken. Fold in beaten egg whites and the reserved 1 cup whipped cream. Pour into center of ring.

(Ingredients continued on page 842)

*1 cup whipped cream
(reserved from the
cream-puff filling)*

Fruit Cakes

There are many types of fruit cakes, ranging from dark and rich to white and delicate. Whatever your preference, there are certain general rules that can be applied to making and baking fruit cakes.

Pans: Fruit cakes may be baked in a variety of shapes and sizes. Loaf pans, tube pans, ring molds, cupcake pans, and coffee cans—all may be used. The important thing to remember is to fill the container not more than three-fourths full. In the recipes that follow, pan sizes have been given as a guide because they influence baking time.

Preparation of pans: Grease the bottom and sides of the pan with soft shortening. Line with several thicknesses of waxed paper or heavy wrapping paper. Allow paper to extend an inch or two above the rim of the pan to protect edges of cake during baking. Grease paper lining well before adding batter.

Baking fruit cakes: Fruit cakes should be baked at a low temperature, usually 250° F. to 300° F. In general, the larger the cake, the lower the temperature should be. Since it is difficult to control ovens at these low temperatures and because of the variations in pan sizes, it is necessary to test the cake for doneness. When a cake is done, a toothpick inserted into the center will come out clean and the top of the cake will spring back easily when touched lightly with a finger. A pan of water placed on a lower rack of the oven during baking will help to keep cakes moist.

Storing fruit cakes: Fruit cakes will cut better and the flavors will mellow and blend if they are made several weeks before using. Cakes must be completely cooled before wrapping and storing. Cool cakes in their pans fifteen to twenty minutes. Lift out cakes and place on cake racks. Pull the paper down from the sides and allow cakes to cool completely. Replace paper and wrap in waxed paper or plastic wrap; overwrap with foil. Store in a tightly covered container in a cool place. A small piece of apple or orange placed in the container with the cake will keep it moist. If desired, pour a little brandy over cakes from time to time during storage. Another method is to wrap the cooled cake in cheesecloth that has been saturated with brandy. Carefully stored fruit cakes will keep for several months. They will keep for a year in the freezer.

Decorating fruit cakes: Fruit cakes may be glazed and decorated as desired with candied fruits, nuts, and cherries just before they are served. For a simple glaze combine ¼ *cup light corn syrup* and *2 tablespoons water.* Bring to a rolling boil; cool to lukewarm. Brush on cold cake; add the desired decoration, and brush again with the warm glaze.

❦ White Fruit Cake

2 cups (1 pound) diced mixed candied fruits and peels
1 cup candied cherries, halved
1 cup (8 ounces) candied pineapple
1 cup golden seedless raisins
1 5-ounce can toasted, slivered almonds
1 3½-ounce can flaked coconut
2 cups sifted all-purpose flour
1½ teaspoons baking powder
1 teaspoon salt
1 cup soft shortening
1 cup sugar
1 teaspoon vanilla extract
5 eggs
½ cup pineapple juice

Prepare two 8½-x-4½-x-2½-inch pans as directed above. Combine the mixed fruits and peels, cherries, pineapple, raisins, almonds, and coconut in a large bowl. Sift together flour, baking powder, and salt. Sprinkle about ¼ cup of the flour mixture over the fruits and toss to coat. Work shortening, sugar, and vanilla together until light and fluffy. Add eggs one at a time, beating well after each addition. Add the remaining dry ingredients alternately with the pineapple juice, blending well after each addition. Pour batter over fruit mixture and blend well. Pour into prepared pans. Heat oven to 275° F. Bake cakes 2 to 2½ hours, or until a toothpick inserted into the center comes out clean. Cool and store as directed on page 842. Makes about 4 pounds of cake.

❦ Extra Rich Dark Fruit Cake

2 cups (1 pound) diced mixed candied fruits and peels
½ cup (4 ounces) candied pineapple
½ cup (4 ounces) candied citron
½ cup (4 ounces) candied cherries
1½ cups seeded raisins
1½ cups seedless raisins

Combine mixed fruits and peels, pineapple, citron, cherries, raisins, and currants in a large bowl. Cut dates, apricots, and prunes into small pieces; combine with candied fruits. Combine whiskey and molasses and pour over fruit mixture. Cover and let stand overnight. In the morning, cover filberts with water; bring to a boil and remove from heat. Drain, rinse in cold water, and slice with a sharp knife. Add to fruits with the pecans and walnuts. Prepare five 8½-x-4½-x-2½-inch or three 9-x-5-x-3-inch pans as directed on page 842. Sift together flour, salt, cinnamon, nutmeg, and allspice. Work

2 cups dried currants
½ cup pitted dates
½ cup dried apricots
½ cup dried pitted prunes
1 cup whiskey
1 cup dark molasses
1½ cups shelled filberts
1½ cups coarsely chopped pecans
2 cups coarsely chopped walnuts
2 cups sifted all-purpose flour
1 teaspoon salt
2 teaspoons ground cinnamon
½ teaspoon ground nutmeg
½ teaspoon ground allspice
1 cup butter or margarine
1 cup firmly packed light brown sugar
¼ cup sugar
8 eggs
1 1-ounce square unsweetened chocolate

butter and sugars together until light and fluffy. Add 3 of the eggs, one at a time, beating well after each addition. Melt the chocolate in the top of a double boiler over simmering water. Add the melted chocolate to the creamed mixture. Add about ⅓ of the flour mixture to the creamed mixture; blend well. Add remaining 5 eggs, one at a time, blending well after each addition. Gradually stir in remaining flour. Add fruit mixture and blend. (The mixture will be very heavy and it may be necessary to mix with the hands until well blended.) Pack mixture into prepared pans, filling each ¾ full. Heat oven to 250° F. Place a pan of hot water on a lower rack of the oven. Bake small loaves about 1½ to 2 hours; large loaves, about 3 hours. Cakes are done when a toothpick inserted into the center comes out clean. Cool and store cakes as directed on page 842. Makes about 8 pounds of cake.

⤳ Bourbon–Pecan Cake

2 cups whole red candied cherries
2 cups golden seedless raisins
2 cups bourbon
2 cups softened butter or margarine
2 cups sugar
2 cups firmly packed dark brown sugar
8 eggs, separated, at room temperature
5 cups sifted all-purpose flour
4 cups pecan halves
1½ teaspoons baking powder
1 teaspoon salt

Combine cherries, raisins, and bourbon in a large mixing bowl. Cover tightly and let stand in the refrigerator overnight. Drain fruits and reserve bourbon. Place butter in the large bowl of an electric mixer and beat on medium speed until light and fluffy. Add sugars gradually, beating on medium speed until well blended. Add egg yolks, beating until well blended. Combine ½ cup of the flour with the pecans. Sift the remaining flour with the baking powder, salt, and nutmeg. Add 2 cups of the flour mixture to the creamed mixture and mix thoroughly. Add the reserved bourbon and the remainder of the flour mixture alternately, ending with flour. Beat well after each addition. Beat egg whites until stiff but not dry; fold gently into cake batter. Add drained fruits and floured pecans to the cake batter; blend thoroughly. Grease a 10-inch tube cake pan; line bottom with waxed paper. Grease and lightly flour waxed

2 teaspoons ground nutmeg
Glaze (optional, recipe
    follows)

paper. Pour cake batter into pan to within 1 inch of the top. (The remaining batter may be baked in an 8½-x-4½-x-2½-inch loaf pan, prepared in the same manner as the tube cake pan.) Place in a 275° F. oven; bake tube cake about 4 hours and loaf cake about 1½ hours, or until a toothpick inserted in the center of cakes comes out clean. Cool cakes in pans on cake rack about 2 to 3 hours. Remove cakes from pans; peel off waxed paper. Wrap cakes in cheesecloth saturated with bourbon; then wrap in aluminum foil or plastic wrap and store as directed on page 842. If desired, glaze cake just before serving. Makes one 10-inch tube cake and 1 small loaf cake.

Glaze

If desired, just before serving cake, beat together 1½ *cups confectioners' sugar, 2 tablespoons hot milk,* and ¼ *teaspoon vanilla extract.* Spread over top of cake, allowing some to run down the sides.

✑ Golden Honey Fruit Cake

1 cup (8 ounces) dried
    golden figs
1 cup dried apricots
2 cups golden seedless
    raisins
1 cup dark seedless raisins
1 cup candied cherries,
    halved
1 cup (8 ounces) diced
    candied orange peel
½ cup (4 ounces) diced
    candied lemon peel
1 cup (8 ounces) diced
    candied citron
2 cups (16 ounces) candied
    pineapple
1 5-ounce can toasted,
    slivered almonds
1 cup coarsely chopped
    pecans
1¼ cups soft shortening
1¼ cups honey

Prepare five 8½-x-4½-x-2½-inch or three 9-x-5-x-3-inch pans as directed on page 842. Cover figs and apricots with 2 cups boiling water; let stand 4 minutes and then drain. Clip stems from figs. Dice the figs and the apricots. Rinse and drain raisins. Combine all the fruits, peels, and nuts in a large bowl. Work shortening and honey together thoroughly. Sift together flour, baking powder, salt, and spices. Add part of the flour to the creamed mixture. Add remaining flour and the beaten eggs alternately; blend well. Pour batter over fruit and stir together. Pour into pans. Fill pans ¾ full. Heat oven to 250° F. Place a pan of hot water on a lower rack in the oven. Bake smaller loaves 1½ to 2 hours, larger loaves about 3 hours. Cakes are done when a toothpick inserted in center comes out clean. Cool and store as directed on page 842. Makes about 8 pounds of cake.

(Ingredients continued on page 846)

2½ cups sifted all-purpose
    flour
 1 teaspoon baking powder
1¼ teaspoons salt
 1 teaspoon ground
    cinnamon
¼ teaspoon ground
    nutmeg
¼ teaspoon ground cloves
 6 eggs, well beaten

✍ Refrigerator Fruit Cake

3 cups whole Brazil nuts (2
    pounds unshelled or 1
    pound shelled)
1 13¾-ounce package
    graham cracker crumbs
1 15-ounce package seedless
    raisins
1 cup (8 ounces) diced mixed
    candied fruits and peels
1 8-ounce jar maraschino
    cherries, drained
2 6¼-ounce packages
    miniature marshmallows
½ cup sweet sherry
¼ cup dark molasses
1 teaspoon vanilla extract
¼ teaspoon ground cinnamon
¼ teaspoon ground nutmeg
¼ teaspoon ground cloves
⅛ teaspoon ground allspice
⅛ teaspoon ground ginger

Prepare one 9-x-5-x-3-inch or two 7½-x-3½-x-2¼-inch loaf pans as directed on page 842. Combine whole nuts, graham cracker crumbs, raisins, mixed fruits and peels, and whole drained cherries in a large bowl. Place marshmallows, sherry, molasses, vanilla, and spices in the top of a double boiler. Stir over boiling water until marshmallows are melted. Pour over nut–fruit mixture and stir until blended. Pack tightly into prepared pan. Cover top with waxed paper and refrigerate at least one week before slicing. Keep unused cake refrigerated. Makes about 4 pounds of cake.

Little Cakes

For tea parties and coffee-and-dessert gatherings, small petits fours or decorated cupcakes make a pretty plate of sweets for nibbling. Any of the one-bowl cakes (pages 823 to 825) make excellent cupcakes. If the cake makes two 8-inch layers, you'll get about twenty-four 2½-inch cupcakes. If the cakes makes two 9-inch layers, you'll get about 30 cupcakes.

✑ Tea Cakes

2½ cups sifted cake flour
  3 teaspoons baking powder
  1 teaspoon salt
 ¾ cup soft shortening
1⅓ cups sugar
1½ teaspoons vanilla extract
  1 cup milk
  5 egg whites, at room temperature
 ⅓ cup sugar
Vanilla Petits Fours Frosting (recipe follows)

Heat oven to 375° F. Grease two 8-inch-square pans; line with waxed paper; grease and flour paper. Sift flour, baking powder, and salt together three times. Cream shortening and the 1⅓ cups sugar in a large bowl; beat until blended. Add vanilla; beat well. Add sifted dry ingredients to shortening mixture alternately with milk. Add about one fourth of the flour mixture at a time; begin and end with it. Beat well after each addition. In another bowl beat egg whites until soft peaks form. Gradually add the ⅓ cup sugar; beat only until stiff peaks form. Fold beaten whites into batter. Pour equal amounts of batter into each of the prepared pans. Bake 30 to 35 minutes, or until top springs back when lightly touched with finger. Remove from oven; cool on a wire cake rack 10 minutes before removing from pans. Prepare Vanilla Petits Fours Frosting. Cut each cake layer into 36 small squares and place on wire racks over cookie sheets. Pour frosting over top and sides of cake squares. Remove frosting that drips on cookie sheets and reheat in top of double boiler over hot water until softened. If desired, a few drops of food coloring may be added to tint all or part of the frosting. Garnish tops of cakes with chocolate pieces, cherries, coconut, or nuts, as desired. Makes 6 dozen cakes.

Vanilla Petits Fours Frosting

4 cups granulated sugar
2 cups water
¼ teaspoon cream of tartar
2 to 3 cups confectioners' sugar
1 teaspoon vanilla or almond extract
Chocolate pieces
Candied cherries
Toasted coconut
Finely chopped nuts

Place granulated sugar, water, and cream of tartar in top of double boiler. Mix and stir over moderate heat (about 250° F.) until sugar is dissolved. Cook without stirring until a candy thermometer registers 232° F. Cool to 110° F. (lukewarm). Gradually add 2 cups of the confectioners' sugar and beat until blended. Stir in vanilla. If frosting is too thin, gradually add the remaining 1 cup confectioners' sugar until frosting is of pouring consistency (about like heavy cream). Place pan over hot water.

CAKES

To frost Petits Fours: Arrange cake pieces on wire rack set on waxed paper or a cookie sheet. Pour frosting over cakes.

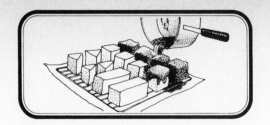

✑ Apricot Party Cakes

1 17-ounce package
  pound cake mix
1 cup dried apricots
1 cup water
¼ cup sugar
½ cup chopped candied
  red cherries
2 teaspoons finely chopped
  candied ginger
¾ cup fluffy frosting mix
  (approximately half a
  6½-ounce package)
¼ cup boiling water

Heat oven to 325° F. Prepare pound-cake batter as directed on package. Pour batter into greased and floured 15½-x-10½-x-1-inch jelly-roll pan. Bake about 25 minutes, until a toothpick inserted in the center comes out clean. Place pan on rack and cool about 10 minutes. Turn cake out on breadboard and cool thoroughly. Combine apricots, water, and sugar in saucepan. Cover and cook over moderately low heat (about 225° F.) about 30 minutes, until apricots are soft. Mash apricots with a spoon and stir in cherries and ginger. Cut pound cake into rounds, using a 1¾-inch fluted or plain cookie cutter. Split rounds. Spread filling lightly between the layers. Prepare fluffy frosting according to package directions, using about half the package and ¼ cup boiling water. Frost tops of filled cakes. Sprinkle with chopped nuts, if desired. Makes 36 party cakes.

✑ Glazed Gingerbread Cupcakes

2½ cups sifted all-purpose
  flour
1½ teaspoons baking soda
1 teaspoon ground
  cinnamon
1 teaspoon ground ginger
½ teaspoon salt
½ cup sugar
1 egg, slightly beaten
½ cup melted butter or
  margarine
½ cup light molasses
½ cup honey

Heat oven to 350° F. Sift together flour, baking soda, cinnamon, ginger, and salt. Combine sugar and egg in a large mixing bowl and beat well. Add melted butter. Combine molasses, honey, and the 1 cup hot water. Add sifted dry ingredients and molasses mixture alternately to butter mixture. Blend well after each addition. Place paper muffin cups in muffin pans. Pour gingerbread batter into paper cups, half-filling each. Bake about 25 minutes, or until top springs back when lightly touched with finger. While cupcakes are baking, combine confectioners' sugar, cocoa, the 1 tablespoon water, and vanilla. Spread frosting on cupcakes while they are still warm. Makes about 2 dozen cupcakes.

1 cup hot water
Paper muffin cups
  ¾ cup sifted confectioners'
    sugar
1½ tablespoons unsweetened
    cocoa
  1 tablespoon hot water
  ¼ teaspoon vanilla extract

Cakes Made from Mixes

The excellent cake mixes on the market make it perfectly possible to turn out a very good cake with very little time and work. And you don't have to sacrifice creativity. Your cake can be an individual creation. In this section you'll find many recipes for a variety of cakes that all start with a mix—including a towering wedding cake.

✎ Angel Food Cake Surprise

1 package angel food cake
  mix
1 3-ounce package
  strawberry-flavored
  gelatin
1¾ cups boiling water
1 2-ounce package whipped
  topping mix

Prepare cake mix; bake and cool in pan according to package directions. Dissolve gelatin in boiling water and chill until slightly thickened. Beat with electric mixer until light and fluffy. Prepare dessert topping mix according to package directions and fold into gelatin. Place cake on serving plate and cut a 1-inch slice from top of cake and reserve. Cut a circle 1 inch from outer edge of cake and to a depth within 1 inch of bottom of cake. Cut a second circle around center of cake. Carefully remove cake to form a shell. Tear the removed cake into small pieces. Pour a layer of strawberry mixture into cake shell. Top with cake pieces. Pour in remaining filling. Chill 1 hour. Place top of cake over filling and chill several hours, until completely set. Serves 12.

✎ Ice-Cream-Filled Cake

1 package chiffon cake mix
1½ quarts vanilla-fudge ice
  cream

Heat oven to temperature called for on cake-mix package. Prepare, bake, and cool cake according to package directions for a 10-inch tube pan. Place cooled cake up-

CAKES

1 4½-ounce container
  frozen whipped topping,
  thawed
2 tablespoons quick
  chocolate-flavored mix
1 tablespoon brandy

side down on a freezerproof serving plate. Cut a horizontal slice about 1 inch thick from the top and set it aside. About 1 inch in from the outer edge of the cake, cut down into the cake to about 1 inch from the bottom. Continue this circular cut all around the cake. Repeat the same cut 1 inch in from the center edge. Using a spoon, carefully scoop out the cake from this cut area. Fill cavity with ice cream; replace top slice. Blend together whipped topping, chocolate mix, and brandy. Frost sides and top of cake. Freeze overnight. Makes one 10-inch cake. Serves 12.

How to fill a tube cake: Place the cooled cake upside down on a serving plate. Cut a horizontal slice about 1 inch thick from the top and set it aside. Starting about 1 inch in from the outer edge of the cake, cut down into the cake carefully, using a sharp-pointed knife; stop at a point about 1 inch from the bottom of the cake. (You determine this both by eye and by "feel.") Continue this circular cut all around the cake. Make a similar circular cuts into the cake 1 inch from the center rim. Using a serving spoon, carefully scoop out the cake from this cut area.

Fill the cavity in the cake with the filling you're using, and run a spatula through the filling to break up air bubbles. Replace the top slice and frost the sides and top.

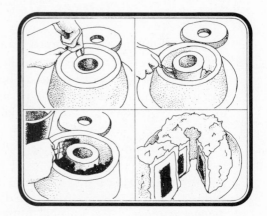

❧ Apricot Trifle

1 package yellow cake mix
¼ to ½ cup sweet sherry
⅓ cup apricot preserves,
  heated
2 3-ounce packages egg
  custard mix
1 cup heavy cream
1 teaspoon vanilla extract
2 teaspoons sugar

Heat oven to temperature called for on cake-mix package. Prepare, bake, and cool cake according to package directions for a 13-x-9-inch cake. When cake is thoroughly cooled, cut down the center of the cake lengthwise to form 2 long halves. Cut each half into 8 pieces approximately 4 x 1½ inches. Arrange these pieces back into the original shape of the cake in a decorative 3-quart casserole. Pour sherry over the cake pieces; spoon on heated apricot preserves. Prepare custard mix according to package directions and pour over all. Chill until the custard is set. Whip cream, vanilla, and sugar together until mixture holds its shape; spread over trifle and decorate as desired. Serves 16.

✺ Broiled Nut-Topped Cake

*1 package yellow cake mix
(1-layer size)
½ cup firmly packed brown
sugar
½ cup flaked coconut
½ cup coarsely chopped nuts
¼ teaspoon ground
cinnamon
¼ cup melted butter or
margarine
2 tablespoons milk
Whipped cream or ice cream

Heat oven, prepare cake as directed. Turn into a greased and floured 8-inch-square cake pan. Bake according to package directions. Meanwhile in a mixing bowl mix together sugar, coconut, nuts, and cinnamon. Stir in butter and milk. When cake is done, remove from oven and immediately spread nut mixture over top. Broil in preheated broiler 4 inches from source of heat 2 to 3 minutes, or until lightly browned. Let cool 5 to 10 minutes on wire rack. Cut into squares and serve warm with whipped cream or ice cream, as desired. Serves 6 to 8.

*Note: If 1-layer-sized package is not available, use a regular-sized cake mix package. Bake two 8-inch layers and freeze one for future use.

✺ Quick Blitz Torte

5 egg whites, at room
temperature
1¼ cups sugar
1 package yellow cake mix
¾ cup sliced blanched
almonds
Velvet Chocolate Filling
(recipe follows)

Heat oven to 350° F. Grease three 9-inch round cake pans and line with waxed paper; grease and flour paper. Beat egg whites with an electric mixer until soft peaks form. Gradually add sugar and beat until stiff peaks form. Prepare cake mix according to package directions. Pour ⅓ of the batter into each pan. Carefully spread meringue evenly over batter in each pan, spreading a small amount at a time. Sprinkle each layer with almonds. Bake 30 minutes. Cool cakes on a wire rack for 8 minutes before removing from pans. Carefully cut around edges of each pan to loosen cake and invert onto a cake rack. Peel off waxed paper; place another cake rack on bottom of layer and turn it right side up. Cool layers thoroughly on cake racks. Stack layers, meringue side up, with Velvet Chocolate Filling between the first and second layers. Leave top of top layer plain. Serves 10.

Velvet Chocolate Filling

2 4-ounce bars sweet cooking
chocolate
7 tablespoons water
5 egg yolks
1 tablespoon butter or
margarine
1 teaspoon vanilla extract

Break chocolate into large pieces and place in top of a double boiler. Add water and place over simmering water until chocolate is melted, stirring occasionally. Beat egg yolks until thick and lemon-colored. Gradually add chocolate mixture and butter; beat until blended. Pour back into top of double boiler and cook over simmering water, stirring constantly, for about 5 minutes, or until filling is smooth and thickened. Stir in vanilla. Cool and spread between layers. Makes 1½ cups.

✑ Quick Dobos Torte

1 package yellow cake mix
⅓ cup sugar
1 can ready-to-spread
   chocolate frosting
1 cup heavy cream, whipped

Heat oven to temperature called for on cake-mix package. Prepare, bake, and cool cake according to package directions for two 8-inch layers. Cut each layer in half horizontally. Place top layer on a cake rack. In a small heavy saucepan and using a wooden spoon, dissolve sugar over moderately low heat (do not use controlled-heat burner; steady heat is required), stirring constantly, until sugar has melted to a rich golden brown syrup, about 15 minutes. Pour and spread quickly over top layer. Working quickly with a heated knife before the syrup hardens, score the cake top into the desired number of serving wedges (8 to 10). In a bowl combine chocolate frosting and whipped cream. Assemble cake with about ½ cup of this mixture between the layers, ending with the scored top layer. Frost sides and decorate top edge of cake with remaining chocolate mixture. Makes one 8-inch cake.

✑ High Boston Cream Pie

1 package yellow cake mix
⅓ cup sugar
3 tablespoons cornstarch
⅛ teaspoon salt
1½ cups milk
1 egg, slightly beaten
¾ teaspoon rum extract
2 1-ounce squares
   semisweet chocolate
1 tablespoon butter or
   margarine
1 egg yolk, slightly beaten
1 tablespoon light corn
   syrup

Heat oven to temperature called for on cake-mix package. Prepare, bake, and cool cake according to package directions for two 8-inch layers. Meanwhile mix together sugar, cornstarch, and salt in a saucepan. Gradually stir in milk. Place over moderately low heat (about 225° F.) and bring to a boil, stirring constantly; boil ½ minute, stirring constantly. Gradually stir some of the hot mixture into beaten egg. Return to mixture in saucepan and cook until thickened, stirring constantly, about 3 to 5 minutes. Remove from heat and stir in rum extract. Turn into a bowl and place a sheet of waxed paper directly on the surface of the cream mixture. Thoroughly chill. Cut each cake layer in half horizontally. Assemble layers with about ⅔ cup cream filling between layers. Melt chocolate and butter in top of a double boiler over simmering water. Beat chocolate mixture into egg yolk. Stir in corn syrup. Spread frosting over top layer. Chill. Makes one 8-inch cake. Serves 8 to 10.

❧ Lord Baltimore Cake

1 package yellow cake mix
½ cup light corn syrup
½ cup sugar
2 egg whites, at room temperature
Few grains salt
¼ teaspoon cream of tartar
1 teaspoon vanilla extract
½ cup dry macaroon crumbs
¼ cup chopped pecans
¼ teaspoon orange extract
¼ cup chopped blanched almonds
12 candied cherries, cut into quarters
1 teaspoon lemon juice
1½ cups dry macaroon crumbs
Red food coloring (optional)
Candied cherry halves (optional)

Prepare cake according to package directions, using two 8-inch round cake pans. Cool cake completely. Combine corn syrup and sugar in a small saucepan. Cook over moderate heat (about 250° F.), stirring constantly, until sugar dissolves and bubbles appear around edge of pan. Remove from heat. Place egg whites, salt, and cream of tartar in a small bowl; beat with rotary beater, or electric mixer set on high speed, until almost stiff. Gradually pour in hot syrup in a thin stream, beating constantly. Add vanilla and beat 3 to 5 minutes, until frosting stands in stiff peaks. In a bowl combine the ½ cup macaroon crumbs, pecans, orange extract, almonds, cherries, and lemon juice. To this mixture add ⅓ of the frosting and mix well. Place one cake layer bottom side up on a large plate. Spread with the macaroon filling. Top with the other layer, right side up. Frost top and sides with remaining frosting. Pat the 1½ cups macaroon crumbs onto side of cake. If desired, frosting may be tinted with a few drops of red food coloring and the top of the cake decorated with additional candied cherry halves.

❧ Chocolate Nut Cake

1 package devil's food cake mix
1 cup miniature marshmallows
½ cup coarsely chopped nuts
½ cup sugar
1 tablespoon milk

Heat oven to temperature called for on cake-mix package. Grease generously and flour a 10-inch Bundt pan or a 10-inch tube pan; set aside. Prepare cake mix according to package directions; stir in marshmallows and nuts and turn into prepared pan. Bake 50 minutes, or until a cake tester or toothpick inserted in the center comes out clean. Cool 5 minutes. Turn out cake onto a wire rack. Mix together sugar and milk and drizzle over top of warm cake. Cool. Makes one 10-inch cake.

❧ Double Chocolate Frosted Cake

4 1-ounce squares semisweet chocolate
1 14-ounce can sweetened condensed milk

Heat oven to temperature called for on cake-mix package. Grease bottom and sides of two 9-inch round cake pans. Line bottom of each pan with waxed paper; grease the paper. In top of a double boiler melt chocolate over

2 tablespoons butter or
margarine
1 package devil's food cake
mix

simmering water over low heat (about 200° F.). Gradually stir in milk. Add butter and heat, stirring constantly, until butter is melted and mixture is well blended. Remove from heat and pour half into each cake pan. Set aside. Prepare cake mix according to package directions and pour batter over chocolate mixture. Bake according to package directions. Cool in pan on a wire rack 10 minutes. Turn one layer upside down on a serving plate; peel off waxed paper. Top with second layer, chocolate side up. Makes one 9-inch cake.

Lemon Bundt Cake

1 package lemon or white
cake mix
1 4-serving-size package
instant lemon pudding
4 eggs
½ cup vegetable oil
1 cup water
1⅓ cups confectioners' sugar
5 tablespoons lemon juice
⅓ cup flaked coconut

Heat oven to just below 350° F. Grease and flour a heavy Bundt pan or a 10-inch tube pan. Place cake mix, instant pudding, eggs, vegetable oil, and the water in the large bowl of an electric mixer. Beat at medium speed for 2 or 3 minutes, scraping the bowl occasionally with a rubber spatula. Pour into prepared pan and bake 35 minutes. Cool on a wire rack for about 5 minutes before removing from pan. Blend together sugar and lemon juice; stir in coconut. Spoon frosting over top and sides of warm cake, covering as much of the cake as possible. Cake will keep moist for several days. Serves 10.

Chocolate-Raspberry Ripple Cake

Butter or margarine
1 17-ounce package
pound cake mix
2 teaspoons vanilla extract
2 squares (2 ounces)
semisweet chocolate,
coarsely grated
¾ cup red raspberry
preserves

Use butter to lightly grease a 9-inch square baking pan. Heat oven to temperature called for on cake-mix package. Prepare cake mix according to package directions. Stir in vanilla and grated chocolate and turn batter into prepared pan. Drop spoonfuls of the preserves over the batter, and with a knife cut through batter several times to create a marble effect. Bake 60 to 65 minutes, until center of cake springs back when touched lightly with a finger. Remove from oven and let cool at least 30 minutes before serving. Cut cake in squares and serve from pan.

Wedding Cake

8 17-ounce packages
pound cake mix

Two or three days before wedding: Grease two or three 13-x-9-x-2-inch cake pans and two or three 9-

Lemon Filling (recipe follows)
Wedding Cake Icing (recipe follows)

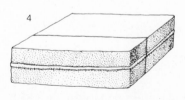

inch-square pans. Line bottoms with waxed paper and grease and flour paper. In a large bowl prepare 3 packages of the pound cake mix, using ingredients and directions called for on the package. In another bowl prepare 2 more packages. Mix batter from both batches together. Measure and pour about 5¾ cups of the batter into each of the larger prepared pans. If only 2 large pans are available, store remaining batter, well covered, in refrigerator while the first 2 cakes are baking. Bake at oven temperature given on cake-mix package for 65 to 70 minutes. Cool on wire rack for about 10 minutes before removing from pans. If there is any leftover batter, bake as soon as possible. Prepare remaining 3 packages of pound cake mix. Measure and pour about 3⅓ cups of the batter into each of the prepared 9-inch-square pans. Keep extra batter chilled if you do not have 3 pans. Bake 55 to 60 minutes. Cool cakes thoroughly; wrap and store in a covered container until ready to ice. There will be 6 cake layers: three 13-x-9-x-2-inch layers and three 9-inch-square layers. Day before wedding: Trim tops of cake layers, if necessary, so that they are all level. Spread Lemon Filling on one of the 13-x-9-x-2-inch layers. Top with another large layer (see drawing 1). Cut remaining large layer in half lengthwise, giving two 13-x-4½-inch layers (see drawing 2); spread one with filling and stack these two layers. Set aside. Spread filling on one of the 9-inch-square layers. Top with another 9-inch square. Cut remaining 9-inch-square layer into quarters (see drawing 3). Put 2 of the quarters together with filling between. Set aside. The two remaining quarters may be used for practice with decorating tube. Place the 13-x-9-inch layers and the 13-x-4½-inch layers side by side to form a 13-inch-square cake on a large tray, heavy cardboard, or a piece of wood (see drawing 4). Frost sides and top with a smooth layer of Wedding Cake Icing. If necessary, smooth with a spatula dipped in boiling water. Place the 9-inch-square layers in center of bottom layer for the second tier (see drawing 5). Frost top and sides. Top with the 4½-inch-square layers for third tier and frost top and sides. With a decorating bag and fancy tips use remaining icing to decorate edges and sides of cake as desired. Add bride and groom figures to top tier, if desired. If necessary, add a little confectioners' sugar to the icing to give proper consistency for pressing through decorating tube. To serve, cut layers separately. Serves 50.

Lemon Filling

3 cups sugar
⅔ cup cornstarch
1½ teaspoons salt
3 cups boiling water
6 tablespoons grated lemon
peel
1½ cups lemon juice
6 tablespoons butter or
margarine

Combine sugar, cornstarch, and salt in a large saucepan. Stir in boiling water, lemon peel, and lemon juice. Bring to a full boil over moderate heat (about 250° F.); reduce heat slightly and boil 1 minute, or until thickened and clear. Stir in butter. Let cool to room temperature before spreading between cake layers. If mixture is not smooth when ready to use, beat with a rotary beater. Makes enough to fill one and a half 13-x-9-inch layer cakes and one and a half 9-inch-square layer cakes.

Wedding Cake Icing

¾ cup soft shortening
¾ teaspoon salt
6 16-ounce packages
confectioners' sugar
8 egg whites (1 cup)
¾ cup milk
1 tablespoon lemon extract

Work shortening and salt together in a large bowl of electric mixer until light and fluffy. Add 1 cup of the sugar and beat until well blended. Add remaining sugar alternately with unbeaten egg whites and milk. Beat until icing is of good spreading consistency. Add lemon extract and additional milk, if necessary, to make icing the right consistency for spreading. While frosting cake keep bowl covered with a damp cloth. Makes enough to frost wedding cake with some icing left over for decorating.

Cake Frostings and Glazes

Butter Cream Frosting

⅓ cup soft butter or
margarine
1 teaspoon vanilla extract
⅛ teaspoon salt
3 cups unsifted
confectioners' sugar
2 to 3 tablespoons milk

Cream together butter, vanilla, and salt. Gradually add 1 cup of the sugar and beat until blended. Add 2 tablespoons milk and the remaining sugar; beat until frosting has a smooth spreading consistency. Add the remaining milk if frosting is too thick to spread. Makes enough frosting to fill and frost two 8- or 9-inch cake layers or one 13-x-9-inch cake or one 10-inch tube cake.

Almond Butter-Cream Frosting

Substitute ½ teaspoon almond extract for vanilla.

Browned Butter-Cream Frosting

Heat butter in a saucepan over moderate heat (about 250° F.) until a delicate brown, before using in Butter Cream Frosting. Increase milk in recipe to 4 to 5 tablespoons to give the proper spreading consistency.

Cherry Butter-Cream Frosting

Stir *2 tablespoons drained chopped maraschino cherries* and *2 drops red food coloring* into frosting.

Chocolate Butter-Cream Frosting

Blend *6 tablespoons unsweetened cocoa* or *two 1-ounce squares melted unsweetened chocolate* into creamed butter; increase milk to 4 to 5 tablespoons.

Coffee Butter-Cream Frosting

Add *2 teaspoons instant coffee powder* with sugar.

Maple-Nut Butter-Cream Frosting

Substitute *½ cup maple-flavored syrup* for vanilla and milk in above recipe; stir in ¼ *cup finely chopped nuts.*

Mocha Butter-Cream Frosting

Blend *¼ cup unsweetened cocoa* and *1 teaspoon instant coffee powder* into creamed butter; use 3 to 4 tablespoons milk.

Orange or Lemon Butter-Cream Frosting

Omit vanilla extract and substitute *orange* or *lemon juice* for milk; stir in *2 teaspoons grated orange peel* or ½ *teaspoon grated lemon peel.*

Peanut Butter-Cream Frosting

Substitute *creamy peanut butter* for butter; increase milk to ¼ to ⅓ cup.

Peppermint Butter-Cream Frosting

Substitute a *few drops peppermint extract* for vanilla in recipe. If desired, add a *few drops green* or *red food coloring.*

CAKES

✑ Caramel Frosting

⅔ cup butter or margarine
1¼ cups firmly packed brown
    sugar
Few grains salt
⅓ cup milk
2 cups confectioners' sugar

Melt butter in a small saucepan over moderately low heat (about 225° F.). Add brown sugar and salt; cook, stirring constantly, until smooth, about 2 minutes. Add milk; continue heating and stirring until mixture boils. Cool to room temperature. Gradually add confectioners' sugar. Beat until well blended with rotary beater or electric mixer. If frosting is too thin, add a little more confectioners' sugar, 1 tablespoon at a time. Makes enough frosting to fill and frost tops and sides of two 8-inch square or round cake layers.

✑ Quick Caramel Frosting

⅓ cup butter or margarine
1 cup firmly packed dark
    brown sugar
2 tablespoons water
3 tablespoons milk
1 teaspoon vanilla extract
3¼ cups confectioners'
    sugar

Mix butter, brown sugar, and water in a saucepan. Place over moderate heat (about 250° F.) and stir constantly until mixture comes to a boil; boil 1 minute. Remove from heat; stir in milk and vanilla. Gradually add sugar, stirring constantly until smooth. Cool to spreading consistency. Makes enough frosting to fill and frost two 9-inch layers.

✑ Four-Minute Fudge Frosting

⅔ cup undiluted evaporated
    milk
1⅔ cups sugar
½ teaspoon salt
1½ cups miniature
    marshmallows
1 6-ounce package
    semisweet chocolate
    pieces
1 teaspoon vanilla extract
1 cup finely chopped nuts

Combine milk, sugar, and salt in a saucepan. Heat to boiling point (do not use temperature-controlled burner), stirring constantly. Reduce heat and simmer 4 minutes. Remove from heat. Add remaining ingredients. Stir until mixture is smooth. Chill to spreading consistency. Fills and frosts two 9-inch layers.

✑ Hungarian Frosting

3 1-ounce squares
    unsweetened chocolate

Melt chocolate in top of a double boiler over hot water. Combine melted chocolate with sugar and the boiling

1½ cups confectioners' sugar
2½ tablespoons boiling water
3 egg yolks
¼ cup soft butter or margarine

water in the small bowl of an electric mixer. Add egg yolks one at a time, beating well after each addition. Add butter, 1 tablespoon at a time. Beat until smooth and the right consistency for spreading. Makes enough frosting to fill and frost tops and sides of two 8- or 9-inch layers.

Lemon Cream-Cheese Frosting

1 3-ounce package cream cheese, at room temperature
5 teaspoons lemon juice
3 cups confectioners' sugar
1 tablespoon finely grated lemon peel

Blend cheese and lemon juice with an electric mixer at low speed or by hand. Gradually add sugar and beat until well blended. Add lemon peel; beat at medium speed until frosting has a smooth spreading consistency. If frosting is too thick, add a little more lemon juice, a teaspoonful at a time. Makes enough frosting to fill and frost two 8- or 9-inch cake layers or one 13-x-9-inch cake.

Swirl Frosting

½ cup light corn syrup
½ cup sugar
2 egg whites, at room temperature
Few grains salt
¼ teaspoon cream of tartar
1 teaspoon vanilla extract

Combine syrup and sugar in a small saucepan. Cook over moderate heat (about 250° F.), stirring constantly, until sugar dissolves and bubbles appear around edge of pan. Remove from heat. Place egg whites, salt, and cream of tartar in a small bowl; beat with rotary beater or electric mixer set on high speed until almost stiff. Gradually pour in hot syrup in a thin stream, beating constantly. Add vanilla and beat 3 to 5 minutes, until frosting stands in stiff peaks and appears less shiny. Makes enough frosting to fill and frost two 8- or 9-inch cake layers.

Maple Swirl Frosting

Substitute *dark corn syrup* for light corn syrup. In place of the 1 teaspoon vanilla extract, use ½ *teaspoon vanilla extract* and ½ *teaspoon maple flavoring*.

White Mountain Frosting

½ cup sugar
¼ cup light corn syrup
2 tablespoons water
2 egg whites, at room temperature

Combine sugar, corn syrup, and water in a small saucepan. Cover and place over moderate heat (about 250° F.) until mixture just starts to boil. Uncover and boil rapidly without stirring until a candy thermometer registers 242° F. (or until a small amount of mixture spins a 6- to

1 teaspoon vanilla extract

8-inch thread). As mixture boils beat egg whites with an electric mixer at medium speed until stiff peaks form. Gradually pour in hot syrup in a thin stream and beat at medium speed until all the syrup is added. Add vanilla and continue beating at high speed until stiff peaks form. Makes enough frosting to fill and frost two 8- or 9-inch cake layers or one 13-x-9-inch cake.

Lady Baltimore Frosting

After preparing White Mountain Frosting, fold in ½ *cup chopped seedless raisins,* ¾ *cup chopped pecans,* and ¼ *cup chopped candied cherries.*

Cocoa Whipped Cream

Sift together ½ *cup confectioners' sugar* and *6 tablespoons unsweetened cocoa.* Stir into *1 pint heavy cream.* Chill at least two hours. Whip until stiff. Makes enough to frost one 10-inch tube cake or to fill and frost two 9-inch layers.

Peppermint Glaze

⅓ *cup water*
1 teaspoon cornstarch
2 cups confectioners' sugar
Few grains salt
½ *teaspoon peppermint*
   extract
Few drops red food coloring

Combine water and cornstarch in a small saucepan. Heat over moderately low heat (about 225° F.), stirring constantly, until clear and thickened. Cool. Stir in sugar, salt, peppermint extract, and food coloring. Spread immediately over cake in a thin layer. Makes enough glaze for one 10-inch tube angel food or sponge cake.

CHAPTER XXIV

COOKIES

The job of having fresh cookies on hand has been so simplified by the packaged mixes, the refrigerated slice-and-bake varieties, and the enormous selection of packaged ready-to-eat cookies that one might wonder why anyone would want to make cookies at home. There are reasons: Cookies are very easy to make, and a fresh, homemade batch can provide a family treat with little effort. For tea parties, for a remembrance from home, for birthdays, and holiday entertaining homemade cookies that have become family favorites are a delightful way to express your individual touch.

Cookie sheets: These are metal baking sheets that have no sides; they do come Teflon-coated so that no greasing is necessary. Do not use a jelly-roll pan for baking cookies; it may warp. Cookie sheets should be at least two inches narrower and shorter than your oven so that heat can circulate freely and cookies will brown evenly. They should be clean and shiny bright (unless Teflon-coated). Since cookies brown more evenly when you bake only one sheet at a time in the middle of the oven, you can get by with one cookie sheet, although it's faster to have two so that you can fill one while the other is baking. Also, placing some types of cookies on a hot baking sheet will spoil their shapes. If you have only one pan, cut several lengths of aluminum foil to fit the baking sheet and arrange unbaked cookies on it—then you can slide foil and all onto the hot pan and put it in the oven.

Mixing cookies: Get out all the ingredients you plan to use before you start mixing. Many cookie recipes call for *soft* shortening. This means to use a solid shortening that has been allowed to stand at room temperature until it will cream easily either by hand or with an electric mixer. If you are mixing by hand, use a wooden spoon with a long handle to make thorough mixing easier.

Baking cookies: The only danger in baking cookies is that they bake in such a short time that it's easy to forget them. If you have a timer with a bell, set it for the least amount of baking time given in the recipe. Without a timer, you'll have to be a clock watcher.

Cooling cookies: Cookies should be cooled on cake racks in a single layer. Never stack cookies until they are completely cool or they may stick together.

Storing cookies: Bar cookies may be stored in their own baking pan; cover them when cool with aluminum foil or plastic wrap. Soft cookies can be stored, when completely cool, in a container with a tight-fitting cover. Crisp cookies will keep best in a container with a loose-fitting cover. Cookies to be wrapped as gifts or mailed should not be packed until completely cool. See our suggestions on pages 891 to 892 for gift wrapping and mailing cookies.

Bar Cookies

These are indeed the easiest cookies to make. They need no shaping, bake in one pan, and are delicious little cakes. If there were no other bar cookies, they would still deserve a category of their own because of brownies.

✑ Fudge Brownies

¾ **cup sifted all-purpose flour**
1 **cup sugar**
7 **tablespoons unsweetened cocoa**
½ **teaspoon baking powder**
¾ **teaspoon salt**
⅔ **cup soft shortening**
2 **eggs**
1 **teaspoon vanilla extract**
1 **tablespoon dark corn syrup**
1 **cup coarsely chopped nuts (optional)**

Heat oven to 350° F. Into the large bowl of an electric mixer, sift together flour, sugar, cocoa, baking powder, and salt. Add shortening, eggs, vanilla, and corn syrup. Mix 2 minutes at medium speed. Stir in nuts. Pour into a greased 8-inch-square cake pan. Bake 40 to 45 minutes. Cool 10 minutes before removing from pan. Cut into 25 squares.

🦢 Peanut Butter–Coconut Brownies

1 cup sifted all-purpose
  flour
¾ teaspoon baking powder
¼ teaspoon baking soda
½ teaspoon salt
3 eggs
1⅓ cups firmly packed brown
  sugar
⅓ cup melted butter or
  margarine
½ cup chunk-style peanut
  butter
1 teaspoon vanilla extract
½ cup flaked coconut

Heat oven to 350° F. Grease and flour a 13-x-9-x-2-inch pan. Sift together flour, baking powder, baking soda, and salt. Beat eggs in a medium-sized bowl until thick and lemon-colored. Gradually add sugar, beating until thick. Add butter, peanut butter, and vanilla; mix well. Fold in sifted dry ingredients and coconut. Pour into prepared pan. Bake 25 to 30 minutes. Cool in pan before cutting into 1⅜-x-2⅜-inch bars. Remove carefully from pan. Makes 30 bars.

🦢 Almond–Jam Bars

1½ cups sifted all-purpose
  flour
½ teaspoon baking powder
½ teaspoon ground
  cinnamon
¼ teaspoon ground cloves
½ teaspoon salt
½ cup softened butter or
  margarine
½ cup sugar
1 egg
¼ cup milk
¼ teaspoon vanilla extract
½ teaspoon almond extract
¾ cup strawberry jam

Heat oven to 400° F. Grease and flour a 9-inch-square cake pan. Sift together flour, baking powder, cinnamon, cloves, and salt. Work butter in a bowl until creamy; add sugar and beat until fluffy. Add egg, milk, and vanilla and almond extracts; beat until blended. Mix in sifted dry ingredients. Spread a third of batter evenly over bottom of pan. Spread strawberry jam over batter for a second layer; top with remaining batter. Bake 25 to 30 minutes, or until lightly browned. Cool in pan and cut into 1⅜-x-2⅛-inch bars. Makes 2 dozen bars.

🦢 Butterscotch–Chocolate Bars

¼ cup softened butter or
  margarine
1 cup sifted all-purpose flour
¼ teaspoon salt
2 eggs
¾ cup firmly packed brown
  sugar

Heat oven to 375° F. Grease an 8-inch-square cake pan; line with waxed paper; grease and flour the paper. Work butter in a bowl until creamy; add the 1 cup flour and the ¼ teaspoon salt and mix until blended. Spread mixture evenly in prepared pan. Bake 15 minutes. Beat eggs well; gradually add sugar and beat until blended. Stir in ¾ cup of the chocolate pieces, coconut, and va-

COOKIES

1 6-ounce package semisweet chocolate pieces
1 teaspoon vanilla extract
½ cup flaked coconut
2 tablespoons flour
¼ teaspoon salt
Orange Frosting (recipe follows)

nilla. Add the 2 tablespoons flour and the ¼ teaspoon salt; mix well. Spread over baked layer and continue to bake 15 minutes. Cool slightly and remove from pan. When cool, frost with Orange Frosting. Melt the remaining chocolate pieces in top of double boiler over hot, not boiling, water. Dip a spatula in the chocolate and draw lines ½ inch apart in one direction on frosting. With a clean spatula or knife draw lines ½ inch apart in the other direction across the chocolate lines to make a decorative pattern. Cut into 1½-x-2½ inch bars. Makes 15 bars.

Orange Frosting

1 tablespoon butter or margarine
½ teaspoon grated orange peel
2 to 3 teaspoons orange juice
¾ cup confectioners' sugar

Blend ingredients together and spread over Butterscotch–Chocolate Bars.

Chocolate–Toffee Bars

½ cup softened butter or margarine
½ cup firmly packed light brown sugar
1 egg
1 teaspoon vanilla extract
½ cup sifted all-purpose flour
½ cup quick-cooking rolled oats
1 6-ounce package semisweet chocolate pieces
½ cup finely chopped nuts

Heat oven to 350° F. Grease and flour a 9-inch-square cake pan. Work butter in a bowl until creamy; add sugar and beat until fluffy. Add egg and vanilla and beat until blended. Add flour and oats; mix well. Spread evenly in prepared pan and bake 20 to 25 minutes. Cool slightly in pan. Melt chocolate pieces in top of double boiler over hot, not boiling, water; spread over top of baked mixture. Sprinkle with nuts. Cool and cut into 1⅜-x-2¾-inch bars. Makes 18 bars.

Dream Bars

½ cup softened butter or margarine
½ cup firmly packed light brown sugar
1 cup sifted all-purpose flour
2 eggs

Heat oven to 350° F. Grease and flour a 9-inch-square cake pan. Work butter in a bowl until creamy; add the ½ cup brown sugar and beat until fluffy. Add the 1 cup flour and mix until crumbly. Pat crumbs firmly into bottom of prepared pan. Bake 20 minutes. Remove from oven and cool slightly. Beat eggs and vanilla well; mix in

1 teaspoon vanilla extract
1 cup firmly packed light
  brown sugar
2 tablespoons flour
½ teaspoon baking powder
¼ teaspoon salt
1 4-ounce can sweetened
  shredded coconut
1 cup chopped pecans

the remaining 1 cup brown sugar, the 2 tablespoons flour, baking powder, and salt. Fold in coconut and pecans; pour over baked layer. Bake 30 to 35 minutes. Cool in pan before cutting into 1⅜-x-2⅛-inch bars. Makes 2 dozen bars.

✍ Fruit Bars

½ cup finely diced dried
  pitted prunes
½ cup finely diced dried
  apricots
1 cup granulated sugar
½ cup dry sherry
¼ cup water
1 cup chopped nuts
1 teaspoon grated lemon
  peel
1 tablespoon lemon juice
1½ cups sifted all-purpose
  flour
1 teaspoon baking soda
¼ teaspoon salt
1 cup firmly packed dark
  brown sugar
1¾ cups quick-cooking rolled
  oats
¾ cup softened butter or
  margarine

Mix prunes, apricots, sugar, sherry, and water in saucepan; bring to a boil and simmer over moderately low heat (about 225° F.) 10 minutes, or until thickened. Remove from heat and add nuts, lemon peel, and lemon juice. Cool. Heat oven to 350° F. Grease and flour a 9-inch-square cake pan. Sift together flour, baking soda, and salt; stir in brown sugar and oats. Add butter and cut in with a pastry blender or two knives until crumbly and evenly mixed. Pour half of crumb mixture into prepared pan; pack tightly over bottom of pan. Spread with fruit mixture; top with remaining crumbs, patting them down firmly. Bake 30 to 35 minutes, or until lightly browned. Cool in pan before cutting into 1⅜-x-2⅛-inch bars. Makes 2 dozen bars.

✍ Lemon–Meringue Bars

½ cup softened butter or
  margarine
½ cup confectioners' sugar
2 egg yolks
1 cup sifted all-purpose flour
¼ cup finely ground almonds
2 teaspoons grated lemon
  peel

Heat oven to 350° F. Grease and flour a 9-inch-square cake pan. Work butter in a bowl until creamy; add confectioners' sugar and beat until fluffy. Add egg yolks, flour, almonds, lemon peel, and salt to creamed mixture; mix well. Spread in prepared pan and bake 10 minutes. Remove from oven and cool slightly. Beat egg whites until soft peaks form. Gradually add granulated sugar and beat until stiff peaks form. Gradually add

¼ teaspoon salt
2 egg whites, at room
   temperature
½ cup granulated sugar
1 tablespoon lemon juice

lemon juice, beating until blended. Spread over baked layer. Bake 25 minutes, or until lightly browned. Cool in pan and cut into 1⅜-x-2⅛-inch bars. Makes 2 dozen bars.

⇜ Raspberry–Crumble Bar Cookies

1⅓ cups sifted all-purpose
    flour
¼ teaspoon baking soda
½ teaspoon ground
   cinnamon
¼ teaspoon salt
¾ cup instant or regular
   whole wheat cereal
⅓ cup firmly packed brown
   sugar
¾ teaspoon grated lemon
   peel
2 3-ounce packages cream
  cheese, at room
  temperature
½ cup softened butter or
   margarine
¾ cup raspberry jam

Heat oven to 350° F. Grease and flour a 9-inch-square cake pan. Sift flour, baking soda, cinnamon, and salt together into a bowl. Stir in cereal, sugar, and lemon peel. Add cheese and butter and cut in with a pastry blender or two knives until crumbly and evenly mixed. Reserve 1 cup of the crumbs. Pour remaining crumbs into prepared pan and pack firmly over bottom of pan. Spread raspberry jam over crumb layer; sprinkle reserved crumbs over jam. Bake 30 minutes, or until crumbs are lightly browned. Cool in pan for 20 minutes before cutting into 1⅜-x-2¾-inch bars. Makes 18 bars.

Drop Cookies

These cookies are quick and easy to make—the best kind to keep in a cookie jar for snacks and lunchtime dessert with a cold glass of milk.

⇜ Vanilla Drop Cookies

2 cups sifted all-purpose
  flour
1½ teaspoons baking powder
¾ teaspoon salt
¾ cup softened butter or
   margarine

Heat oven to 375° F. Sift together flour, baking powder, and salt. Work butter in a bowl until creamy. Add sugar and beat until well blended. Add egg and beat well. Add dry ingredients alternately with milk and vanilla, using ¼ cup of the milk at first, mixing well after each addition. Stir in the additional 4 teaspoons milk if batter is

[866]

1 cup sugar
1 egg
¼ to ⅓ cup milk
1 teaspoon vanilla extract

not the right consistency for dropping. Drop by slightly rounded teaspoonfuls 2 inches apart on greased cookie sheets. Bake 10 to 12 minutes or until edges of cookies are golden brown. Remove to wire cake racks and cool. Makes about 4 dozen cookies.

Chocolate Drops

1¾ cups sifted all-purpose flour
1½ teaspoons baking powder
¼ teaspoon baking soda
⅛ teaspoon ground cloves
¼ teaspoon ground cinnamon
½ teaspoon salt
½ cup soft shortening
1 cup granulated sugar
2 eggs
4 1-ounce squares unsweetened chocolate, melted
1 teaspoon vanilla extract
½ cup milk
Granulated sugar

Heat oven to 375° F. Sift together flour, baking powder, soda, cloves, cinnamon, and salt. Work shortening in a bowl until creamy. Add the 1 cup sugar and beat until well blended. Add eggs one at a time and beat well after each addition. Stir in melted chocolate and vanilla. Add dry ingredients alternately with milk, mixing well after each addition. Drop by slightly rounded teaspoonfuls 2 inches apart on greased cookie sheets. Bake 10 to 15 minutes, until firm to the touch. Remove cookies to a wire rack and sprinkle tops with granulated sugar while they are still hot; or, if preferred, cool completely and frost with a white icing and sprinkle with chopped nuts. Makes about 4½ dozen cookies.

Molasses Drop Cookies

2½ cups sifted all-purpose flour
1 teaspoon ground cinnamon
1 teaspoon ground ginger
¼ teaspoon salt
2 teaspoons baking soda
2 tablespoons hot water
½ cup softened butter or margarine
½ cup sugar
½ cup light molasses
1 egg
6 tablespoons cold water
½ cup dark seedless raisins (optional)

Heat oven to 400° F. Sift together flour, cinnamon, ginger, and salt. Stir baking soda into the hot water and mix until dissolved. Work butter in a bowl until creamy. Add the sugar and molasses and beat until well blended. Add egg and beat well. Stir in baking soda mixture. Add sifted dry ingredients alternately with the cold water, mixing well after each addition. If desired, stir in raisins. Drop by slightly rounded teaspoonfuls, 2 inches apart, on greased cookie sheets. Bake 10 to 12 minutes or until lightly browned. Remove to wire cake racks and cool. Makes about 4½ dozen cookies.

🍃 Coconut Puffs

1 4-ounce can shredded or
  flaked coconut
⅓ cup sweetened condensed
  milk
⅛ teaspoon salt
¼ teaspoon vanilla extract

Heat oven to 350° F. Combine all ingredients in a medium-sized bowl. Stir until well blended. Cover a cookie sheet with brown paper. Drop coconut mixture by teaspoonfuls about 2 inches apart onto brown paper. Bake 15 minutes, or until coconut is lightly browned. Remove cookies immediately from the brown paper with a small spatula; cool on wire rack. Makes about 1½ dozen cookies.

🍃 Coconut Drops

2 eggs
1 cup sugar
3 3½-ounce packages flaked
  coconut
¼ cup sifted all-purpose flour
½ teaspoon almond extract

Heat oven to 350° F. Beat eggs well with an electric mixer or rotary beater. Add sugar; beat until thick. Add coconut, flour, and almond extract; mix until well blended. Drop batter by teaspoonfuls 2 inches apart on well-greased cookie sheets. Bake 10 to 12 minutes, until edges are brown. Remove cookies immediately with a wide spatula and cool on wire racks. Makes about 4 dozen cookies.

🍃 Hazelnut Cookies

1 16-ounce package
  confectioners' sugar,
  sifted
8 egg whites, stiffly beaten
1 pound hazelnuts, finely
  ground
2 teaspoons ground cinnamon
Juice and grated peel of 1
lemon

Heat oven to 350° F. Gradually fold sugar into egg whites. Fold in nuts, cinnamon, lemon juice, and lemon peel. Drop from a teaspoon about 1 inch apart onto greased and floured cookie sheets. Bake 10 to 15 minutes; remove from pans immediately with a wide spatula and cool on wire racks. Makes about 6½ dozen cookies.

🍃 Hermits

1 cup softened butter or
  margarine
2 cups firmly packed light
  brown sugar
2 eggs, slightly beaten
1 cup sour milk or
  buttermilk

Heat oven to 375° F. Work butter in a bowl until soft. Add sugar gradually and beat until well blended. Stir in eggs and sour milk. (Mixture may curdle slightly.) Sift together flour, cinnamon, cloves, and baking soda. Stir gradually into creamed mixture. Beat until smooth. Fold in raisins and nuts. Drop batter by rounded teaspoonfuls 2 inches apart on a greased cookie sheet. Bake about

2⅔ cups sifted all-purpose
    flour
1½ teaspoons ground
    cinnamon
  1 teaspoon ground cloves
  ½ teaspoon baking soda
  1 cup seeded raisins
  ½ cup chopped walnuts

15 minutes. Cool on a wire rack. Makes about 5 dozen 3-inch cookies.

ᵛᶳ Spicy Oatmeal Cookies

¾ cup sifted all-purpose flour
¼ teaspoon baking soda
¼ teaspoon salt
½ teaspoon ground cinnamon
1 egg, well beaten
½ cup sugar
½ cup melted butter or
    margarine
2 teaspoons molasses
2 tablespoons milk
1 cup quick-cooking rolled
    oats
¼ cup dark seedless raisins
¼ cup coarsely chopped nuts

Heat oven to 325° F. Sift together flour, soda, salt, and cinnamon. Combine remaining ingredients in a bowl. Stir to blend. Add sifted dry ingredients and beat until thoroughly mixed. Drop by rounded tablespoonfuls about 2 inches apart on a greased cookie sheet. Bake 10 to 12 minutes, until edges are slightly brown. Cool on wire racks. Makes about 2½ dozen cookies.

ᵛᶳ Praline Drops

1⅔ cups sifted all-purpose
    flour
  ½ teaspoon baking soda
  ¼ teaspoon salt
  ⅔ cup softened butter or
    margarine
  ⅔ cup firmly packed dark
    brown sugar
  1 unbeaten egg
  ½ teaspoon vanilla extract
  ½ teaspoon maple flavoring
  ¾ cup coarsely chopped
    pecans
  ¾ cup pecan halves
Praline Glaze (recipe follows)

Heat oven to 350° F. Sift together the flour, baking soda, and salt. Work butter in a bowl until creamy. Add sugar and beat until light and fluffy. Add egg, vanilla, and maple flavoring; beat thoroughly. Add sifted dry ingredients and mix until smooth. Stir in chopped nuts. Drop batter by rounded teaspoonfuls 2 inches apart onto a greased cookie sheet. Place a pecan half on each cookie. Bake 12 to 14 minutes, until edges are slightly browned. Remove from pan and place on a wire rack. While still warm, spoon a little Praline Glaze over each cookie. Cool and store in an airtight container. Makes about 3½ dozen cookies.

Praline Glaze

In a small saucepan combine ½ *cup firmly packed dark brown sugar, 1 tablespoon dark corn syrup,* and *1 tablespoon water.* Place over moderate heat (about 250° F.) and bring to a boil, stirring constantly. Remove from heat and stir in *1 cup sifted confectioners' sugar* and *1 tablespoon water.* Beat until smooth. Add a few drops of water if necessary to make it pour easily.

Sherry Wafers

¼ **cup softened butter or margarine**
½ **cup sugar**
4 **eggs**
1 **cup sifted all-purpose flour**
2 **teaspoons ground cinnamon**
¼ **teaspoon salt**
¼ **cup dry sherry**

Heat oven to 450° F. Work butter until creamy. Add sugar gradually and beat until well blended. Add eggs one at a time, beating well after each addition. Sift together flour, cinnamon, and salt; add to butter mixture alternately with sherry. Drop rounded teaspoonfuls of batter 2 inches apart onto a well-greased and floured cookie sheet. Bake about 7 to 8 minutes, until edges start to brown. Remove from oven. With a spatula remove cookies from pan while still hot and immediately curl each around the handle of a wooden spoon. If cookies become too brittle to curl, return pan to oven for about 1 minute, until they soften. Makes about 4 dozen cookies.

Molded Cookies

1. To mold crackle tops, shape level tablespoonfuls of dough into round balls with hands. Roll balls in sugar and place 2 inches apart on a lightly greased cookie sheet.

2. To mold crinkle edges, shape level tablespoonfuls of dough into balls. Place 2 inches apart on greased cookie sheets. Flatten tops with a glass dipped in sugar.

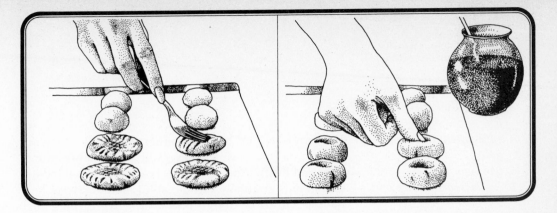

3. For a crisscross top, shape balls with hands; place 2 inches apart on greased cookie sheet. Flatten balls with fork dipped in sugar. Press evenly in both directions.

4. For thumb-print tops, shape cookie dough into round balls; place on greased cookie sheets. Press a hollow into each ball with the thumb. Fill hollow with jam.

Chocolate Pixies

2½ cups sifted all-purpose flour
2 teaspoons baking powder
½ teaspoon salt
½ cup vegetable oil
4 1-ounce squares unsweetened chocolate, melted
2 cups sugar
4 eggs
2 teaspoons vanilla extract
1 cup confectioners' sugar

Sift together flour, baking powder, and salt. Combine oil, chocolate, and sugar. Add eggs one at a time and beat well after each addition. Add vanilla. Add sifted dry ingredients to chocolate mixture and blend thoroughly. Chill several hours or overnight. Heat oven to 350° F. Spread confectioners' sugar in a small, flat pan. Drop dough by rounded teaspoonfuls into confectioners' sugar. With the fingers, coat dough thoroughly with the sugar and shape into balls. Place 2 inches apart on greased cookie sheet. Bake 10 to 12 minutes. Cool on wire racks. Makes 6 dozen cookies.

Butterscotch–Oatmeal Cookies

1 4-serving-size package butterscotch pudding and pie filling
2 cups quick-cooking rolled oats
½ cup chopped pecans

Heat oven to 350° F. Thoroughly blend together all the ingredients in a bowl with the fingers. Shape level tablespoons of dough into balls; place 3 inches apart on ungreased cookie sheets. Flatten balls slightly with a fork. Bake 12 to 15 minutes. Cool on cookie sheet before removing. Makes 2½ dozen cookies.

(Ingredients continued on page 872)

¾ cup soft butter or
   margarine
½ cup sugar
1 teaspoon vanilla extract

✑ Jelly Balls

2⅓ cups sifted all-purpose
   flour
½ teaspoon salt
1 cup softened butter or
   margarine
¼ cup sugar
2 egg yolks
Raspberry or apricot jam

Heat oven to 350° F. Sift together flour and salt. Work butter in a bowl until creamy. Add sugar and beat until light and fluffy. Add egg yolks; beat well. Add sifted dry ingredients gradually and mix until smooth. Shape level tablespoonfuls of dough into balls. Place about 1 inch apart on an ungreased cookie sheet. Press each ball with the index finger, making an indentation. Drop jam into each depression. Bake 18 to 20 minutes, until lightly browned. Cool on wire racks. Makes 3 dozen cookies.

✑ Nut Rolls

2 cups walnuts
1 cup pitted dates
2 cups flaked coconut
1 cup firmly packed dark
   brown sugar
2 eggs, slightly beaten

Heat oven to 350° F. Put nuts and dates through a food chopper, using the coarse blade. Mix with 1½ cups of the coconut, sugar, and eggs. With the hands, shape mixture into rolls about ¾ inch in diameter and 2 inches long. Roll each in the remaining ½ cup coconut. Place about 2 inches apart on greased cookie sheets; bake 10 to 12 minutes, until golden brown. Cool on wire racks. Makes about 3 dozen cookies.

✑ Peanut–Butter Cookies

1½ cups sifted all-purpose
   flour
2 teaspoons baking powder
½ teaspoon salt
½ cup soft shortening
½ cup peanut butter
½ cup firmly packed dark
   brown sugar
½ cup granulated sugar
1 egg
½ teaspoon vanilla extract

Heat oven to 375° F. Sift together flour, baking powder, and salt. Work shortening and peanut butter together in a bowl until creamy. Add sugars and beat until light and fluffy. Add egg and vanilla; beat thoroughly. Add dry ingredients and mix until smooth. Form level tablespoonfuls of dough into balls. Place 2 inches apart on ungreased cookie sheets. Press crosswise with the tines of a fork or flatten with a glass dipped in sugar. Bake 10 to 12 minutes. Cool on wire racks. Makes about 3 dozen cookies.

❧ *Spice Balls*

2¼ *cups sifted all-purpose*
   flour
¼ *teaspoon baking soda*
2½ *teaspoons baking powder*
1 *teaspoon ground*
   cinnamon
½ *teaspoon ground ginger*
⅛ *teaspoon ground cloves*
¼ *teaspoon salt*
¾ *cup soft shortening*
1 *cup granulated sugar*
¼ *cup dark molasses*
1 *egg*
Granulated sugar

Sift together flour, soda, baking powder, cinnamon, ginger, cloves, and salt. Work shortening in a bowl until creamy. Add sugar and beat until light and fluffy. Add molasses and egg; beat well. Add sifted dry ingredients to shortening mixture gradually and mix until smooth. Cover and chill 2 hours. Heat oven to 375° F. Shape level tablespoonfuls of dough into balls. Roll each in granulated sugar to coat evenly. Place balls 2 inches apart on greased cookie sheets. Bake 10 to 12 minutes. Cool on wire racks. Makes about 4 dozen cookies.

Pressed Cookies

Pressed cookies require a cookie press to give them their characteristic shapes. These presses are available in housewares departments of department stores.

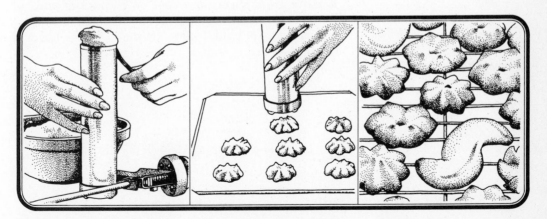

1. Spoon dough into cookie press fitted with desired blade according to manufacturer's directions. Keep dough pliable but not soft. If the room is warm, chill dough.

2. Hold cookie press firmly. Force cookies out onto an ungreased cookie sheet. Cookie sheet must be cold or cookie dough will melt and spread. Space cookies evenly.

3. Bake cookies as directed. When done, cookies will be firm and edges will be delicately browned. Remove cookies from sheet with a spatula and cool on wire cake racks.

❧ Chocolate Pressed Cookies

¾ cup soft shortening
1 cup sugar
1 egg
¼ teaspoon salt
2 1-ounce squares
  unsweetened chocolate,
  melted
2 tablespoons milk
½ teaspoon vanilla extract
2 cups sifted all-purpose
  flour

Work shortening in a bowl until creamy. Add sugar and beat until light and fluffy. Add egg, salt, melted chocolate, milk, and vanilla. Beat thoroughly. Add flour gradually and mix until smooth. Cover tightly and chill 30 minutes. Heat oven to 375° F. Put desired forming plate in cookie press and fill press with dough. Force out shapes about 2 inches apart onto a cold, ungreased cookie sheet. Bake 10 to 12 minutes. Remove from sheets and cool on wire racks. Makes about 5 dozen cookies.

❧ Cream Cheese Spritz

2½ cups sifted all-purpose
  flour
1 teaspoon baking powder
1 cup softened butter or
  margarine
1 3-ounce package cream
  cheese, at room
  temperature
1 cup sugar
1 egg
1 tablespoon lemon juice
1 teaspoon grated lemon
  peel
Lemon Glaze (recipe follows)
Chopped nuts

Sift together flour and baking powder. Work butter and cream cheese in a bowl until creamy. Add sugar and beat until light and fluffy. Add egg, lemon juice, and lemon peel. Beat thoroughly. Add sifted dry ingredients to butter mixture gradually and mix until smooth. Cover and chill 30 minutes. Heat oven to 375° F. Put star plate in cookie press and fill press with dough. Force out 2-inch ribbons in the shape of an S onto cold, ungreased cookie sheets. Bake 10 to 12 minutes, until edges are browned. Remove from sheets and cool on racks. Dip ends of cookies in Lemon Glaze and then in chopped nuts. Place on waxed paper until glaze hardens. Makes about 4 dozen cookies.

Lemon Glaze

Combine *1 cup sifted confectioners' sugar* and *2 tablespoons lemon juice* in a bowl.

❧ Hard-Cooked-Egg Cookies

3 cups sifted all-purpose
  flour
2 teaspoons baking powder
1 cup softened butter or
  margarine

Sift together flour and baking powder. Work butter until creamy; add sugar and beat until fluffy. Press cooked egg yolks through a fine sieve and add to butter with lemon peel, lemon juice, and vanilla. Beat thoroughly. Add sifted dry ingredients to butter mix-

¾ *cup sugar*
6 *hard-cooked egg yolks*
1 *tablespoon grated lemon peel*
3 *tablespoons lemon juice*
1 *teaspoon vanilla extract*

ture and blend. Dough should be stiff enough not to stick to hands; add a little flour if needed. Cover and chill dough. Heat oven to 350° F. Spoon dough into a cookie press and press out in desired shapes about 1 inch apart onto a greased cookie sheet. Bake 15 to 20 minutes, until golden brown. Cool on wire racks. Makes about 5 dozen cookies.

Rolled Cookies

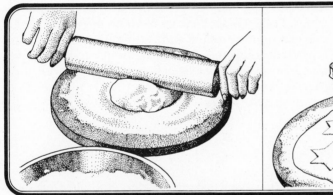

1. Use a lightly floured pastry cloth or board for rolling dough. If cookie dough is very sticky, put a piece of waxed paper over the dough before rolling it out. Roll only a small amount of dough at a time. Keep rest chilled. Roll *evenly* to thickness suggested.

2. Dip cookie cutter into flour; shake off excess flour; cut as many cookies from each rolling as possible. Excessive reworking of the dough will make cookies dry.

3. When cookies have been cut, carefully lift them with a broad, flat spatula and place on a cookie sheet, usually ungreased. The cookies should be placed 2 inches apart.

4. Bake cookies as directed. Perfect rolled cookies will retain cutter shape, have lightly browned edges, and be crisp and thin or soft and thick, depending on the recipe.

COOKIES

❧ Butter Cookies

1 cup softened butter or
    margarine
¾ cup sugar
1 whole egg
1 egg yolk
1 teaspoon vanilla extract
¼ teaspoon almond extract
2¾ cups sifted all-purpose
    flour
1 egg
1 tablespoon water
Chopped nuts, candied
    cherries, and colored
    sugar

Work butter in a bowl until creamy; gradually add sugar and beat until fluffy. Add the whole egg, egg yolk, vanilla, and almond extract; beat thoroughly. Add flour and mix well. Chill at least 2 hours or longer. Heat oven to 350° F. Divide dough into 4 equal portions and roll out 1 portion at a time, leaving remainder in refrigerator. Place dough on floured board; cover with a sheet of floured waxed paper to prevent sticking and roll out ⅛ inch thick. Carefully remove waxed paper and cut dough into desired shapes with a floured cookie cutter. Place cookies 2 inches apart on ungreased cookie sheets. Continue rolling and cutting until all the dough is used. Beat together the egg and water and brush over tops of unbaked cookies before garnishing with nuts, cherries, and colored sugar. Bake 10 to 12 minutes. Cool on wire racks. Makes about 3½ dozen cookies.

❧ Lemon Sugar Cookies

3¾ cups sifted all-purpose
    flour
3 teaspoons baking powder
¼ teaspoon salt
½ cup soft shortening
1 cup granulated sugar
1 egg
½ cup fresh lemon juice
Granulated sugar

Sift together flour, baking powder, and salt. Heat oven to 400° F. Work shortening in a bowl until creamy. Add the 1 cup granulated sugar and beat until well blended. Add egg; beat thoroughly. Add sifted dry ingredients alternately with lemon juice to creamed mixture. Beat until smooth. Cover and chill 1 hour. Roll a small portion of dough at a time on a lightly floured board to a thickness of about ¼ inch. (Keep rest of dough refrigerated.) Cut with a 2-inch cookie cutter. Place cookies 2 inches apart on a lightly greased cookie sheet and sprinkle with granulated sugar. Bake 10 to 12 minutes, until edges are lightly browned. Cool on wire racks. Makes about 4 to 5 dozen cookies.

❧ Molasses Cookies

8½ cups sifted all-purpose
    flour
1 tablespoon ground ginger
1 teaspoon ground cloves
1 teaspoon ground nutmeg
½ teaspoon ground allspice

Sift together flour, ginger, cloves, nutmeg, and allspice. Work shortening in a bowl until creamy. Add sugar and beat until well blended. Combine salt, water, and rum; stir to dissolve salt. Stir soda into molasses and combine with water mixture. Add liquid mixture and sifted dry ingredients alternately to shortening mixture. Mix well

1 cup soft shortening
2 cups sugar
1 tablespoon salt
¾ cup water
¼ cup light rum
2 teaspoons baking soda
2 cups dark molasses

after each addition. Cover and chill overnight. Heat oven to 375° F. Roll a small portion of dough at a time on a floured board to a thickness of about ¼ inch. Cut with a 4-inch cookie cutter, a large brandy snifter, or gingerbread-man cutter, if desired. Bake about 2 inches apart on greased cookie sheets 10 to 12 minutes. Cool on wire racks. Makes about 5 to 6 dozen large cookies.

Sugar Cookie Cutouts

3 cups sifted all-purpose flour
1 cup sugar
1½ teaspoons baking powder
½ teaspoon salt
1 cup softened butter or margarine
1 egg, slightly beaten
3 tablespoons light cream
1½ teaspoons vanilla extract

Heat oven to 400° F. Sift together flour, sugar, baking powder, and salt into a large bowl. Add butter and cut into flour mixture with an electric mixer or a pastry blender until particles are fine. Add egg, cream, and vanilla; blend thoroughly. If desired, chill dough for easier handling. Place ⅓ of the dough on a well-floured board. Place a sheet of floured waxed paper over dough and roll with a rolling pin to a thickness of ⅛ inch. Remove waxed paper. Cut into desired shapes with cookie cutters. Repeat with rest of dough. Place 2 inches apart on ungreased cookie sheets. Bake 5 to 8 minutes, or until lightly browned at edges. Cool on wire racks. When cookies are cool, they may be frosted with a simple sugar icing and decorated as desired. Makes about 6 to 7 dozen cookies.

Tea Wafers

1¾ cups sifted all-purpose flour
¼ teaspoon salt
½ cup softened butter or margarine
1 cup sifted confectioners' sugar
1 teaspoon vanilla extract
½ cup milk
¼ cup finely chopped pecans
1 tablespoon sugar
¼ teaspoon ground cinnamon

Sift flour with salt. Lightly butter two 12-x-15½-inch cookie sheets and chill them thoroughly. (Do not use a Teflon-coated sheet.) Heat oven to 325° F. Cream butter; beat in confectioners' sugar and vanilla. Add sifted dry ingredients to creamed mixture alternately with milk. Beat thoroughly after each addition. Place half the mixture on each of the baking sheets and spread with a spatula almost to the edges of the sheets. With a silver knife, mark batter off into 2-inch diamond shapes. Sprinkle batter on one baking sheet with the chopped pecans. Combine the sugar and cinnamon and sprinkle batter on the other baking sheet with this mixture. Bake about 25 to 30 minutes, or until lightly browned. Remove from the oven, and while still hot, cut through the marked diamonds. Remove from the sheet and cool on wire racks. Makes about 5 dozen cookies.

Filled Cookies

These fat cookies, which may be made with a variety of fillings, are similar to pastry turnovers. They are superb lunch-box cookies

❧ Filled Cookies

6 cups sifted all-purpose
  flour
2 teaspoons baking powder
1 teaspoon baking soda
½ teaspoon salt
1 cup soft shortening
2 cups sugar
2 eggs
1 teaspoon vanilla extract
1 cup commercial sour cream
Prune Filling (recipe follows)
Honey–Coconut Filling
  (recipe follows)
Mincemeat Filling (recipe
  follows)

Sift together flour, baking powder, soda, and salt. Work shortening in a bowl until creamy. Add sugar and beat until well blended. Add eggs and vanilla; blend well. Stir in sour cream. Add dry ingredients a little at a time and mix well after each addition. Cover mixture; chill 1 hour. Heat oven to 425° F. Roll a small portion of dough at a time on a lightly floured board to a thickness of ⅛ inch. Cut with a 3-inch scalloped cutter. Place half the shapes 1 inch apart on an ungreased cookie sheet. Place 1 teaspoon Prune, Honey–Coconut, or Mincemeat Filling in the center of each. Moisten edges with water. Cut out centers of remaining shapes, using a thimble. Top filled shape with cutout shape. Press edges lightly together. Bake 8 to 10 minutes. Cool on wire racks. Makes about 4 to 5 dozen cookies.

Prune Filling

Combine 3 cups chopped, pitted, cooked prunes and ¾ cup sugar. Cook and stir over moderately low heat (about 225° F.) until thick, about 5 minutes. Add 1 teaspoon vanilla extract. Cool.

Honey–Coconut Filling

Combine ½ cup sugar, ⅓ cup honey, ½ cup water, ¼ teaspoon salt, and 2 3½-ounce cans flaked coconut. Stir over moderately low heat (about 225° F.) about 10 minutes. Stir in ½ teaspoon vanilla extract and 1 tablespoon butter or margarine. Cool.

Mincemeat Filling

Combine 1¼ cups canned mincemeat, 1 teaspoon grated orange peel, and 1 tablespoon brandy.

Refrigerator Cookies

These are homemade versions of the familiar commercial slice-and-bake refrigerated cookie rolls. When you have refrigerator cookies on hand you can bake up just a pan at a time to have fresh cookies for a dessert. Also, these can be made ahead and baked at the last minute when you plan to serve cookies for a party.

Butterscotch Cookies

3¼ cups sifted all-purpose flour
½ teaspoon ground cinnamon
1 cup softened butter or margarine
1 cup firmly packed light brown sugar
2 egg yolks
1 cup chopped walnuts

Sift together flour and cinnamon. Work butter in a bowl until creamy. Add sugar and beat until light and fluffy. Add egg yolks and beat well. Add sifted dry ingredients to butter mixture gradually and mix until smooth. Stir in nuts. Cover and chill 30 minutes. Shape dough into a roll about 1½ inches in diameter. Wrap tightly in waxed paper and chill overnight or longer. Heat oven to 350° F. Cut chilled dough into ⅛-inch slices and place about 2 inches apart on ungreased cookie sheets. Bake 10 to 12 minutes, until lightly browned. Cool on wire racks. Makes 8 to 9 dozen cookies.

Chocolate Pinwheels

2 cups sifted all-purpose flour
¼ teaspoon baking powder
½ teaspoon salt
½ cup soft shortening
1½ teaspoons vanilla extract
1 cup sugar
1 egg
1 1-ounce square unsweetened chocolate, melted

Sift flour, baking powder, and salt together. Work shortening in a bowl until creamy. Stir in vanilla. Add sugar gradually and beat until well blended. Add egg and beat thoroughly. Add dry ingredients and beat until smooth. Divide dough in half. Add melted chocolate to half the dough and mix thoroughly. Cut 4 pieces of waxed paper 12 x 8 inches. Roll the chocolate dough between 2 pieces to edges of paper. Repeat with the plain dough. Remove top piece of paper and invert plain layer on top of chocolate layer. Remove paper from plain dough; trim edges. Roll dough like a jelly roll, starting at the wide side; remove paper while rolling. Wrap tightly in waxed paper and chill overnight. Heat oven to 375° F. Cut chilled dough in ¼-inch slices and place about 2 inches apart on greased cookie sheets. Bake 10 to 12 minutes, or until lightly browned. Cool on a wire rack. Makes about 3 dozen cookies.

COOKIES

Date Pinwheels

2¼ cups sifted all-purpose
    flour
½ teaspoon baking soda
¼ teaspoon salt
½ cup softened butter
    or margarine
½ cup firmly packed dark
    brown sugar
½ cup granulated sugar
2 eggs
½ pound (1 cup) pitted
    dates, finely chopped
¼ cup granulated sugar
⅓ cup water
Few grains salt
¼ cup finely chopped
    almonds

To make dough, sift together flour, baking soda, and the ¼ teaspoon salt. Work butter in a bowl until creamy. Add brown sugar and the ½ cup granulated sugar gradually and beat until well blended. Add eggs and beat well. Add sifted ingredients to butter mixture and mix until smooth. Cover and chill 30 minutes.

To make filling, combine dates, the ¼ cup granulated sugar, the water, and the few grains salt in a saucepan. Bring to a boil over moderately low heat (about 225° F.); cook 5 minutes, stirring frequently. Cool. Stir in nuts. Roll chilled dough into a rectangle 10 x 16 inches. Spread with date mixture. Roll up like a jelly roll, starting with a wide side. Wrap tightly in waxed paper and chill overnight or longer. Heat oven to 350° F. Cut roll into ¼-inch slices and place about 2 inches apart on greased cookie sheets. Bake 12 to 14 minutes. Cool on wire racks. Makes about 4½ dozen cookies.

Lemon Slices

2 cups sifted all-purpose
    flour
1 teaspoon baking powder
⅛ teaspoon salt
⅛ teaspoon ground nutmeg
½ cup softened butter or
    margarine
1 cup sugar
2 teaspoons grated lemon
    peel
1 tablespoon lemon juice
1 egg
1 egg white, unbeaten
Thinly shaved Brazil nuts

Sift together flour, baking powder, salt, and nutmeg. Work butter in a bowl until creamy. Add sugar and beat until well blended. Add lemon peel, lemon juice, and whole egg. Beat well. Gradually add sifted dry ingredients to butter mixture and mix until smooth. Chill dough 30 minutes. Shape into a roll about 1½ inches in diameter. Wrap tightly in waxed paper and chill overnight or longer. Heat oven to 375° F. Cut chilled dough into ⅛-inch slices and place about 2 inches apart on ungreased cookie sheets. Brush with unbeaten egg white and sprinkle with nuts. Bake 10 to 12 minutes, until lightly brown. Cool on wire racks. Makes about 6 dozen cookies.

Vanilla Refrigerator Cookies

1¾ cups sifted all-purpose
    flour
½ teaspoon baking soda
¾ teaspoon salt
½ cup soft shortening

Sift together flour, soda, and salt. Work shortening in a bowl until creamy. Add sugar and beat until well blended. Add egg and vanilla; beat well. Gradually add sifted dry ingredients and mix until smooth. Stir in nuts. Cover and chill 1 hour. Turn chilled dough out onto a

1 cup sugar
1 egg
2 teaspoons vanilla extract
½ cup chopped nuts

lightly floured board and shape into a long roll about 1½ inches in diameter. Wrap tightly in waxed paper and chill overnight or longer. Heat oven to 375° F. Remove paper from chilled roll and cut into slices, about ¼ inch thick. Place about 2 inches apart on ungreased cookie sheets and bake 10 to 12 minutes. Cool on wire racks. Makes about 4½ dozen cookies.

Chocolate Refrigerator Cookies

In recipe for Vanilla Refrigerator Cookies, add *3 1-ounce squares melted unsweetened chocolate* to the shortening mixture before adding flour. Use only *1 teaspoon vanilla extract*.

Orange Refrigerator Cookies

In recipe for Vanilla Refrigerator Cookies, add *1 tablespoon grated orange peel* to the shortening mixture before adding the sifted flour mixture. Use *2 teaspoons orange juice* in place of the vanilla extract.

Christmas Cookies

Gingerbread-Cookie Trees

4⅔ cups sifted all-purpose
   flour
1 cup sugar
⅛ teaspoon baking soda
2 teaspoons ground ginger
½ teaspoon ground nutmeg
½ teaspoon ground
   cinnamon
½ teaspoon salt
1 cup soft shortening
1 cup light or dark molasses
Cake and cookie-decorating
   frosting in pressurized
   cans (green, red, yellow,
   or pink)

Sift together flour, sugar, baking soda, ginger, nutmeg, cinnamon, and salt into a large bowl. Add shortening and cut into flour mixture with a pastry blender or two knives until shortening is cut into small pieces. Gradually stir in molasses. Work dough in bowl with lightly floured fingertips until mixture is well blended. Chill in the refrigerator for 1 hour. Heat oven to 375° F. Place a portion of dough on a well-floured board; pat into a rectangle. Place a sheet of floured waxed paper over dough, and roll with a rolling pin to a thickness of ¼ inch. Remove waxed paper. For each Christmas tree, cut one of each of the Christmas-tree patterns (see page 882). Place cutouts on a greased cookie sheet. Roll out remaining dough in same manner. Bake 7 to 8 minutes, or until lightly browned. If center cutouts of Christmas trees bake together, gently separate with a spatula while cookie is still hot. Cool before removing from cookie sheet. If necessary, carefully scrape center cutout of

COOKIES

GINGERBREAD-COOKIE TREE PATTERNS

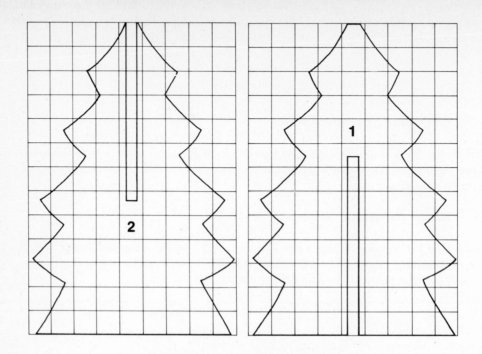

GINGERBREAD-MAN PATTERN

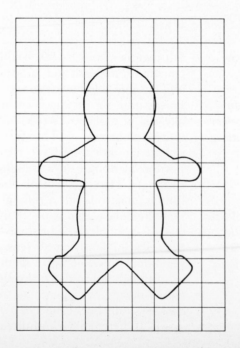

trees with a sharp knife so pattern number 1 fits into pattern number 2 to make a standing tree. Decorate with cake- and cookie-decorating frosting as desired. Makes about 10 trees.

Gingerbread Men

Use gingerbread-cookie recipe on page 881. Cut out gingerbread men with a cookie cutter or use a pattern made from the diagram shown on page 882. Makes about 30 cookies.

Note: To enlarge the patterns, copy each one on a sheet of ½-inch graph paper or heavy paper ruled off into ½-inch squares. Use the squares as a drawing guide. The cookie trees will be 6 inches high; the gingerbread men will be 5 inches tall.

Gingerbread House

Pattern and directions for Gingerbread House courtesy of Grandma's Molasses.

5 cups sifted all-purpose flour
1 teaspoon baking soda
1 teaspoon salt
1 teaspoon ground nutmeg
3 teaspoons ground ginger
1 cup shortening
⅔ cup sugar
1 cup unsulphured molasses
Ornamental Frosting (recipe follows)

To Make Dough
Sift together flour, baking soda, salt, nutmeg, and ginger. Melt shortening in a large saucepan over moderate heat (about 250° F.). Add sugar and molasses; stir well. Remove from heat. Gradually stir in 4 cups of the flour mixture until thoroughly combined. Work in remaining flour mixture with the hands. Divide dough into 3 equal balls.

To Roll Out and Bake Dough
Heat oven to 375° F. Place 1 ball of dough on an ungreased cookie sheet. Wrap the other 2 balls in waxed paper until ready to use. Place a damp towel underneath the cookie sheet to prevent sliding. Roll dough into a ¼-inch-thick rectangle on the cookie sheet. Lay front and back wall patterns on the rolled-out dough. Roll out the other 2 balls of dough separately on 2 cookie sheets in the same manner. On the second rectangle of dough, lay the 2 sides of the house pattern end to end; on the third rectangle, lay out the 2 roof patterns. Using a pointed knife, cut through dough on all lines of the patterns, including windows and door. Do not remove windows or door. Remove all excess dough from around sides of patterns; form excess dough into a ball. Roll out excess dough on another cookie sheet to ¼-inch thickness. Place the other pattern pieces—Santa Claus, chimney pieces, trees and their easels—on rolled-out dough.

COOKIES

Cut out pieces and remove excess dough. Place in oven, 1 sheet at a time, and bake 13 to 15 minutes, or until lightly browned. Each sheet may be baked as soon as the patterns for that sheet have been cut. If it is necessary to reuse a cookie sheet, be sure it is completely cold before rolling another portion of dough. If dough is not used at once, keep it well covered. As soon as a sheet is removed from the oven, retrace the outlines of the windows, door, and adjoining house ends with the point of a knife and carefully remove the door and windows. Save door piece. If necessary, cut house edges to straighten. Do not remove pieces from cookie sheet until completely cooled. Then lift with a spatula to a flat surface.

To Assemble and Decorate House

Prepare Ornamental Frosting according to the recipe. Use a cake decorator or paper cornucopia to put the house together and to decorate. If desired, a portion of the frosting may be colored with food coloring to decorate the trees, the Santa Claus, and the house. Place the house on a board or tray measuring about 26 x 16 inches. Join edge of the back and 1 side of the house by frosting 2 edges and pressing together. Hold in place a few minutes to set. Do the same with remaining side and front pieces. When walls are firm, attach roof, 1 side at a time, by applying frosting on top edges of the 4 walls. Position the roof pieces so that there is about 1 inch of overhang on each side and the roof pieces meet to form a pointed roof. When roof is firm, attach chimney pieces in same fashion with frosting. When frosting is firm, decorate roof, chimney, and windows with Ornamental Frosting. Decorate door and Santa Claus before attaching to house with frosting. Decorate trees with frosting before putting easels on backs. Arrange trees around house. Small cookies and assorted candies may be used to decorate house as desired.

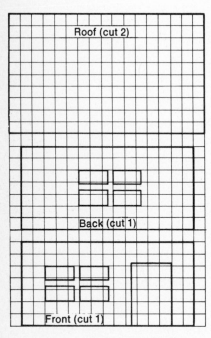

(Patterns continue on page 885)

Ornamental Frosting

2½ cups unsifted
    confectioners' sugar
¼ teaspoon cream of tartar
2 egg whites
½ teaspoon vanilla extract

Sift confectioners' sugar and cream of tartar together into the large bowl of an electric mixer. Add egg whites and vanilla extract; combine on low speed of electric mixer. Beat mixture until very stiff (a knife drawn through mixture should leave a clean-cut path). Cover with a damp cloth until ready to use. Makes about 1½ cups frosting, or enough to assemble and decorate the house simply.

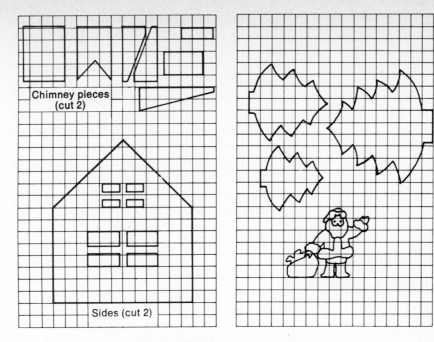

Chimney pieces (cut 2)

Sides (cut 2)

SCALE: 1 SQUARE EQUALS ½ INCH

✑ *Almond Christmas Wafers*

⅔ *cup finely ground blanched almonds*
½ *cup sugar*
½ *cup butter or margarine*
1 *tablespoon flour*
2 *tablespoons milk*

Heat oven to 350° F. Place all 5 ingredients in a skillet. Heat over moderate heat (about 250° F.), stirring constantly, until butter melts and ingredients are well blended. Drop cookie batter by teaspoonfuls, 4 inches apart, onto greased and floured cookie sheets. Bake 8 to 10 minutes, until light golden brown. Cool slightly; remove to wire rack from cookie sheets with a broad spatula. If desired, shape wafers by laying each one across the handle of a wooden spoon or rolling pin while cookies are still warm. If cookies cool and become too crisp to shape, set pan in warm oven with heat turned off for several minutes. Makes about 40 to 50 cookies.

✑ *Anise Drops (Self-Frosting)*

1¾ *cups sifted all-purpose flour*
½ *teaspoon baking powder*
½ *teaspoon salt*

Sift together flour, baking powder, and salt. Place eggs in the large bowl of an electric mixer and beat until very frothy. Add sugar gradually while continuing to beat. Continue to beat for 20 minutes at medium speed. Re-

3 eggs, at room temperature
1 cup plus 2 tablespoons
  sugar
1 teaspoon anise extract

duce speed of mixer and gradually add flour mixture. Beat 3 minutes more. Add anise extract. Drop by slightly rounded teaspoonfuls about 1 inch apart onto a well-greased and -floured cookie sheet, swirling to form a round. (Cookies will spread slightly.) Let cookies stand, uncovered, at room temperature at least 8 hours or overnight to dry. Bake in a preheated 325° F. oven about 15 minutes, or until bottoms of cookies are lightly browned. Cookies will separate into 2 layers. Cool on wire cake racks. Store in an airtight container for at least 10 days. If the cookies should become too dry, place a thick slice of apple in the cookie container. Makes about 7 dozen cookies.

Czechoslovakian Puzzles

1½ cups sifted all-purpose
     flour
  3 tablespoons granulated
     sugar
  ¼ teaspoon salt
  ¼ teaspoon grated lemon
     peel
  3 tablespoons softened
     butter or margarine
  1 egg yolk, slightly beaten
  ⅓ cup light cream
Vegetable oil
Confectioners' sugar

Sift flour, sugar, and salt together into a bowl. Add lemon peel. Cut in butter with a pastry blender or 2 knives. Combine egg yolk and cream; blend into flour mixture. Turn out onto a lightly floured board or pastry cloth and knead 5 minutes. Roll out about ¹/₁₆ inch thick. Cut into elongated diamond shapes 2 x 4 inches. Make a lengthwise slit 2 inches long in center of each and pull 2 opposite corners through the slit. Heat oil in a deep, heavy pan to 375° F. Have oil at least 2 inches deep. Fry a few pieces at a time, about 2 minutes, until light brown. Drain; dust with confectioners' sugar. Makes about 4 dozen cookies.

Florentines

½ cup slivered blanched
   almonds
¾ cup heavy cream
¼ cup sugar
¼ cup unsifted all-purpose
   flour
8 ounces candied orange peel
2 4-ounce bars sweet cooking
   chocolate

Spread almond slivers in a flat pan. Toast in a 300° F. oven about 20 to 25 minutes, turning occasionally. Heat oven to 350° F. Combine the cream and sugar in a bowl; stir until well blended. Gradually stir in flour and mix until smooth. Stir in almonds. Blot orange peel well with paper towels to remove any excess syrup and chop finely. Add peel to cream–sugar batter and stir until well blended. Drop batter by heaping teaspoonfuls 2 inches apart on heavily greased and floured cookie sheets. Flatten each mound of batter slightly with a knife or spatula. Bake 14 minutes, or just until cookies are lightly browned around the edges. Immediately remove cookies from sheets to wire racks. Cookies should be crisp when completely cooled. Melt the chocolate in the top of a double boiler over hot, not boiling, water. Turn cooled cookies upside down on waxed paper; spread melted chocolate to cover bottoms of cookies completely. Place cookies on wire racks and leave at room temperature until chocolate becomes firm. Do not stack cookies. Store in a single layer in a covered container or in refrigerator. Cookies may also be wrapped tightly and frozen. Makes 3½ to 4 dozen cookies.

Greek Crescents

2½ cups sifted all-purpose
   flour
½ teaspoon baking powder
½ pound softened butter or
   margarine
¼ cup granulated sugar
1 egg yolk
2 tablespoons brandy
½ cup chopped pecans
Confectioners' sugar

Sift together flour and baking powder. Heat oven to 375° F. Beat butter in an electric mixer until light and fluffy. Add sugar gradually and beat thoroughly. Beat in egg yolk and brandy. Mix sifted dry ingredients into butter mixture with a wooden spoon. Stir in nuts. Turn out on a lightly floured board and knead gently with floured hands about 2 minutes. Using about 1 tablespoon dough for each, shape into crescents. Place 1 inch apart on an ungreased cookie sheet and bake 25 minutes. Cool slightly and sprinkle heavily with confectioners' sugar. Makes about 3 dozen cookies.

Jan Hagels

1 cup softened butter or
   margarine
1 cup sugar
2 cups sifted all-purpose
   flour
1 egg, slightly beaten
½ cup chopped pecans

Heat oven to 350° F. In the large bowl of an electric mixer, beat butter until creamy. Gradually add sugar and beat until light and fluffy. Add flour gradually and beat until well blended. Pat into an ungreased 15½-x-10½-x-1-inch jelly-roll pan. Brush with egg. Sprinkle top with nuts. Bake 20 to 25 minutes, or until golden brown. Watch carefully during final baking period, as cookies burn easily. Cool slightly until set; then cut with a sharp knife into strips, squares, or diamonds, and remove to wire cake rack to cool completely. Makes about 30 1½-x-2¼-inch cookies.

Lebkuchen

3¼ cups sifted all-purpose
   flour

Sift together flour, baking soda, cinnamon, cloves, allspice, and nutmeg. Combine honey and molasses in a

½ teaspoon baking soda
1 teaspoon ground
  cinnamon
¾ teaspoon ground cloves
1 teaspoon ground allspice
¾ teaspoon ground nutmeg
½ cup honey
½ cup dark molasses
¾ cup firmly packed dark
  brown sugar
1 egg, slightly beaten
1 teaspoon grated lemon
  peel
1 tablespoon lemon juice
⅓ cup finely chopped
  candied citron
½ cup chopped walnuts
1½ cups confectioners' sugar
3 tablespoons hot water
¼ teaspoon vanilla extract

small saucepan and bring to a boil over moderate heat (about 250° F.), stirring occasionally. Remove from heat and pour into a large bowl; cool slightly. Stir brown sugar, egg, lemon peel, and lemon juice into honey–molasses mixture. Gradually add the flour mixture and stir until well blended. Stir in citron and walnuts. Chill, covered, overnight. Heat oven to 400° F. Place about ⅓ of the dough on a well-floured board. Pat into a rectangle. Place a sheet of waxed paper on the dough and roll out to a thickness of ¼ inch. Remove waxed paper; with a knife cut dough into 1½-x-2½-inch rectangles or diamonds. Place 1 inch apart on greased cookie sheets. Roll out remaining dough as above. Bake 8 to 10 minutes, or until lightly browned. Cool on wire racks until slightly warm. In a small bowl combine confectioners' sugar, water, and vanilla and blend well. Spread on slightly warm cookies. Cookies may be stored in a tightly sealed container for several weeks. Makes about 6 dozen cookies.

❧ Moravian Christmas Cookies

3½ cups sifted all-purpose
  flour
½ teaspoon ground
  cinnamon
¼ teaspoon ground nutmeg
¼ teaspoon salt
1 cup softened butter or
  margarine
1½ cups sugar
2 eggs
1 tablespoon brandy

Sift together flour, cinnamon, nutmeg, and salt. Cream butter and sugar together. Add eggs and brandy; beat thoroughly. Gradually add sifted dry ingredients to creamed mixture, mixing well. Cover and chill several hours, or overnight. Heat oven to 400° F. Roll out a small portion of the dough at a time on a floured board, to a thickness of ¼ inch. (Keep remaining dough in refrigerator.) Cut with cookie cutters into desired shapes. Place 2 inches apart on ungreased cookie sheet and bake 12 to 14 minutes. Makes about 4 to 5 dozen cookies.

❧ Pfeffernuesse

4 cups sifted all-purpose
  flour
1 teaspoon ground cloves
1 tablespoon ground
  cinnamon
1 teaspoon ground nutmeg
¼ teaspoon pepper

Sift together flour, cloves, cinnamon, nutmeg, pepper, baking soda, and salt. Stir in anise and cardamom. Cream butter in a mixing bowl; add sugar and beat until blended. Add egg yolks one at a time, beating well after each addition. Add dry ingredients gradually, beating until blended. Stir in grated lemon peel, candied orange peel, and candied citron. Beat egg whites until stiff

1 teaspoon baking soda
1 teaspoon salt
1 teaspoon anise seed
*¾ teaspoon ground
    cardamom seed
¼ cup softened butter or
    margarine
2½ cups unsifted
    confectioners' sugar
5 eggs, separated, at room
    temperature
1 tablespoon grated lemon
    peel
¼ pound finely chopped
    candied orange peel
½ pound finely chopped
    candied citron
Thin Confectioners' Frosting
    (recipe follows)

peaks form and fold into batter. Chill in refrigerator for about 1 hour or until dough is easily handled. Roll teaspoonfuls of dough between floured palms of hands into balls ¾ to 1 inch in diameter. Dough will be slightly soft. Place on cookie sheets covered with waxed paper and let stand uncovered at room temperature overnight to dry. Heat oven to 350° F. To bake, place balls of dough on greased cookie sheets about 2 inches apart. If desired, brush with Thin Confectioners' Frosting. Bake 13 to 15 minutes. Cool on wire cake racks and store in covered airtight containers with a slice of apple. Makes about 6 to 8 dozen cookies.

*Note: If ground cardamom seed is not available, whole cardamom seed may be used. Remove seeds from pods and grind in a mortar or pepper mill.

Thin Confectioners' Frosting

Stir *3 tablespoons hot milk* into *2 cups confectioners' sugar,* mixing until smooth and blended. Stir in *1 teaspoon vanilla extract.* If necessary, add a few drops additional milk to give proper consistency for brushing on dough.

 **Sand Tarts**

1 cup softened butter
2 cups sugar
3 eggs
3½ cups sifted all-purpose
    flour
1 teaspoon salt
2 teaspoons baking powder
1 teaspoon vanilla or lemon
    extract
Milk
3 tablespoons sugar
1 teaspoon ground
    cinnamon

In the large bowl of an electric mixer, beat butter until soft. Add sugar gradually and beat until light and fluffy. Add eggs, one at a time, beating well after each addition. Sift together flour, salt, and baking powder. Gradually add to creamed sugar mixture and blend well. Stir in vanilla extract. Chill dough, covered, overnight. For small thin cookies, heat oven to 350° F.; for large, thicker cookies, heat oven to 325° F. Roll small amounts of dough at a time on a floured pastry cloth. If thin, crisp cookies are desired, roll the dough to a thickness of ⅛ inch. Cut out with cookie cutters. Place on greased cookie sheets about 1 inch apart. Brush tops with milk. Combine sugar and cinnamon in a small dish. Sprinkle tops of cookies lightly with sugar mixture. Bake about 8 minutes, or until lightly browned on edges. If old-fashioned sugar cookies are desired, roll dough ¼ inch thick and cut with a large circular cutter. Brush with milk and sprinkle with sugar mixture. Bake about 15 minutes, or until lightly browned. Watch carefully, as cookies burn easily. Let stand a few seconds before removing from cookie sheet. Cool on wire racks. Makes approximately 14 dozen small, thin cookies.

Springerle

4½ cups sifted cake flour
1 teaspoon baking powder
4 eggs
3½ cups sifted confectioners' sugar
½ teaspoon vanilla extract
2 tablespoons anise seeds

Sift together flour and baking powder. Beat eggs in the large bowl of an electric mixer until lemon-colored. Gradually add sugar and beat until well blended. Stir in vanilla. Add flour mixture gradually and blend thoroughly. Batter will be stiff. Cover and chill 3 to 4 hours. Turn out chilled dough onto a well-floured board. Roll out about ¼ inch thick. Press out designs with a well-floured Springerle rolling pin. Cut cookies apart with a floured, sharp knife. Sprinkle greased cookie sheets with anise seeds. Place cookies 1 inch apart on sheets. Let stand uncovered at room temperature at least 12 hours in order to set the design before baking. Heat oven to 350° F. Bake cookies 12 minutes, until very lightly browned. Cool on a wire rack. Store in airtight container. Makes about 4 dozen cookies.

Spritz Butter Cookies

1 cup softened butter
1 cup softened margarine
1 cup sugar
2 eggs, well beaten
2 teaspoons almond extract
½ teaspoon salt
4 to 4½ cups sifted all-purpose flour

Heat oven to 375° F. Work butter and margarine together until creamy. Add sugar gradually and beat until light and fluffy. Add eggs, almond extract, and salt; blend thoroughly. Stir in enough flour to make a stiff dough. Force through a cookie press onto an ungreased cookie sheet. Place about 1 inch apart. Bake about 12 minutes, until lightly browned. Cool on wire racks. Makes 6 dozen cookies.

Gift Packaging Cookies

All but the most fragile cookies can be mailed successfully. The trick is to pack them in a sturdy, undentable container and to leave no rattling space between the cookies. Small pieces of waxed paper, crumpled tissue, or paper towels can be stuffed between them or use popcorn as an edible stuffer. Several kinds of household containers are sturdy enough to travel; we have tried a cocoa tin, a vegetable-shortening tin with a plastic cover, a coffee tin with a plastic cover, and for a big batch of assorted cookies, a potato-chip tin. Any of these cans may be spray-painted a bright color. They may be trimmed prettily—and flatly—with bands of colored ribbon or strips of solid-color sticky cellophane tape. They may be trimmed with glued-on sequins or bands of rickrack. As with all mailed gifts, it's important to keep trimming flat to allow for a neat, mailable overwrap. Any of those cans with replaceable lids may be covered with gift-wrapping paper, and the smaller sizes make handsome holders for pencils when the cookies are gone. The dark, marbleized, and flocked papers are suitable for a man's desk. An airy print or floral pattern is nice for a woman's. You may also glue bright-colored felt strips or cutouts of white snowflakes on these cans. Trim them with sequins, strips of ribbon, lace, or tiny rickrack, or any one of the decorative trims available in a store's notions department.

Flip-top cracker boxes, shoe boxes, or blouse boxes all may be decoratively covered as described above. These, however, will need a corrugated cardboard and heavy mailing paper overwrap for sending through the mail.

If the gifts are not going through the mail, you may add a number of baubles and bows. Tiny Christmas-tree balls or ornaments will make them look festive. A multicolored strip of gift-wrapping ribbon that picks up the colors of the paper may be taped to the lid to make a "flower" bow. Artificial greens and holly may be taped to the lid. Protect these fancy finishes by putting the completed package in a plastic food-storage bag, securing the top with a ribbon bow.

Children can participate in packaging a bag of cookies for friends. The paper gift bags that come in bright colors need no further trim than the inscribing of a name with glitter or a felt-tipped marking pen. Plain brown paper bags can be made to look like gift-wrapping paper with stick-on gold seals, colored stars, or dots from the stationery store. Tie the bags with a bright bow after the children have decorated them.

COOKIES

A. Vegetable-shortening tin with flat overwrap
B. Baking-powder tin, suitable for a man's desk
C. Baking-powder tin, suitable for a woman's desk
D. Snowflake trim on can with replaceable lid
E. Paper bag with colored tape and stick-on stars
F. Tea tin with "flower" bow-ribbon strips
G. Cocoa tin with ribbon and sequins

CHAPTER XXV

CANDIES
AND CONFECTIONS

Homemade candies are an unusual treat. They're especially nice to have for holiday times and for parties that are a celebration of a big occasion. Popcorn balls and brightly colored lollipops make pretty Christmas-tree decorations that can double as presents for visiting children.

Complicated candy-making is a fine art that takes special equipment and special skills—the recipes you will find in this chapter are not complicated. The first section is a collection of recipes that do not require a candy thermometer. If children want to help, these are the best candies to start them on.

If you can, avoid making cooked candies on a damp, humid day. Cooked sugar is a temperamental ingredient; high humidity can cause it to form crystals that will make the candy grainy.

Storing Candy

Most candies will keep best if they are individually wrapped in waxed paper or clear plastic wrap. They may then be stored in a box or jar or plastic container with a tight seal. Don't refrigerate candies. Chocolates, particularly, will develop a "bloom," a grayed appearance, at cold temperatures.

Easy Candies

❧ Caramel Cashew Turtles

1 1-pound package (about
   54) caramels
2 tablespoons water
¾ pound salted cashew nuts
1 6-ounce package semisweet
   chocolate pieces

Melt caramels in water in top of double boiler over boiling water, about 5 minutes. Stir occasionally. Arrange 36 groups of 4 cashews each, 2 inches apart on greased cookie sheet. Drop a teaspoonful of melted caramel on each group of cashews. (Reheat if it becomes too thick.) Cool 15 minutes. Melt chocolate pieces in the top of a double boiler over hot, not boiling, water. Spoon a teaspoonful on each turtle; spread evenly with spatula. Set in cool, dry place until firm. Makes 36.

❧ Candied Citrus Peel

2 or 3 medium-sized
   oranges
1 large grapefruit
3 or 4 lemons
12 cups water
2½ cups sugar
½ cup honey
1¾ cups boiling water
1 cup sugar

Remove peels from fruit with a sharp knife, cutting as close to the pulp as possible. Cut enough peels into strips ¼ inch wide and 2 inches long to make 1 cup of each fruit peel. (Use fruit pulp for desserts or beverage.) Bring 6 cups of the water to a boil in a large saucepan over moderate heat (about 250° F.). Add the 3 cups citrus peels and return to a boil. Boil, uncovered, 10 minutes. Drain and rinse peels. Repeat with remaining 6 cups water. In a large saucepan combine the 2½ cups sugar, honey, and the 1¾ cups boiling water. Bring mixture to a boil, stirring occasionally, over moderate heat (about 250° F.) and boil 1 minute. Add cooked, drained peels; simmer over moderately low heat (about 225° F.) about 40 to 50 minutes, stirring occasionally. Pour peels into a colander and let stand about 10 minutes to drain well. In a large bowl toss the well-drained peels and the remaining 1 cup sugar to coat pieces well. Spread peels out on waxed paper to dry thoroughly. Cover loosely with waxed paper and let dry overnight at room temperature. Store in tightly covered jars or plastic containers. Makes about 1 pound.

❧ Chocolate–Marshmallow Fudge

2 cups firmly packed dark
   brown sugar
1 cup granulated sugar

Combine sugars, evaporated milk, and butter in a saucepan. Cook over moderate heat (about 250° F.), stirring frequently, until mixture comes to a boil. Boil 15

1 cup undiluted evaporated
  milk
½ cup butter or margarine
1 7-ounce jar marshmallow
  creme (approximately 1¾
  cups)
1 teaspoon vanilla extract
1 12-ounce package (2 cups)
  semisweet chocolate pieces
1 cup coarsely chopped nuts

minutes, stirring occasionally. Remove from heat; add marshmallow creme and vanilla. Stir until the mixture is smooth. Add chocolate pieces and chopped nuts and stir until chocolate is melted. Spread evenly in a buttered 9-inch-square cake pan. Chill until firm. Cut into squares or rectangles, as desired. Makes about 2½ pounds.

Chocolate Bark

2 4-ounce blocks sweet
  cooking chocolate
2 cups coarsely chopped
  walnuts

Melt chocolate in the top of a double boiler over hot, not boiling, water. Remove from heat. Stir in nuts. Spread in a buttered 8-inch-square cake pan. Cool until firm; cut into squares. Makes about 1 pound.

Chocolate Cereal Drops

¾ cup sugar
⅓ cup light cream
¼ cup light corn syrup
Few grains salt
1 6-ounce package semisweet
  chocolate pieces
1 teaspoon vanilla extract
3 cups sugared corn flakes
1 cup flaked coconut

Combine sugar, cream, corn syrup, and salt in a large saucepan. Cook over moderate heat (about 250° F.) until mixture just comes to a boil, stirring constantly. Remove from heat. Add chocolate pieces and vanilla and stir until chocolate melts. Combine cereal flakes and coconut in a large bowl. Add chocolate mixture and stir until blended. Spoon heaping teaspoonfuls onto a foil-lined cookie sheet. Chill until firm. Makes about 3 dozen.

Chocolate–Peanut Balls

1 6-ounce package semisweet
  chocolate pieces
⅔ cup sweetened condensed
  milk
½ cup salted Spanish peanuts
1 teaspoon vanilla extract
Colored sugar (optional)
Candied cherries (optional)

Partially melt chocolate pieces in the top of a double boiler over hot, not boiling, water. Remove from hot water and stir rapidly until chocolate is entirely melted. Stir in milk, peanuts, and vanilla. Drop from a teaspoon onto waxed paper. Chill until firm enough to handle. Shape each into a ball. If desired, decorate with colored sugar or candied cherries. Chill again until firm. Makes about 4 dozen.

CANDIES AND CONFECTIONS

❧ Chocolate Quickies

1 cup chunk-style peanut
butter
⅔ cup sweetened condensed
milk
3 tablespoons unsweetened
cocoa

Heat oven to 350° F. Combine peanut butter, condensed milk, and cocoa. Drop by teaspoonfuls onto greased baking sheet. Bake about 10 minutes. Makes 2½ dozen.

❧ Cereal Gems

⅔ cup soft butter or
margarine
1 cup sifted confectioners'
sugar
1 tablespoon vanilla extract
1 cup diced, mixed, candied
fruits and peels
2 cups quick-cooking rolled
oats

Work butter in a bowl until creamy. Gradually add sugar and continue to beat until fluffy. Add vanilla and mixed fruits and peels; blend thoroughly. Stir in rolled oats. Shape mixture into balls and place on a cookie sheet. Chill until firm. Decorate as desired. Makes about 2 dozen balls.

❧ Date–Nut Candies

¾ cup sugar
2 tablespoons molasses
1 cup chopped pitted dates
2 eggs, slightly beaten
1 teaspoon vanilla extract
1 cup chopped pecans
2 cups corn flakes
1 cup flaked coconut

Combine sugar, molasses, dates, and eggs in a large skillet; place over moderately low heat (about 225° F.) and cook about 5 minutes, stirring constantly, until mixture thickens and leaves sides of pan. Remove from heat; stir in vanilla and pecans. Fold in cereal. Cool slightly. Moisten hands and shape level tablespoonfuls of mixture into balls. Roll in coconut. Chill until firm. Makes 2½ dozen.

❧ Date-and-Pecan Logs

1 tablespoon butter or
margarine
¼ cup light corn syrup
½ teaspoon vanilla extract
3 tablespoons nonfat dry
milk solids
¼ teaspoon salt
2 cups sifted confectioners'
sugar

Blend butter and corn syrup; stir in vanilla. Combine dry milk, salt, and confectioners' sugar; add to corn syrup mixture. Mix and knead with fingers until blended and smooth. Mix in chopped dates and chopped pecans. Stir and knead until thoroughly mixed. Divide mixture into 3 equal portions and shape each portion into a roll about 6 inches long. Wrap in waxed paper and chill 1 hour. Heat caramels and cream in a small saucepan over low heat (about 200° F.) until

1 cup finely cut pitted dates
1 cup chopped pecans
1 14-ounce package vanilla caramels
2 tablespoons cream
1½ to 2 cups pecan halves

caramels are melted. Place a candy roll on a sheet of waxed paper. With a spatula, spread roll with some of the caramel mixture. Press rows of pecan halves into the caramel. Turn roll to coat all sides. Repeat with remaining rolls. Cover and chill until firm. Slice with a sharp knife. Makes about 3 pounds.

No-Cook Fondant

⅓ cup softened butter or margarine
⅓ cup light corn syrup
1 teaspoon vanilla extract
½ teaspoon salt
1 16-ounce package confectioners' sugar

Work butter in a large mixing bowl until creamy; blend in corn syrup, vanilla, and salt. Gradually add confectioners' sugar and mix with spoon until mixture is too stiff to stir. Add remaining sugar and knead with the hands. Turn out onto a board and continue kneading until mixture is well blended and smooth. Wrap fondant tightly in plastic wrap and store in refrigerator 2 or 3 days to ripen. Shape as desired. Fondant may be used to stuff dates or other dried fruits. Store in a cool place. Makes about 1⅓ pounds fondant.

Mint Balls

Substitute *1 teaspoon peppermint extract* for vanilla. Add *a few drops green food coloring.* Shape into small balls and roll in *green sugar* if desired.

Mocha Logs

Add *2 teaspoons instant coffee powder* when adding confectioners' sugar. Shape into 2-x-½-inch rolls. Roll in *chocolate sprinkles.*

Fruited Fondant Rolls

Add *½ cup diced mixed fruits and peels* with the confectioners' sugar. Shape into 3 rolls about 1 inch in diameter and 8 inches long. Roll each in *finely chopped nuts, chocolate sprinkles,* or *nonpareils,* as desired. Wrap tightly in plastic wrap and foil. Chill until firm. Cut into ⅜-inch slices. Makes about 60 slices.

Fondant-Stuffed Fruits

Color all, or portions of, the fondant, if desired. Stuff dried *apricots* by stretching each apricot half slightly to make the surface more moist. Place a small portion of fondant in the center and push apricot up on both sides to form an oval. Stuff *dates* and dried *prunes* by cutting a slit in each and inserting a small portion of fondant. Store in closed container. 1⅓ pounds fondant is enough to stuff about 1¾ pounds fruit.

CANDIES AND CONFECTIONS

❧ Kris Kringles

1 12-ounce package
  semisweet chocolate pieces
¼ pound (16) marshmallows,
  cut in eighths
½ cup small colored
  gumdrops
½ cup coarsely chopped
  walnuts

Melt chocolate in the top of a double boiler over hot, not boiling, water. Cover cookie sheet with double thickness of waxed paper. Spread half the chocolate on it in a 9-x-6-inch rectangle, using a small spatula dipped in warm water. Cover evenly with a layer of marshmallows, gumdrops, and walnuts. Dribble remaining chocolate over top in crisscross fashion. Set in cool, dry place until firm. To serve, cut into squares. Makes 24 squares.

❧ Easy Apricot–Coconut Balls

2 tablespoons softened butter
  or margarine
½ cup light corn syrup
1 tablespoon water
½ teaspoon vanilla extract
¼ teaspoon almond extract
⅔ cup nonfat dry milk solids
2 cups dried apricots,
  coarsely chopped (2
  8-ounce packages)
2 cups flaked coconut
Confectioners' sugar
Candied cherries (optional)

Blend butter and corn syrup in a large bowl. Stir in water, flavorings, and dry milk. Mix apricots and coconut together in a medium-sized bowl; add to corn syrup mixture and knead until thoroughly blended. Form into 1½-inch balls. Roll in confectioners' sugar or garnish with a slice of candied cherry, if desired. Makes about 1½ pounds.

❧ Marshmallows

1 envelope unflavored
  gelatine
⅓ cup cold water
½ cup sugar
⅔ cup light corn syrup
½ teaspoon vanilla extract
½ cup cornstarch
½ cup confectioners' sugar

Soften gelatine in the cold water in the top of a double boiler. Place over boiling water and stir until gelatine is dissolved. Add sugar and stir until sugar is dissolved. Pour corn syrup into the large bowl of an electric mixer. Add gelatine mixture and vanilla. Beat at high speed about 15 minutes, or until mixture becomes thick and of a marshmallow consistency. Combine cornstarch and confectioners' sugar. Coat bottom and sides of an 8-inch-square cake pan with some of the mixture. Reserve remaining cornstarch–sugar mixture. Pour marshmallow mixture into pan and smooth off top with spatula. Let stand in a cool place (not refrigerator) until set, about 1 hour. Sprinkle a board lightly with some of the cornstarch–sugar mixture. Loosen candy around edges of pan with a knife. Turn out onto board. Cut into squares with a serrated knife. Roll squares into cornstarch–sugar mixture to coat thoroughly. Makes about 1 pound.

❧ Quick Marzipan Candies

½ cup warm mashed potato
2 teaspoons soft butter or margarine
Few grains salt
½ cup very finely ground almonds
1 teaspoon vanilla extract
1 teaspoon almond extract
About 6¼ cups sifted confectioners' sugar

Mix warm potato, butter, salt, almonds, vanilla, and almond extract. Gradually add sugar, stirring until thick. Knead mixture with hands, working in more sugar, 2 tablespoons at a time, until candy is no longer sticky. Pull off small rounds of dough and shape into fruits and vegetables about 1 or 2 inches in length. No molds are necessary; just a little practice makes perfect. Let stand about 2 hours before tinting, then follow suggestions given for each fruit. Makes about 2½ pounds.

Apples

Pour a few drops of red food coloring in a cup; dilute with a few drops of water. Apply color with a brush. Cut a small leaf from green paper and attach with piece of green toothpick. Brush apples with Glaze (recipe on page 900) to make them shine.

Peaches

Combine a few drops of yellow and orange food coloring in a cup; dilute with a few drops of water. Apply color with a brush. To give peaches a "blush" spot, paint lightly with diluted red coloring on one side.

Lemons

Pinch a round ball of candy lightly at each end to make it oval. Brush with undiluted yellow food coloring. Insert a clove at one end for stem.

Oranges

Pour a few drops of orange food coloring in a cup; dilute with a few drops of water. Brush color on gently and insert a clove at one end for stem.

Bananas

Brush with undiluted yellow coloring. Add tips and lines with a toothpick dipped in melted unsweetened chocolate. Add a light brushing of diluted green food coloring at both ends, just above the chocolate tips.

CANDIES AND CONFECTIONS

Plums

Pour a few drops of blue and red food coloring in a cup; dilute with a few drops of water. Brush plums lightly with the diluted purple and let dry; then brush color with Glaze (recipe below).

Grapes

Take a small amount of candy and make a thin (⅛ inch) solid base, the shape of a cluster of grapes. Form tiny balls and arrange on base. Press grapes together lightly. Brush with diluted purple coloring used for plums; glaze (recipe below).

Strawberries

Brush generously with Glaze (recipe below). Dip into coarse red sugar. Cut a leaf from green pepper; attach with piece of green toothpick.

Watermelon Slices

Brush outer "rind" with diluted green food coloring. Leave a small space of untinted candy, then brush remainder with diluted red food coloring. Paint on "seeds" with a toothpick dipped in melted unsweetened chocolate.

Carrots

Tint with diluted orange color.

Potatoes

Make "eyes" with tine of fork. Dip in cocoa; brush off excess.

Glaze

Brush fruit with mixture of 1 tablespoon light corn syrup and ¾ teaspoon water.

Peanut Mounds

1 cup peanut butter
2 6-ounce packages
  semisweet chocolate
  pieces
½ cup flaked coconut
½ cup seeded raisins
1½ cups salted Spanish

Place peanut butter and chocolate pieces in the top part of a double boiler. Place over hot, not boiling, water and stir occasionally until mixture is smooth and melted. Fold in coconut, raisins, and peanuts. Spoon a slightly rounded tablespoon of mixture on the top of each graham cracker. Sprinkle with additional coconut, if desired. Makes about 3 dozen.

peanuts
About 36 graham crackers
Coconut (optional)

✑ Peanut Butter–Date Drops

½ cup chunk-style peanut
butter
1 14-ounce can sweetened
condensed milk, undiluted
2 cups packaged graham-
cracker crumbs
1 cup chopped pitted dates
½ teaspoon ground cinnamon
½ teaspoon ground cloves
Flaked coconut (optional)

Combine peanut butter, condensed milk, cracker crumbs, dates, cinnamon, and cloves. Drop rounded teaspoonfuls onto a cookie sheet. Sprinkle with coconut, if desired. Chill until firm. Makes about 4 dozen.

✑ Peanut–Marshmallow Squares

2 tablespoons butter or
margarine
¼ cup peanut butter
8 ounces large marshmallows
(about 32)
2 cups quick-cooking rolled
oats
1 cup salted Spanish peanuts
3 1-ounce squares semisweet
chocolate
3 tablespoons peanut butter

Place butter, the ¼ cup peanut butter, and marshmallows in the top of a double boiler. Place over boiling water and heat, stirring occasionally, until marshmallows are melted and mixture is smooth. Place rolled oats and peanuts in a large mixing bowl. Add marshmallow mixture and combine. Spread mixture with buttered fingers evenly into a buttered 9-inch square cake pan. Place chocolate and the 3 tablespoons peanut butter in the top part of the double boiler and place over boiling water, stirring occasionally, until mixture is smooth and melted. Spread chocolate mixture over cereal mixture. Chill until set. Cut into 1½-inch squares. Makes about 3 dozen.

✑ Scotch Chocolate Drops

1 6-ounce package semisweet
chocolate pieces
1 6-ounce package
butterscotch pieces
1 7-ounce can salted peanuts,
chopped
1 cup cereal (puffed or
shredded type)

Place chocolate and butterscotch pieces in top of a double boiler over hot water; stir until melted. Stir in peanuts and cereal. Drop by rounded teaspoonfuls onto waxed paper; chill until firm. Makes 4 dozen.

Spirit Candy

1 pound pitted dates
1 cup pecans or walnuts
1 4¾-ounce box (about 30) vanilla wafers
¼ cup sugar
¼ cup bourbon
2 tablespoons light corn syrup
2 cups shredded coconut

Put the dates, nuts, and wafers through a food chopper, using a fine blade. Add sugar, bourbon, and syrup; blend well. Form into a layer ½ inch thick on a cookie sheet. Cut into 1-inch squares; coat all sides with coconut. Store in a tightly covered container until ready to use. Makes 4 dozen.

Turkish Paste

2 envelopes unflavored gelatine
½ cup cold water
2 cups sugar
½ cup hot water
½ cup orange juice
2½ tablespoons lemon juice
Grated peel of 1 orange
Grated peel of 1 lemon
Few drops red food coloring
Few drops yellow food coloring
Confectioners' sugar
Granulated sugar

Soften gelatine in the cold water. Combine sugar and the hot water in a saucepan; place over moderately low heat (about 225° F.) and heat to boiling. Stir in dissolved gelatine. Boil slowly 20 minutes. Remove from heat and add fruit juices, grated orange and lemon peels, and food colorings. Let stand 5 minutes. Strain gelatine mixture into an 8-inch-square cake pan. Let stand several hours in a cool place until set. Sprinkle confectioners' sugar over breadboard. Loosen candy from edge of pan with spatula; remove from pan with fingers and place on board. Cut into ¾-inch cubes and roll pieces in granulated sugar. Makes about 3 dozen.

Vanilla-Wafer Fudgies

1 6-ounce package semisweet chocolate pieces
1 3-ounce package cream cheese
¼ cup sifted confectioners' sugar
¼ cup honey
½ teaspoon vanilla extract
⅛ teaspoon salt
2 cups (about 40) finely crushed vanilla wafers
½ cup finely chopped nuts
Chopped nuts or nut halves (optional)

Place chocolate pieces and cream cheese in the top of a double boiler over hot, not boiling, water. Stir until melted. Remove from heat. Blend in confectioners' sugar, honey, vanilla, and salt. Add vanilla wafers and chopped nuts and mix well. Form into 1-inch balls, using 1 level tablespoonful for each. If desired, roll in finely chopped nuts, or press a nut half into the top of each. Chill until firm. (Instead of separate balls, mixture may be pressed evenly into a buttered or foil-lined 8-inch-square cake pan, chilled, and cut into 1½-inch squares.) Makes about 3 dozen balls.

Candies to Make with a Thermometer

A candy-thermometer reading is the most certain test of the doneness of cooked candies that must be brought to just the right degree of cooking. Both the paddle-shaped thermometer and the metal probe with a dial-shaped top come with a clip that fits onto the side of any saucepan. This is necessary because the thermometer tip must be completely covered by the boiling syrup but not be touching the bottom of the pan. When you use the paddle-shaped thermometer, be sure to read it at eye-level. You'll need to watch carefully after the temperature reaches 220° F. (It rises rather slowly to this point but goes up rapidly after that.) When candy has reached the proper temperature, remove it immediately from the heat to stop further cooking. Take out the thermometer and let it cool to room temperature before washing it.

If the recipe calls for cooling the candy before beating it, do it. If you start to beat it before it has cooled to the required temperature (usually 110° F. or until the outside of the pan feels lukewarm when you touch it with your hand), large sugar crystals will form and make the candy grainy. You should even avoid bumping or jarring the pan during this cooling period.

The cold-water test may be used to test doneness of candy if you cannot get a candy thermometer. It is, however, less accurate and subject to experienced judgment. With a clean teaspoon, drop about a half-teaspoon of the hot syrup into a cup of very cold water. Let it stand about thirty seconds. Always remove candy from the heat while you're testing candy by this method; otherwise it may go on cooking past the desired point. All our recipes have a descriptive direction for the cold-water test. At the soft-ball stage, the candy in the water should hold a shape that can be picked up in the fingers. It will be soft and flatten out when it's taken from the water. At the firm-ball stage, the candy will hold a firm shape that doesn't flatten out when it's taken from the water. At the hard-ball stage, it will be very firm but pliable. At the soft-crack stage, the syrup will separate into threads, which will feel hard but not brittle. At the hard-crack stage, threads will be brittle. Always use a clean teaspoon and a fresh cup of cold water for each test. If the recipe calls for the candy to be stirred *after* it starts to boil, wash the stirring spoon each time to avoid stirring any formation of sugar crystals into the candy.

Don't scrape the pan when you turn candy out of it; you may be scraping sugar crystals into the finished candy which will chain-react to make the whole mass grainy. Anyway, you'll probably have someone nearby who will want to lick the pan.

Apricot Candy Roll

3 cups sugar
½ cup peanut butter
1 cup milk
1 cup finely chopped
   dried apricots
½ teaspoon salt
2 teaspoons vanilla extract

Combine sugar, peanut butter, milk, apricots, and salt in a saucepan. Place over moderate heat (about 250° F.) and cook, stirring constantly, until sugar is dissolved and mixture boils. Cook without stirring until a candy thermometer registers 238° F., or a small amount of mixture forms a soft ball when dropped in cold water. Remove from heat. Cool to 110° F. (lukewarm). Add vanilla. Beat until mixture is stiff enough to handle. Turn out on buttered platter and work with hands until very smooth and satinlike. Shape into 2 rolls about 1½ inches in diameter. Wrap in waxed paper; chill at least 3 hours. Cut into slices. Makes 2 pounds.

Butterscotch

2 cups sugar
⅔ cup dark corn syrup
¼ cup water
¼ cup light cream
¼ cup butter or margarine

Combine sugar, corn syrup, water, and cream in a saucepan. Place over moderately high heat (about 300° F.) and cook, stirring constantly, until mixture boils. Continue cooking, stirring occasionally, until a candy thermometer registers 260° F., or a small amount of mixture forms a hard ball when dropped into cold water. Add butter and continue cooking, stirring constantly, until thermometer registers 280° F., or a small amount of syrup separates into threads that are hard but not brittle when dropped into cold water. Quickly pour syrup into a buttered 8-inch-square cake pan. Cool at room temperature. When surface of candy has cooled enough to hold an impression made with a knife, cut into 1-inch squares. When candy is thoroughly hardened, remove from pan and break into pieces along markings. Wrap each piece in plastic wrap or waxed paper. Store candies in a tight container in a cool place. Makes about 5 dozen 1-inch pieces.

Candy Canes

2 cups sugar
½ cup light corn syrup
½ cup water
¼ teaspoon cream of tartar
1 teaspoon peppermint
   extract
1 teaspoon red food coloring

Mix sugar, corn syrup, water, and cream of tartar in saucepan. Cook over moderately high heat (about 300° F.) without stirring, until candy thermometer registers 265° F., or a small amount dropped in cold water forms a very hard ball. Remove from heat; stir in peppermint. Pour out half of syrup onto a greased platter. Stir coloring into remaining portion; then pour out onto another greased platter. When cool enough to handle, pull each with fingers until candy has a satinlike finish and is light in color. Pull into long thin ropes and twist red part around white. Cut in 4-inch lengths and turn one end to shape canes. Place on greased baking sheet until hard. Makes about 24.

❧ Cinnamon-Candied Apples

8 medium-sized red apples
8 6-inch wooden skewers
3 cups sugar
½ cup light corn syrup
½ cup water
1 drop oil of cinnamon
1 teaspoon red food coloring

Wash and polish apples. Remove stems and insert wooden skewers in stem end of apples. Combine sugar, corn syrup, and water in top part of double boiler. Place directly over moderately high heat (about 300° F.). Cook, stirring constantly, until mixture boils. Then cook without stirring until candy thermometer registers 285° F., or a small amount of the syrup separates into threads that are hard but not brittle when dropped into very cold water. In the meantime, heat water in the bottom of the double boiler. Remove syrup from the heat when cooked and add flavoring and coloring. (Oil of cinnamon may be purchased in a drugstore.) Stir only to mix. Place the pan of syrup over the warm water in the bottom of double boiler. Hold each apple by skewer end and quickly twirl apples in syrup, tilting pan to cover apples with syrup. Remove from syrup. Twirl apples to spread syrup smoothly. Place on a lightly buttered cookie sheet to cool. Store in a cool place. Makes 8.

❧ Creamy Caramels

2 cups light cream
2 cups sugar
1 cup light or dark corn syrup
½ teaspoon salt
⅓ cup butter or margarine
1 teaspoon vanilla extract
½ cup coarsely chopped pecans

Heat cream to lukewarm in a large heavy saucepan over very low heat (about 175° F.). Remove 1 cup cream and reserve. Add sugar, corn syrup, and salt to the remaining cream in the saucepan. Cook over moderate heat (about 250° F.) about 10 minutes, stirring constantly. Add the reserved 1 cup cream very slowly so that mixture does not stop boiling. Cook about 5 minutes longer, stirring constantly. Stir in butter, about a teaspoon at a time. Reduce heat to moderately low (about 225° F.) and cook, stirring constantly, until a candy thermometer registers 248° F., or a small amount of mixture forms a firm ball when dropped into cold water. Remove from heat; add vanilla and nuts and mix gently. Allow to stand about 10 minutes. Stir only enough to distribute the nuts and pour into one corner of a lightly buttered 8-inch-square cake pan, letting the mixture flow to its own level in the pan. Do not scrape the saucepan. Cool to room temperature. Turn candy out of pan onto a cutting board. If candy sticks, heat bottom of pan slightly and cool before cutting. Mark off into ¾-inch squares and cut with a large, sharp knife. Wrap each square in waxed paper. Makes about 2 pounds.

◄§ English Toffee

1 cup butter
1 cup sugar
1 6-ounce package semisweet chocolate pieces
1 cup chopped walnuts

Butter well a 9-inch-square cake pan. Combine butter and sugar in a small, heavy saucepan. Cook over moderate heat, stirring constantly, until a candy thermometer registers 310° F. (Do not use temperature-controlled burner; steady heat is required.) At this point the candy should be of caramel color. A small amount of the syrup should form a hard ball when dropped into cold water and be brittle when removed from the water. Remove the candy from the heat while testing. Quickly pour the candy into the greased pan and spread evenly with a spatula. Cool until hardened. Melt half the chocolate pieces in top part of double boiler over hot water and spread over surface of hardened candy in pan. Sprinkle with half the chopped nuts. Cool until chocolate is hardened. Turn candy out of pan onto waxed paper with chocolate layer on the bottom. Melt the remaining chocolate pieces and spread on the top side of the candy. Sprinkle with remainder of nuts. Cool again until this layer of chocolate is hardened. Break toffee into pieces and store in a tightly covered tin for at least 2 days to develop the flavor. Makes 1 pound.

◄§ Fruited Pecans

2 cups sugar
1 tablespoon flour
½ cup plus 2 tablespoons milk
1 tablespoon butter or margarine
Juice of ½ lemon (about 1½ tablespoons)
Juice of 1 orange (about ½ cup)

Combine sugar and flour in a saucepan; add milk and butter. Bring to a boil over moderate heat (about 250° F.). Stir in juices and orange peel. Continue cooking until candy thermometer registers 236° F., or until a soft ball forms when a little of the mixture is dropped into cold water. Place pecans in a 10-inch skillet; pour hot syrup mixture over nuts. Cook over moderate heat (about 250° F.), stirring constantly, until syrup is creamy and nuts tend to separate, about 20 to 25 minutes. Pour

*Grated peel of 1 orange (about
4 teaspoons)*
4 cups pecan halves

nut mixture onto brown paper and separate nuts with 2 forks. Two nut halves may be joined together to make a full-sized nut. Cool and store in a tightly covered jar or other container. Serve as a confection. Makes about 6½ cups, or 1¾ pounds.

Fudge–Peanut Drops

1¼ cups sugar
¼ cup unsweetened cocoa
½ teaspoon salt
¼ cup light corn syrup
½ cup milk
1 teaspoon vanilla extract
¼ cup peanut butter
1 cup salted peanuts
*1½ cups quick-cooking rolled
oats*

Combine sugar, cocoa, and salt in a medium-sized saucepan. Stir in corn syrup and milk. Cook over moderate heat (about 250° F.), stirring constantly, until sugar is dissolved. Continue to cook, stirring occasionally, until a candy thermometer registers 234° F., or a small amount of the mixture forms a soft ball when dropped into cold water. Remove from heat; stir in vanilla, peanut butter, peanuts, and oats. Beat with a spoon until candy begins to thicken. Drop quickly by teaspoonfuls onto waxed paper. Refrigerate. Makes 3 dozen.

Perfect-Every-Time Fudge

*3 6-ounce packages
semisweet chocolate
pieces*
¼ teaspoon salt
1 cup butter or margarine
*1 7-ounce jar marshmallow
creme*
*1 13-fluid-ounce can
evaporated milk*
4½ cups sugar
1 cup chopped walnuts
1 teaspoon vanilla extract

Put chocolate, salt, butter, and marshmallow creme into large bowl. Combine evaporated milk and sugar in large saucepan; place over moderate heat. (Do not use controlled-heat burner; steady heat is required.) Bring to a full, rolling boil and, stirring constantly, boil 13 minutes. If you use a candy thermometer, the temperature should register about 236° F. Pour milk mixture over chocolate mixture and beat until chocolate is melted and blended. Fold in nuts and vanilla. Spread into 2 greased 8-x-8-x-2-inch pans. Refrigerate until candy is firm, and cut into small squares. Makes about 5 pounds.

Chocolate Fudge

1 cup milk
*2 1-ounce squares
unsweetened chocolate*
2 cups sugar
*2 tablespoons light corn
syrup*
Few grains salt

Place milk and chocolate in a heavy saucepan. Place over moderately low heat (about 225° F.) and cook, stirring constantly, until chocolate melts and mixture is smooth. Add sugar, corn syrup, and salt. Stir constantly until mixture boils. Cover and cook 1 minute. Uncover and cook over moderate heat (about 250° F.) until a candy thermometer registers 236° F., or a small amount of

2 tablespoons butter or
  margarine
1 teaspoon vanilla extract
½ cup chopped pecans or
  walnuts

mixture forms a soft ball when dropped into cold water. Add butter and vanilla, but do not stir. Cool to 110° F. (lukewarm). Beat until fudge thickens and loses its gloss. Add nuts and pour into a buttered 8-inch-square cake pan. When firm, cut into squares. Makes about 1 pound.

Peanut-Butter Fudge

2 cups sugar
½ cup light corn syrup
½ cup water
¼ teaspoon salt
1 tablespoon white or cider
  vinegar
2 tablespoons butter or
  margarine
2 tablespoons light cream
⅓ cup peanut butter

Combine sugar, corn syrup, water, salt, vinegar, butter, and light cream in a saucepan. Cook over moderate heat (about 250° F.), stirring constantly, until mixture boils. Continue cooking, stirring occasionally, until a candy thermometer registers 238° F., or a small amount of mixture forms a soft ball when dropped into cold water. Remove from heat. Add peanut butter; do not stir. Cool to 110° F. (lukewarm). Beat until candy thickens enough to hold its shape when a small amount is dropped from a spoon onto waxed paper or until it loses its gloss. Quickly pour into buttered 8-inch-square cake pan. When firm, cut into squares. Makes about 1½ pounds.

Honey Nougat

1½ cups sugar
¼ cup light corn syrup
¼ cup honey
½ cup water
⅛ teaspoon salt
2 egg whites, at room
  temperature
Few grains salt
½ cup chopped candied
  fruits and peels
½ cup chopped walnuts
Candied cherries (optional)
Citron (optional)

Combine sugar, corn syrup, honey, water, and salt in a saucepan. Cook over moderately high heat (about 300° F.), stirring constantly, until sugar is dissolved. Continue cooking without stirring until a candy thermometer registers 290° F., or a small amount dropped in cold water forms a hard ball. Wipe crystals from sides of saucepan with a damp cloth; cool about 2 minutes. Add salt to egg whites and whip with a rotary beater or an electric mixer until stiff peaks form. Slowly pour syrup into egg whites in a long thin stream, whipping constantly. Continue whipping until mixture thickens, loses its glossy appearance, and a small amount dropped from a spoon holds its shape. Fold in fruits and nuts. Drop from a teaspoon onto greased cookie sheet. Top with candied cherries and citron, if desired. Makes about 24.

Lollipops

2 cups sugar
1 cup light corn syrup
½ cup water

Combine sugar, corn syrup, and water in medium-sized saucepan. Cook over moderate heat (do not use temperature-controlled burner), without stirring, until a

½ teaspoon red or green
    food coloring
1½ teaspoons peppermint
    extract
Wooden skewers

candy thermometer registers 300° F., or until a small amount of mixture separates into threads that are hard and brittle when dropped into very cold water. Cool slightly; add coloring and flavoring and blend. Place 2 dozen skewers 4 inches apart on lightly oiled cookie sheets. (If using a Teflon-coated sheet, it is not necessary to oil.) Drop candy mixture from tip of tablespoon over skewers to form 2- to 3-inch disks. If syrup hardens before all the lollipops are made, return pan to low heat long enough to melt syrup. After lollipops have hardened, place on a nonstick-coated cookie sheet or on waxed paper. Store in a cool, dry place, but not in the refrigerator. Makes about 2 dozen lollipops.

✑ Minted Walnuts

1 cup sugar
¼ teaspoon salt
⅓ cup water
1 tablespoon light corn
    syrup
6 large marshmallows
¾ teaspoon peppermint
    extract
2½ cups walnut halves

Combine sugar, salt, water, and corn syrup in saucepan. Cook over moderate heat (about 250° F.) until syrup reaches 236° F. on a candy thermometer, or until a little of the mixture forms a soft ball when dropped into cold water. Remove from heat; add marshmallows and peppermint; stir until marshmallows are melted. Add nuts; stir gently until nuts are evenly coated. Turn out on cookie sheet and separate nuts into a single layer with a fork. When cool, store in tightly covered container. Makes about 3 cups.

✑ Molasses Taffy

⅔ cup light molasses
⅓ cup light corn syrup
1½ cups firmly packed light
    brown sugar
1½ tablespoons white or cider
    vinegar
½ cup water
¼ teaspoon salt
⅛ teaspoon baking soda
¼ cup butter or margarine

Combine molasses, corn syrup, sugar, vinegar, water, and salt in a large saucepan. Cook over moderate heat, stirring constantly until sugar is dissolved. Continue to cook, stirring occasionally, until temperature registers 265° F. on a candy thermometer, or a small amount of the mixture forms a hard ball when dropped in cold water. Remove from heat; stir in baking soda and butter. Pour into a greased, large, shallow pan and allow to stand until cool enough to handle. Butter tips of fingers well. Cut off pieces of mixture and pull and twist until it changes color from brown to bronze. Twist into desired shapes or cut into 1-inch pieces with scissors dipped in cold water. Wrap each piece in waxed paper. Makes about 12 dozen 1-inch pieces.

CANDIES AND CONFECTIONS

✒️ Taffy

2 cups sugar
½ cup light corn syrup
1 cup water
½ teaspoon cream of tartar
2 tablespoons butter or
    margarine
2 teaspoons vanilla extract

Butter well a large shallow platter. Combine sugar, corn syrup, water, and cream of tartar in a saucepan. Bring to a boil over moderately high heat (about 275° F.), stirring constantly, until sugar dissolves. Continue cooking, without stirring, until a candy thermometer registers 260° F., or a small amount of mixture forms a hard ball when dropped into cold water. Remove from heat and stir in butter and vanilla. Pour syrup into the buttered platter. Let stand until cool enough to handle. Pull and twist candy with lightly buttered fingers until it has a satinlike finish and changes from clear to milky-colored. Pull into long strips ¾ inch in diameter. Cut into 1-inch pieces with scissors. Wrap individually in waxed paper. Makes 1 pound candy.

Peppermint Taffy

Add ¼ teaspoon peppermint extract and a few drops red food coloring before pouring into buttered platter.

✒️ Peanut Brittle

½ cup dark corn syrup
¼ cup dark molasses
¼ cup sugar
2 tablespoons butter or
    margarine
1 cup salted peanuts
⅛ teaspoon baking soda

Combine corn syrup, molasses, sugar, and butter in a saucepan. Stir in peanuts. Place over moderate heat and cook until a candy thermometer registers 280° F., or a small amount of the mixture separates into threads that are hard but not brittle when dropped into cold water. (Do not use temperature-controlled burner; steady heat is required.) Stir in baking soda. Pour into a large, shallow, buttered platter. Cool. Run a spatula under candy while it is cooling to prevent it from sticking to platter. When hardened break into irregular-shaped pieces. Store in airtight container. Makes 9 ounces.

✒️ Peppermint Hard Candies

2 cups sugar
1 cup light corn syrup

Combine sugar, corn syrup, and water in a saucepan. Cook over moderately high heat (do not use

½ cup water
6 crushed peppermint sticks
(4 ounces)

temperature-controlled burner), without stirring, until a candy thermometer registers 300° F., or a small amount of the mixture separates into threads that are hard and brittle when dropped into cold water. Cool about 10 minutes. Add crushed peppermint candy and blend. Pour into a buttered jelly-roll pan. When surface of candy is cool enough to hold an impression made with a knife, mark candy into 1-inch squares. Let cool. Turn pan upside down over board or table. Tap bottom sharply to loosen. Break pieces apart. Wrap pieces in squares of plastic wrap and store in cool place. Makes about 1½ pounds.

✑ Penuche

3 cups firmly packed light brown sugar
¼ cup light or dark corn syrup
¾ cup milk
¼ teaspoon salt
2 tablespoons butter or margarine
1 teaspoon vanilla extract
50 pecan halves

Combine sugar, corn syrup, milk, salt, and butter in a saucepan. Cook over moderately high heat (300° F.), stirring constantly, until mixture boils. Continue cooking, stirring occasionally, until a candy thermometer registers 238° F., or a small amount of mixture forms a soft ball when dropped into cold water. Cool to 110° F. (lukewarm). Add vanilla and beat until candy thickens enough to hold its shape when a small amount is dropped from a spoon onto waxed paper or until it loses its gloss. Quickly pour into a buttered 8-inch-square cake pan. Place pecans in rows on top of candy. Chill in refrigerator until firm. When firm, cut candy into 1½-inch squares. Makes about 4 dozen.

✑ Popcorn Balls

2 quarts unsalted popcorn
1 cup light corn syrup
1 teaspoon white or cider vinegar
2 tablespoons butter or margarine
1 teaspoon vanilla extract
Four drops red food coloring (optional)

Place popcorn in a large, greased bowl. Combine corn syrup and vinegar in a small saucepan. Boil slowly over moderately high heat (about 275° F.) until a candy thermometer registers 260° F., or a small amount of syrup dropped in cold water forms a hard ball. Remove syrup from heat and stir in butter, vanilla, and, if desired, food coloring. Pour syrup over popcorn in bowl and toss with 2 forks until corn is well coated. Cool slightly. Shape into balls of desired size and place on buttered plate. Makes about seven 3-inch balls.

↵ *Pralines* I

2 cups sugar
⅔ cup milk
⅓ cup dark corn syrup
¼ teaspoon salt
½ teaspoon vanilla extract
1½ cups whole pecans

Combine sugar, milk, corn syrup, and salt in a saucepan. Place over moderate heat (about 250° F.) and cook, stirring constantly, until sugar is dissolved. Continue to cook, without stirring, until candy thermometer registers 238° F., or a small amount of mixture forms a soft ball when dropped into cold water. Remove from heat and cool to 110° F. (lukewarm). Add vanilla and beat until mixture is thick and creamy. Stir in pecans. Drop from tip of tablespoon onto waxed paper. Shape with a spoon to form a circle and spread pecans so that they are 1 layer deep. Allow the pralines to remain uncovered on the waxed paper several hours, until firm and sugared. Makes 1¼ pounds.

↵ *Pralines* II

2 cups sugar
1 teaspoon baking soda
1 cup buttermilk
2 teaspoons vanilla extract
2 cups pecan halves

Combine sugar, soda, and buttermilk in a medium-sized saucepan. Place over moderate heat (about 250° F.). Cook, stirring occasionally, until a small amount of the syrup forms a soft ball when dropped into cold water, or a candy thermometer registers 236° F. Remove from heat and let cool 5 minutes. Add vanilla and nuts and beat with a wooden spoon until slightly thickened. Drop by heaping tablespoonfuls onto waxed paper. Let stand until set. Makes about 16.

CHAPTER XXVI

PRESERVING FOOD

Preserving food was once the only way a homemaker could provide her family with a variety of nutritious meals through the winter months. Today, preserving food is in most cases a choice, not a necessity. It may be a glass of shimmering rose-geranium jelly to make a special gift for family or friends, or jars of watermelon rind pickles made from leftovers after you've finished the juicy melon. Or it may be bright packages of asparagus or sweet corn-on-the-cob frozen when it's at its briefly tender best. Canning and freezing are the major ways of preserving food at home, both excellent means of taking advantage of a bumper garden crop or low-cost locally raised produce. And both provide a sense of accomplishment and pleasure. There's something very personal about food that's preserved at home.

Freezing

Freezing fruits and vegetables when they are plentiful and lowest in cost and freezing meats and poultry when they're on sale can mean a lot to a food budget. Freezing desserts or appetizers ahead for a party can save you time the day of the party. And no leftovers need go to waste when you have freezer space. Proper freezing will maintain the quality of foods; it will not improve quality.

Nearly any fresh food or prepared dish can be frozen. A few foods, however, are best not frozen: salad greens, raw tomatoes, onions, celery, and green peppers; hard-cooked egg whites; boiled potatoes; custard and cream pies or puddings; mayonnaise and light cream.

If you plan to freeze food for any length of time, it is important to know that the freezer space you use truly freezes. A 0° F.-range temperature is the best for preserving frozen foods. It's all right to use the frozen-food section of a conventional (one-door) refrigerator if you plan to use the food quickly—within a few weeks. Longer storage is not recommended, since the food will deteriorate much more quickly at the 15° to 20° F. temperature that is typical for this compartment.

Many foods require no special preparation for freezing other than packaging in the proper material or container discussed in detail in this chapter. Fresh meats, fish, and poultry and prepared foods fall into this category. In the chart chapter of this book (the freezing charts begin on page 54) you will find specific instructions for packaging and recommended freezing times for these foods. Other foods, notably fresh fruits and vegetables, do require some special handling—usually fruits must be sweetened, vegetables must be blanched (scalded). The basic techniques for these follow.

How to Prepare Fresh Fruits for Freezing

There are four basic ways of packing fruits. Check pages 67 to 70 for methods to use for specific fruits.

Sugar pack: Use for juicy fruits and those that do not darken. Sprinkle sugar over the fruit and mix gently until some juice is drawn out of the fruit and most of the sugar is dissolved. Package, seal, and freeze.

Syrup pack: Use for whole fruits and those that tend to darken (apricots and peaches, for example). Make syrup by heating water and sugar in proportions below to boiling; chill well before using.

Light syrup	2 cups sugar per quart of water
Medium syrup	3 cups sugar per quart of water
Heavy syrup	4¾ cups sugar per quart of water
Very heavy syrup	7 cups sugar per quart of water

To keep fruits from darkening, add ½ teaspoon of ascorbic acid (dissolved in a small amount of water) for each quart of syrup. Add enough syrup to cover fruit in container. Package, seal, and freeze.

Dry pack: Some fruits—raspberries and cranberries, for example—can be frozen successfully without adding sugar. Simply pack into a container; seal and freeze.

Tray pack: Spread a single layer of fruit on shallow trays, freeze, then package promptly. With this method, the food doesn't stick together, so that you can pour out just the amount needed, leaving the rest for later use.

How to Prepare Vegetables for Freezing

Most vegetables that are served cooked lend themselves well to freezing. Some vegetables can be conveniently prepared for freezer storage by the tray-pack or loose-pack methods. However, most vegetables must be blanched (dipped in scalding water), and some must be cooked, before freezing. Blanching inhibits enzyme action and prevents off-flavors, discoloration, and texture changes in freezing. Check pages 62 to 66 for methods to use for specific vegetables.

Water blanching is the most commonly used and easiest method of blanching. Heat the water to a vigorous boil in a *large kettle* or *special scalding kettle*. Use a gallon of water per pound of prepared vegetables (for leafy vegetables, use two gallons of water per pound). Place the vegetables in a wire-mesh basket or in cheese cloth. Plunge vegetables into the water; cover, and immediately start counting the recommended time (times for each vegetable are given in the chart on page 62). When time is up, remove the vegetables and plunge them immediately into a pan of ice water. Change the water as needed until the vegetable feels cool to the touch (this takes about the same amount of time as recommended for blanching). Drain well, then package into any suitable container, seal, and freeze.

Packaging Foods for Freezing

The successful freezing of any food depends on proper packaging to guard against loss of moisture and transfer of flavor. Wrapping materials and containers must be moistureproof and vaporproof.

These wrapping materials are most useful: heavyweight aluminum foil; plastic films such as polyethylene and saran; heavily waxed freezer paper; laminated freezer papers. Ordinary waxed paper and kraft (wrapping) paper are not moistureproof and vaporproof.

Foods wrapped for freezing—usually meats, fish, poultry, and prepared dishes—must have an airtight seal, which you can accomplish with a tight wrap and a seal of either freezer tape (on aluminum foil and freezer papers) or a heat seal (on plastic wraps).

PRESERVING FOOD

To get a neat, airtight package, first pad any meat bones or sharp corners of food with a few layers of wrap. Use a single sheet of wrap large enough to cover the food to be frozen. Place the food in the center of the wrap; bring the wrap up tightly around the sides of the food and use a drugstore fold: Bring opposite sides of the wrap together and fold over about one inch. Continue to fold over and over until the fold is tight against the food. Press air out of package ends; fold each end over twice, then fold up tight against the package. Seal ends tightly to the package with freezer tape or heat-seal plastic film by pressing with a low-temperature iron.

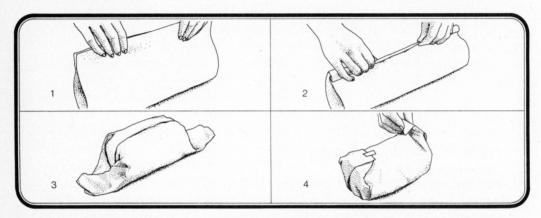

Many containers are suitable for freezer use, although, if you plan to do a great deal of freezing, it is best to select the ones that stack easily and take up the least amount of space. These are the most efficient freezing containers:

Bags: Plastic freezer bags are particularly good for irregularly shaped foods such as poultry. (To prevent punctures, bags can be put in a waxed folding carton.) After filling the bag, press out all air and fasten with a plastic-coated metal closure band. One type of plastic bag is used with a special heat-sealing machine. These pouches are so tightly sealed they can go directly from the freezer into boiling water for thawing and heating the contents.

Plastic containers: Rigid containers, usually polyethylene, in many sizes, can be used for whatever food will fit in them. They stack neatly in the freezer, can be washed and reused indefinitely. (When purchasing these, be sure the label specifies suitability for freezer use.)

Glass freezer jars: For either liquid or dry foods. Leave one-half inch air space at the top of the jar.

Special paper containers: Either waxed or plastic-lined ones are suitable if designed for freezer use. Don't substitute cottage-cheese or ice-cream containers—they are not airtight.

Aluminum or aluminum-foil containers: These are suitable if they can be tightly sealed; also, the container can go from freezer to oven.

Baking dishes: Any baking dish of heatproof material can be used. This is particularly handy for advance preparation of casseroles. Cover with heavy aluminum foil if the dish doesn't have a lid; seal with freezer tape.

Note: Before you store frozen foods—especially those you may keep for some time—do label and date them. There are special freezer marking pencils that will write clearly, and lastingly, on freezer paper or freezer tape. It's frustrating, and wasteful, to find an unknown package or container of food in a corner of the freezer and have no idea what it is or how long it's been there.

Canning

Canning, like freezing, will not improve the quality of food; it will simply preserve food just as it is. Fresh fruits and vegetables should be rushed from the garden to the jar to retain the best of their flavor and nutritive values.

The joy of canning for most people is to preserve a jam, jelly, pickle, or relish that is a family favorite. This is canning on a small scale and, because most recipes of this type have enough sugar or vinegar to keep them from spoiling, these foods involve the simplest methods of home canning. The recipes you will find in this chapter are the kind that are easy to do in a home kitchen with a minimum of extra equipment. However, the principles involved in the methods of sterilization, sealing, and storage are basically the methods involved in all home canning. They must be followed meticulously to prevent spoilage and ensure a good product.

If you want to go into home canning of fruits, vegetables, meats, and poultry on a larger scale, you will need some special equipment and specific instructions for the foods and the equipment you plan to use. The equipment described in the following paragraphs is an introduction to home-canning methods and materials.

Jars and closures for canning: For all foods but jellies and jams, special home-canning jars are absolutely essential. Do not be tempted to use empty jars from commercially prepared foods. They may break during processing; the lid and jar will not seal properly.

Canning jars come in sizes from a half-pint to a half-gallon and in different shapes. The commonest type of lid is made of two pieces: a flat lid with a sealing compound around its rim, and a separate threaded band that holds it firmly in place. Jars and bands (but *not* the flat lids) can be reused.

Kettles and canners: For *open-kettle canning* you can use any kettle of suitable capacity for the food being prepared. This method is used for jellies, jams and some pickles.

For *water-bath processing* of jars, you can use a large deep kettle with a cover, and a rack that will sit inside to hold the jars. Water-bath canning is the method recommended for high-acid foods, such as fruits, pickles, pickled vegetables and most tomatoes. There are special water-bath canners equipped with a rack or basket designed for this purpose. A large steam-pressure cooker can also be used for water-bath processing with the vent open and the cover unfastened.

For *steam-pressure processing,* there is *a special steam canner with a rack* in its base to hold jars. The cover has a vent, a pressure control or dial, a safety valve, and a rubber gasket around the outside of the rim to provide a tight seal. All meat, fish and poultry and vegetables other than those listed above must be processed in a pressure canner.

Steam-pressure canners come in sizes up to 22-quart liquid capacities. A 16-quart canner can process 7 quart jars or 9 pints at one time; a 22-quart canner will process 4 half-gallon jars, 7 quarts, or 18 pints at one time.

If your canning won't be of such magnitude that you want to invest in a pressure canner, you can also use some smaller-size pressure saucepans. Since processing in canning must be done under ten pounds of pressure, the smaller pressure pan must be able to control this amount. A 4-quart saucepan will hold up to 4 pint jars; an 8-quart saucepan will hold up to 7 pint jars or 4 quart jars.

It's important that pressure cookers be kept in accurate working order. The instruction book for the cooker will tell you what parts need periodic maintenance.

Miscellaneous Equipment

Your kitchen may already be supplied with other equipment you'll need: a funnel with a wide opening and a ladle with a lip, for filling jars; a fine sieve, a colander, and a food mill for preparing the foods; tongs and lifters for handling hot lids and jars; measuring cups, including a large quart size. A blender and a food chopper are sometimes useful but not essential. There are special metal gadgets that grip the rim of the jar tightly to lift it out of hot water. You will also need to devise a place for cooling the jars without damaging counter tops or the jars. Some solutions are a large wooden board, layers of thick towels, or sturdy wire racks.

If you want to can foods on a large scale, the following publications will provide you with complete information on home canning:

Ball Blue Book, $1.00. Dept. RB, Post Office Box 2005, Muncie, Indiana 47303.

Kerr Home Canning Book and How to Freeze Foods, $1.00. Kerr Glass Manufacturing Corporation, Post Office Box 97, Sand Springs, Oklahoma 74063.

Bernardin Home Canning Guide, $1.00. Bernardin, Inc., Evansville, Indiana 47705.

Home canning of fruits and vegetables, G-8, 35¢.

Home canning of meat and poultry, G-106, 30¢.

How to make jellies, jams, and preserves at home, G-56, 40¢.

Making pickles and relishes at home, G-92, 45¢.

The last four pamphlets are from: U.S. Department of Agriculture, Office of Communication, Washington, D.C., 20250.

Prices listed are for quantities of booklets; single copies are available at no charge.

A Warning about Botulism

Botulism is a deadly form of food poisoning that can result from careless processing of some canned foods. Although botulism poisoning is rare, incidents have frequently occurred in home-canned foods.

The botulism danger exists whenever you can *low-acid* foods—meats, fish and most vegetables. To destroy any botulism spores, these foods *must* be processed in a pressure canner at a temperature higher than that of boiling-water-bath processing.

Always prepare and process food exactly according to the method, time and temperature recommended for that specific food by a reliable source of canning information. Don't be casual about this advice, or careless about any preparation details. And don't be complacent because you have known someone who has been canning successfully without a pressure canner for years. Botulism poisoning may be rare, but it only has to happen once.

If you have reason to doubt the safety of any low-acid canned foods you have on hand, and you still want to use them, boil them for at least ten minutes. Do *not* taste before boiling. The boiling will destroy botulism toxin, but it will have a bad effect on the texture and nutritive content of canned foods. The best advice—when in doubt, throw out the food.

A special warning: Tomatoes always have been considered a high-acid food, safe for canning by the water-bath method. However, the acidity of tomatoes now varies considerably according to their variety, the kind of soil they are grown in and the degree of ripeness at the time you process them. Botulism poisoning *is* a possibility, however remote, even with canned tomatoes or tomato products. We suggest you contact your county extension office of the United States Department of Agriculture for current canning recommendations for your particular locality.

Pickles and Relishes

Nothing dresses up plain hamburger or leftovers like a homemade relish or pickles. If you have a garden or are near a vegetable stand where you can get quality fruits and vegetables at the peak of their season when prices are the lowest, you can find a great saving and a lot of enjoyment in "putting up" some good pickles and relishes.

The fruits and vegetables you select should be fresh, firm, and free of decaying spots. Use them within twenty-four hours of picking or purchasing, and be sure to wash them thoroughly before preserving them.

Inspect each jar before you use it. Make sure jar has no nicks, cracks, or sharp edges. Lids or caps should be in good condition. Familiarize yourself with the manufacturer's directions for sealing the jars. Then wash both jars and fittings in soapy water and rinse them thoroughly.

To sterilize jars, put clean, rinsed jars on their sides in a pan that is deep enough to completely submerge them with water. Boil five minutes, add lids or caps and rubber rings and boil five minutes more. Keep over low heat till needed. Lift jars out with metal tongs; drain. Fill while hot.

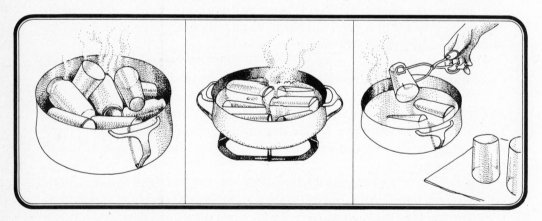

To Get Best Results with Pickles and Relishes

Use proper cooking utensils: Cook pickles and relishes in enamelware, flameproof glass, aluminum, stainless steel, or stoneware utensils. Brass, copper, iron, and galvanized utensils should not be used; they are apt to cause undesirable color changes or may react with acid or salt to produce unwholesome substances.

Use pure ingredients for best results: Recommended salts are pure refined dairy, pickling, or kosher salt. (We used coarse kosher salt in our recipes.) Ordinary table salt tends to cloud the brine.

Use white distilled vinegar unless the recipe calls for another kind. Check the label to see that it has 4 to 6 percent acidity.

Always use fresh spices and herbs for prime flavor. In some recipes the spices must be wrapped in a cheesecloth bag to prevent them from darkening the pickles.

Use soft water in a salt or brine mixture. If the water in your area is hard, boil it for fifteen minutes and let it stand for twenty-four hours. Then remove the scum from the top and ladle the water from the kettle, being careful not to disturb the sediment at the bottom. Add one tablespoon of vinegar to each gallon of boiled water. If vegetables must stand in the salt solution overnight, do not put them in a metal container.

Use white, granulated sugar unless brown sugar is called for.

In all recipes, garlic is optional.

Fill jars one at a time: If using one-piece caps, put the wet rubber ring on the jar before filling it. Ingredients must be boiling hot when packed into sterilized jars. (This applies to recipes that use the open-kettle canning method.) After filling the jar, remove any air bubbles by running a narrow rubber spatula between food and jar. Wipe top and threads of jar with a clean, damp cloth before capping. Now you're ready to remove the next jar from the sterilizer and repeat the operation. If necessary to add more liquid to fill jars, use leftover pickling solution; if there is not enough, add boiling-hot vinegar.

Some of these recipes require water-bath processing. For this you will need a water-bath canner or a large pot. Have it half-filled with hot water and put it on to heat, but do not have water boiling when jars are added. In this procedure, the jars are sterilized in the processing. After filling, wipe jars. With two-piece caps, put the flat lid on the jar, sealing side down, and screw the band tightly into place over it. If you are using a one-piece cap, screw it on tightly; then loosen it about a quarter of an inch. Place filled jars on a rack in the canner. Add enough water to come up 1 or 2 inches over the tops of the jars. Bring to a boil. Reduce heat to hold water at a gentle boil. If water should boil away during processing, add boiling water to cover jars one or two inches over the tops.

Cool and store jars properly: To cool, stand filled jars away from drafts on cake racks, cloths, or a wood surface. Tighten one-piece caps as they cool. Store jars in a dark, dry, cool place. Unless the recipe indicates otherwise, most pickles and relishes are best kept a few months before opening and eating.

About controlled-temperature burners and preserving: In many of the recipes for pickles, jellies, and jams, you will not find a temperature given for use of controlled-temperature burners. We have found that liquids to be kept at a full, rolling boil—an essential step in many preserving recipes—are best done on a source of steady heat.

 ### Crystal Pickle Chips

1 large green pepper
4 large, firm cucumbers, washed and thinly sliced
5 small white onions, thinly sliced
1 large clove garlic
¼ cup coarse salt
2 quarts cold water
14 ice cubes
1½ cups white vinegar
3½ cups sugar
1 tablespoon mustard seed
1 teaspoon celery seed
1 teaspoon ground turmeric

Wash, core, and seed green pepper; put through coarse blade of food chopper. Place green pepper, cucumber, onion, and garlic in a large bowl; add salt. Add water and ice cubes. Cover and chill in refrigerator for about 2 hours. Remove garlic. Drain vegetables. Mix vinegar, sugar, mustard seed, celery seed, and turmeric in a large pot; add vegetables. Bring to a boil over high heat (about 400° F.), stirring occasionally. Remove from heat; pack into sterilized jars, leaving ¼ inch head space. Work out bubbles in jars with a rubber spatula. Add more liquid if necessary to fill jars to proper level. Adjust caps. Makes 3 pints.

Bread-and-Butter Pickles

6 large cucumbers
3 cups water
½ cup coarse salt
3 medium-sized onions, thinly sliced
1 cup white vinegar
1 cup sugar
1 teaspoon celery seed
1 teaspoon mustard seed
¾ teaspoon ground turmeric
½ teaspoon ground ginger
¼ teaspoon pepper

Wash cucumbers and thinly slice. Heat 1 cup of the water and salt together until salt is dissolved; add the remaining 2 cups water and cool. Pour salted water over cucumbers. Add onion and chill 3 hours. Drain and rinse cucumbers in cold water. Bring vinegar, sugar, celery seed, mustard seed, turmeric, ginger, and pepper to a boil over high heat (about 400° F.); add cucumbers and onion and again bring to a boil. Reduce heat to moderately low (about 225° F.) and cook 2 minutes. Pack immediately into sterilized jars, leaving ¼ inch head space. Work out bubbles in jars with a rubber spatula. Add more liquid if necessary to fill jars to proper level. Adjust caps. Makes 4 pints.

Dill Pickles

2 cups white vinegar
2 cups water
6 tablespoons sugar
¼ cup coarse salt
1½ tablespoons mixed pickling spice

Mix vinegar, water, sugar, and salt in a large pot. Place pickling spices on a 5-inch-square piece of cheesecloth; tie ends together to make a bag. Place spice bag in vinegar mixture; bring to a boil and simmer over moderately low heat (about 225° F.) 15 minutes. Pack cucumbers in quart jars; trim if necessary to leave ¼ inch head space.

15 *medium-sized cucumbers*
    (about 6 inches long),
    washed and cut into
    halves lengthwise
Fresh dill heads

Put a few heads of dill in each jar. Heat vinegar mixture to boiling and pour over cucumbers, leaving ¼ inch head space. Work out bubbles in jars with a rubber spatula. Add additional liquid if necessary to fill jars to proper level. Adjust caps. Heat water in a large pot with a rack. Place sealed jars on rack in the hot water and add enough hot water to come 1 or 2 inches over tops of jars. Quickly bring water to a boil, then reduce heat to hold water at a steady, gentle boil. (Do not use controlled-heat burner.) Boil 10 minutes. Remove jars and cool on a wire rack. Makes 4 quarts.

Dilled Beans

2 *pounds green beans*
1 *teaspoon celery seed*
1 *teaspoon mustard seed*
4 *small cloves garlic, cut*
   into halves
Few grains cayenne pepper
8 *heads fresh dill*
2½ *cups water*
2½ *cups white vinegar*
¼ *cup coarse salt*

Wash beans and cut off ends. Pack beans lengthwise in half-pint jars, trimming if necessary to fit into jars with ¼ inch head space. To each jar add ⅛ teaspoon celery seed, ⅛ teaspoon mustard seed, a half clove garlic, few grains cayenne, and a head of dill. Heat the 2½ cups water, vinegar, and salt to boiling; pour over beans, allowing ¼ inch head space. Work out bubbles in jars with a rubber spatula. Add additional liquid if necessary to fill jars to proper level. Adjust caps. Heat water in a large pot with a rack. Place sealed jars on rack in the hot water and add enough hot water to cover them 1 or 2 inches. Quickly bring water to a boil; then reduce heat to hold water at a steady, gentle boil. (Do not use controlled-temperature burner.) Boil 10 minutes. Remove jars and cool on a wire rack away from drafts. Makes eight ½-pint jars.

Mustard Pickles

2 *quarts water*
½ *cup coarse salt*
2 *cups ½-inch crosswise*
   slices of very small
   cucumbers
1½ *cups small*
   cauliflowerettes
1¾ *cups coarsely chopped*
   seeded green pepper
1 *cup coarsely chopped*
   seeded sweet red pepper
3 *medium-sized green*

Heat 1 cup of the water and the salt together until salt is dissolved. Add 7 cups water and cool. Combine cucumbers, cauliflower, green pepper, red pepper, green tomatoes, and onion in a large bowl; pour in salt water and chill in refrigerator 12 to 18 hours. Drain and rinse off salt. Combine sugar, flour, and turmeric in a bowl; gradually add the ¼ cup water, stirring until smooth. Gradually add vinegar and mustard, stirring until blended. Pour into large pot and cook over moderate heat (about 250° F.) until thickened, stirring constantly. Add vegetables; bring to a boil. Reduce heat to a steady boil and cook 15 minutes, stirring frequently. (Do not

tomatoes, cut into ¾-inch
wedges
1 cup thinly sliced onion
¾ cup sugar
¼ cup flour
1½ teaspoons ground
turmeric
¼ cup water
2½ cups white vinegar
¼ cup prepared mustard

use controlled-temperature burner.) Pack into sterilized jars, leaving ¼ inch head space. Work out bubbles in jars with a rubber spatula. Add more liquid to fill jars to proper level. Adjust caps. Makes 3½ to 4 pints.

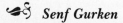

Mixed Vegetable Pickle

1 pound green beans, sliced
2 pounds lima beans,
shelled
½ bunch carrots, peeled and
thinly sliced
2 cups fresh corn kernels
cut off the cob (about 2
ears of corn)
1½ cups sugar
2 tablespoons coarse salt
1 tablespoon dry mustard
½ teaspoon ground turmeric
1½ tablespoons mustard seed
1½ tablespoons celery seed
6 cups white vinegar
1 tablespoon Tabasco
1 pound green tomatoes,
chopped
2 medium-sized seeded
green peppers, chopped
1 pound small white onions,
peeled
1 large head cauliflower,
broken into small
flowerets

Combine green beans, lima beans, carrots, and corn in a large pot with boiling water; bring to a boil and simmer over moderately low heat (about 225° F.) 25 minutes. Drain. Mix sugar, salt, dry mustard, turmeric, mustard seed, celery seed, and vinegar in a large pot; bring to a boil, stirring until sugar is dissolved. Add Tabasco, cooked vegetables, tomato, green pepper, onion, and cauliflower; bring to a boil. Reduce heat slightly to a steady boil and cook 25 minutes, stirring frequently. (Do not use controlled-temperature burner.) Pack into sterilized jars, leaving ¼ inch head space. Work out bubbles in jars with a rubber spatula. Add more liquid if necessary to fill jars to proper level. Adjust caps. Makes 7 pints.

Senf Gurken

6 large ripe yellow cucumbers
9 cups water

Peel cucumbers, cut into quarters lengthwise and then into halves. Remove seeds. Heat 2 cups of the water and

1 cup coarse salt
6 tablespoons mixed pickling
  spice
2 quarts white vinegar
4 cups sugar
2 tablespoons mustard seed
1 sweet red pepper, seeded
  and cut into ½-inch strips
3 small onions, thinly sliced
Fresh dill heads
Bay leaves

the salt together until salt is dissolved. Add the remaining 7 cups water and cool. Pour over cucumbers; cover and chill in refrigerator for about 12 hours. Drain well. Place mixed pickling spices on 5-inch-square cheesecloth; tie ends together to make a bag. Place vinegar, sugar, mustard seed, and bag of spices in a saucepan; heat until sugar is dissolved. Pour ½ inch of the vinegar mixture into a large pot with the spice bag. Arrange cucumbers in a single layer in pot; bring to a boil and remove from heat as soon as boiling point is reached. Pack cucumbers into sterilized jars. Place red pepper, onion, dill, and bay leaves in pot and heat about 1 minute; place a few pieces of each in jar with cucumbers. Remove spice bag from pot and heat remaining vinegar mixture to boiling; pour over pickles in jars, leaving ¼ inch head space. Work out bubbles in jars with a rubber spatula. Add more liquid to fill to proper level. Adjust caps. Makes 3 to 4 pints.

✒ Pickled Watermelon Rind

3 quarts 1-inch pieces
  watermelon rind (dark
  skin and pink flesh
  removed)
6 cups water
¾ cup coarse salt
1½ tablespoons whole cloves
3 cinnamon sticks, broken
  into pieces
2½ tablespoons whole allspice
3 cups white vinegar
3 cups water
6 cups sugar
1 lemon
5 cinnamon sticks

Place watermelon rind in a large bowl. Heat 2 cups of the water and the salt together until salt is dissolved. Add the remaining 4 cups water and cool . Pour salt water over watermelon rind and chill in refrigerator 6 hours or overnight. Drain watermelon; rinse with cold water. Cover with hot water. Bring watermelon to a boil; reduce heat and simmer 10 minutes. Drain. Place whole cloves, the 3 broken cinnamon sticks, and the allspice on a 5-inch-square of cheesecloth; tie ends together to make a bag. Heat vinegar, spice bag, the 3 cups water, and sugar to boiling in a large pot; reduce heat slightly to a steady boil and cook for 10 minutes. Wash lemon and cut off peel. Cut peel into thin strips. Add drained watermelon rind and lemon peel to the vinegar mixture. Bring to a boil; reduce heat slightly and cook about 45 minutes, or until watermelon rind is clear and translucent, stirring frequently. During last 10 minutes of cooking, add the 5 whole cinnamon sticks to watermelon. Remove spice bag. Pack watermelon into sterilized jars, placing a whole cinnamon stick in each jar. Leave ⅛ inch head space. Work out bubbles in jars with a rubber spatula. Add more liquid to fill jars to proper level. Adjust caps. Makes five ½-pints.

Three Quick-to-Make Relishes

❧ Beet-and-Horseradish Relish

About 2 pounds raw beets
2 tablespoons prepared
  horseradish
½ teaspoon salt
⅛ teaspoon black pepper
2 tablespoons sugar
1 tablespoon cider vinegar

Remove leaves and root end from beets. Pare and grind them, using medium blade of meat grinder. You should have about 2½ cups ground raw beets. Add remaining ingredients and blend well. Store, covered, in refrigerator 24 hours before using. Keeps at least 2 weeks in refrigerator. Makes about 2½ cups.

❧ Tangy Vegetable Relish

1 8-ounce can cut green
  beans
1 7-ounce can whole-kernel
  corn
2 tablespoons diced pimiento
¼ cup white vinegar
¼ cup vegetable oil
2 teaspoons instant minced
  onion
¼ teaspoon dry mustard
¼ teaspoon celery seed
1 teaspoon salt
⅛ teaspoon crushed dried red
  pepper (optional)

Combine all ingredients in medium-sized saucepan. Cover and bring to a boil. Reduce heat to moderately low (about 225° F.) and simmer 5 minutes. Let cool; then refrigerate. Serve relish well chilled. Makes 2 cups.

❧ Pickled Celery and Olives

3 stalks celery
1 10-ounce jar stuffed green
  olives
1 clove garlic
⅓ cup olive oil
3 tablespoons cider vinegar
½ teaspoon crushed dried
  oregano leaves

Wash celery. Cut into pieces 3 to 4 inches long. Cut lengthwise if stalks are large. Drain liquid from olives into a mixing bowl. Add garlic, olive oil, cider vinegar, and oregano; stir to blend thoroughly. Place celery sticks and olives in a shallow dish. Pour oil and vinegar mixture over celery and olives. Cover and store in refrigerator overnight. Drain on paper towel before serving. Serves 4 to 6.

Cooked Relishes

✺ Chow-Chow Relish

1 quart coarsely chopped
  cabbage (about ½
  medium-sized head)
3 cups coarsely chopped
  raw cauliflower (about 1
  large head)
2 cups coarsely chopped
  onion (about 4
  medium-sized onions)
2 cups coarsely chopped
  green tomato (about 3
  medium-sized tomatoes)
2 cups coarsely chopped
  seeded green pepper
  (about 2 large peppers)
1 cup coarsely chopped
  seeded sweet red pepper
  (about 1 large pepper)
2½ cups white vinegar
1½ cups sugar
3 tablespoons coarse salt
2 teaspoons dry mustard
1 teaspoon ground turmeric
½ teaspoon ground ginger
2 teaspoons celery seed
1 teaspoon mustard seed

Mix vegetables together in a bowl and chill 4 to 6 hours in refrigerator. Drain well. Combine vinegar, sugar, salt, dry mustard, turmeric, ginger, celery seed, and mustard seed in a large pot; bring to a boil and simmer over moderately low heat (about 225° F.) 10 minutes. Add vegetables; bring to a boil. Reduce heat to a steady boil and cook 10 minutes, stirring frequently. (Do not use controlled-temperature burner.) Spoon into sterilized jars, leaving ⅛ inch head space. Work out bubbles in jars with a rubber spatula. Add more liquid if necessary to fill jars to proper level. Adjust caps. Makes 4 pints.

✺ Corn Relish

1½ dozen ears sweet corn
4 cups finely chopped
  cabbage (about ½
  medium-sized head)
1 cup coarsely chopped
  seeded green pepper
  (about 1 large pepper)
1 cup coarsely chopped
  seeded sweet red pepper
  (about 1 large pepper)
1 cup finely chopped onion
  (about 2 medium-sized
  onions)

Cook corn in boiling salted water for 5 minutes; cool and cut kernels from corn, measuring out 2 quarts to use in recipe. Place measured corn, cabbage, green pepper, red pepper, and onion in a large pot. Add 1 quart of the vinegar. Mix flour and sugar in a bowl; gradually stir in the remaining 1 quart vinegar. Mix dry mustard, cayenne, turmeric, and salt into flour-vinegar mixture. Gradually stir vinegar mixture into vegetables; heat mixture until boiling. Reduce heat slightly to a steady boil and cook 40 minutes, stirring very frequently to prevent sticking. (Do not use controlled-temperature burner.) Spoon into sterilized jars, leaving ⅛ inch head space. Work out bubbles in jars with a rubber spatula. Add

[927]

2 quarts cider vinegar
1 cup flour
6 cups sugar
1½ teaspoons dry mustard
¾ teaspoon cayenne pepper
1½ teaspoons ground
turmeric
½ cup coarse salt

more liquid if necessary to fill jars to proper level. Adjust caps. Makes 4½ pints.

⇥ India Relish

2 large green peppers
2 large sweet red peppers
6 green tomatoes
3 cucumbers, about 6
inches long
1 large onion, peeled
3 tablespoons coarse salt
1 cup finely chopped
cabbage (about ½ small
head cabbage)
1¼ cups sugar
1½ cups white vinegar
1½ tablespoons mustard seed
½ teaspoon ground turmeric
¼ teaspoon ground mace
½ teaspoon ground
cinnamon
½ teaspoon ground ginger
¼ teaspoon chili powder
2 bay leaves

Wash vegetables well. Remove seeds from green and red peppers and cut peppers into wedges. Cut tomatoes, cucumbers, and onion into quarters. Put pepper, tomato, cucumber, and onion through coarse blade of food chopper. Stir in salt. Cover and chill in refrigerator overnight. Strain vegetables. Mix ground vegetables and cabbage in a pot; add remaining ingredients; bring to a boil. Reduce heat to a steady boil and cook 3 minutes, stirring frequently. (Do not use controlled-temperature burner.) Spoon into sterilized jars, leaving ⅛ inch head space. Work out bubbles in jars with a rubber spatula. Add more liquid if necessary to fill jars to proper level. Adjust caps. Makes 4 pints.

⇥ Green-Tomato Pickle

3½ pounds green tomatoes,
washed, cored, and cut
into ⅓-inch slices
4 large onions, thinly sliced
¾ cup coarse salt
9 cups cider vinegar
9 medium-sized green
peppers, washed, seeded,
and thinly sliced
4 medium-sized red sweet
peppers, washed, seeded,

Place tomatoes and onions in a large bowl; stir in the ¾ cup salt and chill in refrigerator for 2 hours. Drain and wash salt off vegetables. Heat vinegar, green pepper, red pepper, garlic, and sugar in a large pot until boiling. Add tomatoes, onions, dry mustard, whole cloves, cinnamon, ginger, celery seed, and the 2½ teaspoons salt and bring to a boil. Reduce heat slightly to a steady boil and cook 45 minutes, stirring very frequently, or until vegetables are translucent. (Do not use controlled-temperature burner.) Pack into sterilized jars, leaving ¼ inch head space. Work out bubbles in jars with a rubber

and diced
8 cloves garlic, minced
3 16-ounce packages light
brown sugar
1½ tablespoons dry mustard
1 tablespoon whole cloves
2 cinnamon sticks, broken
1½ tablespoons ground
ginger
2 teaspoons celery seed
2½ teaspoons coarse salt

spatula. Add more liquid to fill jars to proper level. Adjust caps. Makes 5 pints.

Sweet Pepper Relish

15 cups diced seeded sweet
red pepper (about 15
large peppers)
3 cups diced seeded green
pepper (about 3 large
peppers)
3 cups finely chopped onion
(6 medium-sized onions)
4½ cups peeled and finely
chopped watermelon rind
¾ cup coarse salt
4½ teaspoons mixed pickling
spice
4½ cups white vinegar
8 cups sugar

Mix red pepper, green pepper, onion, and watermelon in a large bowl; stir in salt. Chill in refrigerator 3 to 4 hours. Drain and rinse with cold water. Place mixed pickling spice on a 5-inch-square of cheesecloth; tie ends together to make a bag. Heat vinegar and sugar to boiling in a large pot; add vegetables and spice bag. Bring mixture to full boil; reduce heat slightly to a steady boil and cook 45 minutes, stirring very frequently to prevent sticking. (Do not use controlled-temperature burner.) Remove spice bag. Pack into sterilized jars, leaving ⅛ inch head space. Work out bubbles in jars with a rubber spatula. Add more liquid if necessary to fill jars to proper level. Adjust caps. Makes 5 pints.

Piccalilli Relish

2 quarts finely chopped
green tomatoes (about 12
medium-sized tomatoes)
1 quart finely chopped
cabbage (about ½
medium-sized head)
1 cup finely chopped seeded
sweet red pepper (about 1
large pepper)
1 cup finely chopped seeded
green pepper (about 1
large pepper)

Mix vegetables together in a large bowl; stir in salt. Chill in refrigerator 3 to 4 hours. Drain and press out liquid. Place vinegar, sugar, mustard seed, celery seed, cloves, and horseradish in a large pot; bring to a boil and simmer over moderately low heat (about 225° F.) 15 minutes. Add vegetables and bring to a boil, stirring occasionally. Spoon into sterilized jars. Work out bubbles in jars with a rubber spatula. Add more relish or boiling-hot vinegar if necessary to fill jars to within ⅛ inch of the top. Adjust caps. Makes 4 pints.

(Ingredients continued on page 930)

½ cup finely chopped onion
(about 1 medium-sized
onion)
¼ cup coarse salt
2 cups white vinegar
2 cups firmly packed light
brown sugar
1 tablespoon mustard seed
1½ teaspoons celery seed
1 teaspoon whole cloves
1½ teaspoons prepared
horseradish

Mustard and Chutneys

 Tomato Mustard

8 pounds tomatoes
2 teaspoons crushed, dried
red pepper
1 tablespoon ground ginger
1½ teaspoons ground cloves
1½ teaspoons ground mace
1½ teaspoons ground allspice
2 cloves garlic, minced
¼ cup sugar
¼ cup salt
1 tablespoon pepper
¼ cup dry mustard
½ cup cider vinegar

Wash tomatoes; core, and cut into thick slices. Place tomatoes and red pepper in large saucepot; cover and simmer over moderately low heat (about 225° F.) 1 hour. Strain and press through large strainer. Add ginger, cloves, mace, allspice, garlic, sugar, salt, and pepper. Return to saucepot; cover and simmer over moderately low heat (about 225° F.) 1 hour. Mix mustard and vinegar together; stir into tomato mixture. Boil uncovered 15 to 20 minutes to thicken. (Do not use controlled-temperature burner.) Pour immediately into sterilized jars. Seal at once. Makes about 5 cups.

⊰ Fresh Pear Chutney

5 pounds firm ripe pears
(10 to 12 large)
1 cup finely chopped green
pepper
1½ cups dark seedless raisins
3½ cups sugar
1 cup coarsely chopped
candied ginger
3 cups cider vinegar
½ teaspoon salt
8 whole cloves
8 whole allspice
3 2-inch sticks cinnamon

Peel, core, quarter, and slice pears. (There should be about 10 cups.) In a 6-quart saucepan, combine green pepper, raisins, sugar, ginger, vinegar, salt, and pears. Tie the cloves and allspice in a small square of cheesecloth and add them together with the cinnamon to pear mixture. Bring mixture to a boil, stirring constantly. Reduce heat to a very gentle boil and cook uncovered, stirring occasionally, until pears are tender and mixture is thick, about 30 minutes. (Do not use controlled-temperature burner.) Remove spice bag and cinnamon. Spoon chutney into hot sterilized jars. Seal at once. Serve as a meat accompaniment. Makes about 3 pints.

ᵉᴸ Tomato Chutney

2½ quarts coarsely chopped
  ripe tomatoes (about 15
  medium-sized tomatoes)
1 quart coarsely chopped
  peeled and cored apples
  (about 15 medium-sized
  apples)
2 cups coarsely chopped
  peeled cucumber (about
  1½ medium-sized
  cucumbers)
1½ cups coarsely chopped
  seeded sweet red pepper
  (about 1½ large peppers)
1½ cups coarsely chopped
  onion (about 3 medium-
  sized onions)
1 cup dark seedless raisins
1 clove garlic, crushed
3 cups white vinegar
3 cups firmly packed light
  brown sugar
1 teaspoon chili powder
1 tablespoon ground ginger
1 teaspoon ground
  cinnamon
1 teaspoon coarse salt

Combine all ingredients in a large pot; bring to a boil. Reduce heat to a gentle steady boil and cook 1½ to 2 hours, or until thickened, stirring very frequently to prevent sticking. (Do not use controlled-temperature burner.) Spoon into sterilized jars, leaving ⅛ inch head space. Work out bubbles in jars with a rubber spatula. Add more chutney if necessary to fill jars to the proper level. Adjust caps. Makes 5 to 5½ pints.

Jam- and Jelly-Making

Jam- and jelly-making has been enormously simplified by the availability of manufactured liquid and powdered pectins; you no longer have to rely completely on the natural pectins in fruits to make them jell. These commercial pectins even allow you to make uncooked jellies. You'll find recipes for these on the leaflets that come with the pectin. Since the two forms of pectin are not interchangeable, use the pectin designated in the recipe. Uncooked jellies must be stored in the refrigerator or freezer. Cooked jellies, properly sealed, may be kept on any cupboard shelf.

The equipment needed for making jams and jellies:

A large colander for washing fruit.

A large, wide, flat-bottomed kettle with an 8- to 10-quart capacity. It should be easy to handle, with sturdy handles.

A potato masher for crushing fruits and berries.

A large spoon, preferably wooden, for stirring.

A jelly bag (available in housewares departments) or clean cheesecloth for extracting juice.

Accurate measuring cups and spoons.

A jelly thermometer.

A ladle for filling jars.

Jelly glasses or jars. Standard canning jars and caps are best for lengthy storage. Small glasses with or without covers also may be used if they are sealed with paraffin—½-pint sizes are a practical choice.

A large shallow pan to sterilize glasses and jars.

If paraffin is to be used, a small pan with a pouring lip for melting paraffin, or an empty tin can.

Selecting and preparing the fruit: If fruit pectin is used, select only fully ripe fruit. If fruit pectin is not used, about three-quarters of the fruit should be fully ripe and one-quarter should be underripe.

Plan to make small batches. Do not double recipes.

To wash fruits and berries, place them in a colander and rinse thoroughly but quickly under cold running water. Do not allow fruit to soak in water.

In making jam, the fruit and juice are used together. For jelly, just the juice is used. To extract the juice, use a jelly bag or a large square of cheesecloth dampened with water. The cheesecloth should be at least four layers thick and overlap the colander generously all around. Place the jelly bag or the dampened cheesecloth in a colander resting in a large bowl or pan. Pour the cooked fruit into the bag or cloth, bring the corners together, and while twisting the top, press against the sides of the colander with a masher until all the juice is extracted. This method will give you the greatest yield of juice, but for a clear, sparkling jelly, re-strain the juice through a clean, damp jelly bag or several layers of cheesecloth without squeezing.

General cooking techniques: After the sugar has been added, the jam or jelly should be cooked rapidly. Place over the highest heat and bring to a full rolling boil—one that can't be stirred down. Stir the mixture while it comes to a boil and also as it boils.

When making jams and jellies without the addition of fruit pectin, use a jelly thermometer to arrive at the correct jelling point. For jellies, it is 8° F. above the boiling point of water. For jams, marmalades, conserves, and butters it is 9° F. above the boiling point of water. (At sea level, water boils at 212° F.) The bulb of the thermometer should be completely submerged. Read it at eye level. When fruit pectin is used, it is not necessary to test with a thermometer; follow the directions in the recipe.

Sterilizing jars: (See instructions on page 920).

Filling jars: If jars with two-piece metal caps are used (the best kind), fill them to within ⅛ inch of the top. Seal and invert the jars. When all the jars have been filled, turn them right side up to cool.

For jam, about thirty minutes after the jars have been filled, gently twist them back and forth and up and down to prevent fruit from floating.

If glasses without covers or with non-sealing covers are used, fill them to within ½ inch of the top. Cover at once with ⅛ inch of hot melted paraffin.

Preparing paraffin: To prepare paraffin, melt the paraffin in a tin can placed in a pan of hot, not boiling, water. Pour melted paraffin onto a metal spoon, letting it overflow onto jelly 'till ⅛ inch thick. When set, prick bubbles; pour thin second layer of paraffin. Tip jar to seal; cap.

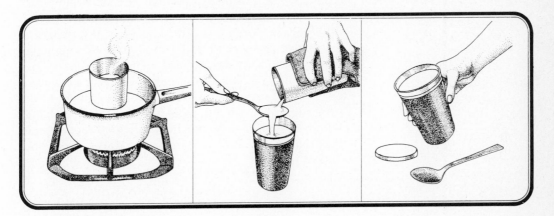

Cooling and storing jams and jellies: Carefully wipe off the tops and sides of the jars or glasses and let them stand at room temperature until completely cooled.

If paraffin-sealed glasses do not have covers, cut rounds of paper to cover the tops and fasten with rubber bands or string.

Store in a dark, dry, cool place that holds a temperature of about 60° F. Jams and jellies should be used within eight to ten months.

Apple Jelly

3½ *pounds tart apples*
Water
Sugar
　2 *tablespoons lemon juice*

Wash apples and cut into large chunks, removing the core. Do not peel. Place in a large kettle. For every pound of prepared apples, add 1 cup water. Over moderately high heat (about 375° F.), bring to a full boil. Reduce heat to moderately low (about 225° F.), cover, and simmer about 20 minutes, or until apples are soft and tender. Strain in a jelly bag or 4 thicknesses of dampened cheesecloth. This should yield about 4 cups juice. In a large kettle, combine ¾ cup sugar with every 1 cup apple juice. Stir in lemon juice. Over high heat (about 400° F.) stir just to dissolve sugar. Bring to full rapid boil; boil to jelling point. Remove from heat. Skim off foam with a metal spoon. Ladle into sterilized jars and seal. Makes three ½-pint jars.

⮌ Grape Jelly

3½ to 4 pounds Concord
    grapes
½ cup water
Sugar

Sort and wash grapes—about ¼ of them should be un-derripe. Place in a heavy kettle. Crush with a potato masher and add water. Over moderately high heat (about 375° F.), bring to a full boil. Reduce heat to mod-erately low (about 225° F.), cover, and simmer 10 min-utes. Strain through a jelly bag or 4 thicknesses of dampened cheesecloth. Refrigerate juice overnight and strain again. This should yield about 4 cups juice. In a large kettle, combine ¾ cup sugar with every 1 cup juice. Over high heat (about 400° F.), stir just enough to dis-solve sugar. Bring to full rapid boil; boil to jelling point. Remove from heat. Skim off foam with a metal spoon. Ladle into sterilized jars and seal. Makes about four ½-pint jars.

⮌ Strawberry–Rhubarb Jam

5 cups (about 1½ pounds)
    unpeeled, sliced (½-inch
    thick) rhubarb
3 cups (about 2 pints) mashed
    firm-ripe strawberries
4 cups sugar

Mix together rhubarb, strawberries, and sugar. Let stand 15 minutes, or until mixture appears to be "juicy," but sugar is not completely dissolved. Over moderately high heat (about 375° F.), boil rapidly to jelling point, about 20 minutes. Stir frequently as jam begins to thick-en. Remove from heat. If necessary, skim off foam with a metal spoon. Ladle into sterilized jars and seal. Makes four ½-pint jars.

⮌ Strawberry Preserves

6 cups firm-ripe
    strawberries, stems
    removed
5 cups sugar
4 whole allspice
⅓ cup lemon juice

Mix together strawberries and sugar. Let stand 4 to 5 hours, or until sugar begins to dissolve, gently stirring occasionally. Combine strawberry mixture with allspice in a large kettle and bring to boil over moderately high heat (about 375° F.), stirring occasionally. Boil 10 to 15 minutes to 220° F. on jelly thermometer. Add lemon juice and boil 5 to 10 minutes longer to 221° F. Remove from heat. Ladle into sterilized jars and seal. Makes five ½-pint jars.

⇜§ Cherry-Pineapple Preserves

4 cups red, sour, pitted
cherries
4 cups granulated sugar
1 29½-ounce can crushed
pineapple, well drained

Grind cherries; put in large kettle with sugar over moderately low heat (about 225° F.); stir until sugar dissolves. Bring to a full boil over moderately high heat (about 375° F.). Add pineapple; boil 20 minutes. Pour into sterilized jars; seal. Makes five ½-pint jars.

⇜§ Peach-and-Plum Preserves

4 cups (about 2 pounds)
diced, unpeeled plums
¼ cup water
2 cups (about 1½ pounds)
diced, peeled peaches
2 tablespoons lemon juice
1 1¾-ounce package
powdered fruit pectin
6½ cups sugar

Combine plums and water in a saucepan. Simmer covered for 5 minutes over moderately low heat (about 225° F.). This should yield 3 cups. Mix together plum mixture, peaches, lemon juice, and pectin in large kettle. Bring to full boil over high heat (about 400° F.), stirring constantly. Add sugar and boil rapidly 1 minute, stirring constantly. Remove from heat. Skim off foam with a metal spoon. Skim and stir alternately for 5 minutes. Ladle into sterilized jars and seal. Makes about seven ½-pint jars.

⇜§ Orange Marmalade

6 medium-sized
thin-skinned oranges,
chilled
1½ cups water
3 cups sugar

To prepare oranges, slice off tops. Remove peel by cutting wide strips from top to bottom, cutting deep enough to remove the white membrane. Slice off bottom. Go over fruit to remove any remaining membrane. Using the tip of a paring knife, remove as much of the white membrane from the peel as possible. Cut peel into 1-inch-long slivers. Measure slivered peel—it should yield 1½ cups. Set aside. Cut each orange into sections by cutting from the outside to the center of the orange along side of dividing membranes. Remove sections over a bowl to catch all the juices. Remove seeds. Sections and juice should measure 2 cups. Set aside. To prepare marmalade, mix together slivered peel and water in a medium-sized saucepan and bring to a full boil over moderate heat (about 250° F.). Reduce heat to moderately low (about 225° F.) and simmer, tightly covered, about 30 minutes or until fork-tender, stirring occasionally. Stir in orange sections with juice; bring back to full boil over moderate heat (about 250° F.). Reduce heat to moderately low (about 225° F.) and simmer, tightly covered, 15 minutes longer, stirring occasionally. Remove from heat and measure—there should be 3 cups. Combine fruit and peel mixture with sugar in a large kettle. Bring to a full boil over high heat (about 400° F.); boil rapidly, stirring frequently, to jelling point, about 10 minutes. Remove from heat. Skim off foam with a metal spoon. Alternately skim and stir for 5 minutes. Ladle into sterilized jars and seal. Makes about four ½-pint jars.

✑ Spiced Peach Marmalade

3½ to 4 pounds peaches
¼ cup lemon juice
½ teaspoon ground
    pumpkin-pie spice mix
7 cups sugar
½ 6-fluid-ounce bottle liquid
    fruit pectin

Peel and pit peaches. Crush enough of the fruit to measure 4½ cups. Mix together peaches, lemon juice, spice mix, and sugar in a large kettle. Bring to full rapid boil over high heat (about 400° F.); boil hard 1 minute, stirring constantly. Remove from heat; stir in pectin. Skim off foam with a metal spoon. Skim and stir alternately for 5 minutes. Ladle into sterilized jars and seal. Makes about eight ½-pint jars.

✑ Peach Conserve

4 pounds (about 16)
    medium-sized peaches
1 unpeeled lemon, halved,
    with seeds removed
1 6-ounce jar maraschino
    cherries
About 4½ cups sugar
1 cup coarsely chopped
    walnut meats

Wash, halve, and pit peaches; grind all fruits. Measure fruit into kettle; add equal amounts of sugar; stir over moderately low heat (about 225° F.) to dissolve sugar. Increase heat to moderately high (about 275° F.); boil 20 minutes. Add walnuts. Pour into sterilized jars. Makes five ½-pint jars.

✑ Cherry Conserve

5 cups stemmed, pitted, and
    halved Bing cherries
    (about 2½ pounds)
⅓ cup lemon juice
5 cups sugar
½ cup shredded coconut
½ cup dark seedless raisins
½ 6-fluid-ounce bottle liquid
    fruit pectin
¼ teaspoon almond extract
    (optional)

Mix together cherries, lemon juice, and sugar in a large kettle. Let stand ½ hour, stirring occasionally. Stir in coconut and raisins. Bring to full rapid boil over high heat (about 400° F.); boil hard 1 minute, stirring constantly. Remove from heat; stir in pectin. Skim off foam with a metal spoon. Skim and stir alternately for 5 minutes. Stir in almond extract. Ladle into sterilized jars and seal. Makes seven ½-pint jars.

CHAPTER XXVII

CASSEROLES

Casseroles are indeed a splendid invention. They save pots and pans and serving dishes; everything cooks in one big baking dish that goes directly to the table. Casseroles are ideal for big parties; most of them can be kept at serving temperature in a warm oven in case guests are late. Also, many of them are fork foods, suitable for eating on a lap.

The casseroles we selected for this chapter are the kind that contain meat, poultry, fish, or eggs. Together with a big green salad and some hot French bread, they make a complete meal. You will find vegetable casseroles in the chapter on vegetables, macaroni casseroles in the chapter on pasta, and so on.

Casseroles come in many decorative colors; choose one that complements your serving plates and bring it confidently from the oven to the table.

Beef Casseroles

 **Beef and Olive Casserole**

12 **small white onions**	Heat oven to 350° F. Peel onions. Melt butter in a heavy skillet over moderately low heat (about 225° F.) and lightly brown onions in skillet. Combine flour, salt, and pepper in a paper bag; add meat pieces, a few at a time, and shake to coat meat evenly. Increase temperature to moderately high (about 300° F.). Add meat to onions
3 **tablespoons butter or margarine**	
¼ **cup flour**	
½ **teaspoon salt**	
⅛ **teaspoon pepper**	

2½ pounds beef chuck, cut
   into 1-inch cubes
1 8-ounce can tomato sauce
½ cup water
1 teaspoon dried rosemary
   leaves
½ teaspoon salt
½ teaspoon paprika
1 cup small stuffed green
   olives
¼ cup chopped fresh parsley
1½ cups cooked mashed
   potatoes

and continue cooking until meat is browned. Arrange meat and onions in a deep 2-quart casserole. Stir tomato sauce and water into drippings in pan. Add rosemary, salt, and paprika; pour sauce over meat. Cover and bake 1¼ hours. Add olives and parsley and continue to bake, covered, 30 minutes longer, until meat is tender. Spoon potatoes into a cake decorating bag and make a border of potato around edge of casserole. Place in a preheated broiler about 3 inches from heat and broil about 5 minutes, until potatoes are browned. Serves 6.

Burgundy Beef and Beans

1 16-ounce package dried
   red, pink, or pinto beans
5 cups water
2 tablespoons vegetable oil
½ cup finely chopped onion
1 clove garlic, minced
2 teaspoons salt
1 pound ground beef
1 egg, slightly beaten
½ cup dry seasoned bread
   crumbs
2 tablespoons butter or
   margarine
1 16-ounce can tomatoes
¾ cup Burgundy wine
2 teaspoons salt
½ 8-ounce package
   mozzarella cheese

Wash beans. Heat water to boiling in a Dutch oven. Add beans, cover, and boil 2 minutes. Remove from heat and let stand, covered, 1 hour. Add vegetable oil, onion, garlic, and the 2 teaspoons salt. Cover and place over moderately low heat (about 225° F.); bring to a boil and simmer 1½ hours, or until almost tender. While beans are cooking, mix beef, egg, and bread crumbs; shape into 1½-inch balls. Melt butter in skillet over moderate heat (about 250° F.) and brown meatballs lightly. Drain liquid from beans. Mix beans, tomatoes, wine, and the 2 teaspoons salt; pour into a deep 3-quart casserole. Arrange meatballs over top. Heat oven to 325° F. Bake 45 minutes. Remove from oven. Slice mozzarella cheese thinly and place on top of meatballs. Bake uncovered about 15 minutes longer, or until cheese is melted and lightly browned. Serves 6 to 8.

Tamale Casserole

1 tablespoon butter or
   margarine
1 pound ground beef chuck
2 teaspoons seasoned salt
1 teaspoon chili powder
½ teaspoon Worcestershire
   sauce

Heat oven to 350° F. Melt butter in skillet over moderate heat (about 250° F.); add meat and cook and stir until lightly browned. Add seasoned salt, chili powder, Worcestershire, and tomatoes. Beat milk and egg together in a large bowl. Stir in cornmeal and corn. Add meat mixture and pour into buttered deep 2-quart casserole. Bake uncovered 1 hour and 10 minutes. Sprinkle top

1 16-ounce can stewed
   tomatoes
1½ cups milk
1 egg
¾ cup yellow cornmeal
2 cups corn, cut from the
   cob or drained canned
   whole-kernel corn
¾ cup (3 ounces) sharp
   Cheddar cheese, coarsely
   shredded

with cheese; bake 10 minutes more or until cheese is melted. Serves 6.

✺ English Beef-and-Kidney Pie

Beef suet (about the size of a
   large egg)
2 pounds beef chuck, cut into
   1½-inch cubes
1 pound trimmed beef
   kidney, cut into 1½-inch
   cubes
¾ cup coarsely chopped onion
1 can condensed beef
   consommé
1 cup water
½ teaspoon salt
Few grains pepper
Few grains cayenne pepper
1½ teaspoons Worcestershire
   sauce
¼ cup cold water
3 tablespoons flour
Enough pastry for a
   single-crust pie or 1 stick
   pastry mix

Place beef suet in a large saucepan or Dutch oven. Place over moderate heat (about 250° F.) until about 3 tablespoons of fat have melted. Remove suet cracklings and discard. Raise heat to moderately high (about 375° F.). Add beef cubes and kidney and cook, stirring occasionally, until meat is thoroughly browned. Reduce heat to moderately low (about 225° F.). Add onion and cook until tender. Add beef consommé, water, salt, pepper, cayenne, and Worcestershire sauce. Stir well. Cover and simmer about 3 hours, or until meat is fork-tender. Drain meat cubes and place in a deep 1½-quart casserole. Measure stock from pan. If necessary, add enough water to make 2 cups; return stock to pan. Gradually stir the ¼ cup water into the flour; blend thoroughly. Combine with stock in pan. Place over moderate heat (about 250° F.) and cook, stirring constantly, until thickened. Pour over meat cubes in casserole. Cool slightly. Roll pastry out on a floured surface into a shape 1 inch wider than the top of the casserole. Place pastry over meat mixture. Roll edges of pastry under to make a standing rim and flute the edges. Cut a few slits in the middle of the crust to permit steam to escape. Place in a preheated 450° F. oven. Bake 10 minutes. Reduce heat to 350° F. and bake about 20 to 25 minutes longer, or until crust is lightly brown. Serves 6.

✺ Pastiche

1 16-ounce package elbow
   macaroni
5 tablespoons butter or
   margarine

Cook macaroni in boiling salted water as directed on package. Drain well. Melt 4 tablespoons of the butter in a skillet over moderately high heat (about 275° F.) and cook until butter begins to brown. Remove from heat.

1 cup grated Parmesan
   cheese
3 tablespoons olive oil
¼ cup chopped onion
3 to 4 cloves garlic, mashed
1 pound ground beef chuck
1 teaspoon salt
1 teaspoon dried oregano
   leaves
4 eggs
1 tablespoon flour
½ cup milk

Add to macaroni with Parmesan cheese. Mix thoroughly. Heat oven to 300° F. Melt the remaining 1 tablespoon butter in a skillet over moderately low heat about 225° F.); add olive oil. Add onion and garlic; cook until onion is golden brown, stirring frequently. Add meat. Cook and stir until meat is browned, stirring frequently. Add salt and oregano. Combine meat mixture with macaroni. Pour into a greased shallow 3-quart casserole. Beat eggs with flour and milk until mixture is well blended. Pour over meat and macaroni mixture in casserole. Bake uncovered 30 minutes. Serves 6.

✑ Beef Pie

½ cup all-purpose flour
2 teaspoons salt
¼ teaspoon pepper
2 pounds stewing beef, cut
   into 1-inch cubes
⅓ cup vegetable oil
2 cups thinly sliced onions
1½ cups coarsely chopped
   celery
3 cups water
1 bay leaf
1½ teaspoons dried basil
   leaves
½ cup finely chopped fresh
   parsley
3 cups cooked and cubed
   potatoes
1½ cups sliced cooked carrots
1 package pie-crust mix

In a small bowl combine flour, salt, and pepper. Roll beef cubes in flour mixture to coat evenly. Reserve any flour mixture not used to coat meat. In a large saucepan or Dutch oven heat oil over moderately high heat (about 300° F.) and add beef. Cook about 5 minutes, or until meat is brown on all sides. Add onions and celery and cook 5 minutes longer. Stir in reserved flour mixture and gradually add water. Cook until sauce begins to thicken. Add bay leaf, cover and simmer over low heat (about 200° F.) about 1½ hours, or until meat is tender. Heat oven to 425° F. Add basil, parsley, potatoes, and carrots to meat. Pour mixture into a shallow 3-quart casserole. Prepare pastry according to package directions. With a 3-inch cookie cutter, cut out 24 rounds. Arrange them around the casserole, overlapping each round slightly. Bake 30 minutes, or until golden brown. Serves 10.

✑ Swedish Casserole

1 tablespoon vegetable oil
¼ cup sliced green onions or
   scallions
1 pound ground beef chuck
¼ cup butter or margarine
¼ cup flour
1½ teaspoons salt

Heat oven to 375° F. In a large skillet heat oil over moderately high heat (about 300° F.); add onion and cook until it begins to brown. Stir in beef and cook, stirring frequently, until meat is no longer pink. Remove meat and onion with a slotted spoon to drain off any excess fat; set aside. In a saucepan over moderate heat (about 250° F.) melt butter and quickly stir in flour, salt, pep-

⅛ teaspoon pepper
¼ teaspoon dried dillweed
2 cups milk
1 cup commercial sour
  cream
1 10-ounce package frozen
  peas and carrots, cooked
  and well drained
1 8-ounce package
  medium-wide egg noodles,
  cooked and well drained
½ cup (2 ounces) sharp
  Cheddar cheese, coarsely
  shredded
Dried dillweed

per, and the ¼ teaspoon dillweed. Gradually stir in milk, blending smooth after each addition. Bring to a boil and boil 1 minute, stirring constantly. Remove from heat and turn into a large bowl. Let cool about 5 minutes. Stir in sour cream. (A wire whip is helpful.) Stir in beef mixture, peas and carrots, and noodles. Turn into a deep 2-quart casserole. Sprinkle with Cheddar cheese and additional dillweed to taste. Bake uncovered 20 minutes, or until bubbling hot and cheese is melted. Serves 6 to 8.

Calico-Bean Hot Pot

½ pound raw bacon, cut into
  1-inch pieces
1 pound ground beef round
½ cup chopped onion
½ cup catsup
½ cup firmly packed dark
  brown sugar
1 teaspoon prepared
  mustard
2 teaspoons white vinegar
½ teaspoon salt
1 16-ounce can pork and
  beans
1 16-ounce can lima beans,
  drained
1 16-ounce can kidney beans,
  undrained

Heat oven to 325° F. Cook bacon in a 10-inch skillet over moderately high heat (about 325° F.) until crisp. Remove from skillet and drain on paper towels. Drain off all but 2 tablespoons of the bacon fat and reserve remaining fat. Add beef to skillet and cook over moderate heat (about 250° F.) until brown and crumbly, stirring occasionally. Remove beef from skillet. Add 2 tablespoons of the reserved bacon fat to the skillet. Add onion and cook until lightly browned. Combine beef and onion with remaining ingredients in a deep 3-quart casserole. Stir mixture to blend well. Bake, uncovered, 1½ hours. Serves 8.

Hamburger-and-Noodles Stroganoff

6 ounces medium egg noodles
  (about 3½ cups raw)
¼ cup butter or margarine
½ cup finely chopped onion
1 4-ounce can sliced
  mushrooms, drained

Cook noodles as directed on package; drain. In a large skillet, melt butter over moderately low heat (about 225° F.). Add onion and mushrooms and cook until tender. Add beef and cook over moderately high heat (about 275° F.), stirring occasionally, until brown and crumbly. Drain off excess fat. Stir in flour and blend well. Add

1 pound ground beef round
1 tablespoon flour
½ teaspoon garlic salt
1 8-ounce can tomato sauce
  with tomato bits
¼ cup Burgundy wine
1 can beef bouillon,
  undiluted
1 teaspoon salt
¼ teaspoon pepper
1 cup commercial sour cream
½ cup grated Parmesan
  cheese

garlic salt, tomato sauce, Burgundy, bouillon, salt, and pepper and blend well. Simmer 10 minutes, over moderately low heat (about 225° F.), stirring occasionally. Blend in sour cream and remove from heat. Arrange alternate layers of beef mixture and noodles in a shallow 2-quart casserole. Sprinkle cheese over top. Bake, covered, in a 375° F. oven 45 to 55 minutes, or until heated through, stirring occasionally as it heats. Serve with additional cheese. Serves 4.

◄§ Lima–Beef Casserole

1 pound fresh lima beans,
  shelled or 1 10-ounce
  package frozen Fordhook
  lima beans
¼ cup olive oil
1½ cups chopped onion
¾ cup chopped green pepper
1 clove garlic, minced
1 pound ground beef
1 teaspoon salt
1 small can tomato paste
½ cup dry sherry
¼ cup fine dry bread crumbs
1 tablespoon grated
  Parmesan cheese

Heat oven to 350° F. Cook beans in boiling water over moderately low heat (about 225° F.) until tender, about 20 minutes, or according to directions on package. Heat oil in heavy skillet over moderate heat (about 250° F.). Add onion, green pepper, and garlic; cook until tender. Add beef and brown quickly over moderately high heat (about 325° F.). Remove from heat. Combine salt, tomato paste, sherry, limas, and beef mixture. Pour into a deep 1½-quart casserole; sprinkle with crumbs and cheese. Bake uncovered 30 minutes. Serves 6 to 8.

◄§ Beef Liver-and-Macaroni Casserole

1 cup elbow macaroni
1 pound beef liver, cubed
1 tablespoon flour
1 teaspoon salt
2 tablespoons vegetable oil
½ cup sliced onion
1 can condensed cream of
  mushroom soup
¾ cup milk
1½ tablespoons steak sauce

Cook macaroni according to package directions; drain. Toss liver cubes with flour and salt in a small bowl, coating pieces well. Heat oil in a skillet over moderate heat (about 250° F.). Add onion and liver and cook until lightly browned on all sides. Pour soup into a deep 2-quart casserole. Add milk and steak sauce and stir to blend well. Fold in macaroni, liver, onion, and corn. Bake, covered, in a 350° F. oven 1 hour. Meanwhile, cook bacon in a 10-inch skillet over moderately high heat (about 325° F.) until partially browned but not

1 8-ounce can whole-kernel
   corn, drained
4 to 6 slices raw bacon

crisp. Place on top of casserole. Bake, uncovered, 30 minutes longer, or until heated thoroughly and bacon is crisp. Serves 4.

Frankfurter Casseroles

❧ Chili Franks

8 slices raw bacon
1 large onion, chopped
1 clove garlic, finely chopped
½ pound frankfurters, sliced
2 teaspoons chili powder
1 teaspoon paprika
¼ teaspoon dried oregano
   leaves
½ teaspoon salt
¼ teaspoon pepper
1 8-ounce can tomato sauce
1 16-ounce can kidney beans,
   drained
½ cup crushed corn chips
¼ cup (1 ounce) sharp
   Cheddar cheese, shredded

Heat oven to 350° F. Fry bacon over moderately high heat (about 325° F.). Drain on paper towel and crumble bacon coarsely. Pour off all but 2 tablespoons of the bacon fat. Add onion and garlic and cook over moderately low heat (about 225° F.) until soft but not brown. Add the crumbled bacon and all remaining ingredients except corn chips and cheese. Heat thoroughly. Pour into a deep 1½-quart casserole. Top with corn chips and shredded cheese. Bake uncovered 25 to 30 minutes, or until cheese is melted and mixture is heated. Serves 4.

❧ Country Franks and Beans

2 cups dried lima beans
¾ teaspoon salt
2 tablespoons butter or
   margarine
1 cup thinly sliced onion
1 12-ounce can
   whole-kernel corn
1½ pounds frankfurters, cut
   into 1-inch pieces
½ cup catsup
¼ cup light molasses
1 tablespoon vinegar
1 teaspoon Worcestershire
   sauce
1½ teaspoons dry mustard

Cover beans with 2 quarts water. Soak 6 hours or overnight. Add salt and simmer over moderately low heat (about 225° F.) in the same water 55 to 60 minutes, until skins loosen and beans are tender. Drain; reserve ½ cup bean liquid. Heat oven to 350° F. Melt butter in a skillet over moderately low heat (about 225° F.). Add onion and cook until tender, about 4 minutes, stirring occasionally. Arrange beans, onion, corn, and frankfurters in layers in a deep 3-quart casserole. Combine remaining ingredients with the ½ cup bean liquid. Pour over beans. Bake, uncovered, 1 hour, stirring twice during baking. Serves 8.

Frankfurter-and-Macaroni Casserole

1 tablespoon butter or
  margarine
⅓ cup thinly sliced onion
2 cans condensed Cheddar
  cheese soup, undiluted
½ cup milk
2 teaspoons prepared spicy
  mustard
½ teaspoon prepared
  horseradish
2 tablespoons chopped
  pimiento
4 cups cooked elbow
  macaroni (8 ounces
  uncooked)
1 pound frankfurters

Heat oven to 400° F. Melt butter in a small saucepan over moderate heat (about 250° F.); add onion and cook until crisp-tender. In a bowl mix together cooked onion, cheese soup, milk, mustard, horseradish, pimiento, and macaroni. Turn into a shallow, rectangular 2-quart casserole. Arrange frankfurters on top. Bake, uncovered, 20 to 25 minutes, or until macaroni is bubbly hot and frankfurters are lightly browned. Serves 4.

Frankfurters and Rice

1½ cups packaged precooked
  rice
1½ cups water
2 teaspoons butter or
  margarine
½ teaspoon salt
1 tablespoon vegetable oil
1 pound frankfurters, cut
  into 2-inch slices
2 8-ounce cans tomato
  sauce
½ cup water
2 tablespoons instant
  minced onion
10 pitted ripe olives, halved
1 10-ounce package frozen
  peas
½ teaspoon salt
Few grains pepper
½ cup (2 ounces) sharp
  Cheddar cheese, coarsely
  shredded

Heat oven to 350° F. Prepare rice as directed on package (using the rice, 1½ cups water, butter, and the ½ teaspoon salt). Heat oil in a skillet over moderately high heat (about 350° F.); add frankfurters and cook until lightly browned on all sides, stirring occasionally. Add tomato sauce, water, and onion; cook over moderate heat (about 250° F.) for 5 minutes. Remove from heat. Add rice, olives, peas, the ½ teaspoon salt and pepper to skillet; mix well. Pour into a greased deep 2½-quart casserole and sprinkle with cheese. Bake, uncovered, 30 minutes. Serves 6.

Luncheon Meat and Canned Meat Casseroles

✑ Noodle Casserole

1 8-ounce package broad
   noodles
2 tablespoons butter or
   margarine
2 tablespoons chopped green
   pepper
1 tablespoon instant minced
   onion
2 tablespoons flour
⅛ teaspoon pepper
½ teaspoon dried oregano
   leaves
½ teaspoon sugar
2 8-ounce cans tomato sauce
1 12-ounce can luncheon
   meat, cubed
1 16-ounce container small-
   curd cottage cheese
Chopped fresh parsley
   (optional)

Heat oven to 350° F. Cook noodles as directed on package. Drain. Melt butter in skillet over moderately low heat (about 225° F.); add green pepper, onion, flour, and seasonings. Stir until well blended. Add tomato sauce; cook over moderately low heat (about 225° F.), stirring constantly, until sauce is smooth and thick. Add meat; remove from heat and fold in cottage cheese. Grease a deep 2-quart baking dish and layer noodles and sauce alternately, ending with sauce. Bake uncovered about 30 minutes, or until thoroughly hot. Garnish with chopped parsley, if desired. Serves 6.

✑ Deviled Ham Tetrazzini

2 cups uncooked spaghetti,
   broken into 2-inch pieces
1½ teaspoons instant minced
   onion
1 can condensed cream of
   chicken soup
⅔ cup milk
1 cup (¼ pound) sharp
   Cheddar cheese, coarsely
   shredded
1 teaspoon Worcestershire
   sauce
1 4½-ounce can deviled
   ham

Heat oven to 350° F. Cook and drain spaghetti as directed on package. Combine spaghetti and remaining ingredients in a deep 3-quart casserole. Stir well to blend. Bake, covered, 20 minutes. Serves 4 to 6.

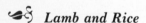 Luncheon Meat Florentine

⅔ cup undiluted evaporated
  milk
½ cup process American
  cheese, coarsely shredded
¼ teaspoon dry mustard
½ teaspoon Worcestershire
  sauce
⅛ teaspoon Tabasco
2 10-ounce packages frozen
  chopped spinach, cooked
  according to package
  directions
1 12-ounce can luncheon
  meat, cut into ¼-inch
  slices
¼ cup soft bread crumbs
1 tablespoon melted butter or
  margarine

Heat oven to 375° F. Mix evaporated milk, cheese, mustard, Worcestershire, and Tabasco in top of a double boiler. Place over simmering water and cook, stirring occasionally, until sauce is smooth. Spoon spinach into a greased shallow, 2½-quart baking dish. Arrange slices of luncheon meat in an overlapping row over spinach; pour cheese sauce over meat. Toss together bread crumbs and butter; sprinkle over cheese sauce. Bake, uncovered, 15 minutes, or until sauce is lightly browned. Serves 4.

Lamb Casseroles

Lamb and Rice

1 tablespoon olive oil
1¾ pounds lamb, cut into
  1-inch cubes
1 medium-sized onion,
  sliced
½ cup chopped green pepper
1 cup uncooked rice
½ teaspoon dried oregano
  leaves
¼ teaspoon dried basil
  leaves
¼ teaspoon paprika
1½ teaspoons salt
⅛ teaspoon pepper
2 beef bouillon cubes
2½ cups boiling water
1 8-ounce can tomato sauce

Heat oil in skillet over moderately high heat (about 325° F.); add meat cubes and cook until lightly browned on all sides. Remove meat from skillet. Reduce heat to moderate (about 250° F.). Add onion and green pepper and cook until just tender. Add rice, oregano, basil, paprika, salt, and pepper; cook over moderately low heat (about 225° F.) until lightly browned. Heat oven to 350° F. Mix meat and rice together and spoon into a deep 1½-quart buttered casserole. Dissolve bouillon cubes in boiling water; stir in tomato sauce. Pour enough of the liquid into casserole to barely cover rice. Cover and bake 1¼ to 1½ hours, stirring every 15 minutes; add the remaining bouillon mixture as liquid is absorbed. If necessary, add boiling water if rice is too dry when all the bouillon mixture has been used. Serves 4 to 6.

◆§ Moussaka

1 pound ground lean lamb
¾ teaspoon salt
Few grains pepper
1 medium-sized eggplant,
 peeled and cut into thin
 slices
1 16-ounce can tomatoes
½ cup fine dry bread crumbs
3 tablespoons melted butter
½ cup grated Parmesan
 cheese

Heat oven to 400° F. Combine lamb, salt, and pepper. Arrange a layer of eggplant in the bottom of a shallow 2-quart casserole, cutting eggplant if necessary to fit in dish. Add a layer of lamb and some of the tomatoes. Repeat layers, ending with a layer of eggplant. Stir together bread crumbs, butter, and cheese; sprinkle over top of eggplant. Bake, uncovered, 40 to 45 minutes. Serves 4.

Pork Casseroles

◆§ Tenderloin–Mushroom Casserole

8 medium-sized white
 onions, about ¾ pound
1 whole pork tenderloin,
 about ¾ pound
2 tablespoons shortening
½ pound medium-sized
 mushrooms
1 tablespoon flour
2 teaspoons sugar
1 teaspoon salt
Few grains pepper
1 8-ounce can tomato sauce
1 tablespoon prepared
 horseradish
2 teaspoons prepared
 mustard
4 toast rounds

Cover onions with water in saucepan, bring to boil over moderate heat (about 250° F.), and cook 15 minutes. Drain and reserve ½ cup of the water. Heat oven to 350° F. Cut tenderloin crosswise into 8 pieces and flatten each with a mallet or a heavy can. Heat shortening in skillet over moderate heat; add meat and mushrooms and brown lightly. Combine meat, mushrooms, and onions in a deep 1½-quart casserole. Blend flour, sugar, salt, and pepper in the skillet. Gradually add the ½ cup onion water and the tomato sauce. Cook over moderate heat, stirring constantly, until thickened. Stir in horse-radish and mustard. Pour over meat. Cover and bake 1 hour. Serve on toast. Serves 4.

◆§ Pork Chop and Potato Scallop *✗ try this –*

1 can condensed Cheddar
 cheese soup
½ cup commercial sour cream
¼ cup water

Combine undiluted soup, sour cream, water, and parsley. In a shallow 2-quart casserole, alternate layers of sliced potatoes, onions, chopped green pepper, and the cheese soup mixture. Sprinkle each layer of potatoes

3 tablespoons finely chopped fresh parsley

4 cups thinly sliced, peeled raw potatoes

2 medium-sized onions, thinly sliced

¾ cup coarsely chopped green pepper

Salt and pepper

6 center-cut pork chops, cut about ¾ inch thick

¼ cup flour

2 tablespoons vegetable oil

Salt and pepper to taste

6 green pepper rings, about ½ inch thick

6 canned spiced crab apples

lightly with salt and pepper. Place, uncovered, in a pre-heated 375° F. oven. Bake 30 minutes. Trim excess fat from pork chops. Roll pork chops in flour to coat thoroughly. Heat oil in a large skillet over moderately high heat (about 375° F.). Place pork chops in the skillet and brown evenly on both sides. Remove casserole from oven and stir potatoes. Sprinkle pork chops on both sides with salt and pepper; place on top of potatoes. Cover casserole and return to oven for 1 hour. Uncover and top each pork chop with a pepper ring and a spiced crab apple. Cover loosely and return to oven for 20 minutes. Serves 4 to 6.

✒ Scalloped Sweets and Pork Chops

3 large raw sweet potatoes, peeled

2 tablespoons melted butter or margarine

2 tablespoons brown sugar

3 tart apples, peeled, cored and sliced

1 large sweet onion, thinly sliced

4 shoulder pork chops, cut about 1½ inches thick

2 tablespoons butter or margarine

2 tablespoons flour

1 teaspoon salt

1 cup beer

Slice sweet potatoes into a greased shallow 3-quart casserole. Sprinkle with the melted butter and sugar. Arrange apples and onions over potatoes. Top with chops. Heat oven to 350° F. Melt the 2 tablespoons butter in a saucepan over moderately low heat (about 225° F.). Stir in flour and salt. Gradually add beer; cook and stir until thickened. Pour sauce over chops. Cover and bake 1¼ hours. Remove cover; bake 30 minutes longer. Serves 4.

Ham Casseroles

✒ Baked Ham Tetrazzini

2 16-ounce packages spaghetti, broken into 2-inch pieces

Cook spaghetti in boiling salted water as directed on package. Drain thoroughly. Heat oven to 375° F. Combine soup and milk; stir until smooth. Add remaining

2 cans condensed cream of
  mushroom soup
2 cups milk
1 tablespoon finely chopped
  onion
2 cups (½ pound) sharp
  Cheddar cheese, coarsely
  shredded
½ teaspoon salt
¼ teaspoon pepper
2 teaspoons Worcestershire
  sauce
¼ cup chopped fresh parsley
¼ cup chopped pimiento
3 cups cubed baked ham
Tomato wedges

ingredients except ham and tomatoes. Pour soup mixture over cooked spaghetti and toss to coat evenly. Arrange layers of spaghetti mixture and cubed ham in a greased deep 2½-quart casserole. Bake, uncovered, 30 minutes until thoroughly heated and bubbly around the edge. Garnish top with tomato wedges. Serves 8 to 10.

✑ Creamed Ham Casserole

2 tablespoons butter or
  margarine
2 medium-sized onions,
  chopped
1 green pepper, chopped
1 4-ounce can sliced
  mushrooms, drained
1 cup cubed cooked ham
1 tablespoon lemon juice
1 cup commercial sour cream
2 cups cooked noodles
⅓ cup fine dry bread crumbs
3 tablespoons melted butter
  or margarine

Heat oven to 350° F. Melt the 2 tablespoons butter in a heavy skillet over moderately low heat (about 225° F.). Add onions, green pepper, and mushrooms; cook until tender, stirring occasionally. Stir in ham, lemon juice, and sour cream. Heat 3 minutes, stirring constantly. Remove from heat. Arrange half the noodles in a greased, shallow 2-quart casserole. Pour in ham mixture. Top with remaining noodles. Mix together the fine dry bread crumbs and the 3 tablespoons butter; sprinkle over noodles. Bake, uncovered, about 30 minutes, until bubbly. Serves 4.

✑ Lima Beans and Ham

2 cups large, dried lima
  beans
2 tablespoons butter or
  margarine
1 cup thinly sliced onions
¼ cup chopped green pepper
1 pound cooked ham, cut
  into 1-inch cubes

Cook beans as directed on the package. Drain and reserve ½ cup of the liquid. Heat oven to 325° F. Melt butter in a skillet over moderately low heat (about 225° F.); add onions and green pepper and cook until tender. Combine onion mixture with lima beans. Arrange alternate layers of beans and ham in a deep 2-quart casserole. Combine catsup, molasses, vinegar, Worcestershire, and mustard with the ½ cup bean liquid. Pour over beans.

½ cup catsup
¼ cup light molasses
1 tablespoon vinegar
2 teaspoons Worcestershire
sauce
1½ teaspoons dry mustard

Bake, uncovered, about 45 minutes, until most of the liquid is absorbed; stir twice during baking. Serves 6.

Sausage Casseroles

✺ Sausage-and-Apple Casserole

1½ pounds bulk sausage meat
1 16-ounce can sliced
apples, drained
1 18-ounce can
vacuum-packed sweet
potatoes, sliced
¼ cup firmly packed brown
sugar
⅛ teaspoon ground
cinnamon

Heat oven to 375° F. Shape sausage meat into 6 or 8 uniform patties. Cook in a skillet over moderately high heat (about 325° F.) until brown on both sides. Pour off fat as it accumulates. Arrange sliced apples and sweet potatoes in a shallow 2-quart casserole; sprinkle with sugar and cinnamon. Place browned patties on top. Cover and bake 30 minutes. Remove cover; bake 15 minutes longer. Serves 4 to 6.

✺ Sausage Noodle Casserole

1 pound bulk sausage
½ medium-sized green
pepper, chopped
1 28-ounce can whole
tomatoes, mashed but not
drained
6 bay leaves
Dash of paprika
½ teaspoon Worcestershire
sauce
1 8-ounce package fine egg
noodles, cooked according
to package directions
Grated Parmesan cheese

Heat oven to 350° F. Crumble sausage and cook in skillet over moderately high heat (about 300° F.) until brown. Remove sausage and drain well. Remove all but 2 tablespoons of the fat from skillet. Add green pepper and cook over moderate heat (about 250° F.) about 5 minutes, or until glossy. Add tomatoes, bay leaves, paprika, Worcestershire, cooked sausage, and noodles; simmer 5 minutes, stirring occasionally. Pour into greased deep 2½-quart casserole. Shake Parmesan cheese generously over top. Bake casserole uncovered 40 to 45 minutes, or until cheese is melted. Top with additional Parmesan. Serves 6.

✑ Pork Sausage Pie

1 pound pork sausage links
½ cup finely chopped onion
¼ cup coarsely chopped green
   pepper
2 16-ounce cans whole
   tomatoes, drained
1 12-ounce can whole-kernel
   corn, drained
1 10-ounce package frozen
   lima beans
½ cup chili sauce
1 teaspoon salt
1 12-ounce package corn
   muffin mix

Place sausage links in a cold, medium-sized skillet over moderate heat (about 250° F.). Cook until browned on all sides. Remove sausage and drain off all but 2 tablespoons of the fat from the skillet. Add onion and green pepper to skillet. Cook until onions are soft. Cut sausages into 1-inch pieces. Add sausages, tomatoes, corn, lima beans, chili sauce, and salt to onion mixture. Cover and simmer over low heat (about 200° F.) for 30 minutes. Pour mixture into a greased deep 3-quart casserole. Heat oven to 400° F. Prepare corn muffin mix as directed on package. Spoon batter over sausage mixture. Bake, uncovered, 20 to 25 minutes, until topping is golden brown. Serves 6 to 8.

✑ Zucchini and Sausage

2 pounds small zucchini
½ pound bulk sausage
¼ cup finely chopped onion
½ cup fine cracker crumbs
2 eggs, slightly beaten
¼ teaspoon ground thyme
½ teaspoon salt
½ cup grated Parmesan
   cheese

Heat oven to 350° F. Wash zucchini; trim off ends. Cook whole in boiling salted water 15 minutes. Drain and chop coarsely. Place sausage and onion in a skillet over moderate heat (about 250° F.); cook and stir frequently until sausage is brown. In a bowl combine zucchini, sausage mixture, crumbs, egg, thyme, salt, and ¼ cup of the cheese. Pour into a shallow 2-quart baking dish. Sprinkle with the remaining ¼ cup cheese. Bake, uncovered, 40 to 45 minutes, until brown. Serves 4.

Veal Casseroles

✑ Veal Baked with Water Chestnuts

2 tablespoons butter or
   margarine
2 tablespoons olive oil
3 pounds stewing veal, cut
   into 1-inch cubes

Heat oven to 375° F. Heat the 2 tablespoons butter and the oil in a heatproof 2½-quart Dutch oven over moderately high heat (about 325° F.) until butter is melted. Add veal cubes and brown quickly on all sides. Remove meat as it browns. Add onion and garlic and cook over

1 medium-sized onion,
  finely chopped
1 clove garlic, crushed
1¼ teaspoons salt
⅛ teaspoon freshly ground
  pepper
¼ cup butter or margarine
1 pound fresh mushrooms,
  sliced
1 cup diluted canned beef
  bouillon
2 5-ounce cans water
  chestnuts, drained and
  sliced
Few grains nutmeg
1 bay leaf
3 tablespoons cornstarch
2 cups heavy cream
¼ cup cognac

moderate heat (about 250° F.) until golden brown, stirring frequently. Stir in salt and pepper. Return meat with juices to Dutch oven. In a large skillet melt the ¼ cup butter over moderately low heat (about 225° F.); add mushrooms and cook until tender. Stir mushrooms into Dutch oven. Add beef bouillon, water chestnuts, nutmeg, and the bay leaf. Cover Dutch oven, place in oven, and bake 1½ hours, or until meat is fork-tender. Place cornstarch in a small bowl and gradually pour in ½ cup cream, stirring constantly until mixture is smooth. Slowly add 1 cup of the hot liquid from the Dutch oven, stirring constantly to prevent lumping. Return cornstarch–cream mixture to Dutch oven. Stir well to blend. Cook over moderately low heat (about 225° F.), gradually adding the remaining 1½ cups cream and stirring constantly until mixture thickens and comes to a boil. Add cognac and cook until thoroughly heated. Serves 6.

❧ Veal Lasagna Romano

6 broad lasagna noodles
2 pounds boneless veal
  shoulder
Instant meat tenderizer
2 tablespoons olive oil
1 can condensed beef broth
2 8-ounce cans tomato sauce
¼ pound mushrooms, sliced
1 clove garlic, minced
¼ teaspoon dried oregano
  leaves
Few grains pepper
½ cup sliced, pitted, ripe
  olives
¼ cup chopped fresh parsley
Dried basil leaves
¼ cup fine dry bread crumbs
2 tablespoons grated
  Romano cheese

Cook noodles in boiling salted water for 10 minutes, until almost tender. Drain and cover with cold water. Brush meat with water and sprinkle with ½ teaspoon tenderizer. Pierce meat with a fork at ½-inch intervals. Repeat on other side. Cut meat into 1-inch cubes. Heat oil in skillet over moderately high heat (about 300° F.); add meat and cook until lightly browned. Remove meat. Add beef broth, tomato sauce, mushrooms, garlic, oregano, and pepper; stir to loosen meat particles in skillet. Pour sauce into a 9-x-9-x-2-inch baking dish. Heat oven to 350° F. Place half the noodles in a layer over the sauce. Arrange half the meat, olives, and parsley over noodles; sprinkle lightly with basil. Repeat noodle and meat layers. Mix bread crumbs and cheese; sprinkle over top. Cover casserole and bake 1½ hours, until meat is fork-tender. Serves 6.

~§ Swiss Veal Casserole

¼ cup all-purpose flour
1 teaspoon salt
⅛ teaspoon pepper
2 pounds boneless veal steak,
  1 inch thick
3 tablespoons vegetable oil
2 medium-sized onions,
  sliced
1 small green pepper, sliced
1 cup tomato juice
1 10-ounce package frozen
  Fordhook lima beans
1 teaspoon salt
Few grains pepper

Heat oven to 350° F. Combine flour, the 1 teaspoon salt, and the pepper in a small bowl and coat veal well with the mixture. Heat oil in a 10-inch skillet over moderately high heat (about 275° F.). Add veal and brown well on both sides. Place veal in a shallow 3-quart baking dish. Add onion and green pepper to skillet and stir to coat with the drippings. Stir in tomato juice and blend well. Pour over veal. Bake, covered with aluminum foil, for 40 minutes. While veal is baking, remove lima beans from freezer, open box, and let beans thaw partially. Separate beans and sprinkle around edge of baking dish. Sprinkle the 1 teaspoon salt and the pepper over the beans. Cover tightly with aluminum foil and bake 40 minutes longer, or until veal is fork-tender. Serves 4.

Chicken (or Turkey) Casseroles

~§ Arroz con Pollo

1 4-pound frying chicken,
  cut up
Salt
Pepper
Paprika
¼ cup olive oil
½ cup finely chopped onion
2 cloves garlic, minced
1 medium-sized green
  pepper, chopped
1 28-ounce can stewed
  tomatoes
2 chicken bouillon cubes
1½ cups water
1¼ cups uncooked rice
1 bay leaf
¼ teaspoon saffron
½ teaspoon dried oregano
  leaves

(Ingredients continued on page 954)

Heat oven to 350° F. Wash and dry chicken. Sprinkle lightly with salt, pepper, and paprika. Heat oil in skillet over moderately high heat (about 325° F.); cook chicken until lightly browned on all sides. Remove chicken and place in a deep 3½- or 4-quart casserole or Dutch oven. Add onion, garlic, and green pepper to skillet and cook until tender over moderate heat (about 250° F.). Add tomatoes and bouillon cubes; cook and stir about 5 minutes to loosen meat drippings. Stir in water, rice, bay leaf, saffron, oregano, and the 1¼ teaspoons salt. Pour over chicken. Cover and bake 25 minutes. Remove from oven and stir to mix rice and sauce. Add additional water if rice seems too dry. Return to oven and bake, covered, 20 minutes. Add peas and stir into rice mixture. Bake, covered, 15 minutes, or until rice and chicken are tender. At end of baking time, gently stir rice. Garnish with strips of pimiento. Serves 6.

1¼ teaspoons salt
1 10-ounce package frozen
    peas, partially thawed
2 pimientos, cut into strips

✎§ Chicken Tetrazzini

1 3- to 3½-pound
    broiler–fryer chicken, cut
    up
2 tablespoons melted butter
    or margarine
1 teaspoon salt
⅛ teaspoon pepper
1 teaspoon paprika
3 tablespoons butter or
    margarine
1½ cups sliced fresh
    mushrooms
¼ cup butter or margarine
¼ cup flour
1 cup canned chicken broth
1 cup heavy cream
1 tablespoon dry sherry
½ teaspoon salt
¼ teaspoon pepper
¼ teaspoon poultry
    seasoning
1 8-ounce package thin
    spaghetti
½ cup grated Parmesan
    cheese

Heat oven to 350° F. Place chicken pieces in a single layer, skin side up, in a shallow 3-quart casserole. Brush chicken with the 2 tablespoons melted butter. Sprinkle with the 1 teaspoon salt, the ⅛ teaspoon pepper, and the paprika. Bake, uncovered, 40 minutes. While chicken is baking, melt the 3 tablespoons butter in a skillet over moderately low heat (about 225° F.). Add mushrooms and cook a few minutes until tender. Melt the ¼ cup butter in a saucepan over moderate heat (about 250° F.); blend in flour. Remove from heat and gradually stir in chicken broth and cream. Place over moderate heat and cook, stirring constantly, until mixture boils. Add sherry, the ½ teaspoon salt, the ¼ teaspoon pepper, and the poultry seasoning. Cook spaghetti according to directions on package. Drain well and combine with the sauce and mushrooms. Remove chicken from casserole. Spread spaghetti mixture over bottom of casserole. Place chicken pieces on top of spaghetti, skin side up. Sprinkle with the Parmesan cheese. Return uncovered casserole to the oven for about 30 minutes, or until chicken is thoroughly baked. Serves 6.

✎§ Chicken Casserole

3 tablespoons butter or
    margarine
¼ cup flour
1 teaspoon grated onion
½ teaspoon salt
⅛ teaspoon pepper
1 6-ounce can sliced broiled
    mushrooms

Heat butter in skillet over moderately low heat (about 225° F.); blend in flour and stir until lightly browned. Add onion, salt, and pepper. Drain mushrooms and add enough milk to mushroom liquid to make 2 cups liquid; gradually add to skillet and cook, stirring constantly, until thickened. Add mushrooms. Layer half of rice, chicken, and asparagus in a deep 1½-quart casserole. Pour in half of the sauce. Repeat layers. Top with

Milk
2 *cups cooked rice*
2 *cups cooked or canned*
   chicken or turkey, diced
1 *10-ounce package frozen,*
   cut asparagus, thawed
½ *cup (2 ounces) shredded*
   sharp Cheddar cheese

cheese. Heat oven to 350° F. and bake, covered, 30 to 35 minutes. Uncover, heat 15 minutes more. Serves 6.

⌘ Sesame Rice with Chicken

2 *tablespoons butter or*
   margarine
¼ *cup sesame seeds*
2 *cups uncooked rice*
2 *12-ounce cans clear*
   chicken broth
1 *teaspoon salt*
½ *cup flour*
1½ *teaspoons paprika*
2 *teaspoons salt*
1 *2½-pound chicken, cut up*
⅓ *cup butter or margarine*
½ *cup water*
⅔ *cup semidry or dry white*
   wine

Heat oven to 300° F. Melt the 2 tablespoons butter in a large skillet over moderate heat (about 250° F.). Add sesame seeds and rice; cook, stirring constantly, until sesame seeds are brown and rice is lightly browned. Add chicken broth and the 1 teaspoon salt. Bring to a boil. Pour into a buttered, deep 2½-quart casserole and cover. Bake 15 minutes. While rice is baking, combine flour, paprika, and the 2 teaspoons salt in a paper bag. Add chicken a few pieces at a time and shake until lightly and evenly coated. Melt the ⅓ cup butter in a large skillet over moderate heat (about 250° F.) and brown chicken lightly on all sides over moderately high heat (about 350° F.). Remove casserole from oven and arrange chicken on rice. Pour the ½ cup water and wine over all. Cover. Bake 40 to 50 minutes, or until chicken and rice are tender. Serves 4.

Chicken-Liver Casseroles

⌘ Beans and Chicken Livers

1 *pound green beans, cut in*
   1-inch pieces
2 *tablespoons butter or*
   margarine
¾ *pound chicken livers,*
   quartered

Cook beans in boiling salted water about 15 minutes, until just tender. Drain. Heat oven to 350° F. Heat butter in a heavy skillet over moderate heat (about 250° F.). Add chicken livers and cook 10 minutes until lightly browned, turning occasionally. Add chicken gravy. Blend thoroughly. Arrange half the beans in a greased

1 10¾-ounce can chicken
gravy
2 tablespoons toasted
almonds

deep 1½-quart casserole. Pour sauce over beans. Arrange remaining beans over sauce; sprinkle with almonds. Bake uncovered 15 to 20 minutes. Serves 4.

⋙ Wild-Rice-and-Chicken-Liver Casserole

1 cup wild rice
1 teaspoon salt
⅛ teaspoon dried thyme
leaves
¼ bay leaf
2 parsley sprigs
2 tablespoons butter or
margarine
1 pound chicken livers
¼ cup flour
½ cup (¼ pound) sweet butter
1 medium-sized onion, finely
chopped
½ clove garlic, minced
½ teaspoon salt
Few grains pepper
2 tablespoons Madeira or
sherry

Cover rice in saucepan with water and bring to a boil; drain. To drained rice in saucepan add 1 quart water, the 1 teaspoon salt, the thyme, bay leaf, parsley, and the 2 tablespoons butter. Bring to boil and simmer, covered, over moderately low heat (about 225° F.) 30 minutes, stirring occasionally. While rice is cooking coat chicken livers with flour. Melt the ½ cup sweet butter in skillet over moderate heat (about 250° F.). Add chicken livers and onion; cook 5 to 10 minutes, until chicken livers are lightly browned and onion is tender. Heat oven to 375° F. Add garlic, the ½ teaspoon salt, the pepper, and the Madeira to the chicken livers. Drain rice thoroughly and remove bay leaf and parsley. Combine chicken livers and rice. Pour into a deep 1½-quart casserole and bake, uncovered, 15 minutes. Serves 6.

Egg Casseroles

⋙ Beef and Egg Casserole

2 cups uncooked elbow
macaroni
2 cans condensed cream of
mushroom soup
1 5-ounce jar sliced, dried
beef
1½ cups cubed Cheddar
cheese
4 hard-cooked eggs, diced
¼ cup finely chopped onion
2 cups milk

Combine macaroni, undiluted soup, dried beef, cheese, eggs, onion, and milk. Pour into a deep 2-quart casserole. Cover and refrigerate 8 hours or overnight. Bake, uncovered, in a 350° F. oven 1 hour, or until mixture bubbles at the edges and is lightly browned on top. Serves 6.

½ cup coarsely chopped
  green pepper
1 tablespoon freeze-dried
  snipped chives
1 teaspoon salt
¼ teaspoon pepper
2 cups crushed corn flakes
1 tablespoon melted butter
  or margarine
¼ teaspoon paprika

❧ Tuna-and-Spinach Casserole

2 tablespoons butter or
  margarine
¼ cup minced onion
3 tablespoons flour
3 cups milk
1 teaspoon salt
Few grains pepper
⅛ to ¼ teaspoon dry mustard
1 teaspoon Worcestershire
  sauce
2 6½-ounce cans water
  packed tuna, drained and
  flaked
1 pimiento, chopped
½ cup chopped celery
1 10-ounce package frozen
  chopped spinach, cooked
  and well drained
2 cups cooked elbow
  macaroni
1 tablespoon drained capers
1 teaspoon lemon juice
2 tablespoons grated
  Parmesan cheese

Over moderate heat (about 250° F.) melt butter in a saucepan and cook onion about 3 minutes. Quickly stir in flour (mixture will appear dry). Gradually stir in milk. Bring to a boil and boil 1 minute, stirring constantly. Stir in salt, pepper, mustard, and Worcestershire and remove from heat. Mix sauce with tuna, pimiento, celery, spinach, macaroni, capers, and lemon juice. Turn into a deep 1½-quart casserole. Sprinkle top with Parmesan cheese. Heat oven to 375° F. and bake casserole 20 to 25 minutes, uncovered, or until the mixture is bubbling hot. Serves 4 to 6.

❧ Shrimp Ramekins

2 tablespoons butter or
  margarine
½ cup sliced celery
1 can condensed cream of
  mushroom soup

Melt the 2 tablespoons butter in saucepan over moderately low heat (about 225° F.); add celery and cook until tender. Remove from heat. Blend in undiluted soup and sour cream until smooth. Slowly stir in milk. Add shrimp. Place 4 to 5 asparagus spears in each of 4 indi-

½ cup commercial sour
    cream
⅓ cup milk
1½ cups cooked shrimp, cut
    up
1 14-ounce can asparagus
    spears, drained
2 tablespoons water
2 tablespoons melted butter
    or margarine
¾ cup fine dry seasoned
    bread crumbs

vidual shallow casseroles. Divide shrimp mixture among the four casseroles. Combine water, the 2 tablespoons melted butter, and bread crumbs; sprinkle about ⅓ cup over each casserole. Bake, uncovered, at 400° F. for 15 minutes, or until hot and bubbly. Serves 4.

---

᪗ Seafood Tetrazzini

¼ cup butter or margarine
¼ cup chopped onion
1 cup sliced fresh
    mushrooms
¼ cup flour
1 teaspoon salt
Few grains pepper
Few grains cayenne pepper
2½ cups milk
¼ cup dry sherry
1 8-ounce package fine egg
    noodles, cooked according
    to directions on package
1½ cups cooked lobster,
    shrimp, or crab meat (or
    use any desired
    combination)
2 tablespoons melted butter
    or margarine
⅓ cup fine dry bread crumbs
2 tablespoons grated
    Parmesan cheese

Heat oven to 375° F. Melt the ¼ cup butter in skillet over moderate heat (about 250° F.). Add onion and mushrooms; cook until lightly browned. Blend in flour, salt, pepper, and cayenne. Gradually stir in milk; cook, stirring constantly, until thickened. Stir in sherry. Combine noodles, sauce, and fish. Pour into buttered deep 2½-quart casserole. Mix the 2 tablespoons melted butter, bread crumbs, and Parmesan cheese. Sprinkle over top. Bake, uncovered, 40 to 45 minutes, or until lightly browned. Serves 4 to 5.

---

᪗ Baked Seafood Salad

1 cup coarsely chopped
    green pepper
½ cup finely chopped onion

Gently mix together all ingredients except potato chips. Pour into a deep 2½-quart casserole. Cover and refrigerate several hours, preferably overnight. About 1 hour

2 *cups coarsely chopped
    celery*
2 *cups mayonnaise*
2 *6½-ounce cans crab meat,
    drained and flaked*
2 *4½-ounce cans shrimp,
    drained*
1 *5-ounce can lobster,
    drained and flaked*
1 *6½-ounce can tuna,
    drained and flaked*
1 *teaspoon Worcestershire
    sauce*
1 *teaspoon salt*
Few grains pepper
Dash of Tabasco
1¼ *cups crumbled potato
    chips*

before serving time, heat oven to 350° F. Sprinkle top of casserole with potato chips. Bake uncovered 40 to 45 minutes or until well heated. Do not overbake. Serves 6 to 8.

CHAPTER XXVIII

SPICES AND HERBS

A knowledge of herbs and spices and how to use them in cooking is considered by many the province of only dedicated, experienced cooks. An air of mystery has somehow grown up around the use of them, and part of that mystery arises from the uncertainty about what they are.

The word *spice* is full of delicious overtones. We often use it in a general way to mean any aromatic flavoring material of vegetable origin. In this broad sense, *spice* includes herbs, seeds, and other seasonings.

Specifically, in the sense that spice adventurers of the past, who set out round the world in search of new spice "treasure islands," used the term, a spice is an aromatic substance obtained from the bark, root, fruit bud, or berry of a perennial, usually tropical, plant. Nutmeg, cinnamon, and cloves are typical spices.

Herbs, which are less exotic in origin, grow closer to home. They are the leaves of low-growing annual and perennial plants from temperate climates. Basil, parsley and oregano are some particularly well-known herbs.

Aromatic seeds also are usually of temperate origin (dill, caraway, and mustard seeds, for example), but some are primarily from warmer climates (cardamom, cumin, and sesame). They are the seeds or fruits of annual plants.

Blends, such as poultry seasoning and chili powder, are mixtures of spices, herbs, seeds, or other flavoring agents.

Other seasonings on the spice shelf include such condiments as Worcestershire sauce and Tabasco, and vegetable seasonings, such as garlic powder, minced onion, and celery salt.

To enhance effectively the dishes they are used in, your spices and herbs must be fresh. An herb or spice is fresh if the odor is strong when you open the jar. If you have to sniff out the aroma or taste the spice more than once, it is probably too stale to use.

Dating your spices when you buy them will help you keep track of their freshness. Whole spices keep much better than ground ones. In fact, ground spices do not retain their full flavor for more than six months. Make sure you keep them in tightly sealed containers, and remember to close them firmly after you use them.

Store all seasonings in a cool, dry place out of direct sunlight. The two worst enemies of herbs and spices are moisture and heat; therefore two places spices shouldn't be stored are over the sink or range. Sunlight also can affect spices and herbs adversely by fading them.

Following this introduction is a shopping list and a use guide for spices, herbs, and related seasonings. The shopping list is divided into three parts: Basic, or most often used; extras to add as you become familiar with the basics; and some extras that are nice to have for special seasoning.

Spice-Shelf Shopping List

Spices
BASIC
Cinnamon (ground)
Cloves (ground and whole)
Ginger (ground)
Nutmeg (ground)
Paprika (ground)
Pepper (black—whole and ground)

TO ADD
Allspice (ground)
Cayenne (ground)
Mace (ground)

NICE TO HAVE
Cinnamon (sticks)
Nutmeg (whole)
Saffron
Turmeric (ground)
Pepper (white—whole and ground)

Herbs
BASIC
Basil (leaves)
Bay (leaves)
Marjoram (leaves or ground)
Oregano (leaves or ground)
Parsley (flakes)

TO ADD
Dillweed (leaves)
Rosemary (leaves)
Sage (leaves or "rubbed")
Thyme (leaves or ground)

NICE TO HAVE
Chervil (leaves)
Mint (flakes)
Savory (leaves or ground)
Tarragon (leaves)

Aromatic Seeds
BASIC
Celery seed

TO ADD
Dillseed (ground or whole)
Mustard seed (ground)

NICE TO HAVE
Anise seed (whole)
Caraway seed (whole)

Cardamom seed (whole or ground)
Coriander seed (whole)
Cumin seed (whole or ground)
Fennel seed (whole)
Mustard seed (whole)
Poppy seed (whole)
Sesame seed (whole)

Italian seasoning
Pumpkin-pie spice
Seafood seasoning
Herb seasoning

Blends
BASIC

Chili powder
Curry powder

TO ADD

Mixed pickling spices
Poultry seasoning

NICE TO HAVE

Apple-pie seasoning
Barbecue seasoning

Seasonings
BASIC

Celery salt
Chives (chopped—dried or freeze-dried)
Garlic powder
Minced onion (dried flakes or instant)
Onion salt
Worcestershire sauce

TO ADD

Garlic salt
Tabasco
Mixed vegetable flakes

Basic Spice-and-Herb Chart

SPICES, HERBS, AND BLENDS	Suggested Uses
Spices	
Cinnamon: The fragrant bark of the cinnamon tree of Southeast Asia. Also called cassia. Available ground or in sticks.	Beef stews, lamb and pork chops, sweet potatoes, pumpkin, squash, broiled grapefruit, fruit pies, puddings, buns, coffee cake, spice cakes, mulled drinks. Use ¼ to 1 teaspoon for 4 servings.
Cloves: The flower buds of the clove tree, a member of the myrtle family. Available whole or ground.	Ham, stews, gravies, gherkins, squash, boiled onions, sweet potatoes, beets, fruit desserts and pies, chocolate mixtures, spice cakes. Use ⅛ to ½ teaspoon for 4 servings.
Ginger: The hot and spicy root of a tuberous tropical perennial. Available whole or ground.	Meats and poultry, stewed fruits, carrots, sweet potatoes, chutney, pickles, puddings, jellies, spice cakes, and cookies. Use ¼ to 1 teaspoon for 4 servings.
Nutmeg: The inner kernel of the nutmeg fruit. (The outer covering is called mace.) Available whole or ground.	Meats, chicken, fish, carrots, cauliflower, spinach, cabbage, stewed fruit, puddings, doughnuts, spice cakes, eggnog. Use ⅛ to 1 teaspoon for 4 servings.

Paprika: The pod of a sweet red pepper. Flavor varies from sweet to mildly pungent. Available ground.

Stews, chicken, fish, shellfish, soups, deviled eggs, potatoes, cabbage, cauliflower, turnips, salad dressings, canapés. Use 2 teaspoons to 2 tablespoons for 4 servings.

Herbs

Basil: A member of the mint family with a strong affinity for tomatoes. Available in dried leaves.

Stews and meat pies, shrimp creole and fish chowders, spaghetti sauces, peas, eggplant, tomatoes, salads. Use ½ teaspoon leaves for 4 servings.

Bay Leaf: The distinctively flavored leaf of the laurel plant. Available in whole dried leaves.

Meats and poultry, halibut, salmon, shellfish, fish chowders, spaghetti sauces, beets, artichokes, tomatoes, squash. Use 1 or 2 leaves for 4 servings.

Marjoram: A milder cousin of oregano. One of the components of poultry and Italian seasonings. Available dried or ground.

Meats and poultry, broiled fish, shellfish, eggs, lima beans, green beans, carrots, mushrooms, zucchini. Use ½ teaspoon for 4 servings.

Oregano: "Wild marjoram." A perennial of the mint family and an essential part of chili powder. Available dried or ground.

Meats and poultry, shellfish, cheese, eggs, spaghetti sauces, chili con carne, pizza, broccoli, eggplant, zucchini, tomatoes. Use ¼ to 2 teaspoons for 4 servings.

Parsley Flakes: Dried form of parsley. One of the mildest herbs.

Stews, soups, shellfish, omelets, sauces, stuffings, salad dressings, vegetables. Use 1 to 2 teaspoons for 4 servings.

Blends

Chili Powder: A blend of ground chili peppers, cumin seeds, oregano, garlic, and salt. Sometimes it includes cloves, allspice, or onion.

Chili con carne and many Mexican dishes, hamburgers, seafood chowders, eggs, cheese rarebits, Spanish rice, corn, eggplant, green beans, tomatoes, bean salads. Use ¼ to 2 teaspoons for 4 servings.

Curry Powder: A mixture that can contain up to 20 ground spices, including allspice, black pepper, red pepper, cayenne, ginger, cinnamon, cardamom, coriander, mustard, nutmeg, saffron, and turmeric.

Curried meats and poultry, eggs, fish, shrimp, seafood chowders, cream of mushroom soup, rice, tomatoes, creamed vegetables, lentils, salted nuts, and pickles. Use ¼ to 3 teaspoons for 4 servings.

Spices

Most of the spices are familiar to many people. They're used frequently in common foods. The basic ones are described in the preceding chart. You may like to know more about the others before you add them to your collection.

Allspice: This pungent spice is not a blend of other spices. It is a separate berry, although its aroma seems to be a mixture of cinnamon, nutmeg, and cloves. It is most commonly used ground though it does come whole. It is used in fruit pies, cakes, cookies, and spiced fruit compotes.

Cayenne pepper: This is a golden red member of the pepper family. It is always ground and should be used sparingly—it's hot.

Cinnamon sticks: These are lengths of cinnamon bark before it is ground. They are used frequently in this country as a flavorful stirrer for hot drinks, such as chocolate and hot toddies.

Mace and nutmeg: Mace is from the same fruit as nutmeg. Nutmeg is the seed of a peachlike fruit and mace is the lacy red membrane surrounding the seed. Whole nutmeg is the dried seed, which is about the size of a peach pit. The difference between freshly ground nutmeg and commercially ground nutmeg is as great as the difference between freshly ground pepper and packaged ground pepper—the flavor and aroma are far greater. Mace comes in dry flakes or ground. It resembles nutmeg in flavor but is more pungent. It is the traditional pound-cake spice, but is also nice in chocolate dishes, fruit pies, and whipped cream.

Saffron: Saffron is golden in both color and cost. It takes the stigmas of 75,000 special crocus blossoms to produce one pound of dried saffron. However, it is a very pungent spice—a few strands of whole saffron will flavor, and color, a whole pot of rice. Powdered saffron is even more expensive, but it too should be used sparingly—a tiny pinch will do. Whole strands of saffron should be crushed and steeped in hot water to use. Saffron is dark orange to reddish brown and turns bright yellow when cooked. Because saffron has a strong, almost medicinal, flavor, it must be used cautiously.

Turmeric: This is a deep yellow spice made from the root of a plant of the ginger family. It is, however, more closely related to saffron than ginger in flavor. It is usually one of the spices in prepared mustard and mustard pickles. It can be used with butter to baste meat, fish and poultry, or in rice.

White pepper: This spice, made from the kernel of the peppercorn, is somewhat milder than black pepper, which is made from the whole corn. White pepper is a nicety to be used when you want to add the spice of pepper to a sauce and don't want the black grains to show. It is available whole or ground.

Herbs

The secret of learning to use herbs is to get acquainted with them one at a time.

Start with the idea of using the herbs you buy to add excitement to everyday cooking. Don't reserve them for special company recipes. There are no hard and fast rules for the use of herbs, but the chart on page 965 will give you a start.

1. The herb flavor should always blend with, never overpower, the other ingredients in a recipe. Start with a little at a time.

2. Except in special cases, only one herb, at the most two, should be used in a recipe. At first always use one at a time so that you can judge its strength and flavor.

3. Certain herbs are especially suited to blend with certain foods—for example, tarragon with fish, rosemary with chicken, basil with tomatoes. For first experiments, use the time-proved combinations.

As you begin to seek out recipes using herbs, you will find *bouquet garni* and *herb butter* used repeatedly. They are classic herb combinations. A *bouquet garni* is a combination of fresh or dried herbs used in stews, soups, and braised meat dishes. It can be varied and individual, but the classic bouquet garni usually contains parsley, thyme, and bay leaf. Basil, chervil, chives, savory, or other herbs may be added. Tarragon is not a good mixer and should not be added. Tie the herbs into a small piece of cheesecloth and remove from sauce before serving.

Herb butter, a favorite dressing for broiled meats and fish, can be made with the herbs of your choice, depending on the food to be flavored. Finely chopped, fresh herbs or dried herbs are combined with sweet, unsalted butter.

The addition of lemon juice accentuates the herb flavor. The usual proportions are ¼ pound softened sweet butter and 1 teaspoon lemon juice creamed with 1 tablespoon finely chopped fresh herb or ½ teaspoon dried or powdered herb. Add salt to taste. Let stand at least one hour at room temperature before using. It may then be kept for several days in the refrigerator in a tightly covered jar.

Basil

Basil is one of the most useful herbs, and one of the easiest to grow either in a pot indoors or in the garden. Its dried leaves are available year-round in grocery stores. Of the many varieties, sweet basil is the best known and liked. The aroma of basil is usually described as being lemony with a slight hint of anise. Its flavor is something like that of cloves. There is a definite affinity of basil for tomatoes, but it can be used with many other foods. Try a few leaves in any canned soup; add fresh or dry leaves to salad greens or to the cooking water of green vegetables; mix it into cottage cheese for a delightful change of flavor. Use it in the basting butter for fish; sprinkle it on roasting meats before cooking.

✎ Herb-Baked Tomatoes

6 medium-sized firm tomatoes
1 tablespoon butter or margarine
¼ cup chopped scallions or green onions
½ cup fine dry bread crumbs
¼ cup chopped fresh basil or 1 teaspoon dried basil leaves
¼ cup chopped fresh parsley
½ teaspoon salt
Few grains pepper
1 cup soft bread crumbs
2 tablespoons melted butter or margarine

Cut tomatoes in halves crosswise. Carefully remove most of the pulp, leaving a shell about ½ inch thick. Chop the pulp coarsely. Melt butter in a skillet over moderately low heat (about 225° F.); add scallions and cook until tender but not brown. Remove from heat and add dry bread crumbs, basil, parsley, tomato pulp, salt, and pepper. Spoon mixture into tomato shells. Toss soft bread crumbs and melted butter together; sprinkle over tomatoes. Heat oven to 400° F. Bake tomatoes about 20 minutes, until crumbs are golden brown. Serves 6.

Bay Leaf

Bay leaf is really the leaf of a laurel tree—the same laurel that was used to weave Julius Caesar's wreaths and was thought to protect the ancient Greeks from ill health. There is no end to the legends about the magical powers of the bay leaf, but in cooking, it gives a distinct pungent flavor to stews, chowders, and soups. Use it sparingly—one leaf will flavor 6 cups of liquid amply. Bay leaf is usually added to cooking liquid at the beginning of the cooking time and discarded before serving the dish.

✎ Fricassee of Beef

½ cup all-purpose flour
1 teaspoon salt
2 pounds lean beef chuck, cut into 1-inch cubes
3 tablespoons vegetable oil
½ cup finely chopped onion

Mix flour and the 1 teaspoon salt together; coat meat with mixture. In a heavy saucepan or Dutch oven, heat oil over moderately high heat (about 300° F.); add meat in a single layer and cook until pieces are browned on all sides. Remove and brown rest of meat. Remove meat from pan. Reduce heat to moderately low (about 225°

3 cups boiling water
1 large bay leaf
2 teaspoons salt
¼ teaspoon pepper
2 cups sliced, peeled carrot
½ cup chopped celery
¾ pound green beans, sliced
About 3 cups hot mashed
    potatoes

F.) and cook onion until tender, stirring occasionally. Return meat to pan and add water, bay leaf, the 2 teaspoons salt, and pepper. Cover and cook 1½ hours, stirring occasionally. Add carrot, celery, and green beans and cook 30 minutes, or until meat and vegetables are tender. Remove bay leaf before serving. If desired, thicken gravy. Serve with mashed potatoes. Serves 6.

Marjoram

Marjoram is an herb of the mint family. It is closely related to oregano, though sweeter and milder than oregano. Traditionally used as a symbol of happiness, sweet marjoram was once used to weave crowns for happy young couples in ancient Greece. It is a versatile herb to be used in meat and fish dishes and to add flavor to eggs or fresh vegetables.

Herbed Spoon Bread

3 cups milk
½ cup yellow cornmeal
2 eggs, separated, at room
    temperature
2 tablespoons butter or
    margarine
½ teaspoon baking powder
1 teaspoon dried marjoram
    leaves
1 teaspoon salt

Heat oven to 350° F. Heat 1½ cups of the milk over moderately low heat (about 225° F.) until small bubbles form around edge of pan; remove from heat. Mix ½ cup of the cold milk and cornmeal together; gradually stir into hot milk. Cook until the consistency of mush, stirring constantly. Remove from heat. Beat egg yolks slightly and stir in the remaining 1 cup milk. Add the egg mixture, butter, baking powder, marjoram, and salt to the cornmeal; stir until butter is melted. Beat egg whites with rotary beater until stiff peaks form; fold into cornmeal mixture. Pour into greased, deep 1½-quart casserole. Bake 60 to 80 minutes, uncovered, or until firm and golden brown. Serves 8.

Oregano

Oregano is known today because of the popularity of pizza—it is the pizza herb. Originally called wild marjoram, oregano is far lustier and more assertive than marjoram. It is good in all tomato dishes, and a touch of it is nice in cheese and egg dishes. It's also excellent used in stuffings for fish.

✑ Italian-Style Tomatoes

4 medium-sized ripe
   tomatoes, peeled and
   chilled
1¼ teaspoons dried oregano
   leaves
Salt and pepper
  1 2-ounce can anchovy
   fillets
  5 tablespoons olive oil
  3 tablespoons wine vinegar
Watercress

Slice tomatoes into ¼-inch slices and arrange on serving platter. Sprinkle with oregano, salt, and pepper. Arrange anchovies over tomatoes. Mix olive oil and wine vinegar and pour over tomatoes. Garnish with watercress. Serves 4 to 6.

Parsley

Parsley may be handsome as a garnish, but using it only in this way is a disservice to an extremely edible, but seldom eaten, plant. Rich in vitamins, parsley is available fresh or dried. There are more than thirty varieties; all have a bitter-sweet flavor. Some have strong, spicy overtones. To keep fresh parsley, wash thoroughly, shake off excess moisture, and pinch off heavy stems. Store in a covered container in the refrigerator. Try chopped fresh parsley or dried leaves in biscuits; use sprigs on all poultry and meats to add flavor when roasting. Parsley butter (see herb butter on page 967) makes a refreshing spread for sandwiches or canapés.

✑ Iced Parsley Soup

2 tablespoons butter or
  margarine
⅓ cup finely chopped onion
1 tablespoon flour
2 cups milk
1 cup chicken consommé or
  1 chicken bouillon cube
  dissolved in 1 cup boiling
  water
1 teaspoon salt
Few grains pepper
½ cup finely chopped fresh
  parsley or 2 tablespoons
  dried parsley

Melt butter in a saucepan over moderate heat (about 250° F.). Add onion and cook until tender but not brown. Stir in flour. Gradually add milk; cook and stir until smooth. Gradually stir in chicken consommé. Cook, stirring constantly, until thickened. Add salt, pepper, and parsley. Cover and chill several hours or overnight. Serves 6.

Dill

Dill is a flavor familiar to most people because of its popular use in pickles. Dill has a pungent flavor, difficult to describe, but since its aroma matches its flavor, it is an easy herb to identify. Dill is often available in fresh form; whenever possible, the leaves and stems should be used fresh because dill loses much of its flavor when dried. However, powdered or whole dillseed or dried dill leaves (called dillweed) are generally available in grocery stores; these will impart much the same flavor to sauces as the fresh leaves. Dill is especially good in potato salad or any of the lentil soups. Add a pinch of powdered seed or some freshly minced leaves to season sour cream or sweet whipped cream. This makes a fine sauce for fresh, sliced cucumbers or any broiled fish. A few dillseeds or leaves sprinkled on freshly boiled potatoes make a superb accompaniment for a roast. As a rule of thumb: For 4 servings, use ⅛ to ½ teaspoon ground dillseed or ½ to 2 teaspoons whole seed or 2 tablespoons fresh chopped leaves and stems.

⌇ Beef Stroganoff

1½ pounds beef top round
2 tablespoons vegetable oil
⅓ cup finely chopped onion
1 4-ounce can sliced mushrooms, undrained
2 beef bouillon cubes
¾ cup hot water
Few grains pepper
4 teaspoons flour
¼ cup cold water
½ cup (4 ounces) commercial sour cream
½ teaspoon powdered dillseed or dried dillweed or 2 tablespoons chopped fresh dill leaves
1 tablespoon flour
About 2½ cups hot cooked noodles

Trim most of the fat from meat and cut meat into narrow strips about ½ inch thick. Melt oil in a heavy skillet or Dutch oven over moderately high heat (about 300° F.). Add meat and brown pieces lightly. Remove meat; add onion and cook until tender. Reduce heat to low (about 200° F.). Add meat, mushrooms, bouillon cubes, the ¾ cup hot water, and pepper. Cover and cook 50 to 60 minutes, until meat is fork-tender. Remove meat from skillet. Blend together the 4 teaspoons flour and ¼ cup cold water; stir into drippings in skillet and cook over moderate heat (about 250° F.) until thickened. Stir together sour cream, dill, and the 1 tablespoon flour. Gradually add about ½ cup of the gravy mixture to the sour cream; then add this mixture to the rest of the gravy. Cook and stir constantly over low heat (about 200° F.) until sauce just starts to bubble. Add meat and heat but do not boil. Serve over hot noodles. Serves 4 to 5.

Rosemary

Rosemary, which has the most romantic herb history, is one of the most favored herbs. As an ancient cosmetic ingredient, it was said to "ensure beauty and make age but a flight of time." As a culinary herb, rosemary has a sweet scent, a rather piny flavor. Rosemary will flourish in a window pot. The fresh lavender-flowered tops or leaves make an aromatic garnish for chilled drinks or fresh fruit cup. The freshly chopped or crumbled dry leaves may be used judiciously in sauces, stews, soups, and over roasts. Because rosemary imparts a delightful but distinct flavor change to foods, it should be used cautiously at first. For example, 1 teaspoon of dried rosemary added to the flour in which a whole frying chicken is coated will make a great flavor change. Use about ¾ teaspoon of dried herb to a 6-pound roast of lamb or pork. As a rule of thumb: For 4 servings, use ½ to 1 teaspoon dried leaves or 1 to 2 teaspoons chopped fresh rosemary leaves.

Rosemary Chicken

2 *2-pound broiler-fryers, cut in half*
2 *cups boiling water*
2 *chicken bouillon cubes*
6 *tablespoons melted butter or margarine*
2 *teaspoons crumbled dried rosemary leaves*
2 *tablespoons flour*
1 *cup hot water*
¼ *cup dry white wine*

Wash chickens and dry thoroughly. Place in a large flat pan. Combine the 2 cups boiling water, bouillon cubes, butter, and 1 teaspoon of the dried rosemary. Pour mixture over chicken and let stand 1 hour, turning chicken frequently. Heat oven to 400° F. Drain chicken and place on a rack in a shallow baking pan. Bake about 40 minutes, until fork-tender; baste several times with a little of the marinade. Remove chicken to serving platter and sprinkle with the remaining 1 teaspoon rosemary. Stir flour into the drippings in baking pan; place over moderate heat (about 250° F.) and gradually add the 1 cup hot water, wine, and any remaining marinade. Cook and stir until smooth and slightly thickened. Serve with the broiled chicken. Serves 4.

Sage

Although the hardy plant is native to the shores of the Mediterranean, it can be grown in all parts of the world, including many American gardens. Sage has a strong, fragrant odor. It is the basic ingredient in poultry seasoning and is used in bread stuffings for poultry, meat, and fish. It is a perfect seasoning for pork. It comes in dried leaf form as well as ground and crushed, or rubbed. As a rule of thumb: For 6 cups of bread, use ¼ teaspoon of sage for stuffing.

❧ Sage Corn Bread Stuffing

¾ cup butter or margarine
1¾ cups finely chopped onion
1½ cups finely chopped celery
1 tablespoon dried rubbed sage
1¾ teaspoons salt
¼ teaspoon pepper
6 cups toasted bread cubes
4 cups crumbled corn bread
¼ cup chopped fresh parsley
½ to ¾ cup hot canned chicken broth

Melt butter in a skillet over moderate heat (about 250° F.); add onion and celery and cook until tender, stirring occasionally. Remove from heat and stir in sage, salt, and pepper. Toss together bread cubes, corn bread, and parsley in a large bowl. Stir in cooked vegetables and butter. Mix in chicken broth. For a dry stuffing, use ½ cup; for a more moist one, ¾ cup. Refrigerate stuffing until ready to use. Use as a stuffing for turkey following directions on page 379. Makes about 10 cups stuffing, or enough for a 10- to 12-pound turkey or two 5-pound chickens.

Thyme

Thyme is a fragrant leaf that was once used by ladies of the Middle Ages to add fragrance to the flower bouquets they clutched in their hands. It is a beautifully versatile herb—traditional in New England fish chowders and popular in creole dishes. It comes in leaf or ground form and is moderately potent. As a rule of thumb: Use ¼ to ½ teaspoon of leaf or ground thyme for a dish to serve 6.

❧ Sautéed Chicken Livers

¼ cup flour
½ teaspoon salt
Few grains pepper
1½ pounds chicken livers
6 tablespoons butter or margarine
½ pound mushrooms, sliced
¼ cup finely chopped onion
½ cup dry sherry
¼ cup water

Mix flour, the ½ teaspoon salt, and pepper together; coat chicken livers with mixture. Heat 4 tablespoons of the butter in a skillet over moderately high heat (about 275° F.); add chicken livers and cook until lightly browned. Remove chicken livers. Reduce heat to moderately low (about 225° F.); add the remaining 2 tablespoons butter and cook mushrooms and onion until tender. Return chicken livers to pan; add sherry, water, thyme, the ½ teaspoon salt, and the pepper. Cover and cook 10 minutes, stirring occasionally, or until chicken

½ teaspoon dried thyme
  leaves
½ teaspoon salt
Few grains pepper
  2 to 3 cups hot cooked rice
  (optional)

livers are cooked through. If desired, serve over cooked rice. Serves 4 to 6.

Chervil

Chervil comes from a plant that has beautiful fernlike leaves. A delicate herb related to parsley, it comes only in whole-leaf form. In French kitchens, it is used as an alternate to parsley in salads and soups. It may also be used to make herb butter for fish and meats. It is mild and can be used lavishly, compared to the more pungent herbs. As a rule of thumb: Use 1 teaspoon to 2 cups of sauce or soup.

Fillet of Sole Cooked in Wine

1½ pounds fillet of sole
⅓ cup dry white wine
  1 tablespoon lemon juice
  2 tablespoons melted butter
  or margarine
  1 teaspoon dried chervil
  leaves
¼ teaspoon salt
Few grains white pepper
½ cup seedless grapes, cut in
  half

Heat oven to 350° F. Arrange fillets in a shallow baking dish. Pour in wine and lemon juice. Brush fillets with melted butter. Sprinkle with chervil, salt, and pepper. Bake 10 minutes; sprinkle grapes over fillets and bake 20 minutes longer, or until fish is easily flaked, basting occasionally with the wine mixture. Serves 4 to 5.

Mint

Mint is an herb familiar to almost every part of the world. Fresh mint of many varieties is easily grown in gardens. The leafy tops or crushed leaves make a tangy, edible garnish for beverages, all fresh fruits, ice creams, and gelatine desserts. Fresh or dried, mint adds a pleasing flavor to boiled carrots or peas and is good on boiled potatoes to be served with roast lamb or veal. Mint leaves added to French dressing make a cool, refreshing addition to fruit salads. Mint tea—made by steeping 2 teaspoons dried mint leaves in ¼ cup boiling water for seven minutes—may be used to flavor frostings, iced tea, fruit juices, or melted jellies to serve with roasts. Substitute mint tea for other liquids if you're using it in such recipes as frostings. As a rule of thumb: For 4 servings, use ¼ to 1 teaspoon crushed dried mint or 1 to 2 tablespoons fresh, chopped mint.

❧ Minted Lamb Patties

1 pound ground lean lamb
2 tablespoons finely chopped
  fresh mint or 1 teaspoon
  crushed dried mint
½ teaspoon salt
Few grains pepper
1 egg, slightly beaten
1 slice white bread, crumbled

Combine lamb, mint, salt, and pepper. Add egg and bread; mix until well blended. Lightly shape into 4 patties about 1 inch thick. Preheat broiler 10 minutes. Arrange patties on broiler rack; broil 3 inches from heat about 7 minutes on each side. Makes 4 patties.

Savory

Savory was one of the favorite herbs of colonial gardeners. It grows in two varieties: summer savory, which is the kind we find on spice shelves, and winter savory, a slightly more pungent herb. Savory is an ingredient in poultry seasoning and is an excellent seasoning for chicken dishes. It is also a favorite herb for beans—green or dried. As a rule of thumb: Use about ¼ teaspoon dried savory per pound of meat or vegetables.

❧ Savory Green Beans

2 10-ounce packages frozen
  French-style green beans
½ cup water
½ teaspoon salt
½ teaspoon instant minced
  onion
3 tablespoons butter or
  margarine
3 tablespoons flour
¾ cup commercial sour cream
¾ teaspoon dried savory
  leaves

Place beans, water, the ½ teaspoon salt, and onion in a saucepan, and cook following directions on package. Drain. Melt butter in a saucepan over moderately low heat (about 225° F.); blend in flour. Stir sour cream, savory, the ½ teaspoon salt, and pepper into butter mixture; cook over low heat (about 200° F.) until sauce is slightly thickened, but not boiling. Fold sauce into beans and pour into a deep 1-quart casserole. Sprinkle with cheese. Place in a preheated broiler about 4 inches from heat until cheese begins to brown. Serves 6.

(Ingredients continued on page 976)

½ teaspoon salt
Few grains pepper
¼ cup coarsely shredded
  Swiss cheese

Tarragon

Tarragon is to some people the most intriguing of the culinary herbs. The slender, pointed, dark green leaves have an astringent, yet sweet, aniselike flavor. For the cook who really wants to know and use herbs, this one is a "must," but it must be used with discretion, and rarely with other herbs, for it will overpower them. It is especially at home in such sauces as Hollandaise, mayonnaise, and tartar and mustard sauces, served with fresh vegetables, fish, or poultry. It is superb used in the basting butter for broiled steaks, fish, or poultry. For an unusually good salad dressing, let ½ teaspoon dried tarragon leaves stand in ¼ cup prepared French dressing an hour before use on fresh salad greens. As a rule of thumb: For 4 servings, use ¼ to ½ teaspoon dried or ½ to 2 teaspoons chopped fresh tarragon.

❧ Tarragon Sauce for Fish

1 cup (8 ounces) commercial
  sour cream
½ teaspoon dried tarragon
  leaves
1 teaspoon seasoned salt
⅛ teaspoon grated onion
½ teaspoon salt

Combine all the ingredients and mix thoroughly. Cover and chill at least 1 hour to blend flavors. Serve with broiled scallops, halibut, sole, or flounder. Makes 1 cup of sauce.

Aromatic Seeds

Celery seed is not related to the celery we eat—it is the seed of a wild celery plant called smallage—but it does add the flavor of celery to soups, sauces, salads, and vegetables. Use the whole celery seed sparingly— about ½ teaspoon to 4 cups of salad.

Mustard seed, whole, is used primarily in pickling and in marinades for meat or shrimp. Powdered mustard, which is the seeds reduced to a powder, is commonly used to flavor mayonnaise and oil-and-vinegar dressing. Oddly enough, mustard does not have any odor or pungency until it is mixed with liquid. Then it is hot. Use it sparingly or as the recipe—and your taste buds—directs. Prepared mustards are usually a mixture of mustard seeds and other ingredients. They range from very mild to very hot.

Anise seeds are always sold whole. Shaped like a comma, they taste like licorice. They are especially good as flavorings for cookies, cakes, and sweet rolls.

Caraway seeds are the pungent seeds used in rye bread. They are popular in much middle-European cookery as a flavoring for sauerkraut and beef stews. They may also be added to cooked vegetables.

Cardamom, a member of the ginger family, is a sweet seed with a lovely fragrance. It is available in whole pods or ground form. The whole pods add an aroma to hot fruit punches. The ground cardamom is especially good in coffee cakes and Danish pastries. It may also be mixed ½ teaspoon to a cup of sugar to sprinkle on hot buttered toast.

Coriander seed, whole or ground, has a taste that's difficult to describe. Some say that it is a combination of lemon peel and sage; others are reminded of caraway and cumin. It is an ingredient of curry powder and is used to spice frankfurters. It is good in fruit pies and in curry sauces.

Cumin seed, available whole or ground, is of Egyptian origin. Although related to the caraway seed, it is distinctly different in flavor. It is an ingredient in both curry and chili powders. It is an extremely versatile seed, which can be used with eggs, meat, fish, and poultry. Get acquainted with it by sprinkling the ground seed over scrambled eggs or rice.

Fennel seed is a member of the parsley family, but its slight licorice flavor is similar to that of anise. It is marketed as a whole seed only. Try it in breads or rolls or over apples in a pie or in spaghetti sauces. Sprinkle seeds over fish before broiling.

Poppy seed, marketed only in its whole seed form, lends a nutlike flavor to vegetables and is a quick way to glamorize brown-and-serve rolls. Brush top with butter and sprinkle on seeds before baking. In case you wondered, the fluid in the bud of the poppy flower—which makes opium—is long since evaporated when the seed is harvested. Crushed poppy seeds are favorite fillings for middle-European holiday pastries and breads.

Sesame seeds are tiny white seeds that have an almond flavor when browned in butter or toasted. They can be used as they come to top any food that will be broiled or baked. To put them into salads, stuffings, or cooked vegetables, they should be toasted first. To toast, spread the white seeds on a cookie sheet or baking pan and toast them for about 20 minutes in a 350° F. oven. Shake the pan occasionally to ensure even browning. They will turn golden and can be used in any way chopped nutmeats would be. Sesame seeds are also known as benne seeds in southern areas of this country.

Blends

Chili powder is a blend of several ingredients: hot red peppers, oregano, cumin, and coriander are usual. Brands vary in their degree of hotness. When you use chili powder, it's best to start with a little and taste as you add more.

Curry powder is a blend of many spices, depending upon the brand. Usually coriander, cumin, fenugreek, cayenne pepper, and turmeric are used. Allspice, cassia, cardamom, cloves, fennel, ginger, mace, mustard, and pepper are typical additions. Discerning chefs may never touch a curry powder blend, preferring to mix their own. Curry powder is not limited to the making of curries; it's a good flavor to add to cream soups, potato salad, meat loaf, and bland vegetables.

All the other blends of spices are obviously named for the use for which they are intended. They have been tested and marketed because they are a blend that suits most tastes.

Seasonings

Celery salt is a blend of ground celery seed (a wild variety of celery called smallage) and ordinary table salt. When you use it, cut down on the salt in the recipe. It will give a mild celery flavor.

Chives are the tender, tubular leaves of a plant belonging to the onion family. They are most frequently used fresh and snipped wherever a mild onion flavor is desirable—in soft cheese; in meat, vegetable, or fish salads; in omelets; in cream sauces; and as a flavorful garnish for soups. They are also available in dried, freeze-dried, or frozen form.

Garlic powder is the dehydrated garlic bud powdered; it contains no salt. *Garlic salt* is salt that has been flavored with fresh garlic. Garlic is also available year-round in fresh form called flowers—the individual buds are called cloves. Garlic is aromatic with a strong flavor that is delicious to some people and not to others. Judging by the popularity of garlic bread, it is a fairly well-loved seasoning. When you use garlic salt, cut down on the amount of table salt in your recipe.

Minced onion comes in flake, instant, and minced instant forms. All are dehydrated onions—the instant is more finely minced than the flaked and the minced instant is tinier still. They are a quick way to add onion to a soup, stew, salad, or other vegetables. If you add them to a salad or want to brown them for a stew, it is necessary to refresh them in water for about five minutes—use equal parts dry onion and water—you can then treat them as fresh onions. Some markets also carry minced frozen onions to use whenever a recipe calls for chopped onion.

Onion salt is table salt flavored with onion. When you use it, cut down on the salt called for in the recipe. *Onion powder* contains no salt. One tablespoon of it is about the equivalent of a medium-sized onion.

CHAPTER XXIX

ABOUT WINES
WITH FOODS

Appreciating wine goes hand in hand with appreciating good food. Each of the many forms—or, more accurately speaking, classes—of wine makes a unique contribution to the enjoyment of a well-prepared dinner. Wine enriches a meal by virtue of its aesthetic appeal too. In colors ranging from pale straw to deep gold and from pink to ruby red, wine served from the bottle or from a decorative decanter will dress up even the simplest occasion when family or friends gather around the dinner table.

Many of today's young adults, however, are beset by confusing and sometimes inhibiting notions about the nature and value of wine, as well as how and when to serve it. The person who walks into a wine shop without knowing which wine to buy or what wine goes best with what kind of food is inevitably confounded by the variety of bottles and labels on display. The American wine-making industry has come far, particularly since World War II, in improving the quality and increasing the quantity of its product. Choosing American wines as an introduction to serving wine with food is easier than trying to choose from the whole world of imported wines.

The following descriptions of wine classes and types, and what each is best suited for, are guidelines to enjoyment.

There are only five classes of wine: (1) appetizer wines; (2) red and (3) white dinner (or table) wines; (4) dessert wines; and (5) sparkling wines.

Within each class of wine there are several types. In the red table-wine class, for example, there is the well-known Burgundy type, so named because it is made from actual descendants of grapes native to the region of Burgundy, France, or because the wines have characteristics similar to certain French wines from Burgundy. In the United States *burgundy* is therefore the *generic* name for a specific type of red table wine, just as *Rhine wine* is the generic name for a certain type of white table wine.

To confuse matters a bit, there are bottles of American wine on the store shelf that are labeled slightly differently, with unfamiliar French or German names. When American wines are produced from more than 51 percent of one particular "breed," or variety, of grape that is highly regarded—such as the Pinot Noir grape originally from Burgundy or the Johannisberger Riesling grape from Germany—they are known as *varietal* wines. Such wines undoubtedly will be labeled prominently *Pinot Noir* or *Johannisberger Riesling*. Their class and type often will be labeled *red* and *Burgundy,* and *white* and *Rhine*, respectively, but in smaller letters. However, there are also native American varietal grapes with more familiar-sounding names—Concord, Delaware, and Niagara, for example—that are prominently labeled as such. These grapes are grown in the eastern and middle-western parts of America, and they too produce excellent varietal wines.

It does get a bit complicated, but once you have become familiar with the basic points and have bought and tasted wines new to you, you will learn to judge which, among certain varietals, you find more to your taste.

Appetizer wines are what their name implies—wines to be taken before dinner, with or without snacks, to stimulate the appetite. The chief appetizer wines are dry sherry and vermouth. A good dry sherry has a nutlike flavor and is generally light to amber in color. Vermouth appetizer wines, or *apéritifs*, are light, dry—"French type"—and sweet—"Italian type." Both are served plain or mixed with another beverage, either chilled or on-the-rocks. A third and increasingly popular appetizer wine is what is called flavored wine, to which fruit, herb, and spice flavors have been added. Wines of this type are variously labeled with catchy trade names, but somewhere else on the label the phrase *natural-flavored* usually is mentioned. They are generally full-bodied, and medium-sweet to sweet. Many people, incidentally, use them as dessert wines.

Red table wines are usually dry (applied to wine, "dry" means "not sweet"), and are meant to accompany main-course dishes, such as steaks, chops, roasts, game, and spaghetti, as well as many highly seasoned casseroles. Within this class of wine are several distinct types, among them Burgundy—deep red and robustly flavored—and claret—lighter in color, medium-bodied, and somewhat drier or tarter. Rosé wine is also in the red wine category; its color is pinkish to clear, light red, and in flavor it ranges from sweet to dry. Some rosés go excellently with seafood and other dishes for which white wine is traditionally recommended. Unlike other red table wines, rosé is served chilled, as is white wine. Added to all these red wine types is another known simply as *vino rosso*. Mellower in flavor and sometimes sweeter, it is very much like Italian table wine. American chianti, another red table wine, resembles its Italian prototype in its full-bodied but slightly tart characteristics.

All but the rosé wines are best served at temperatures of about 60 to 65 degrees, or so-called room temperature—a standard actually established long before the comfortable days of insulated houses and central heating.

White table wines, ranging in color from pale straw to rich, deep gold, vary in taste from dry and tart to sweet; they may be light or full-bodied. All white wines should be served chilled (ideally, at from 40 to 55 degrees), and are an excellent accompaniment to seafood dishes and chicken as well as such light dishes as omelets and soufflés.

The three chief types within the white wine class are sauterne, Rhine, and Chablis. Sauterne may be dry, semisweet (*haut sauterne*), or sweet (*château sauterne*, the sweetest, is often served as a dessert wine. French Sauternes—note the difference in spelling—is always served as a dessert wine). In general, sauterne is deep-yellow colored and is rather fragrantly flavored. Rhine wine is much tarter, drier than sauterne, and its color is pale yellow to slightly greenish gold. Chablis is similar to Rhine wine but is a little less tart, more robust in flavor. Some of the better Chablis wines are not labeled as such, being called white burgundy instead.

Dessert wines all are sweet-tasting and should be served chilled or at very cool room temperature, in small (2½- to 4-ounce) glasses. They go perfectly with light desserts, such as cookies, fruits, nuts, and cheese.

The chief types of dessert wines are port, sweet (or cream) sherry (both should be served at room temperature), and muscatel; the class also includes Tokay and Angelica. Port is a rich and fruity wine in shades ranging from medium red to deep ruby; there also is a white port, which is light to pale gold. *Tawny* port, usually so labeled, should mean that it has been aged longer than regular port; its color is reddish brown as a result. Port goes especially well with cheese. Sweet sherry is dark-amber colored and has a pronounced "nutty" flavor. Muscatel, in colors all the way from gold and dark amber to red, is more full-bodied than sweet sherry, and has a noticeable fruity flavor.

This class of wine often is used in cooking as a basting sauce for some meats and for making wine jellies. In addition, many fruit desserts are enhanced by a light dousing with a dessert wine. These dessert wines usually have a higher alcohol content than the other classes of wine. By law, alcohol content must be noted on the label.

Sparkling wine, the aristocrat of the wine family, is good with any or all parts of a meal. This class includes white and pink champagne as well as sparkling Burgundy. It should be noted, however, that those bottles carrying only the "sparkling wine" label—with no mention of champagne—are actually carbonated wines. They are made in a different way and do not pretend to be true champagnes.

In the mysterious world of wine nomenclature, the driest champagne is called *nature*, the very dry champagne, *brut*. As its sweetness increases, champagne successively is called extra-dry, dry, or *sec* (which is medium-sweet), *demi-sec* (sweeter still), and sweet or *doux* (the sweetest in the group).

In general, pink champagne, also known as champagne rosé, is medium-dry to sweet; sparkling Burgundy is about the same.

Sediment rarely forms in bottles of American wine. But if you think some sediment has collected in a bottle that you have stored for several years, take these precautions before serving it. Lift the bottle gently and, keeping it in the same position, place it in a wine basket; open it with a good, leverage-operated corkscrew with a rounded, "worm" edge. Or you may prefer to *decant* the wine; transfer it to a decanter, pouring it very slowly so that the sediment is not shaken up and absorbed into the wine. Both wine basket and decanter are acceptable for taking to the table—and they are highly decorative, too.

Unopened wine bottles may be kept over long periods in a dry area, not too brightly lighted, where the temperature is constant—anywhere from 50 to 60 degrees. Many ingenious storage areas have been improvised behind stairways, in kitchen cabinets, and on closet shelves. Whether you select special wine racks or make your own shelves or bins, you must remember to store all corked bottles on their sides; this keeps the cork moist. Wine bottles with screw caps may stand upright; this applies to champagne bottles with plastic corks.

Leftover table wines may be stored in the refrigerator for several days and still be palatable, but you must be sure that they are tightly closed. Leftover dessert and appetizer wines can be stored for much longer periods.

Chilling wines in advance of serving them is advised for all white wines (at least one hour in the refrigerator or 20 minutes in a bucket of ice) and sparkling wines (several hours, or overnight, if you find that easier, but don't let it get below 40 degrees). If you find you must get red table wine down to "room temperature," it is suggested that you quick-chill a bottle for about 15 minutes before serving. This should not interfere with the recommended suggestion of uncorking red wine about an hour before serving, in order to let it "breathe."

How to Choose the "Right" Wine

There is only one rule for choosing the right wine: have the one that suits your taste; it's the right one for the occasion. The guides given here are simply wine services that have become customary because most people, over a period of time, have agreed that certain wines taste best with certain foods.

As a cocktail: With appetizers or soup, sherry or vermouth is usually chosen. They're both served slightly chilled; both come in sweet or dry form. Your preference will depend upon whether you like a sweet or dry drink. In addition, any of the wines are frequently used in mixed drinks for cocktails such as:

Port Cocktail

For each drink, measure *1½ ounces port, ½ ounce dry vermouth, ½ ounce orange juice, 1 drop Angostura bitters* over *2 ice cubes.* Stir to blend and chill. Strain into a cocktail glass.

As a party drink: For afternoon or after-dinner parties, the sparkling wines—champagne or sparkling Burgundy—or the sweet wines—red or white port, Tokay, muscatel, or cream sherry—are usually served. With them, you can have any of the salted nibbling foods, cookies, cheese, fruit, sandwiches, or cake. Here again, any of the wines can be served in mixed drinks or punch. Tall, cool ones, such as the Claret Float, make easy, inexpensive drinks to serve to a crowd for an evening party.

Claret Float

Fill a tall glass half full of *lemonade.* Add *cracked ice.* Slowly pour *3 ounces claret* down side of glass. Decorate with *lemon slice.*

As an accompaniment to food: The seven domestic wines most commonly served with food are called table wines. They are all dry. Three are red—claret, Burgundy, and Chianti; three are white—sauterne, Rhine, and Chablis. Rosé is a pink wine that goes safely with all food.

With beef or game, most people like the red wines best, since they are hearty in flavor and complement the heavier-flavored meats.

With lamb or veal, use either red or white table wine.

With fish, fowl, or eggs, the white wines are usually preferred because they don't overpower the delicate flavors of the food.

With cheese and spaghetti dishes, let the choice depend upon the seasonings in the food. If the seasonings are heavy, choose red wine; if they are bland and light, a white wine is preferred.

How Much to Buy

One fifth bottle of table wine will pour 6 servings of 4 ounces each.

When serving wine for a cocktail or appetizer, count on getting from fourteen to sixteen glasses from a fifth bottle.

To plan champagne for a wedding or other large occasion, count on one case of twelve bottles to serve twenty to twenty-five guests.

Wineglasses

The ideal all-purpose glass in which to serve wine holds about nine ounces. It should be of clear glass with a slim stem, its bowl tapering slightly inward at the top. Colored glasses are not desirable for wines because they hide the wine's color. If you use an all-purpose glass rather than a special one for each class of wine, it shouldn't be more than half full for table wines, and not more than a quarter full for appetizer or dessert wines.

Any small glass may be used for wines. You need not be rigid about choice. Generally a four- to six-ounce glass is desirable for wines served with a meal; smaller (two- to three-ounce) glasses are chosen for appetizer or sweet party wines. Shallow or hollow-stemmed glasses show off the bubbles of sparkling wines best.

Wines in Mixed Drinks and Punch

Wine coolers are refreshing, light, inexpensive drinks to serve before dinner, especially in summertime.

Champagne Punch

1 pint raspberry sherbet
1 fifth rosé, chilled
⅓ cup frozen lemonade
    concentrate
1 fifth champagne, chilled
Berries (optional)
Fresh mint (optional)

Combine sherbet, rosé, and lemonade in punch bowl; stir until raspberry sherbet is partially thawed. Pour in champagne. Garnish with berries or fresh mint if desired. Makes 16 ½-cup servings.

❧ Peach Bowl

1 10-ounce package frozen
sliced peaches, thawed
¼ cup sugar
1 fifth Rhine wine

Combine peaches, sugar, and half of the wine in a large bowl. Cover and refrigerate overnight. At serving time, half-fill a punch bowl with ice; add wine–fruit mixture and rest of wine. Makes 10 to 11 ½-cup servings.

❧ Fruited Burgundy Cooler

1 fifth Burgundy wine
¼ cup lemon juice
1 cup sugar
1 orange, thinly sliced
1 lemon, thinly sliced
2 cups chilled carbonated
water

Combine wine, lemon juice, sugar, orange, and lemon slices in a large bowl. Cover and chill 3 to 4 hours. Just before serving, add carbonated water; stir well. Pour into ice-filled glasses. Makes about 10 ½-cup servings.

❧ Cranberry Cup

1 pint (16 fluid ounces)
bottled cranberry juice
cocktail
½ cup Burgundy wine
¼ cup sugar
6 whole strawberries

Combine cranberry juice, wine, and sugar in a cocktail shaker. Add a generous amount of cracked ice; shake vigorously. Strain into chilled champagne glasses. Garnish with berries. Makes about 6 ½-cup servings.

❧ Sherry Cooler

2 cups dry sherry
2 cups lemon–lime soda
Lime slices

Pour wine into a large pitcher. Add soda and stir to mix. Pour into ice-filled glasses; garnish with lime slices. Makes 8 ½-cup servings.

❧ Wine Spritzer

12 ice cubes
2 cups Concord grape wine*
2 cups carbonated water

In each of 4 tall, chilled glasses place 3 ice cubes. Add ½ cup wine and ½ cup carbonated water. Stir ingredients with a long-handled teaspoon to combine. Serve immediately. Makes 4 servings.

*Note: Chablis, Rhine wine, sauterne or any other wine may be substituted for the grape wine.

❧ Vermouth Cassis

½ ounce (1 tablespoon)
Crème de Cassis
3 ounces dry vermouth
Carbonated water

Put the Crème de Cassis in a 5- to 7-ounce glass. Pour the dry vermouth over it and add 2 or 3 ice cubes. Fill the glass with a small amount of carbonated water. Stir. Makes 1 serving.

Note: Kir, another cool summer cocktail, is made just like Vermouth Cassis except that Chablis is used instead of vermouth.

Wines and Cooking

If you can cook, you can cook with wine. As a rule of thumb, use the dry wines with main dishes and the sweet wines with desserts or fruit. If you are serving nondrinkers or children, don't worry about the alcoholic content in foods cooked with wine. Any alcoholic beverage loses its alcohol content when cooked—only the flavor remains.

You can start experimenting with the added flavor of wines used in cooking with the following suggestions and the recipes that follow.

Add 1 tablespoon of sherry to 1 cup of Cream Sauce (recipe page 481).

Use red wine for half of the water in beef stews.

Use half dry white wine and half water to poach fish. Use the resulting bouillon as the liquid to make a sauce for the fish.

Use 2 ounces (¼ cup) white wine for final basting of roast chicken or turkey.

Add 1 tablespoon of red wine to a cup of spaghetti (tomato) sauce.

Add 1 tablespoon of dry sherry to each cup of egg mixture for Baked Custard (recipe page 737).

Add 1 tablespoon of port wine to 1 cup grated Cheddar cheese. Mix and pack in an empty juice can and refrigerate over night. Open the remaining end of the can; push out the cylinder of cheese. Slice to serve on crackers.

Drizzle sherry over the sugar in baked apples before baking.

Moisten 1 cup of soft bread cubes with ¼ cup Burgundy wine. Mix with 1 pound of ground beef round to make hamburgers.

Soak lady fingers in dry sherry, use them to line dessert dishes, and pour vanilla pudding over them.

Toss apples for pie with ½ cup of Chablis before putting them in the crust to bake.

Serve freshly poached peach halves or chilled, canned peach halves in sherbet glasses with champagne poured over them.

To Season Soups with Wine

Stir wine into soup just before serving; otherwise you will lose the delicate flavor of the wine. Follow these rules of choice to flavor soups with wine.

For *clear* soups, add 1 tablespoon of claret or Burgundy wine for each cup of soup.

For *cream* soups, add 1 tablespoon dry sherry.

For *rich broth* soups, such as French onion, use 1 tablespoon of sauterne. Do not use wine in heavy vegetable soups.

✌ Wine French Dressing with Blue Cheese

1 teaspoon salt
1 teaspoon sugar
½ teaspoon paprika
2 tablespoons lemon juice
2 tablespoons cider vinegar
½ cup sauterne
1 cup vegetable oil
2 to 3 ounces blue cheese, mashed
1 small cut clove garlic

Place all ingredients except garlic in a large bowl and blend with rotary beater. Add the cut clove garlic. Let the mixture stand several hours to blend flavors. Remove garlic. Toss with a mixed green salad. Makes about 2¼ cups dressing.

Avocado Variation

Omit paprika and blue cheese from recipe above and add *1 sieved or finely mashed avocado* and *1 more tablespoon lemon juice.* Blend as above and serve with pear salad or a tossed fresh fruit salad.

Herb Chili Sauce Variation

Omit blue cheese and add *½ cup chili sauce, 1 teaspoon dried salad herb blend* and *1 teaspoon dried basil leaves.* Mix and blend as above. Serve with a tomato tossed salad, endive, watercress, or mixed greens.

✌ Wine Marinade for Veal, Lamb, Steaks, or Broiling Chicken

*½ cup dry sherry
¼ cup vegetable oil
1 medium-sized grated onion

Combine all ingredients and blend. This is enough marinade for one 3½- to 4-pound chicken or 2 pounds of meat. Pour the sauce over meat and let stand at room temperature for about 2 hours or overnight in the re-

*Note: For beef marinade use Burgundy wine.

1½ teaspoons Worcestershire
    sauce
 1 tablespoon dry mustard
 ¾ teaspoon dried thyme
 ¾ teaspoon dried marjoram
 ¾ teaspoon dried oregano
 ½ teaspoon salt
 ¼ teaspoon garlic salt
 ½ teaspoon pepper

frigerator. To broil: place the drained meat on a broiler rack and broil in a preheated broiler 3 inches from heat; turn and baste occasionally with the marinade. Broil to the desired degree of doneness. Makes about 1 cup of marinade.

✒ Wine Sauce for Meat, Chicken, or Fish

*2 chicken bouillon cubes and
   2 cups boiling water or 2
   cups Chicken Stock (recipe
   on page 211)
 ¾ cup light cream
 3 tablespoons flour
 ¼ teaspoon salt
 3 tablespoons butter
 ¼ cup dry sherry or sauterne

Dissolve bouillon cubes with boiling water in a saucepan or heat Chicken Stock. Shake together cream, flour, and salt. Stir into hot bouillon. Stir constantly over moderately low heat (about 225° F.) until smooth and thickened. Add butter and sherry. Blend. Makes 3 cups.

*Note: For beef or veal use beef bouillon cubes.

✒ Wine Jelly

2 cups dry sherry
2 cups sauterne or muscatel
3 cups sugar
½ 6-fluid-ounce bottle fruit
   pectin

Combine the sherry and sauterne or muscatel in a saucepan. Add 3 cups sugar. Mix well and heat over moderate heat (about 250° F.), stirring constantly, for 2 minutes. Remove from heat and quickly stir in fruit pectin. Pour quickly into 5 or 6 jelly glasses. Serve as a meat accompaniment.

✒ Orange Gelatine

1 envelope unflavored
   gelatine
¼ cup cold water
¼ cup boiling water
⅓ cup sugar
⅛ teaspoon salt
¾ cup sauterne

Sprinkle gelatine over cold water. In a small saucepan, combine boiling water, sugar, salt, and ¼ cup of the sauterne. Bring to a boil and stir in gelatine. Add remaining sauterne and other ingredients. Blend and pour into 4 individual molds; chill until firm. Serves 4.

(Ingredients continued on page 990)

ABOUT WINES WITH FOODS

2 tablespoons lemon juice
½ cup orange juice
1 teaspoon grated orange
    peel

_____

❧ Pudding Sauce

2 egg yolks, beaten
½ cup sugar
¾ cup dry or cream sherry
2 egg whites, at room
    temperature
2 tablespoons sugar
½ teaspoon of grated lemon
    peel

In top of double boiler, over rapidly boiling water, combine egg yolks, ½ cup of the sugar, and the sherry. Heat, stirring until smooth and slightly thickened. Beat egg whites until soft peaks form; add the remaining 2 tablespoons of the sugar and beat until very stiff. Pour sherry mixture over egg whites; beat 1 minute. Stir in lemon peel. May be served warm or chilled. If chilled, beat until smooth before serving. Serve over sponge-cake slices, steamed puddings, or gelatine desserts. Makes about 3 cups sauce.

_____

❧ Burgundy Whip

1 cup hot water
1 3-ounce package
    lemon-flavored gelatin
1 cup Burgundy wine

Pour hot water over the gelatin in a bowl and stir until gelatin is dissolved. Add Burgundy and chill until slightly thickened. Pour half of the mixture into a 1-quart mold; chill well. Whip remaining half with a hand or electric beater until it is light and fluffy. Pour this over the plain, unwhipped layer and chill again. When ready to serve, unmold quickly, but carefully, onto a chilled dessert plate. Makes 6 generous servings.

_____

❧ Pears in Port

4 to 5 large, firm pears
½ cup sugar
½ cup water
1 cup port
6 whole cloves

Peel, halve, and remove cores from pears. In a large shallow pan or heavy skillet, combine sugar, water, port, and cloves. Bring to a boil over moderately low heat (about 225° F.), stirring. Add pears. Simmer, covered, 10 minutes or until pears are barely tender. Remove pears from syrup. Boil the syrup again over moderately high heat (about 350° F.) until half its original volume remains. Pour over pears and chill. Serves 4 to 5.

৺ Frozen Wine Frappé

2 cups sweet sauterne
¼ cup sugar
1 6-ounce can frozen fresh
    unsweetened pineapple
    juice, unthawed
2 cups crushed ice
3 maraschino cherries

Place wine, sugar, pineapple juice and crushed ice in the container of an electric blender. Cover and blend at high speed for 30 seconds. If pineapple juice is not entirely blended in, stir mixture with a rubber spatula and blend another 30 seconds. Pour mixture into 3 tall, chilled glasses and garnish each with a maraschino cherry. Serves 3.

CHAPTER XXX

ABOUT FOOD AND NUTRITION

Although much has been written and said about the subject of nutrition, far too many people in the affluent countries of the world choose the foods they eat with neither a consciousness nor a conscience. Yet what you eat can affect the length and quality of your life. It can be one of the factors that determine whether you live to a healthy and productive old age or suffer premature disease.

What a female child eats today may have an effect on the kind of pregnancy she may have years from now.

What a pregnant mother eats may have an effect on her child's mental and physical growth and development.

What a child eats affects the way that young person grows and develops and it also can affect the size of the medical and dental bills parents pay.

Yet the food we eat is one of the factors of good health over which we can exert considerable control by thoughtful selection and preparation.

There is a great deal we don't know about food. Many nutrition authorities estimate that the body of knowledge still to be discovered about nutritional needs is far greater than the body of knowledge we now possess. But we know enough to realize that good nutrition is preventive medicine and that selecting good food, preparing it well and enjoying it has a direct relationship to our well-being.

Nutrition—What It Is

Nutrition, very simply stated, is the process by which our bodies use nutrients from the food we eat. We eat to live, to grow, to keep healthy and to get energy for work and play. You really don't need a computer nor do you need to develop an obsession about health foods to feed yourself or others an adequate diet. You do need to be aware of foods and know which ones supply which important nutrients. Then combine them creatively in daily meals—including between-meal snacks. They count too.

The body needs prescribed amounts of some 40 to 50 food nutrients to function properly and, happily, all of these can be supplied by eating the right foods.

The three major nutrients, called macronutrients by nutritionists, are proteins, carbohydrates, and fats. Few foods are all carbohydrate or all protein or all fat. The common ones are table syrups and sugar (all carbohydrate); cooking and salad oils (all fat); and plain unflavored gelatine (nearly all protein). However, almost all the foods we eat contain a combination of two or all of the macronutrients. For weight control and for guiding you to proper food selection, it is important to understand the function of these major nutrients, in which foods you will find them and how much you need of them.

Protein

Protein is essential to life; every living organism depends upon it, especially for growth and repair. Protein from food can't be used directly by our bodies; it is broken down into amino acids (of which at present 22 have been identified). All but eight of these can be manufactured by healthy adult human bodies as they are needed; hence these eight are called "essential" amino acids.

It also is important to know that these essential eight are interdependent. Unless all are present within the body at the same time, a complete body protein cannot be constructed. This is why you'll hear about complete protein foods (they contain a good balance of all eight amino acids) and incomplete ones (foods in which one or more essential amino acids are lacking or in poor supply). In general, animal proteins (meats, fish, poultry, eggs, milk, and cheese) provide a better balance of essential amino acids than the vegetable proteins (lentils, dried beans and peas, nuts, and cereals).

Proteins in the body are responsible for three fourths of our body structure and many of the internal workings, including the production of enzymes, which play a large part in the digestion of food, and of hormones, which act as a kind of signal system in the body.

The RDA (Recommended Daily Allowance) of protein for adults is individually calculated. Multiply your weight by 0.364. The result is the number of grams of protein you need daily. (Even if you are overweight, your body needs this amount of protein for proper nutrition.) More protein is recommended for growing children. Pregnant women should add about ten extra grams and nursing mothers about 20. It is possible for persons to get along on less than the recommended daily allowance, but very low protein reducing diets simply will not sustain growth or body repair. You'll use body reserves and lose muscle, not fat. High-protein diets, based primarily on meat, are an expensive way to get energy into the body, since the extra proteins are utilized in the form of energy.

Carbohydrates

The primary sources of energy in the body are carbohydrates and fats, and in that role they are interchangeable. But the body has a specific need for carbohydrates as a source of energy for the brain and for certain other specialized purposes. Adaptation to diets very low in carbohydrates is possible, but in individuals accustomed to normal diets, at least 100 grams (a little more than three and a half ounces) of carbohydrates per day appear to be needed.

Carbohydrates in food come primarily from starchy foods and sugars. There is little problem in getting the proper amount of carbohydrates in a normal diet, but several popular reducing diets call for less daily carbohydrate intake, and these should be avoided for any prolonged period of time. With low carbohydrate intake you'll be missing needed vitamins. But in the eating patterns of many persons an excess of carbohydrates in the form of snack foods is a greater problem.

Fats

Not only is fat the most concentrated source of food energy but also it carries the fat-soluble nutrients, including vitamins A, D, E, and K, and produces needed fats known as essential fatty acids. Nutritionists estimate that about one third of our daily caloric intake should be in fats. Extremely low fat diets, except as prescribed by a doctor, should be avoided. A diet low in fat tends to be dull and unappetizing and may be lacking a fatty acid essential, linoleic acid. Overeating of fats may lead to overweight. By many indications this problem may be related to heart disease; many doctors and nutritionists believe that polyunsaturated fats (in general, those liquid at room temperature) should be substituted wherever possible for saturated fats (those solid at room temperature—including the fat on meats).

Vitamins and Minerals

Depending upon how you make the count (and different nutrition authorities do it differently), you now are familiar with ten of the 40 to 50 nutrients: carbohydrates, fats and the eight essential amino acids of protein. All the others are vitamins and minerals—called *micronutrients*—and these are the major components of the food supplements we buy at drug counters. With minor exceptions they are in the foods we eat if we choose variety in proper amounts from the carbohydrate, protein and fat groups.

It is important to know that some of the vitamins (B and C) are soluble in water and some are soluble in fat (A, D, E and K).

The vitamins that are fat-soluble can be stored in the body; the water-soluble vitamins cannot. Amounts of the water solubles taken in excess of body needs are simply eliminated through urine.

The charts that begin on the page 998 are a guide to the foods that provide important vitamins and minerals.

What Foods Provide Good Nutrition

If you study the charts beginning on page 998 and wonder how you can tell whether you consume 800 milligrams of calcium every day, it's a good question. If you're curious, research-minded and don't mind juggling figures, there are government booklets that tell you the amounts of nutrients in common foods. (See Facts-About-Nutrition references at the end of this chapter.)

There is a way to get most of the necessary nutrients you need, however, that avoids the arithmetic, but it requires careful meal planning and shopping. It is commonly referred to as the "Basic Four"—a method of buying those foods that will provide a sound diet. By making selections in the proper quantity from the *variety* in each of these groups each day, and by cooking and handling them properly, there should be little or no need for mineral or vitamin supplements. A key word is *variety*. Never or seldom to serve a dark-green vegetable such as broccoli or spinach or a deep-gold vegetable or fruit such as carrots or apricots from the vegetable and fruit group deprives you of essential nutrients.

The Basic Four food groups are:

I. THE MILK GROUP

You may choose from several types of milk: fluid whole, evaporated, skim, dry or buttermilk. Yogurt, cheeses such as cottage and Cheddar, or ice cream may be substituted for part of the milk. Milk is a main source of calcium; it also provides protein, riboflavin, vitamin A and other nutrients.

Daily amounts needed:
School child—2 or 3 servings
Adult—2 or more servings
A serving is:
 1 cup milk or yogurt
 1½ cups cottage cheese
 2 or 3 scoops ice cream
    About a 1-inch cube of Cheddar or other hard cheese

II. THE HIGH PROTEIN (OR MEAT) GROUP

Here you may choose from any meats—beef, veal, lamb, pork—poultry or fish (including shellfish). Liver, kidneys and brains are valuable protein sources. Eggs, dried beans or peas, soybeans, lentils, nuts or nut butter may be substituted for a portion of meat. This group not only is valued for its protein, but also provides iron, thiamine, riboflavin and niacin.

Daily amounts needed:
School child—1 or 2 servings
Adult—2 or more servings
A serving is:
 3 ounces of any meat, fish or poultry
 2 eggs
 1 cup dried beans or peas, lentils, soybeans
 4 tablespoons nut butter
 60 nuts
    Cheese may be used as a meat substitute if it is not counted in Group I as a milk substitute

III. THE VEGETABLE-FRUIT GROUP

This is where variety is important. It is a big group and is easier, we think, to break into three subgroups. Choose one serving from each of the three subgroups and then one more, preferably from the first two subgroups.

(a) Deep-green or deep-yellow vegetables, such as broccoli, carrots, sweet potatoes

(b) Citrus fruits, tomatoes and other fruits rich in vitamin C, such as strawberries, melons and blackberries, or vegetables such as green peppers, cauliflower and asparagus

(c) Potatoes and other fruits and vegetables such as pineapples, apples, bananas, beets, lima beans and corn

This group is a primary source of vitamins and minerals.

Daily amounts needed:

Everyone: 4 or more servings, to include 1 or more from each of the three subgroups

A serving is:

½ cup raw or cooked fruit or vegetable

6 ounces citrus juice

A normal serving unit such as 1 apple or banana or orange, half a grapefruit

IV. THE BREAD–CEREAL GROUP

Here you choose from whole-grain or enriched breads, cereals, pastas (including spaghetti, noodles and macaroni), rice, cornmeal, grits. Cookies, cakes, crackers, muffins and biscuits, pancakes and waffles fall in this category. Curb these if you're counting calories, but don't eliminate all foods from this group. They provide iron, vitamins, carbohydrates and proteins.

Daily amounts needed:

Everyone: 3 to 4 servings

A serving is:

1 slice bread

1 ounce ready-to-eat cereal

½ to ¾ cup cooked cereal, cornmeal, grits

2-inch biscuit or muffin

3-inch cookie or piece of cake

Obviously fats and sugars are not included in the Basic Four food groups except as they occur naturally in foods. It is expected that you will use some butter or fortified margarine on breads or vegetables. Mayonnaise, salad dressing and oils used in cooking also will contribute to necessary fats in the diet. (A serving is a tablespoon, and three to five servings are recommended for everyone.) Sugar, a source of energy but containing no nutrients, may be added to coffee, fruit and cereal and be substantially present in jams, jellies and honey.

THE MICRONUTRIENTS

WHAT THEY ARE	WHAT THEY DO FOR YOU	GOOD FOOD SOURCES	RDA*
THE FAT-SOLUBLE VITAMINS			
Vitamin A	Helps to form and maintain healthy functioning of eyes, skin, hair, teeth, gums, various glands and mucous membranes. It also is involved in fat metabolism. High deficiency results in impaired vision.	Deep-yellow foods (carrots, sweet potatoes, apricots, peaches, cantaloupes, Cheddar cheese) and fortified margarine, butter and fortified dark-green vegetables (spinach, mustard greens, Swiss chard). It's easy to determine Vitamin A presence by food color.	5,000 IU.** *Warning:* Daily doses of more than 50,000 IU can be toxic.
Vitamin D	Promotes absorption of calcium and phosphorus from digestive tract—these minerals are essential for building strong bones and teeth.	Simple exposure to sunshine may fill required needs. Fish liver oils are a good source. Because of vitamin D scarcity in food, 400 IU of vitamin D has been added to all forms of fluid milk.	400 IU for children, pregnant women and nursing mothers. Probably less for adults unless there is no exposure to sunlight. *Warning:* Amounts in excess of 1,800 IU per day may be hazardous to children. (A quart of fortified milk contains 400 IU of vitamin D. For other foods, check labels.) Children drinking fortified milk as well as fortified-milk flavorings, fruit drinks, cereals and candy can consume too much vitamin D.
Vitamin E (A-tocopherol)	Its *known* function is to prevent the oxidation of certain needed fatty acids. It protects vitamin A from destruction by oxidation. There are no known advantages to large intakes of vitamin E except in cases of malabsorption of fat.	Vegetable oils, legumes, nuts, meats, eggs, leafy vegetables, wheat germ and sprouts, whole grains.	Infants: 10 IU. Adults: 30 IU. Evidence of toxic overdose levels is scarce.
Vitamin K	Is essential for normal liver functioning. Prevents prolonged blood-clotting time.	Green leafy vegetables, liver, soy oil, egg yolk, cabbage and cauliflower.	None except in therapeutic adult needs to be dictated by a physician. (Single doses of 1 milligram may be given to infants to prevent hemorrhagic disease.)
THE WATER-SOLUBLE VITAMINS			
Thiamine (B₁)	Helps keep nerves in a healthy condition. Aids appetite and digestion. High deficiency produces beriberi.	Meat (especially pork), fish, poultry, eggs, whole-grain or enriched breads and cereals, dried peas and beans, wheat germ.	Ranges from 0.2 milligram for infants to a high of 1.5 for male adolescents.

	Function	Food Sources	Daily Allowance*
Riboflavin (B₂)	Functions in the body's use of carbohydrates, proteins and fats, particularly to release energy to cells. Keeps eyes and skin around mouth and nose healthy.	Milk, cheese, ice cream, liver, fish, poultry and eggs. Enriched and whole-grain breads and cereals.	Ranges from 0.4 milligram for infants to a high of 2 milligrams for nursing mothers.
Niacin (nicotinic acid, nicotinamide)	Acts as a component of two important co-enzymes. Unlike the other water-soluble vitamins, niacin can be stored to some extent in the liver. High deficiency produces pellagra and mental disorders.	Nut butters, meat, liver, fish (especially canned tuna), poultry, milk, enriched or whole-grain breads and cereals.	RDA for niacin is expressed in equivalents because in addition to the niacin in foods, amino acid tryptophan can be converted into niacin by the body. Ranges from 5 milligram equivalents for infants to a high of 20 milligrams for adolescents and nursing mothers.
Biotin	Involved in the formation of certain fatty acids and the production of energy from glucose. Essential for the working of many chemical systems in the body.	When other B vitamins are sufficiently present in foods, so is biotin. Also, intestinal bacteria in healthy people manufacture enough to supply requirements.	0.3 milligram
Choline	Part of several compounds necessary in certain aspects of nerve function and fat metabolism.	Egg yolk, beef liver, all meats, whole grains, legumes, vegetables and milk.	None.
Folacin (folic acid, pteroylmonoglutamic acid)	Involved with a number of metabolic processes. Deficiencies usually occur only when there is impaired absorption, metabolic derangements or an excessive demand by tissues of the body.	In a wide variety of foods of animal and vegetable origin, particularly in glandular meat, yeast and green leafy vegetables.	0.4 milligram, from dietary sources. Women using an oral contraceptive should ask their doctors about the need for folacin.
Pantothenic Acid	A key substance in body metabolism —involved in changing carbohydrates, fats and protein into molecular forms needed by the body.	Widely distributed in animal tissue, whole-grain cereals and legumes.	None. A daily intake of 5 to 10 milligrams is probably adequate for children and adults.
Vitamin B₆ (pyridoxine)	Aids in the formation of red blood cells and proper functioning of the nervous system, including brain cells.	Since B₆ is not a single substance but a collection of them, it is available from both animal and plant sources. Liver, ham, lima beans and corn are good sources.	Ranges from 0.2 milligram for infants to 2.0 milligrams for adults and 2.5 milligrams for pregnant women and nursing mothers.

*Recommended Daily Allowance
**International Units—a standard vitamin measurement for vitamins A, D, E.

THE MICRONUTRIENTS (Continued)

WHAT THEY ARE	WHAT THEY DO FOR YOU	GOOD FOOD SOURCES	RDA*
THE WATER-SOLUBLE VITAMINS (Continued from preceding page)			
Vitamin B₁₂ (cyanocobalamin)	Essential for normal functioning of all body cells, including brain and other nerve cells, as well as tissues that make red cells.	Predominantly in foods of animal origin; since it is bound to protein, this vitamin can be a problem for strict vegetarians.	5 micrograms for adults, 8 micrograms for pregnant women and 6 micrograms for nursing mothers.
Vitamin C (ascorbic acid)	This vitamin has multiple functions to do with blood vessels, hemoglobin, iron deposits, wound healing and resistance to infection. (This is where the prevalent theory about prevention or cure of the common cold derives.)	Citrus fruits, strawberries, cantaloupe, tomatoes, green peppers, broccoli, raw-greens, cabbage, potatoes. This is the dangerously lacking vitamin for followers of the all-grain diets.	Ranges from 35 milligrams for infants to 60 for adult males, pregnant women and nursing mothers.
Inositol now is not thought to be a vitamin, although it is often sold as a food supplement. Nutritionists believe we make all we need in our bodies; it is also amply available in a balanced diet.		Vitamin P is nonexistent. The substance once thought to be this vitamin is now called a bioflavinoid (found chiefly in the white pulp and connective tissue of citrus fruits). It has no known need.	
MINERALS			
Calcium	A major constituent of the body for bones and teeth. A small percentage of it is utilized for control of nerve functions. Helps muscles function normally and recover from fatigue.	Milk, cheese and green leafy vegetables. Without a daily intake of 2 or more glasses of milk or 2 or more servings of cheese, adequate calcium is difficult to get.	1 gram for adults.
Phosphorus	Along with calcium, the major constituent of bones and teeth. Works with calcium for normal nerve response and muscle contraction.	Available in major calcium sources, also in meats and cereals. Adequate amounts are easy to get.	1 gram for adults.
Copper	Present in many organs. Part of important proteins, including certain enzymes involved in brain and red cell functions. Aids utilization of iron.	Ordinary diets provide 2 to 5 milligrams per day.	2 milligrams for adults.

			RDA*
Fluoride	Incorporated in the structure of bones and teeth and necessary to the resistance of tooth decay.	Fish, cheese, milk are good sources, though not enough to prevent tooth decay. Water supplies that have been treated to bring the fluoride concentration to 1 part per million are.	None, but water fluoridation is recommended where fluoride level is low.
Iodine	Important to the healthy functioning of the thyroid gland. Iodine deficiency may cause goiter.	Seafoods. Use of iodized table salt will preclude deficiency.	Ranges from 25 micrograms for infants to 150 for adolescent males.
Iron	A constituent of hemoglobin and a variety of enzymes. Now considered the most lacking nutrient, especially among women.	Red meats, whole grains, wheat germ, prunes, raisins, molasses and dark-green vegetables.	10 milligrams for males. 18 milligrams for females over 10 years of age.
Magnesium	An important constituent of all soft tissue and bone and an activator of many enzymes.	Deficiency in a balanced diet is unlikely.	400 milligrams for adults
Sodium, Potassium and Chloride	These minerals are often called electrolytes. They maintain an inner balance of body fluids and contribute to cellular enzyme function.	All are readily available in common foods. In fact, sodium (table salt) intake can be harmfully high.	None.

THE TRACE MINERALS

Chromium, Cobalt, Manganese, Molybdenum, Selenium, Zinc and possibly others.	In minute amounts these minerals serve essential body needs.	Green leafy vegetables, whole grains, organ meats and lean meats.	None, except for Zinc: 15 milligrams
Water	Water is not usually counted as a nutrient, but it is well-known that we can survive without food much longer than we can without water.	Water or other fluids.	None, but 1 to 2 quarts of fluid daily is recommended.

Of all the known minerals the body needs, widespread deficiencies exist only in calcium and iron. In some geographic areas, iodine and fluoride supplies are low.

*Recommended Daily Allowance.

Food Handling and Preparation: Its Importance to Nutrition

The proper storage and preparation of food is essential to preserve the natural nutrients in them. Vegetables are particularly perishable and can lose a lot of vitamins and minerals from the time they're harvested until they reach the dinner table. Modern industrial handling methods are designed to cut down on vitamin losses, especially the perishable vitamin C, which is subject to oxidation at room temperature or higher. When well handled, perishable vegetables are rushed from the field through a quick wash and are cooled—sometimes even wrapped and put into refrigerator cars for shipment—within a few hours after they're harvested.

What happens with vegetables until and after they reach the retailer is often another problem. Sidewalk or in-store deliveries may not be refrigerated immediately, sometimes not at all. If you want vegetables with the maximum number of vitamins in them, don't buy them from a nonrefrigerated display case. Tests have shown, for example, that green beans lose 25 per cent of their vitamin C in 72 hours at room temperature but only 5 per cent in 96 hours in an ice refrigerator and 10 per cent in 96 hours on the shelf of a home refrigerator. But you can do a great deal to preserve what you buy.

1. Wash—don't soak—vegetables quickly, and only when necessary. For example, there's no need to wash beets, peas in pods or tomatoes before storage.

2. Refrigerate as soon as possible in a plastic bag; place in vegetable crisper.

3. Peel vegetables only when necessary. Good vitamins and minerals are stored next to the skin.

4. Don't cut or tear leafy vegetables or other C-vitamin vegetables such as broccoli and cauliflower before time to use. An enzyme action begins that immediately starts reducing the vitamin C content.

5. Time cooking of vegetables so they can be served immediately

6. Serve many vegetables raw. Raw cauliflowerettes, zucchini rounds and green pepper strips are a good relish dish.

Since you know that the B and C vitamins are water-soluble, choose cooking methods that use as little water as possible. Baking is an excellent way to prepare many vegetables. Stir-frying or crisp-cooking will preserve nutrients. Braising also is a good method. Steam vegetables by putting them on a rack over boiling water. This keeps the liquid completely away from the vegetables. All of these cooking methods are described fully on pages 497 to 499. Reheating vegetables results in more than half the nutrient loss. It's better to use leftover vegetables in salads or sandwich fillings.

Canned vegetables do sustain some vitamin and mineral loss because of solubility. However, if you pour the can liquid into a pan and cook it down to a small amount before adding the vegetables, you will have retrieved a good number of the vitamins to serve as a sauce over the vegetables.

There is relatively little nutrient loss in the freezing of vegetables. However, frozen vegetables should never be defrosted before cooking. When a choice of methods is given on the package directions, choose the one that uses the least liquid.

Nutrition Labels

There's much you can learn about packaged foods that must, by law, be on the label. An ingredients listing, including additives, must be on all but a few "standardized" products such as catsups and mayonnaise. Ingredients must be listed in descending order of predominance by weight. A can of soup may list its ingredients as follows: water, potatoes, cooked beef, tomatoes, carrots, onions, peas, beef fat, potato starch, salt, enriched wheat flour, modified food starch, sugar, yeast extract, hydrolyzed milk proteins, caramel color, spices, flavoring and lactic acid. This means there is more water than potatoes in the soup, more potatoes than beef, more carrots than onions or peas, and so on.

Some fruit and vegetable products carry a "grade" on the label, such as Grade A. These grades, set by the U.S. Department of Agriculture on the basis of appearance, are not based on nutritional value. Grade A on milk or milk products is based on sanitary standards for the processing and production of the products. The grade is not based on nutritional value.

But many foods—and for any claiming to be "enriched" or "fortified" it's mandatory—do carry nutrition labels. Look for them when you shop. They will always tell how many calories are in a serving and give the gram count of protein, carbohydrates, and fats plus the U.S. Recommended Daily Allowance of important vitamins and minerals. Nutrition information can help you plan better meals and also help you get better value for your money.

Vegetarian Eating and Nutrition

For a variety of reasons many people are turning to a largely vegetarian diet, which, of course, includes fruits and grains. With few exceptions (B_{12}, calcium and phosphorus), their nutrition problem is one of getting ample complete proteins. When one's own diet does not meet the basic protein needs through meat, poultry and fish intake, there is no margin for error. A careful calculation must be made to be sure the eight essential amino acids are eaten in the proper proportions at the same time.

Strict vegetarians have to rely heavily on lentils, soybeans, dried peas and beans, nuts, seeds, whole-grain breads and cereals and the newer meat substitutes, also called meat analogues, in canned or frozen form. Meat analogues are made largely from soybeans and other grain flours that can be textured and flavored to taste like meats.

A lacto-vegetarian diet, allowing the addition of milk and related products such as cheese, ice cream and yogurt to a vegetarian diet, makes the problem of getting sufficient protein much less critical and minimizes the calcium-phosphorus needs. When eggs are added (this diet usually is referred to as ova-lacto-vegetarian), all the problems are reduced.

If the desire to follow a vegetarian diet is based neither on religious conviction nor the desire to oppose all killing of animals, a vegetarian regime that includes light servings of poultry, fish and lean meats in addition to protein-rich vegetables can easily meet all nutritional needs and should contribute to a permanent as well as a temporary feeling of well-being.

In this book you will find several recipes that have been carefully calculated to be part of meatless meals yet provide protein quality similar to that of meat. These ten sample menus will supply at least one third of the protein needs for a day.

MENU #1
*Brazilian Black Beans and
Rice with Salsa
Green Salad
Corn Sticks and Butter
Sliced Fresh Oranges
*Recipe on page 555

Per person yield is approximately 25 grams protein (0 grams animal, 25 grams vegetable), 843 calories, 25 grams fat, 131 grams carbohydrate. Estimates are based on 1 serving Brazilian Black Beans and Rice with 1 serving Salsa; 1 serving Green Salad; 2 corn sticks, 1 teaspoon butter or margarine; 1 orange.

MENU #2
*Two-Cheese Rice Balls
Steamed Fresh Broccoli
Lettuce and Tomato Salad
Vanilla Ice Milk Sprinkled
with Ground Espresso
*Recipe on page 566

Per person yield is approximately 35 grams protein (23 grams animal, 12 grams vegetable), 842 calories, 46 grams fat, 77 grams carbohydrate. Estimates are based on 1 serving Two-Cheese Rice Balls; 1 cup cooked broccoli; 1 serving lettuce leaves plus half a tomato; ½ cup vanilla ice milk sprinkled with ½ teaspoon ground espresso coffee or instant coffee powder or granules. Dieters may omit dessert (100 calories, 3 grams protein).

MENU #3

Chinese Egg Drop Soup
*Sukiyaki with Noodles
and Sesame Seeds
Fresh Pineapple with Yogurt,
Honey and Toasted Almonds

*Recipe on page 570

Per person yield is approximately 26 grams protein (7 grams animal, 19 grams vegetable), 719 calories, 27 grams fat, 96 grams carbohydrate. Estimates are based on 1 cup chicken broth, ½ egg, 2 teaspoons minced scallions; 1 serving Sukiyaki with Noodles and Sesame Seeds; ¾ cup fresh or juice-packed pineapple chunks, ½ cup plain low-fat yogurt, 1 teaspoon honey, 2 tablespoons chopped toasted almonds. Dieters may omit honey and almonds (112 calories, 3 grams protein).

MENU #4

*Linguini with Walnut Sauce
Green Salad
Sesame Bread Sticks
Fresh Fruit Compote

*Recipe on page 571

Per person yield is approximately 31 grams protein (12 grams animal, 19 grams vegetable), 906 calories, 39 grams fat, 121 grams carbohydrate. Estimates are based on 1 serving each of *Linguini* with Walnut Sauce, Green Salad and Fresh Fruit Compote; 3 sesame bread sticks.

MENU #5

Hot Clam-Tomato Broth
*Cheese-and-Potato Pie
Watercress, Romaine and
Red Onion Salad
Fresh Fruit Compote
and Sherbet

*Recipe on page 538

Per person yield is approximately 36 grams protein (24 grams animal, 12 grams vegetable), 738 calories, 30 grams fat, 87 grams carbohydrate. Estimates are based on 1 cup clam-tomato broth; 1 serving Cheese-and-Potato Pie; 1 serving Watercress Salad made with watercress and romaine lettuce with 2 thin slices peeled red onion; ½ serving Fresh Fruit Compote with ½ cup sherbet. Dieters may omit sherbet (118 calories, 1 gram protein).

MENU #6

*Lentil-Potato Soup
Rye Bread and Butter
Romaine Salad with
Swiss Cheese and Walnuts
Fresh Oranges

*Recipe on page 554

Per person yield is approximately 25 grams protein (10 grams animal, 15 grams vegetable), 576 calories, 16 grams fat, 72 grams carbohydrate. Estimates are based on 1 serving Lentil-Potato Soup; 1 slice rye bread with 1 teaspoon butter or margarine; 1 serving Romaine Salad, ¼ cup grated Swiss cheese and 1 tablespoon chopped walnuts; 1 orange.

ABOUT FOOD AND NUTRITION

MENU #7
*Steamed Vegetables
with Cheese
Whole Wheat Bread and
Peanut Butter
Escarole Salad
Vanilla Ice Milk Topped
with Hot Applesauce

*Recipe on page 549

Per person yield is approximately 32 grams protein (18 grams animal, 14 grams vegetable), 661 calories, 32 grams fat, 62 grams carbohydrate. Estimates are based on 1 serving Steamed Vegetables with Cheese: 1 slice whole wheat bread with 1 tablespoon peanut butter; 1 serving Escarole Salad; ½ cup each vanilla ice milk and applesauce. Dieters may omit peanut butter (95 calories, 4 grams protein) and ice milk (100 calories, 3 grams protein).

MENU #8
*Chinese Slivered Eggs
and Mushrooms
Brown Rice
Chocolate Ice Milk
with Ginger Preserves
and Chopped Peanuts

*Recipe on page 465

Per person yield is approximately 24 grams protein (12 grams animal, 12 grams vegetable), 759 calories, 27 grams fat, 95 grams carbohydrate. Estimates are based on 1 serving Chinese Slivered Eggs and Mushrooms with 1 cup cooked brown rice; 1 cup chocolate ice milk with 1 tablespoon ginger preserves and 2 tablespoons roasted, salted peanuts.

MENU #9
*Sweet and Pungent Chick-Peas
Cracked Wheat Pilaf
Green Salad with
Chopped Egg
Frozen Bananas and Yogurt

*Recipe on page 557

Per person yield is approximately 25 grams protein (7 grams animal, 18 grams vegetable), 641 calories, 20 grams fat, 95 grams carbohydrate. Estimates are based on 1 serving Sweet and Pungent Chick-Peas; ½ cup cooked cracked wheat or bulgur; 1 serving Green Salad with half a chopped hard-cooked egg; 1 small banana and ½ cup low-fat plain yogurt.

MENU #10
*French Bean Pot
Toasted French Bread
Green Salad
Gruyère or Cheddar Cheese
Fresh Pears

*Recipe on page 556

Per person yield is approximately 35 grams protein (14 grams animal, 21 grams vegetable), 772 calories, 32 grams fat, 92 grams carbohydrate. Estimates are based on 1 serving French Bean Pot; 1 slice enriched French bread; 1 serving Green Salad; 2 ounces cheese; 1 pear. Dieters may substitute 1 cup buttermilk for the cheese, for a menu total of 30 grams protein (9 grams animal, 21 grams vegetable), 632 calories, 14 grams fat, 102 grams carbohydrate.

Nutrition and Food Supplements

Food supplements are primarily vitamins and minerals (the micronutrients) in pill, capsule or liquid form. For individual deficiencies or periods following shock or stress, doctors often will recommend a temporary intake of a particular food supplement. But by far the largest amount of food supplements being used today are self-prescribed. If you never eat a vegetable or a piece of fruit, it is likely you will end up with a few deficiencies. But if your diet is that limited or your food attitudes so individual, it would be much better to consult a doctor who is also a nutritionist than to clutter your breakfast table with an assortment of pills.

It is indeed a blessing that we have vitamins and minerals in easy-to-take forms to meet specific needs, but it's much cheaper to get the nutrients you need in the food itself rather than in pill form.

Also it is a far happier experience to sit down to a beautifully prepared meal of delicious poached chicken, a crisp green salad, a pure-white steamed potato, a gorgeous piece of fruit and a handful of nuts than it is to gulp a pill.

To enjoy what you eat by preparing food so that it tastes good, selecting it for color and presenting it so that mealtime is a relaxed, happy interval, is one of the great by-products of good nutrition.

Facts-About-Nutrition References

From the Superintendent of Documents, U.S. Government Printing Office, Washington, D.C. 20402:

"Nutritive Value of Foods, Home and Garden Bulletin, #72." Tells you (in grams) what portions of common foods are carbohydrate, protein or fat and lists some of the vitamins and minerals in common foods. Also a short table of Recommended Daily Allowances. 85 cents a copy.

"Nutrition Labeling, Tools For Its Use, Agriculture Information Bulletin #382." Gives the same information as Home and Garden Bulletin #72 (above), but it expresses the food nutrient portions in percentages of the Recommended Daily Allowances. $1.15 a copy.

"Nutrimeter." For choosing foods that provide the nutrients you need. For use with the Nutrition Labeling book above. 70 cents a copy.

"Agriculture Handbook, #8." Composition of foods—raw, processed, prepared. Covers the nutrient composition of a far greater list of foods; however, data is presented in 100-gram edible portions or in 1 pound of food as purchased. More arithmetic but more information. $2.85 a copy.

ABOUT FOOD AND NUTRITION

From the National Academy of Sciences, 2101 Constitution Avenue, Washington, D.C. 20418:

"Recommended Dietary Allowance," eighth edition (1974). Gives a large amount of scientific data on all nutrients and describes the findings that have led to the committee's arrival at RDAs for specific nutrients. $3.00 a copy.

From the U.S. Department of Agriculture, Washington, D.C. 20250:

"Conserving the Nutritive Value in Foods, G-90." Single copies are free.

"Family Fare, A Guide to Good Nutrition, HG-1." Single copies are free.

In bookstores:

Food Values of Portions Commonly Used, by Bowes and Church (eleventh edition), J. B. Lippincott Company. Gives nutrient values and essential amino-acid values of foods in normal serving portions. $5.40 a copy.

INDEX

À la king, 4
  tuna, 439
À la mode, 5
  cranberry pears, baked, 728
  pears streusel, 729
À la Rousse, stuffed eggs, 462
Acorn squash, 544
  baking, 544
  custard, 545
  See also Squash, winter
Alaska ribbon pie, 805
Alexander cocktail, 272
Allspice, 966
Almond(s)
  butter-cream frosting, 856
  cabbage amandine, 511
  -cherry angel cake, 131
  -chicken mousse, 617
  -chicken soup, 234
  -chocolate
    -dipped, for Continental grapes, 705
    filling, for cream torte, 838
    pie, 798
    torte, 837
  cream, for chocolate torte, 839
  fillet of sole amandine, 402
  garnish for main dish, 154
  ice cream, 757
  -jam bars, 863
  meringue layers for strawberry torte, 840
  pastry shell, 787
  pole beans amandine, 504
  raisin-nut pie, 796
  soufflé, 765
  stir-fried turkey with zucchini and, 388
  wafers, Christmas, 885
Ambrosia, 104, 720
American cheese
  and corn pie, 476
  -stuffed baked potatoes, 536
  vegetable chowder, 475
Anadama bread, rapid-mix method, 670
Anchovy
  sauce
    -butter, for broiled fish steaks, 403
  tartlets, 189
Angel food cake, 827
  surprise, 849
Anise drops, 885
Anise seeds, 977
Antipasto, 192
Appearance of foods, 150-161
Appetizers, 162-209
  anchovy tartlets, 189
  antipasto, 192
  artichokes
    with Hollandaise sauce, 200
    lemon-marinated, 191
  asparagus-ham pinwheels, 175
  avocado dip, 163

bacon
  and cheese whirls, 184
  curls, 171
  and egg circle sandwiches, 179
  hot onion snacks, 171
barbecue dip, 199
barbecued spareribs, 205
bean sprout and curried egg sandwiches, 182
beef
  corned, glazed, 203
  dried, and watercress canapés, 181
  meatballs and mushrooms, 190
  roast, with horseradish-whipped cream dip, 163
  shish kabobs, 201
  tartare, 166
  teriyaki, tiny, 177
bologna wedges, cheese-stuffed, 172
canapés, 178-187
  cold, 178-183
  hot, 184-187
caviar roll, 209
celery, crunchy stuffed, 173
chafing dish, 190-191
cheese
  assorted pastry hors d'oeuvre, 187
  and bacon whirls, 184
  California rolls, 170
  cream, and sardine canapés, 182
  crisp, 172
  deviled cream balls, 170
  dip, 198
  dip, for butterfly shrimp, 418
  -dipped pretzels, 176
  holiday ball, 168
  log, 169, 206
  molded Roquefort crème, 170
  -olive puffs, 184
  puffs, 184
  sherry dip, 164
  and shrimp spread, 206
  sticks, 188
  straws, 188
  -stuffed bologna wedges, 172
  -stuffed deviled eggs, 172
  stuffed Gouda, 169
  -stuffed mushrooms, 173
  Swiss pie, 189
  -wine spread, 199
chicken
  creamed, 207
  creamed, with profiteroles, 207
  -ginger spread, 167
  sesame bites, 174
  wings, cocktail, 202
chicken liver
  and mushroom canapés, 178
  pâté, 209
  rumaki, 200
chick-pea dip, 164
chili dip, for butterfly shrimp, 418

chili peanuts, 176
clams
  baked, Casino, 195
  creamy canapés, 185
cornucopias, 188
crab meat
  cocktail, 195
  diamonds, 178
  dip, hot curried, 163
  fondue, hot, 207
  puffs, 185
  quiche, 189
  and rolled shrimp sandwiches, 183
  spread, 201
cucumbers, stuffed, 173
curried
  crab meat dip, hot, 163
  egg and bean sprout sandwiches, 182
  -green onion dip, 199
  ham turnovers, 175
  pastry bites, 180
  vegetable dip, 165
deviled ham filling for pinwheel sandwiches, 205
dinner first courses, 192-196
dips, 163-166, 198-199
eggplant spread, 204
eggs
  bacon and, circle sandwiches, 179
  curried, and bean sprout sandwiches, 182
  deviled, 203
  deviled, cheese-stuffed, 172
  deviled canapés, 179
  filling for pinwheel sandwiches, 205
  en gelée, 193
  and radish filling for glazed party canapés, 180
finger hors d'oeuvre, 171-178
frankfurters
  in blankets, 187
  butterfly, 201
  sweet-and-sour cocktail, 191
French radish tartine, 182
fruits with spiced sour cream dip, 165
general data on, 162
ginger-chicken spread, 167
ginger-pear, 193
glazed corned beef, 203
glazed party canapés, 180
  radish and egg filling, 180
  shrimp filling, 180
green onion-curry dip, 199
ham
  -asparagus pinwheels, 175
  -curry turnovers, 175
  deviled, filling for pinwheel sandwiches, 205
  orange-glazed baked, 208
  and peanut spread, 198
  roulades, 175

Appetizers—*Continued*
  tartlets, 185
jalapeño bean dip, hot, 164
for a large party, 196-209
  general data on, 196-197
lemon-marinated artichokes, 191
meat loaf, country, 194
meatballs
  and mushrooms, 190
  Swedish, for a crowd, 190
menu
  elaborate, 197
  simple, 197
mushrooms
  cheese-stuffed, 173
  and chicken liver canapés, 178
  and meatballs, 190
  squares, 185
  stuffed caps, 199
mustard dip for butterfly shrimp, 418
nuts, hot buttered, 176
olive-cheese puffs, 184
oysters on the half shell, 195
party mix, 175
pastry, 187-190
  anchovy tartlets, 189
  assorted cheese, 187
  cheese sticks, 188
  cheese straws, 188
  cornucopias, 188
  crab meat quiche, 189
  curried bites, 180
  franks in blankets, 187
  liver pâté, 188
  rich, 188
  Swiss cheese pie, 189
pâté
  au porto, 197
  chicken liver, 209
  liver pastries, 188
  liver ribbon sandwiches, 181
  liver spread, 167
  party, 167
  tuna, 193
peanuts
  chili, 176
  and ham spread, 198
pear, ginger-, 193
pinwheel sandwiches, 205
pizza whole wheat canapés, 187
poppy-seed morsels, 177
pretzels, cheese-dipped, 176
radish tartine, French, 182
Reuben sandwiches, miniature, 198
rumaki, 200
salmon pinwheels, 181
sardine
  -cream cheese canapés, 182
seafood tartlets, hot, 203
sesame chicken bites, 174
sesame crisps, 177
sherried strawberries, 193
shish kabobs, beef, 201
shrimp
  and cheese spread, 206
  coconut, 208
  and cucumber sandwiches, rolled, 183
  filling for glazed party canapés, 180
  Italian pickled, 177
  marinated, 196
  paste, 168
  seafood tartlets, hot, 203
  toast, 186

sour cream dip, low calorie, 166
spreads, 166-168
strawberries, sherried, 193
Swedish meatballs for a crowd, 190
sweet-and-sour cocktail
  frankfurters, 191
teriyaki, tiny, 177
toothpick hors d'oeuvre, 171-178
tuna
  puffs, 186
  spread, 202
vegetable dip, 198
  curried, 165
vegetable relishes, stuffed, 174
vegetables, fresh raw, 198
  with low calorie dip, 165
watercress sandwiches, rolled, 183
Apple(s), 34-36, 694-696
  baked
    freezing, 55
    glazed, 695
    rosy, 695
    wine in, 987
  breakfast parfait, 696
  bread, nut, 640
  brown Betty, 724
    brandy butter for, 724
  buying, 75, 694
  cinnamon-candied, 905
  conversion chart, 32
  coring whole, 694
  crepes, 774
  dried, 717
    general data on, 717
  dumplings, rosy, 725
  equivalent amounts, 26
  filling for blintzes, 774
  freezing, 55, 67
  fritters, -ring, 645
  garnish for main dish, 154
  general data on, 34-36, 694-695
  grape ade cooler, 255
  jelly, 933
  kuchen, quick, 725
  marzipan, 899
  nut bread, 640
  pancakes filled with, 649
    German, 650
  pandowdy, 724
  parfait, breakfast, 696
  pie
    -honey, 794
    perfect, 789
    wine in, 987
  -plum sauce, spiced, pork loin roast with, 313
  preparing sliced, 694-695
  red cinnamon rings, 696
  roll, Mrs. Chandler's, 726
  salad
    -celery, 112
    piquant, 118
  -and-sausage casserole, 950
  selecting, 34-36
  storing, 72, 694
  tart
    flaming, 806
    warm, 800
  using, 34-36
  varieties of, 34-36
Applesauce
  freezing, 55
  strained, 695
Apricot(s), 696-697
  buying, 75, 696-697
  candy roll, 904

  -coconut balls, 898
  conversion chart, 32
  curried fruit, hot, 728
  dried, 717
    general data on, 717
  flip, 255
  fondant-stuffed, 897
  freezing, 67
  general data on, 696-697
  -glazed ham, 102
  jelly balls, 872
  nut bread, 640
  nutritive values, 998
  parfait, 697
  party cakes, 848
  preparing, 697
  sauce for beignets soufflés, 780
  shortcake, delight, 112
  storing, 72
  streusel coffeecake, 638
  trifle, 850
Aromatic seeds, 976-978
Arrowroot, substitutions for, 28
Arroz con pollo, 953
Artichokes, 499-501
  buying, 40
  general data on, 499-500
  with Hollandaise sauce, 200
  Jerusalem, 500
    creamed, 501
  lemon-marinated, 193
  -and-orange salad, 591
  savory butter sauce for, 501
  Swiss-style, 501
Asparagus, 502-503
  buying, 41, 75, 502
  cooking
    slices, 502
    stalks, 502
  freezing, 62
  general data on, 502
  -ham pinwheels, 175
  Polonaise, 502
  salad, 592
  soufflé, 458
  soup, iced, 235
  storing, 74
  -tomato bisque, 233
  vinaigrette, 502
Aspic
  tomato, 103, 616
  vegetable, 616
Au gratin, 5
Au jus, 5
Au pistou, 224
Avocado(s), 697-698
  buying, 75, 697
  conversion chart, 32
  dip, 163
  dressing
    cream, 629
    wine French, 988
  freezing, 67
  general data on, 697-698
  guacamole, 105
  preparing, 698
  salad
    stuffed with crab meat, 606
    -and-tuna, molded, 622
    -tuna luncheon plate, 610
  soup, green goddess, 240
  storing, 72, 697-698
  and wine French dressing, 988

Baba au Fraises, 780
Bacardi cocktail, 271

Bacon, 328-329
appetizers
and cheese whirls, 184
curls, 171
and egg circle sandwiches, 179
hot onion snacks, 171
breakfast muffins, 634
buying, 76
-cheese custards, 460
chicken livers with peppers and, 125
croutons, 660
dressing for spinach salad, hot, 596
-and-egg salad, 462
freezing, 59
garnish for vegetables, 159
general data on, 328-329
piquant glazed Canadian, 328
shirred eggs with, 460
storage of, 73
Baked Alaska, 759
Baked beans, *see* Beans, baked
Baking, 5
Baking powder, substitution for, 28
Banana(s), 698-699
baked, 699
dessert, 699
breakfast shake, 254
buying, 75, 698-699
cake, 824
conversion chart, 32
cream pie, 797
flambé, 699
freezing, 67
general data on, 698-699
marzipan, 899
mousse, 745
pecan muffins, 634
preparing, 699
raisin bread, 640
-rum cream cake, 120
shake, breakfast, 254
storing, 72, 699
-strawberry dessert, 122
in stuffed pineapple, 714
tidbits for curried eggs, 466
vegetable-fruit blend, 257
Bar syrup for whiskey sour, 268
Barbecue(d)
beef
flank steak, 290
ribs, 293
chicken, 364
frankfurters, oven-, 354
ham steaks, 326
lamb
patties, 337
spareribs, 336
pork
ribs, 205, 318
sauce
bastings, 491-494
dip, 199
glaze, 364
veal, breast of, 340
Barbecuing, 5
Barley-lamb soup, 220
Basil, 965, 967-968
Bass
à la Franey, 408
baked stuffed, 405
cold poached, with watercress sauce, 408
Basting, 5
sauces, 491-494
deluxe, 491

diable, 492
jiffy, 493
lemon, 492
marmalade, 492
pungent barbecue, 493
Batter, 5
breads, 671-673
cheese, 672
oatmeal, 673
raisin, 672
white, 671
coating, for deep-fat-fried chicken, 362
Bauernwurst, 352
Bay leaf, 965, 968-969
Beans
baked
Boston, 552
with frankfurters, 353
freezing, 57
Italian, 553
buying, 41, 75
calico-hot pot, 941
and chicken livers, 955
dried
Burgundy, 552
Burgundy, with beef, 938
country franks and, 943
general data on, 43, 551-552
succotash, 518
See also Black beans; Green beans; Jalapeño beans; Kidney beans; Lima beans; Wax beans
Béarnaise sauce
for beef tournedos, 287
classic, 489
less-rich, 494
quick, for beef fondue, 294
salmon steaks with, 411
stuffed salmon turbans with, 409
swordfish steaks with, 411
Beating, 5, 13
Béchamel sauce, 478-481
Chantilly, 480
cream, 480
long method, 480
Mornay, 482
Newburg, 480
onion, 481
short method, 480
Beef, 275-278,281-310
à la mode, 285
appetizers
corned, glazed, 203
dried, and watercress canapés, 181
meatballs and mushrooms, 190
roast, with horseradish-whipped cream dip, 163
shish kabobs, 201
tartare, 166
teriyaki, tiny, 177
basic retail cuts, 295-298
boiled
brisket with horseradish sauce, 296
brisket with mustard sauce, 296
New England dinner, 297
brisket of, boiled
with horseradish sauce, 296
with mustard sauce, 296
broiling timetable, 50
Burgundy, 300
buying, 75-76
calorie counts, 81-82
casseroles, 937-943

Burgundy, and beans, 938
calico-bean hot pot, 941
corned beef-macaroni, 128
egg and, 956
English beef-and-kidney pie, 939
hamburger-and-noodles Stroganoff, 941
-lima bean, 942
liver-and-macaroni, 942
and olive, 937
pastiche, 939
pie, 940
Swedish, 940
tamale, 938
corned
glazed, 203
hash, 297
-macaroni casserole, 128
egg drop soup, 230
fondue, 293-296
Béarnaise sauce, quick, 294
Cumberland sauce, 295
curried mayonnaise, 296
curry sauce, 294
general data on, 293
horseradish-chive sauce, 295
mushroom-catsup sauce, 296
oriental, 295
tomato sauce, 294
freezing, 58, 59
fricassee, 968
goulash
easy, 305
Hungarian, 300
paprikash, 306
ground *see* hamburger; meat loaf; meatballs
hamburger, 302-307
broiled, 303
cheese-stuffed, 303
with garlic butter, 303
general data on, 302
hash, 307
juicy, 302
-and-noodles Stroganoff, 941
pan-fried, 303
Salisbury steaks, 304
Stroganoff, 305
heart, baked stuffed, 346
kidneys
buying, 76
English beef pie and, 939
and steak pie, 349
liver
-and-macaroni casserole, 942
menu for, 95
and onions, smothered, 346
meat loaf, 307-310
freezing, 59
general data on, 307-308
our best, 308
with textured protein, 310
variations, 308-310
meatballs
and mushroom appetizer, 190
and spaghetti with tomato sauce, 574
Swedish, 304
Swedish, for a crowd, 190
oxtail
ragout, 301
soup, 223
pie, 940
English kidney and, 939
pilaf, 306
Polynesian, 307

INDEX

Beef—*Continued*
pot roasts, 283-286
  à la mode, 285
  basic, 283
  boeuf en daube, 285
  carne Mechada, 284
  general data on, 283
  menu for, 97
  oven, 284
  sauerbraten, 286
rib(s)
  barbecued, 293
  entrecôte with watercress garnish, 288
  German-style, 301
  lentils and, 555
  roast, standing, 281
  vegetable soup with liver balls and, 225
roast, 281-283
  cubed, with horseradish-whipped cream dip, 163
  general data on, 281
  gravy for, 281
  menu for, 97
  standing rib, 281
  Wellington, 282
roasting chart, 44-46
roulades, 291
sauce, 574
shish kabobs, 201
soup, egg drop, 230
Southwest chili, 305
steaks, 286-293
  au poivre, 288
  barbecued flank, 290
  broiled, 286
  chuck de luxe, 290
  entrecôte with watercress garnish, 288
  flank, barbecued, 290
  general data on, 286
  kabobs, 292
  -and-kidney pie, 349
  London broil, skillet, 289
  marinade, wine for, 988
  menu for, 96
  minute Diane, 124
  mock filet mignon with broiled Parmesan toast, 289
  pepper, 288, 292
  porterhouse, 286
  roulades, 291
  Salisbury, 304
  sirloin, 286
  sirloin pepper, 292
  sliced, with wine sauce and glazed onions, 288
  sukiyaki, 292
  Swiss, 289
  T-bone, 286
  tenderloin tips Deutsch, 291
  wine marinade for, 988
  wine sauce for, 293
stew, 298
  carbonade, 299
  menu for, 95
  old-fashioned, 298
  in wine, 299, 987
stock, 211
Stroganoff, 971
tartare, 166
tenderized, 281
teriyaki, tiny, 177
Texas soup, 222
tongue

deviled, 350
general data on, 278
with raisin sauce and vegetables, 114
smoked, with raisin sauce, 350
tournedos, with Béarnaise sauce, 287
Wellington, 282
wine sauce for, 989
See also Frankfurters
Beet(s), 506-507
baked, 507
buttermilk, 258
buying, 41, 75, 506
cooking, 506
flower garnish for main dish, 55
freezing, 62
general data on, 506
Harvard, 506
-and-horseradish relish, 926
jellied salad, 615
shredded, 506
storing, 74
Beet greens
buying, 42
freezing, 64
Beignets soufflés with apricot sauce, 779
Bel Paese cheese, 470
Belgian waffles, 777
Belgian endive, 521-522
braised, 522
  with walnuts, 522
buying, 41, 521
general data on, 521-522, 585
with mustard dressing, 148
Roquefort cream sauce for braised, 522
salad with chiffonade dressing, 594
Benedict
eggs, poached, 459
ham and eggs crepes, 654
tomatoes, 546
Berries, 700-701
buying, 75, 700
equivalent amounts, 26
freezing, 67
general data on, 700-701
preparing, 700
storing, 72
See also names of berries
Beurre noir, 138
Beverages, 242-272
apricot flip, 255
buttermilk beet, 258
  -strawberry frosted, 257
calorie counts, 77
carbohydrate gram counts, 87
cereal, 243
champagne punch, 985
chocolate
  Brazilian cooler, 254
  caffè Borgia, 246
  coffee, Brazilian-, 248
  Coffee, Mexican, 245
  coffee mocha frosted, 247
  French, 252
  hot, 252
  hot, Mexican, 253
  hot mocha froth, 253
  ice cream soda, 245
  minted cola punch, 261
  -spice shake, 254
claret float, 984
cocktails, 266-272
  Alexander, 272

Bacardi, 271
bar syrup, 268
bloody Mary, 268
champagne, 270
choosing wine for, 984
daiquiri, 270
daiquiri (frozen), 270
gimlet, 270
gin fizz, 271
grasshopper, 271
John Collins, 269
Manhattan, 267
martini, 267
mint julep, 269
old-fashioned, 269
port, 984
Rob Roy (sweet), 271
rum Collins, 269
Scotch sour, 268
screwdriver, 267
shandygaff, 269
sidecar, 271
stinger, 272
Tom Collins, 268
vodka Collins, 269
whiskey sour, 268
wine as, 984
cocoa
hot, 251
-hot rum, 253
syrup for hot or iced, 252
coffee, 242-248
brands of, 243
Brazilian-chocolate, 248
buying, 243
café brûlot, 245
café Chantilly, 246
café au lait, 245
caffè Borgia, 246
caffè cappuccino, 245
caffè cioccolaccino, 246
creamed cinnamon, 248
decaffeinated, 243
demitasse, 244
espresso, 244
grinds of, 243
iced, 247
iced spiced, 247
instant, 243
Irish, 246
jelly, 743
making, 243-244
Mexican, 245
mocha frosted, 247
mocha froth, hot, 253
substitutes, 243
tropicale, 247
Viennese, 245
cranberry cup, 986
frosted, 255
fruit shrub, 256
fruited burgundy cooler, 986
grape ade cooler, 255
honey-peanut butter shake, 256
ice-cream soda, 258
  basic, 258
  black and white, 258
  chocolate, 258
  strawberry, 258
lemonade, 255
  -rhubarb, 257
minted chocolate cola punch, 261
peach thaw, 256
pineapple cress, 256
port cocktail, 984
punch, 259-266, 985-987

Beverages—*Continued*
bourbon, 265
California, 262
Caribbean bowl, 264
champagne, 262, 985
children's candy stick, 259
cranberry-lemon, 260
fruit syllabub, 260
fruited burgundy cooler, 986
holiday eggnog, 264
holiday wine, 264
Kris Kringle, 260
La Fonda sangría, 263
minted chocolate cola, 261
mock pink champagne, 261
orange eggnog, 261
peach, 986
snowy eggnog, 263
tea, festive hot, 250
Texas, 265
Tom and Jerry, 265
vermouth cassis, 987
wassail bowl, 265
wine spritzer, 986
wine syllabub, 263
raspberry fruit refresher, 257
razzberry yogurt, 254
rhubarb-lemonade, 257
sherry cooler, 986
strawberry
-buttermilk frosted, 257
milk, 256
tea, 248-251
cinnamon, hot, 249
iced, 250
iced by the pitcher, 250
iced spiced, 251
instant, 249
making, 249
midnight, 249
punch, festive hot, 250
vegetable-fruit blend, 257
vermouth cassis, 987
wine spritzer, 986
Biotin, nutritive values and sources,
999
Biscuit tortoni, 753
Biscuit(s), 631-633
basic rolled, 631
basic shortcake, 730
crust for chicken pot pie, 372
general data on, 630-631
orange tea, 632
parsley, 631
-pecan coating for oven-fried
chicken, 363
poppy seed spirals, 632
rolled cheese, 632
watercress, 631
Bisque
crab, 231
seafood, 218
tomato, 229
tomato-asparagus, 233
Black and white
ice cream soda, 258
Black bean
Brazilian, and rice, 555
soup, 227
buttered, 232
Black butter sauce, 490
Blackberries
freezing, 67
general data on, 700
in melon surprise, 707
Black-bottom pie, 797

Blanching, 5
Blender Hollandaise sauce, 489
Blending, 5
Blintzes, 773
apple filling, 774
blueberry filling, 774
cheese filling, 774
Blitz torte, quick, 851
Blond (velouté) sauce, 482-483
long method, 482
short method, 483
smitaine, 483
supreme, 483
Bloody Mary, 268
Blue cheese, 469
French dressing, 626
with wine, 988
mayonnaise, 626
Blueberry(ies)
conversion chart, 32
filling for blintzes, 774
freezing, 67
general data on, 700
muffins, 634
pie, 791
Bluefish à la Franey, 408
Blutwurst, 352
Boeuf en daube, 285
Bohemian kolacky, 688
nut filling for, 689
Boiling, 5
Bologna, 351
cheese-stuffed, 172
garnish for cold meat platters, 157
storing, 73
Bombe
glacée, 760
jubilee ice cream, 760
mocha, 754
Bordelaise sauce, 485
Borscht, 227
cold, 241
jellied, 235
Ukrainian vegetable, 219
Boston baked beans, 552
Boston cream pie, 822
high, 852
Bouillabaisse, 214
quick, 413
Bouquet garni, 5, 967
Bourbon
-pecan cake, 844
punch, 265
Boysenberries
conversion chart, 32
freezing, 67
general data on, 700
Brains, calf's
au beurre noir, 351
general data on, 278
Braise, to, 5, 280-281
Bran
date muffins, 634
raisin muffins, 634
Brandy butter, for apple brown Betty,
724
Bratwurst, 352
Brazilian
black beans and rice, 555
coffee-chocolate, 248
cooler, 254
cream puffs, 769
Bread, to, 5
Bread crumbs, equivalent amounts,
26
Bread-and-butter pickles, 922

Bread(s)
calorie counts, 77
carbohydrate gram counts, 87-88
pudding
custard, 735
deluxe chocolate, 735
queen of, 735
spoon
herbed, 969
Southern, 602
storing, 71
Breads, quick, 630-660
apple nut, 640
apricot nut, 640
banana raisin, 640
biscuits, 631-633
basic rolled, 631
general data on, 630-631
orange tea, 632
parsley, 631
poppy seed spirals, 632
rolled cheese, 632
watercress, 631
cheese, 641
coffeecakes, 636-639
apricot streusel, 638
basic, 636
crunch topping for, 637
date nut surprise rolls, 638
general data on, 636
jam topping for, 637
lemon ball, 639
old-fashioned, 637
Sally Lunn, 639
corn, 642-643
crisps, 643
general data on, 642
muffins, 642
skillet, 643
southern spoon, 582
sticks, 642
stuffing, crown roast pork with,
312
stuffing for poultry, 394
stuffing, sage, 973
cranberry orange, 641
crepes, 652-656
basic, 653
cheese fondue, 654
chicken livers in Madeira sauce,
655
creamed spinach, 655
general data on, 652
ham-and-egg Benedict, 654
salmon velouté, 656
croutons, 659-660
bacon, 660
baked, 660
cheese, 660
garlic, 659
general data on, 659
herbed, 660
doughnuts, 646-647
general data on, 646
lemon crullers, 647
rich, 646
dumplings, 643-644
basic, 644
general data on, 643
parsley, 644
for soup, 644
freezing, 54
French toast, 656-657
basic, 656
crispy, 657
general data on, 656

Breads, quick—*Continued*
  strawberry whipped butter for, 657
  fritters, 644-646
    apple-ring, 645
    basic, 645
    clam, 645
    corn, 645
    crunchy tuna, 646
    general data on, 644
    oyster, 645
  general data on, 630-631
  graham cracker, 641
  loaves, 639-642
    apple nut, 640
    apricot nut, 640
    banana raisin, 640
    cheese, 641
    cranberry orange, 641
    graham cracker, 641
  muffins, 633-635
    bacon breakfast, 634
    banana pecan, 634
    basic, 633
    blueberry, 634
    bran, 634
    cheese, 634
    cornmeal, 642
    date bran, 634
    general data on, 633
    ginger, 634
    orange, 634
    raisin bran, 634
  nut
    apple, 640
    apricot, 640
  orange cranberry, 641
  pancakes, 647-652
    apple-filled, 649
    basic, 648
    chicken, with sour cream sauce, 651
    chicken-curry, 651
    crab-filled, 652
    fruit, 649
    fruit syrup for, 649
    general data on, 647-648
    German apple, 650
    maple butter, whipped, for, 649
    rich, 649
    vanilla butter syrup for, 650
    yeast, 650
  popovers, 635
  scones, 635-636
    general data on, 635
    griddle, 636
  waffles, 657-659
    basic, 658
    cornmeal brunch, 659
    deluxe, 658
    general data on, 657-658
    raisin oatmeal, 659
    sour cream, 658
Bread(s), yeast, 661-692
  anadama, rapid-mix method, 670
  batter, 671-673
    cheese, 672
    oatmeal, 673
    raisin, 672
    white, 671
  Bohemian kolacky, 688
    nut filling for, 689
    poppy seed filling for, 689
  bowties, cinnamon, 704
  bran whole wheat, 677
  brioches, 685

buns
  egg glaze for, 683
  honey, 681
  hot cross, 682
cereal *see* whole grain
cheese batter, 672
Christmas stollen, 689
cinnamon
  bow ties, 683
  rolls, 681
coffeecake, Moravian, 687
cool-rise, 673-675
  rolls, 678
  white, 674
  whole wheat, 674
Cornell, 676
cracked-wheat, 677
croissants, French, 685
currant oatmeal, 675
Czechoslovakian kolacky, 688
  nut filling for, 689
  poppy seed filling for, 689
descriptive phrases used in recipes, 662-665
dough
  basic sweet, 680
  kneading, 13, 663
egg-whole wheat, 676
fastnacht, 686
freezing, 55
French
  grùyere, onion soup with, 229
  rapid-mix method, 670
French croissants, 685
garlic cubes for chef's salad, 587
general data on, 661-662
honey buns, 681
hot cross buns, 683
  egg glaze for, 683
ingredients of, 661-662
Italian Easter, 690
kolacky, 688
kuchen, 687
kulich, 691
  lemon icing for, 692
Moravian sugar cake, 687
oatmeal
  batter, 673
  currant, 675
old-fashioned homemade, 665-667
  rye, 667
  white, 665
  whole wheat, 666
raisin batter, 672
rapid-mix, 667-671
  anadama, 670
  French, 670
  rolls, 678
  rye, 669
  white, 668
  whole wheat, 668
rolls, 678-682
  cinnamon, 681
  cool-rise, 678
  dough, basic sweet, 680
  honey buns, 681
  icing, white, for, 681
  rapid-mix, 678
  shaping, 679-680
Russian kulich, 691
  lemon icing for, 692
rye
  conventional method, 667
  rapid-mix method, 669
Santa's, 688
  confectioners' glaze for, 688

schnecken, 684
shaping loaves, 665
Swedish coffee ring, 682
sweet, 682-692
white
  batter, 671
  conventional method, 665
  cool-rise method, 674
  rapid-mix method, 668
whole grain, 675-678
  Cornell, 676
  cracked-wheat, 677
  currant oatmeal, 675
  nutritive values, 998, 999, 1001
  See also whole wheat
whole wheat
  bran, 677
  conventional method, 666
  cool-rise method, 674
  cracked-wheat, 677
  -egg, 676
  rapid-mix method, 668
Brick cheese, 469
Brie cheese, 470
Brioches, 685
Broccoli, 507-508
  beurre noir, 138
  buying, 41, 75, 507
  freezing, 63
  general data on, 507
  with lemon sauce, 508
  nutritive values, 1000
  soup, 226
  storing, 74
  timbales, 508
Broiling, 6
Brown (Espagnole) sauce, 484-486
  Bordelaise, 485
  diable, 485
  long method, 484
  mushroom, 485
  piquant, 485
  Robert, 486
  short method, 484
Brownies
  fudge, 862
  peanut butter-coconut, 863
Brunswick stew, 371
Brushing, 6
Brussels sprouts, 508-509
  buying, 41, 75, 508
  in celery sauce, 147
  with cheese, 509
  cooking, 508
  freezing, 63
  general data on, 508
  preparing, 508
  with sour cream sauce, 122, 509
  storing, 74
Bûche de Noël, 148
  quick, 835
Buckwheat groats
  general data on, 580
  kasha varnishkis, 583
Buffet, Continental, 101-104
Bulgur, 580
  salad, 581
Bundt cake, lemon, 854
Buns
  honey, 681
  hot cross, 683
    egg glaze for, 683
Burgundy beans, 552
  with beef, 938
Burgundy whip, 990
Butter

Butter—*Continued*
  beurre noir, 138
  brandy, for apple brown Betty, 724
  buying, 76
  cakes, 817-822
    Boston cream, 822
    carrot, 819
    choco-chip lovelight, 818
    chocolate marmalade, 820
    dark devil's food, 818
    devil's food, 817
    general data on, 817
    gold, 819
    marble, 820
    pound, 821
    special tips, 813-815
    spice, 821
    techniques for, 812-813
    white, 817
  clarified, 490
  cookies, 876
    spritz, 890
  equivalent amounts, 26
  freezing, 60
  garlic sauce
    hamburgers with, 303
    mussels with, 435
    for spaghetti, 576
  herb, 967
    lamb chops with, 331
  maple, whipped, for pancakes, 649
  mocha, for bûche de Noël, 149
  nutritive values, 998
  pastry, for warm apple tart, 800
  pecan ice cream, 757
  sauce, 490-491
    -anchovy, for broiled fish steaks, 403
    black, 990
    clarified, 490
    garlic, hamburgers with, 303
    garlic, mussels with, 435
    garlic, for spaghetti, 576
    herb, 490
    lobster tails in, 424
    maître d'hôtel, 491
    nuts, hot, 176
    -parsley, new potatoes in, 123, 535
    savory, for artichokes, 501
    -wine, for broiled fish steaks, 403
  storing, 71
  strawberry whipped, for French toast, 657
  syrup, vanilla, for pancakes, 650
Butter-cream frosting, 856
  almond, 856
  browned, 857
  cherry, 857
  chocolate, 857
  coffee, 857
  lemon, 857
  maple-nut, 857
  mocha, 857
  orange, 857
  peanut, 857
  peppermint, 857
Butterfly
  franks, 201
  shrimp, 417
    dips for, 418
Buttermilk
  -strawberry frosted, 257
  substitute for, 29
Butterscotch
  candy, 904

-chocolate bars, 863
  cookies, 879
  meringue pie, 801
  -oatmeal cookies, 871
  sauce, for ice cream, 763

Cabbage, 509-511
  amandine, 511
  braised, 510
  buying, 41, 75, 509
  Chinese
    freezing, 63
    general data on, 585
  cooking, 509-510
  freezing, 63
  general data on, 509-510, 585
  nutritive values, 998, 1000
  red
    general data on, 509-510
    sausage and, 321
    with wine, 511
  savoy, 510
  slaw, 594
    blender, with sour cream dressing, 594
    hot, 511
    with pineapple and mustard dressing, 128
  steamed buttered, 510
  storing, 74
Caciocavallo cheese, 469
Caesar salad, 588
Café
  brûlot, 245
  Chantilly, 246
  au lait, 245
Caffè
  Borgia, 246
  cappuccino, 245
  cioccolaccino, 246
Cakes, 810-860
  angel food, *see* foam
  apricot party, 848
  banana-rum cream, 120
  bûche de Noël, 148
  butter, 817-822
    Boston cream, 822
    carrot, 819
    choco-chip lovelight, 818
    chocolate marmalade, 820
    dark devil's food, 818
    devil's food, 817
    general data on, 817
    gold, 819
    marble, 820
    pound, 821
    special tips, 813-815
    spice, 821
    techniques for, 812-813
    white, 817
  calorie counts, 78
  carbohydrate gram counts, 88
  cheese, 829-832
    fruit glaze for, 831
    general data on, 829
    pineapple, 831
    Hawaiian pineapple, 100
    supreme, 830
    velvet, 830
  cherry-almond angel, 131
  chiffon, *see* foam
  chocolate refrigerator, 751
  cream, banana-rum, 120
  cutting, 816
  foam, 826-829
    angel food, 827

    daffodil, 828
    feather sponge, 827
    golden chiffon, 827
    maple pecan chiffon, 829
    special tips, 826
    sugared orange chiffon, 828
  freezing, 55
  frostings, 856-860
    almond butter-cream, 856
    butter-cream, browned, 876
    butter-cream, 856
    caramel, 858
    caramel (quick), 858
    cherry butter-cream, 857
    chocolate butter-cream, 857
    cocoa whipped cream, 860
    coffee butter-cream, 857
    four-minute fudge, 858
    general data on, 815-816
    Hungarian, 858
    Lady Baltimore, 860
    lemon butter-cream, 857
    lemon cream-cheese, 859
    maple swirl, 859
    maple-nut butter-cream, 857
    mocha butter-cream, 857
    orange butter-cream, 857
    peanut butter-cream, 857
    peppermint butter-cream, 857
    swirl, 859
    vanilla petits fours, 847
    white mountain, 859
  fruit, 842-846
    baking, 842
    bourbon-pecan, 844
    decorating, 843
    extra rich dark, 843
    general data on, 842-843
    golden honey, 845
    pans for, 842
    refrigerator, 846
    storing, 842
    white, 843
  general data on, 810-812
  glazed gingerbread cupcakes, 848
  glazes
    for bourbon pecan cake, 845
    for chocolate marmalade cake, 820
    peppermint, 860
    pineapple, 832
  little, 846-849
    apricot party, 848
    glazed gingerbread cupcakes, 848
    tea, 847
  mocha mousse coronet, 747
  Moravian sugar, 687
  one-bowl, 823-825
    banana, 824
    devil's food, 823
    gingerbread, 824
    golden yellow, 824
    Lady Baltimore, 823
    quick spice cake, 825
    tomato soup, 825
    white, 823
  pineapple chiffon, 104
  potato, Swiss, 538
  quick-mix, 849-856
    angel food surprise, 849
    apricot trifle, 850
    blitz torte, 851
    Boston cream, high, 852
    broiled nut-topped, 851
    chocolate nut, 853
    chocolate raspberry ripple, 854

Cakes—*Continued*
  dobos torte, 852
  double chocolate frosted, 853
  ice-cream-filled, 849
  lemon bundt, 854
  Lord Baltimore, 853
  special tips, 813-815
  wedding, 854
  rolled, 832-835
    bûche de Noël, 148
    bûche de Noël, quick, 835
    chocolate cream, 832
    Christmas log, 835
    general data on, 832
    peppermint cream, 833
    pineapple, 834
    raspberry jelly, 834
    rum-banana cream, 120
  sponge, *see* foam
  storing, 71
  sugar, Moravian, 687
  tea, 847
  tortes, 837-841
    blitz, quick, 851
    chocolate cream, 838
    chocolate-almond, 837
    dobos, quick, 852
    general data on, 837
    meringue strawberry, 839
    mocha, 839
    St. Honoré, 840
  upside-down, 835-837
    cherry, 836
    chocolate, 836
    pineapple, 836
  wedding, 854
  See also Coffeecake; Shortcake
Calcium, nutritive values and sources,
    1000
Calf's brains
  au beurre noir, 351
  general data on, 278
Calf's liver
  broiled, 346
  pan-fried, 346
Calico-bean hot pot, 941
California
  cheese rolls, 170
  punch, 262
Calorie counts, 77-87
Camembert cheese, 470
  soufflé, 454
Canadian bacon, piquant glazed, 328
Canapés, *see* Appetizers
Candy, 893-912
  calorie counts, 78-79
  carbohydrate gram counts, 90
  easy, 893-902
    apples, marzipan, 899
    apricot-coconut balls, 898
    bananas, marzipan, 899
    caramel cashew turtles, 894
    carrots, marzipan, 900
    cereal gems, 896
    chocolate bark, 895
    chocolate cereal drops, 895
    chocolate drops, Scotch, 901
    chocolate marshmallow fudge,
      894
    chocolate peanut balls, 895
    chocolate quickies, 896
    citrus peel, candied, 894
    date-nut, 896
    date-and-pecan logs, 896
    fondant, no-cook, 897
    fruited fondant rolls, 897

    fruits, fondant-stuffed, 897
    glaze for marzipan, 900
    grapes, marzipan, 900
    Kris Kringles, 898
    lemons, marzipan, 899
    marshmallows, 898
    marzipan, 899
    mint fondant balls, 897
    mocha fondant logs, 897
    nut-date, 896
    oranges, marzipan, 899
    peaches, marzipan, 899
    peanut butter-date drops, 901
    peanut marshmallow squares,
      901
    peanut mounds, 900
    pecan-and-date logs, 896
    plums, marzipan, 900
    potatoes, marzipan, 900
    Scotch chocolate drops, 901
    spirit, 902
    strawberries, marzipan, 900
    Turkish paste, 902
    vanilla-wafer fudgies, 902
    watermelon slices, marzipan, 900
  general data on, 893, 903
  to make with a thermometer,
    903-912
    apricot roll, 904
    butterscotch, 904
    candy canes, 904
    caramels, creamy, 905
    chocolate fudge, 907
    cinnamon-candied apples, 905
    fudge, perfect-every-time, 907
    fudge-peanut drops, 907
    general data on, 903
    honey nougat, 908
    lollipops, 908
    minted walnuts, 909
    molasses taffy, 909
    peanut brittle, 910
    peanut butter fudge, 908
    pecans, fruited, 906
    penuche, 911
    peppermint hard, 910
    peppermint taffy, 910
    popcorn balls, 911
    pralines I, 912
    pralines II, 912
    taffy, 910
    toffee, English, 906
    walnuts, minted, 909
  storing, 893
Candying, 6
Cannelloni
  cream sauce for, 579
  homemade, 578
  meat filling for, 578
Canning, 917-935
  chutney, 931
    pear, 930
    tomato, 930
  conserves
    cherry, 936
    peach, 936
  general data on, 917-920
  jam, 931-936
    general data on, 931-936
    strawberry-rhubarb, 934
  jelly, 931-935
    apple, 933
    general data on, 931-936
    grape, 934
  mustard, tomato, 930
  pickles, 920-925

    bread-and-butter, 922
    crystal chips, 922
    dill, 922
    dilled beans, 922
    general data on, 920-921
    green-tomato relish, 928
    mixed vegetable, 924
    mustard, 923
    senf gurken, 924
    watermelon rind, 925
  publications on, 918-919
  preserves
    cherry-pineapple, 935
    peach-and-plum, 935
    strawberry, 934
  relishes, 920-921
    beet-and-horseradish, 925
    chow-chow, 927
    corn, 927
    general data on, 920-921
    green-tomato pickle, 928
    India, 928
    piccalilli, 929
    pickled celery and olives, 926
    sweet pepper, 929
    vegetable, tangy, 926
    vegetable bowl, 127
Cannoli, 778
  cheese filling for, 778
Cantaloupe(s)
  buying, 75
  freezing, 69
  and ham salad, 604
  with lime sherbet, 126
  in melon surprise, 707
  nutritive values, 998, 1000
  selecting, 39
  using, 39
Caramel
  cashew turtles, 894
  creamy candy, 905
  crème, 736
  crème frite, 779
  frosting, 858
    quick, 858
  syrup, 841
    for crème frite, 779
Caramelizing, 6
Caramelized sugar, 733
Caraway seeds, 977
Carbohydrate gram counts, 87-91
Carbohydrates, nutritive values and
    sources, 994
Cardamom, 977
  cream dressing for fruit salad, 590
Caribbean
  fish soufflé, 404
    lemon-curry sauce for, 405
  punch bowl, 264
Carne mechada, 284
Carp, baked stuffed, 405
Carrot(s), 512-513
  baked shredded, 512
  buying, 41, 75
  cake, 819
  freezing, 63
  garnish
    curls, 154
    flower, 155
    for main dish, 154
    for soup, 154
  general data on, 512
  glazed
    Lyonnaise, 147
    orange, 512
  marzipan, 900

Carrots—*Continued*
in mixed vegetable pickles, 924
nutritive values, 998
orange glazed, 512
peas with ring of, 531
-rice casserole, 566
soup, cream of, 226
and spinach timbales with nutmeg
    sauce, 513
storing, 74
Casabas
in melon surprise, 707
selecting, 39
using, 39
Cashew nuts
caramel turtles, 894
rice with peppers and, 565
-tuna casserole, 120
Casserole(s), 937-961
apple and sausage, 950
beef, 937-943
    Burgundy, and beans, 938
    calico-bean hot pot, 941
    egg and, 956
    English beef-and-kidney pie, 939
    hamburger-and-noodles
        Stroganoff, 941
    -lima bean, 942
    liver-and-macaroni, 942
    and olive, 937
    pastiche, 939
    pie, 940
    Swedish, 940
    tamale, 938
cheese
    and shrimp, 958
    spaghetti, six-, 477
chicken, 953-955
    arroz con pollo, 953
    sesame rice, 955
    Tetrazzini, 954
chicken liver, 955-957
    beans and, 955
    wild-rice-and, 956
chili franks, 943
corn, Southern, 518
corned beef-macaroni, 128
country franks and beans, 943
crab meat
    -mushroom, 957
    -and-rice, 957
deviled ham Tetrazzini, 945
egg, 956-957
    baked noodles and, 957
    beef and, 956
    deviled, 463
    green island, 464
    -salad, 466
eggplant, moussaka, 947
frankfurter, 943-944
    chili, 943
    country, and beans, 943
    -and-macaroni, 944
    and rice, 944
freezing, 56
general data on, 937
green bean, 504
green island, 464
ham, 948-950
    baked, tetrazzini, 948
    creamed, 949
    deviled, Tetrazzini, 945
    lima beans and, 949
lamb, 946-947
    moussaka, 947
    and rice, 946

lasagna veal Romano, 952
lobster rock, 425
luncheon meat, 945-946
    Florentine, 946
    ham, deviled Tetrazzini, 945
    noodle, 945
macaroni
    and beef liver, 942
    -corned beef, 128
    and frankfurters, 944
    -tuna, 958
Marie-Blanche, 568
measurements of, 12
moussaka, 947
mushroom
    and crab meat, 957
    -tenderloin, 947
noodles
    baked, and eggs, 957
    baked vegetable, 569
    garden, 569
    -hamburger Stroganoff, 941
    with luncheon meat, 945
    Marie-Blanche, 568
    and sausage, 950
    veal lasagna Romano, 952
pork, 947-948
    chop, 111
    chop and potato scallop, 947
    chop, scalloped sweets and, 948
    sausage pie, 951
    tenderloin-mushroom, 947
    See also Ham; Sausage
potato
    and pork chop scallop, 947
    scalloped sweets and pork chops,
        948
rice, 563
    arroz con pollo, 953
    -carrot, 566
    crab meat and, 957
    frankfurters and, 944
    lamb and, 946
    sesame seeds with chicken or
        turkey, 955
    wild, and chicken livers, 956
sausage, 950-951
    -and-apple, 950
    noodle, 950
    pork, pie, 951
    zucchini and, 951
seafood, 957-961
    baked salad, 960
    mixed, 415
    Tetrazzini, 960
shrimp
    -and-cheese, 958
    ramekins, 959
spaghetti, six-cheese, 477
spinach and tuna, 959
Swedish, 940
tuna
    -cashew, 120
    macaroni, 958
    -and-spinach, 959
turkey, 953-955
    arroz con pollo, 953
    sesame rice, 955
    Tetrazzini, 954
turnip
    -and-onion, 549
    whipped, 141
veal, 951-953
    lasagna Romano, 952
    Swiss, 953
    with water chestnuts, 951

vegetable
    baked noodle, 569
    medley, 103
    zucchini and sausage, 951
Catsup-mushroom sauce, for beef
    fondue, 296
Cauliflower, 513-514
    buying, 41, 75, 513
    cooking, 513
    freezing, 63
    garden, 514
    general data on, 513
    in mixed vegetable pickles, 924
    Mornay sauce for, 482
    nutritive values, 998
    old-fashioned slaw, 595
    steamed with Salsa Verde, 514
    storing, 74
Caviar roll, 209
Cayenne pepper, 966
Celeriac, *see* Celery root
Celery, 514-515
    -apple salad, 112
    braised, 515
    buying, 41, 75, 514
    cooking, 515
    crunchy stuffed, 173
    freezing, 63
    garnish for cold meat platter, 156
    general data on, 514
    au gratin, 515
    and olives, pickled, 926
    sauce, Brussels sprouts in, 147
    storing, 74
    Victor, 595
    vegetable relish bowl, 127
Celery root, 515-516
    buying, 41, 515
    celeriac salad, 516
    general data on, 515-516
Celery salt, 978
Celery seed, 976
Cereals, 580-583
    beverages, 243
    calorie counts, 78
    candy gems, 896
    carbohydrate gram counts, 88
    chocolate drops, 895
    nutritive values, 993, 997
    storing, 72
Cervelat, 351
Champagne
    cocktail, 270
    mock pink, 261
    punch, 262, 985
Chantilly sauce, 480
Chard, 522
    freezing, 64
    nutritive values, 998
    storing, 74
Cheddar cheese, 468
    golden buck, 474
    rum tum tiddy, 474
    soufflé, 453
    soup, 475
    spaghetti casserole, 477
    strata, 476
    Welsh rarebit, 473
    Yankee fondue, 473
Cheese, 29-32, 467-477
    appetizers
        assorted pastry hors d'oeuvre,
            187
        and bacon whirls, 184
        California rolls, 170
        cream, and sardine canapés, 182

INDEX

Cheese—*Continued*
crisp, 172
deviled cream balls, 170
deviled eggs stuffed with, 172
dip, 198
-dipped pretzels, 176
holiday ball, 168
log, 169, 206
molded Roquefort crème, 170
olive puffs, 184
puffs, 184
sherry dip, 164
and shrimp spread, 206
sticks, 188
straws, 188
-stuffed bologna wedges, 172
-stuffed deviled eggs, 172
stuffed Gouda, 169
-stuffed mushrooms, 173
Swiss pie, 189
-wine spread, 199
-bacon custards, 460
Bel Paese, 470
Blue, 469
French dressing with, 626
wine, 988
biscuits rolled, 632
bread, 641
batter, 672
Brick, 469
Brie, 469
broiled toast, 289
Brussels sprouts with, 509
caciocavallo, 469
cakes *see* cheesecakes
calorie counts, 83
Camembert, 470
carbohydrate gram counts, 88
casserole, spaghetti, six-, 477
Cheddar, 468
chowder, vegetable-, 475
cooking, 472
-corn pie, 476
cream
cloud nine, 720
coeur à la crème, 720
deviled balls, 170
lemon frosting, 859
-sardine canapés, 182
spritz, 874
croutons, 660
dip, for butterfly shrimp, 418
-dipped pretzels, 176
Edam, 469
eggplant with, 519
equivalent amounts, 26
filling
for blintzes, 774
for cannoli, 778
fondue, 472
crepes, 654
Yankee, 473
freezing, 60-61
French dressing with, 626
with wine, 988
garnish for soups, 154
general data on, 467-472
golden buck, 474
Gouda, 469
Gruyère, 469
hamburgers
-stuffed, 303
hard, 468-469
caciocavallo, 469
Cheddar, 468
Edam, 469

Gouda, 469
Gruyère, 469
Provolone, 469
Swiss, 468
-lemon crepes, 775
Liederkranz, 471
Limburger, 471
-lobster custard, 476
macaroni
freezing, 56
salad, 598
mayonnaise with, 626
Mozzarella, 471
Muenster, 470
muffins, 634
nutritive values, 993, 998-1001
-olive puffs, 184
onion soup with, 229
Parmesan toasts, 289
parsnips au gratin, 529
pastry, 787
pear salad stuffed with, 591
pie, corn and, 476
Port du Salut, 470
and potato pie, 538
process, 471
provolone, 469
quiche Lorraine, 474
for Continental buffet, 101
quick, 474
rice balls, 566
ricotta, 471
Romano, 468
rum tum tiddy, 474
sapsago, 468
sauce
for braised endive, 522
eggs with, 464
semisoft, 469-470
Bel Paese, 470
blue, 469
brick, 469
Muenster, 470
Port du Salut, 470
-shrimp
casserole, 958
soufflé, 455
spread, 206
six, spaghetti casserole, 477
soft, 470-471
Brie, 470
Camembert, 470
Liederkranz, 471
Limburger, 471
Mozzarella, 471
Neufchâtel, 471
ricotta, 471
soufflés, 453-455
Camembert, 454
Cheddar, 453
-shrimp, 455
Swiss-parmesan, 454
soup, 475
spaghetti casserole, six-, 477
-spinach mousse ring, 615
storage of, 71-72, 472
strata, 476
stuffed baked potatoes with, 536
Swiss, 468
varieties of, 29-32
veal Parmigiana, 341
-vegetable chowder, 475
very hard, 468
Parmesan, 468
Romano, 468

sapsago, 468
Welsh rarebit, 473
wine, 987
zucchini Parmigiana, 549
See also names of cheese
Cheesecakes, 829-832
fruit glaze for, 831
general data on, 829
pineapple, 831
Hawaiian, 100
supreme, 830
velvet, 830
Chef's salad, 587
Cherry(ies), 701-702
-almond angel cake, 131
baked fruit compote, 717
-brandy mousse, 746
butter-cream frosting, 857
buying, 75, 701
cake, upside-down, 836
conserve, 936
conversion chart, 32
coronet salad, 613
curried fruit, hot, 728
floating island, 701
freezing, 67
general data on, 701
pie, 790
cobbler, 113
-pineapple preserves, 935
pitting, 701
sauce, for jubilee ice-cream bombe, 761
storing, 701
Chervil, 974
Chesapeake crab imperial, 427
Chestnut(s)
boiled, 392
-chicken soup, 231
custard crepes, 775
and mushrooms, creamed, 525
stuffing, 382, 393
for roast goose, 391
for roast turkey, 382
Chicken, 357-378
-almond mousse, 617
appetizers
creamed, 207
creamed, with profiteroles, 207
ginger spread, 167
liver and mushroom canapés, 178
liver pâté, 209
rumaki, 200
sesame bites, 174
wings, cocktail, 202
baked
crunchy, 121
with herb gravy, 110
herbed, 363
orange, 366
barbecued, 364
basting with wine, 987
breasts
baked in tarragon cream, 375
baked in mushroom cream sauce, 373
how to bone, 373
moo goo gai pien, 374
scaloppine, 375
in wine, 374
broiled, 363
barbecue sauce glaze, 364
herb glaze, 364
menu for, 94
wine glaze, 364
wine marinade for, 988

Chicken—*Continued*
  broiling timetable, 52
  buying, 76
  cacciatore, 367
  calorie counts, 86
  carbohydrate gram counts, 89-90
  carving, 383-385
  casseroles, 953-955
    arroz con pollo, 953
    sesame rice, 955
    Tetrazzini, 954
  coq au vin, 366
  Cornish hens
    general data on, 357-358
    roast with rice stuffing, 377
    on a spit, 377
  curried
    cold creamy, 602
    Hawaiian, 98
    pancakes, 651
  egg drop soup, 230
  freezing, 56, 59
  fricasseed, lemon, 370
  fried
    basic, 360
    batter coating for, 362
    biscuit-pecan coating for, 363
    corn flake crumb coating for, 362
    deep-fat, 361
    herb-flour coating for, 362
    Kansas, 360
    Maryland, 361
    menu for, 95
    oven-, 362
    potato coating for, 362
    sesame seed coating for, 363
    sour cream coating for, 363
  garnish for soups, 154
  general data on, 357-359
  giblets, 358-359
  and ham mousse, 617
  hibachi, 365
  Kiev, 386
  legs, with skillet macaroni, 376
  lemon-fricasseed, 370
  Marengo, 368
  Mexican, 369
  mousse
    -almond, 617
    and ham, 617
  orange marmalade souce for, 365
  pancakes with sour cream sauce,
    651
  parts of, 372-373
  Polynesian, 368
  pot pie, 371
    crust and topping for, 372
  Raphael Weill, 369
  roast
    carving, 383-385
    general data on, 358, 359
    gravy, 360
    menu, 95
    menu (holiday), 132-139
    pineapple-glazed, 136
    savory, 359
    stuffed, 359
  roasting timetable, 51-52
  rosemary, 972
  salad, 602
    -almond mousse, 617
    cold creamy, curried, 602
    cold with walnut sauce, 621
    ginger-cream, 602
    and grape salad, 619
    -and-ham mousse, 617

  Malibu, 604
  sautéed, with forty cloves of garlic,
    367
  -seasoned rice, 126
  simmered in stock, 372
  soufflé, 457
  soup
    -almond, 234
    -chestnut, 231
    and-dumpling, 221
    egg drop, 230
    petite marmite, 234
  on a spit, with pineapple, 365
  stew
    Brunswick, 371
    with matzo balls, 370
  stock, 211
  terrapin, 348
  Véronique, 366
  wine baste for, 987
  wine marinade for, 988
  wine sauce for, 989
  wings
    cocktail, 202
    oriental, 376
Chicken liver
  with bacon and peppers, 125
  casseroles, 955-957
    beans and, 955
    wild-rice-and, 956
  crepes, in Madeira sauce, 655
  and mushroom canapés, 178
  omelet, French, 450
  pâté, 209
  rumaki, 200
  sautéed, 973
  savory, 377
Chick-pea(s)
  falafel, 556
  and rice salad, chilled, 598
  sweet and pungent, 557
  and tabouli salad, 599
Chicory, general data on, 585
Chiffon cake
  golden, 827
  maple pecan, 829
  orange, sugared, 828
  pineapple, 104
Chiffon filling, for St. Honoré cake,
    841
Chiffon pies, 802-805
  chocolate-peppermint, 802
  eggnog, 803
  general data on, 802
  lemon, 803
  lime, 803
  pumpkin, 804
  raspberry, 804
Chiffonade dressing, Belgian endive
    salad with, 594
Children's candy stick punch, 259
Chili
  dip, for butterfly shrimp, 918
  franks, 943
  freezing, 56
  peanuts, 176
  Southwest, 305
Chili powder, 965, 978
Chili sauce herb dressing, 988
Chilling, 6
Chinese
  brown rice, 562
  pork tenderloin, 317
  slivered eggs, 465
  spareribs, 318
  spinach soup, 214

Chinese cabbage
  freezing, 63
  general data on, 585
Chive(s)
  garnish for soup, 153
  -horseradish sauce for beef fondue,
    295
Chloride, nutritive values and sources,
    1001
Choco-chip lovelight cake, 818
Chocolate
  -almond pie, 798
  bars
    -butterscotch, 863
    -toffee, 864
  beverages
    Brazilian cooler, 254
    caffè Borgia 246
    coffee, Brazilian, 248
    coffee, Mexican, 245
    coffee mocha frosted, 247
    French, 252
    hot, 252
    hot, Mexican, 253
    hot mocha froth, 253
    ice cream soda, 245
    minted cola punch, 261
    -spice shake, 254
  bread pudding deluxe, 735
  butter-cream frosting, 857
  cake
    choco-chip lovelight, 818
    cream roll, 832
    devil's food, 817
    devil's food, dark, 818
    devil's food, one-bowl, 823
    double frosted, 853
    marmalade, 820
    nut, 853
    -raspberry ripple, 854
    refrigerator, 751
    upside-down, 836
  candy
    bark, 895
    cereal drops, 895
    fudge, 907
    fudge, perfect-every-time, 907
    -marshmallow fudge, 894
    peanut balls, 895
    quickies, 896
    Scotch drops, 901
    toffee, English, 906
    vanilla-wafer fudgies, 902
  -cinnamon mousse, 108
  cookies
    -butterscotch bar, 863
    drop, 867
    (molded) pixies, 871
    pinwheels, 879
    pressed, 874
    refrigerator, 881
    -toffee bar, 864
  -cream crepes, 775
  -cream pie, 798
  -crumb pie shell, 794
  -dipped almonds, for Continental
    grapes, 705
  -drop cookies, 867
  éclairs, frozen, 770
  filling
    -almond, for cream torte, 838
    for frozen éclairs, 771
    chiffon, for St. Honoré cake, 841
    velvet, for blitz torte, 851
  fondue, 771
  French icing, for bûche de Noël, 149

Chocolate—*Continued*
ice cream, 777
chip, 757
rum nut, 761
ice-cream soda, 258
black and white, 258
-strawberry, 258
minted cola punch, 261
mousse, 748
nesselrode pudding, 734
pancakes with peppermint whipped
cream, 772
pastry shell, flaky, 787
pears supreme, 722
pie
-almond, 798
cream, 798
crumb shell, 794
heavenly, 806
-peppermint chiffon, 802
pinwheels, 899
pixie cookies, 871
pot-de-crème, 733
pressed cookies, 874
pudding
bread, deluxe, 735
steamed, 739
refrigerator cookies, 881
sauce
bittersweet, 762
for coconut soufflé, 764
fudge, 762
rum, 762
soufflé, 764
froid au, 748
-spiced shake, 254
substitution for, 28
torte
-almond, 838
cream, 837
turnover custards, 116
Choline, nutritive values and sources,
999
Chop suey, 319
freezing, 56
Chopping, 6
Chorizo, 352
Choucroute, quick, 541
Chow mein, shrimp, 419
Chow-chow relish, 927
Chowder
corn, quick, 221
Manhattan clam, 217
New England clam, 217
New England fish, 216
tomato-fish, 216
vegetable-cheese, 475
Christmas
cookies, 881-890
almond wafers, 885
anise drops, 885
Czechoslovakian puzzles, 886
Florentines, 886
gingerbread house, 883
gingerbread men, 883
gingerbread trees, 881
Greek crescents, 887
Jan Hagels, 887
lebkuchen, 887
Moravian, 888
pfeffernuesse, 888
sand tarts, 889
springerle, 890
spritz butter, 890
log, 835
melons

selecting, 39
using, 39
menus, 131-149
plum pudding, 740
pudding, English, 741
stollen, 689
Chutneys, 931
pear, 930
tomato, 931
Cinnamon, 964, 966
bow ties, 683
-candied apples, 905
-chocolate mousse, 108
coffee, creamed, 248
red apple rings, 696
rolls, 681
white icing for, 681
tea, hot, 249
whipped cream, coconut pancakes
with, 772
Cioppino, 414
Citrus peel, candied, 894
Citrus salad, 138
with creamy dressing, 129
Clam(s), 430-432
appetizers
baked, Casino, 195
creamy canapés, 185
baked stuffed, 431
in bouillabaisse, 214
quick, 413
buying, 430
chowder
Manhattan, 217
New England, 217
-and-corn soufflé, 436
freezing, 60
fried, 431
fritters, 645
general data on, 430
preparing, 430
roasted, 431
steamed, 431
-tomato soup, 232
white sauce, 575
Claret float, 984
Clarified butter, 490
Clarifying, 6
Cloud nine cream, 720
Cloves, 964
Coating, 6
Coating a spoon, 6
Coatings, for fried chicken, 362-363
Cocktails, 266-272
Alexander, 272
Bacardi, 271
bar syrup, for whiskey sour, 268
bloody Mary, 268
champagne, 270
choosing wine for, 984
daiquiri, 270
daiquiri (frozen), 270
gimlet, 270
gin fizz, 271
grasshopper, 271
John Collins, 269
Manhattan, 267
martini, 267
mint julep, 269
old-fashioned, 269
port, 984
Rob Roy, sweet, 271
rum Collins, 269
Scotch sour, 268
screwdriver, 267
shandygaff, 269

sidecar, 271
stinger, 272
Tom Collins, 268
vodka Collins, 269
whiskey sour, 268
wine as, 984
Cocoa
beverages
hot, 251
-hot rum, 253
syrup for hot or iced, 252
whipped cream, 860
Coconut(s), 702
-apricot balls, 898
conversion chart, 32
cookies
drop, 868
puffs, 868
equivalent amounts, 26
freezing, 68
general data on, 702
grating, 702
-honey filling for cookies, 878
ice cream, toasted, 757
opening, 702
pancakes with cinnamon whipped
cream, 772
-peanut butter brownies, 863
puffs, 868
shrimp, 208
soufflé with chocolate sauce, 764
storing, 702
toasted, 746
toasted shell for pie, 793
Cod
fillet, poached, 404
with mustard caper sauce, 404
fish and chips, 411
steaks, poached, 410
mustard sauce for, 411
Coddling, 6
Coeur à la crème, 720
Coffee, 242-248
brands of, 243
Brazilian-chocolate, 248
butter-cream frosting, 857
buying, 243
café brûlot, 245
café Chantilly, 246
café au lait, 245
caffè Borgia, 246
caffè cappuccino, 245
caffè cioccolaccino, 246
cream puffs, 769
creamed cinnamon, 248
crème, for Brazilian cream puffs,
769
decaffeinated, 243
demitasse, 244
espresso, 244
hot mocha froth, 253
grinds of, 243
ice cream, cognac-, 757
iced, 247
iced spiced, 247
instant, 243
Irish, 246
jelly, 743
making, 243-244
boiled, 244
drip, 244
espresso, 244
filtered, 244
instant, 244
percolated, 243
steeped, 244

Coffee—*Continued*
  vacuum-type, 243
Mexican, 245
mocha
  frosted, 247
  hot froth, 253
substitutes, 243
tropicale, 247
Viennese, 245
Coffee ring, Swedish, 682
Coffeecakes, 636-639
  apricot streusel, 638
  crunch topping for, 637
  date nut surprise rolls, 638
  general data on, 636
  jam topping for, 637
  lemon ball, 639
  Moravian, 687
  old-fashioned, 637
  Sally Lunn, 639
Coleslaw, *see* Slaw
Collards
  buying, 42
  freezing, 64
Compote
  baked fruit, 717
Concord grape pie, 790
Confectioners' frosting for Christmas
    cookies, 889
Confectioners' glaze for Santa's
    Bread, 688
Conserves
  cherry, 936
  peach, 936
Consommé
  jellied garden, 239
  julienne, 231
  à la Ritz, 236
  tomato, 230
Continental buffet, 101-104
Cookies, 861-892
  baking, 862
  bar, 862-866
    almond-jam, 863
    butterscotch-chocolate, 863
    chocolate-toffee, 864
    dream, 864
    fruit, 865
    fudge brownies, 862
    general data on, 862
    lemon-meringue, 865
    peanut-butter-coconut brownies,
      863
    raspberry-crumble, 866
    using press, 873
  Christmas, 881-890
    almond wafers, 885
    anise drops, 885
    Czechoslovakian puzzles, 886
    Florentines, 886
    gingerbread house, 883
    gingerbread men, 883
    gingerbread trees, 881
    Greek crescents, 887
    Jan Hagels, 887
    lebkuchen, 887
    Moravian, 888
    pfeffernuesse, 888
    sand tarts, 889
    springerle, 890
    spritz butter, 890
    thin frosting for, 889
  cookie sheets, 861
  cooling 862
  -crumb shell, 793
  drop, 866-870

chocolate, 867
coconut, 868
coconut puffs, 868
general data on, 866
hazelnut, 868
hermits, 868
molasses, 867
praline, 869
praline glaze, 870
sherry wafers, 870
spicy oatmeal, 869
vanilla, 866
filled, 878
  general data on, 879
  honey-coconut, 878
  mincemeat, 878
  prune, 878
freezing, 55
general data on, 861-862
gift packaging, 891
mixing, 861-862
molded, 870-873
  butterscotch-oatmeal, 871
  chocolate pixies, 871
  crackle tops, 870
  crinkle tops, 870
  crisscross tops, 871
  general data on, 870-871
  jelly balls, 872
  nut rolls, 872
  peanut-butter, 872
  spice balls, 873
  thumb-print top, 871
pie shell, 793
pressed, 873-874
  chocolate, 874
  cream cheese spritz, 874
  general data on, 873
  hard-cooked-egg, 874
refrigerator, 879-881
  butterscotch, 879
  chocolate, 881
  chocolate pinwheels, 879
  date pinwheels, 880
  general data on, 879
  lemon slices, 880
  orange, 881
  vanilla, 880
rolled, 875-877
  butter, 876
  cutting, 875
  general data on, 875
  lemon sugar, 876
  molasses, 876
  rolling, 875
  sugar cutouts, 877
  tea wafers, 877
storing, 862
Cooking, 3-24
  appearance of prepared food, and
    table, 150-161
  equipping a kitchen, 16-20
  high altitude, 24
  measuring accurately, 11-12
  metric measurements, 15-16
  mixing, 12-13
  pan size, choosing, 12
  recipes
    changing quantities, 4, 14-16
    equivalent amounts, 26-27
    how to use, 3-4
    ingredient substitutions, 27-29
  terms, definitions of, 4-11
  timing the dinner
    for company, 113-122
    for two, 110-113

holiday dinners, 131-149
last-minute meals, 122-131
shopping and preparing wisely,
  20-24
See also Food; Menu planning;
  Nutrition
Cooking terms, guide to, 4-11
Cooling, 6
Copper, nutritive values and sources,
  1000
Coq au vin, 366
Coquille
  crab, 437
  scallop, 433
Coriander seed, 977
Corn, 516-518
  buying, 516
  -cheese pie, 476
  chowder, quick, 221
  -and-clam soufflé, 436
  cooking on-the-cob
    baking, 517
    barbequing, 517
    boiling, 517
  freezing, 63-64
  fritters, 645
  general data on, 516
  in mixed vegetable pickles, 924
  nutritive values, 999
  on-the-cob leftover, 517
  oysters, 517
  pudding, 517
  relish, 927
  Southern casserole, 518
  storing, 74
  succotash, 518
Corn bread, 642-643
  crisps, 643
  general data on, 642
  muffins, 642
  skillet, 643
  sticks, 642
  stuffing
    crown roast of pork with, 312
    for poultry, 394
    sage, 973
Corn flakes
  coating for oven-fried chicken, 362
  -crumb shell, 793
Corn meal, 580
  brunch waffles, 659
  equivalent amounts, 26
  mush, 581
    fried, 582
  Southern spoon bread, 582
Corned beef
  glazed appetizer, 203
  hash, 297
  -macaroni casserole, 128
Cornell bread, 676
Cornish hens
  general data on, 357-358
  roast, with rice stuffing, 377
  on a spit, 377
Cornstarch, substitution for, 28
Cornucopias, 188
Country franks and beans, 943
Country meat loaf, 194
Crab(meat), 425-428
  appetizers
    cocktail, 195
    diamonds, 178
    fondue, hot, 207
    puffs, 185
    quiche, 189
    spread, 201

INDEX

Crab(meat)—*Continued*
avocado stuffed with, 606
bisque, 231
in bouillabaisse, 214
buying, 75, 426
casseroles
divan, 129
mixed seafood, 415
-mushroom, 957
-and-rice, 957
coquille, 437
deviled, 436
divan, 129
filling for Mexican turnovers, 106
freezing, 60
fried soft-shelled blue, 426
general data on, 425
imperial, Chesapeake, 427
Louis, 607
in New Orleans seafood gumbo, 215
pancakes filled with, 652
preparing, 426
salad
avocado stuffed with, 606
Louis, 607
in seafood bisque, 218
in seafood casserole, mixed, 415
soufflé, 427
stuffed lobster tails, 424
Cracked wheat, 580
bread, 677
Crackers
calorie counts, 77-78
equivalent amounts, 26
Cranberry(ies), 702-703
buying, 702
clafouti, 732
conversion chart, 33
cup, 986
freezing, 68
frost, 145
frosted beverage, 255
garnish for main dish, 154
general data on, 702-703
hearts, 263
-lemon punch, 260
-nut stuffing for any poultry, 395
orange bread, 641
pears, baked, à la mode, 728
pie, 790
preparing, 703
relish, 703
salad
molded, 613
-Waldorf, with fruit dressing, 142
Cranshaw melons
freezing, 69
selecting, 39
use of, 39
Cream
equivalent amounts, 26
freezing, 61
gravy, 360
storing, 73
substitution for, 28
See also Whipped cream
Cream cheese
deviled balls, 170
garnish for cold meat platter, 157
lemon frosting, 874
-sardine canapés, 182
spritz, 874
Cream pie
banana, 797
chocolate, 798

Cream puffs, 768-771
Brazilian, 769
coffee, 769
dough, for St. Honoré cake, 841
freezing, 55
general data on, 768
sundae-sauce, 768
swans, 770
Cream sauce, 481
for cannelloni, 598
mushroom, chicken breasts baked in, 373
sherried, 987
Creaming, 6, 13
Creamy dressing, citrus salad with, 129
Crème, coffee, for Brazilian cream puffs, 769
Crème brûlée, 732
Crème caramel, 736
Crème caramel frite, 779
Crème de menthe parfaits, 753
Creole
shrimp, 420
squash, 544
Crepes, 652-656
basic, 653
cheese fondue, 654
chicken livers in Madeira sauce, 655
creamed spinach, 655
dessert, 774-776
apple, 774
chestnut custard, 775
chocolate-cream, 775
lemon-cheese, 775
Suzette, 776
general data on, 652
ham-and-egg Benedict, 654
salmon velouté, 656
Suzette, 776
Crimping, 6
Croissants, French, 685
Croquettes, fish, 440
Croutons, 659-660
bacon, 660
baked, 660
buttered for garnish, 154
cheese, 660
garlic, 659
general data on, 659
herbed, 660
Crullers, lemon, 647
Crumbing, 6
Crunch topping for coffeecake, 637
Cubing, 6
Cucumber(s), 518-519
buying, 41, 75, 518
cooking, 519
dressing, 628
freezing, 64
fried rounds, 519
garnish
flower, for cold meat platters, 156
for main dish, 154
for soup, 153
general data on, 518-519
and shrimp sandwiches, 183
rolled, 183
salad, 596
Mexican, 107
ring, filled with turkey, 620
in sour cream, 596
with tangy sour cream dressing, 130
soup
cream of, 236

icy, 240
storing, 74
stuffed, 173
turkey salad in ring of, 620
Cumberland sauce for beef fondue, 295
Cumin seed, 977
Cupcakes, 846-847
glazed gingerbread, 848
Currant(s), 703, 718
bread, oatmeal, 675
conversion chart, 33
equivalent amounts, 27
freezing, 68
general data on, 703, 718
pink dressing, 626
storing, 718
Curry(ied)
appetizers
crabmeat dip, hot, 163
egg and bean sprout sandwiches, 182
-green onion dip, 199
-ham turnovers, 175
pastry bites, 180
vegetable dip, 165
chicken
cold creamy, 602
Hawaiian, 98
pancakes, 651
cream dressing, for poached turkey, 387
eggs, 466
fruit, hot, 728
ham turnovers with, 175
lamb, 337
mayonnaise for beef fondue, 296
pancakes, chicken-, 651
pastry bites, 180
pears, fresh, 713
Polynesian salad, 618
rice ring, 618
sauce
for beef fondue, 294
lemon, for Caribbean fish soufflé, 405
shrimp, 421
soup
East Indian, 236
Senegalese cream, 239
Curry powder, 965, 978
Custard
baked, 737
bread pudding, 735
cheese-bacon, 460
chestnut crepes, 775
chocolate turnover, 116
cream puff filling, 769
freezing, 55
lobster-cheese, 476
pie, 795
sauce, for Christmas plum pudding, 740
sherried, baked, 987
squash, 545
vanilla sauce, for date nut torte, 738
Cutting in, 7
Czechoslovakian
Christmas puzzle cookies, 886
kolacky, 688
nut filling for, 689
poppy seed filling for, 689
soup pot, 223

Daffodil cake, 828
Daiquiri cocktail, 270

Daiquiri cocktail—*Continued*
  frozen, 270
Dandelion greens
  buying, 42
  freezing, 64
Dash, 7
Date(s), 717
  bran muffins, 634
  conversion chart, 33
  equivalent amounts, 26
  fondant-stuffed, 897
  freezing, 68
  general data on, 717
  -nut candies, 896
  -nut surprise rolls, 638
  -nut torte, 737
  -peanut butter drops, 901
  -and-pecan logs, 896
  -pecan pie, 795
  pinwheels, 880
  spirit candy, 902
  storing, 717
  sweet raisin kugel, 716
Decaffeinated coffee, 243
Deep-fat fry, to, 7
Demitasse, 244
Desserts, 719-781
  ambrosia, 720
  apple
    brown Betty, 724
    crepes, 774
    dumplings, rosy, 725
    kuchen, quick, 725
    pandowdy, 724
    roll, Mrs. Chandler's, 726
  apricot
    curried fruit, hot, 728
    sauce for beignets soufflés, 780
  baba au fraises, 780
  baked Alaska, 759
  banana
    fruits mandarin, 721
    mousse, 745
  beignets soufflés with apricot sauce, 779
  Belgian waffles, 777
  biscuit tortoni, 753
  blintzes with assorted fillings, 773
  calorie counts, 81
  cannoli, 778
  caramel crème frite, 779
  caramelized sugar for floating island pudding, 733
  cherry
    brandy mousse, 746
    curried fruit, hot, 728
    floating island, 701
  chocolate
    cake, refrigerator, 751
    crepes, -cream, 775
    éclair filling, 771
    éclairs, frozen, 770
    fondue, 771
    ice cream, 756
    ice cream, -chip, 756
    ice cream, rum nut, 756
    mocha mousse coronet cake, 747
    pancakes with peppermint whipped cream, 772
    pears supreme, 722
    pot-de-crème, 733
    pudding, deluxe bread, 735
    pudding, nesselrode, 734
    pudding, steamed, 739
    sauce, bittersweet, 762
    sauce, fudge, 762

  sauce, rum, 762
  soufflé, 764
  soufflé froid au chocolat, 748
Christmas
  plum pudding, 740
  pudding, English, 741
cloud nine cream, 720
coeur à la crème, 720
coffee
  cognac ice cream, 757
  crème for Brazilian cream puffs, 769
  jelly, 743
cottage pudding with sauce, 736
cranberry
  clafouti, 732
  pears, baked, à la mode, 728
cream puffs, 768-771
  Brazilian, 769
  coffee, 769
  dough, 841
  freezing, 55
  general data on, 768
  sundae-sauce, 768
  swans, 770
crème brûlée, 732
crème caramel, 736
crème de menthe parfaits, 753
crepes
  apple, 774
  chestnut custard, 775
  chocolate-cream, 775
  lemon-cheese, 775
  Suzette, 776
custard
  baked, 737
  bread pudding, 735
  chestnut crepes, 775
  cream filling for sundae-sauce cream puffs, 769
  sauce, vanilla, for date nut torte, 738
éclairs, frozen chocolate, 770
  chocolate filling for, 771
English Christmas pudding, 741
fondue, chocolate, 771
freezing, 55
frozen, 753-755
  biscuit tortoni, 753
  chocolate éclairs, 770
  crème de menthe parfaits, 753
  fruit-studded log, 753
  lemon-crunch freeze, 754
  mocha bombe, 754
  plum pudding, 755
fruit, 719-732
  Betty, 728
  cream, exotic, 720
  curried, hot, 728
  flan, 726
  fluff, low calorie, 723
  hot, 724-730
  ice cream, 757
  mandarin, 721
  shortcakes, 730-732
  -studded log, 753
gelatine, 742-745
  coffee jelly, 743
  fruit fluff, low calorie, 723
  general data on, 742-743
  orange cream in orange cups, 743
  snow pudding, 744
  strawberry charlotte Russe, 744
general data on, 719
grapefruit, in fruits mandarin, 721
ice cream, 755-757, 759-761

  almond, burnt, 757
  baked Alaska, 759
  bombe glacée, 769
  bombe, jubilee, 760
  butter pecan, 757
  cake filled with, 849
  chocolate, 756
  chocolate chip, 757
  chocolate heavenly pie, 806
  chocolate rum nut, 756
  coconut, toasted, 757
  coffee cognac, 757
  flavor variations, 756-757
  freezing, 61
  fruit, 757
  general data on, 755
  peanut ripple, 119
  peppermint stick, 757
  refrigerator tray, 756-757
  ribbon Alaska pie, 805
  rainbow meringue glacé, 761
  sweet tart shell for, 807
  tub-churn, 755-757
  vanilla refrigerator-tray, 756
  vanilla tub-churn, 775
ice-cream sauces, 761-763
  butterscotch, rich, 763
  chocolate, bittersweet, 762
  chocolate fudge, 762
  chocolate rum, 762
  maple-nut, 763
  pineapple, 763
  pineapple mint, 763
  strawberry, 763
ices
  lemon, 758
  raspberry, 758
Indian pudding, baked, 738
lemon
  -cheese crepes, 775
  -crunch freeze, 754
  ice, 758
  mousse, 746
  sherbet, 758
lime, key, 751
meringues, 750-751
  general data on, 750
  nests, 751
  shell, 750
mocha
  bombe, 754
  mousse coronet cake, 747
mousses, 745-749
  banana, 745
  cherry-brandy, 746
  au chocolat, soufflé froid, 748
  cinnamon-chocolate, 108
  general data on, 745
  lemon, 746
  mocha coronet cake, 747
  nesselrode pudding, 734
  orange Grand Marnier, 748
  peanut brittle, 747
  raspberry-macaroon, 749
  strawberry festival, 749
  strawberry, fresh, 748
omelets, flaming, 451
orange(s)
  ambrosia, 720
  in Cointreau, 721
  cream in orange cups, 743
  crepes Suzette, 776
  fruits mandarin, 721
  Grand Marnier, 748
  sauce, foamy, 767
  sherbet, 759

INDEX

Desserts—*Continued*
 soufflé, 766
 pancakes, 772-774
  blintzes, 773
  chocolate with peppermint
   whipped cream, 772
  coconut with cinnamon whipped
   cream, 772
  Swedish, flaming, 773
 peach
  cottage pudding with peach
   sauce, 736
  crisp, 729
  fruit flan, 726
  melba, 723
 peanut brittle mousse, 747
 pears
  chocolate, supreme, 722
  cranberry, baked, à la mode, 728
  Hélène, 722
  streusel à la mode, 729
 Piedmont pudding, 739
 pineapple
  cloud nine cream, 720
  curried fruit, hot, 728
  sponge shortcake, 731
  syrup, 763
  syrup, mint, 763
 plum
  pudding, Christmas, 740
  pudding, frozen, 755
 puddings, 732-742
  bread, chocolate, deluxe, 735
  bread, custard, 735
  bread, queen of, 735
  chocolate pot-de-crème, 733
  chocolate steamed, 739
  Christmas plum, 740
  cottage, with peach sauce, 736
  crème brûlée, 732
  crème caramel, 736
  custard, baked, 737
  custard bread, 735
  date nut torte, 737
  English Christmas, 741
  floating island, 733
  Indian, baked, 738
  lemon, baked, 738
  nesselrode, 734
  Piedmont, 739
  plum, Christmas, 740
  plum, frozen, 755
  queen of bread, 735
  rhubarb, baked, 729
  rice, 739
  rice, brown, 734
  rum, refrigerator, 752
  zabaglione, 734
 raspberry
  dream, 723
  ice, 758
  -macaroon mousse, 749
  peach melba, 723
 refrigerator, 751-752
  chocolate cake, 751
  Key lime, 751
  rum pudding, 752
  toffee, 752
 rhubarb
  fruit Betty, 728
  pudding, baked, 729
 rice
  pudding, 739
  pudding, brown, 734
 rum
  baba au fraises, 780

 pudding, refrigerator, 752
 sherbet
  emerald milk, 757
  freezing, 56
  lemon, 758
  lime, cantaloupe with, 126
  orange, 759
  strawberry Dolley Madison, 759
 shortcakes, fruit, 730-732
  biscuits, basic, 730
  cranberry clafouti, 732
  pineapple sponge, 731
  strawberry, old-fashioned, 731
 snow pudding, 744
 soufflé
  fresh strawberry, 748
  froid au chocolat, 748
 soufflés, hot, 764-767
  almond, 765
  chocolate, 764
  coconut with chocolate sauce, 764
  orange, 766
  strawberry, 748
  vanilla, 767
 strawberry
  baba au fraises, 780
  charlotte russe, 744
  coeur à la crème, 720
  fruit Betty, 728
  fruit fluff, low calorie, 723
  fruited cream, exotic, 720
  mousse, festival, 749
  sauce, 763
  sherbet Dolley Madison, 759
  shortcake, old-fashioned, 731
  soufflé, fresh, 748
 Swedish pancakes, flaming, 773
 vanilla
  custard sauce for date nut torte,
   738
  ice cream, refrigerator tray, 756
  ice cream, tub-churn, 755
  soufflé, 767
 waffles, 776-778
  Belgian, 777
  graham with fudge sauce, 777
  sweet, 776
 zabaglione, 734
 See also categories of desserts
Deutsch tenderloin tips, 291
Deviled crab, 436
Deviled egg(s), 203
 canapés, 179
 casserole, 463
 with cheese, 174
 mold, 621
Deviled ham
 filling, 205
 Tetrazzini, 945
Devil's food cake, 817
 chocolate nut, 853
 dark, 818
 double chocolate frosted, 853
 one-bowl, 823
Dewberries, freezing, 67
Diable sauce, 485
 basting, 492
Dicing, 7
Dill, 971
 garnish for vegetables, 159
 lima beans with, 505
 pickles, 922
Dilled
 beans, 923
 MacTurkey, 388
Dips, *see* Appetizers

Dissolving, 7
Dobos torte, quick, 852
Dough
 cream puff, 841
 kneading, 663
Doughnuts, 646-647
 general data on, 646
 lemon crullers, 647
 rich, 646
Dream bars, 864
Dredging, 7
Dressing, 7
Dressings, 623-629
 avocado, 988
  cream, 629
 bacon for spinach salad, hot, 596
 blue cheese
  French, 626
  French with wine, 988
  mayonnaise, 626
 brown rice, roast duckling with, 147
 calorie counts, 79
 cardamom cream, for fruit salad,
  590
 chef's, 587
 chiffonade, Belgian endive salad
  with, 594
 cooked
  basic, 628
  general data on, 623
  mustard, 628
  sour cream, 628
 cream-based
  avocado, 629
  cucumber, 628
  general data on, 623
  orange, 629
 creamy, citrus salad with, 129
 cucumber, 628
 curry cream, for poached turkey,
  387
 French
  basic, 626
  blue cheese, 626
  garlic, 627
  general data on, 623
  honey, 627
  lime, 626
  mint, 627
  olive oil, 627
  sherry, 626
 fruit, cranberry Waldorf salad
  with, 142
 general data on, 623
 green goddess, 625
 Hawaiian, 100
 herb, roast pork with, 311
 honey-lime, 625
 Italian, 627
 mayonnaise
  basic, 623
  blender, 624
  blue cheese, 626
  curried, for beef fondue, 296
  general data on, 623
  green goddess, 625
  honey-lime, 625
  pink currant, 626
  Russian, 624
  storing, 73
  strawberry cream, 625
  Thousand Island, 624
 mustard, 628
  Belgian endive with, 148
  slaw with pineapple and, 128
 orange cream, 629

Dressings—*Continued*
  pecan, turkey breast with, 386
  pink currant, 626
  rice, brown, for roast duckling, 147
  Russian, 624
  sour cream, 628
    for coleslaw, 595
    tangy, cucumber salad with, 130
  spinach, half-crown roast of pork
    with, 312
  storing, 73
  strawberry cream, 625
  Thousand Island, 624
  vinaigrette, 627
  wine
    with avocado, 988
    with blue cheese, 988
    with herb chili sauce, 988
Dried beans, 551-552
  Burgundy, 552
    with beef, 938
  country franks and, 943
  general data on, 43, 551-552
  preparing for cooking, 552
  succotash, 518
Dried fruits, 717
  baked fruit compote, 717
  preparing, 717
  rice with, 565
  storing, 717
  See also names of fruits
Dried lentil(s), 551-552
  baked, 555
  -frankfurter stew, 354
  general data on, 551-552
  preparing for cooking, 552
  and short ribs, 555
  -and-split pea soup, 215
Dried pea(s), 551-552
  general data on, 43, 551-552
  preparing for cooking, 552
  rarebit, 553
  savory supper dish, 554
  soup, 228
    with lentils, 215
Duckling, 390-391
  buying, 76
  freezing, 59
  general data on, 390
  roast
    with brown rice dressing, 146
    with green grape stuffing, 390
    holiday menu, 143-149
    orange-glazed, 390
  roasting timetable, 54
Dumplings, 643-644
  apple, rosy, 725
  and-chicken soup, 221
  fruit, shaping, 726
  general data on, 643
  parsley, 221, 644
  for soup, 644
Dusting, 7

East Indian curry soup, 236
Easter
  bread, Italian, 690
  eggs, colored, 691
Eclairs
  chocolate, frozen, 770
  freezing, 55
Edam cheese, 469
Egg(s), 442-466
  appetizers
    bacon and circle sandwiches, 179
    deviled, 203

  deviled, cheese-stuffed, 172
  deviled canapés, 179
  filling for pinwheel sandwiches,
    205
  en gelée, 193
  and radish filling for glazed party
    canapés, 180
  and bacon sandwiches, 179
  baking, 447
  Benedict
    ham and, crepes, 654
    poached, 459
  buying, 442-444
  calorie counts, 83
  carbohydrate gram counts, 88
  casseroles, 956-957
    baked noodles and, 957
    beef and, 956
    deviled, 463
    green island, 464
    -salad, 484
  with cheese sauce, 464
  cheese-bacon custard, 460
  Chinese slivered, 465
  cookies, hard-cooked, 874
  cooking
    in egg cookers, 446
    hard, 446
    soft, 446
  curried, with banana tidbits, 466
  deviled, 203
    canapés, 179
    casserole, 463
    with cheese, 174
    mold, 621
  diluted white or yolk, 7
  for dinner dishes, 463-466
  Easter, colored, 691
  equivalent amounts, 26
  filling for pinwheel sandwiches, 205
  foo yung, 461
    sauce 438
    shrimp, 438
  frying, 445-446
    in electric skillets, 446
    -steam, 446
    traditional 445
    without fat, 446
  gadgets for cooking, 444
  general data on, 442-448
  glaze, for hot cross buns, 683
  golden buck, 474
  grades of, 442-443
  ham and
    crepes Benedict, 654
    scallop, 464
  hard-cooking, 446
  lobster Newburg with, 465
  for luncheon, 459-461
    cheese bacon custards, 460
    foo yung, 461
    poached, Benedict, 459
    Scotch woodcock, 460
    shirred with bacon, 460
  nutritive values, 993, 998, 999
  omelets, 449-451
    chicken liver, 450
    flaming dessert, 451
    fluffy, 450-451
    French, 449-450
    general data on, 449, 450-451
    making, 449
    mushroom, 450
    plain, 449
    Spanish, 450
    spinach, 450

  peeling hard-cooked, 447
  for picnics, 461-462
  poaching, 447
  and radish filling for glazed party
      canapés, 180
  salad, 462
    bacon and, 462
    casserole, 466
    salmon salad and, platter, 608
  Scotch woodcock, 460
  scrambled, 448
    baked, 448
    creamy, 448
  separating, 444
  shell color, 443
  shirred, with bacon, 460
  sizing, 443
  sliced with tarragon and mushroom
      sauce, 463
  soft-cooking, 446
  soufflés, *see* Soufflés
  for special breakfasts, 459-461
    cheese-bacon custards, 460
    foo yung, 461
    poached, Benedict, 459
    Scotch woodcock, 460
    shirred, with bacon, 460
  storing, 72, 447
    leftover yolks and whites, 445
  stuffed
    à la Russe, 462
    special, 461
  stuffing for flounder Florentine,
      407
  substitution for, 28
  use in cooking, 445-448
  utensils to use, 443-444
  whites
    beating, 452
    diluting, 7
  yolks, diluting, 7
Egg drop soup, 230
Eggnog
  children's candystick punch, 259
  holiday, 264
  orange punch, 262
  pie, 803
  sauce for baked rhubarb pudding,
      730
  snowy punch, 263
Eggplant(s), 519-521
  buying, 41, 75
  freezing, 64
  general data on, 519
  herb-broiled, 520
  in moussaka, 947
  parmigiana, 519
  Provençale, stuffed, 521
  in ratatouille, 520
  spread, 204
  storing, 74
  -and-tomato scallop, 520
Elderberries, freezing, 67
Emerald milk sherbet, 757
Endive, *see* Belgian endive
English
  beef-and-kidney pie, 939
  Christmas pudding, 741
  grill, 332
  toffee, 906
Entrecôte with watercress, 288
Equipment, 14-17
  measuring utensils, 10-11
  oven, 17
  preparing, 16-17
  storing, 16

Equipment—*Continued*
top of range, 17
Equivalent amounts table, 26-27
Escarole, general data on, 585
Espagnole sauce, *see* Brown
(Espagnole) Sauce
Espresso, 244

Falafel, 556
Farina
gnocchi Romano, 582
Fastnacht, 686
Fats
calorie counts, 79
carbohydrate gram counts, 88-89
nutritive values and sources,
994-995
Fennel seed, 977
Fettucine, 569
Few drops, 7
Few grains, 7
Figs, 703, 718
conversion chart, 33
dried, 718
freezing, 68
general data on, 703, 718
preparing, 703
Filling
apple, for blintzes, 774
blueberry, for blintzes, 774
cheese
for blintzes, 774
for cannoli, 778
chocolate
-almond, for cream torte, 838
chiffon, for St. Honoré cake, 841
for frozen éclairs, 771
mocha butter, for bûche de Noël,
149
velvet, for blitz torte, 851
coconut-honey, for cookies, 878
crab meat, for Mexican turnovers,
106
custard cream, 769
egg
for pinwheel sandwiches, 205
and radish, for glazed party
canapés, 180
ham, deviled, 205
lemon, for wedding cake, 856
meat, for cannelloni, 578
mincemeat, for cookies, 878
nut
for kolacky, 689
poppy seed, for kolacky, 689
prune, for cookies, 878
radish and egg, for glazed party
canapés, 180
shrimp, for glazed party
canapés, 180
spinach, for ravioli, 580
Finnan haddie, creamed, 441
Fish, 397-441
baked stuffed, 404
bass
à la Franey, 408
baked stuffed, 415
cold poached, with watercress
sauce, 408
batter-fried, 401
bluefish à la Franey, 408
bouillabaisse, 214
quick, 413
broiled, 402
broiled marinated, 403
buying, 75-76, 397-398

calorie counts, 79-80
canned, 435-441
carbohydrate gram counts, 88-89
carp, baked stuffed, 405
and chips, 411
cioppino, 414
cod
fillet, poached, 404
fish and chips, 411
steaks, poached, 410
cooking, 399-400
croquettes, 440
fillets
baked, sweet-and-sour, 406
batter-baked, 407
in bouillabaisse, 214, 413
cioppino, 414
flounder, baked, sweet-and-sour,
406
flounder Florentine, 406
gumbo, 414
mackerel, mustard-broiled, 410
with Marguéry sauce, 412
poached, 432
poached in wine, 987
poached with mustard
caper/sauce, 404
sautéed, 401
sole *see* Sole
finnan haddie, creamed, 441
freezing, 59-60
fried, menu for, 96
general data on, 397
gumbo, 414
haddock,
fillets, in tomato-fish chowder,
216
steaks, poached, 410
halibut
in bouillabaisse, 214
in cioppino, 414
steaks, poached, 410
herring
kippered, 441
salad, 611
mackerel
buying, 75
fillets, mustard broiled, 410
meunière, 402
New England chowder, 216
nutritive values, 993, 998, 999, 1001
pan-fried whole, 400
perch, in bouillabaisse, 413
red snapper
à la Franey, 408
baked stuffed, 405
vegetable-stuffed baked whole,
406
salmon
Béarnaise, 411
buying, 76
crepes, velouté, 656
croquettes, 440
loaf, sauced, 440
pinwheels, 181
salad and eggs platter, 608
stuffed turbans, with Béarnaise
sauce, 409
sole, fillet of
amandine, 402
baked, stuffed with lobster, 409
bonne femme, 412
in cioppino, 414
cooked in wine, 974
in mixed seafood casserole, 415
in seafood bisque, 218

stuffed salmon turbans with
Béarnaise sauce, 409
Véronique, 413
with white wine sauce, 123
Soufflé, Caribbean, 404
steaks
anchovy-butter sauce for, 403
broiled, 403
mustard sauce for, 411
poached, 410
poached in wine, 987
salmon Béarnaise, 411
salmon turbans, stuffed, with
Béarnaise sauce, 409
swordfish, broiled marinated, 403
swordfish Béarnaise, 411
stock, 212
storing, 73, 398-399
swordfish
Béarnaise, 411
broiled marinated, 403
tarragon sauce for, 976
tartar sauce for, 401
-tomato chowder, 216
trout
broiled, 402
meuniére, 402
tuna
à la king, 439
-cashew casserole, 120
-chip bake, 438
croquettes, 440
fritters, crunchy, 646
-macaroni casserole, 958
-potato skillet pie, 439
puff/appetizers, 186
salad, 610, 611, 622
-and-spinach casserole, 959
spread, 202
wine sauce for, 989
See also Seafood; Shellfish
Flaking, 7
Flambé, 7
Flaming apple tart, 806
Flaming dessert omelet, 451
Floating island, 733
cherry, 701
Florentine
Christmas cookies, 886
flounder, 406
luncheon meat casserole, 946
soufflé, 454
Flounder
in bouillabaisse, 214
fillet of, Florentine, 406
in New England fish chowder, 216
sweet-and-sour baked, 406
Flour
buying, 76
equivalent amounts, 27
measuring, 11
storing, 72
substitution for, 28, 29
Fluffy omelets, 450-451
Fluoride, nutritive values and sources,
1001
Fluting, 7
Folacin, nutritive values and sources,
999
Folding in, 7
Folic acid, *see* Folacin
Fondant
fruited rolls, 897
mint balls, 897
mocha logs, 897
no-cook, 897

Fondant—*Continued*
-stuffed fruits, 897
Fondue
  beef, 293-296
    Béarnaise sauce, quick, 294
    Cumberland sauce, 295
    curried mayonnaise, 296
    curry sauce, 294
    horseradish-chive sauce, 295
    mushroom-catsup sauce, 296
    tomato sauce, 294
  cheese, 472
    crepes, 654
    Yankee, 473
  chocolate, 771
  crab, hot, 207
  oriental, 295
Foo yung
  eggs, 461
  sauce, 438
  shrimp, 438
Food, 25-91
  appearance of, 150-161
  buying, 20-24
    for two, 75-76
  calorie counts, 77-87
  carbohydrate gram counts, 87-91
  cheese, principal varieties of, 29-32
  equivalent amounts table, 26-27
  freezing, 54-70
    fruits, 56, 67-70
    packaging for, 915-917
    vegetables, 62-66
  fruits, fresh, 32-40
    conversion chart, 32-34
    freezing, 56, 67-70, 913-915
    selecting, 34-40
    using, 34-40
  ingredient substitution table, 27-29
  meat broiling timetables, 50-51
    beef, 50
    lamb, 51
    pork, smoked, 50-51
    poultry, 52
  meat roasting timetables, 44-49
    beef, 44-46
    lamb, 48-49
    pork, fresh, 46-47
    pork, smoked, 47-48
    poultry, 51-54
    veal, 49
  preparing wisely, 20-24
  storing, 19-20, 70-75
    equipment for, 16
  vegetables, dried, 43
  vegetables, fresh, 40-43
    buying, 40-43
    freezing, 62-66, 915
  See also Cooking; Nutrition
Four-bean salad, 593
Frankfurter(s), 351-355
  appetizers
    in blankets, 187
    butterfly, 201
    sweet-and-sour, 191
  baked beans and, 353
  barbecued, 354
  buying, 76
  casseroles, 943-944
    chili, 943
    country and beans, 943
    -and-macaroni, 944
    and rice, 944
  German-style and, potato salad, 606
  Knackwurst-with-sauerkraut
    dinner, 353

Lyonnaise potatoes and, 355
-potato puff, 355
stew, -lentil, 354
on a stick, 354
storing, 73
Freezing, 54-70, 913-917
  fruits, 56, 67-70, 913-915
  packaging for, 915-917
  vegetables, 62-66, 915
French
  au pistou, 224
  bread
    Grùyere with Onion Soup, 229
    rapid-mix method, 670
  croissants, 685
  chocolate beverage, 252
  chocolate icing for bûche de Noël,
    149
  fried onion rings, 125, 528
  omelets, 449-450
    chicken liver, 450
    making, 449
    mushroom, 450
    Spanish, 450
    spinach, 450
  peas, 530
  radish tartine, 182
  strawberry pie, 799
  toast, 656-657
    basic, 656
    crispy, 657
    general data on, 656
    strawberry whipped butter for,
      657
French dressing
  basic, 626
  blue cheese, 626
  garlic, 627
  general data on, 623
  honey, 627
  lime, 626
  mint, 627
  olive oil, 627
  sherry, 626
    with avocado, 988
    with blue cheese, 988
    with herb chili sauce, 988
French endive, *see* Belgian endive
Fricassee, 7
Fritters, 644-646
  apple-ring, 645
  basic, 645
  clam, 645
  corn, 645
  crunchy tuna, 646
  general data on, 644
  oyster, 645
Frizzle, to, 7
Frostings, 856-860
  butter-cream, 856
    almond, 856
    browned, 857
    cherry, 857
    chocolate, 857
    coffee, 857
    lemon, 857
    maple-nut, 857
    mocha, 857
    orange, 857
    peanut, 857
    peppermint, 857
  caramel, 858
    quick, 858
  cocoa whipped cream, 860
  confectioners', thin, 889
  four-minute fudge, 858

general data on, 815-816
Hungarian, 858
Lady Baltimore, 860
lemon cream-cheese, 859
orange, 864
ornamental, 884
swirl, 859
  maple, 859
thin confectioners', for
  pfeffernuesse, 888
vanilla petits fours, 847
white mountain, 859
Fruit(s), 32-40, 693-718
  ambrosia, 720
  Burgundy cooler, 986
  buying, 75, 76, 693-694
  cakes, 842-846
    baking, 842
    bourbon-pecan, 844
    decorating, 843
    extra rich dark, 843
    general data on, 842-843
    golden honey, 845
    pans for, 842
    refrigerator, 846
    storing, 842
    white, 843
  calorie counts, 80-81
  canned, 694
  carbohydrate gram counts, 88-89
  compote, baked, 717
  conversion chart, 32-34
  cookie bars, 865
  desserts, 719-732
    baked, 699
    Betty, 728
    cream, exotic, 720
    curried, hot, 728
    flambé, 699
    flan, 726
    fluff, low calorie, 723
    hot, 724-730
    ice cream, 757
    mandarin, 721
    shortcakes, 730-732
    -studded log, 753
  dressing, cranberry Waldorf salad
    with, 142
  dried, 717
    baked compote, 717
    buying, 717
    preparing, 717
    rice with, 565
    storing, 717
  fondant rolls, 897
  fondant-stuffed, 897
  freezing, 56, 67-70, 913-915
  fresh, 32-40, 693
    conversion chart, 32-34
    freezing, 56, 67-70, 913-915
    selecting, 34-40
    using, 34-40
  frozen, 693
  general data on, 693-694
  glaze
    for bourbon-pecan cake, 845
    for cheesecake, 831
  hot curried, 728
  ice cream, 757
  ice cubes, 261
  ice ring, 261
  ices
    freezing, 56
    lemon, 758
    raspberry, 758
  juices

INDEX

Fruits—*Continued*
  calorie counts, 80-81
  carbohydrate gram counts, 89
  storage of, 73
nutritive values, 996, 1000
pancakes, 648
parfait
  apricot, 697
  breakfast, 696
rice with, 565
salad
  with cardamom cream dressing,
    590
  citrus, 138
  citrus, with creamy dressing, 129
  five cup, 590
  fresh, 124
  fresh, with wine-gelatin cubes,
    600
  frozen, 592
  plate, 600
  twenty-four-hour, 590
sausage stuffing, roast goose with,
  145
selecting, 34-40
shortcake, 730-732
  biscuit, basic, 730
  cranberry clafouti, 732
  pineapple sponge, 731
  strawberry, old-fashioned, 731
shrub drink, 256
with spiced sour cream dip, 165
storing, 72
-studded log, 753
stuffing
  for poultry, 394
  sausage, roast goose with, 145
syllabub punch, 260
syrup, for pancakes, 649
using, 34-40
-vegetable blend drink, 257
watermelon filled with, 707
See also names of fruits
Fruited
  Burgundy cooler punch, 986
  exotic cream, 720
  fondant rolls, 897
  pecans, 906
  pork roast, 313
Frying, 7
  deep-fat, 7
  pan-, 8
  sautéing, 9
Fudge
  brownies, 862
  chocolate, 907
    perfect-every-time, 907
    -marshmallow, 894
    sauce, 762
  four-minute frosting, 858
  peanut butter, 908
  -peanut drops, 907
  sauce
    graham waffles with, 777
    for pears Hélène, 722
  vanilla-wafer, 902

Game, freezing, 59
Garbanzo beans, in four-bean salad,
  594
Garlic
  bread cubes for chef's salad, 587
  butter
    hamburgers with, 303
    mussels with, 435
    sauce, for spaghetti, 576

croutons, 659
French dressing, 627
sautéed chicken with forty cloves of,
  367
Garlic powder, 978
Garlic salt, 978
Garnishes
  for cold-meat platters, 156-158
  for main dishes, 154-156
  for sandwiches, 156-158
  for soups, 153-154
  for vegetables, 158-159
Garnishing, 7
Gazpacho, 237
  jellied, 134
Gelatin
  freezing, 56
  -wine cubes, 600
Gelatine
  desserts, 742-745
    coffee jelly, 743
    general data on, 742-743
    orange cream in orange cups, 743
    snow pudding, 744
    strawberry charlotte russe, 744
  equivalent amounts, 27
  freezing, 56
  orange, 989
German
  apple pancakes, 650
  potato salad, baked, 597
    franks and, 606
  short ribs, 301
Giblet(s), 358-359
  gravy, 360, 382
  stuffing for poultry, 394
  turkey, cooked, 383
Gift packaging cookies, 891
Gimlet cocktail, 270
Gin fizz, 271
Ginger, 964
  -chicken spread, 167
  -cream chicken salad, 602
  muffins, 634
  -pear appetizer, 193
Gingerbread
  cake, 824
  Christmas cookies
    house, 883
    men, 883
    ornamental frosting for, 884
    patterns for, 882
    trees, 881
  cupcakes, glazed, 848
Gingersnap-crumb shell, 793
Glacé, rainbow meringue, 761
Glacée, bombe, 760
Glaze
  apricot, 102
  barbecue sauce, 364
  for bourbon-pecan cake, 845
  cake
    peppermint, 860
    pineapple, 832
    See also Cake, frostings
  for cheesecake, 832
  for chicken
    barbecue sauce, 364
    herb, 364
    pineapple, 137
    wine, 364
  for chocolate marmalade cake, 820
  confectioners', for Santa's bread,
    688
  egg, for hot cross buns, 683
  for fruit flan, 727

for gingerbread cupcakes, 848
for ham, 102, 208, 323
lemon, for cream cheese spritz, 874
for marzipan, 900
orange, for carrots, 512
pie top, 788
praline, for drop cookies, 870
Glazing, 8
Gnocchi, Romano, 582
Gold cake, 819
Golden buck, 474
Golden chiffon cake, 827
Golden honey fruit cake, 845
Golden yellow cake, 824
Goose, 391-392
  freezing, 59
  general data on, 391
  roast
    with chestnut stuffing, 391
    holiday menu, 143-149
    with sausage-fruit stuffing, 145
  roasting timetable, 54
Gooseberries
  conversion chart, 33
  freezing, 68
  general data on, 700
Gouda cheese, 469
  stuffed, 169
Goulash
  beef
    easy, 305
    Hungarian, 300
    paprikash, 306
Graham cracker
  bread, 641
  -crumb shell, 792
  waffles with fudge sauce, 777
Granola, Rachel's, 583
Grape(s), 38, 704-705
  ade cooler, 255
  buying, 75
  and chicken salad, 619
  chicken Véronique, 366
  continental, 705
  conversion chart, 33
  freezing, 68-69
  frosted, 158
    apricot-glazed ham with, 102
    garnish for cold meat platters,
      158
    roast fresh ham with, 141
  in fruit-filled watermelon, 707
  general data on, 38, 704-705
  green, stuffing roast duckling, with,
    390
  jelly, 934
  marzipan, 900
  pie, 790
  selecting, 38
  storing, 72, 705
  in stuffed pineapple, 714
  using, 38
  varieties, 38
Grapefruit, 704
  buying, 704
  in candied citrus peel, 894
  conversion chart, 33
  freezing, 68
  fruits mandarin, 721
  general data on, 704
  honey-baked, 704
  preparing, 704
  salad
    citrus, 138
    citrus with creamy dressing, 129
    molded, 613

Grasshopper cocktail, 271
Grasshopper pie, 798
Grating, 8
Gravy
  cream, 360
  giblet, 360, 382
  herb, baked chicken with, 110
  milk, 311
  roast chicken, 360
  for standing rib roast, 281
Greasing, 8
Greek Christmas cookie crescents, 887
Green bean(s), 503-504
  buying, 41, 75, 503
  casserole, 504
    and chicken livers, 955
  dilled, 923
  freezing, 62
  with fried onions and thyme, 503
  general data on, 503
  pole, amandine, 504
  salad, 593
    four-bean, 593
  savory, 503, 975
  storing, 74
Green goddess dressing, 625
Green goddess soup, 240
Green grape stuffing, roast duckling
    with, 390
Green island casserole, 464
Green onion(s)
  -curry dip, 199
  general data on, 526
Green peas, see Peas
Green pepper(s), 539-540
  buying, 42, 75, 539
  chicken livers with bacon and, 125
  freezing, 57, 65
  garnish for vegetables, 158
  general data on, 539
  Italian-style, 539
  in mixed vegetable pickles, 924
  nutritive values, 1000
  and onions, scalloped, 528
  preparing for use, 539
  in ratatouille, 520
  relish
    piccalilli, 929
    sweet, 929
  rice with cashews and, 565
  sirloin steak with, 292
  storing, 74
  stuffed, 539
  veal with, 344
  See also Red peppers
Green tomato pickle, 928
Greens, 522-524
  buying, 523
  cooking
    boiling, 523
    steaming, 523
  freezing, 64
  general data on, 522-523, 603-605
  mustard, in sour cream, 523
  spinach
    creamed, 523
    Swiss, 523
  storing, 74
  See also names of greens
Griddle scones, 636
Grilling, 8
Grinding, 8
Grits, hominy, 580
  soufflé, 581
Groats, buckwheat
  kasha varnishkis, 583

Gruyère cheese, 469
  fondue, 472
  onion soup with, 229
Guacamole, 105
Gumbo
  fish, 414
  New Orleans seafood, 215

Haddock
  fillets in tomato-fish chowder, 216
  steaks, poached, 410
Halibut
  in bouillabaisse, 214
  in cioppino, 414
  steaks, poached, 410
Ham, 322-328
  appetizers
    -asparagus pinwheels, 175
    baked orange-glazed, 208
    and curry turnovers, 175
    deviled filling, 205
    and peanut spread, 198
    roulades, 175
    tartlets, 185
  apricot-glazed, 102
  barbecued steak, 326
  -bologna, 352
  broiled
    with mustard pickles, 130, 325
    steak, 325
  buying, 76
  calorie counts, 90
  casseroles, 948-950
    baked, Tetrazzini, 948
    creamed, 949
    deviled Tetrazzini, 945
    lima beans and, 949
  and chicken mousse, 617
  in crust, 324
  deviled
    filling, 205
    Tetrazzini, 945
  and eggs
    crepes Benedict, 654
    scallop, 464
  freezing, 59
  garnish for soups, 154
  general data on, 322-323
  glazed baked, 323
    steak, 325
  glazed meatballs, 327
  glazes for, 323
  glazing, 155
  honey-broiled steak with sweet
      potatoes, 326
  meat loaf, 309
  meatballs with sour cream-mustard
      sauce, 327
  menu for baked, 96
  orange-glazed, 208, 323
    loaf, 327
  pecan-topped picnic, 324
  roast fresh
    with frosted grapes, 142
    holiday menu, 139-143
  salad
    -and chicken mousse, 617
    holiday mold, 619
    -macaroni loaf, 605
    and melon, 604
  stuffed slices, 326
Hamburgers
  broiled, 303
  cheese-stuffed, 303
  with garlic sauce, 303
  general data on, 302

  hash, 307
  juicy, 302
  -and-noodles Stroganoff, 941
  pan-fried, 303
  Stroganoff, 305
  in wine, 987
Hard sauce, for English Christmas
    pudding, 742
Harvard beets, 506
Hash
  corned beef, 297
  hamburger, 307
Hawaiian
  cheesecake, pineapple, 100
  curried chicken, 98
  fried rice, 99
  luau, 97
  pork kabobs, 99
  salad, 99
  scallops and shrimps sautéed, 98
  sweet potatoes, 121
Hazelnut drop cookies, 868
Head cheese, 352
Heart
  Andalouse, 347
  beef, baked stuffed, 346
  freezing, 58
  general data on, 278
Herb(s), 962-979
  basic chart, 964-965
  bouquet garni, 967
  broiled eggplant, 520
  butter, 967
    lamb chops with, 331
    sauce, 490
  buying, 76
  chili sauce with wine French
      dressing, 988
  dressing, roast pork with, 311
  -flour coating for fried chicken, 363
  fresh, substitution for, 28
  general data on, 962-979
  glaze for broiled chicken, 364
  gravy, baked chicken with, 110
  mushrooms and, 525
  shopping list, 963-964
  stuffing for poultry, 393
  See also names of herbs
Herbed
  baked chicken, 363
  baked tomatoes, 968
  croutons, 660
  peas and onions, 530
  spoon bread, 969
  roast leg of lamb, 329
Hermit cookies, 868
Herring
  kippered, fried, 441
  salad, 611
Hibachi chicken, 365
High altitude cooking, 24
Holiday dinners, 131-149
Holiday punch
  eggnog, 264
  wine, 264
Hollandaise sauce, 488-489
  artichokes with, 200
  blender, 489
  classic, 488
    Béarnaise, 489
  jiffy, 507
  less-rich, 488
    Béarnaise, 489
Hominy grits
  soufflé, 581
Honey

Honey—*Continued*
-apple pie, 794
-baked grapefruit, 704
-broiled ham steak with sweet
    potatoes, 326
buns, 681
-coconut filling for cookies, 878
French dressing, 627
fruit cake, golden, 845
-lime dressing, 625
nougat, 908
-peanut-butter shake, 256
storing, 73
Honeyballs
selecting, 39
using, 39
Honeydews
buying, 75
freezing, 69
in melon surprise, 707
-and-pear cup, 114
selecting, 39
using, 39
Hoppin' John, 566
Hors d'oeuvre, *see* Appetizers
Horseradish
-and-beet relish, 925
-chive sauce for beef fondue, 295
-sauce for boiled brisket of beef, 296
-whipped cream dip, cubed roast
    beef with, 163
Hot cross buns, 683
egg glaze for, 683
Huckleberries, freezing, 67
Hulling, 8
Hungarian
beef goulash, 300
cake frosting, 858

Ice cream, 755-757
almond, burnt, 757
butter pecan, 757
cake, 849
chocolate, 756
coconut, toasted, 757
coffee cognac, 757
desserts, 759-761
    baked Alaska, 759
    bombe, jubilee, 760
    bombe glacée, 760
    rainbow meringue glacé, 761
flavor variations, 756-757
freezing, 61
fruit, 757
general data on, 755
nutritive values, 999
peanut ripple, 119
pecan, butter, 757
peppermint stick, 757
pies, 805-806
    chocolate heavenly, 806
    ribbon Alaska, 805
refrigerator tray, 756-757
sauces, 761-763
    butterscotch, rich, 763
    chocolate, bittersweet, 762
    chocolate fudge, 762
    chocolate rum, 762
    maple-nut, 763
    pineapple, 763
    pineapple mint, 763
    strawberry, 763
    tub churn, 755-757
soda, 258
    basic, 258
    black and white, 258

chocolate, 258
strawberry, 258
vanilla, 258
    refrigerator-tray, 756
    tub-churn, 755
Ice cubes
cranberry hearts, 263
fruit, 261
Ice ring, 261
Iced coffee, 247
Ices
freezing, 56
lemon, 758
raspberry, 758
Icing
for chocolate marmalade cake, 820
French chocolate, for bûche de
    Noël, 149
lemon, for Russian kulich, 692
wedding cake, 856
white, for cinnamon rolls, 681
India relish, 928
Indian pudding, baked, 738
Ingredient substitutions, 27-29
Instant coffee, 243
Iodine, nutritive values and sources,
    1001
Irish coffee, 246
Iron, nutritive values and sources, 1001
Italian
baked beans, 553
dressing, 627
Easter bread, 690
pickled shrimp, 177
-style green peppers, 539
tomatoes, 970
veal cutlets, 126

Jalapeño bean dip, hot, 164
Jam(s), 931-936
-almond bars, 863
general data on, 931-933
storing, 73
strawberry-rhubarb, 934
topping for coffeecake, 638
See also Conserves; Jelly;
    Marmalades; Preserves
Jan Hagel Christmas cookies, 887
Japanese shrimp soup, 226
Jellied
borscht, 235
garden consommé, 239
gazpacho, 237
Jelly, 931-935
apple, 931
balls, 872
coffee, 743
general data on, 931-933
grape, 934
storing, 73
wine, 989
See also Conserves; Jam;
    Marmalades; Preserves
Jelly rolls
raspberry, 834
rolling, 832
Jerusalem artichokes, 500
creamed, 501
Jiffy basting sauce, 493
John Collins cocktail, 269
Jubilee ice cream bombe, 760
Julienne, to, 8

Kabobs
lamb and kidney, 337
pork, Hawaiian, 99

scallop, 434
shish
beef, 201
lamb, 333
steak, 292
Kale
buying, 42
freezing, 64
storing, 74
Kansas fried chicken, 360
Kasha varnishkis, 583
Key lime dessert, 751
Kidney beans
in calico-bean hot pot, 741
in four-bean salad, 593
Mexican salad, 107
-and-rice salad, 601
Kidneys
beef
    English beef pie and, 939
buying, 76
general data on, 278
lamb
    broiled, 348
    English grill, 332
    fondue oriental, 295
    kabobs, 337
    steak-and-kidney pie, 349
veal, savory, 349
Kielbasa, 351
Polish sausage ring, 352
Kippered herring, fried, 441
Kir, 987
Knackwurst, 352
quick choucroute, 541
-with-sauerkraut dinner, 353
Kneading, 13
Kneading dough, 13, 663
Kohlrabi, 524
buying, 42, 524
cooking, 524
freezing, 64
general data on, 524
Kolacky, Czechoslovakian or
    Bohemian, 688
nut filling for, 689
poppy seed filling for, 689
Kris Kringle punch, 260
Kris Kringles, 898
Kuchen, 687
apple, quick, 725
Kulich, Russian, 691
lemon icing for, 692
Kumquats, 705
flower garnish for main dish, 155
general data on, 705
preparing, 705
storing, 705

La Fonda sangría, 263
Lady Baltimore cake, 823
Lady Baltimore frosting, 860
Lady Curzon soup, 232
Lamb, 329-338
barbecued
    patties, 337
    spareribs, 336
-barley soup, 220
basic retail cuts, 275-278
breast of
    baked with pears, 335
    barbecued spareribs, 336
    riblets with orange sauce, 335
broiling timetable, 51
buying, 76
calorie counts, 82

Lamb—*Continued*
  casseroles, 946-947
    moussaka, 947
    and rice, 946
  chops
    baked, 332
    braised shoulder, 332
    English grill, 332
    with herb butter, 331
    menu for, 95
  curry, 337
  freezing, 58
  general data on, 329
  heart Andalouse, 347
  kabobs, 337
  kidneys
    broiled, 348
    buying, 76
    English grill, 332
    fondue oriental, 295
    kabobs, 337
    steak-and-kidney pie, 349
  with lemon sauce, 338
  meat loaf, 309
  menu for, 95
  minted patties, 975
  moussaka, 947
  mousse, 619
  patties, barbecued, 337
  roast
    crown of, 330
    grilled butterfly leg of, 330
    leg of, herbed, 329
    marinated, 331
  roasting chart, 48-49
  salad, mousse, 679
  shanks
    braised, 334
    de luxe, 334
  shish kabob, 333
  spareribs, barbecued, 336
  steaks, spicy, 333
  stew
    South American, 117
    spring, 336
  wine marinade for, 988
Larding, 8
Lasagna, 572
  tomato sauce for, 572
  veal Romano, 952
Lebanon bologna, 352
Lebkuchen, 887
Leek(s), 524
  buying, 524
  general data on, 524
  -vegetable soup, 233
Lemon(s), 706
  artichokes marinated in, 193
  ball coffeecake, 639
  basket for garnish, 155
  -braised veal steak, 341
  bundt cake, 854
  butter cream frosting, 857
  in candied citrus peel, 894
  -cheese crepes, 775
  conversion chart, 33
  cookie bars
    meringue, 865
    slices, 880
    sugar, 876
  -cranberry punch, 260
  cream-cheese frosting, 859
  crullers, 647
  -crunch freeze, 754
  drop freeze, 115
  equivalent amounts, 27

filling for wedding cake, 856
-fricasseed chicken, 370
garnish
  basket, 155
  for main dish, 155
  for soup, 154
general data on, 706
glaze for cream cheese spritz, 874
ice, 758
icing for Russian kulich, 692
lemonade, 255
marzipan, 899
-meringue
  bars, 865
  pie, 801
  quick, pie, 802
mousse, 748
nutritive values, 1000
pie
  angel, 799
  chiffon, 803
  meringue, 801
  quick meringue, 802
preparing, 706
pudding, baked, 738
-rhubarb beverage, 257
sauce
  basting, 492
  broccoli with, 508
  -curry, for Caribbean fish soufflé, 405
  lamb with, 338
  steamed holiday pudding with, 143
sherbet, 758
sugar cookies, 876
Lemon peel, equivalent amounts, 27
Lentil(s)
  baked, 555
  general data on, 43, 551-555
  nutritive values, 993, 996, 999
  and short ribs, 555
  soup,
    potato, 554
    -spinach, 227
    -and-split pea, 215
Less-rich sauce
  Béarnaise, 489
  Hollandaise, 488
Lettuce
  buying, 42, 75
  general data on, 584-586
  storing, 74
Level, 8
Liederkranz cheese, 471
Lima bean(s), 504-506
  -beef casserole, 942
  buying, 504
  in calico-bean hot pot, 941
  continental, 505
  cooking, 504-505
  country franks and, 943
  with dill 505
  freezing, 62
  general data on, 504
  and ham casserole, 949
  in mixed vegetable pickles, 924
  nutritive values, 998, 999
  salad, marinated, 593
  Spanish, 505
  storing, 74
  succotash, 518
Limburger cheese, 471
Lime(s), 706
  buying, 706
  conversion chart, 33

cream salad, 614
equivalent amounts, 27
French dressing, 626
general data on, 706
-honey dressing, 625
Key dessert, 751
pie, 803
salad, cream, 614
sherbet, cantaloupe with, 126
Linguine with walnut sauce, 571
Liquids, measuring, 11
Liver
  balls, vegetable soup with beef ribs and, 225
  beef
    broiled, 346
    -and-macaroni casserole, 942
    menu for, 94
    and onions, smothered, 346
  buying, 76
  calf's
    broiled, 346
    pan-fried, 346
  chicken
    with bacon and peppers, 125
    beans and, 955
    casseroles, 955-957
    in Madeira sauce crepes, 655
    and mushroom canapés, 178
    omelet, 450
    pâté, 209
    sautéed, 973
    savory, 377
    wild-rice-and, casserole, 956
  freezing, 58
  general data on, 278
  nutritive values, 998, 999
  paté
    chicken, 209
    party, 167
    pastries, 188
  ribbon sandwiches, 181
  spread, 167
Liver cheese, 352
Liverwurst, 352
Lobster, 422-425
  baked 423
  baked fillet of sole stuffed with, 409
  boiled, 422
  in bouillabaisse, 214
    quick, 413
  broiled, 423
  buying, 75, 442
  -cheese custard, 476
  in cioppino, 414
  freezing, 60
  general data on, 422
  mousse, 620
  Newburg, 112
    -and-egg, 465
    sauce, 410
  in seafood bisque, 218
  and shrimp, baked, 437
  soufflé, 456
Lobster tails
  broiled, 423
  in butter sauce, 424
  casserole, 425
  stuffed, 424
Loganberries
  freezing, 67
  general data on, 700
Lollipops, 908
London broil, skillet, 289
Lord Baltimore cake, 853
Lukewarm, 8

INDEX

Luncheon meat casseroles, 945-946
  Florentine, 946
  noodle, 945
Lyonnaise carrots, glazed, 147
Lyonnaise potatoes, frankfurters and, 355

Macaroni
  baked, 590
  casseroles
    and beef liver, 942
    -corned beef, 128
    and frankfurters, 944
    pastiche, 939
    -tuna, 958
  and cheese
    freezing, 56
    salad, 598
  equivalent amounts, 27
  freezing, 56
  salad
    and cheese, 598
    -ham loaf, 605
    and shrimp, 609
  skillet, 573
    chicken legs with, 376
    -tuna casserole, 958
Macaroons
  biscuit tortoni, 753
  raspberry mousse, 749
Macchinetta, 244
Mace, 966
Mackerel
  buying, 75
  fillets, mustard-broiled, 410
Madeira sauce, chicken livers in crepes, 655
Magnesium, nutritive values and sources, 1001
Maître d'hôtel butter, 491
Making omelets
  fluffy, 450
  French, 449
Malibu chicken salad, 604
Mandarin fruits, 721
Mandarin oranges, 709
  sundae sauce, 709
Mangoes, 706
  general data on, 706
  preparing, 706
  storing, 706
Manhattan clam chowder, 217
Manhattan cocktail, 267
Manicotti, 571
Maple
  butter, whipped, 649
  -nut butter-cream frosting, 857
  -nut syrup, 763
  pecan chiffon cake, 829
  swirl frosting, 859
Marble cake, 820
Marengo, chicken, 368
Margarine freezing, 60
Marguéry sauce, fish fillets with, 412
Marie-Blanche casserole, 568
Marinate, to, 8
Marjoram, 965, 969
Marmalades
  orange, 935
    basting sauce, 492
    sauce for hibachi chicken, 365
  peach, spiced, 936
Marshmallow
  candy, 898
  chocolate fudge, 894
  fluffy stuffed sweet potatoes, 137

Kris Kringles, 898
  -peanut squares, 901
Martini cocktail, 267
Maryland fried chicken, 361
Marzipan, 899
  apples, 899
  bananas, 899
  carrots, 900
  glaze for, 900
  grapes, 900
  lemons, 899
  oranges, 899
  peaches, 899
  plums, 900
  potatoes, 900
  strawberries, 900
  watermelon slices, 900
Mashing, 8
Masking, 8
Matzo balls, 370
  chicken stew with, 370
Mayonnaise
  basic, 623
  blender, 624
  blue cheese, 626
  curried, for beef fondue, 296
  general data on, 623
  green goddess, 625
  honey-lime, 625
  pink currant, 626
  Russian, 624
  storage of, 73
  strawberry cream, 625
  Thousand Island, 624
Meal, measuring, 11
Measuring ingredients, 10-12
  equivalent weights and measures, 14
Measuring utensils, 10-11
Meat loaf
  appetizer, country, 194
  freezing, 59
  general data on, 307-310
  and mushroom-wine sauce, 102
  our best, 308
    with textured protein, 310
    variations, 308-310
  wine-mushroom sauce for, 102
Meatballs
  beef
    and mushroom appetizer, 190
    and spaghetti with tomato sauce, 573
    Swedish, 304
    Swedish, for a crowd, 190
  pork
    glazed, 327
    with sour-cream-mustard sauce, 327
Meats, 273-355
  appearance of fresh, 274
  basic retail cuts, 275-278
  broiling timetables, 50-51
    beef, 50
    lamb, 51
    poultry, 52
    smoked pork, 50-51
  buying, 75-76
  calorie counts, 81-82
  carbohydrate gram counts, 89-90
  cooking, 279-281
    frozen, 280
  grading, 273
  labeling, 273
  market labels, 273-274
  nutritive values, 993, 996, 998-1001

roasting timetables, 44-49
  beef, 44-46
  fresh pork, 46-47
  lamb, 48-49
  poultry, 51-54
  smoked pork, 47-48
  veal, 49
  storing, 73, 279
  tenderizers, 281
  variety, see Brains; Heart; Kidneys; Liver; Sweetbreads; Tripe; Tongue
  wine sauce for, 989
  See also names of meats
Mediterranean tuna sauce, spaghetti with, 575
Melon(s), 706-708
  buying, 75
  freezing, 69
  general data on, 39, 706-707
  and ham salad, 604
  preparing, 707
  selecting, 39
  storing, 707
  surprise, 707
  using, 39
  varieties, 39
  See also names of melons
Melting, 8
Menu planning, 92-108, 109-149
  classic mates, 94-97
  for company, 97-108, 113-122
    Continental buffet, 101-104
    Hawaiian luau, 97-101
    Mexican Fiesta, 104-108
  holiday dinners, 131-149
  last-minute meals, 122-131
  vegetarian, 1004-1006
  See also Nutrition
Meringue(s), 750-751
  almond layers for strawberry torte, 840
  freezing, 56
  general data on, 750
  -lemon bars, 865
  nests, 751
  rainbow glacé, 761
  shell, 750
  -strawberry torte, 839
  -topped pies, 800-802
    butterscotch, 801
    general data on, 800-801
    lemon, 801
    lemon, quick, 802
Metric measurements, 15-16
Mettwurst, 351
Mexican
  bean salad, 107
  chicken, 369
  coffee, 245
  cucumber salad, 107
  fiesta, 105-108
  foam soup, 234
  Guacamole, 105
  hot chocolate, 253
  Paella, 105
  tostadas, 107
  turnovers, 106
Milk
  calorie counts, 83
  carbohydrate gram counts, 87, 90
  equivalent amounts, 27
  freezing, 61
  gravy, 311
  nutritive values, 993, 996, 998-1001
  storing, 73

Milk—*Continued*
strawberry, 256
substitution for, 28, 29
Mincemeat
filling for cookies, 878
pie, 791
Mincing, 8
Minerals, nutritive values and
sources, 995, 1000, 1001
Minestrone, 213
Mint, 974
fondant balls, 897
French dressing, 627
garnish for vegetables, 159
pineapple syrup, 763
Mint julep, 269
Minted
chocolate cola punch, 261
lamb patties, 975
walnuts, 909
Mrs. Chandler's apple roll, 726
Mixing, 12-13
Mocha
bombe, 754
butter, for bûche de Noël, 149
butter-cream frosting, 857
cream, for torte, 839
fondant logs, 897
frosted coffee, 247
froth, hot, 253
mousse coronet cake, 747
torte, 839
Mock pink champagne punch, 261
Molasses
cookies, 876
drop, 867
nutritive values, 1001
taffy, 909
Molded salads, 612-622
general data on, 612
Moo goo gai pien, 374
Moravian
Christmas cookies, 888
sugar cake, 687
Mornay sauce, 482
Mortadella, 352
Moussaka, 947
Mousses
chicken
-almond, 617
-and-ham, 617
dessert, 745-749
banana, 745
cherry-brandy, 746
chocolat, soufflé froid au, 748
cinnamon-chocolate, 108
general data on, 745
lemon, 746
mocha coronet cake, 767
orange Grand Marnier, 748
peanut brittle, 747
raspberry-macaroon, 749
strawberry festival, 749
strawberry, fresh, 748
lamb, 619
lobster, 620
spinach-cheese ring, 615
Mozzarella cheese, 471
rice balls, 566
Muenster cheese, 470
Muffins, 633-635
bacon breakfast, 634
banana pecan, 634
basic, 633
blueberry, 634
bran, 634

cheese, 634
cornmeal, 642
date bran, 634
general data on, 633
ginger, 634
orange, 634
raisin bran, 634
Mush, corn meal, 581
fried, 582
Mushroom(s), 524-526
appetizers
cheese-stuffed, 173
and chicken liver canapés, 178
and meatballs, 190
squares, 186
stuffed caps, 199
baking, 525
broiling, 525
brown sauce, 485
buying, 42, 75, 524
cheese-stuffed, 173
and chestnuts, creamed, 525
crab meat casserole, 957
creamed, with chestnuts, 525
freezing, 64
frying, 525
general data on, 524-525
and herbs, 525
omelet, French, 450
sauce, 485
brown, 485
-catsup, for beef fondue, 296
cream, chicken breasts baked in,
373
-cream, for chicken soufflé, 457
-pork tenderloin casserole, 947
-tarragon, sliced eggs with, 463
-tomato, for Italian veal cutlets,
126
-wine, for meat loaf, 102
sautéing, 525
soufflé, fresh, 458
turkey scaloppini with ham, cheese
and, 387
Muskmelons, freezing, 69
Mussels, 434-435
cold marinated, 435
with garlic butter, 435
general data on, 434
Mustard, 930
-broiled mackerel
fillets, 410
dip for butterfly shrimp, 418
dressing, 628
Belgian endive with, 148
slaw with pineapple and, 128
pickles, 923
broiled ham with, 130
sauce
boiled brisket of beef with, 296
for fish steaks, 411
onions in, 528
pork chops with, 315
-sour cream, pork meatballs with,
327
sweet-and-sour, for glazed
corned beef, 204
tomato, 930
Mustard greens
buying, 42
freezing, 64
nutritive values, 998
in sour cream, 523
Mustard seed, 977

Nectarines, 708

freezing, 69
general data on, 708
preparing, 708
storing, 708
Nesselrode pudding, 734
Neufchâtel cheese, 471
New England
boiled dinner, 297
clam chowder, 217
fish chowder, 216
New Orleans seafood gumbo, 215
Newburg
lobster, 112
lobster and egg, 465
sauce, 480
lobster, for, baked fillet of sole
stuffed with lobster, 410
shrimp, on toast, 420
Niacin, nutritive values and sources,
999
Nicoise, salad, 601
Noodle(s)
casserole, 945
and eggs, baked, 957
garden, 569
-hamburger Stroganoff, 941
with luncheon meat, 945
Marie-Blanche, 568
and sausage, 950
veal lasagna Romano, 952
vegetable, baked, 569
equivalent amounts, 27
fettucine, 127, 569
freezing, 56
fried, 569
homemade, 576, 595
Romanoff, 569
spinach, 125
veal riblets with, 340
Nougat, honey, 908
Nuts(s)
apple bread, 640
apricot bread, 640
buttered hot, 176
calorie counts, 83-84
carbohydrate gram counts, 90
chocolate cake, 853
-cranberry stuffing for poultry, 395
-date candies, 896
-date surprise rolls, 638
-date torte, 737
equivalent amounts, 27
filling
for Bohemian kolacky, 688
for Czechoslovakian kolacky, 688
-maple butter-cream frosting, 857
-maple syrup, 857
nutritive values, 993, 998
pastry, 787
pie shell, 794
pine, rice with, 562
-raisin pie, 796
rice with, 565
rolls, 872
squash topped with, 544
storing, 73
-topped cake, broiled, 850
See also names of nuts
Nutmeg, 964, 966
buttered spinach with, 123
sauce, carrot and spinach timbales
with, 513
Nutrition, 94, 992-1008
calorie counts, 77-87
carbohydrate gram counts, 87-91
carbohydrates, 994

INDEX

Nutrition—*Continued*
defined, 993
fats, 994-995
food preparation and, 1002-1003
food sources of, 995-1001
food supplements and, 1007
importance of, 992-993
information, references for,
1007-1008
and labeling, 1003
menu planning and, 94
minerals, 995
functions and food sources of,
1000, 1001
protein, 993
vegetarian eating and, 1003-1006
vitamins, 995
functions and food sources of,
998, 999

Oatmeal
bread
batter, 673
currant, 675
cookies
-butterscotch, 871
spicy drop, 869
Rachel's granola, 583
raisin waffles, 659
Oils
calorie counts, 79
equivalent amounts, 27
nutritive values, 993, 998
storage of, 71
Okra, 526
buying, 42, 526
cooking, 526
freezing, 64
general data on, 526
gumbo
fish, 414
New Orleans seafood, 215
Old-fashioned cocktail, 269
Olive(s)
and beef casserole, 937
and celery, pickled, 926
-cheese puffs, 184
garnish
for main dish, 154
for soup, 154
loaf, 351
Olive oil French dressing, 627
Omelets, 449-451
fluffy, 450-451
flaming dessert, 451
making, 450
plain, 449
French, 449-450
chicken liver, 450
making, 449
mushroom, 450
plain, 450
Spanish, 450
spinach, 450
Onion(s), 526-529
bacon snacks with, hot, 171
beef liver and, smothered, 346
buying, 42, 75, 526
cooking, 526
creamed, 137, 527
creamy spinach, 130
equivalent amounts, 27
freezing, 65
fried
and green beans with thyme, 503
rings, French, 125, 528

garnish
for main dish, 154
for soup, 154
general data on, 526-527
glazed, 528
sliced steak with wine sauce and,
288
green
-curry dip, 199
general data on, 526
minced, 979
in mixed vegetable pickles, 924
in mustard sauce, 528
and peas, herbed, 530
and peppers, scalloped, 528
in ratatouille, 520
red, 527
rings, French fried, 125, 528
and sage stuffing for poultry, 395
sauce, 481
soup
with Gruyère cheese, 229
petit marmite, 234
Spanish, 527
storing, 74
stuffed, in tomato sauce, 527
-and-turnip casserole, 549
Onion powder, 979
Onion salt, 979
Orange(s) 40, 708-709
ambrosia, 720
-and-artichoke salad, 591
biscuits, tea, 632
broiled, 709
butter-cream frosting, 857
buying, 75, 708
cake, sugared chiffon, 828
calorie counts, 81
candied citrus peel, 894
carbohydrate gram counts, 89
chicken, baked, with, 368
in Cointreau, 721
conversion chart, 33
cranberry bread, 641
cream dressing, 629
cream in orange cups, 742
crepes Suzette, 776
eggnog punch, 262
equivalent amounts, 27
freezing, 68, 69
frosting for butterscotch-chocolate
bars, 864
fruit-filled watermelon, 707
fruits mandarin, 721
garnish for vegetable, 159
gelatine, 989
general data on, 40, 708
-glazed carrots, 512
-glazed ham, 323
baked, 208
loaf, 327
-glazed pork chops, 314
-glazed roast duckling, 390
Grand Marnier mousse, 748
mandarin, 709
in cherry coronet salad, 613
general data on, 709
sundae sauce, 709
marmalade, 935
glaze, 820
sauce for basting, 492
sauce for hibachi chicken, 365
marzipan, 899
muffins, 634
peeling, 708
refrigerator cookies, 881

salad
citrus, 138
citrus, with creamy dressing, 129
sauce
foamy, for orange soufflé, 767
lamb riblets with, 335
mandarin sundae, 709
sectioning, 708
selecting, 40
sherbet, 759
soufflé, 766
squash-filled, 146
storing, 708-709
strawberries, flavored, 700
in stuffed pineapple, 714
sweet potatoes, 538
tarts, 808
tea biscuits, 632
temple, 709
using, 40
varieties, 40
Orange marmalade, 935
sauce
for basting, 492
for hibachi chicken, 365
Oregano, 965, 969
Oriental
chicken wings, 376
fondue, 295
Ornamental frosting for gingerbread
cookies, 884
Osso buco, 345
Oxtail
ragout, 301
soup, 223
Oyster plant, *see* Salsify
Oyster(s), 428-429
buying, 428
freezing, 60
fritters, 645
general data on, 428
on the half shell, 195
preparing, 428-429
Rockefeller, 429
scalloped, 429
stew, 228
stuffing
for poultry, 393
for roast turkey, 382

Paella, 105
Pan-broil, to, 279-280
Pancakes, 647-652, 772-774
breakfast, 648-650
apple, German, 650
apple-filled, 649
basic, 648
fruits, 649
maple butter, whipped for, 649
rich, 649
syrup, fruit, for, 649
syrup, vanilla butter, for, 649
yeast, 650
dessert, 772-774
blintzes with assorted fillings, 773
chocolate with peppermint
whipped cream, 772
coconut with cinnamon whipped
cream, 772
Swedish, flaming, 773
luncheon or supper, 650-652
chicken, with sour cream sauce,
651
chicken-curry, 651
crab-filled, 652
potato, 537

Pan-fry, to, 8
Pantothenic acid, nutritive values and
    sources, 999
Papayas, 710
    general data on, 710
    preparing, 710
Paprika, 965
    garnish
        for main dish, 154
        for soup, 153
    goulash, 306
Parboiling, 8
Parching, 8
Paring, 8
Parfaits
    apricot, 697
    breakfast, 696
    crème de menthe, 753
Parmesan cheese, 468
    broiled toast, 289
    Brussels sprouts with, 509
    eggplant Parmigiana, 519
    six-cheese spaghetti casserole, 477
    soufflé, -Swiss, 454
    veal with, 341
    zucchini Parmigiana, 543
Parmigiana
    eggplant, 519
    zucchini, 543
Parsley, 965, 970
    biscuits, 631
    -butter sauce, new potatoes in, 123,
        535
    dumplings, 221, 644
    flakes, 965
    garnish, 154, 159
    soup, iced, 970
Parsnips, 529-530
    au gratin, 529
    buying, 42, 529
    freezing, 65
    fried, 529
    general data on, 529
Party Mix, 175
Pasta, 9, 567-580
    basic method for cooking, 568
    calorie counts, 78
    cannelloni
        cream sauce for, 579
        homemade, 578
        meat filling for, 578
    carbohydrate gram counts, 88
    general data on, 567-568
    homemade, 576-580
    lasagna, 572
        tomato sauce for, 572
        veal Romano, 952
    linguine with walnut sauce, 571
    macaroni
        baked, 572
        and beef liver, 942
        and cheese, freezing, 56
        and cheese salad, 598
        -corned beef, 128
        equivalent amounts, 27
        and frankfurters, 944
        freezing, 56
        pastiche, 939
        salad, and cheese, 598
        salad, ham loaf, 605
        salad, and shrimp, 609
        skillet, 573
        skillet, chicken legs with, 376
        -tuna, casserole, 958
    manicotti, 571
    noddles

baked egg and, casserole, 957
    baked vegetable casserole, 569
    casserole Marie-Blanche, 568
    equivalent amounts, 27
    fettucine, 127, 569
    fettucine-stuffed veal rolls, 342
    freezing, 56
    fried, 569
    garden casserole, 569
    -hamburger Stroganoff,
        casserole, 941
    homemade, 576-577
    luncheon meat casserole, 945-946
    Romanoff, 567
    and sausage casserole, 950
    spinach, 125
    sukiyaki with sesame seeds and,
        570
    veal lasagna Romano casserole,
        252
    veal riblets with, 340
ravioli, 579
    freezing, 57
    spinach filling for, 580
spaghetti
    casserole, six-cheese, 477
    equivalent amounts, 27
    freezing, 56
    and meatballs, with tomato sauce,
        573
    with Mediterranean tuna sauce,
        575
spaghetti sauces, 573-576
    garlic butter, 576
    meat, 574
    spicy, 575
    summer salad, 574
    tomato, basic, 574
    white clam, 575
vermicelli, baked, 570
Paste, 9
Pastiche, 939
Pastry, 782
    almond, 787
    appetizers, 187-190
        anchovy tartlets, 189
        assorted cheese, 187
        cheese sticks, 188
        cheese straws, 188
        cornucopias, 188
        crab meat quiche, 189
        curried bites, 180
        franks in blankets, 187
        liver pâté, 188
        rich pastry for, 188
        Swiss cheese pie, 189
    butter, for warm apple tart, 800
    cheese, 787
    chocolate, 787
    curried bites, 180
    edgings
        fluted, 786
        fork, 786
        how to make, 786
        leaf, 786
        rope, 786
    fitting into a plate, 785
    flaky liquid-shortening, 787
    flaky solid-shortening, 786
        almond, 787
        cheese, 787
        chocolate, 787
        nut, 787
        two-crust, 787
    general data on, 782
    glazed top, 785

lard shell, 789
    lattice top, 788
    mixing, 783-784
    nut, 787
    rolling, 784
    sealing, 785
    shaping, 785
    tart shells, 807
        sweet, 807
    topping for chicken pot pie, 372
    tops
        glazed, 788
        lattice, 788
        trellis, 788
Pâté
    chicken liver, 209
    liver pastries, 188
    liver ribbon sandwiches, 181
    liver spread, 167
    party, 167
    tuna, 193
Pea(s), 530-531
    buying, 42, 75, 530
    ring of carrots with French, 530
    cooking, 530
    dried
        general data on, 43, 551-552
        rarebit, 553
        savory supper dish, 554
        soup, 228
        soup, with lentils, 215
    freezing, 65
    French, 530
        with ring of carrots, 531
    general data on, 530
    nutritive values, 993, 999
    and onions, herbed, 530
    snow, braised tenderloin with, 317
    soup
        frosted, 240
        potage St. Germain, 219
        tomato boullion medley, 233
        turtle and, 232
        -vegetable, 233
    storing, 74
Peach(es)
    buying, 75
    chilled, with wine, 987
    conserves, 936
    conversion chart, 33
    cottage pudding with peach sauce,
        736
    crisp, 729
    dried, 717
        general data on, 717
    flambées, 711
    in fruit flan, 726
    general data on, 710
    marmalade, spiced, 936
    marzipan, 899
    Melba, 723
    peeling, 710
    pie, continental, 807
    -and-plum preserves, 935
    poached, 711
        with wine, 987
    punch bowl, 986
    salad, spiced, 614
    sauce, cottage pudding with, 737
    slicing, 710
    storing, 72, 710-711
    thaw drink, 256
Peanut
    butter-cream frosting, 857
    candy mounds, 900
    chili, 176

INDEX

Peanut—*Continued*
-chocolate balls, 895
-fudge drops, 907
and ham spread, 198
-marshmallow squares, 901
ripple ice cream, 119
Peanut brittle, 910
mousse, 747
Peanut butter
-coconut brownies, 863
cookies, 872
-date drops, 901
fudge, 908
-honey shake, 256
ice cream, 119
Pear(s), 36-37, 712-713
baked breast of lamb with, 335
buying, 75
cheese-stuffed, fresh salad, 591
chocolate supreme, 722
chutney, 931
conversion chart, 33
cooking, 712
cranberry, baked, à la mode, 728
curried fresh, 713
dried, 717
  general data on, 717
freezing, 69
general data on, 36-37, 712
-ginger appetizer, 193
Hélène, 722
-honeydew cup, 114
in port, 990
ripening, 712
salad
  cheese-stuffed, fresh, 591
selecting, 36-37
serving, 712
storing, 72, 712
streusel à la mode, 729
using, 36-37
varieties, 36-37
in wine, 712
Pecan(s)
banana muffins, 634
-biscuit coating for oven-fried
    chicken, 363
-bourbon cake, 844
-bread stuffing for poultry, 395
-and-date logs, 896
dressing, turkey breast with, 386
fruited, 906
ice cream, butter, 757
maple chiffon cake, 829
nutted rice, 565
pastry shell, flaky, 789
pie
  -date, 795
  shell, 794
  Southern, 795
pralines, 912
  glaze for drop cookies, 869
sweet potatoes stuffed with, baked,
    532
-topped picnic ham, 324
Peeling, 9
Penuche, 911
Peperoni, 352
Pepper, 966
cayenne, 966
white, 966
Pepper(s)
rice with cashews and, 565
veal and, 344
See also Green pepper(s); Red
    pepper(s)

Pepper pot soup, 222
Pepper steak, sirloin, 292
Peppermint
butter-cream frosting, 857
-chocolate chiffon pie, 802
cream roll, 833
glaze, 860
hard candies, 910
ice cream, 757
taffy, 910
whipped cream, chocolate pancakes
    with, 772
Perch, in bouillabaisse, 413
Persian melons
freezing, 69
selecting, 39
using, 39
Persimmons, 713
buying, 713
freezing, 69-70
general data on, 713
storing, 713
Petite marmite, 234
Petits fours frosting, vanilla, 847
Pfeffernuesse, Christmas cookies, 888
Phosphorus, nutritive values and
    sources, 1000
Piccalilli relish, 929
Piccata, veal, 342
Pickle-and-pimiento loaf, 351
Pickles, 920-925
bread-and-butter, 922
celery and olives, 926
crystal chips, 922
dill, 922
dilled beans, 922
general data on, 920-921
green-tomato, relish, 928
mixed vegetable, 924
mustard, 923
  broiled ham with, 130
senf gurken, 924
watermelon rind, 925
Piedmont pudding, 739
Pies, 782-809
almond-chocolate, 798
apple
  -honey, 794
  perfect, 789
banana cream, 797
beef, 940
  English kidney and, 939
black-bottom, 797
blueberry, 789
Boston cream, 822
  high, 852
butterscotch meringue, 801
calorie counts, 78-79
carbohydrate gram counts, 90
cheese and corn, 476
cherry, 790
  cobbler, 113
chicken pot, 371
  crust, for, 372
chiffon, 802-805
  chocolate-peppermint, 802
  eggnog, 803
  general data on, 802
  lemon, 803
  lime, 803
  pumpkin, 804
  raspberry, 804
chocolate
  -almond, 798
  cream, 798
  crumb shell, 794

heavenly, 806
  -peppermint chiffon, 802
Concord grape, 790
cookie crumb, 793
corn-and-cheese, 476
cranberry, 790
cream
  banana, 797
  chocolate, 798
crumb crust
  general data on, 792
  shaping, 792
  chocolate, 794
  cookie, 793
  corn-flake, 793
  gingersnap, 793
  graham-cracker, 792
  meringue, 793
  nut, 794
  toasted coconut, 793
custard, 795
date-pecan, 795
eggnog chiffon, 803
freezing, 56, 57-58
French strawberry, 799
general data on, 782
gingersnap crumb shell, 793
graham-cracker crumb shell, 792
grasshopper, 798
honey-apple, 794
ice-cream, 805-806
  chocolate heavenly, 806
  ribbon Alaska, 805
lemon
  angel, 799
  chiffon, 803
  meringue, 801
  quick meringue, 802
lime chiffon, 803
meringue crumb shell, 793
meringue-topped, 800-802
  butterscotch, 801
  general data on, 800
  lemon, 801
  quick lemon, 802
mincemeat, 791
nut crumb shell, 794
one-crust, 791-806
  apple tart, warm, 800
  apple-honey, 794
  banana cream, 797
  black-bottom, 797
  chocolate-almond, 798
  chocolate cream, 798
  custard, 795
  date-pecan, 795
  French strawberry, 799
  general data on, 791-792, 794
  grasshopper, 798
  honey-apple, 794
  lemon angel, 799
  pecan-date, 795
  pumpkin, 138
  raisin-nut, 796
  Southern pecan, 795
  strawberry, French, 799
  sweet-potato, 796
  toasted coconut crumb shell, 793
  variations, 791-792
peach continental, 807
pecan
  -date, 795
  Southern, 795
pumpkin, 138
  chiffon, 804
purple plum, 715

Pies—*Continued*
  raisin-nut, 796
  raspberry chiffon, 804
  rhubarb-strawberry, 791
  sausage, 322, 951
  shaping crumb shell, 792
  skillet potato-tuna, 439
  steak-and-kidney, 349
  storing, 74
  strawberry
    French, 799
    -rhubarb, 791
  sweet-potato, 796
  Swiss cheese, 189
  tart shells, 807
    sweet, 807
  tarts, 806-809
    apple, flaming, 806
    orange, 808
    peach, continental, 807
    shaping, 808
    strawberry-vanilla, 809
  See also Quiche; Tartlets; Tarts
Pilaf
  beef, 306
  rice, 564
    Eastern, 564
  wheat, 580
Pimiento-pickle loaf, 351
Pine nuts, rice with, 562
Pineapple(s), 713-714
  baked fruit compote, 717
  buying, 75, 713
  cake
    roll, 834
    upside-down, 836
  cheesecake, 831
    Hawaiian, 100
  -cherry preserves, 935
  chicken on a spit with, 365
  chiffon cake, 104
  cloud nine cream, 720
  conversion chart, 34
  cress beverage, 256
  curried fruit, hot, 728
  freezing, 70
  in fruit-filled watermelon, 707
  garnish for main dish, 154
  general data on, 713-714
  glaze, 832
  -glazed roast chicken, 136
  peeling, 714
  preparing, 714
  removing the eyes, 714
  sauce
    for cheesecake, Hawaiian, 100
    ice cream, 763
    mint, 763
  slaw with mustard dressing, 128
  sponge shortcake, 731
  storing, 713
  stuffed, 714
  syrup, 763
    mint, 763
Pinwheel sandwiches, 205
Pipe, to, 9
Piquant
  apple salad, 118
  glazed Canadian bacon, 328
  sauce, 485
Pitting, 9
Pizza whole wheat canapés, 187
Plum(s), 715
  -apple sauce, spiced, pork loin roast
    with, 313
  buying, 75, 715

Christmas pudding, 740
  conversion chart, 34
  freezing, 70
  frozen pudding, 755
  general data on, 715
  marzipan, 900
  -and-peach preserves, 935
  pie, 715
  storage of, 72, 715
Poaching, 9
Pole Beans *see* Green Beans
Polish
  sausage, 351
    ring, 352
Polynesian
  beef, 307
  chicken, 368
  curry salad, 618
Pomegranates, 715
  general data on, 715
Popcorn balls, 911
Popovers, 635
  general data on, 635
Poppy seed, 977
  appetizer morsels, 177
  filling for Czechoslovakian or
    Bohemian kolacky, 689
  rice pudding, 118
  spirals, 632
Pork
  bacon, 328-329
    breakfast muffins, 634
    buying, 76
    Canadian piquant glazed, 328
    -cheese custards, 460
    and cheese whirls, 184
    chicken livers with peppers and,
      125
    croutons, 660
    curls, 171
    and egg circle sandwiches, 179
    -and-egg salad, 462
    freezing, 59
    general data on, 328
    hot dressing for spinach salad,
      596
    hot onion snacks, 171
    piquant glazed Canadian, 328
    shirred eggs with, 460
    storing, 73
  barbecued
    ribs, 205, 318
  basic retail cuts, 275-278
  broiling timetable, 50-51
  buying, 76
  calorie counts, 82-83
  casseroles, 947-948
    chop, 111
    chop and potato scallop, 947
    chop, scalloped sweets and, 948
    sausage pie, 951
    tenderloin-mushroom, 947
  chop suey, 319
  chops
    braised, 314
    casserole, 111
    menu for, 96
    with mustard sauce, 315
    orange-glazed, 314
    and potato scallop, 974
    scalloped sweet potatoes and, 948
    stuffed, 315
    and sweet potatoes, 316
    sweet-sour, 316
  fondue oriental, 295
  freezing, 58, 59

general data on, 310-311
  ground patties, 319
  ham, 322-328
    apricot-glazed, 102
    -asparagus pinwheels, 175
    baked, glazed, 323
    baked, Tetrazzini, 948
    barbecued steak, 326
    -bologna, 352
    broiled, with mustard pickles,
      130
    broiled steak, 352
    buying, 76
    calorie counts, 82-83
    casseroles, 948-950
    creamed casserole, 949
    in crust, 324
    curry turnovers, 175
    deviled, filling, 205
    deviled, Tetrazzini, 945
    -and-egg crepes Benedict, 654
    -and-egg scallop, 464
    freezing, 59
    general data on, 322
    glazes for, 323
    ground, 327-328
    honey-broiled steak with sweet
      potatoes, 326
    lima beans and, 949
    meatballs, glazed, 327
    meatballs with sour
      cream-mustard sauce, 327
    and melon salad, 604
    menu for baked, 96
    orange-glazed, 323, 208
    orange-glazed baked, 208
    orange-glazed loaf, 327
    and peanut spread, 198
    pecan-topped, 324
    roast fresh, with frosted grapes,
      140
    roast fresh, holiday menu,
      139-143
    roulades, 175
    salad and chicken mousse, 617
    salad holiday mold, 619
    salad macaroni loaf, 605
    steak, barbecued, 326
    steak, broiled, 325
    steak, glazed baked, 325
    steak, honey-broiled with sweet
      potatoes, 326
    stuffed slices, 326
    tartlets, 185
    turkey scaloppine with
      mushrooms, cheese, and, 387
  heart Andalouse, 347
  hocks, with sauerkraut, 320
  kabobs, Hawaiian, 99
  meat loaf
    appetizer, country, 194
    our best, 308
    variations, 308-309
  meatballs
    glazed, 327
    with sour-cream-mustard sauce,
      327
  nutritive values, 998, 999
  pie, sausage, 322, 951
  ribs
    barbecued, 205, 318
    Chinese sheet, 318
    general data on, 317-318
    glazed, 318
  roast, 310-314
    crown of, with corn bread

INDEX

Pork—*Continued*
stuffing, 312
fruited, 313
general data on, 310-311
half-crown, with spinach dressing, 312
with herb dressing, 311
loin, with spiced apple-plum sauce, 313
menu for, 96
milk gravy for, 311
shoulder, 313
roasting charts
fresh, 46-47
smoked, 47-48
sausage, 321-322
-and-apple casserole, 950
buying, 76
calorie counts, 83-84
casseroles, 950-951
and apple, 950
noodle, 950
pie, 951
zucchini, 951
English grill, 332
freezing, 58
fruit stuffing for roast goose, 145
general data on, 310-311, 351-352
noodle casserole, 950
pie, 322, 951
Polish ring, 352
poultry stuffing, 393
and red cabbage, 321
-rice stuffing, for roast chicken, 136
storing, 73
zucchini and, casserole, 951
steaks
braised, 314
sweet-and-sour, 320
chops, 316
tenderloin
braised, with snow peas, 317
Chinese, 317
mushroom casserole, 947
Port cocktail, 984
pears in, 990
Port du salut cheese, 470
Portugaise sauce, 486-487
Potage St. Germain, 219
Potassium, nutritive values and sources, 1001
Potato(es), 534-539
baked, stuffed, 536
baking, 534
buying, 42, 75
and cheese pie, 538
cheese-stuffed baked, 536
chip-tuna bake, 438
chips, fish and, 411
coating for oven-fried chicken, 362
creamy mashed, 535
crisp-baked halves, 538
Duchess, 537
equivalent amounts, 27
freezing, 65-66
general data on, 534-535
hashed brown, 536
Lyonnaise, with frankfurters, 355
marzipan, 900
mashed, creamy, 535
new
general data on, 534
in parsley-butter sauce, 123, 535
nutritive values, 998

O'Brien, 537
pancakes, 537
pan-roasted, 141
and pork chop scallop, 947
puff, frankfurter-, 355
salad, 597
German style, baked, 597
German style franks and, 606
hot meat and, 606
scalloped, 535
soup, 229
-lentil, 554
Vichyssoise, 238
Vichyssoise, emerald, 238
storing, 74
stuffed baked, 536
with cheese, 536
Swiss cake, 538
-tuna skillet pie, 439
See also Sweet Potatoes
Pot-roasting, 9, 280
Poultry, 356-396
broiling timetable, 52
buying, 356
calorie counts, 86
carbohydrate gram counts, 89-90
five kinds of, 356
freezing, 59
general data on, 356
general stuffings for, 392-396
chestnut, 393
classic herb, 393
corn bread, 394
cranberry-nut, 395
fruit, 394
giblet, 394
oyster, 393
pecan-bread, 395
sage and onion, 395
sausage, 393
vegetable, 395
nutritive values, 993,998,999
roasting timetable, 51-54
storing, 73, 356-357
trussing, 380
See also Chicken; Duckling; Goose; Turkey
Pound cake, 821
Powdered ingredients, measuring, 11
Praline(s), 912
glaze for drop cookies, 869
Precooking, 9
Preheating, 9
Preparation equipment, 16-17
Preserves
cherry-pineapple, 935
peach-and-plum, 935
storage of, 73
strawberry, 934
See also Conserves; Jam; Jelly; Marmalade
Preserving, 913-935
general data on, 913, 917-919
See also Canning; Freezing
Pretzels, cheese-dipped, 176
Profiteroles with creamed chicken, 207
Proteins, nutritive values and sources, 993-994
Provençale
stuffed eggplant, 521
tomatoes, 547
Provolone cheese, 469
six-cheese spaghetti casserole, 477
Prune(s)
conversion chart, 34

dried, 717
general data on, 717
filling for cookies, 878
fondant-stuffed, 897
freezing, 70
fresh, 715
general data on, 715
kugel, sweet raisin, 718
nutritive values, 1001
Puddings
bread
chocolate, deluxe, 735
custard, 735
queen of, 735
calorie counts, 79
corn, 517
dessert, 732-742
chocolate bread, deluxe, 735
chocolate pot-de-crème, 733
chocolate steamed, 739
Christmas plum, 740
cottage, with peach sauce, 736
crème brulée, 732
crème caramel, 736
custard, baked, 737
custard bread, 735
date nut torte, 737
English Christmas, 741
floating island, 733
Indian, baked, 738
lemon, baked, 738
nesselrode, 734
Piedmont, 739
plum, Christmas, 740
plum, frozen, 751
queen of bread, 735
refrigerator rum, 752
rice, 739
vanilla, and wine, lady fingers with, 987
zabaglione, 734
freezing, 56
plum, 740
frozen, 751
rhubarb, baked, 729
rice, 739
poppy seed, 118
sauce for, 990
snow, 744
steamed holiday, with lemon sauce, 142
Yorkshire, 635
Pumpkin(s), 540
buying, 43
cooking, 540
freezing, 66
general data on, 540
pie, 138
chiffon, 804
roasted seeds, 540
Punch, 259-266, 985-987
bourbon, 265
California, 262
Caribbean bowl, 264
champagne, 262, 985
children's candy stick, 259
cranberry-lemon, 260
fruit syllabub, 260
holiday eggnog, 264
holiday wine, 264
Kris Kringle, 260
La Fonda sangría, 263
minted chocolate cola, 261
mock pink champagne, 261
orange eggnog, 262
peach bowl, 986

Punch—*Continued*
snowy eggnog, 263
tea, festive hot, 250
Texas, 265
Tom and Jerry, 265
wassail bowl, 265
wine syllabub, 263
Pungent barbecue sauce, 493
Puréeing, 9

Queen of bread
puddings, 735
Quiche
crab meat, 189
Lorraine, 474
miniature, 101
quick, 474
Quince(s), 716
baking, 716
buying, 716
conversion chart, 34
general data on, 716
poaching, 716
storing, 716

Rachel's granola, 583
Radish(es), 540
buying, 43, 540-541
cooking, 541
and egg filling for glazed party
canapés, 180
finger sandwiches, 610
freezing, 66
garnishes
for main dish, 155
for cold meat platters, 157
general data on, 540-541
storing, 74
tartine, French, 182
vegetable relish bowl, 127
Rainbow meringue glacé, 761
Raisin(s), 718
banana bread, 640
batter bread, 672
bran muffins, 634
conversion chart, 34
equivalent amounts, 27
general data on, 718
kugel, sweet, 718
-nut pie, 796
nutritive values, 1001
oatmeal waffles, 659
sauce
smoked tongue with, 350
tongue with vegetables and, 114
storing, 718
Raphael Weill chicken, 369
Rarebit
split pea, 533
Welsh, 473
Raspberry(ies)
-chocolate ripple cake, 854
conversion chart, 34
-crumble bar cookies, 865
dream, 723
freezing, 70
fruit refresher, 257
fruit shrub, 256
general data on, 700
ice, 758
jelly
balls, 872
roll, 834
-macaroon mousse, 749
in melon surprise, 707
in peach melba, 723

pie, 804
soup, iced, 237
yogurt, razzberry, 254
Ratatouille, 520
Ravioli, 579
freezing, 57
spinach filling for, 580
Recipes, *see* Cooking
Red cabbage
general data on, 509-510
sausage and, 321
with wine, 511
Red onions, 527
Red pepper(s)
chicken livers with bacon and, 125
freezing, 65
general data on, 539
relish, 929
storage of, 74
See also Green peppers
Red snapper
à la Franey, 408
baked stuffed, 405
vegetable-stuffed baked whole, 406
Reducing, 9
Rehydrating, 9
Relish(es), 920-921
beat-and-horseradish, 926
bowl, 127
chow-chow, 927
corn, 927
cranberry, 703
general data on, 920-921
green-tomato pickle, 928
India, 928
piccalilli, 929
pickled celery and olives, 926
storing, 74
sweet pepper, 929
vegetable, 174
vegetable, tangy, 926
vegetable relish
bowl, 127
Rendering, 9
Reuben sandwiches, miniature, 198
Rhubarb, 716
buying, 716
conversion chart, 34
freezing, 70
fruit Betty, 728
general data on, 716
lemonade, 257
pie, strawberry-, 791
preparing, 716
pudding, baked, 729
eggnog sauce for, 730
stewed, 716
storing, 716
-strawberry
jam, 934
pie, 791
Ribbon Alaska pie, 805
Riboflavin, nutritive values and
sources, 999
Ribs
beef
barbecued, 293
German-style, short, 301
lentils and, 555
roast, standing, 281
vegetable soup with liver balls
and, 225
buying, 76
lamb
barbecued, 336
with orange sauce, 335

pork
barbecued, 205, 318
Chinese sheet, 318
general data on, 317-318
glazed, 318
veal, and noodles, 340
Rice, 559-567
baked, 561
balls, two-cheese, 566
basic cooking method for, 561
beef pilaf, 306
Brazilian black beans and, 555
brown, 560
Chinese, 562
pudding, 734
roast duckling with dressing of,
147
salad, minted, 598
with cashews and peppers, 565
casserole, 563
arroz con pollo, 953
-carrot, 566
crab meat and, 957
frankfurters and, 944
lamb and, 946
sesame seeds with chicken or
turkey, 955
wild, and chicken livers, 563
chicken-seasoned, 126
Chinese fried, brown, 562
curried
dressing, roast duckling with, 147
ring, 618
with dried fruit, 565
equivalent amounts, 27
frankfurters and, 944
freezing, 56
fried, Hawaiian, 99
general data on, 559-561
hoppin' John, 566
nutted, 565
parboiled (converted), 560
pilaf, 564
beef, 306
Eastern, 564
with pine nuts, 562
precooked, 560
pudding, 739
poppy seed,
risotto, 564
salad
and chick-peas, chilled, 598
curried ring, 618
with fresh herbs, 608
kidney-bean-and, 601
minted brown, 598
and stuffed eggs, 607
sesame, with chicken or turkey, 955
Spanish, gourmet, 563
stuffing
Cornish hens with, 377
sausage, for roast chicken, 136
white, regular milled, 559
wild, 560
casserole, 563
-and-chicken-liver casserole, 956
Ricotta cheese, 471
Risotto, 564
Roast, to, 9, 279, 280
Rob Roy cocktail (sweet), 271
Robert, sauce, 486
Rolling, 9
Rolls, *see* Bread(s), yeast
Romano cheese, 468
six-cheese spaghetti casserole, 477
Roquefort cheese, 469

INDEX

Roquefort cheese—*Continued*
  cream sauce, for braised endive, 522
  molded crème appetizer, 170
Rosemary, 972
  chicken, 972
Roulades
  beef, 291
  ham, 175
Roux, 9
Rum
  baba au fraises, 780
  -banana cream cake, 120
  -cocoa, hot, 253
  nut chocolate ice cream, 756
  pudding, refrigerator, 752
  sauce
    chocolate, 762
    for pears Hélène, 722
Rum Collins cocktail, 269
Rum tum tiddy, 474
Rumaki, 200
Russian
  dressing, 624
  kulich, 691
    lemon icing for, 692
Rutabaga, *see* Turnips, yellow
Rye bread
  conventional method, 667
  rapid-mix method, 669

Saffron, 966
Sage, 972-973
  stuffing, for roast turkey, 135
    corn bread, 973
    onion, 395
St. Honoré cake, 840
Salad(s), 584-622
  almond-chicken mousse, 617
  apple
    -celery, 112
    piquant, 118
  artichoke-and-orange, 591
  asparagus, 592
  aspic
    tomato, 616
    vegetable, 616
  avocado
    stuffed with crab meat, 606
    -and-tuna, molded, 622
    -tuna luncheon plate, 610
  bacon and egg, 462
  baked seafood, 960
  bean, 107
    four, 593
    green, 543
    lima, marinated, 593
  beat, jellied, 615
  Belgian endive
    with chiffonade dressing, 594
    with mustard dressing, 148
  Bulgur, 581
  Caesar, 588
  celeriac, 516
  celery
    -apple, 112
    Victor, 595
  chef's, 587
  cherry coronet, 613
  chicken, 602
    -almond mousse, 617
    cold creamy curried, 602
    cold, with walnut sauce, 621
    ginger-cream, 602
    and grapes, 619
    -and-ham mousse, 617

Malibu, 604
  tonnato, 603
chick-pea
  and rice, chilled, 598
  -and-tabouli, 599
citrus, 138
  with creamy dressing, 129
classic green, 586
coleslaw *see* slaw
crab meat
  avocado stuffed with, 606
  Louis, 607
cranberry
  molded, 613
  -Waldorf, with fruit dressing, 142
cucumber, 596
  Mexican, 107
  ring filled with turkey, 620
  in sour cream, 596
  with tangy sour cream dressing, 130
delicate tossed, 588
dressings, *see* Dressings
egg, 462
  bacon and, 462
  casserole, 466
  deviled mold, 621
  stuffed, with rice, 607
endive, *see* Belgian endive
four-bean, 593
fruit, 124
  with cardamom cream dressing, 590
  five-cup, 590
  fresh with wine gelatin cubes, 600
  frozen, 592
  plate, 600
  twenty-four-hour, 590
garden, molded, 615
garlic bread cubes for, 587
general data on, 584-586
grape and chicken, 619
grapefruit
  citrus, 138
  citrus with creamy dressing, 129
  molded, 613
green bean, 593
green, classic, 586
ham
  -and-chicken mousse, 617
  holiday mold, 619
  -macaroni loaf, 605
  and melon, 604
Hawaiian, 99
herring, 611
Holiday ham mold, 619
honeydew and pear cup, 114
hot tossed, 589
jellied beet, 615
kidney bean and rice, 601
lamb
  mousse, 619
lima bean, marinated, 593
lime cream, 614
lobster mousse, 620
macaroni,
  -and-cheese, 598
  -ham loaf, 605
  and shrimp, 609
main dish, 600-612
melon and ham, 604
Mexican bean, 107
mimosa, 588
molded, 612-622
  general data on, 612-613
  main dish, 617-622

Nicoise, 601
orange
  -and-artichoke, 591
  citrus, 138
  citrus with creamy dressing, 129
peach, spiced, 614
pear
  cheese-stuffed, 591
  and honeydew cup, 114
  piquant apple, 118
Polynesian curry, 618
potato, 597
  baked, German style, 597
  German style, franks and, 606
  hot meat-and, 606
radish finger sandwiches for, 610
rice
  brown, 598
  and chick-pea, chilled, 598
  curried ring, 618
  with fresh herbs, 608
  kidney-bean-and, 601
  and stuffed eggs, 607
salmon
  and egg platter, 608
shrimp, 609
  and macaroni, 609
slaw, 594
  blender, with sour cream dressing, 594
  hot, 511
  old-fashioned cauliflower, 595
  with pineapple and mustard dressing, 128
spinach
  -cheese mousse ring, 615
  with hot bacon dressing, 596
  special, 589
summer, 605
tomato
  aspic, 103, 616
tossed green, 586-589
  Caesar, 588
  chef's, 587
  classic, 586
  delicate, 588
  hot, 589
  mimosa, 588
  special spinach, 589
tuna, 611
  -and-avocado, molded, 622
  -avocado luncheon plate, 610
  hot, 611
turkey
  in cucumber ring, 620
vegetable
  aspic, 616
  garden, molded, 615
  medley, 116
Waldorf, 591
  -cranberry, with fruit dressing, 142
Salami, 352
Salisbury steaks, 304
Sally Lunn coffeecake, 639
Salmon
  Béarnaise, 411
  buying, 76
  crepes, velouté, 655
  croquettes, 440
  loaf, sauced, 440
  pinwheels, 181
  salad and eggs platter, 608
  stuffed turbans with Béarnaise sauce, 409
  velouté crepes, 655

Salsa, 526
  verde for steamed cauliflower, 514
Salsify, 541
  buying, 43, 541
Salt
  garlic, 978
  onion, 979
Sand tarts, 889
Sandwiches
  freezing, 58
  garnishes for, 156-158
  pinwheel, 205
  radish finger, 610
  Reuben, miniature, 98
  watercress, rolled, 83
Sangría, La Fonda, 263
Santa Claus melons
  selecting, 39
  using, 39
Santa's bread, 688
  confectioners' glaze for, 688
Sapsago cheese, 468
Sardine appetizers
  -cream cheese canapés, 182
Sauces, 478-494
  anchovy
    -butter, for broiled fish steaks,
      403
  apple-
    freezing, 55
    -plum, spiced, pork loin roast
      with, 313
    strained, 695
  apricot, beignets soufflés with, 780
  barbecue, 491-494
    deluxe, 491
    diable, 492
    glaze for broiled chicken, 364
    jiffy, 493
    lemon, 492
    marmalade, 492
    pungent, 493
  basting, 491-494
    deluxe, 491
    diable, 492
    jiffy, 493
    lemon, 492
    marmalade, 492
    pungent barbecue, 493
  Béarnaise
    classic, 489
    less-rich, 489
    quick, for beef fondue, 294
    salmon with, 411
    stuffed salmon turbans with, 409
    swordfish with, 411
  béchamel, 478-480
    Chantilly, 480
    cream, 481
    long method, 480
    Newburg, 480
    onion, 481
    short method, 480
  beef, 574
  blond (velouté), 482-483
    long method, 482
    short method, 483
  Bordelaise, 485
  brown (Espagnole), 484-486
    Bordelaise, 485
    diable, 485
    long method, 484
    mushroom, 485
    piquant, 485
    Robert, 486
    short method, 484

butter, 490-491
  -anchovy, for broiled fish steaks,
    403
  black, 490
  clarified, 490
  garlic, for spaghetti, 576
  herb garlic, 490
  lobster tails in, 424
  maître d'hôtel, 491
  -parsley, new potatoes in, 123,
    535
  savory, for artichokes, 501
  -wine, for broiled fish steaks, 403
butterscotch, 763
calorie counts, 86
catsup-mushroom, for beef fondue,
  296
celery, Brussels sprouts in, 147
Chantilly, 480
cheese
  for braised endive, 522
  eggs with, 464
cherry, for jubilee ice cream bombe,
  761
chili herb with wine French
    dressing, 988
chocolate
  bittersweet, 762
  coconut soufflé with, 764
  fudge, 762
  rum, 762
clam, white, 575
cream, 481
  for cannelloni, 579
Cumberland, for beef fondue, 295
curry, for beef fondue, 294
custard, for Christmas plum
    pudding, 740
custard, vanilla, 738
diable, 485
  basting, 492
eggnog, for baked rhubarb
    pudding, 730
Espagnole (brown), see brown
    (Espagnole)
foo yung, 438
freezing, 56, 57
fudge
  graham waffles with, 777
  for pears Hélène, 722
garlic butter, for spaghetti, 576
general data on, 478
hard, for English Christmas
    pudding, 742
Hollandaise, 488-489
  artichokes with, 200
  blender, 489
  classic, 488
  jiffy, for broccoli, 507
  less-rich, 488
horseradish
  for boiled brisket of beef, 296
  -chive for beef fondue, 295
ice cream, 761-763
  bittersweet chocolate, 762
  butterscotch, rich, 763
  chocolate fudge, 762
  chocolate rum, 762
  maple-nut, 763
  pineapple, 763
  pineapple mint, 763
  strawberry, 763
lemon
  broccoli with, 508
  -curry, for Caribbean fish soufflé,
    405

lamb with, 338
  steamed holiday pudding with,
    143
lobster-Newburg, 410
Madeira, crepes with chicken livers
    in, 655
mandarin orange sundae, 709
Marguéry, fish fillets with, 412
Mediterranean tuna, spaghetti with,
    575
meat, 574
Mornay, 482
mushroom, 485
  brown, 485
  -catsup, for beef fondue, 296
  -cream, chicken breasts baked in,
    373
  -creamy, for chicken soufflé, 457
  -tarragon, sliced eggs with, 463
  -tomato, for Italian veal cutlets,
    126
  -wine, for meat loaf, 102
mustard
  boiled brisket of beef with, 296
  for fish steaks, 411
  onions in, 528
  pork chops with, 315
  -sour cream, ham balls with, 327
  sweet-and-sour, for glazed
    corned beef, 204
Newburg, 480
  -lobster, for baked fillet of sole
    stuffed with lobster, 410
nutmeg, for carrot and spinach
    timbales, 513
onion, 481
orange
  foamy, for orange soufflé, 767
  lamb riblets with, 335
  mandarin sundae, 709
orange marmalade
  for basting, 492
  for hibachi chicken, 365
parsely-butter, new potatoes in,
    123, 535
peach, cottage pudding with, 737
pineapple
  for cheesecake, 100
  ice cream, 763
  mint, 763
  piquant, 485
Portugaise, 486-487
for pudding, 990
raisin
  smoked tongue with, 350
  tongue with vegetables and, 114
Robert, 486
Roquefort cream, for braised
    endive, 522
rum, for pears Hélène, 722
Salsa, 556
Salsa verde, for steamed
    cauliflower, 514
Smitaine, 483
sour cream
  Brussels sprouts with, 122, 509
  chicken pancakes with, 651
  -mustard, pork meatballs with,
    327
spaghetti, 573-576
  garlic butter, 576
  Mediterranean tuna, 575
  meat, 574
  spicy, 575
  summer salad, 574
  tomato, basic, 574

Sauces—*Continued*
white clam, 575
wine in, 987
summer salad, for spaghetti, 574
sundae
cream puffs, 768
mandarin orange, 709
supreme, 483
strawberry, 763
tarragon
for fish, 976
-mushroom for sliced eggs, 463
tartar, 401
tempura, 419
tomato
basic, for meatballs and spaghetti, 574
for beef fondue, 294
for lasagna, 572
and meat, 574
-mushroom, for Italian veal cutlets, 126
Portugaise, 486-487
stuffed onions in, 527
tuna, Mediterranean, spaghetti with, 575
vanilla
custard, 738
for English Christmas pudding, 742
velouté, *see* blond
walnut
for cold chicken, 621
linguini with, 571
watercress, for cold poached bass, 408
white, *see* Béchamel
white clam, 575
wine
-butter, for broiled fish steaks, 403
fillet of sole with, 123
for fillet of flounder Florentine, 407
for meat, chicken, fish, 989
-mushroom, for meat loaf, 102
sliced steak and glazed onions with, 288
for steak kabobs, 293
veal birds with, 342
yogurt, for falafel, 557
Sauerbraten, 286
Sauerkraut, 541
cooking, 541
general data on, 541
knackwurst dinner with, 353
pork hocks and, 320
quick choucroute, 541
Sausage, 321-22, 351-355
buying, 76
calorie counts, 83
carbohydrate gram counts, 90
casseroles, 950-951
-and apple, 950
noodle, 950
pork pie, 951
zucchini and, 951
English grill, 332
freezing, 58
general data on, 321
meat loaf
appetizer, country, 194
beef and, 309
pie, 322, 951
Polish, ring, 352
and red cabbage, 321
smoked, varieties of, 351-352

storing, 73
stuffing
fruit, for roast goose, 195
for poultry, 393
-rice, for roast chicken, 136
Sautéing, 9
Savory, 975-976
green beans, 503,975
Savoy cabbage, 510
Scald, to, 9
Scallions, *see* Green onions
Scallop
egg and ham, 464
eggplant-and-tomato, 520
onion-and-pepper, 528
potato, 535
and pork chops, 947
Scallops, 432-434
batter-fried, 433
in bouillabaisse, 214
broiled, 432
buying, 75, 432
coquille, 433
freezing, 60
kabobs, 434
general data, 432
in seafood bisque, 218
in seafood casserole, mixed, 415
and shrimps sautéed, Hawaiian, 98
Scaloppine
chicken, 375
veal, 341
Scampi, shrimp, 421
Schnecken, 684
Scones, 635-636
general data on, 635
griddle, 636
Scotch
chocolate drops, 901
woodcock, 460
Scotch sour cocktail, 268
Scrambling, 9, 448
Screwdriver cocktail, 267
Seafood
bisque, 218
bouillabaisse, 214
calorie counts, 82
carbohydrate gram counts, 88-89
casseroles, 952-961
baked salad, 960
crab meat mushroom, 957
crab-rice, 957
mixed, 415
shrimp-cheese, 958
shrimp ramekin, 959
-spinach, 959
Tetrazzini, 960
tuna-macaroni, 958
New Orleans gumbo, 215
nutritive values, 1001
tartlets, 203
See also names of seafood
Searing, 10
Seasoning, 10
Sectioning, 10
Senegalese cream soup, 239
Senf gurken, 924
Serving dishes, 151-152
Sesame seeds, 977
chicken bites with, 174
coating for oven-fried chicken, 363
crisp appetizer, 177
rice with chicken and, 955
toasting, 978
Shakes
banana breakfast, 254

chocolate-spice, 254
honey-peanut butter, 256
Shandygaff cocktail, 269
Shallots, 542
buying, 43
general data on, 542
Shellfish, 415-438
buying, 75
carbohydrate gram counts, 88-89
freezing, 59-60
general data on, 415-416
See also names of shellfish
Sherbet, 757-759
emerald milk, 757
freezing, 56
lemon, 758
lime, cantaloupe with, 126
orange, 759
strawberry Dolley Madison, 759
Sherry
cheese dip, 164
cooler, 986
French dressing, 626
shrimp, 418
strawberries, 194
wafers, 870
Shirring, 10
Shish kabobs
beef, 201
steak, 292
lamb, 333
Shortcake
apricot delight, 112
fruit, 730-732
basic biscuits for, 730
cranberry clafouti, 732
pineapple sponge, 731
strawberry, old-fashioned, 731
Shortening
buying, 76
to cut in, 13
equivalent amounts, 27
measuring, 12
storing, 71
Shredding, 10
Shrimp, 416-422
appetizers
and cheese spread, 206
coconut, 208
and cucumber sandwiches, rolled, 183
filling for glazed party canapés, 180
Italian pickled, 177
marinated, 196
paste, 168
seafood tartlets, hot, 203
toast, 186
batter-fried, 433
boiled, 417
in bouillabaisse, 214
quick, 413
broiled, 432
Italian-style, 421
butterfly, 417
cheese dip for, 418
chili dip for, 418
mustard dip for, 418
buying, 76
casseroles
-and-cheese, 958
mixed seafood, 415
ramekins, 959
-cheese soufflé, 455
-cheese spread, 206
chow mein, 419

Shrimp—*Continued*
  Creole, 420
  curry, 421
  filling, for glazed party canapés, 180
  foo yung, 438
  freezing, 60
  general data on, 416
  Hawaiian, sautéed with scallops, 98
  Japanese soup, 226
  lobster and, baked, 437
  in New Orleans seafood gumbo, 215
  Newburg, on toast, 420
  preparing, 416-417
  Ramekin, 959
  salad, 609
    and macaroni, 609
  and scallops sautéed, Hawaiian, 98
  scampi, 421
  in seafood bisque, 218
  sherried, 418
  soufflé, and cheese, 455
  soup, Japanese, 229
  sweet-and-pungent, 116
  sweet-and-sour, 421
  tempura, 419
Sicilian squash, 542
Sidecar cocktail, 271
Sifting, 10
Simmering, 10, 280
Singeing, 10
Skewering, 10
Slaw
  cabbage, 594
    hot, 511
    with pineapple and mustard
        dressing, 128
    with sour cream dressing, 594
  cauliflower, 595
Slitting, 10
Smelts, buying, 75
  pan-fried whole, 400
Smitaine sauce, 483
Snipping, 10
Snow peas, braised tenderloin with,
    317
Snow pudding, 744
Snowy eggnog punch, 263
Sole, fillet of
  amandine, 402
  baked, stuffed with lobster, 409
  bonne femme, 412
  in cioppino, 414
  cooked in wine, 974
  mixed seafood casserole, 415
  seafood bisque, 218
  stuffed salmon turbans with
      Béarnaise sauce, 409
  Véronique, 413
  with white wine sauce, 123
Sodium, nutritive values and sources,
    999
Soufflés, 452-459
  almond, 765
  asparagus, 458
  cheese, 453-454
    Camembert, 454
    Cheddar, 453
    Swiss-Parmesan, 453
  chicken, 457
  chocolate, 764
  clam-and-corn, 456
  coconut with chocolate sauce, 764
  crab, 427
  dessert, 764-767
    almond, 765
    chocolate, 764

coconut with chocolate sauce, 764
  orange, 766
  strawberry, 748
Florentine, 454
hominy grits, 581
lobster, 456
making, 452
mushroom, fresh, 458
orange, 766
shrimp-cheese, 455
strawberry, 748
turnip, 548
Soups, 210-241
  asparagus
    cold, 235
    -tomato bisque, 233
  au pistou, 224
  bisque
    asparagus-tomato, 233
    crab, 231
    seafood, 218
    tomato, 229
  black bean, 227
    buttered, 232
  borscht, 227
    cold, 241
    jellied, 235
    Ukrainian vegetable, 219
  bouillabaisse, 214
    quick, 413
  broccoli, 226
  calorie counts, 86
  carbohydrate gram counts, 90
  carrot, cream of, 226
  cheese, 475
  chicken
    -almond, 234
    -chestnuts, 231
    -dumpling, 221
  Chinese spinach, 214
  chowder
    corn, 221
    Manhattan clam, 217
    New England clam, 217
    New England fish, 216
    tomato-fish, 216
    vegetable-cheese, 475
  clam
    Manhattan chowder, 217
    New England chowder, 217
    tomato, 232
  cold, 235-241
  consommé
    jellied garden, 239
    julienne, 231
    à la Ritz, 236
    tomato, 230
  corn chowder, quick, 221
  crab bisque, 231
  creamed
    carrot, 226
    cucumber, 236
    Senegalese, 239
  cucumber
    cream of, 236
    icy, 240
  curried East Indian, 236
  Czechoslovakian pot, 223
  dumplings for, 644
  egg drop, 230
  freezing, 58
  garnishes for, 153-154
  gazpacho, 237
    jellied, 134
  general data on, 210
  green goddess, 240

gumbo
  fish, 414
  New Orleans seafood, 215
Japanese shrimp, 229
Lady Curzon, 232
lamb-barley, 220
leek-vegetable, 233
lentil
  -potato, 554
  -spinach, 227
  -and-split-pea, 215
Mexican foam, 234
minestrone, 213
onion with Gruyère cheese, 229
oxtail, 223
oyster, 228
parsley, iced, 970
pea
  frosted, 240
  potage St. Germain, 219
  -vegetable, 233
pepper pot, 222
petite marmite, 234
potage St. Germain, 219
potato, 229
  Vichyssoise, 238
  Vichyssoise, emerald, 238
  and watercress, iced, 239
quick-supper, 220
raspberry, iced, 237
seafood bisque, 218
seasoning with wine, 988
Senegalese cream, 239
shrimp, Japanese, 229
spinach
  Chinese, 214
  emerald Vichyssoise, 238
  -lentil, 227
split-pea, 228
  with lentils, 215
stocks, 211-212
  beef, 211
  chicken, 211
  fish, 212
  general data on, 211
  veal, 212
Texas beef, 222
tomato
  -asparagus bisque, 233
  bisque, 229
  bouillon medley, 233
  in cake, 825
  -clam, 232
  consommé, 230
  fish chowder, 216
  iced, 237
turtle
  Lady Curzon, 232
  and pea, 232
vegetable
  au pistou, 224
  borscht, Ukranian, 219
  -cheese chowder, 475
  Czechoslovakian pot, 223
  fresh, 230
  -leek, 233
  with liver balls and beef ribs, 225
  -pea, 233
  Vichyssoise, 238
    emerald, 238
  watercress, iced, 239
Sour cream
  coating for oven-fried chicken, 363
  cucumbers in, 596
  dressing, 628
    coleslaw with, 594

Sour cream—*Continued*
 tangy, cucumber salad with, 130
 garnish, for soup, 153
 mock, 612
 mustard greens in, 523
 sauce
  Brussels sprouts with, 122, 509
  chicken pancakes with, 651
  -mustard, pork meatballs with, 327
 spiced dip, fruits with, 165
 waffles, 658
Souse, 352
South American lamb stew, 117
Southern
 corn casserole, 518
 pecan pie, 795
 spoon bread, 582
 sweet potatoes, fried, 532
Southwest chili, 305
Spaghetti
 casserole, six-cheese, 477
 equivalent amounts, 27
 freezing, 56
 sauces, 573-576
  garlic butter, 576
  Mediterranean tuna, 575
  meat, 574
  spicy, 575
  summer salad, 574
  tomato, basic, 574
  white clam, 575
  wine in, 987
Spanish
 lima beans, 505
 omelet, 450
 onions, 527
Spanish melons
 selecting, 39
 using, 39
Spareribs, *see* Ribs
Spice balls, 873
Spice cake, 821
 quick, 825
Spice-chocolate shake, 254
Spices, 962-979
 basic chart, 964-965
 blends, 978
 buying, 76
 general data on, 962-967
 seasonings, 978-979
 shopping list, 963-964
 storing, 72
Spicy oatmeal cookies, 869
Spinach
 buttered, with nutmeg, 123
 buying, 42, 43, 75
 and carrot timbales, with nutmeg sauce, 513
 -cheese mousse ring, 615
 creamed, 523
  crepes with, 655
 creamy onion, 130
 dressing, half-crown roast of pork with, 312
 filling, for ravioli, 580
 freezing, 64
 general data on, 585
 -lentil soup, 227
 noodles, 125
 nutritive values, 998
 omelet, 450
 salad
  -cheese mousse ring, 615
  with hot bacon dressing, 596
  special, 589

savory, 142
soufflé Florentine, 454
soup
 Chinese, 214
 emerald Vichyssoise, 238
 -lentil, 227
 storing, 74
 -and-tuna casserole, 959
 Swiss, 523
Spirit candy, 902
Split pea(s)
 general data on, 551-552
 rarebit, 553
 savory supper dish, 554
 soup, 228
  with lentils, 215
Sponge cake, feather, 827
Spoon bread
 herbed, 969
 Southern, 602
Spreads, *see* Appetizers
Springerle, 890
Spritz butter cookies, 890
Squash
 buying, 43, 75, 542, 543
 freezing, 66
 orange cups filled with, 146
 storing, 74
 summer, 542
  buying, 542
  cooking, 542
  general data on, 542
  Sicilian, 543
  zucchini, baked stuffed, 542
  zucchini Parmigiana, 543
  zucchini, sautéed, 542
 winter, 543-545
  baking, 544
  boiling, 543
  buying, 543
  Creole, 544
  custard, 545
  general data on, 543-544
  nut-topped, 544
Staples, choosing a stock of, 18-19
Steaks
 beef, 286-293
  au poivre, 288
  barbecued flank, 290
  broiled, 286
  chuck de luxe, 290
  entrecôte with watercress, 288
  flank, barbecued, 290
  general data on, 286
  kabobs, 292
  -and-kidney pie, 349
  London broil, skillet, 289
  marinade, wine for, 988
  menu for, 96
  minute, Diane, 124
  mock filet mignon with broiled Parmesan toast, 289
  pepper, 288, 292
  porterhouse, 286
  roulades, 291
  Salisbury, 304
  sirloin pepper, 292
  sliced, with wine sauce and glazed onions, 288
  sukiyaki, 292
  Swiss, 289
  T-bone, 286
  tenderloin tips Deutsch, 291
  wine marinade for, 988
  wine sauce for, 293
 fish

  broiled, 403
  broiled, anchovy-butter sauce for, 403
  broiled marinated swordfish, 403
  poached, 410
  salmon Béarnaise, 411
  salmon turbans, stuffed, with Béarnaise sauce, 409
  swordfish Béarnaise, 411
  wine-butter sauce for, 403
 ham
  baked glazed, 325
  barbecued, 326
  broiled, 325
  honey-broiled with sweet potatoes, 326
  stuffed, 326
 lamb, spicy, 333
 pork
  braised, 314
 veal, lemon-braised, 341
Steaming, 10
Steam-baking, 10
Steeping, 10
Stewing, 10, 280
Stews
 beef, 298
  carbonade, 299
  menu for, 95
  old-fashioned, 298
  in wine, 299, 987
 chicken
  Brunswick, 371
  with matzo balls, 370
 frankfurter, with lentils, 354
 freezing, 56, 58
 lamb
  South American, 117
  spring, 336
 oyster, 228
 paella, 105
 veal, 345
Stinger cocktail, 272
Stirring, 13
Stocks, 211-212
 beef, 211
 chicken, 211
 fish, 212
 general data on, 211
 veal, 212
Stollen, Christmas, 689
Storage of foods, 19-20, 70-74
 equipment for, 16
Strawberry(ies)
 -almond jam bars, 863
 baba au fraises, 780
 -banana dessert, 122
 -buttermilk frosted, 257
 charlotte russe, 744
 conversion chart, 34
 coeur à la crème, 720
 creme dressing, 625
 freezing, 70
 French pie, 799
 in fruit Betty, 728
 in fruit fluff, low calorie, 723
 in fruited cream, exotic, 720
 in fruit-filled watermelon, 707
 general data on, 700
 ice cream soda, 258
 marzipan, 900
 in melon surprise, 707
 meringue torte, 839
 milk, 256
 mousse, 748
  festival, 749

Strawberry(ies)—*Continued*
nutritive values, 1000
pie
French, 799
-rhubarb, 791
preserves, 934
-rhubarb jam, 934
Romanoff, 700
sauce, 763
sherbet Dolley Madison, 759
sherried, 194
shortcake, old-fashioned, 731
soufflé, 748
syrup, 259
-vanilla tarts, 809
whipped butter for French toast, 637
Stroganoff
beef, 971
hamburger-and-noodles, 941
Stuffing
chestnut, 382, 393
roast goose with, 391
roast turkey with, 381
corn bread
crown roast of pork with, 312
for poultry, 394
sage, 973
egg, for fillet of flounder
Florentine, 407
green grape, roast duckling with, 390
oyster
for poultry, 393
for roast turkey, 382
for poultry, 392-396
chestnut, 393
classic herb, 393
corn bread, 394
cranberry-nut, 395
fruit, 394
fruit-sausage, 145
giblet, 394
oyster, 393
pecan-bread, 395
sage and onion, 395
sausage, 393
sausage-fruit, 145
sausage-rice, 145
vegetable, 395
rice
Cornish hens with, 377
-sausage, for roast chicken, 136
sage, 135
corn bread, 973
onion, 395
sausage
-fruit, roast goose with, 145
for poultry, 393
-rice, for roast chicken, 136
Succotash, 518
Sugar
buying, 76
cake, Moravian, 687
calorie counts, 87
caramelized, 733
carbohydrate gram counts, 90
cookie cutouts, 877
equivalent amounts, 27
lemon cookies, 876
measuring, 12
nutritive values, 993, 994
storing, 72
Sukiyaki, 292
with noodles and sesame seeds, 570
Summer salad sauce, for spaghetti, 574

Summer squash, *see* Squash, summer
Sundae sauce
cream puffs, 768
mandarin orange, 709
Supreme sauce, 483
Swedish
casserole, 940
coffee ring, 682
meatballs, 304
for a crowd, 190
pancakes, flaming, 773
Sweet potato(es), 531-534
baking, 532
boiling, 532
buying, 42, 75, 531
candied, 532
fluffy stuffed, 137, 533
freezing, 65-66
fried, Southern-style, 532
general data on, 531-532
glazed, 533
Hawaiian, 121
honey-broiled ham steak with, 326
nutritive values, 998
orange, 533
pecan-stuffed, baked, 532
pie, 796
pork chops and, 316
scalloped, and pork chops, 948
Southern-style fried, 532
Sweet-and-pungent
chick-peas, 557
shrimp, 116
Sweet-and-sour
baked flounder fillets, 406
frankfurter appetizers, 191
mustard sauce, 204
pork, 320
chops, 316
shrimp, 421
Sweetbreads
chicken terrapin, 348
general data on, 278
in wine, 347
Swirl frosting, 859
maple, 859
Swiss
artichokes, 501
-cheese fondue, 472
fondue crepes, 654
-potato cakes, 538
spinach, 523
steak, 289
veal casserole, 953
Swiss chard, buying, 42
Swiss cheese, 468
fondue, 472
-lobster custard, 476
-Parmesan Soufflé, 454
pie, 189
six-cheese spaghetti casserole, 477
See also Quiche
Swordfish
Béarnaise, 411
broiled marinated, 403
Syrup
bar, 268
caramel, 841
for crème frite, 736
cocoa, 252
equivalent amount, 27
fruit, for pancakes, 645
maple-nut, 763
pineapple, 763
mint, 763
storing, 73

strawberry, for ice cream soda, 259
vanilla butter, for pancakes, 645

Table settings, 159-160
colors, 153-159
party, 151-153
patterns, 151
shapes, 151
Tabouli and chick-pea salad, 599
Taffy, 910
molasses, 909
peppermint, 910
Tamale casserole, 938
Tangelos, 717
general data on, 717
Tangerines, 716-717
general data on, 716-717
preparing, 717
storing, 717
Tarragon, 976
cream, chicken breasts in, 375
sauce
for fish, 976
-mushroom, sliced eggs with, 463
Tartar sauce, 401
Tartlets
anchovy, 189
ham, 185
seafood, 203
Tarts, 806-809
apple
flaming, 806
warm, 806
continental peach pie, 807
orange, 808
sand, 889
shells for, 807
shaping, 808
sweet, 807
strawberry-vanilla, 809
Tea, 248
bags, 248
festive hot, 250
hot cinnamon, 249
iced, 250
by the pitcher, 250
from bags, 251
from loose, 250
spiced, 251
instant, 249
loose, 249
making, 249
midnight, 249
Tea biscuits, orange, 632
Tea cakes, 847
Tea wafers, 877
Temple oranges, 709
Tempura, 419
sauce, 419
Tenderizing, 10
Tenderizers, 281
Teriyaki appetizers, 177
Texas
beef soup, 222
punch, 265
Textured protein, meat loaf with, 310
Thermometer, candy, 903
Thiamine, nutritive values and sources, 999
Thousand Island dressing, 624
Thuringer, 352
Thyme, 973-974
green beans with fried onions and, 503
Timbales
broccoli, 508

INDEX

Timbales—*Continued*
carrot and spinach with nutmeg sauce, 513
Toast
broiled Parmesan, 289
French, 656-657
basic, 656
crispy, 657
general data on, 656
strawberry whipped butter for, 657
shrimp, 186
Newburg on, 420
Toasting, 10
Toffee
-chocolate bars, 864
English, 906
refrigerator dessert, 752
Tom Collins cocktail, 268
Tom and Jerry punch, 265
Tomato(es), 545-547
à la Provençale, 547
-asparagus bisque, 233
aspic, 616
for Continental buffet, 103
baked halves, 546
Benedict, 546
bisque, 229
bouillon medley, 233
broiled halves, 546
buying, 43, 75
chutney, 931
consomme, 230
cooking, 546
-and-eggplant scallop, 520
equivalent amounts, 27
fish chowder, 216
freezing, 66
garnish
for cold meat platter, 158
flower, 155
for main dish, 155
general data on, 545-546
green pickle relish, 928
hearty stuffed, 547
herb-baked, 968
Italian style, 970
in mixed vegetable pickles, 924
mustard, 930
nutritive values, 1000
in ratatouille, 520
salad
aspic, 103, 616
sauce
for beef fondue, 294
for lasagna, 572
and meat, 574
meatballs and spaghetti, 573
-mushroom, for Italian veal cutlets, 126
Portugaise, 486-487
stuffed onions in, 527
wine in, 987
soup
-asparagus bisque, 233
bisque, 229
bouillon medley, 233
in cake, 825
-clam, 232
consommé, 230
-fish chowder, 216
iced, 237
storing, 74
stuffed, hearty, 547
Tomato juice, freezing, 66
Tongue

deviled, 350
general data on, 278
with raisin sauce and vegetables, 114
smoked, with raisin sauce, 350
Tortes, 837-841
blitz, quick, 851
chocolate almond, 838
chocolate cream, 837
date nut, 737
dobos, quick, 852
general data on, 837
meringue strawberry, 839
mocha, 839
St. Honoré, 840
Tossing, 10
Tostadas, 107
Tripe
breaded, 349
general data on, 278
pepper pot soup, 222
Trout
broiled, 402
meunière, 402
Trussing, 10
Tuna
à la king, 439
appetizers
puffs, 186
spread, 202
casserole
-cashew, 120
-macaroni, 958
-and-spinach, 959
-chip bake, 438
croquettes, 440
fritters, crunchy, 646
-potato skillet pie, 439
salad, 611
-and-avocado, molded, 622
-avocado luncheon plate, 610
hot, 611
Turkey, 378-389
basted with wine, 987
breast, with pecan dressing, 386
broiled, 385
buying, 378
carving, 383-385
casseroles, 953-955
arroz con pollo, 953
sesame rice, 955
Tetrazzini, 954
dilled MacTurkey, 388
freezing, 56, 59
fried, 385
frozen, 378
garnish for soups, 154
general data on, 378-381
giblets, 383
Kiev, 386
leftovers, 385
legs Milanese, 389
parts of, 385
poached, cold, with curry cream dressing, 387
roast
with chestnut and oyster stuffings, 381
general instructions, 378
giblet gravy for, 382
holiday menu, 132-139
preparing for the oven, 380-381
with sage stuffing, 135
roasting timetable, 52, 53
salad, in cucumber ring, 620
scallopini with mushrooms, ham,

and cheese, 387
stir-fried, with almonds and zucchini, 388
stuffing, general instructions, 379
terrapin, 348
trussing, 379-380
wine baste for, 987
Turkish candy paste, 902
Turmeric, 966
Turnip(s)
buying, 43, 75
freezing, 66
garnish, 155, 156, 158
general data on, 547-548
mashed, 548
patties, 548
storing, 74
white, 547
yellow, 548-549
mashed, 548
-and-onion casserole, 549
patties, 548
soufflé, 548
whipped, casserole of, 141
Turnip greens
buying, 42
freezing, 64
Turnovers
ham-and-curry, 175
Mexican, 106
Turtle soup
Lady Curzon, 232
and pea, 232

Ukrainian vegetable borscht, 219
Upside-down cakes, 835-837
cherry, 836
chocolate, 836
pineapple, 836
Utensils
choosing right size, 12
for eggs, 443-444
measuring, 10-11

Vanilla
butter syrup, 649
cookies
drop, 866
refrigerator, 880
custard sauce, 866, 738
ice cream
refrigerator-tray, 776
tub-churn, 775
petits fours frosting, 847
pudding and wine, ladyfingers with, 987
sauce
custard, 738
for English Christmas pudding, 742
soufflé, 767
spirit candy, 902
-strawberry tarts, 809
-wafer fudgies, 902
Veal, 338-342
basic retail cuts, 275-278
birds, with wine sauce, 342
blanquette, 344
breast of
barbecued, 340
riblets and noodles, 340
stuffed rolled, 339
buying, 76
calorie counts, 83
casseroles, 951-953
lasagna Romano, 952

Veal—*Continued*
Swiss, 953
with water chestnuts, 951
chops
broiled, 343
zesty, 343
cutlets
Italian, 126
piccata, 342
fondue oriental, 295
freezing, 59
general data on, 338
heart Andalouse, 347
kidneys, savory, 349
lasagna Romano, 952
lemon-braised steak, 341
marinade, wine for, 988
meat loaf
and beef, 309
our best, 308
osso buco, 345
Parmigiana, 341
and peppers, 344
piccata, 342
riblets and noodles, 340
roast
leg or loin, 339
menu for, 96
roasting chart, 49
rolls, stuffed, 342
scaloppine, 341
shanks, osso buco, 345
soup, pepper pot, 222
stew, 345
stock, 212
sweetbreads
chicken terrapin, 47
in wine, 347
Swiss casserole, 953
and water chestnut casserole, 951
wine marinade for, 984
See also Calf's brains; Calf's liver
Vegetable(s), 40-43, 495-558
aspic, 616
baking, 498
beef tongue with raisin sauce and, 114
boiling, 498
braising, 498
broiling, 498
buying, 40-43, 76, 495-496
canned, 496
dried, 43
fresh, 495
frozen, 496
calorie counts, 84-86
carbohydrate gram counts, 90-91
casserole
baked noodle, 569
medley, 103
-cheese chowder, 475
cooking
canned, 499
dehydrated, 499
fresh, 497-499
frozen, 499
dip, 198
curried, 165
freezing, 62-66, 915
French frying
fresh raw appetizer, with low calorie dip, 165
-fruit blend drink, 257
garnishes for, 158-159
general data, 495
medley, 550

nutritive values, 996, 998-1001
pan-cooking, 498
pan-frying, 499
pickles, mixed, 924
platters, 549-551
braised mixed, 550
foil-baked, 550
medley, 550
tempura, 551
pressure-cooking, 498
relish, tangy, 926
relish bowl, 127
salad
aspic, 616
medley, 116
molded garden, 615
soup, 230
au pistou, 224
borscht Ukranian, 219
-cheese chowder, 475
Czechoslovakian pot, 223
fresh, 230
-leek, 233
with liver balls and beef ribs, 225
pea, 233
steaming, 497-498
stir-frying, 498
storing, 74-75, 496-497
canned, 75, 497
dehydrated, 497
fresh, 496-497
frozen, 497
leftovers, 497
-stuffed baked whole fish, 406
stuffed, relishes, 174
stuffing for poultry, 395
tempura, 551
Ukrainian borscht, 219
See also names of vegetables
Vegetable juices, calorie counts, 84
Vegetable oil, equivalent amounts, 27
Vegetarian eating, 1003-1007
Velouté sauce, 482-483
long method, 482
short method, 483
Vermicelli, baked, 570
Vermouth cassis, 987
Vichyssoise, 238
emerald, 238
Viennese coffee, 245
Vinaigrette dressing, 627
See also French dressing
Vitamins, nutritive values and sources, 995, 998-1000
fat-soluble, 994-995, 998
A, 998
D, 998
E, 998
K, 998
water soluble, 995, 998-1000
B_6, 999
B_{12}, 1000
biotin, 999
C, 1000
choline, 999
folacin, 999
niacin, 999
pantothenic acid, 999
riboflavin (B_2), 999
thiamine (B_1), 999
Vodka Collins cocktail, 269

Wafer(s)
almond Christmas, 885
sherry, 870
tea, 877

-vanilla fudgies, 902
Waffles, 657-659
basic, 658
cornmeal brunch, 659
deluxe, 658
dessert, 776-778
Belgian, 777
graham with fudge sauce, 777
sweet, 776
general data on, 657-658
raisin oatmeal, 659
sour cream, 658
Waldorf salad, 591
-cranberry, with fruit dressing, 142
Walnuts
braised endive with, 522
chocolate bark, 895
minted, 909
pastry shell, flaky, 787
sauce, linguiné with, 471
sauce for cold chicken, 621
squash topped with, 544
Wassail bowl, 265
Water chestnuts, veal baked with, 951
Watercress
biscuits, 631
canapés, dried beef and, 181
entrecôte with garnish of, 288
garnish for soup, 154
general data on, 585
pineapple beverage, 256
rolled sandwiches, 183
sauce, for cold poached bass, 408
soup, iced, 239
vegetable relish bowl, 127
Watermelon(s)
freezing, 69
fruit-filled, 707
in melon surprise, 707
pickled rind, 925
selecting, 39
slices, marzipan, 900
using, 39
Wax beans, 503-504
buying, 41, 75
in four-bean salad, 593
See also Green beans
Wedding cake, 854
Wedging, 10
Weights and measures, equivalent, 14
Welsh rarebit, 473
Whipping, 11, 13
Whipped cream
cinnamon, coconut pancakes with, 772
cocoa, 860
garnish for soup, 153
-horseradish dip, cubed roast beef with, 163
peppermint, chocolate pancakes with, 772
Whiskey sour cocktail, 268
White bread
batter, 671
conventional method, 665
cool-rise method, 674
rapid-mix method, 668
White cakes
butter, 817
fruit, 843
one-bowl, 823
White icing for cinnamon rolls, 681
White mountain frosting, 859
White pepper, 966
White sauce, *see* Béchamel
Whole grain bread, 675-678

INDEX

Whole grain bread—*Continued*
Cornell, 676
cracked wheat, 677
currant oatmeal, 676
whole wheat, *see* Whole wheat bread
Whole wheat bread
bran, 677
conventional method, 666
cool-rise method, 674
cracked wheat, 677
-egg, 676
rapid-mix method, 668
Wild rice, 560
casserole, 563
-and-chicken-liver casserole, 956
Wine
Burgundy whip, 990
-cheese spread, 199
chicken breasts in, 374
cog au vin, 366
fillet of sole cooked in, 974
frappé, 991
French dressing
with avocado, 988
with blue cheese, 988
with chili herb sauce, 988
-gelatin cubes, 600
glaze for broiled chicken, 364
holiday punch, 264
jelly, 989
marinade for veal, lamb, or chicken, 988
orange gelatine, 989
pears in, 712

pears in port, 990
red cabbage with, 511
sweetbreads in, 347
syllabub, 263
Wine sauce
-butter, for broiled fish steaks, 403
fillet of sole with, 123
for flounder Florentine, 407
for meat, chicken, fish, 989
-mushroom, for meat loaf, 102
sliced steak and glazed onions with, 288
for steak kabobs, 293
veal birds with, 342
Wines, 980-991
buying, 985
chilling, 983
choosing, 984
as a cocktail, 984
cooking with, 987
decanting, 983
five classes of, 980
as a food accompaniment, 984
general data on, 980-983
glasses for, 985
in mixed drinks and punch, 985-987
champagne punch, 985
claret float, 984
cranberry cup, 986
fruited Burgundy cooler, 986
peach bowl, 986
port cocktail, 984
sherry cooler, 986

vermouth cassis, 987
wine spritzer, 986
as a party drink, 984
seasoning soup with, 988
storing, 983
See also Cocktails
Winter squash *see* Squash, winter

Yams
See Sweet potatoes
Yankee cheese fondue, 473
Yeast, 661-662
pancakes, 650
See also Breads, yeast
Yellow cake, golden, 824
Yogurt
razzberry, 254
sauce for falafel, 557
Yorkshire pudding, 635
Youngberries, freezing, 67

Zabaglione, 734
Zucchini
baked stuffed, 542
buying, 43, 75, 542
general data on, 542
Parmigiana, 543
in ratatouille, 520
and sausage casserole, 951
sautéed, 542
stir-fried turkey with almonds and, 388

A GUIDE TO THE MOST

There are many cuts of meat that may be oven-roasted;
pictured here are 28 of the most popular. They
represent a wide price range and each of them can be
beautifully succulent. The names of the roasts
shown here are meat industry standards but individual

ILLUSTRATED BY BARNEY LINE

BEEF

Standing Rib

Rib Eye

Tenderloin

LAMB

Boneless Shoulder

Cushion Shoulder

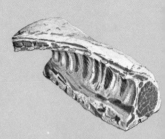

Rib (Rack)

PORK

Blade Boston Shoulder

Arm Picnic Shoulder

Boneless Arm Picnic Shoulde

Crown

Leg, Whole

Leg, Rump Half, left
Shank Half, right

Boneless Whole Leg